Post-Reformation
Reformed Dogmatics

Post-Reformation Reformed Dogmatics

*The Rise and Development of Reformed
Orthodoxy, ca. 1520 to ca. 1725*

VOLUME THREE
The Divine Essence and Attributes

RICHARD A. MULLER

Baker Academic
Grand Rapids, Michigan

Published by Baker Academic
a division of Baker Publishing Group
P.O. Box 6287, Grand Rapids, MI 49516-6287
www.bakeracademic.com

Second printing, June 2006

Printed in the United States of America

Library of Congress Cataloging-in-Publication Data
Muller, Richard A. (Richard Alfred), 1948–
    Post-Reformation reformed dogmatics : the rise and development of reformed orthodoxy, ca. 1520 to ca. 1725 / Richard A. Muller—[2nd ed.].
        p.   cm.
    Includes bibliographical references and indexes.
    Contents: v. 1. Prolegomena to theology — v. 2. Holy Scripture — v. 3. The divine essence and attributes — v. 4. The triunity of God.
    ISBN 10: 0-8010-2617-2 (v. 1 : cloth)
    ISBN 978-0-8010-2617-1 (v. 1 : cloth)

    ISBN 10: 0-8010-2616-4 (v. 2 : cloth)
    ISBN 978-0-8010-2616-4 (v. 2 : cloth)

    ISBN 10: 0-8010-2294-0 (v. 3 : cloth)
    ISBN 978-0-8010-2294-4 (v. 3 : cloth)

    ISBN 10: 0-8010-2295-9 (v. 4 : cloth)
    ISBN 978-0-8010-2295-1 (v. 4 : cloth)
    1. Reformed Church—Doctrines—History—16th century. 2. Reformed Church—Doctrines—History—17th century. 3. Reformed Church—Doctrines—History—18th century. 4. Protestant Scholasticism. I. Title.
BX9422.3 .M85 2002
230'.42'.09—dc21   2002026165

Contents

PART 2   THE REFORMED ORTHODOX DOCTRINE OF GOD

Preface

This preface and the briefer one in volume four of *Post-Reformation Reformed Dogmatics* mark a moment of relative closure in an unfinished discussion. I come to the formal completion of a project that has, in varying degrees of concentration, occupied me since 1978. In that time, I have written on other subjects, but the analysis of sixteenth- and seventeenth-century Reformed understandings of prolegomena and *principia* has remained a primary interest and focus of my research. Completion of the project comes, however, with the recognition that the investigation has barely scratched the surface of the subject. Even though the last twenty-five years have seen an increase of scholarly interest in the intellectual history of Protestantism in the late sixteenth and the seventeenth centuries, a host of issues contributing to the course of Protestant orthodoxy and a vast mass of documents belonging to its history remain either superficially examined or utterly unexamined. The very fact that only prolegomena and the doctrines of Scripture and God have been studied here indicates an enormous amount of work to be done, on a scale similar to that undertaken in the present work, but with other historical and doctrinal emphases, before we can begin to have a comprehensive picture of Reformed orthodoxy. Further study of the history of exegesis, the piety, and the homiletics of the era, with attention to the contexts of theological discourse and the interrelationships of academic study and popular religion, is required before we have full closure to the discussion. In addition, despite the length of the present study, I am more aware than ever of the need for the study of individual thinkers, of the varieties of doctrinal formulation among the Reformed orthodox, and of the issues debated between the Reformed orthodox and their various opponents. Often essays and monographs are needed on points that occupy barely a paragraph or two in the present study. Many of the topical sections in each of the four volumes survey issues that were the subject of vast treatises in the seventeenth century.

Just stating the needs of scholarship in this way offers an indication of why the older nineteenth- and twentieth-century dogmatic scholarship, given both its phobia for and misdefinition of scholasticism and its attachment to variations of the central dogma theory, was so egregiously wrong in its assessment of the late sixteenth- and the seventeenth-century materials. Beyond and underlying this basic historiographical problem, moreover, is the fact that the theologians of the nineteenth and twentieth centuries wrote in a context that was largely cut off from the orthodox and scholastic dogmatics of Protestantism — and that, even when they examined its materials, they typically did so by way of less-than-representative compendia, like Heppe's *Reformed Dogmatics*, and in the context of modern philosophical perspectives that hardly coincided with the philosophical perspectives, not to mention the shifting world-view of the sixteenth and seventeenth centuries. Modern theological critics of this older Protestant theology typically misunderstand the ideas and formulae that they attack — sometimes because the misunderstanding is shared by the modern "defenders" of orthodoxy. The point is perhaps best illustrated by the discussion of divine simplicity in the present volume: many of the defenders as well as detractors of the doctrine assume (incorrectly) that it permitted no distinctions in the Godhead. The greatest difficulty that confronts the modern writer in dealing with this material is, thus, learning its vocabulary and, via its vocabulary, its meaning.

Nevertheless, this study of the prolegomena and the two *principia* of the Reformed system offers, even taken by itself, a suitable basis for the discussion and partial reappraisal of scholastic and orthodox Protestant thought. These three *loci* taken together offer a glimpse into the presuppositions and methods of seventeenth-century theology. A survey of the contents of two of the doctrines — Scripture and God — identified by the orthodox as *principia*, and arguably, most important to the Protestant orthodox mind, illustrates the ways in which definitions, approaches, and methods outlined in the prolegomena came into play in doctrinal formulation. Even more than the prolegomena and the doctrine of Scripture, the Protestant orthodox doctrine of God — the divine essence, attributes, and Trinity — gives evidence of the character of post-Reformation Reformed dogmatics. The doctrine is profoundly biblical, highly philosophical, utterly situated in its seventeenth-century exegetical and philosophical context, yet eminently traditional and never very far from piety. It is Protestant in its confessional recognizance and catholic (in an ecumenical sense!) in its scholastic method, its patristic foundations, and its classical philosophical roots. It shares an existential, homiletical, and kerygmatic tendency, as well as a trinitarian orthodoxy, with the theology of the Reformers — but it also shares a dialectical and philosophical acuity and, indeed, an interest in the intra-trinitarian relations, with the theology of the medieval doctors. The division of the subject into two volumes, one dealing with essence and attributes, the other dealing with the doctrine of the Trinity, does not, moreover, indicate a separation of the topics, which the Reformed orthodox understood as a unity. The division is merely a concession to the increasing length of the project.

The character of the Protestant orthodox doctrinal statements evidences a genuine concern for biblical norms, confessional boundaries, and catholicity of formulation that renders the identification of scholastic Protestant dogmatics as a form of rationalism quite impossible. One ought not to dismiss the Reformed orthodox as rationalists any more than one ought to dismiss the Reformers as blind fideists — and although it is quite clear that the theologians of the seventeenth century were more willing to engage in doctrinal discussions of a more metaphysical nature than were the Reformers of the first and second generations of Protestantism, it is also fairly certain that such discussions belong to the framing of full-scale theological system and were not entered upon lightly by the orthodox.

The biblicism of Reformed orthodoxy or, more precisely, the intimate connection between exegesis and dogmatic formulation characteristic of seventeenth-century theology is also, therefore, a theme in volumes three and four. A reasonable case can be made that the Reformed orthodox doctrine of God was highly exegetical — and that the portion of the *locus* concerned with the doctrine of the Trinity was predominantly exegetical. This theme, moreover, stands as a continuation and documentation of the point made in volume two concerning the use of *dicta probantia*. There, the thesis was offered that these "proof texts" were not biblical verses wrenched out of their context and used to justify a non-exegetical, dogmatic theology — here the thesis is illustrated by comparison of the work of various commentators with the doctrinal formulations of the Reformed orthodox. Similarly, the connection between exegesis, dogmatics, and piety is illustrated by the citation of sermons and "popular" commentaries (usually resulting from sermons preached in series) as well as technical commentaries and systems of theology. Thus, despite its systematic organization, the volume also illustrates and argues the broader impact of Reformed orthodoxy beyond the university classroom. (I also note that I have had to be selective in the biblical texts examined: I have attempted to select representative texts that either evidence the positive exegetical basis of the doctrine or provide documentation of the polemic with various anti-trinitarians. There was no possibility, however, given the length of the study, that all of the exegetical arguments could be surveyed.)

As in previous volumes, I have identified and corrected the biblical citations given in the various works cited, without indication of corrections made. Many of the citations, particularly in works published before 1560, are merely to chapters, given the novelty of versification in the sixteenth century. Where possible, I have indicated the verses. Readers ought also to be aware that significant differences in versification continued into the seventeenth century (and in some cases remain to this day): thus the versification of the Authorized Version is often different from that of the *Statenvertaling* where, among other differences, the superscriptions of the Psalms are consistently identified as the first verse. In such cases, where the different versification is a correct reading, I have made no change. I have also standardized the abbreviations of biblical books and the typography of citation of book numbers, chapters, and verses. Quotations of biblical text usually follow the form of the words given in the sixteenth- or seventeenth-century sources. I have translated Latin citations directly into English and done so in consultation with several of the sixteenth- and seventeenth-century translations. When it was necessary to provide a citation of a biblical text not provided in full by the theological text being examined, I have followed older translations, given that their language conforms to the usage of the era and, more importantly, they are all translations of the so-called Textus Receptus, then in use as the normative basis for translation.

My profound thanks go to colleagues and friends at the University of Utrecht — especially Willem Van Asselt, Eef Dekker, Anton Vos, and Andreas Beck — who have been my dialogue partners on several significant portions of the text and whose penetrating analyses helped me to refine my views. I am particularly indebted to our discussions of simplicity, infinity, and middle knowledge in seminars held in Utrecht in spring 1997 and to the extended discussions that we had in the *Onderzoeksgroep oude Gereformeerde Theologie*, during my tenure as the Belle van Zuylen Professor in the Faculty of Theology at the University of Utrecht in spring 1999. So also, I extend my thanks to the faculty and students at Talbot Seminary in La Mirada, CA for their cogent response to penultimate versions of several of the chapters in this volume, presented in 1996 as the Lyman Stewart Lectures. A long-awaited word of thanks also goes to Diane Bradley, who entered the first electronic version of this work from my often nearly illegible handwritten pages.

Finally, my thanks and deepest appreciation go, as always, to Gloria, who has constantly supported and encouraged my research and writing and who, more importantly, is my support and companion when the writing is done.

Richard A. Muller
May 16, 2002

PART 1

Introduction

1

The Doctrine of God from the Twelfth to the Fifteenth Century

1.1 Scholarship and Perspectives on the History of the Doctrine of God

A. Toward a History of the Doctrine of God — with emphasis on the Sixteenth and Seventeenth Centuries

1. Limitations and directions of the present study. The doctrine of God found in Reformed thought during the era of orthodoxy (ca. 1565-1725) has occupied a central place in the criticism of post-Reformation theology and has, typically, distinguished from the doctrine of the Reformers on the basis of its scholastic and Aristotelian content. Despite this reasonably prominent critique, the doctrine itself has been little studied — there are a few monographs and essays on the views of individual thinkers, but no extensive examination of the development and spectrum of Reformed teaching on the subject. The critiques, moreover, have largely been dogmatic rather than historical, have judged the views of the older dogmaticians on the basis of twentieth-century dogmatic constructs, and have resorted to rather vague claims: the doctrine of the orthodox writers was "rigid," "arid," "abstract," characterized by "scholasticism" and "Aristotelianism."[1]

---

1. Thus, e.g., Charles S. McCoy, "Johannes Cocceius: Federal Theologian," in *Scottish Journal of Theology*, XVI (1963), pp. 352-370; Basil Hall, "Calvin Against the Calvinists," in *John Calvin: A Collection of Distinguished Essays*, ed. Gervase Duffield (Grand Rapids: Eerdmans, 1966), pp. 19-37; Brian G. Armstrong, *Calvinism and the Amyraut Heresy: Protestant Scholasticism and Humanism in Seventeenth Century France* (Madison: University of Wisconsin Press, 1969); Cornelis Graafland, "Gereformeerde Scholastiek V: De Invloed van de Scholastiek op de Gereformeerde Orthodoxie," in *Theologia Reformata*, 30 (1987), pp. 4-25; cf. Bert Loonstra, "De leer van God en Christus in de Nadere Reformatie," in Th. Brienen, et al. *Theologische Aspecten van de Nadere Reformatie*

A full history of the doctrine of God, even granting its limitation to developments in thought from the twelfth through the seventeenth or early eighteenth century, would be a massive undertaking: what follows this and the next chapter is an outline of major developments and a critical approach to some of the literature — specifically with reference to the trajectories of thought that have bearing on the development of the doctrine in Reformation and post-Reformation Reformed theology. During these centuries the doctrine of God was established as a full-scale dogmatic formulation by the writers of the high scholastic era of the Middle Ages, given a critical turn by the writers of the fourteenth and fifteenth centuries, transformed again by the soteriological and exegetical emphases of the Reformation, and reformulated on a vast scale by the Protestant scholastics of the post-Reformation period — not to mention the development of doctrine within Roman Catholicism after the Council of Trent, under the impact of the late Renaissance revival of Aristotelianism and scholasticism. In addition, the philosophical labors of the entire medieval scholastic era were sharply criticized by the Reformers and then reassessed by the Protestant scholastics in their attempt to fashion a new system of doctrine in the light both of the Reformation and of the insights of the earlier doctors of the church, both patristic and medieval. All that can be presented here is a survey of these developments as a prelude to the topical discussion of the Reformed orthodox doctrine of the essence and attributes and of the triune nature of God. We leave aside, moreover, developments in Roman Catholic and Lutheran theology in the sixteenth and seventeenth centuries except where they impinge on the thought of the Reformed.

Virtually the same chronological pattern is observed here as in the two preceding volumes — an early orthodox era extending roughly from 1565 to 1640, divided into two phases by the Arminian controversy and the Synod of Dort; a high orthodox era extending from 1640 to 1725, also divided into two phases by the shift in the philosophical sensibilities, the exegetical and critical perspectives, and the political fortunes of Protestantism that was broadly noticeable ca. 1685; and an era of late orthodoxy extending from 1725 to 1775. As previously, although several late orthodox theologians are fairly consistently referenced, the emphasis of the study remains on the early and late orthodox eras, ca. 1565-1725.[2]

2. The present state of the inquiry. As noted in the preceding volume,[3] the character and emphases of the secondary literature differ considerably from one topical concern to another: examination of the history and development of prolegomena is sparse, but fairly objective; of the doctrine of Scripture and the history of exegesis, sizeable but much invested in theological issues and problems. In the case of the doctrine of God, there is a vast literature on the medieval views of divine essence and

---

(Zoetermeer: Boekencentrum, 1993), pp. 99-150.

2. See the discussions of the chronology in Richard A. Muller, *Post-Reformation Reformed Dogmatics*, I, 1.1 (A.2); 1.3 (A-D), hereinafter cited as *PRRD*; and in Richard A. Muller, *After Calvin: Studies in the Development of a Theological Tradition* (New York: Oxford University Press, 2002), chapter 1.

3. *PRRD*, II, 1.1.

attributes, less on the Trinity in the Middle Ages, and still less on either of these topics in the eras of the Reformation and orthodoxy. The important exception to this pattern of decreasing interest are the efforts of historians of philosophy to present the developments of the seventeenth century and the work that has been done on antitrinitarianism in the sixteenth and seventeenth century.[4]

Unfortunately, moreover, there appears to be very little crossover between the historians of philosophy and historians of theology: each group can be faulted bibliographically for not examining the other's investigations. What is more, there is a strong modern philosophical interest in the classical or traditional views of divine essence and attributes, too much of which manifests little concern for historical detail. The philosophers appear to have even more interest than the various schools of modern theologians in using (and frequently distorting) the history for contemporary ends: a typical pattern of argument is the presentation of a partial picture or of a caricature of the scholastic teaching for the sake of more easily dismissing it in favor of a modern alternative.[5] An important exception to both of the generalizations in this paragraph is the recent work of the research groups at the University of Utrecht.[6]

Scholarship on the historical development of the doctrine of God has been partial at best. Several major histories of doctrine — like Schwane's *Histoire des Dogmes*, Seeberg's *History of Doctrines*, and the *Handbuch der Dogmengeschichte* of Grillmeier, Schmaus, and Scheffczyk — do offer surveys of the work of major thinkers; Pelikan's *Christian Tradition* offers reflections on the Trinity, but not the doctrine of the divine essence and attributes; and the extensive essay by Chossat in *Dictionnaire de théologie catholique* offers a sound synopsis of developments in the medieval period.[7] Similarly,

---

4. Two of the best points of access to the bibliography on the history of seventeenth century philosophy are Daniel Garber and Michael Ayers, eds., *The Cambridge History of Seventeenth-Century Philosophy*, 2 vols. (Cambridge: Cambridge University Press, 1998), and the *Encyclopédie philosophique universelle*, publié sous la direction d'André Jacob, 4 parts in 5 vols. (Paris: Presses Universitaires de France, 1989-1998). I will take up the discussion of trinitarian and antitrinitarian thought in *PRRD* IV.

5. E.g., Nicholas Wolterstorff, "God Everlasting," in *God and the Good: Essays in Honor of Henry Stob*, ed. Clifton Orlebeke and Lewis Smedes (Grand Rapids: Eerdmans, 1975), pp. 181-203; idem, "Divine Simplicity," in *Philosophical Perspectives, 5, Philosophy of Religion*, ed. James Tomberlin (Atascadero, CA: Pidgeview Publishing, 1991), pp. 531-552; and Alvin Plantinga, *Does God Have a Nature?* (Milwaukee: Marquette University Press, 1980); for a defense of the more traditional doctrine, see Ronald H. Nash, *The Concept of God: An Exploration of Contemporary Difficulties with the Attributes of God* (Grand Rapids: Zondervan, 1983).

6. E.g., John Duns Scotus, *Contingency and Freedom. Lectura I 39*, Introduction, translation, and commentary by A. Vos, H. Veldhuis, A. H. Looman-Grasskamp, E. Dekker, and N. W. den Bok (Dordrecht, 1994); Antonie Vos, *Johannes Duns Scotus* (Leiden, 1994); Eef Dekker, "Does Duns Scotus Need Molina? On Divine Foreknowledge and Co-causality," in *John Duns Scotus (1265/6-1308): Renewal of Philosophy*, ed. E. P. Bos (Amsterdam: Rodopi, 1998), pp. 101-11 and idem, "The Reception of Scotus' Theory of Contingency in Molina and Suárez," in *Via Scoti*, ed. Sileo, pp. 445-54.

7. Joseph Schwane, *Histoire des Dogmes*, trans. A. Degert, 5 vols. (Beauschesne, 1906); Reinhold Seeberg, *Text-book of the History of Doctrines*, trans. Charles E. Hay, 2 vols. (Grand Rapids: Baker Book House, 1977); A. Grillmeier, M. Schmaus, and L. Scheffczyk, eds., *Handbuch der Dogmengeschichte*, (Freiburg: Herder, 1956ff.); Jaroslav Pelikan, *The Christian Tradition: A History of the Development of*

though not in as great detail, the older histories of doctrine by Neander and Hagenbach offer surveys of the doctrines of God and Trinity in each of the major eras of the church.[8] Two older studies also deserve mention: Gillett's *God in Human Thought*[9] and Gwatkin's *The Knowledge of God in Its Historical Development*.[10] The former is a work that is notable for its scope and, granting its time, for its objectivity. It still serves as a useful finding-list of materials, particularly with reference to the natural theology of the seventeenth and early eighteenth centuries. Gillett must be criticized, however, for not establishing a clear criterion for the inclusion or exclusion of works on natural theology and, in his discussion of the seventeenth century, for simply following out the lines of Deist and rationalist philosophy rather than attempting to examine the broader subject rational theism. The latter is a rather sketchy series of lectures notable for its bias against scholastic developments, whether medieval or post-Reformation, for its rather shallow philosophizing, and for its frequent neglect of the sources. Beyond these works, the doctrine is also surveyed, albeit from another perspective, in the various major histories of philosophy, notably Ueberweg and Copleston.[11] Also worthy of note are the short survey of the doctrine of God by Kaiser and the collection of excerpts from a series of significant essays and monographs on aspects of the doctrine of God throughout Western history gathered by Fortman under the title *Theology of God*. Fortman's collection is far to general to be of use in this study and Kaiser's work, unfortunately, repeats stereotypes concerning the era of orthodoxy without evidence of any research into the actual documents of the era.[12]

Nor could we pass from a survey of the broader accounts of the doctrine of God without some mention of the massive discussion of the subject found in Barth's *Church Dogmatics* and the lengthy survey, often based on Barth, found in Weber's *Foundations of Dogmatics*.[13] Barth's presentation is one of the most detailed extant, and it is filled with reflections on the logic of the older dogmatics that have frequently influenced twentieth-century scholarship on Reformed orthodoxy. It suffers, however, like most

---

Doctrine, 5 vols. (Chicago: University of Chicago Press, 1971-1989); M. Chossat, "Dieu. Sa nature selon les scholastiques," in *Dictionnaire de théologie catholique*, vol. 4/1, cols. 1152-1243.

8. Johann August Wilhelm Neander, *Lectures on the History of Christian Dogmas*, 2 vols. (London: Bohn, 1858); Karl R. Hagenbach, *A History of Christian Doctrines*, 3 vols. (Edinburgh: T. & T. Clark, 1880-1881).

9. Ezra Hall Gillett, *God in Human Thought; or, Natural Theology Traced in Literature, Ancient and Modern, to the Time of Bishop Butler*, 2 vols. (New York, Scribner, Armstrong, 1874).

10. Henry Melvill Gwatkin, *The Knowledge of God in Its Historical Development*, 2nd ed., 2 vols. (Edinburgh: T. & T. Clark, 1907).

11. Friedrich Ueberweg, et al., *Friedrich Ueberweg's Grundriss der Geschichte der Philosophie*, 5 vols. (Berlin: E. S. Mittler & Sohn, 1923-1928); also idem, *A History of Philosophy from Thales to the Present Time*, 2 vols. (New York: Scribner, 1872-1874); and Frederick Copleston, *A History of Philosophy*, 9 vols. (Westminster, Md.: The Newman Press, 1946-1974; repr. Garden City: Image Books, 1985).

12. Christopher B. Kaiser, *The Doctrine of God: an Historical Survey*, rev. ed. (Eugene, Or.: Wipf & Stock, 2001); Edmund Fortman, *The Theology of God: Commentary* (Milwaukee: Bruce, 1968).

13. Karl Barth, *Church Dogmatics*, ed. G. W. Bromiley and T. F. Torrance, 4 vols. (Edinburgh: T. & T. Clark, 1936-1975), II/1, pp. 322-677; Otto Weber, *Foundations of Dogmatics*, trans. Darrell Guder, 2 vols. (Grand Rapids: Eerdmans, 1981-1982), I, pp. 397-460.

of Barth's dogmatic excurses, from a willingness to use the older materials as a foil for his own argument: for all its detail, it cannot be viewed as an attempt to enter the mind of the traditional doctrine on its own terms. Barth's discussion of *scientia media* is exemplary— his comments on divine immutability are problematic. His presentations must be studied carefully but also warily. So also in the case of Weber is there much detail and understanding but also much theologized misunderstanding.

Whereas, in general, individual thinkers in the early scholastic era have received little attention,[14] the doctrine of God in Anselm's work had been well and widely discussed.[15] The literature on the high scholastic doctrine is, however, massive, and only a few representative studies can be noted in this summary. Individual studies of Aquinas' doctrine of God abound,[16] and there has been some significant work comparing Bonaventure and Thomas.[17] Here, however, as in the general remarks made at the outset of this chapter, there is a distinct problem caused by the use of Aquinas for modern philosophical purposes, apart from historical examination of his ideas in their medieval context of interpretation — indeed, as if often the case, the examination of portions of his *Summa theologiae* apart from the larger corpus of his writings, not to mention their historical context. The assumption of much of this writing appears to be that Aquinas is the representative thinker par excellence of medieval theology and that the *Summa theologiae* is the most complete expression of his thought on nearly all points, when in fact, his views often exemplify only one position in a major medieval debate and the fullest exposition of his ideas occurs in another document, such as his commentary on the *Sentences*. This problem is nowhere more evident than in the modern debate over the doctrine of divine simplicity.

---

14. But note Donald F. Duclow, "Pseudo-Dionysius, John Scotus Eriugena, Nicholas of Cusa: An Approach to the Hermeneutic of Divine Names," in *International Philosophical Quarterly*, 12 (1972), pp. 260-278; Ivan Boh, "Divine Omnipotence in the Early Sentences," in Tamar Rudavsky (ed.), *Divine Omniscience and Omnipotence in Medieval Philosophy: Islamic, Jewish, and Christian Perspectives*, (Dordrecht: Riedel, 1985), pp. 185-211.

15. E.g., Gillian Evans, *Anselm and Talking About God* (Oxford: Clarendon Press, 1978); John Moreall, "The Aseity of God in St. Anselm," in *Studia Theologica: Scandinavian Journal of Theology*, 36/1 (1982), pp. 37-46; William Courtenay, "Necessity and Freedom in Anselm's Conception of God," in *Analecta Anselmiana*, 4/2, ed. H. Kohlenberger (1975), pp. 39-64.

16. E. g., Robert L. Patterson, *The Conception of God in the Philosophy of Aquinas* (London: Allen & Unwin, 1933); Karl Albert, "Exodusmetaphysik und Metaphysische Erfahrung," in *Thomas von Aquino: Interpretation und Rexeption*, ed. Willehad Eckert (Mainz: Matthias-Grünewald-Verlag, 1974), pp. 80-95; P. Fontan, "Dieu, premier ou dernier connu, de Spinoza á St. Thomas d'Aquin," in *The Thomist*, 74 (1974), pp. 244-278; Gerhard Ebeling, "The Hermeneutical Locus of the Doctrine of God in Peter Lombard and Thomas Aquinas," in *Journal for Theology and the Church*, 3 (1967), pp. 70-111; L.-B. Geiger, "Les idées divines dans l'oeuvre de S. Thomas," in *St. Thomas Aquinas, 1274-1974; Commemorative Studies*, foreword by Etienne Gilson, 2 vols. (Toronto: Pontifical Institute of Mediaeval Studies, 1974), vol. I, pp. 175-209; W. J. Hankey, *God in Himself: Aquinas' Doctrine of God as Expounded in the Summa Theologiae* (New York: Oxford University Press, 1987).

17. Cf. Thomas A. Fay, "Bonaventure and Aquinas on God's Existence: Points of Convergence," in *The Thomist*, 41 (1977), pp. 585-595; Anton Pegis, "The Bonaventurean Way to God," in *Medieval Studies*, 29 (1967), pp. 206-242.

The theology of Henry of Ghent has been reassessed in the twentieth century by Paulus and Pegis as offering a distinctive and significant contribution to the doctrine of God in the context of late thirteenth century critiques of Aristotelianism. Among other things, Henry recognized more fully that any of his predecessors that Aristotelian arguments from motion, particularly in their original form, do not yield as a necessary conclusion that there is only one God. Henry therefore preferred a Platonic understanding of God and, beyond that, the metaphysics of Avicenna.[18]

Beginning with the monographs of Seeberg and Minges, Duns Scotus' theology has gradually come to be viewed as a positive and constructive rather than as a purely critical work destructive of the thirteenth-century synthesis of theology and philosophy.[19] Recent scholarship, most notably that of Allan Wolter and Antonie Vos, has directed increasingly positive attention to Duns Scotus' doctrine of God.[20] Similarly, the theology of William of Ockham, once viewed as a negative and excessively critical influence on Christian doctrine, has been significantly reappraised in recent years, and the philosophical side of his doctrine of God has been minutely examined.[21] Among other studies of the thinkers of the later Middle Ages, Hoenen's work on Marsilius of Inghen on divine knowledge offers a considerable advance in the discussion and, from our perspective here, an analysis of a major element of the medieval background to Reformation and post-Reformation views of the *scientia Dei*, particularly with reference the distinction of divine attributes, the extent of divine knowledge, and the problem of the divine foreknowledge of future contingents.[22]

---

18. J. Paulus, *Henri de Gand. Essai sur les tendances de sa métaphysique* (Paris: J. Vrin, 1938); Anton Pegis, "Toward a New Way to God: Henry of Ghent," in *Medieval Studies*, 30 (1968), pp. 226-247, and 31 (1969), pp. 93-116; idem, "Four Medieval Ways to God," in *Monist*, 54 (1970), pp. 317-358; idem, "Four Medieval Ways to God," in *Monist*, 54 (1970), pp. 317-358.

19. Reinhold Seeberg, *Die Theologie des Johannes Duns Scotus. Eine dogmengeschichtliche untersuchung* (Leipzig: Dieterich, 1900); Parthenius Minges, *Der Gottesbegriff des Duns Scotus* (Vienna, 1907); and idem, *Ioannis Duns Scoti Doctrina Philosophica et Theologica*, 2 vols. (Quaracchi: Collegium S. Bonaventurae, 1930).

20. Allan B. Wolter, "Duns Scotus on the Existence and Nature of God," in *Proceedings of the American Catholic Philosophical Association*, XXVIII (1954), pp. 94-121; idem, "Duns Scotus on the Natural Desire for the Supernatural," in *The New Scholasticism*, XXIII (1949), pp. 281-317; idem, "Duns Scotus on the Nature of Man's Knowledge of God," in *Review of Metaphysics*, 1/2 (Dec. 1947), pp. 3-36; idem, "The 'Theologism' of Duns Scotus," in *Fransiscan Studies*, 7 (1947), pp. 257-273, 367-414; idem, *The Transcendentals and Their Function in the Metaphysics of Duns Scotus* (St. Bonaventure, New York: The Franciscan Institute, 1946); Allan B. Wolter and Marilyn McCord Adams, *The Philosophical Theology of John Duns Scotus* (Ithaca: Cornell University Press, 1990).

21. Gordon Leff, *William of Ockham: The Metamorphosis of Scholastic Discourse* (Manchester: The University Press, 1975); Marylin McCord Adams, *William Ockham*, 2 vols. (Notre Dame: University of Notre Dame Press, 1987); Armand Maurer, *The Philosophy of William of Ockham in the Light of Its Principles* (Toronto: Pontifical Institute of Mediaeval Studies, 1999); also note Allan B. Wolter, "Ockham and the Textbooks: On the Origin of Possibility," in *Franziskanische Studien*, 32 (1950), pp. 70-96.

22. M. J. F. M. Hoenen, *Marsilius of Inghen: Divine Knowledge in Late Medieval Thought* (Leiden: E. J. Brill, 1993).

There are also a host of essays on various problems debated in the doctrine of God from the twelfth through the fourteenth centuries — like those of Sweeney, Wass, and Catania on divine infinity,[23] the essays by several authors on the problem of the *potentia Dei absoluta* and *potentia Dei ordinata*,[24] studies of individual divine attributes and the implications of language about them,[25] and numerous studies of the doctrine of God in the work of various medieval theologians.[26] Sweeney, in particular, must be noted as having shown that the notion of divine infinity cannot simply be taken for granted as characteristic of traditional Christian theism — and that it was the subject of intense discussion in the thirteenth century, with some theologians positing

---

23. Leo Sweeney, "Divine Infinity, 1150-1250," in *The Modern Schoolman*, 35 (1957-1958), pp. 38-51; idem, "Divine Infinity in the Writings of Thomas Aquinas" (Ph.D. diss.: University of Toronto, 1954); idem, "Lombard, Augustine and Infinity," in *Manuscripta*, 9 (1958), pp. 24-40; idem, "Some Medieval Opponents of Divine Infinity," in *Medieval Studies*, 19 (1957), pp. 233-245; also Leo Sweeney and Charles Ermatinger, "Divine Infinity according to Robert Fishacre," in *The Modern Schoolman*, 35 (1957-1958), pp. 191-235; Sweeney's essays are gathered together in his *Divine Infinity in Greek and Medieval Thought* (New York: Peter Lang, 1992); Meldon C. Wass, *The Infinite God and the Summa Fratris Alexandri* (Chicago: Franciscan Herald Press, 1964); F. L. Catania, "Divine Infinity in Albert the Great's Commentary on the Sentences of Peter Lombard," in *Medieval Studies*, 22 (1960), pp. 27-42.

24. E. g., Heiko A. Oberman, "Some Notes on the Theology of Nominalism with Attention to Its Relation to the Renaissance," in *Harvard Theological Review*, 53 (1960), pp. 47-76; Francis Oakley, "Pierre D'Ailly and the Absolute Power of God: Another Note on the Theology of Nominalism," in *Harvard Theological Review*, 56 (1963), pp. 59-73; Felix Alluntis and Allan B. Wolter, "Duns Scotus on the Omnipotence of God," in *Stud Phil Hist Phil*, 5 (1970), pp. 178-222; M. A. Pernoud, "The Theory of the *Potentia Dei* according to Aquinas, Scotus and Ockham," in *Antonianum*, 47 (1972), pp. 69-95; Kathleen Ashley, "Divine Power in the Chester Cycle and Late Medieval Thought," in *Journal of the History of Ideas*, 39 (1978), pp. 387-404; Edward Grant, "The Condemnation of 1277, God's Absolute Power and Physical Thought in the Late Middle Ages," in *Viator*, 10 (1979), pp. 211-244; Laurence Eldredge, "The Concept of God's Absolute Power in the Later Fourteenth Century," in *By Things Seen: Reference and Recognition in Medieval Thought* (Ottawa: University of Ottawa Press, 1979), ed. David L. Jeffrey (1979), pp. 211-226.

25. Armand Maurer, "John of Jandun and the Divine Causality," in *Medieval Studies*, 17 (1955), pp. 185-207; Girard J. Etzkorn, "John Reading on the Existence and Unicity of God, Efficient and Final Causality," in *Fransiscan Studies*, 41 (1981), pp. 110-221; Matthew J. Kelly, "John Went, O. F. M., and Divine Omnipotence," in *Franciscan Studies*, 47 (1987), pp. 138-170; idem, "Power in Aquinas," in *The Thomist*, 43 (1979), pp. 474-479; Leonard A. Kennedy, "Divine Omnipotence and the Contingency of Creatures, Oxford, 1330-1350 A.D.," in *The Modern Schoolman*, 61 (1983/84), pp. 249-258.

26. E.g., A. John Badcock, "Aspects of the Medieval Idea of God," in *London Quarterly and Holborn Review*, 177 (1952), pp. 86-97; Ebeling, "Hermeneutical Locus of the Doctrine of God," pp. 70-111; Konrad Fischer, "Hinweise zur Gotteslehre Bonaventuras," in Alphonso Pompei, ed. *San Bonaventura Maestro di Vita Francescana e di Sapienza Cristiana*, 3 vols. (Rome: Pontifica Facolta Teologica San Bonaventura, 1976), vol. I, pp. 513-525; L. Hodl, "Die philosophische Gotteslehre des Thomas von Aquin, O.P. in der Diskussion der Schulen um die Wende des 13. zum 14. Jahrhundert," in *Rivista di Filosofia Neo-scholastica*, 70 (1978), pp. 113-134; Mark G. Henninger, "Henry of Harclay's Questions on Divine Prescience and Predestination," in *Franciscan Studies*, 40 (1980), pp. 167-243; Etzkorn, "John Reading on the Existence and Unicity of God,", pp. 110-221; Hankey, *God in Himself: Aquinas' Doctrine of God*.

a finite divine essence in view of the association of infinitude with quantity and, therefore, from an Aristotelian perspective, with imperfection.[27]

Unfortunately, the theology of the Reformation and post-Reformation Protestantism has been less well served on such matters than that of the Middle Ages. The doctrine of God is discussed, of course, in the various studies of major Reformers like Luther,[28] Zwingli,[29] and Calvin;[30] and there are essays on the doctrine of God as taught by these and other Reformation-era thinkers.[31] In the case of Calvin, the most extended discussion the doctrine of God is still the study by Warfield. Together with the companion essays on Calvin's doctrines of the knowledge of God and of the Trinity, it constitutes a major monographic effort still to be reckoned with.[32] Nonetheless, with a few notable exceptions, the continuity and discontinuity between Reformation and medieval concepts of God has been seldom studied in depth.[33]

Studies of the doctrine of God developed by post-Reformation Protestant thinkers remain relatively few, given the number of thinkers and span of years to be discussed — and they divide into three basic categories. First, there is an older scholarship characterized by dogmatic generalization and use of the nineteenth-century central

---

27. Sweeney, Divine Infinity, pp. 337-63.

28. Julius Köstlin, The Theology of Luther in its Historical Development and Inner Harmony, 2 vols. trans. Charles E. Hay (Philadelphia: Lutheran Publication Society, 1897; repr. St. Louis: Concordia, 1986); Paul Althaus, The Theology of Martin Luther, trans. Robert C. Schultz (Philadelphia: Fortress, 1966).

29. Gottfried W. Locher, Die Theologie Huldrych Zwinglis im Lichte seiner Christologie, I, Die Gotteslehre (Zürich: EVZ Verlag, 1952); W. P. Stephens, The Theology of Huldrych Zwingli (Oxford: Clarendon Press, 1986).

30. Émile Doumergue, Jean Calvin, les hommes et les choses de son temps, 7 vols. (Lausanne: G. Bridel, 1899-1917); Wilhelm Niesel, The Theology of Calvin, trans. Harold Knight (London: Lutterworth, 1956; repr. Grand Rapids: Baker Book House, 1980); François Wendel, Calvin: The Origins and Development of His Religious Thought, trans. Philip Mairét (N.Y.: Harper and Row, 1963).

31. E.g., R. T. L. Liston, "John Calvin's Doctrine of the Sovereignty of God" (Ph.D. diss.: University of Edinburgh, 1930); John Murray, Calvin on Scripture and Divine Sovereignty (Grand Rapids: Eerdmans, 1960); Garret A. Wilterdink, "Irresistible Grace and the Fatherhood of God in Calvin's Theology." Ph.D. dissertation, University of Chicago, 1974; idem, "The Fatherhood of God in Calvin's Thought," in Reformed Review, 30/1 (fall 1976), pp. 9-22; idem, Tyrant or Father? A Study of Calvin's Doctrine of God, 2 vols. (Bristol, In.: Wyndham Hall Press, 1985); Richard Kyle, "The Divine Attributes in John Knox's Concept of God," in Westminster Theological Journal, 48/1 (1986), pp. 161-172.

32. Benjamin Breckinridge Warfield, "Calvin's Doctrine of the Knowledge of God," "Calvin's Doctrine of God," and "Calvin's Doctrine of the Trinity," in Samuel Craig (ed.), Calvin and Augustine, (Philadelphia: Presbyterian and Reformed Publishing Company, 1956), pp. 29-130, 133-185, 189-284.

33. E. g., Otto Hermann Pesch, The God Question in Thomas Aquinas and Martin Luther, trans. Gottfried Kroedel (Philadelphia: Fortress, 1972); David C. Steinmetz, "Calvin and the Absolute Power of God," in Calvin in Context (New York: Oxford University Press, 1995), pp. 40-52; Susan E. Schreiner, "Exegesis and Double Justice in Calvin's Sermons on Job," in Church History, 58 (1918), pp. 322-338; idem, Where Shall Wisdom be Found? Calvin's Exegesis of Job from Medieval and Modern Perspectives (Chicago: University of Chicago Press, 1994).

dogma theory,[34] in which writers like Beza and Zanchi have been described as formulators of deductive system of doctrine contrary to the tendencies of Reformation thought. There are also studies of a more philosophical interest not typically rooted in the generalizations of the older dogmatic scholarship in which the works of the seventeenth-century Reformed are examined,[35] and there is, third, the recent scholarship of reappraisal, that pays more attention to the historical context and the rather diverse background of the documents, and that has set aside the central dogma model.[36] There is a clear overlap between the latter two categories. There is also a survey of the Lutheran doctrine of God in the era of orthodoxy,[37] with no comparable analogue in studies of Reformed orthodoxy.

There is also a sizeable body of work on the history of philosophy that has bearing on the subject. Wolfson's study of Spinoza remains the most detailed analysis of any particular thinker's doctrine of God in the seventeenth-century![38] Here, again, there is far better coverage devoted to the philosophers of the seventeenth century and, unfortunately, this literature seldom examines the theology of the age either as a

---

34. Cf. Otto Gründler, "Thomism and Calvinism in the Theology of Girolamo Zanchi, 1516-1590," (Th.D. dissertation, Princeton Theological Seminary, 1961); and idem, *Die Gotteslehre Girolami Zanchis und ihre Bedeutung für seine Lehre von der Prädestination* (Neukirchen: Neukirchner Verlag, 1965); Heiner Faulenbach, *Die Struktur der Theologie des Amandus Polanus von Polansdorf* (Zurich: EVZ Verlag, 1967); and note the relevant chapter in Antonie Hendrik Haentjens, *Remonstrantsche en calvinistische dogmatiek: in verband met elkaar en met de ontwikkeling van het dogma* (Leiden: A.H. Adriani, 1913).

35. Frederik Gerrit Immink, *Divine Simplicity* (Kampen: J. Kok, 1987); Gijsbert van den Brink, *Almighty God: A Study of the Doctrine of Divine Omnipotence* (Kampen: J. Kok, 1993); Luco Johan van den Brom, *Divine Presence in the World: a Critical Analysis of the Notion of Divine Omnipresence* (Kampen: Kok Pharos, 1993); and note the essays in Gijsbert van den Brink and Marcel Sarot eds., *Understanding the Attributes of God* (Frankfurt: Peter Lang, 1999); Aza Goudriaan, *Philosophische Gotteserkenntnis bei Suárez und Descartes in Zusammenhang mit die niederländischen reformierten Theologie und Philosophie des 17, Jahrhunderts* (Leiden: E. J. Brill, 1999); idem, "Die Rezeption des cartesianischen Gottesdankens bei Abraham Heidanus," in *Neue Zeitschrift für systematische Theologie und Religionsphilosophie*, 38/2 (1996), pp. 166-197.

36. John Platt, *Reformed Thought and Scholasticism: The Arguments for the Existence of God in Dutch Theology, 1575-1650* (Leiden: Brill, 1982); Richard A. Muller, *God, Creation and Providence in the Thought of Jacob Arminius: Sources and Directions of Scholastic Protestantism in the Era of Early Orthodoxy* (Grand Rapids: Baker Book House, 1991); Carl R. Trueman, *The Claims of Truth: John Owen's trinitarian Theology* (Carlisle: Paternoster Press, 1998); idem, "John Owen's *Dissertation on Divine Justice*: An Exercise in Christocentric Scholasticism," in *Calvin Theological Journal*, 33 (1998), pp. 87-103; Andreas Beck, "Gisbertus Voetius (1589-1676): Basic Features of His Doctrine of God," in Willem Van Asselt and Eef Dekker, eds., *Reformation and Scholasticism: An Ecumenical Enterprise* (Grand Rapids: Baker Book House, 2001), pp. 205-226; Harm J. M. J. Goris, "Thomism and Zanchi's Doctrine of God," in ibid., pp. 125-126.

37. Robert D. Preus, *The Theology of Post-Reformation Lutheranism*, 2 vols. (St. Louis: Concordia, 1970-1972), vol. 2, pp. 52-163. Note also the selection of texts in Heinrich Schmid, *Doctrinal Theology of the Evangelical Lutheran Church*, trans. Charles E. Hay and Henry Jacobs (Minneapolis: Augsburg, n.d.).

38. Harry Austryn Wolfson, *The Philosophy of Spinoza*, 2 vols. (Cleveland and New York: World, 1958).

backdrop or as a dialogue partner of the philosophy, despite the clear interrelationship of the theological and philosophical literature of the era. Jolley's philosophically excellent essay in the recent *Cambridge History of Seventeenth-Century Philosophy* is a case in point: despite its intention to discuss the relationship of the seventeenth-century philosophers to theology, virtually no theologians of the era are mentioned.[39]

B. The Doctrine of God in Reformed Orthodoxy: Toward a Thesis

1. The general problem: identifying trajectories, continuities, and discontinuities. It can be argued with significant reference to this body of secondary literature that the historical problem of the doctrine of God in its development from the Middle Ages to the Reformation and post-Reformation eras has not only been studied partially but has also, because of the partial character of the study, not been sufficiently or clearly analyzed in terms of the great doctrinal continuities or, indeed, in terms of the genuine changes and discontinuities that both characterize its development. Most studies of the medieval doctrine of God have emphasized the philosophical and speculative character of the doctrine, with comparatively little interest in the traditionary elements that carried over from the patristic into the medieval period and with virtually no interest in the relationship between doctrinal or systematic theological formulation and the history of exegesis. By contrast, the few studies that have appeared dealing with the doctrine of God during the Reformation have tended to ignore the traditionary elements, to emphasize the relationship of Protestant teaching to Scripture (without, however, clear reference to the continuities of the exegetical tradition), and to stress in addition the early Reformation antipathy to scholastic argumentation and to philosophy. The majority of discussions of the Protestant orthodox doctrine of God have taken as their point of departure the rise of scholastic method, the return of a more positive approach to and use of philosophy, and therefore the contrast between the doctrine of the Reformers and that of the Protestant scholastics — without any examination of the exegetical tradition employed by the Reformers and by their scholastic successors and, in addition, without any detailed comparison of the Protestant with the medieval scholastics with a view to continuities and discontinuities in method and in doctrinal formulation.

When these neglected factors of tradition and exegesis are taken into consideration and, moreover, when the Protestant scholastic doctrine of God is compared not only to the teaching of the Reformers but also, in some detail, to that of the medieval doctors, several previously unnoticed but highly significant points can be made concerning both the development of the doctrine of God and the nature and character of Protestant scholastic theology. First, an underlying agreement in the interpretation of numerous key biblical *loci* appears and, with it, a strong element of continuity between medieval, Reformation, and post-Reformation theology. Second, it becomes

---

39. Nicholas Jolley, "The Relation Between Theology and Philosophy," in Daniel Garber and Michael Ayers (eds.), *Cambridge History of Seventeenth-Century Philosophy*, 2 vols. (Cambridge: Cambridge University Press, 1998), I, pp. 363-392.

apparent that, despite the clear methodological differences between the work of the Reformers and that of their successors brought on by the reintroduction of scholastic method, the theology of the Protestant orthodox held for the most part quite firmly to the exegetical tradition of which the Reformers were a part.

Third, the comparison of Protestant with medieval scholasticism indicates that the Protestant theologians of the late sixteenth and of the seventeenth century did not simply return to a form of medieval scholasticism. Scholastic method had itself altered and developed during the fourteenth, fifteenth, and sixteenth centuries — and, what is more, the Protestant scholastics retained in their theology both an element of the Reformation distrust for philosophical speculation and a high degree of concern for the biblical basis of theology. As indicated in the first part of this study, the Protestant scholastics adopted the terms "scholastic" and "scholasticism" advisedly, identifying them with a particular disputative form and method of theology used in the academic context and distinct from exegesis, catechetics, and even "positive" doctrinal exposition. Accordingly, the philosophical or metaphysical elements of their doctrine of God evidence an eclectic approach to philosophy and an effort, paralleled by the work of the academic philosophers and logicians of the era, to develop a contemporary philosophy in dialogue with theology. This philosophy can be called "Christian Aristotelianism" only with qualification: specifically, the Reformed thinkers of the era of orthodoxy engaged in an ongoing debate and dialogue with the older tradition, its late Renaissance manifestations, with various classical options — notably Platonism, Stoicism, and Epicureanism — that had been revived in the Renaissance, and with the newer forms of skepticism and deism born in the sixteenth century. Declamations made in the sixteenth and seventeenth centuries against classical philosophies and, equally, appeals to them ought to be understood as encounters with contemporary problems.[40]

Attention to the exegetical tradition, moreover, carries forward one of the central methodological and theological themes of this study considered as a whole. In the second volume, we examined the doctrine of Scripture not only from a dogmatic or systematic perspective but also, as indicated by the scholastic Protestant theological systems themselves, from an interpretive or hermeneutical perspective. By continuing to examine the issue of biblical interpretation, now through the lens of the doctrine of God, we are in a position to examine both the relationship between the Protestant doctrine of Scripture and the rest of theological system and the impact of the hermeneutical aspects of the Protestant doctrine of Scripture on doctrinal formulation in the era of Protestant orthodoxy in general.

Just as exegesis must not be ignored, so also must the relation of theology to piety, particularly as indicated in the dogmatic works of Protestant orthodox theologians and carried forward in the homiletical literature, not be forgotten. The dogmatics of post-Reformation Protestantism did not develop in a vacuum and was not formulated simply for the sake of classroom exercises in speculative thinking — it was a churchly

---

40. Cf. *PRRD*, I, 1.3 (A.4-5); 4.1 (B); 8.1 (A-C).

dogmatics that reflected the concerns of religion. This characteristic of the orthodox dogmatics is most clearly evidenced in the Dutch and English theology of the late sixteenth and the seventeenth centuries, and to the extent that Heppe, for example, cites thinkers like Mastricht from a purely dogmatic perspective, without clear indication of their consistent interest in the direct relation of the doctrine of the divine essence, attributes, and Trinity to piety, the older Protestant doctrine of God has been misrepresented. Even so, to the extent that older scholarship has ignored both the positive, integral relationship of Reformed orthodoxy in the Netherlands to the piety of the *Nadere Reformatie*, the so-called Dutch Second Reformation, and the relationship of the central, Reformed trajectory of English Puritanism to continental Reformed theology, the close relationship between dogma and piety that existed, sometimes in tension, but often in profound and mutually supportive formulation, has been overlooked and ignored, again misrepresenting the nature and character of Reformed orthodoxy. In this relationship, moreover, the orthodox writers illustrate their more typical definitions of theology as either both practical and speculative or as largely practical: their interest in the piety of the attributes arises directly from their sense of theology as a discipline directed toward the goal of salvation.[41]

2. **Some specifics.** The doctrine of God taught by Reformed Protestants in the sixteenth and seventeenth centuries presents a diverse and varied trajectory. Examination of the materials of the history demonstrates that, contrary to the typical perception of the secondary literature, the orthodox or scholastic theology of the era did not have a monolithic structure. Given the diversity of the materials, moreover, the trajectories that lead from the later Middle Ages through the Reformation into the era of orthodoxy also manifest diversity and subtleties in transmission and development — a point that appears to have been lost on much of the older scholarship.

An example that will be addressed at the very outset of the topical section of this study is the use of arguments for the existence of God where, contrary to much received opinion, the Reformers did not scorn the issue and the later orthodox did not revert to a purely Thomistic exposition of the five ways. Rather both the Reformers' and the later orthodox writers' use of these arguments offers evidence of the changing patterns of logic and rhetoric characteristic of the movement from the later Middle Ages into the Renaissance — parallel to the relative shift from the demonstrative mode of the medieval disputation and *quaestio* to the more rhetorically-couched form of *loci communes*.[42]

Theologians within the Reformed orthodox camp also differed concerning the order and organization of the divine attributes — as they did concerning the nature and character of the attribution itself. Specifically, they neither universally followed the pattern of incommunicable and communicable attributes typically identified as the standard older paradigm nor did they agree among themselves on the nature of the

---

41. Cf. *PRRD*, I, 7.3 (A-B).

42. See the discussion in Richard A. Muller, *The Unaccommodated Calvin: Studies in the Formation of a Theological Tradition* (New York: Oxford University Press, 2000), pp. 102-111; and *PRRD*, I, 4.1 (A.1).

distinctions within the Godhead indicated by the attributes and the persons of the Trinity. There was not universal agreement over the meaning of divine simplicity.

There are also a series of issues related to the doctrine of God on which there was a high degree of consistency among the Reformed orthodoxy but also on which the standard wisdom of the secondary literature has entirely missed the point of the sixteenth- and seventeenth-century discussion. By way of example: we do not find here a doctrine of an unrelated deity. The doctrine of eternity expressed by the Reformed orthodox does not readily characterize as a doctrine of divine timelessness, under the terms of which an everlastingly changeless and atemporal being does not relate directly to the temporal order. The older orthodox doctrine of eternity not only posits a radical relationship of God to the world, it also assumes the immediate and intimate relationship of God to temporal beings. Rather than identifying God as "timeless," it argues that God encompasses time. On an equally striking note, the Reformed orthodox conception of divine impassibility does not argue a God who lacks love, mercy, anger, hate, or (indeed!) pleasure, but who has all of these relations to the world order. The exclusion of "passions" from the divine being never implied the absence of "affections."

Not only does the older orthodox assume the relationship between eternal God and his world, and argue it in terms of a substantial series of divine affections, it also assumes (contrary to much received "wisdom") that God is utterly free in his willing — fully capable of not willing to create the world and, willing to create, fully capable of willing a world entirely different from the one that we have, albeit equally good. This conception of the radical divine freedom is certainly part of the late medieval heritage and, as in the case of the medieval language of *potentia Dei absoluta*, it carries with it epistemological as well as ontological implications, notably the limitation of the powers of reason to deal with questions concerning the nature and the work of God.

Finally, in virtually all aspects of the doctrinal exposition, the sixteenth- and seventeenth-century Reformed writers evidence a significant interrelation, even interplay, between the doctrine of God and the other topics of their theology. The identification of God as the *principium essendi* of theology, far from generating a theological system deduced from the doctrine of God, actually produced a theological system in consistent dialogue with the doctrine of God, often to the extent that aspects of the doctrine of God derive from concerns at the heart of other *loci*, notably Christology, soteriology, and eschatology.

1.2 Scripture, Tradition, and Philosophy in the Scholastic Doctrine of God

A. The Early Scholastic Contribution: From Anselm of Canterbury to Peter Lombard

1. Lines of historical development. The scholastic doctrine of God — of the divine essence, attributes, and Trinity — had its beginnings in the theology of the late eleventh and early twelfth centuries, most notably in the work of Anselm of Canterbury. Before Anselm, Western theology possessed all of the elements of its doctrine of God: it knew the language of divine essence, it understood the concept of divine simplicity, it could draw on a lengthy list of divine attributes argued by the way of negation (*via negationis*) and by the way of eminence (*via eminentiae*), and it had at its disposal a massive structure of trinitarian argumentation. All of this had been passed on to the teachers of the Middle Ages in the writings of the fathers. The patristic materials, however, were hardly systematized. Of the great patristic thinkers, only Origen had attempted anything like a cohesive theological system — and his *De Principiis*, both because of its early date (ca. 230 A.D) and because of the highly individualistic character of its speculations, failed to provide the church with a normative statement of Christian doctrine. From Augustine, the Middle Ages received a vast but not always clearly organized source of formulations concerning the Godhead, its essence, and its attributes and, of course, trinitarian language. What Anselm attempted, in the late eleventh and early twelfth century, was to draw together the threads of patristic teaching — chiefly the teaching of Augustine — into a coherent fabric.

Anselm's efforts, in the *Monologium*, the *Proslogium*, and the treatise *On the Procession of the Holy Spirit against the Greeks*, all follow a logical or dialectical path toward a statement of doctrine based not — as was the usual pattern — on the authority of Scripture and tradition without any distinction being made between the traditio-exegetical and the dogmatic task, but on a rational exposition of the logic of the doctrine and its constituent concepts. Anselm clearly identified the dogmatic task as the rational argumentation of a doctrinal point. This point is important inasmuch as Anselm himself did not offer a clearly stated distinction between *sacra pagina* and *sacra theologia* as would his successors,[43] although it is obvious that Scripture is the ultimate norm for doctrine in his theology and that both the truths directly expressed in Scripture and those that arise by necessary conclusions from examining the text are to be "received with certainty."[44]

There is no small irony in the continuing interest in Anselm's great treatises, the *Monologion* and the *Proslogion*, as repositories of proofs of the existence of God, inasmuch as the treatises, although they do contain significant attempts to formulate such proofs and, in the case of the *Proslogion*, the uniquely Anselmic ontological argument, are primarily treatises on the logic of the doctrine of God. The preface or prologue to the *Monologion* offered numerous works of the subsequent generations, including Lombard's *Sentences*, the many commentaries on it, and the great *summas* of the thirteenth century, a foundational insight into the object and method of theology.[45] The intention, indeed, of both of Anselm's treatises on God is to draw together into a coherent whole the issues of the divine existence, essence, attributes

---

43. On this distinction, see PRRD, II, 1.2 (A.2; B.1).

44. Anselm, *De processione Spiritus Sancti*, ii, in *Opera*, II, p. 209; and see the discussion in Jasper Hopkins, *A Companion to the Study of St. Anselm* (Minneapolis: University of Minnesota Press, 1972), pp. 46-48.

45. Cf. Ebeling, "Hermeneutical Locus of the Doctrine of God," pp. 85-87.

and trinity— to identify the fundamental purpose of theological discourse as a meditation on the nature of God, whether considered "absolutely" as such in the thought of Alexander of Hales, Bonaventure, Aquinas, and Duns Scotus or considered "relatively" as Creator, Redeemer, and Glorifier in the work of such thinkers as Giles of Rome, Gregory of Rimini, and Durandus of Sancto Porciano.[46]

Thus, the impact of these treatises on the development of scholastic doctrine was in the codification and internal argumentation of the doctrine of God, including, of course, the proofs, but going far beyond them, indeed, identifying their context within the doctrine of God and manifesting the logic and interrelation of the various elements of the doctrine as a whole. Even those, like Aquinas, who did not accept Anselm's ontological argument, stand in the line of his influence on the nature of language about God and, in particular, the assumption that God is what he has and that the essence of God is such that God must exist. In addition, the argumentation of both treatises determined the shape of the *locus* on God for one of the major trajectories of theological system: an argument beginning with the fact of God and proceeding toward the faithful contemplation of God as Trinity.

Although Anselm's genius certainly assured the ultimate victory of philosophical realism in the debates of the eleventh and twelfth centuries, the outcome was not, at the time, sufficiently clear nor was the superiority of Realism sufficiently manifest to prevent alternative views from appearing and from having their influence, whether positive or negative, on the formulation of doctrine. Two controversies of the twelfth century exemplify the diversity of early scholastic formulation and the need, perceived by many of the teachers of the era, to establish a normative language concerning God and the attributes. The earlier of these two debates concerned Abelard's views on the relationship between God's goodness and the work of creation, as addressed by the Synods of Soissons (1121) and Sens (1140). The second debate was over the view of the divine essence and attributes reportedly advanced by Gilbert de la Porrée and condemned at the synods of Paris (1147) and Rheims (1148).

In reaction to the heightened realism of the school of Chartres and its conception of creation as an emanation out of the divine, Abelard argued a clear distinction between God and world in creation and identified creation as the result and the revelation of God's goodness. This fundamentally orthodox corrective to the pantheistic tendencies of the day led Abelard, however, to a series of conclusions that challenged the concept of God's freedom in creation: given that God is absolutely good and must always, therefore, act for the best, he must create the world and, in fact, must create this particular world: Abelard states explicitly that "it is necessary that God wills and makes the world, nor does he exist at leisure, like one who, before he makes [something] is able not to make it."[47] Attacked by the Cistercians Bernard of Clairvaux and William of St. Thierry, Abelard's views were condemned at the Synods of Sens

---

46. Chossat, "Dieu. Sa nature selon les scolastiques," col. 1153-1154.

47. Peter Abelard, *Theologia christiana*, V, in J. P. Migne, ed. *Patrologia Latina Cursus Completus* [hereinafter *PL*], 221 vols. (Paris: Vivès, 1844-55), vol. 187, col. 1321; cf. Leo Scheffczyk, *Creation and Providence* (New York: Herder and Herder, 1970), p. 127.

and Soissons. Subsequent medieval approaches to the question insisted on the freedom of God and, consequently, the contingency of the world order.

Of particular importance to the development of the scholastic doctrine of God was the controversy surrounding the teaching of Gilbert de la Porrée concerning the distinction of persons and of attributes in the Godhead. Gilbert, a student and follower of Anselm who was bishop of Poitiers from 1142 to 1154, was construed by his contemporaries as teaching that the divine persons and the divine attributes, as representing distinct ideas in the mind that conceives them, must also be distinct within the divine essence. Specifically, in raising via Boethius the question of the relationship of goodness and being, Gilbert had recourse to the formula *diversum est esse, et id quod est* — existence is different from what a thing is, or, existence is different from essence. Gilbert, following out the distinction, was reported as making a real distinction between essence and existence, even in God, and as positing real distinctions between one and another divine attribute, between each of the attributes and the divine essence, among the persons, and between each of the persons and the divine essence. His critics concluded that he had taught that God was a composite being.[48]

The Synod of Paris (1147) condemned a series of propositions attributed to Gilbert on the basis of reports of his commentary on Boethius' *De Trinitate*. Inasmuch as Gilbert claimed to have understood Boethius differently and inasmuch as the council did not have direct access to his book, the abbot Gottschalk of St. Eligius was commissioned to review the book and document its erroneous propositions. Gilbert, in his turn, was able to demonstrate how his own understanding of the propositions was not at all heretical and thereby to avoid condemnation: he did not, he argued, extend the logic of a distinction between essence and existence to infinite Being, who has his being according to his essence and not by participation. God is simple Being and is all that he has: it is not merely the case that God is powerful and wise, God is his power and is his wisdom. Gilbert escaped condemnation but, as Chossat points out, failed to resolve the basic question of the basis for making distinctions among divine attributes.[49]

More importantly, the problems posed by the debate over Gilbert's theology became a focus of further discussion at the Synod of Rheims (1148), which, in the presence of Pope Eugene III, affirmed as dogma a series of propositions formulated by Bernard of Clairvaux, heard further explanations and retractions from Gilbert, and thereby formalized the outlines of the doctrine of divine simplicity in its relationship to the fundamental trinitarian definitions. The conciliar decision is not a matter of abstruse speculation and is certainly not a denial of any and all manner of distinctions in God. The propositions of the council stand primarily as arguments that (1) there may be no distinction between divinity and God such as might imply that God was one being in a genus and therefore somehow subordinate to the idea of Deity, (2) that the threeness of person does not divide the divine essence or substance, (3) that the various relations or properties — that is, personal or essential properties — associated with

---

48. Cf. "Gilbert de la Porrée," s.v. in *Dictionnaire de théologie catholique*; with Schwane, *Histoire des Dogmes*, IV, p. 191; and with Chossat, "Dieu. Sa nature selon les scolastiques," cols. 1165-7.

49. Chossat, "Dieu. Sa nature selon les scolastiques," col. 1166.

God are not separable from God, and (4) that incarnation does not divide the Godhead.[50] The council, therefore, hedged the concept of divine simplicity both positively and negatively — positively as an affirmation of the absolute ultimacy and priority of God and negatively as a concept that neither undermines the threeness of the Trinity nor prevents the identification of attributes in God.

The medieval conciliar teaching did not extend beyond the teaching already present in the writings of the fathers.[51] Specifically, with relation to the problem of the predication of divine attributes, the issue remained precisely where the Christian Platonism of the fathers has placed it: the divine attributes, considered as ultimate exemplars of the good, the true, the righteous, and so forth, could no longer be understood as ideas having a real existence *extra mentem Dei* and, therefore, prior to God, as would have been the case with the Platonic Demiurge. So, too, the eternal exemplars of temporal things must subsist *in mente Dei* and must subsist in such as way as to respect the ultimacy of God as the source of all that is and, therefore, of all that is good, or true, or righteous, and so forth.[52]

The next major stage in the formulation of the medieval doctrine of God appears in the work of the various writers of "summas" and books of "sentences": in the mid-twelfth century, Honorius of Autun, Hugh of St. Victor, Peter of Poitiers, Robert Pulleyn, Alain of Lille, and Peter Lombard moved to codify the topical discussion of theology (as distinct from the running commentary or "gloss") into a separate course of study. Whereas Hugh of St. Victor's *De sacramentis* and *Summa sententiarum* adopted a fundamentally neo-platonic approach to the doctrine of God and world, understanding the creation as an emanation of being out of God and developing his doctrine of God by way of God's self-manifestation in creation and redemption, Lombard's *Sentences* begins with the doctrine of God, returning to the Anselmic sense of God as the primary object of theology but with far fewer Platonic or neoplatonic emphases than either Anselm or Hugh.[53] Where Lombard differs methodologically from several of his most important predecessors, like Anselm and Hugh, is in his emphasis on the rootage of doctrine directly in Scripture and the fathers: his work stands as a theological textbook that emphasizes the sources of theology and derives all discourse from them rather than develop a more speculative or philosophical approach to the materials. This methodological difference may also account for a difference in order of discussion: Lombard departs from the method of Anselm by

---

50. In Bernard of Clairvaux, *Libellus contra capitulum Gilberti*, in PL, 185, col. 609; cf. Schwane, *Histoire des Dogmes*, IV, p. 193. For the trinitarian implications of the argument and the text of the propositions, see *PRRD*, IV, 1.2 (A.4).

51. Thus, e.g., Gregory of Nyssa, *Orat.cat.* praef., in Migne, J. P., ed. *Patrologia Graeca Cursus Completus* [hereinafter, *PG*], 161 vols. (Paris: Vives, 1857-66), vol. 45, col. 12); Augustine, *Ennarationes in Psalmos*, CXXXIV.3-4; *De civitate Dei*, XI.x.2-3; *Sermo* 341, cap. 6.8.

52. Cf. F. G. Immink, *Divine Simplicity* (Kampen: J. H. Kok, 1987), p. 61 with William P. Tolley, *The Idea of God in the Philosophy of Saint Augustine* (New York: R. R. Smith, 1930), p. 44.

53. On the development of "systematic theology" in the twelfth century, see Marcia L. Colish, *Medieval Foundations of the Western Intellectual Tradition, 400-1400* (New Haven and London: Yale University Press, 1997), pp. 277-288.

beginning his doctrine of God with the doctrine of the Trinity and the discussion of concepts of essence and attributes folding into the discourse as a whole.[54] In Lombard's model, the Augustinian distinction between sign and thing, *signum* and *res*, provided the argumentative shape for the entirety of his theological presentation in the *Sentences*. The result of this approach was, among other things, the integration of theological and philosophical questions in the doctrine of God, the understanding of God as the ultimate reality (*summa res*) and the fruition of all things, and, therefore, of the doctrine of God as the foundational statement and interpretive key for all subsequent theological discourse.[55]

2. The divine attributes in early scholastic theology. We can potentially distinguish two approaches to the medieval discussion of divine attributes — again representing the difference between Anselm's and Lombard's methods. In the case of Anselm's theology, whether in the *Monologion* or the *Prosolgion*, the attributes were developed in terms of logic of God-language, assuming the identity of God either as the infinite Being or as the Being than which none greater can be conceived and proceeding to enumerate attributes by way of deduction. This logical approach was carried forward in the next generation by Hugh of St. Victor. On the other hand, in the form given to it by Peter Lombard, the discussion of divine attributes was fundamentally biblical and patristic, content to present the stated doctrines of the church, rather than develop the attributes as a matter of rational speculation. It also needs to be noted that although this deductive approach to the attributes was fundamental to the early scholastic argumentation, it cannot be said to rest either on a Platonic or on an Aristotelian model, given that the early scholastic era knew Plato only through the *Timaeus* and Aristotle only through the logical *Organon* — and the early scholastic knowledge of Neoplatonism was derived largely from the church fathers (most notably Ambrose, Augustine, and Gregory the Great) and Pseudo-Dionysius.[56] The philosophy underlying the process of deduction, thus, was for the most part a form of realism, but it was mediated largely by the earlier Christian tradition and not a result of direct access to classical philosophical argumentation.

3. Divine simplicity. Among the divine attributes one stands forth as a governing concept which determines the way in which theology discusses the attributes and their relation to the divine essence: the divine simplicity. Here we encounter the basic question of the difference between God and his creatures and of the relation of universals to God. Indeed, the question of the reality of universals and of the relation of universals to the object of which they are predicated defines the problem of the divine attributes: what are attributes when they are predicated of God? When we say God is infinite, omnipotent, omniscient, just, good, loving, and so forth have we exhaustively described the divine essence? And in doing so, have we conceived of

---

54. Cf. Peter Lombard, *Sententiae in IV libris distinctae*, editio tertia, 2 vols. (Grottaferrata: Collegium S. Bonaventurae ad Claras Aquas, 1971-1981), lib. I, d. 2, cap. 1.

55. See Ebeling, "Hermeneutical Locus of the Doctrine of God," pp. 73-87.

56. Chossat, "Dieu. Sa nature selon les scolastiques," col. 1158.

God in a composite way, as we conceive of creatures — as a sum of properties or parts? And is this description legitimate?

The doctrine of divine simplicity is among the normative assumptions of theology from the time of the church fathers,[57] to the age of the great medieval scholastic systems,[58] to the era of Reformation and post-Reformation theology, and indeed, on into the succeeding era of late orthodoxy and rationalism. Recent studies of divine simplicity, notably those that have appeared since the major essay by Stump and Kretzman,[59] have taken rather different directions. Davies, for example, argues (with specific reference to Aquinas) that "from first to last the doctrine of divine simplicity is a piece of negative or apophatic theology and not a purported description of God," certainly not a concept that stands in the way of the positive doctrines concerning

---

57. Cf. e.g., Melito of Sardis, fragment 14, in *Melito of Sardis On Pascha and Fragments*, Texts and translations ed. Stuart G. Hall (Oxford: Clarendon Press, 1979), p. 81; Irenaeus, *Against Heresies.*, II.xiii.3-5; cf. IV.xxxviii.4, in *The Ante-Nicene Fathers: Translations of the Writings of the Fathers down to A.D. 325*, ed. Roberts and Donaldson, 10 vols. (Grand Rapids: Eerdmans, 1950-1951), I, pp. 373-374, 522 (hereinafter ANF); Clement of Alexandria, *Stromata*, IV.xxv; V.xii (ANF, II, pp. 438, 463-464); Origen, *On First Principles*, trans. G. W. Butterworth (New York: Harper & Row, 1966), I.i.6 (p. 10); Lactantius, *Divine Institutes*, I.ix (ANF, 7, p. 54); Eusebius Pamphilius, *The Theophaneia or Divine Manifestation of Our Lord and Saviour Jesus Christ*, trans. Samuel Lee (Cambridge: Cambridge University Press, 1843), I.27-9 (pp. 17-19); Athanasius, *Against the Heathen*, xxviii, in *A Select Library of the Nicene and Post-Nicene Fathers of the Christian Church*, ed. Schaff and Wace, 2 series in 28 vols. (Grand Rapids: Eerdmans, 1956), 2nd ser., IV, pp. 18-19 (hereinafter, NPNF); idem, *Defense of the Nicene Definition*, xi (NPNF, 2nd ser., IV, p. 157); idem, *To the Bishops of Egypt*, xvi (NPNF, 2nd ser., IV, p. 231); idem, *Against the Arians*, IV.1 (NPNF, 2nd ser., IV, p. 433); Gregory of Nyssa, *Answer to Eunomius*, I.19 (NPNF, 2nd ser., V, p. 57); idem, *Answer to Eunomius' Second Book*, II (NPNF, 2nd ser., V, pp. 254-255); idem, *Great Catechism*, I, in ibid., pp. 474-476; Basil the Great, Letter 134, to Amphilochius (NPNF, 2nd ser., VIII, p. 274); Augustine, *De Civitate Dei*, XI.10; idem, *De Trinitate*, VI.iv-iv; XV.v.8 (NPNF, 1st ser., III, pp. 100-101, 203); Rufinus, *On the Apostles' Creed*, 4 (NPNF, 2nd ser., III, p. 544); cf. W. J. Hill, "Simplicity," s.v. in *New Catholic Encyclopedia*, vol. 12; Basil Krivocheine, "Simplicity of the Divine Nature and the Distinctions in God, According to St. Gregory of Nyssa," in *St. Vladimir's Theological Quarterly*, 21/2 (1977), pp. 76-104; idem, "Simplicité de la nature divine et les distinctions en Dieu selon S. Grégoire de Nysse," in *Studia Patristica* 16/2 (1985), pp. 389-411; Eric Osborne, *The Beginnings of Christian Philosophy* (Cambridge: Cambridge University Press, 1981), pp. 31-78; Christopher Stead, "Divine Simplicity as a Problem for Orthodoxy," in Rowan D. Williams (ed.), *The Making of Orthodoxy: Essays in Honor of Henry Chadwick* (Cambridge: Cambridge University Press, 1989), pp. 255-269; and Katherin Rogers, "The Traditional Doctrine of Divine Simplicity," in *Religious Studies*, 32 (1996), pp. 165-186.

58. Cf. Lombard, *Sententiae in IV libris distinctae*, editio tertia, 2 vols. (Grottaferrata: Collegium S. Bonaventurae ad Claras Aquas, 1971-1981), I, d. 8, cap. 5-8; Alexander of Hales, *Summa theologica*, 4 vols., (Quaracchi: Collegium S. Bonaventurae, 1924-1948), pars I, inq. I, tract. 1, qu. 3, cap. 1-3; Thomas Aquinas, *Summa theologiae cura fratrum in eiusdem ordinis*, 5 vols. (Madrid: Biblioteca de Autores Cristianos, 1962-1965), 1a, q. 3; Bonaventure, *In Sent.*, I, q. 8, in *Opera omnia*, (Quaracchi: Collegium S. Bonaventurae, 1882-1902), vol. I; Duns Scotus, *Ordinatio.*, I, d. 8, q. 1; Ockham, *In Sent.*, I, d. 8, q. 1, in *Opera philosophica et theologica*, (St. Bonaventure, New York: The Franciscan Institute, 1967-1986), vol. I. On Aquinas' doctrine of simplicity, see Brian Davies, *The Thought of Thomas Aquinas* (Oxford: Clarendon Press, 1992), pp. 44-57.

59. Eleonore Stump and Norman Kretzman, "Absolute Simplicity," in *Faith and Philosophy*, 2 (1985), pp. 353-382.

revealed attributes and the Trinity. Similar conclusions have been reached by Immink.[60] Mann, by way of contrast, understands the doctrine in an affirmative (as distinct from an apophatic) sense and also as a denial of all distinction in the divine essence: he neither indicates a variety of formulation nor acknowledges the possibility of distinctions in a simple being — and he defends this doctrine as valid.[61]

Other modern writers, notably and Wolterstorff and Plantinga, however, have understood simplicity as ruling out all distinctions in God (including the distinction of persons in the Trinity), but, unlike Mann, go on to conclude that divine simplicity is contradictory or unintelligible, specifically in the form given to the doctrine by Aquinas.[62] The traditional conception of simplicity, with its denial of composition, argues Plantinga, yields the conclusion that God "is identical with his nature and [with] each of his properties." This conclusion in turn means that "if God is identical with each of his properties, then each of his properties is identical with each of his properties, so that God has but one property"; beyond this, "if God is identical with each of his properties, then, since each of his properties is a property, he is a property — a self-exemplifying property."[63] Such doctrine undermines any claim that God's power is distinct from his mercy — as, indeed, it undermines the assumption that God is a "person" as distinct from a "mere abstract object." "No property," Plantinga notes, "could have created the world." He concludes, "So taken, the simplicity doctrine seems an utter mistake."[64] Indeed, so taken, the doctrine is a mistake — but it is arguable

---

60. Brian Davies, "Classical Theism and the Doctrine of Divine Simplicity," in Brian Davies (ed.), *Language, Meaning and God: Essays in Honor of Herbert McCabe, OP* (London: Cassell, 1987), p. 59; also see F. Gerrit Immink, "The One and Only: The Simplicity of God," in Brink and Sarot (eds.), *Understanding the Attributes of God*, pp. 115-117; also see Christopher Hughes, *On a Complex Theory of a Simple God* (Ithaca: Cornell University Press, 1989); and note Nash, *Concept of God*, pp. 85-97.

61. William Mann, "Divine Simplicity," in *Religious Studies*, 21 (1982), pp. 451-471; and idem, "Simplicity and Immutability in God," in *The Concept of God*, ed. Thomas V. Morris (Oxford and New York: Oxford University Press, 1987), pp. 253-267.

62. Thus, Plantinga, *Does God Have a Nature?*, pp. 46-47; Wolterstorff, "Divine Simplicity," pp. 531-552.

63. Plantinga, *Does God Have a Nature*, pp. 46-47; note that Plantinga's language here does not at all reflect Aquinas' meaning: Aquinas assumes that the divine attributes are distinguishable and, therefore, not identical in every way. The scholastic understanding of "identity" assumes various levels of identity, e.g., essential identify and formal identity — so that the term "identity" does not indicate radical equation in every sense possible. The phrase "self-exemplifying property," moreover, does not rightly describe Aquinas' thought or, indeed, the thought of any other scholastic, inasmuch as in the traditional scholastic sense, no "property" or "attribute" could be, in itself, an *individuum*: see *aequalitas, attributum, individuum, proprietas*, s.v. in Roy J. Deferrari et al., *A Lexicon of St. Thomas Aquinas based on the Summa theologica and selected passages of his other works, by Roy J. Deferrari and M. Inviolata Barry, with the collaboration of Ignatius McGuiness* (Washington: Catholic Univ. of America Press, 1948); and *aequalitas, attributum, identitas, priprium*, s.v., in Fernandez Garcia, *Lexicon Scholasticum Philosophico-Theologicum* (Quaracchi: Collegium S. Bonaventurae, 1910); also see Geoffrey G. Bridges, *Identity and Distinction in Petrus Thomae, O. F. M.* (St. Bonaventure, N. Y.: Franciscan Institute, 1959), pp. 31-42 on the hierarchy of different levels of identity and/or distinction; also Henri Grenier, *Thomistic Philosophy*, trans. J. P. E. O'Hanley, 3 vols. (Charlottestown: St. Dunstan's University, 1948), I, pp. 137-140.

64. Plantinga, *Does God Have a Nature*, p. 47.

that few thinkers in the Christian tradition ever took it to mean this, given that the tradition has consistently affirmed not only divine simplicity but also the Trinity, the meaningful identification of divine attributes, and the creation of the world by God.[65] The various modern readings of simplicity as indicating an utter absence of distinction in the Godhead misinterpret the traditional doctrine. Most modern writers have assumed a uniformity of argument in the Middle Ages, whereas there was in fact a massive debate — and the debate was not over the implications of a distinctionless notion of simplicity but over the precise nature of the distinctions that, arguably, belong to the Godhead.

According to traditional orthodoxy, there *are* distinctions in God, but they are distinctions that in no way detract from or impugn the non-compositeness and, therefore, the ultimacy of the divine essence. By way of example, the doctrine of the Trinity indicates that there are personal or relational distinctions in the Godhead — but, as the patristic doctrine of the Trinity (affirmed in toto by the scholastic tradition) indicates, threeness of person does not conflict with oneness of essence.[66] The three persons participate in the one essence without dividing it into three parts: Christianity is monotheistic, not tritheistic. Nor is the existence of the three persons prior to the existence of the one God, as if the one God were a result of some activity on the part of the persons; or, indeed, as if the Trinity were the secondary essence or genus to which the three persons belong. In the doctrine of the Trinity — the classic conception of the unity and distinction of the persons — the issue is not merely to identify the distinction of persons, but to find a way to argue a certain manner of distinction (for the sake of manifesting the three) while at the very same time denying other kinds of distinction (for the sake of confessing the One). A similar point must be made concerning the divine attributes and the Reformed orthodox discussion of distinctions between them: the point was not merely either to affirm or to deny distinctions, but to identify the kinds of distinctions that could not be present in the Godhead and the kinds of distinctions that could be present, for the sake of affirming both the genuineness of the divine attributes and the oneness of God.[67] The doctrine of divine simplicity, then, belongs to the full *locus de Deo*, the larger topics of essence, attributes, and Trinity — and it belongs there as having the specific function, not of ruling out distinctions per se, but of allowing only those distinctions in the Godhead that do not disrupt the understanding of the ultimacy and unity of the One God. With very few exceptions in the history of the doctrine, discussion of simplicity, in the context of the full *locus*, provides the place at which the datum of divine oneness is coordinated with one level of distinction *ad intra*, corresponding with the distinction of attributes, and

---

65. Cf. Immink, "The One and Only," pp. 115-17 and idem, *Divine Simplicity*, pp. 127-145.

66. Cf. G. L. Prestige, *God in Patristic Thought*, 2nd ed. (London: S.P.C.K., 1952), pp. 254-264, 282-291; Bertrand de Margerie, *The Christian Trinity in History*, trans. Edmund J. Fortman (Still River, Mass.: St. Bede's, 1975), pp. 126-134, 143-146 et passim; and Seeberg, *History*, I, pp. 228-231, 238-243.

67. See below, 4.3 (D).

another level of distinction *ad intra*, corresponding with the necessarily different distinctions among the three divine persons.

Once this has been said, however, it is necessary to note that the doctrine of divine simplicity has not always been understood in the same way or received the same emphasis in theology. Stead has pointed out, for example, that the concepts of simplicity found in classical philosophy and in the church fathers should not easily be reduced to a "neat antithesis of simple and compound," given that an "object which has no parts need not be wholly undifferentiated."[68] He nonetheless queries how this approach can cohere, given that the fathers, notably the Cappadocians, assume that the three persons can be distinguished and that there are energies and relations in the Godhead at the same time that it is a "simple undivided essence."[69] Some of this problem is dispelled in Krivocheine's examination of Gregory of Nyssa's theology, where the notion of simplicity is seen to be the exclusion only of compositeness and division, not of other kinds of distinction, notably the distinction between divine hypostases and divine energies or powers.[70]

Similarly, Augustine affirmed the divine simplicity on the ground that God is not composite and is devoid of accidents and did so primarily in the context of the doctrine of the Trinity as an affirmation of the fundamental unity and uniqueness of the Godhead.[71] Nonetheless, Augustine indicated that (in addition to the distinction of the persons in the Trinity), there was some distinction of attributes: he spoke of God as "both simple and manifold," having a "simple multiplicity or multifold simplicity" and held that the notion of simplicity undergirded and protected orthodox, post-Nicene trinitarianism.[72] He also argued distinct ideas — the eternal exemplars of things — in the essence or mind of God. Augustine also assumed that God knows these distinct ideas as distinct ideas.[73] Unfortunately, Krivocheine did not look farther than Gregory and, without examining later sources or, indeed, Augustine, assumed that medieval views of simplicity ruled out distinctions in the Godhead.[74] What, arguably, he would have found had he taken the time to do look, is that the medieval writers, far from rendering the notion of divine simplicity problematic through speculation, actually took a patristic conception that, in its most strict forms, could stand in a problematic or paradoxical relationship to the distinction of divine attributes and the doctrine of

---

68. Stead, "Divine Simplicity as a Problem for Orthodoxy," in Rowan D. Williams, ed., *The Making of Orthodoxy: Essays in Honor of Henry Chadwick* (Cambridge: Cambridge University Press, 1989), p. 261. Stead does not recognize that the juxtaposition of simplicity with compositeness does not rule out the coincidence of simplicity with distinctions other than those that imply partition.

69. Stead, "Divine Simplicity as a Problem for Orthodoxy," p. 267.

70. Krivocheine, "Simplicité de la nature divine," pp. 394-405; idem, "Simplicity of the Divine Nature," pp. 88-99.

71. Augustine, *De trinitate*, V.ii.3-v.6; x.11-xi.12 (*NPNF*, 1 ser., III, pp. 88-9, 92-3).

72. Augustine, *De trinitate*, VI.iv, vi (*NPNF*, 1ˢᵗ ser., III, pp. 100, 101); cf. Lewis Ayres and Michel R. Barnes, "God," s.v., in Allan D. Firzgerald, ed., *Augustine Though the Ages*, esp. pp. 387-388.

73. Augustine, *De trinitate*, V.ii.3; xi.12; VI.iv.6; vi.8; *Confessions*, I.vi.9; *De ideis*, 2

74. Krivocheine, "Simplicité de la nature divine," p. 410; cf., idem, "Simplicity of the Divine Nature," p. 104.

the Trinity,[75] and worked to develop a more nuanced and flexible concept that could rule out composition while at the same time allowing for the "operational complexity" of the Godhead.

Medieval thinkers consciously continued the patristic meditation and, even more fully than the fathers, argued that the identification of "simplicity" as uncompounded-ness did not rule out either the distinction of divine persons or the distinction of divine attributes. Indeed, it would be one of the burdens of scholastic argumentation to identify precisely what kinds of distinction there might be in the simplicity or uncompoundedness of the Godhead. Anselm transferred the discussion from the fundamental location in the doctrine of the Trinity to a location in the discussion of the divine essence, and argued the point a bit more fully, again on the assumption that composition is an indication of incidental properties or accidents and a violation of the divine self-identity: "nothing that is truly said of the supreme Being is accepted in terms of quality or quantity, but only in terms of *what* it is; for ... either quality or quantity would constitute another element."[76] This exclusion of composition functions primarily as a foundational statement of the necessary self-existence or aseity of God: God is ultimate, sole, underived and no other aspect of the doctrine of God (particularly not the doctrine of the Trinity) ought to be formulated in such as way as to undermine that truth.[77] God's unique existence, which is such that not only must it be, but it must also be the way it is, contains a vast richness of attributes that are the foundation of the attributes of created being.[78] Still, it should not be concluded that Anselm's effort to give structure to the discussion amounted to either a division of the topic of God into two separate topics (i.e., essence-attributes and Trinity) or to a removal of the theme of simplicity from the realm of trinitarian discussion. In Anselm, as in the fathers, simplicity serves to safeguard trinitarianism from tritheistic implications.[79]

Several interpretations of divine simplicity are already observable among the scholastics of the late twelfth century. Anselm, without great elaboration, stated a traditional doctrine of divine simplicity according to which the attributes belong to God essentially, not accidentally or as incidental properties: in Anselm's example, it is the same for God to be just and to be justice itself, given that the justness or righteousness of God is not a separable property as righteousness is in human beings. This must be so, Anselm argues, inasmuch as God is just through himself, not through or on the basis of a prior justice in another. The divine attributes are not, therefore, descriptions of how God is or of what sort of being God is but are, specifically, statements of "what" God is.[80] God is not a composite being. Still, Anselm appears

---

75. The phrase "operational complexity" is from Stead, *Divine Substance*, p. 175. Stead, ibid., pp. 109, 163-164, 185-189, is also the source of my sense of the difficulties underlying the patristic usage of simplicity.

76. Anselm, *Monologion*, 17; cf. 25; cf. Immink, *Divine Simplicity*, pp. 27, 115-122.

77. Cf. John Moreall, "The Aseity of God in St. Anselm," pp. 37-46.

78. Anselm, *Monologion*, 16; cf. *Proslogion*, 5; and Immink, "One and Only, pp. 114-115.

79. Cf. Anselm *Prosolgion*, 23 with Anselm, *On the Incarnation of the Word*, iv-v.

80. Anselm, *Monologion*, XVI.

to understand that the various attributions have meaning, namely, that they are not merely synonyms. He does not, however, elaborate on the point.

The debate over the theology of Gilbert de la Porée posed and saw the rejection of a theory of real distinctions among the divine attributes and the affirmation of a basic doctrine of divine simplicity, without however, answering the question of whether the attributes are merely distinct *ad extra* and in our human comprehension or are distinct in some manner *ad intra* apart from consideration by a human knower. Alain of Lille offered a solution that leaned strongly toward the former option: like the earlier tradition and echoing the Synod of Rheims, he argued that everything in God is God, allowing no essential distinction between the various divine attributes and affirming the utter simplicity of the divine being. The distinction of the attributes, therefore, is not in God himself but in the effects of God's work *ad extra*. Nonetheless, given that these attributes are evident to us by way of causality, they are not merely names or terms applied by us to God but are in fact proper designations of the divine substance.[81]

In the standard definition of Lombard, the divine simplicity excludes all manner of composition, whether in terms of substance and accident, matter and form, parts, or attributes, and asserts the essential identity of God with all of his attributes or qualities. The attributes of God are not accidents or modifications of the divine being.[82] In the structure of Lombard's argument, moreover, the obvious purpose of this doctrine of simplicity is the affirmation of the full divinity of each of the persons of the Trinity, each of whom possesses the divine essence indivisibly. The divine attributes, therefore, belong to the persons not in their distinction but in their unity, as God — the persons are distinct according to their personal properties and not on the ground that they have differing divine attributes or, indeed, the same divine attributes in differing measures.[83]

4. Various attributes. As inherited from the fathers, the doctrine of the early scholastic writers placed a strong emphasis on such attributes as the unity, spirituality, simplicity, immutability, self-sufficiency, eternity, omnipresence, omniscience, omnipotence, and justice of God. The early scholastic doctrine of God and his attributes, contrary to what has been sometimes alleged, advanced the discussion of individual attributes.

Still, particularly in the case of Anselm's two major treatises on the subject, the early scholastic thinkers did contribute a more synthetic approach to the discussion of divine essence and attributes that showed, beyond the patristic statement of the various attributes, a certain logic to the discussion of essence and attributes as a whole. In Anselm's case, this logic was clearly tied to the notion of necessary being and, as most clearly indicated in the famous "proof" of the *Proslogion*, the inseparability in God of essence and existence. Anselm assumed that not only was the existence of God demonstrable from the concept of God, but that the various divine attributes

---

81. Chossat, "Dieu. Sa nature selon les scolastiques," col. 1169.
82. Lombard, *Sententiae*, I, dist. 8, cap. 3.
83. Cf. Marcia L. Colish, *Peter Lombard*, 2 vols. (Leiden: E. J. Brill, 1994), I, pp. 245-247.

were also demonstrable — an assumption that would be met with considerable opposition from theologians of the fourteenth and fifteenth centuries.

An example of this development is the doctrine of divine simplicity, which, in its basic content, advanced very little beyond the patristic statement of the case — but which also was drawn into relation with more detailed discussion of other attributes in a more formal and logical manner than can be found among the church fathers. We do not find here a sudden shift from a patristic notion of God as non-composite to a monistic philosophical notion of a radical identity of the attributes. In fact, the early scholastic doctrine of divine simplicity largely leaves open the question of how the attributes are distinct: what is ruled out is composition in the Godhead and, therefore, real distinctions between the divine essence and divine attributes and among the attributes — while at the same time the attributes are not reduced to mere synonyms. The rule for understanding the issue was expressed by Anselm's dictum that, apart from the "opposition of relation" that distinguishes the divine persons, "anything which is said about the one God, who is wholly whatever He is, is said about the whole of God."[84] Discussion of the nature of the distinctions among the attributes was left for the next several generations of theologians.

The doctrine of divine immutability is of particular interest because of its correlation with other attributes, like simplicity, eternity, and omnipresence. In the case of Anselm's exposition in the *Monologion*, immutability correlates with these other attributes and in fact follows them in order of exposition without, however, being deduced from them.[85] Hugh of St Victor, however, understood immutability as following logically on simplicity, given that the identification of the attributes as belonging essentially and without any composition to God implies the absence of change, normally understood as the mutation or alteration of properties. This conclusion, in turn, leads to the attributes of eternity and omnipresence or immensity.[86] Lombard, however, inverted the order and discussed immutability prior to simplicity. As Chossat points out, what is not found here, either in Hugh or in the Lombard, is the later notion of divine immutability as the immoveability of the first mover.[87] Thus neither the philosophical content associated with later Christian Aristotelianism nor a definitive pattern of argument is to be found among the early scholastics.

The concept of divine freedom is also present in the early scholastic understanding of God and his attributes, particularly in view of the assumption of divine sufficiency or aseity and the creation of the world ex nihilo.[88] Still the question remained as to whether God, given his nature, must create: one of the lingering results of John Scotus

---

84. Anselm, *On the Procession of the Holy Spirit*, I (p. 85).

85. Anselm, *Monologion*, XXV; cf. XVI-XVII (simplicity), XVIII-XIX (eternity), XX-XXIV (omnipresence).

86. Hugh of St. Victor, *De sacramentis*, I.iii.13 (*PL*, 183, col. 220); idem, *Eruditio didascalia*, VII.xix (*PL*, 183, col. 827).

87. Lombard, *Sententiae*, I, dist. 8, cap. 2; cf. Chossat, "Dieu. Sa nature selon les scolastiques," col. 1160.

88. See Courtenay, "Necessity and Freedom," pp. 39-64 and Moreall, "The Aseity of God in St. Anselm," pp. 37-46.

Erigena's pantheism was the theory of the necessity of the world — a teaching that, from the perspective of the early scholastics militated against the freedom of God. Abelard, for one, could argue that even though the world was created out of nothing, nevertheless God necessarily created it as a result of his goodness and his need to reveal his goodness. Hugh of St. Victor had combated this view, maintaining the freedom of God in his creative work, defining creation as the totally free manifestation of God's goodness in the communication or gift of being.[89]

B. The High Scholastic Doctrine of God: Theologians of the Thirteenth Century

Once scholastic theology has been arranged in a definitive form, such as Peter Lombard's *Sentences* became for the thirteenth, fourteenth, and fifteenth centuries, theologians were able to examine more closely the individual subtopics of theology — Lombard's "distinctions" — together with the issues proposed or adumbrated by those subtopics. It would be difficult to underestimate the formal significance of Lombard's work: not only did the *Sentences* provide the standard format for theological discussion for centuries, it also provided with this standard format a set of topics which, because of their order and coherence in virtually all basic lectures on theology, could be compared, contrasted, and constantly reworked by each succeeding generation of theological teachers. The tradition of lecturing on the *Sentences* made possible a tradition of discussion that easily incorporated and brought forward for discussion the insights and problems of the theological tradition, whether ancient, more recent, or contemporary. This internal development of debate was not as apparent in the topics belonging to the prolegomena (including the doctrine of Scripture), granting that Lombard did not develop a preliminary discussion of theology and its principles in and for his *Sentences*, but it becomes quite apparent in the high scholastic doctrine of God.

1. The comprehensibility of God. The scholastic investigation of the relation of faith and reason, theology and philosophy, and of the grounds of theological discourse raised almost immediately — one might well say, necessarily — the fundamental questions underlying the doctrine of God. And it is, conversely, the Christian perception of the essence, attributes, and trinitarian nature of God that most clearly presses these issues of the ways of knowing. As the fathers after Origen had recognized, God is at once the supreme object of theology and also the most difficult object to know. The medieval scholastic doctrine of God proceeded with the recognition that we cannot know God in the same way that we know things — given that the being or essence of God is not available to sense perception and does not fit into our normal categories of comprehension. It is also, therefore, not immediately clear how we can say of God the things we wish to say about him: that he is good, just, powerful, and so forth. Likewise, it is not immediately apparent just how the things that faith and revelation tell us about God — that he is good, just, powerful and so forth — fit into our normal

---

89. Hugh of St. Victor, *De sacramentis*, I.iv.

rational use of those terms. After all, what God is, the essence of God, is not at all like what we are.

In the immediate context of the scholastic development of the doctrine of God, so often characterized as highly speculative in the modern sense of the term, therefore, there was also a powerful sense of the limits of human comprehension. The point is important to the broader study of the "scholastic" doctrine of God — and we need to return to it in later discussion of late sixteenth- and seventeenth-century scholasticism. Where Anselm had indicated that the divine is ultimately beyond our comprehension, Albert the Great distinguished carefully between the intellectual attainment of the divine and the creaturely comprehension of God: the former, he commented, was possible, the latter impossible.[90] A similar, and related, point concerning the scholastic approach to God concerns the intimate connection between the objective statements concerning knowledge of God found in the more systematic or dogmatic expositions of theology and the piety and "subjectivity" of knowledge: a contrast can be made between the more objectivising "outer way" of knowing that moves from sense perception, through a process of rational abstraction, to knowledge, and the "inner way" that moves deeply into the intellect of the knowing subject for its foundations of knowledge. The latter pattern, more characteristic of Bonaventure than of Aquinas, ought not to be severed from our understanding of scholastic method in theology.[91]

With specific reference to the ways in which God may be known, the scholastics offered a series of "paths," or *viae*, that not only describe the rational patterns of gaining some knowledge of God but that also provide categorizations of the divine attributes. Thus, Alexander of Hales could indicate that God is known *per modum positionis* and *per modum privationis*, by way of positive argument and by way of removal or negation: according to the former pattern, we know "what God is," according to the latter, "what God is not." The negative path is necessary since, in an ultimate sense, "the divine substance, in its immensity, is not knowable by the rational soul according to a positive understanding, but by a privative understanding."[92] There is, moreover, a variant of the positive way, an inward *via eminentiae*, that moves by way of the image of God in the soul, through intellect, memory, and will, to the knowledge of God as the highest Good and as ultimate Truth.[93] There is, in fact, a major divide among the medievals on this point: in the Bonaventurean perspective, this model of inward intellectual ascent toward knowledge of God yield not a full but nonetheless an essential knowledge of the divine. Aquinas, on the other hand, stressed the transcendence of God and the necessity of the negative or privative way. Granting this sense of the limitation of human knowledge of God and the principle of his teacher, Albert, that the intellect

---

90. Albert the Great, *Summa theol.*, I, tract. IV, qu. 18, memb. 3.

91. Cf. Cousins, "St. Bonaventure, St. Thomas, and the Movement of Thought in the 13th Century," pp. 395-398.

92. Alexander of Hales, *Summa theol.*, I, q. 2, memb. 1, art. 2.

93. Cousins, "St. Bonaventure, St. Thomas, and the Movement of Thought in the 13th Century," p. 400.

can attain to God but cannot ultimately comprehend him, Aquinas concluded that human beings have no natural or purely rational knowledge of God *in se*, specifically, no ultimate essential or "quidditative" knowledge of God (*cognitio Dei quidditativa*) apart from grace — and that this is gained by revelation rather than by inward illumination.[94]

2. The "proofs" of God's existence. One of the as yet only partially answered questions concerning the nature and character of medieval scholastic theology relates to the purpose and place of the proofs of God's existence. Modern philosophical discussion of the proofs has, more often than not, isolated them from their context in the scholastic theology and has asked the simple, logical question of their viability: do they succeed in proving or demonstrating the existence of God? Yet, when their context has been examined, questions can be raised about the very nature of the demonstration and, most definitely, concerning the presumed audience of the proofs. Given that Anselm's ontological argument is situated in a treatise that takes the form of prayer, it does not appear to be purely rational argument nor does it appear to be an argument that was intended for use either as a beginning point for a purely rational theism or as the linchpin of an apologetic.[95] Indeed, in the context of Anselm's foundational assumption that "I believe in order that I might understand," the precedence of faith over reason in even the proof is clear. What is more, given Anselm's profound attachment to the theology of Augustine and the fact that virtually all of the elements of the proof can be extracted from Augustine's meditation on Psalm 14 and his *De Trinitate*, there are motives present in Anselm's formulation that stand above and apart from the issue of simple, rational proof of the existence of the Deity. The ontological argument certainly cannot be understood apart from its location in the larger treatise — which includes lengthy discussion of the divine essence, attributes, and trinity and which can best, perhaps, be described as an exercise in the internal logic of God-language. A different perspective, more in accord with the proofs in Anselm's *Monologion*, is found in Lombard's *Sentences*, in which our knowledge of God is identified as an indirect or mediate knowledge, resting on God's works or effects and not on an immediate apprehension of the being (or Persons) of God.[96] Given the nearly exclusive use of Lombard's *Sentences* as the basic text in theology during the later Middle Ages, the impact of this assumption on the formulation of the proofs was considerable.

The medieval approaches to the proofs, moreover, virtually never accord with the modern understanding of demonstrations as a matter of apologetics and/or as necessary a prelude or prolegomenon to "revealed theology" resting on "natural theology." Thus, by way of example, Aquinas' "five ways" belong to theology, specifically, to the faithful exercise of reason rather than to the realm of a purely rational apologetic: in response to the initial rational objections to the existence of God noted at the outset of his question, Aquinas' *sed contra* reads, "On the contrary, it is said in the person of God,

---

94. Aquinas, *Summa theol.*, Ia, q. 12, art. 12.

95. Cf. Schwane, *Histoire des Dogmes*, IV, pp. 161-162.

96. Lombard, I *Sent.*, d. 3, 1.

'I am who I am' (Ex. 3:14)."[97] Apart from any other conclusion we might draw from this pattern of rebuttal, we ought at least to recognize that Aquinas does not at all ratify the claim that scholasticism was a fundamentally rationalistic endeavor. Nor, indeed, does this initial gambit of the proofs of the existence of God document the often heard claim that the proofs are an example of a purely rational theology. Rather, Thomas' basic pattern of argument, even in the proofs, assumes the fundamental Augustinian and Anselmian model of "faith in search of understanding." The citation of Exodus is, for Aquinas, a citation of the highest authority against the objectors — and, given the authority of the biblical text, a suitable ground on which he can base his own precise logical and theological rejoinder to the objections.[98] Nor, of course, were Aquinas' five ways the sole model for developing the proofs in the high scholastic era. Whereas Bonaventure did accept the a posteriori proofs, which he recognized as belonging to the Augustinian tradition of meditation on the knowledge of God, he also drew out of that tradition two other patterns of argument, one resting on the implanted inward desire for goodness and truth and on the assumption of an inward illumination, the other resting on the ultimate divine ground of knowing and yielding a form of the ontological argument.[99]

3. The being and attributes of God. For the teachers of the thirteenth century there was no particular problem in the identification and basic definition of specific divine attributes. The attributes were capable of being known either directly from Scripture or from the tradition of the church's meditation on Scripture — or from a rational examination of the traditional language about God, as Anselm had well shown. Thus, the more nominally philosophical of the attributes, like simplicity, eternity, infinity or omnipresence, were easily recognized as indicated or implied by the text of Scripture, as stated precisely by the fathers of the first five centuries and argued rationally by earlier generations of scholastics, like Anselm, Hugh of St. Victor, or Peter Lombard. The teachers of the high scholastic era, from Alexander of Hales to Henry of Ghent and Duns Scotus, identified the central problem of the doctrine of God as an epistemological and linguistic one: they recognized the problem of predicating attributes of a transcendent being as central to the discussion of the doctrine of God.

---

97. Aquinas, *Summa theol.*, Ia, q. 2, art. 3. It would be far beyond the scope of the present study to cite anything like a full bibliography on the proofs of the existence of God, even from a historical perspective. A good basis for further study can be found in Bernardino M. Bonansea, *God and Atheism: A Philosophical Approach to the Problem of God* (Washington, D.C.: Catholic University of America, 1979); also note Joseph Owens, *St. Thomas Aquinas on the Existence of God: Collected Papers of Joseph Owens, C. Ss. R.*, ed. John R. Catan (Albany: State University of New York Press, 1980); William Bryar, *St. Thomas and the Existence of God: Three Interpretations*, (Chicago: Henry Regnery, 1951).

98. See my comments in Richard A. Muller, "The Dogmatic Function of St. Thomas' Proofs: a Protestant Appreciation," in *Fides et Historia*, XXIV (1992), pp. 15-29 and cf. G. de Broglie, "La vraie notion thomiste des 'praeambula fidei,'" in *Gregorianum*, 34 (1953), pp. 341-389.

99. Cf. Pegis, "Bonaventurean Way to God," pp. 210-211, 223-225, with Cousins, "St. Bonaventure, St. Thomas, and the Movement of Thought in the 13th Century," p. 397; also note Thomas A. Fey "Bonaventure and Aquinas on God's Existence: Points of Convergence," in *The Thomist*, 41 (1977), pp. 585-595.

If God is unlike the finite creation, if terms drawn, even by negation or by way of eminence — like infinitude and omniscience — from the created order cannot be predicated of God in the same way that attributes can be predicated of creaturely beings, how is language about God possible, and what does that language mean when we use it? Beginning with Alexander of Hales, the medieval doctors addressed in considerable depth the problem of the predication of divine attributes: Alexander recognized, in the first place (in accord with the Synod of Rheims), that the doctrine of God must assume the divine simplicity.

On this point in particular, there was much discussion in the high and late scholastic eras: far from being a settled point, the doctrine of divine simplicity received much discussion, particularly from the perspective of the kind of distinctions that might obtain in the being of a non-composite God. Against Islamic and Jewish philosophy, the medieval scholastic theologians were pressed to argue that the doctrine of the Trinity did not render God composite and that the distinctions between the persons were not divisions of the divine essence.[100]

It is true, to a certain extent, that the discovery of Aristotle's metaphysical works and of the writings of the Arabian philosophers by the West led to a vast and highly philosophical elaboration of the doctrine of God, including the examination of questions of existence and essence. Nonetheless, it must also be remembered that these questions, as evidenced by Anselm's work, not only existed in the West before the rediscovery of Aristotle, but were imbedded in the patristic heritage of the Western church. What is more, certain aspects of these questions and, certainly, the way in which discussion of these questions developed in the scholastic era rested on the exegetical tradition of the church.

Etienne Gilson makes the very pointed remark, in *The Spirit of Medieval Philosophy*, that the great source and starting-point of all medieval discussion of the being and essence of God is not Greek philosophy in general or Aristotle in particular, but Moses — in Exodus 3:14: "God said to Moses, 'I am who I am.'"[101] Nor ought we to attribute the use of Exodus 3:14 as a reference to the being of God as a result of ignorance of Hebrew and dependence on the *sum qui sum* of the Latin Vulgate. We read, for example, in the *Guide for the Perplexed* of Moses Maimonides,

God taught Moses how to teach them and how to establish amongst them the belief in the existence of Himself, namely, by saying *Ehyeh asher Ehyeh*, a name derived from the verb *hayah* in the sense of "existing," for the verb *hayah* denotes "to be," and in Hebrew no difference is made between the verbs "to be" and "to exist." The principle point in this phrase is that the same word which denotes "existence" is repeated as an attribute.... This is, therefore, the expression of the idea that God exists, but not

---

100. Giles of Rome, *Errores philosophorum*, critical text with notes and intro. by Josef Koch, trans. John O. Riedl (Milwaukee: Marquette University Press, 1944), IV.7 (pp. 20-23: Averroes); XII.1-4 (pp. 58-61: Maimonides).

101. Etienne Gilson, *The Spirit of Medieval Philosophy*, trans. A. H. C. Downes (New York: Scribner, 1936), p. 51.

in the ordinary sense of the term; or, in other words, He is "the existing being which is the existing Being," that is to say, the Being whose existence is absolute.[102]

Of the Holy Name, Maimonides adds, "the tetragrammaton ... is not an appellative; it does not imply anything except His existence. Absolute existence includes the idea of eternity, i.e., the necessity of existence."[103] The point must be made, with respect to Gilson's remarks, that however much the classical philosophical heritage influenced scholastic formulation, the form that the influence took and, indeed, the medieval interpretation of the classical sources, was in large measure determined by biblical exegesis — and that, granting the Greek philosophical sources of medieval Jewish and Christian conceptions of God, those sources, taken by themselves, do not by themselves account for either the theology or the metaphysics of the medieval thinkers.[104]

We must take exception to often-uttered claims that descriptions of God in terms of "substance" and "essence" lead ineluctably "to the unfruitful abstractions of the conception of God in Greek philosophy," or that language such as that of Aquinas concerning God as "supremely existent" (maximè ens) is a "Grecian" as opposed, presumably, to a "religious conception of God."[105] Such claims assume, first, that discussion of the divine essence is a fundamentally Greek enterprise (if Gilson and Maimonides are correct, it is not) — and second, quite arbitrarily, that abstraction is both characteristically Greek and quite "unfruitful" and, in addition, is somehow divorced from the "religious conception of God." We ought not to accept any of these comments uncritically, nor ought we to suppose that the medieval development of concepts of God as willing, as thinking, as loving, and as, by nature, spirit (none of which are without "religious" implication), can be severed in a facile manner from the issue of the divine being or essence.

If, then, it is Scripture that gives us the definition of God as the one "who is" and points us to the identification of God as absolute existence or absolute being, the problem of the essence and attributes of God in the medieval systems can be seen as an issue of both faith and reason — an issue brought forth by the revelation and explained rationally, with the aid of philosophy. It would be a mistake, therefore, to infer from the presence of the proofs just prior to the discussion of the divine essence and attributes that essence and attributes, like the proofs, belong to the realm of natural reason or natural theology — just as it would be a mistake to infer from the discussion of scripture just prior to the proofs that the proofs are in fact revealed theology. Gilby notes, with characteristic lucidity, "These five ways lead immediately to five different

102. Moses Maimonides, *The Guide for the Perplexed*, trans. M. Friedlaender (London: George Routledge, 1956), pp. 94-5.

103. Maimonides, *Guide for the Perplexed*, p. 95.

104. On the classical and Arabian backgrounds of Maimonides thought, see Julius Guttmann, *Philosophies of Judaism: A History of Jewish Philosophy from Biblical Times to Franz Rosenzweig*, trans. David Silverman (New York: Schocken Books, 1973), pp. 178-194.

105. Seeberg, *History*, II, pp. 106-108.

truths under the same name of *God*, but they are drawn together in a subsequent argument when the revelation *I am who am* is set in the philosophy of Pure Act."[106]

Once God is identified as the one who is — who is the existent one — it is not a matter of excessive logical abstraction to describe God in the language of being, essence, and existence. The words are forbidding only because they are not part of our normal vocabulary, not, at least, in the strict sense in which they are used in scholastic theology and philosophy. Being and existence are roughly synonymous: existence, which translates the Latin *esse*, simply indicates the real or actual being of a thing. To speak of the existence of God or the being of God is to say no more and no less than Exodus 3:14, that God really or actually is. "Essence" is merely a term derived from the verb *esse*, "to be," which points to the nature of a given being. Essence, simply defined, is the quiddity or "whatness," the nature of a being. Quiddity, as an exact synonym of essence, simply indicates "that which answers the question '*Quid sit*?' — 'What is it?'"[107]

From Avicenna, the greatest of the eastern Moslem philosophers, William of Auvergne (d. 1249) adopted and developed the distinction between essence and existence, in Copleston's words, making this distinction the basis of an "explanation of the creature's finitude and dependence" over against the infinitude and independence of God.[108] The issue is simply this: the essence or nature of things is not identical with their existence. For instance, our essence, "humanity," is not identical with any individual human being. Human nature, according to which individual human beings are recognized, cannot be reduced simply to the aggregate of individuals, nor does knowledge of human nature necessarily imply the actual being of individual humans at any particular moment. The coincidence of essence and existence, in the case of finite things — like people — indicates that God has created individual instances of human nature or, in other words, given real or actual being to his idea of humanity.

There is only one exception to this argument: God himself. The existence of God, according to William, is identical with the divine essence. This must be so if God is "He who is." Since God is identified as the self-existent or necessary being who cannot not be, it is of the essence of God that God is — or, more precisely, has actual being. The separation of essence or "whatness" and existence in finite creatures arises from the fact that it is not of their very nature or "whatness" to exist in and of themselves: their existence is dependent not on what they are, but on the will of another. God's existence, however, is inseparable from what God is: if God did not or could possibly not exist, he would not be God.

---

106. Gilby, *Philosophical Texts*, p. 36, note 1.

107. On the importance of Exodus 3:14 to the medieval development of God-language, see Gilson, *Spirit of Medieval Philosophy*, p. 51; and Karl Albert, "Exodusmetaphysik und Metaphysische Erfahrung," in *Thomas von Aquino: Interpretation und Rezeption*, ed. Willehad Eckert (Mainz: Matthias-Grünewald-Verlag, 1974), pp. 80-95.

108. Copleston, *History of Philosophy*, II, p. 219.

4. Divine simplicity. The early scholastic understanding of divine simplicity was maintained with little fundamental modification in its high scholastic development. The scholastics of the thirteenth century understood the doctrine, in continuity with the fathers and their immediate predecessors as an exclusion of compoundedness from the Godhead and as a significant corollary of both the unity and trinity of God. Bonaventure, for example, noted that the eternal ideas or exemplars cannot be essentially or really distinct from one another (as if the divine intellect were composite) but that they are distinct *secundum rationem intelligendi* — with the result that "in knowing himself [God] knows also all ways in which His divine essence can be mirrored externally."[109] Alexander of Hales and Albert the Great went into considerable detail to deny composition in God — neither in a physical, nor a metaphysical, nor a logical manner is God composite. If God were composed of parts or predicates, these parts or predicates would be prior in some way to God — so that God would be conceived as potentially the result of a combination and, subsequently, as the actual result. But any such conclusion of a movement in God (even a logical, a temporal movement) from potency to act destroys the definition of God as the necessary being, as absolute being.[110] Attributes of God, therefore, are identical with the being and essence of God and are human ways of describing the divine dignity: whereas humans have attributes properly predicated of them in a composite way, God does not. We say a person is just — and we are able to subtract or exclude the justice and still have a human body. The same may be said of human goodness, human finitude, human power. But God is not only just, God is justice; not only good, but goodness; not only all powerful, but omnipotence itself. What is more, God's justice, goodness, and omnipotence are identical with his essence in its simplicity.[111] The point is that the doctrine of divine simplicity prevents us from saying that God *has* goodness, justice, power, life, and so forth and insists that God *is* goodness, justice, power, life and insists also that these attributes cannot be separated out of the divine essence.

Still, at this point in the scholastic development of the concept of simplicity, great pains were taken to indicate that this "simplicity of substance" in no way removed distinction of persons. Thus Alexander argues that the denial of substantial, accidental, and formal composition is not at all a denial of the relational distinctions among the divine persons, just as the distinction of the persons in no way implies composition in the Godhead.[112]

Thomas Aquinas addressed the concept of divine simplicity as fundamental to the understanding of God, giving it more relative importance in his doctrine of the attributes than his predecessors had done and addressing the issue of distinctions in the Godhead other than the distinctions between the persons. Thomas begins by arguing that God is beyond our positive powers of knowing — and that our knowledge

---

109. Copleston, *History of Philosophy*, II, p. 261.

110. Albert the Great, *Summa theol.*, I, tract. 4, q. 20, memb. 1-3; Alexander of Hales, *Summa theol*, pars. I, inq. I, tract. 1, q. 3, cap. 1, 3; cf. Schwane, *Histoire des Dogmes*, IV, p. 194.

111. Alexander of Hales, *Summa theol*, pars. I, inq. I, tract. 1, q. 3, cap. 2.

112. Alexander of Hales, *Summa theol*, pars. I, inq. I, tract. 1, q. 3, cap. 1, ad. 2; cap. 2, ad. 2, 3.

of him is restricted to three modes or types of argument: 1. how God is not (*via negativa*); 2. how God is known by us (epistemology); and 3. how God is named (revelation). He begins by discussing how God is not: we cannot know the divine essence directly, so as to state what or how God is, but we can argue indirectly by excluding from our conception anything not "befitting" God: how God is not. Thus we exclude composition and, by extension, *motion* considered as motion from potency to act. By removal of the idea of composition, we come to simplicity.[113]

First, God is clearly the same as his essence or nature — whereas a man is not quite the same as his humanity. God not only lives but he is life itself: his living and life cannot be distinguished. Moreover, whereas humanity does not have the individual matter that defines the person as individual, divinity and the divine essence are inseparable: there is no form of God apart from God, and no divine "material" separable from the idea of God. "Since, then, God is not composed of matter and form, He must be His own Godhead, His own Life, and whatever else is so predicated of Him." From this it follows that, in the second place, God is identical to his nature or essence. Since he is the first being (as established in the proofs), he cannot exist posterior to anything — and all composites are posterior to their parts; and similarly, a composite must have a cause joining its parts and God has no cause.[114]

Aquinas initially poses the issue as part of his discussion of "how God is not" and raises the question, "whether God is in some way composite (*quocumque modo compositus*), or wholly simple (*totaliter simplex*)," firmly lodging the discussion in his examination of the doctrines of the divine essence and attributes.[115] Article 7 of the question asks "whether God is utterly simple" (*omnino simplex*), then cites Augustine to the effect that God is "truly and wholly simple" (*vere et summe simplex*), and proceeds to argue "that God is utterly simple" (*quod Deum omnino esse simplicem*).[116] The later phrase has been rendered "the absolute simplicity of God," and interpreted as if it understands the divine essence as radically devoid of all kinds of distinction[117] — when the text of the article indicates no more than the denial of composition in God, *totaliter simplex* standing as the opposite of *compositus* in Aquinas' question.

Aquinas, it should be observed, does not use the phrase "absolute simplicity" — indeed, *simplicitas absoluta* is not a term that one often encounters in traditional presentations of the doctrine of simplicity. What is more, when he comes to discuss the doctrine of the Trinity, Aquinas explicitly states that there are distinctions in God, indeed that "there must be a real distinction in God, not, indeed, according to that which is absolute — namely, essence, wherein there is supreme unity and simplicity

---

113. Aquinas, *Summa theologiae*, Ia, q. 3, art. 1-8; cf. *Summa contra gentiles*, I.18, where again, the issue is to rule out "composition" not to exclude distinction.

114. Aquinas, *Summa theologiae*, Ia, q. 3, art. 3.

115. Aquinas, *Summa theologiae*, Ia, q.3, prol.

116. Aquinas, *Summa theologiae*, 1a, q.3, a.7, sed contra & resp.

117. Cf. Wolterstorff, "Divine Simplicity," pp. 533-535; Mann, "Simplicity and Immutability," pp. 255-260; idem, "Divine Simplicity," pp. 451-471. Although Mann defends the concept, he neither indicates variety of formulation nor argues the possibility of distinctions in a simple being. Note the definitions in Copleston, *History of Philosophy*, II, pp. 219, 349, 360-361, 508-509, 529.

— but according to that which is relative."[118] Thus, the paternity, filiation, and, procession are real relational or relative distinctions, but they are not real essential distinctions such as subsist between things and other things or such as would imply composition in one thing.

We understand the distinction of the attributes differently — by a process of analysis (*ratio ratiocinata*) with a foundation in the thing (*cum fundamento in re*) — because, as Aquinas later tells us, the attributes are distinct in God as the foundation of the things of the finite order, insofar as they preexist in God. We conceive of God by means of "conceptions proportional to the perfections flowing from God to creatures, which perfections preexist in God unitedly and simply, whereas in creatures, they are received, divided, and multiplied." The divine attributes all "signify the one thing" (*unam rem*), namely, God, but "they signify him under diverse and multiple concepts, which are not synonyms."[119] Attributes or perfections, thus, are truly in God, but their distinction cannot be a real distinction, namely, the kind of distinction that subsists between things and other things; nor is it a purely rational distinction made only from our point of view for our comprehension — instead it is a distinction resulting from the human understanding of the object, a rational distinction *cum fundamento in re*.

Aquinas is still clearer on the point in the more extended discussion found in his commentary on Lombard's *Sentences*: he asks the question "whether there is a plurality of attributes in God" — the very form of which assumes the positive answer! Aquinas responds to various negatives (negatives based on the unity and simplicity of God), that "a plurality of attributes in no way prejudices the highest unity" given that the plurality is *secundum rationem* and not *secundum rem*.[120] This notion of a plurality *secundum rationem* is clarified in the body of the question, where Aquinas makes clear that the rational distinction of attributes is not merely the *ad extra* understanding of multiplicity belonging to a finite mind incapable of comprehending the infinite. Aquinas notes that in God there are such attributes as wisdom, goodness, and so forth: "all of these [attributes] are one thing" yet, "the concept (*ratio*) of wisdom is not the concept of goodness" — so it appears, Aquinas states, that there are diverse concepts (*rationes*) in God. These distinctions are not merely made on the part of the one doing the reasoning, but also on the basis of the properties of the thing, namely, God.[121] God

---

118. Aquinas, *Summa theol.*, Ia, q. 28, art. 3.

119. Aquinas, *Summa theol.*, Ia, q. 13, art. 4: "nomina Deo attributa, licet significent unam rem, tamen, quia significant eam sub rationibus multis et diversis, non sunt synonyma"; cf. *Summa contra gentiles*, I, cap. 35. Note that the identification of God as "one thing" or "reality," namely as a single *res*, belongs also to the normative trinitarian language of the scholastics: see *PRRD*, IV, 1.2 (B.2).

120. Thomas Aquinas, *In quattuor libros sententiarum*, in *S. Thomae Aquinatis Opera omnia, ut sunt in indice thomistico: additis 61 scriptis ex aliis medii aevi auctoribus*, curante Roberto Busa (Stuttgart-Bad Canstatt: Frommann-Holzboog, 1980), I, d.2, q.1, art. 2, ad. 1: "dicendum quod pluralitas attributorum in nullo praejudicat summa unitati ... pluralitas tantum secundum rationem."

121. Aquinas, *In quattuor libros sententiarum*, I, d.2, q.1, art. 2, corpus: "quod in deo est sapientia, bonitas, et huiusmodi, quorum quodlibet est in ipsa divina essentia, et ita omnia sunt unum re, et quia unumquodque est in deo secundum sui verissimam rationem, et ratio sapientiae non est ratio bonitatis ... relinquitur quod sunt diversas rationes, non tantum ex parte ipsius ratiocinantis sed ex proprietate

is one simple or uncompounded *res* in whom there can be no distinctions made *realiter*, yet the attributes are genuinely distinct in God as *rationes*, and thus distinct in a conceptual or formal sense in God himself.[122]

Note that, here, as in all scholastic references to "real" distinctions or a "real" presence, the terms "real" (*realis*) and "really" (*realiter*) are related to the "thing" or *res* — with the result that "real" does not mean "genuine" but rather "thingish" or "substantial." To argue that a rational distinction can have a basis in the properties of a thing presses the question of the relationship between logical being and real being: Aquinas' notion of a rational distinction founded in the thing assumes that our attributions reflect actual properties and are not merely rational distinctions made for the convenience of the human knower. What Aquinas does not do, at least not to the satisfaction of later scholastics, is make clear precisely what kind of distinction there may be in the thing that is reflected in the distinction made by reason concerning the thing.

This dilemma is reflected in the article of the *Summa* immediately following Aquinas' discussion of simplicity, where Aquinas takes up the problem of divine perfections and indicates that just as an effect "preexists virtually" in its efficient cause, so must "the perfections of all things preexist in God in a more eminent way."[123] In addition, God has knowledge of "singular things" and knows them "as they are distinct from each other" inasmuch as he contains in himself the perfections of all things and is the cause of all things.[124] Aquinas certainly assumes that there are what might be called ideational distinctions or, indeed, in the traditional language, rational distinctions of some sort in God. This argument, by the way, is not Aristotelian, but rather builds on the views of Augustine noted above. When one turns to the question of attributes, moreover, Aquinas surely did not intend to exclude distinctions from God, but only such distinctions as would render God composite: his language reflects the Augustinian assumption that the exemplars of all things are in the mind of God and are known

---

ipsius rei." See the similar conclusions in Robert L. Richard, *The Problem of an Apologetical Perspective in the trinitarian Theology of St. Thomas Aquinas* (Rome: Gregorian University, 1963), pp. 64-67; and cf. Lemaigre, B. M. "Perfection de Dieu et multiplicité des attributs divins. Pourquoi S. Thomas a-t-il inséré la dispute des attributs divins (I Sent., d. 2, q. 1, a. 3) dans som commentaire des Sentences," in *Revue des sciences philosophiques et théologiques*, 50 (1966), pp. 198-277 for a survey of Aquinas' doctrine and a synopsis of medieval debate on the subject.

122. See *ratio*, s.v. in Deferrari, et al., *Lexicon of St. Thomas Aquinas*: Deferrari indicates that *ratio*, used to indicate a concept is synonymous with *formalitas* in Thomas.

123. Aquinas, *Summa theol.*, Ia, q.4, art.3.

124. Cf. Aquinas, *Summa theol.*, Ia, q.14, a.6 with a.11; note that this formulation is intimately related to Aquinas' argument that God alone is Being and that in God, essence and existence are inseparable — whereas creatures, in whom essence and existence are separable, must exist by participation in the being of God: just so are our attributes separable from our being, whereas in God the attributes remain inseparable, albeit distinguishable: Aquinas' whole point is to show how creaturely multiplicity is somehow grounded in and proceeds from the unity of God. See Robert L. Patterson, *Conception of God*, p.189; Geiger, "Les idées divines dans l'oeuvre de S. Thomas," vol. I, pp. 175-209; and Immink, "One and Only," pp. 116.

by God as distinct ideas.[125] Indeed, this is precisely the interpretation given to Aquinas' teaching by Cajetan, who argues that, according to Aquinas, the attributes are distinct *eminenter* or *virtualiter* in God.[126] Thus, "simplicity," by definition, means *not* an absence of distinctions, but only and strictly an absence of composition (and of the kind of distinctions that indicate composition).[127] In effect, Aquinas argues that if the attributes of God are distinct only on grounds of our reasoning process (*ratio rationans*), namely, only in our minds, then we gain no true knowledge of God from his manifest attributes — and by extension we might be pressed to deny anything but a merely rational distinction between the Father as unbegotten, the Son as begotten, and the Spirit as proceeding — since no such distinctions could be predicated of the simple essence of God. And this is absurd: there must be distinctions in God.

According to the traditional vocabulary of philosophy, whether medieval or early modern, the entire intent of positive predication is to assert material or essential identity of subject and predicate and, at the same time, their difference or distinction in some other sense.[128] Essential identity does not indicate an utter convertibility of subject and predicate: the proposition that "God is goodness" does not permit the conclusion that "goodness is God," certainly not in any sense of a full rational or formal equivalency. Nor does the statement that, essentially, God's goodness is identical with his omnipotence allow the claim either that goodness is omnipotence and omnipotence of goodness — for stated in this latter way we have perfect tautologies that assume not only essential but also utter identity, whether according considered *rationaliter, formaliter, virtualiter*, or *eminenter*. Thus, given the basic rules of traditional predication (and not merely a set of special considerations concerning God), to indicate that the divine attributes are essentially identical is necessarily to indicate also that they are distinct in another sense, namely, formally, rationally, virtually, or eminently. As Aquinas indicates, the various names and attributes of God all "signify one thing" but they are, nonetheless, "not synonymous."[129] Thus Aquinas could argue that, as in a human knower, "the conception of the intellect, which is the intellectual likeness, is distinct from the knowing intellect," so also "the representation of the divine intellect, which is God's Word, is distinct from Him who produces the Word, not with respect to substantial existence, but only according to the procession of one from the other."[130]

---

125. See. John L. Farthing, "The Problem of Exemplarity in St. Thomas," in *The Thomist*, 49/2 (April, 1985), pp. 183-222.

126. Thomas de Vio, Cardinal Cajetan, *Commentary on Being and Essence (In De ente et Essentia d. Thomas Aquinatis)*, trans., with and intro by Lottie H. Kendzierski and Francis C. Wade (Milwaukee, Marquette University Press, 1964), p. 245ff., 251, 256, on the question of "Whether the perfections existing in God are in some way distinct independent of every act of the intellect?"

127. See *simplicitas*, s.v. in Deferrari, *Lexicon of St. Thomas Aquinas*: Deferrari notes that *simplicitas* is synonymous with *indivisibilitas* and the opposite of composition.

128. See Grenier, *Thomistic Philosophy*, I, pp. 138-9; cf. Davies, "Classical Theism and the Doctrine of Divine Simplicity," p. 59.

129. Aquinas, *Summa theol.*, I, q. 13, art. 4.

130. Thomas Aquinas, *Compendium of Theology*, I.52.

Given these considerations, Plantinga's and Wolterstorff's readings of Aquinas on this issue (and, by extension, of the classic doctrine of divine simplicity) certainly fall short of the mark. Mann's counterargument falls short as well, at least from a historical perspective: simplicity did not indicate the utter absence of distinctions to a majority of the theologians in the patristic, medieval, and post-Reformation eras, and the broader tradition would not have defended such a concept. In addition, other scholars, who have tended to look only at Aquinas, have not seen the full implication of the denial of composition and, therefore, specifically, of real distinctions in the Godhead, nor have they dealt fully with either later Thomistic understandings of Aquinas himself or with the non-Thomistic versions of the doctrine of divine simplicity found in the later medieval and post-Reformation scholastic traditions.[131] Leaving aside differences of formulation found throughout the tradition, the basic doctrinal point is plain: in God there is an essential or substantial simplicity but there are distinctions — and these distinctions can be represented on the analogy of distinctions in the intellect.

5. **Various approaches to the attributes and to the logic of their formulation.** If there is a certain degree of uniformity among the scholastic teachers of the thirteenth century concerning the basic concepts of the eternity, simplicity, immutability, infinity, and various other of the divine attributes, there are also significant nuances of argument on which they differ. For Alexander of Hales, the key to understanding the doctrine of the divine essence and attributes was certainly the immensity or immeasurability of God. Divine immensity is the immediate conclusion drawn from the discussion of the incommunicability and simplicity of God's essence — and it is the basic concept from which arise the divine infinity, incomprehensibility, omnipresence, and eternity, given that, if truly immeasurable, God is infinite, and is transcendent in relation to space, to time, and to knowing.[132] If, by way of contrast, one understands the apologetic argumentation of Aquinas' *Summa contra gentiles* as proceeding through the divine attributes in as logical a manner as Aquinas thought possible, then certainly eternity is the more fundamental concept for Aquinas, followed logically by utter actuality and spirituality, with simplicity standing as a conclusion from these three concepts rather than as the root concept — and infinity as a rather distant conclusion, after goodness and unity or oneness.[133] Alternatively, if one consults the *Summa theologiae*, Aquinas moves from simplicity as root concept to the related concept of perfection, thence to goodness, infinity, immutability, and only then eternity, in what also appears to be a more or less deductive order.[134]

The various scholastic teachers of the thirteenth century also offered significant refinements with regard to the doctrine of divine eternity. Whereas the Boethian definition of eternity as the "simultaneous and perfect possession of interminable life" is common to all of the scholastic teachers, most from Alexander of Hales onward

---

131. See below, 1.3 (B.3) and 4.3 (C-D).

132. *Summa theol.*, lib. I, pars. I inq. 1, tract 2. See Wass, *Infinite God*, p. 47 and Sweeney, *Divine Infinity*.

133. Aquinas, *Summa contra gentiles*, I.15-18, 37-43.

134. Aquinas, *Summa theologiae*, Ia, qq. 3-10.

insist that eternity is also an endless duration and then proceed, often by way of the basic definition, to argue precisely the divine duration differs from that of creatures, even from that of those creatures that have no end.[135] Bonaventure recognized that the traditional conception of divine eternity, inherited from the fathers and given definition by Boethius, given its assumption of the simultaneous knowing by God of all things, past, present, and future, could be misinterpreted in such a way as either to deny time by implying the presence of all things, past, present, and future, to one another. Rather, therefore, than defining God's "foreknowledge" as merely a successionless, divine knowledge of all things as present, Bonaventure argued that the concept of divine foreknowledge must preserve the futurity of things — not as a futurity for God, but as futurity belonging to the things themselves in relation to one another. God's foreknowledge, then, is the simultaneous or eternal divine knowledge of all things, including the way in which things succeed each other in time. Just as futurity is a relationship belonging to the things known and not to God, so is the "presentiality" (*praesentialitas*) of the divine knowing a characteristic of the knowing, not of the things known. God knows all things, in all time, as present to him — but he also knows them as not present to one another. Without being in the sequence of events, God knows the sequence of events.[136]

The divine freedom both in creation and over against the created order remained a significant issue for the scholastic teachers of the thirteenth century. If not Erigena's, then certainly Abelard's formulations of the necessity of the creation remained a concern even after Hugh of St. Victor's and Lombard's critiques. Alexander of Hales added to the critique of Abelard the thought that the perfection of the world order was the free gift of God, who did not have to create this "best of all possible worlds" but freely chose to reach the limit of perfection within the possibilities of a created order.[137] But the issue of the relation of the divine creative willing to the created order received its fullest treatment from Aquinas — and it was Aquinas, therefore, in whom the teaching concerning the divine freedom and the argument against Abelard reaches its fruition.

Aquinas makes a basic distinction between the necessity to create and the necessity, once the work of creation is viewed as belonging definitively to the will of God, of creating the world in a certain manner. He also divides this second necessity into two questions relating to ends and means. Thus, first, the divine determination to bring the world to its full realization — the eternal idea which God has in his mind concerning the world — is a counsel freely formed, an idea freely conceived. The object and end of God's willing is his own goodness — the glory of God rests in a sense on his power to create or not to create. In a derivative sense, however, creation is necessary

---

135. Alexander of Hales, *Summa theol.*, lib. I, pars. I, inq. 1, tract. 2, q. 4, especially memb. 3-4; cf. Wass, *Infinite God*, pp. 76-78, 86-88.

136. Bonaventure, *I Sent.*, d. 39, a. 2-3; cf. Aquinas, *Summa contra gentiles*, I.lxvi.7; and see Copleston, *History of Philosophy*, II, pp. 261-262.

137. Alexander of Hales, *Summa theol.*, lib. II, qu. 21, memb. 3, art. 1-2; cf. Schwane, *Histoire des Dogmes*, IV, p. 284.

even if no necessity is placed on the will of God from without. Since discrete ideas cannot be separated out of the mind or essence of God — so that the content of the divine mind is simple and equal to God himself — the eternally free will to create and the eternally realized idea of the creation must result in the world itself. For God's eternal mind and will are immutable: the world must necessarily exist, but this is a necessity of the consequence or of supposition, resting upon the divine counsel or decision to create.[138]

Second, there is in any will a certain necessity and a certain freedom. Aquinas looks to the analogy of the human will. Certain things are willed necessarily or governed by the nature and the end, the goal, of the person — yet the person freely chooses the means by which he effects that end. This argument also applies to God: for in the act of creation God necessarily wills his own absolute goodness as the end or goal of all his willing. Yet God freely chooses, without any necessity, the means by which he will communicate his goodness to creation. He freely chooses those things and means which lie outside of his nature and refer to the contingent order of nature. We need to make a distinction, then, between absolute necessity (*necessitas absoluta*) and the necessity of the consequences (*necessitas consequentiae*) or conditional necessity: the former applies to creation, not to God; the latter applies to God insofar as, *de potentia ordinata*, God has bound himself to the counsel of his will.[139] The question of whether a *necessity of nature* (*necessitas naturae*) applied to God was debated — positively by Thomists, negatively by Scotists.

The divine beatitude and felicity constitute a topic that was both exegetically and dogmatically significant in medieval theology, especially in the Augustinian tradition — given in particular the juxtaposition of texts like 1 Tim. 1:11 and 6:15, Romans 9:5, and 2 Cor. 1:3 and 11:31 with Boethius' classic definition, "beatitude is the state made perfect by the aggregation of all good things" and the Augustinian definition of God as the *summum bonum*.[140] In Lombard's *Sentences*, Boethius' definition appears by way of the initial meditation on the themes of "use" and "enjoyment" from Augustine's *De doctrina christiana*, and in subsequent meditations on the essential goodness of God and on the cause of evil as outside of God.[141] Aquinas argues that blessedness must belong to God in "the highest degree" inasmuch as blessedness or beatitude is "the perfect good of an intellectual nature." The divine beatitude, moreover, respects the pure and perfect actuality of the divine being — so that the term is not predicated of God in the way that it is predicated of humans: divine beatitude is neither an accident nor a reward of virtue.[142] Even so, the all-embracing

---

138. Aquinas, *Summa theol.*, Ia, q. 19, art. 3; note also art. 5, which concludes that the will of God has no cause prior to it; cf. *Summa contra gentiles*, I, cap. 80-81, 87; cf. Schwane, *Histoire des Dogmes*, IV, p. 285.

139. Aquinas, *Summa theol.*, Ia, q. 19, art. 3.

140. Cf. Boethius, *De Consolatione*, IV; and note Etienne Gilson, *Christian Philosophy of St. Augustine*, trans. L. E. M. Lynch (New York: Vintage, 1960), pp. 138-142.

141. Lombard, *Sententiae*, I, dist.1, cap. 3.4-7; dist. 34, cap. 3; dist. 46, cap. 7.2; Cf. Augustine, *De doctrina christiana*, I.xxii, xxxi, xxxiii and note Aquinas, *Summa theol.*, I, q. 26, art. 1.

142. Aquinas, *Summa theol.*, I, q. 26, art. 1.

divine beatitude can be understood as a "contemplative happiness" or joy, for God "possesses a continual and most certain contemplation of Himself and of all else ... He possesses joy in Himself and all things else for his delight."[143]

1.3   Late Medieval Contributions to the Doctrine of God

A. Alterations of Perspective in Late Medieval Theology — Decline or Development?

1. The role of Duns Scotus, Durandus, and their contemporaries. It is certainly the case that the particular synthesis of revelation and reason, theology and philosophy offered by Thomas Aquinas and more or less followed by the thinkers of the *via antiqua* in the later Middle Ages was disputed by large numbers of later medieval thinkers, including Scotus, Durandus, Aureole, Ockham, Holcot, and Biel. Some of the older scholarship, including the significant work of Lortz on the background to the Reformation, regarded much of the effort of these thinkers as a sign of decadence and disintegration. Other, typically more recent, schools of thought on the later Middle Ages, argue that this opposition to Aquinas' "synthesis" of theology and philosophy hardly renders its rather varied proponents decadent — nor does it offer evidence of a major shift away from a grand synthesis of theology and philosophy toward intellectual and spiritual collapse. Aquinas' model for the relationship of philosophy and theology was not universally accepted beyond his order — and it never, certainly, became a major option within either the Franciscan or the Augustinian orders.[144] Accordingly, the intellectual movement of the fourteenth century can be seen neither as an assault on a synthesis nor as a decline, but rather as a significant alteration of approach to the basic issues of faith and reason and, by extension, to the way in which the not only the doctrine of God but also the language concerning God was to be construed.

The rather different perspective on the relationship of faith to reason or of theology to philosophy that is broadly characteristic of the medieval tradition from the time of Scotus onward has led historians of theology and philosophy to raise with regularity a series of questions concerning the continuity and/or discontinuity of the thought of the later Middle Ages with the thought both of the preceding and the following eras. On the one hand, given the critique of the various thirteenth-century attempts at synthesis of theology and philosophy that is characteristic of the fourteenth century, its thinkers have often been regarded inaugurators of a "decline," indeed, of a decadence and "collapse" of scholastic thought.[145] In the view of Josef Lortz, it was this decadence

---

143. Aquinas, *Summa theol.*, I, q. 26, art. 4.

144. See Heiko A. Oberman, "Fourteenth-Century Religious Thought: A Premature Profile," in *The Dawn of the Reformation: Essays in Late Medieval and Early Reformation Thought* (Edinburgh: T. & T. Clark, 1986), pp. 4-5.

145. Etienne Gilson, *Reason and Revelation in the Middle Ages* (New York: Scribner, 1938), pp. 85-91; Maurice DeWulf, *An Introduction to Scholastic Philosophy, Medieval and Modern*, trans. P. Coffey (New York: Dover, 1956), pp. 145-154; Émil Bréhier, *The History of Philosophy*, trans. Wade Baskin and Joseph Thomas, 7 vols. (Chicago: University of Chicago Press, 1965), III, p. 183; Schwane,

that prepared the way for the Reformation, inasmuch as (in his view) the chief characteristics of the Reformation were the mistaken rejection of the entire tradition of scholastic theology based on an equation of this problematic later medieval theology and philosophy with the Catholic faith.[146]

As is often indicated in histories of theology and philosophy, Johannes Duns Scotus can be regarded as the most significant of the transition figures who led Christian thought away from the high scholastic syntheses of faith and reason, theology and philosophy, that were more or less characteristic of the thirteenth century — and certainly evident in the major efforts of Alexander of Hales, Bonaventure, Albert the Great, and Thomas Aquinas. While at the same time wrestling more thoroughly and positively with elements of Christian Aristotelianism than his Franciscan predecessors had, Scotus maintained their stress on an Augustinian approach to philosophical and epistemological issues. Implicit in much of his thought, therefore, is a critique of Aquinas and several followers of Aquinas' approach, coordinated with a refinement of the various Augustinian models: in the doctrine of God, this attitude is clear in the discussion of proofs of God's existence, in the discussion of the divine attributes and the simplicity of God, and in the doctrine of the Trinity as well. Thus, if Scotus' view of God represents a critical stance over against the approaches of Aquinas and Henry of Ghent, it also represents a positive point of departure for much later medieval doctrine, particularly in view of Scotus' sense of the divine transcendence as identified by the concept of absolute power.[147] Granting that he observed a strict separation between theology and metaphysics, the difficulties he had observed in the a priori proofs of God's existence did not stand in the way of Scotus' use of concepts like first and final causality in his theological doctrine of God.

A similar role was played by the critically minded Dominican, Durandus of Sancto Porciano. Durandus' differences with both Albert the Great and Thomas Aquinas over the relationship of individuals to species, in particular his denial of the priority of species, not only led to his condemnation and intellectual ostracization within his order but also to his identification by various historians of philosophy as "the first of the nominalists" of the later Middle Ages.[148] There are, it is true, certain resemblances: Durandus did undermine the Thomist assumption of the intelligibility of species as

---

Historie des Dogmes, IV, pp. 142-149.

146. Josef Lortz, *The Reformation in Germany*, 2 vols., trans. Ronald Walls (London and New York: Herder & Herder, 1968), I, pp. 67-77, 193-210.

147. This is certainly the assumption of Karl Werner in his *Die Scholastik des späteren Mittelalters*, 4 vols. in 5.(Vienna, 1881-1887; repr. New York: Burt Franklin, n.d.), as particularly noted in vol. 2, *Die nachscotistische Scholastik*, pp. 1-30, with reference to the doctrine of God, pp. 221-231; cf. E. Randi, "A Scotist Way of Distinguishing between God's Absolute and Ordained Powers," in *From Ockham to Wyclif*, ed. Hudson and Wilks, pp. 43-50.

148. Thus, Bréhier, *History of Philosophy*, III, p. 193; similarly, Schwane, *Historie des Dogmes*, IV, pp. 137-139; J. L. Neve, *A History of Christian Thought*, 2 vols. (Philadelphia: United Lutheran Publication House, 1943), I, p. 211; cf. P. Godet, "Durand de Saint-Pourçain," in *Dictionnaire de théologie catholique*, IV, col. 1964-1966; and the more measured assessment in Copleston, *History of Philosophy*, III, pp. 25-28.

a foundation of our knowing of individuals, he denied strictly "scientific" character to theology, grounding it on faith rather than on evidence, and he did argue, in anticipation of Gabriel Biel, the radical freedom of God to accept a "half" or "proportionate merit" as the basis of any temporal or spiritual blessings,[149] but Durandus' epistemology, his doctrine of the divine essence and attributes, and his trinitarian theory are so profoundly different from the thought of Ockham that it is difficult to identify him as a founder of the movement with which Ockham is so profoundly associated.

Durandus, whose work would be read with favor in the era of early Reformed orthodoxy by Daneau and others, identified, beyond the twofold path of knowledge of God indicated by Alexander of Hales and Aquinas, a threefold way: the *via eminentiae*, the *via remotionis*, and the *via causalitatis*.[150] Whereas this understanding draws on several elements of the earlier Thomist model and, indeed, refines its vocabulary, other elements of Durandus' doctrine of God, such as his understanding of the radical freedom of God, look more in the direction of Scotus and Ockham.

2. Developments after Scotus and Durandus: the problems of "nominalism" and the *via moderna*. After Scotus, moreover, the face of theology and philosophy changed. The more critical use of philosophy and the less optimistic epistemology that were characteristic of this thought became the springboard for further, highly critical developments, as well as for speculation concerning the ultimate or absolute power of God beyond the grasp of theological or philosophical reason. Given the changing face of scholarship on the later Middle Ages, anyone who would use such terms as "nominalism," "Ockhamism," and "via moderna" as descriptors of these developments must do so with some slight fear and trepidation.[151] At very least, the term "via moderna" must be used in a most general fashion, without importing to the term itself particular theological or philosophical implications: it can, certainly, be used relative to differences between trajectories and styles of teaching within particular orders. Thus, without passing judgment as to the applicability of other specifiers — like "nominalism" — it is surely useful to identify a thinker like Gregory of Rimini as representing the *via moderna* to the Augustinian order, in contrast to thinkers like Giles of Rome and Thomas of Strasbourg, who have been associated with an Augustinian *via antiqua*.[152]

"Ockhamism" is, admittedly, quite another matter. As Boehner has pointed out, the late fourteenth-century author of the *Centiloquium* identified a group of thinkers,

149. Thus, Carl Feckes, *Die Rechtfertigungslehre des Gabriel Biel und ihre stellung innerhalb der nominalistischen Schule* (Münster: Aschendorff, 1925), pp. 96-101, as cited in É. Amann and P. Vignaux, "Occam, Guillaume de," in *DTC*, II/1, col. 885.

150. Durandus, *In Sent.*, I, d. 3, qu. 1.

151. See William J. Courtenay, "Nominalism in Late Medieval Religion," in Charles E. Trinkaus and Heiko A. Oberman, eds., *The Pursuit of Holiness in Late Medieval and Renaissance Religion*. (Leiden: E. J. Brill, 1974), pp. 26-59.

152. Cf. Oberman, *Dawn of the Reformation*, pp. 8-11; with E. L. Saak, "Scholasticism, Late," s.v. in Allan D. Fitzgerald, ed., *Augustine Through the Ages: An Encyclopedia* (Grand Rapids: Eerdmans, 1999), especially pp. 756-757.

called by him *moderni*, who were followers of Ockham.[153] This particular usage not only offers evidence of "Ockhamist" teachings, but also provides ground for our previous caution concerning the use of *via moderna* — what it does not do, however, as Boehner was very much aware, is place Ockham in the center of a vast theological movement responsible, as was once claimed, for "the breakdown of scholasticism."[154] In addition, as Boehner himself details, on the important questions of the formal character of logic and the viability and use of the *distinctio formalis*, quite a few of the thinkers once identified as "Ockhamist" — notably Adam Wodham, Gregory of Rimini, and Robert Holcot — stand a varied distances from Ockham's perspective.[155] Nonetheless, granting modifications and refinements of interpretation concerning all of the thinkers involved, Pierre D'Ailly and Gabriel Biel can still be understood as theologians who drew inspiration from Ockham, albeit certainly not, any more than Ockham himself, as contributors to a "breakdown" or "decadence" in scholasticism, and not in so precise a manner as to be easily called Ockhamists. It can still be consistently argued that Ockham, D'Ailly, and Biel are united by their use of the distinction between *potentia absoluta* and *potentia ordinata* as a means of preserving the divine freedom against "Graeco-Arabian necessitarianism," although D'Ailly and Gregory of Rimini also appear to use the distinction as a way of explaining departures from the normal or ordained course of events, such as miracles.[156]

Finally, "nominalism" — a term that, several decades ago, was probably viewed as the clearest of the three and as most applicable to the larger theological and philosophical tendencies of the later Middle Ages. The term certainly cannot be used any longer as a broad and indiscriminate category for labeling the dominant theology of the later Middle Ages without attention to the details of the views of individual thinkers. Its application in the field of logic and metaphysics, however, to a critical temper that emphasized knowledge as a knowledge of particulars and refused to grant either the real, extra-mental existence of universals or the "real existence of the universal in individuals," remains, I think, unchallenged.[157] The question, then, of

153. Philotheus Boehner, "On a Recent Study of Ockham," in Boehner, *Collected Articles on Ockham*, ed. Eligius M. Buytaert (St. Bonaventure, N.Y.: Franciscan Institute, 1958), pp. 39-41.

154. Boehner, "On a Recent Study of Ockham," p. 42, a critique aimed directly at Erwin Iserloh, "Um die Echtheit des Centiloquium. Ein Beitrag zur Wertung Ockhams und zur Chronologie seiner Werke," *Gergorianum*, 30 (1949), pp. 78-103, 309-346. And note the very detailed work of Katherine Tachau, *Vision and Certitude in the Age of Ockham: Optics, Epistemology and the Foundations of Semantics, 1250-1345* (Leiden: E. J. Brill, 1988), which indicates broad areas of investigation in the later Middle Ages — including problems of cognition noted in commentaries on the *Sentences* — that, contrary to received opinion, were utterly untouched by Ockham's critical approach to the problem of knowledge.

155. Boehner, "The Medieval Crisis of Logic and the Author of the Centiloquium attributed to Ockham," in *Collected Articles*, pp. 370-372.

156. Cf. Courtenay, "Nominalism and Late Medieval Religion," in Trinkaus and Oberman, eds., *Pursuit of Holiness*, pp. 40-43, 50 with Francis Oakley, *Omnipotence, Covenant, & Order: An Excursion in the History of Ideas from Abelard to Leibniz* (Ithaca and London: Cornell University Press, 1984).

157. Cf. Boehner, "The Realistic Conceptualism of William of Ockham," in *Collected Articles*, p. 159, with the somewhat pointed comments of Paul Oskar Kristeller, "The Validity of the Term:

the usability of "nominalism" as a term of reference to types of late medieval theology and philosophy has a great deal to do with the implications of the nominalistic emphasis on particulars for theological and philosophical construction and with the potential relationship of these implications to other characteristics of the thought of writers of the era — by way of example, to a particular way of using the distinction between *potentia absoluta* and *potentia ordinata*.[158]

By way of establishing that connection, it is certainly legitimate to note that both the nominalist understanding of universals and the distinction, used by many if not all of the theologians usually identified as nominalists, between *potentia ordinata* and *potentia absoluta*, have a similar, limiting, effect on metaphysics and on the metaphysical portions of theological system. On the one hand, the critical epistemology of nominalism focussed thought on present reality and the particular and turned philosophy away from optimistic argumentation concerning the hierarchy of being and the construction of a metaphysics grounded on analogy. On the other hand, the emphasis on what Oberman has called "the dialectic of the two powers," the *potentia ordinata* and *potentia absoluta*, pressed the point that "our world, is contingent, not an ontologically necessary outflow or reflection of eternal structure of being, but the result of a decree, a contract, a *pactum Dei*."[159]

We can also affirm, albeit with cautions similar to those just noted about basic terms like "nominalism," that the impact of the late medieval debates over formal logic in its application to the Trinity, over the existence and character of genus and species, over the location and identity of universals, over the problem of the relation of reason and metaphysics to theology, over the question of authority in theological discourse, and over the implications of the distinction between *potentia absoluta* and the *potentia ordinata*, did have an impact not only on the teaching of the Reformers, but also and sometimes much more clearly on the theology of their Protestant scholastic successors.

B. Specific issues.

1. The knowability of God and the proofs of God's existence. The general absence of proofs of God's existence from Reformation theologies (the sole exception in the early Reformation being Melanchthon) can potentially be traced to the late medieval severing of faith and reason, although few of the Reformers can be identified as fully

---

'Nominalism'," in Trinkaus and Oberman, eds., *Pursuit of Holiness*, pp. 65-66. We could debate, endlessly, the question of whether or not to replace "nominalism" with "terminism" or with a less-known but highly accurate identifier like Boehner's characterization of Ockham's thought as "realistic conceptualism," but the prudent course is probably to retain the standard term, with qualifications such as those noted above.

158. Cf. Oberman, "The Shape of Late Medieval Thought: the Birthpangs of the Modern Era," in Trinkaus and Oberman, eds., *Pursuit of Holiness*, pp. 12-15, with idem, "Some Notes on the Theology of Nominalism with Attention to Its Relation to the Renaissance," in *Harvard Theological Review*, 53 (1960), pp. 47-76.

159. Oberman, "Shape of Late Medieval Thought," pp. 12-13; cf. idem, *Harvest*, pp. 3-47.

nominalist in their philosophical inclinations.[160] The issue is not so much that the Reformers looked to Scripture and found there a God unlike the God described in Thomas Aquinas' proofs: they surely did not doubt that God is the first and final cause of all things, or that God is perfect and necessary Being. Rather, the Reformers were heirs to the increasingly critical discussions of the knowledge of God that characterized both the Scotist and nominalist forms of *via moderna* theology — and they tended to assume a separation of faith and reason and the inability of the a posteriori proofs to support faith.

Scotus argued a clearer and stricter separation of rational and revelational knowing than had Aquinas, including making a strict distinction between the way in which God is the object of metaphysics and the way in which God is the object of theology. Although there is, according to Scotus, no intuitive or immediate knowledge of God in this life, reason can attain a limited knowledge of God through God's effects and, therefore, can produce a series of a posteriori proofs of God's existence and, indeed, a nuanced form of the ontological argument, but these arguments are properly theological, given that theology understands God as its proper object, whereas metaphysics takes as its proper object Being as such.[161] The metaphysician can know some of the essential attributes of God, like unity, infinity, simplicity, and goodness, given that they are the attributes of Being — such attributes, however, as omnipotence, immensity, omnipresence, truth, mercy, and providence (both general and special) are truths of faith not known to metaphysics. Theology, therefore, given its focus on God and its patterns of faithful argumentation, will have a rather different approach to proofs of God's existence and can, in fact, offer a modified version of the so-called ontological argument, resting on a prior justification of Anselm's definition as itself not involving a contradiction — establishing in other words the possibility of the greatest conceivable being before arguing its actuality.[162] The Anselmic argument then stands less as a demonstration of the divine existence than as an exercise in the logic of language about God. The boundary between metaphysics and theology, reason and revelation, has shifted and the province of metaphysics grown smaller. So also is the triunity of God known only to theology.[163]

---

160. Luther is certainly the main exception to this generalization: see Martin Brecht, *Martin Luther: His Road to Reformation, 1483-1521*, trans. James Schaaf (Philadelphia: Fortress, 1985), pp. 35-37.

161. Minges, *Doctrina philosophica et theologica*, II, pp. 14-16.

162. Cf. Bernardino M.Bonansea, "Duns Scotus and St. Anselm's Ontological Argument," in C. Balic, ed., *De Doctrina Ioannis Duns Scoti*, 4 vols. (Rome: Congressus Scotisticus Internationalis, 1968), II, pp. 461-475.

163. See further Séraphin Belmond, "L'existence de Dieu d'après Duns Scot," in *Revue de philosophie*, 8, vol. XIII (1908), pp. 241-268, 364-381; idem, "La connaissance de Dieu d'après Duns Scot," in *Revue de philosophie*, 10, vol. XVII (1910), pp. 496-514; and idem *Études sur la philosophie de Duns Scot. Dieu, existence et cognoscibilité* (Paris: Beauschesne, 1913); Felix Alluntis, "Demonstrability and Demonstration of the Existence of God," in *John Duns Scotus*, ed. John Ryan and Bernardine Bonansea, pp. 133-170; also note Copleston, *History of Philosophy*, II, pp. 518-529.

Leff points to two central principles or operations in Ockham's discussion of doctrine. First, on the rational side of doctrine related to the argument of natural and revealed theology manifest in Aquinas' theology, Ockham would rule out all teaching that could not be demonstrated. Second, on the fideistic side of doctrine — in the area of church dogmas — Ockham would press reason out of the court of argument by resting dogmatic constructions on the absolute power of God (*potentia absoluta*) to effect his will.[164] The best example of Ockham's assault on rational theology is his critique of the proofs of God's existence. Ockham denies that reason can demonstrate the God of the Bible. We cannot know things in themselves, naturally, unless we grasp them intuitively, argues Ockham: our natural ability provides us with no intuitive knowledge of God. By intuitive knowledge, Ockham means immediate apprehension of a thing and the knowledge that comes by immediate apprehension. The expression also covers what later writers would identify as innate knowledge of primary truths. We might paraphrase the idea by speaking of knowledge founded on immediate experience. We have, argues Ockham, no immediate experience, no innate apprehension of God: our sense, our natural ability, do not provide a knowledge of God in his immediacy.

But what does this argument have to do with the proofs? All of Aquinas' a posteriori demonstrations move by regress toward God: they do not point to a divine immediacy but, instead, rise through mediate or proximate movers or causes or perfections to God. It is precisely here that Ockham attacks — the method of regress toward a mover or cause is illegitimate and no demonstration at all. It is tendentious in the extreme. The argument from causality assumes that God can be identified as an efficient cause, indeed, as the ultimate efficient cause of all things. Yet efficient causes are known only insofar as they are experienced as present prior to their effects. The relation of cause and effect is purely sequential, known only by experience. But we have no intuitive, experiential knowledge of God, no immediate apprehension of the divine presence prior to any given effect. Therefore we cannot know God as efficient cause. The procedure of argument by regress simply assumes any number of unexperienced and therefore unknown and non-demonstrable causes.

Ockham can add to this argument, in a moment of perverse humor, that human reason might just as well assume that heavenly bodies — the moon, planets, the stars — are the first efficient cause of the world and thus dispense with the idea of God as first cause. We do, says Ockham, experience heavenly bodies as causes of actual effects in our world, and we have absolutely no experience of a cause of the heavenly bodies![165] Beyond this, theories of causal regress do not arrive at a single first cause any more logically than at a multiplicity of first causes: the causal argument can produce polytheism as easily and logically as monotheism.

Similarly, the argument for the existence of God as final cause is also found insufficient. As Maurer argues,

164. Gordon Leff, *Medieval Thought: St. Augustine to Ockham* (Baltimore: Penguin, 1958), p. 286.
165. Armand Maurer, *Medieval Philosophy* (New York: Random House, 1962), p. 270.

The term "final cause" in this context means that God foreordains and wills creatures to act as they do. But neither experience nor any evident proposition convinces us that the heavenly Intelligences or natural agents act in view of an end intended by God. True, natural agents act uniformly, but they would act in this way whether God intended it or not; they act by natural necessity and not for an end.[166]

Scotus, too, had seen the weaknesses in Aquinas' arguments — particularly their inability to reach beyond the world of causes and effects to a transcendent being, their inability to produce, at the end of a logical sequence, the God of Christian theology. Having seen this, Scotus attempted his own proof based on the univocity of the term "being" and the proposition that "some being is producible." Infinite series here is no problem because Scotus' desire is to argue for an infinitely superior, infinitely perfect being with infinite causal power who produces "producible being." Ockham argues that Scotus has simply hypothesized, arbitrarily, an infinite being extrinsic to the infinite series of finite causes and effects — a hypothesis not at all necessary. What Ockham admits is that reason establishes the probability of God's existence. Conviction that God does indeed exist comes only from faith.

2. Divine power, will, and freedom. The distinction of *potentia absoluta* and *potentia ordinata* was, of course, not new to the thinkers of the fourteenth century.[167] The eleventh-century fideist Peter Damian had used the concept as a means of asserting the divine freedom and the absolute transcendence of God while also affirming the constancy and irrevocability of the ordained order of the universe. Hugh of St. Victor understood the ultimate power of God as limited only by the principle of non-contradiction.[168] The terminological distinction between *potentia absoluta* and *potentia ordinata* can, moreover, be found in Aquinas' insistence on the freedom of the divine willing from any determination to do the particular things that God does: considered in itself the divine power is absolute and can do anything that has "the nature of being" — considered as "it is carried into execution," the divine power is ordained, namely, ordered by God's own just willing. Thus it is correct to state "that God can do other things by his absolute power than those he has foreknown and preordained he would do."[169] Duns Scotus and Durandus used the concept in a similar manner: God could, if he chose, dispense with his ordinances. Still, there was a shift in emphasis and in the use of the concept as the language of *potentia ordinata* and *absoluta* moved into the later Middle Ages and became associated with the intellectual development known as the *via moderna*.

---

166. Maurer, *Medieval Philosophy*, p. 270.

167. See the discussions in Oberman, "Some Notes on the Theology of Nominalism," pp. 56-68; Vignaux, *Nominalisme*, in *DTC*, IX, col. 764-765; Francis Oakley, "Pierre D'Ailly and the Absolute Power of God, pp. 59-73; and William Courtenay, "The Dialectic of Omnipotence in the High and Late Middle Ages," in Tamar Rudavsky, ed., *Divine Omniscience and Omnipotence in Medieval Philosophy: Islamic, Jewish, and Christian Perspectives* (Dordrecht: Riedel, 1985), pp. 243-269; and idem, *Capacity and Volition: A History of the Distinction of Absolute and Ordained Power* (Bergamo: P. Lubrina, 1990).

168. Hugh of St. Victor, *De sacramentis*, I, cap. 22 (*PL* 176, col. 214).

169. Aquinas, *Summa theol.*, Ia, q. 25, art. 5.

The *via antiqua* approach related directly to the larger part of the patristic language of divine omnipotence, where the confession of the almighty power of God stands in a direct relationship to the providential care of God for the created order.[170] In the Thomist approach to the concept of divine *potentia* or *omnipotentia*, the emphasis was upon the enactment of God's power and will in the order of the world, although the freedom of God was maintained in the assumption that God's unlimited power was not bound by the world order and certainly not determined by it. Thus, Aquinas was able to speak of an absolute power of God, the *potentia absoluta*, but did not identify this as a power radically different in extent or potential objects from the ordained power of God — instead, he used the concept as one way of identifying his own views over against the arguments of earlier writers, like Scotus Erigena and Abelard, who had argued that necessarily God made the best possible world and, indeed, could have made no other. Aquinas refused both the imposition of necessity on God and the removal of ultimate contingency from the created order.[171]

Beginning with Duns Scotus, the distinction between *potentia absoluta* and *potentia ordinata* became increasingly used as a way of identifying the transcendence of the ultimate divine power over any and all aspects of the world order ordained and sustained by God. In addition, in contrast to the use of the distinction by Aquinas, thinkers of the fourteenth century assumed that God not only can but has, in fact, acted outside of the bounds of his ordained will.[172] Theologians of the *via moderna* like Robert Holcot and Adam Woodham argued that, according to his absolute power, God could lie or undo his promises — yet it remains a matter of debate whether this form of speculation actually removed all limits from the divine power.

Ockham is often identified as taking the notion a step further in terms of the large-scale use of the concept of *potentia absoluta* in the service of his doctrines of divine transcendence and the ultimate unknowability of God. Leff comments that "where Duns had utilized" the *potentia absoluta/ordinata* distinction "to assert the radical contingency of all created forms, Ockham uses it with devastating effect to show the impossibility of discussing matters of faith" — although it certainly must be added that Ockham did not set aside the Scotistic use of the concept to indicate the contingency of the created order.[173] All things of faith, according to Ockham, rest upon the divine decree. Christian morality, the distinction of right from wrong, cannot

---

170. Note that this accent is found throughout the tradition, notably in the church fathers: see André de Halleux, "Dieu le Père tout-puissant," in *Revue Théologique de Louvain*, 8 (1977), pp. 401-22.

171. Thomas Aquinas, *Summa theol.*, Ia, a. 25, q. 5; idem, *De potentia Dei*, q.1, a.5; and idem, *Summa contra gentiles*, II, cap. 23-30; cf. Steinmetz, "Calvin and the Absolute Power of God," in *Calvin in Context*, p. 40.

172. Cf. David B. Burrell, "Creation, Will and Knowledge in Aquinas and Scotus," in *Pragmatik*, I, ed. H. Stachowiak (Hamburg: Felix Meiner, 1985), pp. 246-257 with Felix Alluntis and Alan B. Wolter, "Duns Scotus on the Omnipotence of God," in *Studies in Philosophy and the History of Philosophy*, 5 (1970), pp. 178-222.

173. Leff, *Medieval Thought*, p. 289; cf. Vignaux, *Nominalisme*, in *DTC*, XI, col. 764; Courtenay, "Dialectic of Omnipotence," p. 255.

be rationally deduced. In a relative sense — distinct from the unalterable nature of God — all concepts of good, evil, of merit and reward become contingent upon the divine will. Final reward can be dispensed by God without reference to the present temporal order. God, following the acceptance of Ockham's distinction, could not be bound by reason nor faith by experience. The unbounded divine possibility made natural theology incapable of reaching a knowledge of God — given that divine acts belong to the ordained power. In the realm of morality, however, Ockham assumed that God could command anything that did not violate the law of noncontradiction and that all things commanded by God are by definition "good." In Ockham's thought, therefore, the utterly free will of God establishes all things and defines all norms.[174]

This logic of the *potentia absoluta* placed the essence and attributes of God beyond reason and natural theology. Ockham goes beyond Scotus in refusing to allow that the divine infinitude and oneness can be rationally known. In general, the divine attributes can be known only to faith. Note that the inaccessibility to reason of the divine infinity and oneness stands as a corollary to Ockham's denial of the a posteriori proofs. Recent studies have indicated that neither Scotus nor Ockham claimed an utter arbitrariness and unboundedness of the divine will or power: they assumed, specifically, that even the absolute power was limited by the divine nature itself, as understood in and through the other attributes of God, and that God's was limited by the logically contradictory.[175] Indeed, in Courtenay's view, the notion of God acting absolutely was a development of fourteenth-century thought after Ockham.[176]

3. Divine simplicity. An approach to the problem of divine simplicity related to Aquinas' solution was offered by Henry of Ghent (d. 1293) at the close of the thirteenth century. Henry argued that divine attributes represent something more than ideas or predicates arising from the relation of God to the world, founded on God's essence, but not truly in it. Attributes are predicated of God by similitude and by eminence: they have a certain likeness to the excellencies of God's creatures insofar as those creaturely perfections are included in and founded on the perfection of God.[177] God is one and simple, but the attributes, as representing different ideas and different relations *ad extra*, must also represent genuine distinctions in God. There exist in God,

---

174. See David W. Clark, "Voluntarism and Rationalism in the Ethics of Ockham," in *Franciscan Studies*, 31 (1971), pp. 72-87 and cf. E. Randi, "Ockham, John XII and the Absolute Power of God," in *Franciscan Studies*, 46 (1986), pp. 205-216.

175. See the survey of scholarship in M. A. Pernoud, "The Theory of the *Potentia Dei* according to Aquinas, Scotus and Ockham," in *Antonianum*, 47 (1972), pp. 69-95. Also see the discussions of the topic in Adams, *William Ockham*, II, pp. 1065-1083; and Allan B. Wolter, *The Philosophical Theology of John Duns Scotus*, ed. Marylin McCord Adams (Ithaca and London: Cornell Universty Press, 1990).

176. Courtenay, "Dialectic of Omnipotence," p. 257; cf. Eldredge, "The Concept of God's Absolute Power in the Later Fourteenth Century," pp. 211-226.

177. Thus, Henry of Ghent, *Summa quaestionum ordinariarum theologi recepto praeconio solennis Henrici a Gandavo, cum duplici repertorio, tomos prior-posterior*, 2 vols. (Paris, 1520; repr. St. Bonaventure, N.Y.: The Franciscan Institute, 1953), art. XXXII, q. 2, resp (vol. I, fol. CLCCCIX, K-L).

Henry argued, genuine distinctions of various sorts. After all, the persons in the Trinity are distinct and are traditionally said to be distinct *realiter*. Since, moreover, attributes of power, understanding, and will relate to these persons in their working, these attributes also are distinct in God: goodness, justice, power, understanding, will are distinct from one another — even apart from their distinction as manifest in God's relation to the world. Certainly, if the blessed in heaven are able to know God as good, just, and wise, these attributes must be distinguishable in God apart from God's relationship to the world — given that the blessed in heaven know God immediately rather than by means of God's relations to the world order. Following Aquinas, Henry understands the divine attributes as distinct by reason of analysis founded in the thing (*distinctiones rationis ratiocinatae quae habent fundamentum in re*) or, in his distinctive language, having their "root" (*radix*) in the thing. These are not merely rational distinctions made by our mind (*ratio rationans*) but distinctions which state some truth about God — the attributes are rationally distinct in God, as indicated by the "similitude" or resemblance that they have in the created order, given that creatures possess these attributes by participation in God's being and God possesses such attributes by way of eminence. If this were not the case, Henry notes, and the divine attributes merely the result of rational distinctions on our part, not rooted in the thing, then the attributes noted by theology would be mere figments of the imagination.[178]

Henry concludes, moreover, that he can argue three levels of distinction which do not disrupt the essential simplicity of the one God: (1) distinctions in external relation revealed to us in the manifold ways God appears to his creatures — that is, an exterior distinction recognized in the "vestiges" of God's handiwork: the *via vestigii*; (2) a plurality of attributes which we infer from perfections in the created order and from the resemblance between creaturely and divine perfection, and which we refer to God by way of eminence (*via eminentiae*) as existing in God; (3) the trinity of persons distinct within the divine essence — but, of course, representing no division essential or substantial of it.[179]

This view of the inward distinction of divine attributes was unacceptable to the subtle Doctor, Duns Scotus, who saw it as begging the question: distinction of attributes based on the divine essence but not truly in it, based on our analysis of God's relation to us and correct in a sense from our side, but not from God's side, where simplicity, without an identifiable kind of distinction still reigned even if the distinctions we apprehend are somehow founded on the reality of the one, absolute, divine essence. Scotus launched a critique of this position — chiefly of Henry of Ghent, indirectly of Aquinas — but strove to maintain the noncomposite character of the divine essence. God, for Scotus, is perfect being, and therefore can be characterized neither by composition nor by potency. Whereas Aquinas and Henry proposed three types of distinction, (1) real, (2) by reason of analysis and resting on the thing, and (3) purely

---

178. Henry of Ghent, *Summa quaestionum*, art. LI, q.1, resolutio; q. 3, responsio (vol. II, fol. LII verso- LIII recto).

179. Henry of Ghent, *Summa quaestionum*, art. LI, q.3, ad.2 (vol. II, fol. LV verso, F); Cf. Schwane, *Histoire des Dogmes*, IV, p. 195.

rational, Scotus added a fourth, the "formal distinction residing in things" (*distinctio formalis a parte rei*). According to this *distinctio formalis a parte rei*, the divine attributes are really or substantially the same — the same in the thing (*in re*) — but in a formal sense they are distinct, so that truth, formally, is not goodness and goodness, formally, is not power or justice or wisdom.[180]

That these eternal ideas are in some sense distinct both from one another and from the divine essence as such — without, however, disturbing the essential simplicity of God, was argued at length by Duns Scotus, who held both the formal distinction of the divine ideas from the divine essence and the formal distinction of the divine ideas from one another. (The essence and its attributes or essential properties are, therefore, logically prior to the divine ideas, although the attributes, too, are formally distinct from one another and from the divine essence as well.) With regard to the attributes as well, Scotus set himself in opposition to the views of Aquinas and of Henry of Ghent. According to Henry, the distinction of attributes rests on the way in which the minds of composite creatures must understand the infinitely rich perfection of the non-composite divine essence, yielding the idea of a rational distinction of attributes nonetheless grounded or "rooted" in the thing. Even more pointedly than Henry, the late-medieval nominalists held the attributes to be concepts created in the mind in order to describe the perfection of the divine essence, without any ultimate correspondence to anything in God.[181]

Over against such views, but equally intent on affirming the distinction of attributes within God, Scotus' *distinctio formalis* attempted to find an alternative to the idea of a rational or ratiocinative distinction between attributes, with a basis "in the thing," that is, in God, particularly given its use in Thomas Aquinas' doctrine of the analogical predication of names or attributes of the divine essence and Henry of Ghent's seeming insistence on the equivocal character of terms predicated both of God and of creatures. There are no real distinctions in God, Scotus argued, but, equally so, it is insufficient to explain the divine attributes to argue that they are rationally or ratiocinatively distinct.[182] Scotus' point, certainly, is to try to identify the nature of the distinction in God, based on the assumption that the reasoning mind makes predications by apprehending the formal properties in things: it is not as if the logical realm simply

---

180. Duns Scotus, *Ordinatio*, I, d.8, pars1, q.4 [193]: "est igitur aliqua non-identitas formalis sapientiae et bonitatis, in quantum earum essent distinctae definitiones... Definitio autem non tantum indicat rationem causatam ab intellectu, sed quiditatem rei" and [209] "Ista autem non-identitas formalis stat cum simplicitate Dei, quia hanc differentiam necesse est inter essentiam et proprietatem." Cf. Etienne Gilson, *Jean Duns Scot: Introduction à ses positions fondamentales* (Paris: J. Vrin, 1952), pp. 248-53; Wolter, *Philosophical Theology of John Duns Scotus*, pp. 35-38; and Copleston, *History of Philosophy*, II, pp. 360-362, 529-530.

181. Cf. David C. Steinmetz, *Misericordia Dei: The Theology of Johannes von Staupitz in its Late Medieval Setting* (Leiden: Brill, 1968), pp. 42-43.

182. Cf. Aquinas, *Summa theol.*, Ia, q.13, art. 2 & 4 with Copleston, *History of Philosophy*, II, pp. 352-353, 472, 503-505 and with the citations of Scotus in Minges, *Doctrina philosophica et theologica*, II, pp. 56-60; also note the use of Scotus' view in Henry of Harclay: Mark G. Henninger, "Henry of Harclay on the Formal Distinction in the Trinity," in *Franciscan Studies*, 41 (1981), pp. 254-256, 287-288.

transfers into the real, but rather that the logical attributions we make are grounded in the diverse forms present in the reality of the thing.

According to Scotus, the attributes are formally distinct — as concepts genuinely distinct from other concepts, not as things distinct *realiter* from other things. The divine attributes are, thus, formally or conceptually distinct, implying neither accidents in God nor a composite divine nature but also allowing a distinction to exist in some genuine sense in God, so that, for example, divine goodness is genuinely different from divine omnipotence and a valid distinction is made in theology when these attributes are juxtaposed.[183] Scotus held that formally distinct concepts or attributes remain formally distinct when they are understood as infinite. Thus infinite justice is formally distinct from infinite goodness in the same way that finite justice is distinct from finite goodness. Such distinctions in God do not in any way impugn the essential simplicity of God.[184]

God does not have attributes in the way that created objects have accidents or qualities — rather God as simple being, as the thing or object of theological consideration, has attributes which are each singly and all together identical with his essence, yet even with God these attributes are formally or objectively distinct. The distinction is formal, in that it truly exists between goodness and wisdom insofar as they are objects of thought but are "absolutely inseparable from the thing in which they are apprehended — they cannot exist without the thing and the thing does not exist without them" and from the point of view of the thing itself they do not represent essential divisions or distinctions.[185] "Form" in the Aristotelian sense of the term refers to the essential nature of a thing, indicating determination of that nature as of a certain kind. In this sense, a "formal distinction" is a distinction belonging to the essential nature of a thing but also, in a sense, a non-substantial distinction, a distinction unlike that between one substance and another, one essence and another, one thing and another thing. In developing the idea of a formal distinction, Scotus was postulating a distinction less ultimate than a real or essential distinction, yet a distinction nonetheless inherent in the very nature of a thing. The distinction can be less than real but more than simply rational — more, indeed, than a purely rational distinction based upon our (valid but external) analysis of the thing.

---

183. On the formal distinction in Scotus, see Efrem Bettoni, *Duns Scotus: the Basic Principles of his Philosophy* (Washington: Catholic University of America Press, 1961), pp. 78-81; Wolter, *Philosophical Theology of John Duns Scotus*, pp. 27-41. Also see Bridges, *Identity and Distinction in Petrus Thomae, O. F. M.*, pp. 100-116.

184. Duns Scotus, *Ordinatio*, I, d.8, pars 1, q.4 [193]: "est igitur aliqua non-identitas formalis sapientiae et bonitatis, in quantum earum essent distinctae definitiones... Definitio autem non tantum indicat rationem causatam ab intellectu, sed quiditatem rei" and [209] "Ista autem non-identitas formalis stat cum simplicitate Dei, quia hanc differentiam necesse est inter essentiam et proprietatem." Cf. Gilson, *Jean Duns Scot*, pp. 248-253; P. Raymond, "Duns Scot," in *DTC*, 4/2, col. 1876-1877; Wolter, *The Philosophical Theology of John Duns Scotus*, pp. 35-38; Copleston, *History of Philosophy*, II, pp. 360-362, 529-530.

185. Cf. P. Coffey, *Ontology or the Theory of Being: An Introduction to General Metphysics* (New York: Peter Smith, 1938), p. 154.

In response to such critique (or, perhaps, development) of the Thomist position, the fourteenth-century defender of Aquinas, John of Paris, insisted that the distinction of attributes *ratio ratiocinata* did not leave God devoid of attributes when there were no finite subjects to distinguish them. Indeed, he states explicitly that simplicity rules out "real distinction" (and therefore composition) but not rational distinction: "on the contrary, to the extent that something is simple, it will comprehend in itself multiple *rationes*."[186] Cajetan's reading of Aquinas argued a similar point.[187]

If Scotus' critique of Henry of Ghent's position demanded a fuller sense of distinctions within the Godhead than that offered by either Henry or Aquinas, the nominalist approach to the problem of divine simplicity and the distinction of attributes pressed away from Aquinas in the other direction. Ockham raised the issue of the attributes its most radical form, denying any transfer between the logical and the real, on the ground that forms or ideas are not *in things* but only in the mind of the knower — arguing in effect that the attributes are merely our finite and composite conception of God *ad extra*, identical with the divine essence and therefore with one another, pressing home the point that their essential identity ruled out formal distinction. Indeed, Ockham could argue that the idea of "divine attributes" was a recent doctrine, in contrast with the more correct traditional approach to "divine names."[188] This rejection of the formal distinction coupled with a denial of conceptual distinctions in God carries over into such late medieval thinkers as Adam Wodeham, Gregory of Rimini, and Marsilius of Inghen.[189] In the case of Gregory, at least, the conclusion of distinction *ad extra* only was intended to avoid speculation concerning the Godhead in itself.[190]

Once the rational deductibility of the attributes is denied and fideism asserted, the only problem that remains is the problem of predication. An attribute, argues Ockham, is something predicated, or, more precisely, a predicate. Now that which is predicated is a term, a name, not an independent reality. A term is that which stands for something, a "supposition" about the thing. General suppositions — terms used as universals — are mere words and have only a conceptual reference. Personal suppositions, however, refer to individuals. Only personal suppositions have true significance, that is to say, reference to existent reality. The divine attributes, according to Ockham, are "personal suppositions" — terms or names — which concern God. When we say, "God is good," good stands for God (and is therefore a supposition), and it also signifies God (so that it is a personal supposition). Of course, "God" is a reality and "good" is a term — so that the attribute is not identical with God. It is merely a way of signifying God. This argument carries over to all the attributes. They

---

186. John of Paris, *Commentaire sur les Sentences*, lib. I, q. ii (d. 2, q. 3).

187. Cajetan, *Commentary on Being and Essence*, pp. 245-247, 251, 256.

188. Vignaux, *Nominalisme*, in DTC, 11/1, col. 755, 758.

189. Cf. Hoenen, *Marsilius of Inghen*, pp. 56-59 with Gordon Leff, *Gregory of Rimini: Tradition and Innovation in Fourteenth-Century Thought* (Manchester: Manchester University Press, 1961), pp. 82-84.

190. Leff, *Gregory of Rimini*, p. 84.

are distinct concepts which signify God. Since the divine essence is perfect and indivisible, the attributes are ultimately identical with the essence.

Perhaps echoing and responding to Aquinas' phrase in the commentary on Lombard's *Sentences*, that the concepts of the divine attributes are distinct not only on the part of the thinking or conceptualizing subject but also *"ex proprietate ipsius rei,"* by way of the property of the thing being considered, namely, God,[191] Ockham went on to argue that the divine perfections cannot be distinguished on the basis of the nature of the thing (*ex natura rei*) from the divine essence but are really identical (*idem realiter*) with the divine essence. There is, therefore, in God neither a formal nor a rational distinction between the attributes — as Vignaux points out, Ockham's radical conception of divine simplicity is posed not only against Scotus but also against Aquinas. In Ockham's doctrine, the attributes are only a series of diverse names applied to God by the finite intellect — in himself, in the divine reality there is "one perfection without real or rational distinction" (*uns perfectio indistincta re et ratione*), there is not, in Vignaux's words, "a plurality of attributes, there is but a single perfection."[192] Ockham views the Thomist and Scotist discussions of predication as violations of the divine simplicity because they make the distinction of attributes more than a mere distinction between our concepts. Ockham will allow neither the formal distinction nor the (Thomist) rational distinction founded in the thing by reason of analysis.[193]

Ockham notes three types of distinction: (1) distinctions between things — the real distinction; (2) distinctions between concepts — the purely rational distinction; and (3) the distinction between things and concepts.[194] This ordering of distinctions rests upon the most economical application of the principle of noncontradiction. When Scotus says that wisdom and goodness are formally distinct from the divine essence as well, he unwittingly destroys the ground of real distinctions. Once we admit a formal distinction in real things, we have no reason for stating that a man and an ass are really and not merely formally distinct! Against Aquinas, Ockham will not allow that conceptual distinctions can be founded in the reality of the thing. A thing gives basis for a single concept only — many concepts refer to many things. The many attributes or concepts we frame about God are meaningful to us only as they refer to many individual things. We understand the terms because they refer to distinct qualities in the created order, in which things *are* composite. This means that the multiplication of attributes — even those known by faith in revelation — does not really increase our knowledge about God as he is in himself. This conclusion, which appeared to deny any and all distinctions in the Godhead (or, at very least to remain agnostic on the issue), did, of course, run aground on the doctrine of the Trinity, where Ockham clearly recognized the inability of reason to penetrate the mystery: he retained his denial of

---

191. Aquinas, *In quattuor libros sententiarum*, I, d.2, q.1, art. 2, corpus.

192. Ockham, *In Sent.*, I, dist. 2, q. 2, A, F, cited in Vignaux, *Nominalisme*, in *DTC*, 11/1, col. 755-756.

193. Cf. Adams, *William Ockham*, II, pp. 941-944.

194. Cf. Maurer *Medieval Philosophy*, p. 272, and note the discussion in Marylin McCord Adams, "Ockham on Identity and Distinction," in *Franciscan Studies*, 36 (1976), pp. 5-74.

distinctions in the divine essence and also upheld the orthodox doctrine of the Trinity on the ground that faith and reason do not have equal authority. Reason cannot grasp the doctrine of the Trinity and must yield to faith.[195]

4. Various attributes: their order and arrangement. If the medieval doctors were generally in agreement concerning the identification of the divine attributes, they offered highly varied approaches to the definitions of individual attributes and also to the logic and order of the attributes. The shift from a more optimistic synthesis of faith and reason characteristic of the teachers of the thirteenth century and of the ongoing *via antiqua* to the more critical perspectives of Durandus, Scotus, Ockham, and the later medieval *via moderna* was evidenced by an increased unwillingness to view the attributes as logically deducible, whether from the basic conception of God or from one another, and by an increased unwillingness to view God as capable of being understood. At the root of this change was, certainly, the increased emphasis on the *potentia absoluta* and *potentia ordinata* — but the change also embodied a series of related issues, including a dissatisfaction with many of the demonstrative arguments found, for example, in the theology of Aquinas.

For Scotus, the fundamental concept of God involved the recognition of the existence of God as *primum ens*, or ultimate being, and the recognition that the ultimate being is infinite. Scotus insists that there must be a first or highest being in the orders of efficient and final causes and in the order of perfection or eminence such that it cannot fail to be acknowledged as existing and as infinite — thus linking his unique form of the proof of God's existence with a concept of the triple primacy of God that, in turn, governs his teaching on the divine essence and attributes. Divine infinity becomes the key to understanding Scotus' doctrine and identifying also its distinctive character: in contrast to Aquinas, Scotus does not understand infinity merely as a relational term indicating absence of limitation, nor does he understand it as an attribute derived from the divine simplicity.[196] The essential concept of God for Scotus is "infinite being." In Raymond's words, this fundamental infinity "is the essential, distinctive, and primordial characteristic of God" in the Scotist view, beyond even the "formal infinity" of each of the divine attributes which is rooted in the radical and fundamental infinity of the divine essence as such.[197] This focus on divine infinity as the foundational concept in the doctrine of God surely reflects the earlier Franciscan tradition, notably the thought of Alexander of Hales.

In his discussion of the various divine attributes, Scotus also distinguishes between those attributes that stand as the ultimate, intrinsic modes of the divine essence,

---

195. See Vignaux, "Nominalisme," in *DTC*, 11/1, col. 776-779 and further, *PRRD*, IV, 1.3 (B.2).

196. Scotus, *God and Creatures*, q. 5.1, 10 (pp. 108, 111-112); cf. Richard Cross, *Duns Scotus* (New York: Oxford University Press, 1999), p. 40.

197. Raymond, "Duns Scot," in *DTC*, 4/2, col. 1874-1875, citing Scotus, *Opus Oxoniense*, IV, d. 13, q.1, n.31, and *Opus Oxoniense*, I, d.10, 13; cf. Minges, *Doctrina philosophica et theologica*, I, p. 46; Emmanuel Freitas, "De argumentatione Duns Scoti pro infinitate Dei," in *De Doctrina Ioannis Duns Scoti*, edited by C. Balic, vol. II, pp. 427-433; and Felix Alluntis, "Demonstrability and Demonstration of the Existence of God," in John Ryan and Bernardino M. Bonansea, eds., *John Duns Scotus, 1265-1965* (Washington: CUA Press, 1965), p. 134.

namely, perfection, infinity, simplicity, immutability, eternity, invisibility, and ineffability or incomprehensibility — and those attributes that stand as the acts or actions of the divine life *ad intra*, specifically, intellect or intelligence and will, with its related attribute of omnipotence. Like the concept of divine simplicity,[198] immutability also derives from the infinitude of God. God is absolutely immutable, being subject to no change, whether of form, time, or place.[199]

Eternity follows from the attributes of perfection, infinity, and immutability. In Scotus' view of eternity, moreover, there is a development past Aquinas. Whereas Aquinas, arguably, left the concept of eternity over against time with the paradox that, given the simultaneity of all temporal events with eternity, there is a sense in which temporal events might be thought of as simultaneous with one another,[200] Scotus added a qualifier. He points out that this seeming simultaneity of all temporal events with one another when conceived in relation to eternity would hold only if the eternal divine being were not limitless. Like Alexander of Hales, he defined eternity as a subcategory of divine *immensitas*. This argument allows Scotus to argue that all things are eternally present to God but also to deny that these temporal things have an eternal existence, in Cross' words, "all temporal things are present to eternity" but not "temporally present" — God's limitless existence coexists with all of the divisions or parts of time without compromising their temporality.[201]

Similarly, the divine immensity or omnipresence is also a logical consequence of the divine infinity: since God has no limit he is understood to be in and through all things according to essence. Unlike Aquinas, however, Scotus does not think that the divine omnipresence can be demonstrated, on the ground that one cannot infer essential presence from the presence of divine power — against Aquinas' denial that God's power is such that it acts immediately, Scotus counters that God can, presumably, operate across distances or at least that such operation ought not to be considered a diminution of power.[202]

Scotus' discussion of the attributes of divine life — principally, intellect and will — had a significant formal impact on later dogmatics, particularly given the way in which Scotus can distinguish between the fundamental actuality of the divine essence

198. Scotus, *On God as First Principle*, iii, conclusio 10 (pp. 134-139).

199. Scotus, *On God as First Principle*, iii.

200. Cf. Anthony Kenny, "Divine Foreknowledge and Human Freedom," in A. Kenny, ed., *Aquinas: A Collection of Critical Essays* (London: Macmillan, 1969), p. 264, with Davies, *Thought of Thomas Aquinas*, pp. 103-109, who argues (I believe) convincingly that Aquinas also saw past the problem with a conception of divine *duratio*. See further, 4.4 (D.3-4).

201. See Richard Cross, "Scotus on Eternity and Timelessness," in *Faith and Philosophy*, 14/1 (1997), pp. 12, 16; cf. Scotus, *God and Creatures*, VI.32-37. Also note Edith Wilks Dolnikowski, *Thomas Bradwardine, a View of Time and a Vision of Eternity in Fourteenth-Century Thought* (Leiden: E. J. Brill, 1995).

202. Scotus, *Opus Oxoniense*, I, d. 37, n. 1, and *Reportata Parisiense*, I, d. 37, art. 6; cf. Minges, *Doctrina philosophica et theologica*, II, pp. 38-39; and note Aquinas, *Summa theol.*, I., q. 8, a. 1, ad. 3.

and its operation.[203] Like Aquinas and other earlier thinkers, Scotus insisted that the primary and utterly adequate object of divine knowledge must be the divine essence itself, and that all finite objects are known by God, not in and through the imperfect medium of finite being, but through the divine essence itself. Scotus' own approach to the problem differs from Aquinas' view in arguing that God does not merely know by means of the ideas of things in the divine essence but that the finite order is known by means of the divine essence in such a way that the divine knowledge actually terminates on finite objects: there is a primary act of the divine intellect by which God knows his own essence and a second "instant" or act of the divine intellect by which its knows objects *ad extra* directly. Scotus also differed with Aquinas over the nature of the divine ideas themselves — for Aquinas they are aspects of the divine essence itself, for Scotus they are concepts formed by the divine intellect: according to Scotus, God does not merely know all possibilities, God produces them by an action of his intellect.[204]

Even so, God knows future events by means of his decree, including future conditionals. Scotus can argue in this way given his assumption that the necessary divine knowledge or knowledge of simple intelligence is not merely a knowledge of infinite discrete possibles but of all the interrelations of all possibles and of all the results of those interrelations. God thus knows all conditionals in his infinite knowledge of possibility prior to his decree — and he knows all actual future events, including all instances of free choice, as a result of his decree.[205] A somewhat different solution with similar result is found in the thought of Gregory of Rimini, who (despite his strongly predestinarian inclinations) rested his teaching on the divine eternity: given that all things are present to God, whether past, present, or future, God knows them all with certainty in a single act of knowing — moreover, with respect to the temporal relations of things, God knows as future to particular points in time those things that, at that moment, do not yet exist. God knows actual things in their temporal relationality.[206]

Scotus' view of divine knowledge points toward the underlying voluntarism of his theology: in his view the *voluntas Dei* is absolutely free — free even in relation to the divine understanding, defined only in terms of the love or delight that he has in himself, for the possibilities that he forms in his intellect, and for the actualities that he intends to bring into being.[207] In one sense, Scotus notes, this willing is necessary. God must love himself as the most perfect object — "there is a simple necessity both in the act by which God loves himself and by which he spirates the Love that proceeds, i.e., the Holy Spirit." There is a "necessity of immutability" in all divine willing of objects *ad*

---

203. Cf. the discussion in Muller, *God, Creation, and Providence*, pp. 119-120, 124-127, 143-145, 168.

204. Raymond, "Duns Scot," in *DTC*, 4/2, col. 1879, citing *Opus Oxoniense*, I, d. xxxv; *Reportata Parisiense*, I, dist. xxxv. Cf. Adams, *William Ockham*, II, pp. 1042-1043.

205. Raymond, "Duns Scot," in *DTC*, 4/2, col. 1879, citing *Opus Oxoniense*, I, d. xxxix, n.23; II, d. xxxvii, q. 2, n. 14..

206. Leff, *Gregory of Rimini*, pp. 108-109.

207. See Pietro Scapin, "Il significato fondamentale delle libertà divina secondo Giovanni Duns Scoto," in Balic, ed., *De Doctrina Ioannis Duns Scoti*, II, pp. 519-566.

extra, given that the divine will does not experience successive states such as would imply a change in God. Such necessity, however does not exclude the utter freedom of the divine will inasmuch as, in the first instance, there is no constraint on the divine willing and in the second instance there is no "necessity of inevitability or determination, which not only excludes change or succession but rules out that the divine will could have willed other than it has."[208] Scotus insists that "the divine will contingently wills the goodness or existence of another."[209] This freedom in the divine willing and loving is also characterized by a distinction between the simple love of delight (*amor complacentiae simplicis*) that God has for all the possibilities he conceives and the efficacious love of delight (*amor complacentiae efficaci*) that God has for the possibilities that he creates — indicating that God is ultimately content in the contemplation of all possibilities that arise from his essence and, therefore, also, that the movement from the possible to the actual rests on the freedom of God.[210]

Scotus' views on the divine and its freedom, taken together with his grounding of all possibility in God's intellect, give a significant accent to his understanding of divine omnipotence. Scotus connects the concept of omnipotence to possibility and defines the possible as the causable — neither as the mere opposite of impossible nor as a producible result in opposition to that which is necessarily existent: "Omnipotence is that active power or potency whose scope extends to anything whatsoever that can be created."[211] Given the identity of all that can be created (or caused) with the full range of possibility and the grounding of possibility in the working of the divine intellect, the only limitation on the divine power is God himself, and specifically the divine production of possibility. God, in a primary moment of his understanding, intellectively produces all possibility in the generation of the intelligible essences of things and all of their possible interrelationships — and then God freely wills one particular concatenation of possibilities into actuality. Whereas Aquinas understood the contingency of the created order as its non-necessary existence, Scotus added to this the notion that the order is also contingent because it could have been configured entirely differently.[212]

The omnipotence of God is such that he might have created an entirely different world — and that the contingency of the world order is that, although known immutably and certainly by God, it could be otherwise.[213] This model also has affinities

---

208. Scotus, *God and Creatures*, q. 16.5, 27-28.

209. Scotus, *God and Creatures*, q. 16.33.

210. *Reportata Parisiense*, I, d. 47, q.2, n.2, cited in Minges, *Doctrina philosophica et theologica*, II, p. 129-130. Also see below, 6.5 (B.3-4) for the use of these categories among the Reformed orthodox; divine freedom is discussed in 5.4 (C).

211. Scotus, *God and Creatures*, q. 7.8.

212. Cf. David B. Burrell, "Creation, Will and Knowledge in Aquinas and Scotus," in *Pragmatik*, I, ed. H. Stachowiak (Hamburg: Felix Meiner, 1985), p. 248, with Antonie Vos, "Always on Time: The Immutability of God," in Gijsbert van den Brink and Marcel Sarot, eds., *Understanding the Attributes of God*, pp. 66-67.

213. Vos, "Always on Time: the Immutability of God," p. 66. At greater length, see Antonie Vos, et al., eds., *John Duns Scotus: Contingency and Freedom: Lectura I/39* (Dordrecht and Boston: Kluwer,

with that found somewhat later in Gregory of Rimini: against Ockham's contention that contingency belongs to futures only, Gregory insisted that although in the composite sense it is impossible for something to be and not be at the same time, in the same place, and in the same way, in the divided sense, it is true that any contingent thing both exists and can be nonexistent.[214]

Much of Ockham's doctrine of God stands as a rejection or partial rejection of his predecessors' views, particularly those of Aquinas and Scotus. As already noted, Ockham (and after him Gregory of Rimini) rejected Aquinas' assumption that really or essentially identical divine attributes could be rationally distinct, and he rejected Scotus' formal distinction as well. He accordingly also rejected any *ad intra* distinction of divine attributes. Similarly, Ockham rejected Scotus' notion of "instants" or "moments" in the divine essence or nature. All of Ockham's discussions of divine attributes, therefore, are understood by him as discussions only of our conceptions concerning God.[215]

This means, by extension, that Ockham could not follow Scotus and the Franciscan tradition generally in arguing the primacy of the will in God: given the absence of distinctions in God, no primacy of one attribute over another is conceivable.[216] Still, Ockham could declare unreservedly that the divine will is the cause of all things — meaning, of course, that God as such is the cause of all things. In addition, the divine will stands as the ground of all *ad extra* goodness and righteousness, and if one asks the question of a rule or standard for the operation of the divine will, Ockham must answer that there is none, given the identity of the divine act of willing with the divine will and the divine will with the divine essence itself. Of course, given the identity of the divine will with the divine intellect and the divine goodness, neither could Ockham understand the divine will as irrational or less than good.

Ockham acknowledged the divine omniscience and divine omnipotence — and he debated their implications at length — but, at the same time, he disavowed the various demonstrations of these attributes. By way of example, Aquinas had argued the divine omniscience on the ground that God is the efficient and final cause of all things and therefore must be understood as also knowing all things as caused by himself. Ockham countered that it could not be demonstrated that God is the efficient cause of everything, nor could it be demonstrated either that God is the final cause of all temporal things or that the ordering of all things to an end implies perfect knowledge of them on the part of the orderer — the subsequent demonstration of omniscience must fail as well.[217]

1994). Also see Leonard A. Kennedy, "Divine Omnipotence and the Contingency of Creatures, Oxford, 1330-1350 A.D.," in *The Modern Schoolman*, 61 (1983/84), pp. 249-258; and idem, "Early Fourteenth-Century Franciscans and Divine Absolute Power," in *Franciscan Studies*, 50 (1990), pp. 197-233.

214. Leff, *Gregory of Rimini*, p. 110.

215. Cf. Adams, *William Ockham*, II, pp. 941-942; Leff, *Gregory of Rimini*, pp. 85-86.

216. Vignaux, "Nominalisme," in *DTC*, XI, col. 762.

217. Ockham, *In Sent.*, I, d.35, q.2; d.42, q. unica.

As for divine omnipotence, Ockham followed a similar line of argument, given Aquinas' logical grounding of the concept in the assumption of the universal divine efficient causality.[218] As Adams comments, the numerous objections leveled by modern writers against Ockham's conception of divine omnipotence are a bit curious inasmuch as the doctrine itself was an aspect of the normative Christianity that Ockham confessed in accord with the entire tradition, and inasmuch as Ockham did not claim that God could either bring about logical impossibilities or make unmakeable or impossible things.[219] Still, Ockham and various other thinkers of his era did raise questions concerning the extent of divine omnipotence that pressed the doctrine toward paradox — could God, for example, command a person not to love him and would obedience to such a command imply love of God?[220]

The difficulty with Ockham's thought on the point, at least from the perspective of various objectors, lay in the way in which he distinguished between the absolute power (*potentia absoluta*) and the ordained power (*potentia ordinata*) of God and the appearance of a radically arbitrary divine power hovering behind all of the works of God. Here too, however, further analysis of his thought has removed many of the perceived problems. In the first place, neither Ockham nor other nominalists like Aureole argued two distinct powers in the Godhead, but only that the distinction could be made *ad extra* concerning God's relation to the world. Second, Ockham did not claim that these powers worked by turns, as if God made some things "ordinately" and others absolutely or "inordinately": God makes nothing inordinate or set apart from what he has ordained.[221] In the view of Vignaux and Oberman, the distinction between ordained and absolute power ought to be understood in terms of the definition of possibility: the possible can be understood in terms of the way God has ordered the world or in terms of the ability of God to do anything that does not include a contradiction — in the former, restricted sense, the possible is what can occur under the ordained power of God, in the latter, far broader sense, the possible is that which can occur under the absolute power of God. The distinction concerns, moreover, the relationship between ultimate possibility and actuality, between what God is able to do (*potest facere*) and what God in fact wills to do (*vult facere*). The distinction is intended, therefore, among other things, to identify the radical freedom of God and the radical contingence of the entire created order. God is free not only not to have created the world but, given his absolute power, to have created an entirely different world.[222]

---

218. Ockham, *In Sent.*, I, d.35, q.2; d.42, q. unica.

219. Adams, *William Ockham*, II, pp. 1151-1156.

220. Cf. Leonard A. Kennedy and Margaret E. Romano, "John Went, O.F.M. and Divine Omnipotence," in *Franciscan Studies*, 47 (1987), pp. 138-170.

221. Vignaux, "Nominalisme," in *DTC*, XI, col. 764, citing Ockham, *Quodlibet* VI, q. 1; cf. Peter Aureole, *Sententiae*, I, d. 44, a. 5.

222. Vignaux, "Nominalisme," in *DTC*, XI, col. 764; Oberman, "Some Notes on the Theology of Nominalism," p. 58; and cf. the discussion of *potentia absoluta* and *ordinata* in Oberman, *Archbishop Thomas Bradwardine: A Fourteenth-Century Augustinian. A Study of his Theology in Its Historical Context* (Utrecht: Kemink & Zoon, 1957), pp. 35-40; also note Leff, *Gregory of Rimini*, pp. 91-92.

The effect of this distinction in nominalist theologies, as Oberman has noted, was to emphasize the sovereignty and immediacy of God as well as create a rift between faith and reason. The radical contingency of the created order stood in the way of chains of reasoning that led from perceptions of the world to conclusions concerning the nature of God — yet, contrary to the possible inference that this rift between faith and reason turned God into a cipher: "in his quest for certainty, the Nominalist makes a clear distinction between the revelation of God Himself and human conclusions, but the revelation in creation and in Christ is not attacked or undermined."[223] From the perspective of the doctrine of God, the nominalist model represents an utter rejection of the Scotist interest in the distinction of attributes and, therefore, in the inward order of the divine life or, indeed, in the "psychology of God"[224]: where Scotus argued the freedom of the divine will in its ordered relation to the divine intellect, Ockham refused the concept of an order in the name of divine simplicity, strictly identifying essence, intellect, and will in God.

---

223. Oberman, "Some Notes on the Theology of Nominalism," pp. 56-57.
224. Vignauz, "Occam, Guillaume," in *DTC*, XI , col. 881.

2

The Doctrine of God from the Sixteenth to the Early Eighteenth Century

2.1 The Doctrine of God in the Reformation

A. Views on God at the Beginning of the Reformation

1. Luther and Melanchthon. Discussions of the Reformers' views of the doctrine of God frequently begin with Luther's negation of the view of God proposed by a rationalistic *theologia gloriae* and then, with reference either to the medieval scholastic doctrine of God or to the doctrine of the Protestant orthodox, proceed to drive a wedge between the Reformation and traditional theological system, specifically on the issue of the divine essence and attributes. Once the polemic of Luther's early theology is taken as a norm for understanding the nature of the Reformation as a whole, then it becomes a very easy matter to drive another wedge between Reformation and orthodoxy. After all, the appearance of the orthodox theological systems is not at all like the appearance of early Reformation treatises, and, indeed, the subjects treated as well as the detail of the treatment could, on superficial examination, appear to be a return to the medieval scholastic models.

It is certainly true that Luther objected strenuously to the late medieval scholastic approach to the doctrine of God. The evidence that can be gathered from his early marginalia on Lombard's *Sentences* indicate a distaste for the lengthy discussion of divine attributes in a speculative manner, divorced from the doctrine of the Trinity — indeed, Luther seems to have preferred a pattern of theological system that began with Trinity and did not separate out the discussion of the divine attributes as the fundamental way of approaching the doctrine of God. This, at least, appears to have been his view at a very early point in his teaching career.[1] In addition, the polemic found in the Heidelberg Disputation against the *theologia gloriae*, together with Luther's positive identification of the *theologia crucis*, indicates a strong suspicion on the part of the Reformer that a rational ascent toward the divine had no relation to the chief purpose of Christian theology, the right teaching of Christ and the gospel.[2] The problem of the *theologia gloriae* can probably be understood as a soteriological and christological intensification of Luther's fundamentally nominalistic doubts concerning the validity of rational speculation concerning the doctrine of God — and, therefore, primarily as a point made not so much about the *content* of traditional theological system as about the proper approach to theological issues.

Nonetheless, a "theology of Luther" culled from the vast corpus of his works and arranged in a more or less systematic order offers the picture, somewhat surprising, given Luther's reservations concerning traditional theological system, of a nearly complete discussion of the divine attributes.[3] These reflections in no way diminish Luther's originality: Luther certainly did not reverse his views on metaphysics and engage in speculation concerning the divine essence and attributes; he assumed the ultimate hiddenness of the divine Being, and he was consistently guided in his discussions of the attributes both by his biblical exegesis and by his view that God is known in relation, particularly in saving relation, to the world. It is not the case, however, that Luther's perceptions concerning the character of true theology excised consideration of the divine omnipotence, majesty, omnipresence, or of an examination of the tetragrammaton that, in a rather traditional manner, yielded up consideration of the eternity and absoluteness of divine Being.[4]

The way in which Luther's concern for the right approach to theology actually relates to the problem of constructing a system of Protestant theology and, specifically, a

---

1. See Paul Vignaux, *Luther, Commentateur des Sentences* (Paris: J. Vrin, 1935), pp. 24-30, and see the description of Luther's work as *Sentence*-commentator in Richard P. Desharnais, "Reason and Faith, Nature and Grace: A Study of Luther's Commentaries on the *Sentences* of Lombard," in *Studia Int. Filosofie*, 3 (1971), pp. 55-64.

2. See especially Gerhard Ebeling, *Luther: An Introduction to His Thought*, trans. R. A. Wilson (Philadelphia: Fortress, 1970), pp. 226-227; cf. the discussion in Paul Althaus, *The Theology of Martin Luther*, trans. Robert C. Schultz (Philadelphia: Fortress, 1966), pp. 20-34. In the following, Luther's works are cited from Martin. D. *Martin Luthers Werke. Kritische Gesamtausgabe*, 66 vols. (Weimar: Hermann Böhlaus Nachfolger, 1883-1987), hereinafter, *WA*; or from the translation, *Luther's Works*, ed. Jaroslav Pelikan and Helmut Lehmann, 56 vols. (St. Louis: Concordia / Philadelphia: Fortress, 1955-86), hereinafter, *LW*.

3. E.g., Julius Köstlin, *The Theology of Luther in Its Historical Development and Inner Harmony*, 2 vols., trans. Charles E. Hay (Philadelphia: Lutheran Publication Society, 1897; repr. St. Louis: Concordia, 1986), II, pp. 274-310. This culling process took place already in the sixteenth century, as evidenced by numerous sets of *loci communes theologici* complied from Luther: see Robert A. Kolb, *Martin Luther as Prophet, Teacher, and Hero: Images of the Reformer, 1520-1620* (Grand Rapids: Baker Book House, 1999). Note the lengthy presentations of the essence and attributes of God in *Loci communes D. Martini Lutheri, viri Dei & Prophetae Germanici, ex Scriptis ipsius Latinis forma gnomologica & aphoristica collecti, & in qinque classis distributi*, a M. *Theodosio Fabrico, ecclesiae Gorringensis pastore* (London: R. H. & W. E., 1651), I.i-ii, xii-xiii, xv, xix-xxii.

4. Köstlin, *Theology of Luther*, II, pp. 276-280.

Protestant *locus de Deo*, is very subtle. As noted in a previous volume,[5] the early Reformation rejection of scholasticism involved the rejection of the speculative excesses of a method and the rejection of certain doctrinal conclusions, particularly concerning the doctrines of salvation and the church. Other doctrines, like the doctrines of God, creation, and providence were never the objects of direct debate. Luther's comments about theology have been taken by some as a demand for the thorough recasting of theology, whereas other scholars — in the absence of any such attempt on Luther's part — have understood them as references to a theological approach, the effect of which can be clearly identified only in certain primarily soteriological and ecclesial topics and which may not have any great effect on other doctrinal issues. On many theological topics, Luther appears to have held — and to have continued to hold throughout his life — fairly traditional views. This appears to have been the case, despite Luther's polemic against the *theologia gloriae*, with the doctrine of God.

Köstlin refers directly to this problem in his classic study of Luther's theology:

> we shall be compelled to pass rapidly over many subjects which in a complete system of theology would demand more extended treatment. These will be found to be, in part, subjects in the treatment of which Luther adopts largely traditional formulas, having found no occasion to recast them in the light of the newly-fixed central point of saving doctrine. Among such subjects may be mentioned the Trinity, angels, Creation, etc. They are in part, also, doctrinal points and questions in regard to which the peculiarity of Luther's position lay precisely in his refusal to enter upon their consideration in such a way as may be appropriate in a dogmatic system. This, again, is susceptible of various interpretations. Thus, for example, we find among the very frequent references of the Reformer to the divine attributes, some of which throw a new and thoroughly characteristic light upon this important subject, no attempt anywhere to classify, or group, the separate attributes with precision. The reason for this, is, as intimated, a lack of interest in formal and systematic arrangement.[6]

We cannot easily infer how Luther would have constructed a system of theology or a doctrine of the divine attributes — nor can we infer that he opposed such construction. There is evidence that he did not follow out the polemic against the *theologia gloriae* toward a denial of the possibility or the propriety of any discussion of the divine attributes, just as there is some evidence that he had new insight into the way in which some of the attributes might be discussed. Nor can we easily infer how Luther would have regarded the question of the distinction of the attributes — although there is a high probability that he would have followed the nominalist explanation and understood them as conceptually distinct *ad extra* only. The latter two points, moreover, must be taken into consideration not only when comparing Luther's thought with the thought of the Protestant orthodox, but also when comparing it with the thought of other Reformers, most of whom were not nearly as creative as Luther in their approach to theology.

---

5. Cf. *PRRD*, I, 2.3 (A.1) with the discussion in Muller, *Unaccommodated Calvin*, pp. 39-58.
6. Köstlin, *Theology of Luther*, II, p. 274.

In accord with the antispeculative thrust of Luther's reformatory theology, Melanchthon's earliest *Loci communes* omitted all discussion of what seemed to be speculative topics divorced from the saving message of the gospel or of what could be classified as "exalted topics" beyond human comprehension, such as the doctrines of God and the Trinity. In later editions of the *Loci* (1536, 1543), the doctrine of God has returned in the form of an introduction to the topic, a traditional definition of God, referring to the essence, attributes, and Trinity, followed by extended meditation on the Trinity.[7] Melanchthon also lectured on logic, ethics, and various topics in the area of natural philosophy, including the doctrine of the soul. In these efforts, he emphasized the remnants of the natural light that remained in human beings following the Fall and, although he recognized that the full and necessary relationship with God provided by faith in the teachings of Scripture was in no way available to philosophy, he indicated that philosophy did know of the existence of God, the identification of the good with God's will, and the duty of worshiping God. In this context, it is hardly surprising that proofs of God's existence began to appear in Protestant theology, as early as Melanchthon's *Loci communes* of 1536. Nor is it surprising that the Protestant proofs often took the form of rhetorical or persuasive arguments rather than purely logical demonstrations, given the role of Melanchthon in the development of rhetoric in the sixteenth century.[8]

2. Zwingli. At the very wellsprings of Reformed theology, however, in the thought of the scholastically and humanistically trained Ulrich Zwingli, we find a clear and strong precedent for a highly developed and quite traditional doctrine of God that evidences ties to the older Christian tradition and to classical philosophy. Stephens makes the point well that "the centre of Zwingli's theology is God — not God as opposed to Christ, but as opposed to all that is not God."[9] In contrast to Luther, moreover, Zwingli offers a well-developed doctrine of God which, despite Zwingli's stated distaste for philosophical speculation and for the intrusion of philosophical categories into the doctrine of God, is quite traditional. Any attempt to argue discontinuity between the Reformation and the Reformed orthodox doctrine of God will need to sever Zwingli from the Reformation.

It is entirely incorrect to claim that Zwingli "presents the doctrine of God in the form of the doctrine of providence and predestination."[10] There is, to be sure, a discussion of providence in Zwingli's doctrine of the knowledge of God as found in the *Commentarius de vera et falsa religione*. There is, however, no discussion of predestination at this point in the *Commentarius* but only a reference to the subsequent

---

7. Melanchthon, *Loci communes* (1521), in *Opera quae supersunt omnia*, ed. C. G. Bretschneider and H. E. Bindseil, *Corpus Reformatorum*, vols. 1-28 (Brunswick: Schwetschke, 1834-1860), 21, col. 83-84 (hereinafter CR); cf. *Loci communes* (1536), in CR, 21, col. 255-269; *Loci communes* (1543), in CR, 21, col. 607-637.

8. See below, 3.2 (B.2-4).

9. W. P. Stephens, *The Theology of Huldrych Zwingli* (Oxford: Clarendon Press, 1986), p. 80.

10. Weber, *Foundations of Dogmatics*, I, p. 464.

discussion of that doctrine in the chapter on merit.[11] The crucial characteristic of Zwingli's doctrine in the *Commentarius*, that explains both his lengthy discussion of natural and philosophical knowledge of God and his discussion of the doctrine of providence is his concentration in the third and fourth sections of the *Commentarius* on the juxtaposition of the "knowledge of God" and the "knowledge of man" — a theme that would be echoed by Calvin's *Institutes*. Nor, indeed, do we find a doctrine of God developed at length in Zwingli's treatise on providence — although Zwingli offers evidence here of a traditional view of the essence and attributes of God, and evidences some scholastic and philosophical background in his interest in arguing providence from the simplicity, perfection, truth, and goodness of the supreme being.[12]

Zwingli begins his doctrine of God with the statement that "*What* God is is perhaps above human understanding, but not *that* God is."[13] The existence of God, Zwingli notes, is seldom disputed. Philosophers and the "heathen" in general acknowledge it "in widely different ways." But this diversity itself indicates the problem of general or natural knowledge: "*what* God is, we have as little knowledge from ourselves as a beetle has of what man is."[14] The fundamental problem confronting human beings in their attempt to gain knowledge of God is the utter disproportion between the infinite perfection of God and the imperfection of finite creatures. God, writes Zwingli, is a hidden God. Here as well, Zwingli evidences his relationship to the scholastic background, potentially to the Scotist or nominalist line of late medieval thought — although, clearly, the form and method of his discourse are not at all scholastic. Indeed, he protests against philosophical attempts to understand the divine nature and declares all such speculation false. Rather than beginning with philosophy or reason, theology ought to begin with the biblical revelation of God's "absolute being" in Exodus 3:13-16 followed by the revelation of the goodness of God in creation.[15] Indeed, both in the *Commentarius* and in his treatise on providence, Zwingli evidences a strong sense of the necessary connection between being and goodness. Here also is an adumbration of the doctrine of God in later orthodoxy — the traditionary background is obvious, but the point is based primarily on exegesis rather than philosophy.[16]

B. The Doctrine of God in the Work of the Second-Generation Codifiers

1. Calvin, Viret, and Bullinger. When we turn to the group of what can be called second-generation codifiers, Reformation-era writers who were a decade or more

---

11. Ulrich Zwingli, *Commentary on True and False Religion*, ed. Samuel Macauley Jackson and Clarence Nevin Heller (Philadelphia, 1929; repr. Durham, N.C.: Labyrinth Press, 1981), pp. 70, 271, 272, 274.

12. Zwingli, *On Providence*, in *On Providence and Other Essays*, ed. John W. Hinke (Durham, N.C.: Labyrinth Press, 1983), pp. 133-134, 137-138, 147-148.

13. Zwingli, *Commentary on True and False Religion*, p. 58.

14. Zwingli, *Commentary on True and False Religion*, pp. 59-61.

15. Zwingli, *Commentary on True and False Religion*, pp. 61-62; further, below, 4.2 (B.2-3, 5).

16. As Stephens indicates, *Theology of Huldrych Zwingli*, pp. 6-7, the roots of Zwingli's thought are difficult to distinguish: some elements appear to have nominalist or Ockhamist frames of reference, whereas other may be Scotistic, and still others, Thomistic.

younger than Luther, Bucer, and Zwingli, who approached the Reformation as a movement under way, and who began the work of developing and codifying the theology of Reform into systems of theology — *loci communes* and other more formal bodies of doctrine — we enter a rather different phase of the development of Reformed theology, one in which the doctrinal and exegetical continuities between Reformed doctrine and the teachings of previous centuries become more formally apparent.

Calvin registered the problem of order and organization in his 1539 redaction of the *Institutes*, noting that "our wisdom, in so far as it ought to be deemed true and solid wisdom, consists almost entirely of two parts: the knowledge of God and of ourselves," but that "it is not easy to determine which of the two precedes and gives birth to the other."[17] Still, the literary necessity of coming to terms with the problem of arrangement, led Calvin to assert the priority of the knowledge of God: "But though the knowledge of God and the knowledge of ourselves are bound together by a mutual connection, due arrangement requires that we treat of the former in the first place, and then descend to the latter."[18] Like Melanchthon's exposition, but more attuned to the controversies of the day, Calvin's discussion of God in the *Institutes* is, in large part, an exposition of the doctrine of the Trinity, albeit prefaced with a discussion of the infinite, spiritual essence of God.[19]

Calvin appears not only to have despised philosophical speculation into theological matters, but also to have avoided any lengthy discussion of the divine essence or of the attributes, either their order and arrangement or their number and definitions, in his *Institutes*. This approach has led some scholars, most notably Niesel, to argue that "Calvin does not use his knowledge of Scripture to produce any description of the being of God," and then proceed to discuss only Calvin's views on the Trinity and omit any discussion of the divine essence and attributes.[20] It may even be wrongly inferred that Calvin had a fundamental objection to the doctrine of the divine essence and attributes as presented in traditional, scholastic dogmatics. As many passages in Calvin's commentaries reveal — particularly the commentaries on the Old Testament

---

17. John Calvin, *Institutio christianae religionis nunc vere demum suo titulo respondens* (Strasbourg: Rihel, 1539), I, fol. 2r; cf. John Calvin, *Institutio christianae religionis, in libros quatuor nunc primum digesta, certisque distincta capitibus, ad aptissimam methodum: aucta etiam tam magna accessione ut propemodum opus novum haberi possit* (Geneva: Robertus Stephanus, 1559), I.i.1. In citing the 1559 *Institutes*, I have consulted both *Institutes of the Christian Religion*, trans. Henry Beveridge, 2 vols. (Edinburgh, 1845; repr. Grand Rapids: Eerdmans, 1994) and *Institutes of the Christian Religion*, ed. John T. McNeill, trans. Ford Lewis Battles, 2 vols. (Philadelphia: Westminster, 1960), hereinafter referenced as "Calvin, *Institutes*." Calvin's shorter tracts and treatises are cited from *Selected Works of John Calvin: Tracts and Letters*, ed. Henry Beveridge and Jules Bonnet, 7 vols. (Grand Rapids: Baker Book House, 1983); John Calvin, *Treatises Against the Anabaptists and Against the Libertines*, trans. and ed. Benjamin Wirt Farley (Grand Rapids: Baker Book House, 1982); John Calvin, *Concerning the Eternal Predestination of God*, trans. with an intro. by J.K.S. Reid (London: James Clarke, 1961); and *Calvin's Calvinism: Treatises on the Eternal Predestination of God and the Secret Providence of God*, trans. Henry Cole (London, 1856; repr. Grand Rapids: Reformed Free Publishing Association, n.d.).

18. Calvin, *Institutio* (1539), I, fol. 2r; cf. *Institutes* (1559), I.i.3.

19. Calvin, *Institutes* (1559), I.xiii.1.

20. Niesel, *Theology of Calvin*, p. 54.

that appeared in the latter half of his career — Calvin had an abiding interest in the divine attributes and an ever increasing interest in such issues as the power of God. The absence of certain doctrinal topics from the *Institutes* ought to be explained either because there was no great controversy over the topics — as is certainly the case with the doctrine of God — or from the fact that Calvin (who was not trained in theology) built the *Institutes* gradually over many years without asking precisely which topics ought to be included in order for the originally catechetical work to be transformed into a manual for theology. Thus, Calvin not only omits discussion of the divine attributes from the *Institutes*, he also omits discussion of creation ex nihilo and of the doctrine of covenant — issues that he presents in detail in his commentaries.[21] Calvin does, then, offer extended discussion of the divine attributes, albeit not in the *Institutes*. What remains a matter of more uncertainty is the issue of the distinction of the attributes: Calvin's understanding, as we will note below, is susceptible of a nominalist interpretation.

Viret's approach is rather different from Calvin's: his language concerning God (particularly concerning the Trinity) has more explicit roots in the patristic and medieval tradition than Calvin's. Like Calvin, he engages in a discussion of the problem of the knowledge of God, more clearly indicating the divine infinitude as the ground of the problem, and he does offer discussion of various divine attributes in his *Instruction chrestienne*, albeit not in one place as a unified doctrinal topic.[22] Viret thus describes God as eternal, simple, free, immutable, impassible, infinite in power, the fountain of all good, the efficient and final cause of all things, but also as jealous, loving, merciful, kind, and gracious. In addition, Viret accents the creative work of God and, against the deists and atheists of his time, offers what has been called a natural theology emphasizing the revelation of God in nature and in the human being.[23]

---

21. Cf. Calvin, *Commentary upon the Book of Genesis*, Gen. 1:1 (*CTS Genesis*, I, p. 70). N.B., I have cited Calvin's commentaries from *Commentaries of John Calvin*, 46 vols. (Edinburgh: Calvin Translation Society, 1844-55; repr. Grand Rapids: Baker Book House, 1979). The set is abbreviated as CTS, followed by the biblical book and, when applicable, the volume number of the commentary on that particular book. I have also consulted John Calvin, *Sermons of Maister Iohn Calvin, upon the Book of Iob*, trans. Arthur Golding (London: George Bishop, 1574; repr. Edinburgh: Banner of Truth, 1993); *Sermons of M. John Calvin, on the Epistles of S. Paule to Timothie and Titus*, trans. L. T. (London: G. Bishop, 1579; repr. Edinburgh: Banner of Truth, 1983); and *The Sermons of M. Iohn Calvin upon the Fifth Booke of Moses called Deuteronomie*, trans. Arthur Golding (London: Henry Middleton, 1583; repr. Edinburgh: Banner of Truth, 1987). Latin and French texts of Calvin's commentaries, sermons, and treatises, unless otherwise noted will be cited from *Ioannis Calvini opera quae supersunt omnia*, ed. G. Baum, E. Cunitz, and E. Reuss (Brunswick: Schwetschke, 1863-1900), hereinafter, CO.

22. And see Georges Bavaud, *Le réformateur Pierre Viret (1511-1564): Sa théologie* (Geneva: Labor et Fides, 1986), pp. 49-54.

23. Pierre Viret, *Instruction chrestienne en la doctrine de la Loy et de l'Évangile*, 2 parts (Geneva, 1564), II, pp. 68, 85, 453, 502, 575, 596-597; idem, *Exposition familière sur le Symbole des Apostres* (Geneva, 1560), pp. 5, 60; cf. the assessment of Charles Schnetzler in *Pierre Viret d' après lui-même*, pages extraites des oeuvres du Réformateur ... par Charles Schnetzler, Henri Vuilleumier, et Alfred Schroeder, avec la collaboration d' Eugène Choisy et de Philippe Godet (Lausanne: Georges Bridel, 1911), p. 256.

Bullinger, who is generally thought to be a far less formal or rigid thinker than Calvin, devoted far more space to the discussion of the names, attributes, and essence of God than did the Genevan. Indeed, the example of Bullinger adds still more weight to the contention that the amount of space devoted to such traditional discussions by the Reformers has less to do with a theological choice on the part of some to avoid such topics than with the fact of more theological training in the personal history of others: Bullinger was, after all, trained in patristic and scholastic theology in Cologne.[24] Thus, in the final section of his fourth *Decade*, Bullinger notes that, up to this point, his sermons had dealt with "the word of God" and its "lawful exposition," with "the Christian faith, the love of God and our neighbor." His arguments, he intimates, had all been premised on a view of God, of Christ, of the Holy Ghost, and of the church which must now be discussed at greater length. He begins, appropriately, with a sermon, "Of God; of the true knowledge of God, and of the diverse ways of knowing him; that God is one in substance, and three in persons."[25] In his shorter *Compendium*, Bullinger briefly enumerates the divine attributes that believers ought to consider in their study of the faith: God is spirit, infinite and immense, incomprehensible, omnipresent, omniscient, almighty, eternal, righteous, truthful, bountiful, loving, faithful, merciful, and good — indeed, the source of all goodness.[26] Bullinger, thus, may be viewed as more comfortable with the tradition than Calvin, though surely his theology is stylistically, in its approach to Scripture and to the exposition of doctrine, far closer to Calvin than it is to the teaching of the late medieval doctors.

2. Hyperius, Musculus, Vermigli, and Hutchinson. Even more telling are the examples of Andreas Hyperius' *Methodus theologiae*, Wolfgang Musculus' *Loci communes*, and Peter Martyr Vermigli's *Loci communes*, in which the doctrine of God receives a full and massive elaboration, indicating a clearer continuity with the scholastic tradition than either Calvin's *Institutes* or Bullinger's *Decades*, and offering a significant basis in the theology of the second-generation Reformers for the scholastic development of the Reformed doctrine of God. Hyperius' treatment is not as vast, but it gives ample evidence of the continuity between the traditional teaching concerning divine existence, essence, and attributes — replete with patristic references, use of Lombard's *Sentences*, and dialogue with the medieval tradition on such issues as the proofs.[27] Musculus devoted a full nineteen chapters of his *loci* to the doctrine of God, fourteen of which are devoted specifically to the discussion of the divine names and attributes — namely, to the divine names, nature, sufficiency, omnipotence, will, truth, goodness, love, mercy, power and dominion, justice (or righteousness), foreknowledge, wrath,

---

24. On Bullinger's education, see Fritz Blanke, *Der junge Bullinger, 1504-1531* (Zürich: Zwingli-Verlag, 1942).

25. Heinrich Bullinger, *The Decades of Henry Bullinger*, trans. H.I., edited by Thomas Harding, 4 vols. (Cambridge: Cambridge University Press, 1849-1852), IV, sermon iii.

26. Heinrich Bullinger, *Compendium christianae religionis* (Zürich, 1556), II.ii.

27. Andreas Gerardus Hyperius, *Methodus theologiae, sive praecipuorum christianae religionis locorum communium, libri tres* (Basel, 1568).

and judgments.[28] Vermigli's *Loci communes*, drawn together posthumously from his commentaries and treatises by Robert Masson, offers a discussion of the divine names and attributes prior to its extensive doctrine of the Trinity.[29]

Significant here also is the treatise by the English theologian Roger Hutchinson, *The Image of God or laie mans booke* (1550).[30] Hutchinson's work is a treatise intended for laity in which the entire doctrine of God, essence, attributes, and Trinity is developed as a foundation for religion and a bulwark against heresies. The work is significant in that it surveys the entire doctrine of God in fairly simple terms, presuming the framework of traditional doctrine but never moving into technical language — while at the same time assuming that a right understanding of essence, attributes, and Trinity is proof against such heresies as transubstantiation, anthropomorphism, the sacrifice of the Mass, universal salvation, the Epicurean doctrine of an absent deity, the primacy of Peter, denials of hell, Arianism, and Manicheeism.

If, therefore, the magisterial reformers sometimes exhibited a certain reticence in developing a full-scale doctrine of God, they nonetheless adhered to the framework of the theology of the Western tradition.[31] This is not the case in the writings of the more dissident thinkers of the time, particularly those who are remembered generally as antitrinitarians. Their theologies, although focused on the doctrines of the Trinity and the Person of Christ,[32] also contained elements of protest against the traditional views of the church concerning divine essence and attributes. This is perhaps most notably the case in the thought of Lelio and Fausto Socinus, where the language of God focuses on judicial and moral concepts and excludes some attributes, such as omnipresence and omniscience, as insupportable.[33] Had either of the Socini published their ideas widely at an early date, their teachings on the divine nature would certainly have become objects of controversy during the Reformation. The full impact of their

---

28. Wolfgang Musculus, *Loci communes sacrae theologiae* (Basel, 1560; 3rd ed., 1573), cap. 41-55, omitting cap. 52, *De providentia* as not, strictly, dealing with an attribute. The *Loci communes* were translated as *Commonplaces of Christian Religion* (London, 1563; 2nd ed., 1578). See the discussion in Robert B. Ives "The Theology of Wolfgang Musculus (1497-1562)" (Ph.D. diss.: University of Manchester, 1965), pp. 135-142.

29. Peter Martyr Vermigli, *P. M. Vermilii loci communes* (London, 1576; 2nd ed., 1583); and in translation, *The Common Places of Peter Martyr*, trans. Anthony Marten (London, 1583), I.xii.

30. *The Image of God or laie mans booke, in which the right knowledge of God is disclosed, and diverse doutes besydes the principal matter* (Cambridge, 1550), reissued by the Parker Society (Cambridge: Cambridge University Press, 1542).

31. Cf. the similar conclusion in Richard Kyle, "The Divine Attributes in John Knox's concept of God,"in *Westminster Theological Journal*, 48/1 (1986), pp. 161-162, 172.

32. Because of the division of the topic, more detailed discussion of the various antitrinitarians is reserved for *PRRD*, IV, 2.1 (B).

33. Cf. the discussion in Johann August Wilhelm Neander, *Lectures on the History of Christian Dogmas*, trans. John Ryland, 2 vols. (London: Bohn, 1858), pp. 644-645, with Otto Zöckler, "Socin und der Socianismus" in *Realencyclopaedie für protestantische Theologie und Kirche*, 3rd ed., 24 vols. (Leipzig: J. C. Hinrich, 1896-1913), 18, pp. 459-480 (hereinafter, *RE*); and note especially, Otto Fock, *Der Sozinianismus nach seiner Stellung in der Gesamtentwickelung des christlichen Geistes, nach seinem historischen Verlauf und nach seinem Lehrbegriff dargestellt*, 2 vols. (Kiel, 1847; repr. Aalen: Scientia Verlag, 1970), II, pp. 414-454.

teachings on the doctrine of God would become apparent, however, only in the era of orthodoxy.

C. The Doctrine of God in the Reformed Confessions

1. Confessions of the sixteenth century. We ought not to expect and certainly do not find any revolutionary ideas or even any doctrines related specifically to the Reformation in the chapters of our confessions which deal with the unity and Trinity of God.[34] This is one of the places where the Reformed most clearly manifest their catholicity and confess, together with all genuine representatives of the Christian church on earth, the universal truth of one God in three persons. Most of the Reformation-era confessions, from the Augsburg Confession and Zwingli's *Christianae fidei expositio* to the great national confessions of the mid-sixteenth century, like the Gallican and the Belgic Confessions, the Thirty-nine Articles, and the Irish Articles, direct our attention toward this catholicity or universality of our faith through their explicit reference to the Apostles', the Nicene, and the Athanasian Creeds or to the consensus of the fathers of the church during the first five centuries.[35] The ancient creeds stand as clear statements of biblical truth and, precisely because they are biblical in their teaching, may be accepted as guides for faith.[36] The major exceptions to this rule are the Tetrapolitan Confession and the Second Helvetic Confession, both of which confess faith in the triune God in terms of the threeness of person and oneness of essence, but which also refrain from pointing to the creeds of the early church as subordinate norms of doctrine, even though they offer no disrespect for the teaching of the fathers.[37]

The earliest Reformed confessions, notably the Tetrapolitan Confession (1530) and the First Helvetic Confession (1536), offer an article on God, but address primarily the trinitarian question. This does yield the statement that God is one in essence and three in person and, in the case of the First Helvetic Confession, the assertion that the one God is omnipotent.[38] This approach is changed in the great national confessions of the mid-sixteenth century in which a fuller statement of the doctrine of God appears — in the Gallican and Belgic confessions, moreover, as the first article of the confession.

---

34. Texts of the Reformed confessions are found in H. A. Niemeyer, ed., *Collectio confessionum im ecclesiis reformatis publicatarum*, 2 parts (Leipzig: J. Klinkhardt, 1840); texts, with translations, in Philip Schaff, *The Creeds of Christendom, with a History and Critical Notes*, 6th ed., 3 vols. (New York, 1931; repr. Grand Rapids: Baker Book House, 1983).

35. Augsburg Confession, I.i, in Schaff, *Creeds*, III, pp. 7-8; Gallican Confession, V; Belgic Confession, XI; Thirty-nine Articles, VIII; Irish Articles, 7; cf. Zwingli, *Exposition of the Christian Faith*, I.i; II.iv, vii, etc. in *On Providence and other Essays*, trans. William John Hinke (Durham, N.C.: Labyrinth Press, 1983), pp. 235-293, where the Apostles' Creed is used an organizing principle and continual point of reference and note the prominent use of the Athanasian Creed in Zwingli's *Fidei ratio* or *Account of the Faith*, in ibid., p. 36. Cf. the discussion of the early Reformation view of trinitarian language and speculation in ch. 9, §159

36. Cf. Thirty-nine Articles, VIII; Irish Articles, 7.

37. Cf. Tetrapolitan Confession, II; Second Helvetic Confession, III.

38. First Helvetic Confession, vi.

The Gallican begins with the statement that "We believe and confess that there is but one God, who is one sole and simple essence. Spiritual, eternal, invisible, immutable, infinite, incomprehensible, ineffable; who can do all things; who is all-wise, all-good, all-righteous, and all-merciful."[39] Further on, the confession declares its faith in "the Father, first cause, principle and origin of all things. The Son, his Word and eternal wisdom. The Holy Spirit, his virtue, power and efficacy."[40] The Belgic Confession, in virtually the same terms, also presents both essential attributes of God and the properties manifested by the three persons in their intratrinitarian relationships and their common work *ad extra*.[41] Similarly, the Second Helvetic Confession identifies the oneness of God in essence and nature, his self-subsistence and all-sufficiency, infinity and eternity, and various other attributes, including wisdom, mercy, justice, and truth.[42]

It is also the typical pattern of the confessions to move from a declaration of the unity of God in his essence and attributes to the presentation of the doctrine of the Trinity. This pattern is found in the Gallican Confession, the Belgic Confession, the Scots Confession, the Thirty-nine Articles, the Second Helvetic Confession, the Irish Articles, and the Westminster Confession. All of these confessions, including that production of the scholastic era, the Westminster Confession, refrain from developing speculative statements concerning the divine essence and attributes, but several, notably the Gallican, the Belgic, and the Westminster Confessions, do present lists of the divine the attributes, without elaboration, for consideration by the faithful. This pattern of doctrinal declaration reflects the Reformed view that presentation of attributes like the unity, simplicity, omnipotence, omnipresence, and eternity of God is a profoundly scriptural exercise and not at all the result of philosophical argumentation or natural theology, neither of which have any place in confessions of the church. Indeed, that most elaborate of the confessions, the Westminster Confession of Faith, in its virtually exhaustive list of the divine attributes, provides a clear scriptural reference for each in what may be the closest scriptural argumentation in the entire confession.

2. Confessions in the era of orthodoxy. In the era of early orthodoxy, the Irish Articles of 1615 echo the interest of the confessions of the mid-sixteenth century in offering a basic but brief doctrine of God, stating the oneness of essence and the divine attributes prior to a discussion of the Trinity in the same article:

---

39. Gallican Confession, i.

40. Gallican Confession, VI.

41. Cf. Scots Confession, I; Thirty-nine Articles, I; Irish Articles, 8.

42. Second Helvetic Confession, III.i; cf. the discussion in Joachim Staedke, "Die Gotteslehre der *Confessio Helvetica posterior,*" in *Glauben und Bekennen: Vierhundert Jahre Confessio Helvetica Posterior, Beiträge zu ihrer Geschichte und Theologie,* edited by J. Staedke (Zürich: Zwingli Verlag, 1966), pp. 251-257. Staedke makes too much of the purported problem of patristic and medieval theology emphasizing the oneness of God to the expense of the threeness and the seeming correction in the confession — a conclusion that is certainly unavailable given the brevity of the confessional statement.

> There is but one living and true God, everlasting, without body, parts, or passions; of infinite power, wisdom, and goodness; the maker and preserver of all things, both visible and invisible. And in unity of this Godhead, there be three persons of one and the same substance, power, and eternity: the Father, the Son, and the Holy Ghost.[43]

The language here is noteworthy, particularly the phrase "without body, parts, or passions," which is taken over directly into the Westminster Confession.

The presentation of the attributes in the Westminster Confession is so complete and clear as to merit citation *in extenso* together with its scriptural documentation:

> There is but one only (Deut. 6:4; 1 Cor. 8:4, 6) living and true God (1 Thess. 1:9; Jer. 10:10), who is infinite in being and perfection (Job 11:7, 8, 9; 26:14), a most pure spirit (John 4:24), invisible (1 Tim. 1:17), without body, parts (Deut. 4:15, 16; John 4:24; Luke 24:39), or passions (Acts 14:11, 15), immutable (James 1:17; Mal. 3:6), immense (1 Kings 8:27; Jer. 23:23, 24), eternal (Psalm 90:2; 1 Tim. 1:17), incomprehensible (Psalm 145:3), almighty (Gen. 17:1; Rev. 4:8), most wise (Rom. 16:27), most holy (Isa. 6:3; Rev. 4:8), most free (Psalm 115:3), most absolute (Exod. 3:14), working all things according to the counsel of his own immutable and most righteous will (Eph. 1:11), for his own glory (Prov. 16:4; Rom. 9:36); most loving (1 John 4:8, 16), gracious, merciful, longsuffering, abundant in goodness and truth, forgiving iniquity, transgression and sin (Exod. 34:6, 7); the rewarder of them that diligently seek him (Heb. 11:6); and withal most terrible in his judgments (Neh. 9:32, 33); hating all sin (Psalm 5:5, 6); and who will by no means clear the guilty (Nahum 1:2, 3; Exod. 34:7).[44]
>
> God hath all life (John 5:26), glory (Acts 7:2), goodness (Psalm 119:68), blessedness (1 Tim. 6:15; Rom. 9:5), in and of himself; and is alone in and unto himself all-sufficient, not standing in need of any creatures which he hath made (Acts 17:24, 25), nor deriving any glory from them (Job 22:2, 23), but only manifesting his own glory in, by, unto, and upon them: he is alone the foundation of all being, of whom, through whom, and to whom are all things (Rom 9:36); and hath most sovereign dominion over them, to do by them, for them, or upon them whatsoever he pleaseth (Rev. 4:11; 1 Tim. 6:15; Dan. 4:25, 35). In his sight are all things open and manifest (Heb. 4:13); his knowledge is infinite, infallible, and independent upon the creature (Rom. 9:33, 34; Psalm 147:5); so as nothing to him is contingent or uncertain (Acts 15:18; Ezek. 11:5). He is most holy in all his counsels, in all his works, and in all his commands (Psalm 145:17; Rom. 7:12). To him is due from angels and men, and every other creature, whatsoever worship, service, or obedience, he is pleased to require of them (Rev. 5:12-14).[45]

Although we might wonder, occasionally, why the Westminster Assembly proposed certain texts and not others, there is no question that the texts provide a firm biblical ground for the confession and that the exegetical tradition followed by the English Reformed divines had, in numerous commentaries on the texts and the books of

---

43. Irish Articles, 8.
44. Westminster Confession, II.i
45. Westminster Confession, II.ii; cf. Gallican Confession, i; Belgic Confession, i.

Scripture from which they come, argued the doctrines so perspicuously declared by the confession.[46]

2.2   Protestant Scholasticism and the Doctrine of God: The Early Orthodox Achievement (1565-1640)

A. Toward Revision of Perspective.

1. Theological and historical biases of modern approaches to the material. Twentieth-century theological reaction to the orthodox Protestant doctrine of God is fairly well encapsulated in Otto Weber's comments on the history of the doctrine:

> The doctrine of God in the early Church, in the Middle Ages, and in orthodoxy is a curious mixture of Greek, especially Neo-Platonic, and biblical ideas. Since the Reformation showed little interest in the traditional doctrine of God, it survived the fiery ordeal of the Reformation's reworking of all tradition far more unscathed than was really good. For this reason, Protestant Orthodoxy on the whole maintained the traditional mixture of non-Christian and biblical statements.[47]

Weber's comments are worth citing if only in order to manifest the ahistorical, dogmatic bias characteristic of many contemporary approaches to the Protestant orthodox doctrine of God. The claim that the doctrinal amalgam of classical philosophy and biblical theology characteristic of Christian thought from the time of the early church virtually down to the present is "curious" itself embodies a certain element of curiosity, as does the distinction between "non-Christian" and "biblical" statements — as if the only kind of statements a Christian theology can make are strictly biblical ones. This language arbitrarily rules out a host of traditionary materials that belong to the Christian theological enterprise and stand below Scripture in the usual hierarchy of authorities — namely, the ecumenical creeds, churchly confessions, and the broader tradition of the church.

From a historical point of view, moreover, Weber's statement stands as an argument on the ground of silence: in Weber's view, the Reformers failed to take the traditional doctrine properly to task, leaving their successors open to all of its problems. Yet this assessment, as we have already begun to show, is inaccurate on three counts. First, Weber's assumption that the Reformation proposed a "reworking of all tradition" is simply incorrect. Second, as indicated in the preceding section, the Reformers did show some interest in the traditional doctrine of God, albeit not a negative interest such that Weber might have appreciated enough to note. Third, given the elements of traditional doctrine found throughout their works and their adherence to traditionary patterns of exegesis in addressing the divine essence and attributes, the relative lack of elaboration of the doctrine by the Reformers ought to be construed in favor of the traditional doctrine. Most "curious" here is Weber's implication that the Protestant scholastic language against which he so strenuously objects is in fact the language of

---

46. See the discussion in *PRRD*, II, 7.5 (B) and below, beginning with 4.3.
47. Weber, *Foundations of Dogmatics*, I, pp. 397-398.

the tradition of Christian orthodoxy from the patristic period onward — and that his alternative to Protestant orthodoxy, whatever it may be, is not the language of the church's great tradition.

A similar and more historically couched example of this rather artificial severing of the Reformers' doctrine of God from the later orthodox teaching is found in Heppe's comment that "the doctrine of the divine attributes is touched upon but with quite scanty remarks by Calvin and his immediate pupils, as well even by Virellus and the German-Reformed emanating from the school of Melanchthon and is carefully illustrated for the first time not until Hyperius and Danaeus."[48] This statement too is riddled with historical and theological problems. In the first place, Heppe completely ignores the work of Wolfgang Musculus, who was born some eleven years before Calvin and who died in 1563, the year before Calvin's death: Musculus' *Loci communes* contain a highly elaborate treatment of the divine attributes. The doctrine was, thus, "carefully illustrated" by a contemporary of Calvin. Hyperius, whose extended discussion of the attributes Heppe does mention, was also a contemporary of Calvin and not a later dogmatician. As noted above, moreover, Bullinger did discuss the attributes, albeit not in the same detail as Musculus. We do, therefore, find a full discussion of the attributes fairly early on in the development of Reformed theology — though certainly not by all writers. What is more, individual attributes are discussed exegetically, as they appear in the text of Scripture, throughout the period.

As for Calvin's "immediate pupils," we do have a discussion of the attributes from the pen of Franciscus Junius, although not from the much-misrepresented Theodore Beza. Indeed, when Beza's works are examined in comparison with those of contemporaries like Ursinus, Olevianus, and Zanchi, he is easily seen to be far less the dogmatician than these other early orthodox writers and of far less impact on the doctrinal *loci* of later orthodoxy.[49] Danaeus or Daneau,[50] moreover, though not an

---

48. Heinrich Heppe, *Reformed Dogmatics Set Out and Illustrated from the Sources*, revised and edited by Ernst Bizer, trans. G. T. Thomson (London, 1950; repr. Grand Rapids: Baker Book House, 1978), p. 57 (hereinafter cited as Heppe, *Reformed Dogmatics*).

49. A significant body of Beza's writings is collected in Theodore Beza, *Tractationes theologicae*, 3 vols. (Geneva, 1570-82). Among Beza's specifically doctrinal works are his *Confession de la foy chrestienne* (Geneva, 1558), in Latin, *Confessio christianae fidei, et eiusdem collatio cum Papisticis Haeresibus ... adjecta est altera brevis eiusdem Bezae fidei Confessio* (Geneva, 1560; London, 1575); and the *Quaestionum et responsionum christianarum libellus, in quo praecipua christianae religionis capita kat epitome proponunter* (Geneva, 1570; second part, Geneva, 1576), in translation as *A Booke of Christian Questions and Answers* (London, 1572) and *The Other Parte of Christian Questions and answeres, which is Concerning the Sacraments* (London, 1580). Beza's most influential work was certainly his *Jesu Christi Nostri Novum Testamentum, sine Novum Foedus, cuius Graeco contextui respondent interpretationes duae . ... Eiusdem Theod. Bezae Annotationes* (Geneva, 1582, 1589, 1598; Cambridge, 1642). The *Propositions and Principles of Divinitie Propounded and Disputed in the University of Geneva.under M. Theod. Beza and M. Anthonie Faius*, trans. John Penry (Edinburgh, 1595) offer an index to early orthodox thought in the Genevan Academy, albeit only an indirect testimony to Beza's theology.

50. Lambert Daneau, *Christianae isagoges ad christianorum theologorum locos communes*, 5 parts (Geneva, 1583-1588); also note idem, *Compendium sacrae theologiae seu erotemata theologica, in quibus totius verae theologiae christianae summa breviter comprehense est* (Montpellier, 1595).

"immediate pupil" certainly ought to be considered among the linear descendants of the Genevan theology. On the Melanchthonian side of the development, we also have several examples of lengthy discussion of the attributes: Ursinus presented a full discussion of attributes in his fragmentary *Loci communes*[51] and in his lectures on the Heidelberg Catechism.[52] Hyperius, who also discoursed on the attributes at length, must also be regarded as standing in the line of Melanchthon. Similarly, on the Lutheran side, pupils of Melanchthon like Chemnitz and Strigel also developed fairly lengthy discussions of the attributes.[53] In the same generation, moreover, we must place the vast treatise on the essence and attributes of God by Jerome Zanchi, who was a mere five years Calvin's junior — and three years Beza's senior.[54]

2. Grounds of revision. Examination of the works of the Reformers and their successors indicates a continuity of the doctrine of God, not in style of exposition and not always in detail of exposition, but rather in basic theological and philosophical framework. The underlying assumptions governing the doctrine of God during the eras of the Reformation and Protestant orthodoxy are very little different from those governing the discussion during the Middle Ages. Discontinuity can be measured, however, in terms of the overt biblicism of the Reformers and their successors in contrast with the more theological and philosophical interest of the medieval writers; and certainly, the rise of Protestant orthodoxy brought with it a revival and modification of the dogmatic and philosophical approaches of the past, often in the light of Reformation-era biblicism — so that elements of discontinuity can be identified between the theology of the Reformers and that of their successors. What must be emphasized, however, is the relationship of these elements of discontinuity to the literary genre of the documents examined and the presence of a significant continuity of intellectual framework or assumption concerning the doctrine that far outweighed any discontinuities in detail. It is not merely problematic, it is fundamentally absurd, to attempt to "save" the Reformers for neoorthodoxy by apologizing for the traditional

---

51. Zacharias Ursinus, *Loci theologici*, in *Opera theologica quibus orthodoxae religionis capita perspicue & breviter explicantur*, ed. Quirinius Reuter, 3 vols. (Heidelberg, 1612), vol. I.

52. Zacharias Ursinus, *Doctrinae christianae compendium* (Leiden: Iohannes Paetsius, 1584; also, Oxford, 1585); edited and augmented as *Explicationes catecheseos*, in *Opera*, vol. 1; note the influential seventeenth-century Dutch translation, *Schat-Boeck der Verklarigen over den Nederlandtschen Catechismus, uyt de Latijnshe Lessen van Dr. Zacharias Ursinus, op-gemaecht van Dr. David Paraeus, vertaelt, ende met Tafelen, &c. Verlicht, door Dr. Festus Hommius, nu van nieuws oversien ... door Johannes Spiljardus*, 2 parts (Amsterdam: Johannes van Revensteyn, 1664); also *The Commentary of Dr. Zacharias Ursinus on the Heidelberg Catechism*, trans. G. W. Williard, intro. by John W. Nevin (Columbus, Ohio, 1852; repr. Phillipsburg, New Jersey: Presbyterian and Reformed Publishing Co., 1985). The rather convoluted text history of the catechetical lectures is recounted in T. D. Smid, "Bibliographische Opmerkingen over de Explicationes Catecheticae van Zacharias Ursinus," in *Gereformeerd Theologisch Tijdschrift*, 41 (1940), pp. 228-243.

53. Martin Chemnitz, *Loci theologici*, 3 vols. (Frankfurt and Wittenberg, 1653); in translation, *Loci theologici*, trans. J. A. O. Preus, 2 vols. (St. Louis: Concordia, 1989); Victorinus Strigellus, *Loci theologici Strigelli, quibus loci communes Melanchthonis illustrantur* (Neustadt, 1582-1583).

54. Jerome Zanchi, *De natura Dei, lib.* I, in *Operum theologicorum D. Hieronymi Zanchii*, 10 vols. in 9 (Geneva: Samuel Crispin, 1617-1619).

foundations of their theology, by arguing a case for their disagreement or potential disagreement with the traditional teachings of the church on the basis of their silence, or by claiming a high degree of discontinuity between the Reformation and Protestant orthodoxy on the basis of topics omitted from such documents as Calvin's *Institutes*.

A major mark of continuity between Reformation and orthodoxy in the development of the doctrine of God, moreover, is the emphasis on the biblical divine "names" as a point of departure for the discussion of the essence and attributes. This pattern is characteristic of the theologies of Bullinger, Vermigli, Musculus, and Hyperius,[55] and it continues to be a primary issue in the works of such early writers as Zanchi, Perkins, Gomarus, Walaeus, Maccovius, Downame, Spanheim, the Leiden Synopsis, and Alting,[56] among the high orthodox in the works of Hottinger, Turretin, Leigh, Heidegger, Pictet, and Mastricht,[57] and, in the late orthodox era in the work of Ridgley and Brown.[58] This was not, typically, a pattern reminiscent of the medieval scholastic systems: there, in the case of Ockham's preference for the term *nomina Dei* over *attributa Dei* was not a recourse to the biblical names of God but an identification of divine properties such as omnipotence and omniscience as "names" rather than "attributes." Rather, this pattern in the Reformed orthodox must be understood as an indication

---

55. Cf. Bullinger, *Decades*, IV.iii; Vermigli, *Loci communes*, I.xi. 2 [*Commonplaces*, I.xii.2]; Musculus, *Commonplaces*, pp. 875-878; Hyperius, *Methodus theologiae*, I (pp, 89-91).

56. William Perkins, *A Golden Chaine*, ii, in *The Workes of ... Mr. William Perkins*, 3 vols. (Cambridge, 1612-1619), I, p. 11, col.1; Thomas Nichols, *An Abridgement of the Whole Body of Divinity, extracted from the Learned Works of that ever-famous and reverend Divine, Mr. William Perkins* (London, 1654), p. 2; Franciscus Gomarus, *Disputationes*, iii, in *Opera theologica omnia*, 3 vols. (Amsterdam, 1644), vol. I; Antonius Walaeus, *Loci communes s. theologiae* (Leiden, 1640), also in Walaeus' *Opera omnia* (Leiden, 1643); Johannes Maccovius, *Loci communes theologici* (Amsterdam, 1658), xiv; John Downame, *The Summe of Sacred Divinitie briefly and methodically propounded: and then more largely and cleerly handled and explaned* (London: W. Stansby, 1625; 1628), i (pp. 7-27); Friedrich Spanheim, *Disputationum theologicarum syntagma. Pars prima: Disputationum theologicarum miscellanearum; Pars secunda: Anti-Anabaptistica controversia* (Geneva, 1652), part 1, IX (*de Deo I*).v-xix; X (*de Deo II*).i-xiv; *Synopsis purioris theologiae, disputationibus quinquaginta duabus comprehensa ac conscripta per Johannem Polyandrum, Andream Rivetum, Antonium Walaeum, Antonium Thysium.* (Leiden, 1625), VI.x-xi; Jacob Alting, *Methodus theologiae didacticae*, iii, in *Opera omnia theologica: analytica exegetica, practica, problematica: & philogogica*, 5 vols. (Amsterdam, 1687), vol. 5.

57. Johann Heinrich Hottinger, *Cursus theologicus methodo Altingiana expositus* (Duisburg: Adrian Wyngaerden, 1660); Francis Turretin, *Institutio theologiae elencticae*, 3 vols. (Geneva, 1679-1685), III.iv.4-5, 13, 17; Edward Leigh, *A Treatise of Divinity* (London, 1646), II.ii-iii; idem, *A Systeme or Body of Divinity* (London, 1662), II.ii-iii; Johann Heinrich Heidegger, *Corpus theologiae christianae ... adeoque sit plenissimum theologiae didacticae, elenchticae, moralis et historicae systema*, 2 vols. (Zurich: David Gessner, 1700); Benedict Pictet, *Theologia christiana ex puris ss. literarum fontibus hausta* (Geneva, 1696), II.ii; Petrus van Mastricht, *Theoretico-practica theologia, qua, per capita theologica, pars dogmatica, elenchtica et practica, perpetua successione conjugantur, praecedunt in usum operis, paraleipomena, seu sceleton de optima concionandi methodo*, 2 vols. (Amsterdam, 1682-1687), II.iv.3.

58. Thomas Ridgey, *A Body of Divinity: Wherein the Doctrines of the Christian Religion are Explained and Defended, being the Substance of Several Lectures on the Assembly's Larger Catechism*, 2 vols. (London, 1731-33), I, pp. 135-136; John Brown of Haddington, *A Compendious View of Natural and Revealed Religion. In seven books* (Glasgow, 1782; second ed. revised, Edinburgh, 1796; reissued, Philadelphia, 1819), II.i (pp. 99-130).

of the importance of the text of Scripture and the interpretation of its original languages to theological formulation — that is, as a characteristic brought to theology by the biblical and exegetical interests of the Reformers. The exegetical emphasis of the Reformation, on this point at least, cannot be regarded as a denial of theological system but, as we have indicated with regard to other points of doctrine, a pressure toward the development of a distinctively Protestant theological system.[59]

It is important also to emphasize the variety of Reformed formulations: the developing doctrine of God in Reformed theology drew on antecedents and models as diverse as those present in the training of the Reformers themselves. Within the group of theologians identified as "orthodox" Reformed, there are Thomist, Scotist, and nominalist accents, elements of the later medieval *via antiqua* and *via moderna*, moments of dialogue and debate with variant streams of Renaissance philosophy, including the renewed scholasticism of the late Renaissance. This yields, within the Reformed development itself, different readings of classifications of attributes, debate over the understanding of some attributes as "communicable," differing readings of the doctrine of divine simplicity and of the distinction of attributes in God, differing sensibilities as to which attributes (if any) ought to provide the primary categories for understanding or framing the doctrine of the divine essence, and different emphases in the discussion of individual attributes as well.

In moving from the prolegomena and doctrine of Scripture to the doctrine of God, moreover, we have come to a point in the discussion at which the premises and principles noted in our analyses of these previous *loci* can begin to be illustrated from the process of doctrinal formulation. Specifically, the orthodox approach to the doctrine of the divine essence, attributes, and Trinity evidences both a respect for the broader and fundamental definition of Scripture as *principium cognoscendi*, and the more hermeneutical understanding of the text of Scripture as providing *principia* or *axiomata* from which conclusions could be deduced, as indicated in the Westminster Confession, "The whole counsel of God, concerning all things necessary for his own glory, man's salvation, faith, and life, is either expressly set down in Scripture, or by good and necessary consequence may be deduced from Scripture."[60] Thus, the deductive aspect of positive theological formulation points toward the logical process of drawing conclusions from principles, axioms, or propositions — but also toward the assumption that the firm ground of theological conclusions lies not in the logical process per se, but in the instrumental use of logic or reason to understand the implications of the biblical *principium*, which must be the source of the individual *principia* or *axiomata*

---

59. Those few of the Reformed, however, who argued a nominalist approach to divine simplicity and the distinction of divine attributes, notably Heidanus, do approach Ockham's understanding of the divine "nomina," while at the same time offering a highly exegetical reading of the biblical names of God: see Abraham Heidanus, *Corpus theologiae christianae in quindecim locos digestum*, 2 vols. (Leiden, 1687), I (pp. 55-56) and below, 4.2 (B.1).

60. Westminster Confession, I.6, cf. Donald W. Sinnema, "Antoine De Chandieu's Call for a Scholastic Reformed Theology (1580)," in W. Fred Graham, ed., *Later Calvinism: International Perspectives*, (Kirksville, MO: Sixteenth Century Journal Publishers, 1994), pp. 176-179, with Muller, *PRRD*, I, 9.3 (A.2); II, 7.4 (C.5).

used in theological argumentation. The point takes on specific direction from the scholastic assumption that, when syllogistic arguments are employed, theological conclusions can be drawn only when the minor premiss contains a theological truth.[61]

We are pressed by this data toward the conclusion that the Reformed orthodox doctrine of the divine attributes, while clearly reflecting the traditional scholastic doctrine as taught by the medieval doctors, also reflects views present in the era of the Reformers and partakes of a fairly continuous and unbroken development of those views toward full systematic statement. There is, in particular, a strong continuity at a biblical and exegetical level with the theology of the Reformers, and, by way of the Reformers with the exegetical tradition of the fathers and the medieval doctors: the dogmatic systems of the early orthodox clearly reflect the exegetical tradition and, equally clearly, indicate the way in which theological problems were often dealt with by the Reformers themselves in the context of exegetical *loci* and subsequently incorporated in theological system.

The underlying problem of virtually all of the extant studies of the trajectory of Reformed thought from the time of the Reformation into the era of orthodoxy is that they ask, in one way or another, whether the orthodox or scholastic theological formulations or whatever doctrine may be under consideration are as satisfactory or as suitable as Calvin's — and at the same do not ever pose the issue of establishing the criterion that makes a doctrine "satisfactory." In fact, most seem to argue that the doctrinal formulation that most clearly fulfills a particular dogmatic criterion (e.g., "Christocentrism") is best[62] — whereas the sole criterion available to the seventeenth-century theologian was the positive relationship of doctrinal formulation to exegetical result! This means that even the studies that most accurately and with the least bias discuss the trajectory of opinion on the point between the Reformers and later Reformed writers but that also omit the exegetical dimension have not examined the best indices of the doctrine and have not, in fact, understood where the roots of the actual continuity and/or discontinuity lie.

It is also evident, with reference to the doctrine of God, as in the case of the concept of divine permission typically incorporated into the Reformed doctrine of predestination, Calvin is not always the primary antecedent and did not consistently provide the systematic model for later Reformed doctrine. Often his greatest influence derived from his exegetical works, not from the *Institutes*. Moreover, we must look to the works of Musculus, Vermigli, Bullinger, and Hyperius and, after that, to the writings of such transitional figures as Ursinus, Danaeus, and Junius, who, together with that great theorist of the divine attributes, Jerome Zanchi, account for the development of Reformed theology toward its early orthodox expression. What is more, the early

---

61. Cf. *PRRD*, I, 8.3 (B.2).

62. E.g., Otto Gründler, *Die Gotteslehre Girolami Zanchis und ihre Bedeutung für seine Lehre von der Prädestination* (Neukirchen: Neukirchner Verlag, 1965) and idem, "Thomism and Calvinism in the Theology of Girolamo Zanchi (1516-1590)" (Th.D. dissertation, Princeton Theological Seminary, 1961), from which the monograph was translated: see Gründler, "Thomism and Calvinism," pp. 21-23, 70-72, 158-159.

orthodox thinkers appear to have recognized not only the polemical necessity of developing a scholastic theology over against the Roman Catholic dogmatics of the day, they appear to have recognized also, albeit without negative comment on the work of their theological forebears, that many of the formulations of theologians like Bullinger and Calvin failed completely either to explain issues or to resolve theological problems. Thus, while it is clear that Calvin intended to deny that God is the author of sin and to affirm the existence of secondary causes, contingency, and human freedom or responsibility, his difficulty with the language of divine permission and his lack of recourse to established language of divine *concursus* left places in which his theology is unclear on such issues. The introduction into Reformed theology and the careful interpretation of scholastic distinctions in the new context of Reformed confessional dogmatics by the early orthodox writers brought to Reformed thought a clarity of definition and, in addition, a capability of balanced and nuanced formulation not possible in earlier theology. (Of course, this introduction and use of distinctions itself was a gradual process, evident already on the thought of contemporaries of Calvin, like Musculus and Hyperius, but furthered considerably in the work of the next generation by such thinkers as Zanchi, Ursinus, and Danaeus.)

Just as a close examination of the *loci de theologia* and *de Scriptura* manifested, not a rigid uniformity of statement among the Reformed orthodox, but rather a certain degree of diversity within the bounds of a technically controlled scholasticism — a feature typical the baroque — so does a survey of the discussions of the divine essence and attributes present a picture of considerable variety within the established forms and patterns of discussion. In particular, we note a wide variety of arrangement of the attributes within the scholastic systems and a considerable diversity of opinion concerning which attributes are to be included in the discussion.

B. The Beginnings of Early Orthodoxy and the Aristotelian Revival of the Late Renaissance.

1. Early orthodox thinkers and the revival of scholastic argumentation. Prominent among the expositions of the doctrine of the divine essence, attributes, and Trinity belonging to the first phase of early orthodoxy are the work of Ursinus, both in his commentary on the Heidelberg Catechism and in his unfinished *Loci communes*, the relevant sections of Olevianus' exposition of the creed,[63] Aretius' *Theologiae problemata*,[64] Daneau's major essays in theological system, the confession of faith and the extended *De tribus Elohim* and *De natura Dei* of Zanchi,[65] and the major

---

63. Caspar Olevianus, *Expositio symboli apostolici sive articulorum fidei: in qua summa gratiuti foederis aeterni inter Deum et fideles breviter & perspicué tractatur* (Frankfurt, 1584), translated as An *Exposition of the Symbole of the Apostles* (London, 1581).

64. Benedictus Aretius, *S. S. theologiae problemata, seu loci communes, et miscellaneae quaestiones*, editio quarta (Geneva, 1589).

65. Jerome Zanchi, *De tribus Elohim, aeterno Patre, Filio. Et Spiritu Sancto* (Frankfurt am Main: Georgius Corvinus, 1573); *De natura Dei seu de divinis attributis* (Heidelberg: Jacob Mylius, 1577). Both works are also found in volumes 1 and 2, respectively, of Zanchi's collected works: *Operum*

doctrinal efforts of the next generation of writers, namely, Junius,[66] Polanus, Keckermann,[67] Perkins, Ames, Ainsworth,[68] Ussher,[69] and their contemporaries. These works consistently evidence the interrelationship of exegesis, doctrine, instruction, and piety that would be characteristic of Reformed orthodoxy in the seventeenth century.

Scholastic elements also appear in Ursinus' adaptation of the catechetical questions to the form of a dispute, in which the questions are subdivided into series of questions belonging to the topic, objections are states, and replies given. In the case of the doctrine of God, he follows the catechetical question, "Since there is but one divine essence, why speakest thou of Father, Son, and Holy Spirit?" with a series of eight questions, each one receiving a substantial portion of his exposition. Of the eight, the first three deal strictly with God as one, the latter five with the doctrine of the Trinity. The fourth contains a lengthy discussion of "essence." Thus:

I. From what does it appear that there is a God?
II. What is the character of that God whom the church acknowledges and worships, and in what does he differ from heathen idols?
III. Is he but one, and in what sense do the Scriptures call creatures gods?
IV. What do the terms Essence, Person, and Trinity signify, and in what do they differ?[70]

The first question permits Ursinus to introduce a series of proofs of the existence of God, and the second provides place both for a contrast of a purely philosophical or rational definition of God and a definition based on revelation and for a significant

theologicorum D. Hieronymi Zanchii, 8 vols. (Heidelberg: Stephanus Gamonetus and Matthaeus Berjon, 1605) and Operum theologicorum D. Hieronymi Zanchii, 8 vols. in 3 (Geneva: Samuel Crispin, 1617-1619). I have consulted the first editions, but the column numbers in citations refer to the 1605 edition; the main citations to book, chapter, question, and/or section function for all editions. Zanchi's confession is the De religione christiana fides (Neustadt: Matthaeus Harnisch, 1585), also in Opera, vol. VIII, and in translation as H. Zanchius, his Confession of Christian Religion (London, 1559).

66. Franciscus Junius, Theses theologicae quae in inclyta academia Ludgunobatava ad exercitia publicarum disputationum [Theses Leydenses] and Theses aliquot theologicae in Heidelbergensi academia disputatae [Theses Heidelbergenses], in Opuscula theologica selecta, ed. Abraham Kuyper. Amsterdam: F. Muller, 1882), pp. 103-289, 289-327, respectively.

67. Bartholomaus Keckermann, Systema sacrosanctae theologiae, tribus libris adornatum (Heidelberg, 1602; Geneva, 1611); also found in Opera omnia quae extant, 2 vols. (Geneva, 1614), appended to vol. II, separate pagination.

68. Henry Ainsworth, The Orthodox Foundation of Religion, long since collected by that judicious and elegant man Mr. Henry Ainsworth, for the benefit of his private company: and now divulged for the publike good of all that desire to know that Cornerstone Christ Jesus Crucified, ed. Samuel White. (London: R. C. for M. Sparke, 1641). On Ainsworth's exegesis, see Muller, After Calvin, pp. 156-174. Ainsworth's major exegetical efforts are all found in his Annotations upon the Five Books of Moses, the Book of Psalms, and the Song of Songs, 7 vols. (London: Miles Flesher, 1626-27), each volume titled separately by book, e.g., Annotations on Genesis, etc..

69. James Ussher, A Body of Divinity, or the Sum and Substance of Christian Religion, sixth edition (London, 1670).

70. Ursinus, Commentary on the Heidelberg Catechism, p. 121 (reserving the last four questions for the discussion of the Trinity).

exposition of the divine attributes. The third question, abbreviated in the text of the commentary to read, "From what does the Unity of God appear?" offers discussion of the biblical and rational grounds for identifying God as one and sole.[71]

With Zanchi especially, we encounter the entrance of scholastic categories into the domain of Reformed theology.[72] Whereas Zanchi's Christology, soteriology, and even his doctrine of predestination evidence only relative alterations in terminology and method, his doctrine of God presents an enormous alteration of theological and philosophical attitude, if only in the detail in which each issue is addressed. Not only has nominally Aristotelian language become a foundation for the discussion of metaphysical categories, Thomas Aquinas is present as a guide to the appropriation of philosophical categories to theology. What is more, the discussion of the divine nature and attributes follows a scholastic locus method of exposition that presents in succession the concept of God as *ens simplicissimus* and then the various *proprietates essentiales*. In form and in content, this is a genuinely "scholastic" exposition, although it certainly differs from the medievals in its consistent interest in exegesis and in the original languages of the biblical text. In its positive use of philosophy and of traditional theological method, it stands in contrast to the thought of Calvin and Bullinger in the previous generation and, indeed, in its detail, even to the somewhat more traditional work of Musculus, Vermigli, and Hyperius.

Still, the approach of Zanchi is not at all equivalent to that of his medieval models. Whereas Gründler rightly points out that, unlike Aquinas, Zanchi does not begin his doctrine of God with proofs, he omits to mention that Zanchi actually began his discussion of God one whole folio volume prior to the *De natura Dei*, with a massive discussion of the Trinity. Nor does Gründler do justice either to the biblicism or to the order and arrangement of Zanchi's initial discussion of divine names: Gründler focuses on Zanchi's reading of Exodus 3:14 and its essentialist understanding of "I am who I am," commenting that, in Zanchi's view, as in Aquinas' understanding, this is the name "most appropriately attributed to God," and offering only Zanchi's reference to the Septuagint as exegetical justification.[73] Zanchi, in matter of fact, begins with a lengthy discussion of the names of God and the problem of predication and then passes on, not to a discussion of the name "I am," but to chapters on Elohim and Jehovah, pronouncing Jehovah to be "the proper and essential name of God."[74] Nor, indeed, are Aquinas and the Septuagint the only precedents for Zanchi's reading of Exodus 3:14![75] And Zanchi does not move, as Gründler implies, directly from the

---

71. Ursinus, *Commentary on the Heidelberg Catechism*, pp. 128-129.

72. Cf. John Patrick Donnelly, "Calvinist Thomism," in *Viator*, 7 (1976), pp. 441-455; idem, "Italian Influences on the Development of Calvinist Scholasticism," in *Sixteenth Century Journal*, VII/1 (1976), pp. 81-101; and Richard A. Muller, *Christ and the Decree: Christology and Predestination in Reformed Theology from Calvin to Perkins* (Durham, N.C.: Labyrinth Press, 1986; repr. Grand Rapids: Baker Book House, 1988), pp. 110-125.

73. Gründler, "Thomism and Calvinism," pp. 96-97.

74. Zanchi, *De natura Dei*, I.xii (Elohim), xiii (Jehovah), xiv (I am); cf. col. 31, Jehovah as the "proprium & esentiale nomen Dei."

75. See below, 4.2 (B.5).

discussion of "I am" to the divine simplicity as a central concept: the former appears in *De natura Dei*, I.xiv, and is followed by five chapters and a transition from book I to book II before simplicity is discussed in *De natura Dei*, II.ii. The highly philosophical and Thomistic reading offered by Gründler falls rather short: Zanchi's doctrine is not rooted in simplicity per se, rather it is rooted in a highly traditionary, essentialist reading of the divine names which, in turn, yields such doctrines as simplicity, eternity, and immutability — and, what is more, it is formulated with reference to Scripture, exegetical questions, and patristic materials as much to the medieval tradition, and, more often than not, each *locus* concludes with a discussion of practical "use" of the doctrinal point.[76] Nor, as Gründler claims, can one easily read through Zanchi's *De natura Dei* and not find christological considerations.[77]

Aretius, the philologist, exegete, and theologian of Bern following the death of Musculus, produced a gathering of *loci communes* and miscellaneous questions, the *Theologiae problemata*,[78] in which he offered disquisitions on such topics as the natural knowledge of God available to the Gentiles, the One God and the name "Father," the deity of Christ, the Holy Spirit, and providence — in no way a full body of doctrine, but work significant for its detailed discussions and its wide ranging use of classical and patristic sources. In the latter three topics noted, Aretius contributed massively to the Reformed doctrine of the Trinity, but unlike his major contemporaries, he produced no discussion of the divine essence and attributes.

From the same era, we have also Lambert Daneau's larger *Christianae isagoges* and his *Compendium*.[79] Whereas the *Compendium* offers a brief prolegomenon before entering on the discussion of God, the *Christianae isagoges* begin directly with the *locus de Deo*, discussing first "the term God," the divine essence (*Quid sit Deus*), then — curiously — whether God exists (*An sit Deus*), of what sort is the true God (*Qualis sit verus Deus*), the distinction of divine attributes, the individual divine attributes, whether there are incidental properties in God, the unity and Trinity of God, the divine essence and persons — in some twenty-three chapters. Daneau manifests particular care in his discussion of the attributes to offer categories and rules for understanding them: the attributes, in the first place, are given to God by Scripture and are divided into two different categories, *proprietates* or essential attributes of God and *accidentia* or temporal relationships into which God comes. The former are truly in God, the latter are not

---

76. See the discussion of the sources and method of Reformed orthodoxy in Richard A. Muller, *After Calvin: Studies in the Development of a Theological Tradition* (New York: Oxford University Press, 2002), chapters 2 and 3.

77. Contra Gründler, "Thomism and Calvinism," p. 159 et passim; note, e.g., the discussion of the distinction between Christ's divinity and humanity that alone occupies some thirty columns in the *locus* on divine immensity: Zanchi, *De natura Dei*, II.vi, q. 4 (cols. 107-138), or the highly christological and soteriological conclusion to the *locus* on divine blessedness, ibid., II.viii (col. 160); or the discussion of incarnation and immutability, ibid., II.vi, q. 2.2 (col. 79).

78. Benedictus Aretius, *S. S. theologiae problemata, seu loci communes, et miscellaneae quaestiones.* (Bern, 1573; editio quarta, Geneva, 1589).

79. On Daneau's theology, see Olivier Fatio, *Méthode et théologie. Lambert Daneau et les débuts de la scholastique réformée* (Geneva: Droz, 1976).

and do not in any way alter the divine being.[80] It is also of interest that his initial "essence" discussion, *Quid sit Deus*, is brief and non technical and reserves the greater portion of the discussion of the divine essence to the doctrine of the Trinity. Characteristic of Daneau's work is his rich citation of the fathers, medievals, and sixteenth-century Reformers. He offers evidence of the way in which Protestant theologians of his generation sought to affirm the catholicity of the Reform and to develop a theology at once biblical and traditionary.

An index both to the development of the Reformed doctrine of God and to the impact of Ramism on early orthodoxy is found in the work of William Perkins and the Hungarian theologian, Stephanus Szegedinus (Istvan Kis). Perkins, certainly the most famous of the English Ramist theologians, presented his doctrine of God in two forms — one developed in a neat propositional form and suited to the tight Ramist organization of his treatise on the working out of the divine decree, *A Golden Chaine*, the other in a more discursive manner in his extended *Exposition of the Creede*. The first of these expositions of the doctrine offers a full doctrine of God, briefly stated, organized according to careful divisions of the topic, suited to the Ramist approach to argument and organization.[81] The latter exposition offers less evidence of the Ramist divisions and is couched in highly practical and hortatory language, emphasizing the "duties" and "consolations" arising from the confession of God as Father, and stressing the doctrine of the Trinity rather than the doctrine of the essence and attributes — indeed, dealing only with the one creedal attribute, almightiness or omnipotence.[82] Szegedinus' *Theologiae sincerae loci communes de Deo et Homine*, develops, in the form of detailed Ramist charts, a full series of divine names and attributes together with a definition of the *natura Dei* but, curiously, no doctrine of the Trinity.[83] That topic Szegedinus reserved for another vast Ramist exercise, his *Confessio verae fidei de uno vero Deo Patre, Filio, et Spiritu Sancto*.[84] Both in the works of Perkins and in those of Szegedinus, the reader is impressed not so much with any originality of basic doctrine as with the power of the Ramist technique in the organization of the material. A similar point can be made of Ames' famous *Medulla* or *Marrow*.[85]

Several other writers of the era can be noted as instrumental in the formulation of the early Reformed orthodox doctrine of God: Scharpius, Fenner, Trelcatius the

---

80. Daneau, *Christianae isagoges*, I.v (fol. 8r-v); cf. I.viii (fol. 20v-21r).

81. William Perkins, *Golden Chaine*, ii-v, in *Workes*, I, pp. 11-15.

82. William Perkins, *Exposition of the Symbole or Creede*, in *Workes*, I, pp. 129-144.

83. Stephanus Szegedinus, *Theologiae sincerae loci communes de Deo et Homine perpetuis Tabulis explicati et scholasticorum dogmatis illustrati* (Basel, 1585; editio secunda, 1588).

84. Stephanus Szegedinus, *Confessio verae fidei de uno vero Deo Patre, Filio, et Spiritu Sancto, libris duobus comprehensa, & perpetuis tabulis illustrata* (Basel, 1588), printed in *Theologiae sincerae*, pp. 507-665.

85. William Ames, *Medulla ss. theologiae* (Amsterdam, 1623; London, 1630); also note *The Marrow of Theology*, trans. with intro. by John Dykstra Eusden (Boston: Pilgrim, 1966; repr. Durham, N.C.: Labyrinth Press, 1984).

Younger, Bucanus, Wollebius,[86] and Polanus. Of these, Amandus Polanus von Polansdorf is certainly the most remarkable, whether for the detail of his doctrinal statements, his full use of the patristic and medieval tradition, or his Ramist attention to the architectonic issues of theology.[87] Whereas the other writers just noted wrote shorter systems, notable for definition and organization, Polanus produced not only a finely defined and organized work, but also a summation of Reformed doctrine vast in its proportions. In particular, Polanus shares the Ramist architectonic sensibility with Szegedinus and Perkins, a characteristic eminently evidenced in his *Partitiones theologicae* and in their subsequent use as the synoptic table prefaced to his *Syntagma theologiae*.[88] Where Polanus goes beyond his predecessors is in his detail of definition and in the vast mass of patristic material and of references to the scholastic tradition that illustrate and augment his own definitions and arguments. With specific reference to the doctrine of God, his *Syntagma* certainly represents the most highly developed system of its era, exceeded in length only by Zanchi's *De tribus Elohim* and *De natura Dei*.

The question that must be asked of these early orthodox writers is not simply whether or not they introduced a change in the terminology and method of the Reformed doctrine of God or brought about the use of a traditional scholastic language of being in their discussion of the nature and unity of God — for they did all of this — but rather what these changes brought about within Reformed theology, how they related to the over arching issue of the structure and implication of that theology, and how they served to convey the body of Reformed doctrine to yet another generation of thinkers. At the most fundamental level, this development of terminology and method did not actually alter the basic intellectual framework of Protestant theology — if only because of the continuity of certain basic theological, philosophical, and logical usages so standard or assumed that they were never questioned.[89] The content

---

86. Johannes Scharpius, *Cursus theologicus in quo controversia omnes de fide dogmatibus hoc seculo exagitate*, 2 vols. (Geneva, 1620); Dudley Fenner, *Sacra theologia sive veritas qua est secundum pietatem ad unicae et verae methodi leges descripta* (London, 1585; Geneva 1589); Lucas Trelcatius Jr., *Scholastica et methodica locorum communium institutio* (London, 1604; Hanau, 1610), idem, *A Briefe Institution of the Commonplaces of Sacred Divinitie* (London, 1610); Gulielmus Bucanus, *Institutiones theologicae seu locorum communium christianae religionis* (Geneva, 1602); idem, *Institutions of the Christian Religion, framed out of God's Word*, trans. R. Hill (London, 1606; 1659); Johannes Wollebius, *Compendium theologiae christianae* (Basel, 1626; Oxford, 1657).

87. The sole monograph on Polanus, with specific reference to his doctrine of God, Heiner Faulenbach, *Die Struktur der Theologie des Amandus Polanus von Polansdorf* (Zurich: EVZ Verlag, 1967), is rendered problematic by its highly theologistic analysis, its recourse to the central dogma theory, and its excessively generalized notions of Aristotelianism. A more balanced assessment is found in Robert Letham, "Amandus Polanus: A Neglected Theologian?" in *Sixteenth Century Journal*, 21/3 (1990), pp. 463-476.

88. Amandus Polanus, *Partitiones theologiae christianae*, Pars I-II (Basel, 1590-1596); also note *The Substance of the Christian Religion* (London, 1595), a translation of part I of the *Partitiones*; and the *Syntagma theologiae christianae*, 2 parts (Hanau, 1609; folio, Geneva, 1617).

89. See Charles B. Schmitt, *The Aristotelian Tradition and Renaissance Universities* (London: Variorum Reprints, 1984); idem, *Aristotle and the Renaissance* (Cambridge, Mass.: Harvard University

of their theology in general and of specific topics — essence, attributes, Trinity — not only has been drawn from the larger tradition but evidences clear continuities with the thought of second-generation codifiers like Calvin, Musculus, Bullinger, Vermigli, and Hyperius. Nor, indeed, did the development of a more scholastic terminology diminish commitment to the Reformation emphasis on the authority of Scripture or alter the patterns of biblical interpretation developed during the eras of the Renaissance and Reformation. Thus, alongside the more overtly scholastic exercise there is also a clear continuity both in basic doctrinal implication and in the interpretation of key biblical texts or *loci* traditionally related to the formulation of the doctrine of God.

2. Suárez, Molina, and the new metaphysics of modified Thomism. The decade following 1590 was as crucial for the development of the scholastic Protestant doctrine of God as it was for the development of theological prolegomena — and for much the same reason. The rise of prolegomena, as evidenced by Junius' magisterial treatise *De vera theologia*, signaled an interest among Protestants in the clear and precise definition of theology and in the identification of specifically Protestant theology as a legitimate *scientia* in the classic Aristotelian sense, in and for its study in the universities.[90] Directly related to this development was the beginning of a Protestant interest in prolegomena, the enunciation of *principia*, and specifically in some of the preliminary questions of the nature of the discipline itself — notably as found in an earlier form in the older scholasticism and, indeed, in the tradition of Christian Aristotelianism. By way of example, we now see discussion of theology as a *scientia* or study of first principles and of the conclusions that can be drawn from them. We also see the establishment of a Protestant, indeed a Reformed, discussion of metaphysics, as evidenced by the appearance of the first Protestant textbooks on the subject. Indeed, the Protestant theologians and philosophers of this generation viewed Aristotelian metaphysics as a crucial source for definitions and arguments needed in the construction and defense of their theological systems.[91] And there is certainly evidence that Protestant theologians and philosophers were aware of the trajectories of thought

---

Press, 1983).

90. Franciscus Junius, *De vera theologia*, in *Opuscula theologica selecta*, pp. 39-101. Cf. the arguments in Muller, *After Calvin*, pp. 137-155, and *PRRD*, I, 2.4 (A.3), 5.1 (B), 5.2 (A, C).

91. Cf. Ernst Lewalter, *Spanisch-jesuitisch und deutsch-lutherische Metaphysik des 17. Jahrhunderts* (Hamburg, 1935; repr. Darmstadt: Wissenschaftliche Buchgesellschaft, 1968), pp. 19-20, 36-42, with Lohr, "Metaphysics," in Charles B. Schmitt, Quentin Skinner, and Eckhard Kessler, eds., *The Cambridge History of Renaissance Philosophy* (Cambridge: Cambridge University Press, 1988), pp. 625-627; and idem, "Jesuit Aristotelianism and Sixteenth-Century Metaphysics," in *Paradosis: Studies in Memory of Edwin A. Quain*, ed. G. Fletcher and M. B. Schuete (New York: Fordham University press, 1976), pp. 203-220. Also see Hans Emil Weber, *Die philosophische Scholastik des deutschen Protestantismus in Zeitalter der Orthodoxie* (Leipzig: Quelle & Meyer, 1907) and idem, *Der Einfluss der protestantischen Schulphilosphie auf die orthodox-lutherische Dogmatik* (Leipzig: Deichert, 1908).

that flowed out of the later Middle Ages into the Renaissance and Reformation eras — whether the Thomistic, Scotistic, or the nominalistic lines of argument.[92]

Nonetheless, the Aristotelianism that influenced the language, structure, and contents of the early Protestant scholastic doctrine of God was not identical with the Aristotelianism of the last three medieval centuries in any of its varieties and certainly not identical with the metaphysics of Aristotle.[93] The Renaissance had brought about alterations in philosophical perspective and a post-Reformation revival of Aristotelian thought which was itself innovative and in some discontinuity with medieval models. The Protestant theologians, moreover, were highly eclectic, particularly inasmuch as they had no commitment to any single school of earlier thought but were able to draw together perspectives on various theological and philosophical issues from earlier Protestant sources as well as from a wealth of classical and medieval materials at their disposal in early-modern printed editions. Specifically, the nominalist, Scotist, Thomist, and Augustinian backgrounds of the Reformers themselves could be blended with and augmented by older materials to produce a highly traditionary but also distinctively Protestant theology in dialogue with the broader philosophical currents of the time.

The appearance of Suárez' *Disputationes metaphysicae* in 1597 marked a epoch in the history of Aristotelianism both in view of its organization and in view of its mastery of medieval and Renaissance sources. Suárez had recognized that Aristotle's *Metaphysics* lacked logical organization (indeed, the *Metaphysics* is merely a collection of related works of Aristotle) and that scholastic philosophy had tended to follow out Aristotle's order and simply comment on the text. Suárez's *Disputationes metaphysicae* took the revolutionary step of departing from Aristotle's order and finding a logical arrangement of the various topics included in metaphysics.[94] Because of its superior arrangement and masterful argumentation, Suárez's work rapidly became the standard text on metaphysics and the basis for other metaphysical argumentation throughout Europe, including Protestant lands.[95]

Suárez's major impact on the doctrine of God may well be what has been called his "theoretical reversal" of the philosophical conception of God as "being" — rather than follow the Thomistic assumption of an analogy of being between the divine and the human, Suárez held that the concept of "being" was used univocally of God and

92. See Stanislav Sousedík, "Arriagas Universalienlehre," in Tereza Saxolvá and Stanislav Sousedík, eds., *Rodrigo de Arriaga (+1667): Philosoph und Theolog* (Prague: Univerzity Karlovy, 1998), pp. 41-49, for a discussion of the nominalism of Petrus Hurtado de Mendoza and Rodericus de Arriaga, whose works were well known to the Protestant scholastics.

93. See the discussion of "Aristotelianism" in *PRRD* I, 8.1 (B-C).

94. Franciscus Suárez, *Disputationes metaphysicae* (Salamanca, 1597), also in *Opera omnia*, 26 vols. (Paris: Vives, 1856-1877), vols. 25-6.

95. Cf. Karl Eschweiler, "Die Philosophie der spanischen Spätscholastik auf dem deutschen Universitäten des siebzehnten Jahrhunderts," in H. Finke (ed.), *Gesammelte Aufsätze zur Kulturgeschichte Spaniens* (Münster: Aschendorff, 1928), p. 283, with Cyril Vollert, "Introduction," in Francis Suárez, *On the Various Kinds of Distinctions*, (Milwaukee: Marquette University Press, 1947), pp. 7-8. Also note Max Wundt, *Die deutsche Schulmetaphysik des 17. Jahrhunderts* (Tübingen: J. C. B. Mohr, 1939), pp. 41-47, 66-71, 102-104, 269-272.

creatures, in effect, replacing the Thomist with a Scotist view in what was basically Thomistic metaphysics.[96] Suárez also departed from the Thomistic assumption that the divine essence contains the exemplars of finite being, which derives from God and has its being by participation — rather Suárez held that created *essences* have their own internal coherence and that God creates, in the strictest sense, not essences but existences. So too, God knows the possibilities of being, not on the ground of his creative power, but because of the range of possibilities inherent in being in general.[97]

We must not assume that Suárez' conclusions were universally accepted — but, given the profound influence of his metaphysics, they were certainly the cause of much reconsideration of the language of God and creation in seventeenth-century philosophy and theology. Indeed, the stance of many of the Reformed philosophers of the day, notably Keckermann and Maccovius, that God does not belong within the category of being in general and that rational metaphysics, therefore, does not discuss the concept of God, ought to be understood as a direct opposition to Suárez.[98] On the other hand, Jacchaeus could follow Suárez in offering a basic division of philosophy into the consideration of infinite and finite being and thereby allow a discussion of God within the purview of metaphysics.[99] This was not a neutral development or a simple "advance" as one might gather from histories of philosophy — rather we are noting a significant point of contention in the theological and philosophical battles of the era.

In addition to Suárez' work, a major contribution to the metaphysical discussion of the age was made by Louis Molina, whose *Concordia liberi arbitrii cum gratiae donis, divina praescientia, providentia, praedestinatione et reprobatione* (1588) had offered a revision of Thomist metaphysics to include a separate category of divine knowledge of future contingents (*scientia media*) and a considerably altered view of the divine concurrence with free secondary causes.[100] Whereas Suárez' thought influenced the development of Reformed theology both positively and negatively, the influence of Molina was primarily negative. The debate over *scientia media* that began following the publication of Molina's *Concordia* in 1588 was but a prelude to the intense debates

---

96. Jean-Luc Marion, "The Idea of God," in Daniel Garber and Michael Ayres, eds., *The Cambridge History of Seventeenth-Century Philosophy*, 2 vols. (Cambridge: Cambridge University Press, 1998), I, p. 267; cf. John P. Doyle, "Suarez on the Analogy of Being," in *The Modern Schoolman*, 46 (1969), pp. 219-249, 323-341; and idem, "The Suarezian Proof for God's Existence," in *History of Philosophy in the Making: A Symposium of Essays to Honor Professor James D. Collins on his 65th Birthday*, ed. Linus J. Thro (Washington, D.C.: University Press of America, 1982), pp. 105-117.

97. Marion, "Idea of God," p. 267.

98. Bartholomaus Keckermann, *Scientiae metaphysicae brevissima synopsis*, in *Opera omnia quae extant*, I, col. 2015; Johannes Maccovius, *Metaphysica, ad usum quaestionum in philosophia ac theologia adornata & applicata* (Leiden, 1658), pp. 2-3, 6.

99. Gilbertus Jacchaeus, *Primae philosophiae institutiones* (Leiden, 1616).

100. Luis de Molina, *Concordia liberi arbitrii cum gratiae donis, divina praescientia, providentia, praedestinatione et reprobatione*, ed. Johann Rabeneck (Onia and Madrid: Collegium Maximum Societatis Jesu, 1953). See E. Vansteenberghe, "Molina, Louis," in *DTC*, vol. 10/2, cols. 2090-2092; and idem, "Molinisme," s.v. in *DTC*, vol. 10/2, cols. 2094-2187; also note the historical background offered in Paul Dumont, *Liberté humaine et concours divin d'après Suarez* (Paris: Beauchesne, 1936).

over the views of Vorstius, the Socinians, and eventually of Remonstrant theologians like Episcopius and Curcellaeus. Whereas there had been considerable trinitarian debate in the sixteenth century and very little over the question of the divine essence and attributes, the seventeenth century saw both the continuation and the intensification of the trinitarian polemic and the inauguration of a series of major debates over the identity of God and over the character and manner of predication of the divine attributes.

Granting that the most prominent and influential positive use of Molinist arguments on *scientia media* and the divine *concursus* among Protestants during the era of early orthodoxy was in the theology of Arminius,[101] and that Arminius' use of these concepts was directed primarily toward the establishment of a different relationship between God and the world than that found in early orthodox Reformed dogmatics,[102] Arminius' theology occupies a significant, albeit somewhat negative, place in the development of the Reformed doctrine of God: on the one hand, the shape and structure of his doctrine, with its emphasis on the divine life as distinguished into the faculties of intellect and will, belongs to the central line of the Reformed development — while, on the other, his revision of the conception of *scientia media* alone Molinist lines sets him apart from the Reformed development.[103]

3. Among the Protestants: God and the new philosophical perspectives. Several strands of late Renaissance or early modern philosophical thought had considerable impact on the development of early orthodox Reformed theology, with specific reference to the Reformed doctrine of God. Noteworthy is the impact of skepticism, of the revived and revised Aristotelian metaphysics, and of various eclectic strains of Renaissance philosophy that can be identified, for lack of a better term, as Platonic. First the influence of contemporary skepticism: already in the time of Calvin and Viret, there had been a rise of skeptical literature, variously identified as atheistic, deistic, or rationalistic in tone.[104] Viret noted the phenomenon explicitly in his *Instruction*

---

101. Jacobus Arminius, *Opera theologica* (Leiden, 1629); the preferred translation is *The Works of James Arminius*, trans. James Nichols and William Nichols, with an intro. by Carl Bangs, 3 vols. (London, 1825, 1828, 1875; repr. Grand Rapids: Baker Book House, 1986).

102. See Richard A. Muller, *God, Creation and Providence in the Thought of Jacob Arminius: Sources and Directions of Scholastic Protestantism in the Era of Early Orthodoxy* (Grand Rapids: Baker Book House, 1991), pp. 153-166, and idem, "God, Predestination, and the Integrity of the Created Order: A Note on Patterns in Arminius' Theology," in Graham, ed., *Later Calvinism*, pp. 431-446.

103. Cf. William L. Craig, *The Problem of Divine Foreknowledge and Human Freedom from Aristotle to Suarez* (Leiden: E. J. Brill, 1980), and idem, "Middle Knowledge: A Calvinist-Arminian Rapprochement?" in *The Grace of God and the Will of Man*, ed. Clark H. Pinnock (Grand Rapids: Zondervan, 1989), pp. 141-164 with Richard A. Muller, "Grace, Election, and Contingent Choice: Arminius's Gambit and the Reformed Response," in Thomas Schreiner and Bruce Ware, eds., *The Grace of God and the Bondage of the Will*, 2 vols. (Grand Rapids: Baker Book House, 1995), II, pp. 251-278.

104. See, e.g., Don Cameron Allen, *Doubt's Boundless Sea: Skepticism and Faith in the Renaissance* (Baltimore: Johns Hopkins, 1964); Lucien Febvre, *The Problem of Unbelief in the Sixteenth Century: The Religion of Rabelais*, trans. Beatrice Gottlieb (Cambridge, Mass.: Harvard University Press, 1982); George T. Buckley, *Atheism in the English Renaissance* (New York: Russell and Russell, 1965).

chrestienne of 1564, speaking of "deists" who confessed the existence of God, the eternal creator but who denied that salvation was to be found in Christ. Such persons, he continued were to be identified as "atheists" in the same sense that the Apostle Paul referred to pagans as atheists — deniers of the true God.[105] The identity of these "deists" is almost impossible to determine with precision, apart from their failure to fit into the category of orthodox theists, whether Protestant or Roman. They may have been antitrinitarians or perhaps theists who leaned toward views of God resting on the classical philosophical tradition. In any case, they were not deists in the same sense as the Deists of the eighteenth century.[106]

Not only, moreover, did the theological debates of the age concerning standards of truth and certainty inspire a literary skepticism such as that of Rabelais and Montaigne, they also prompted several varieties of philosophical skepticism, notably the refutation of Aristotelian theories of knowing by Francisco Sanchez, *Quod nihil scitur* (1581) and the attack on atheism, paganism, Judaism, Mohammedanism, and Protestantism, *Les Trois Veritez* (1594) by Pierre Charron. Charron's arguments against Protestant theology, focused on the apologetic work of Mornay, had emphasized the infinitude of God and the lowliness of human knowing to the point of denying the ability of human beings to know anything about God — unless, of course, they accepted the authority of church and tradition. As for the atheists, their denials of the existence of God rest on feeble human definitions and are, therefore, as worthless as the nonauthoritative claims of the Protestants.[107]

Another work of the era, significant for its expression of the broad value of natural religion and its skepticism concerning the dogmas of any and all faiths, is Jean Bodin's unpublished but widely circulated *Colloquium heptaplomeres* or *Colloque entre sept scavans*, written ca. 1593.[108] There has been debate over which of the seven savants in Bodin's dialogue represents Bodin, with plausible arguments, on the basis of the ability and intelligence of two of the sages, that Bodin either leaned toward a Jewish

---

105. Pierre Viret, *Instruction chrestienne en la doctrine de la loy de de l'Évangile, et en la vraye philosophie et théologie naturelle et supernaturelle des chrestiens*, 3 pts. (Geneva: J. Rivery, 1564), the unpaginated letter to the church at Montpellier, prefaced to pt. 2; the text is available in *Pierre Viret d' après lui-même*, pp. 233-236.

106. Thus, C. J. Betts, *Early Deism in France: From the So-called 'Déistes' of Lyon (1564) to Voltarie's 'Letres philosophiques' (1734)* (Den Haag: Martinus Nijhoff, 1984), pp. 6-17.

107. See Richard H. Popkin, *The History of Scepticism from Erasmus to Descartes* (New York: Harper & Row, 1968), pp. 57-66.

108. Jean Bodin, *Colloque entre sept scavans qui sont de differens sentimens des secrets cachez des choses relevees*, texte presente et etabli par Francois Berriot et al., *Travaux d'humanisme et Renaissance*, 204 (Geneve: Librairie Droz, 1984); in translation, *Colloquium of the seven about secrets of the sublime [Colloquium heptaplomeres de rerum sublimium arcanis abditis]*, trans. with intro., annotations, and critical readings, by Marion L. Kuntz (Princeton, N.J.: Princeton University Press, 1975); also note Bodin's *Vniversae naturae theatrum: in quo rerum omnium effectrices causae & fines quinque libris discutiuntur* (Lugduni: Apud Iacobum Roussin, 1596). On Bodin, see Gottschalk Eduard Guhrauer, *Das Heptaplomeres des Jean Bodin; zur Geschichte der Kultur und Literatur im Jahrhundert der Reformation* (Berlin, 1841; repr. Geneve: Slatkine Reprints, 1971).

or Judaizing view or toward a purely philosophical or natural theological theism.[109] However this question is answered, Bodin clearly understood the fundamental truth of religion to be the monotheism held by the ancient sages of the Biblical narrative, Adam, Abel, Enoch, and Noah, prior to the beginnings of Judaism. These truths were available by means of "right reason" and the natural religion implanted in the mind of all people. This religion was carried forward by the patriarchs, Moses, the prophets, Christ and, as well, by the ancient monotheistic philosophers, Greek and Roman — at its center is belief in one eternal God, the ultimate Being endowed with infinite goodness, power, and wisdom. Bodin critiques those philosophers who would explain the world without recourse to God — and all religious confessions that appeal to authorities such as tradition or sacred books in order to create narrowly specific systems of belief.

These philosophical developments were not without their impact on the Reformed theology of the era and, specifically, on the Reformed approach to the doctrine of God. The early orthodox era saw the publication of several major apologetic treatises by Reformed authors in which the existence and oneness of God began the roster of truths to be demonstrated against various kinds of atheists and infidels. Perhaps the most eminent of these is Du Plessis-Mornay's *Traité de la verité de la religion chrétienne* (1581), which argued the existence of God largely on cosmological grounds, moved on to the divine essence, including an argument for the Trinity based on ancient philosophy, the creation of the world ex nihilo, the sovereign concern of God for the welfare of humanity, and therefore the necessity of true religion. From these topics Mornay moves on to a refutation of polytheism, an identification of Scripture as the Word of God and the only true revelation, followed by arguments for the divine Sonship and sole mediatorship of Christ.[110] Also of note is the uncompleted project of Martin Fotherby, bishop of Sarum, *Atheomastix*, which projected arguments on the existence of God, the oneness of God, the identity of Jehovah as the one God, and the authority of Scripture as the Word of God, in four books, but covering, in its three hundred and sixty pages, only two out of eight proposed "books" on the existence of God. As his predecessors, Fotherby cited Aquinas' *Summa contra gentiles*, Raymond of Sebonde's *theologia naturalis*, Bradwardine's *De causa Dei*, and Valesius' *De sacra philosophia*, complaining that these works, although worthy, had only presented their arguments "Scholastically, by way of Logicall Arguments, which doe not *influere*" and therefore "cannot affect, nor leave any great impression in the mind of a man." He notes his preference for Ludovicus Vives' *De veritate fidei christianae*, Mornay's treatise, and

---

109. Thus, Paul Lawrence Rose, *Bodin and the great God of nature: the moral and religious universe of a Judaiser*, Travaux d'humanisme et Renaissance, 179 (Geneve: Librairie Droz, 1980); cf. the discussion in Harald Höffding, *A History of Modern Philosophy: A Sketch of the History of Philosophy from the Close of the Renaissance to our own Day*, trans. B. E. Meyer, 2 vols. (London: Macmillan, 1935), I, pp. 60-64.

110. Philippe Du Plessis-Mornay, *Traité de la verité de la religion chrétienne contre les Athées, Epicures, Payens, Juifs, Mahumedistes, et autres Infideles* (Antwerp, 1581); trans. as *A Worke concerning the Trunesse of the Christian Religion ... Against Atheists, Epicures, Paynims, Iewes, Mahumetists, and other Infidels*, trans. Philip Sidney and Arthur Golding (London: George Potter, 1587; 1604; etc.).

Zanchi's *De operibus Dei* as models for his own refutation of "Infidels, Epicures, and Atheists."[111] In the work both of Mornay and of Fotherby, the apologetic assumption was not only that theism could be asserted against a generalized atheism, but that a Protestant, Reformed theism could be argued against all forms of infidelity — by implication, supported by a form of Christian natural theology or Christian metaphysics in which various forms of apologetic argumentation concerning the truth of traditional conceptions of the divine essence and attributes could be shown as supporting the Reformed faith.

The concurrent revival of a more traditional Aristotelianism is evidenced in the thought of a series of Reformed teachers of philosophy and metaphysics during this era — whose exponents not only drew heavily on new editions of Aristotle and, eventually, on the work of Suárez. Several of the Reformed writers, moreover, also opposed many of Suárez's alterations of the Thomistic model, with significant impact on Reformed approaches to the doctrine of God. This development can be observed in the philosophical works of Gulielmus Xylander,[112] Bartholomaus Keckermann,[113] J. H. Alsted, and Johannes Maccovius. Xylander marks an early turn to Renaissance Aristotelianism at Heidelberg. The three latter thinkers tended toward a Thomistic view of the analogy of being over against the Suárezian conception of the univocity of being, with Keckermann and Maccovius denying that God was a topic in metaphysics, given that God cannot be construed as a subcategory of "being in general." A more positive approach but nonetheless critical to Suárez can be seen in the thought of the Leiden philosopher and logician, Franco Burgersdijk. His *Idea philosophiae naturalis* (1622) and *Institutiones metaphysicae* (1640) evidence the progress of an eclectic alternative — we may even say a Reformed alternative — to the fully Suárezian approach to the divine being and knowledge, adding to the Suárezian distinction between infinite and finite being a more Thomistic language of "being of itself" and "being by participation," as a basis for allowing proofs of the existence of God and discussion of the essential properties of God to enter his metaphysics.[114] Burgersdijk's approach was carried forward by his highly influential pupil and successor, Adriaan Heereboord, whose logic, ethics, and metaphysics were influential not only on the continent but also in Britain.[115]

---

111. Martin Fotherby, *Atheomastix: Clearing foure Truthes, Against Atheists and Infidels: 1. That, There is a God. 2. That, There is but one God. 3. That, Jehovah, our God, is that One God. 4. That, The Holy Scripture is the Word of that God* (London: Nicholas Okes, 1622), preface to the reader, fol. A5 verso - A6 recto.

112. Gulielmus Xylander, *Institutiones aphoristicae logices Aristotelis* (Heidelberg, 1577).

113. See W. H. Zuylen, *Bartholomaus Keckermann: Sein Leben und Wirken* (Leipzig: Robert Noske, 1934).

114. Cf. E. P. Bos, and H. A. Krop, eds., *Franco Burgersdijk (1590-1635): Neo-Aristotelianism in Leiden* (Amsterdam: Rodopi, 1993).

115. Adriaan Heereboord, *Meletemata philosophica in quibus pleraeque res Metaphysicae ventilantur, tota Ethica κατασκευαστικως καὶ ἀνασκευαστικως explicatur, universa Physica per theoremata & commentarios exponitur, summa rerum Logicarum per Disputationes traditur*, editio nova (Amsterdam: Henricus Wetstenius, 1680); idem, *Philosophia naturalis, cum Commentariis Peripateticis anthaec edita*

Another evidence, both of the impact of streams of later medieval thought mediated to the Reformed orthodox by the traditions of their own teachers and by the reading of the editions of major medieval writers like Aquinas, Scotus, Durandus, and Gregory of Rimini and by the Protestant reading of more recent Roman Catholic theologians like Cajetan and Suárez, is the rise of a somewhat varied reading of the concept of divine simplicity. The early orthodox writers, followed by the high orthodox, consistently raise the question of the character of predications made concerning God, the viability of language concerning divine "properties" and "attributes," and the character of the distinctions among the attributes — whether such distinctions are made only *ad extra* or, if made *ad intra*, the kind of distinction that can be made in a non-composite or simple being. It is important, moreover, to recognize that the assumption of divine simplicity was not merely inherited from the Reformers; it was also lodged in the confessional theology of the Reformed churches.[116] It was this confessional stance, prepared for dispute by examination of the older tradition, that the orthodox defended against the Vorstian and Socinian denials of divine simplicity.

Conrad Vorstius also occupies a significant, but nearly entirely negative, place in the development of Reformed orthodox doctrine of the divine attributes. After his successful defense of two of his works, *De sancta trinitate* (1597), and *De personis et officio Christi* (1597), before the Heidelberg faculty, he was called in 1610 to Leiden as the successor of Arminius. There, the revised edition of his 1602 *Disputationes decem de natura et attributis Dei* brought rapid condemnation from the Dutch Reformed, notably Sibrandus Lubbertus, and from the faculty at Heidelberg. Vorstius was dismissed from his professorship but paid his salary until his condemnation as a heretic by the Synod of Dort. Vorstius' treatise on the divine nature and attributes attempted to modify the concepts of divine simplicity, infinity, and immensity in such as way as to allow distinctions in the divine nature.[117]

The problems of middle knowledge and the Vorstian understanding of divine attributes, coupled with a rising interest in Platonism — not merely the writings of Plato but also of middle- and neoplatonism, together with a sampling from the Hermetic literature — were evident to English Reformed as well as to the continental divines. The inroads of the new views were most noticeable in the highly developed *Treatise of the Divine Essence and Attributes* (1628) written by Thomas Jackson, an Oxford scholar and Dean of Peterborough. Notable among the erudite defenders of Protestant orthodoxy against these variant views was William Twisse, whose eminence would earn him, at the very end of his career, the position of prolocutor of the Westminster Assembly.[118] Although, like Owen after him, Twisse did not write a theological system,

---

(London: Wilmot & Crosley, 1684).

116. Thus, Gallican Confession, I; Belgic Confession, I; cf. Thirty-nine Articles, I; Irish Articles, 8; Westminster Confession, II.1.

117. Conrad Vorstius, *Tractatus theologicus de Deo, sive, de natura et attributis Dei* (Steinfurt, 1610).

118. See Sarah Hutton, "Thomas Jackson, Oxford Platonist, and William Twisse, Aristotelian," in *Journal of the History of Ideas*, 39 (1978), pp. 635-652; also Peter White, *Predestination, Policy and Polemic: Conflict and Consensus in the English Church from the Reformation to the Civil War* (Cambridge:

his treatises on divine grace, power, and providence, on middle knowledge, and on predestination, together with his massive refutation of Jackson on the divine essence and attributes, both reached a level of detail and penetration nearly unparalleled in his time.[119] Twisse's debates with Jackson and others gave him a clearer perception than many of his contemporaries of the significance of Aristotle for traditional orthodoxy and, in his view, of the problematic character of Platonism — not to mention his sense of the positive relationship between the great medieval doctors and the Reformed tradition. Twisse's citations of Aquinas, Scotus, Durandus, Vasquez, and Suárez show him to have been a master of the scholastic materials, old and new.

2.3 The Doctrine of God in the High Orthodox Era (1640-1685)

A. The Transition to High Orthodoxy

1. Thinkers and Issues. The first phase of the high orthodox era brought both a further codification and considerable change to the Protestant scholastic doctrine of God. On the one hand, the variety of positive formulation that we have seen during the early orthodox era has hardly disappeared — at the same time there is an identifiable continuity of doctrine in its main outlines, a continuance and even clarification of various trajectories of doctrinal nuance (often identifiable in terms Thomist, Scotist, and nominalist accents either mediated through the Renaissance Reformation or recovered by the Protestant scholastics from the older sources), and a continuity of exegetical trajectories. Granting the distinctions made by the orthodox writers among contrasting types or genres of theology, namely, the positive or didactic, the polemical, the catechetical or ecclesial, the homiletical, and the scholastic, differences of genre within the field of dogmatic or "systematic" theology account for much of the variety. By way of example, high orthodoxy, particularly among the British writers of the time of the Westminster Assembly, saw a plethora of catechetical and homiletical works with a systematic form. The Scots theologian Hugh Binning developed a homiletical theology notable for its rootage in the technical theology of the era as well as for its

---

Cambridge Univ Press, 1992), pp. 256-271; and M. E. Van der Schaaf, "The Theology of Thomas Jackson (1579-1640): An Anglican Alternative to Roman Catholicism, Puritanism and Calvinism" (Ph.D. diss., University of Iowa, 1979).

119. William Twisse, *Vindiciae gratiae, potestatis, ac providentiae Dei hoc est, ad examen libelli Perkinsiani de praedestinatione modo et ordine, institutum a J. Arminio, responsio scholastica* (Amsterdam, 1632); idem, *Dissertatio de scientia media tribus libris absoluta* (Arnheim, 1639); idem, *The Doctrine of the Synod of Dort and Arles* (London, 1650/1); and idem, *A Discovery of D. Jacksons Vanitie. Or, a Perspective glasse, whereby admirers of D. Jacksons profound discourses, may see the vanitie and weaknesse of them* (London, 1631).

piety.[120] Thomas Watson,[121] John Flavel,[122] and David Dickson[123] all produced expansive catechetical theologies grounded on the Westminster standards, the two former writers offering positive catechetical systems, Dickson offering a polemical or disputative expansion of the Confession.

On a more technical level but remaining firmly within the genre of devotional and homiletical theologies, the English writers Richard Baxter and Stephen Charnock wrote extensively on the divine attributes, with particular emphasis on the practical "use" of their doctrine.[124] Such works, like the homiletical commentaries of the era, evidence the connection made between the more academic or scholastic theology taught in the universities and the more popular theology of the time, intended for the laity. These works stands in some contrast, in style and in level of technical detail, with the major systematic efforts of continental dogmaticians like Cloppenburg, Wendelin, Burman, Essenius,[125] Spanheim, Marckius,[126] Turretin, and Heidegger, with the sets

120. Hugh Binning, *The Common Principles of the Christian Religion*, in *The Works of the Rev. Hugh Binning, M. A.*, collected and ed. M. Leishman (Edinburgh, 1858; repr. Ligonier, Pa.: Soli Deo Gloria, 1992).

121. Thomas Watson, *A Body of Practical Divinity* (London, 1692); idem, *Discourses on Important and Interesting Subjects: Being the Select Works of the Rev. Thomas Watson*, 2 vols. (Glasgow, 1829; repr. Ligonier, PA: Soli Deo Gloria, 1990).

122. John Flavel, *An Exposition of the Assembly's Catechism with Practical Inferences from Each Question*, in *The Works of John Flavel*, 6 vols. (London: Baynes and Son, 1820), VI, pp. 138-317.

123. David Dickson, *The Summe of Saving Knowledge, with the Practical Use Thereof* (Edinburgh: George Swintoun, 1671); idem, *Truths Victory over Error. Or, an Abridgement of the Chief Controversies in Religion ... between those of the Orthodox Faith, and all Adversaries whatsoever* (Edinburgh: John Reid, 1684). Note also Dickson's efforts as biblical exegete: *A Brief Exposition of the Evangel of Jesus Christ according to Matthew* (London: Ralph Smith, 1647); *A Brief Exposition of the Psalms*, 3 vols. (London, 1653-55); reissued as *A Commentary on the Psalms*. 2 vols. (London: Banner of Truth, 1965); *An Exposition of all St. Pauls Epistles together with ... St. James, Peter, John, and Jude* (London: R. I. for Francis Eglesfield, 1659); *A Short Explanation of the Epistle of Paul to the Hebrews* (Dublin: Society of Stationers, 1637).

124. Stephen Charnock, *The Works of the late learned Divine Stephen Charnock, B.D.*, 2 vols. (London: Printed for Ben Griffin, and Tho. Cockeril, 1684); also *Discourses upon the Existence and Attributes of God*, 2 vols. (New York: Robert Carter, 1853).

125. Johannes Cloppenburg, *Opera theologica* 2 vols. (Amsterdam, 1684); idem *Exercitationes super locos communes theologicos*, in *Opera*, vol. I; Marcus Friedrich Wendelin, *Christianae theologiae systema majus duobus libris comprehensum* (Cassel, 1656), also published as *Christianae theologiae libri duo* (Amsterdam, 1657); Franz Burman, *Synopsis theologiae et speciatim oeconomiae foederum Dei*, 2 parts (Geneva, 1678; Den Haag, 1687); Andreas Essenius, *Synopsis controversiarum theologicarum, et index locorum totius s. scripturae, quibus adversarii ad errores suos confirmandos, et veritatem impugnandum vel declinandum, praecipue abuti solent: ubi tum adversarii, qui iis abutuntur, tum singulae eorum collectiones brevi methodo proponuntur* (Utrecht: Meinardus a Dreunen, 1677); idem, *Systematis theologici pars prior -tomus tertius: I. De natura theologia, de fide, de S. Scriptura, de Deo, de personis divinis, dedecreto Dei, de creatione, de providentia, de foedere legali, & de peccato. II. De foedere evangelico, de Christo mediatore, de salutis impetratione, de vocatione & regeneratione, de justificatione, reconciliatione, & adoptione. III. De sanctificatione, de conservatione & corroboratione, de obsignatione, de glorificatione, & de Ecclesia*, 3 vols. (Amsterdam: Johannes Ansonius, 1659-1665).

126. Johannes Marckius, *Christianae theologiae medulla didactico elenctica* (Amsterdam, 1690); idem, *Compendium theologiae christianae didactico-elencticum* (Groningen, 1686).

of dogmatic theses produced by Amyraut and his colleagues at Saumur or by Le Blanc at Sedan.[127] Still, these differences in style do not indicate, as some writers have argued, a less-systematic British approach and a more-systematic continental approach. On the one hand, the fully scholastic and polemical works of British divines like Leigh, Twisse, Rutherford, Baxter, and Owen equaled the technical mastery and expansive development of argument found in the works of continental divines. On the other hand, the British homiletical and catechetical "systems," are rather similar (as one might expect) to the catechetical and homiletical systems of their continental counterparts, like Alsted or Cocceius.[128] There is also a significant relationship between the devotional emphases of these English theologies and the work of various proponents of the *Nadere Reformatie* or Dutch "Second Reformation," notable among them Wilhelmus à Brakel,[129] Simon Oomius, and Petrus van Mastricht. Nor, indeed, do these works evidence a major rift either in method or in content between the Saumur theologians and those of Sedan or Geneva or, for that matter, between Voetians and the Cocceians. In point of fact, the methodological contrast between the more scholastic and less scholastic models ought to be made on grounds of literary genre rather than theological position in the internal debates of orthodoxy, as illustrated by various works of a theologian like Baxter — with the strict scholastic model evidenced in his *Catholike Theology* or his *Methodus theologiae christianae* and the practical application exemplified in the first part of his treatise on *The Divine Life*, where he offers an extensive discussion of the existence and attributes of God from the perspective of piety.[130] So too, Cocceius'

---

127. Moyse Amyraut, Louis Cappel, and Josue La Place, *Syntagma thesium theologicarum in Academia Salmuriensi variis temporibus disputatarum*, editio secunda, 4 parts (Saumur: Joannes Lesner, 1664; second printing, 1665); Ludovicus Le Blanc, *Theses theologicae, variis temporibus in Academia Sedanensi editae et ad disputandum propositae* (London: Moses Pitt, 1675).

128. Johann Heinrich Alsted, *Theologia catechetica, exhibens sacratiaaimam novitiolorum christianorum scholam, in qua summa fidei et operum ... exponitur* (Hanau, 1622); Johannes Cocceius, *Explicatio catecheseos Heidelbergensis*, in *Opera omnia theologica, exegetica, didactica, polemica, philologica*, 12 vols. (Amsterdam, 1701-1706), vol. 7, second pagination, pp. 1-72.

129. Wilhelmus à Brakel, *ΛΟΓΙΚΗ ΛΑΤΡΕΙΑ, dat is Redelijke Godsdienst in welken de goddelijke Waarheden van het Genade-Verbond worden verklaard ... alsmede de Bedeeling des Verbonds in het O. en N.T. en de Ontmoeting der Kerk in het N. T. vertoond in eene Verklaring van de Openbaringen aan Johannes*. 3 parts. Dordrecht, 1700; second printing, Leiden: D. Donner, 1893-94); in translation, *The Christian's Reasonable Service in which Divine Truths concerning the Covenant of Grace are Expounded, Defended against Opposing Parties, and their Practice Advocated*, trans. Bartel Elshout, with a biographical sketch by W. Fieret and an essay on the "Dutch Second Reformation" by Joel Beeke, 4 vols. (Ligonier, PA: Soli Deo Gloria Publications, 1992-95).

130. Richard Baxter, *Catholike Theologie: Plain, Pure, Peaceable; for Pacification of the Dogmatical Word-Warriours* (London, 1675); idem, *Methodus theologiae christianae* (London, 1681); and idem, *The Divine Life in Three Treatises: first, The Knowledge of God, and the Impression it Must make upon the Heart ... second, The Description, Reasons, and Reward of the Believer's Walking with God ... third, The Christian's Converse with God* (London, 1664).

doctrine of God bears all of the characteristics of the scholastic model,[131] as do the expositions of doctrine in Cocceian thinkers like Heidanus and Burman.[132]

In addition, the major biblical commentators of the era — whether British exegetes like the authors of the Westminster Annotations[133] or authors of individual, sometimes massive commentaries, like Adams, Jenkyn, Durham, Greenhill, or Caryl,[134] or continental exegetes, like the authors of the *Statenvertaling* or "Dutch Annotations,"[135] or major exegetes like Cocceius — continued and even developed the tradition of the *locus* method by identifying theological topics throughout their commentaries. Here also the outlines of the orthodox doctrine of God can be found, not, of course, argued systematically, but identified in its various elements — whether in discussions of who or what God is, of various individual attributes, of the relationship between God and world, of divine affections, or of the Trinity — in the course of their exegesis of individual texts.

On the other hand, the philosophical and theological problems encountered by the orthodox formulators have changed. The debate over the theories of Vorstius had only intensified, given the apparent acceptance of some of his views on the divine essence and attributes by later Socinian and Remonstrant thinkers. The Socinian threat itself had intensified, given the exegetical efforts of a series of significant Socinian theologians.[136] Perhaps more subtle, but equally significant, was the shift in philosophical

---

131. Johannes Cocceius, *Aphorismi per universam theologiam breviores*, in *Opera*, vol. 7, pp. 3-16; idem, *Aphorismi per universam theologiam prolixiores*, in *Opera*, vol. 7, pp. 17-38; and idem, *Summa theologiae ex Scriptura repetita* (Geneva, 1665; Amsterdam, 1669); the *Summa* is also in *Opera*, vol. 7, pp. 131-403. See Willem J. van Asselt, "Johannes Cocceius Anti-Scholasticus?" in van Asselt and Dekker (eds.), *Reformation and Scholasticism*, pp. 227-251; also note idem, *The Federal Theology of Johannes Cocceius (1603-1669)*, trans. Raymond A. Blacketer (Leiden: E. J. Brill, 2001), pp. 94-105.

132. Cf. Heidanus, *Corpus theologiae*, II (pp. 53-207); Burman, *Synopsis theologiae*, I.ii.14-29;

133. *Annotations upon all the Books of the Old and New Testament, wherein the Text is Explained, Doubts Resolved, Scriptures Parallelled, and Various Readings observed*, by the Joynt-Labour of certain Learned Divines (London, 1645; 2nd ed., 1651; 3rd ed. 1657), hereinafter cited as *Westminster Annotations*, from the 1645 edition, unless otherwise noted.

134. Thomas Adams, *A Commentary on the Second Epistle General of St. Peter* (London, 1633; reissued, Edinburgh: James Nichol, 1839); William Jenkyn, *An Exposition upon the Epistle of Jude*; revised and corrected by James Sherman (Edinburgh: James Nichol, 1863); James Durham, *A Commentarie Upon the Book of Revelation. Wherein the Text is explained ... together with some practical Observations, and several Digressions necessary for vindicating, clearing, and confirming weighty and important Truths* (London: Company of Stationers, 1658); William Greenhill, *An Exposition of Ezekiel*, 5 vols. (London, 1665-67; reissued in one volume, Edinburgh: James Nichol, 1863); Joseph Caryl, *An Exposition with Practicall Observations upon ... the Booke of Iob*, 12 vols. (London: G. Miller and M. Simmons, 1644-1666).

135. *The Dutch Annotations upon the Whole Bible: Or, All the holy canonical Scriptures of the Old and New Testament ... as ... appointed by the Synod of Dort, 1618, and published by authority, 1637*, 2 vols., trans. Theodore Haak (London, 1657).

136. E.g., the works of Socinus, Crell, Schlichting, and others, gathered in the *Bibliotheca fratrum polonorum quos Unitarios vocant*, 6 vols. (Eleutheropolis [Amsterdam]: n.p., 1656); also note Johann Crell, *The Expiation of a Sinner in a Commentary upon the Epistle to the Hebrews.* (London, 1646); idem, *The Two Books of John Crellius Francus, touching one God the Father wherein many things also concerning the nature of the Son of God and the Holy Spirit are discoursed of* (Kosmoburg [London: s.n.],

perspective away from the early seventeenth-century debates between varieties of Aristotelianism to debates between the proponents of an eclectic Aristotelianism and the proponents of a variety of philosophical alternatives, from a revived neoplatonism to the new rationalist and mechanistic philosophies of the day, from Descartes, Gassendi, and Lord Herbert of Cherbury, to the Cambridge Platonists, Geulincx, Hobbes, Malebranche, Spinoza, and Leibniz. The patterns and trajectory of the doctrine of God in the theological works of the seventeenth century cannot be separated from this philosophical development or, indeed, intellectually subordinated to it: as Popkin has observed from the side of the history of philosophy, the interplay of revelation and reason, theological categories and the new rationalist philosophies is evident in the writings of the major and minor philosophers of the era, whose thought is separated from that of the Enlightenment rationalists by their advocacy of and intellectual involvement in theological and religious developments.[137] Given the traditional alliance of theology and philosophy and the dependence of theology on terms and models of discourse shared with philosophy, the dependence and interrelationships consistently took the opposite direction as well.

If the early orthodox doctrine of the divine essence and attributes can be understood as standing in some continuity both with the medieval and the Reformation perspectives — specifically, in continuity with the Reformation granting both its profoundly biblical content and reference and its indebtedness to and its unwillingness to alter the medieval perspective on fundamental definitions of essence, attributes, and Trinity — so also can the high orthodox doctrine be recognized as part of a continuous development. Here, however, more than in the early orthodox era we do encounter a somewhat more rationalistic and philosophical orientation — albeit not without attention to the problem of revelation and its relation to philosophy. The primary difference between the high orthodox and the early orthodox teaching, in this as in other *loci*, lies in the tendency of high orthodoxy not to develop new ideas but merely to repeat and defend in more detail what had been formulated during the era between 1565 and 1640, now, however, with increasingly less aid from an agreed upon philosophical system and in the face of altering patterns of hermeneutics.

2. Controversy and change: specific developments. During this era, the doctrine of God was the subject of numerous and far reaching controversies. In the face of a

---

1665). Much of this theology and exegesis is summarized in the text and seventeenth-century notes of *The Racovian catechisme: wherein you have the substance of the confession of those churches, which in the kingdom of Poland and Great Dukedome of Lithuania, and other provinces appertaining to that kingdom, do affirm, that no other save the Father of our Lord Jesus Christ, is that one God of Israel, and that the man Jesus of Nazareth, who was born of the Virgin, and no other besides, or before him, is the onely begotten Sonne of God* (Amsterdam: For Brooer Janz, 1652), also *The Racovian Catechism*, with notes and illustrations, trans. Thomas Rees (London: Longman, Hurst, 1609; reprint, London, 1818).

137. Richard H. Popkin, "The Religious Background of Seventeenth-Century Philosophy," in Popkin, ed., *The Third Force in Seventeenth-Century Thought* (Leiden: E. J. Brill, 1992), pp. 268-284. See also the discussion of Leibniz's theological roots in Leroy E. Loemker, *Struggle for Synthesis: The Seventeenth Century Background of Leibniz's Synthesis of Order and Freedom* (Cambridge, Mass.: Harvard University Press, 1972).

declining Aristotelianism and a rising rationalism, both in the form of Cartesian philosophy and of Deism, Reformed orthodoxy revisited the problem of the rational knowledge of God and its relation to theological system. Continuing controversy with the Arminians, Jesuits, and Socinians brought intense examination of the question of divine knowledge of contingent events, specifically the question of *scientia media*, the divine foreknowledge of future contingents lying outside of the divine willing. Related debate over the theological and philosophical speculations of Conrad Vorstius, whose ideas on divine simplicity, infinity, immensity, and eternity were taken up by some Arminian thinkers, on the one hand, and by Socinian theologians, on the other, continued throughout the era of orthodoxy — most notably over Vorstius' assumption of sequence in God. Equally profound were the debates between the Reformed orthodox and the Socinians over the question of punitive or vindicatory justice in God and, consequently, over the necessity of punishment for sin. And, of course, the Socinian and neo-Arian approaches to the doctrine of the Trinity caused vast controversies during the seventeenth century, carrying forward the problems first raised in the mid-sixteenth century by Servetus and the Italian antitrinitarians, Blandrata and Gentile.[138]

In the seventeenth century, moreover, not only did the Reformed orthodox have to contend with the Molinist conception of a dialogical divine knowing dependent on the foreknowledge of future contingencies, they also were confronted by an even more radical Socinian perspective: whereas Molina assumed the infinity, simplicity, eternity, and omniscience of God, the Socinians increasingly denied an essential infinity, argued incidental properties in the divine being, assumed the sequential nature of divine knowing, and argued that future contingencies could not be known by God. The reason given by the Socinians for this conclusion was, moreover, related to a more or less traditionary concern. Just as the orthodox tradition had generally acknowledged that God is to be understood as omnipotent and yet unable to do what is absolutely impossible (given that doing something utterly impossible would involve a contradiction), so the Socinians argued that God ought not to be viewed as any less divine if he were incapable of knowing future contingencies, inasmuch as these contingencies are unknowable and knowing them would involve a contradiction.[139]

In the Socinian view, all events and things that occur either freely or contingently are so because they are not determinate in their causality. Indeterminate and therefore uncertain causality, they further argue, cannot be known with certainty. Thus, a human being, given that he has the freedom of contrary choice, may either act or not act, act one way or act differently, in a given circumstance: such choices, springing as they do from human freedom, can never be foreknown as certain — and, given that an uncertain foreknowledge is no genuine foreknowledge, simply cannot be foreknown. A future event that is known as certain cannot belong to the free choice of the moment. God must, therefore, have a limited foreknowledge of the future, lacking knowledge

---

138. See *PRRD*, IV, 2.1 (B-C); 2.2 (B).

139. Turretin, *Inst. theol. elencticae*, III.xii.7, citing Socinus, Crellius, and Smalcius, among the Socinians; cf. Herman Venema, *Institutes of Theology*, part I, trans. Alexander Brown (Edinburgh: T. & T. Clark, 1850), VI (p. 150) for a late orthodox reading of the continuing debate.

of the results of free and contingent circumstances. What God can do is understand the range of future possibilities, recognizing that, in the future, some things cannot happen while others either may or may not happen.[140]

Each of these controversies was understood by the orthodox writers as a threat not merely to a traditional doctrine of God but to the entirety of Christian doctrine. The Cartesian definition of truth as clear and distinct knowledge accessible to unaided reason, particularly coupled as it was with the principle of doubt, seemed to fly in the face of the Christian doctrine of revelation and Scripture and, by extension, to undermine the orthodox understanding of philosophy and reason as necessarily subordinate or ancillary tools in theological formulation.[141] The Arminian and Jesuit claim of a divine "middle knowledge" not only offered a new and more refined way of stating the case for a semi-Pelagian doctrine of salvation, but also raised questions concerning the relationship between God and the entire order of finite being: how could God know future contingents lying outside of his will unless there were actualities not brought into being by God? Vorstius' claim of sequence in God appeared to undermine all traditional conception of divine ultimacy, unity, and sovereignty — and the Socinian denial of an essential punitive justice threatened the logic of orthodox atonement theory.

B. Reformed Orthodoxy and the Rise of Rationalism.

Following 1640, the Reformed orthodox doctrine of God encountered a series of different, if not entirely new, philosophical problems in the various new strains of rationalism. Indeed, whereas the philosophical debates of the early orthodox era consisted largely in arguments over the appropriation or critique of the renewed and often revised Christian Aristotelianism of the Renaissance or over the use of the highly variegated medieval sources then available, the philosophical debates of the high orthodox era chart the decline of the older Aristotelianism and debates over the validity of a series of new philosophical systems, namely, the various rationalist philosophies of the seventeenth century, as advanced by Descartes, Lord Herbert of Cherbury, Leibniz, Hobbes, and Spinoza.

---

140. Owen, *Vindiciae evangelicae*, in *The Works of John Owen*, ed. William H. Goold, 17 vols. (London and Edinburgh: Johnstone and Hunter, 1850-1853), XII, pp. 116-117, citing Socinus, Smalcius, and Biddle; cf. Venema, *Institutes*, VI (p. 150): "They do not deny that [God] has a conjectural knowledge of future contingent events — of what the creature in certain given circumstances will freely do, but they deny that these events can be certainly foreknown by him, because they are not certainly future.".

141. Cf. the analysis of Cocceius' negative approach to this aspect of Cartesianism in Van Asselt, *Federal Theology*, pp. 77-78.

1. Descartes and the Cartesians.[142] As in the case of the use and appropriation of Suárez' thought, the results of the encounter were mixed. One cannot, moreover, argue that the Cartesianism of the era is a reformist wave of the future and that the theological and philosophical opposition to it represents a kind of counter-reformation mentality.[143] This approach is, among other things, an over-simplification that minimizes the large areas of shared assumptions: like the theologically "orthodox" philosophical perspectives of Reformed thinkers like Voetius, the Cartesian philosophies of the seventeenth century held a host of basic doctrinal premises concerning God that had deep traditionary roots — notably divine simplicity and immutability, the uncaused and nonreactive nature of the divine knowledge of the finite order, and the existence of all things by reason of the divine will or decree. In addition, Descartes' proof of the existence of God stood in relation to the long tradition of Anselm's so-called ontological argument — a point not only evident to his contemporaries but also problematic, in view of the more or less Christian Aristotelian or modified Thomistic trajectory along which much of the orthodox theology of the time had developed.

The difficulty that the Reformed orthodox had with Cartesian philosophy, whether in rejecting it or in adapting or appropriating one or another of its elements was, therefore, not that it was in most of its claims radically different either from traditional philosophy or from theological orthodoxy, but that in so many ways it was similar and, moreover, grounded on a common scholastic ancestor. By way of example, Descartes held the infinite spiritual perfection of God and argued that this entailed such attributes as eternity, omniscience, omnipotence, goodness, and truth. Even so, God must be acknowledged as "the source of all goodness and truth, creator of all things."[144] Descartes also assumed both the fundamental freedom of human beings and the ultimate divine foreordination of all things, the former as a presupposition even of the *Cogito*, the latter as a result of his meditations on the nature of God subsequent to the proof of the existence of God. In his *Principles of Philosophy*, moreover, he made no effort to reconcile the two points, commenting that the solution to our problem lay in the difference between our finitude and God's infinitude and that "we should soon be involved in great difficulties if we undertook to make his preordinations

---

142. Citations from the writings of Descartes follow either *The Philosophical Works of Descartes*, trans. Elizabeth S. Haldane and G. R. T. Ross, 2 vols. (London: Cambridge University Press, 1931), hereinafter cited as *Works*, or *The Philosophical Writings of Descartes*, trans. John Cottingham, Robert Stoothoff, Dugald Murdoch, and Anthony Kenny, 3 vols. (Cambridge: Cambridge University Press, 1985-1991), hereinafter cited as *Writings*.

143. See Josef Bohatec, *Die cartesianische Scholastik in der Philosophie und reformierten Dogmatik des 17. Jahrhunderts* (Leipzig: Deichert, 1912); Ernst Bizer, "Die reformierte Orthodoxie und der Cartesianismus," in *Zeitschrift für Theologie und Kirche* (1958), pp. 306-372; Thomas A. McGahagan, "Cartesianism in the Netherlands, 1639-1676; the New Science and the Calvinist Counter-Reformation" (Ph.D. dissertation, University of Pennsylvania, 1976). The above point stands contrary to the central thesis of McGahagan, but in no way diminishes the significance of his survey of historical materials. On the scholastic elements in Cartesian thought, see Marjorie Glicksman Grene, *Descartes Among the Scholastics* (Milwaukee: Marquette University Press, 1991), and Roger Ariew, *Descartes and the Last Scholastics* (Ithaca and London: Cornell University Press, 1999).

144. Descartes, *Principles of Philosophy*, xxii, in *Works*, I, p. 228).

harmonize with the freedom of our will, and if we tried to comprehend them both at one time."[145]

To some of the Reformed, notably several of the Cocceian thinkers (Heidanus and Burman) and several of the Genevans (Tronchin and Chouet), Cartesian philosophy represented a new philosophical theism of potential use to Christian theology. Burman went in search of Descartes, questioned the philosopher on a series of theological issues, and published a transcript of the conversation.[146] Burman and Heidanus drew directly on Descartes' views of God and truth, not without a certain reserve. Neither writer produced a fully Cartesian theology — certainly not to the point that Cartesian views of deductive argumentation yielded a purely rational theology, nor to the point that Cartesian views of substance had any real impact on their doctrine of divine spirituality or Trinity.[147] To others, however, it seemed on a whole series of points, from its definitions of knowledge and the foundation of certainty, to its deductive rationalism, to its understanding of God, divine providence, and the created order, to represent a philosophy fundamentally incompatible with Christian orthodoxy — and, we might add, from the perspective of many thinkers of the day, theologians and philosophers alike, fundamentally unconvincing.[148] In particular, the mid-seventeenth century saw a series of debates between the Reformed and the Cartesians over the relationship between God and finite causality, with specific reference to the issue of *concursus*,[149] and a confrontation over the understanding of spirit or spiritual substance.[150]

In the academic philosophy of the day, Adriaan Heerboord of Leiden exemplified the eclectic approach that was increasingly characteristic of Protestant thinkers: his initial academic program opposed the Roman Catholic scholastics and demanded a return to the sources of philosophy, notably to the text of Aristotle as distinct from later Aristotelianism. Although not a Cartesian, Heerboord was favorable toward

---

145. Descartes, *Principles of Philosophy*, xl-xli, in *Works*, I, p. 235.

146. *Descartes' Conversation with Burman*, trans. with an introduction and commentary by John Cottingham (Oxford: Clarendon Press, 1976).

147. Cf. Aza Goudriaan, "Die Rezeption des cartesianischen Gottesdankens bei Abraham Heidanus," in *Neue Zeitschrift für systematische Theologie und Religionsphilosophie*, 38/2 (1996), pp. 166-197.

148. See Theodorus Verbeek, *Descartes and the Dutch: Early Reactions to Cartesian Philosophy, 1637-1650* (Carbondale: Southern Illinois University Press, 1992), and note the chapter on Descartes in the Netherlands in Geneviève Rodis-Lewis, *Descartes: His Life and Thought*, trans. Jane Marie Todd (Ithaca and London: Cornell University Press, 1998), pp. 143-187.

149. Gisbertus Voetius, *Testimonium Academiae Ultrajectinae, et Narratio Historica qua defensae, qua exterminatae novae Philosophiae* (Utrecht, 1643); also see *La Querelle d'Utrecht*, texte établi et traduites avec une introduction et notes par Theodorus Verbeek (Paris: Impressions Nouvelles, 1988) and the discussion by Johan A. van Ruler, "New Philosophy to Old Standards: Voetius' Vindication of Divine Concurrence and Secondary Causality," in *Nederlands Archief voor Kerkgeschiedenis*, 71 (1991), pp. 58-91. Also see Margaret J. Osler, *Divine Will and the Mechanical Philosophy: Gassendi and Descartes on Contingency and Necessity in the Created World* (Cambridge: Cambridge University Press, 1994).

150. Cf. Pictet, *Theol. Chr.*, II.iii.3, where there is a hint of Cartesianism in the identification of spirituality with thought, with Mastricht, *Theoretico-practica theologia*, II.vi.8, who explicitly attacks this understanding; and further, below, 4.3 (E.2).

Descartes' thought: he preferred a method of disputation to that of meditation, but in his disputations he argued, among other points, that Cartesian doubt was not antithetical to Aristotelian philosophy. His physics denied the Aristotelian theory of four basic elements but also refused the Cartesian approach, arguing instead a form of atomism. Also, against one of the philosophical tendencies of his day, Heerboord denied the theory of double truth and argued the necessary unity of truth in theology and philosophy.[151]

Some attempt to understand and, indeed, come to terms with various aspects of Cartesian philosophy can be seen in Descartes' recorded "Conversation" of 1648 with the young Franz Burman: not only was Descartes quite forthcoming on a series of issues raised by his philosophy, but his comments are clearly related to objections raised by the Reformed on such issues as proofs of God's existence, the truthfulness, eternity, simplicity, and perfection of God, and the identity or nature of substance.[152] In addition, Descartes expressed himself on divine causality in such as way as to give the impression that he preferred Reformed predestinarianism to the Molinism of the Jesuits. From Burman's perspective, the conversation offers evidence of the increasing interest of Reformed theologians in the way in which a Cartesian approach modified discussion of such divine attributes as eternity and truthfulness, even when the anti-Cartesian polemic is not particularly obvious in their theologies — and it also offers indications of an otherwise almost undetectable Cartesian influence in some of the later Reformed theologians.

The debates over Cartesian philosophy and, specifically, Cartesian theology, are particularly significant insofar as they point toward the trials of theological orthodoxy in the eighteenth century and, perhaps more importantly, identify specific points at which the importation of a new metaphysic radically changes the shape of theological formulations. Cartesian notions of substance as either thought or extension together with the denial of substantial forms on the part of many Cartesians rendered traditional language of God difficult, if not impossible. As the debates among the Reformed make clear, the reduction of spiritual being to unextended thought was viewed as a denial of divine omnipresence akin in its implications to Socinian teachings concerning the finitude of divine being and the identification of omnipresence as a universal exercise of power. So also did the Cartesian language cause problems for the doctrine of the Trinity.[153] In addition, taken to its logical conclusions, the Cartesian philosophy would

151. See Claude Weber, "Heerboord ou Heerboort, Adriaan," in *Encyclopédie philosophique universelle*, publié sous la direction d'André Jacob, 4 parts in 5 vols. (Paris: Presses Universitaires de France, 1989-1998), III/1, pp. 1191-1192; and note Adriaan Heereboord, *Meletemata philosophica* (Leiden, 1654; new edition, 1680); *An vera philosophia contrietur S. Theologia, et vicissim* (in the *Meletemata*).

152. *Descartes' Conversation with Burman*, pp. 19-23, 25, 30, 35, 43, 50. On the problem of "substance" in seventeenth-century thought, also see W. von Leyden, *Seventeenth Century Metaphysics: An Examination of Some Main Concepts and Theories* (London: Duckworth, 1968), pp. 129-144, 162-163, et passim.

153. See the discussion in *PRRD*, IV, 2.3 (B.2); 3.2 (A.3).

lead to a denial of genus and species and to a full-blown metaphysical determinism repugnant to the Reformed understanding of God and world.[154]

An example of the impact of Cartesian thinking on an entire system of nominally Reformed theology is Poiret's *L'Oeconomie divine, ou système universel* (1687): in its subtitle, the work indicates that it demonstrates and explains the origin of Christianity and offers metaphysically certain statement of the "principles and truths of nature and grace, philosophy and theology, reason and faith, natural morality and Christian religion" together with a resolution of "the great and thorny difficulties of predestination, freedom, universal redemption, and providence."[155] Here we actually have a theology that begins with the problem of Pyrrhonistic skepticsm, asserts the certitude of self-existence on the ground of the Cartesian *cogito*, and proceeds from the existence of certainty to the existence of God.[156] From these arguments, Poiret passes on to a discussion of "the fundamental idea of the divine essence" and "the nothingness of ideas by themselves," to a positing of "the origin of ideas through the decree of God in his discretionary understanding."[157] The eternal decree, according to Poiret, is the firm resolve of God "to give birth to ideas in his understanding, and beyond himself to things corresponding to his ideas."[158] The doctrine of the Trinity is to be understood by inference from the tripartite character of the soul — with the Father as "infinitely living Thought," the Son as "image" and "light," and the Spirit as "joy" and activity.[159] The problem of predestination is resolved in the declaration "that all those who have and who will participate in human nature are all predestined by god to life eternal" on the ground that the god who is infinite thought and who, in the execution of his decree, has realized his own ideas in the finite order, could not decree to create the most admirable creature in his own image and then consign it to eternal death.[160] The irony of Poiret's formulation is that this sole "decretal" system produced in the seventeenth century rests on Cartesian, not Aristotelian, principles and deduces apokatastasis from the eternal counsel of God! And, by Reformed orthodox standards, Poiret's decretal Cartesianism had certainly produced heresy.

2. **The Reformed orthodox and Spinozism.** Yet another Rationalist alternative that deeply troubled the orthodox theological mind was the teaching of Spinoza —

---

154. Cf. Theo Verbeek, "Descartes and the Problem of Atheism: The Utrecht Crisis," in *Nederlands Archief voor Kerkgeschiedenis*, 71/2 (1991), pp. 211-223.

155. Pierre Poiret, *L'Oeconomie divine ou système universel et deémontré des oeuvres de des desseins de dieu envers les hommes. Où l'on explique & prouve d'origine, avec une évidence & une certitude métaphysique, les principes & les vérités de la nature & de la grace, de la philosophie & de la théologie, de la raison % de la foi, de la morale naturelle & de la religion Chrétienne: et où l'on resoud entiérement les grandes & épineuses difficultés sur la prédestination, sur la liberté, sur l'universalité de la redemption, & sur la providence, &c.* 7 vols. (Amsterdam, 1687); Latin trans. 2 vols. (Frankfurt, 1705).

156. Poiret, *Oeconomie divine*, I.i.3-5 (I, pp. 2-5).

157. Poiret, *Oeconomie divine*, I.ii-iv (I, pp. 44-81), especially I.iv: "Naissance des idées par le decret de dieu dans son concept arbitraire."

158. Poiret, *Oeconomie divine*, I.v.1 (I, p. 82).

159. Poiret, *Oeconomie divine*, II.xiv.1-5 (II, pp. 363-367).

160. Poiret, *Oeconomie divine*, II.xxviii.2, 4 (II, p. 716-717, 728).

which, despite attacks and censorship, made significant inroads into Reformed circles in England and the Netherlands in the late seventeenth century.[161] As in the case of Descartes philosophy, the difficulty caused by Spinozism arose not because it was so radically different from the older philosophical tradition or from theological orthodoxy but because of its grounding in the older tradition and its frequent recourse to the common language of traditional philosophy and theological orthodoxy, but with highly different results.[162]

The chronology of Spinoza's published works is of importance to understanding their reception. His *Reni Descartes principiorum philosophiae*, with its appended *Cogitata metaphysica* (1663), was the first of Spinoza's works to be published — a work that set him clearly into the Cartesian camp but that also evidenced the radical nature of this thought on God. The only other work of Spinoza to appear during his life was the *Tractatus theologico-politicus* (1670). His other major works, among which the *Ethica ordine geometrico demonstratione* proved the most objectionable to orthodox theism, were published posthumously in 1677 in his collected works.[163] Reaction from other philosophers and from theologians came in stages — first, to the Cartesian premises and to Spinoza's early views on God, then to the exegetical and interpretive approaches of the *Tractatus theologico-politicus*, and only later, after Spinoza was no longer living, to the full-scale development of his metaphysical views in the *Ethica*.

In common with the broader philosophical and theological tradition, Spinoza's earliest published work defined God as the necessary being who understands himself and, in or through himself, all things; who created all things in the "absolute freedom of will."[164] God is eternal, one, absolutely infinite in perfection, immense, immutable, simple or non-composite, life in himself, utterly omniscient, absolutely powerful. Spinoza even makes the standard distinction between the absolute and ordained power of God as a distinction between God's power as such, in itself, and God's power understood as the decree that brings all things into existence. All things are created and sustained by one eternal act of God.[165] The shared conceptual foundation is clear — shared not only with the rationalist philosophers of his day but with the older scholastic philosophical and theological tradition.

---

161. See the essays in Wiep Van Bunge and Wim Klever (eds.), *Disguised and Overt Spinozism Around 1700* (Leiden: E. J. Brill, 1996).

162. The traditionary background of Spinoza is still best explored in Harry Austryn Wolfson, *The Philosophy of Spinoza*, 2 vols. (Cleveland and New York: World, 1958); also note Guttmann, *Philosophies of Judaism*, pp. 301-324 , 516-518.

163. I have followed the versions of the *Tractatus* and the *Ethica* found in *The Chief Works of Benedict de Spinoza*, trans., with an intro. by R. H. M. Elwes, 2 vols. (London: George Bell & Sons, 1883; repr. New York: Dover, 1955). I have also consulted Baruch Spinoza, *Earlier Philosophical Writings: The Cartesian Principles and Thoughts on Metaphysics*, trans. Frank A. Hayes, intro. by David Bidney (Indianapolis: Bobbs-Merrill, 1963) and idem, *Spinoza's short Treatise on God, Man, and Human Welfare*, trans. Lydia Robinson (Chicago: Open Court, 1909).

164. Spinoza, *Thoughts on Metaphysics*, I, in *Earlier Philosophical Writings*, p. 112.

165. Spinoza, *Thoughts on Metaphysics*, II.i-x (pp. 127-149).

His early understanding of omnipresence, however, given its denial of corporeality and therefore of extension to God, rested on the universally extended power and concurrence of God, not on a doctrine of ontic ubiquity.[166] As for the divine omniscience, Spinoza not only held (one might say, quite Thomistically!) that God knows all things through himself, but also that "no object of God's knowledge exists outside of God" given that there is no material order external to God and that God has only one single and simple idea of himself, which includes the variety of all individuals. There is, moreover, according to Spinoza, no distinction in God whatsoever between intellect, will, and power: such distinctions exist only in the thought of the finite knower.[167] In the posthumous *Ethica*, moreover, it became clear that this removal of all distinction from the Godhead meant also the removal of any and all analogy between divine intellect and will and those faculties in finite creatures. Creation is the necessary flowing of all things from the infinite perfection of the divine nature. Indeed, although God is the free cause of all things, neither intellect nor free will belong to the divine essence in the sense of purpose or choice — so that God necessarily creates a particular world, knowing of no other possibilities, and creating a world without any contingencies. Specifically, "nothing in the universe is contingent, but all things are conditioned to exist and operate in a particular manner by the necessity of the divine nature."[168]

The fears held by various Reformed orthodox thinkers concerning Descartes' view on God and their removal both of divine freedom and of all contingent or secondary causality were fully realized in the philosophy of Spinoza. Howe's lengthy attack on Spinozism in part two of *The Living Temple*, together with his consistent sense of the deficiency of Cartesian speculation, offers indication of the high orthodox conviction that the new philosophies could not serve Christian theology in the positive way that the waning Christian Aristotelian and Platonic models had done.[169] Parallel arguments are found among the English in the work of William Carroll and, in the Netherlands, Leonardus Rijssenius and Jacobus Leydekker.[170] Similar assumptions clearly underlay — and with some justice — the anti-Cartesian views of Voetius and Mastricht. Voetius in particular found Cartesian thought to be an unsuitable vehicle for balancing out

---

166. Spinoza, *Principles of the Philosophy*, II, prop. ii, scholium, in *Earlier Philosophical Writings*, pp. 59-60.

167. Spinoza, *Thoughts on Metaphysics*, II.vii-viii (pp. 139-143).

168. Spinoza, *Ethics*, I, prop. 29 (*Works*, II, p. 68); cf. prop. 17, note; prop. 33, note 1 (*Works*, II, pp. 60-61, 70-71).

169. See John Howe, *The Living Temple, or, A Designed Improvement of that Notion, that a Good Man is the Temple of God. Part I. Concerning God's Existence and His Conversableness with Man against Atheism, or the Epicurean Deism* (1676). *Part II. Containing Animadversions on Spinoza, and a French Writer Pretending to Refute Him* (1702), in *The Works of the Rev. John Howe, M.A.*, 3 vols. (London: William Tegg, 1848; repr. Ligonier, Pa.: Soli Deo Gloria Publications, 1990), vol. I, pp. 1-344.

170. Leonardus Rijssenius, *De Oude Rechtsinnige Waerheyt verdonkert, en bedeckt door DesCartes, Cocceijus, Wittich, Burman, Wolzogen, Perizon, Groenewegen, Allinga, &c. En nu weder Op-geheldert, en ondeckt* (Middelburgh: Benedictus Smidt, 1674); Jacobus Leydekker, *De blyde Spinosist en de bedroefde Christenleeraar, over de wysgeerige verhandelinge van de Natuure Gods* (Rotterdam: R. van Doesburg, 1719).

the primacy of divine causality with the existence of individual secondary causes in a system of concurrence and cooperation.[171]

3. Other forms of seventeenth-century rationalism and their impact. In addition to the various forms of Cartesian rationalism and the increasingly rationalistic theology of the Socinians, Reformed orthodoxy was confronted, particularly in Britain, by the broad, irenic rationalism of Anglican writers like Chillingworth and Stillingfleet and by the highly diverse philosophical rationalism of thinkers like Robert Greville, Robert Fludd, Francis Bacon, Lord Herbert of Cherbury, the Cambridge Platonists, and Thomas Hobbes.

Francis Bacon wrote little concerning theology per se, positively or negatively, but he did offer a high view of revelation and sacred theology as "the haven and sabbath of all human contemplations."[172] He also regarded revealed or sacred theology as a form of *scientia*, but as quite distinct from "first philosophy," metaphysics, and natural theology. Bacon's "first philosophy" dealt with the concepts of being and non-being and the fundamental concepts or axioms of philosophy — whereas natural theology deals with the existence and nature of God insofar as that can be learned from the light of nature.

A highly platonized alternative to Bacon's philosophy was offered by Robert Fludd's *Philosophica Mosaica* (1638) and Robert Greville's *Nature of Truth* (1640) — preparing the way for the speculations of the Cambridge Platonists. Greville advanced a theory of the inward divine light as a basis for philosophical and theological knowing, and Fludd offered a philosophy of divine opposites — opposite attributes or properties in God — that explained the diversity and contradiction in the finite order. According to Fludd, God is both darkness and light, utterly hidden in himself but manifest as the light and wisdom of the world order. The light of God is the source of good in the world, the darkness, the source of opposition and hate, as paralleled and reflected in human nature itself, which is both the image of God and the microcosm of the universe as a whole.[173]

Among the Cambridge Platonists, Cudworth in particular evidenced a careful reading of Descartes at the same time that he argued for a rather different form of rationalist philosophy: Cudworth adopted a rather ambivalent stance toward the Cartesian assumption that the existence of God can be deduced from the idea of God — just as he distanced himself pointedly from the Cartesian notion of ultimate divine

---

171. See Johan A. van Ruler, *The Crisis of Causality. Voetius and Descartes on God, Nature, and Change* (Leiden: E. J. Brill, 1995), pp. 261-301.

172. Francis Bacon, *De augmentis scientiarum*, III.1; cf. Copleston, *History of Philosophy*, III, p. 295.

173. See Robert Greville, second Baron Brooke, *The Nature of Truth, its Union and Unity with the Soule, in a Letter* (London: R. Bishop for S. Cartwright 1640); and Robert Fludd, *Philosophia Moysaica: in qua sapientia & scientia creationis & creaturarum sacra vereque Christiana ... ad amussim & enucleate explicatur, authore, Rob. Flud, alias De Fluctibus* (Gouda: Petrus Rammazenius, 1638); trans. as *Mosaicall philosophy: grounded upon the essentiall truth or eternal sapience* (London: s.n., 1659); also note Fludd's *Tractatus theologo-philosophicus in libros tres distributus, quorum i. de vita. ii. de morte. iii. de resurrectione. Cui inseruntur nonnulla sapientiæ veteris, Adami infortunio superstitis, fragmenta* (Oppenheim: Hieronymus Gallerus, 1617).

arbitrariness: it is absurd to claim, with Descartes, that God could have two times two not to have been four![174] Cudworth also offered an extended discussion of the various forms of atheism both in the ancient world and in his time, together with critiques of the various atheistic arguments. Henry More developed an extensive view of God and the divine attributes that, like the somewhat earlier arguments of Thomas Jackson, departed from the traditional scholastic models and on a series of issues, including the character of divine causality, opposed the Reformed approach — but this was hardly his major polemic: even beyond Cudworth's hesitations, More became critical of Cartesianism, seeing it as antagonistic to Christian beliefs.[175]

Hobbes' philosophy caused difficulties for the Reformed on several fronts — notably its understanding of substance as corporeal and its determinism. Still, there are various points of continuity between Hobbes and the Reformed theology of his time that must be noted: on the one hand, Hobbes' understanding of causality had affinities with the Aristotelian tradition of the seventeenth century, specifically as found in the scholastic manuals of the era, whether Suárez, Alsted, or Keckermann.[176] On the other hand, although his determinism did not please the Reformed orthodox of the era, Hobbes himself viewed it as rooted in the theology of the Reformation.[177]

C. The Full Development of the Reformed Orthodox Doctrine of God

1. The British theologians. Following the mid-seventeenth century, a series of Protestant thinkers — including a notable series of British writers[178] — saw the need

---

174. Ralph Cudworth, *The True Intellectual System of the Universe: the first part; wherein, all the reason and philosophy of atheism is confuted; and its impossibility demonstrated* (London: Printed for Richard Royston, 1678). I have followed idem, *The True Intellectual System of the Universe*, 2 vols. (Andover, Mass., 1837-38), II, pp. 48, 140-144. See the discussion of Cudworth's relationship to Descartes in Copleston, *History of Philosophy*, V, pp. 58-60, 62-63; cf. Richard Popkin, "Cudworth," in *Third Force in Seventeenth-Century Thought*, pp. 347-349.

175. Henry More, *Divine Dialogues, containing sundry Disquisitions & Instructions concerning the Attributes of God and His Providence in the World*, 2 vols. (London, 1668), I, p. 411. On More and Descartes, see Copleston, *History of Philosophy*, V, p. 60, and John Tulloch, *Rational Theology and Christian Philosophy in England in the Seventeenth Century*, 2 vols. (Edinburgh: Blackwood, 1872), II, pp. 372-385.

176. Cees Leijenhorst, "Hobbes's Theory of Causality and its Aristotelian Background," in *The Monist*, 79 (July 1996), pp. 426-447.

177. Thus, Leopold Damrosch, Jr., "Hobbes as Reformation Theologian: Implications of the Free-Will Controversy," in *Journal of the History of Ideas*, 40 (1979), pp. 339-352.

178. Thus, Seth Ward, *A Philosophical Essay towards an Eviction of the Being and Attributes of God. The Immortality of the Soule. The Truth and Authority of Scripture* (Oxford, 1652); John Pearson, *Lectiones de Deo et attributis* (ca. 1661), in *The Minor Theological Works of John Pearson, D.D.* (Oxford: Oxford University Press, 1844), I, pp. 1-267; William Bates, *The Harmony of the Divine Attributes in the contrivance and accomplishment of man's redemption by the Lord Jesus Christ, or, Discourses: wherein is shewed how the wisdom, mercy, justice, holiness, power, and truth of God are glorified in that great and blessed work* (London: J. Darby, 1674); Samuel Clarke, *A Discourse Concerning the Being and Attributes of God, the Obligations of Natural Religion, and the Truth and Certainty of Christian Revelation. In Answer to Mr Hobbes, Spinoza, the Author of the Oracles of Religion, and Other Deniers of Natural and Revealed Religion*, in *The Works of Samuel Clarke* (London, 1738), vol. II.

to develop what can only be called a "contemporary" philosophical and theological approach to the question of the being and attributes of God. Two thinkers of the mid-seventeenth century, William Twisse and Samuel Rutherford, both members of the Westminster Assembly, belong to a group of internationally known Reformed writers who grappled with the issues of the predication and distinction of divine attributes, middle knowledge, and the establishment of a suitable philosophical foundation for Reformed theology — and both were broadly published on the continent as well as in Britain. Twisse's work belongs largely to the era of early orthodoxy, but Rutherford's career extends from the time of the Westminster Assembly into the high orthodox era.[179]

John Owen stands out as one of the most erudite of the British Reformed orthodox after Twisse. His several defenses of the doctrine of God, the divine attributes (most notably the righteousness or justice of God), and the Trinity against the Socinians evidence a mastery of the history and literature of Socinianism as well as a power of exegesis and theological argument unexcelled in his time. Like Twisse, Owen viewed Socinianism as the great heresy of the age and as the abyss of error into which the other, milder, seventeenth-century forms of heterodoxy all tended. Owen's *Brief Declaration and Vindication of the Doctrine of the Trinity* (1669) was translated into Dutch and cited with favor by Vitringa,[180] and his writings testify generally to the interchange between the Reformed theologians on the continent and the major English Reformed writers. Beyond this, his *Death of Death in the Death of Christ* (1647) and *Dissertation on Divine Justice* (1653) bring to bear on the subject of the divine attributes a scholastic detail and subtlety uncommon even in the era of Protestant scholasticism. These latter two treatises, moreover, offer documentation of the internal Reformed debate over divine justice and of a shift in Owen's own perspective on the doctrine — namely, from grounding Christ's satisfaction in the will of God to grounding it in the essential justice or righteousness of God.[181] As Owen himself recognized, his shift in perspective took

---

179. Samuel Rutherford, *Disputatio scholastica de divina providentia, variis praelectionibus, quod attinet ad summa rerum capita ... Adjectae sunt disquisitiones metaphysicae de ente, possibili, dominio Dei in entia & non entia, & variae quaestiones* (Edinburgh: George Anderson, 1649); idem, *Exercitationes apologeticae pro divina gratia, in quibus vindicatur doctrina orthodoxa de divinis decretis, & Dei tum aeterni decreti, tum gratiae efficacis operationis, cum hominis libertate consociatione & subordinatione amica* (Franecker: Johannes Dhüiringh, 1651); idem, *The covenant of life opened, or, A treatise of the covenant of grace: containing something of the nature of the covenant of works, the soveraignty of God, the extent of the death of Christ ... the covenant of grace ... of surety or redemption between the Lord and the Son Jesus Christ, infants right to Jesus Christ and the seal of baptisme: with some practicall questions and observations.* (Edinburgh: Andro Anderson, 1655).

180. Campegius Vitringa, *Doctrina christianae religionis, per aphorismos summatim descripta*, 8 vols. (Arnheim: Johannes Möeleman, 1761-1786), VI, p. 6

181. See Dewey Wallace, *Puritans and Predestination: Grace in English Protestant Theology, 1525-1695* (Chapel Hill: University of North Carolina Press, 1982), pp. 152-153; Hans Boersma, *A Hot Peppercorn: Richard Baxter's Doctrine of Justification in Its Seventeenth-Century Context of Controversy* (Zoetermeer: Boekencentrum, 1993), pp. 130-131; and Carl Trueman, "John Owen's *Dissertation on Divine Justice*: An Exercise in Christocentric Scholasticism," in *Calvin Theological Journal*, 33 (1998), pp. 87-103. Cf. the discussion, below, 6.1 (B.7).

him from an agreement with Augustine, Calvin, Musculus, Twisse, and Rutherford to an agreement with Paraeus, Piscator, Du Moulin, Lubbertus, Rivetus, Junius, Cameron, Maccovius, and the Saumur theologians, including Amyraut. Again, we find evidence that the neat bifurcation between orthodox "scholastics" like Owen, Du Moulin, and Maccovius, on the one hand, and opponents of orthodoxy, on the other, does not represent the case.[182]

Baxter needs also to be noted here as one who both mastered the intricacies of scholastic argumentation and adapted many of its insights to the language and life of piety. Thus, his *Divine Life* not only addresses concerns of piety but also draws the pious mind to consider, in devotional form, the contents of the proofs of the existence of God.[183] Baxter's *Catholike Theologie*, moreover, although not a full system of theology, addresses a series of complex theological topics in debate in the later seventeenth century, among them the middle knowledge, the divine decrees and operations, and providence.[184] And Baxter also wrote major theological system, the *Methodus theologiae christianae*.[185] In these latter two works there is evidence both of an ongoing debate with other thinkers of the age, like Twisse and Owen, but also of a profound indebtedness to the theology of the later Middle Ages.

Nor was Baxter alone in his assumption that the traditional doctrine of the divine attributes could and ought to be used as a basis for Christian piety and meditation. Much the same perspective can be found in William Bates' *Harmony of the Divine Attributes* (1674), Ezekiel Hopkins' *On Glorifying God in His Attributes* (ca. 1680), and Stephen Charnock's famous *Discourses upon the Existence and Attributes of God* (1682).[186] All three works are series of sermons subsequently developed into treatises by their authors. In Hopkins' work, an orthodox doctrine of the attributes is set forth as a foundation of piety, each attribute having by turns a providential, a soteriological, or a christological point of reference that offers a basis for meditation on the fact that believers are dependent on God — indeed the entire discussion, replete with nominally scholastic definitions of the divine essence and attributes takes its point of departure from 1 Cor. 6:19-20, "Ye are not your own: for ye are bought with a price: therefore glorify God in your body, and in your spirit, which are God's."[187]

---

182. Owen, *Dissertation on Divine Justice*, in *Works*, 10, pp. 488-489, 585-586, 594-595, 607ff.; cf. Trueman, "John Owen's *Dissertation*," p. 91, note 1, and the argument in *PRRD*, I, 1.3 (B.1-2); II, 2.3 (A.2).

183. Baxter, *Divine Life*, I.ii (pp. 14-17).

184. Baxter, *Catholike Theologie*, I, §12 (middle knowledge); §13 (divine will and decrees in general); §15-24 (divine decrees with respect to predestination and providence).

185. Richard Baxter, *Methodus theologiae christianae* (London, 1681).

186. William Bates, *The Harmony of the Divine Attributes in the Contrivance and Accomplishement of Man's Redemption* (London: J. Darby, 1674; repr. Philadelphia: Presbyterian Board of Publication, n.d.); Ezekiel Hopkins, *On Glorifying God in His Attributes*, in *The Works of Ezekiel Hopkins, successively Bishop of Raphoe and Derry*, ed. Charles W. Quick, 3 vols. (1874; repr. Morgan, Pa.: Soli Deo Gloria Publications, 1995-1998), vol. 2, pp. 590-708.

187. Hopkins, *On Glorifying God in His Attributes*, p. 590.

Also of considerable significance as both a contribution to the English Reformed theology of the seventeenth century and as a codification of doctrine evidencing the broad resources and major opponents of the Reformed position is Charnock's *Discourses upon the Existence and Attributes of God*. Originally delivered as lectures to his congregation, Charnock's *Discourse* certainly stands as one of the more elaborate and detailed treatises on the subject written in the seventeenth century and, although discursive and tending toward the copious in its style, partakes of the careful distinctions and definitions that belong to the scholastic theology of the era. It also evidences the exegetical and practical character of the Protestant theology of the era, with consistent references to the texts of Scripture on which its teaching is based and equally consistent attention to the churchly and pious "use" of each doctrinal point. Charnock's work, remarkable for its grasp of the scholastic materials and for its ability to turn those materials to homiletical use, also invariably turns toward christological and soteriological issues — perhaps most notably following the discussion of the attribute of spirituality with an entire homily on spiritual worship.[188] Although, for the most part lacking in the polemical or elenctical aspect of the Reformed theology of the day, Charnock's treatise echoes the fourfold concern for exegetical, doctrinal, polemical, and practical emphases exemplified in a continental work like Mastricht's great *Theoretico-practica theologia*.

2. The continental Reformed. The doctrine of the divine essence and attributes found its major Reformed elaboration at the hands of the orthodox and scholastic writers of the latter part of the seventeenth century. For the most part, these thinkers held to the more traditional Christian Aristotelianism as a philosophical foundation for their thought, but a smaller number either drew on or adapted elements of the Cartesian thought of the era. On the one side of the argument, thinkers like Wendelin, Maresius,[189] Essenius, Cloppenburg, Hoornbeeck, the elder Spanheim, Voetius, Marckius, Turretin, Witsius,[190] Le Blanc, Rijssen,[191] Heidegger, and Mastricht continued the main lines of the Reformed development, taking up both the exegetical and the traditionary understandings of earlier writers like Junius, Trelcatius, Polanus, Ames, the authors of the Leiden *Synopsis*, and Maccovius, and developing them into a still

188. Charnock, *Discourses upon the Existence and Attributes of God*, I, pp. 204-275.

189. Samuel Maresius, *De abusu philosophiae Cartesianae in rebus theologicis et fidei* (Groningen: T. Everts, 1670); idem, *Collegium theologicum sive systema breve universae theologiae comprehensum octodecim disputationibus*. Groningen, 1645; 1659); idem, *Theses theologicae de judice controversiarum* (Paris, 1625).

190. Herman Witsius, *Exercitationes sacrae in symbolum quod Apostolorum dicitur. Et in Orationem dominicam* (Amsterdam, 1697); translated as *Sacred Dissertations on what is commonly called the Apostles' Creed*, trans. D. Fraser, 2 vols. (Edinburgh: A. Fullarton/Glasgow: Kull, Blackie & Co., 1823) and *Sacred Dissertations on the Lord's Prayer*, trans., with notes, by William Pringle (Edinburgh: Thomas Clarke, 1839); idem, *De oeconomia foederum Dei cum hominibus libri quattuor* (Leeuwarden, 1685; Utrecht, 1694); translated as *The Oeconomy of the Covenants between God and Man. Comprehending a Complete Body of Divinity*, 3 vols. (London: Edward and Charles Dilly, 1763; second edition, revised and corrected, 1775).

191. Leonhardus Rijssenius, *Summa theologiae didactico-elencticae* (Amsterdam, 1695; Edinburgh, 1698; Frankfurt and Leipzig, 1731).

more cohesive statement, particularly with reference to doctrinal adversaries like Vorstius and the Socinians. On the other side of the argument, several fairly significant thinkers — Heidanus, Burman, Tronchin, and, to a lesser extent, Pictet — drew on Cartesian notions of clarity and truth and evidenced use of Descartes' proof of the existence of God in their theologies.

The work of Gisbertus Voetius demands particular notice inasmuch as Voetius, perhaps more than any of the other Reformed scholastics, mastered the vast and difficult bibliography on the doctrine of God and incorporated into Reformed thought detailed and heavily documented examinations of such topics as the unity and simplicity of God, the presence and distinction of ideas in the divine mind, the divine knowledge of all possibility and actuality, and virtually all of the divine attributes.[192] Voetius, who served as professor of theology at Utrecht from 1636 until his death in 1676, provides a significant index to the Reformed reception of philosophy in the mid-seventeenth century. Together with his colleague, Martinus Schoock, professor of philosophy at Groningen, Voetius came to oppose Cartesian philosophy in the name of a more traditional (but nonetheless contemporary) modification of the older Aristotelianism. The dispute was complicated by several prior relationships: first, Voetius entered the debate with a certain respect for Mersenne (already a colleague of Descartes) but had corresponded with Mersenne, indicating a favorable reception of the latter's writings against atheism.[193] Second, Descartes had several significant colleagues and supporters in Utrecht — notably, the professor of philosophy, Henricus Reneri, and the professor of medicine and botany, Henricus le Roy (Regius). After hearing the highly Cartesian funeral oration of Reneri, Voetius set a disputation *De atheismo*, in which he attacked new philosophy, with its seeming claims of the virtual omniscience of human reason. As of 1641, Descartes and Regius returned the favor and accused their opponents of atheism. The ensuing debate focused on the Cartesian denial of substantial forms and its implications for the Christian view of human nature, the resurrection, and the world order, with ramifications for the doctrine of God, the authority of Scripture, and the principial use of reason by the Cartesians.[194]

These issues, particularly debate over the definitions of substance and of spiritual essence, carry over into the thought of the high and late orthodox writers. We see

---

192. Cf. Gisbertus Voetius, *Selectarum disputationum theologicarum*, vol. I, disp. 13 (*De Unica et Simplicissima Dei Essentia*), disp. 14 (*De Essentia Dei*), disp. 15-18 (*De conditionata seu Media in Dei Scientia, partes IV*), disp. 19-21 (*De Jure et Justitia Dei*), disp. 22-25 (*De Potentia Dei, partes IV*); vol. V/2, pp. 48-147 (*Problemata de Deo*). Also note Gisbertus Voetius, *Syllabus problematum theologicorum, quae pro re natâ proponi aut perstringi solent in privatis publicisque disputationum, examinum, collationum, consultationum exercitiis* (Utrecht: Aegidius Romanus, 1643). On Voetius' doctrine of God, see Andreas Beck, "Gisbertus Voetius (1589-1676): Basic Features of His Doctrine of God," in Willem J. van Asselt and Eef Dekker, eds., *Reformation and Scholasticism: an Ecumenical Enterprise* (Grand Rapids: Baker Book House, 2001), pp. 205-226.

193. E.g., Marin Mersenne, *L'impieté des Déistes, Athées, et Libertins de ce temps, combattu et renversée* (Paris, 1624).

194. On the debate, see A. C. Duker, *School-gezag en eigen-onderzoek: historisch-kritisch studie van den strijd tusschen Voetius en Descartes* (Dissertation: Leiden, 1861); Verbeek, *Descartes and the Dutch*, pp. 13-33; van Ruler, *Crisis of Causality*, pp. 261-301.

such issues reflected quite clearly in the language of theological works like Turretin's *Institutio*, Pictet's *Theologia christiana*, Mastricht's *Theoretico-practica theologia* — with Turretin holding the traditional view of divine substance without specific anti-Cartesian polemic, Pictet evidencing minor sympathies for the Cartesian approach, and Mastricht arguing, with noticeable hostility, for a careful distinction between spiritual being and thought. In Mastricht, moreover, the exegetical trajectory of the Reformed doctrine of God was also maintained, by the incorporation of extended exegesis of the *loci classici* into his theological system. Brakel, Mastricht, and other theologians associated with the *Nadere Reformatie* also echo the British writers' sense of the relationship between meditation on the divine attributes and the life of piety — rendering rather odd the claim that theirs was a purely abstract representation of a divine being utterly removed from relation to the world.[195]

3. Issues in formulation and debate. The positive formulation of the orthodox Protestant doctrine of God in the high orthodox era stands on a trajectory of development that has its explicit roots in the older tradition of catholic orthodoxy, notably in the thought of the church fathers and medieval doctors as well as in the work of the Reformers. These influences are detectable not in a vast revision of the doctrine, but in the finer nuances of its formulation. The Reformation, after all, did very little to revise the dogmatic content of the doctrine of God. For influences of the Reformation on the later orthodox formulation, we ought to look to the biblicism and the soteriological emphases of the Reformers and then be prepared to recognize significant changes in the shape of argumentation in the doctrine of God, even in its most "scholastic" formulations. Briefly, there are at least three points to be noted: first, the Protestant orthodox doctrine of God is built far more consistently and profoundly on the text of Scripture and on the results of exegesis than medieval formulations — and this grounding has subtle impact on the way in which issues are formulated, even when the broad definitions of doctrinal points remain relatively unchanged. Second, in a very specific development, resting on the biblicism of the Reformation, the Protestant orthodox discussions of the doctrine of God frequently rest the locus, not on an initial discussion of the divine essence, but on a lengthy analysis of the divine names found in the text of Scripture — and then move from the names, particularly the tetragrammaton, to the discussion of the essence of God according to the standard list of divine attributes. Third, many of the orthodox theologians, perhaps most notably Mastricht and Brakel, insist on relating each doctrinal topic to the Christian life: discussions of the divine essence, simplicity, eternity, immutability, and so forth are not merely abstract doctrinal expositions, but each offers an approach for piety to the God of salvation.

---

195. C. Graafland, "Gereformeerde Scholastiek V: De Invloed van de Scholastiek op de Gereformeerde Orthodoxie," in *Theologia Reformata*, 30 (1987), pp. 4-25; idem, "Gereformeerde Scholastiek VI: De Invloed van de Scholastiek op de Nadere Reformatie," in *Theologia Reformata*, 30 (1987), pp. 109-131; 313-340; cf. Bert Loonstra, "De leer van God en Christus in de Nadere Reformatie," in T. Brienen, et al., *Theologische Aspecten van de Nadere Reformatie* (Zoetermeer: Boekencentrum, 1993), pp. 99-150.

On the exegetical front, particularly toward the end of the century, both the increasingly critical and now historical tendencies in exegesis and an increasingly literal, non-typological approach to the meaning of the text caused increasing difficulty for the traditional association of key *loci* or *sedes doctrinae* with agreed upon dogmatic results. Works like Grotius' *Annotationes*,[196] the text and critical apparatus of the great London Polyglot, and Richard Simon's *Histoire critique du Vieux Testament* raised virtually insuperable problems for the traditional use of certain texts — while, at the same time, the critical and historical approaches pioneered in these works were used by Socinian and later Arminian exegetes with significantly nontraditional doctrinal result. This critical development did not, of course, indicate a sudden, radical break with either the interpretive models of pre-critical exegesis or the older, positive relationship between exegesis and Christian doctrine. The major Reformed philologists, exegetes, and commentators of the era did not view their linguistic or even their text-critical skills as undermining orthodox theological conclusions.[197] The main lines of the older exegetical tradition continued to be evident in such massive compilations as Diodati's and Tossanus' annotations on the Bible,[198] the annotations to the authorized Dutch translation or *Statenvertaling*, the so-called *Westminster Annotations*, the major works of Matthew Poole,[199] and the commentary of Matthew Henry.[200]

Related to these debates over the exegesis of the Bible were a series of debates over the understanding of divine attributes, particularly over the nature of the biblical testimony to the attributes and, indeed, over the nature of the biblical testimony itself and its potential relationship to theology.[201] As in the later Middle Ages, so also in the seventeenth century was the concept of divine simplicity a primary index differences the understanding of the divine attributes and the meaning of biblical attributions to the Deity, even among the orthodox writers. Heavy polemic continued to be directed against Vorstius and the Socinians, who had denied divine simplicity — but the more subtle debate, often unaccompanied by any direct polemics, was among the orthodox

---

196. Hugo Grotius, *Annotationes ad Vetus Testamentum*, in *Opera omnia theologica* (3 vols., Amsterdam, 1679), vol. 1; *Annotationes in quatuor Evangelia & Acta Apostolorum*, in *Opera*, vol. 2, part 1 [i.e., pp. 1-668]; and *Annotationes in epistolas Apostolicas & Apocalypsin*, in *Opera*, vol. 2, part 2 [i.e., pp. 669-1238].

197. See the discussion in *PRRD*, II, 2.3; 7.1-7.2.

198. Jean Diodati, *Pious and Learned Annotations upon the Holy Bible, plainly Expounding the Most Difficult Places Thereof* (London, 1641); Paulus Tossanus, *Biblia, das ist die gantze Heilige Schrifft durch D. Martin Luther verteutscht: mit D. Pauli Tossani hiebevor ausgegangenen Glossen und Auslegungen*, 4 vols. (Frankfurt, 1668).

199. Matthew Poole, *Synopsis criticorum aliorumque sacrae scripturae interpretum et commentatorum, summo studio et fide adornata*, 5 vols. (London, 1669-1676). Poole also produced, on the basis of this larger work, *Annotations on the Holy Bible*, 2 vols. (London, 1683-1685; reissued in 3 vols., London: Banner of Truth, 1962), hereinafter cited as Poole, *Commentary*.

200. Matthew Henry, *An Exposition of the Old and New Testament: wherein each chapter is summed up in its contents: the sacred text inserted at large, in distinct paragraphs; each paragraph reduced to its proper heads: the sense given, and largely illustrated; with practical remarks and observations*, new edition, revised and corrected, 6 vols. (London: James Nisbet, n.d)

201. Cf. *PRRD*, II, 2.3 (C).

writers themselves over the precise meaning of simplicity, specifically, over the question of whether or not there were distinctions of attributes or properties in God and, if so, of what sort these distinctions might be. Through out the discussion, the various approaches continued to reflect the differences noted in the later Middle Ages among Thomists, Scotists, and nominalists — including differences in the interpretation of biblical predications, namely, whether they were descriptions of the way that God in fact is, or merely descriptions of his relations *ad extra*.

Among the Reformed themselves, given the various understandings of simplicity, there were differences concerning the distinction of divine attributes. This debate took place entirely within the bounds of the confessions and does not appear to have been a matter of any angry controversy, so that it registers rather low on the decibel scale of seventeenth-century discussion. Still, it is a significant index to the character of the theology itself and, equally importantly, to the reception of the philosophical tradition on the part of the Reformed. A large number of the Reformed assumed some distinction of attributes *ad intra*, drawing on the Thomist language of a "distinction by reason of analysis with a foundation in the thing" and recognizing the importance of identifying the attribute as an essential property of the Godhead *ad intra*, apart from any relationship to the world order. By way of contrast, a not insignificant group of Reformed thinkers held to a most nominalistic pattern of explanation, arguing that the attributes are distinct only in our conceptions of the work of the Godhead *ad extra* — while nonetheless insisting on the real distinction of the divine persons *ad intra*. The absence of polemic here is, from one perspective, quite remarkable. The Reformed, at the same time, were in debate with Vorstius and the Socinians over the doctrine of divine simplicity.

Characteristic of the majority of the Reformed, who insisted on a distinction of attributes in the Godhead, was also the insistence on defining many, if not all, of the attributes of God in an *ad intra* and in an *ad extra* sense. This characteristic points toward several important elements of the Reformed doctrine. It serves to underline the typical definition of the distinction of attributes as by reason of analysis founded in the thing — and to identify the foundation in God as the attribute *ad intra*, apart from any relation to the finite order. The outward exercise of the attributes is, therefore, not arbitrary nor is it so distanced from the divine identity that it does not serve to reveal God in truth.

Debate over the nature and limits of the *voluntas Dei* also continued, with specific reference to Arminian theology. On this point, moreover, there was a general consensus among the Reformed against the Arminian position, particularly on the issue of the hidden and revealed will of God and the antecedent and consequent will. Indeed, contrary to what one might expect from the Saumur theologians (given the older scholarship concerning their purported opposition to scholastic "orthodoxy"), their published disputation on the divine will not only began with an extended reference to the errors of Arminius, it also reveals a positive doctrine in full accord with the teaching emanating from such places as Sedan, Utrecht, and Geneva.[202]

The high orthodox era was also the time of the decline of classical philosophy, particularly of the Aristotelian perspective that had for so long and so fruitfully supplied the doctrine of God with metaphysical language. In this sense, high orthodoxy experienced the difficulty of maintaining the traditional God-language as its philosophical underpinnings were being swept away. This difficulty is evidenced in several ways: it can be seen in a movement away from the large-scale use of philosophical categories and a definition of theological truth and certainty exclusive of the philosophical categories of the day, such as is seen in the theology of Francis Turretin. And it is evident as well in the highly polemical advocacy of the older metaphysics against all comers as witnessed in the works of Voetius, Maresius, and Mastricht as they turned to defend the faith — and the philosophy — against nominally orthodox but philosophically innovative theologians like Heidanus and Wittich.[203] Equally so, following out the increasingly Cartesian model pressed by Heidanus, the famous published conversation between Burman and Descartes also evidences the shifting terrain of philosophical discussion among the Reformed.[204] And still further evidence is offered by the trend toward Cartesianism in Geneva in the work of Tronchin and Chouet, by the sudden waning of interest in Aristotelian metaphysics in the British universities, and in the search for a new philosophical paradigm among the English theologians, culminating in the somewhat unsuccessful theological metaphysics of Samuel Clarke in the early eighteenth century.

This difficulty of maintaining the philosophical dimension of the doctrine thus became a profound issue for Reformed dogmatics during the transition between high orthodoxy and late or rationalistic orthodoxy, both among those Reformed theologians who were affected by the pietist approach to theology and the *Nadere Reformatie*, and among the greater number, who belong more or less clearly in the category of "transitional" thinkers — such writers as the orthodox but somewhat rationalistic Pictet, the strongly pious Brakel, and the highly irenic and considerably less orthodox J. A. Turretin.[205] In the case of Brakel, where the underlying interest of the doctrinal exposition is the relationship between doctrine and piety, there is very little of what might be called philosophical or metaphysical argumentation — although Brakel in

---

202. Moyse Amyraut, Louis Cappel, Josue La Place, *Syntagma thesium theologicarum in Academia Salmuriensi variis temporibus disputatarum*, editio secunda, 4 parts (Saumur: Joannes Lesner, 1664; second printing, 1665), IV.viii.2-3; contra Armstrong, *Calvinism and the Amyraut Heresy*, pp. 31-41, 179-180, et passim.

203. On Wittich, see Bizer, "Die reformierte Orthodoxie und der Cartesianismus," pp. 306-372.

204. Cf. *Descartes' Conversation with Burman*, with the rather different picture presented in McGahagan, "Cartesianism in the Netherlands, 1639-1676."

205. On J. A. Turretin, see Martin I. Klauber, *Between Reformed Scholasticism and Pan-Protestantism: Jean-Alphonse Turretin (1671-1737) and Enlightened Orthodoxy at the Academy of Geneva* (Selinsgrove: Susquehanna University Press, 1994); and John W. Beardslee III, "Theological Developments at Geneva under Francis and Jean-Alphonse Turretin, 1648-1737" (Ph.D. diss.: Yale University, 1956).

no way sets himself apart from the main stream of traditional dogmatics. Indeed, it is characteristic of the Voetian line of the *Nadere Reformatie* that the tradition of scholastic orthodoxy was closely wedded to Christian piety. In Pictet, the attachment to traditional Aristotelian metaphysics has waned still further than it had in the thought of Francis Turretin while the Cartesian line that had been advocated by Chouet and Tronchin cannot be seen to have borne any great fruit.[206] Indeed, by the end of the seventeenth century, the Cartesian high tide had passed — theologians and philosophers alike were looking for another perspective.[207] Pictet's doctrine of the divine essence and attributes lacks the strongly philosophical dimension of a Zanchi or a Polanus in the early orthodox period or of a Mastricht, a Maresius, or a Heidegger in the high orthodox era. Yet, in the context of this eclectic and almost nonphilosophical mixture, there are elements both of the older Aristotelianism and of the newer Cartesian models.

2.4 Orthodoxy, Theism, and Rationalism in the Late Seventeenth and the Eighteenth Centuries

A. Continental Developments

1. Leibniz and the beginnings of rapprochement between rationalism and orthodoxy. It was also in the early eighteenth century that the new forms of philosophical expression generated by Spinoza and Leibniz began to affect the language of theology. In the case of Spinoza, there was initially and there remained a nearly universal abhorrence among the orthodox theologians of the era. In the cases of Leibniz, however, the conscious affinities of his philosophical and theological language with the tradition made the transition possible to rationalist forms of orthodoxy — a gambit accepted by a few orthodox theologians of the eighteenth century.

In view of his training among the Herborn encyclopedists, Leibniz entered the philosophical arena not only equipped with a sound knowledge in the metaphysics and physics of the first half of the seventeenth century, but also with a broad knowledge of the theology taught by the Reformed and Lutheran orthodox of his day.[208] Leibniz' works, moreover, manifest deep immersion not only with the problems and issues related to the specifically philosophical questions of the era, but also quite consistently with the broader theological and philosophical arena.[209] The result of this breadth was a

---

206. On the development of Reformed Cartesianism in Geneva, see Michael Heyd, "From a Rationalist Theology to a Cartesian Voluntarism: David Derodon and Jean-Robert Chouet," in *Journal of the History of Ideas*, 40 (1979), pp. 527-542; Klauber, *Between Reformed Scholasticism and Pan-Protestantism*, pp. 37-45, 55-56.

207. See Richard A. Watson, *The Downfall of Cartesianism, 1673-1712*, International Archives of the History of Ideas, 2, (Den Haag: Nijhoff, 1966); idem, *The Breakdown of Cartesian Metaphysics* (Atlantic Highlands, N.J.: Humanities Press, 1987).

208. See Loemker, *Struggle for Synthesis*; and idem, "Leibniz and the Herborn Encyclopedists," in *Journal of the History of Ideas*, 22 (1961), pp. 323-338.

209. Gottfried Wilhelm Leibniz, *Opera philosophiae quae extant*, ed. J. E. Erdmann, 2 vols. (Berlin, 1840) remains the best source of most of the Latin works. There is no complete translation. I have

doctrine of God and a set of meditations on the Trinity that places Leibniz into a closer dialogue with the theological orthodoxy of his time than had been the case with Descartes. Leibniz was also deeply involved in ecumenical discussions.[210]

Thus, whereas it is not at all incorrect to follow the lines of most Leibniz scholarship and note his relationships in commentary and dialogue with the rationalist philosophers of the seventeenth century, notably Descartes, Foucher, Spinoza, Arnauld, Malebranche, Clarke, and Locke, this line of argument, taken by itself, ignores the common ground of discourse between philosophers and theologians in the seventeenth century and the theological rootage of many of the issues and even basic definitions argued by Leibniz. This point is nowhere more clearly illustrated than in Leibniz's teachings on God: he understands God as the necessary and utterly simple being in whom are attributes of power, intellect, and will — and he argues that these attributes are in God both perfectly and infinitely. Leibniz also characterizes the divine knowledge or understanding as a knowledge of all possibility and therefore as the knowledge on which all actuality depends as willed by God, the *scientia necessaria* and *scientia voluntaria* of the scholastics.[211] Leibniz views on the divine knowledge of "future" contingents, moreover, appears quite compatible with the orthodox Lutheran and Reformed doctrine in opposition to the Jesuit, Arminian, and Socinian versions of *scientia media*.[212] A similar point can be made for Leibniz doctrine of the Trinity, formulated in dialogue particularly with the English debates of the late seventeenth and early eighteenth century.[213] When such examples are multiplied, it becomes clear that not only was there a relationship between the developing rationalism and the older orthodoxy but, more specifically, that some of the compatibility between various forms of rationalism and the transitional theologies of the early eighteenth century reflects not only the increasingly rationalistic perspective of the theology but also the orthodox theological background of much of the philosophical language.

Lines of argument similar to those taken by Leibniz in the application of new philosophical and scientific models to theistic questions can be discerned in the treatise

---

consulted *Discourse on Metaphysics, Correspondence with Arnauld, Monadology*, intro. by Paul Janet, trans. George R. Montgomery (Lasalle, Ill.: Open Court, 1902, repr. 1980); *Monadology and Other Philosophical Essays*, trans. Paul Schrecker and Anne Martin Schrecker (Indianapolis: Bobbs-Merrill, 1965); *Philosophical Papers and Letters*, ed. with an intro. by Leroy E. Loemker, 2 vols. (Chicago, University of Chicago Press, 1956); *The Philosophical Works of Leibniz*, trans. George Martin Duncan, second edition (New Haven: Tuttle, Morehouse & Taylor, 1908); and *Theodicy: Essays on the Goodness of God, the Freedom of Man, and the Origin of Evil*, intro. by Austin Farrer, trans. E. M. Huggard (London: Routledge & Kegan Paul, 1951; repr. Chicago: Open Court, 1985).

210. See G. W. Leibniz, *A System of Theology*, trans. Charles William Russell (London: Burns and Lambert, 1850).

211. Leibniz, *Monadology*, §43, 45, 47, 48.

212. Leibniz, *Discourse on Metaphysics*, VIII.

213. Masterfully presented in Maria Rosa Antognazza, *Trinità e Incarnazione: Il rapporto tra filosofia e teologia rivelata nel pensiero di Leibniz* (Milan: Vita e Pensiero, 1999); also, idem, "Leibniz de Deo Trino: Philosophical Aspects of Leibniz's Conception of the Trinity," in *Religious Studies*, 37 (2001), pp. 1-13.

of the Dutch physicist, Paulus Buchius.[214] Buchius attempted to develop a doctrine of the divine essence and attributes that respected the teaching of Scripture and natural theology but which drew on the philosophical vitalism and monadology of the younger Van Helmont. Given the fundamental intention of the vitalist philosophy to provide an alternative to the mechanistic approach of the Cartesians and the materialism of Hobbes, the result is quite similar to Leibniz's efforts on the same subject, albeit far less traditional in its result.[215] Buchius objects to the wedge driven in his own time between theology and philosophy on the ground that Scripture, reason, and "all Natural things" come from God and that, therefore, there can be no disagreement between true theology and genuine philosophy. In his own time, however, theology is divided by sectarian debate, and philosophy has so emphasized the material that it cannot account for either the spiritual side of human beings or the relationship "betwixt things Divine and Natural." For Buchius, "deliverance" from both of these problems is to be found in Van Helmont's philosophy.[216] This recourse to rational philosophy as a release from dogmatic dispute was, we remember, also a foundation of Meijer's pleas against theological exegesis of Scripture and, arguably, a model for various of the more irenic of the transitional theologians, such as J. A. Turretin — in any case, it was not only a common, but also a telling argument in the debates of the era between the older orthodoxy and rationalism.[217]

Buchius addresses such issues as the relationship of the infinity and immutability of God to the creation of the universe, arguing against the materialism of his day that the creation of an extended order does not result either in a change in God or, specifically, in a greater extension of divine being to coincide with the extended universe. He then defends divine eternity and immutability and overcomes the Cartesian dualism of thought and extension and the materialism of Hobbes by denying a strict creation ex nihilo: God, in his omniscience, has all things eternally present to him, inasmuch as he himself is "the original" of all things. The "ideas," moreover, that God has of things are not "nothing" — they are the divine essence. And it is out of this essence, making visible and material what was invisible and immaterial, that God creates the world, as, Buchius insists, is taught in Hebrews 11:3.[218] A rather standard reading of arguments for the existence of God and of various of the divine attributes, wedded to an alternative philosophy, produces results rather different from those attained by theology in dialogue with the traditional Christian Aristotelianism!

2. The "Transitional Theology" and the movement toward rationalism. The shift away from the traditional Protestant theology of the high orthodox era toward

---

214. Paulus Buchius, *The Divine Being and its Attributes Philosophically Demonstrated from the Holy Scriptures and the Original Nature of Things. According to the Philosophical Principles of F. M. B. of Helmont* (London: Randal Taylor, 1693).

215. On F. M. van Helmont and his relation to Leibniz, see Copleston, *History of Philosophy*, III, pp. 268-269.

216. Buchius, *Divine Being and its Attributes*, preface to the reader, unpaginated.

217. On Meijer, see PRRD, II, 2.3 (C.2); 5.4 (B.5).

218. Buchius, *Divine Being and its Attributes*, §14-16, 27 (pp. 13-14, 20-22, 46-50).

the rationalistic eighteenth-century theology of late orthodoxy was not only gradual but also was distinctive enough in its character for several historians of doctrine to identify it as the era of Pietism and of the "Transitional" or "Transition Theology," or as a time of latitudinarianism in Christian thought.[219] Characteristic of this theology was its adherence to the doctrinal definitions of traditional orthodoxy at the same time that it absorbed some of the pietistic critique of the older scholastic dogmatics and leaned toward the new rationalist philosophies of the day, notably those of Descartes, Malebranche, and Leibniz. This latter relationship ought not to be viewed as unusual, given the strongly orthodox theological interests of the latter two philosophers in particular.[220] And although the term "Transitional Theology" is typically applied to the Lutheran context of the early eighteenth century, the shift in theological style occurred among the Reformed as well.[221] Among the Swiss Reformed, the rationalistic tendency was paralleled and supported by a rising indifference toward the complexities of the older polemics and, indeed, toward the more technical and disputative aspects of Protestant scholasticism, as evidenced in the writings of J.-A. Turretin, Osterwald, and, in the next generation, the highly rationalistic Vernet.[222] Even in the writings of Pictet, who remained more consistently within the boundaries of confessional orthodoxy than his younger contemporaries, a positive use of elements of Cartesian thought is evident.

3. **Reformed orthodoxy and Wolffian philosophy.** If the search for a new metaphysical foundation for a scholastic form of orthodox dogmatics was relatively unsuccessful among the British, Dutch, French, and French-speaking Swiss Reformed, a new philosophical alliance was rapidly forged between the Wolffian philosophy and a series of German Reformed and German-speaking Swiss Reformed dogmaticians, most notably Daniel Wyttenbach of Marburg and Johann Friedrich Stapfer of Basel. These writers are of significance for their attempt to maintain a fully orthodox body of doctrine and at the same time offer a new philosophical underpinning.

219. See, e.g., J. H. Kurtz, *Church History*, trans. John Macpherson, 3 vols. (New York: Funk & Wagnalls, 1890), pp. 146-147; Bengt Hägglund, *History of Theology*, trans. Gene Lund (St. Louis: Concordia, 1968), pp. 343-344.

220. On Malebranche, see: Beatrice K. Rome, *The Philosophy of Malebranche: A Study of his Integration of Faith, Reason, and Experimental Observation* (Chicago: Henry Regnery, 1963); Daisie Radner, *Malebranche: A Study of a Cartesian System* (Assen: Van Gorcum, 1978); on Leibniz, Philibert Secretan, "À propos de Dieu de Leibniz," in *Freiburger Zeitschrift für Philosophie und Theologie*," 27 (1980), pp. 24-35; Jacques Jalabert, *Le Dieu de Leibniz*, Publications de la Faculté des lettres et sciences humaines, Universite de Grenoble, v. 23 (Paris: Presses Universitaires de France, 1960; repr. New York: Garland, 1985); Catherine Wilson, *Leibnitz's Metaphysics: A Historical and Comparative Study* (Princeton: Princeton University Press, 1989).

221. Cf. *PRRD*, I, 1.3 (C).

222. See Martin I. Klauber, "The Eclipse of Scholasticism in Eighteenth-Century Geneva: Natural Theology from Jean-Alphonse Turretin to Jacob Vernet," in John B. Roney and Martin I. Klauber (eds.), *The Identity of Geneva: The Christian Commonwealth, 1564-1864*, pp. 129-42; and idem, "Theological Transition in Geneva from Jean-Alphonse Turretin to Jacob Vernet," in Carl Trueman and R. Scott Clark, eds., *Reformed Scholasticism: Essays in Reappraisal* (Carlisle: Paternoster Press, 1999), pp. 256-70.

Wyttenbach classes, certainly, as a Reformed Wolffian scholastic.[223] His theology takes its philosophical grounding from Wollfian rationalism, to the point of utilizing the principle of sufficient reason as a foundational premise of the entire system and to the point of arguing that natural theology necessarily precedes a theology based on supernatural revelation — given that a supernatural theology, in Wyttenbach's understanding, assumes, without proving, the existence of God. This approach leads, in Wyttenbach's *Tentamen theologiae*, to an extended meditation on the existence and attributes of God prior to his entry into the realm of traditional biblically grounded dogmatics.

Stapfer, like Wyttenbach, was an orthodox Wolffian. He was the author of three major essays in systematic form — his German-language positive theology and its compend, plus his massive Latin polemical theology.[224] His shift to the vernacular in dogmatic theology not only mirrors the gradual shift of orthodoxy in the eighteenth century away from its Latinate forms, but also the Wolffian pattern of presenting philosophy in the vernacular as well as in Latin.[225] Stapfer's doctrine of God takes on, particularly in his apologetic or polemical system, a highly rationalistic tone, fully employing the Wolffian principle of sufficient reason as the basis for its argumentation. Still, one can see significant continuities with the older orthodoxy: Stapfer and Wyttenbach both affirm the traditional categories of divine knowing, the *scientia necessaria* and the *scientia voluntaria*, and deny the Molinist and Socinian *scientia media*. Stapfer engages, moreover, in a discussion of the necessary knowledge not merely as a knowledge of all possibles, but fills out the discussion along lines indicated among the orthodox by Twisse and Rutherford, arguing that God does not merely know unassociated possibilities in an absolute sense, but knows them as "systems of possible things" or possible worlds."[226] Of course, the immediate source of Stapfer's language was as much Leibniz and Wolff as it was the Protestant orthodox tradition — but Leibniz and Wolff, after all, had drawn the language out of the preceding theological and philosophical tradition.

4. Remnants of traditional orthodoxy in the eighteenth century. It would be a mistake to assume that more traditional patterns of Reformed orthodoxy, rooted in the approaches of the seventeenth century, were utterly absent from the eighteenth century. We can certainly speak of various forms of late orthodoxy continuing through the eighteenth century — but it is clear that these forms offer little evidence of broad

223. Daniel Wyttenbach, *Praelectio inauguralis de iis, quae observanda sunt circa theologiam et dogmaticam et elenchticam docendam. Habita 17. Novemb. 1746* (Frankfurt, 1749); *Tentamen theologiae dogmaticae methodo scientifico pertractatae*, 3 vols. (Frankfurt, 1747-1749); *Theses theologicae praecipua christianae doctrinae capita ex primis principiis deducta continentes ... publicé defenderunt Isaacus Sigfrid ... & Daniel Wyttenbach* (Frankfurt, 1747).

224. Johann Friedrich Stapfer, *Grundlegung zur wahren Religion*, 12 vols. (Zürich, 1746-1753); *Auszug aus der Grundlegung zur Wahren Relgion*, 2 vols. (Zürich, 1754); *Institutiones theologiae polemicae universae, ordine scientifico dispositae*, fourth edition, 5 vols. (Zurich, 1756-1757).

225. Wolff was one of the first major continental writers to develop a vernacular language of philosophy: note his *Vernunftige Gedanken von Gott, der Welt und der Seele des Menschen* (1725).

226. Stapfer, *Inst. theol. polemicae*, I.iii, §336-40.

or uniform confessionality and little sense of a cooperative effort between traditional theology and a clearly ancillary philosophy. After 1725, the traditional Reformed orthodox model was, certainly, attenuated. Still, the basic orthodox and confessional teaching did remain a norm for a fairly large number of theologians throughout the eighteenth century. The orthodox model remained among the teachers associated with the *Nadere Reformatie*. Here, the line of the older orthodoxy, particularly that of Voetius and of the modified federalism of Witsius, carried over into the theology of Gürtler[227] and Francken — while the Cocceian line was represented in the writings of Lampe, Vitringa, and van der Kemp.[228] A fully orthodox, albeit somewhat rationalistic, model — to all intents and purposes, a bibliographical summing-up of orthodoxy — is found in Vitringa's *Doctrinae christianae religionis* and De Moor's massive commentary on Marckius' *Compendium theologiae*.[229] These writers typically identify two sources of our knowledge of God, natural and supernatural, and strictly limit the former to non-soteriological issues — whether the essence and essential attributes of God, creation, providence, the law of nature, God's sovereignty over humanity, or some of the implications of human misery.[230] In specific relation to the doctrine of God, the impact of the *Nadere Reformatie* and of Puritan piety was to produce a traditional orthodoxy, characterized by an exegetical foundation and a full scholastic development of doctrinal points, blended with a strong sense of the practical impact of the doctrine — indeed, of each of the doctrinal subtopics — on Christian life. Following out the approach of Mastricht, this perspective on theology was often coupled with a distrust and a pointed polemic against the rationalist philosophy of the era. In all of these theologies, one finds a traditional doctrine of God, posed against the various adversaries of the time.

Both in the doctrine of the divine essence and attributes and in the doctrine of the Trinity, the late orthodox era saw many changes and adaptations, not the least

227. Nicholaus Gürtler, *Institutiones theologicae ordine maxime naturali dispositae ac variis accessionibus auctae* (Marburg: Müller, 1732) and idem, *Synopsis theologiae reformatae* (Marburg: Müller, 1731).

228. Friedrich Adolf Lampe, *Compendium theologiae naturalis* (Utrecht, 1734); idem, *Melk der waarheit volgens aanleydinge van den Heidelbergschen Catechismus: ten nutte van de leer-begeerige jeugdt opgesteld ... door Frederik Adolf Lampe*, 2nd ed. (Amsterdam: Antony Schoonenburg, 1725); Johannes van der Kemp, *De Christen geheel en al het Eigendom van Christus* (Rotterdam: R. van Doesburg, 1717); translated as *The Christian Entirely the Property of Christ, in Life and Death, Exhibited in Fifty-three Sermons on the Heidelberg Catechism*, trans. John M. Harlingen, 2 vols. (New Brunswick: Abraham Blauvelt, 1810; repr. Grand Rapids: Reformation Heritage Books, 1997); and idem, *De Heid. Catechismus kortelyk geopened en verklaard by wyze van Vragen en Antwoorden*, ed. D. van der Kemp (Rotterdam: P. Losel & J. Bosch, 1746).

229. Campegius Vitringa, *Doctrina christianae religionis*; also note idem, *Korte stellingen: in welke vervat worden de grondstukken van de christelyke leere* (Amsterdam: Balthazar Lakeman, 1730); Bernhard de Moor, *Commentarius perpetuus in Joh. Marckii compendium theologiae christianae didactico-elencticum*, 7 vols. in 6 (Leiden, 1761-1771).

230. E.g., Aegidius Francken, *Kern der Christelijke leer: dat is de waarheden van de Hervormde godsdienst, eenvoudig ter nedergesteld, en met de oefening der ware Godzaligheid aangedrongen* (Dordrecht: J. van Braam, 1713; Groningen: O.L. Schildkamp, 1862), q. 26-27.

of which was the impact of various forms of theistic rationalism, even among the non-Wolffian thinkers. Reformed dogmaticians like Van Til, and, later, Vitringa and Venema reflect a strongly rationalistic tendency in their dogmatics — Van Til in his recourse to natural theology as a prolegomenon to revealed theology, Vitringa and Venema in their inclusion of reason in the principial structure of dogmatics. These alterations in perspective were not without profound effect on the doctrine of God, evidenced in particular by the new relationship established between a purely rational discussion of the divine attributes and the exposition of the doctrine of divine essence and attributes within the system of revealed dogma. In the case of Van Til's theology, the weight of the exposition falls fairly equally upon the shoulders of reason or nature and revelation, with the natural theology offering an extended presentation of the essence and attributes of God, the revealed theology providing a doctrine of God consisting in the divine names, the essence and attributes, and the Trinity. Van Til assumed that reason could elicit the basic philosophical conception of God as ultimate simple being, having a series of essential properties including life, intellect, will, and various "virtues," but that the divine names and the doctrine of the Trinity were inaccessible to reason. He also assumed that revealed theology, in the contest of the divine names and the doctrine of the Trinity, would provide also a full discussion of the divine attributes, based directly on Scripture, mirroring and even expanding upon the list given by natural theology.[231]

Allowing for the inroads of a somewhat rationalistic natural theology, a form of orthodoxy is also found in Venema's *Institutes* and in Klinkenberg's lengthy theological instruction and biblical commentary as well.[232] Although Venema's thought is influenced by a rather bland and eclectic rationalism, his doctrinal statements remain fully orthodox, his exegesis stands in continuity with the older tradition, and his identification of Socinian and fully rationalist teachings as inimical to his orthodoxy stands well within the bounds of the older confessional theology. Whereas his exegesis tends to follow out the lines of the traditional or precritical model in its understanding of the theological implications of texts, Klinkenberg's theology moves through a discussion of natural revelation, arguments for the existence of God, a discussion of God as creator, exposition of the doctrine of God and his attributes, the spirituality and immortality of the soul, and human nature from the perspective of the light of nature prior to engaging revealed theology from the perspective, not of the traditional *loci*, but of the flow and history of the biblical narrative. The impact of rationalism is seen not only in Klinkenberg's massive interest in the cosmic order as proof of God's

---

231. Cf. Van Til, *Theologiae utriusque compendium ... naturalis* (Leiden, 1704; second edition, 1719), I/1.i-iii; with Van Til, *Theologiae utriusque compendium ... revelatae* (Leiden, 1704; second edition, 1719), II.i-iii.

232. Venema, *Institutes of Theology*; Jacob van Nuys Klinkenberg, *Onderwys in den godsdienst*, 11 vols. (Amsterdam: J. Allart, 1780-1794); Jacob van Nuys Klinkenberg and Ger. Joh. Nahyus, *De Bijbel, door beknopte Uitbreidingen, en ophelderende Aenmerkingen, verklaerd*, 27 vols. (Amsterdam: Johannes Allart, 1780-1790).

existence but in the complete separation achieved in his theology between the doctrine of the divine essence and attributes and the doctrine of the Trinity.[233]

B. Declining Reformed Theology in the British Isles

1. Rationalism and latitudinarianism in British theology. As noted briefly above, a philosophically different but parallel quest for a new metaphysics, a metaphysics supportive of theological system, can be seen in the work of Samuel Clarke, both in his correspondence with Leibniz and in his work on the doctrine of God.[234] Beyond the philosopher Clarke, the various forms of rationalism — whether Cartesian, Hobbesian, Spinozistic, or Leibnizian — began also to have an effect on the language of British theology similar to the effect of the new rationalism on the continental Reformed: traditional usages became difficult to maintain, and the more orthodox of the theologians evidence a search for vocabulary, sometimes critiquing but also sometimes adopting or adapting the altered language of the contemporary philosophy. In the wake of the Deist controversy, moreover, the more orthodox side of eighteenth-century English theology developed the genre of rationalistic apologetics or of theistic evidences and began to merge the topics of natural religion and natural theology more comfortably into the broader system of Christian thought. The most typical division of the subject was into two sections; first, the evidences of natural religion and, second, the evidences of revealed religion, both internal and external.

Among the somewhat rationalistic and latitudinarian English systems that attempted to address this problem is Richard Fiddes' *Theologia speculativa* (1718) and *Theologia practica* (1720).[235] Taken together, the two volumes form a full system of "natural and revealed religion" divided equally into discussions of "principles" and "duties." Noteworthy is Fiddes' initial discussion of the divine existence and, to a certain extent, the divine essence and attributes, as a rational and apologetic exercise rather than as a churchly doctrinal exposition — albeit with a fairly traditional result. Fiddes was concerned particularly to argue that the God of true religion could not be either a material being or "the one substance of Spinoza."[236] As points of reference, throughout

233. Klinkenberg, *Onderwys*, I.i.7-8, §58-72, where, unlike the discussions of essence and attributes among the early and high orthodox, the doctrine of the Trinity is not even mentioned in relation to the question of the way in which the attribute belongs to the persons.

234. Samuel Clarke, *A Demonstration of the Being and Attributes of God. More Particularly in answer to Mr. Hobbes, Spinoza, and their followers. Being the substance of eight sermons preached in the year 1704 at the lecture founded by the honourable Robert Boyle, Esquire*, ed. Ezio Vailati (Cambridge: Cambridge University Press, 1998); also (title altered), *A Discourse Concerning the Being and Attributes of God, the Obligations of Natural Religion, and the Truth and Certainty of Christian Revelation. In Answer to Mr Hobbes, Spinoza, the Author of the Oracles of Religion, and Other Deniers of Natural and Revealed Religion*, in *The Works of Samuel Clarke*, 4 vols. (London, 1738; repr. New York: Garland, 1978).

235. Richard Fiddes, *Theologia speculativa: or, The First Part of a Body of Divinity ... wherein are Explain'd the Principles of Natural and Revealed Religion* (London, 1718); idem, *Theologia Practica: or, The Second Part of a Body of Divinity ... wherein are Explain'd the Duties of Natural and Revealed Religion* (London, 1720).

236. Fiddes, *Theol. spec.*, I.i.4.

these arguments, Fiddes drew on classical philosophers and, in his debate with Spinoza, on Clarke and Cheyne among his contemporaries — rather than either on Scripture or on the teachers of the early and medieval church or the orthodox Protestant thinkers of the sixteenth and seventeenth centuries. Neither is Fiddes overtly Aristotelian, but quite eclectic. Even so, his discussion of the divine attributes draws both on Scripture and philosophy, although the tendency of the discourse is to remain in the realm of rational argument — as is indicated by the placement of the existence, essence, and attributes prior to the discussion of revelation and separated by the major *loci* of revelation and Scripture,[237] and creation and providence[238] from the exposition of the creed in which Fiddes offers his doctrine of the Trinity.[239] Here we see, finally, the identification of essence and attributes as a topic belonging to natural theology and of Trinity as revealed theology that the Reformed orthodox had never advocated: the doctrines expressed are still nominally orthodox, but the form and method of scholastic orthodoxy has been lost. The doctrine of essence and attributes belongs to the rational argumentation for "the existence and unity of God" against the "Atheists and Polytheists" while the doctrine of the Trinity is offered "with a peculiar regard to Christians ... considering what they are to believe concerning God" based on revelation and the patristic tradition.[240]

Although the division of the discussion of revealed religion into internal and external evidences draws directly on the rationalizing tendency already present in the seventeenth-century scholastic discussions of the intrinsic and extrinsic arguments for the divinity of Scripture, a major philosophical shift has occurred in the transition from high orthodoxy to this eighteenth-century theological apologetic. The English theistic apologists, very much like their continental rationalist contemporaries, adopted philosophical premises concerning the sufficiency and capability of reason that were foreign to the theology of seventeenth-century orthodoxy and which were, in fact, akin to the presuppositions of their opponents, the Deists and the rationalist philosophers. The resultant structure of apologetics argued reason and natural theology as the foundation upon which revealed or supernatural theology could be based — or, at least, as a highly constructive dialogue partner in the reformulation of theology for their time.

Prominent examples of this development can be found in the work of Robert Boyle and in the thought of the various philosophical theists and theologians who contributed to the famous Boyle Lectures. Boyle himself had written on the question of the limitation of reason and on the "veneration" owed to God's wisdom and power,[241] and he inaugurated a series of monthly lectures on natural and revealed religion. In the

---

237. Fiddes, *Theol. spec.*, II.i-ii.
238. Fiddes, *Theol. spec.*, III.i-ii.
239. Fiddes, *Theol. spec.*, IV.i.2.
240. Fiddes, *Theol. spec.*, IV.i.2.
241. Robert Boyle, *A Discourse of Things Above Reason, Inquiring whether a Philosopher should admit that there are any such* (London: F. T. & R. H., 1681); idem, *Of the High Veneration Man's Intellect Owes to God; Peculiarly His Wisedom and Power* (London: M.F., 1685).

fourth and fifth years' lectures, John Williams, chaplain to William III, addressed the issues of revelation, reason, and the authority and certainty of Scripture, and in the seventh year, John Harris broached the subject, later to be taken up by Samuel Clarke, of the divine essence and attributes against the various forms of "atheism" in his time.[242] Both in intention and effect, the lectures did not so much further the cause of traditional doctrinal or dogmatic theism but rather affirmed the validity of theism in the face of what appeared to be the atheistic or the theistically nonproductive avenues of the newer philosophies and science.

Of the Boyle lecturers, Samuel Clarke certainly had the greatest immediate and most lasting impact. A scholarly graduate of Cambridge, well versed in English rationalism, Cartesianism, and Newtonian physics, Clarke intended his *Discourse Concerning the Being and Attributes of God* (1704-1705) and his subsequent *Scripture Doctrine of the Trinity* (1712) as defensive arguments against the problematic views on the divine essence, attributes, and Trinity generated by Cartesian, Spinozist, and Hobbesian thought.[243] His work was immediately attacked by proponents, both Anglican and Nonconformist, of a more traditional doctrine. His thought exemplifies the way in which the rationalist approach to doctrine and to Scripture, even when specifically orthodox in intentionality, could result in the troublesome alterations of the orthodox model — consequently, he is a pivotal figure in the development of eighteenth-century English theology, crucial to an understanding of the polemics of late orthodoxy.

The full title of Clark's Boyle Lectures gives a sense of their scope and purpose: *A Demonstration concerning the Being and Attributes of God, the Obligations of Natural Religion, and the Truth and Certainty of the Christian Revelation, in Answer to Mr. Hobbs, Spinoza, the Author of the "Oracles of Reason", and Other Deniers of Natural and Revealed Religion.*" Clarke's purpose in his lectures was to uphold true religion against its rationalist detractors, with a particular emphasis upon the "atheism" of Thomas Hobbes, Baruch Spinoza, and other rationalists of the age. The method he employed, however, to uphold both natural and revealed religion was thoroughly rationalistic itself: he would demonstrate rationally the truth of his position and manifest all Christian doctrine to be "not unreasonable." Leslie Stephen commented of Clarke, with a characteristic zest for pointing out the problematic elements in the thought of his historical subjects, "Hobbes and Spinoza are named as adversaries on the title page; but he might be more accurately described as following the argument of Spinoza up to the point where its logic becomes irreconcilable with the ordinary theism."[244]

Clarke's famous proof of God's existence is not exactly a proof in the traditional sense but rather an argument derived from the idea of a contingent world and the maxim *ex nihilo nihil fit.* Clarke begins by elaborating the assertion that "something has existed from eternity," namely, an unchangeable and necessary being, as the basis

---

242. John Harris, *The Atheistical Objections, against the Being of a God, and His Attributes, Fairly Considered and Fully Refuted in Eight Sermons* (London: J. L., 1698).

243. Samuel Clarke, *The Scripture Doctrine of the Trinity*, in *Works*, vol. IV.

244. Sir Leslie Stephen, *History of English Thought in the Eighteenth Century*, preface by Crane Brinton, 2 vols. (New York: Harcourt, Brace and World, 1962), I, p. 101.

for anything existing in time.[245] The argument becomes interesting and quite original when Clarke discusses time and space in relation to his view of God. If God is an immutable, independent, and necessary being who has attributes of eternity and omnipresence, namely, in Clarke's view, infinite time and infinite space, being limited by neither, then time and space are neither substances nor categories of substances. Instead, they are the eternity and immensity of God's being understood from a finite perspective. Clarke's logic neatly stands the *analogia entis* on its head and, at the same time, obliges the Newtonian notion of absolute time and absolute space: when time and space are understood as absolutes, raised to the level of infinity, they are attributes of God.[246]

The theological significance of Clarke's view of time and space cannot be underestimated. On the one hand, his rationalism reaches out toward Spinoza's pantheism, attaining perhaps a panentheistic view of the relationship of God and world. All things exist in time and space and, therefore, are in an absolute sense sustained within the attributes of God — and the attributes, as Clarke still maintains, are identical with the divine essence. Whereas the scholastic identification of attributes with the incomplex divine essence, paired with the *via negativa* approach to such attributes as infinity and immensity, had the effect of arguing God's utter transcendence of the finite order, Clarke's identification of the attributes of space and time with the divine essence, apart from the use of the *via negativa* or any other means of breaking the univocal relationship between divine space and human space, divine time and human time, has the effect of arguing a concept of divine imminence.

On the other hand, of still greater impact for the future of theology, Clarke's acceptance of the Newtonian view of space and time as absolutes represents the ultimate break between theology and the Aristotelian world view. As Burtt well argues,[247] space, time, and the other categories utilized by modern science were foreign to the medieval world-view — not that the medieval scholastics failed to apprehend relationships of space and time, but rather that they apprehended place and time as relations not as things and that they viewed relations as predicables or incidental properties of things. The medieval view, based on Aristotle's categories, reflects a world-view in which nature is open to the active inspection of the mind and in which things as such, together with their attributes, can be known directly. The modern scientific view embodies a conception of a far less easily known world in which relations like space and time have been reified and in which the intellect no longer can achieve such a direct perception of reality. Clarke's theology manifests the loss of the Aristotelian categories of the older scholasticism and represents, as it were, a rescholasticization of theology in the academy of modern science or, more precisely, in the courtyard of the Royal Society. The very book in question was Clarke's Boyle Lectures.

---

245. Clarke, *Demonstration*, ii-iii (Vailati, pp. 10-29).

246. Clarke, *Demonstration*, iv (Vailati, pp. 30-31); cf. Clarke, *Answer to Butler's Fifth Letter*, in ibid., pp. 110-111; and Clarke, *Answer to a Sixth Letter*, in ibid, p. 115.

247. Edwin A. Burtt, *The Metaphysical Foundations of Modern Science*, revised ed. (New York: Humanities Press, 1951), pp. 18, 26-27, 239-264.

Clarke was no Deist as Matthew Tindal alleged, but neither was he orthodox by any standard acceptable to his more traditional contemporaries. He stands somewhere between orthodoxy and Deism, having espoused the rationalist philosophy and all its methods but being unwilling entirely to divest himself of the traditional doctrines of Christianity. Clarke's doctrine, then, retains the old formulae but states their meaning in an overly rationalistic manner. He can hardly be said to deviate in doctrine, however, from a truly churchly position, since the teachers of doctrine in his day were departing generally from the older philosophical synthesis and, as a result from the doctrinal structures explained and undergirded by it. The dying Aristotelianism of the seventeenth century and the orthodoxy associated with it have been replaced in Clarke's thought, as in the thought of the continental rationalist theologians, by a new metaphysic and a profoundly altered view of the basic doctrines of Christianity.

2. The remnants of orthodoxy in the eighteenth century. From the same era that produced Francken, the elder Vitringa, and Venema in the Netherlands, British theology saw the production of several more traditional theological models: Edwards', Ridgley's, and Boston's theologies represent an attempt to follow the orthodoxy of the Westminster standards with a detailed but somewhat less scholastic theology than that of the seventeenth century. Edwards' *Theologia reformata* stands as the summation of an orthodox approach, born of controversy in the declining years of the Commonwealth and the troubled times of the Restoration.[248] Edwards' major works against Socinianism and his apologetics for the existence of God mark a late development of English Reformed theology, facing the major debates of the era: his systematic statement is a fully orthodox and somewhat retrospective defense of broad synthesis no longer possible within the narrow compass of English Dissent and fading also in Edwards' own circle of conforming but theologically Reformed thinkers.[249] His extended *Theologia Reformata* contains, in a more or less catechetical model, a highly traditionary view of the divine existence, essence, attributes, and Trinity. Both of the latter writers offer commentaries on the Westminster catechisms, Boston on the shorter, Ridgley on the larger catechism — and both reflect the older tradition of orthodoxy on the divine essence and attributes, manifesting a connection with the same exegetical tradition as the Reformers and the seventeenth-century orthodox and, particularly

---

248. John Edwards, *Theologia Reformata: or, the Body and Substance of the Christian Religion, comprised in distinct discourses or treatises upon the Apostles Creed, the Lord's Prayer, and the Ten Commandments*, 2 vols. (London: John Lawrence, et al., 1713); and idem, *Theologia reformata, or, Discourses on those graces and duties which are purely evangelical : and not contained in the moral law, and on the helps, motives, and advantages of performing them, being an entire treatise in four parts, and if added to the two former volumes, makes a compleat body of divinity* (London: T. Cox, 1726).

249. John Edwards, *A demonstration of the existence and providence of God, from the contemplation of the visible structure of the greater and the lesser world in two parts, the first shewing the excellent contrivance of the heavens, earth, sea, &c., the second the wonderful formation of the body of man* (London: Jonathan Robinson and John Wyat, 1696); idem, *A preservative against Socinianism shewing the direct and plain opposition between it, and the religion revealed by God in the Holy Scriptures* (Oxford: Henry Clements, 1693); and idem, *The Socinian creed, or, A brief account of the professed tenents and doctrines of the foreign and English Socinians wherein is shew'd the tendency of them to irreligion and atheism, with proper antidotes against them* (London: J. Robinson and J. Wyat, 1697).

in Boston's case, few of the controversies beginning to best the traditionary view of Scripture and its exegetical results. Ridgley, perhaps because of the greater length of his exposition, does note more of the "adversaries," most notably the Socinians, and does also engage in rebuttal. Both also accept the incommunicable/communicable distinction of attributes, with Boston reading it through the concept of *via negationis* and *via eminentiae*.[250]

The theology of John Gill represents the remnants of the older scholasticism in its clear and consistent reference to the major Reformed thinkers of the seventeenth century and in its efforts to maintain an exegetical continuity with the older tradition.[251] Indeed, Gill's primary dialogue partners in his work of biblical interpretation and theological construction are the orthodox of the seventeenth century rather than his own contemporaries. On the other hand, his theology is certainly a product of the loss of broad confessionality among the Reformed and fits into a picture of theologically fragmented dissent: on the issue of infant baptism, Gill is overtly negative concerning the older Reformed tradition; his conceptions of election, covenant, and justification have a fundamentally antinomian tendency; and his eschatology, although not beyond the pale, still echoes the millennial splintering of the tradition rather than the main confessional positions. It similarly reflects the loss of connection with the philosophical tradition: there is no attempt to return to the older Christian Aristotelianism but, equally, no use for the rationalist perspectives of its own time. Still, Gill's work, both in his massive commentary on the whole Bible and his *Body of Divinity*, stands as perhaps the most erudite of the eighteenth-century Dissenting theologies in the tradition of the older orthodoxy.[252]

---

250. See Ridgley, *A Body of Divinity*; also published as *Commentary on the Larger Catechism; Previously Entitled A Body of Divinity*, revised, with notes by John M. Wilson (1855; repr. Edmonton: Still Waters Revival Books, 1993); and Thomas Boston, *An illustration of the doctrines of the Christian religion, with respect to faith and practice, upon the plan of the assembly's shorter catechism. Comprehending a complete body of divinity. Now first published from the manuscripts of ... Thomas Boston*, 2 vols. (Edinburgh: John Reid, 1773; 1853), cited as *Body of Divinity* from the 1853 edition.

251. See Richard A. Muller, "John Gill and the Reformed Tradition: A Study in the Reception of Protestant Orthodoxy in the Eighteenth Century," in *The Life and Thought of John Gill (1697-1771): A Tercentennial Appreciation*, ed. Michael A. G. Haykin (Leiden: E. J. Brill, 1997), pp. 51-68.

252. John Gill, *An Exposition of the New Testament*, 3 vols. (London, 1746-8); *An Exposition of the Old Testament*, 6 vols. (London, 1748-63); *Complete Body of Doctrinal and Practical Divinity: or A System of Evangelical Truths Deduced from the Sacred Scriptures*, with *A Dissertation Concerning the Baptism of Jewish Proselytes*, 2 vols. (1769-70; reissued, London: Tegg & Company, 1839; repr. Grand Rapids: Baker Book House, 1978).

PART 2

The Reformed Orthodox Doctrine of God

3

The Unity of Existence, Essence, and Attributes in God

3.1 The Order and Arrangement of the Doctrine of God in Reformed Orthodox Theology

A. Method and Order in the Era of the Reformation

1. Reformation era "ways though" the *locus de Deo*. An important element of the rise of Reformed orthodoxy was the development of coherent models for the discussion of the topics of Christian doctrine — a development that began early on in the Reformation with Melanchthon's various suggestions for determining a *methodus* or "way through" the basic theological topics and with the use of various credal, confessional, and catechetical forms for the organization of larger theological works by thinkers like Bullinger and Calvin.[1] There were also, in the era of the Reformation, at least two Reformed theologians who offered some explicit instruction for organizing the doctrine of God: Musculus and Hyperius. Musculus' *Loci communes* evidence a basic distinction between the doctrine of God and the doctrine of God's works that would become a standard organizational device in later orthodoxy, as well as a pattern of movement from the question of the existence of God, to a general definition of what (or who) God is and a brief adumbration of the doctrine of the divine attributes, to the doctrine of the Trinity.[2] Hyperius' discussion not only moves from a preliminary presentation of Scripture as the basis for Christian doctrine and passes on to the *locus de Deo* by way of proofs of God's existence, it also understands the *locus* as a unity.

---

1. See *PRRD*, I, 4.1 (A.1) and Muller, *Unaccommodated Calvin*, pp. 102-117, 119-139.

2. Note the explicit precedent of Musculus, *Loci communes*, I-III (*De Deo; De divinitate Christi; De divinitate Spiritus Sancti*) and IV (*De operibus Dei*); cf. the discussion in Robert B. Ives, "The Theology of Wolfgang Musculus (1497-1562)," (Ph.D. diss., University of Manchester, 1965).

Hyperius begins with a discussion of the oneness of God and moves to an initial discussion of the divine essence under the rubrics *Quid sit Deus* and *Qualis sit Deus*.[3] He then presents an exposition of the biblical names of God and of the doctrine of the Trinity,[4] and a discussion, nearly unique among the Reformed of the sixteenth and seventeenth centuries, on the "similitudes" in the created order that declare the mystery of the Trinity.[5] He then presents, first, the personal properties that distinguish the Father, Son, and Spirit, and then, second, the divine attributes or essential properties possessed equally by all three persons.[6] Calvin did not state the logic of his arrangement of the topics as overtly as Musculus and Hyperius, but his result was, arguably, quite similar, moving from a discussion of the problem of the knowledge of God, to the universal knowledge of God's existence and the absence of excuse for idolatry, to a lengthy statement of the doctrine of the Trinity prefaced by notice of the divine essence and attributes.[7] These models, moreover, would be echoed in the writings of the Reformed orthodoxy — and, in fact, explained in some detail.

2. **Modern critiques: misapprehensions and misrepresentations of the order and arrangement of the *locus de Deo*.** Many of the difficulties associated by modern writers with the Reformed orthodox doctrine of God — namely, that it is a reversion to medieval scholasticism, a form of rationalism, a large-scale intrusion of natural theology into Christian dogmatics, and a major deviation from the humanistic and "christocentric" thought-world of the Reformation — are theological or dogmatic claims made initially by systematic theologians and later adopted on less than historical grounds by various historians of Reformation and early modern-era Christian thought. These theological critiques of the historical materials are, in large part, based on a mistaken reading of the problem of natural revelation in sixteenth- and seventeenth-century Reformed thought and on the order and arrangement of doctrines in the older dogmatics, notably the arrangement of the *locus de Deo* that moves from proofs of God's existence, to the doctrine of the divine essence and attributes, and then to the doctrine of the Trinity.[8]

Perhaps the most blatant and ill-founded of the critiques is Brunner's claim that the orthodox writers diminished the significance of the "Name of God" in Protestant theology and, in their proofs of God's existence, reintroduced natural theology into Protestantism and effected a complete reversion to the "medieval metaphysic."[9] He also speaks of "the metaphysical, speculative perversion of the doctrine of God ... in the dogmatic treatment of the Attributes of God" and then proceeds to erect contrasts

---

3. Hyperius, *Methodus theologiae*, I (pp. 80-89).

4. Hyperius, *Methodus theologiae*, I (pp. 89-108).

5. Hyperius, *Methodus theologiae*, I (pp. 109-111).

6. Hyperius, *Methodus theologiae*, I (pp. 111-135 and 135-269, including a discussion of predestination as perdicated of God).

7. See Calvin, *Institutes*, I.i-xiii.

8. See the discussion of natural revelation in *PRRD*, I, 6.1-6.2.

9. Emil Brunner, *The Christian Doctrine of God; Dogmatics: vol. I*, trans. Olive Wyon (Philadelphia: Westminster, 1950), p. 131.

between the Reformers and the Protestant scholastics: Calvin, according to Brunner, "firmly rejects the scholastic idea of Omnipotence," while the Protestant scholastics affirm it; the Reformers strongly associated divine omniscience with providence, understood as the "loving sympathy" of God for the world, and with election, while the later scholastics generally "ignored" the doctrine of omniscience.[10] Did Brunner ever read sixteenth- and seventeenth-century documents? One wonders. The exposition of Reformed doctrine that follows will not only show clear continuities between the Reformers and the orthodox, it will indicate among other things the affinities between Calvin's view of omnipotence and the scholastic teaching and indicate that not only the Reformers but the Reformed orthodox as well meditated extensively on divine omniscience in relation to providence. This Brunnerian view is echoed in Armstrong's definition of Protestant scholasticism as evidencing "a pronounced interest in metaphysical matters, and abstract speculative thought, particularly with reference to the doctrine of God" and in Gründler's similar statement that a christocentric theology of revelation was set aside by a causal metaphysic.[11]

Barth also has claimed an implicit problem in the standard ordering of subtopics in the traditional doctrine of God, namely, proofs of God's existence, essence, attributes, Trinity, which arrives only third in line to what he views as the distinctively Christian identification of God — and he notes the important exceptions of Lombard's *Sententia* and Bonaventura's *Breviloquium*, both of which set Trinity first among doctrines in order of analysis. And he points to Luther's trinitarian objections to the altered shape of late-medieval commentaries on Lombard. According to Barth, these medieval thinkers point to a crucial issue in dogmatics that was identified by Calvin and Melanchthon at the beginning of Protestant dogmatics and recognized the confessions of the Reformed and Lutheran churches, but subsequently overlooked by the orthodox dogmaticians of the seventeenth century. Barth writes:

> It is ... hard to see how what is distinctive for this God can be made clear if, as has constantly happened in Roman Catholic and Protestant dogmatics both old and new, the question who God is, which it is the business of the doctrine of the Trinity to answer, is held in reserve, and the first question to be treated is that of the That and the What of God, as though these could be defined otherwise than on the presupposition of the Who.[12]

As is often the case with Barth's reviews and critiques of the tradition, his argument is directed more toward the justification of his own position than toward a genuine understanding of the past. In a similar vein, Weber indicates that the movement from essence and attributes to Trinity is a movement from a "general" doctrine of God to

---

10. Brunner, *Christian Doctrine of God*, I, pp. 203, 293, 297, 299.

11. Armstrong, *Calvinism and the Amyraut Heresy*, p. 32; Gründler, "Thomism and Calvinism," p. 159.

12. Barth, *Church Dogmatics*, I/1, pp. 300-301; Barth's argument is reproduced by T. F. Torrance in "The Distinctive Character of the Reformed Tradition," in *Reformed Review*, 54/1 (Autumn 2000), pp. 5-6.

the "special Christian doctrine of God" — an approach that he declares to be "dangerous" to Christian theology.[13]

The order of the older dogmatics, in moving from proofs to essence and attributes and then to Trinity, was not a movement from "that" (or more properly, "whether"), to "what," to "who" (or in Torrance's version, from "what," to "that" or "whether," to "what sort"), but from "whether" (*an sit?*) to "what" (*quid*) to "what sort" (*qualis*) — with the "whether" (Barth's "that") corresponding to the proofs; the "what" corresponding to the essence and essential properties (attributes of the "first order") and, in the arrangement of some of the orthodox writers, to the Trinity as well, not as Barth would seem to imply, to the essence and the attributes generally; and the "what sort" referring to the relational attributes (attributes of the "second order") and, in other of the orthodox, to the Trinity. The *locus* does not segment Trinity off from the discussion of essence and attributes: the issue addressed by this order is not a movement from an extended philosophical or speculative discussion of "what" God is to a biblicistic, trinitarian definition of "who" God is, but the movement from a statement of "what" (or "who") the existent One is, namely, God, to a lengthy discussion in terms of attributes and Trinity, of precisely "what sort" of God has been revealed, namely, a triune God who is simple, infinite, omnipotent, gracious, merciful, and so forth. Among the Reformers themselves, this understanding of the order of the questions is particularly evident in Musculus, who understood the doctrine of the Trinity as the identification of *qualis* or "what sort" rather than of "what" (*quid*) or "who" (*quis*) God is.[14] The order, here, follows out the standard logical and rhetorical order of discussion, according to which the existence of something ought to be attested prior to any discussion of the thing. The order was not intended to deflect discussion away from concentration on the uniquely Christian content of the doctrine of God but to expedite the discussion.

Even so, Torrance's comment that the movement from *an sit*, to *quid sit*, to *quale* or *qualis sit* is a "stereotyped medieval" approach is fundamentally mistaken: this set of questions, albeit used by the medieval scholastics, is actually derived from classical rhetoric and was available to the Reformers both from ancient handbooks like Quintilian's *Institutiones oratoriae* and also from humanist manuals like Melanchthon's *Elementa rhetorices*.[15] It is found, in the era of the Reformation, in the order of discussion of Musculus' *Loci communes* and Hyperius' *Methodus theologiae*.[16] Nor is the approach foreign to Calvin. Calvin, it is true, argued that "Those, therefore, who, in considering this question [of the knowledge of God], propose to inquire what God is (*quid sit Deus*), only delude us with frigid speculations; it being much more our interest to know what

---

13. Weber, *Foundations of Dogmatics*, I, p. 350.

14. Musculus, *Loci communes*, i-iii (*Commonplaces*, pp. 1-18).

15. Cf. Torrance, "Distinctive Character," p. 5, where Torrance mistakes the order of the questions, placing "*quid sit*" before "*an sit*," and then using the less usual *quale* rather than *qualis*.

16. Musculus, *Loci communes*, ii, xlii (*Commonplaces*, p. 5, col. 2; p. 886, col. 2 - p. 887, col. 1); Hyperius, *Methodus theol.*, I (pp. 83-91).

kind of being God is (*qualis sit*), and what things are agreeable to his nature."[17] But this is hardly what Torrance claims, a "reversal" of the medieval questions, the "rejection" of an "essentialist approach," and the insistence that the "primary question" now must be "Who is God."[18]

In the first place, Calvin does not at all pose the question, "Who is God?" — as if this were really a different question from "What is God?" From a purely grammatical perspective, a turn from "what" to "who" is not a turn from *quid* to *qualis* — rather it would be from the first person singular neuter nominative interrogative, *quid*, to the first person singular masculine nominative interrogative, *quis*. Calvin does not once ask "*quis sit?*" Rather he moves away from this basic question on the ground that, when it is asked, it becomes too speculative and detached from the present reality of God as the "author of every good" — whether phrased as "what" or as "who" — to ask the next question in order, *qualis* or "what sort." The ground of the anti-speculative point is clear: Calvin has previously indicated that unless human beings find their complete happiness in God, they will never truly give themselves to him.[19] He then reinforces the point rhetorically by declaring that those who ask the question *Quid sit Deus* are missing this truth and engaging in useless speculation. Calvin is still concerned with the basic content of the traditional discussion: God is a being infinite and spiritual in his essence. Calvin thus assumes the traditional answer and refuses the speculative discussion: he specifically includes the traditional identification of the divine essence in his doctrine of God as foundational to the teaching of the Bible and as distinctively Christian. He merely refrains from speculative elaboration..

What is more, as is clear from his text, Calvin does not reject discussion of "What God is" because of an aversion to the classical (whether medieval scholastic or classic rhetorical) order of questions and its purportedly Aristotelian implications: his polemic here makes no mention of the scholastics but addresses the Epicureans — and presumably the Epicureanism of various Renaissance philosophers — whose speculations portray God as distant and uninvolved.[20] Once Calvin has made his point against the problem of Epicureanism and stressed his primary interest in "what kind" or "sort" of God we seek to know, he moves to a series of rhetorical arguments drawn largely from Cicero, indicating that God exists,[21] to a lengthy discussion of the problem of the natural knowledge of God and the Scriptural revelation,[22] to a discussion of the one God, his names, and his attributes as revealed in Scripture,[23] to a very brief statement that the "essence" of God is "infinite and spiritual" (*quid sit Deus*!!!),[24] to his discussion of the doctrine of the Trinity, in which he also sets forth various divine

---

17. Calvin, *Institutes*, I.ii.2.
18. Torrance, "Distinctive Character," pp. 5-6.
19. Calvin, *Institutes*, I.ii.1.
20. Calvin, *Institutes*, I.ii.2.
21. Calvin, *Institutes*, I.iii.1-2.
22. Calvin, *Institutes*, I.iv-ix.
23. Calvin, *Institutes*, I.x.1-3.
24. Calvin, *Institutes*, I.xiii.1.

attributes as evidences of the divinity of the Son and the Spirit.[25] Thus, even as he has polemicized against the view of God found in certain kinds of "profane philosophy" (specifically, against Epicureanism and the Stoicism of Seneca) and even as he has emphasized, from the beginning to the end of his discussion, "what sort" of being God is, he has still followed the standard order of *an sit, quid sit,* and *qualis sit.*[26] (It is also quite clear that the issue of essence is not avoided but in fact made prominent in the various confessions of the era on which Calvin had some influence,[27] and that the so-called essentialist understanding of God belongs to Calvin's exegesis of Exodus 3:14.)[28] To this it should be added that Calvin does appeal to the question *qualis sit Deus* or, more precisely, identify Paul as beginning a rational discourse with it, precisely in a context where the use of Scripture was unwarranted (the Areopagus in Athens) and the issue was to identify precisely what and what sort of being God is, given the confused notions of divinity held by the Greeks.[29]

Arguably, the entire traditional discussion of essence, attributes, and Trinity is devoted to answering the question of "who" (or "what") God is, not merely the presentation of the Trinity. This hypothesis is reinforced in the Reformed orthodox dogmatics by the fact that the traditional order of proofs, essence, attributes, and Trinity has, typically, been altered — and what appears in a large number of the orthodox Reformed theological systems is an order that moves from the proofs and a discussion of the knowledge of God to a statement concerning the divine essence in its unity and independence, to an extended analysis of the divine names, and only then to the doctrines of the attributes and the Trinity. Mastricht, for one, placed the discussion of the names prior to his discussion of the question, "Quid sit," thereby setting the issue of fundamental divine identity at the beginning of his formal presentation of the doctrine of God.[30] Prior to the attributes, and close to the beginning of the formal doctrine of God, thus, the Reformed orthodox offer a discussion of the names of God — specifically, of the individual identity of God as revealed in and through his names, and then pass on to the more traditional questions of essence and attributes.

From the perspective of the older orthodoxy, to restrict "who" to Trinity — or to claim that the doctrine of the Trinity is all that is specifically Christian in the doctrine of God — would be a major error in theology. Rather, the traditional ordering of doctrine begins with the primary datum of the biblical revelation, the oneness of God, and then, on the basis of this biblical monotheism, moves on to the mystery of the

---

25. Calvin, *Institutes,* I.xiii.2-29.

26. On Calvin's rhetorical "proofs," see below, 3.2 (B.3).

27. See Gallican Confession, i; Belgic Confession, i; and see further, above, 2.1 (C.1). Note John Platt's discussion of the editing of the *Belgic Confession* and its implication in *Reformed Thought and Scholasticism: The Arguments for the Existence of God in Dutch Theology, 1575-1650* (Leiden: Brill, 1982), pp. 104-110.

28. See John Calvin, *Mosis libri in formam harmoniae,* in CO 24, col. 43-4 (CTS *Harmony,* I, pp. 73-4); cf. the comments in Muller, *Unaccommodated Calvin,* pp. 153-154, 156-157.

29. Calvin, *Commentary on Acts,* 17:24 (CTS *Acts,* II, pp. 157-158 = CO 46, col. 410).

30. Mastricht, *Theoretico-practica theol.,* II.ii.1; cf. Amyraut, et al., *Syntagma thesium theologicarum,* I.xiii.2.

threeness of the one God. This ordering of doctrine, moreover, makes clear that all of the divine attributes belong equally to each of the divine persons in their essential oneness — and, via the resultant argument that the work of the Trinity *ad extra* is the common work of the three divine persons, opens the doctrine of God outward toward the doctrine of creation and the other *loci* of the system: the divine identity is not merely a matter of the doctrine of the three divine persons, but of the identity of those persons as the infinite, omnipotent, merciful, and gracious God.[31] The assumption that the discussion of the divine essence and attributes is a matter for "natural theology" whereas the doctrine of the Trinity belongs to "supernatural theology" is a major misunderstanding of the Reformed orthodox theology: Barth, uncritically followed by Weber and Torrance, missed the point.

B. Order, Method, and the Construction of Early Orthodox Reformed Dogmatics

1. Early orthodox models: Ramist architectonics and problems of priority. The Ramist division of theology into two parts, faith and works, followed by subsequent divisions that serve to set the body of Christian teachings in order under the doctrine of God, is characteristic of the early orthodox era and its attempt to develop a clear architecture of theological system.

> There are two divisions of Christian theology: the first concerning faith (*de fide*), the second concerning good works (*de bonis operibus*).
> The divisions of the doctrine of faith are two: first concerning God (*de Deo*), second concerning the Church (*de Ecclesia*).[32]

It is important to remind ourselves of what has preceded these divisions and definitions. The "theology" that has here been divided into the categories of faith and works is not theology in general, theology ideally considered, or the ultimate theology known to God, the *theologia archetypa*. This theology is the finite ectypal theology of revelation, after the Fall, in the individual subject, the theology that Junius and his successors identified as "imperfect," albeit sufficient to the task of teaching the doctrines of salvation.[33] Such theology must rest on a special revelation, namely on Scripture, which

---

31. Trelcatius, *Schol. meth.*, I.iii (p. 19) specifically assigns "quid" to the question of God's nature or essence according to the names of God (from whence he derives Trinity) and "quis" to the discussion of the attributes.

32. Polanus, *Syntagma*, *Synopsis libri II*; cf. John Stoughton, *A Learned Treatise in Three Parts: 1. The Definition; 2. The Distribution of Divinity; 3. The Happinesse of Man: As it was Scholastically Handled* (London: Richard Hodgkinson, 1640), pp. 63-67, where theologies making an initial distinction between faith and works or faith and obedience are understood as distinct from theologies that make a basic distinction between doctrines concerning God and those concerning the works of God — alternatively, the distinctions may be seen as belonging to the same sequence, as in Polanus. Also note Flavel, *An Exposition of the Assembly's Catechism*, in *The Works of John Flavel*, 6 vols. (Edinburgh: Banner of Truth, 1968), VI, p. 144.

33. Junius, *De vera theologia*, xvii, in *Opuscula theologica selecta*; cf. Heidegger, *Corpus theol*, I.67-70; De Moor, *Commentarius*, I.x; also, *PRRD*, I, 5.5 (C.2).

stands as the postlapsarian form of *theologia revelata in hac vita* and as the ideal of theology, the *theologia viatorum absolutè dicta*, over against the imperfect forms that fallen human beings derive from it.[34] As for its basic division into faith and works — it ought to be clear that this imperfect, finite, and fallen theology is directed primarily toward the needs of its subjects, namely, a right knowledge of faith and works! And faith comes first, inasmuch as it is the "principle" from which "all obedience flows."[35]

The twofold partition of theology into doctrines of faith and doctrines of obedience is also found in Perkins' *Golden Chaine*. In view of the purpose of his treatise, the description of the *ordo salutis* rather than the presentation of a compend of theology, it is not surprising that Perkins gives a prominence to the doctrine of God over the definition of theology and the brief doctrine of Scripture that precede it — a prominence not characteristic of the early orthodox systems generally. Nevertheless, both the ordering of the treatise and its exposition of the doctrine of God are significant for the development of theology in the early orthodox period and must be examined along with Perkins' discussion of divine unity and Trinity in his *Exposition of the Symbole*. There, as in *A Golden Chaine*, Perkins makes very clear the placement of the doctrine of God at the head of the system is a result of the identification of God as *principium essendi*.[36] Scharpius notes the problem in his transition from the doctrine of Scripture to the doctrine of God: "in the order of nature," he comments, "there is nothing prior to God, since he is the essential foundation of all things" — nonetheless, the order of knowing has required that Scripture be discussed first.[37]

The initial division between faith and works intentionally reflects the definition of religion as consisting in the knowledge and worship of God.[38] Although it might be considered an issue to be discussed in the prolegomena, under the definitions of theology and religion, it typically appears after the prolegomena, indeed, in Polanus' case after both the prolegomena and the doctrine of Scripture, as the introductory division of the system proper. The thrust of the entire series of introductory distinctions, as they appear in Polanus' *Syntagma* is to identify, first, two branches of theology based on the goals of religion and then to focus the first part of theological system, the teachings concerning the knowledge of God or, as they can also be identified, faith in an objective sense, on God and the works of God:

> There are two divisions of the faith concerning God: first concerning the essence of God (*de essentia Dei*), second concerning his works (*de operibus ipsius*).
>
> The essence of God is considered either *communiter* or *singulariter*. In the very same sense, it is said that the divine essence is to be considered either *indistinctè* or *distinctè*.

---

34. Polanus, *Syntagma theol.*, I.xiii; Owen, *Theologoumena*, I.iii.3.

35. Flavel, *Exposition of the Catechism*, in *Works*, vol. 6, p. 144.

36. Perkins, *Golden Chaine*, i-ii (p. 11), and cf. Perkins, *Exposition of the Symbole*, in *Workes*, I, pp. 130-131.

37. Scharpius, *Cursus theol.*, col. 170.

38. Wollebius, *Christianae theol. comp.*, praecognita, §2; cf. Polanus, *Syntagma theol.*, II.1; idem, *Substance of the Christian Religion*, p. 1; Alting, *Methodus theol.*, III.1; Ames, *Medulla theologica*, I.ii.1-2; Marckius, *Chr. theol. medulla*, I.xxxiv; also see *PRRD*, I, 3.2 (B); 3.4 (A-B).

And once again in the very same sense, it is said that the divine essence is to be considered either *absolutè* or *relatè*.

The faith concerning the essence of God falls into two parts: first concerning the attributes of God; second concerning the persons of the Godhead (*de personis Deitatis*).[39]

Only, moreover, after he has finished his entire discussion of the doctrine of God and is ready to move from the Trinity to the "works of God" does Polanus state, "thus far concerning the essence of God, the works of God follow" — reinforcing his initial assumption that the *locus de Deo*, indeed, the *locus de essentia Dei*, is a topic including both attributes and Trinity.[40]

This set of divisions or bifurcations provides us with pattern and logic for the order and organization of the *locus de Deo*. Polanus accepts the Ramist division of theology, also taught by Perkins and Ames,[41] between the basic categories of faith and obedience, that is, between Christian doctrine and Christian life or ethics. This division itself is important insofar as it represents an overview of Christian theology which not only distinguishes intellectually between doctrine and ethics but which also unites the two, considered as reciprocal halves of "living to God" or of "the science of living blessedly forever," into one theological system. This division and conjunction expressed in terms of "faith" and "good works" also manifests the typical reformed emphasis on the *sola fide* of salvation and upon the good works that must flow from faith if faith is genuine. This model was preserved during the era of orthodoxy and is evident in Wendelin's *Christianae theologiae libri duo* in the mid-seventeenth century and in Mastricht's *Theoretico-practica theologia* (1682-1689) at the end of the era of orthodoxy.[42]

2. Other early orthodox approaches. Examination of the early orthodox theological systems, moreover, evidences a certain level of debate concerning the order of the first several *loci* of theological system. Gulielmus Bucanus' *Institutiones* begin with a brief statement relating to God and his revelation and then proceeds to treat, first, the doctrine of God and then the doctrine of Scripture before developing the doctrine of providence and creation.[43] This problem of placement had already been put into focus, moreover, in the Gallican Confession and the Belgic Confession, which had offered brief definitions of God and then noted the two sources, natural and supernatural, of the knowledge of God before moving on to discuss Scripture and the Trinity.[44] Beza's *Quaestionum et responsionum*, perhaps more clearly echoing the model of the Gallican Confession, begins by identifying God as the source and goal of the

---

39. Polanus, *Syntagma*, Synopsis Libri II; cf. Hottinger, *Cursus theologicus*, III.i and canon.

40. Polanus, *Syntagma*, Synopsis Libri III, ad fin; cf. Gürtler, *Synopsis theol.*, v.1, and note that Moyse Amyraut, *De mysterio trinitatis, deque vocibus ac Phrasibus quibus tam Scriptura quam apud Patres explicatur, Dissertatio, septem partibus absoluta* (Saumur: Isaac Desbordes, 1661) begins with a discussion of the divine essence and attributes.

41. Perkins, *Golden Chaine*, i-ii (p. 11); Ames, *Medulla theologica*, I.ii.1.

42. Wendelin, *Christianae theologiae libri duo*, I.i.3; Mastricht, *Theoretico-practica theol.*, II.i (*De fide salvifica*), set immediately prior to *De existentia & cognitione Dei* (II.ii), and the entire dogmatic project proper standing prior to *Idea theologiae moralis*, with I.i as *De obedientia fidei, & obedientia*.

43. Thus, Bucanus, *Institutiones*, cap. i-iii (God), iv (Scripture), v (creation).

44. Cf. *Gallican Confession*, I-VI; *Belgic Confession*, I-XI.

life of believers, moves on to discuss Scripture as the place where God reveals himself to us, and then, at length, develops the doctrine of God, emphasizing the Trinity[45]: following the order of the confessions, both Beza and Bucanus place an identification of the *principium essendi* first, as a preliminary issue and as the basis of the *principium cognoscendi*. Bucanus also recognizes the claim of the epistemological problem to a priority in order. The structure noted in Bucanus' *Institutiones* may also be observed in the Westminster catechisms and the systems built on them and even in a system as late as Gill's *Body of Divinity*. This pattern was, to a certain extent, adumbrated also in Calvin's *Institutes*: first the establishment of a general human knowledge of God, the recognition of the insufficiency of this knowledge for salvation and the necessity of a revealed Word of God; then the definition of Scripture as that Word; and finally a return via the revelation to the questions concerning what and who God is.[46]

Trelcatius introduces his *locus de Deo* by arguing that "the second *principium* of sacred theology is God."[47] This is to be understood not according to "the order of Nature," but in an epistemological sense:

> as the Scripture is the first Instrument of every healthful knowledge concerning God: so God is the first, and supreme Principle of the being of those things which serve this knowledge, on whom all things immediately depend. Now concerning God (whom to be both nature and reason hath sufficiently taught the natural man to make him inexcusable, as also the Scripture and Faith hath sufficiently taught the Christian man to his salvation:) we must know two things; first, what he is, to wit, his Nature: secondly, who he is, that is his Attributes.[48]

In the period of early orthodoxy we also find, in several theologians, a reluctance to separate the problems of the unity and the Trinity of God. Bucanus prefaces his discussion of the attributes with a trinitarian description of God drawn from Chalcedon, and Trelcatius goes so far as to discuss the Trinity first, prior to the attributes. We also see an adumbration of this order in Zanchi, whose *De natura Dei seu attributis* presupposes the doctrine of the Trinity and sees the attributes in terms of trinitarian and christological issues. Not only does Zanchi's *De tribus Elohim* precede his *De natura Dei seu attributis* in the order of his collected works, the form and pattern of argument in the *De natura Dei* assumes the doctrine of the Trinity as underlying the discussion both of the divine nature in general and of the attributes in particular;[49] and there are continual references, throughout the work, to the way in which the various attributes must be understood in a trinitarian context. Thus, Zanchi argues that he has shown, in the former treatise, *De tribus Elohim*, who (*quis*) God is — Father, Son, and Spirit — he must next discuss what manner or sort (*qualis*) of being God is: this,

---

45. Beza, *Quaestionum et responsionum*, in *Tractationes theol.*, I, pp. 654-656; cf. Beza, *Booke of Christian Questions and Answers*, fol. Bi, r-v.

46. *The Larger Catechism*, qq. 1-11; cf. Calvin, *Institutes*, I.iii-xiii.

47. Trelcatius, *Schol. meth.*, I.iii (p. 49).

48. Trelcatius, *Schol. meth.*, I.iii (p. 50).

49. Cf. Zanchi, *De natura Dei*, I.i, in *Opera*, II, col. 1.

he argues, is the burden of the doctrine of the divine essence or nature and attributes.[50] A similar understanding of the attributes as answering the question "Of what sort" is found in the theses debated in Geneva under Beza, where the discussion of divine attributes also follows that of the Trinity.[51]

Perhaps the most interesting of the early orthodox variants in order is Bartholomaus Keckermann's *Systema s.s. theologiae*. There, following a brief first *locus* on the definition and method of theology, Keckermann adopts an analytical approach, presenting the essence of God and its triunity, the distinction of the persons, the divine attributes, including the decretive will of God, and the doctrine of Scripture as Word. The order demonstrates the close relationship between the early orthodox prolegomena and the *locus de Deo*. Even more than Trelcatius, Keckermann unites the *loci* concerning God as one with those concerning the Trinity and to them, as a result, joins the doctrine of Scripture: the two *principia theologiae*, God and his Word, are here joined in a single preliminary "book" *continens disciplinae theologicae principia*.[52]

More common among the seventeenth-century theologians, even those who did not overtly use Ramist patterns of organization, was the division between God and his works, followed by a division of the topic of God into discussions of essence, names, attributes, and persons. As Maccovius states the issue, "the nature or essence of God ... is considered either absolutely or according to its manner of subsisting (*cum modo subsistendi*),"[53] which is to say either according to its attributes or according to the personal relations in the essence. Wendelin's division of the topic also assumes the fundamental unity of the doctrine of the triune God: there is an initial division into a discussion of God *in se* and of God *in operibus suis* and then a second division identifying the doctrine of God *in se* as presenting God "*1) quoad Naturam ... 2) quoad Proprietates naturae; 3) quoad Personas*."[54] Similarly, Spanheim notes a division of the topic into the discussion of God essentially and the discussion of God personally — and then indicates the subdivision of these two basic topics into discussions of the divine essence as such, the essential attributes, the divine persons, and the personal attributes, yielding four basic areas for consideration as parts of the larger *locus de Deo*.[55] Furthermore, the discussion of God follows a pattern of moving from God absolutely considered (the divine essence) to God relatively considered, namely, in his personal relations and acts (the Trinity), while the discussion of each of these primary divisions moves from *onomatologia*, the consideration of names, to *pragmatologia*, the discussion of substance or issues.[56] In simplified form, the model remains in Rijssen's late seventeenth-century synopsis: "We know four things of God, 1. Names. 2. Essence.

50. Zanchi, *De natura Dei*, I.i.

51. Beza et al., *Propositions and Principles*, V.

52. Bartholomaus Keckermann, *Systema S.S. Theologiae*, in *Opera*, vol. II, separate pagination at end of volume, p. 67.

53. Maccovius, *Loci communes*, xv (p. 120).

54. Wendelin, *Christianae theologiae libri duo*, I.i.3-4.

55. Spanheim, *Disp. theol.*, IX (*de Deo* I).iii.

56. Spanheim, *Disp. theol.*, IX (*de Deo*).iv.

3. Persons. 4. Works."[57] As a preamble to the problem of the divine names and essence, Rijssen justifies the terminology he plans to use: *essence, substance, subsistence, persons, Trinity, homoousios* — Can they rightly be predicated of God? Such terms can be used of God if they are used correctly as descriptions of truths stated in Scripture: Rijssen refers his readers to Calvin's argument.[58] In sum, the discussion does not pass from a rational and philosophical discussion of essence to a revelational discussion of Trinity: there is, in effect, one doctrine of God in the orthodox systems, distinguished, but not separated, into two basic topics, both of which are addressed in the context of faith.

3.2 The Existence and Knowledge of God

A. Knowledge of God and the Divine Incomprehensibility

1. The sources and the limitations of our knowledge of God. Many of the larger orthodox theological systems preface their doctrines of God with a discussion of the knowledge of God, including both a general discussion of the sources and the character of our knowledge of God and a more specific discussion of the proofs of God's existence.[59] This discussion provides the Reformed orthodox with an initial framework for developing the doctrine of God — specifically for understanding the relationship of innate apprehensions of the divine both to rational discernment of God's handiwork in nature and to the biblical revelation in a unified doctrine of God. As can also be argued of the proofs of God's existence, the more general discussion of the knowledge of God offers an initial justification for a doctrine of God that is both biblical and rational — on the assumption that biblical revelation was neither irrational nor incongruous, but instead normative for rational, human presentations of doctrine, and normative in such a way as to respect the demands both of reason and of piety.[60]

The tacit assumption found in much modern discussion of Protestant orthodoxy, that the Protestant orthodox were unaware of the difficulties involved in theological formulation, is a misconception of considerable proportion. That this is the case appears with the greatest clarity in the orthodox statement of the problem of the knowledge of God. "This is the chief point of saving knowledge," wrote Binning, "to know God; and this is the first point or degree of the true knowledge of God, to discern how ignorant we are of him, and to find him beyond all knowledge."[61] God is and must remain incomprehensible to us: we cannot know God "in himself," but we see only

---

57. Rijssen, *Summa theol.*, III.ii.

58. Rijssen, *Summa theol.*, II.iii, controversia I; cf. Calvin, *Institutio* (1559), I.xiii.5.

59. E.g., Beza, et al., *Propositions and Principles of Divinitie*, I.i-v; Heidanus, *Corpus theologiae*, II (pp. 54-55); Burman, *Synopsis theologiae*, II.xiv.1-6; Maresius, *Collegium theologicum*, II.1-2; Leigh, *Body of Divinity*, II.i (pp. 144-147); Mastricht, *Theoretico-practica theologia*, II.ii; Turretin, *Inst. theol. elencticae*, III.i.4-5; on the knowledge of God in the teaching of the Reformers, see *PRRD*, I, 6.1 (A); 6.3 (A).

60. Cf. Richard A. Muller, "The Dogmatic Function of St. Thomas' Proofs: A Protestant Appreciation," in *Fides et Historia*, XXIV (1992), pp. 15-29.

61. Binning, *Common Principles*, VIII, in *Works*, p. 40.

as in a mirror or in a mystery.[62] The Reformed orthodox make this point initially in their prolegomena, in the distinction between the divine archetypal theology and the various forms of ectypal theology found among creatures, including the human nature of Christ and the angels.[63] The point is reinforced in the doctrine of God either in introductory discussions of essence and attributes, in the occasional placement of "incomprehensibility" among the attributes, or as an inference from such attributes as divine infinity, omniscience, or wisdom.[64]

Knowledge of God is possible, but only on the basis of divine revelation. Even this revelation, moreover, does not conform to the demands of natural reason:

> The Lord gives a definition of himself, but such an one as is no more clear than himself to our capacities; a short one indeed, and such you may think it says not much — "I am." What is it that may not say so, "I am that I am?" The least and most inconsiderable creature hath its own being. ... you would think the superlatives of wise, good, strong, excellent, glorious, and such like, were more beseeming his majesty; an yet there is more majesty in this simple style than in all others; but a "natural man" cannot behold it, for it is "spiritually discerned."[65]

A regenerate mind is requisite for drawing correct theological and practical conclusions from the biblical text.[66]

God is not known through his essence — but "through his effects and his names, by which he wills to reveal his virtues to us."[67] The nature of God can be known, then, "according to the manner of divine Revelation, and the measure of our knowledge" and is to be discussed in terms of the name of God and in terms of the definition. The exposition of doctrine, moreover, proceeds on the premises that whatever is said or predicated of God is not God himself — for God is ineffable — but rather what the human mind in its limitation can apprehend about God. Indeed, a distinction must be made between "comprehension" and "apprehension," inasmuch as we cannot have an "adequate" idea of God in the sense that we know and understand God fully or are able "fully to describe" the divine perfections, but we can have "some imperfect or inadequate ideas of what surpasses our understanding and we can have "a full conviction that God hath those infinite perfections, which no creature can

---

62. Le Blanc, *Theses theol.*, *De Dei simplicitate*, ii, citing 1 Cor. 13:12.

63. Cf. *PRRD*, I, 5.2 (C); 5.5 (A).

64. Thus, Ridgley, *Body of Divinity* (1855), pp. 90-91; cf. Flavel, *Exposition of the Catechism*, in *Works*, 6, pp. 147, 150.

65. Binning, *Common Principles*, VIII, in *Works*, pp. 40-41.

66. Gillespie, *A Treatise of Miscellany Questions*, in *The Works of Mr. George Gillespie*, 2 vols. (Edinburgh: Ogle, Oliver, and Boyd, 1846) p. 101; cf. Thomas Gataker, *Shadowes without Substance, or Pretended New Lights: Together with the Impieties and Blasphemies that Lurk Under Them* (London, 1646), p. 82; note also that the point is made by Zanchi, *Praefatiuncula*, cols. 417-418; William Whitaker, *A Disputation on Holy Scripture, against the Papists, especially Bellarmine and Stapleton*, trans. and ed. by William Fitzgerald (Cambridge: Cambridge University Press, 1849), IX.5 (pp. 470-471); Rijssen, *Summa theol.*, II.xii, xvii; and see the discussion in *PRRD*, II, 7.4 (A.1).

67. Cocceius, *Summa theol.*, III.ix.1.

comprehend."[68] Thus, language about God proceeds cautiously, frequently according to a negative manner; as when God is called "incomprehensible" or "infinite." These identifications of God are intended to "remove far from him the imperfections of creatures."[69] When God is named affirmatively the language is either essential or relative.[70]

2. Ways of knowing God and the piety of theology. Knowledge of God is, for the creature, at best incomplete — and theology or the "word about God" is difficult to formulate:

> God being infinite and our understanding finite, betwixt the two there is no proportion: who knows the things of God save the Spirit of God? A created understanding can no more comprehend God than a vial-glass can contain the waters of the sea.[71]

Our theology is, at best, imperfect.[72] Nevertheless, as the Reformed orthodox learned from the older tradition, potentially from Durandus, there are three ways of approach to the problem of knowledge of and language concerning God, the *via causationis* or *causalitatis*, the *via eminentiae*, and the *via negationis*. The "way of causation" understands that a cause can be known in some manner from its effects and that "we can ascend from secondary causes to the first cause, Ps. 94:9: 'He that planted the ear, shall he not hear, and he that formed the eye, shall he not see.'"[73] By the "way of eminence" we attribute eminently to God all of the "perfections" known from creatures — while by the "way of negation we remove from God the imperfections known from creatures."[74] In Leigh's words,

> (1) All perfections which we apprehend, must be ascribed unto God, and that after a more excellent manner than can be apprehended; as that he is in himself by himself and of himself: that he is one, true, good, and holy.
> (2) We must remove from him all imperfections whatsoever; he is Simple, Eternal, Infinite, Unchangeable.
> (3) He is the supreme cause of all.[75]

Thus, the *via eminentiae* gathers the "positive attributes" of God, the *via negativa* the "negative attributes," and the *via causalitatis* the "relative attributes" that indicate the way in which God relates to his creatures.[76] To the scholastic mind, therefore, the doctrine of the divine attributes is clearly not a matter of abstract speculation but rather a basic statement of the way of knowing God, in the case of the *via causalitatis*,

---

68. Ridgley, *Body of Divinity* (1855), p. 91.

69. Trelcatius, *Schol. meth.*, I.iii (pp. 50-51).

70. Trelcatius, *Schol. meth.*, I.iii (p. 52).

71. Leigh, *Treatise*, II.i (p. 2); cf. Binning, *Common Principles*, VIII, in *Works*, p. 41.

72. Gomarus, *Disputationes*, I.xlvi; Cocceius, *Summa theol.*, i.5; Burman, *Synopsis theol.*, I.ii.30, 38; Heidegger, *Corpus theol.*, I.; cf. the discussion of ectypal theology in *PRRD*, I, 5.2 (C.3).

73. Turretin, *Inst. theol. elencticae*, III.ii.8.

74. Turretin, *Inst. theol. elencticae*, III.ii.8.

75. Leigh, *Treatise*, II.i (p. 2).

76. Turretin, *Inst. theol. elencticae*, III.ii.8.

a way rooted in the temporal reality of the created order. Nor is it the case that these three ways of approach to God are purely philosophical: the Reformed orthodox typically correlate the rational exercise with biblical arguments and thereby approach the three ways more as patterns of classification than as a basis for deduction.[77]

Indeed, the orthodox recognize an intimate relationship between the various approaches to the knowledge of God and true religion or piety: despite the difficulty of knowing God, these doctrines are necessary "because man was made for that end, that he might rightly acknowledge and worship God, love and honor him." Moreover, that doctrine or "divinity" which takes Scripture as its rule and which teaches "of God and his works" is "the end of all divine Revelation, *John* 5:39." Ignorance of God is the misery of alienation from him.[78]

If God is difficult to know and cannot be known fully, he nevertheless appears clearly to belief — and at a fundamental level, his existence is in need of no proof:

> That God is, is the most manifest, clear, evident, ungainsayable truth in the world. It is the first verity, and the principal verity, from which all other truth hath its original and it is the foundation of all true goodness and religion truly to believe it; so saith the Author to the Hebrews, *He that cometh to God*, to do him any service or to receive any benefit from him, *must believe*, that is, be firmly and undoubtedly persuaded, *that God is*.[79]

It is, however, necessary to seek after God in Christ and in "his word" and, indeed, to believe certain truths such as "the doctrine of the Trinity [and] the Mediator."[80] Thus, the Protestant orthodox approach to the problem of the knowledge of God, typically presented in connection with the proofs in the *locus de Deo*, returns to the issue stated in the prolegomena, that religion is the true knowledge and worship of God.

3. Supernatural theology, natural theology, and metaphysics — relation and distinction in Reformed thought in the era of orthodoxy. There were differences among the Reformed as to the character and foundations of natural theology: whereas various of the later writers simply declared that reason was the *principium* of natural theology, the early orthodox, notably Alsted, argued that reason, universal experience, and Scripture were the *principia* of natural theology, creating considerable common ground between the disciplines. This assumption of a common ground, together with the sense that natural theology was a partial and lesser form of the truth, but nonetheless truth, enabled the Reformed orthodox to draw on natural theology and metaphysics as ancillary disciplines — under the rules for the use of reason philosophy

---

77. See further below, 3.3d.

78. Leigh, *Treatise*, II.i (p. 2).

79. Leigh, *Treatise*, II.i (p. 3), citing Heb. 11:6.

80. Matthew Poole, *Synopsis criticorum aliorumque sacrae scripturae interpretum et commentatorum, summo studio et fide adornata*, 5 vols. (London, 1669-1676), in loc.

in general — or, at least, to use reason in their exposition of supernatural theology in a manner cognate to the use of reason in natural theology and metaphysics.[81]

In the most generalized sense, the rational discussion of God and world that appears in natural theology is virtually identical to that which appears in metaphysics understood, in the traditional sense, as *prima philosophia*. Nonetheless, the two disciplines come at the topic from somewhat different angles: natural theology understands its object as God, rationally and experientially addressed on the basis of natural revelation, and accepts the division of the subject into the discussion of God and God's works, whereas metaphysics understands its object as Being, addressed rationally. Since metaphysics is not theology, it does not rest on revelation and, unlike the natural theology defined by Alsted, would not draw on Scripture as a *principium*. God is to be understood as the object of metaphysics insofar as God is included under the general definition of Being — namely, the primary category in the division of Being into infinite and finite or into "being of itself" (*Ens a se*) and "being by participation" (*ens per participationem*).

It was precisely on this point that the early orthodox era evidences, not a universal acceptance of metaphysics as an adjunct of theology, but a debate over the relationship of theology and metaphysics and an interest in the delimitation of metaphysics as a discipline.[82] Neither Keckermann nor Maccovius, for example, discussed God as a topic in their metaphysics: for although discussion of the divine essence and attributes is nominally meta-physical, it is not part of the science of metaphysics as understood by the Reformed. According to Keckermann, God is not discussed in metaphysics in as much as God is "above being" in the sense that God is "beyond all substance and accident." It is sufficient, he declares, for metaphysics to acknowledge "the dependence of all substance on God, inasmuch as [God is] the foundation and source of all substance."[83] Maccovius notes that "the efficient cause and the goal of being in general is God alone," but the proper subject of metaphysics is being in general (*Ens in genere*) or being understood as being (*Ens, quatenus Ens*): God considered as God, therefore, is not discussed in metaphysics — nor is metaphysics the category to which the doctrine of God belongs.[84] Still, the point is not that metaphysics has no bearing on the discussion of God. Rather, as in the cases of reason and philosophy in general, so also in the case of metaphysics, theology occupies the prior place and its *principia* remain both cognitively and essentially above the *principia* of other forms of knowing.

---

81. Cf. Keckermann, *Systema ss. theologiae*, I.ii (p. 69, col. 1); cf. Beza et al., *Propositions and Principles*, I.iii-iv.

82. Thomas Barlow registered the debate in his *Exercitationes aliquot metaphysicale, de Deo: quod sit objectum metaphysicae* (London, 1637); cf. William Ames, *Adversus metaphysicam* (Franecker, 1625).

83. Keckermann, *Scientiae metaphysicae brevissima synopsis*, in *Opera*, I, col. 2015. Still, despite these reservations, Keckermann did predicate *substantia* of both God and creatures, distinguishing between infinite and finite substance, see his *Systema logicae minus*, I.iii, in *Opera*, I, col. 175-176.

84. Maccovius, *Metaphysica*, pp. 2-3, 6; cf. Hottinger's denial that God's unity of being is a unity either of genus or species: *Cursus theologicus*, III.iv, canon C.

Metaphysics, therefore, can serve theology — and God's existence and being cannot be fully or properly explained without metaphysics.[85]

This determination to reserve the doctrine of God, strictly understood, for theology, if argued by some of the Reformed, was not the universal approach to metaphysics in the seventeenth century. Neither Suárez nor Campanella removed consideration of God from metaphysics but, once having observed a division of the subject into finite and infinite being, incorporated natural theology into their metaphysics.[86] An approach among the Reformed that developed in dialogue with the Suárezian model can be found in the thought of Alsted, Burgersdijk, and Heereboord. Alsted and Burgersdijk divided the subject of Being (*Ens*) into the discussion of Being of itself (*Ens a se*) and Being from another (*Ens ab alio*), namely God and creatures — further distinguished, following Suárez and in a somewhat Thomistic fashion, into *Ens per essentiam* and *Ens per participationem*,[87] necessary, infinite Being and contingent, finite being.[88] Neither Alsted, nor Burgersdijk, nor Heereboord, moreover, drew on biblical categories, discussed divine attributes such as love, mercy, or righteousness in their metaphysical treatises, or moved past the logic of infinite spiritual being to draw doctrinal conclusions concerning the Trinity.

At least in the understanding of the Reformed orthodox, therefore, their doctrine of God was not, in the strictest sense, a matter of metaphysics, nor could metaphysics account for the entire doctrine of God — although, clearly, the Reformed metaphysicians did understand their discussions of the divine essence, simplicity, infinity, intellect, and will as supportive of orthodoxy. This relationship between the disciplines meant that the exercise of reason in the doctrine of God would produce, in the systems of Christian doctrine written in the seventeenth century, discussions of the proofs of God's existence, the divine essence, and the essential properties, namely, the attributes of simplicity, spirituality, immensity, infinity, eternity, omnipresence, intellect, and will that reflected arguments found in the natural theologies and the metaphysics of the era — but in the context of a use of Scripture as the primary source for the doctrine of essence and attributes; in the interpretive context of other attributes, namely, divine virtues and affections that were not usually identified as a subject for either natural theology or metaphysics; and in relation to the doctrine of the Trinity and of the soteriological issues of the system as a whole, none of which belonged to the realm of natural theology or metaphysics. The *theological*, as distinct from

---

85. Keckermann, *Praecognitorum philosophicorum*, col. 37A.

86. Cf. Francis Suárez, *Disputationes metaphysicae: posteriorem partem ... in quibus et universa naturalis theologia ordinate traditur*, in *Opera omnia*, vol. 26; with Tomasso Campanella, *Universalis philosophiae, seu metaphysicarum rerum* (Paris, 1638), Lib. VII: "Unitatem importare primitatem, divinitatem, & entitatem supremam, simpliciter, vel in genere, vel ex nostro instituto..." (Pars. II, pp. 111-240).

87. J. H. Alsted, *Metaphysica [Methodus metaphysicae] tribus libris tractata; per praecepta methodica:theoremata selecta: & commentariola dilucida* (Herborn, 1613), pp. 24, 32-3; Franco Burgersdijk, *Institutiones metaphysicae libri duo* (Leiden: 1640), II.iii.1-3; cf. Heereboord, *Meletemata philosophica, De ente infinito*, ii (p. 48); on Suárez, see Copleston, *History of Philosophy*, III, 22.7.

88. Burgersdijk, *Institutiones metaphysicae*, II.iii.4-5.

philosophical, exposition was, consistently, an exposition of biblical materials through the use of accepted categories of rational argumentation. In addition, as opposed to the metaphysical contemplation of God as Being, Reformed orthodox theology explicitly sought to understand God in this life, as an anticipation of and preparation for the life eternal: the interest is practical rather than purely contemplative.[89]

B. Nature, Reason, and the Problem of the Proofs of the Existence of God in Reformed Theology

1. The form and character of the proofs in Reformed orthodoxy.

The question of the existence of God (*existentia Dei*) does not appear in all of the Reformed scholastic systems and, when it does appear, has an apologetic and polemical function rather than a substantive or formative one in the course of theological system.[90] In neither the early nor the high orthodox eras do we find the proofs stated as a basis in rational philosophy or natural theology upon which the system of revealed doctrine can build: the use of the proofs and of natural theology as a prologue to a system of revealed doctrine occurs only in the eighteenth century under the impact of Wolffian rationalism. Indeed, apart form the very real apologetic concern to refute both "theoretical" and "practical" atheism, the proofs serve only an interest in systematic completeness. Just as the *locus de theologia* began with the question *An sit?* — whether there might be such a thing as theology to discuss — so does the *locus de Deo* also begin with the logically first question, that of the existence of God.[91] Of course, the question has been already answered by faith in the preceding *loci*, and the proofs appear primarily as the answer of faith to the atheists.

What was also apparent to the Reformed orthodox was that the logic of the proofs, albeit taken from philosophy or from a more philosophical form of theology, was nonetheless a logic that both reflected some of the concerns of Scripture and supplied some of the needs of piety. Their discussions of the proofs recognize fully that believers fundamentally and ultimately need no proof precisely because they are believers — but also that believers do need, mediately, as it were, tools and weapons for their spiritual arsenals. The proofs fill a need in a world where doubts arise and atheists abound. They reflect the assumption of Scripture itself that "he that cometh to God must believe that He is" (Hebrews 11:6) and that God is He "who is" (cf. Exodus 3:14 and Revelation 1:4, 8, 11, 18; 21:6), the source of all being, the *fons essendi*. These proofs, then, are not only manifestations of a partial return to scholastic argumentation — they are also evidences of the presence in Protestant thought of a tradition of piety and of biblical interpretation in which the logic of the proofs was echoed at a series of levels, many of which depart from the strictly philosophical, and relate the proofs to the concerns of faith and doctrine. This limitation of the function of the proofs as well as their association with issues of faith and doctrine draws, moreover, on the

---

89. *Synopsis purioris theol.*, VI.ii.
90. The foundational study of this issue remains Platt, *Reformed Thought and Scholasticism*.
91. Cf. Le Blanc, *Theses theol.*, *Quibus demonstratur Deum esse*, ii.

assumption of the incomprehensibility of God and on the recognition that *principia* are indemonstrable in any a priori sense and, at most, can be inferred from their effects or results.

We have no preliminary divisions to cite from Polanus, who omits the proofs from his basic *partitiones* but includes a rather cursory treatment of them in the larger *Syntagma*. Calvin, Vermigli, Beza, Zanchi, Perkins, Trelcatius, and Gomarus do not note the standard "proofs" or, strictly speaking, the demonstrative arguments. Musculus, Calvin, Ursinus, Perkins, Cloppenburg, Turretin, Le Blanc, Pictet, Leigh, Mastricht, and Charnock all present arguments, but as we shall see, do not state them in strictly logical forms — the treatment is rhetorical and hortatory, particularly in the works of the English theologians, and tends not to distinguish between truly logical arguments, like the cosmological and teleological proofs, and purely rhetorical arguments, like that from the common consent of mankind (*e consensu gentium*). The question *An sit Deus* is profane and unnecessary inasmuch as the principle "that God exists" is not proved but presupposed by Christians. Yet, both the subjective "light of the mind" and the objective "light of being" demonstrate the truth of what conscience already knows. The "antitrinitarians," thus, err when they deny an innate knowledge of God.[92] Of the Reformed orthodox, only those with Cartesian sympathies — notably, Burman and Heidanus — appear to allow the ontological argument: the others either reject it or simply do not mention it.

2. The Reformers and the proofs: Melanchthonian beginnings. The increasing interest in the proofs of the existence of God evidenced in the Reformed systems of the mid- and late sixteenth century cannot simply be accounted for in terms of the increased reliance of Protestant writers on the methods and tools of the older scholasticism or in terms of the resurgence of Aristotelian metaphysics in the second half of the century. The claim of the proofs to refute atheists, specifically, "practical," as distinct from metaphysical or "speculative," atheists, presupposes the existence of adversaries, and these adversaries were present during the early decades of the Reformation: the Renaissance and Reformation had resulted in an intellectual pluralism in religion and philosophy such that "freethinkers" and "Deists" were capable of spreading their ideas even when censorship laws frequently forbade the publication of their writings.[93] Calvin's colleague and close friend Pierre Viret recognized the presence of these early "deists" and warned against them.[94]

The first statement of proofs of the existence of God in Protestant theology occurs, most probably, in the 1535 edition of Melanchthon's *Loci communes*. Melanchthon had not noted the proofs in the earlier edition of the *Loci* (1521). He had, in fact, there

---

92. Spanheim, *Disp. theol.*, IX (*de Deo* I).ii.

93. Cf. J. M. Robertson, *A History of Freethought, Ancient and Modern to the Period of the French Revolution*, fourth edition, revised and expanded (1936; repr., London: Dawsons, 1969), with Lucien Febvre, *The Problem of Unbelief in the Sixteenth Century: The Religion of Rabelais*, trans. Beatrice Gottlieb (Cambridge, Mass.: Harvard University Press, 1982).

94. Pierre Viret, *Instruction chrestienne*, pt. II, prefatory letter; cited in *Pierre Viret d'aprè lui-même*, pp. 233-236; cf. *PRRD*, I, 1.3 (A.4).

indicated a distrust of those who would argue the existence of God by means of syllogisms.[95] It is a vast overstatement of a point, however, to argue that Luther's polemic against abuses in late medieval theology had somehow banned consideration of the proofs from Protestant theology and that Melanchthon's *Loci* of 1535 represent a radically new point of departure: there were no objections heard from Luther over Melanchthon's 1535 *Loci communes*, despite various differences that had begun to appear between his thought and Melanchthon's. More importantly, in 1535, we are still at a stage of initial formulation when Protestants were developing their theological positions based upon the materials provided both by the Reformation and by the earlier tradition.[96] On this particular issue, moreover, Melanchthon's intention was not to offer a rational foundation for theological system but to indicate that there was available to humanity in general, in the created order itself, a fundamental, non-saving knowledge of God. The argument arose in the context of the exegesis of Romans 1:18, and it had much in common with Luther's own views on the general knowledge of God, as found in his 1535 commentary on Galatians.[97]

The systematic placement and the logical forms of Melanchthon's proofs are also significant. Melanchthon assumed that the existence of God did not need proof and placed the arguments into his doctrine of creation as a way of moving from the existent creator, by way of the forms of divine activity and by way of human recognition of that activity, to the doctrine of creation. This placement and use of the proofs is evident in the *Loci communes* of Melanchthon's greatest pupil, Martin Chemnitz,[98] and it carries over into Reformed theology in the thought of yet another important Melanchthon student, Zacharias Ursinus. In both Chemnitz' and Ursinus' work, however, there are substantive changes: Chemnitz refers to elements of the proofs in his *locus* on creation largely because he is commenting on Melanchthon — but he also transferred his major discussion of the proofs to his preliminary section on the general and special knowledge of God.[99] Ursinus, similarly, argues the proofs first in his introduction to the doctrine of God and then restates elements of the proofs as part of a philosophical argument, secondary to and supportive of arguments drawn from Scripture, "that the world was created, and that by God."[100] We are impressed, here, as in the proofs offered by Melanchthon and Chemnitz, with an absence of logical rigor and philosophical elaboration and with the mixture of logical and philosophical with purely rhetorical arguments.

3. **Calvin and the proofs.** Calvin, like Viret, spoke of atheists in his time, singling out for debate those who held to the theory that religion originated, not from a

---

95. Melanchthon, *Loci communes* (1521), in CR 21, col. 119; cf. Platt, *Reformed Thought*, p. 13.

96. On the nature and limits of Melanchthon's "rationalism" see Clyde L. Manschreck, "Reason and Conversion in the Thought of Melanchthon," in Franklin H. Littell, ed., *Reformation Studies: Essays in Honor of R. H. Bainton* (Richmond: John Knox, 1962), pp. 168-180.

97. Cf. Platt, *Reformed Thought*, pp. 14-15.

98. Chemnitz, *Loci communes*, iv.2, 6 (Preus, pp. 157-158, 172).

99. Chemnitz, *Loci communes*, i.1(Preus, pp. 52-53).

100. Ursinus, *Commentary*, pp. 121-123, 142-143.

rudimentary knowledge of the divine, but out of the desire of a few subtle and crafty individuals, who themselves believed nothing, to subject "simple folk" to their authority. "I confess," Calvin writes,

> that in order to hold men's minds in greater subjection, clever men have devised very many things in religion by which to inspire the common folk with reverence and to strike them with terror. But they would never have achieved this if man's minds had not already been imbued with a firm conviction about God, from which the inclination toward religion springs as from a seed.[101]

Calvin makes this point concerning the general knowledge of God available to all human beings in the early portion of his argument on the knowledge of God, before he incorporates biblical materials into his argument.[102]

Whereas it is correct that Aquinas' proofs of the existence of God are not found in Calvin's *Institutes*, there is no ground for claiming that such proofs "do violence to the motive of [Calvin's] theology."[103] Nor does Calvin's argument at his point indicate a massive discontinuity with "scholastic Calvinism." It is probable that Calvin's choice of a discursive, rhetorically determined form of exposition for the *Institutes* generally led him to use rhetorical rather than demonstrative arguments: he therefore presses the Ciceronian point of the universal belief in God, the rhetorical argument *e consensu gentium*.[104] Calvin also appeals to the terrors of the guilty conscience — again, a persuasive rather than a demonstrative argument.[105] In addition, "men of sound judgment" accept the fundamental sense of divinity, while only the "impious" reject it, perhaps a form of the rhetorical argument *ad verecundiam*, an appeal to accepted values.[106] The order and workmanship of the world provide proofs or examples (*documenta*) of the existence of God, specifically noting the movement of the heavens, the premise of the cosmological argument.[107] Human beings are not, moreover, the source of their own existence, and it is "preposterous" to ignore the Author of the gifts we receive in the world, given that "he from whom all things draw their origin

---

101. Calvin, *Institutes*, I.iii.2; cf. Josef Bohatec, *Budé und Calvin: Studien zur Gedankenwelt des französischen Frühumanismus* (Graz: Herman Böhlaus, 1950), pp. 149-240.

102. Cf. Calvin, *Institutes*, I.ii-iii, where there is an emphasis, by way of citation, on pagan sources, with *Institutes*, I.iv-v, where the emphasis shifts to biblical sources.

103. Contra T. H. L. Parker, *The Doctrine of the Knowledge of God: A Study in Calvin's Theology*, revised ed. (Grand Rapids: Eerdmans, 1959), p. 9, note 1; cf. Benjamin B. Warfield, "Calvin's Doctrine of the Knowledge of God," in Samuel Craig, ed., *Calvin and Augustine* (Philadelphia: Presbyterian and Reformed Publishing Company, 1956), p. 41, note 8.

104. Calvin, *Institutes*, I.iii.1.

105. Calvin, *Institutes*, I.iii.2.

106. Calvin, *Institutes*, I.iii.3.

107. Calvin, *Institutes*, I.v.1-2; cf. Aquinas, *Summa theol.*, Ia, a. 2, q. 3 (the "third way"). Calvin's language is of interest: he notes (*Institutes*, I.v.9) that "elaborate demonstration" (*laboriosa demonstratione*) of the divine majesty is needed given the numerous "testimonies" (*testimonia*) to the fulness of God's glory in nature. He also uses the term *documentum*, example or proof. The issue broached by Calvin is hardly the unsuitability of "proofs" of God's existence — but rather the more specific question of literary genre and a preference for rhetorical argument over logical demonstration.

must be eternal and have beginning from himself" — a rhetorical form of the argument for a necessary being on the basis of contingent existence.[108] If, then, the *Institutes* does not contain demonstrations of the existence of God, it certainly contains arguments to the point, several of which relate to the traditional proofs. Both these less logically stated forms of the logical proofs and Calvin's rhetorical and hortatory arguments find, moreover, precise parallels in the Reformed orthodox systems, in which rhetorical arguments stand alongside the logical proofs and in which the logical proofs often take on rhetorical rather than purely demonstrative forms.[109]

The *Institutes*, moreover, does not contain all of Calvin's views on demonstrations of God's existence. In his commentary on Acts, Calvin returns to the theme of Romans, chapter 1 — that, although faith rests on the Word, still human beings are left, in the midst of God's handiwork and providential care, without excuse for their unbelief. At Lystra, Paul and Barnabas argue the existence of God from evidences in nature: they did not argue "subtly ... after the manner of the philosophers," given that this was an "unlearned" audience, but nonetheless they took as their "principle (*principium*), that in the order of nature there is a certain and clear manifestation (*manifestationum*) of God" and that "the wonderful workmanship of nature manifestly shows the providence of God."[110] Calvin indicates that Paul drew "proofs" (*probationes*) from nature because, confronted by pagans, he could not rest on the authority of Scripture,[111] that a person can be "brought to acknowledge God" by "contemplating the heavens" — given that these revelatory characters are "large and bright" to be "read with the greatest ease,"[112] and that God "meets us everywhere in the fabric of the world."[113]

4. Bullinger, Musculus, and Hyperius on the proofs. Like many later thinkers, Bullinger begins by discussing false and deficient ideas of God held by the pagan philosophers: in the words of Tertullian, the "philosophers are the patriarchs of heretics." The opinions of Plutarch and others derive

> from none other fountain than from the boldness and unskillfulness of men, which are not ashamed of their own device and brain to add and apply to God the things from which he is most far and free. ... who, I pray you, is able with his understanding to conceive the being (*essentiam*) of God, when as indeed no man did ever fully understand of what fashion the soul of man is.... There are given many reasons of natural philosophy; but the work of God doth still abide more great and wonderful than that the wit or speech of men is able to comprehend or express it.[114]

---

108. Calvin, *Institutes*, I.i.1; v.6; cf. Aquinas, *Summa theol.*, Ia, a. 2, q. 3 (the "fifth way").

109. See the excellent discussion of the proofs in various early orthodox compendia of Calvin's *Institutes*, in Platt, *Reformed Thought*, pp. 34-43. A general overview of the compendia is available in Olivier Fatio, "Présence de Calvin à l'époque de l'orthodoxie réformée: Les abrégées de Calvin à la fin du 16e et au 17e siècle," in W. Neuser, ed., *Calvinus Ecclesiae Doctor* (Kampen: J. H. Kok, 1978), pp. 171-207.

110. Calvin, *Commentary on Acts*, 14:17 (CTS Acts, II, pp. 19-20 = CO 46, col. 328).

111. Calvin, *Commentary on Acts*, 17:24 (CTS Acts, II, pp. 158-159 = CO 46, col. 410).

112. Calvin, *Commentary on the Psalms*, 19:1 (CTS Psalms, I, pp. 308, 313).

113. Calvin, *Commentary on the Psalms*, 104:4 (CTS Psalms, IV, p. 146).

114. Bullinger, *Decades*, IV.iii (p. 124).

No one can attain any certainty about the existence and nature of God from either his own thoughts or the theories of others: "God cannot be rightly known but by his word."[115]

Still, neither reliance on the Word nor the deficiencies of pagan philosophy lead Bullinger to reject other sources of knowledge of God:

> Now since this God doth in his word, by the workmanship of the world, by the holy scriptures, and by his oracles uttered by the mouth of the patriarchs, prophets, and apostles, yea, in the very minds and consciences of man, testify that he is, therefore did the kingly prophet David say with good reason: "The fool hath said in his heart, There is no God." For he must needs be an ass or a fool, which denieth the thing that is evident to all men in the world ... namely, that there is a God.[116]

All know that God exists, but to go further in description of God is difficult and, indeed, dangerous to the overly curious: believers ought to understand "that his eternal and incomprehensible power and unspeakable majesty cannot be defined, and cannot be comprehended in any name whatsoever."[117]

Still, there are several paths to the knowledge of God: God is best known through his revealed names, through the language of Scripture, and through the Son, but he is also known in a fourth way — through his works:

> Lo, the power and Godhead of God are these invisible things of God; and yet they are understood by the consideration of God's works: therefore even God himself is known by the works of God.[118]

These works are to be considered in two ways: first, the great works of creation, providence, and government, the works of God "laid before us to be beheld in things created" and, second, "the works of God ... in man, the very lord and prince of all creatures: not so much in the workmanship or making of man ... as in the works which toward man, or in man, or by man, the Lord himself doth finish and bring to pass."[119] God is manifest in his punishment of sin and his rewarding of the good.

God is also known, Bullinger argues, by comparison with the excellent things of the world — given that God is to be preferred above all finite good. By what is, in effect, the *via eminentiae*, God may be known as the "chief good." As an example of this form of our knowledge of God, Bullinger cites much of the fourteenth chapter of Isaiah, remarking that such descriptive passages as "Behold, all people are in comparison of him as a drop of a bucket" and "he shall cast out the isles as the smallest crumb of dust" are close in form to the imagery or visionary language of the *prosopopeial* passages examined as part of the second form of divine knowledge. A final way of knowing God

---

115. Bullinger, *Decades*, IV.iii (p. 125).

116. Bullinger, *Decades*, IV.iii (p. 125).

117. Bullinger, *Decades*, IV.iii (p. 126).

118. Bullinger, *Decades*, IV.iii (p. 150); cf. Calvin, *Commentary on Romans*, 1:20 (*CTS Romans*, p. 70).

119. Bullinger, *Decades*, IV.iii (pp. 151-152).

is through recourse to the sayings of the prophets and apostles which define God as most wise and merciful, as just and righteous. "Therefore we say that God is a savior, a liberal giver of all good things, an upright judge, and assured truth in performing his promises."[120]

An impetus similar to that underlying Melanchthon's inclusion of the proofs in his *Loci communes* can be identified in Musculus' *Loci communes* and Hyperius' *Methodus theologiae*. The traditionary rootage of Musculus' theology together with his Scotist and nominalist training led him to formulate a detailed doctrine of God and to state, not so much the proofs themselves, but the rationale for the proofs. It is eminently probable that Musculus was, for philosophical as well as theological reasons, wary of the proofs in their Thomistic form. Hyperius was perhaps the most consistent formulator of his generation, overtly pressing the questions of theological system, method, and dogmatic formulation: like Musculus, he understood the need to draw critically on traditional forms in order to produce a Protestant, but also churchly theology.

After his initial statement of the problem and the bounds of our knowledge of God, Musculus, in a rather scholastic fashion, poses the question "Whether there is a God?"[121] The question of the existence of God is one that would not have to be asked, he notes, were not "the heart of man ... sometimes assaulted with this kind of impiety." Musculus cites Cicero's *Of the Nature of the Gods* as giving the opinions of Protagoras, Diagoras Melius, and Theodorus Cyrenaicus: the first doubted the existence of God, the others denied it. Beyond that they had put forth the idea that belief in God was the invention of wise men devised to restrain those who could not be made obedient by reasonable argument. And then there is the fool of Psalm 14. We must first ascertain, therefore, that there is a God if our religion is not to be vain. It is first necessary "to believe that God is" and then to state "what essence of God we believe him to be."[122] Hyperius, perhaps somewhat more formally, begins his doctrine of God with the question "Whether God exists?" — noting that it is necessary to move from the discussion of the Scriptures as *principium* to the discussion of the author and *principium* of all things, and that it is fitting to begin with the question of God's existence. His exposition echoes Musculus, citing Psalm 14 and Cicero's reference to Diagoras.

Both Hyperius and Musculus argue that opinions and doubts, such as those of the ancient skeptics and atheists (and, by extension, their sixteenth-century followers), are placed in the mind by Satan. It is therefore necessary that all who would be saved confirm themselves in the knowledge of God's existence:

> For this cause and the authority of the Apostle, we have first proposed this question, whether there be a God, to admonish all them that be studious of Divinity, what not only they themselves shall firmly hold for the principal point of our Religion, but also what they shall as most assured instruct and beat into other men's heads, without which they can proceed not one step onward toward godliness, which is, that there is a God.[123]

---

120. Bullinger, *Decades*, IV.iii (pp. 152-154).
121. Musculus, *Loci communes*, I (*Commonplaces*, p. 2, col. 1).
122. Musculus, *Commonplaces*, I.i, p. 2, col. 2.
123. Musculus, *Commonplaces*, I.i, p. 2, col. 2; cf. Hyperius, *Methodus theologiae*, I (pp. 73-74).

In fact, the existence of God is so inscribed on the human heart that all men believe — or would believe were not doubts instilled in them by Satan. For all men are created in the image of God and "indeed with the light of reason."[124]

Unlike Musculus, who offers no further detail, Hyperius presents a fairly elaborate series of grounds for belief in the existence of God, the order of which is quite significant. First, he notes the secret or immediate revelation of God to certain holy people, namely, Adam, Seth, Enoch, Noah, Abraham, the other patriarchs, and the prophets. Second, he points to the Word of God in its unwritten and written forms.[125] Third, there is the testimony of God's "conservation and preservation of the world," which declares to all his eternal power and divinity and leaves unbelievers without excuse. Hyperius distinguishes here between arguments based on the magnitude and splendor of the universe in all its individual parts (as witnessed in Job 9, Psalm 19, Acts 14, and Hebrews 11) and the "perpetual movement" of all things as they pass into being, mutate, change their place, and pass out of existence, from which the existence of a first mover can be inferred (as witnessed in Job 9 and as taught by the Damascene, Aquinas, and Aristotle).[126] So, too, the existence of God can be inferred from the "ordinary movement of causes and effects," which points toward the existence of a most powerful and most wise being: this is the implication of Psalms 104 and 134, of Acts 14, and Job 5, 9, and 12 — and it was also recognized by Cicero.[127] Fourth, there are extraordinary events or miracles which also argue the existence of God. Fifth and sixth, the nature of the human being, made, according to Scripture, in the image of God and the admirable understanding of law and governance characteristic of human society both testify to the existence of God. These arguments, Hyperius concludes, have been widely recognized by theologians and philosophers and can be confirmed from the Word of God.[128]

5. The direction of the proofs: logical and rhetorical approaches and the problems of "speculative" and "practical" atheism. The rather diverse approach to the proofs and/or to various elements of the proofs, already identified, among the Reformers carried over into the early orthodox era. Lambert Daneau, who had studied in the Academy of Geneva, offered an interesting amalgam of the Thomistic five ways, other scholastic formulae, rhetorical arguments, and various testimonies. He introduces the proofs with the standard scholastic question, "Whether God exists?" Daneau then proceeds to offer arguments, as Fatio characterizes them, from external evidences, inward evidences, Scripture (miracles and the immortality of the soul), and natural

---

124. Musculus, *Commonplaces*, I.i, p. 3, col. 1.

125. See the discussion of unwritten and written Word in *PRRD*, II, 3.4 (A.2).

126. Hyperius, *Methodus theologiae*, I (pp. 75-77), citing John of Damascus, *De fide orthodoxa*, I.iii-iv; Aquinas, *Summa theol.*, I. q. 2, art. 3; and Aristotle, *Physica*, lib. 6-7.

127. Hyperius, *Methodus theologiae*, I (p. 77), citing Cicero, *De natura deorum*, II.2, 4.

128. Hyperius, *Methodus theologiae*, I (pp. 77-80), citing Psalm 104; Tertullian, *Apologia*, 17; Greqogy of Nazianzus, *Orationes*, 2; Pseudo-Augustine, *De cognitione verae vitae*; John of Damascus, *De fide orthodoxa*, I.iii-v; Aquinas, *Summa theol.*, I, q. 2, art. 3; commentaries on Romans 1, "principally" that of Melanchthon; and finally Cicero, *De natura deorum*, II.

reason, with favorable citations of Aquinas' approach as preferable to Ockham's, of Aristotle's *Metaphysics*, and Anselm's *Monologion*, plus references to Plato, Hermes Trismegistus, Augustine, Cicero, and Tertullian.[129] Another product of the Genevan academy, Franciscus Junius took an entirely different approach to the proofs: both in his early Heidelberg *Theses theologicae* and in his major efforts in Leiden, Junius consciously adopted Aquinas' five ways — without modification, either by way of philosophical nuances reflecting non-Thomistic trajectories of earlier thought or by way of adding the rhetorical arguments found in Calvin, Melanchthon, Ursinus, or Daneau.[130] Junius' colleague, the elder Trelcatius, offered no fully developed proofs, indicating only that the existence of God is undeniable, given both inward and outward evidences and the common assent of all humanity.[131]

Arguments for the existence of God, including such more strictly rhetorical statements of the common belief of all mankind, generally occur in two places in the orthodox systems. A few thinkers include them in the prolegomena prior to discussion of saving knowledge[132] while the larger number place them in the *locus de Deo* as part of the necessary refutation of atheism.[133] The prolegomena to the orthodox systems manifest a variety of opinion on the proofs from positive use, to simple neglect, and finally to outright antagonism. As Turretin wrote, the proofs have limited usefulness in the system of theology: "this question is rendered necessary by accursed madness of the Atheists, who have arisen in great numbers in this corrupt age."[134] The proofs do not relate to matters of salvation — and believers should take the existence of God for granted apart form proof.[135] Among the early orthodox, Ames, Polanus, Maccovius, and Wollebius either neglect or specifically exclude the proofs from Christian theology. Even so, some of the Reformed orthodox do not offer a separate discussion of the divine essence in its unity, but move directly to a foundational discussion of the divine names — thus Maccovius and Gomarus.[136]

The use of rhetorical arguments as well as logical proofs, together with the evangelical and hortatory thrust of the arguments presented by Calvin, Musculus, and Hyperius, also carries over into the era of Reformed orthodoxy. Indeed, the impact of Renaissance rhetoric, which accounts for the alteration of the mode of the proofs

---

129. Lambert Daneau, *Christianae isagoges ad christianorum theologorum locos communes, libri II* (Geneva, 1583), III (fol. 3r-5r); cf. Fatio, *Méthode et théologie*, pp. 158-159.

130. Junius, *Theses theologiae Heydelbergensis, De Deo: seu, Deum esse*, 20-37; and see Platt, *Reformed Thought*, pp. 131-143.

131. Lucas Trelcatius Sr., *Compendium locorum communium s. theologiae*, in *Opuscula theologia omnia* (Leiden, 1614), locus II; cited in Platt, *Reformed Thought*, p. 127.

132. Bucanus, *Institutions*, I (p. 1); Pictet, *Theol. chr.*, I.i.3-9.

133. Turretin, *Inst. theol. elencticae*, III.i; Marckius, *Compendium theologiae*, IV.x; Leigh, *System*, II.i; Charnock, *Discourse* I ("The Existence of God") and II ("On Practical Atheism); also note that this model appears as well in the Remonstrant theology: Phillip van Limborch, *Theologia christiana ad praxin pietatis ac promotionem pacis christiana unice directa* (Amsterdam, 1735), I.ii.

134. Turretin, *Inst. theol. elencticae*, III.i.3.

135. Pictet, *Theol. chr.*, I.ix. ; cf. Turretin, *Inst. theol. elencticae*, III.i.4.

136. Maccovius, *Loci communes*, xiv (p. 116ff.); Gomarus, *Disputationes*, iv-v.

in the teaching of the Reformers, is evident as well in the proofs as presented by the Reformed orthodoxy. This formal shift also indicates a different understanding of the proofs than is found among the medieval doctors: the rhetorical form indicates, among other things, that the primary force of the proofs is not so much to *demonstrate* as to *persuade* the opponent of the existence of God. The Reformed orthodox version of the proofs, therefore, neither operates at a primarily theoretical level nor serves to ground their theological systems in a rational foundation. The proofs are directed primarily against those who, for a variety of reasons, ignore the reality of God's power and grace in human life and act as if God were an absent deity.

Just as we saw in our earlier survey of theological prolegomena, the Reformed orthodox, very much like the Reformers, were sensitive to the interrelationship of the problem of knowledge and the problem of sin. Knowledge of God was viewed as both rational and saving — or, to state the issue in another way, questions of knowledge and of faith were recognized by the Protestant orthodox as distinct but not truly separable.[137] This conjunction of issues is perceivable even in the exposition of the proofs — and particularly in the way the exposition of the proofs identifies and argues against "atheism," specifically, against "practical atheism." In addition, the apologetic approach to the proofs of God's existence carries over, in a disputative system like Turretin's, into the entire *locus de Deo*, where the proofs properly so called are a demonstration of the existence of God against the atheists, the discussion of the nature or essence and attributes of God is identified as a demonstration of what God is against the heathen, and the doctrine of the Trinity as a demonstration of who God is against the Jews.[138]

Although the proofs are posed "against the atheists," the Reformed orthodox frequently argue that there are no "atheists properly so called," or, at least, very few.[139] The Reformed orthodox writers typically understood "atheist" in a very broad sense, designed to include all who denied the true God. "There are many kinds of Atheists," wrote Bucanus, for some entirely deny the existence of God, others worship "feigned gods," and still others acknowledge the "true God," but not "as he is," rather, "as they fancie him to be."[140] Given this broad sense of the term, the Reformed tend also to direct their arguments against the majority of atheists, namely, against those who do not deny God absolutely, but whose understandings of God are in need of major revision. The homiletical and hortatory dimension of the Reformed proofs is particularly clear in Charnock's initial identifications of atheists and atheism. The problem of atheism is not primarily philosophical but hamartiological: "though some few may choke in their hearts the sentiments of God and his providence, and positively deny them, yet there is something of a secret atheism in all, which is the foundation of the evil

---

137. Cf. John Flavel, *The Reasonableness of Personal Reformation and the Necessity f Conversion*, I.1-6, in *Works*, VI, pp. 472-475.

138. Turretin, *Inst. theol. elencticae*, III.i.2.

139. Turretin, *Inst. theol. elencticae*, III.ii.

140. Bucanus, *Institutions*, I (p. 6).

practices in their lives, not an utter disowning of the being of a God, but a denial or doubting of some of the rights of his nature."[141]

Whereas, then, there are either no or virtually no "speculative atheists," those who directly and expressly deny the existence of any superior Being and have absolutely no "sense and belief of deity," there are many people who have inward doubts concerning the identity of God or may deny to God such attributes or qualities — as providence or justice — that are necessary to any being rightly called God. In addition, they recognize the existence of "practical atheists."[142] Thus the text of the Psalm (14:1), "The fool hath said in his heart, there is no God," is not a philosophical text but a "description of man's corruption."[143] The point resonates strongly with Calvin's exegesis of the text.[144] Charnock continues,

> Practical atheism is natural to man in his corrupt state. It is against nature as constituted by God, but natural, as nature is depraved by man: the absolute disowning of the being of a God is not natural to men, but the contrary is natural; but an inconsideration of God, or misrepresentation of his nature, is natural to man as corrupt. A secret atheism, or a partial atheism, is the spring of all the wicked practices in the world.[145]

Charnock points out that the "fool" speaks in his "heart," not in his "head":

> Men may have atheistical hearts without atheistical heads. Their reasons may defend the notion of a Deity, while their hearts are empty of affection to the Deity.[146]

They have "unworthy imaginations" concerning God, engage in "debasing the Divine nature" through idolatry, and exalt human nature unduly.[147] If we are the question of who these practical atheists are, the probable answer is the "cultured despisers of religion" in Charnock's day, many of whom fit the description of Viret's "Deists."

Baxter, as much as Charnock, recognized the importance of the logic of the proofs to piety and to the refutation of the foolish and malicious attempt on the part of Satan to lead Christians "to question the being of [their] God." The existence of God, he indicates, following Hebrews 11:6, is "the first thing to be imprinted upon the soul": "He that cometh to God," the text reads, "must believe that God is." The fundamental nature of this knowledge, moreover, is obvious from the order of creation and providence:

> As sure as the streams come forth from the fountain, and as sure as Earth and Stones, and Beasts, and Men did never make themselves, nor do uphold themselves, or continue the course of nature in themselves and others, nor govern the world, so sure is there

---

141. Charnock, *Discourse* I, "The Existence of God," p. 24.

142. Turretin, *Inst. theol. elencticae*, III.ii.2-3.

143. Charnock, *Discourse* I, "The Existence of God," p. 24.

144. Calvin, *Commentary upon the Book of Psalms*, 14:1 (CTS *Psalms*, I, pp. 190-191).

145. Charnock, *Discourse* I, "The Existence of God," p. 25; cf. *Discourse* II, "On Practical Atheism," pp. 89-175.

146. Charnock, *Discourse* II, p. 89.

147. Charnock, *Discourse* II, pp. 138-141, 155-158.

an Infinite eternal Being that doth this. Every Atheist that is not mad must confess that *there is an Eternal Being*, that had *no beginning* or *cause*; the question is only, which this is! ... Certainly it is that Being that hath *being* it self from none that is the first cause of all other *beings*: and if it *caused* them, it must necessarily be every way *more excellent* than *they*, and contain all the good that it hath *caused*; For none can *give* that which it *hath not* to *give*; nor *make* that which is *better* than it self.... It could not have put *strength* and *power* into the Creatures, if it had not it self *more strength* and *power*. It could not have put *Wisdom* and *Goodness* into the Creature, if it had not *more Wisdom* and *Goodness* than all they. Whatever it is therefore that hath *more Power, Wisdom* and *Goodness* than all the world besides, that is it which *we* call God.[148]

Baxter wonders that "Democritists will ascribe all this to *Atomes*, and think that the *Motes* made the Sun."[149] The logic of the proofs — here an amalgam of the cosmological and causal arguments and the argument from perfection — was learned by Baxter from a close reading of scholastic sources, both medieval and post-Reformation. Baxter's arguments emphasize the relation of doctrine to piety — the proofs underline the fundamental recognition of the existence of God on the part of the human soul. If there is a distinction, there is certainly no separation, between the more speculative aspects of the theological discipline and the more practical application. Not only does the more speculative aspect here serve the practical, but clearly it can be seen to describe logically the fundamental apprehension of the divine: "the holy soul discerneth that the *Beginning* and the *End* of his Religion, the *substance* of his hope, is the *Being* of *Beings*, and not a shadow; that his faith is not a fansie."[150]

C. Proofs of the Existence of God in Reformed Orthodox Theology

1. The character and typologies of the proofs. The presence of proofs of God's existence in the theology of the Reformed orthodox ought not to be taken as an indication that they held God to be comprehensible or they believed the proofs to be an easy point of entry into the doctrine of God. The opposite is, in fact, the case. Their presentations of the various logical and rhetorical arguments for the existence of God are often prefaced by disclaimers indicating that we "can never comprehend" God and that the proofs only serve to provide "certain characters of his being, as will severally, or together, distinguish him from all things else."[151] Here especially one must proceed with reverence and not "rashly pry into the secrets" that God reserves for himself. So too, is the existence of God something that religion assumes and does not need to prove — which is why, in Cocceius' view the proofs follow the prolegomena and the doctrine of Scripture.[152]

---

148. Baxter, *Divine Life*, I.ii (pp. 14-15).
149. Baxter, *Divine Life*, I.ii (p. 15); cf. the nearly identical argument in Le Blanc, *Theses theol., Quibus demonstratur Deum esse*, xxxii.
150. Baxter, *Divine Life*, I.ii (p. 15).
151. Howe, *Living Temple*, I.ii (p. 27).
152. Turretin, *Inst. theol. elencticae*, I.iii.1, 3; Cocceius, *Summa theol.*, II.viii.12.

Still, as Cocceius indicates, the soul needs to be firmly grounded in the knowledge that God exists in order for it to grasp the great truths of the love of God and the hope of eternal life. Such knowledge comes only from revelation (whether natural or supernatural) — even so, Moses began his account of God's covenant with the words, "In the beginning God created the heavens and the earth"; God began his covenant with Abraham with the words, "I am your God"; and Paul begins his argument in Romans by identifying "that which may be known of God ... for God hath showed it unto them." There must always be a basic demonstration of God's existence, such as these, in order for there to be religion or theology.[153] These demonstrations must, moreover, be distinguished from the knowledge of God based solely on rational use of the light of nature, knowledge such as provides the basis for philosophy and that fails to reach the true God.[154]

Arguably, the purpose of the proofs in the Reformed orthodox systems was not to provide a logical or principial foundation for the doctrine of God on the basis of philosophy, but, within the context of a biblical and rational Christian theology, to point to certain attributes and qualities that can be predicated only of God, "whatever his being may contain more, or whatsoever other properties may belong to it, beyond what we can as yet compass in our present thoughts of him."[155] In addition, the proofs belong to the Reformed insistence, against the Socinians, that there is, in fact, a minimal *sensus divinitatis* and a genuine natural revelation.[156] They serve, therefore, an apologetic purpose against the atheists who disbelieve in God and disrespect Scripture and against the deniers of natural revelation. This apologetic purpose and the identity of those to whom the apology is addressed explain the emphasis on reason rather than on Scripture found in the larger number of traditionary proofs.[157]

Various of the Reformed orthodox theologians offer typologies of the proofs, with two rather distinct results. Burman, evidencing his Cartesian tendencies, indicates that the "idea of God" must be connected with the existence of God — and that this connection can be demonstrated both in an a priori and an posteriori manner. The *a priori* demonstration shows that the essence of God necessarily implies, indeed, "at the same time contains [his] existence." The a posteriori approach is twofold: first, on the ground that the idea of God requires a cause, namely, God; second, because we could not have the idea as we have it if the existence of God were not possible.[158] Burman clearly prefers the a priori argument, and he offers it in a form that follows closely Descartes' language: the idea of God demonstrates the existence of God

---

153. Cocceius, *Summa theol.*, II.viii.1-3; similarly, Martin Fotherby, *Atheomastix: Clearing foure Truthes, Against Atheists and Infidels: 1. That, There is a God. 2. That, There is but one God. 3. That, Jehovah, our God, is that One God. 4. That, The Holy Scripture is the Word of that God* (London: Nicholas Okes, 1622), pt. 1, I.i.1-3; Ward, *Philosophicall Essay*, I.ii (pp. 4-11).

154. Cocceius, *Summa theol.*, II.viii.8.

155. Howe, *Living Temple*, I.ii (p. 27).

156. Heidanus, *Corpus theol.*, I (p. 9); Turretin, *Inst. theol. elencticae*, I.iii.4; iv.1; Venema, *Inst. theol.*, ii (pp. 11-12); Wyttenbach, *Tentamen theol.*, III, §214.

157. Thus, Fotherby, *Atheomastix*, preface, fol. B5 recto.

158. Burman, *Synopsis theol.*, I.xiv.7.

inasmuch as whatever is clearly and distinctly perceived to be contained in the idea of a thing must be affirmed concerning it — and necessary existence is clearly and distinctly perceived to be contained in the idea of an infinite being. This perception is as certain as the perception that extension and divisibility are included in corporeal being. "Nor is it as if my cogitation bring this about ... but rather because the nature of God and the thing itself determines me to this understanding (*quia natura Dei & res ipsa ad hoc cogitandum me determinet*)."[159] By way of contrast, the other theologian of this generation with distinct Cartesian tendencies, Heidanus, avoids large-scale development of the proofs and argues the existence of God on the basis of Scripture as divine testimony and innate idea of God as the one than whom a greater cannot be conceived.[160]

The majority of the Reformed argue only the a posteriori rational proofs. Cloppenburg, for example, indicates that the existence of God is known in five ways: 1) from the interconnectedness of all things; 2) from their motion; 3) from the order of causes in the world; 4) from the governance of all things, which points toward the necessary existence of a prime mover and first efficient cause; and 5) from the sole rule (*monarchia*) of the entire universe, understood as "the procession of all causality, of secondary causes from the first efficient cause to the final and ultimate cause," inasmuch as it indicates the existence of infinite being (*ens infinitum*).[161]

The Reformed orthodox also note that the existence of God as the "first essence" that, of its very nature, "must be" is confirmed both by "testimony" and by "reason," thus posing what, in their view, were two sorts of proof.[162] This distinction between proofs of testimony and proofs of reason arises, at least in Cloppenburg's theology, out of his sense of the relationship of natural to revealed theology: against Socinus, he allows a "natural knowledge of God, part inborn (*congenita*) and part acquired," but notes that this is not a "distinct and explicit" knowledge of God such as is given in Scripture but rather a rough or unformed knowledge, "that tells of the existence of Deity in a confused and indistinct way" on the basis of the "light" resident in nature.

---

159. Burman, *Synopsis theol.*, I.xiv.8; cf. Descartes, *Meditations on the First Philosophy*, v, in *Philosophical Works*, I, p. 181: "from the fact that I cannot conceive of God without existence, it follows that existence is inseparable from Him ... not that my thoughts can bring this to pass, but, on the contrary, because the necessity which lies in the thing itself, i.e., the necessity of the existence of God determines me to think in this way."

160. Heidanus, *Corpus theol.*, I (p. 8).

161. Cloppenburg, *Exercitationes super locos communes*, II.i.5. Note that this set, despite some significant overlap, is quite different in its general tendency from the "five ways" of Aquinas' *Summa theologiae*, namely, 1) motion to the unmoved Being; 2) from effects and lesser causes to the first cause; 3) from contingency to the necessary Being; 4) from varying degrees of perfection to the perfect Being; 5) from the order of the world to an ordering Principle. Cloppenburg omits Aquinas' third and fourth way, begins with Aquinas' fifth way, then as second and third rehearses Aquinas' first and second. Cloppenburg's fourth way is a modification of the two preceding that draws motion and causality together into one argument — and his fifth way is both cosmological and teleological, both order and goal being at issue. Cf. the summary of Aquinas' proofs in Davies, *Thought of Thomas Aquinas*, pp. 28-31.

162. Leigh, *Treatise*, II.i (pp. 3-4).

Albeit indistinct and confused, this "inborn ... universal apprehension" does lead to a "demonstration of the necessary existence of God from his effects."[163] Demonstrative proof is therefore possible, but it will have a lower status than proof grounded in direct testimony.

This relative devaluation of demonstrative argument is certainly one of the grounds for the Reformed orthodox writers' high valuation of the rhetorical arguments for the existence of God — they are, in effect, a form of a posteriori testimony. In Turretin's model, the proofs divide into rational and rhetorical categories. He speaks of four foundations of demonstration: 1) the "universal voice of nature"; 2) contemplation of the human being; 3) the "testimony of conscience"; and 4) the general "consent of peoples."[164] The first of these categories contains all of the standard a posteriori arguments with the exception of Aquinas' third way (which is omitted by Turretin). The second could be viewed as a form of causal argument, but the third and fourth are purely rhetorical.

Leigh's and Mastricht's analysis of proofs divides them into two basic categories: proofs according to "testimony" and proofs according to "reason," these latter being drawn by Leigh both from "effects" and from contraries. Rational proofs will be a posteriori. This remains the case despite Leigh's identification of two kinds of demonstrations or "proofs":

(1) A demonstrating of the effects by their causes, which is a proof *a priori*. Principles cannot be demonstrated *a causa* and *a priori* because they have no superior cause.
(2) A demonstrating of causes by their effects: which is a proof drawn *a posteriori*. So principles may be demonstrated. All principles being *prima*, and *Notissima* of themselves are thereby made indemonstrable [i.e. in an *a priori* sense].[165]

This typology of proofs, unlike Burman's, rules out use of the ontological argument, given the orthodox writers' acceptance of the definition of *principia* as both self-evident and indemonstrable: there can be no rational a priori proof of God, given the identity of God as ultimate *principium*.[166]

Leigh allows only one valid a priori demonstration of the existence of God — that which comes from "testimony," namely, the self-demonstration or revelation of the First Principle:

---

163. Cloppenburg, *Exercitationes super locos communes*, II.i.4-5.

164. Turretin, *Inst. theol. elencticae*, III.i.5; cf. Maresius, *Collegium theol.*, II.3.

165. Leigh, *Body of Divinity*, II.i (p. 4); cf. Philip du Plessis Mornay, *A Worke concerning the Trunesse of Christian Religion*, trans. Philip Sidney and Arthur Golding (London: George Potter, 1604), i (pp. 1-2); Mastricht, *Theoretico-practica theol.*, II.ii.4, 12; Le Blanc, *Theses theol.*, *Quibus demonstratur Deum esse*, viii; also note Cocceius, *Summa theol.*, II.viii.34-125.

166. Cf. Louis Cappel, *The Hinge of Faith and Religion; or, A Proof of the Deity against Atheists and Profane Persons, by Reason, and the Testimony of Scripture: the Divinity of which is Demonstrated*, trans. Philip Marinel (London: Thomas Dring, 1660), pp. 9-10.

The weightiest Testimony only that can be brought to prove that *there is a God*, is to produce the Testimony of God speaking in his own word. None other in the world can have equal authority, *John 8:13, 14*.[167]

This is the fundamental truth of religion — which is as entitled to its *principium* as any other way of knowing, so much so, indeed, that it ought to be forbidden to call God's existence into question.[168] The a priori order of the typical orthodox Reformed theological system rests on the testimony of God to his own existence — on a biblical a priori — and not on the ability of the theologian to argue the existence of God. (This model contrasts with Burman's Cartesian approach and, in the course of the development of orthodoxy, with the fully rationalist approach found in the eighteenth-century Wolffian systems, in which the doctrine of God in "supernatural theology" must be preceded by the demonstration of God's existence in "natural theology."[169] This rationalist alternative was identified and opposed in Burman's time by Voetius and others of the Reformed orthodox who opposed the Cartesian claim of an innate idea of God as the cognitive underpinning of their proofs.)[170]

2. Proofs from testimony: revelation and the rhetorical arguments. Given that the primary testimony to the existence of God is God himself speaking in Scripture, there is a relative priority of the proofs from "testimony," including the rhetorical proofs, over the rational demonstrations in Reformed orthodox thought. This priority coincides, moreover, with the frequent denial of the existence of a genuine speculative atheism and the focus of the discussion on "practical atheism." The true "speculative atheists" will deny the proof from testimony: "For as they deny that *there is a God*, so they deny likewise that the Scripture is his word."[171] The primary testimony, as already noted, is the divine revelation:

he that testifieth of himself, either by word or writing, is. God hath written a Book to us, in which he affirms of himself that he is. Every page almost, and line of Scripture point to God. He begins his Book himself, saying, *In the beginning God made heaven and earth*. He concludes this Book with himself, saying, *if any man shall take ought from this prophesy, God shall take away his part out of the Book* of life. In every particular prophecy, he testifieth the same thing, saying, *thus saith the Lord*.[172]

To the primary testimony, God's own revelation, may be added the secondary testimony, that of human beings. Both this form of testimony and the a posteriori

---

167. Leigh, *Treatise*, II.i (p. 4); cf. Bucanus, *Institutions*, i (pp. 1, 3-4); Mastricht, *Theoretico-practica theol.*, II.ii.14; also Henry Ainsworth, *The Orthodox Foundation of Religion, long since collected by that judicious and elegant man Mr. Henry Ainsworth*, ed. Samuel White (London: R. C. for M. Sparke, 1641), p. 8.

168. Mornay, *Trunesse of Christian Religion*, i (p. 2); cf. Beza et al., *Propositions and Principles*, I.iv.

169. See the discussion in *PRRD*, I, 6.3 (B.4).

170. Cf. Verbeek, "Descartes and the Problem of Atheism," p. 214.

171. Leigh, *Treatise*, II.i (p. 4), citing Fotherby, *Atheomastix*, pt. 1, I.ii; Turretin, *Inst. theol. elencticae*, III.i-ii; Charnock, *Discourse*, I-II (pp. 23-175) on the problem of atheism.

172. Leigh, *Treatise*, II.i (p. 4); Bucanus, *Institutions*, i (pp. 3-4); Cocceius, *Summa theol.*, II.viii.122-124.

arguments function in the case of God, given that the divine *principium* of theology is not only given by special revelation in the Word but is also taught by the very nature of things, as Romans 1:20 and Job 12:6 indicate.[173] First among the secondary teztimonies, many of the Reformed use the argument *e consensu gentium*, "from the consent of all nations" — for there is no nation so barbarous that it fails to acknowledge the existence of some god. Many of the Reformed orthodox, like Calvin, echo or cite Cicero on this point; Turretin also notes the testimony of the Neoplatonic philosopher Iambilichus and the arguments of John of Damascus.[174] Precisely echoing the Damascene is Leigh's statement,

> All commonwealths had always something, which they worshiped, and called in their language, "God"; this principle is written by God himself in the table of every man's soul. That which is written in the hearts of all men, which with one mouth all acknowledge, must needs be a truth, seeing it is the voice of reason itself.[175]

Second, in a modification of the argument from universal consent, Leigh can also speak of "An implanted knowledge which is in every man's conscience, a natural ingrafted principle about God, *O anima naturaliter Christiana*! said Tertullian."[176] Thus, not only all of mankind but also each individual man bears the testimony of God within him. Turretin notes several explanations of this implanted knowledge — nature itself, common conceptions belonging to all people, and (surprisingly, given its Cartesian sound) "the idea of God as the most perfect being impressed upon our minds."[177]

Third, along similar rhetorical lines, the Reformed orthodox also point directly to the voice of conscience. "Whence those terrors of conscience, trembling at more atrocious wickedness," writes Turretin, "unless from the sense of some avenger and judge whom, not seeing, it everywhere feels ... they who appeared to have divested their minds of the sense of deity, tremble at an angry God."[178] Like Calvin, Mornay, Turretin, Cappel, and Mastricht appeal to the example of Caligula.[179] Thus,

> The most pregnant and undeniable proof of the God-head with the Heathen, was the voice of conscience. The Scripture showeth that the wicked were much terrified in

---

173. Le Blanc, *Theses theol.*, *Quibus demonstratur Deum esse*, iv.

174. Turretin, *Inst. theol. elencticae*, III.i.16-17; Bucanus, *Institutions*, i (pp. 2-3); Mornay, *Trunesse of Christian Religion*, i (p. 9); Fotherby, *Atheomastix*, I.iii.3; iv.1-5; Cappel, *Hinge of Faith*, pp. 117-119; Mastricht, *Theoretico-practica theol.*, II.ii.13; Venema, *Inst. theol.*, ii (p. 11); Klinkenberg, *Onderwys*, I.i1, §12; cf. Calvin, *Institutes*, I.iii.1, with Egil Grislis, "Calvin's Use of Cicero in the Institutes I:1-5 — a Case Study in Theological Method," in *Archiv für Reformationsgeschichte*, 62 (1971), pp. 5-37.

175. Leigh, *Treatise*, II.i (p. 5); so also Perkins, *Golden Chaine*, ii (p. 11, col. 1); Nichols, *Abridgement of Perkins*, p. 1; cf. John of Damascus, *On the Orthodox Faith*, I.i (NPNF 2 ser., vol. IX, p. 1).

176. Leigh, *Treatise*, II.i (p. 2); cf. Fotherby, *Atheomastix*, I.iii.1-2.

177. Turretin, *Inst. theol. elencticae*, III.i.18.

178. Turretin, *Inst. theol. elencticae*, III.i.14; Nichols, *Abridgement of Perkins*, p. 2; Cocceius, *Summa theol.*, II.viii.120.

179. Cf. Turretin, *Inst. theol. elencticae*, III.i.14; Cappel, *Hinge of Faith*, p. 91; Mornay, *Trunesse of Christian Religion*, i (p. 9); Mastricht, *Theoretico-practica theol.*, II.ii.12, with Calvin, *Institutes*, I.iii.2.

their consciences, after the committing of heinous sins, *Rom* 2:15; *Isaiah* 57:20, 21; *Mark* 6:14, 16. ... Conscience proclaims a Law in every heart, and denounceth a punishment for the breach of God's Law. Conscience is a natural ability of discerning the condition and state of our actions, whether good or bad; and that not alone is respect of men, but of some other thing above men: for when one hath done things unlawful, though such as no man can accuse us of because no man doth know, yet ... then he hath something in him threatening, arraigning, accusing, and terrifying, a Deputy of God, sitting within him. ... A man must therefore confess, there is a higher power to whom that conscience of his is an officer, and a Supreme Judge.[180]

Fourth, a related argument is the identification of the human being as the *microcosmos*. This might be identified as a form of rational argumentation, given its resemblance to arguments from causality and degrees of perfection and its teleological dimension, but it is mounted primarily as a form of testimony, akin in form to the argument from conscience: the human being, looking inward, should recognize a wisdom of construction, a "mutual interconnection" of members and faculties, a spiritual dimension blessed with intellect and will — in short, an image that points to its maker, God himself.[181] The argument can also be grounded, perhaps more convincingly, on the existence and immortality of the soul:

> The Nobility and Excellence of the soul, showeth plainly, that it is of Divine Original; it being Spiritual and Incorporeal, could not but proceed from that which is Incorporeal. The effect cannot be *toto genere* better than the cause.[182]

3. Proofs from reason: the a posteriori demonstrations. The other form of argument used by the Reformed orthodox consists in a series of versions of the standard *a posteriori* proofs of the existence of God. The formulations, however, are not nearly as precisely structured as the "five ways" of Aquinas and, in fact, evidence much the same interest in a rhetoric of persuasion that obtains in the testimonies and more strictly rhetorical arguments used by the orthodox. What is more, the variations in formulation of the proofs indicate, as Platt has shown, sources as much in the contemporary philosophy of the early seventeenth century as in the original medieval forms of the arguments.[183]

First, the argument from cause and effect has a certain preeminence among the Reformed orthodox. Examination of the world as it presently exists proves the existence of God, inasmuch as "nothing can be the cause of itself" or, in a positive form,

---

180. Leigh, *Treatise*, II.i (p. 6); cf. Perkins, *Golden Chaine*, ii (p. 11, col. 1); Nichols, *Abridgement of Perkins*, p. 1.

181. Turretin, *Inst. theol. elencticae*, III.i.13; Cocceius, *Summa theol.*, II.viii.104; Mornay, *Trunesse of Christian Religion*, i (pp. 6-9); at great length, Fotherby, *Atheomastix*, pt. 1, book III; cf. E. M. W. Tillyard, *The Elizabethan World Picture* (New York: Vintage: 1942), pp. 91-94.

182. Leigh, *Treatise*, II.i (p. 10); cf. Perkins, *Golden Chaine*, ii (p. 11, col. 1); Nichols, *Abridgement of Perkins*, p. 1; Fotherby, *Atheomastix*, pt. 1, book IV, entire; Cappel, *Hinge of Faith*, pp. 77-90.

183. Platt, *Reformed Thought*, pp. 139-176.

"everything that exists owes its existence to a cause."[184] When the cause of existence is not in the object itself — that is, when it is not "self-caused" and eternal — it must have a cause beyond itself:

> The world must needs be eternal or must be made by itself or by something which was before it, and therefore also was far better than it. But it could not make itself, for what maketh worketh, what worketh is, but what is made is not till it be made. Now nothing can be and not be at the same time. ... Neither could it be eternal, for a thing compounded out of parts must needs have those parts united together by some other thing beside itself, and above itself.[185]

Granting that created things must have a maker and that this contingent world as a whole must have a causal principle, it also appears that the sum of finite things must have a creator who is prior to them, which is to say, from eternity. Thus the creation itself proves God to exist.[186] Among the late orthodox Wolffian dogmaticians, the basic causal argument is modified to show that the finite universe, as contingent, cannot provide the "sufficient reason" for its own existence.[187]

The arguments employed to manifest from creation the existence of God can be applied also to the examination of human beings: even as the world is created and ordered, so is the individual "framed" in his mother's womb:

> Each particular man in the world, may reason from his own being, thus: either there must be an infinite number of men, or else there must be a first man, which was the beginning of all men; but an infinite number of particular men is impossible ... for every number begins with a unity, and is capable of being made greater by addition of a unity: therefore there cannot be an infinite number of particular men. Therefore we must come to some first man; and that first man could not make himself, nor be made by any inferior thing ... therefore it must be made by something more excellent than itself, *viz.* one infinite thing, from which all particulars had their original.[188]

The argument against an infinite series of particular men is, in fact, the same as the argument against an infinite series of contingent causes and effects, and — when understood as such — can be a fairly telling argument. Leigh's argument has two basic points; first, that an infinite temporal series of particular men or, as Turretin defines it, "an infinite series in producing causes," is inconceivable; and second, that a

---

184. Turretin, *Inst. theol. elencticae,* III.i.6; Bucanus, *Institutions,* i (p. 2); Venema, *Inst. theol.,* ii (p. 15); Nichols, *Abridgement of Perkins,* p. 1; Le Blanc, *Theses theol., Quibus demonstratur Deum esse,* x-xi.

185. Leigh, *Treatise,* II.i (p. 7); cf. Cocceius, *Summa theol.,* II.viii.34, 66, 89-90; Cappel, *Hinge of Faith,* pp. 10-12; Venema, *Inst. theol.,* ii (p. 15); Klinkenberg, *Onderwys,* I.i1, §10-11.

186. Mastricht, *Theoretico-practica theol.,* II.ii.5; cf. Venema, *Inst. theol.,* ii (p. 16).

187. Thus, Wyttenbach, *Tentamen theol.,* III, §211; Stapfer, *Inst. theol. polemicae,* I.iii, §287-296.

188. Leigh, *Treatise,* II.i (pp. 10-11); Le Blanc, *Theses theol., Quibus demonstratur Deum esse,* xxiv; Cappel, *Hinge of Faith,* pp. 13-14.

contingent creature cannot ultimately be self-producing but must have a ground for its being.[189]

Second, the Reformed orthodox also argue the existence of God from the contingent nature of the world order, an argument that attains prominence among the late orthodox Wolffian dogmaticians: given that the world is not necessary but contingent, the world itself did not have to exist. There could have been other worlds: other possible series of things and events could exist. Our particular world, moreover, does not contain within itself the reason or foundation for its own existence — and, therefore, there must be a necessary cause, indeed, a necessarily existent being that causes, the existence of the world. There must be a God who exists necessarily and *a se ipso*, of himself.[190]

Third, the argument from the order of the universe is also present, expressed in more or less causal terms — albeit here too the structure of argument tends to be more persuasive or rhetorical than demonstrative: "When we see the glorious frame of heaven and earth; the excellence, magnitude, and multitude of natural things; the beautiful order and harmony; so great variety; we cannot but conclude that there is a God, who made and ordereth all these things."[191] Here, too, there are parallels among the Reformers — in Musculus and Hyperius, as noted above — and with Calvin who both declares that the right examination of the natural order yields belief in the eternal God, and that this God is the "first cause" of all things, who consistently works by means of "secondary causes."[192] Indeed, all of the causal arguments assume a multi-layered universal causality, in which God is first cause or "supreme agent" and under whom the vast array of finite causes, including angels, human beings, and lesser creatures is arrayed — and arrayed in such a way that some things occur by necessity, others contingently, and still others through the agency of free choice on the part of rational creatures.[193]

Another version of argument, again capable of reference to the views of Calvin and Bullinger, can be drawn from the fact of the providential conservation and governance of the world. (In the form of the argument offered by Mastricht, conservation and government are distinguished into two proofs.)[194]

> The preservation and continuance of the world ... maketh it manifest that there is a God which preserveth and ordereth it. For either it must be preserved, ruled, and ordered by itself or by some more excellent thing than itself: not by itself, for what could

189. Cf. Turretin, *Inst. theol. elencticae*, III.i.6; Le Blanc, *Theses theol.*, *Quibus demonstratur Deum esse*, xiii; Mastricht, *Theoretico-practica theol.*, II.ii.4.

190. Wyttenbach, *Tentamen theol.*, I, §12-17.

191. Leigh, *Treatise*, II.i (p. 8); cf. Bucanus, *Institutions*, i (p. 2); Turretin, *Inst. theol. elencticae*, III.i.10; Le Blanc, *Theses theol.*, *Quibus demonstratur Deum esse*, xiv; Klinkenberg, *Onderwys*, I.i1, §14.

192. Cf. Calvin, *Commentary on Romans*, 1:20 (*CTS Romans*, p. 70), with Calvin, *Commentary on Genesis*, 1:11 (*CTS Genesis*, I, p. 82).

193. Cf. Richard Holdsworth, *Praelectiones theologicae* (London: Jacob Flesher, 1661), I.xxxii (p. 278); with Westminster Confession, III.i; V.ii.

194. Mastricht, *Theoretico-practica theol.*, II.ii.6-7.

not make itself cannot of itself keep and uphold itself, seeing no less power is required to its continuation than to its constitution. ... That which is effected by the constant, orderly, and subordinate working of innumerable particulars for one common end, whereof no one of them hath any knowledge or acquaintance, must needs be wrought by some common Ruler and Governor which knows the motion and working of each, and rules all. ... What upholds the world is; but God upholds the world; therefore God is.[195]

It ought to be obvious that the nonrational portion of creation must be governed, together with the rational, by a higher mind or understanding which rules them all.[196]

In what can stand as a variant of the argument from universal order, Mornay examines the hierarchy of the world order, noting that there are things that have being, but in themselves no life, sense, or reason; other things that have being and life, lacking sense and reason; still others that have being, life, and sense; and finally those that have all four properties, including reason. Not only is there such an order, but, marvelous to see, the lowest forms, earth, water, and air, that have only being, serve and support the life of the higher forms. Plants, which have being and life, take nourishment from the earth and the air; beasts, which have being, life, and sense, are nourished by the elements and the plants; human beings, which have being, life, sense, and reason, "injoyeth the elements, liveth of the Plants, commandeth the Beasts, & discourseth of all things both above and beneath him." Such an order demands belief in a necessary, almighty being who governs the "unequall partition" of this world order and holds it "in concorde."[197] It also follows that since none of the things that have being, life, sense, or reason exists forever, "Notbeeing, Notliving, Notsensible, and Notreasonable" precede Being, Living, Sensation, and Reason — and that none of these four all-embracing categories of things, nor all the categories together, can account for itself. There must therefore be a being, namely, God, who can bring all things into existence out of nothing.[198]

Fourth, the orthodox writers also offer a cosmological version of the "fourth way," a proof based on the degrees or grades of perfection in the universe but arguing its case from the beauty of the universal order: "if order requires wisdom and intelligence, the most perfect necessarily supposes the most perfect and infinite Wisdom that we call God."[199] Nor is it possible that there be more than one most perfect being.[200] Only a blind person could fail to see the beauty of the order around him, the concord and harmony of all things, whether in the heavens, or in the grass, or in the oceans. Such

---

195. Leigh, *Treatise*, II.i (p. 8); cf. Perkins, *Golden Chaine*, ii, in *Workes*, I, p. 11, col. 1; Cocceius, *Summa theol.*, II.viii.93; and note Calvin, *Institutes*, I.v.2.

196. Leigh, *Treatise*, II.i (p. 9); Nichols, *Abridgement of Perkins*, p. 2; Le Blanc, *Theses theol.*, *Quibus demonstratur Deum esse*, xvi-xvii; Cappel, *Hinge of Faith*, pp. 21-23, 40-45; Cocceius, *Summa theol.*, II.viii.34, 98.

197. Mornay, *Trunesse of Christian Religion*, i (p. 3).

198. Mornay, *Trunesse of Christian Religion*, i (p. 4).

199. Turretin, *Inst. theol. elencticae*, III.i.10; cf. Le Blanc, *Theses theol.*, *Quibus demonstratur Deum esse*, xv.

200. Cocceius, *Summa theol.*, II.viii.109.

beauty and harmony could not arise merely by chance, given that chance does not yield arrangement, certainty, constancy, or similarity. To claim that chance might produce order is, as Cicero, commented, to think that a random scattering of the letters of the alphabet might actually produce a readable copy of the *Annals* of Ennius.[201]

Fifth, the arguments from causality and universal order are typically supplemented by the teleological argument toward the existence of an ultimate final cause of all things. All "natural beings" work toward a goal, and nature as a whole does "nothing in vain." If all nature works toward a goal, then it must either know its own goal or receive its direction from another — but, given the presence of inanimate things and of living things that are not endowed with reason, it is clear that nature as a whole cannot understand its own goal. There must be, therefore, a divine being who orders the whole toward its end.[202]

Sixth, to the standard arguments for the existence of God from the created order, Leigh, Turretin, and Mastricht add a note on miracles as proofs of God. The occurrence of miracles is attested not only in Scripture but also in the "profane histories" of the world. Given that miracles are events that cannot be produced by nature but require a power higher than nature, the true miracle presupposes the existence of God.[203] Or as Leigh comments, "the worker of a Miracle, is he that can lift Nature off the Hinges as it were, and set it on again as seemeth best to himself; and therefore is above the course of nature, and so is the Author of all things under himself ... and that is none but God."[204]

Furthermore, there are proofs "from the contrary" — from the existence of opposition to God — from devils and "from the slightness of reasons brought to disprove" the existence of God. The first of these Leigh draws "from the being of Devils":

> There is a Devil, an Enemy to God, which sets himself against God and desires, and strives, and prevails in many places to be worshipped as God. Therefore it must needs be there is a God to whom service and honor is due...which these do unduly seek. Again the Devil is a creature for strength, wisdom, nimbleness, able to destroy all mankind quickly, and out of his Malice and Fury very willing to do it. Yet he cannot do it; it is not done. Of this restraint there is some cause: therefore there must be something which..overrules him, and that can be no other than a God; that is, something of Higher Power, and in wisdom far beyond him.[205]

The second proof or, in fact, series of proofs "from the contrary" rest on "the slightness of the reasons brought to disprove this truth, or to show the Contrary," for any

201. Turretin, *Inst. theol. elencticae*, III.i.10-11.

202. Turretin, *Inst. theol. elencticae*, III.i.12.

203. Mastricht, *Theoretico-practica theol.*, II.ii.11.

204. Leigh, *Treatise*, II.i (pp. 11-12), citing Exodus 15:11; Psalm 72:18; 136:4; cf. Turretin, *Inst. theol. elencticae*, III.i.19.

205. Leigh, *Treatise*, II.i (pp. 12-13).

reasonable person can recognize that "what is opposed alone by weak and false reasons is a truth." Thus,

> i. If there were a God, some man should see him, and sensibly converse with him. This is a brutish reason: [if] what cannot be seen is not, then man hath not a soul. God is above sense, more excellent than to be discerned by so poor, weak, and low a thing as sense is. [Moreover] God daily makes himself visible after a sort to men by his works.
> ii. If there were a God, he would not suffer wicked men to prosper, and oppose better men than themselves; nor himself to be so blasphemed as he is. Those things that to us seem most unjust and unfit, if we could see the whole tenor of things from the beginning to the ending, would appear wise and just.
> iii. All Divine Religion (say the Atheists) is nothing else than a human invention, artificially excogitated to keep man in awe; and the Scriptures are but the device of man's brain, to give assistance to Magistrates in Civil Government. This objection strikes at the root and heart of all Religion & opposeth two main principles at once: (1) that there is a God; (2) that the Scripture is the word of God.[206]

"The perpetuity of religion" also indicates its divine origin. As for the claim that Scripture was invented to buttress the Magistrates and the Government, "Nothing crosseth human wisdom more than the whole Scripture from beginning to end." Christ came poor into the world, into humble circumstances: he was not the son of an emperor. Christ also "chose ... unlearned men to propagate the Gospel" and denied the claims of "great Doctors" — he attacked the ceremonial law and outworn traditions. This is hardly a prop to the established classes![207]

The form and the function of the proofs of God's existence in the Reformed orthodox systems, thus, also provide evidence against the claim that this theology is a form of rationalism. On the one hand, these proofs do not function as the necessary and proper foundation of the doctrine of God. They do not typically serve, as they did in Aquinas' *Summa*, a demonstration of the ability of reason to point toward the same conclusion as is given by revelation, and therefore of the ability of reason to venture into theological discussion. Their primary purpose is to attack skepticism and atheism on the basis of a fundamental, but non-saving natural knowledge, including the innate knowledge of God or immediate *sensus divinitatis* shared by all people. This approach does not indicate the creation of an independent and/or prior natural theology, as Barth once claimed.[208]

Occasionally, it is true, a Reformed theologian will place the proofs in such a way as to show their positive relationship to theological system. Thus, Cloppenburg can indicate that the results of the proofs conform, in a particular manner, to the teachings of Scripture: the necessary existence of God, apart from a prior principle or cause, is witnessed by Isaiah, who identifies God as "the first and the last," "before whom there

---

206. Leigh, *Treatise*, II.i (pp. 12-13).

207. Leigh, *Treatise*, II.i (pp. 13-14).

208. Cf. Barth, *Church Dogmatics*, II/1, p. 127, pointing at the Belgic Confession as a cause of the purported problem; note the rebuttal by Pierre Courthal, "Karl Barth et quelques points des confessions de foi Reformées," in *La Revue Reformée*, 9 (1958), pp. 1-29.

is no God" (Isa. 44:6, 7; 43:10).[209] Indeed, Cloppenburg appears to understand the testimonies of Scripture to the existence and attributes of God as consistently mirroring the logic of the attributes that can be developed from the proofs, pointing positively to the existence and attributes where the proofs had indicated a more negative way, by the removal of imperfection.[210] And we have seen Baxter and Charnock use the logic of the proofs to support piety against both genuine and "practical" atheism. On the other hand, at least in the early and high orthodox eras, the proofs do not take on the form and function given to theistic proof by the various rationalist philosophies of the age. The Cartesian form of the ontological argument is scorned, and the more empirical patterns of argument found in the a posteriori rational theism of writers like Lord Herbert of Cherbury are not applied with any rigor nor are they used, as typical of rationalism, to argue the soundness of natural reason and natural theology as an independent and morally or soteriologically significant form of the knowledge of God.

The historical context of argumentation is crucial for an understanding of the development of proofs for the existence of God in Reformed theology in the sixteenth and seventeenth centuries. Clues to the altered historical context can be found in the location of the proofs, the reference to *principia* and principial knowledge found in many of the expositions, the alteration of the relationship of rhetoric and logic characteristic of Renaissance and early modern thought, and the connection between the proofs and the polemic against atheism and skepticism that they embody. In relation to these issues, even the Thomistic "five ways" take on a character not at all familiar to their famous author: they are now rhetorically, not demonstratively, framed, and they are presented together with and as having the same status as the standard rhetorical arguments like *e consensu gentium*. Such presentation concedes, from one perspective, the nominalist and even the more historically proximate Pyrrhonist, skeptic, or "atheist" critique, admitting the existence of God is indemonstrable. From another perspective, however, it steps past the critique by declaring God principial and therefore undeniable, using the rhetorical form of the arguments to press home the point.[211] This formulation is not specifically Thomistic — nor is it Scotistic, given the absence of a reframed ontological argument from all but the thinkers of a Cartesian affiliation.[212] Rather, the formulation is an example of how a philosophically eclectic orthodoxy adapts elements of a tradition to a new situation.

4. Transformation of the proofs in the late orthodox era. It was a clear indication of a transformation of orthodox theology, specifically on the point of the relationship between reason and revelation for Van Til and Venema, or for Wolffians like Wyttenbach and Stapfer, in the mid-eighteenth century, to begin their consideration

---

209. Cloppenburg, *Exercitationes super locos communes*, II.i.6.

210. Cloppenburg, *Exercitationes super locos communes*, II.i.6-8.

211. Notably in Mornay, *Trunesse of Christian Religion*, i (pp. 1-2).

212. On Descartes' relation to Scotism, see Calvin Normore, "Meaning and Objective Being," in A. O. Rorty, ed., *Essays on Descartes' Meditations* (Berkeley: University of California Press, 1986), pp. 223-240; Roger Arieu, *Descartes and the Last Scholastics* (Ithaca and London: Cornell University Press, 1999), pp. 45-57.

of theology with a discussion of the proofs of the existence of God than for a seventeenth-century Protestant scholastic to do so: unlike their seventeenth-century predecessors, Van Til, Venema, Wyttenbach, and Stapfer have acknowledged the principial function of reason in theological system. The proofs now lose their purely apologetic function and become a positive prologue offered by reason to the system of revelation. Here, for the first time in the development of Reformed theological system, natural or philosophical theology provides a foundation on which revelation can build: we have lost the inherent fideism of the seventeenth century Protestant scholastics.

In the case of Wyttenbach in particular, the proofs of God's existence have begun to take their place in a genuinely deductive approach to theology. Indeed, Wyttenbach provides one of the earliest evidences that we have seen of a movement toward the exposition of theology on the basis of a single self-evident principle from which all else can be (more or less!) deduced. The *Theses theologicae praecipua christianae doctrinae capita ex primis principiis deducta*, delivered by Wyttenbach and his associate Isaac Sigfrid, begin with the Wolffian assumption that "nothing exists or may exist in the world without sufficient reason."[213] From this principle, it is evident that everything that exists must have a cause: and we may therefore note of ourselves, that we are either self-caused or caused by something outside of ourselves. If the former case, we would be necessary beings, notes Wyttenbach — which is certainly not true, inasmuch as we can cease to exist. The same is true of the things that we experience beyond ourselves in our world. Moreover, in seeking a valid cause *extra nos*, it is clear that we cannot regress toward infinity, granting that there is no sufficient reason to guarantee the existence of the infinite chain. We must postulate a first cause that is necessarily existent in and of itself and that cannot not exist *(non potest non existere)* — and this self-existent, necessary being is God.[214]

The importance of Wyttenbach's argument is certainly not its originality — the argument derives indirectly from the scholastic tradition, courtesy of Christian Wolff, who transformed the argument by supplying the notion of the "principle of sufficient reason." The historical importance of Wyttenbach's form of argument lies in its optimistic assumption that an entire system of theology, beginning with a rational proof for the existence of God, can rest deductively on a single principle. Neither the early nor the high orthodox Reformed theologians had accepted so large a role for reason. The clearest theological precedent for this Wolffian deductive system is the Cartesian system of Poiret at the end of the seventeenth century, but this too was hardly a product of Reformed orthodoxy.[215] Wyttenbach evidences the genuine inception of a fully rationalist attempt at orthodoxy — characteristic of the eighteenth, not of the seventeenth, century. We see here also the beginning of the deductive logic that would

---

213. Wyttenbach, *Theses theologicae*, §i.
214. Wyttenbach, *Theses theologicae*, §ii-iii.
215. Cf. above, chapter 2.4 (B.2).

ultimately lead to the notion of central dogmas.[216] What ought to be evident, simply in the contrast between Wyttenbach's approach to doctrine and that of his Reformed orthodox predecessors, is that this highly deductive model is not at all reflective of the approach of seventeenth-century Reformed systems of theology.

3.3 The Problem of Predication and the Attributes of God in General

A. The Problem of Predication

1. Predication and the difficulty of God-language: some orthodox preliminaries. If the orthodox systems are characterized by lengthy expositions of the doctrine of the essence and attributes of God, they are also characterized by rather circumspect descriptions of the difficulties entailed upon such expositions. This is hardly metaphysics run rampant; even toward the close of the orthodox era, the English theologian Thomas Ridgley could begin his extended discussion of the catechetical question "What is God?" — *Quid sit Deus?* — with a carefully worded qualification of the entire doctrine:

> Before we proceed to consider the divine perfections ... let it be premised, 1. That it is impossible for anyone to give a perfect description of God, since he is incomprehensible; therefore no words can fully express, or fully set forth his perfections.... 2. Though God cannot be perfectly described, yet there is something of him that we may know, and ought to make the matter of our study and diligent inquiries. When his glory is set forth in Scripture, we are not to look upon the expressions there made use of as words without any manner of Ideas affixed to them; for it is one thing to have adequate ideas of an infinitely perfect being, and another thing to have no Ideas at all of him; neither are our ideas of God to be reckoned, for this reason, altogether false, though they may be imperfect; for it is one thing to think of him in an unbecoming way, not agreeable to his perfections, or to attribute the weakness and imperfection to him which do not belong to his nature, and another thing to think of him, with the highest and best conceptions we are able to entertain, of his infinite perfections, while, at the same time, we have a due sense of our own weakness, and the shallowness of our capacities. When we thus order our thoughts concerning the great God, though we are far from comprehending his infinite perfections, yet our conceptions are not to be concluded erroneous, when directed by his word; which leads us to consider how we may conceive aright of the divine perfections.[217]

The difficulty of the problem of language concerning God is offset for the orthodox only by the fact of revelation: the divine attributes, then, are the perfections according to which God manifests himself to us and overcomes "the defect of our capacity, who are not able to understand that which is known of God under one name or act of understanding."[218] As Turretin indicates, the way in which God is what he is in the simplicity of the divine essence cannot be known by the human mind, granting that

---

216. Cf. the comments of Hermann Bauke, *Die Probleme der Theologie Calvins* (Leipzig: J. C. Hinrichs, 1922), pp. 22, 30-31 with the discussion in *PRRD*, I, 6.3 (B.4); 9.3 (B.2).

217. Ridgley, *Body of Divinity*, q. vii (p. 53, cols. 1-2).

218. Leigh, *A System*, II.i (p. 160).

the human mind knows things only by composition and composite attribution — nonetheless, we are given to know the divine attributes or essential properties by revelation and rational reflection on revelation in such a way that God's nature is truly known by means of the revealed attributes.[219]

Pictet, even more carefully, prefaces his discussion of the attributes in such a way as to avoid a spirit of extreme rationalism and to acknowledge the epistemological difficulties involved in the doctrine:

> We are sensible indeed that the infinite nature of God cannot be perfectly comprehended by finite beings. Nevertheless, there are many things revealed concerning it in the Scriptures, which we are permitted to examine.[220]

We see here, immediately, two issues crucial to the Reformed exposition of the divine attributes: first, the principle of the absence of proportion between the finite and the infinite and the conclusion drawn from it that the finite cannot grasp or comprehend the infinite; and, second, the effect of interrelationship between this more or less philosophical principle and the strong biblical sense of divine sovereignty and transcendence found in the Reformed theologies of the sixteenth and seventeenth centuries.

Beyond the necessary distinction between the personal properties of the Father, Son and Spirit and the attributes belonging to the entire Godhead, the Protestant orthodox also inherited from the medieval doctors and, to a certain extent, from the Reformers as well, the recognition that the idea of an "attribute," or "predicate," like the idea of a "nature," does not comport with the concept of God — at least not in precisely the same manner that attributes or predicates are spoken of finite things.[221] God, to borrow from Augustine, is all that he has.[222] God, as traditionally understood, cannot be described, nor can God be understood or comprehended. The logical difficulty is signaled, in part, by the terms used in Protestant orthodox writings: many of the orthodox writers speak of divine attributes, but others write of "properties" or "perfections." Late in the era of Protestant orthodoxy, Van Til preferred to identify the "attributes" as the "excellencies" of the divine essence, while Francken spoke of "perfections" (*volmaaktheden*) "in the being of God" as essential or most intimate properties (*eigenschappen*).[223] In its most strict use, the term "attribute" very nearly avoids the problem of predication inasmuch as "attribution" is a logical task performed by a rational subject that does not raise the question of the actual properties of the object under consideration. The terms "property" and "perfection" do, however,

---

219. Turretin, *Inst. theol. elencticae*, III.v.1-2.

220. Pictet, *Theol. chr.*, II.iii.

221. Cf. Davies, "Classical Theism and the Doctrine of Divine Simplicity," p. 58 with Rogers, "The Traditional Doctrine of Divine Simplicity," p. 170-171, 174.

222. Augustine, *De civitate Dei*, XI.10.

223. Van Til, *Theol. revelata comp.*, I.ii; cf. Francken, *Kern der Christelijke Leer*, III, q. 24-25 (p. 57).

indicate that the predicate in question actually belongs to the object under consideration.

This logical problem of predication is, thus, also directly related to the ontological question of precisely how the divine attributes or properties belong to the divine essence if we are unable to predicate them of God in the ways that we usually predicate attributes of the finite things we encounter in the world. There are, in other words, two profoundly related problems to be addressed in the preliminary discussion of divine attributes. First, both Scripture and reason lead us to affirm certain things of God and to deny certain things of God: God is good, righteous, almighty, omnipotent; God is not finite, measurable, or physical. But we do not make the attribution "God is good" in quite the same way that we make the attribution "Saul is good." Second, once we have been led by Scripture and reason to affirm and deny certain things of God, we are led to the further question of the meaning of the attribution: does it indicate an intrinsic or an extrinsic characteristic of the object under consideration and how does the attribute or predicate belong to the thing as one of its actual properties. The point is no longer simply subjective, namely, how we affirm a predicate of a thing, but objective, how the predicate, considered as a property, belongs to the thing. The interrelationship between the two questions is grounded in the formal identity of the categories of predication with the categories of being: the older philosophy assumes correspondence between *ens rationis* or logical being, things as they are conceived and *ens reale* or real being, things as they are.[224] As Keckermann pointed out, "Logica est ars dirigens mentem in cognitione rerum" — "logic is the art that directs the mind in its understanding of reality."[225]

2. Rules of predication. In order to understand the Reformed orthodox approach to both of these problems, we must step back from the doctrine of the divine attributes and note briefly rules of predication.[226] "Predication" is the logical act of attribution by which a subject is united with a predicate. The act of predication assumes some relationship between a given subject and that which is being attributed to it: an affirmative predication assumes positive relation, indeed, material identity of subject and predicate. There must be something that is materially the same, but also formally different, about both subject and predicate in order for there to be an affirmative predication that is not merely a tautology. The subject and the predicate, the thing

---

224. See P. Coffey, *Ontology or the Theory of Being: An Introduction to General Metphysics* (New York: Peter Smith, 1938), pp. 42-43.

225. Keckermann, *Systema logicae minus*, in *Opera*, I, col. 167.

226. E.g., in Alsted, *Metaphysica*; Bartholomaus Keckermann, *Scientiae metaphysicae compendiosum systema*, in *Opera*, I, col. 2007ff.; idem, *Systema logicae tribus libris adornatum*, in ibid, col. 542ff.; and Johannes Maccovius, *Opuscula philosophica omnia* (Amsterdam, 1660), containing his brief *Logica* and *Dictata de usu logica*; idem, *Distinctiones et regulae theologicae et philosophicae* (Amsterdam, 1656); and idem, *Metaphysica, as usus quaestionum in philosophia ac theologia* (Leyden, 1658). Cf. the review of the subject in Henri Grenier, *Thomistic Philosophy*, trans. J. P. E. O'Hanley, 3 vols. (Charlottestown: St. Dunstan's University, 1948), I, pp. 157-167, 176-183; II, pp. 31-63; Coffey, *Ontology*, pp. 32-50, 114-251; and R. P. Phillips, *Modern Thomistic Philosophy: An Explanation for Students*, 2 vols. (New York: Newman Press, 1959), II, pp. 174-179.

and its attribute, are, therefore, not convertible: the affirmative predications "God is love" and "God is goodness" do allow the inference that "Love is God" and "Goodness is God." The entire traditional language of the divine attributes, therefore (despite what has sometimes been claimed concerning divine simplicity), presumes a *real* or entitative identity but also a *formal* difference between the divine subject and its predicates and, in addition, between the various predicates as well — as would be the case in any predication that is not tautological. A negative predication assumes difference and distinction in reality.[227]

Beyond these basic considerations, traditional logic assumes a classification of predicates. In the order of entitative reality (*ens reale*), the classification describes the modes of finite being; in the order of logical reality (*ens rationis*), the classification identifies the categories or genera of predicates or attributions. These predications either belong to the essence of a subject or do not belong to its essence, viz., are incidental to the subject. This basic division of the topic yields "substance" as the first genus of predication — predicates which belong essentially to the subject. The predicates that do not belong absolutely to the essence of the subject, but inhere in it in a secondary or incidental sense. These "accidents" or incidental properties are either intrinsic or extrinsic. The intrinsic predicates are quantity (*quantitas*), quality (*qualitas*), and transcendental or real relation (*relatio secundum esse*); the extrinsic are action (*actio*), passion (*passio*), "where" or place (*ubi seu locus*), posture (*situs seu positio*), "when" or time (*quando seu tempus*), and habit (*habitus*). One qualification is necessary, moreover, to define and distinguish the intrinsic and extrinsic categories: if an attribute indicates an immanent "action" — like intellectual activity — it would be identified not as *actio*, but as *qualitas*: *actio* refers to a transitive, not to an intransitive, activity.[228] There is an immediate problem here when God is the subject of predication: God is not extrinsically determined, nor does God have incidental properties in any sense of the term.

The traditional language of divine attributes stands, therefore, both in an intimate relationship to the rational or logical categories of attribution or predication, but also to assumptions concerning the way in which these categories offer a reflection on the real order and its division into finite and infinite being. Attribution is, strictly speaking, an ascription of something to another thing, based on a variety of grounds. Namely, attribution can occur on the assumption of an inherent quality in a thing, the identification of a cause, or simply as a result of the act of classifying a thing. Predication, similarly, involves the affirmation or denial of an attribute, quality, or property of a particular subject. Given that attribution and predication does not terminate in a merely logical exercise (a matter of rational classification), but demands also a metaphysical dimension (a matter of the modes of finite being), discussion of divine "attributes" or "predication of properties" consistently addresses not only the fact of attribution or predication but also the grounds for it. Thus, the divine

227. Cf. Grenier, *Thomistic Philosophy*, I, p. 157.
228. Grenier, *Thomistic Philosophy*, I, pp. 176-183.

"attributes" are not simply logical attributions, they are attributions or predicates that assume an intrinsic quality or property in God.

The problem of the predication of attributes is not simply one of logical *praedicamenta* but also of metaphysical *praedicamenta*, that is, not simply an issue of orderly classification but an issue of the modes of being. In order to make the point clear, the Reformed orthodox prefer to use the terms "property," "essential property," or "perfection" rather than the term "attribute" or, when they use "attribute," they make very clear that the term indicates a property or mode of the divine being and not merely an "attribution" on the part of human beings. The logical difficulty of the predication of attributes is not merely the issue of classification — more than that, it is the difficulty of moving from metaphysical predication, which refers to the modes of finite being, to a predication concerning infinite being. And infinite being, by definition, is not proportionate to finite being.

3. **Attributes and essential properties: issues of analogy and disproportionality.** The problem of predication, with specific reference to God, is simply that of the transition, both metaphysical and logical, from finite to infinite being: the logical *praedicamenta*, namely, the orderly classification of attributes or predicates according to the categories of properties and accidents, do reflect the metaphysical *praedicamenta*, but these are "the real modes of finite being."[229] The difficulty for theology lies in the problem of applying the logic of predication to the discussion of the *modes of infinite being*, given that, as the Reformed orthodox insist, there is no proportion between the finite and the infinite.

Thus Zanchi would carefully define an attribute as "something that we attribute to God on our part" rather than as an incidental or separable property of the divine nature.[230] Zanchi's discussion set the stage for subsequent Reformed scholastic analysis of the problem of the attributes with its clear declaration that there are no accidents or natural passions in God, and that there is no diversity or division in the divine essence. God has simply chosen to accommodate his revelation in the Scriptures to our way of knowing, revealing there a series of attributes that are applied to him by way of similitude or analogy and not *realiter*, as they would be applied to beings in the created order. More precisely, Zanchi holds that the attributes are not predicated directly of God, but are identified through their effects in the created order.[231]

Others of the early orthodox would press the point still further by offering the term *proprietates essentiales* not merely as a substitute for the term *attributa* but as a term for a class of attributes that represented those characteristics most properly attributed to God. According to Wendelin, "the properties (*proprietates*) of the divine nature or essence are the essential attributes of God, by which the verity and majesty of the divine essence becomes known to us, and by which it is distinguished from all others."[232] The notion of *perfectiones divinae* points toward properties or characteristics of the

---

229. Grenier, *Thomistic Philosophy*, I, p. 177.

230. Zanchi, *De natura Dei*, II.ii.

231. Zanchi, *De natura Dei*, II.i; cf. Fiddes, *Theol. spec.*, I.ii.1 (p. 66).

232. Wendelin, *Systema*, as cited by Leigh, *Treatise*, II.i.

divine essence that belong to it in a manner different from the imperfect and separable manner in which the attributes of finite being inhere in individual creatures. Quite a few of the orthodox point to this term, together with the term *proprietates essentiales* as clarifying the language of divine attributes: "attributes," argues Turretin, "are not properly (*proprie*) ascribed to God, as something *epuosiodes*, that is accidentally in a subject, that completes it, and that is distinct *realiter* from it, but improperly (*improprie*) by presumption, seeing that they are called essential perfections of the divine nature."[233]

Thus, the principle taken over by the Reformed from the late medieval scholastics and mediated to the orthodox by the Reformers, in particular by the second-generation codifiers, *finitum non capax infiniti* or, in its medieval form, *finiti ad infinitum dari proportio non potest*, appears as a specifically epistemological rather than, as one modern author has rather naively argued, a concept reflecting "crudely naive spatial categories" and a "quantitative" notion of the divine and the human.[234] As Binning indicated,

> We can find no name to name him; or what can you call him when you have said, "He is light?" You can form no other notion of him but from the resemblance of this created light. But alas! that he is not; as he infinitely transcends that, and is distant from it, as if he had never made it according to his likeness. His name is above all these names; but what it is himself knows and knows only. ... though we may compare one creature with another, and find different degrees of perfection and excellency, while we are comparing them among themselves; but once let the glorious brightness of God shine upon the soul, and in that light all these difference shall be obscured, all their differences unobserved. An angel and a man, a man and a worm, differ much in glory and perfection of being: but oh! in [God's] presence there is no such reckoning. Upon this account all things are alike, God infinitely distant from all, and so not more or less. Infiniteness is not capable of such terms of comparison.[235]

Indeed, the Reformed use of the concept of disproportionality, whether in the era of the Reformation or that of orthodoxy, between finite and infinite, albeit sometimes attended by spatial metaphors, looks directly toward the medieval maxim, typically cited from Albert the Great, that it is utterly impossible to comprehend God (*Deum comprehendere*) but within the realm of the possible to attain to God (*Deum attingere*): Brakel expressly cautions,

> we are very unfit to comprehend anything about God who is an infinite Spirit. Can a small bottle contain an entire ocean? How then can a finite being comprehend an infinite Being? ... Truly, to perceive that God is incomprehensible and to acquiesce in and lose one's self in this; to pause and reflect in holy amazement ... that constitutes knowledge of God and is the best frame to increase in this knowledge.[236]

---

233. Turretin, *Inst. theol. elencticae*, III.v.2; cf. Beza et al., *Propositions and Principles*, V.i-ii.

234. Cf. E. David Willis, *Calvin's Catholic Christology: The Function of the So-Called* Extra Calvinisticum *in Calvin's Theology* (Leiden: Brill, 1966), pp. 74-75; also Muller, *Christ and the Decree*, pp. 21-22; and cf. *PRRD*, I, 5.2 (C.2).

235. Binning, *Common Principles*, vii-viii, in *Works*, pp. 38, 41.

236. Brakel, *Redelijke Godsdienst*, I.iii.48; cf. Calvin, *Sermons sur Job* (CO, 33, col 96), of the secret justice of God: "elle est plus haute que tout ce que nous pouvons comprendre en nostre entendement,

Given, moreover, the tendency of seventeenth-century Reformed metaphysics to exclude the doctrine of God from discussion, on the ground that God is the foundation and source of being in general and, therefore, not to be considered together with "being in general," and their concomitant refusal to follow Roman Catholic metaphysicians like Suárez in distinguishing being into infinite and finite as a basic division of the topic, recourse to the principle *finiti ad infinitum dari proportio non potest* probably also implies that the Reformed would not accept the univocal predication of being of God and of the finite order. This, at least, is a probable conclusion. This declaration of an absence of proportion between the finite and the infinite does not, however, rule out an analogical understanding of God-language in general or of the divine attributes in particular. Rather, the principle rules out some forms of analogical predication while at the same time affirming others.

4. Revelation, reason, and the identification of the attributes. Writers like Mastricht, Turretin, and Pictet make clear that, even at this late stage, Reformed orthodoxy was not conducting a strictly metaphysical or speculative inquiry into the divine attributes, but that the inquiry was generated in large part by Scripture and limited both by the bounds of the scriptural revelation and by the epistemological problems implicit in the attempt to understand, even in a limited way, the nature of transcendent deity.[237] This is not to deny the presence of nominally Aristotelian categories in the orthodox theology and certainly not to deny that, over the course of centuries of development of scholastic theology and philosophy, there had developed a close relationship between the understanding of scriptural language concerning the divine attributes and the corresponding philosophical categories — but only to note that the Aristotelian world-view of the orthodox needed to be, by their own express declaration, modified and guided by the content of revelation. In addition, as the specifically Aristotelian philosophical model lost ground in the face of the rise of modern science and rationalism, the orthodox attempted to maintain the older scholastic approach to the attributes by arguing the familiar patterns of attribution within the context of the language of Scripture. (The basis of this relationship had, of course, been prepared by the fathers of the first five centuries and, moreover, was latent in the fundamental agreement between religious and philosophical monotheism in their approach to the identity of God.)

Typically, then, the Protestant orthodox assume a dual attestation of the attributes — both by revelation and by rational inquiry — with the revelational basis being taken as prior even in the discussion of the more metaphysical or nominally philosophical of the attributes. In the high orthodox era, Rijssen in particular attempts to derive the attributes by proof from Scripture, invariably prefacing his arguments with a series of texts. Of course, most of these texts had been established as "proof-texts" by a lengthy exegetico-theological tradition reaching back into the patristic period, so that

---

il n'y a nulle proportion."

237. Thus, e.g., Mastricht, *Theoretico-practica theol.* II.vii.1; viii.1; ix.1; Turretin *Inst. theol. elencticae*, III.vii.7; viii.5; Pictet, *Theol. chr.*, I.iii-iv; II.ii-iii.

we ought not to infer much new or original exegesis on this point by the Protestant orthodox.[238] It is nonetheless the case that the orthodox did, frequently, scrutinize these texts carefully both in exegetical discussions in the longer theological systems and in their commentaries on the texts. Thus, the systems of Burman and Mastricht offer detailed discussion of the Greek and the Hebrew texts of various "proofs," often with considerable insight into the implications of the original languages for theology.[239] As Donnelly observed of Zanchi, the discussion of the divine attributes in the systems of the Protestant orthodox is distinguished from the discussion found in the medieval scholastic systems by the Protestants' continual recourse to Scripture,[240] in particular, to the divine "names" as a basis for the entire doctrine of God. Indeed, in the case of Gomarus' *Disputationes*, we find no separate discussion of attributes and no interest whatsoever in metaphysical and rational argumentation, but rather a restriction of the doctrine of God to an analysis of the biblical "names" of God and the doctrine of the Trinity.[241]

Thus, too, Pictet's frequent recourse to rational argumentation in his exposition of the attributes serves two primary purposes in and for his system: in the first place, the argumentation is intended to manifest the reasonableness of the Christian doctrine of God, but in the second place to declare clearly, in the context of theological system, the insufficiency of reason to provide a complete view of the divine essence and perfections. This twofold use of reason and philosophy serves to separate even the somewhat rationalistic Pictet from a full-blown philosophical rationalism, despite his tendency to derive succeeding attributes logically from preceding ones — and all of the attributes, ultimately, from the spirituality of God.[242]

Leigh's discussion of the problem both carries forward this logic into the high orthodox era and offers a representative statement of the mid-seventeenth century orthodox teaching. He provides seven general rules for the attribution of "properties" or "essential properties" to God:

> 1) they are all essential to God; for in him is no accident at all; whatsoever is in God the same is God. All these are also one in him: his Mercy is his Justice, and his Justice is his Mercy, and each are his essence, they differ only in our apprehension.
>
> 2) they are all absolute properties in God, and so distinguished from those respective properties whereby every person in the Trinity hath his own subsistence.
>
> 3) they are all equal to all the three Persons, and alike affirmed of all.
>
> 4) these Attributes are altogether in God alone, and that in the highest degree and measure, yea above all degree and measure; they are eternal and infinite in him. He alone is good, Matt. 19:17; and only wise, Rom. 16:27; and King of Kings, 1 Tim. 6:15. They are affirmed of him both in the concrete and abstract: he is not only wise and

---

238. Cf. the discussion of *dicta probantia* in PRRD, II, 7.5 (B).

239. See, e.g., Burman, *Synopsis theol.* I.xv.4; xvi.3-29; xvii.1, 4, 7, etc.; Mastricht, *Theoretico-practica theol.*, II.iii.2; iv.1-11; v.2.

240. Donnelly, "Calvinist Thomism," pp. 454-455; cf. idem, "Italian Influences," pp. 90, 91.

241. Cf. Gomarus, *Disputationes*, iii-iv.

242. Cf. Pictet *Theol. chr.*, II.iii.

good, but wisdom and goodness itself, life and justice itself [margin: John 8:12; 1 John 1:5; 4:16].

5) they are all actually and operatively in God ... his holiness makes us holy.

6) all these are in God objectively and finally: our holiness looks upon his holiness, as the face in the looking-glass on the man whose representation it is; and our holiness ends in his.

7) the attributes of God are everlasting, constant, and unchangeable, forever in him, at one time as well as another. This may minister comfort to God's people; God's attributes are not mutable accidents, but his very essence. His love and mercy are like himself, infinite, immutable, eternal [margin: Psalm 105:8; James 1:17; Psalm 100:5; 117:2; 136:1; Numb. 23:10].[243]

These criteria both state the basic orthodox argument and point toward one of its central problems — namely, the distinction of attributes. Leigh even appears to pose a possible contradiction: on the one hand he states that the attributes are identical to the divine essence and "differ only in our apprehension," even augmenting this definition with the marginal comment, "these Attributes differ not among themselves, nor from the divine essence," while, on the other hand, he states that the attributes are "actually and operatively in God," which, like the larger part of his analysis, seems to posit distinctions between the attributes. Leigh's approach to this particular point represents, moreover, only one of several approaches to the problem found among the Reformed orthodox.[244]

At the heart of these rules and underlying the problem of predication of the attributes is the foundational distinction between the essential or necessary existence of God and the contingent, caused, and composite nature of creatures. This difference between identification of creaturely and identification of divine attributes is neatly summed up by Maccovius: "The attributes that are spoken of God are God himself," so that "Nothing is in God that is not God."[245] Similarly, when Ridgley proceeds to examine the problem of the attributes or perfections by noting one of the philosophical methods for identifying the attributes, the *via eminentiae*, and relating it to the problem of predication, he also qualifies the method on the assumption that it correlates with his scriptural premises:

1) We must first take an estimate of finite perfections, which we have some Idea of ... such as power, wisdom, goodness, faithfulness, &c.

2) Then we must conceive that these are eminently, though not formally, in God; that is, there is no perfection in the creature, but we must ascribe the same to God, though not in the same way ... not in such a finite, limited, or imperfect way, as it is in the creature.

3) When the same words are used that import a perfection in God, and in the creature, *viz.*, wisdom, power &c. we must not suppose that these words import the same thing in their different application; for when they are applied to the creature ...

---

243. Leigh, *Treatise*, II.i (pp. 21-22).
244. See further, below, section 4.4 (C-D).
245. Maccovius, *Loci communes*, xv.1, 2 (pp. 120-121).

they are, at best, but finite, and have many imperfections attending them, all which we must separate or abstract in our thoughts, when the same words are used to set forth any divine perfection: thus knowledge is a perfection of the human nature, and the same word is used to denote a divine perfection; yet we must consider, at the same time, that *the Lord seeth not as man seeth* (1 Sam. 16:7).[246]

These basic considerations concerning the divine attributes lead to two final rules governing the discussion and the patterns of predication:

1) there is nothing in common between God and the creature, that is, there is nothing which belongs to the divine nature that can be attributed to the creature; and nothing proper to the creature is to be applied to God: yet there are some rays of the divine glory, which may be held as shining forth, or displayed in the creature, especially in the intelligent part of the creation, angels, and men, who are, for that reason, represented as made after the divine image.

2) Let us never think or speak of the divine perfections but with the highest reverence, lest we take his name in vain, or debase him in our thoughts; *Shall not his excellency make you afraid, and his dread fall upon you?* (Job. 13:11).[247]

We note here a point of connection and continuity between the Reformed orthodox doctrine of God and the basic principles for the formulation of theology set forth in the prolegomena to the Reformed orthodox systems. The prolegomena, particularly with reference to the definitions of *theologia* and of the divine *sapientia* and *scientia*, made a distinction between the divine archetype and the finite ectype. In theology itself, in the formulation of its language, even granting the rather direct sense of revelation found in the orthodox doctrine of Scripture, there can be no absolute grasp of the ultimate reality of the divine: theological language, at its best, is an ectypal reflection of the divine archetype, a finite and imperfect statement about an infinite and perfect being.[248] The orthodox doctrine of the attributes of God reflects these qualifications — both in its general statement of the problem of predication and in the strictures that it will place on the concept of "communicable attributes."

Turretin addresses the issue at several points by indicating the "inadequacy" of human thought and language: the attributes, like the divine names, are necessarily an "inadequate" representation of God, offered "not according to its total relation, but now under this perfection, then under another, for what we — as being finite — cannot take in by one adequate conception, we divide into various inadequate conceptions so as to obtain some knowledge of him." This, Turretin adds, "is not a proof of error in the intellect, but only of imperfection."[249] The modern reader is likely to miss Turretin's point: by "inadequate" he does not mean either unsuitable or capable of being improved upon in any way. His point rests on the broadly Aristotelian

---

246. Ridgley, *Body of Divinity*, p. 53, col. 2.

247. Ridgley, *Body of Divinity*, p. 54, col. 1.

248. Cf. Junius, *De vera theologia*, iv; Polanus, *Syntagma theol.*, Synopsis libri I; Turretin, *Inst. theol. elencticae*, I.i.9 with the discussion in PRRD, I, 5.2 (A, C).

249. Turretin, *Inst. theol. elencticae*, III.v.3; cf. III.iii.8.

definition of truth as "the adequation of the mind to the thing," i.e., the establishment of a conceptual likeness in it of the mind to the form of the thing known. In the case of God, such "adequation" is impossible inasmuch as there can be no proportion between infinite God and the finite mind. Our thoughts cannot be adequated to the divine reality — they necessarily remain "inadequate." Thus, concludes Turretin, "omnipotence is the divine essence itself apprehended as free from every obstacle in acting; eternity is the essence of God as without limit in duration; and so of the rest."[250] We cannot, however, grasp the incomplex essence of God in its infinite fulness: our theology, as Heidegger wrote, must remain "imperfect."[251]

Yet, despite the imperfection of our knowledge of God and the profound difficulty of understanding the way in which God possesses the revealed "attributes" or "properties," the doctrine of the divine attributes is no mere speculation and no mere exercise in academic theology. As Owen points out,

> God hath not only revealed his being unto us in general, but he hath done it in many distinct properties, all of them suited to promote in our minds our whole duty towards God, and this or that duty in particular. And he often distinctly presseth upon us the consideration of those properties, for to stir us up unto those distinct duties which they direct unto. ... So in places innumerable doth he mind us of his power and greatness; that upon our thoughts and apprehensions of them we might be stirred up to fear him, to trust in him, to get our hearts filled with a due reverence of him.[252]

Thus, the right understanding of the divine attributes in general and of each attribute in particular will be related directly to Christian piety. Each attribute, as defined in the Reformed orthodox system, will have its "practical use" — an issue directly addressed in many of the orthodoxy systems and consistently reflected in commentaries, sermons, and practical treatises.

B. The Reformers on the Divine Attributes

1. The problem of the divine attributes in the era of the Reformation. As we noted in the preliminary discussion of the order and arrangement of the *locus de Deo*, the Protestant orthodox were not unaware of issues relating to the order of theological system and to the way in which order affects meaning. Not only did the influence of Ramism on early Reformed orthodoxy assure that a close attention would be paid to the architectonics of theological system, it is also true that several of the most influential of the systematic and exegetical essays of the second-generation codifiers of the Reformation had a major impact on the way in which the early orthodox moved to construct fully developed systems of Reformed doctrine.

Calvin's discussions of the knowledge of God and of the scriptural revelation of God in the first book of his *Institutes* are often noted as examples of the lack of interest

---

250. Turretin, *Inst. theol. elencticae*, III.v.3.

251. Heidegger, *Corpus theol.*, I.70; cf. the discussion in PRRD, I, 5.5 (C).

252. John Owen, *An Exposition of the Epistle to the Hebrews*, ed. William H. Goold, 7 vols. (London and Edinburgh: Johnstone and Hunter, 1855), vol. IV, p. 365 (on Heb. 4:12-13).

of the Reformers in a speculative or metaphysical discussion of the divine attributes — and, by extension, as a major point of distinction between Calvin's thought and that of the later Reformed tradition. Not only is it the case that, among Calvin's contemporaries, Musculus, Bullinger, and Vermigli provided a clearer model for later discussion of the divine attributes than did Calvin, it is also the case that Calvin hardly provides an unequivocal argument against the discussion of divine attributes in Reformed theological system. As we have argued elsewhere, Calvin's *Institutes* is not to be considered as a fully developed system of theology in the modern sense of the term but rather as an expanded set of *loci communes* and *disputationes*, based on a catechetical exposition, augmented by polemic, and rearranged with a clearer vision of the requirements of a body of doctrine than, for example, Bullinger's *Compendium*.[253]

Calvin himself viewed the *Institutes* as a gathering of the "dogmatic disputations" that he chose, for reasons of style, not to include in his commentaries. He therefore notes that the *Institutes* offers a basic summary of the faith, a "road" toward the larger part of his "program of instruction" in the commentaries.[254] Nonetheless, despite these stylistic and philosophical limits, Calvin did offer a significant listing of the attributes, including all of the more philosophical concepts, such as simplicity and infinity, and assuming a traditional division of the attributes into the categories of essential and personal.[255] Thus, in the *Institutes*, Calvin often lists groupings of attributes: "fatherly goodness and beneficently inclined will";[256] kindness, goodness, mercy, justice, judgement, power, might, holiness, and truth, as identified in the divine names, Jehovah and Elohim;[257] infinity and spirituality;[258] glory, eternity, self-existence, omnipotence, wisdom, and righteousness;[259] unity and simplicity.[260] His commentaries, moreover, particularly the Old Testament commentaries written in the latter part of his career, by way of contrast to the *Institutes*, offer extended discussions of the divine attributes — and in the *Institutes* itself, where the discussions are brief, he points us toward the lengthier discussions in the commentaries.[261] Indeed, a full-scale doctrine of God and the divine attributes can also be elicited from Calvin's sermons.[262] What Calvin clearly

---

253. Muller, *Unaccommodated Calvin*, pp. 101-117.

254. Cf. Calvin, *Institutes*, "John Calvin to the Reader," pp. 4-5 (N.B., these particular words were part of Calvin's prefatory address from 1539 onward).

255. On simplicity and infinity, see Calvin, *Institutes*, I.xiii.1 and xiii.2, respectively; cf. the discussion in Warfield, "Calvin's Doctrine of God," pp. 167-171.

256. Calvin, *Institutes*, I.x.1.

257. Calvin, *Institutes*, I.x.2.

258. Calvin, *Institutes*, I.xiii.1.

259. Calvin, *Institutes*, I.xiv.3.

260. Calvin, *Institutes*, I.xiii.20.

261. Cf. e.g., the commentaries on Exodus 3:14; Psalm 50, 93, 106, 145; Isaiah 42:8; 49:8; 55:1. Cf. *Institutes*, I.x.2, where Calvin cites Ps. 145 as a source of the doctrine of the attributes, and note Muller, *Unaccommodated Calvin*, pp. 28-29, 140-143, 148-152, on the relationship of the *Institutes* to the commentaries.

262. Cf. Richard Stauffer, *Dieu, la création et la Providence dans la prédication de Calvin* (Bern and Frankfurt: Lang, 1978).

disliked was excessive metaphysical speculation into the doctrine of the divine attributes — a dislike well described and qualified by his statement concerning the character of the proper knowledge of God,

> What is God? Men who pose this question are merely toying with idle speculations. It is more important for us to know of what sort he is and what is consistent with his nature.[263]

If we can take Calvin at his word, he has little sympathy with discussions of "what God is" — "*quid sit Deus*," which is to say, with abstruse discussions of the divine essence or quiddity, but he has a profound interest in discussions of "what sort God is" — "*qualis sit Deus*," which is to say discussions of the so-called communicable attributes that describe the relation of God to the world.

Granting this division of the topic and this distaste for one of its parts, Calvin did not often discuss either the problem of the relation of the attributes to the essence of God or the problem of predication of attributes — but he did provide a considerable mass of materials for the biblical discussion of the divine attributes. And, in several places, he quite clearly indicates a very traditional view of the attributes as indivisibly and irreducibly belonging to the divine essence: we can arrive, Calvin indicates, at a conception of the "eternal power and divinity" of God, which in turn leads to the recognition that God is "without beginning and from himself." Calvin then continues, "When we arrive at this point, the divinity becomes known to us, which cannot exist except accompanied with all the attributes of God, since they are all included under that idea."[264] Indeed, had Calvin not written his *Institutes* separate from the commentaries but — like Vermigli — had it compiled for him out of the commentaries, we can easily imagine a rather vast discussion of divine attributes!

It is also of some importance to note here that Calvin's method of presenting the attributes, both in his *Institutes* and in his *Instruction* or catechism of 1537, obliges a view of natural revelation that assumes the truth of God's revelation through his works of the natural order and that assumes also that the regenerate have access to this revelation.[265] Accordingly, in both places, Calvin divides the divine attributes into two categories, those derived from contemplation of "the operation of the world," and those revealed in the Scriptures.[266] The attributes are, indeed, "more intimately and vividly revealed in the Word" than in the created order. Nonetheless, Calvin can state that "the knowledge of God set forth for us in Scripture is destined for the very same goal as the knowledge whose imprint shines in his creatures, in that it invites us first to fear God, then to trust in him."[267] A similar approach is found in Viret, who indicates

263. Calvin, *Institutes*, I.ii.2.
264. Calvin, *Commentary on Romans*, 1:20 (*CTS Romans*, p. 70).
265. Cf. the discussion in *PRRD*, I, 5.3.
266. Calvin, *Institutes*, I.x.1; cf. Warfield, "Calvin's Doctrine of God," pp. 171-172, n. 105.
267. Calvin, *Institutes*, I.x.2.

that God cannot be known in himself but ought to be sought where he has manifested his will, namely, in his works of creation and redemption.[268]

Calvin also appears to accept the fairly standard rule in discussing the divine attributes that they are not known in themselves or in the divine essence but through their effects in the word: he writes concerning the divine Logos, "Now the design of the Evangelist is, as I have already said, to show that no sooner was the world created than the Word of God came forth into external operation; for having formerly been incomprehensible in his essence, he then became publicly known by the effect of his power."[269] Calvin indicates, therefore, no methodological barrier to the discussion of the attributes both as they can be inferred from nature and as they are given in Scripture in Reformed theological system. In contrast to Calvin's approach in the *Institutes*, moreover, perhaps because of their broader acquaintance with the medieval tradition, Hyperius and Musculus acknowledged the importance not only of an initial discussion of the existence of God and our knowledge of it and of a subsequent approach to the problems of the divine essence and subsistence.[270] The early Reformed tradition offered several models for constructing theology, all of which (including Calvin's) provided extended discussion of the divine essence and attributes — including several models that presented the discussion in its more or less traditional place. It is simply an error in historical interpretation of the Reformation that claims such doctrinal discussion was categorically removed from Reformed theology by its founding teachers.

2. Does God have a "nature"? A critical question from Musculus. The "nature of God" is a most difficult subject, yet a necessary one if religion is to be rightly understood. "Surely," Musculus writes,

> the knowledge of all things is such that unless their nature is known, they cannot be truly and perfectly known. ... So it is concerning the knowledge of God. ... The knowledge of God cannot be plain and perfect unless his nature is known.[271]

The nature of God must be the beginning of the study of God, particularly of the study of the divine attributes, "lest we should say anything incautiously about the majesty of God."

Yet, there is a problem in the attribution of a "nature" to God inasmuch as the term is usually applied to creatures. Musculus cites several definitions of "nature," including that offered by Augustine in *De spiritu et anima*, but favors Lactantius' definition found in the *Divine Institutes* — itself a reflection of the definition found in Aristotle's *Physics*:

---

268. Viret, *Exposition familière sur la symbole*, pp. 51-52; cf. the discussion in Bavaud, *Le réformateur Pierre Viret*, pp. 50-51, 54-56.

269. Calvin, *Commentary on John*, 1:3 (CTS *John*, I, p. 30). Note that Calvin rendered "logos" as *sermo*, not as *verbum*, leading the translators to render his Latin as "Speech" rather than as "Word" — yet his reference here is to the second person of the Trinity, rendered here as "Word."

270. Hyperius, *Methodus theologiae*, I, pp. 71-91, 135-220.

271. Musculus, *Loci communes*, XLII (*Commonplaces*, p. 886, col. 2 - p. 887, col. 1).

nature is derived from the Latin word *nascendo*, which relates to birth. My opinion is not that the "nature" is the thing itself, but the power peculiar or proper to the thing imparted naturally to it in its origin, wherefrom it receives its individual character or quality not only of being, but also of doing, bearing, begetting, etc.[272]

Insofar, moreover, as "*natura*" indicates something that is given, imparted, or begotten, it cannot be applied to God: nature must always be, in some sense, the work of a creator and is in created things only, as both containing and governing the thing whose nature it is.

By extension beyond it normal reference, *natura* may, then, be used to identify qualities that belong to God and are considered to be "naturally" in him, such as goodness, love and kindness, mercy and honor, faithfulness and truth.[273] God is also said to be by nature "indifferent" or impartial and "not a respecter of persons"; he is just and opposed to all wickedness; he "abhorrs the proud and embraces the humble"; he is "patient and slow to anger ... wise and foreseeing." Since, moreover, God is all of these things "neither by reason of some other being nor by chance, but by nature and of himself, it follows that the same nature must forever and unchangeably be in him, a fact that brings incredible comfort to the faithful." Thus also, the "quality of his nature" cannot be altered, even though at some times, under special circumstances, God may appear to deal strangely with the world or to abridge the normal order of events.[274] As already indicated in the foregoing comments, Musculus' interest in an extended discussion of the "nature" and attributes of God is inseparably bound to his interest in Christian piety: we have not come very far from Calvin's insistence that our knowledge of God emphasize "what sort" of God stands in relation to us — we have only stated the interest in piety in a way conducive to a more traditional view of the divine attributes.

As a final element in his initial discussion of the divine nature, Musculus raises the question of the greatness of God. This, he notes, is not a question of "bodily quantity, but of the majesty of God": God, after all, has no body but is nonetheless exceedingly great in his goodness, wisdom, power, and glory — and is, moreover, eternal. Even used in their superlative forms, such words apply best to human beings, since they admit of a "certain comparison" with others who are good, wise, and so forth. God's greatness, like God's nature, is not analogous to creatures, so that the simple expedient of using superlatives in reference to God does not solve the problem of predication: "We must forbear all comparisons, and acknowledge that his goodness, wisdom, greatness, majesty, power, glory, are incomparable." His goodness appears in his providential care of creation, his loving kindness in the sending of his Son into

---

272. Musculus, *Loci communes*, XLII (*Commonplaces*, p. 887, col. 2), citing Lactantius: see *Divine Instiutes*, I.ix (in ANF, VII, p. 53); cf. Aristotle, *Physics*, II.1 (192b, 10-25), and Grenier, *Thomistic Philosophy*, I, pp. 299-300.

273. Musculus, *Loci communes*,I [III].4 (*Commonplaces*, p. 17, col.1).

274. Musculus, *Loci communes*,I [III].4 (*Commonplaces*, p. 17, col. 2).

the world, the "excellency of his strength and power" in the work of creation by the Word, and his "infinite wisdom" in the "marvellous ordering of all things."[275]

Although Calvin favored the use of the term "nature" as indicating what is knowable concerning God, as distinguished from the divine essence, God in himself, which must remain incomprehensible,[276] he also evidenced a concern over the usage. "I admit," he wrote,

> indeed that the expression "Nature is God," may be piously used, if dictated by a pious mind; but as it is inaccurate and harsh, (Nature being more properly the order which has been established by God,) in matters which are so very important, and in regard to which special reverence is due, it does harm to confound the Deity with the inferior operations of his hands.[277]

Theology, nevertheless, uses the term "*natura Dei*" when it argues that "Christ is by nature the Son of God" or that "there are two natures in him, the divine and human natures."

In Musculus' view, a somewhat different definition is needed, then, when the term "nature" is applied to God:

> there is in God some quality whereby he differs from all created things ... and seeing that this quality does not arise by chance or accident, nor is acquired from another being, nor is it mutable, but is natural, proper, and unchangeable, it follows that God has a nature.[278]

It must be observed from the very outset of discussion, therefore, that there is a distinction between created and uncreated nature: God can, indeed, must be said to have a nature, but it is an uncreated nature.

A nature or a thing can be described according to what it is or according to what it is not. The definition of the nature of God as distinct from all created nature points theology toward the second, the negative, pattern: "this is the first degree of the knowledge of God, to understand before all else what he is not, so that we do not reverence anything that is not God." Following out the logic of the negative way, Musculus concludes that, over against composite character of the world order, God's nature is "simple and void of all composition" — yet God is also distinguished into three persons, Father, Son, and Holy Spirit, and therefore distinguished also into three properties, the unbegottenness of the Father, the begottenness of the Son, and the

---

275. Musculus, *Loci communes*, I [III].5 (*Commonplaces*, p. 18, cols. 1-2); cf. the similar issues raised in Amyraut et al., *Syntagma thesium theologicarum*, I.xvii.4. Following this point, Musculus moves on to a discussion of the works of God and of creation. He returns to the discussion of the problem of the divine "nature" and of the predication of attributes at the beginning of his subsequent discussion of the divine attributes.

276. Calvin, *Institutes*, I.ii.2.

277. Calvin, *Institutes*, I.v.5.

278. Musculus, *Loci communes*, xlii (*Commonplaces*, p. 888, col. 2).

procession of the Spirit, which nonetheless must be understood to subsist in the one divine nature.[279]

Gregory of Nazianzus was correct when he observed "that the nature of God cannot be perceived" and that, therefore, we can have no "full and perfect" knowledge of God's nature. We can distinguish, however, between those things that are proper to God's nature and those things that are alien or strange to it, such as God's alien work (*opus alienum*) of wrath and destruction, identified in Isaiah 28:21. Some knowledge of God's nature can be gained from his works, but this knowledge is imprecise and imperfect apart from Scripture, which reveals God's proper intention, his true purpose toward the human race. Scripture, thus, can be said to reveal the "quality" of God's nature — that is, to identify "what sort" of being God is. This quality is not defined in the way that logicians define quality, in terms of habit or disposition, natural power or lack of power, affection, form, and so forth. Rather, "quality," as belonging to God, is that which distinguishes the nature of God from all other natures and identifies God as surpassing all created things in majesty, power, goodness, and wisdom, and having the power to govern and preserve all things.[280]

God does not communicate his nature to his works; whatever God makes or creates does not partake of his Godhead, inasmuch as the act of creation is utterly different from bearing or begetting. Even man, who was called by the apostle the child or image of God, and who has a rational soul, does not partake of the divine nature in any degree: that is reserved for Christ alone, who is the "only-begotten Son of God."[281] The elect, who are "of God" by "the grace of election and predestination," partake not of God's nature but of God's grace. Christ alone is Son by nature: human beings are sons and heirs by grace alone. Nor is the human nature of Christ deified in such a way as to change the human into a divine nature. Christ's humanity, in its union with the second person of the Trinity, remains truly human: rejecting the premises of Lutheran Christology, Musculus argues that the nature of God cannot be communicated to any creature.[282]

A related argument is found in the chapter dealing with the divine unity and Trinity in Vermigli's *Loci communes*. As a whole, from the editorial pen of Masson, the chapter tends to present the doctrine of God as a unity, not separating out the doctrine of divine essence and attributes from the doctrine of the Trinity of Persons. It begins, however, with a piece of a posteriori logic that bears witness both to Vermigli's sense of the remoteness of God and of the need for revelation and to his Thomistic leanings:

> Since the nature of God is infinite, it cannot be comprehended under any one of the titles by which he is known ... nonetheless, his special properties are to be inferred from his effects and works, and from these we understand something of the divine nature and power, so that even though we cannot comprehend the whole, we may at least

---

279. Musculus, *Loci communes*, xlii (*Commonplaces*, p. 899, cols. 1-2).

280. Musculus, *Loci communes*, XLII (*Commonplaces*, pp. 891-892).

281. Musculus, *Loci communes*, XLII (*Commonplaces*, pp. 893-894).

282. Musculus, *Loci communes*, XLII (*Commonplaces*, pp. 895-897).

arrive at a partial knowledge of God. ... Even so, men can in some sense perceive the nature and infinite substance of God, knowing him by these aspects and titles — not as if God is composite, but because we come to an understanding of his power and infinite greatness through his effects and through our composite knowing. The titles by which he is known are manifold: as when he is called merciful, constant, just, good, the God of hosts, and so forth.[283]

(The a posteriori aspect of this argument so rests on Scripture that it involves the theological premise of a necessary body of revelation and in no way conflicts with Vermigli's earlier hesitance concerning the *analogia entis*.)[284]

C. The Divine Attributes in the Theology of Reformed Orthodoxy

1. Basic issues of exposition: the importance of the discussion of attributes and its biblical and traditionary foundations. Granting this ontological and epistemological distance between the divine and the human — according to which even the word "nature" cannot be applied univocally to both and according to which the divine "nature," which is non-composite or simple, can be known only in a composite way (i.e., in a way that does not correspond at all to the way in which it is in itself, but that corresponds to our way of enumerating and explaining attributes and persons)[285] — the early orthodox Reformed theologians received from the hands of the second generation theologians of the Reformation a major problem in the construction of a *locus de Deo*, specifically in the discussion of the divine attributes.[286] If the Reformers did not offer their successors a fully developed doctrine of the divine attributes or even a full systematic discussion of the problem of predication, they did provide them with a fairly clear indication of where they stood in relation to the paradigms and models found in the scholastic tradition. The Reformed orthodox, accordingly, were pressed to draw critically upon the extant scholastic paradigms for the predication, enumeration, and discussion of the attributes, with a view toward the construction of the complete *locus* under terms consistent with the basic insights of the Reformation concerning the transcendence and the relationality of God.

The problem of the relationship of revelation and reason, theology and philosophy, very naturally arises in the context of this enumeration and discussion. On the one

---

283. Vermigli, *Loci communes*, I.xii.1.

284. Cf. *PRRD*, I, 5.1.

285. Cf. Grenier, *Thomistic Philosophy*, II, p. 31: "properties of being are explained by the fact that being is virtually multiple and superabundant, and therefore cannot be attained completely by a single concept of the intellect. But, given the concept of being, we can have other concepts of being under different aspects. These concepts presuppose the concept of being ... and therefore are said to express the properties of being."

286. Some exception must be taken to Alvin Plantinga, *Does God Have a Nature* (Milwaukee: Marquette University Press, 1980) where the notion of the essential identity of properties in God is taken as ultimately the identification of God as a property. See the critique of Davies, "Classical Theism and the Doctrine of Divine Simplicity," pp. 53-59, 64-66 and Robert M. Burns, "The Divine Simplicity in St. Thomas," in *Religious Studies*, 25, pp. 271-272, especially note 1.

hand, many, indeed, most of the attributes are available from the reading of Scripture, either by direct citation or by logical inference — so that the exposition of the attributes falls well within the bounds of the orthodox hermeneutic.[287] On the other hand, the Protestant scholastics drew on a long tradition of discussion of the attributes in their relation, positive (*via eminentiae*) or negative (*via negativa seu negationis*) to the created order. Although this latter approach to the problem belongs, when examined in isolation from its history, to the purely philosophical or rational discussion of the idea of God, its use in the scholastic tradition, particularly by the Thomistic school, so influential in the development of Protestant orthodoxy, assumed the analogical relationship of God as creator to the created order — with the result that the scriptural language about God was assumed to cohere with the more rational discussion of the divine attributes based on an examination of the divine handiwork in the created order. From this perspective, the language of eminence, negation and cause used by philosophy stood in a necessary relation to the language of Scripture, which, as language, could hardly fail to evidence the same patterns of relationship between the divine and the creature. These traditionary categories, as used by the Reformed orthodoxy, were no longer patterns of purely rational deduction of attributes but rather categories of analysis or organization into which biblically revealed attributes were gathered for purposes of exposition.

The orthodox are clear in their assumption that the divine attributes, as known by revelation and by reason, are crucial to the understanding of God, God's works, and God's will. Since the attributes are, for the most part, either given directly or indirectly, by logical inference, in Scripture, they are accepted as indicators both of the way in which God relates to the world and — with the proper epistemological cautions noted — of the way God is in himself. Thus, Leigh begins his discussion of the attributes with a definition based on the arguments of Zanchi and Wendelin:

> God may be known by his attributes and essential properties, of which some show what he is in himself, [others] what he is to us. They are called attributes because they are rather said to be attributed to God (that we might by them better conceive what he is) than to be in him. They are the one most pure God diversely apprehended, and the same with the divine essence, but for the weakness of our capacity they are diversely distinguished. They are called properties, because they are peculiar to his majesty, and are so in him as they are not in any creature: *Attributum est Divinae simplissimae essentiae pro diversa agendi ratione diversa, & vera habitudo & conceptio nobis expressa.*[288]

Somewhat more simply, "Attributa Dei sunt perfectiones eius, quae declarent qualis sit" — "the attributes of God are his perfections, which declare what sort [of being] he is."[289] Granting, moreover, that God is infinite and eternal, he must also have

---

287. Cf. *PRRD*, II, 5.3 and 5.7.

288. Leigh, *Treatise*, II.i (pp. 20-21); cf. Brakel, *Redelijke Godsdienst*, I.iii.6; Le Blanc, *Theses theol.*, *De Dei simplicitate*, xvi.

289. Rijssen, *Summa theol.*, III.iv.

innumerable attributes, so that the theological discussion cannot possibly claim to exhaust the divine identity, but only to examine reverently what has been revealed.[290]

We also encounter in the writings of the Reformed orthodox, despite the increasingly elaborate discussions of the attributes, a sense of limits and boundaries related to the strictures leveled by the Reformers against the development of a more speculative theology — and related also, therefore, to the limits imposed on rational knowing by Scotist and nominalist theologies of the later Middle Ages. Ursinus, for one, carried reservations like those of Musculus concerning the attribution of a "nature" to God into the next generation of Reformed theology. God, Ursinus comments, is "different from all creatures and things." Thus, "God is not nature itself, nor matter, nor form, nor any part of nature, but the efficient cause of all things; neither is his essence mixed or blended with other things; it is different and unlike everything else."[291]

In addition, our knowledge of the divine attributes must vary with the variations of our relationship to God — namely, humanity knows God differently under the covenant of grace than under the covenant of works, or, to put the point in slightly different language, the knowledge of the attributes gained from natural revelation or creation, even prior to the fall, is different from the knowledge of the attributes gained by special revelation under grace. Thus, under the covenant of works, the attributes related to the creation and preservation of the world, such as God's wisdom, power, goodness, bounty, and justice were most clearly known — whereas under the covenant of grace, attributes "such as mercy which regards the creature in misery, and longsuffering which respects the creature as offending and provoking God to wrath" are revealed to the greater glory of God.[292] Not that God's attributes change, but rather "upright man was not a qualified object for pardoning mercy and longsuffering patience, but lapsed man was a qualified object for these attributes."[293] (Here, again, the point must be made that we are not dealing with an a priori logic that deduces theology from the essence and attributes but rather an analysis of the attributes grounded in soteriological issues and concerns.)

2. Attributes, accidents, properties, and essential perfections: terminological distinctions in the doctrine of the "attributes." There was also some attempt among the Reformed theologians of the era of orthodoxy to clarify the terminology of the "attributes" — specifically, by distinguishing between *attributa, accidentia, proprietates* and *proprietates essentiales*, and also to clarify the concept of attributes through the use of alternative terms, like *proprietates* and *perfectiones*. Simply put, an attribute is strictly a characteristic or quality attributed to or predicated of an object, whereas a property is a characteristic that belongs to an object. Properties can be either incidental to the nature of a thing or intrinsic to it: incidental, changeable, or removable properties are called "accidents" or *accidentia*; intrinsic characteristics that belong to

290. Rijssen, *Summa theol.*, III.ix.

291. Ursinus, *Explicationes catecheseos* (*Commentary*, p. 125).

292. Patrick Gillespie, *The Ark of the Testament Opened: or, the Secret of the Lords Covenant Unsealed in a Treatise of the Covenant of Grace* (London: R.C., 1661), I.vi.5-6.

293. Gillespie, *Ark of the Testament Opened*, I.vi.6.

the very nature of a thing and that cannot be removed or abstracted without altering the thing are "essential properties," *proprietates essentiales.*[294] To say that God has "attributes," in the strictest sense, is simply to state that various characteristics have been attributed to or predicated of God — to identify the attributes as "properties," which is the typical orthodox approach, is to indicate that they are genuinely in God in some sense. Since, moreover, God is understood to be ultimate, self-sufficient, and immutable, God cannot be said to have incidental, but only essential properties.

The point had arisen in medieval scholastic discussion that the distinguishing characteristics of the three divine persons were of a different order than the divine attributes properly so called: the attributes belong equally and indivisibly to the three divine persons, inasmuch as the three are coessential in the undivided deity of the Godhead — but the *proprietates personales* are the characteristics that distinguish the three persons one from another, "personally" but not essentially. The Father, thus, is unbegotten and neither begotten nor proceeding; the Son or Word, begotten, and neither unbegotten nor proceeding; the Spirit, proceeding, and neither unbegotten nor begotten. All three, however, are eternal, simple, infinite, omnipotent, omniscient, righteous, loving, and so forth — as the Athanasian Creed reminds us, "and yet there are not three eternals: but one eternal..., [because] there are not three gods: but one God."[295] As Alexander of Hales, had argued, there cannot be any *distinctio realis* between the attributes — nor can there be such a "real distinction" between the divine persons and the divine essence — but the persons, as identified by the *proprietates personales*, must be distinct from one another, indeed, really *(realiter)* distinct.[296]

The distinctions made by the orthodox between properties, essential properties, attributes, and affections of the will relate also to the exceeding diversity of the Reformed orthodox systems in their enumeration of the attributes. Thus, Daneau speaks of attributes or properties, distinguishing between "common" and personal properties of the Godhead, and contrasts them with accidents, which pertain to God only in the sense of external relations spoken of figuratively or anthropopathically.[297] Polanus identifies the attributes as either "proper" or "figurative," the proper attributes as essential properties, divine names, or personal properties.[298] Leigh argued a traditional scholastic distinction between "attributes ... which belong to the Essence, and Properties to the Persons themselves," but he also noted the identification of the attributes

---

294. Zanchi, *De natura Dei*, II.i (col. 50); cf. Thomas Spencer, *The Art of Logick delivered in the precepts of Aristotle and Ramus* (London: John Dawson, 1628), I.xi (pp. 57-61).

295. Cf. *Symbolum quicunque (The Athanasian Creed)*, in Schaff, *Creeds*, II, p. 67: "Aeternus Pater: aeternus Filius: aeternus Spiritus Sanctus. Et tamen non tres aeterni: sed unus aeternus. Sicut non tres increati; nec tres immensi: sed unus increatus: et unus immensus. ... Et tamen non tres dii: sed unus est Deus."

296. See Alexander of Hales, *Summa theol.*, pars I, inq. I, tract. 2, q. 2; and see further, below, 6.2 and N.B., that a "real distinction" is the sort that appears between "things" and other "things": cf. DLGT, s.v., *"distinctio"* for a discussion of the various kinds of distinctions in their distinction from one another.

297. Daneau, *Christianae isagoges*, I.7-8.

298. Polanus, *Syntagma theol.*, Synopsis libri III.

themselves as "essential properties."[299] What must be recognized throughout the discussion of the Reformed orthodox doctrine of divine attributes, then, is the presence of diversity without fundamental disagreement, the grounding of that diversity as much in questions of genre and method as in the issue of substance, and (from the perspective of historical study of these systems) the necessarily composite character of any list of attributes discussed by the Reformed orthodox. A similar diversity will appear when the question of the order and arrangement of the *locus* is raised.

D. Patterns of Classification

1. Toward understanding the paradigms. As a final step toward resolution of the issue of predication, the orthodox raised the question of basic paradigms for setting forth the attributes. In Reformed theology, this question typically arose first in the era of early orthodoxy — although it is also broached by Hyperius already in the era of the Reformation, with reference to patristic sources, notably Gregory of Nazianzus and John of Damascus.[300] The point is important to an understanding of their teaching, just as modern misapprehensions of their approach provide barriers to understanding the meaning of the divine attributes, both in general and individually.[301] Whereas the Reformed orthodox manifest relative agreement on the problem of predication of attributes, following out a Thomist pattern of argument modified with Scotistic accents, they disagree quite strongly over the patterns of classification of the attributes. There appears never to have been an internal Reformed controversy over this subject — certainly the level of disagreement fell far short of the rancor of the debates over covenant theology, hypothetical universalism, or the mediate imputation of sin — but the disagreement is obvious, not only in the varying organization of systems but also in the fairly pointed critique of alternative patterns that frequently appears in the Reformed systems.

What is more, these variant patterns of exposition are hardly distributed at random among the theologians. Instead, several schools or trajectories of thought are clearly identifiable. There is, of course, the well-known distinction into incommunicable and communicable attributes, somewhat mistakenly viewed by Heppe and others as the dominant model from early on in the development of Reformed orthodoxy.[302] Major objections to this paradigm had been raised by Zanchi and were repeated throughout the era of orthodoxy. Edward Leigh noted, without much sense of preference (and

---

299. Leigh, *Treatise*, II.i (pp. 20-21).

300. Hyperius, *Methodus theologiae*, I, pp. 90-1.

301. There is a massive misunderstanding in Weber, *Foundations of Dogmatics* I, pp. 397-399, 438-439: Weber even invents the notion of "majesty attributes" as a category for understanding the older dogmatics—a point for which there is no basis in the documents. Similarly, Brunner, *Christian Doctrine of God*, p. 191, claims that the older dogmatics divided the attributes up into categories of "metaphysical attributes" and "ethical attributes," the former being "Greek" and the latter biblical. As in the case of Weber's claim, this paradigm, is not supported by the documentary evidence of sixteenth- and seventeenth-century Reformed dogmatics.

302. Heppe, *Reformed Dogmatics*, pp. 60-62; cf. Louis Berkhof, *Systematic Theology*, p. 55.

also without reference to the incommunicable-communicable distinction), several patterns of classification: attributes can be classified according to the ways of knowing God, the *via eminentiae* and *via negativa*, but they may also be arranged as "absolute," describing God as he is in himself apart from any relation to the creature, and "relative," describing God in his relations *ad extra* — or, similarly, according to his "sufficiency" (almighty, infinite, perfect, unchangeable, eternal) and his "efficiency" (powerful, just, good, patient, just, and merciful).[303]

The several models are, moreover, not mutually exclusive: the distinction between *via eminentiae* and *via negativa*, sometimes with the added language of a *via causalitatis*, was often used in connection with other patterns of classification. Similarly, the absolute-relative and incommunicable-communicable distinctions can be used in conjunction with one another or as a way of clarifying the distinction between attributes of essence and attributes of life.[304] Quite a few of the orthodox theologians take elements from one classification over into another.

2. Divine names, essential or absolute attributes (attributes of the first order), relative attributes and divine affections (attributes of the second order). Zanchi had classified the attributes into categories of absolute and relative, a priori and a posteriori and had noted that the alternative classification into incommunicable and communicable was untenable, inasmuch as none of the divine *perfectiones essentiales* can be communicated to creatures.[305] In an argument that had broad significance for the later Reformed orthodox exposition of the divine essence and attributes, Zanchi pointed out that, since God is most simple essence, not being composite or having accidents and separable qualities, the so-called attributes of God are intended to indicate this most simple essence without essential or real distinction between them: the essence itself is good, powerful, just, merciful, and so forth. The way in which this difficult issue can best be understood, Zanchi indicates, is to begin the discussion, not with the attributes themselves, but with the divine names, the foremost of which is "Jehovah," indicating eternity and simplicity of essence.[306] This insistence on divine simplicity as a governing concept in the doctrine of God is retained throughout the orthodox era and on into the early eighteenth century — after the demise of Aristotelianism.[307] Even so, the discussion of the divine names, Zanchi argues, places the essential identity of God as Jehovah first and then, by way of the other names, leads to a further discussion of divine attributes either as faculties or powers (*facultates & dynameis*) natural to God, such as *voluntas* and the *potestas agendi*; or as *qualitates* analogous to the human virtues, such as *bonitas, justitia*, and *veritas*; or as affections, such as *amor, ira, odium*, and *misericordia*.[308]

---

303. Leigh, *Treatise*, II.I (p. 22).

304. Cf. *Synopsis purioris theol.*, VI.xxiii, with Mastricht, *Theoretico-practica theol.*, II.v.8-9.

305. Zanchi, *De natura Dei*, I.i

306. Zanchi, *De natura Dei*, I.i.

307. Cf. Fiddes, *Theol. spec.*, I.ii.1 (p. 67), with Wyttenbach, *Tentamen theologiae dogmaticae*, III, § 227-8; and Stapfer, *Institutiones theologiae polemicae*, vol. I, III.301, 305-308.

308. Zanchi, *De natura Dei*, II.i.

After his book-length presentation of the meaning of the divine names, Zanchi begins his discussion of the attributes in book II of the *De natura Dei* by setting forth those essential properties of God that do not necessarily imply any external relation of the Deity: simplicity, eternity, immutability, life or aseity, infinity, immensity, perfection, and beatitude. Book III takes up the discussion of the attributes which, as faculties or powers of God, will be the ground of his self-expression: omnipotence, wisdom, truth, and will. Book IV discusses attributes as affections manifested in God's dealings with his creatures: goodness, grace, love, mercy, righteousness, anger, hate, rule. Finally, in his fifth book, Zanchi discusses providence and predestination as they are attributed to God. There are significant reflections here of Aquinas' *Summa* — notably the foundational use of simplicity and the discussion of providence and predestination toward the end of the list of predications.

Zanchi's work is determined by its foundational discussion of the divine names prior to the discussion of the attributes and his division of the attributes into absolute and relative categories or, as several later writers describe the distinction, between attributes of the first and attributes of the second order or genus — an approach echoed variously in the works of later Reformed writers like Polanus, Cartwright, Gomarus, Maccovius, Voetius, Cocceius, Burman, Heidanus, Mastricht, Edwards, and Van Til.[309] Zanchi also departs from Aquinas not only in the order of the remaining attributes but also in their logic: whereas Aquinas understood goodness as a fundamental attribute in relation to simplicity and perfection, Zanchi places it among the affections. Zanchi also evidences a far greater interest in the divine affections than does Aquinas — reserving the entire fourth book of his *De natura Dei* to the affections.[310] Owen also held this to be the most suitable way of classifying the attributes:

> The properties of God are either *absolute* or *relative*. The absolute properties of God are such that they may be considered without the supposition of any thing else whatever, towards which their energy and efficacy should be exerted. His relative are such as, in their egress and exercise, respect some things in the creatures, though they naturally and eternally reside in God.[311]

In both cases, the purpose of the classification is to manifest, even in the order of discussion, the identity of God *in se* and in relation to the world order.

---

309. Polanus, *Syntagma theol.*, II.viii, xiv, cf. ibid, Synopsis libri II; Thomas Cartwright, *A Treatise of the Christian Religion, or the Whole Bodie and Substance of Divinitie* (London: Felix Kyngston, 1616), iii (pp. 6, 8); Gomarus, *Disputationes*, IV-V; Maccovius, *Loci communes*, XIV-XXIV; Maccovius, *Distinctiones et regulae*, IV.xiii; Voetius, *Syllabus problematum*, II (fol. D1r, D2v, D4v, E3v); Cocceius, *Summa theol.*, III.ix-x; Burman, *Synopsis theol.*, I.xx; Heidanus, *Corpus theologiae*, II (pp. 58-70); Mastricht, *Theoretico practica theol.*, II.iv; Edwards, *Theologia Reformata*, I, p. 44; Van Til, *Theol. revelata comp.*, I.i.

310. Zanchi, *De natura Dei*, IV.i-viii, treating in order, goodness, grace, love, mercy, justice, wrath, hate, and dominion; cf. the similar development in Polanus, *Syntagma*, II.xx-xxxi, goodness, grace, love, mercy, patience, clemency, justice, truth, holiness, power, freedom, glory; Aquinas, *Summa theol.*, I, qq. 3-23.

311. Owen, *Vindiciae evangelicae*, in *Works*, XII, p. 93.

Cocceius' variant of the pattern both serves to illustrate the way in which divine names provide a fundamental category for the development of divine attributes and to illustrate the variety and interrelationship of the various paradigms. His discussion of the divine attributes is rooted in a doctrinal and exegetical presentation of the biblical names of God, with Jehovah standing first and foremost as the proper name of God. Cocceius next argues — in the same chapter of his *Summa* — the incommunicable attributes, beginning with divine simplicity, as the category of attribution that, like the names, serves to distinguish God from creatures.[312] The communicable attributes follow in a further chapter, yielding a pattern very much like that of names, absolute attributes, and relative attributes. A structurally similar categorization of attributes is found, later, in Burman's *Synopsis theologiae* — a movement from names, to attributes identifying the actuosity of the divine essence, to attributes identifying the mode of the divine essence over against the created order — where it is presented as an advance over the incommunicable-communicable classification, by implication, over that of Burman's mentor, Cocceius.[313] The absolute/relative classification also appears in the late eighteenth century in Klinkenberg, who finds it most appropriate after having reviewed distinctions between proper and improper, positive and negative, quiescent and active, natural and moral, incommunicable and communicable.[314]

3. Attributes of essence, life, intellect, and will. There is also the distinction, often related to the former and resting in part on Aquinas' *Summa* and on Scotus' discussions of the divine attributes, but primarily reflecting the fairly standard analogy of the faculty psychology, and found particularly among the Leiden theologians of the late sixteenth and early seventeenth centuries — Junius, Arminius, Polyander, Ames, and Walaeus — between the attributes of the divine essence considered in its primary actuality and the attributes of the divine life in its operations, intellect and will, or intellect, will, and the affections.[315] This particular point, the identification of the divine life in the intellect and will as divine operation, may be an indication of a Scotist accent.[316]

Not only is this the standard division in several of the early seventeenth-century Leiden theologies, it also carries over as an element of the approach to divine attributes in several of the federal theologians. Despite his primary division of the subject into

---

312. Cocceius, *Summa theol.*, III.ix. 34-46.

313. Burman, *Synopsis theologiae*, I.xix.16-17; and on Burman's classification, see 3.3, E.5 of this volume.

314. Klinkenberg, *Onderwys*, I.i.8, §62-63.

315. Cf. Junius, *Theses Leydenses*, viii.27; Arminius, *Disputationes privatae*, XV.iii-iv, vii-ix; XVI.v-vi; *Synopsis purioris theologiae*, VI.xxii, xxxi-ii; Ames, *Marrow*, I.iv.52; and Walaeus, *Loci communes*, p. 170, col. 1, with Aquinas, *Summa theol.*, I, q. 18, prol. and art. 2, corpus: "Sometimes, however, life is used less properly for the operations from which its name is taken, and this the Philosopher says (*Ethics*, ix.9) that to live is principally to sense or to understand"; cf. Richard A. Muller, *God, Creation and Providence in the Thought of Jacob Arminius* (Grand Rapids: Baker Book House, 1991), pp. 113-123. Also note Cocceius, *Summa theol.*, X.6-9, 14; Burman, *Synopsis theol.*, I.xx.2, 5; and the discussion in Heppe, *Reformed Dogmatics*, pp. 69-70, 81.

316. Cf. Minges, *Doctrina philosophica et theologica*, II, pp. 143-144.

divine names, incommunicable attributes, and communicable attributes, Cocceius also has recourse to the faculty psychology in his classification of attributes: he distinguishes the communicable attributes into those concerning life (*vita*), those concerning virtue or excellency (*virtus*), and those related to the divine power (*potentia*). The attributes of the divine life Cocceius further divides into attributes of intellect and attributes of will.[317]

The identification of certain attributes as indicating the divine *actus primus* and others as indicating the *actus secundus* or living operation *ad intra* is, admittedly a somewhat improper or at least unusual use of the *actus primus-actus secundus* distinction, which typically refers to a faculty or *habitus* in itself apart from its operation or activity (i.e., as merely present, even dormant) and the same faculty or habit in its operation — namely, the intellect as resident faculty and the intellect as operatively knowing something or as engaged in reasoning. Van Til also obliged this model, distinguishing, however, between attributes of essence (sufficiency, infinity, simplicity, and immutability) and attributes of existence (eternity, omnipresence) before coming to the *vita Dei* and its division into intellect and will. Burman also uses this model as a subdivision of his larger classification.[318]

4. Classification into the *via negativa* and *via eminentiae* or into a priori and a posteriori attributes. Early on in the Reformed tradition, this classification was discussed favorably by Hyperius, who noted the transcendence of God and the inability of the intellect to grasp divinity — and argued the usefulness of a discussion of God by way of "remotion," that is, the *via negativa* as well as through the statement of affirmative attributes. Still, Hyperius did not view this as a complete classification, given the attributes of relationship to the world order and attributes indicating the actions or activity of God.[319] Polanus rejected the classification of attributes into incommunicable and communicable, preferring the division of attributes into categories of affirmative and negative predications, the so-called *via eminentiae* and *via negativa* or *negationis*, followed by a distinction between proper and figurative attributes.[320] In the first and basic division of attributes, he both echoes and alters the Thomistic pattern: Aquinas had first, in view of the epistemological problem, argued negatively "what God is not" and only subsequently developed the affirmative pattern.[321] Sometimes the model is expanded to include attributes by way of causality in addition to the ways of eminence and negation.[322] Others among the early orthodox, like Alting, adopted the Thomistic ordering, moving from negative to affirmative.[323]

---

317. Cocceius, *Summa theol.*, III.x.5-6; cf. Burman, *Synopsis theol.*, I.xx.4, and note xx (*vita*), xxi (*intellectus & scientia*), xxii (*voluntas*).

318. Van Til, *Theol. revelata comp.*, I.ii.

319. Hyperius, *Methodus theologiae*, I, pp. 90-91.

320. Polanus, *Syntagma, Symopsis libri II*; cf. Le Blanc, *Theses theol.*, *De Dei simplicitate*, iv.

321. Cf. Aquinas, *Summa*, Ia, q.3, prol.

322. E.g., Ainsworth, *Orthodox Foundation*, p. 9.

323. Alting, *Methodus theol.*, III (p. 76, col. 2).

Similarly, Trelcatius and Hottinger could argue that the *proprietates essentiales* of the Godhead are to be classed either as a priori or as a posteriori, with the former grouping being divided either into attributes considered "negatively, as infinitives" or "affirmatively" as conclusions from the divine simplicity, and the latter group being understood either as attributes predicated "properly, as those things that are in God principally and by themselves as power, knowledge and will" or as predicated "improperly, as those things which are spoken of God metaphorically ... according to the similitude of human passion or affection, as love, anger, and so forth."[324] The model is virtually identical to that of Polanus and, in its primary division into a priori and a posteriori attributes, but akin in spirit to the absolute-relative and incommunicable-communicable distinctions used by other theologians of Trelcatius' time.

This agreement of models becomes clear in Trelcatius' elaboration of the paradigm. Those attributes, he continues, "which are in God a priori are assigned to God solely according to his own essence, actuality and operation, and they are said to be incommunicable, as simplicity and infinitude."[325] Thus, God is simple inasmuch as he is indivisible and absolute, "admitting neither diversity or composition of parts, accidents, neither in himself, nor in the persons, nor in his works." This is so of God in himself, since his essence is one with his being or existence, "for God is the principle, first and pure act, of whom all things are wrought, and by whom all things are capable of movement."[326] This applies also to the persons of the Godhead, because all three participate equally in the divine essence — and to the works of God as well, since the divine activities of willing and of executing that will in the temporal order are identical with the divine essence. God is understood, therefore, as self-sufficient, with all things deriving from him as the "pattern and cause of all perfection, nature and grace."[327] The a posteriori attributes belong to God "principally and of themselves, but are communicated to creatures according to the proportion of his act and use," which is to say that they belong to God essentially and "immovably," whereas they are in creatures as accidents, "by participation" and on the ground of the divine movement of creatures from potency to actuality. To this category of attributes belong the power, knowledge, and will of God.[328]

5. Essential properties, attributes of divine actuosity, and attributes of divine relationality. Burman, writing in the middle of the seventeenth century, attempted a variation on several of the earlier typologies. He noted, as one possibility, a threefold distinction between essential attributes, attributes of intellect, and attributes of will, favored (but clearly not developed) by other Reformed writers with Cartesian

324. Trelcatius, *Schol. meth.*, I.iii; cf. Hottinger, *Cursus theologicus*, III.vi.
325. Trelcatius, *Schol. meth.*, I.iii.
326. Trelcatius, *Schol. meth.*, I.iii.
327. Trelcatius, *Schol. meth.*, I.iii.
328. Trelcatius, *Schol. meth.*, I.iii; cf. Brakel, *Redelijke Godsdienst*, I.iii.16.

sympathies.[329] For his own use, Burman preferred a threefold division of the attributes into a primary set of essential properties including the aseity, ultimacy, and oneness of God, the divine names, the spirituality, and invisibility and, finally, the infinity and perfection of God. These, he appears to argue, provide a series of interrelated governing concepts for the understanding of the other attributes.[330] Beyond this primary set, the attributes can be divided into two subordinate categories, the former identifying the internal and absolute attributes of God that explain actuality or actuosity of the divine essence, the latter identifying external and relative attributes that describe God's manner of existing either positively in relation to externals or negatively in terms of the denial of the imperfections of creatures. In the former category belong the life, intelligence, will and omnipotence of God; in the latter, the eternity, omnipresence, immutability and simplicity.[331] If the underlying argument here is much the same as that which in the era of early orthodoxy generated the categories of negative and affirmative or absolute and relative attributes, Burman's logic nonetheless produced significantly different groupings of attributes and must also be regarded as the most radical use of the distinction already noted between essential properties and a lesser order of attributes.

6. **Attributes arranged argumentatively:** *quid, quantus, & qualis.* At the very end of the high orthodox period, another theologian strongly influenced by federalism, Petrus van Mastricht, offered a fourfold division of the attributes, in some aspects reminiscent of Burman, as part of a qualification or qualified rejection of the incommunicable/communicable distinction. It is true, as Heppe notes, that Mastricht does discuss the incommunicable/communicable distinction and notes its usefulness in Reformed theology, particularly as a way of opposing the Lutheran view of the *communicatio idiomatum*, once the so-called communicable attributes are recognized as not "univocally communicable" but as belonging to creatures by analogy.[332] Mastricht nonetheless offers a series of further qualifications and, in the end, develops a somewhat different pattern of classification. After discussion the essence and knowledge of God, Mastricht places the topics of the essence, independence and names of God prior to the discussion of "attributes in general," echoing Burman's interest in a set of governing principles.[333] Then, rather than simply divide the attributes into categories of absolute and relative, incommunicable and communicable, Mastricht offers a tripartite grouping

---

329. Thus, e.g., Heidanus, *Corpus theol., syllabus,* fol. *2v and II (pp. 110, 114, 127) or, later, by the Wolffian, Stapfer, *Inst. theol. polemicae,* I, iii (2-4), at §297, 321, 371. The model is akin to the third approach noted here, lacking, however, the initial bifurcation into essence and life.

330. Burman, *Synopsis theol.,* I.xvii.1.

331. Burman, *Synopsis theologiae,* I.xix.17.

332. Heppe, *Reformed Dogmatics,* p. 62, citing Mastricht, *Theoretico-practica theol.,* II.iv.12.

333. Without claiming a "school" of thought here, it is significant that Burman was a Cocceian who modified the covenantal structure away from Coccceius' concept of gradual abrogation to approximate the typical orthodox model, while Mastricht was an orthodox writer of the Utrecht faculty who nonetheless developed a significant covenantal structure at the heart of his theology. A major contrast remains, however, between Burman's openness to Cartesianism and Mastricht's heated rejection of the philosophy.

of attributes corresponding to the questions "*Quid,*" "*Quantus,*" and "*Qualis*" — "What," "How great," and "Of what sort." The first group — *quid* — clearly identifies essential properties, that is, those relating directly to the question of quiddity, spirituality, simplicity, and immutability, attributes closely related to the previously discussed issues of essence and independence. The discussion of attributes under the rubric *quantus* leads Mastricht to identify God as one, infinite, great, immense, omnipresent, and eternal, a grouping which, when placed together with the first set, corresponds roughly to the internal and absolute attributes of Burman's classification. The final grouping, *qualis,* includes attributes of life — intellect, will, and affections — plus majesty, glory, and blessedness, corresponding roughly with the category of relative or communicable attributes.[334] As in the case of Burman's classification, Mastricht's stands not as a model opposed to the basic premise of the incommunicable-communicable classification but as a qualification that looks toward a more precise vocabulary for defining the classes of attributes given the problem with language of communicability.

7. **Incommunicable and communicable attributes.** The distinction between incommunicable and communicable attributes appears early on in the Reformed orthodox theologies, seldom as the basic pattern of classification, but given the kind of reservations stated by Zanchi, as a collateral way of stating the basic typology of affirmative and negative, proper and improper or figurative attributes offered by Polanus, Trelcatius, and others of their generation.[335] Bucanus, however, uses the classification after explaining it as a distinction between "absolute" and "relative" attributes, and the theses debated in Geneva adopt it with the standard qualifications.[336] What is more, granting that the term "communicable" attributes was understood as applicable only in a limited, proportionate, and, in a sense, improper manner, it was met with strenuous objections on the part of several of the Reformed scholastics of the early and high orthodox eras. Alting, rather briefly and pointedly, noted the distinction as referring "not to the properties themselves, but to their effects, inasmuch as some of the properties of God come to have an analogy in man, created after the image of God, while others have no analogy, inasmuch as man is not God." The distinction is therefore "obscure and ambiguous since the properties of [the divine] nature are incommunicable," that is, all of the attributes are essentially incommunicable. Alting concludes by expressing his preference for the distinction, already noted from Polanus, between negative and affirmative attributes.[337] Although Cocceius favored the distinction,[338] his follower Burman rather sarcastically notes, against the incommunicable-communicable distinction, that the *scientia Dei* agrees as much with human wisdom as the constellation Canis agrees with the barking animal of the same

---

334. Cf. Mastricht, *Theoretico-practica theol.,* I.xii-xxiii; cf. ibid., *Methodica dispositio totius operis,* fol. **2r.

335. Cf. Trelcatius, *Schol. meth.,* I.iii, with Zanchi, *De natura Dei,* I.i.

336. Bucanus, *Institutions,* i (p. 7); Beza et al., *Propositions and Principles,* V.i.

337. Alting, *Methodus theol.,* III (p. 76, col. 2).

338. Cocceius, *Aphorismi prolixiores,* IV.17-18; V.1; *Summa theol.,* III.ix.34; x.1.

name! The distinction can only be used insofar as some of the divine attributes have remote analogical relationships to creaturely properties, while those categorized as incommunicable lack even the remote analogy.[339] Maccovius and Pictet similarly dismiss the distinction.[340] Heidanus and Hottinger also reject the distinction, on grounds of their basically nominalistic view of the differentiation of attributes.[341]

Turretin, Marckius, Heidegger, Rijssen, Pictet, Boston, Ridgley, and various other high and late orthodox writers tended to accept the qualifications offered by Burman and Mastricht, but attempted to define the *communicabilia* in such a way as to overcome the logical and philosophical problems of the classification. Heidegger and Turretin modify the model to present the divine names before engaging in the discussion of incommunicable and communicable attributes. In the case of Heidegger, moreover, the communicable attributes are discussed as attributes of life in its subdivisions of intellect, will, and the affections — manifesting an affinity for the approach of Zanchi, Cocceius, and others who had emphasized the divine names as the basis for discussion of the attributes and who used divine life as a basis for identifying attributes of divine activity and relationality.[342] Marckius comments that "the attributes are distinguished into Proper and Metaphorical, Negative and Positive, Absolute and Relative, Internal and External, and, optimally, into Communicable and Incommunicable."[343] "Communication," according to Turretin, Marckius, and Rijssen, may be understood in two ways — either as the essential and formal communication of qualities intrinsic to the being of things or as a similitude or analogy according to the effects or operations of things. The denomination of divine attributes as communicable indicates only the latter understanding of communication. Such attributes are, thus, termed communicable neither univocally nor equivocally, but analogically. They exist in God *originaliter, independenter,* and *essentialiter,* but in creatures secondarily, *accidentaliter,* and *participative.*[344] Indeed, Pictet can observe that God is beyond measure in all of his attributes — citing Job 11:7-9 — and conclude, over against any notion of actual communicability of attributes that "all the arguments ... which prove God to be an all-perfect, prove him to be an infinite Being," and therefore utterly transcendent.[345] The attributes taken together, moreover, lead to the same conclusion:

---

339. Burman, *Synopsis theol.,* I.xix.16. The denial of analogy and therefore communicability of attributes using the comparison of the constellation and the actual dog is also found in Spinoza, *Ethics,* I, prop. xvii, corollary 2, note (Elwes, II, p. 61), which, although only published in 1677, was circulated as early as 1674: Burman's *Synopsis* appeared in 1678.

340. Maccovius, *Distinctiones et regulae,* IV.xiii; Pictet, *Theol. chr.,* II.xii.6. Cartwright does not mention the distinction, but defines all divine attributes as incommunicable, *Treatise of Christian Religion,* iii (p. 8).

341. Heidanus, *Corpus theologicae,* II (p. 70); Hottinger, *Cursus theologicus,* III.vi, canon C.

342. Heidegger, *Corpus theologiae,* III.iii, iv, xi; Turretin, *Inst. theol. elencticae,* III.iv, vi.

343. Marckius, *Christianae theol. medulla,* IV.xix.

344. Cf. Turretin, *Inst. theol. elencticae,* III.vi.2-4, with Marckius, *Compendium theol.,* IV.xix; Rijssen, *Summa theol.,* III.v; Brakel, *Redelijke Godsdienst,* I.iii.7, 16; Van der Kemp, *Christian Entirely the Property of Christ,* I, p. 174.

345. Pictet, *Theol. chr.,* II.viii.

From these attributes and perfections result the supreme glory and majesty of God; which he possesses in himself from eternity; and which he displays to creatures in time, unfolding and illustrating before them his excellencies in his works. ... All of God's attributes are wholly incommunicable to the creatures; yet there are traces of some of them in the creatures, which therefore are improperly termed by the scholastics communicable.[346]

Ridgley goes even farther and speaks of "an infinite disproportion" between the communicable attributes as they are in God and their creaturely analogues — although he maintains the classification and remains willing to argue some analogy between God and creatures.[347]

Among the high orthodox, the division into incommunicable and communicable attributes appears, indeed, to have become the most frequently used model — and not without a touch of internal irony: Turretin, for example, argues strongly for the incommunicable-communicable distinction while at the same time arguing that attributes are predicated, not *realiter*, but *virtualiter* and *eminenter*, the latter term pointing directly toward an alternative model for classification, the distinction between the *via eminentiae* and *via negativa*.[348] The term "communicable" applies to the attributes predicated by way of eminence insofar as it reflects the fundamentally Thomistic doctrine of the existence of creatures by participation in the essential goodness of God: it is not the divine attribute itself that is communicated and certainly not the divine essence — rather there is a communication, grounded in the superabundant divine goodness, of the power or potency for being, and — because of the communication of and resultant participation in the essential goodness of God — an impartation of attributes resembling those of infinite being to finite being. "That cause," Baxter wrote, "that hath communicated to all things else, the being, power, and all the perfections which they have, is the God whom we acknowledge and adore."[349] The relationship of God's communicable attributes to the attributes of creatures parallels the relationship of God as creator to human beings made in the divine image and likeness — human beings, as created good, reflect in their being some of the attributes of the divine being, but without being essentially equal to God or, in the strictest sense, partakers of the divine being.[350]

In the view of all of these writers, the term incommunicable is reserved as a term for those attributes proper to God which have neither a similitude or analogy nor an image or vestige in God's creatures,[351] but represent the difference or "opposition" between God and the creature: "thus when we speak of him as infinite, incomprehensible, unchangeable, without beginning, independent, & c. these perfections contain

---

346. Pictet, *Theol. chr.*, II.viii; cf. Boston, *Body of Divinity*, I, pp. 79-80.
347. Ridgley, *Body of Divinity*, p. 54, col. 1.
348. Cf. Turretin, *Inst. theol. elencticae*, III.v.5; so also Boston, *Body of Divinity*, I, pp. 79-80.
349. Baxter, *Divine Life*, p. 131 (I.ii) and see below, 6.1.
350. Brakel, *Redelijke Godsdienst*, I.iii.7.
351. Turretin, *Inst. theol. elencticae*, III.vi.3.

in them an account of the vast distance between God and the creature, or how infinitely he exceeds all other beings, and is opposed to everything that argues an imperfection in them."[352] The so-called incommunicable attributes, therefore, ultimately recall the *via negativa*.

The remoteness of the analogy, together with the need to avoid equivocity in predication, leads Turretin to note that, strictly speaking, attributes are predicated of the divine nature neither univocally, analogically, or equivocally, but rather "denominatively."[353] The divine attributes are set forth as "names" of God and, as such, do not stand in a precisely determinable relation to the use of those terms as attributes of other beings: that is, the omnipotence and omnipresence of God are not to be understood as standing in any definable proportion to or in an absolutely equivocal disjunction with the creaturely attributes of power and presence. (This argument also identifies the reason for the prominence of the discussion of the biblical "names" of God in the Protestant orthodox system and indicates the formative character of this discussion for analyses of the attributes.)

Yet another variation of the model is apparent in the early eighteenth-century theology of Fiddes, who distinguished between "incommunicable" attributes (simplicity, immutability, eternity, immensity, and unity); "vital" attributes (life, happiness, knowledge, wisdom, will, and power); and "moral" attributes (holiness, justice, veracity, and goodness).[354] Here, quite clearly, the difficulty inherent in the notion of "communicable" attributes has led to the alternative classification of the relational or transitive properties that adopts the basic distinction between ultimate attributes of the divine essence or nature and attributes concerning the divine life. Fiddes revises the model further in identifying a final division, which in fact contains virtues of the will, as "moral attributes."

---

352. Ridgley, *Body of Divinity*, p. 54, col. 1.
353. Turretin, *Inst. theol. elencticae*, I.v.3.
354. Fiddes, *Theol. spec.*, I.ii.2, 7, 13.

4

The Divine Essence, Names, and "Essential" Attributes

4.1 The Essence, Independence, and Unity of God

A. The Doctrine of the Divine Essence

1. Basic issues and approaches in the Reformed discussion of the divine essence. The structure of the orthodox Reformed doctrine of the divine essence follows out several of the patterns and models already observed in the discussion of the *locus de Deo* in general. As Polanus' division of the topic demonstrates, the *locus* is constructed as a unified discussion in which the understanding of divine essence includes both analysis of the divine attributes and of the doctrine of the Trinity:

> The essence of God is considered either *communiter* or *singulariter*. In the very same sense, it is said that the divine essence is to be considered either *indistinctè* or *distinctè*. And once again in the very same sense, it is said that the divine essence is to be considered either *absolutè* or *relatè*.
> The faith concerning the essence of God falls into two parts: first, concerning the attributes of God; second, concerning the persons of the Godhead (*de personis Deitatis*). The divine attributes are, in the first place, either affirmative or negative; in the second, either proper or figurative.
> The distributions of the proper attributes of God are principally two: First, the proper divine attributes (*attributa divina propria*) are either divine names (*nomina divina*) or essential properties of God (*proprietates Dei essentiales*).[1]

There is considerable variety in the patterns and structures of argument followed not only by the Reformers but also by the orthodox — although all understand the

---

1. Polanus, *Syntagma theol.*, Synopsis libri II; cf. Wollebius, *Compendium*, I.i.3, prop. 1-3. N.B., the doctrine of the Trinity is reserved for *PRRD*, volume IV.

issue of "essence" as that of basic definition. It is not a "speculative" issue. Of the Reformers who wrote theological systems or *loci communes*, Musculus and Hyperius both devote space to the discussion of the divine essence, while Musculus expresses reservations concerning the language of divine "nature."[2] Bullinger's *Decades* raises the issue briefly in connection with the question of the knowledge of God, with specific reference to God's revelation to Moses.[3] Others among the first and second generations of the Reform do discuss the divine essence and, of course, the divine attributes in their biblical commentaries — whether as a result of the *locus* method of exegesis or simply because of the consistent reference to the many predicates of God throughout the Bible, particularly in the Psalms and the prophets. Continuities in the exegetical tradition, therefore, need to be balanced against discontinuities in the developing dogmatic or systematic style and content of Reformed theology. Among the orthodox, Polanus, Voetius, and Mastricht define "essence" at some length,[4] while others, from Zanchi to Wendelin, prefer the term *natura* and tend to avoid extended discussion of the problem of the divine essence. In all cases, whether Calvin among the Reformers or Wendelin among the orthodox, however, the term *essentia* is readily applied to God and presumed to be a legitimate element of the language of the doctrine God and, indeed, an element directly indicated by the language of certain texts in Scripture. The implied but not debated question concerns, simply, how much attention need be given to the concept and to what degree the metaphysical elements of the tradition ought to be drawn into the discussion.

2. In the era of the Reformation. Having discussed the existence of God and knowledge of him, Musculus moves on to the question, "Who is God?" or as he puts it in the body of the question, "Who it is that is this God?", that is, the God whose revelation has just been noted.[5] Just as in a kingdom we first acknowledge that there is a king (who can be known) and then proceed to ask who this king is, in theology we must ask as a second question, "Who is God?", in order that we do not worship a false or feigned God. In ancient times man sought vainly after God and identified such things as the sun, stars, fire, air, and water as God. The question cannot relate to the problem of distinguishing between like things, since the true God must be "one alone, and hath none like to him in nature and condition." This is so obvious that the pagans could have been held back from true knowledge of God only by their own blindness of heart: there is no obscurity or darkness in the one true God.[6]

> There is no readier way for us to know who is God than to be very wary that we take nothing that hath been created, either in Earth, either in Heaven, corporal or spiritual, for God: and so let us with a godly imagination and fearful heart pass over all things

---

2. Musculus, *Loci communes*, xlii (*Commonplaces*, p. 886, col. 2 - p. 887, col. 1); Hyperius, *Methodus theol.*, I (pp. 83-91), and see the discussion above, 3.3 (B.2).

3. Bullinger, *Decades*, IV.iii (III, p. 146).

4. Polanus, *Syntagma theol.*, II.v; Voetius, *Selectarum disputationum theologicarum*, I, xiii; Mastricht, *Theoretico-practica theol.*, II.iii.

5. Musculus, *Loci communes*, I.ii (*Commonplaces*, p. 5, col. 2).

6. Musculus, *Loci communes*, I.ii (*Commonplaces*, p. 6, col. 1).

created, as well visible as invisible, and procede to the contemplation of him, having most certain trial that he is, and yet of that sort, that it may by no means be brought within the compass of any creature, whether it be corruptible or incorruptible. Neither can we yet this way thoroughly attain to the certain knowledge who is God, and to call him by any proper name. For his name is right marvellous and unspeakable.[7]

Musculus' argument is not polemically stated, but it does imply a denial of the *analogia entis* and, potentially indicates a Scotist or nominalist inclination. Even so, God refuses to give his name to Jacob and speaks obliquely to Moses (Ex. 3) "because ... the same description of name was not proper, nor containing the very substance of him." God says to Moses,

"I am he that I am," or as some say, "I will be who I will be. Thus thou shalt say to the children of Israel: he that is sent me to you." Thereby was signified to him, that the being of God was of such sort, that he cannot nor ought not to be called his proper name. ... God declareth himself who he is, true and living, not by any proper name, but by such lively strength and working, as cannot be ascribed to any, but unto the true God. And therefore it is unnecessary to demand who God is.[8]

Similarly, the question of essence arises when, rather than be caught in the worship of a false God, men ask, "What God is." The question may be considered in three ways: first, etymologically. The Latin word "Deus" derives from the Greek *theos*, "which signifieth piercing or running through: derived out of the verb ... because God by his presence and power doth never cease to pass through, move and govern the whole mass of this world and all that is in it."[9] Second, the question may be answered in terms of the essence or being of God. Both Christians and "Gentile" philosophers agree that the essence of God is inconceivable:

The judgment of Plato is, that the definition of God is not to be sought. The Thomists say that God hath no definition. ... A definition might serve, if we spake of a thing finite or that have an end: but God being infinite, it is not possible to define him by any manner or reason.[10]

Nevertheless, despite these initial qualms about defining the essence of God, Musculus will devote much space to this concept later on: he views the essence and attributes of God as genuine topics for theology and, unlike Calvin, emphasizes the usefulness of a positive exposition which includes some debate with the great medieval schools of thought, particularly the Scotist and the nominalist. Yet, if the structure and order of exposition in his *Loci communes* is any indication, he does not view the essence and attributes of God as a point of departure for theology: the existence, unity, and trinity of God are the fundamental doctrines on which the system rests — the essence and attributes appear only later, after God is known as creator, ruler, and redeemer.

---

7. Musculus, *Loci communes*, I.ii (*Commonplaces*, p. 6, col. 2).

8. Musculus, *Loci communes*, I.ii (*Commonplaces*, p. 7, col. 1).

9. Musculus, *Loci communes*, I.iii (*Commonplaces* p. 7, col. 2).

10. Musculus, *Loci communes*, I.iii (*Commonplaces*, p. 7, col. 2.-p. 8, col. 1).

If, however, we leave off attempting to define God's essence and look to his works, definition becomes more easy:

> The office and work of God is to be the maker and preserver of all things, such a one as without him nothing can be, nothing continue. Thus is reported of God in holy scripture. And in our belief we call him maker of heaven and earth. ... And God doth report these things of himself in Isaiah 46, saying: "I made, I bear, I sustain and preserve all."[11]

God also works salvation and all governance, so that judgment and justice are his in the punishment of the wicked and the reward of the godly. Thus, knowledge of God's works is sufficient to the needs of faith and godliness: as Augustine noted of Varro, "it availeth thee nothing, if thou know that there is a God, his name, and his being: if thou know not that he is the maker, saviour, and governor of all things."[12] Thus the question of "What God is" should conduce to knowledge and to an understanding that leads to piety and godliness, and not be an avenue for curiosity.

Musculus next raises traditional questions that lead to the discussion of various divine attributes: "Of what quality God is" and "Of what manner or sort God is in the consideration of his Essence." Such questions are usually asked of things, specifically, material, composite things. Since God is a spirit, such qualities as color or temperature do not apply to him. This is the problem of anthropomorphism. Nevertheless there are some "things in God" which help to define "what manner of sort he is" as the ideas of his "essence of being," "substance and nature." These things are utterly "unsearchable in God, but yet some part there is of them necessary to know, and is expressed in Scriptures by the spirit of revelation":[13]

> Of the Essence or Being of God, beside that it is the fountain and beginning of all things that be, first it may be said that it is only one, having none like neither in heaven neither in the earth: and therefore make the one only God. ... to this place belongs that which is read in holy scriptures of the unity of God, as in the 6. of Deuteronomy: "Hear Israel, the Lord thy God is one God." And the 44. and 45. of Isaiah: "Besides me," he says, "there is no other God." ... This unity of God the philosophers of the Gentiles did acknowledge. Plato manifestly defends the Monarchy or sole governance of God. Aristotle witnesses that one mind and understanding governs the world.[14]

Clearly, the maker is greater than his creation and, indeed, perfect in all things: thus he must be also one and all-powerful, for more than one God or a weak God implies imperfection. The essence of God, therefore, is one — and it follows also that it is

> simple and pure. With simplicity it agreeth that he is spirit: with pureness that he is called a light in which there is no darkness. [He] is also without a body, occupying no place, incomprehensible, immutable, indivisible, impassible, incorruptible, immortal,

---

11. Musculus, *Loci communes*, I.iii (*Commonplaces*, p. 8, col. 2).
12. Musculus, *Loci communes*, I.iii (*Commonplaces* pp. 8-9), citing *De Civ Dei*, IV.xxii.
13. Musculus, *Loci communes*, I.iv (*Commonplaces*, p. 9, col. 2-p. 10, col. 1).
14. Musculus, *Loci communes*, I.iv (*Commonplaces*, p. 10, cols. 1-2), citing Cicero, Virgil, Ovid.

unspeakable, perfect and everlasting: which all appertaineth to the consideration of God's essence or being.[15]

Such attributes, Musculus comments, surpass the understanding.

3. The Reformed orthodox on the divine essence. In moving on to the consideration of Protestant orthodox doctrine, it is worth noting that the orthodox themselves vary considerably over the emphasis placed on essence language in their doctrine of God: indeed, we may argue almost as much variety among the orthodox as among the second-generation Reformers. Theologians like Maccovius and Gomarus, usually denominated as "speculative" thinkers, together with their colleague, Walaeus, disappoint the creators of stereotype by not discussing the divine essence at any great length: all three emphasize, instead, the development of a doctrine of God on the basis of the divine names, and all three speak of the divine essence in terms of the names Jehovah, Ehyeh, and Jah.[16] Similarly, Thysius' discussion of the nature and attributes of God in the *Synopsis purioris theologiae* and Binning's meditation in his *Common Principles* derive the language of essence from a discussion of the divine names.[17]

A different pattern is found in Polanus' *Syntagma*, where the first topic following the proofs of God's existence is a fairly extensive discussion of the *essentia Dei*,[18] indicating a correlation between the broadly Thomistic influence leading to an exposition of the proofs and the discussion of divine essence by the Reformed orthodox. This correlation occurs not only in Polanus, but also in Mastricht and to a certain extent in Turretin.[19] As in Aquinas, demonstration of *esse* precedes and in a sense permits discussion of *essentia*: Mastricht explicitly notes the order of his discussion as necessarily proceeding from the divine *esse* to the divine *essentia* and thence to the divine *operationes*, inasmuch as God is first known to be, and then to be sufficient to his own existence, and then to be capable of communicating that *esse* to creatures.[20] There is, of course, some agreement between these two patterns, insofar as the former often includes some reference to the proofs, and the latter typically does discuss the divine names, but the latter is surely more interested in the language of *esse* and *essentia* than the former.

Having stated the truth that God exists and manifestly so, the orthodox move to define what God is in brief prior to the greater definition contained in the explication of the attributes. It is necessary to the right understanding of the *locus de Deo* that we remind ourselves at this point of the import of Polanus' argument that "the faith concerning the essence of God falls into two parts: first, concerning the attributes of God; second concerning the persons of the Godhead."[21] The *locus* does not fall either

---

15. Musculus, *Loci communes*, I.iv (*Commonplaces*, p. 11, col. 2).

16. Cf. Maccovius, *Loci communes*, XIV, with Gomarus, *Disputationes*, IV, and Walaeus, *Loci communes*, III.i (pp. 151-156).

17. *Synopsis purioris theologiae*, VI.xix-xxi; Binning, *Common Principles*, VII, in *Works*, pp. 35-38.

18. Polanus, *Syntagma theol.*, II.v.

19. Mastricht, *Theoretico-practica theol.*, II.ii.1; Turretin, *Inst. theol. elencticae*, III.i, iv-v.

20. Mastricht, *Theoretico-practica theol.*, II.ii.1.

21. Polanus, *Syntagma theol.*, Synopsis libri II.

into three distinct parts, essence, attributes, and Trinity, or into two separate discussions, essence/attributes and Trinity. The *locus* offers a discussion of the essence or whatness of God considered, first, according to attributes and then, second, according to persons or personal relations. Just as the various theologians insist that all of the attributes belong essentially to each of the persons, so do they understand the *locus* itself as a unity.

Thus, in answer to the question of "What" or "Who" God is, the orthodox set themselves first to describe the "nature" or "essence" of God and to encompass in the discussion the topics of the divine essence, the divine attributes, and the Trinity. There is a single topic, namely, the doctrine of God, which is divided for purposes of discussion— as the basic definitions of the orthodox indicate:

> God is a most simple, immutable, immense, eternal, most living, wise, just, free, powerful, and blessed Spirit: and he is Father, Son, & Holy Spirit. ... The essence of God is Deity itself or the divine nature, one in number but three in the community of persons: known to us both by names or by distinct properties.[22]

Burman's basic definition of God similarly evidences the Reformed orthodox sense of the interrelationship of the doctrines of divine essence and divine Trinity despite the topical separation of these doctrines in theological system: God, he writes "is most simply defined" as "infinite or most perfect being (*ens infinitum, seu perfectissimum*), or indeed, infinite Spirit, having life from himself (*a se ipso vivens*), Father Son, and Holy Spirit."[23]

Typically, the language of the topical division either moves from the divine "nature" to an initial discussion of essence and attributes and then to the doctrine of the Trinity or from a statement concerning the divine essence to the doctrine of the divine attributes and then to the doctrine of the Trinity. The difference between the two models is minimal, resting on the decision of some of the writers to use the disputed term, "nature," and of others to omit it. Thus, in Leigh's case, the discussion of the divine "nature" or "What God is" has two divisions, first, the divine essence and, second, the "Distinction of Persons in that Essence,"[24] indicating a trinitarian approach to the essence and attributes of God, despite the separation of issues for purposes of discussion.

The word "God" can be applied properly only to the one who is "essentially God," and it can be applied "either personally, commonly, without a determination of certain person" (cf. John 4:24), or it can be applied "singularly to some one person by Synecdoche, John 3:16; Acts 20:28; 1 Tim. 3:16." The word "God" can, however, even in Scripture be applied improperly "to those who by nature are not God, 1 Cor. 8:5; Gal. 4:8." This improper predication occurs either by God's own ordination in

---

22. Hottinger, *Cursus theologicus*, III.ii, iv; cf. the definitions in Westminster Confession of Faith, II.i-iii; Belgic Confession, I, VIII; also Olevianus, *Exposition of the Symbole*, pp. 62-63; Beza et al., *Propositions and Principles*, I.v; and Ainsworth, *Orthodox Foundation*, pp. 8-9.

23. Burman, *Synopsis theol.*, I.vii.3.

24. Leigh, *Body of Divinity*, II.ii (p. 158).

reference to a "Dignity and Excellency of their office, as to Angels (Ps. 8:6), to Magistrates (Ps. 82:6), to Moses (Exod. 4:16); or from their own unjust persuasion, as to the Devil, who is called, the *God of the World* (2 Cor. 4:9), or from the erroneous persuasion of men, as to Idols (1 Cor. 8:4, 5)."[25]

The name God, rightly defined and capable of application to the true God either in general or with reference to the divine persons, indicates,

> an Infinite Essence which is of Himself, and gives being to all other things. ... God is a Spirit, a being void of all Dimensions, Circumscriptions and Divisiblenesse of parts. Other Spirits are compounded of Substance and Accidents at least, and exist in a place by limitation of Essence, by which they are here and not there; but God is an Essence altogether simple and immaterial, utterly free from all manner of composition any way, in whom are no qualities, nor any limitation of Essence. He is a Spiritual, Simple, and Immaterial Essence. His essence is substantial, an Essence which hath a being in it self, not in another, simply and wholly Immaterial (He is one most Pure and meer Act) but Incomprehensible. ... so that we cannot comprehend his Essence, nor know it as it is. He onely perfectly knows himself, but he may be known in some sort.[26]

Following out the medieval tradition, Mastricht rests the doctrine of the essence and independence of God on Exodus 3:13-14, specifically on God's answer to Moses' question concerning his name: Mastricht renders the answer, "ero qui ero," "I will be who I will be," noting that the Hebrew might also be rendered "sum qui sum."[27] His sensitivity to the implications of the Hebrew verb reflects the arguments of Reformers like Bullinger and Musculus and of early orthodox writers like Zanchi and Polanus,[28] just as his doctrinal conclusions echo the results of exegesis in his time: Diodati, for example, interpreted the text as saying "I am the only true God, truly subsisting, & not only through the opinion of men as Idols are; I am he that have an everlasting beeing, unchangeable, subsisting of its self, not depending from others, infinite, most simple, the author and cause of the beeing of all things: not a borrowed, changeable, finite, dependent, and compounded being & c. as all other creatures have."[29] Similar readings, resting both on philological analysis and on rabbinic exegesis appear in the commentaries of Willet and Ainsworth. Willet notes that *Eheje* "signifieth ... all the difference of time, both past, present, and to come; as this name is expounded, *which was, which is, and which is to come*, Rev.1.8." The name *Eheje*, thus, is not "a divers name in effect from the name *Iehovah*, which the Lord proclaimeth afterward, as thinketh *Aquinas*: for they are both derived from the future tense of the word *Hajah*, which signifieth to be." The Lord "here describeth himself, by his everlasting being,

---

25. Leigh, *Body of Divinity*, II.ii (pp. 158-159).

26. Leigh, *Body of Divinity*, II.ii (p. 158); cf. Howe, *Living Temple*, I, p. 27.

27. Mastricht, *Theoretico-practica theol.*, II.iii.1; cf. Thomas Gataker, *De nomine tetragrammato dissertatio* (London: R. Cotes, 1645), pp. 7-10, summarizing the various suggestions for translating the phrase from Jerome to Piscator, Olearius, and Junius.

28. Cf. Zanchi, *De natura Dei*, I.xii-xiv, with Polanus, *Syntagma theol.*, II.v.

29. Diodati, *Pious and Learned Annotations*, on Ex. 3:14 (p. 38); cf. Poole, *Commentary*, in loc.; Henry, *Exposition*, in loc.

who is of himselfe, and giveth being to all other things, which propertie of being is most peculiar unto god (as best shewing what hee is) of all other attributes which are given unto him."[30] Ainsworth adds that "the Rabbins do also explain this name ... The blessed God said unto Moses, say unto them, I that have been, and I the same now, and I the same from time to come" and relates the explanation to New Testament texts such as Revelation 16:5 ("he that is, and that was, and that will be") and Hebrews 13:8 ("Jesus Christ, the same yesterday, today, and forever").[31]

The divine essence, as identified in Exodus 3:14, must be understood as "imperceptible," by which he means "what the divine essence is in itself must be inaccessible to our intellect."[32] When God says "sum qui sum" in answer to the question of his identity, he does not answer but, in fact, rejects the question itself — manifesting nothing other than the incomprehensibility and ineffability of his essence. Even so, we read in the New Testament (1 Tim, 6:16), that God dwells in inaccessible light and that no one can or ever will see him — not with the eyes of the flesh and not even with the "eyes of the mind." This conclusion relates directly to the doctrine of the simplicity of God, inasmuch as he is one, most simple, and most pure actuality (*simplicissimus ac purissimus actus*); for the text of 1 Timothy should be understood as indicating "light" in the abstract and not a bright substance (*substantia lucens*) in the concrete.[33] The biblical imagery of light does not draw the divine essence into the realm of created things: "among all the sensible creatures of God, the creation of light hath the first place, for the manifestation of his glory," nonetheless,

> Our thoughts of God should be higher, larger, more purified from bodily apprehensions and all imperfections, than our thoughts of created light are, when we look upon the light illuminating all the world at once; for as the garment of a king showeth his majesty, and yet is no part of his substance or essence, and in its nature is much inferior to his worth; so is the light nothing but God's creature, serving to show forth his glory, and is infinitely inferior to him, *who covereth himself with light, as a garment.*[34]

The utter simplicity of the divine unity corresponds to nothing within the comprehension of the creature and cannot be defined in any way by the creature.

Similarly, the conclusion of imperceptibility and incomprehensibility comport with the divine infinity, granting that God "cannot be comprehended or perceived by the finite intellect."[35] These considerations mark a crucial point of contention between the Reformed and the Cartesians. According to Mastricht, the Cartesians reason as follows: the divine essence consists in nothing other than "infinite thought," the idea,

30. Andrew Willet, *Hexapla in Exodum* (London, 1608), p. 32; cf. Ainsworth, *Annotations upon Exodus*, in loc.

31. Ainsworth, *Annotations upon Exodus*, in. loc.

32. Mastricht, *Theoretico-practica theol.*, II.iii.3.

33. Mastricht, *Theoretico-practica theol.*, II.iii.4.

34. David Dickson, *A Brief Exposition of the Psalms*, 3 vols. (London, 1653-55); reissued as *A Commentary on the Psalms*, 2 vols. (London: Banner of Truth, 1965), II, pp. 225-226 (on Ps. 104:1-4).

35. Mastricht, *Theoretico-practica theol.*, II.iii.4.

thus, of an "infinite entity" that the mind can and does conceive. Indeed, the Cartesian emphasis on the ontological argument for the existence of God could, in this context, appear to make comprehensibility a fundamental attribute of the divine: the Cartesians hold, therefore, a "positive concept of God's essence" that can be clearly and distinctly perceived by the mind. Mastricht strenuously denies this view, since all that discussion of the divine essence can provide is an understanding of what God is not, rather than what God is in himself. The conception we have of the divine essence is, first and foremost, negative rather than positive.[36] The Cartesians reduce all substance to thought and extension: this is as inadequate a description of the world order as is the description of the soul as merely thought and of the body as nothing more than extension.[37] Even so, although the Reformed acknowledge that the divine thoughts are one with the divine essence in its simplicity, they deny that God is merely thought.[38]

In the traditionary interpretation of Exodus 3:14, the name of God designates the One God as *ho on*, *existens*, and *to on*, *ens*, and therefore as *absolutè primum et independens*. The essence of God admits no prior cause, whether efficient, material, formal, or final. It is, thus, the great *ero qui ero*, *sum qui sum*, *ero qui sum*, or *sum qui ero* who is and who has essence and in whom all times coexist — which is to say, the essential designation of God also implies his eternity. As the Apocalypse testifies, Jehovah is the beginning and the end (1:8), both the *principium et finis* (21:6) and the *primus et ultimus* (22:13).[39] God is *ens à se* and *per essentiam absolutè primum*, the one on whom all things depend for their being: for otherwise we would have to assume an infinite regression of dependency and contingent being. Such a regression involves a contradiction, however, inasmuch as it proposes that all things both produce and are produced, both in a sense exist and do not exist, in a circular fallacy of creation and dependency. Obviously, no thing can, either directly or indirectly, be the cause of itself.[40]

That God is *ens à se* also appears by examination of the ground of the divine attributes: the divine essence, aseity, independence, and primacy make possible the derivation, by induction, of the other attributes of the divine nature: the *unitas Dei*

---

36. Mastricht, *Theoretico-practica theol.*, II.iii.7. Much of the difference between Mastricht's discussion of the divine essence and of Exodus 3:14 and the Reformation-era discussion found in Musculus' *Loci communes* lies not in the basic exegesis of the text but in Mastricht's adoption, by way of further explanation, of a traditional language of divine essence strongly reminiscent of Aquinas' adaptation of the Pseudo-Dionysian *via negativa*: we know first what God is not.

37. Mastricht, *Theoretico-practica theol.*, II,iii.20.

38. Mastricht, *Theoretico-practica theol.*, II.iii.19.

39. Mastricht, *Theoretico-practica theol.*, II.iii.13-14; note the similar comparison or conference of texts in Willet, *Hexapla in Exodum*, p. 32; Poole, *Commentary*, in loc.: "Heb. *I shall be what I shall be*. He useth the future tense.... Because that tense in the use of the Hebrew tongue comprehends all times.... Of this name of God, see. Rev. 1:4, 8; 16:5"; Ainsworth, *Annotations upon Exodus*, in. loc.: "The Hebr. *Ehjeh asher ehjeh*, properly signifieth, *I will be that I will be*: the Gr. translateth, *I am he that Is*. And God is called, 'he that is, and that was, and that will be,' Rev. xvi.5; where this name *Ehjeh*, is opened."

40. Turretin, *Inst. theol. elencticae*, III.iv.5; Mastricht, *Theoretico-practica theol.*, II.iii.15.

follows directly from the discussion of God's essence, since the *ens absolutè primum* cannot but be *unum*.[41] Similarly, God must be immutable, since any change must be caused by another and thus denies the absolute and essential primacy of God; and infinite, since finitude implies external limitation and a limitation to perfection. Similarly, the idea of *ens absolutè primum* also implies simplicity, since any composite can have an equal, composed of the same elements. It also implies life, since the concept of life in itself involves no imperfection. Intellect, will and omnipotence follow from the idea of perfection, as do the attributes of holiness, wisdom, goodness and graciousness.[42]

Still, it would be mistaken to conclude that, in such arguments, the philosophy of essence has overruled the scriptural motive behind Protestant orthodox theological formulation: Mastricht recognized that philosophical considerations of the implication of essence might be construed as extra-biblical or even non-biblical in implication and, in order to avoid the potential problem, inquired whether or not the language and meaning of Scripture would in fact sustain such an interpretation and whether the term *essentia* may be accurately employed by theology in describing God. He notes polemically that the Remonstrants, who are little more than crypto-Socinians, deny to God this language of essence. This denial, he comments, serves only the purpose of subverting the doctrine of the Trinity.[43] If only by way of controversy, therefore, the orthodox were more sensitive than the medieval doctors to the exegetical problem of applying the language of philosophy to the teachings found in Scripture.

There are a series of exegetical warrants for the use of essence language. In the first place, the Hebrew word translated as "wisdom" in Prov. 8:14 signifies "essence."[44] It is worth noting here that this reading of the text comes directly out of the exegetical tradition and that Mastricht and other of the orthodox who assume this construction were not so much "proof-texting" in the very negative sense of that term as pointing toward what they took to be one of "the assured results of exegesis," to borrow a phrase from the critical present: Mastricht here specifically follows the *Statenvertaling*.[45] Thus, on this verse, "Counsel is mine, and sound wisdom: I am understanding...," Poole comments,

> *Sound wisdom:* all solid, and substantial, and useful, yea, essential wisdom, is natural and essential to me, for the word properly signifies *essence. I am understanding*, by my nature and essence, as was now said.[46]

A still firmer case can be made on the basis of the Greek New Testament for the attribution of essence to God and for the identification of God as *ens*. Paul in Rom.

---

41. Mastricht, *Theoretico-practica theol.*, II.iii.16; Turretin, *Inst. theol. elencticae*, III.iv.5.

42. Mastricht, *Theoretico-practica theol.*, II.iii.16; cf. Leigh, *Treatise*, II.vi.

43. Mastricht, *Theoretico-practica theol.*, II.iii.17-18.

44. Mastricht, *Theoretico-practica theol.*, II.iii.18.

45. Haak, *Dutch Annotations*, Prov. 2:7 and 8:14, in loc.

46. Poole, *Commentary*, II, p. 227; cf. Poole, *Synopsis criticorum*, in loc. "Ego sum prudentia, sive intelligentia."

1:20 speaks of *theiotes* or *divinitas* with reference to God himself, and in Col. 2:9 of *theotes* or *deitas* with reference to the divinity of Christ. Galatians 4:8 contains the term *theia physis, divina natura*. Furthermore, the name of God, Jehovah, is implied in Rev. 1:4,8 and is there equated with *ho on*, from which *essentia* can be directly inferred. (Here too, we are not encountering a rank proof-texting, but rather an application of the older hermeneutic whereby either direct declarations of Scripture or conclusions capable of being drawn from the text are understood as the basis of vaild teaching.) By way of a qualification reminiscent of John of Damascus, the *essentia Dei* is so different from the *essentia creaturarum* that it might well be called *hyperousion* or even *ousion hyperousion*.[47]

Once the identification of God's essence with being itself has been noted, we are also to understand that this identification is not either purely nominal (*nominaliter*) or simple (*simpliciter*) but rather by participation (*participialiter*), granting that God cannot be understood as not necessarily existing: God is *ens actu existens*, taken not in the concrete sense of a finite composite of existence and essence, but in the abstract as one whose essence and existence are identical. "We consider God to be Being according to essence; or conversely, we consider his existence to be from his own essence."[48] It is impossible to conceive of the most perfect essence as not existing: the *essentia* and the *esse* of God, the essence and the existence, are inseparable. Nor ought we to conceive of *ens a se* as self-producing and self-caused, as this may imply a contradiction: rather we ought to understand the divine aseity as a self-grounded essence not produced by another. The divine essence may, therefore, be defined by saying that God "is spirit having life from itself," simply and perfectly. As in Zanchi's argument, Mastricht roots his point in extended exegesis.[49] This argument stands in significant parallel with the confessions, notably the Second Helvetic Confession, in which the identification of God as one essence *per se subsistens* leads, by way of a list of divine attributes, to a series of biblical citations identifying the oneness and ultimacy of God.[50]

Nor ought we to view this doctrine of the divine essence as entirely speculative and out of contact with piety: our teaching of God as the one whose essence is his existence and who must necessarily be, is a doctrine that brings great consolation to the faithful. Think of the sorrow and anguish of soul, writes Mastricht, that comes

---

47. Mastricht, *Theoretico-practica theol.*, II.iii.18; cf. Poole, *Synopsis criticorum*, on Rom. 1:20; Col. 2:9; Gal. 4:8; and Rev. 1:4, 8, in loc.; in the latter text, Poole explicitly notes that "who is and was and is to come" is not a series of participles but the name of God: the Apostle, he indicates, here reflects on Exodus 3:14, where God, the "one who is," is revealed as the *fons essendi*.

48. Mastricht, *Theoretico-practica theol.*, II.iii.17; cf. Amyraut, *De mysterio trinitatis*, I, p. 31.

49. Mastricht, *Theoretico-practica theol.*, II.iii.17; Zanchi, *De natura Dei*, I.xiv.3; II.iii.2-3 (cols. 42-43, 65-67); cf. Howe, *Living Temple*, I.iv (pp. 89-90). Note Gründler, "Thomism and Calvinism," pp. 97-103, on Zanchi's discussion of the identity of essence and existence.

50. Second Helvetic Confession, III.i-ii, citing Deut. 6:4; Exod. 20:2, 3; Isa. 45:5, 21; Exod. 36:6. Cf. Staedke, "Die Gotteslehre der *Confessio Helvetica posterior*," pp. 251-252, where the connection of the technical language with the scholastic tradition is noted and then biblicism noted, lest it be concluded that Bullinger held to a "theoretical monotheism" like that of the scholastics!

upon us when that which we would have to be is not: as Jeremiah wrote, "Rachel weeps for her children, and they are not." How great a remedy to our anguish is this God who "*per essentiam & exochos est.*"[51] This doctrine manifests as reprehensible all those who deny the existence and essence of God, those who infringe upon the aseity and independence of the divine essence, and who would rest the predestining will and grace of God on man's free will or on man's faith and unbelief! Even so, this doctrine unmasks those who by their practices rail at the independence of God, as if he needed assistance to attain his ends, and those who would either limit God or dare to work against his counsel.[52] Finally, we learn to attribute all glory to God and to stand in humility before him, setting our own will to nought and living in faith under the will of the One who lives, who gives life, and in whom we live.[53]

B. Divine Independence and Unity

1. **The independence of God.** God is essentially absolute in all senses — his essence and eternity preclude any coexistent being and manifest God to be utterly independent both in existence and operation,[54] having absolutely "no limit of being."[55] Thus, "the primacy or independence of God is [that attribute] by which all that God is derives from no other and by which all creatures that exist are from him"; or, alternatively, "independence is the property of God according to which his essence, subsistence and actions depend on no external cause, inasmuch as he is from himself."[56] Thus, first, God is utterly independent in his being. God is also independent in his power, having received it from no other being and having the capacity to exercise it apart from the will of any other being — no creature, therefore, can alter or set aside his will and power. So also are the goodness and bountifulness of God independent, given that they derive from no other being and are communicated by God to his creatures without either necessity or constraint: thus, the act of creation is most free and the work of grace most merciful.[57]

The "independence" of God can be considered an attribute by way of negation, paralleled in the positive series of attributes by the self-existence (aseity) and all-sufficiency of God. God is independent both in his existence and in his activity — in existence because, unlike created things, the reason for his existence is not outside of himself; in activity because all that is actual, apart from himself, exists by his will alone.[58] Thus, "with respect to this primacy, God is said to exist *a se ipso*, which is to be understood more correctly in the negative, since he has his existence from no other,

51. Mastricht, *Theoretico-practica theol.*, II.iii.25.

52. Mastricht, *Theoretico-practica theol.*, II.iii.26.

53. Mastricht, *Theoretico-practica theol.*, II.iii.27.

54. Mastricht, *Theoretico-practica theol.*, II.iii.17.

55. Howe, *Living Temple*, I.iv (p. 91).

56. Rijssen, *Summa theol.*, III.xiii; Wendelin, *Systema theol.*, I.

57. Ridgley, *Body of Divinity* (1855), I, p. 82; Ward, *Philosophicall Essay*, I.iii (pp. 25-26).

58. Wyttenbach, *Tentamen*, III, §224, 278-279.

than positively, as if he were his own cause, since this implies a contradiction, as if he could be both prior and subsequent to himself."[59]

This is to say that God's "being and perfections are underived and not communicated to him ... therefore he is self-existent, or independent, which is one of the highest glories of the divine nature, by which he is distinguished from all creatures, who live, move, and have their being in and from him." The "attribute of independency," moreover, is not an isolated concept but rather "belongs to all his perfections: thus his wisdom, power, goodness, holiness, &c. are all independent."[60]

As an illustration of the "independency" of all the perfections of God, Ridgley comments that

> with respect to his knowledge or wisdom, he doth not receive *Ideas* from any object out of himself, as all intelligent creatures do, and, in that respect, are said to depend on the object; so that if there were no such objects, they could not have the knowledge or *Idea* of them in their minds; therefore the object known must first exist, before we can apprehend what it is. But this must not be said of God's knowledge, for that would be to suppose the things that he knows antecedent to his knowing them. The independency of his knowledge is elegantly described in scripture; *Who hath directed the Spirit of the Lord, or, being his counsellor, has taught him? With whom took he counsel, and who instructed him, and taught him in the path of judgment, and taught him knowledge, and shewed to him the way of understanding?* (Isaiah 40:13, 14).[61]

The central point, that God knows externals not on the basis of externals but in and through the divine essence, certainly derives from Aquinas. Some of the argument, here, might seem over subtle, and it might be ground for making the claim that orthodoxy debated metaphysical points unrelated to piety and beyond the bounds of exegetical findings were it not for the fact that this point in particular is necessary to the scriptural understanding of God as creator.

The independence of God as related to his power, similarly, is a doctrine that has immediate bearing upon piety and, more importantly, on the structure and understanding of soteriology and is not, therefore, to be dismissed as a speculative excess:

> He is independent in power, therefore, as he receives strength from no one, so he doth not act dependently on the will of the creature, who hath injoined him his way (Job 36:23); and accordingly, as he received the power of acting from no one, so none can hinder, turn aside, or control his power, or put a stop to his methods of acting.[62]

---

59. Rijssen, *Summa theol.*, III.xiv; cf. Wendelin, *Systema theol.*, I, and Ridgley, *Body of Divinity*, p. 55, col. 1.

60. Ridgley, *Body of Divinity*, p. 55, col. 2.

61. Ridgley, *Body of Divinity*, p. 55, col. 2.

62. Ridgley, *Body of Divinity*, p. 55, col. 2; cf. Joseph Caryl, *An exposition with practicall observations upon .... the booke of Iob*, 12 vols. (London: G. Miller and M. Simmons, 1644-1666), 22:2; 36:23, in loc. (VII, p. 7; XI, p. 345).

By extension, God must also be conceived of as independent in his goodness and bounty, since "he communicates blessings not by constraint, but according to his sovereign will." God's creation and providence, thus, represent his good pleasure and cannot be conceived of as acts determined by any internal necessity.[63]

> God is *Independent*, Is. 44:6; Rev. 1:8, 21:6; 22:13; Rom. 11:35-36. Every creature as a creature, is dependent, and hangs upon some other thing than itself, and owes its being and continuance to another, Neh. 9:6. It hath causes of its being, from which, of which, and by which, and for which it is; and further than these causes did and do contribute to its being, it cannot be. The Angels have an efficient cause and end, and they do as such stand indebted to God for their being and continuance as the poorest worm. ... but God is altogether independent of himself, by himself, for himself; he hath no causes. ... He is what he is without help from any other thing, as himself shows in his name, *I am that I am*.
>
> There are many things which have a beginning from some other thing; there must be something therefore that is of itself. ... God's being is neither *ab alio*, *ex alio*, *per aliud*, nor *propter aliud*. We should acknowledge God to be a necessary and Independent essence.[64]

There is also a certain logical necessity underlying the idea of the primacy or independence of God: all created things depend upon him and are by nature not necessary but contingent —

> If therefore all things depend on God, it is the greatest absurdity to say that God depends on any thing, for this would be to suppose the cause and effect to be mutually dependent on, and derived from each other, which infers a contradiction.[65]

Dependence, moreover, implies inferiority and is at odds with the very nature of God:

> If God depends on any creature, he does not exist necessarily; and if so, then he might not have been; for the same will by which he is supposed to exist, might have determined that he should not have existed. If therefore God be not independent, he might not have been, and, according to the same method of reasoning, he might cease to be; for the same will, that gave being to him, might take it away at pleasure, which is altogether inconsistent with the *Idea* of a God.[66]

God is thus necessarily independent — and all creatures necessarily dependent: "let us conclude that all our springs are in him, and that all we enjoy and hope for is from him, who is the author and finisher of our faith, and the fountain of all our blessedness."[67] On this point, Zanchi explicitly echoes Aquinas — "all things can be said to exist from God by participation in the divine existence."[68]

---

63. Ridgley, *Body of Divinity*, pp. 55-56.
64. Leigh, *Treatise*, II.v (p. 56); cf. Poole, *Synopsis criticorum*, Rev. 1:4, 8; 21:6, in loc.
65. Ridgley, *Body of Divinity*, p. 56, col. 1.
66. Ridgley, *Body of Divinity*, p. 56, col. 1.
67. Ridgley, *Body of Divinity*, p. 56, col. 2.
68. Zanchi, *De natura Dei*, II.i, thesis 3 (col. 55); cf. Gründler, "Thomism and Calvinism," p. 107.

2. The unity of God. The unity or oneness of God is by its very nature a concept central to the biblical message and the system of Christian theology, but its placement in the *locus de Deo* depends more on its derivation than its importance. For an early orthodox writer like Trelcatius, the divine unity arose conceptually from the basic consideration of the divine essence:

> The *Essence* is that whereby God both is and exists by himself and of himself absolutely: for he alone is that thing which is, and who is, that is, a being not leaning upon any other. The manner of [God's] unity is not of knitting together, nor of the general, nor of the special, nor of consent, but of number, because there cannot be many Gods.[69]

Similarly, for Turretin and Pictet, unity was the primary concept derived, on the one hand, from Scripture and, on the other, from the concept of God: both therefore placed it immediately after their statements of the existence of God.[70] Mastricht treats unity as one of the attributes which follows naturally from the spirituality, simplicity, and immutability of God — indeed, as a necessary conclusion from his discussion of the divine essence.[71] Leigh placed the doctrine under the category of greatness in nature and works, as a correlate of the necessity and independence of God, just prior to discussion of the divine intellect and will, but like Pictet, viewed the doctrine as a necessary implication of the biblical language about God.[72] Others touch on the doctrine only tangentially among the attributes and leave discussion of the divine unity until the doctrine of the Trinity — whereas the rationalistic orthodox of the eighteenth century tend to take the soleness and unity of God as their point of departure.[73]

For Pictet, the concept of God as one was the logical outcome of his inquiry into the doctrine of Scripture:

> 1) Since it has pleased God to make himself known to men in the scriptures, the order of [theological] discussion requires, that, having established the authority which is due to the sacred writers, the faith and reverence which must be given to their books, we should examine what these holy scriptures teach concerning God. 2) Now there is nothing which they teach, first, more clearly, than that there is one God only; the passages are numerous and well known; "Hear, O Israel, the Lord our God, is one Lord" (Deut. 6:4.); "See now that I, even I, am he, and there is no God with me" (Deut. 33:39) which is confirmed by Deut. 4:35 and Isaiah 33:6. "To us there is but one God, the Father" (1 Cor. 8:4-6); "There is one God, and one Mediator" (1 Tim. 2:5; [cf.] Eph. 4:6). 3) Reason itself also teaches us this; for whosoever has any thought and

---

69. Trelcatius, *Schol. meth.*, I.iii (pp. 53-54).

70. Turretin, *Inst. theol. elencticae*, III.iii; Pictet, *Theol. chr.*, II.i; so also Heidanus, *Corpus theol.*, II (pp. 73-78); Burman, *Synopsis Theol*, II.xv.

71. Mastricht, *Theoretico-practica theol.*, II.vi-viii.

72. Leigh, *Treatise*, II.vi.

73. Ridgley, *Body of Divinity* (1855), pp. 127-135, on q. 8 of the *Larger Catechism*; Watson and Vincent similarly follow the catechetical order, namely, of the *Shorter Catechism* at q. 4; also Owen, *Vindication of the Doctrine of the Trinity*, in *Works*, II, pp. 381, 401; Venema, *Inst. theol.*, v, ix (pp. 137, 195-196); cf. the rationalist model in Klinkenberg, *Onderwys*, I.i7, §58, and note his citations of anti-Deistic rationalists like Leland and Warburton as well as Vernet and the Wolffian Stapfer.

sense of deity, must acknowledge that only to be deity, than which nothing can be conceived better, more sublime, and more perfect; but of such a nature as this, there can be only one; for if such a being could have an equal, we could conceive of some more perfect Being, having none equal to himself, and possessing all the perfections of that other deity in himself alone.[74]

This is a significant adaptation of Anselm's ontological argument: it is not here a proof of God's existence but of his unity. It proves not that there is a God but that the God already known to the mind must be one and unique.[75]

Here, as in the rational arguments for the Trinity used by Keckermann and Alsted and cited by Burman, we observe the openness of orthodoxy to the older tradition. The difference between the orthodox and the early formulators of Reformed thought on this point is, of course, one of degree: for we have only to glance briefly at the *Institutes* to see the formative use of Augustine by Calvin and a cursory examination of Calvin's or Ursinus' Christology manifests their appreciation of Anselm's meditation on the necessity of the God-man as mediator in the *Cur Deus homo?* Yet the rationality of the ontological argument, even adapted as we find it here, is typical of the scholastic view of God in a way that the Reformed adaptation of Anselmic atonement theory is not: for here we do not describe a necessity imposed on man by the very nature of his plight but a rational necessity devised for the description of the "unsearchable" divine nature.

The Reformed also explicitly borrow patristic arguments: there can, logically, be only one supreme being: "Phebadius, bishop of Agenna, rightly observes [in his] book against the Arians, 'If God is neither one nor true, there is no God.'"[76] Furthermore, God is one and also a unity, both *unus* and *unicus*. Thus,

God is called one: 1) Not only because he is undivided in himself *(indivisus in se)*, and separated *(divisus)* from everything else, as an individual human being is numerically one, rather God is called one to the *exclusion* of all others. He is one *(unus)*, which is to say sole or only *(unicus)*, just as the Sun is referred to as one, because it is the only one. 2) He is *unus* not according to a numerical unity of person, but of essence; given the plurality of persons in the one essence.[77]

The issue of "numerical unity" is significant: threeness of person does not contradict numerical unity of essence — there is no class of beings (whether genus or species) identifiable as "god" to which the divine persons belong and the divine unity is not a composite unity such as belongs to the several members of a genus or species.[78]

---

74. Pictet, *Theol. chr.*, II.i.1-3.

75. Cf. Pictet, *Theol. chr.*, II.xiii.1, 5-6, on the necessary equality, as God, of the three persons of the Trinity with Turretin, *Inst. theol. elencticae*, III.iii.3, 9.

76. Pictet, *Theol. chr.*, II.i.4.

77. Rijssen, *Summa theol.*, III.ix, controversia II.

78. Ames, *Medulla*, I.iv.42; Bucanus, *Institutions*, i (p. 5); Hottinger, *Cursus theologicus*, III.iv, canon C. See further, PRRD, IV, 3.2 (A.4-5); 4.1 (C.2). Note that both "genus" and "species" can refer to what is identified as "secondary essence" in classical philosophy, namely the class of essentially

Were this not so, it would imply a contradiction of those passages in Scripture which declare God's oneness and a contradiction also of the divine perfection, eternity, and infinity: there cannot be two perfect, eternal, and infinite beings. As Justin Martyr, Prudentius, and Lactantius indicate, some of the wisest pagan philosophers — specifically Aristotle, Plato, Epictetus, Cicero, and Seneca — held to belief in one God, but in general the pagans, in their idolatry, failed to conceive of God properly, whether in his infinite essence to the exclusion of lesser deities, or in his relation to the creation.[79] The biblical revelation teaches that

> God is wholly one, Deut. 6:4; Gal. 3:20; 1 Tim. 2:5; Hos. 13:4; Mal. 2:10. All creatures are subject to multiplication; there may be many of them and many; many Angels, men, stars, and so in the rest. Not one of them is singular and only one so; but one might conceive that there should be more; for he that made one of them, can make another and another, and as many as he pleaseth; but God is simply one, singular, and sole Essence; there neither is, nor can be more than one God, because he is the first and best Essence; and there can be but one first, and one best. He is Infinite, and there cannot be but one Infinite.[80]

It would be impossible, moreover, for a "plurality" of divine beings together to compose an infinite perfection, inasmuch as "many finites can never make one infinite; much less can many broken parcels or fragments of perfection ever make infinite and absolute perfection."[81] If one attempts to attribute perfection to a series of gods, like Jupiter, Neptune, and Apollo, one cannot conceive of all of them as simultaneously and equally most perfect, for then they would identical and not distinct gods: it is contradictory to claim two infinitely perfect beings. Nor, if their distinction is emphasized, and some perfections accorded to Jupiter, others to Neptune, and so forth, can any one of them be identified as most perfect, given that they each lack something. In order to be most perfect, a being would necessarily have to be infinitely perfect and, therefore, also unique.[82] Thus, from a biblical or exegetical perspective,

> Some places of Scripture simply deny other gods; and others exclude all but this one God; *Though there be gods many, and lords many*; that is, that are so called, and reputed by men, who deceive themselves in their own imaginations, yet *to us* (in the Church)

---

like things as composed of individuals. Strictly, "genus" would indicate a universal or form, incompletely expressing essence, that can be predicated of "specifically distinct" subjects, i.e., of a series of subjects distinct in species; "species" indicates a universal or form, completely or properly expressing essence, that can be predicated of a series of subjects distinct in number. Things belonging to a "genus" are distinct both in species and number. Both genus and species, in this sense, therefore, are composites. See Grenier, *Thomistic Philosophy*, I, pp. 164-165.

79. Cf. Amyraut, *De mysterio trinitatis*, I, pp. 8-14, with Pictet, *Theol. chr.*, II.i.5, and Rijssen, *Summa theol.*, III.ix, controversia II, argumenta, and III.x.

80. Leigh, *Body of Divinity*, II.vi (p. 188), citing (margin), Psalm 18:31, 45; Deut. 4:35, 39; 32:39; Ephes. 4:5, 6; 1 Peter 2:9; Mark 12:2; 19:32, 1 Cor. 8:5; John 17:3; 2 Sam. 2:2; Isaiah 11:12; 42:36; 44:1, 6, 8; 45.5, 21, 48; cf. Amyraut, *De mysterio trinitatis*, I, pp. 28-29.

81. Howe, *Living Temple*, I.iv (p. 107); cf. Ward, *Philosophicall Essay*, I.iii (p. 27-30).

82. De Moor, *Commentarius perpetuus in Joh. Marckii compendium*, IV.xxiii (I, p. 604).

there is but one God, 1 Cor.8:4, 5, 6; Zech. 14:9; after Christ shall come, the Gentiles with the Jews shall worship one and the same true God.[83]

The philosophical problem of the meaning of "infinity" also enters the system at this point: "there cannot be but one Infinite, because [if there were, hypothetically, more than one] either of them should include the other, and so the included must needs be finite, or not extend to the other, and so itself not be Infinite."[84] Of course, the argument stated in so blunt a fashion implies that interpenetration and "extension" need be understood in a spatial sense — and does not answer the deeper question of whether or not the infinite spirituality of God can be juxtaposed with an infinite materiality, as posed by the Cartesian dualism of thought and extension. The Reformed orthodox discussion of the divine infinity as an attribute will, therefore, need to develop greater precision on the point — as is notably seen in the distinction between an extrinsic infinity, like that just noted, and an intrinsic infinity, infinity understood as a positive attribute denoting the absolute "fulness of being."[85] Leigh, in fact, points toward the distinction in his subsequent comment, "that which is perfect in the highest degree can be but one; because that one must contain all perfections."[86]

Nor do these rather philosophical arguments stand in the way of piety. Confession of the absolute unity of God leads to "tranquillity of soul" beyond the discord and strife of our temporal existence: in God and in those who are joined to God there is concord.[87] The entire mode of Christian worship is similarly grounded in the unity of God, against all idolatry.[88] Even so, the scriptural mandate to obey God in all things indicates, via its relationship to the divine omnipotence, that there is but one God alone —

> if one can do all things, what need is there of many gods; if there were more gods than one, we might and ought to do service to more than one, to acknowledge them, praise, and love them, and be at least in mind ready to obey them, if they should command us anything, and we might lawfully seek to them for what we need, and give thanks to them, for what we received. But the Lord professeth himself to be a jealous God, and cannot endure any Copartner in worship.[89]

Scripture also emphasizes the oneness of God and the denial of existence to other gods in its reference to Gentile polytheists as "atheists" (Eph. 2:12): "not worshipping him which is the only true God. They worshipped none, Gal. 4:8."[90]

---

83. Leigh, *Body of Divinity*, II.vi (pp. 188-189), citing Heb. 1:6; Ps. 86:2; 97:7; 2 Cor. 4:4; Eph. 4:5-6.

84. Leigh, *Treatise*, II.vi (p. 57).

85. Howe, *Living Temple*, I.iv (p. 97); and see below, 4.4 (B) et passim.

86. Leigh, *Treatise*, II.vi (p. 57).

87. Mastricht, *Theoretico-practica theol.*, II.viii.11.

88. Mastricht, *Theoretico-practica theol.*, II.viii.12.

89. Leigh, *Treatise*, II.vi (pp. 57-58), citing Matt. 4:10.

90. Leigh, *Treatise*, II.vi (p. 59); cf. Mastricht, *Theoretico-practica theol.*, II.viii.6.

If there be many Gods, then either they must all be Subordinate, one being Superior; or else Coordinate each being equal to the other. If one be inferior to another, that which is at the command of another or exceeded by another is not God; if coordinate and equal, then one of them may cross another or many may hinder one, and what can be hindered in its working is not God.[91]

The divine unity, in its theological and religious dimension, thus transcends a purely rational notion of numerical unity insofar as it utterly denies even the hypothetical conception of another God: "for unity, as it denotes number, leaves also a place for a second or third, at least in apprehension." God's oneness means not only that he is "one" but that he is the "only one" and can have no equal or "copartner" in worship: "God is not only *unus* but also *unicus*, or to use Saint Bernard's word, *unissimus*." Furthermore, the divine unity is not the unity of a mathematical point — for, although a point is one and indivisible (as God is also defined), a mathematical point cannot be infinite nor can it be distinguished into three persons![92] Thus, God's oneness needs be considered "transcendentally as *Ens and unum* are counted only one, solely and alone God: there cannot be two Infinities in essence, for then one should not have all the other hath."[93] In addition to inferring God's oneness thus, from his "singularity" we can also infer it from

the *purity* and *simplicity* of his substance, which is not compounded with anything else. For that is most truly and properly one, which is nothing but itself, and hath no other thing mixed with it.[94]

Leigh also notes, on this point, the similar opinions of ancient philosophers, notably Socrates, Plato, and Pythagoras.[95]

This unity receives the uniform testimony of Scripture both of the Old and New Testament and, over against the Socinian tendency toward tritheism, in no way interferes with or is compromised by the doctrine of the Trinity.[96] The "essential perfection" of each of the persons of the Trinity must, thus, be something held in common: as there cannot be two or more infinite, perfect beings. The Godhead is one in its perfection: "Through this *Identity* of Essence in the persons, or most single ... unity, Christ is said to be in the Father and the Father in Christ (John 14:10)," as the fathers of the Church call it, "a union of the persons."[97]

This Essence which is one in number and individual, is improperly said to be communicated from one person to another, ... and in respect of it, the three persons

---

91. Leigh, *Treatise*, I.vi (p. 60); cf. De Moor, *Commentarius perpetuus in Joh. Marckii compendium*, IV.xxiii (I, p. 604)

92. Amyraut et al., *Syntagma thesium theologicarum*, I.xv.7.

93. Leigh, *Treatise*, II.vi (p. 58).

94. Leigh, *Treatise*, II.vi (p. 58).

95. Leigh, *Treatise*, II.vi (p. 59).

96. Mastricht, *Theoretico-practica theol.*, II.viii.8-10; cf. Howe, *Living Temple*, I.iv (p. 107).

97. Leigh, *Treatise*, II.vi (pp. 54-55).

of the Godhead are of themselves God: but most properly it is said to be common to the three persons, not as the universal to the particular, but as the accident to the subjects, not as the cause to the Effects, but as the whole to the parts: lastly, not as one thing to others, but as the thing to its proper manners, which are in the thing, for the persons are the manners of subsisting of the divine Essence; from which they are distinguished, not by the respect alone, nor by the real distinction, but by the degree and manner of the thing.[98]

4.2 The Names of God

A. Doctrinal Discussion of the Divine Names in the Era of the Reformation

1. The divine names and the Reformers' doctrine of God. From the time of Zwingli onward, with very strong precedent being offered in the next generation in the writings of Calvin, Bullinger, Musculus, Vermigli, and Hyperius, the names of God provided the Reformed with a primary source and focus for the *locus de Deo*.[99] Neither among the Reformers nor among the Reformed orthodox, however, does this development appear to arise from a nominalist or Ockhamist interest in divine "names" as a term preferable to divine "attributes": the Reformed motive in developing a doctrine of the divine names is fundamentally exegetical and does not at all relate to a theory of attributes as mere terms or concepts grounded not in the thing but in our perception only. Rather the Reformed interest in divine names, whether among the Reformers themselves or among the later orthodox, relates to a fundamental biblicism and to the assumption that the names offer a primary way of approach to the identity of God. This biblicism and its attendant sense of the importance of the biblical names of God is apparent not only in the theological manuals or systems of the Reformers but also in their commentaries. If, moreover, Calvin did not offer an elaborate doctrine of the essence, attributes, or names of God in the *Institutes*, he did discuss the divine names at length in his commentaries, particularly the commentaries on the Psalms, Isaiah, and Job, and in his sermons, most notably the sermons on Job. In these places, Calvin offered considerable exegetical support for the development of the Reformed doctrine of God, specifically, the doctrine of the divine names and the doctrine of the attributes.[100]

Musculus' *Loci communes* in particular evidence the formal as well as substantial importance of the language of divine names for early Reformed theology — and they offer a significant precedent for the organization of several of the early orthodox systems. The initial discussion in the second major division of Musculus' *Loci* deals first with the "name" and only subsequently with the "nature" of God as an introduction to an extended discussion of the attributes, a pattern reflected, notably, in Gomarus' and Maccovius' theologies. His discussion is at times highly metaphysical in character and

---

98. Leigh, *Treatise*, II.vi (p. 55).

99. Cf. Zwingli, *Commentary on True and False Religion*, pp. 62-64; Calvin, *Institutes*, I.x.2; Bullinger, *Decades*, IV.iii with Musculus, *Loci communes*, xli (*Commonplaces*, pp. 875-878) and Vermigli, *Commonplaces*, I.xii.2; Hyperius, *Methodus theol.*, I (p. 89).

100. Cf. Calvin's commentaries on Genesis 17:1; Ex. 3:13; 6:4; Isa. 42:8.

approaches the language and style of the scholastics — not, however, to the exclusion of practical or religious application: this balance of the theoretical and practical remained characteristic of much later orthodox theology.

Musculus understood the interpretation of the name of God as the most fundamental of categories for the full exposition of the doctrine of God: the name of God is a central issue in all right religion: believers must take care to use God's name "lawfully, truly, and religiously" and to "beware of the profanation and dishonoring thereof" — as the third precept of the Decalogue makes clear. The balancing of the speculative with the practical — indeed, this emphasis on the practical typical of Reformed theology as it moved toward and entered the era of orthodoxy[101] — is evident in the threefold division of the subject:

1. What the name of God is.
2. What it means to do anything in God's name.
3. To whom it belongs to do anything in God's name, and to whom not.[102]

It should be clear that a name is given to everything, "with the intent that every thing might be known as what it is, and that not only the general qualities, but also the special, might be discovered": the name of a thing, rightly understood, points toward the whatness or essence of the thing.[103] The name of God, therefore, will be fundamental to the understanding of the divine essence or nature. Bullinger similarly understands the divine names, including the holy name, as a more direct way of access to the doctrine of God: the names given to God in Scripture, he argues, reflect the infinitude of God's virtue, wisdom, goodness, justice, and power and are, thus, "the chief way of knowing God."[104] Given the unity and simplicity of the divine essence, Hyperius declares, the diversity of divine names offers insight into the fulness of the Godhead and into the activity or "acts" of God.[105]

Nonetheless, Musculus recognizes an underlying difficulty with the entire discussion: the consideration of names is, typically, a consideration of the nature of finite things:

> whether the majesty of God may be drawn into this consideration of "names" may be doubted: for it appears that since God, according to the essence of his deity is no manifold or diverse thing, but is utterly singular and a unity, no such thing [as a name] can be determined for him.[106]

As with Calvin,[107] so also in Musculus' teaching, the transcendence of God makes difficult any form of attribution — a potential sign of a nominalist accent in both thinkers.

---

101. Cf. *PRRD*, I, 7.3 (B).
102. Musculus, *Loci communes*, xli (*Commonplaces*, p. 875, col.1).
103. Musculus, *Loci communes*, xli (*Commonplaces*, p. 875, col.1).
104. Bullinger, *Decades*, IV.iii (p. 130).
105. Hyperius, *Methodis theologiae*, I, p. 89.
106. Musculus, *Loci communes*, xli (*Commonplaces*, p. 875, col. 2).
107. Cf. Calvin, *Institutes*, I.x.2.

The Reformers themselves, therefore, establish a precedent for the later development of the Reformed orthodox doctrine of God. We noted previously that Zanchi, on this point a clear transition figure to the orthodox approach, viewed the revealed names of God as the ground for all discussion of the essence and attributes — indeed, even of the Trinity — and that the supralapsarian Gomarus reduced his entire doctrine of God to a discussion of the names of God and a formulation of the doctrine of the Trinity.[108] This pattern of emphasis is maintained by the orthodox, who, with few exceptions, treat of the names of God immediately prior to and as a ground of the discussion of the individual attributes of God. Mastricht explicitly makes the methodological and formal point that the "names" are a category of attribution prior to the other categories of property predicated of God.[109] The divine names present a biblical point of entry into the rather abstruse and necessarily metaphysical discussion of the essence and attributes — indeed, as far as the Protestant orthodox were concerned, the names of God, the biblical identifiers of who and what God is, provided the natural point of contact between the biblical language of God and a more strictly philosophical discussion. Thus, the discussion of the divine names by the second-generation codifiers of the Reformation, as much and perhaps more than their analysis of various attributes directly stated by Scripture, pointed toward the fully articulated language of divine attributes typical of the Protestant scholastic systems. This particular pattern of continuity between Reformation and orthodoxy, moreover, points to a fairly consistent difference between the Protestant and the later medieval scholastics — one clearly traceable to the biblicism and the exegetical interest of the Reformation.

2. The "proper name" of God: Jehovah. Even so, God does not need a "proper name" inasmuch as proper names are used to separate or distinguish individuals from other individuals of the same kind — and, as the scholastics were wont to say, there is no genus "god." Nonetheless, God does give to himself a proper name in Scripture: "as in Exodus, where he says, 'And my name Iehovah, I have not made known unto them' (Ex. 6:4); and in Isaiah he says, 'I am Iehovah, this is my name' (Is. 42:8)." This particular name does indeed identify God in a unique way — but still with the limitations belonging to all human knowledge about God: "although this name does so properly belong to God that it may not be communicated to any creature, it is not such that, by it, we may attain a knowledge of the entire essence and substance of his majesty, the knowledge whereof is utterly incomprehensible."[110] This name, Iehovah, is the most excellent name of God since it alone of the divine names is not "derived from effects." It is, instead, an "express name" by which the very essence or "substance of the creator" is signified, manifesting the difference between God and his creatures. Such a name, granting that it has "nothing in common" with the creature or with creaturely names, is utterly unsearchable: it cannot, as far as Musculus is concerned, become the basis for extended theological discussion. He turns, therefore, to an

---

108. Cf. above, 2.1 (B); 2.2 (A.2, B.1); 3.1 (C.2).

109. Mastricht, *Theoretico-practica theol.*, II.iv.1.

110. Musculus, *Loci communes*, xli (*Commonplaces*, p. 875, col. 2), and see below, 6.2 (C) on the "majesty of God."

extended discussion of those names which impart some knowledge of God to theology because they have some creaturely analogue.[111]

Among other of Musculus' contemporaries, however, the tendency to move from the holy name in a more traditional manner toward discussion of the essence and self-existence of God was more the typical practice — perhaps because the nominalist tendencies evident in Musculus' thought were shared by few of the second-generation codifiers. The "most excellent" of the divine names, Bullinger declares, is the so-called tetragrammaton or "four-lettered name ... compounded of the four spiritual letters" and pronounced *Jehovah*.[112] Bullinger does not elaborate on his rather Cabbalistic-sounding comment about "four spiritual letters" but rather launches into an exposition of the meaning of *Jehovah*, that — given its emphasis on the concept of divine being and essence — echoes Zwingli and differs but little from the language of the early orthodox systems:

> *Jehovah* ... is derived from the verb-substantive *Hovah*, before which they put *Jod* and make it *Jehovah*, that is to say, "Being" or "I am"; inasmuch as he is *autousia*, a being of or from himself, having his life or being not from any other but from himself; requiring no assistance to make him be, but giving being to all manner of things; to wit, eternal God, without beginning or ending, in whom we live and move, and have our being.[113]

This is precisely the meaning of Exodus 3:14:

> "And God said to Moses, I am that I am; or I will be that I will be: and he said, Thus shalt thou say to the children of Israel, I am, or Being, or I will be, hath sent me to you." That is, I am God that will be, and he who hath sent me is himself Being, or Essence, and God everlasting.[114]

The combination of the syllables *Jah* and *Hu* given as a name of God in Isaiah 42:8 reflects not only the identification of God with Being but also the assumption that the highest being is the source and goal of all things: "these words are also derived from [the concept of] being, and teach us that God is always like himself, an essence that is of itself eternally and that gives being to all things that exist: since it is he by whom, in whom and to whom all things are, being himself a perpetual and most absolute *entelecheia*."[115]

The relationship between the verb "to be" and the tetragrammaton, together with the use of the verb form *Ehjeh* as a name is also registered by Hyperius,[116] and discussed at some length by Vermigli:

---

111. Musculus, *Loci communes*, xli (*Commonplaces*, p. 876, col.1).

112. Bullinger, *Decades*, IV.iii (p. 130).

113. Bullinger, *Decades*, IV.iii (pp. 130-131); cf. Zwingli, *Commentary on True and False Religion*, pp. 62-63.

114. Bullinger, *Decades*, IV.iii (p. 131); cf. Zwingli, *Commentary on True and False Religion*, pp. 63-64; Calvin, *Harmony on the Four Last Books of Moses*, (CTS Harmony I, pp. 73-74).

115. Bullinger, *Decades*, IV.iii (p. 132).

116. Hyperius, *Methodus theologiae*, I, p. 89.

he is called *Iehova* from *Haia,* that is, 'to be.' And this name belongs properly to God since God is Essence or Being in such a way that all things depend on him, nor could they exist without his power and assistance. Further, [his people] also have promises from him, both to be and to be performed. Wherefore, the name *Iehova* is properly attributed to God.[117]

"*Iehova,*" Vermigli adds, "signifies the chief Being," Plato's *to on* or essence. Vermigli is clear, however, that this essentialist understanding of God is not a matter of metaphysical or rational speculation, and that the revelation of the divine name makes a crucial theological point concerning the divine faithfulness: "there is no creature that may say 'I will be,' for if God draws back his power, all things will immediately perish; but God, doubtless, may truly say so, because he cannot fail or forsake himself." This *Jehovah,* furthermore, is known by his name to be entirely spiritual: the rabbis argue that the letters of the holy name indicate a spirit and that they also signify "rest" or "quietness" or "felicity," inasmuch as these blessings can be found only in God.[118]

A similar essentialist reading (and a rather intractable text for those who argue philosophical discontinuity between Calvin and the later Reformed) can be found in Calvin's commentary:

The verb in Hebrew is in the future tense, "I will be what I will be"; but it is of the same force as the present, except that it designates the perpetual duration of time. This is very plain, that God attributes to himself alone divine glory, because he is self-existent and therefore eternal; and thus gives being and essence to every creature. Nor does he predicate of himself anything common, or shared by others; but he claims for himself eternity as peculiar to God alone, in order that he may be honored according to his dignity. Therefore, immediately afterwards, contrary to grammatical usage, he used the same verb in the first person as a substantive, annexing it to a verb in the third person; that our minds may be filled with admiration as often as his incomprehensible essence is mentioned. But although philosophers discourse in grand terms of this eternity, and Plato constantly affirms that God is peculiarly *to on*; yet they do not wisely and properly apply this title, viz., that this one and only Being of God absorbs all imaginable essences; and that, thence, at the same time, the chief power and government of all things belong to him. ... Wherefore, rightly to apprehend the one God, we must first know, that all things in heaven and earth derive at his will their essence or subsistence from the One who truly is. From this being all power is derived; because, if God sustains all things by his excellency, he governs them also at his will.[119]

Calvin here demonstrates that he belongs as much to the theological tradition, with its interest in the divine essence and in its understanding of Scripture as containing references to the divine being, as any of the later Reformed writers: this is not a biblicistic Calvin who avoids the traditional essentialist reading of Exodus 3:14 —

---

117. Vermigli, *Commonplaces,* I.xii.2.

118. Vermigli, *Commonplaces,* I.xii.2.

119. Calvin, commentary on Exodus 3:14 (*CTS Pentateuch,* I, pp. 73-74); cf. the similar comments in Zwingli's *On the Providence of God,* p. 147.

and his successors deviate not a hair's breadth from his thought when they look to this text as the basis for the more metaphysical considerations belonging to the *locus de Deo*.[120]

Calvin does evidence a caution about metaphysical speculation concerning the tetragrammaton that was not always present either in the earlier or later exegetical tradition in his comment on the name of God in Psalm 8:1: Calvin cautions against speculative use of God's holy name and demands, as he states elsewhere in other terms, an examination of God's revealed nature rather than God's incomprehensible essence:

> The name of God, as I explain it, is here to be understood of the knowledge of the character and perfections of God, in so far as he makes himself known to us. I do not approve of the subtle speculations of those who think the name of God means nothing else but God himself. It ought rather to be referred to the works and properties by which he is known than to his essence. David, therefore, says that the earth is full of the wonderful glory of God.[121]

Even here, Calvin's emphasis on the relationship between God and his people that is indicated by the holy name stands in continuity with the later Reformed emphasis on the practical or homiletical application of exegesis and of doctrine. Nor does Calvin intend by these comments to rule out an essentialist understanding of the divine name when that understanding is developed exegetically, without philosophical speculation: of the phrase "thy name Jehovah" in Psalm 83:18, Calvin writes, "this implies that *being*, or *really to be*, is in the strict sense applicable to God alone," implying the traditional view of the inseparability of essence and existence in God.[122]

3. Other names of God. Beyond the tetragrammaton, other biblical names of God also play a role in the movement of early Reformed theology toward a full exposition of the divine attributes: two of these divine names signify the divine power and lordship. The foremost of these is *Adonai,* rendered into Latin as *Dominus.* This divine name is used by the Jews in place of the tetragrammaton, since they regard the holy name *Jehovah* as set respectfully beyond utterance. *Adonai* signifies that God is "Lord of all things, both visible and invisible." This point is also made by another of the divine names: God is called *Dominus Sabaoth,* indicating "the Lord of powers" or "the Lord of hosts." In his host are all angels, "all evil spirits, all men, kings and princes, all creatures, both visible and invisible: and all these," Bullinger adds, "he uses according to his own pleasure, yea, according to his own good and just will."[123] Other appellations point directly toward various attributes: God is called "king, creator, governor,

---

120. Contra Gründler, "Thomism and Calvinism," pp. 103-104, who argues that Calvin's real concern, unlike that of his successors, is *Deus erga nos*, passing lightly over the traditionary metaphysical assumptions belonging to Calvin's as well as to Zanchi's thought and ignoring the highly soteriological *usus* that belongs to each of Zanchi's topics. Also note the alternative explanation of Calvin's approach, below, 4.3 (B.1).

121. Calvin, *Commentary on the Psalms*, 8:1 (*CTS Psalms*, I, p. 94).

122. Calvin, *Commentary on the Psalms*, 83:18 (*CTS Psalms*, III, p. 350); cf. idem, *Commentaries on Hosea*, 12:5 (*CTS Minor Prophets*, I, pp. 420, 422).

123. Bullinger, *Decades*, IV.iii (pp. 132-133); cf. Hyperius, *Methodus theologiae*, I, p. 89.

immortal, invisible, consuming fire, glory, hope, strength, courage, defender, God of gods, Lord of lords, righteousness, good, merciful."[124]

The name of the Lord is also sometimes connected with the word *Elyon*, meaning "high," and God is sometimes called *El* because of his strength. Related to both of these names is *Elohim*, indicating the presence and unfailing power of God. Bullinger remarks that *Elohim* is a plural form and can be referred to "angels, to judges, and to men in authority: because God is always present with them ... and works by their ministry things that he himself wills."[125] When the plural form, *Elohim*, takes a singular verb, however, it refers to God alone and, in effect, adumbrates the doctrine of the Trinity.[126] Calvin, who did not accept the trinitarian exegesis of the passage, argued that "a title is here ascribed to God, expressive of that power which was previously in some way included in his eternal essence."[127] Hyperius, too, holds that the names *El* and *Elohim* are titles that signify divinity — to be translated as *Deus*.[128]

In Calvin's view, other divine names also reveal much concerning the identity, power, and salvific intention of God. Thus,

> The Hebrew noun *El*, which is derived from power, is here put for God. The same remark applies to the accompanying word *Shaddai*, as if God would declare, that he had sufficient power for Abram's protection: because our faith can only stand firmly, while we are certainly persuaded that the defense of God is alone sufficient for use and can sincerely despise everything in the world which is opposed to our salvation. God, therefore, does not boast of that power which lies concealed within himself; but of that which he manifests towards his children.[129]

Musculus comments, "The Hebrews use the word *shadai*, which is in the holy Scriptures applied unto God, and has a signification of sufficiency, and is never found spoken but of God only. God only say they, depends on none other, neither in substance nor in qualities, but he with all his appurtenances is clear ... from all dependence."[130] *Shaddai*, according to Hyperius, is an indication of the power of God.[131]

Bullinger also noted the importance of the name *Shaddai*. This name, as used in Genesis 17:1, indicates the "sufficiency" of God, following Maimonides' derivation over against the interpretation of *Shaddai* as "destroyer" or "just revenger." Granting Maimonides' reading, the name identifies God as "he who suffices for himself and is the sufficiency or fulness of all things."[132] The same point is made even by non-biblical and pagan names for the deity: the German *Gott* means "good or best" because "as

---

124. Hyperius, *Methodus theologiae*, I, pp. 89-90.

125. Bullinger, *Decades*, IV.iii (p. 134).

126. Bullinger, *Decades*, IV.iii (p. 135).

127. Calvin, *Commentary on Genesis*, 1:1 (*CTS Genesis*, I, p. 72)

128. Hyperius, *Methodus theologiae*, I, p. 89.

129. Calvin, *Commentary on Genesis*, 17:1 (*CTS Genesis*, I, pp. 442-443).

130. Musculus, *Loci communes*, xliii (*Commonplaces*, p. 901, cols. 1-2).

131. Hyperius, *Methodus theologiae*, I, p. 89.

132. Bullinger, *Decades*, IV.iii (p.135); cf. Bullinger, *Decades*, II.ii (pp. 215-216).

he is full of all goodness, so does he bestow on the human race all manner of good things" — and even the pagan *Saturnus* derives from *saturando*, "satisfying or filling." God, thus, is universally understood as self-sufficient and therefore, as having all good in himself, and the ability, as well, to bestow it on his creatures for their sustenance and fulfillment. Thus, in Exodus 6, the Lord uses the names *Jehovah* and *Shaddai* together to indicate the self-sufficiency of his essence or eternal being and to declare that he is "immutable, true," and ever faithful to his promise.[133]

Vermigli, more than Bullinger, though not in as elaborate a form as Musculus, viewed the divine names as giving form and structure to the doctrine of God: "some of the names of God," he argued, "are derived from his substance, and others from some property." Thus, *Jehovah* and *Ehi* are "substantial" names signifying "I will be" in an an ultimate sense, as no creature can claim to be. Other names refer to various attributes: *El* to the power of God; *Kadosh* to his holiness; *Shaddai* to his sufficiency — not, however, in the sense of accidents or incidental properties, but as belonging intrinsically to the one God.[134]

Musculus, whose exposition of the names and attributes of God adumbrates the large-scale argumentation of the orthodox era, never loses sight of the elements of piety that belong to the doctrine of the divine attributes — a feature of Reformed theology that carried over into Zanchi's *De natura Dei* and into many of the Reformed orthodox theologies. Such names as "Almighty" and "Lord," Musculus remarks, lead directly to the praise of God: the latter name reminds us that, in addition to the attributes of power and might, God is "our judge, just, merciful, gracious and favorable." The uttering of the divine names itself is an act of piety,

> For what is the praise and glory of God but that which is religiously and honorable thought and reported of him, as that he is good, merciful, just, true and almighty? Wherefore it is sung in the Psalm, "according to thy name, so is thy praise also" (Ps. 48).[135]

Therefore, to do anything in the name of God is to work for God's glory: all things (1 Cor. 10; Col. 3) ought to be done to the glory of God. Furthermore, "to do a thing in the name of God is to do it in the trust of God's name," trusting not in our own strength but in the strength of God, "whom we know to be Almighty and a defender of his people."[136] Finally, "to do anything in the name of God is to do it in the person, stead, and power of God." — as his minister and by his commission. From this it follows that it is not for all people to use the name of God, surely not the ungodly. Nor should all things be done in God's name. Rather all actions should be carefully considered

---

133. Bullinger, *Decades*, IV.iii (pp. 135-136).

134. Vermigli, *Commonplaces*, I.xii.2 (*Loci communes*, I.xi.2).

135. Musculus, *Loci communes*, xli (*Commonplaces*, p. 876, col. 1).

136. Musculus, *Loci communes*, xli (*Commonplaces*, p. 876, col. 2).

and only those things which "serve to the glory of his name" done while pronouncing the name of God.[137]

B. Reformed Orthodox Discussion of the Divine Names

1. The divine names in general: patterns of classification and discussion. The orthodox writers evidence considerable diversity both of extent and of detail in their discussions of the divine names, but they virtually all indicate the importance of the topic to theological system, because of the manner in which the discussion was capable of moving from exegesis to doctrinal formulation. Some of the early orthodox understood the *locus de Deo* as either initially or primarily a treatise on the divine names.[138] Others, accepting a division between "names" and "properties," divide the discussion, giving priority to the names and then offering some categorization of the properties as, for example, absolute and relative, first and second order.[139] Van Til, citing Bisterfeld, states that "the names of God are a summary of all theology and the key to all of Scripture."[140] This assumption concerning the importance of the names leads, in the case of Spanheim, to a significant interrelation of the topics *de Deo* and *de Trinitate* given the pressure exerted by antitrinitarians on the understanding of the biblical names of God.[141] For the same reasons, Downame focuses his entire discussion of the essence and attributes on the name "Jehovah."[142] This interest not only stands in continuity with the work of the second-generation codifiers of the Reformation, it also stands in continuity with and builds upon the work of the Protestant exegetical tradition, in which the desire for strict verbal equivalency in translation and for the identification of meaning through careful interpretation of Hebrew words had led to lengthy discussion of the various divine names.[143]

---

137. Musculus, *Loci communes*, xli (*Commonplaces*, p. 877, cols. 1-2). Musculus adds at this point a lengthy discussion (pp. 878-886) of the manner of "things to be done," the Christian *agenda*: whether such things ought to be commanded expressly in Scripture or not; that such things must be done faithfully as tending toward our redemption. Musculus touches briefly on preaching and teaching of the Word of God.

138. Cf. Gomarus, *Disputationes*, IV-V; with Spanheim, *Disp. theol.*, IX (*de Deo* I).v-xix; X (*de Deo* II).i-xiv; and, from the perspective of Reformed piety, note John Howe, *The Right Use of that Argument in Prayer from the Name of God*, in *Works*, III, pp. 207-239.

139. Thus, Polanus, *Syntagma*, Synopsis libri II; Wollebius, *Compendium*, I.i.1, prop. 4, 5; 2, prop. 1, 2; Cocceius, *Summa theol.*, II.ix-x; Gürtler, *Synopsis theol.*, v.5-13, 16.

140. Van Til, *Theol. rev. compendium*, II.i (p. 26).

141. Spanheim, *Disp. theol.*, X (*de Deo*).ix, xiii-xiv.

142. Downame, *Summe*, i (pp. 7-27).

143. Cf. Ainsworth, *Annotations upon Genesis*, 1:1 [Elohim]; 2:4 [Jehovah]; 17:1 [Shaddai] (pp. 1-2; 11-12, 89); idem, *Psalms*, 2:4 [Adonai]; 3:3 [Elohim] (pp. 411, 414); Jeremiah Burroughs, *An Exposition of the Prophecy of Hosea*, 4 vols. (London, 1643-51; reissued in one volume, Edinburgh: James Nichol, 1865), 12:6 [Jehovah] (pp. 523-4); William Greenhill, *An Exposition of Ezekiel*, 5 vols. (London, 1665-67; reissued in one volume, Edinburgh: James Nichol, 1863), 1:28 [Jehovah] (pp. 67-88).

"Scripture," Pictet notes, "does not simply teach that God is one, but describes this highest being with various names."[144] From a polemical perspective — against the "heathens," "tritheists," and Socinians — the orthodox stressed that "the variety of divine names and attributes does not argue a plurality of gods" or a divisibility or compoundedness in the one God.[145] As in the case of the attributes, the many names of God "are used to connote the perfection of the one God in order that by many inadequate conceptions we might comprehend in some measure what we could not by a single adequate one."[146] So, too, does this understanding protect against the Socinian and Vorstian attempt to undermine divine simplicity and transcendence: the Socinians in particular attempted to argue that the name of God, Jehovah, was not peculiar to the divine being and was in fact communicable to creatures.[147] Spanheim indicates, moreover, that discussion of the divine names must observe a distinction between humanly given and divinely given names — names that merely refer to God and names that both refer to and are from God — the latter category being reserved for those names given to God in the Old and New Testaments.[148]

Several paradigms were used by the Reformed scholastics, offering either a twofold or threefold categorization of the names. Fairly representative summary statements of the twofold models are offered by Polanus and Leigh. Polanus provides a neat Ramist division of the subject:

> The divine names (nomina divina) are either from the Old or from the New Testament. Of those in the Old Testament, some designate the essence of God (essentiam Dei) others what is proper to his essence (essentiae propria).
> The designations of the essence of God are Iehova, Iah, and Eheie.
> The designations of the essential properties of God are El, Elohim, Schaddai, Adonai, Helion, etc.
> The most frequent [names] in the New Testament are Theos and Kyrios.
> These also occur: Hyphistos, Pater ton Photon, Abba, Kyrios Sabaoth.[149]

In addition, the name or names of God are used in several distinct ways in Scripture, each with significant for the formulation of the doctrine of God:

> The Name of God is used five ways in Scripture: First, essentially for God himself, Isaiah 30:27. Secondly, for the power and efficacy which comes from God, Psalm 118:10, 11, 12. Thirdly, for the command and authority of God, 1 Sam. 17:45. Fourthly, passively for those actions whereby he is acknowledged by us, Matt. 18:19; that is, nothing but worshipping and calling upon the Father, Son and Holy Ghost for

---

144. Pictet, Theol. chr., II.ii.1-2.
145. Turretin, Inst. theol. elencticae, III.iii.8.
146. Turretin, Inst. theol. elencticae, III.iii.8.
147. Turretin, Inst. theol. elencticae, III.iv.1-19.
148. Spanheim, Disp. theol., IX (de Deo I).v.
149. Polanus, Syntagma, Synopsis libri II.

assistance. Lastly, for that Word whereby he is distinguished from creatures, and by which we are to have our thoughts directed about him.[150]

In the early orthodox era, Trelcatius proposed a threefold division of the "names" that both underlines the direct relationship of the Protestant orthodox doctrine of God to that of the Reformers — at least to that of Vermigli and Bullinger — and clearly identifies the direction taken by orthodoxy in establishing a relationship between the discussion of the names and subsequent discussion of the attributes. His use of the term "names" as indicating all denominations of the Godhead and not only the actual names, like Jehovah or El Shaddai, found in Scripture echoes the late medieval nominalist approach to the doctrine. The essential names of God, Trelcatius argues, may be either proper, improper, or relative. The first type of name, like "that proper and essential name of God, Iehova," cannot be attributed to creatures, not even analogically. The second type, given to God improperly or "commonly" either as descriptions of the excellence of God — such as "King, Good, Wise" — or as descriptions of God as a cause — such as "Creator, Redeemer" — may also be given to human beings and, thus, apply to God "not in respect of his essence, but of its effects."[151] The third kind of name or attribute, the relative or metaphorical names of God, is given "either after human affection or passion ... or else by a congruency or similitude" — for example, as when God is called Angry or Loving. This category of relative names appears to be identical with the list of affections of the divine will and follows out a logic similar to that of the so-called communicable attributes and is, typically, merged with the discussion of the individual attributes, with only the categories of "proper" and "improper" names, as they designate either the divine essence directly or some "essential property" discussed under the topic of divine names.[152] (This overlapping of the category of "names" with the category of "attributes" reflects the problem of predication discussed above — specifically the question of whether the attributes are predicated merely denominatively.)[153]

Among the later orthodox, Mastricht also proposed a threefold division of the divine names based on a somewhat different set of considerations: the names, he argues, reflecting the covenantal orientation of his theology, are either "essential," or "personal," or "federal." "Jehovah" is the fundamental essential name of God, rendered

---

150. Leigh, *Treatise*, II.i (p. 20); cf. the identical model in Wollebius, *Compendium*, I.i.1, prop. 5. Leigh's points correspond fairly closely to the interests of Reformed exegesis in his day: thus, on the first usage, cf. Tossanus, *Biblia*, in loc.: "[des Herrn Name] Das ist, seine macht und herrlichkeit, oder Gott selbst"; and cf. Poole, *Synopsis criticorum*, in loc.: "*Ecce nomen Dei* (i.e., vel, 1. ipse Jehova: ut dicimus *Maiestas regia* ... vel, 2. potentia Domini ...); on the second, Tossanus, *Biblia*, in loc. "[in Namen des Herrn] ... den Herrn als meinen nothhelfe verlassen"; on the third, Poole, *Synopsis criticorum*, in loc.: "Dei nomen hic in duas partes distribuitur. Pars prior denotat potentiam Dei: pars posterior voluntatem Dei, benignumque ipsius animum erga populum suum"; and on the fourth, Diodati, *Pious and Learned Annotations*, Matt. 18:19-20, in loc.

151. Trelcatius, *Schol. meth.*, I.iii.

152. Trelcatius, *Schol. meth.*, I.iii.

153. See above, 3.3 (D.7); cf. 3.3 (A.2-3).

customarily as *Dominus*, but indicating rather the *aseitas*, the absolute perfection, the faithfulness and truthfulness of God, his constancy and faithfulness, and his performance of all that he has promised. The preeminent personal name of God is "Elohim," rendered *Deus*, and indicating in its plural form in the Hebrew the *tribus personis subsistens*. Finally, the federal names of God are those names that represent him as *Deus Patrum vestrorum*, God our Father, the God of Abraham, of Isaac, and of Jacob.[154] Mastricht's identification and discussion of the names, therefore, adumbrates not only his entire doctrine of God — Trinity as well as essence and attributes — but also a central soteriological motif of his system. In addition, the "essential" characteristics of God relating to the name "Jehovah" are hardly a uniformly abstract, metaphysical set — they provide a foundation for both the theoretical and the practical sides of his system in the very being of God. Despite differences with Mastricht over elements of meaning and over the categories of names, eighteenth-century orthodox writers like Brakel and Franken continue to give prominent place to the divine names, in Francken's case, for the very same reason — that the names provide a basis for the practical as well as the more dogmatic or speculative elements of the doctrine of God and, indeed, indicate the intimate relationship of those elements.[155]

Similarly, after establishing their doctrine of the oneness of God, Turretin, Rijssen, and Pictet embark on a discussion of the divine names, arguing that the names — in Turretin's case, the name Jehovah in particular — stand as a primary issue in theological system inasmuch as they contain God's revelation of himself to his church and are, by divine revelation, to be considered as the beginning of knowledge about God.[156] Examination of the name or names of God is also one of the foundations of the relationship between doctrine and piety in the *locus de Deo*: after all, we pray in the first petition of the Lord's Prayer that God's name be hallowed or reverenced by us. Indeed, there is considerable overlap between the Reformed orthodox discussions of the first petition and their discussions of the divine names in theological systems.

2. Jehovah Elohim. The first and foremost definition of God, according to many of the Reformed orthodox, comes from the compound Hebrew name, "Jehovah Elohim," as it is given in Exodus 3:15. Although there is no noticeable difference among the theologians and exegetes over the understanding of "Jehovah," the juxtaposition with Elohim receives some different treatment — Perkins and Trelcatius understand the compound name as a brief but full revelation of the divine essence and trinity: "Jehovah Elohim (Exod. 6:2 & 3:15), the Lord God, that is, one Essence of three persons."[157] Others do not invoke the Trinity at this point.[158] Perkins thus begins his

---

154. Mastricht, *Theoretico-practica theol.*, II.iv.2; cf. Cocceius, *Summa theol.*, III.ix.3; Benjamin Austin, *Scripture Manifestation of the Equality of the Father, Sonne, and Holy Ghost* (London: P. W. and John Wright, 1650), I.iii (p. 5); Nichols, *Abridgement of Perkins*, p. 2.

155. Francken, *Stellinge God-Geleertheyd*, pp. 145-154.

156. Cf. Pictet, *Theol. chr.*, II.ii; cf. Turretin, *Inst. theol. elencticae*, III.iii.5; iv.1ff.

157. Trelcatius, *Schol. meth.*, I.iii (p. 53); cf. Perkins, *Golden Chaine*, ii (p. 11, col. 1).

158. E.g., Diodati, *Pious Annotations*, Ex. 3:15, in loc.; Ainsworth, *Annotations upon Exodus*, Ex. 3:15, in loc. — although Ainsworth elsewhere argues the trinitarian understanding of the name

discussion of the doctrine of God in *A Golden Chaine* with the simple declaration, "God is Jehovah Elohim" — the name offered to Moses in Exodus 3:15. Both the declaration and its recourse to Scripture offer insight into the character of the early orthodox theological enterprise: Perkins had begun his chapter with a brief a posteriori statement concerning the existence of God as evident from nature, civil order, and the temporal order — but the fundamental ordering of the discussion of the divine nature, like the ordering of Perkins' entire treatise is synthetic and a priori. In order to move in this fashion, Perkins has primary recourse, not to rational argumentation, but to revelation — indeed, to the highly specific revelation of the identity of God to Moses, "God is Jehovah Elohim."[159]

"Jehovah" signifies "I am" and therefore, comments Perkins, denotes the "most lively and most perfect essence." The name "Jehovah," therefore, directs the attention of theology toward "the perfection of the nature of God," which is "the absolute constitution thereof, whereby it is wholly complete within itself," whereas the plural form of Elohim, points toward the mystery of the Trinity.[160] Thus, "Jehovah Elohim" is descriptive of the entire doctrine of God, given that,

> of this description there are two members, the one of the *Essence*, and the *Unity* of the Essence: the other of the *Persons* and the *Trinity* of the persons, which two can neither be separated from the declaration of the divine Nature, nor ought to be confounded in the same: for as there is an exceeding great and indivinable unity of the divine Essence in the plurality of the persons: (for the Essence of the Father is the Essence of the Son and the holy Ghost:) so is there a real and different *Distinction* of the persons in the unity of Essence (so to be the Father is not to be the Son or the Holy Ghost.)[161]

This use of the plural form "Elohim" to point toward the doctrine of the Trinity is typical of the theology of the sixteenth and seventeenth centuries, most clearly echoing, perhaps, the great treatise by Zanchi, *De Tribus Elohim*. In any case, the revealed name of God provides access for quite a few of the early orthodox and high orthodox writers, not only to the doctrine of the divine essence and existence, but to the entire *locus de Deo*, both essence and attributes and Trinity.

3. The tetragrammaton: *Jahve* **or** *Jehovah*. Generally speaking, there can be no word "full enough, perfectly to express what God is."[162] Thus, Scripture indicates in several places that the name of God is "secret" and a "name which none can tell"(Judg. 13:18; Prov. 30:4). This is true also of the name of the Son — it is a name that none can tell (Prov. 30:4) and a name above every other name (Phil. 2:9). God, who is one

---

Elohim: see Ainsworth, *Annotations upon Genesis*, Gen. 1:1, in loc.

159. Perkins, *Golden Chaine*, ii (p. 11, col. 1).

160. Perkins, *Golden Chaine*, ii (p. 11, col. 1); cf. Wollebius, *Compendium*, I.i.1, prop. 5, canones i and iii.

161. Trelcatius, *Schol. meth.*, I.iii (p. 53).

162. Flavel, *Exposition of the Catechism*, in *Works*, 6, p. 297; cf. Hottinger, *Cursus theologicus*, III.v, canon A.

and sole, cannot be named by us — the church has referred to him consistently with the names that he himself has revealed.[163] In signifying the one God, therefore, Jehovah is the name of the full Godhead, Father, Son, and Holy Spirit, not the name of the Father alone.[164] Thus, the text of Exodus 3:13-15, the one place in Scripture where God does in fact specifically offer his name, is of paramount importance and forms the basis of nearly all the discussions of the divine name or names among the Reformed orthodox. The exegetes nearly invariably note the probable relationship between the verb *ejeh* in verse 14 and the name *Jahve* or *Jehovah* in verse 15.[165] They also are well aware of the problem of establishing a proper pronunciation and of the fact the "Jehovah" is a traditionary but probably not original rendering of the Hebrew, resulting from the insertion of the vowels of "Adonai" into the unpointed holy name — thus, the typical seventeenth-century recourse to the term "tetragrammaton" as indicating the four Hebrew consonants.[166] Indeed, Pictet notes that we are ignorant of the proper pronunciation of the tetragrammaton, JHWH. He suggests "Jahve" and "Jahave," offering also an "ancient Greek" form, "Jao," and the frequently heard, "Jehova."[167]

This name is often given in Scripture as the peculiar name of God (cf. Isa. 42:8) and denotes God as the one, in the words of the apostle John, "who is, who was, and who is to come" (Rev. 1:4). It is, moreover, this text in Revelation, more than the Septuagint rendering of Exodus 3:14, that sanctioned the traditional essentialist understanding of the text.[168] Since God alone is such a being, the name Jehovah "belongs to God alone" and "is never given, either properly or improperly, to any creature." Thus "in Isaiah 42:8, after the words, 'I am Jehovah, that is my name' the text adds, 'and my glory I will not give to another.'"[169]Pictet here echoes Calvin precisely: "*Hu* is sometimes taken for a substantive, so as to be a proper name of God; but I explain it in a more simple manner, 'It is my name,' that is, 'Jehovah is my own name, and cannot lawfully be given to any other.'"[170] It is, therefore, the sole "proper" name of God.[171] This interpretation of the meaning of Jehovah, moreover, stands in continuity with the exegetical tradition, with the views of the Reformers and also Calvin's reading, both in the *Institutes* and in his commentary on Exodus 3:14 — God's

---

163. Pictet, *Theol. chr.*, II.ii.1-2.

164. Zanchi, *De natura Dei*, I.xiii (col. 30).

165. Cf. Gataker, *De tetragrammato*, pp. 5-6; Ainsworth, *Annotations upon Exodus*, in loc.; Poole, *Commentary*, I, p. 122; Henry, *Exposition*, in loc.; and note Calvin, *Harmony of the Four Last Books of Moses*, Ex. 3:14 and 6:3 (CTS *Harmony*, I, pp. 74, 126-127).

166. Gataker, *De tetragrammato*, pp. 38-39, 74.

167. Pictet, *Theol. chr.*, II.ii.3; cf. Cocceius, *Summa theol.* III.ix.4; Gataker, *De tetragrammato*, p. 67.

168. Zanchi, *De natura Dei*, I.xiii.3 (col. 33); Pictet, *Theol. chr.*, II.ii.3. The text also figures significantly in the arguments for the full divinity of the Son: see the discussion and references to the exegetical tradition in PRRD, IV, 4.2 (B.4).

169. Pictet, *Theol. chr.*, II.ii.4.

170. Calvin, *Commentary on Isaiah*, 42:8 (CTS *Isaiah*, III, p. 296).

171. Hottinger, *Cursus theologicus*, III.v, canon D; cf. Francken, *Kern der Christelijke Leer*, III, q. 5 (p. 54).

"eternity and self-existence are announced by that wonderful name," declares Calvin in the *Institutes*.[172]

That Jehovah is an "incommunicable" or "proper" name of God" appears from the words of the prophet Amos, "Jehovah is his name" (5:8; 9:6) and from Psalm 83:18, "That men may know, that thou, whose name alone is Jehovah, art the most high over all the earth."[173] This, writes Ridgley, "is never said of any other divine names, which are, in a limited sense, sometimes given to creatures; and, indeed, all creatures are expressly excluded from having a right hereunto."[174] The fact that Jehovah means "I AM" and that the Lord speaks of this particular self-disclosure (Ex. 3:14) as his "memorial unto all generations" also manifests that the name Jehovah is peculiar to God as an indication of "all the perfections of the divine nature."[175] These theological arguments, moreover, are confirmed by the grammar of the Hebrew Scriptures:

> the word *Jehovah* has no plural number, as being never designed to signify any more than the one God; neither has it any emphatical particle affixed to it, as other words in the *Hebrew* language have; and particularly several of the other names of God, which distinguishes him from others, who have those names sometimes applied to them; and the reason of this is, because the name *Jehovah* is never given to any creature.[176]

Even so, the Jewish practice of never pronouncing the name of God, but using circumlocutions such as "that name" or "that glorious name" or "that name that is not to be expressed" testify to the peculiarity of the holy name, as does the verbal replacement of the name with Adonai by readers of the Hebrew text. So also the Septuagint shows a similar respect by replacing "Jehovah" with "Kyrios," the Greek translation of "Adonai."[177]

A highly exegetical and traditionary reading of the divine name, with concern for the meaning and derivation of the Hebrew, is found in Ainsworth's annotations on the Psalms:

> *Iehovah*] This is the chiefest name of the Eternal and most blessed God, so called of his Essence, being, or existence, which is simply one, Deut. 6.4. The force of this name the holy Ghost openeth up *He that is, that was, & that wil be,* or, *is to come,* Rev. 1.4,8, & 4.8, & 11.17, & 16.5. and the forme of the Hebrue name, implieth so much *Ie,* being

---

172. Calvin, *Institutes*, I.x.2; cf. xiii.23, and Calvin, commentary on Exodus 3:14 (CTS *Pentateuch*, I, pp. 73-74).

173. Turretin, *Inst. theol. elencticae*, III.iv.4; cf. Zanchi, *De natura Dei*, I.xiii.4 (cols. 34-35); Mastricht, *Theoretico-practica theol.*, II.iv.6 and Ridgley, *Body of Divinity*, p. 135, col. 1; Van Til, *Theol. revelatae comp.*, I.i.

174. Ridgley, *Body of Divinity*, p. 135, col. 1.

175. Ridgley, *Body of Divinity*, p. 135, col. 2.

176. Ridgley, *Body of Divinity*, p. 135, col. 2; cf. Gale, *Court of the Gentiles*, pt. 4, II.iii.1.

177. Cf. Ridgley, *Body of Divinity*, p. 135, col. 2-p. 136, col. 1, with Cocceius, *Summa theol.* III.ix.4; Turretin, *Inst. theol. elencticae*, III.iv.17; Mastricht, *Theoretico-practica theol.*, II.iv.8; and Ainsworth, *Psalmes*, annotation on Ps. 83:19 (p. 221), who argues on the basis of the translation of the divine name as *Aionios*, rather than its rendition as *Kyrios*, in the Greek text of the history Baruch that at an earlier time the Jews did in fact pronounce the holy name.

a signe of the time to come, *Ieheveh, he wil be; ho,* of the time present, *Hoveh, he that is;* and *vah,* of the time past, *Havah, he was.* It importeth that God *Is,* and hath his *being* of himself from before all worlds, Isa. 44.6, that he giveth *being* or existence unto al things, and in him al are and consist, Act. 17.25, that he giveth *being* unto his word, effecting whatsoever he hath spoken, whether promises Exod. 6.3, Isa. 45.2, 3 or threatenings, Ezek. 5.17 & 7.27. It is in effect the same that *Ejheh, I wil be,* or, *I am,* as God calleth himself, Exod. 3:14.[178]

The Reformed orthodox draw various conclusions from the exegesis, offering a series of theological implications of God's name. The name Jehovah means three things, writes Pictet,

> 1) An *ens aeternum* that exists of itself and that is independent of all others, and hence is simply called *ho on.* 2) A being from which all others have their being. 3) A being immutable and constant in its promises, in the sense of Exodus 6:3.[179]

The *Dutch Annotations* indicate that the text (Ex. 3:14), identifies a God who "is eternal in his being, faithful in his promises, and Almighty in the performance thereof."[180] In Gale's view, Jehovah signifies four things — first, the eternity of God "that eminently comprehendeth al differences of time, as John expounds it, Rev. 1:4, 8; second, the simplicity of the divine essence and the identity of God as "Being it self"; third, the efficacy and causality of God in "giving being and Existence to al his Creation"; and fourth, the omnipotence and veracity of God "in giving being and effect to his promisses, and word."[181] The latter point is seen in the fact that the Holy Name was first revealed to Moses (cf. Ex. 6:3), "because he had not fulfilled and given effect to the promise made to [Abraham, Isaac, and Jacob], and thence not opened his name."[182] At great length, Binning elaborates on the implications of unsearchableness, unchangeableness, and absoluteness that can be drawn from the divine name.[183] In all these instances, the argument offers an example of the hermeneutical model of drawing necessary conclusions from the text,[184] even as it evidences considerable dogmatic and exegetical continuity between the Reformed orthodoxy and much of the earlier Christian tradition.

4. Socinian objections to the tetragrammaton as sole name of God. As part of their exegetical polemic against traditional theism, seventeenth-century Socinians

---

178. Ainsworth, *Psalmes,* annotation on Ps. 83:19 [i.e., 83:18] (p. 221).

179. Pictet, *Theol. chr.,* II.ii.3; Amyraut et al., *Syntagma thesium theologicarum,* I.xvii.7.

180. Haak, *Dutch Annotations,* Ex. 3:14, in loc.

181. Gale, *Court of the Gentiles,* part 4, II.iii.1 (p. 241); similarly, Diodati, *Pious and Learned Annotations,* Ex. 3:14 and 6: 3, 6, in loc.; Cocceius, *Summa theol.* III.ix.9-10.

182. Gale, *Court of the Gentiles,* part 4, II.iii.1 (p. 241); cf. Haak, *Dutch Annotations,* Ex. 6:2, in loc.

183. Binning, *Common Principles,* VII, in *Works,* pp. 38-9; cf. Francken, *Kern der Christelijke Leer,* III, q. 7, 1-4 (p. 54).

184. Cf. the extended treatment of this hermeneutical point in George Gillespie, "That necessary consequences from the written word of God do sufficiently and strongly prove the consequent of conclusion," in *Treatise of Miscellany Questions, Works,* II, pp. 100-104, with the analysis in *PRRD,* II, 7.3B.

argued that Jehovah cannot be a proper name for God inasmuch as it is applied to Christ and is, in a sense, communicated to creatures. The orthodox argue to the contrary that any use of the name Jehovah that does not point directly to God is a metonymy and a mystery pertaining to the covenant — used absolutely and without any figurative implication, the name can apply only to God himself. As it is written in Isaiah 42:8, "Ego sum Jehovah, hoc est nomen meum." The name itself implies God's eternity and independence *quatenus Deus independenter per se existit* and thus also his causality and his efficiency in causing all creatures to exist. It also signifies his immutability and his constancy in his promises.[185] (As will be even more evident below in the discussion of the attributes, the Protestant orthodox do not separate the divine immutability from the idea of God's constancy and faithfulness: immutability is never simply a philosophical concept.) The orthodox also warn that the revelation of the name and the interpretation of its significance in no way remove the transcendence of God — God's proper name does not make his essence any the less incomprehensible, nor does it show him to be an individual distinct, as a species from others of the same genus: it only evidences the way in which God will become known to us as utterly distinct from his creatures.[186]

The Socinian objections are easily overcome: their chief purpose in arguing that Jehovah is not the incommunicable name of God is to prove that its predication of the Son does not prove the Son's divinity. Accordingly, they distort the meaning of texts to suit their doctrinal ends. Thus, they argue that the name Jehovah is given to places and things: Moses' altar is called "*Jehovah nissi,*" "the Lord is my banner" (Ex. 17:15); Gideon's altar is called "*Jehovah shalom*" (Judg. 6:24); Abraham's altar for the sacrifice of Isaac, "*Jehovah jireh*" (Gen. 22:14); and Jerusalem itself is called by Exekiel, "*Jehovah shammah*" (Ezek. 48:35). Moreover, in Psalm 47:5, the phrase "Jehovah is gone up with a shout" refers to the Ark of the Covenant.[187]

In none of these examples, the orthodox counter, is the name of God predicated of a place or a thing. In the case of Moses' altar, the words *Jehovah nissi* do not represent the name of the altar in a strict sense but rather signify "to the faith of those that came to worship there, that the Lord was their banner": the name itself, therefore, pointed to God himself rather than to the altar. The same argument applies to Gideon's altar: the name given signifies that the God worshiped there was the "God of peace."[188]

---

185. Rijssen, *Summa theol.*, III,iii, controversia 2; cf. Van Til, *Theol. revelatae comp.*, I.i.

186. Mastricht, *Theoretico-practica theol.*, II.iv.3.

187. *Racovian Catechism*, iv.1 (pp. 76-77), cf. 3.1 (pp. 34-6); cf. Ridgley, *Body of Divinity*, p. 136, col. 2.

188. Ridgley, *Body of Divinity*, p. 136, col. 2-p. 137, col. 1; cf. the exegesis in Calvin, *Harmony of the Four Last Books of Moses*, Ex. 17:15, in loc (CTS *Harmony*, I, pp. 294-295); Diodati, *Pious and Learned Annotations*, on Ex. 17:15 (pp. 48-49): "*Called God's name*] not to attribute Gods incommunicable name to the Altar, but to make it beare this *Motto* ... or because he would now make this profession of his thankfulnesse.... See Iudges 6:24"; Poole, *Commentary*, I, p. 153: "*The name of it*, viz. of the altar, which he calls so metonymically, because it was a sign and monument of *Jehovah-nissi*; even as circumcision is called God's *covenant*, Gen. xvii.13, and the lamb, the *passover*, Exod. xii.11."

Similarly, in the instance of Abraham's place of sacrifice, the real name of the place was Mount Moriah, and the phrase *"Jehovah jireh,"* "God will provide," indicates the gift of the lamb in place of Isaac: "So that the place was not really called *Jehovah*; but Abraham takes occasion, from what was done here, to magnify him ... whom alone he calls *Jehovah*."[189] Even so, Ezekiel's name for Jerusalem, *Jehovah shammah*, "the Lord is there," does not name Jerusalem with the name of God but signifies God's preeminent place in that city in the time of its final glory: "it is one thing to be and be called Jehovah; another for Jehovah to be and to dwell somewhere" — and it is the latter that is intended in the passage.[190]

The Psalmist's statement that "Jehovah is gone up with a shout," does refer to the progress of the ark into the city of David, but it hardly names the ark itself "Jehovah." There are parallels to this text in Ps. 24:7 and Ps. 68:1 — and in the latter the point is made very clear: "Rise up Jehovah, and let thine enemies be scattered," refers, as do the other passages to the taking up of the ark into battle or for a ceremonial purpose. Such apostrophes are directed to the ark but to God "of whose presence the ark was a symbol and pledge."[191] The Psalmist meant to indicate that "God had ordained that the mercy seat over the ark should be the immediate seat of his residence, from whence he would condescend to converse with men."[192]

> But since none are so stupid to suppose that inanimate things can have the divine perfections belonging to them, therefore, the principal thing, contended for in this argument is, that the ark was called *Jehovah*, because it was a sign and symbol of the divine presence; and from thence they conclude, that the name of God may be applied to a person that has no right to divine glory, as the sign is called by the name of the thing signified thereby.[193]

Again, however, the ark itself was not called Jehovah — rather the divine majesty or presence focused so on the ark that it could be referred to as Jehovah.[194]

---

189. Ridgley, *Body of Divinity*, p. 137, col. 1; cf. Turretin, *Inst. theol. encticae*, III.iv.14; and note Calvin, *Commentary on Genesis*, 22:14, in loc. (CTS Genesis, I, p. 571).

190. Turretin, *Inst. theol. elencticae*, III.iv.13; cf. Ridgley, *Body of Divinity*, p. 137, cols. 1-2; and note the exegesis in Diodati, *Pious and Learned Annotations*, Ez. 48:35, in loc.; and Poole, *Commentary*, Ez. 48:35, in loc. (II, p. 810): Poole places this name of Jerusalem into the context of Ezekiel's former vision of the glory of the Lord departing from the temple and writes of the eschatological vision of Ezekiel, "from the day of the Lord's restoring this people and rebuilding their city ... it shall be said of Jerusalem, *The Lord is there....* Such is the case of every true sincere believer, who may, wherever he is in his way of duty, still write, Jehovah-shammah, My God is here; and it is best to be where he is, till he bring me within the gates of the glorious city, where inconceivable light and love from the immediate presence of God give everyone a demonstration that *Jehovah shammah*. To him be glory for ever."

191. Turretin, *Inst. theol. elencticae*, III.iv.15.

192. Ridgley, *Body of Divinity*, p. 137, col. 2; cf. Poole, *Commentary*, II, p. 76.

193. Ridgley, *Body of Divinity*, p. 137, col. 2; cf. Turretin, *Inst. theol. elencticae*, III.iv.3; Calvin, *Commentary on Psalms*, Ps. 47:5, in loc. (CTS Psalms, III, p. 211); Diodati, *Pious and Learned Annotations*, Psalm 47:5, in loc.

194. Ridgley, *Body of Divinity*, p. 138, col. 1.

Another set of Socinian arguments against the sole predication of the name Jehovah of God look to the Old Testament passages concerning the "Angel" or "Messenger of the Covenant." This angel does indeed receive the divine name and says of himself, "I am the God of thy fathers, the God of Abraham, the God of Isaac, and the God of Jacob" (Ex. 3:6): or, to state the issue more accurately, "the Angel of the Lord" and "the Lord" seem to be one and the same in the text. The Reformed orthodox note in response that the name Jehovah is not applied indiscriminately to angels, but only to this particular "Angel of the Lord," who is evidently divine and not distinguished from Jehovah essentially, but only personally — not a created angel, but the Son of God, "in a prelude to his incarnation."[195] This angel was identified, moreover, by the ancient Jewish thinkers as the Word of the Lord, a point argued at length by Allix,[196] or as the archangel Michael, frequently associated in the Christian exegetical tradition, in such passages as Genesis 32:24, Daniel 10:21, Jude 9, and Rev. 12:7, with Christ.[197] "That it was the person of the Sonne ... rather than of the Father or of the Holy Ghost," Willet comments, "is thus shewed; the Father is never said to be an Angell, that is, a messenger or sent: nor is yet the holy Spirit in scripture called by that name, but the Sonne is called the Angell of the Covenant, *Malach, 3.1* in respect of his incarnation to come, when he was sent of his Father into the world ... which name of Angell given unto Christ is a title of office, not shewing his nature."[198] Drawing on Allix, Ridgley notes that an angel appeared to John (Rev. 22:8-9) and refused the divine honor accorded to the Angel of the Lord — a fact that supports the contention that the Angel of Exodus 3:2 and Malachi 3:1 was in fact "a divine Person."[199] The orthodox, recognizing the validity of the traditional reading of these texts as theophanic, typically added a christological interpretation as well, on what they assumed were sound exegetical grounds. "The angel of the Lord," Poole comments, was

> not a created angel, but the Angel of the covenant, Christ Jesus, who then and ever was God, and was to be a man, and to be sent into the world in our flesh, as a messenger from God. And these temporary apparitions of his were presages or forerunners of his more solemn mission and coming, and therefore he is fitly called an Angel. That this Angel was no creature, plainly appears by the whole context, and specially by his saying, *I am the Lord, &c.* The angels never speak that language in Scripture, but, *I am sent from God,* and, *I am thy fellow servant, &c.*[200]

Similarly, the exegetical tradition, including the exegesis of the Reformers, favored the reading of the reference in Malachi 3:1 to "the angel" or "messenger of the

195. Turretin, *Inst. theol. elencticae*, III.iv.7-8; cf. Ridgley, *Body of Divinity*, p. 138, cols. 1-2.

196. Pierre Allix, *The Judgment of the Jewish Church against the Unitarians* (London: R. Chiswell, 1699), ch. xiii-xvi on the "Angel of the Lord."

197. Cf. Ainsworth, *Annotations upon Genesis*, Gen. 32:42, in loc., with Ainsworth, *Annotations upon Exodus*, Ex. 3:2, in. loc. for a review of the Jewish exegesis as adapted to christological purposes; and note Willet, *Hexapla in Exodum*, p. 28.

198. Willet, *Hexapla in Exodum*, p. 28.

199. Ridgley, *Body of Divinity*, p. 138, col. 2.

200. Poole, *Commentary*, I, p. 120; cf. Diodati, *Pious and Learned Annotations*, in loc.

covenant, whom ye delight in" as a reference to Christ as Lord in his office of Mediator — "God manifested in the flesh" and, at the same time, "God's minister and interpreter" in the confirmation of the covenant.[201]

5. Hayah — the "I AM." Related to the name Jehovah there is, potentially, another name, *Hayah*, which also "denotes the divine essence." Most of the Reformed thinkers from Zwingli onward tend to discuss the "I AM" in relation to the tetragrammaton rather than identify it as a distinct name, but a few writers separate out the discussion. Thus, Pictet notes that it is disputed among the learned whether or not *"hayah"* is actually a name, but it is clear from the text of Exodus 3:14 "that the same one is designated by this word, as is understood by the name YHWH."[202] The "learned" to whom Pictet refers included some of the most noted Hebraists and exegetes of the day — among them Sixtus Amama, Drusius, Johannes Buxtorf the younger, and Thomas Gataker — all of whom wrote extensively on the problem of the divine names, specifically on the tetragrammaton and its relationship with the verb to be. Some of the writers of the seventeenth century even take the time to note that Lyra's fifteenth-century editor, Paul of Burgos, denied that *hayah*, or, specifically, the *ehjeh* of Exodus 3:14 was a name.[203] There is an awareness in all of these writers that the Hebrew language functions rather differently than Greek or Latin, but an equal awareness that the close association between the divine name and the verb "to be" demands that existence and being be somehow identified as peculiarly belonging to God.[204] The orthodox theologians, many of whom were themselves exegetes well versed in ancient languages, stood in this case, as in most others, firmly in an established exegetical tradition in which the relationship had already been strongly established between the verb, *hayah* and the divine name, *Jahve* or *Jehovah*. The text of Exodus 3:14 does, after all, present the phrase "I am who I am" or "I will be who I will be" as an answer to the question, "Moses said unto God, Behold, when I come unto the children of Israel and say unto them, the God of your fathers hath sent me unto you; and they shall say unto me, What is his name, what shall I say unto them?" — "Thus shalt thou say unto the children of Israel, I AM hath sent me unto you."

The simple sense of the text is that "I AM" is the name of God.[205] The basic religious significance of the name is "the reality of his being, in opposition to idols, which are

---

201. Calvin, *Commentaries on the Prophet Malachi*, in loc. (CTS *Minor Prophets*, V, pp. 568-570); cf. Luther, *Lectures on Malachi*, in loc. (LW, 18, pp. 408-409); Poole, *Commentary*, II, p. 1025; Diodati, *Pious and Learned Annotations*, in loc.

202. Pictet, *Theol. chr.*, II.ii.5.

203. E.g., John Trapp, *A Commentary on the Old and New Testaments*, 5 vols. (London: Richard Dickinson, 1856-68), in loc. (I, p. 185).

204. Cf. Johannes Buxtorf the Younger, *Dissertatio de nominibus Hebraicis* in *Dissertationes philologico-theologicae* (Basel, 1645); Thomas Gataker, *Dissertatio de nomine Tetragrammato*; Nicholas Fuller, *Miscellaneorum theologicorum ... libri tres* (London: John Bill, 1617), II.vi.

205. Thus, Flavel, *Exposition of the Catechism*, in *Works*, vol. 6, p. 298; cf. Ainsworth, *Annotations upon Exodus*, Ex. 3:14, in loc.; Poole, *Commentary*, Ex. 3:14, in loc. (I, p. 122); Trapp, *Commentary*, in loc. (I, p. 185); Hottinger, *Cursus theologicus*, III.v, canon C.

but imaginary and fantastic things."[206] The Hebrew, as many of the orthodox exegetes
and theologians indicate, is a future tense and best translates as "I will be who [or what]
I will be." This literal reading yields a sense of the constancy of the divine "nature,
will, and word" inasmuch as the God who made his promises to Abraham remains
the same and delivers the substance of his promises to later generations. Poole argues
two possible theological implications of this use of the future:

> He useth the future tense; either, 1. Because that tense in the use of the Hebrew tongue
> comprehends all times past, present and to come, to signify that all times are alike to
> God, and all times are present to him; and therefore what is here, *I shall be*, is rendered,
> *I am*, by Christ, John 8:58. See Psalm 90:4; 2 Peter 3:8. Or, 2. To intimate, though
> darkly ... the mystery of Christ's incarnation. *I shall be what I shall be*, i.e., God-man;
> and I who come now in an invisible, though glorious, manner to deliver you from this
> temporal bondage, shall in due time come visibly and by incarnation, to save you ...
> from your sins, and from the wrath to come. Of this name of God, see Rev. 1:4, 8;
> 16:5.[207]

6. Elohim: generic but plural. "Elohim," note the orthodox, is a name that simply
indicates "God" in the most general sense and is applied also, therefore, to "God's
viceregent's on earth," to angels, magistrates, and even to "false gods."[208] The name
Elohim, therefore, corresponds with the Greek *theos* and the Latin *deus*. The orthodox
raise questions, moreover, concerning the category to which the name belongs: it does
not function as a proper name for God, certainly — but does it even belong to the
other category of essential names, the "common" names for God? Rijssen and Mastricht
note that it can be understood as an indication of divine work (*officium*) rather than
a designation of the *deitas* or essence of God. It is in this fashion, after all, that the
Jews interpret those passages in Scripture which can be interpreted as referring to Christ
or to the Holy Spirit as Elohim: they are identified under the name "God" inasmuch
as they belong to the work of God. Thus, Jehovah alone designates God himself and
no other, while Elohim is applied analogically to other beings.[209] More problematic
still, from the orthodox perspective, was the Socinian appropriation of this pattern
of Jewish exegesis:

> The word God is two wayes chiefly used in Scripture. The first is, when it denoteth
> him, who both in the heavens, and on the earth, doth so rule and exercise dominion
> over all, that he acknowledgeth no superior, and is so the Author and Principall of

---

206. Flavel, *Exposition of the Catechism*, in *Works*, vol. 6, p. 298; cf. Poole, *Commentary*, Ex. 3:14,
in loc.

207. Poole, *Commentary*, Ex. 3:14, in loc.

208. Zanchi, *De natura Dei*, I.xii (col. 29); Ainsworth, *Orthodox Foundation*, p. 8; Pictet, *Theol.
chr.*, II.ii; Van Til, *Theol. rev. comp.*, I.i: citing Gen. 1:1 (God); Ps. 8:5; Heb. 2:7 (angels); Ps. 82:6;
Jn. 10:34-35 (princes and magistrates).

209. Rijssen, *Summa theol.*, III.iii, controversia iii; Mastricht, *Theoretico-practica theol.*, II.iv.15; Cf.
Calvin, *Commentary on Genesis*, 20:13; 35:7 (*CTS Genesis*, I, p. 531; II, p. 239), in both instances
rendering *Elohim* as "angels" because of the plural verb; cf. Ainsworth, *Annotations upon Genesis*, 1:1,
in loc.

all things, as that he dependeth on none. The other is, when it designeth him who hath some sublime dominion from that one God, and so is in some sort partaker of his Deity. Hence it is that Scripture calleth that one God the *God of Gods*, or the most *high God*. Ps. 50:1; Heb. 7:1. And in the latter signification, the Son of God is in certain places in the Scripture dignified with the title of a God.[210]

This particular argument serves, among other things, to link the initial discussion of divine names with the discussion of the Trinity — in the initial discussion, presenting the problem of the legitimate application of the name to God and its plurality to the adumbration of the Trinity, in the later discussion specifically raising the issue of the title "Son of God" and its implication for such categories of the doctrinal discussion as the full divinity, specifically the *aseity* of the Son. The Socinian exegesis of Elohim/God also raised, tangentially, the issues of Christian exegesis of the Old Testament and of the character of the appropriation of Jewish exegesis by the Reformed of the seventeenth century.[211]

With reference to the doctrine of God and the divine names, this argument is somewhat difficult to counter, insofar as the Reformed agree with it in general in terms of the identification of angels, false gods, and other heavenly beings as *Elohim*. Nonetheless, in those cases in which the word must be translated as referring to the true God — including those places where it appears to refer to Christ or the Spirit — it is not at all applied analogically, but is used as a reference to the absolute rule or *dominium* of God, to his *justitia* and *judicium* just as El typically refers to his strength or *fortitudo*. Again, as in the case of the name *Jehovah*, this echoes the reading of the Reformers: "power and might are contained under the title *Elohim*," wrote Calvin.[212] Indeed, if *Elohim* indicates nothing more than a divine work or discharge of a divine duty, Mastricht queries, what work or duty might that be? He notes that other names denoting duties invariably correspond with the name of the duty — as *rex* with *regendo* and *Dominus* with *dominando*; but neither *Elohim* nor its Greek equivalent, *theos*, have such a word corresponding with them.[213] *Elohim*, translated as *Deus*, and in the abstract as *deitas*, denotes, according to Rijssen, *natura Entitas perfectissimi* and is synonymous with the term *natura vel forma Dei*.[214]

The peculiarity of the plural form, *Elohim*, was also the subject of debate. In general, the Protestant orthodox, Reformed and Lutheran alike, followed the tradition in affirming the plural form as an indication of the plurality of persons in God: Mastricht cites Zanchi, Martyr, Junius, Mercer, Danaeus, and Drusius as advocating this view.[215]

---

210. Racovian Catechism (1652), Of the Knowledge of God, i (p. 19).

211. On the Reformed interest in Judaica see the references in *PRRD*, II, 7.1 (B.2); trinitarian exegesis of the Old Testament and the specific problem of the divinity of the Son are discussed in *PRRD*, IV, 4.2 (A-B); 6.1 (B.1; C.1-2).

212. Calvin, *Institutes*, I.x.2.

213. Mastricht, *Theoretico-practica theol.*, II.iv.15.

214. Rijssen, *Summa theol.*, III.iii, controversia iii, arg. 4.

215. Mastricht, *Theoretico-practica theol.*, II.iv.16; cf. Zanchi, *De natura Dei*, I.xii (cols. 29-30). Also see Polanus, *Syntagma theol.*, I.iii.3; Bucanus, *Institutions*, i (p. 5); Austin, *Scripture Manifestation*,

The Socinians, to the contrary, assume not only a oneness of essence, but also a oneness of person in God, and insist that the plural form indicates either a plurality of powers or of attributes and virtues. If, counters Mastricht, the word *Elohim* indicates a unity of person and a plurality of powers, why the plural verb in Gen. 1:26? Nor can the use of *Elohim* in this passage be interpreted as attributing creative powers to angels: this is shown to be false by Jer. 10:10-11.[216] Rijssen adds that the name *Elohim*, though it allows the doctrine of the Trinity, does not provide ground for a deduction of that doctrine either etymologically or by reason of the plural form of the noun — trinitarian implications derive from the context, and from "the subject and circumstances" of the use of the term. Thus, *Elohim* does not always signify Trinity.[217] Indeed, in the early eighteenth century, Francken appears to have given up the trinitarian reference and fastened on the creative and federal relationships of the name *Elohim*, breaking somewhat with the paradigm of his predecessor, Mastricht.[218]

7. **Shaddai and El Shaddai.** Zanchi, Cocceius, Mastricht, Pictet, and various other Reformed writers also understand the names *Shaddai* and *El Shaddai* as having considerable importance for the doctrine of God. They also offer several derivations of *Shaddai*: it might derive from the verb *sdd*, indicating "he makes waste" or "empty". In this case, *Shaddai* would refer to the power of God, "by which God has created all things and is capable of reducing them to waste." Pictet notes that it is this derivation that probably lies behind the Septuagint translation of *Shaddai* as *pantokrator* or *ho ta panta poiesas* — ruler or maker of all things. Some have derived the name, however, from the noun *sd*, a female breast, indicating a meaning similar to the pagan representations of Diana, Isis, and Ceres as large-breasted (*mammosa*) — namely, as "nourishing all things" — an etymological point known to the Reformers as well as to the later orthodox.[219] The probable majority of writers favors, however, a derivation of the name from *dy* (dalet yod), indicating sufficiency or *autarchia*:

> If this last derivation is the correct one, we understand why God, revealing himself to Abraham (Gen. 17:1), calls himself by this name: in order to intimate that he did not covenant with him as if he needed Abraham's help or resources; on the contrary, [he calls himself by this name in order to indicate] that he is so abundant in goodness that he can fulfill all of the promises that he so rightly set forth in his covenant.[220]

Zanchi cites rabbinic exegesis in justification of the point.[221] Others render *Shaddai* as "Almighty" and *El Shaddai* as "God Almighty."[222]

I.iii (p. 5).

216. Mastricht, *Theoretico-practica theol.*, II.iv.16; cf. Cocceius, *Summa theol.* III.ix.25-30.

217. Rijssen, *Summa theol.*, IV.xv; cf. Hottinger, *Cursus theologicus*, III.v, canon E.

218. Francken, *Stellinge God-Geleertheyd*, p. 150.

219. Cf. Calvin, *Harmony of the Four Last Books of Moses*, Ex. 6:2 (*CTS Harmony*, I, p. 126).

220. Pictet, *Theol. chr.*, II.ii.9; cf. Zanchi, *De natura Dei*, I.xv (col. 44); Cocceius, *Summa theol.* III.ix.15; Mastricht, *Theoretico-practica theol.*, II.iv.11; also, Van Til, *Theol. revelatae comp.*, I.i.

221. Zanchi, *De natura Dei*, I.xv (col. 44).

222. Cf. Francken, *Kern der Christelijke Leer*, III, q. 13 (p. 55).

8. Other names of God. Pictet and several of the other orthodox writers add a brief discussion of the names *Yah* and *El*, the former signifying either "to be fit" or "to be suitable" and the latter "strength or might" thereby indicating that God is omnipotent, having all power, virtue, and efficacy.[223] *El*, moreover, translates as Θεός or *Deus*.[224] Pictet concludes his examination of the names of God with a review of several other biblical designations of God — *Adonai, Sabaoth, Elyon, Theos, and Kyrios*. *Adonai*, Lord, indicates dominion and identifies God as the "one who subjects all things to himself" and was used in various forms by the ancient pagan nations.[225] In this sense, moreover, the name has trinitarian implications and may refer not merely to the Godhead but either to the Father or the Son, understood personally, or indeed to the Trinity. Thus, in the theophany of Isaiah 6:1-6, the "Lord sitting upon a throne" can refer either to

> 1. God the son, who frequently appeared to the patriarchs and prophets, and that sometimes in the form of a man. Or, rather, 2. The Divine Majesty as he subsisteth in three persons, as may be gathered from the plural number *us*, used of this Lord, ver. 8, and comparing other scriptures; for God the Father is described as sitting upon a throne, Can. 7:9, 13, and elsewhere; and the glory of God here manifested is said to be Christ's glory, John 17:41, and the words of the Lord here following are said to be spoken by the Holy Ghost, Acts 28:25.[226]

Sabaoth is not properly a name of God, but rather a designation added to the name of God that implies the exercise of divine lordship over many people — much as the pagan Bacchus was called *sabasiou* by his worshipers.[227] Similarly, *Elyon* is not a name, but an epithet signifying exalted status or supremacy, like the Greek, *heliou*.[228] To these Hebrew terms, the two principle Greek names of God must be added: *Theos* and *Kyrios*. Pictet notes that the former name denotes the nature of God while the latter, meaning "Lord," is frequently used to translate *Jehovah* but is "especially ascribed to Christ the Redeemer, who is called 'Lord of Lords.'" Since, moreover, *Kyrios* translates the Hebrew *Adonai*, its use as a divine name is largely exhausted by the discussions of *Jehovah* and *Adonai* — including, as we have seen, its christological implication as well. The term is also sometimes attributed *improprie* to creatures.[229]

God is also called "Father," *Pater*. Both the Reformers and the Reformed orthodox were aware that the name "Father" is given to God in several ways: there is the "essential" understanding of the name, which refers to the one God as Creator — and

---

223. Pictet, *Theol. chr.*, II.ii; cf. Cocceius, *Summa theol.* III.ix.18; Francken, *Kern der Christelijke Leer*, III, q. 12 (p. 55).

224. Zanchi, *De natura Dei*, I.xvi (col. 45).

225. Pictet, *Theol. chr.*, II.ii.10.

226. Poole, *Commentary*, in loc. (II, p. 337); cf. Diodati, *Pious and Learned Annotations*, Isa. 6:8, in loc.; Cocceius, *Summa theol.* III.ix.13-14.

227. Pictet, *Theol. chr.*, II.ii.11.

228. Pictet, *Theol. chr.*, II.ii.12; cf. Francken, *Kern der Christelijke Leer*, III, q. 14 (pp. 56-57).

229. Pictet, *Theol. chr.*, II.ii.13; cf. Mastricht, *Theoretico-practica theol.*, II.iv.14.

there is the "personal" understanding of the name, which refers to the first person of the Trinity. Leaving aside the "personal" or hypostatic understanding,[230] the "essential" meaning of the name also bears a double implication. Calvin, for example, is famous for his assertion that God is revealed in general as Creator and is only known as Father in through Christ — that in the present "ruin" of the world, God is not experienced as father apart from Christ.[231] Still, in the subsequent discussion of the general revelation of God in nature, Calvin reminds his readers that the apostle Paul cited the pagan poet Aratus as calling God "Father" and identifying human beings as God's "offspring." Calvin comments, "in the same way also, from natural instinct, and, as it were, at the dictation of experience, heathen poets called him the Father of men." There is, therefore, a general sense in which all people understand God as father and themselves as his progeny — but there is also the full and proper sense, resting on redemption in Christ and the Spirit of adoption.[232]

The Reformed orthodox also allow this general sense of the name "Father" to be applied to God in order to identify the entire Godhead according to essence or nature. The usage, they note is biblical: the phrase "the will of God and our Father" (Gal. 1:4) is often taken as a general reference, "not excluding the Son."[233] All human beings in general revere God as Creator and preserver. It is in this sense that Malachi wrote, "Have we not all one father? Hath not one God created us?" God is also called "the Father of Spirits."[234] So also is God recognized to be the benefactor of all humankind: the Psalmist refers to him as "the Father of the fatherless" (Ps. 68:5), a father who pities his children (Ps. 103:13).

Beyond this broadest application of the name, however, there is the more special sense in which believers or the covenant people refer to God as father. Poole echoes Calvin precisely in his comment on Acts 17:29: all human beings are the "offspring" of God and bear his image, but those who have the Spirit of adoption recognize the divine parentage more fully.[235] By extension, therefore, "God our Father" and "Father" in the general or non-trinitarian sense, and "the God of Abraham, of Isaac and of Jacob" are, according to Mastricht and others, to be identified as "federal names" of God — names that identify God as the One who wills and pledges to be "our God." The point can be made easily from Deuteronomy 32:6, "Do ye thus requite the Lord, O foolish people ... is he not that father that hath bought thee."[236]

---

230. Cf. PRRD, IV, 5.1, A.2.

231. Calvin, Institutes, I.ii.1; cf. II.vi.1.

232. Calvin, Institutes, I.v.3; cf. Calvin, Commentary on Acts, 17:26, (CTS Acts, II, pp. 164, 170).

233. Poole, Commentary, Gal. 1:4, in loc (III, p. 640).

234. Ridgley, Body of Divinity (1855), II, p. 603, citing Mal. 2:10 and Heb 12:9; cf. Poole, Commentary, Heb 12:9, in loc (III, p. 870).

235. Poole, Commentary, Acts 17:29, in loc (III, p. 443).

236. Mastricht, Theoretico-practica theol., II.iv.2; cf. Ridgley, Body of Divinity (1855), II, p. 603.

4.3 Simplicity, Spirituality, Immutability, and Related Attributes

A. *Quid sit Deus*: Essential Attributes of the Primary Order

The essential attributes or properties of God (*proprietates Dei essentiales*) belong to a twofold order: some are primary, others are secondary.

The essential attributes of the primary order are both simplicity and perfection (*simplicitas & perfectio*); and infinity and immutability (*infinitas & immutabilitas*).

The infinity of God is both eternity (*aeternitas*) and immensity (*immensitas*).

The immutability of God is both of essence (*essentiae*) and of nature or of essential properties (*naturae seu proprietatem essentialem*) and of the decrees and promises of God (*decretorum & promissionum Dei*).[237]

The first series of attributes treated in many of the Reformed orthodox theologies, spirituality, simplicity, invisibility, immutability, and perfection, follow directly from the principle of the essential unity of God, from his independence, from the implications of the discussion of the divine names, and by way of conclusions drawn from a series of biblical texts. Simplicity, spirituality, and invisibility, moreover, stand together in many of the Reformed orthodox systems as a triad of related attributes — so related, indeed, that they imply each other and, at times, demand virtually the same definition. For that reason, we deal with them as a distinct group. Spirituality, for example, indicates non-composite existence and indivisibility — which is precisely the characteristic of spiritual as opposed to material existence — and spiritual things are, by definition, invisible. Given this interrelated structure of argument, the order of the terms varies from one treatise or system to another.

Ursinus' extended definition of God began with the statement that "God is a spiritual essence," and his discussion of the attributes likewise began with the identification of God as "spiritual," albeit with no indication of the rationale for the order.[238] Wendelin echoes this model in the rather straightforward and simple statement with which he opens his discussion of the divine nature, "God is by nature spirit, which is to say, of an utterly incorporeal substance or essence."[239] Spirituality is also the first attribute to be considered in the Westminster standards and therefore in Watson's, Boston's and Ridgley's systems, all of which are commentaries on the catechism — and for various thinkers provides the basis for at least a partial derivation of the other divine perfections.[240] Ward's largely a posteriori philosophical "eviction" of the attributes infers God from creation and then understands eternity as the basis for understanding the divine attributes.[241] Perkins, in contrast, begins with the concept of simplicity and from the arguments on the simplicity of the divine nature, concludes

---

237. Polanus, *Syntagma*, Synopsis libri II.

238. Ursinus, *Commentary*, pp. 123, 125.

239. Wendelin, *Christianae theologiae libri duo*, I.i.5, citing John 4:24.

240. Cf. Westminster Confession, II.i.; Larger Catatechism, VII; Watson, *A Body of Practical Divinity*; Boston, *Body of Divinity*, I, pp. 77-80; and Ridgley, *Body of Divinity*, p. 54, col. 2 - p. 55, col. 1; Mastricht, *Theoretico-practica theologia*, II.vi.

241. Ward, *Philosophical Essay*, I.iii (p. 22)

that God's nature is "immutable and spiritual." Like simplicity, immutability implies God "is void of all composition, division, and change."[242] God's spirituality, in turn, indicates his incorporeal and invisible nature.[243] Spanheim assumes that simplicity and perfection ought to be discussed first in order, followed by infinity, which then leads to the discussion of eternity and immensity.[244]

In Mastricht's order, the first three of these attributes, spirituality, simplicity, and immutability, together with the divine aseity, belong to a "primary class" of divine attributes and answer the basic question, *Quid sit Deus?*[245] Spirituality is treated first on the understanding that the other terms follow from the biblical truth that "God is Spirit, and they that worship him must worship him in spirit and in truth" (John 4:24) — the text that provides Mastricht with his exegetical foundation for the discussion. Indeed, simplicity follows among the *consectaria* of spirituality, stated as a second theorem of the *locus* with no new exegetical point of departure. (Immutability follows, in clear logical relation, but with a new exegetical foundation, namely, James 1:17.)[246]

Pictet, by way of minor contrast, assumes that the divine perfection is not only the first of the series, but also (with perhaps a slight Cartesian accent) "the first idea that we form in our minds concerning God." The remainder of the attributes, therefore, are "divine perfections." Thus, God

> is a perfect Being, devoid of all imperfections. And Scripture confirms this, everywhere proclaiming the divine perfections. A general declaration of the perfection of God is taught by Christ, Matt. 5:48, *Be ye perfect, even as your Father which is in heaven is perfect.* But the sacred writings do also set forth his perfections particularly and singly.... These perfections are so great that nothing can be added to them, or taken from them; they are immutable and never contrary to each other, although the effects of them may be so, and they are altogether identified with the essence of God.[247]

Pictet then considers the perfection of spirituality or immateriality of the divine essence, but clearly understands that it implies simplicity and immutability:

> For since all matter is extended, and all that is extended is composed of parts, divisible, imperfect, liable to change, senseless and inert, which cannot be set in motion, except impelled by something else...; this cannot be attributed to God, without arguing imperfection in him, and it is the height of absurdity, to attribute [such] imperfection to a Being whom we conceive to be most perfect.[248]

---

242. Perkins, *Golden Chaine*, ii (p. 11, col. 2), citing James 1:17 and Malachi 3:6.
243. Perkins, *Golden Chaine*, ii (p. 11, col. 2), citing John 4:24; 2 Cor. 3:17; 1 Tim. 1:17; Col. 1:15.
244. Spanheim, *Disp. theol.*, XIII.iv; Le Blanc, *Theses theol.*, *De Dei simplicitate*, v.
245. Mastricht, *Theoretico-practica theol.*, II.vi-vii.
246. Mastricht, *Theoretico-practica theol.*, II.vii.
247. Pictet, *Theol. chr.*, II.iii.1.
248. Pictet, *Theol. chr.*, II.iii.3.

There is, again, a Cartesian accent in the identification of matter with extension — although Pictet does not follow the fully Cartesian route to the conclusion that all substance is either thought or extension, a conclusion that would have had particular ramifications for the concepts of divine spirituality and immensity.

B. The Reformers on Divine Simplicity

1. The early Reformers. When we turn to the theologies of the Reformers and the Protestant orthodox, we find little difference in substance: the Reformed scholastic systems do not so much disagree with the Reformers on the point as exceed them in detail. In fact, we find a highly traditional approach to divine simplicity. Zwingli understood divine simplicity to be fundamental to right teaching and necessarily characteristic of God as the one who is "good by nature and good in the highest degree" — for Zwingli, simplicity denoted the changelessness and non-compositeness of God.[249] Farel similarly begins his summary of the Christian faith with the statement that "God is a simple Essence, spiritual, indivisible, and incomprehensible, who cannot be comprehended or understood by any created intellect that tries to consider him simply and in himself."[250]

Melanchthon's theology evidences a development on this issue: his earliest *Loci communes* do not address either the doctrine of God or the doctrine of the Trinity and, therefore, omit also discussion of divine simplicity. The need to deal with traditional formulations concerning God and Trinity, however, brought change in the *Loci communes*. In the later editions of his *Loci*, Melanchthon engaged in a rather lengthy statement concerning simplicity, noting that the attributes or virtues of God are not "accidental qualities": human beings and angels, he notes, possess goodness, righteousness, and wisdom as incidental properties that can change. The attributes of God, however, "are not to be distinguished or separated from his essence" — nor, Melanchthon adds, "is the attribute one thing and the essence another." Rather all of the divine attributes are the divine essence itself, inseparable from it.[251]

2. Calvin and Musculus. Calvin could state without elaboration that "under the name of God is understood a single and simple essence" (*unicam et simplicem essentiam*).[252] Although he indicates no interest whatsoever in speculating about doctrine of divine simplicity, Calvin clearly could confess it when necessary as an underpinning of the Christian understanding of God, and the related concept of divine aseity was of considerable importance to him, particularly in his trinitarian theology.[253]

---

249. Zwingli, *On Providence*, i (pp. 131-132).

250. Guillaume Farel, *Sommaire: c'est une brieve declaration d'aucuns lieux for necessaires à un chacun Chrestien, pour mettre sa confiance en Dieu, & à ayder son prochain*, in *Du Vraye Usage de la Croix de Iesus-Christ par Guillaume Farel suivi de divers écrits du même auteur* (Geneva: Fick, 1865), p. 209.

251. Melanchthon, *Loci communes*, I (Preus, p. 20).

252. Calvin, *Institutes*, I.xiii.20; cf. Calvin, *Sermons on Job*, p. 415, col. 1:42-9 (CO 34, col. 340) and idem, *Concerning the Eternal Predestination of God*, pp. 182-183.

253. Cf. Calvin, *Expositio impietatis Valen. Gentilis*, in CO, 9, col. 368 with Calvin, *Institutes*, I.xiii.2, 17-18, 23; and note Warfield, "Calvin's Doctrine of the Trinity," p. 237, and Muller, *Christ and the*

For Calvin, divine simplicity functions not as a philosophical ground for discussion of the divine essence and attributes, but as a biblically revealed divine attribute and as a basic rule of God language identifying God as non-composite, particularly for the sake of a right understanding of the doctrine of the Trinity and of the unity and consistency of the divine power and justice.[254]

Indeed, we can easily conclude from the rather diverse comments of Calvin concerning the nature of the Godhead that he held one or another of the late medieval conceptions of divine simplicity, assumed a genuine enumeration and distinction of divine attributes in the biblical revelation, and also recognized — in view of the doctrine of the Trinity — that there are distinctions in the divine essence itself.[255] Whether Calvin assumed distinctions other than the trinitarian distinction, however, may be questioned. In addressing the meaning of the divine name, Jehovah, Calvin commented that:

> Many take the name of God simply for God himself; but, as I have observed in my remarks on a preceding psalm, I think something more is expressed by this term. As God's essence is hidden and incomprehensible, his name just means his character, so far as he has been pleased to make it known to us."[256]

It is typical of Calvin's discussions of various divine attributes that he refrains from identifying them in the divine essence but speaks of the relationship between God and the world order. One finds a similar accent in the thought of Viret.[257] There is, therefore, a potentially nominalistic accent in Calvin's and Viret's understanding of the divine attributes as identifiable only *ad extra*, an accent that carries over into some of the Reformed orthodox definitions of divine simplicity.[258] (Despite his assumed

---

Decree, pp. 29-31, 192 n. 103.

254. Calvin, *Institutes*, I.xiii.2: "lest anyone should dream of a threefold God, or think that the simple essence is divided by the three Persons"; cf. Calvin, *Harmony of the Evangelists*, Matt. 6:10 (CTS *Evangelists* I, p. 320); *Commentary on Jeremiah*, 50:44 (CTS *Jeremiah*, V, pp. 192-193); *Sermons of Maister Iohn Calvin, upon the Book of Iob*, trans. Arthur Golding (London: George Bishop, 1574), p. 415, col. 1:42-49 (CO, 34, col. 340).

255. Cf. Calvin, *Commentary on Genesis*, 1:3 (CTS *Genesis*, I, p. 75), with Calvin, *Commentary on Ezekiel*, 1:25-6; 18:23 (CTS *Ezekiel*, I, pp. 95-102; II, p. 247); *Commentary on Isaiah*, 44:15-17 (CTS *Isaiah*, III, pp. 375-376); and John Calvin, *Secret Providence of God*, in *Calvin's Calvinism*, trans. Henry Cole (London, 1856; repr. Grand Rapids: Reformed Free Publishing Association, n.d.), p. 307 (resp. to art. VII).

256. Calvin, *Commentary on the Psalter*, 9:10, in CO , col. (CTS *Psalms* I, p. 120).

257. Pierre Viret, *Exposition familière sur le symbole*, pp. 51-52; I disagree on this point with Bavaud, *Le réformateur Pierre Viret*, p. 51, who notes that Viret does not use the term "analogy," but then construes Viret's statement that the attributes are known in their manifestation as analogical.

258. Jelle Faber, "Nominalisme in Calvijns preken over Job," in *Een sprekend begin*, ed. R. ter Beek, et al. (Kampen: Uitgeverij Van den Berg, 1993), pp. 68-85, raises this question in another context — and answers it negatively. Gründler, "Thomism and Calvinism," p. 104, understands Calvin's interest in the manifestation of attributes *ad extra* largely as a matter of piety, not recognizing that the contrast with Zanchi on this point may indicate a different philosophical point of departure. See further, below, 4.3 (D.3).

"Scotist" leanings, Calvin does not appear to have ever claimed a formal distinction among the divine attributes — nor does his usage have any affinities with that of Aquinas or Henry of Ghent — among the nominalists, it may have affinities with the view of Gregory of Rimini.)[259] The brevity of Calvin's comments on divine simplicity is counterbalanced somewhat by his pronounced emphasis on the correlative concept of *aseitas*, including the radical aseity of the divine persons.[260]

Musculus, too, deals with the concept of divine simplicity with brevity: quite in contrast to the extended discussions of other attributes, simplicity appears as a fundamental aspect of the divine nature, noted in the discussion of the *natura Dei*. And, like Calvin, Musculus understands the concept both in its basic sense as a denial of "composition" in the Godhead and in its trinitarian application. God, Musculus comments, is devoid of composition but nevertheless is distinguished into three persons. The persons are distinguished by the trinitarian relations of unbegottenness, begottenness, and procession, yet there is only one Godhead: thus, "there are three properties of the divine nature that are distinguished from one another according to the distinction of the persons, but there is only one essence." Or, again, "this Trinity is one and the same nature; for these three are one, and each of them is God ... immutable, everlasting, without beginning or end."[261] We need also to remember that the concept of a "sole and simple essence" of God was also understood by the Reformed as so basic a truth that it was early on ensconced in the confessions of the Reformed churches.[262] Although the language offered by Calvin, Musculus, and the confessions is neither speculative nor philosophical, it offers a framework for understanding the doctrine of God that is little changed from that of the medieval doctors.

C. The Reformed Scholastics on Divine Simplicity

1. Simplicity as absence of composition. Although the concept of divine simplicity was held by virtually all of the orthodox theologians of the sixteenth and seventeenth centuries, it was not invariably discussed as a separate attribute in their theological systems — nor was it always given the same prominence. Thus, Maccovius, Gomarus, Binning, Charnock, Ridgley, and Gill omit it as a separate category; Polanus, the *Synopsis purioris*, Alting, Hottinger, Leigh, Cocceius, Turretin, and Mastricht identify it as a primary defining category discussed immediately after the presentation of the problem of divine attributes in general; Brakel and Wyttenbach include it in a preliminary grouping of essential attributes but do not present it as the primary defining category; while Burman and Pictet place it toward the end of their lists. In a few cases, the reason for the placement is clear: Turretin places simplicity first because the genre of his system is polemic and he is concerned to refute, first in order, the teaching of Vorstius and the Socinians that he finds so disruptive to the doctrine of God. Polanus

---

259. Cf. Leff, *Gregory of Rimini*, p. 84 and above, 1.3 (B.3).
260. Cf. further, below, 5.2 (A.1).
261. Musculus, *Loci communes*, XLII (*Commonplaces*, p. 889, cols. 1-2).
262. Gallican Confession, i; Belgic Confession, i.

and Mastricht, by way of contrast, appear to be concerned primarily with the positive and objective division of the *locus* into primary, secondary, and tertiary categories for the sake of clarity and order in exposition. Omissions in the exercises of Charnock and Gill can be explained in part by the originally homiletical purpose of their works.

If some of the late patristic and scholastic expositions of the doctrine class as philosophical and perhaps speculative, the basic concept is not: from Irenaeus to the era of Protestant orthodoxy, the fundamental assumption was merely that God, as ultimate Spirit is not a compounded or composite being. It is also the case that, from the time of the fathers onward, divine simplicity was understood as a support of the doctrine of the Trinity and as necessarily defined in such a manner as to argue the "manifold" as well as the non-composite character of God.[263] Wyttenbach could therefore announce, in the twilight of Reformed orthodoxy, without expectation of any significant objection, that God is *ens simplex* and that, therefore, *in Deo nullum est accidens*.[264] The objection that this potentially philosophical point might not be easily rooted in the text of Scripture (or, once understood, that it should fail to be an integral part of Christian teaching), was never taken particularly seriously by the orthodox tradition — given, as Wyttenbach indicates, that the alternative to the doctrine of divine simplicity is so bizarre as to be neither amenable to any exegetical result nor acceptable to reason. It belongs to the very nature of composite things that they come into being and perish — and Scripture certainly indicates that God cannot either be made or destroyed![265] Various opponents of the doctrine, therefore, like Vorstius, the Socinians, and various Remonstrant theologians, were viewed as heterodox in the extreme.[266]

The basic definitions of the concept offered by the Reformed orthodox remain quite consistent throughout the late sixteenth and the seventeenth centuries, despite some variety of language. Perkins views the divine simplicity, together with infinity, as an immediate and necessary corollary of God's perfection. He offers the following definition:

> The Simpleness of his Nature, is that by which he is void of all Logical relation in arguments. He hath not in him subject or adjunct, "As the Father hath life in himself, so hath he given to the Son to have life in himself" (John 5:26): conferred with John 14:6, "I am the way, the truth, and the life." "But if we walk in his light, as he is light" (1 John 1:7): conferred with verse 5, "God is light, and in him is no darkness." Hence it is manifest that to have Life, and to be Light, in God are all one. Neither is

263. E.g., Gregory of Nyssa, *Answer to Eunomius*, I.19, in *NPNF*, 2 ser. V, p. 57; and idem, *Answer to Eunomius' Second Book*, II, in *NPNF*, 2 ser. V, pp. 57, 254-255; idem, *Great Catechism*, I, in ibid., pp. 474-476; Basil the Great, Letter 134 (to Amphilochius), in *NPNF*, 2 ser, VIII, p. 274; also note Augustine, *De trinitate*, VI.vi.8. The correlation of simplicity with Trinity in the theology of the Cappadocians is an element of patristic trinitarianism carefully neglected by modern so-called social Trinitariaism.

264. Wyttenbach, *Tentamen theologiae dogmaticae*, III, §227-228.

265. Wyttenbach, *Tentamen theologiae dogmaticae*, III, §227.

266. Turretin, *Inst. theol. elencticae*, III.vii.1.

God subject to generality or specialty: whole, or parts: matter, or that which is made of matter: for so there should be in God divers things, and one more perfect than another. Therefore, whatsoever is in God is his essence, and all that he is, he is by essence. The saying of Augustine in his 6th book and 4th chapter of the Trinity, is fit to prove this; "In God" (saith he) "to be, and to be just, or mighty are all one: but in the mind of man, it is not all one to be, and to be mighty, or just: for the mind may be destitute of these virtues, and yet a mind."[267]

It follows that God cannot be destitute of these virtues and still be God: which, again, is the meaning of the dicta that the attributes are identical with the divine essence and that the divine essence is simple.[268] The key issue is that God must never be conceived as if "there should be in God divers things, and one more perfect than another" — rather God is understood as always and necessarily who and what he is, with the result that "whatsoever is in God is his essence, and all that he is, he is by essence."[269] In the creature, by contrast, essence and existence, nature and subsistence, are distinct and separable.[270]

God, according to the orthodox writers, is *ens simplicissimum:* thus God is recognized to be "void of all composition, mixtion and division, being all essence; whatsoever is in God is God."[271] As Pictet states, the *simplicitas Dei* is "nothing more than ... the intimate connection and entire unity of all the attributes of God" and "their unity or identity" with the divine essence.[272] Or, as De Moor indicates, simplicity, positively understood, is "the most perfect unity of divine essence and attributes, excluding all real composition."[273] As a property in God (or characterization of the divine essence) this *simplicitas* is utterly without analogy in the creature. This absence of analogy is illustrated by the description of simplicity by way of negation from creaturely composition: it is seen that

God is simple, by removing from him all kinds of composition, which are five:
(1) of quantitative parts, as a body.

---

267. Perkins, *Golden Chaine,* ii (p. 11, col. 2) cf. Nichols, *Abridgement of Perkins,* pp. 2-3; Amyraut, *De mysterio trinitatis,* II, p. 99; Edwards, *Theologia Reformata,* I, p. 50.

268. Note that here, in addition to the association of the language of essence with the revealed nature of God, we encounter an almost paradigmatic example of the use of reason and of hermeneutical principles in the orthodox theological system: Perkins' argument evidences how the mutual interpretation of biblical texts followed by logical deduction from the texts provides the basis for a dogmatic formulation. The tradition of the church, which here agrees with the result of the interpretive process, is stated in confirmation of the argument.

269. Perkins, *Golden Chaine,* ii (p. 11, col. 2); cf. Beza et al., *Propositions and Principles,* V.iii.

270. Le Blanc, *Theses theol., De Dei simplicitate,* vii-viii.

271. Leigh, *Treatise,* II.iii (p. 25); Le Blanc, *Theses theol., De Dei simplicitate,* x; Cocceius, *Summa theol.,* III.ix.35; Ward, *Philosophicall Essay,* I.iii (pp. 23-24).

272. Pictet, *Theol. chr.,* II.xii.1 (p. 96); cf. Voetius, *Selectarum disputationum theologicarum,* I. xiii; Amyraut et al., *Syntagma thesium theologicarum,* I.xvii.4.

273. De Moor, *Commentarius perpetuus in Joh. Marckii compendium,* IV.xxiii (I, p. 604); cf. Owen, *Vindiciae evangelicae,* in *Works,* XII, p. 71, noting that the notion of simplicity is a "pure negation" that nonetheless "denotes ... a most eminent perfection of the nature of God."

(2) of essential parts, matter and form, as a man consists of soul and body.

(3) of a genus and difference, as every species.

(4) of subject and accidents, as a learned man, a white wall.

(5) of act and power, as the Spirits.[274]

Thus, in Rijssen's words. "The simplicity of God is [the property] according to which we conceive the divine nature not only as devoid of all composition and division, but, indeed, incapable of componibility and divisibility."[275]

The language here clearly mirrors the language of the so-called transcendental properties of being, according to which being as such is understood to be one, true, and good in and of itself. And whether the definition removes "logical relation in argument ... subject [and] adjunct ... generality ... specialty ... parts" (Perkins), "sensible" or physical and "metaphysical composition" (Le Blanc), "all composition" (Leigh, Turretin, Mastricht), "real distinction" (Howe), or "real composition" (De Moor), the specific object of the definition is to address those kinds of distinction related to accidents in the real order or to the non-substantial and particularly to the transitive categories in the logical order: namely, quantity, quality, relation, action, passion, place, posture, time, and habit. The point is to deny properties that are accidental or incidental predicates, not to exclude essential properties that are immanent in and intrinsic to God, and certainly not to deny any and all distinction between these essentially identical properties: "for simplicity does not mean, generally, the absence of all multitude, nor does it exclude either all distinctions or all plurality."[276] Indeed, the entire force of the Reformed scholastic argument is to deny in God *only* those distinctions that imply composition, namely, real distinctions and, therefore, to point toward the *proper* distinctions that do subsist among the attributes and between the attributes and the divine essence.[277]

The divine simplicity appears also as a conclusion from the *independentia, unitate,* and *perfectione Dei* — all these conceptions of God preclude composition by precluding dependency, mutability, plurality.[278] Furthermore, the *actuositate Dei,* according to which God may be described as *actus purus,* applying his attributes in the abstract and without qualification — life, light, truth — militates against the idea of composition

---

274. Leigh, *Treatise,* II.iii, in margin, "Simplex proprie dicitur quod compositum ex diversis non est" (p. 25); similarly, John Davenant, *The Determinationes; or Resolutions of Certain Theological Questions, publicly discussed in the University of Cambridge,* trans. Josiah Allport (London: Hamilton, Adams, 1846), xxiv (pp. 344-346); *Synopsis purioris theol.,* VI.xxiv; Turretin, *Inst. theol. elencticae,* III.vii.5; Le Blanc, *Theses theol., De Dei simplicitate,* vi-x, xv, xvii.

275. Rijssen, *Summa,* III.x (note that in this edition of Rijssen, "Locus III" lacks a "*propositio xi,*" moving from "x" to "xii.")

276. Heereboord, *Meletemata philosophica, Disputatio XXI, de simplicitate Dei,* i (p. 115). On the problem of identity and distinction in scholastic thought, see Bridges, *Identity and Distinction in Petrus Thomae,* pp. 140-165; and cf. Grenier, *Thomistic Philosophy,* I, pp. 137-140, 157-160; II, pp. 35-36.

277. Cf. Turretin, *Inst. theol. elencticae,* III.vii.5 with ibid., III.vi.5-10 with Heereboord, *Meletemata philosophica, Disputatio XXI, de simplicitate Dei,* i-viii (pp. 115-118).

278. Turretin, *Inst. theol. elencticae,* III.viii.4.

as incompleteness.[279] To this it is objected by the Socinians and particularly strenuously by Vorstius that the plurality and apposition of divine attributes contradicts the concept of divine simplicity. To this objection, the Reformed reply in terms of their definition of the attributes: "*Ut sunt in Deo, omnia unum & idem sunt*, quae nos cogimur diversis conceptibus nobis imaginari."[280] Similarly, they argue that, were God simple in essence, the power to decree could not exist — but the very essence of God is itself the *actio decernens* and, as such, cannot *not* be![281] Even so,

> in God, existence and essence (*esse & essentia*) are identical, as also are the fact of living and life itself (*vivens & vita*), since God does not have life through the agency of another essence beyond his own, but has life in himself (*in seipsa*) and is identical with that life (*& est ipsa vita*); he lives by and through himself (*vivit à seipso & per seipsum*).[282]

Several of the orthodox writers do in fact use the term "absolute simplicity," but this usage does not alter the import of the doctrine:

> God is absolutely Simple; he is but one thing, and doth not consist of any parts; he hath no accidents; but himself, his essence, and attributes are all one thing, though by us diversely considered and understood. If he did consist of parts, there must be something before him, to put those parts together; and then he were not eternal; he is one most pure and mere act (Isaiah 43:10). In God to be, to will, and to do are the same (John 15:26 compared with John 14:6); and 1 John 1:7 compared with 1 John 1:5, where to have life, and be life; to be in the light, and be light, are the same. God is therefore called in the abstract, light, life, love, truth (John 14:6; 1 John 4:8).[283]

So too does Pearson speak of "absolute simplicity" — but he defined the term as indicating specifically the absence of "composition."[284] It is also the case, that the absence of any "real distinction" between the divine essence and its attributes stands in the way of any full communication of divinity to a creature: since "the essential properties do not indeed differ from the essence," the essential attributes or properties "cannot be communicated to any creature; and therefore no creature can be, or can be said to be, for example, omnipotent simply."[285]

2. Simplicity and the presence of distinctions in the Godhead. There was also a certain caution voiced concerning the concept of divine simplicity among the Reformed orthodox and some diversity of language in definition, typically related to the recognized need for theology to acknowledge both the distinction of persons and

---

279. Rijssen, *Summa theol.*, III.x, controversia I, argumenta; cf. Ward, *Philosophicall Essay*, I.iii (p. 24).

280. Rijssen, *Summa theol.*, III.x, controversia I, obj. 1 & resp; Le Blanc, *Theses theol.*, De Dei *simplicitate*, xvi.

281. Rijssen, *Summa theol.*, III.x, controversia I, obj. 2.

282. Leigh, *Treatise*, II.iii (p. 26, margin); cf. Francken, *Kern der Christelijke Leer*, III, q. 26-27 (p. 57).

283. Leigh, *Treatise*, II.iii (p. 27); cf. Amyraut et al., *Syntagma thesium theologicarum*, I.xvii.4.

284. Pearson, *Lectiones de Deo*, V, in *Minor Theol. Works*, I, p. 44.

285. Zanchi, *De religione christiana fides*, II.iv.

the distinction of attributes in the godhead.[286] Howe notes that "God hath not by his word taught us to ascribe to him universal, absolute simplicity." Specifically, "the word" simplicity is not "among his *attributes* mentioned in the Holy Scriptures" — and although the "thing" signified by the word, when rightly understood, can and should be applied to our understanding of God, it is obvious that Scripture does not identify God as "in every respect most absolutely simple."[287] Any concept of "absolute or omnimodus simplicity" that removes the distinctions between the persons of the Trinity must be rejected. Thus,

> whatsoever simplicity the ever-blessed God hath, by any express revelation, claimed to himself, or can by evident and irrefragable reason be demonstrated to belong to him, as a perfection, we ought humbly and with all possible reverence and adoration, to ascribe to him. But such simplicity as he hath not claimed, as is arbitrarily ascribed to him by overbold and adventurous intruders into the deep and most profound arcana of the divine nature ... such as would prove an imperfection and a blemish, would render the divine nature less intelligible, ... as would ... make our apprehensions of his other known perfections less distinct, or inconsistent...; we ought not ... to ascribe to him such simplicity.[288]

On the other hand, Mastricht indicates that divine simplicity, as following from spirituality, is not "participative and restrictive," as in the case of created spirits, but "original and omnimodal" inasmuch as God "is spirit in himself and univocally." God, Mastricht indicates (reflecting the same basic definition as Howe), is utterly devoid of all such composition as obtains between one thing and another.[289]

(The differences of expression here can be accounted for, at least in part, by the different adversaries: Howe is particularly concerned to argue against the philosophical monism of Spinoza, whereas Mastricht directs his attention to the Socinian and Vorstian denials of simplicity. Spinoza was seen as pressing simplicity to the point of denying both Trinity and real distinction between God and world; the Socinians and Vorstius as denying simplicity as part of an antitrinitarian assault on traditional God language.[290] The term "omnimodus simplicity" itself, as used by Mastricht, has a long history, going back at least as far as Alexander of Hales, in which it is used to indicate a ruling out of *all manner* of composition — Howe's usage reflects the Spinozistic appropriation of the traditional vocabulary to a radically altered understanding of divine substance which understood a "mode" as an "alteration of substance" and therefore denied not only composition but also "modes" of subsistence in God. Spinoza also denied any and all distinction of attributes in God.[291] The doctrine of divine simplicity,

---

286. See *PRRD*, IV, 4.2, B.2, for discussion of the point relative to the persons of the Trinity.

287. John Howe, *An Inquiry into the Possibility of a Trinity in the Godhead*, in *Works*, II, p. 536.

288. Howe, *Inquiry*, in *Works*, II, pp. 530, 531.

289. Mastricht, *Theoretico-practica theol.*, II.vi.20, 22.

290. Cf. Mastricht, *Theoretico-practica theol.*, II.vi.23-24 with Howe, *Inquiry*, in *Works*, II, pp. 533-534.

291. Spinoza, *Thoughts on Metaphysics*, V.3-4 in *Earlier Philosophical Writings*, pp. 136-137.

thus, placed the late seventeenth-century orthodox on the horns of a theological dilemma. Right definition was a matter of great moment.)

As Howe makes clear, "absolute simplicity" should rightly indicate not the absence of all distinctions, but the absence of real distinctions:

> we easily apprehend by reflecting ourselves, that, without multiplying the subject, these [viz., power, wisdom, goodness] may all reside together in the same man. But our difficulty is greater to conceive what is commonly taught, that these without real distinction, or with formal only, as contradistinguished from the difference of thing from thing, are in the abstract affirmable of God, that he is power, wisdom, goodness: that to his being belongs so absolute simplicity, that we must not look upon these things as really distinguishable, *there*, from one another, but as different conceptions of the same thing.[292]

The language here is highly significant, inasmuch as it represents, at the very end of the era of orthodoxy, an explicit continuity with the earlier tradition: Howe refuses both the *distinctio realis* between attributes and the purely rational *distinctio formalis*. From the perspective of identifying God as the *res* or "thing" within which the distinctions are found, the attributes do not have the distinction or "difference of thing from thing," but are, in fact, "different conceptions of the same thing." Howe also refers negatively to the exclusion of all forms of distinction whatsoever: this he speaks of as "the notion of most absolute omnimodus simplicity," which must be incompatible with the Christian conception of God."[293] The Reformed orthodox, like the ancient fathers and the medievals, were sensitive to the fact that divine simplicity — the absence of composition — cannot be defined as a denial of what one modern author has called the "operational complexity" of the Godhead.[294]

Since the *simplicitas Dei* is the natural corollary of the *spiritualitas* and the *unitas Dei*, the orthodox come into very real conflict with their contemporaries, Vorstius and the Socinians, both of whom deny the simplicity of God and view the attributes as real distinctions in the divine essence. Rijssen explicitly connects this denial of simplicity with the Socinian attempt to subvert the doctrine of the Trinity.[295] Trelcatius and Keckermann indicate that the persons are *not distinct* in essence, degree, condition, or dignity, but they *are distinct* in order, number, manner of working, personal names, and personal properties.[296] Cocceius expressly declares that "the simplicity of God in no way contradicts the trinity of divine persons and their *perichoresis*."[297] Similarly, Marckius notes that the distinction of person in the Godhead in no way opposes the

---

292. Howe, *Inquiry*, in *Works*, II, p. 536; cf. Amyraut et al., *Syntagma thesium theologicarum*, I.xvii.4; Mastricht, *Theoretico-practica theol.*, II.vi.22.

293. Howe, *Inquiry*, in *Works*, II, p. 538.

294. Stead, *Divine Substance*, p. 175.

295. Rijssen, *Summa theol.*, III.x, controversia I.

296. Cf. Trelcatius, *Schol. meth.*, I.iii (p. 56), with Wendelin, *Christianae theologiae libri duo*, I.ii.3 (1).

297. Cocceius, *Aphorismi prolixiores*, IV.9.

notion of simplicity: since the persons are distinguished "not as things, but as modes of subsistence, not composing, but modifying the divine essence."[298] Moreover, the claim of real distinctions between attributes proves just as dangerous to Trinity as the utter denial of distinctions, inasmuch as it allows for no higher level of distinction within the divine essence by which the persons can be distinguished at the same time as the unity of the Godhead is preserved. It is crucial to the doctrine of God to maintain a level of distinction between the persons that "cannot be less than is sufficient to sustain distinct predicates or attributions," but not "so great as to intrench upon the unity of the Godhead."[299]

Once again, there is an interpenetration of doctrinal issues: it is not as if the orthodox can really separate consideration of the divine essence from the analysis of God as Trinity — the doctrines are interdependent. Rijssen points out that this issue is not, as the Remonstrants would have it, a purely metaphysical question.[300] Whereas the Remonstrants, following Episcopius, defined theology as entirely practical, the Reformed insisted that it was both practical and theoretical, clinging to certain metaphysical questions as necessary to the correlation of the nature of God with the manner of his working[301] — thus, what the Remonstrants could call *mere metaphysicam* appeared to the Reformed as, indeed, metaphysical in the most general sense but nevertheless of enormous significance to the doctrines concerning the divine *oeconomia*, and certainly not — in the Reformed view — a topic belonging to the philosophical discussion of metaphysics as the source of being in general.[302]

In short, the plurality of persons in God does not contravene the divine simplicity, but can even be said to imply it.[303] As far as the seventeenth-century orthodox are concerned, moreover, the doctrine of divine simplicity is a corollary and support of the doctrine of the Trinity: in the polemics of the day, in fact, the Vorstian and Socinian denials of simplicity were directly connected with the affirmation of an alternative, seemingly tritheistic view in Vorstius' case and with an overt antitrinitarianism in the case of the Socinians. Rijssen thus argues that "the persons are not collected out of the essence, inasmuch as they are not separate entities (*entia realia*) brought into existence by composition out of a fourth [entity], and therefore having a single essence in common, but solely modifications (*tantum modificationes*) according to which the [divine] essence is understood as subsisting in three persons."[304] The three divine persons are not, then, three numerically distinct essences, but three persons conjoined in a unity of essence: for although the term "three persons" as applied to human beings

---

298. Marckius, *Christianae theol. medulla*, IV.xxiv.

299. Howe, *Inquiry*, p. 531.

300. Rijssen, *Summa theol.*, III.x, controversia I.

301. Episcopius, *Institutiones theologicarum*, I.ii (*Opera*, I, pp. 4-5).

302. See above, 3.2 (A.3)

303. Cf. Hottinger, *Cursus theologicus*, III.vi, canon A; xviii, canones G, H; cf. George Bull, *The Doctrine of the Catholic Church for the First Three Ages of Christianity, concerning the Blessed Trinity, considered, in opposition to Sabellianism and Tritheism* [1697], in *English Theological Works*, p. 374.

304. Rijssen, *Summa*, III.x, controversia I, obj. 3 & resp.; see further *PRRD*, IV, 3.2 (B).

indicates three human beings who are numerically distinct, with each instance of the essence subsisting as a finite individual, "three persons" as applied to the Godhead indicates the communicability of the sole, infinite, individual, and singular divine essence to these three without division.[305]

This point is to be stressed against Vorstius, who explained the distinction of persons as a distinction of "really diverse beings," each of which has its own "proper essence," and who also claimed that Scripture indicated "that one thing and another thing (*aliud et aliud*) are in God, namely, subject and accident, or the agent and the action."[306] Clearly, "simplicity and triplicity" are mutually exclusive and cannot subsist together, but the orthodox doctrine of the Trinity is not a claim of divine triplicity: against Vorstius and the Socinians, the orthodox insist in accord with the tradition that "simplicity and trinity" can subsist together in the same being inasmuch as "they are said in different respects" — simplicity with respect to essence, trinity with respect to persons.[307] The point here is quite similar to the argument concerning the distinction of attributes, which "differ both from his essence and mutually from one another as is evident from the diversity of conceptions."[308]

All composition is therefore excluded from the conception of God, not only in the sense of physical composition as implied by anthropomorphism, but also in the sense implied by the Platonists, who define God as the *anima mundi*, and by the Manichees, who believe that all creatures are propagated out of the divine essence.[309] Thus, simplicity implies that God is utterly distinct from creatures and is immutable and incorruptible — all of which is denied by the Platonic and Manicheean views.[310] To this position there are two objections: first, that all things are from God (cf. Rom. 11:36) — but this text is not to be understood *hylikos & materialiter*, as if God supplied from himself the material substratum of things, but rather *demiourgikos & efficienter*, given that God is the creative cause of all. Second, the statement (Acts 17:28) that we are the offspring of God indicates "not by participation in the same essence, but by a similitude of image; by efficient causality (*efficienter*), not essentially (*non essentialiter*).[311]

This divine simplicity, moreover, does not contravene either the manifold fulness of the wisdom of God or of God's Word:

> The Gospel and the ways of it are not Simple, as Simplicity is opposed to the depth
> of wisdom (for therein is made known the manifold wisdom of God, Eph. 3:10), but

---

305. N.B., the divine "essence" is therefore understood only in the sense of the "primary essence" or individual, not in the sense of the "secondary essence" or genus — that is, not a form or concept that can be applied to or shared by different beings. See further, *PRRD*, IV, 3.2 (A.3).

306. Cf. Vorstius, *Tractatus theologicus de Deo*, nota ad Disp. III (p. 191), with De Moor, *Commentarius perpetuus in Joh. Marckii compendium*, IV.xxiii (I, pp. 606-608).

307. Turretin, *Inst. theol. elencticae*, III.vii.9.

308. Turretin, *Inst. theol. elencticae*, III.vi.8.

309. Rijssen, *Summa theol.*, III.x, controversia II.

310. Rijssen, *Summa theol.*, III.x, controversia II, argumenta.

311. Rijssen, *Summa theol*, III.x, controversia II, objectiones.

as Simplicity is opposed to mixture. Every thing the more simple (in this sense) the more excellent.[312]

Nor is this a doctrine so speculative as to be devoid of practical use: "the simplicity of God should make us know the imperfection and vanity of all the creatures that are compounded things; and so should help to alienate us from them," wrote Baxter. Human knowledge is "mixed with much ignorance, ... humility ... with pride, ... love with selfishness ... but in God is none of all this mixture, but pure uncompounded good."[313] Christian piety learns to "leave then the compounded, self-contradicting creatures, and adhere to the pure, simple Deity."[314]

D. The Distinction of Attributes in Non-composite Being

1. Properties of Being and distinctions in Being: preliminary considerations. Since the contention that God is "simple" does not typically mean that the divine essence is utterly devoid of distinctions — and given that Scripture consistently distinguishes between the various divine attributes, as it also does between the persons of the Trinity,[315] the question naturally arises as to the kind of distinctions that can be properly said to be in God. The Reformed solutions to this problem are varied, complex, and rooted in a long history of debate over the problem of distinctions.[316]

A primary consideration governing the problem of distinctions between the essential properties of God derives from the traditional understanding of the properties of being. It is here, in the properties of being as such (as opposed to the properties of individual finite things), that traditional theology finds a partial solution to the problem of the predication of properties of God. The properties of being, identified frequently as "transcendental properties" or "transcendentals," are those properties which must be predicated of all and, therefore, also of each and every being. They are called "transcendentals" inasmuch as being, simply understood, is transcendent: being as such is the ultimate principle and/or category of all things, beyond the distinction between infinite and finite, beyond all categories in the sense that it encompasses all

---

312. Leigh, *Treatise*, II.iii (p. 26).

313. Baxter, *Divine Life*, I.vi.2 (p. 144).

314. Baxter, *Divine Life*, I.vi.2 (p. 144).

315. Mastricht, *Theoretica-practica theol.*, II.v.5-7; vi.24; xii.12; cf. Stead, "Divine Simplicity as a Problem for Orthodoxy," pp. 256-60.

316. See the historical discussions, above, 1.2 (B.4) ; 1.3 (B.2); and cf. Francis Suárez, *On the Various Kinds of Distinctions*, trans., with an intro. by Cyril Vollert (Milwaukee: Marquette University Press, 1947), with Gisbert Voetius, *Disputatio philosophico-theologica, continens quaestiones duas, de distinctione attributorum divinorum, et libertate voluntatis* (Utrecht, 1652). I owe my knowledge of this disputation to Drs. Andreas Beck of the University of Utrecht: it was not included by Voetius in his *Selectae disputationes theologicae*, 5 vols. (Utrecht, 1648-1669). It stands as a separate disputation propounded by Engelbertus Beeckman and presided over by Voetius. As Beck points out, it does not, therefore, belong as clearly to the theology of Voetius as those disputations propounded by him and his students, edited by him, and eventually published in the five volumes of selected topics. The disputation does, however, offer significant documentation of the Reformed approach to the problem of predication in the mid-seventeenth century.

categories. Whereas there is a real (i.e., a substantive or "thingish) distinction between things and other things, there can be no real distinction between any real things and being itself — given that being in its general sense is not a thing. The properties of being are transcendental inasmuch as they belong necessarily to being as such, but, unlike the properties of individual things, they are inseparable from it. The transcendental properties of being, like being itself, are not subsumed under the categories but rather pertain to all categories.[317] The transcendentals are, unlike the separable attributes of finite things or individual instances of being, universal predicates: they belong, without any real distinction, to being itself and they belong inseparably to all individual beings.

There are six universal predicates, at least three of which are traditionally identified as transcendental properties of being: *ens, res, aliud* or *aliquid, unum, verum,* and *bonum* — thus a being (*ens*) is a "thing," namely a substance or essence, has otherness or distinction, oneness or unity, truth, and goodness.[318] Because it would be redundant to speak of "being" as a property of being and, similarly, because "being" understood as a noun is identical in meaning to *res* or thing, the first two predicates, *ens* and *res*, are not normally understood as transcendental properties of being. It is and must be "other," in that being in general is distinct from nonbeing and inasmuch as any particular being is divided from all other particular beings — being is necessarily a subject or a substance. When the property of being as "other (*aliud*)" is understood as being "something (*aliquid*)," as *substantia*, we again encounter the problem of redundancy — it is synonymous with *ens* and *res* — leaving three irreducible and inseparable properties of being in general, namely, that it is one, true, good. This remaining set of three irreducible properties of being is characteristic of the Reformed metaphysics of the late sixteenth and the seventeenth centuries, which identifies *unitas, veritas,* and *bonitas* as the threefold primary *modus* of being (*ens*) or substance (*substantia*): a being is "one" in itself as distinct from other beings, "true" in that it corresponds with the end or goal for which it was intended and is knowable as such, "good" because it in fact tends toward its goal.[319]

Once it is recognized that the notion of inseparable properties that cannot be distinct *realiter* from their subject is a fundamental issue in the older logic and metaphysics,

---

317. Keckermann, *Compendium metaphysicae,* iii; cf. Grenier, *Thomistic Philosophy,* II, pp. 18, 31-32 with R. P. Phillips, *Modern Thomistic Philosophy: An Explanation for Students,* 2 vols. (New York: Newman Press, 1959), II, pp. 159-160, 174-175.

318. To which are added the standard "categories" of predication: see Gideon Harvey, *Archeologia Philosophica Nova, or, New Principles of Philosophy. Containing Philosophy in General. Metaphysicks or Ontology. Dynamilogy, or a Discourse of Power. Religio Philosophi, or Natural Theology. Physicks, or Natural Philosophy* (London: J. H. for Samuel Thomson, 1663), pt. I, II.xv.1-2 (p. 55). Note the application of this argument to the discussion of the attributes and their essential identity in Junius, *Theses theol. Leydenses,* IX.2; Arminius, *Disp. priv.,* XV.vii; Mastricht, *Theoretico-practica theol.,* II.viii.5; xiv.5; xvi.3.

319. Cf. Keckermann, *Compendium metaphysicae,* iii; Maccovius, *Metaphysica,* I.v-viii; Harvey, *Archeologia Philosophica,* pt. I, II.xv-xix (pp. 56-68); and note the discussion in Phillips, *Modern Thomistic Philosophy,* II, pp. 174-179 and Grenier, *Thomistic Philosophy,* II, pp. 36-63.

it also becomes clear that the notion of divine simplicity, the absence of "real" distinctions or "composition" from the Godhead is not a concept peculiar to theology nor, indeed, peculiar to the problem of the predication of divine attributes. It is merely one of the basic issues to be addressed when one raises the question of the properties and predicates of any and all being. The point of the traditional discussion of the divine attributes is, first of all, to recognize that God, as the ultimate Being, possesses all his properties as constituent principles — not merely his unity, truth, and goodness, but all his properties — and that none of the properties of the divine essence can be distinct *realiter* or, literally, "thingishly" from the divine essence.

The Reformed orthodox (as was typical in the theology and philosophy of the seventeenth century) followed the scholastic tradition in recognizing a series of different kinds of distinctions, some of which clearly cannot refer to God, others of which may, and still others which certainly do.[320] Maccovius offers four levels of distinction: real, formal, modal, and rational — which, as we shall see, cover the entire range of possible distinctions.[321] Others, like Ames and Maresius, indicate other traditional terms for rather discrete kinds of distinction that fit within the broader paradigm, namely, eminent and virtual.[322] There are, in the first place, what the scholastics called "real distinctions" — distinctions *between* one *res* and another *res*, one thing and another thing. These real distinctions can obtain between different things of different essences (e.g., between a flower and a table), or between two things of the same essence (e.g., between two tables), or between the separable parts of a composite thing (e.g., between the tabletop and the legs of the table). Since there is only one God and since God is one and non-composite or simple, this kind or level of distinction does not apply to God.

There are, second, also distinctions *in* things, identified variously by the scholastics as "formal," "modal," "eminent," and "virtual" distinctions. There are, thus, distinctions that do not separate a particular thing from other things or render the thing composite but which indicate the ways "by which a thing is differentiated within itself."[323] These are not, therefore, distinctions of essence but less-than-essential distinctions within an essence or, indeed, within a thing, such as the formal distinctions between the woodiness and the hardness of a table, or the formal distinctions between the volitional and the intellectual capacities of a human being. In the case of the trinitarian relations and divine attributes, such distinctions can and do apply to God.

Third, there are rational distinctions concerning things, what the scholastics call distinctions "by reason of analysis (*ratio ratiocinata*) founded in the thing" — which can be viewed as pointing toward such inward distinctions as those identified by the

320. Cf. Descartes, *Meditations*, III, in *Philosophical Works*, I, p. 166; *Principles of Philosophy*, I.lx-lxii, in ibid., I, pp. 243-245.

321. Johannes Maccovius, *Logica*, I.xx, ad init., in *Opuscula philosophica omnia* (Amsterdam, 1660), p. 20.

322. Ames, *Medulla*, I.iv.26; cf. Maresius, *Collegium theologicum*, II.xi.

323. Maccovius, *Logica*, I.xx, ad init. (p. 20).

terms "eminent" and "virtual."[324] As implied in the preceding paragraph, this understanding of rational distinctions was typical of the thought of Aquinas and subsequent Thomists. And, fourth, there are purely rational (*ratio rationans*) distinctions made with reference to the externally perceived relationships of things to other things — both of which can be illustrated like the so-called formal distinction, given the philosophical problem that the qualities or formalities identified in the distinction may belong more to the mind performing the analysis than to the thing being analyzed.

In summary, a distinction made *realiter* invariably indicates a distinction such as obtains between things and other things or between a thing taken as a whole and its removable parts. Its presence indicates, therefore, either two things or a composite thing. The remainder of the terms indicate various kinds of distinctions *within* things. A distinction made *formaliter* belongs to the primary actuality of a substance or essence, whereas a distinction made *eminenter* identifies the causal foundation or ground in one thing of some other thing, effect, or attribute outside of the thing itself. Attributes that are identified *per eminentiam* and are understood as distinct *eminenter* may be understood as a class or subset of those that are distinct *formaliter*, given that all attributes are not causal. A distinction made *virtualiter* identifies a quality belonging not to the primary actuality of a thing but to its potency or power — and is, therefore, similar to a distinction made *eminenter*, but can be understood as an *ad extra* exercise of power rather than an *ad intra* causal foundation. A distinction made *rationaliter*, when it assumes a foundation in the thing, is an ideational distinction (nonetheless genuine) that, unlike the formal, eminent, and virtual distinctions, does not specify the nature of its foundation.

2. Reformed orthodoxy and the problem of distinctions in the divine essence. The Protestant orthodox returned to the problem of the attributes, particularly to the issue of the *distinctio formalis* and of distinctions *per eminentiam*, specifically in order to identify distinctions that can be said to subsist not *realiter*, but *formaliter, eminenter, virtualiter,* or *rationaliter*. The Reformed orthodox attempted to deal with a fairly extensive debate over the essence and attributes of God — and, in so doing, to retain the extra-mental conceptual objectivity of the attributes and the legitimacy of their predication, without implying any "real" distinction in the divine essence itself. Thus, they tended to accept the Thomist and nominalist arguments against Scotus, but remain dissatisfied with the nominalist and, at times, with the original Thomist solution. Specifically, the definition of perfections as being "in" God "eminently, though not formally"[325] represents a rejection, often found explicitly among the Reformed orthodox, of the language of the Scotist *distinctio formalis* — yet, in rejecting (and sometimes misunderstanding) the term, the Reformed orthodox also accept some of its implication,

---

324. Note that Barth, *Church Dogmatics* II/1, p. 329, rightly identifies this language in the older orthodoxy and then proceeds, incorrectly, to argue "an explanation of what is to be understood by this *fundamentum* has never been vouchsafed." It is one of the burdens of this section to indicate that the Reformed orthodox did precisely this — namely, to explain how the attributes or properties are distinguished in God as well as in our conception of God.

325. Ridgley, *Body of Divinity*, p. 53, col. 2.

if only by way of later clarifications of the Thomistic model at the hands of John of Paris and Cardinal Cajetan. The influence of Thomist, Scotist, and nominalist thought on the orthodox doctrine of the attributes was, thus, of enough importance that the orthodox needed to define their position over against that of the great medieval systems with great care: they accepted the Scotist and nominalist assumption of a disproportion between the finite and the infinite, but they were at the same time unwilling to press the distinction to the point that the principle of analogy utterly disappeared — as also they were unwilling to press the argument over the precise manner of distinction to be found between the divine attributes to the point of insisting categorically that the attributes must be eminently or rationally, rather than formally, distinct or, indeed, rather than distinct only *ad extra*.

The resulting hybrids, scholastic Protestant approaches to the distinctions between divine attributes, were framed at least in part by a reaction to the modified version of the formal or modal distinction by the foremost metaphysician of the time, Francis Suárez, and by the adoption of other, variant views by Vorstius, the Socinians, and the Cartesian rationalists of the day. There was considerable pressure on the orthodox to identify a philosophical language that was capable of supporting the basic assumptions of the Reformed system concerning the divine attributes and the simplicity of God. Suárez had contended that "whatever extends beyond the essential definition of a thing is in some sense really distinct from it; but many elements extend beyond the essence of a thing without being themselves distinct from the thing in question; therefore it is a distinction in the real order that is less than a real distinction."[326] Such distinctions, according to Suárez, are not rational distinctions (which, by definition, do not belong to the *real* order), but formal or, as Suárez preferred to denominate them, modal distinctions, having to do with the way or manner of the being. The Socinians, following the views of Conrad Vorstius, went even farther, claiming that a real distinction could be argued between the divine essence and the power or *virtus* of God.[327] Some of the *ad extra* attributes, therefore, like vindicative or punitive justice, would then not be intrinsic or necessary to the divine being and, therefore, would not necessarily be exercised by God.[328] Under this view, attributes might be understood as separable from God — and the divine essence could be understood as a composite.

Thus, Marckius explicitly states that by "simplicity" the orthodox indicate, against the Socinians and Vorstius, that "in the singular essence [of God] there can be no *real composition (compositio realis)*, whether physical, or logical, or metaphysical,"[329] and points toward, "the perfect unity of the divine essence and attributes excluding all *real composition*," whether physical (material and formal), logical (genus and differentia, substance and accident), or metaphysical (act and potency, essence and

---

326. Suárez, *Disp. metaph.*, VII.15; in translation, *On the Various Kinds of Distinctions*, trans., with an intro. by Cyril Vollert (Milwaukee: Marquette University Press, 1947), p. 26.

327. Cf. Vorstius, *Tractatus de Deo*, with Mastricht, *Theoretico-practica theol.*, II.v.10.

328. See John Owen, *Dissertation on Divine Justice* (1653), in *Works*, vol. 10, pp. 481-642.

329. Marckius, *Christiana theol. medulla*, IV.xxiv; cf. Le Blanc, *Theses theol.*, De Dei simplicitate, vi-vii.

existence).[330] Keckermann assumes the distinction of attributes *eminenter* or *virtualiter* and cites Cajetan as the source of his argument.[331] This solution then passed over into the writings of such thinkers as Walaeus, Maresius, Twisse, Le Blanc, Voetius, and Turretin.[332] Thus, Voetius identifies the distinction of the attributes from one another *eminenter* as the equivalent of a distinction *ratio ratiocinata*, but now identifying more fully how that rational distinction is founded "in the thing" or "in the nature of the thing" by way of eminence. He also accepts the traditional assumption that the persons are identical *essentialiter* but distinct *personaliter* — and that the relational distinction between the persons is a *distinctio realis*.[333] Voetius also uses the "formal distinction" but tends to assimilate it to the distinction *ratio ratiocinata*.[334]

3. Varieties of Reformed orthodox formulation: echoes of traditionary debate.[335] In the light of these contemporary questions and in the light of the traditional discussion of the kinds of distinctions that could legitimately be posited among the divine attributes, the Reformed argued, not one, but at least three somewhat different ways of understanding the distinction of divine attributes, each of which reflects one of the major medieval approaches to the problem — in summary: first, the attributes are essentially one in God, but known to reason as distinct in their operation *ad extra*; second, the attributes are essentially one in God, are understood by us as distinct *ratio ratiocinata cum fundamento in re*, but are also recognized to be distinct in God *eminenter* or *virtualiter* and, according to some of the Reformed writers, distinct *realiter* in their effects; third, in a slight variant or elaboration of the second, the attributes are essentially identical in God, externally distinct *ratinaliter* or *formaliter*, as known in their operations, and distinct in the Godhead itself *eminenter* or *virtualiter*.

First, the distinction of attributes *ad extra*, with emphasis on their purely rational distinction in relation to effects: here, perhaps is the echo of Ockham, given that the formulation, as found in Bucanus, Alting, Hottinger, Maccovius, Owen, Heidanus, and Mastricht indicates a rational or conceptual distinction but does not offer the modification, "founded on the thing." Alting, for example, states without any elaboration that the attributes "do not differ from the essence, nor among themselves

---

330. Marckius, *Compendium theologiae*, IV.xxiii-xxiv; cf. Voetius, *Disputatio philosophico-theologica, continens quaestiones duas de distinctione attributorum divinorum, & libertate voluntatis* (Utrecht, 1652); and Aquinas, *Summa theol.*, Ia, art. 11, q.4.

331. Keckermann, *Metaphysica*, I.i.

332. Thus, Walaeus, *Loci communes*, p. 162; Maresius, *Collegium theologicum*, II.xii.; Twisse, *Discovery*, pp. 71-2, 75; Le Blanc, *Theses theol.*, *De perfectione et infinitate Dei*, ix-xi; Turretin, *Inst. theol. elencticae*, III.v.9.

333. Voetius, *Selectarum disputationum theologicarum*, I, 13; cf. ibid., V, p. 59.

334. Cf. Voetius, *Syllabus problematum*, fol. D4r: "An attributa divina insint Deo virtualiter tantum & eminentur, an v. etiam formaliter? A. post" and, a few lines farther on, "An attributa Dei inter se & ab essentia distinguantur distinctione solummodo ratiocinante an v. etiam ratione ratiocinata? A. post."

335. Note that the discussion in Heppe, *Reformed Dogmatics*, pp. 57-60, is quite defective inasmuch as it assumes only one position among the Reformed, viz., a rational distinction founded in the thing (*ratio ratiocinata*) but relating merely revealed effects of God in the world.

... but only according to our conception."[336] So also are the attributes to be understood as "equal ... in God" inasmuch as all are infinite and "one infinite cannot exceed another," when the infinites in question are essentially the same, nonetheless, "in their Exercise and Effects" the attributes "shine with different glory."[337] Owen, similarly, argues a distinction of divine attributes or properties by means of their effects, but he does not specifically state a view concerning the *ad intra* distinction of properties: his primary concern is to argue that, given the infinite distance between God and human beings, God in himself must remain utterly incomprehensible to us and known only in his external representation.[338]

Maccovius, quite explicitly, argues that there is no distinction of attributes in God, but only in our conception,[339] while Heidanus argues at length that there are no properties, attributes, or accidents in God and that what we identify as attributes are not distinguished from the divine essence, nor differentiated among themselves, but only distinguished "according to our conception" — leading in Heidanus' case to a pointed denial of the notion of communicable attributes.[340] This perspective echoes the approach of the medieval nominalists, but it certainly did not merely appear without notice in the middle of the seventeenth century: it probably derives from the medievals by way of Suárez, who was concerned to argue through the medieval categories and who, in his own resolution of the problem, allowed no distinction of attributes in the divine essence itself, but only in our perceptions.[341] In Heidanus' case, moreover, it is a point shared with Descartes and other rationalist writers of the era,[342] and it is a view that carries over into the highly rationalist theology of the late orthodox.[343]

In somewhat more detail, perhaps modeling his definitions on the tripartite description offered by Descartes, Burman posits three levels of distinction: the greatest, *realis*; the median, *modalis* or *formalis*; and the least, *rationis*.[344] The first level of distinction is ruled out immediately by Burman in order to cancel out the Socinian

336. Alting, *Methodus theol.*, III (p. 76B); cf. Bucanus, *Institutions*, p. 5; Hottinger, *Cursus theologicus*, III.vi, canon A; Wollebius, *Compendium*, I.i.2, prop. 1, canones i-ii. Note that this definition of the attributes as distinct *ad extra* does not in any way prejudice the result of the discussion of the distinction of persons: Alting and Hottinger define the persons as distinct from one another *realiter*: see *Methodus theol.*, III (p. 77B); Bucanus, *Institutions*, p. 11; also Hottinger, *Cursus theologicus*, III.xviii, canones G, H.

337. William Bates, *The harmony of the divine attributes in the contrivance and accomplishment of man's redemption by the Lord Jesus Christ* (London: J. Darby, 1674), p. 143.

338. Owen, *ΧΡΙΣΤΟΛΟΓΙΑ*, pp. 65-67.

339. Johannes Maccovius, *Distinctiones et regulae theologicae et philosophicae*, (Amsterdam, 1656), IV.x-xiii.

340. Heidanus, *Corpus theologiae*, II (pp. 69-70); as also in the teaching of the English Arminian Thomas Jackson, *Treatise of the Divine Essence*, (London, 1627), I.iv.1-6.

341. See above, 1.3 (B.2) and note Suárez, *Disp.metaph.*, XXX.vi.19.

342. Cf. Descartes, *Principles of Philosophy*, I.lvi (*Philosophical Works*, I, pp. 241-242), with Spinoza, *Principles of the Philosophy of Descartes*, I, prop. xvii (p. 50); *Thoughts on Metaphysics*, II.v (pp. 135-137).

343. Cf. Klinkenberg, *Onderwys*, I.i.8, §62

344. Descartes, *Principles of Philosophy*, I.lx-lxii (*Philosophical Works*, I, pp. 243-245).

position: divine attributes do not differ *realiter* from one another or from the divine essence, and there is no diversity or composition in the divine essence. The mind, thus, cannot distinguish the attributes of God from God himself: for the mind cannot conceive of God without his justice or without his mercy, as indeed it can conceive of a man without the qualities of justice and mercy.[345] Similarly, the idea of modal or formal distinctions in God — which, comments Burman, was the Jewish Cabbalists' explanation of the attributes — must be rejected, even as the thought of an alteration or modification of the divine essence is repugnant to the idea of God.[346] As Burman further argues, with probable reference to Suárez's argument, for a distinction to exist "formally," it must also exist really and objectively somewhere in something — that is, exist somehow in the real order — but such a distinction of attributes *in Deo ex natura rei* appears to Burman to be too much like a so-called real distinction.[347]

The distinction of attributes *rationaliter*, however, by a process of mental abstraction is both acceptable and necessary, Burman concludes, even as it is both possible and useful to consider the justice or righteousness of God apart from the mercy of God — all the while realizing that the essence of God cannot be conceived of as lacking either.[348] This is not to say, of course, that God is not in fact good, just, merciful, wise, and so forth, inasmuch as the distinctions made concerning him are founded on his true revelation of himself. Burman takes seriously the qualifying clause typically attached to the notion of a *distinctio ratio ratiocinata* by the medieval scholastics, notably Aquinas and Henry of Ghent, *cum fundamento in re* — which, incidentally, is echoed by Descartes[349] — but reads it in what can only be called an Ockhamist or nominalist manner. The rational distinction of attributes in God, he notes, is not at all arbitrary or solely a product of the mind's own power of abstraction, for it is grounded partly in us but also and primarily partly outside of us (*extra nos*) in the diverse objects, effects, and operations of the divine essence.[350]

Mastricht, similarly, adapts the *distinctio ratio ratiocinata* to the discussion not of distinctions in the divine essence, but of distinctions both necessary to our

---

345. Burman, *Synopsis theol.*, III.xix.8-9.

346. Burman, *Synopsis theol.*, III.xix.10; cf. III.xix.6; and cf. Mastricht, *Theoretico-practica theol.*, II.v.7.

347. Burman, *Synopsis theol.*, III.xix.6.

348. Burman, *Synopsis theol.*, III.xix.11.

349. Descartes, *Principles of Philosophy*, in *Works*, I, p. 245: "the distinction of reason is between substance and some one of its attributes without which it is not possible that we should have a distinct knowledge of it, or between two such attributes of the same substance."

350. Burman, *Synopsis theol.*, III.xix.12; cf. the different nuancing of the terms in Turretin, *Inst. theol. elencticae*, III.v.9-11, 14. Strehle notes, correctly, but without explanation the occasional nominalist accent found in Reformed orthodox theology: see his *Calvinism, Federalism, and Scholasticism* (Bern: Peter Lang, 1988); part of the explanation, surely, is the ongoing philosophical debate of the sixteenth and seventeenth centuries in which the nominalist position continued to be referenced — and the other part is the reappropriation of nominalist assumptions as in the case of Suárez's understanding of distinctions in the Godhead: see Michael V. Murray, "The Theory of Distinctions in the Metaphysics of Francis Suárez" (Ph.D. diss., Fordham University, 1944).

conceptualization of the divine perfection and accurately descriptive of the way in which God is discerned in his operations and effects, that is, in the objects of his work. (Given his philosophical proclivities, despite the similarity to Burman's definition, Mastricht's sources are certainly not Cartesian!) Thus, God may be said to hate some things and to love others, according to an attribution of properties by way of eminence, based on the similitude of the effect of his working to the effect of the working of creatures possessing those attributes or properties.[351]

According to the second view found among the Reformed orthodox, the attributes are understood as genuinely and observably distinct *ad extra*, in the way in which God addresses the distinct creatures of his finite universe. Indeed, the effects of the various attributes may be understood as distinct *realiter*. The distinction is neither *realis* in God (as if the attributes were distinct as things from other things) nor simply *rationalis* according to our way of understanding, but *eminenter* or *virtualiter* in God and founded on the diverse objects and effects of God upon the world.[352] It is noteworthy here that these theologians identify the attributes as in God in the sense of *perfectiones* or *proprietates essentiales* — the terminology is consciously plural: God is not spoken of as undifferentiated *perfectio* or as having a single *proprietas*, namely, perfection, as in the medieval nominalist model. God is, therefore, described both concretely and abstractly by his attributes: he is good and he is goodness itself, essentially so. There is no real or substantive difference between his goodness, his power, his eternity, and his infinity — essentially, his goodness is his power, his power is his eternity, and so forth — but in the world of finite objects, there is a real difference between the effects that lead us to identify God as good or as powerful or as just or as wise, and therefore to recognize that there is goodness, power, justice, and wisdom in God and that these are conceptually different in God himself. Thus, Walaeus comments that heat and light are distinct *virtualiter*, but not *realiter* in the rays of the sun.[353]

Ames and Maresius argue in a similar vein: the divine attributes "are distinguished from the essence and among each other not only *ratio rationans* but also *ratio ratiocinata* ... in such a way that the *fundamentum* of the distinction is in God himself."[354] The divine attributes are not, moreover, distinguished *realiter* either from the divine essence or from one another — as, Maresius indicates, the Socinians, some Scotists, and the Cabbalists would have it — but are distinguished only by reason (*ratione tantum*). Nonetheless, this rational distinction is not merely a product of reason itself (*non simpliciter ratiocinante*) but rests on analysis (*ratiocinata*): if it is not a distinction on the part of the thing itself, it is nevertheless a distinction that "has its foundation in

351. Mastricht, *Theoretico-practica theol.*, II.v.7; cf. Turretin, *Inst theol. elencticae*, III.v.9.

352. Rijssen, *Summa theol.*, III.vii; cf. Fiddes, *Theol. spec.*, I.ii.1 (p. 66); Turretin, *Inst. theol. elencticae*, III.v.9.

353. Walaeus, *Loci communes*, p. 162; cf. Le Blanc, *Theses theol.*, *De perfectione et infinitate Dei*, viii-xiv; Rijssen, *Summa theol.*, III.vi.

354. Ames, *Medulla*, I.iv.28; cf. Maresius, *Collegium theologicum*, II.xi-xii; also Burgersdijk, *Institutiones metaphysicae*, II.v.6; Heereboord, *Meletemata philosophica*, *Disputatio XXI*, *de simplicitate Dei*, ix (pp. 118-119); probably also indicated in Beza et al., *Propositions and Principles*, V.iv.

the thing, namely in the effects and objects of God."[355] What is more, these "diverse concepts of ours, which are really distinct among themselves, correspond to diverse concepts objectively belonging to God, which although in actuality are in God indivisible, are nonetheless eminently and virtually distinct."[356]

Thus, "when we conceive the justice of God to be an attribute really distinct from his mercy or goodness, our faculties do not deceive us; because tho' these attributes are individually the same in principle, yet in the diversity of operations flowing from that principle, they are truly understood and defin'd, as so many different attributes."[357] Wendelin summarizes the argument:

> the properties (*proprietates*) of angels and men, such as goodness, holiness, wisdom, power, and so forth, are accidents (*accidentia*), which are not only in their subjects, that is, in angels and men, but which also differ *realiter* among themselves and, together with their subjects determine their composite character; the properties of God, however, are not accidents, but are the divine essence itself ... as conceived by us according to the manner of a property (*per modum proprietatis ... a nobis concepta*). Thus the righteousness of God is God himself righteous, the mercy of God is God himself merciful, the wisdom of God, God himself wise, and so forth. Neither is righteousness one thing in God, mercy another, wisdom yet another: rather they are a single and most simple actuality (*unus sunt et simplicissimus actus*), which is identified by various names or terms in view of its effects and diverse [external] objects.[358]

Yet, these properties or attributes are genuinely distinct, Wendelin argues, and genuinely distinct not merely in the mind of the human knower but distinct *virtualiter* (not *realiter*) in God.[359] As Davenant makes the point, the attributes "are applicable to God, in regard to the qualities signified by them, since God has these qualities preeminently in his own essence" nonetheless, "they are not appropriate to God as to the mode expressing that signification; because the qualities are not in God as any thing distinct from, or only accidentally conjoined unto His essence."[360] This second approach to the problem clearly follows the Thomist understanding of the distinction of attributes in God and even indicates an awareness (as documentable in Keckermann's discussion of the problem) of Cajetan's reading of Aquinas.

A differently nuanced view of the "eminent" distinction of attributes was advanced in detail by Twisse. Rather than exclude the distinction of persons in the Godhead from the discussion of the distinction of the attributes by identifying it as an entirely separate issue, Twisse (like Zanchi before him) saw the trinitarian distinctions as central to the argument:

355. Maresius, *Collegium theologicum*, II.xi.

356. Maresius, *Collegium theologicum*, II.xii.

357. Fiddes, *Theol. spec.*, I.ii.1 (p. 68).

358. Wendelin, *Systema*, I.i, thesis 6, explicatio ii; cf. Polanus, *Syntagma*, II.vii (p. 141); Owen, *Hebrews*, IV, p. 365.

359. Wendelin, *Systema*, I.i, thesis 6, explicatio v; cf. Turretin, *Inst. theol. elencticae*, III.v.5-6; Forbes, *Instructiones hist.*, I.xxxiv.3.

360. Davenant, *Determinationes*, xxiv (p. 347).

though the Father be not the Sonne, nor the H. Ghost, &c. Yet they are not really distinct from one another. In the Trinity there is *alius & alius*, not *aliud & aliud*.[361]

Even so, against Jackson's understanding of a radical absence of distinctions in the Godhead and an inwardly undifferentiated "totality of perfection," Twisse comments "to say that God is all his perfections eminently, doth not hinder his formall unitie; as likewise his formall unitie doth nothing to prejudice his perfection's eminent pluralitie."[362] On the one hand, we recognize that God's nature is not divisible into parts. On the other hand, we acknowledge that it "conteynes all entities, *not fomally*, but vertually, or eminently, or exemplarily."[363] The statement that attributes are in God eminently or *per eminentiam*, moreover, reflects the two ways of approaching the attributes, the *via negativa* and the *via eminentiae*: as noted, divine simplicity reflects primarily the *via negativa* and is only one side of the discussion. The declaration of simplicity is designed to rule out by negation any and all composition in God, not to rule out according to eminence any and all distinctions.[364]

As his subsequent argument shows, Twisse has a rather different understanding of the formal distinction than Burman did and, moreover, a very different reason for rejecting it. The difference between a real or formal "containing" of entities and a virtual, eminent, or exemplary containing or "comprehension" of entities lies in the possibility of exhausting the former "by particulars." As Twisse explains, "exhaustinge formally by particulars derived from them, belongs to natures that conteyne the particulars formally; as a bushell of wheat by subtraction of graynes may be exhausted," but such "exhausting by particulars derived from them" does not belong "to natures, that conteyne particulars eminently." Thus, Twisse continues,

> to say that God is being itselfe, or perfection, dothe not exclude pluralitie in my judgement, and that for this reason. Humanitie is humanitie itselfe, yet this hindereth not, but that many thousands may be partakers of humanitie. In like sort, thoughe the divine perfection be perfection itselfe, yet this hindereth not, but that many may be partakers of Divine perfection.[365]

---

361. Twisse, *Discovery*, p. 75; cf. Zanchi, *De natura Dei*, II.ii.4 (cols. 67-69).

362. Twisse, *Discovery*, p. 71, apostrophe added for clarity; cf. Jackson, *Treatise of the Divine Essence*, I.iv.3; and note the discussion in Sarah Hutton, "Thomas Jackson, Oxford Platonist, and William Twisse, Aristotelian," in *Journal of the History of Ideas*, 39 (1978), pp. 635-652; cf. Strehle, *Calvinism, Federalism, and Scholasticism*, pp. 104-107, who mistakenly identifies Twisse as holding a nominalist view of the divine simplicity, presumably on the basis of Twisse's voluntarism; and see above, 1.3 (B.3) on the nominalist understanding of simplicity.

363. Twisse, *Discovery*, p. 72, italics mine; cf. Le Blanc, *Theses theol.*, *De perfectione et infinitate Dei*, xiii; Ridgley, *Body of Divinity*, p. 53, col. 2.

364. This is a highly interesting reversal of the Suárezian perspective, which understood the distinctions as arising only according to the *via negativa*, and therefore as not arguable *per eminentiam* in God: cf. Suárez, *Disp metaph.*, XXX.vi.19.

365. Twisse, *Discovery*, p. 72; cf. Zanchi, *De natura Dei*, II.ii.4 (col. 69).

There are in the divine essence "denominations personall" which are partakers of the divine perfection.[366] The point carries also for the attributes or individual divine perfections. For the distinction of attributes, Twisse, again echoing Zanchi, draws on Aquinas:

> as for the perfections of being which are founde without God ... life, and sense, and reason: as they are not like unto God according to any univocall notion of Species, or kind, but only analogicall, which as Aquinas sheweth, is this, that God is entitie by essence, and every other thing is entitie only by participation. So likewise their perfections cannot be said to be in God univocally, but only analogically, as the effect is said to be in the Agent, in as much as he hathe power to produce it. ... God is wise, good, powerfull; these attributes are conveniently given to men and angells. Yet these denominations, in admitting whereof bothe God and creatures doe agree, are different in respect of God and the creatures.[367]

The attributes are, then, in God in a manner different from the way they are in creatures — yet, the implication is that the presence of attributes *per eminentiam* in God has some analogy to the participation of all finite beings in the divine being. Again, even in the supralapsarian Twisse, the Thomistic model is ratified.

Turretin's argument — the third approach — draws on the language of eminent and the language of formal distinction, arguing an *ad intra* application of the eminent or virtual distinction and an *ad extra* application of the formal distinction. The attributes, Turretin indicates, are not distinct either from the divine essence or from one another *realiter* but, nonetheless, "the may properly be said to be distinguished both intellectually as to the diverse formal conception and objectively and effectively as to the various external objects and effects." Yet, like his Reformed contemporaries, Turretin is quite unwilling to argue a distinction that is purely or entirely *ad extra* — and ready to argue an *ad intra* distinction of attributes that borrows on the language of the distinction *per eminentiam*. Turretin continues, "it is evident that this distinction is neither simply real [as] between things and things, nor formal (which is only in our manner of conception), but eminent (which although it does not hold itself on the part of the thing as between thing and thing, yet has a foundation in the thing on account of the diversity of objects and effects)."[368] In Turretin's language, the mind isolates attributes by a "praecisive abstraction" that is simple and negative, but neither exclusive nor privative — we conceive of the divine goodness by abstracting it or mentally isolating it from other attributes, like power, but not by arguing God to be good as opposed to his being merciful or just.[369]

---

366. Twisse, *Discovery*, p. 72.

367. Twisse, *Discovery*, p. 82; Zanchi, *De natura Dei*, II.vii, q. 2.2 (col. 141); cf. B. M. Lemaigre, "Perfection de dieu et Multiplicité des Attributs Divins," in *Revue des Sciences Philosophiques et Théologiques*, 50 (1966), pp. 198-225.

368. Turretin, *Inst. theol. elencticae*, III.v.9.

369. Turretin, *Inst. theol. elencticae*, III.v.4.

The language here is both curious and significant: the *distinctio formalis* is denied, but on the ground that it was purely rational — that is, identical with the *distinctio rationalis* or *rationis rationans* — which was certainly not the intention of Scotus' usage. (Indeed, Turretin appears to reverse Burman's mistake, removing the formal distinction from the real order rather than identifying it too closely with a real distinction.)[370] In addition, an "eminent distinction" is affirmed as having a "foundation in the thing," echoing the language of the *distinctio rationis ratiocinatae cum fundamento in re*, but following out the line of argument we have seen Keckermann draw from Cajetan. At the same time, Turretin associates this more Thomistic language with a sense of intellectual distinctions that can be made concerning the divine essence resting on our "diverse formal conception" of the divine acts *ad extra*.[371] Turretin thus appears, like Voetius, to draw on elements of Scotist vocabulary while using a fundamentally late Thomistic paradigm for the basic distinction of attributes.[372]

Similar statements are also found in Maresius, Ames, and Le Blanc, indicating a formal distinction — but not necessarily in its root Scotistic sense. The attributes, Maresius argues, are essentially identical "on the part of the thing signified," but are genuinely distinguished "according to the manner of signifying" them, with the result that both our concepts and their objects are formally distinct.[373] In the case of Le Blanc, we find a distinction between those divine attributes that are in some sense analogous to attributes present in creatures accidentally or "in a certain respect" (*secundum quid*), such as attributes of perception, like seeing and hearing; and those attributes that God has absolutely or *simpliciter*. The first cannot be in God "formally and properly," given that their presence would signify an imperfection: God does not see and hear as creatures do, but he does know and perceive all things. What is in God is the power (*vis*) of knowing and perceiving — and thus, he is said to have such attributes *virtualiter* or *eminenter*. Other attributes, namely, divine perfections, do belong to God *proprie et formaliter*, namely, those attributes that belong to God properly according to his essence — among which are life, intellect, will, wisdom, goodness, and justice — given that God does not merely have these but is essentially living, knowing, willing, wise, good, and just.[374] Such perfections *vere sunt intra essentiam divinam*.[375]

By way of summary, we have found three basic solutions to the question of the distinction of attributes: all of the Reformed orthodox assume the simplicity of the divine essence, and all understand the attributes as in some sense distinct. Some, like

---

370. Behind this problem — whether as seen in Burman, Twisse, or Turretin — may well be a confusion caused by Suárez' attempt to redefine the Scotistic language.

371. Turretin, *Inst. theol. elencticae*, III.v.9

372. Turretin, *Inst. theol. elencticae*, III.v.8-9; cf. Voetius, *Selectarum disputationum theologicarum*, I, 13; cf. ibid., V, p. 59.

373. Maresius, *Collegium theologicum*, II.xiii; cf. Voetius, *Syllabus problematum*, fol. D4r; Ames, *Medulla*, I.iv.26: "attributa divina insunt Deo, non tantum virtualiter, et eminenter, sed etiam formaliter."

374. Le Blanc, *Theses theol, De perfectione et infinitate Dei*, xi-xiv.

375. Le Blanc, *Theses theol, De perfectione et infinitate Dei*, xv.

Alting, Burman, Owen, and Mastricht, argue the essential identity of the attributes and point to their rational distinction *ad extra* on the basis of their effects, and echo elements of the Ockhamist solution to the problem, albeit without drawing the conclusion that God, in an ultimate sense is perfection, without any "attributes" or "properties" in the usual sense. Maccovius and Heidanus clearly follow the nominalist solution, denying distinction of attributes *ad intra* — in Heidanus' case, surely grounded in his appreciation of Cartesianism. Many, including Ames, Maresius, Leigh, Wendelin, and Twisse, argue in continuity with the medieval discussion that distinctions between attributes can be defined *ad intra*, whether as eminent or virtual, following a more or less late Thomistic pattern of argument, resembling the views of John of Paris and Cajetan. Others, notably Turretin and Voetius, argue a slight variant — namely, an eminent distinction of the attributes, but, adopting a slightly Scotistic accent, allow a formal distinction of the attributes in their *ad extra* conception in the mind. Le Blanc may go so far as to argue a formal presence and distinction of attributes in God.

This insistence of the majority on an essential identity with an eminent or virtual distinction *intrinsic* to the divine essence, reflected in the distinction of attributes in their operation *ad extra* is also born out in the structure of the discussion of individual attributes, notably in the distinctions between infinity, immensity, and omnipresence, or between infinity, eternity, and everlasting duration.[376] The proponents of the rational distinction *ad extra*, moreover, pose no explicit objections to the distinction *per eminentiam*, reserving their polemic for the Socinians, and may differ with their Reformed contemporaries only because of the relative brevity of their statements — and their unwillingness to posit the nature of the *fundamentum in re* of the distinction of attributes. And, most probably the reason that a series of definitions affirming the way in which positive distinctions can be made in God does not always appear (notably being absent from the writers noted in the first view) in the doctrine of divine simplicity is that the doctrine belongs to the *via negativa* and is designed to indicate that God is non-composite — whereas the distinctions appear along the lines of the *via eminentiae*, as indicated by the language of the distinctions itself (i.e., *per eminentiam* and *eminenter*).

In addition, beyond the purely philosophical and linguistic issues addressed by these formulations of a basic rule for understanding the divine attributes lies a crucial question of the logic of theological system — of the theological reason for formulating the rule in this particular way. Those modern writers who take the concept as purely philosophical and therefore miss the point of the traditional treatment, which always assumed that the denial of composition was made for the sake of the right understanding of the doctrine of the Trinity and of the divine attributes. Aquinas himself, like Alexander of Hales and like many theologians in the subsequent tradition, recognized the potential for misunderstanding caused by a juxtaposition of divine simplicity with the doctrine of the Trinity: the assumption of "threefold personality ... in God," inasmuch as it indicates number and, given that "number always follows

---

376. See below, 4.4 (A.1; C.1-2; D.3-4).

division," appears to contradict the notion of "supreme simplicity" in God,[377] unless as has been consistently the case in the Christian tradition, the notion of divine "persons" is carefully defined to avoid the analogy with human persons or distinct "centers of consciousness."[378] Yet, neither Aquinas nor later writers, whether Roman Catholic or Protestant, were ready to give up either of these points of doctrine (simplicity or Trinity) that had been so intimately related in patristic orthodoxy — indeed, virtually all theologians we will examine on this point, whether medieval scholastics like Aquinas, Reformers like Calvin and Musculus, or subsequent Protestant scholastic writers like Perkins, Turretin, Howe, and Rijssen, held to the patristic assumption that, far from contradicting the doctrine of the Trinity, the notion of divine simplicity offered profound support to an orthodox doctrine of the triune God. In its affirmation that God is one and also three, the church consistently assumed that God was one in essence and three in persons or hypostases — one in one way and three in another — and that personal distinction was to be necessarily correlated with essential identity.

We recognize in the first place that the Reformed orthodox version of the rational distinction of attributes conforms to the general structuring of the orthodox system around the epistemological problem of the *finitum non capax infiniti* and its resolution in the explication of the eternal decree and its execution of the sovereign will of God in and for the temporal economy. Here we see both a statement of the *non capax* and an approach to the divine relatedness: the mind cannot conceive of the way in which the attributes belong to the utter simplicity of the divine essence; nonetheless, the distinct attributes are correctly distinguished by reason in the effects and operations of God in the world — and these effects and operations rightly and genuinely reveal the identity of God, indeed, the indivisible essence of the utterly simple Godhead. The effect of this distinction, like the effect of the distinction between the decree and its execution, is to direct attention away from the divine essence toward the divine economy: this in the reputedly speculative doctrine of the divine attributes! In practical terms, this economic direction of the language points directly toward the Protestant orthodox insistence that all of the attributes have implications for piety and toward the intensely practical sections found not only in the English Puritan discussions of the divine attributes but also in many of the continental Reformed presentations of the attributes.

E. Spirituality and Invisibility

1. The teaching of the Reformers.[379] The Reformed orthodox discussion of the attributes stands in substantive continuity with the thought of the Reformers, although, as in other examples we have encountered, the Reformers tend to refrain from detailed discussion, whereas the Reformed orthodox develop the issue at length: the style and

---

377. Thomas Aquinas, *Compendium of Theology*, I.51.
378. See further, *PRRD*, IV, 2.3, B.2; 4.2, B.3
379. Cf. the discussion of God as Spirit in *PRRD*, IV, 7.1.

method of argument and the detail of discussion have changed, but the intellectual framework is unaltered. Thus, in his comment on John 4:24, "God is a Spirit," Calvin writes that "this is a confirmation," namely, of the preceding statement of the evangelist that worship ought to be spiritual, "drawn from the very nature of God." Calvin adds that, although this passage was often cited by the fathers in order to prove the divinity of the Holy Spirit, it in fact is Christ's simple declaration "that his Father is of a spiritual nature."[380] Similarly, Calvin clearly held, without great elaboration, the traditional corollary of spirituality, the divine invisibility. He comments on the text, "who is the image of invisible God," that "the sum is this — that God in himself, that is, in his naked majesty, is invisible, and that not to the eyes of the body merely, but also to the understandings of men, and that he is revealed to us in Christ alone, that we may behold him as in a mirror."[381] In addition, against the libertines, Calvin clearly distinguished between uncreated and created spirit, and insisted that "souls and heavenly spirits" were not of the divine "substance."[382]

Musculus cites John 4:24 as a primary point of reference in his introductory comments on God. When Christ said that God is a spirit, Musculus indicates, he did not intend thereby to define "God" exhaustively but only to admonish his hearers to spiritual worship: indeed by "so saying, he expressed more what God is not, than what God is."[383] "Spirit" in the sense employed by Christ indicates things which by nature are not "earthly and gross" like "angels, winds, and the souls as well of man as of beast." Pagans like Pythagoras, Cato, and Virgil called God spirit, in that they — presumably with some insight — viewed God as "mind and understanding."[384]

2. The Reformed orthodox view of divine spirituality. These same assumptions can be found in the extended discussions of the subject found among the Reformed orthodox. Several different patterns of discussion can, moreover, be noted. Ridgley, for example, describes the attribute of spirituality according to his proposed *via eminentiae*, examining first the quality of spirituality among creatures.[385] By way of contrast, Pictet argues a *via negativa* approach with a hint of Cartesian vocabulary, first negating the possibility that God could be conceived of as in any way material, given the imperfections and divisibility of all extension, the asserting that God must be conceived of as immaterial or spiritual.[386] Charnock, in what is perhaps the most fully exegetical and homiletical of his discourses on the attributes, simply takes his point of departure from the biblical statement and then elaborates the principle positively toward its doctrinal content and then its practical conclusion, namely, the

---

380. Calvin, *Commentary upon the Gospel According to John*, 4:24, in loc. (CTS *John*, I, p. 164).

381. Calvin, *Commentaries on the Epistles ... to the Philippians, Colossians, and Thessalonians*, Col. 1:15, in loc. (CTS, pp. 149-150).

382. Calvin, *Against the Libertines*, xi (pp. 230-233).

383. Musculus, *Loci communes*, I.iii (*Commonplaces*, p. 8, col. 1).

384. Musculus, *Loci communes*, I.iii (*Commonplaces*, p. 8, col. 2).

385. Ridgley, *Body of Divinity*, p. 54, col. 2.

386. Pictet, *Theol. Chr.*, II.iii.3.

necessity of spiritual worship. But he, like Pictet, also views "spirit" as necessarily understood "by way of negation."[387]

Thus, "God in respect of his nature is a *Spirit*; that is, a substance or essence altogether incorporeal: this the Scripture expressly witnesseth, John 4:24; 2 Cor. 3:17."[388] That this is, at least in the view of many of the orthodox writers, a product of the *via negativa*, can be seen from a basic definition:

> Spirituality is the attribute according to which God is without materiality [and] is all that he is. *Spiritualitas est attributum, quo Deus sine mole est, id omne quod est.*[389]

Thus, spirituality indicates, first and foremost, that God "is not a body" and does not consist in "various parts, extended one ... beyond another." Nor indeed, as spirit, is God like angels and souls, "but infinitely higher."[390] This view alone does justice to the text of Scripture and also to reason, which (when rightly exercised) joins with revelation in asserting the essential spirituality of God. On this issue, not few "heathens" and several writers of the Church have in fact erred — Tertullian being a case in point.[391]

Still, the use of the term "spirit" to identify angels and souls yields, for some of the Reformed orthodox, including Charnock, the need to expand the definition beyond mere affirmation of a "way of negation":

> God is called a Spirit (1) Negatively, because he is not a body. (2) Analogically, or by a certain likeness because there are many perfections in spiritual substances, which do more shadow forth the divine nature than any bodily thing can.[392]

There is a certain likeness established between created spirits (angels and the human soul) and the uncreated divine spiritual nature:

> Whatsoever is affirmed of God, which is also communicable to the creatures, the same must be understood by a kind of excellence and singularity above the rest. Angels are Spirits, & the souls of men are spirits, but God is a spirit by a kind of excellence or singularity above all spirits, the God of spirits, Num. 16:22; the Father of spirits, Heb. 12:9; the Author of spirits, and indeed the spirit of spirits.[393]

Just as our soul is nobler than our body, so also must we "conceive of [God] by the perfections of our souls, without the vileness of our bodies" and "raise our thoughts of God according to the noblest part" of the divine image in us.[394]

---

387. Charnock, *Existence and Attributes*, III (p. 181); cf. IV, on "Spiritual Worship."
388. Leigh, *Treatise*, II.iii (p. 23); Le Blanc, *Theses theol.*, *De Dei simplicitate*, xiv.
389. Rijssen, *Summa*, III.ix.
390. Charnock, *Existence and Attributes*, III (p. 182).
391. Charnock, *Existence and Attributes*, III (p. 182).
392. Leigh, *Treatise*, II.iii (p. 23); cf. Ames, *Medulla*, I.iv.34 (nearly identical).
393. Leigh, *Treatise*, II.iii (p. 23).
394. Charnock, *Existence and Attributes*, III (p. 183).

Some distinction, therefore, may be made in usage, particularly in the pattern of the language of the *imago Dei* — applied to God the term indicates his ultimate essence, applied to creatures, it takes on a derivative sense:

> The word spirit in Greek *pneuma*, in Hebrew *Ruach*, is used chiefly of God, and secondarily of creatures; when it is used of God, it is used either properly or metonymically; properly, and so first essentially, then it signifieth the Godhead absolutely as John 4:24, or more restrictively the divine nature of Christ, Heb. 9:14; 1 Pet. 3:18, secondly, personally for the third person in the Trinity, commonly called the Holy Spirit or Ghost, 1 Cor. 2:11. If the word be taken metonymically, it signifieth sometimes the effects of grace, either the common graces of God's spirit, prophetical (1 Sam. 10:6, 10), miraculous, or the sanctifying graces, Ephes. 5:18.[395]

Nonetheless, the identification of God as "spirit" does not place God in a class or genus with other spiritual beings or indicate that "God and angels" have a "common nature" — it merely identifies God as invisible and incorporeal.[396] Spirituality also implies efficacy and activity (Ezek. 1:20) and perfect simplicity: the essence of God and the faculties attributed to God are not divisible or capable of real distinction, given that only material reality can be divided in this manner.

We do not know precisely, comments Ridgley, "what our own spirits, or souls, are" much less what angelic spirits are, and least of all what spirituality means when it is attributed to God as a perfection.[397] Nevertheless some clarification of the term "spirit" is possible, beginning with finite spirits: "let it be observed,

> 1) That a Spirit is the most perfect and excellent being; the soul is more excellent than the body, or indeed than anything that is purely material; so Angels are the most perfect and glorious part of the creation, as they are spiritual beings in some things excelling the souls of men.
>
> 2) A Spirit is, in its own nature, immortal; it has nothing in its frame and constitution that tends to corruption, as there is in material things, which consist of various parts, that may be dissolved or separated, and their form altered, which is what we call corruption; but this belongs not to Spirits, which are liable to no change in their nature; but by the immediate hand of God, who can, if he pleases, reduce them again to their first nothing.
>
> 3) A Spirit is capable of understanding, and willing, and putting forth actions agreeable thereunto, which no other being can do: thus, though the sun is a glorious and useful being; yet, because 'tis material, 'tis not capable of thought, or any moral action, such as angels, and the souls of men, can put forth.[398]

Moving beyond the realm of finite spirit, Ridgley goes on to describe God as Spirit:

395. Leigh, *Treatise*, II.iii (pp. 23-24).
396. Brakel, *Redelijke Godsdienst*, I.iii.13.
397. Ridgley, *Body of Divinity*, p. 54, col. 2.
398. Ridgley, *Body of Divinity*, p. 54, col. 2.

1) As spirits excel all other creatures, we must conclude God to be the most excellent and perfect of all beings, and also that he is *incorruptible, immortal,* and *invisible,* as he is said to be in scripture (Rom 1:23 and 1 Tim 1:17). Moreover, it follows from hence, that he has an understanding and will, and so we may conceive of him as the creator and governor of all things; this he could not be if he were not an intelligent and sovereign being, and particularly a Spirit.[399]

2) The difference between other spiritual substances and God, is, that all their excellency is only comparative, *viz.* as they excel the best of all material beings in their nature and properties; but God, as a Spirit, is infinitely more excellent, not only than all material beings, but than all created spirits. Their perfections are derived from him, and therefore he is called, *the Father of spirits* (Heb. 12:9); and *the God of the spirits of all flesh* (Num. 16:22); but his perfections are underived: other spirits are, as we have observed, in their own nature, immortal, yet God can reduce them to nothing; but God is independently immortal, and therefore 'tis said of him, that *he only hath immortality* (1 Tim. 6:16).[400]

Here, the balance of rational argumentation with biblical material remains evident in the late orthodox doctrine of the attributes is apparent: there is no obvious movement here either into metaphysics strictly so called or into natural theology. The rational argument remains within the framework of the biblical language, as understood in the exegetical tradition of the church. This approach may be contrasted with the tendency toward a more philosophical or rationalistic doctrine of God typical of eighteenth-century latitudinarian works and of Wolffian orthodoxy. In the latter dogmatics, a summary statement concerning the essence and attributes of God could be elaborated as part of the *theologia naturalis,* leaving the full doctrine of God, particularly the doctrine of the Trinity, for the *theologia supernaturalis.*[401] During the period of high orthodoxy, however, the linkage between the doctrine of the attributes and scriptural revelation continued to hold.

3. The divine invisibility. The spirituality of God implies his invisibility or "insensibility," and, indeed, the reverse is also true: God's invisibility implies his spirituality. The orthodox cite, in particular, Luke 24:39; Col. 1:15; John 1:18; 1 Tim. 1:17, arguing that the latter text, more than any other, makes clear that God, as spirit, is not an object of sense. God is identified by 1 Tim. 1:17 as "eternal, immortal, invisible": "if he had a body," comments Charnock, "and hid it from our eyes, he might be said not to be seen, but could not be said to be invisible." Charnock concludes, "if he be invisible, he is also spiritual."[402]

The eternal power and majesty of God is evidenced in all of the divine works, whether of creation or providence — but in all of these things, God is never directly

---

399. Ridgley, *Body of Divinity,* p. 54, col. 2 - p. 55, col. 1.

400. Ridgley, *Body of Divinity,* p. 55, col. 1.

401. Cf. Christian Wolff, *Theologia naturalis methodo scientifica pertractata* (Frankfurt and Leipzig, 1739-41), with Wyttenbach, *Tentamen theologiae,* I, § 24-58 (*theologia naturalis*), with ibid., III, § 210-388 (*De Deo prout in Scriptura Scara exhibetur*).

402. Charnock, *Existence and Attributes,* III (p. 185).

seen, "not only because he is invisible in his nature, but because ... the manner of his working is invisible." In some of his works, God works evidently, with the result that godly people identify the hand or finger of God at work — "but in other things he workes so secretly, that the spirituall man is not able to see where the finger of God is, unless upon the acknowledgment that the finger of God is everywhere."[403] And even in his evident works, God is not seen.

4. Debate over divine spirituality and invisibility in the era of orthodoxy. These definitions stand quite specifically against a series of errors and objections. In the era of orthodoxy, the typical opponents are identified as "Anthropomorphites." The argument could become particularly pointed inasmuch as not only various rational philosophies of the day raised questions concerning the usefulness of traditional conceptions of substance and, in the case of Hobbes, equated substance with corporeality, but also because of the popular ramifications of the debate.[404] Thomas Edwards, for example, cites a pamphlet arguing "that God hath a bodily shape and proportion" given that "man was made according to the likeness of God in personall shape, and God the Creator beareth the same form in shape and person which man hath."[405] On the more technical level, the orthodox named Tertullian (for his more or less Stoic assumption of the materiality of "spiritual being"), Conrad Vorstius, the Socinians, and sometimes (in the high orthodox era) the Cartesians, and Thomas Hobbes as specific adversaries on the issue.[406]

The usual objections to divine spirituality, moreover, are both biblical and rational or philosophical in character and are variously treated in the different Reformed orthodox theologies. Thus, first, it can be objected that the term *spiritus* is only "improperly" predicated of God and does not indicate an essential property. For Mastricht, this appears to be the fundamental objection inasmuch as it reflects both an erroneous reading of the biblical language and a series of fundamental theological and philosophical errors. The point of the objection is that "spirit" does not indicate an essential or substantial nature but that it indicates the fact of being spirated or breathed.

Second, it is objected that Scripture itself indicates that God has often appeared to human beings.[407] These appearances, the orthodox respond, are precisely that — appearances, not of God *in se*, but of God in some visible form taken for the sake of revelation. When we read in Genesis 3:8 that God was "walking in the garden in the

---

403. Caryl, *Exposition of Iob*, 23:9, in loc. (VII, p. 366).

404. See also the discussion of "substance" in *PRRD*, IV, 2.2D and 4.2B; and see Amos Funkenstein, "The Body of God in 17th Century Theology and Science," in R. Popkin (ed.) *Millenarianism and Messianism in English Literature and Thought, 1650-1800* (Leiden: Brill, 1988), pp. 149-175.

405. Thomas Edwards, *The Third Part of Gangraena or, A new and higher Discovery of the Errors, Heresies, Blasphemies, and indolent Proceedings of the Sectaries of these times; with some Animadversions by way of Confutation upon many of the Errors and Heresies named* (London: Ralph Smith, 1646), p. 2.

406. See Mastricht, *Theoretico-practica theologia*, II.vi.8; Edwards, *Theologia Reformata*, pp. 48-49.

407. Ursinus, *Commentary*, p. 125 (obj. 1).

cool of the day," we ought to assume that God appeared in human shape. Henry even speculates that "he who judged the world now was the same that shall judge the world at the last day, even *that man whom God has ordained*."[408] Thus, God appears as he chooses and to whom he chooses. Nor are his appearances "natural," given that he is not visible "in himself" — rather his appearances are "voluntary" and belong to privileged moments.[409] These appearances are either in bodily form, as when God appeared to Abraham (Gen. 18:1), or they are representations made to "the inward sense and imagination," as in the case of Micah and Isaiah (1 Kg. 22:19; Isa. 6:1) — but in no case are these appearances or representations to be understood as moments in which the divine substance or essence became visible: "the substance of God was not seen, no more than the substance of angels was seen in their apparitions to men."[410]

Similarly, third, God is said to have been seen and is promised to be seen by believers in the kingdom, "face to face."[411] With reference to Genesis 32:30, where Jacob states that he has seen God "face to face," Poole comments that this does not mean that Jacob saw the divine essence, "for so *no man ever saw God*, John 1:18, nor yet in a dream or vision, but in a most evident, sensible ... manifestation of himself."[412] Other interpreters make similar statements and go on to juxtapose the text with others, like Isaiah 8:17, where God is said to be a God who "hides himself" and with 1 Timothy 6:16, where God is said to be one who "dwells in unapproachable light."[413] Even so, these texts do not mean "that God was perceptible to the natural eye, but that there was a clear perception of him by the mind."[414]

Fourth, "the Scriptures frequently attribute to God various parts and members of the human body."[415] But Scripture also states specifically that angels, as spirits, have no flesh and bone (Luke 24:39): "how much more should this apply to God," argues Rijssen, who is called Spirit (Jn. 4:24) and the Father of spirits (Heb. 12:9)."[416] Furthermore, as Isaiah declares (40:18) none is like unto God: God, therefore, is unlike his corporeal creation.[417]

> This confutes (1) Tertullian (*Adversus Praxeas*; *de Anima*) who held God to be corporeal, then he should consist of matter and form; (2) the Anthropomorphites who ascribed to God the parts and members of a man; they alledge that place, Gen. 1:27 ... yet a man was not said to be made after the Image of God in respect of his corporal figure,

---

408. Henry, *Exposition*, in loc.
409. Caryl, *Exposition of Iob*, 23:9, in loc. (VII, p. 367).
410. Charnock, *Existence and Attributes*, III (p. 185); cf. Ursinus, *Commentary*, p. 125.
411. Ursinus, *Commentary*, p. 125 (obj. 2).
412. Poole, *Commentary*, in loc. (I, p.76); cf. Henry, *Exposition*, in loc.
413. Trapp, *Commentary*, in loc. (I, p. 124).
414. Ursinus, *Commentary*, p. 125.
415. Ursinus, *Commentary*, p. 125; cf. Charnock, *Existence and Attributes*, III (p. 188).
416. Rijssen, *Summa*, III.ix, controversia, arg. 1.
417. Rijssen, *Summa*, III.ix, controversia, arg. 2.

but in respect of knowledge, righteousness, and holiness, Ephes. 4:23; Col. 3:10; not in respect of his substance, but qualities.[418]

There is, moreover, a fundamental question raised here concerning the nature of revelation itself: the Reformed orthodox continue to affirm, as Calvin had, the accommodated character of biblical truth:

> Nor must it be thought strange, that God is everywhere in the scripture represented like a man, having the members of the human body ascribed to him; for that is done to assist the weakness of our comprehension, and must be explained in a manner consistent with the divine nature. In short, by those members the scripture intends to point out the divine attributes; and it is to be observed also, that only those members of the human frame are attributed to God, which are either the principle of those human actions which are best known ... or which are instruments of those actions that are most worthy of man. ... The *heart* is mentioned as the principle of vital actions; the *hands*, because by them we perform many things; the *eyes*, because through them we gain the knowledge of many things.[419]

All those places in Scripture which describe God anthropomorphically simply set forth those powers which God has spiritually but which by analogy are found in creatures and are exercised corporeally. When "viscera, eyes, and hands are ascribed to God," we understand that such attributions "are by *anthropopatheia*, granting that God works by his spiritual powers much as human beings operate according to corporeal powers."[420] When John writes that we shall see God as he is (1 John 3:2) he indicates that we shall see Christ with the eyes of the flesh but God with the eyes of the mind.[421] Since God has no body, he cannot be seen — and clearly cannot have eyes or hands or any corporeal parts.[422]

> And thus these members represent the mercy, the power, the knowledge, the omnipresence, and other perfections of God. It must be observed also, that such members are ascribed to God, as perform extraordinary things: thus the scriptures give him eyes, but eyes which penetrate men's hearts and see all things; ears, which hear the inner echoes of the heart, and listen to all men, at one and the same time. And so of the other members.[423]

Here we have moved from the philosophical notion of immateriality and unmoved actuality to a more scriptural argument — one which does no injustice to the text of the Old Testament and which, arguably, conveys its meaning exceptionally well. We observe, thus, not an unscriptural Aristotelianism or an anti-philosophical biblicism,

---

418. Leigh, *Treatise*, II.iii (p. 24).
419. Pictet, *Theol. chr.*, II.iii.4; cf. Burman, *Syn. theol.*, I.xvii.6.
420. Rijssen, *Summa*, III.ix, controversia, obj. 1-3.
421. Rijssen, *Summa Theol.*, III.ix, controversia (I).
422. Cf. Leigh, *Treatise*, II.iii (p. 25).
423. Pictet, *Theol. chr.*, II.iii.4.

but an attempt to integrate a philosophically sound view of God with the scriptural revelation.

As a fifth objection to divine spirituality, the orthodox note that some appeal to the biblical statement that human beings were made "in the image of God."[424] This objection is refuted by appeal to the correct doctrine of the *imago Dei*, which teaches that the image according to which human beings were created was not their bodily form but the "essence of [their] soul, in its powers and integrity."[425] Henry's commentary provides a classic definition of the *imago Dei*:

> God's image upon man consists of those three things, 1) In his *nature* and *constitution*, not those of his body, (for God has not a body), but those of his soul. This honor, indeed, God has put upon the *body* of man, that the Word was made flesh, the Son of God was clothed with a body like unto ours, and will shortly clothe our's with a glory like unto his. ... But it is the soul ... that does especially bear God's image. The soul is a spirit, an intelligent immortal spirit, an influencing active spirit, herein resembling God, the Father of spirits, and the Soul of the world. *The spirit of man is the candle of the Lord* [Ps. 20:27]. The soul of man, considered in its three noble faculties, understanding, will and active power, is perhaps the brightest, clearest looking-glass in nature, wherein to see God. 2) In his *place and authority. Let us make man in our image, and let them have dominion.* As he has the government of the inferior creatures, he is, as it were, God's representative, or viceroy, on earth.... Yet [man's] government of himself, by the freedom of his will, has in it more of God's image than his government of the creatures. 3) In his *purity and rectitude*. God's image upon man consists in knowledge, righteousness, and true holiness, Eph. iv. 24; Col iii.10. He was upright, Eccl. vii. 29. ... His understanding saw divine things clearly and truly, and there were no errors or mistakes in his knowledge: his will complied readily and universally with the will of God, without reluctancy or resistance: his affections were all regular, and he had no inordinate appetites or passions. ... All the inferior powers were subject to the dictates and directions of the superior, without any mutiny or rebellion. Thus holy, thus happy, were our first parents, in having the image of God put upon them.[426]

As a final element in their discussions of divine spirituality, the orthodox consistently argue its relationship to the nature of religion and worship. Since God is Spirit, he has "immediate power" over our spirits: as the "Father of Spirits" he is both the guide and the judge of our spiritual existence. This ought to lead Christians to "take heed of the sins of the heart and spirit; pride, unbelief, insincerity, 2 Cor. 7:1; 1 Thess. 5:22, such as not only arise from, but are terminated in the spirit" since such sins are "most abhorred by God."[427] Even as God loves acts or thoughts of spiritual rectitude, so does he hate "spiritual iniquities." Here we encounter a thought most eloquently expressed by Milton in his characterization of Satan's throne as a "bad eminence": since spiritual good is eminently good, so must the fall of spirit from the good be the deepest and

---

424. Cf. Ursinus, *Commentary*, p. 125.
425. Cf. Ursinus, *Commentary*, p. 125.
426. Henry, *Commentary*, in. loc.
427. Leigh, *Treatise*, II.iii (p. 26).

furthest fall and the resultant spiritual evil be eminently evil.[428] Writes Edward Leigh, "Spiritual evils make us most like the Devils, who are spiritual wickedness."[429]

Pictet notes that "reason dictated even to heathen that God is a spirit" and that several pagan thinkers opposed images of God for this very reason. "What reason argues," moreover, "Scripture confirms in Christ's own words, 'God is a spirit,' John 4:24." Pictet argues further, on the basis of a view of progressive revelation, that these words of Christ supercede and interpret correctly the anthropomorphisms of the Old Testament.

> Since, therefore, the nature of God is spiritual, we ought to worship him in spirit, except he himself shall otherwise command, as he did under the Old Testament, where he exacted a worship, for the most part, of a carnal nature, although he did enjoin spiritual worship also. But now, Christ says, the time is come, when that ceremonial worship demanded of the fathers is abrogated; now God requires a worship suitable to his nature, thereby teaching men that he is a spirit.[430]

The spirituality of God is a chief ground of religion among men: "The very Heathen," comments Leigh, "made this inference, *Si Deus est animus, sit pura mente colendus*." Our spirits are called upon to worship the spiritual God — as Christ himself taught (John 4:24) or as the Psalm says, "Bless the Lord, O my soul" (Psalm 103:1, 2) and Paul speaks of serving God in the Spirit (Rom. 7:6, 8:14).[431] "Since God is a Spirit, it follows that he is invisible," argues Pictet, adducing as scriptural proof two verses from I Timothy: "To the King, eternal *invisible*" (1:17) and "Whom no man hath seen or can see" (6:16) and one from Exodus (33:20), "There shall no man see me and live."[432] There are, of course, "many passages in which it is said that God has been seen; and others, in which God promises that he will give sight of himself to men in the future world," but these are either "visions" of Christ as preludes to his incarnation or prophecies of his appearance on the last day; or they are testimonies of God's presence and clear manifestation — as when Moses saw him "face to face" or when in eternity the redeemed have "perpetual and intimate communion with God, and the enjoyment of the divine favor and love" and, in addition, are given "perfect knowledge of God, as great as a finite creature can attain; as when it is said that we shall 'see God face to face' (1 Cor. 13:12)."[433]

Like the divine spirituality, invisibility is also a ground of piety and comfort: "God, though invisible in himself, may be known by things visible: He that seeth the Son,

---

428. Milton, *Paradise Lost*, Bk. II, line 6. From *Paradise Lost*, II, ll. 1-9: "High on a throne of Royal State, which far / Outshon the wealth of Ormus and of Ind, ... / Satan exalted sat, by merit rais'd / To that bad eminence; and from despair / Thus high uplifted beyond hope, aspires / Beyond thus high, insatiate to pursue / Vain Warr with Heav'n."

429. Leigh, *Treatise*, II.iii (p. 26).

430. Pictet, *Theol. chr.*, II.iii.3.

431. Leigh, *Treatise*, II.iii (p. 25).

432. Pictet, *Theol. Chr.*, II.iii.v.

433. Pictet, *Theol. Chr.*, II.iii.vi.

hath seen the Father, John 14:9. We should praise God as for other excellencies, so for his invisibility, 1 Timothy 1:17." There is virtually no difference of even development between the Reformation and orthodoxy on this point. The universal assumption of Scripture is that human eyes cannot see God and the explicit declaration of a series of texts is that God is "invisible." From this it can be inferred that believers ought to "learn to walk by faith, as seeing him who is invisible, Heb 11:27" and "Labor for pure hearts, that we may see God hereafter, Matth 5:8."[434] Furthermore, "Here is comfort against invisible enemies; we have the invisible God and invisible Angels to help us."[435] And the lesson drawn from the doctrine is also the same as that noted by the Reformers: Calvin comments that "in calling him invisible, [the Apostle] shows that is does not belong to us to seek out God utterly or to sound out his secret and hidden things: for the more that men inquire into the secrets of God ... the more they ... become fools."[436]

F. Divine Immutability

1. Immutability in recent historiography. The conception of divine immutability is certainly a mark of continuity between the Reformers and the Protestant orthodox — indeed, it is a mark of continuity in the thought of the church from the time of the fathers through the seventeenth century. For Augustine, immutability was a necessary corollary of the divine self-existence declared in Exodus 3:14: "That which is called 'IS' and not only is called such, but also is so, is unchangeable: it remains forever, it cannot be changed, it is in no part corruptible."[437] This intimate relationship between the divine self-existence and the assumption of immutability, moreover, remained at the heart of the doctrine in both the era of the Reformation and the era of orthodoxy.

In recent literature, the concept of immutability has been criticized as a departure from scriptural verity particularly in view of this Aristotelian language of God as "First Mover" and the finite order as "moved" from potency to actuality. Barth, among others, devoted considerable space to the critique of this orthodox conception of the "immovable" God.[438] But, as in the case of other modern criticisms of traditional theological definitions, the question which needs to be asked here is not the question of scholasticism per se (or whether Ambrose and Augustine are "proto-scholastic"!), but rather how the doctrine is rightly defined and whether Barth's critique actually understands the traditional point. In fact, Barth appears to have confused the notion of an ultimate, necessary, and, therefore, "unmoved" Being with ideas of inaction, physical stasis, and immobility — whereas the traditional notion of the "unmoved"

---

434. Leigh, *Treatise*, II.iii (p. 25).

435. Leigh, *Treatise*, II.iii (pp. 25-26).

436. John Calvin, *Sermons on the Epistles of S. Paule to Timothy and Titus*, trans. L. T. (London: G. Bishop, 1579), p. 91, col. 1.

437. Augustine, *In epistolam Joannis ad Parthos*, IV; cf. Tolley, *The Idea of God*, pp. 107-108. Also see Ambrose, *De Fide*, I.ii.14 in *NPNF*, II, vol. X, p. 203.

438. Barth, *Church Dogmatics*, II/1, pp. 492-494.

Being of God indicates only that God has not been "moved" from potency into actuality, and in no way implies that God is *inactive*.[439]

Barth indicates the various biblical passages that were used by the orthodox in their discussion but then indicates that Polanus' definition of immutability transports the reader "to quite a different world," from that of the texts.[440] Polanus argues (not as his initial, but as his sixth proof of divine immutability) that, since God himself is "the primary mover and effector of all good" and since his "unmoved being is the cause of the motion of all other things," God must be considered as immutable.[441] Now, of course, this is philosophical language unlike the language of the text of Scripture, but Barth's conclusion that, unlike the related and active God of Scripture, this language indicates a "pure *immobile*" incapable of having "any relationship between Himself and a reality distinct from Himself,"[442] is a far cry from the intention and implication of Polanus' definition. God, in Polanus' traditional language is "unmoved" because, unlike beings in the created and contingent order, he does not pass in and out of existence or experience any development from potency to actuality. Prior to making this point, moreover, Polanus had argued for immutability on the basis of biblical texts, citing James 1:17, Psalm 102:29, Isaiah 46:10, Romans 11, and Hebrews 6:17, understanding immutability of the divine being as necessary to the immutability of God's will or counsel. Only then does Polanus go on to state *rationes* that demonstrate divine immutability: arguments from the divine name Jehovah, the divine aseity, simplicity, infinity, eternity, perfection, and the work of God as *principium* and first mover — so that, in context, Polanus' argument from the identity of God as the first mover was hardly the sole or even the primary reason for arguing divine immutability, nor was it stated in isolation from Scripture.[443] Ironically, Barth recognized the orthodox point some hundred pages before when he praised Polanus' identification of divine mercy with the divine essence, indicating that Polanus "is right to the extent that ... he wishes to avoid the conception of a God who can be moved and stirred from without."[444] It is also ironic that, once Barth's somewhat polemical approach to the classical notion of divine immutability has been thus defused, his own teaching appears quite close to that of orthodoxy.

It is worth noting here that the Reformed orthodox theologians do not typically argue "impassibility" as an attribute. The term *impetibilitas* and its other forms, *impatibilitas* and *impassibilitas*, is not found in the lists and classifications of divine attributes developed by any of the major late sixteenth- and seventeenth-century

---

439. See Antonie Vos, "Always on Time: The Immutability of God," in Brink and Sarot, eds., *Understanding the Attributes of God*, pp. 53-73; and idem,"Immutabilitas Dei," in *Nederlands Theologisch Tijdschrift*, 35 (1981), pp. 111-133.

440. Barth, *Church Dogmatics*, II/1, p. 492.

441. Polanus, *Syntagma theol.*, II.xiii (p. 151, col. 1); cf. Barth, *Church Dogmatics*, II/1, p. 492, citing the 1609 edition of Polanus, col. 967.

442. Barth, *Church Dogmatics*, II/1, p. 494.

443. Polanus, *Syntagma theol.*, II.xiii (p. 151, col. 1).

444. Barth, *Church Dogmatics*, II/1, p. 370.

Reformed theologians whose works I have examined: Junius, Polanus, Perkins, Ames, Maccovius, the *Synopsis purioris*, Maresius, Burman, Heidanus, Leigh, Charnock, Turretin, Mastricht, Ridgley, Van Til, or Wyttenbach, all of whom write of divine *immutability*, not *impassibility*. Arminius, however, does use the term *impatibilitas* to indicate the absence of divine *passiones*, as distinct from *immutabilitas*, the absence of all change.[445] At one level, there is arguably no great difference between the terms, and those writers who refrain from using the term *impassibilitas* are also quite adamant in stating that God has no *passiones*. Nonetheless, at another level, the choice of the term indicates the source and direction of the usage: the Protestant orthodox rooted their conception in the traditional notion of a God who does not mutate or is not "moved" from potency to actuality, and not in the ancient Stoic notion of an uninvolved or unrelated God.[446] The modern writers who argue against the doctrine of divine impassibility as if it were little more than the uncritical importation of a Stoic concept are beating, not a dead, but a nonexistent horse.

What is more, in the usages found in the Christian tradition, immutability (or, indeed, impassibility, when the term is actually used) in no way implies an absence of relatedness, love, long-suffering, compassion, mercy, and so forth. Impassibility, when attributed to God in the Christian tradition and, specifically, in medieval and Protestant scholastic thought, indicates, not a Stoic notion of *apatheia*, but an absence of mutation, distress, or any other sort of negative *passiones*.[447] The meaning and connotation of the terms *passio*, *patibilitas* and *passivitas* in the Western and Christian philosophical tradition is quite important here: as Wéber points out, "passion signifies, together with passivity, and in correlation with 'action/activity,' the property of a subject which, through an action exerted by an exterior agent, receives a determinate quality and, in the reception, is altered by it."[448] Indeed, among the church fathers, Nyssa has indicated that "passion" conduces to sin.[449] Certainly the denial of *passiones* to God, as the denial of *patibilitas* or *passivitas* and the occasional use of the term *impassibilitas*, has primarily to do with the assumption that finite creatures do not alter

---

445. Arminius, *Disputationes publicae*, IV.xiii, xvii; Arminius, *Disputationes privatae*, XV.vii.

446. The point can also be argued with reference to patristic theology, where "impassibility" is a more frequently used term: the fathers are not indicating that God has no relation to the world order but rather that the essence or being of God does not receive new (and problematic!) qualities in its relation to the world order — indeed, the fathers typically affirm impassibility or immutability as foundational to the redemption of the passible, which God draws to himself in the incarnaton: cf. Ignatius, *Ephesians*, 7:2; *Polycarp*, 3:2; Justin, *I Apol.*, 13:4; 25:2; Athanasius, *Contra Arianos*, I.39.

447. Cf. Origen, *Homiliae in Ezecheliam*, vi.6 (attributing *passibility* to God, specifically in the sense of "affection") with idem, *Homiliae in Numeros*, xxiii.2 (denying *passiones* and mutation), with Augustine, *De patientia*, §1, 26. See below, 6.3 on the Reformed orthodox view of divine affections, and note the definitions in Arminius, *Disputationes publicae*, IV.xiii, xvii; Arminius, *Disputationes privatae*, XV.vii.

448. Edouard Wéber, "Passio, Passivitas," in *Encyclopédie philosophique universelle*, II/2, p. 1871; cf. *impassibilitas* and *passio* s.v., in J. F. Niermeyer, *Mediae Latinitatis Lexicon Minus* (Leiden: Brill, 1976) and Deferrari, *Lexicon of St, Thomas Aquinas*.

449. Gregory of Nyssa, *Against Eunomius*, VI.iii in *NPNF*, 2 ser., vol. 5, p. 186.

the divine being or add new properties to it — and not at all with a denial of relationality to God. Indeed, in the standard Aristotelian categories of predication, there is a distinction made between quality and relation as indications of different sorts of predicates: the denial of a particular quality, therefore, does not impinge at all on the issue of relationality.

2. The teaching of the Reformers. As in the case of other essential attributes not discussed at length by the Reformers, divine immutability belongs to the framework of their thought and, although not elaborated, is certainly assumed over against the heresy of a mutable God. Zwingli makes the point as incontestable, associating divine immutability with the doctrines of divine goodness, truth, and simplicity. God is the "supreme good," the only being that is absolutely and perfectly "good by nature." As "the philosophers" recognized, the ultimate good must also be true — and for this to be so, God must be also "pure, genuine, clear, complete, simple, and unchangeable." That which changes cannot retain these other attributes.[450]

Calvin, likewise, insists pointedly on the doctrine — and he does so in defense of the Trinity against those who would define the Logos as having a beginning:

> Here an outcry is made by certain men, who, while they dare not openly deny his divinity, secretly rob him of his eternity. For they contend that the Word only began to be when God opened his sacred mouth in the creation of the world. Thus, with excessive temerity, they imagine some change in the essence of God. For as the names of God, which have respect to external work, began to be ascribed to him from the existence of the work (as when he is called the Creator of heaven and earth), so piety does not recognize or admit any name which might indicate that a change had taken place in God himself.[451]

In addition, Calvin appeals to the texts cited traditionally in favor of the doctrine — Numbers 23:19; Malachi 3:6; and James 1:17:

> But to God, nothing of this sort occurs; for he is neither deceived, nor does he deceitfully promise anything, nor, as James says, is there with Him any 'shadow of turning' (James 1:17). We now understand to what this dissimilitude between God and men refers, namely, that we should not travesty God according to our own notions, but, in consideration of his nature, should remember that he is liable to no changes, since He is far above all heavens.[452]

And similarly,

> Under the name Jehovah, God reasons from his own nature ... nor is it a wonder that God here disclaims all inconsistency, since the impostor Balaam was constrained to celebrate God's immutable constancy — "For he is not a God," he says, "who changes"

---

450. Zwingli, *On Providence*, i (pp. 131-132).

451. Calvin, *Institutes*, I.xiii.8; cf. Vermigli, *Commonplaces*, I.xii.21-23, and further below, on divine repenance, 6.3 (A.1-2).

452. Calvin, *Commentaries on the Four Last Books of Moses*, Num. 23:19, in loc. (*CTS Harmony*, IV, p. 211); cf. Calvin, *Commentary on James*, 1:16-17, in loc (*CTS Catholic Epistles*, p. 291).

or varies, "like man" (Num. 23:19). We now understand the force of the words, *I am Jehovah* ... that God continues in his purpose and is not turned.... God denies that anything of this kind can take place in him, for he is *Jehovah, and changes not.*"[453]

Clearly, for Calvin, immutability stands together with eternity as one of the attributes that must be confessed as belonging to God if fundamental Christian truth is to be maintained — to the point that he notes that such limitations that appear to be ascribed to God in predications resting on the divine work *ad extra* belong not to God but to the works, notably, creation. This line of argument is continued throughout Calvin's commentaries. In the case of Malachi 3:6 ("I am the Lord, I change not") Calvin can even argue that God draws a lesson from his own "nature," moving from his essential immutability to his constancy. Calvin similarly assumes the divine immutability in his discussions of "anthropopatheia" in the Old Testament.[454] Traditional assumptions concerning divine immutability are also evident in the thought of Calvin's contemporaries, perhaps most notably, John Knox,[455] but also in such diverse writers as Bullinger, Vermigli, Hutchinson, and Hyperius, often stated in connection with the problem of divine affections. Immutability is also one of the attributes noted in the Gallican and the Belgic Confessions.[456]

3. The Reformed orthodox view of divine immutability: definitions. These premisses concerning the relationship of various texts that seem to indicate change in God to the doctrine of God's immutability stand in strong continuity with the teachings of the Protestant scholastics — and once again evidence the continuity of the exegetical tradition, in this case not merely between the Reformers and the orthodox, but from the patristic era through the seventeenth century. Pictet thus defines the question:

> From the simplicity of God follows his immutability, which denotes nothing else than such a state of the divine essence and attributes, as is not subject to any variability. We argue this immutability ... since whatever possesses all perfection, such is incapable of mutation.[457]

This assertion of immutability is to be understood absolutely denying every sort of mutation, including corruption, alteration, changes in knowing and willing, changes

---

453. Calvin, *Commentaries on Malachi*, 3:6, in loc. (*CTS Minor Prophets*, V, p. 579); note the use of Mal. 3:6 in Aquinas, *Summa theol.*, Ia, q. 9, art 2, contra; and of Num. 23:19, in ibid., Ia, q. 19, art 7, contra.

454. Calvin, *Commentaries on Malachi*, 3:6, in loc. (*CTS Minor Prophets*, V, p. 574); cf. Calvin, *Commentary upon the Book of Genesis*, 6:6, in loc. (*CTS Genesis*, I, p. 249); *Harmony of the Last Four Books of Moses*, Num. 23:18, in loc. (*CTS Harmony*, IV, p. 211).

455. Kyle, "The Divine Attributes in John Knox's Concept of God," pp. 164-168.

456. Bullinger, *Decades*, IV.iii (III, pp. 136, 148-149); Vermigli, *Loci communes*, I.xi.22-23; Hutchinson, *Image of God*, iv (pp. 25-28); Hyperius, *Methodus theol.*, I (pp. 135-136; Gallican Confession, i; Belgic Confession, i.

457. Pictet, *Theol. chr.*, II.xii.3.

in and of attributes, and changes of place involving "local motion."[458] Thus, attributes that indicate the accomplishment of effects *ad extra* and which, therefore, seem to have "a beginning in time" do not imply any change or "accident" in God,[459] but only in the thing effected.

Nor is the divine immutability mere changelessness, to be classed with the changelessness of various finite beings. It is an essential changelessness of the goodness and perfection of the Godhead in all its attributes. Thus, the immutability of the fallen angels and the reprobate in their wickedness or even of the holy angels in their perfection cannot be understood as analogues: the former is not a perfection or an excellence, and the latter is a "conferred" immutability.[460] In short, God's immutability is "God's perfection according to which He remains what He is," in all of his attributes and excellencies.[461] In summary form, it is an immutability in being, knowledge, and will.[462]

> There is no mutation in God; neither in his essence, nor in his eternity, nor in his understanding, nor in his will. Therefore, there is no mutation, &. c. Thus, the minor is proved: not in his *essence*, for being *first*, he cannot be superceded by any prior being; being *all-powerful*, he cannot be injured by any; being most *simple*, he can be corrupted by none; being *immense*, he cannot be augmented or diminished; being *eternal*, he cannot fail. Nor in his eternity, for where there is no succession, there is no mutation. And so forth. Nor in his *understanding*, for the knowledge of God is all-perfect. Nor in his *will*, for the will of God is all-wise, to which nothing unforeseen can happen, so as to compel him to change his intentions for the better. Again, nothing can prevent and resist his will; he does, indeed, will the various changes of things, but his will itself remains unchangeable. ... This immutability of God is the fulcrum of our faith and the foundation of our hope.[463]

4. Immutability and Scripture: the exegetical argument. In the structure of this topic, Turretin, Pictet, and Rijssen and various other orthodox writers set out their scriptural proofs prior to giving the argument from reason, showing that reason fulfills its ancillary role and is not in conflict with revelation.[464] Echoing, moreover, the traditional exegesis of the Reformers, they examine a fairly standard series of biblical texts to argue divine immutability — and, as in the case of eternity, the argument for divine immutability does not rest merely on the several texts that deny change

---

458. Cf. Maccovius, *Distinctiones et regulae*, IV.xiv.

459. Beza et al. *Propositions and Principles*, V.x.

460. Ridgley, *Body of Divinity* (1855), I, p. 88.

461. Francken, *Kern der Christelijke Leer*, III, q. 40 (p. 59); cf. Rijssen, *Summa theol.*, III.xxi, controversia et argumenta: "*Immutabilitas Dei est, qua Deus nunquam aliud est, nec esse potest, quam quod est.*"

462. Ridgley, *Body of Divinity* (1855), I, pp. 88-89.

463. Pictet, *Theol. chr.*, II.xii.3.

464. Turretin, *Inst. theol. elencticae*, III.xi.3-4; Pictet, *Theol. chr.*, II.xii.3; Rijssen, *Summa theol.*, III.xxi, arg. 1-2; so also, e.g., Leigh, *Treatise*, II.v (pp. 44-45); Brakel, *Redelijke Godsdienst*, I.iii.14; Mastricht, *Theoretico-practica theol.*, II.xvii.1-4; Ridgley, *Body of Divinity* (1855), I, pp. 88-90.

in God, but on a broad grouping of texts that not only deny change in the most basic sense, but that also speak of the stability or changelessness of God's knowledge, counsel, will, purpose, and promises. As Zanchi argues, the texts indicate a twofold immutability — the immutability of God in his essence or nature, as taught in Psalm 102:26-27, and the immutability of the divine will, decrees, promises, and counsels, as taught in Malachi 3:6, Isaiah 46:10, and Romans 11:29.[465]

First, there are the simple declarations of changelessness, found negatively expressed in Malachi 3:16 and James 1:17 and affirmatively in Exodus 3:14-16, Psalm 102:27, and Hebrews 1:11-12.[466] James 1:17, Turretin comments, not only denies change but any hint or "shadow" of change in God: even the sun, that "fountain of immaterial light," can be obscured by clouds and eclipses, but God's influence cannot be impeded. He is the father of lights, immutable beyond the seeming changelessness of all created luminaries.[467]

Second, such texts as Isaiah 46:10, "My counsel shall stand, and I will do all my pleasure," and Proverbs 19:21, "The counsel of the Lord shall stand" (cf. Psalm 33:11; Prov. 21:30; Isa. 14:24; Heb. 6:17), indicate the changelessness of God's counsel, and therefore of his knowledge and will or decree.[468] This is confirmed in such passages as 2 Corinthians 1:18-20, where the truth of God and the promise of the gospel are shown to be "infallible," and "inviolable."[469] In the case of Matthew 5:18, "Till heaven and earth pass, one jot or one tittle shall in no wise pass from the law, till all be fulfilled," the text reflects the identification of the law as "the certain and unchangeable will of God concerning reasonable creatures."[470] This in turn implies the changeless essence or nature of the one who has such counsel.[471]

Third, God is not subject to changes in will, such as are usually identified with repentance: Numbers 23:19 and 1 Samuel 15:29. The orthodox writers know, of course, that these texts can be juxtaposed with declarations that God repents (e.g., Genesis 6:6), but they draw on the larger array of texts concerning immutability and eternity to argue the case for viewing the texts concerning divine repentance as anthropopathisms. They also can point out the different status of the texts: whereas there are a few texts in which God is said to repent, in no text does God declare that he repents. On the other hand, God does specifically declare that he does not repent. The text presents, above all, God's constancy "in his mercifull promises" — directing our attention to one of the "names and essentiall properties of God, whereby he is known to be God,

---

465. Zanchi, De natura Dei, II.iv (col. 77).

466. Zanchi, De natura Dei, II.iv.2 (col. 78); cf. Leigh, Treatise, II.v (pp. 43-44); Venema, Inst. theol., vi (p. 143); Ridgley, Body of Divinity (1855), I, pp. 88-89.

467. Turretin, Inst. theol. elencticae, III.xi.3.

468. Rijssen, Summa, III.xxi, argumenta; cf. Turretin, Inst. theol. elencticae, III.xi.3; cf. Dutch Annotations, Ps. 33:11, in loc.; Day, Exposition of Isaiah, 42:10, in loc.; Henry, Exposition, Is. 14:24, in loc.

469. Henry, Exposition, 2 Cor. 1:18-20, in loc.

470. Poole, Commentary, Matt. 5:18, in loc. (III, p. 22); cf. Henry, Exposition, in loc.

471. Rijssen, Summa, III.xxi, argumenta; cf. Turretin, Inst. theol. elencticae, III.xi.3.

who is unchangeably good, unchangeably holy, unchangeably just and mercifull, and is found firme and faithfull in all his promises."[472] Here Scripture speaks "properly" concerning the nature of God, as it also does in 1 Samuel 15:29 — in contrast to those places where it speaks "unproperly and figuratively for our capacity." "The change is not in GOD, but in his worke," as the general sense of Scripture indicates, consistently identifying him as unchangeable "in all his waies, words, and works," in his decrees, judgments, mercies, and goodness.[473] As in the case of Calvin's teaching, the orthodox reading of the doctrine of immutability has specific reference to the constancy of God in all that he wills, most especially to the work of salvation.

Fourth, such texts as Psalm 90:2, 102:26, and 110:4 indicate the divine eternity in terms of its contrast with the changeableness of temporal things — in the first instance, the earth and mountains, in the second, human repentance. So also does the divine name, Jehovah, imply both the eternity and the immutability of God.[474]

5. Immutability and reason: theological argumentation and philosophical support for the traditionary exegesis. Underlying the more philosophical or rational component of the orthodox discussion of divine immutability, there is the understanding of a necessary difference between God and his creatures, particularly given the variability, mutability, and fallibility of the creatures:

A reasonable creature may be changed five ways: (1) In respect of existence, if it exist sometimes and sometimes not. (2) In respect of place, if it be moved from one place to another. (3) In respect of accidents, if it be changed in quantity or quality. (4) In respect of the knowledge of the understanding, as if it now think that to be true, which before it judged to be false. (5) In respect of the purpose of will, if it now decree to do something, which before it decreed not to do. God is not changed in any of these ways.[475]

By way of contrast, God cannot cease to exist. Neither does God alter in his essential properties — as most clearly indicated by his omniscience and his eternal purpose. The confession of God's infinite essence and power implies the immutability of God and the eternity, "for he that is infinite can neither be moved nor changed ... and ... cannot be extended, neither concerning Essence, nor concerning work."[476] Similarly, the spirituality of God implies immutability, as opposed to materiality and all its accompanying *predicamenta*, in particular that of "movability" or "motion." These assumptions lead to the rational argument:

---

472. William Attersoll, A *commentarie upon the fourth booke of Moses, called Numbers; containing the foundation of the church and common-wealth of the Israelites, while they walked and wandered in the wildernesse ... Wherein the whole body of divinity is handled touching matters dogmatical ... ceremoniall ...[and] polemicall* (London: William Jaggard, 1618), 23:19, in loc. (p. 951).

473. Attersoll, *Commentarie upon Numbers*, 23:19, in loc. (pp. 951-952).

474. Brakel, *Redelijke Godsdienst*, I.iii.14; on "Jehovah," see above, 4.2 (B.2-3).

475. Leigh, *Treatise*, II.v (pp. 44-45); Cocceius, *Summa theol.* III.ix.46.

476. Trelcatius, *Schol. meth.*, I.iii (pp. 66-67).

It may be demonstrated rationally [that God is immutable], for God can neither change for the better, since he is the best, nor for the worse, since he cannot cease to be most perfect. Granting this, such causes of mutation as dependence on something prior or passive potency, error of mind or inconstancy of will are also not to be attributed to God.[477]

Further, the immutability of God may be argued from the divine names and other divine attributes: Jehovah, which identifies God as *ipsum Ens*, being itself, existing always and of itself — and, therefore, immutable, given that mutability arises from having a created nature that comes from nothing. The divine simplicity argues immutability, inasmuch as mutation belongs to composite being, arising specifically from the composition of essence and existence, actuality and potency (which, of course, are excluded from God). The infinity and immensity of God indicate immutability as they exclude change of place — as eternity excludes temporal change. God alone, then, is immutable inasmuch as all other things are created *ex nihilo* and, as created, cannot be simple, infinite (in the eminent sense that God is), or eternal.[478] God's immutability can also be argued "from his perfection: all change is a kind of imperfection; there is indeed a change corruptive and perfective; but the perfective alteration supposeth the Subject to be imperfect" — or, in a negative statement of the same logic,

> If God should change, then either he must change for the better, and then he was not best and perfect before; or for the worse, and then he is not best now [i.e., subsequent to the change].
>
> If he should be changed, it must be from some other thing stronger than himself, and there is none such. Nothing without him can change him, because he is omnipotent; and nothing within him, for there is no ignorance in his mind, inconstancy in his will, nor impotency in his power.[479]

These arguments are not countered by the fact that God creates, "since, by this act, God is possessed of nothing in himself other than what he previously had, rather he only adds a new relation to himself."[480] Nor does it imply mutability to claim that "when God first began to act Externally, there was a Change in him," even when the argument claims that there was a time before the creation of the world when God was not creating and that he began creating in time. This is a "Relative change" that "implies no Imperfection."[481] God is certainly the agent of creation, but change occurs in an agent only when, in the accomplishment of its act, it becomes different from what it was before the act. But this is not the case in creation: nothing new can be said to occur to God in creation, given that he eternally wills it. There is a change, brought about by creation, relative to the creature, which has passed from nonexistence

---

477. Rijssen, *Summa theol.*, III.xxi, argumentum 2; cf. Venema, *Inst. theol.*, vi (p. 143).

478. Zanchi, *De natura Dei*, II.iv, qq. 1.3, 2.1 (col. 77-79).

479. Leigh, *Treatise*, II.v (pp. 45-46).

480. Rijssen, *Summa theol.*, III.xxi, resp. and obj. 1.

481. Edwards, *Theologia Reformata*, I, pp. 134-135.

into existence — so that there is a "new relation" *ad extra* between God and the now-existent creature. Since, however, the act of creation is not an immanent act in the Godhead, but a "transient" act, passing over from God to the creature, the change is *ad extra*, not *ad intra*.[482] (Note that the orthodox do not deny that, from a temporal perspective, God enters into new relations — they only deny that such "accidental" properties as external relations belong to the divine being. Since they are not "in" God, their alteration indicates no change in the divine being.)[483]

God eternally and changelessly wills many different things to occur at different times. God institutes and then permits the abrogation of the covenant of works. He inaugurates the covenant of grace to be administered under various temporal economies.[484] God also changelessly willed to create the world in time and later to destroy it by a flood. Nor does the divine "institution" and subsequent "abrogation" of the Levitical code pose a change in God. Even the incarnation does not indicate a change in God, inasmuch as the Logos was incarnate by "conversion" into flesh — rather the flesh was assumed by the person or hypostasis of the Word, as God eternally willed. As implied by the denial of "passive potency" to God, the *potentia Dei* does not by its operation add anything to God, but only brings about new relations *ad extra* as it operates to actualize the finite order: "It is one thing to alter the will, another to will the mutation of some thing" — "Aliud est *mutare voluntatem*, aliud *velle* alicujus rei *mutationem*."[485]

> And so in all the Changes that happen in the World, in the several Ages of it, the case is the same. It is the permanent, and unchangeable Will of God, that he will act and influence on his Creatures, especially Men, as there is occasion. It is his immutable Decree that he will produce such and such alterations in the World, and at such a time. God himselfe is Immoveable and Unchangeable though he moveth and changeth all things. We move, not God. We are changed, not He.[486]

6. Objections to divine immutability. The affirmation of immutability confronts several obstacles. A first obstacle to the concept of divine immutability is the attribution of "affections" (*affectus*) to God — which occurs throughout Scripture and which, given its exegetical significance, forms a large part of the orthodox doctrine of the divine attributes.[487] A second objection concerns the divine freedom and the variation of acts of the divine will: there is a profound difference, Turretin argues, between liberty and mutability. In God, the former arises out of the ultimate indifference of the divine will prior to the decree and from the absence of any compulsion on God. The eternal decree is utterly free but, once decreed, immutable. The Reformed insist that God,

---

482. Turretin, *Inst. theol. elencticae*, III.xi.5.

483. Daneau, *Christianae isagoges*, I.7-8.

484. Edwards, *Theologia Reformata*, I, p. 135. Note that the *pactum salutis* serves, among other things, to manifest the eternal foundation of the temporal administrations of the covenant.

485. Turretin, *Inst. theol. elencticae*, III.xi.6-7; Rijssen, *Summa theol.*, III.xxi, obj. 2.

486. Edwards, *Theologia Reformata*, I, p. 135.

487. See further, below, 6.3 (A.1).

in his eternity, "could have determined himself to other objects than those he has decreed" but pointedly deny that the decree, once willed, can be rescinded. Variations of divine willing appear because of the varied objects of the divine will — objects that are mutable — not because of mutations in the will itself, nor is the ground of mutability (*principium mutabilitatis*) in the divine will, but in the objects themselves.[488]

A third objection encountered by the orthodox is the concept of a finite God advanced by Conrad Vorstius and the Socinians — the Socinians adding that God is a composite of qualities. Both of these obstacles to the doctrine imply mutability, and in particular a mutability according to place: can God change his location? The issue is important, granting that the orthodox position had been challenged by Vorstius, who argued the finitude of the divine essence and its location in heaven, while the Socinians so argued the finitude of God that they understood him as moving from place to place! Mastricht counters that the biblical assumption that in God there is no shadow of change extends to the issue of place as well, granting that the divine essence is infinite, omnipresent, immense — as Scripture often states — filling heaven and earth.[489] When Scripture says that God is in heaven, it does not mean that he is only in heaven; rather, it identifies him as exalted and sovereign. Even so must references to his ascending and descending be interpreted in accordance with his infinitude and omnipresence as indicating "*praesentiam suam extraordinariam, ad finem & opus extraordinarium, extraordinario modo patefacit*," namely, an extraordinary presence directed toward a specific end, not a change of place, and not referring at all to his essence.[490]

The concept of divine immutability also led the orthodox to clarify the work of the Word in creation: it is not as if God began to "speak" and thus changed inwardly or intrinsically. Rather, God "spoke from eternity" in his essential wisdom concerning the temporal creation. "Creation is nothing but God's will from eternity, that the world should exist in time, so that the creature hath something now, which it had not before, but God's will hath not" anything new added to it.[491] The Reformed understanding of this attribute, moreover, far from being a purely philosophical or metaphysical category unrelated to Christian doctrine, becomes in the working out of system the ontological ground of soteriological argument:

> The Lord hath revealed himself to be one and unchangeable, as in nature so in will, Heb. 13:8. [So also] Rom. 3:29, shewing that God is one in nature, truth and constancy,

---

488. Turretin, *Inst. theol. elencticae*, III.xi.9-10; and see below, 4.3 (F.3, 5).

489. Mastricht, *Theoretico-practica theol.*, II.vii.8 citing, Jer. 23:24; Josh. 2:11; Ps. 139:7-10; Acts 7:49; 17:24-28; cf. Leigh, *Treatise*, II.v (pp. 44-45); Watson, *Body of Divinity*, p. 27; and see below, 4.4 (C.2-3).

490. Mastricht, *Theoretico-practica theol.*, II.vii.8, and note the identical interpretation in Calvin, *Harmony of the Four Last Books of Moses*, Ex. 3:8; 19:12; Deut. 12:7; Ex. 34:5 (CTS *Harmony*, I, pp. 68, 325; II, p. 132; III, p. 385); cf. Owen, *Vindiciae evangelicae*, in *Works*, 12, pp. 89-91, contra Biddle, *Duae catecheses* (London: s.n., 1664), II, pp. 26-8.

491. Leigh, *Treatise*, II.v (p. 47); cf. Wendelin, *Christ. theol.*, I.i.

and that as well toward the Gentiles as toward the Jews, so he would justify both the circumcision and the uncircumcision.[492]

A similar approach to the doctrine is found in the theology of John Owen, particularly in his *The Doctrine of the Saints Perseverance Explained and Confirmed*.[493]

7. *Usus practicus*: piety and the confession of divine immutability. The concept of divine immutability therefore also carries with it a series of lessons for faith:

(1) This is terrible to wicked men: God is unchangeable which hath threatened to curse them and bring destruction upon them; they must change, or else there is no repealing of the curse [1 Sam 15:18].

(2) It comforts the godly, to whom he hath made many promises, Num. 23:19-20; Heb. 13:5. He is constant and will perform them. He told *Adam* that the seed of the woman should break the Serpent's head. He was long, but sure, for it was fulfilled at the last. His Covenant is everlasting, Isaiah 55:3; [He says], "I am God and I change not, therefore you are not consumed, Mal. 3:6; we should labor for God's love: it is a freehold, and like himself immutable; whom he loves once, he loves forever. God's people shall never fall from grace, shall never be wholly overcome of temptations.

(3) We should imitate God's Immutability in a gracious way, be constant in our love to God and men, in our promises and good purposes.... We should pray for the establishment of our faith and patience [Gal. 6:9; 2 Tim. 3:14; 1 Cor. 15:58].

(4) We should admire the glorious nature of God; for what an Infinite Glorious God must he be, which hath had all that happiness and glory from eternity. [Further, we should] worship the true God, because he is Immutable, and we shall be so hereafter, being made most like to him, Psalm 102:27.

(5) It confutes the Eutychians, and Ubiquitarians which held that the God-head became flesh; can a Spirit be a body, and both visible and invisible.[494]

Here, where Aristotelianism and metaphysics, not to mention philosophical rationalism, might easily have made great inroads, we encounter generally restrained discussion of the attributes: God's immutability is not a springboard for speculation but a ground of Christian faith and hope in the God whose nature and therefore whose intention and will cannot change: "believers," writes Brakel, should "be comforted by the immutability of the Lord, for all the promises of which [they] are the heirs will most certainly be fulfilled."[495] So, too, ought the sinner to look to the divine immutability and recognize that the divine "threatenings and judgments" will fall on him unless he repents.[496] Mastricht similarly notes that the immutability of God is a foundation for belief and piety.[497] The continental theologians' insistence on the

---

492. Leigh, *Treatise*, II.viii (p. 142); cf. Olevian, *Exposition of the Symbole*, p. 65.

493. Owen, *Doctrine of the Saints Perseverance*, in *Works*, vol. XI, pp. 1-666.

494. Leigh, *Treatise*, II.v (pp. 47-48).

495. Brakel, *Redelijke Godsdienst*, I.iii.15 (*Reasonable Service*, I, p. 101); cf. Baxter, *Divine Life*, I.vi.3; and note Preus' remarks on the Lutheran doctrine in *Theology of Post-Reformation Lutheranism*, vol. II, pp. 100-101.

496. Brakel, *Redelijke Godsdienst*, I.iii.15.

497. Mastricht, *Theoretico-practica theol.*, II.vii.9-14.

practical implication of the concept of divine immutability was shared by British Reformed divines of the orthodox era: Binning writes that "when we think on his unchangeableness, let us consider our own vanity, whose glory and perfection is like a summer flower.... To be one thing, and then another thing, is a property of sinful and wretched man." Therefore, we ought not to put our ultimate trust in finite things, but in "God, 'who changeth not.'"[498]

G. Perfection and Necessity

1. Perfection. The concepts of divine perfection and divine necessity stand as corollaries, inasmuch as perfection stands over against the imperfection of contingent existence. They are also variously treated by the Reformed — sometimes as distinct attributes identified for individual treatment, sometimes as implications of the discussion of other attributes, sometimes in conjunction, sometimes separately. Divine perfection, moreover, was certainly an integral element of Reformed teaching from Zwingli onward.[499] By way of basic definition,

> God is absolutely and simply perfect, because he hath all things which are to be desired for the chiefest felicity. He is perfect first, in the highest degree of perfection, simply without any respect or comparison; secondly he is perfect in all kinds, 1 John 1:5. John saith he is light in which there is no darkness; that is, Perfect and Pure without the least mixture of the contrary, the Author and cause of all perfections in the creatures, [these perfections] are all in him, but more perfectly and in a more perfect manner. God is most absolutely Perfect, Job 22:2; Psalm 16:2; Matt. 5:48. The words in Scripture which signify this are, (1) *Schaddai*, which is as much as one sufficient to help himself, or one that gives nourishment to all other things, and therefore, Gen. 17:1, when God was to make a Covenant with Abraham, to leave all earthly things, and so trust in him only, he brings this argument, that he was such a sufficient God. (2) *Gomer*: the verb is used five times in the Psalms (7:10; cf. 7:6-8; 137:9; 53:3; 11:1). (3) *Tamim*, Job 37:16: it signifieth both Simple and Perfect.[500]

The orthodox differ in their understanding and placement of the concept of divine perfection. On one hand, divine perfection can be defined as a "derivative" rather than as an ultimate or "primitive" attribute of the divine essence.[501] On the other hand, perfection can be understood as not merely one among other divine attributes, but, in language reminiscent of nominalism, of the divine essence itself — although the Reformed tendency to speak of "perfections" rather than of a sole, undifferentiated "perfection," stands in the way of a strictly Ockhamist approach to the problem of

---

498. Binning, *Common Principles*, in *Works*, p. 46; cf. Baxter, *Divine Life*, I.vi.3.

499. Zwingli, *Commentary on True and False Religion*, pp. 65, 67.

500. Leigh, *Treatise*, II.vi (p. 49); cf. Le Blanc, *Theses theol.*, *De perfectione et infinitate Dei*, xix, on the meaning of Shaddai.

501. Mastricht, *Theoretico-practica theol.*, II.xxi.1; cf. II.v.9.

the attributes.[502] "Perfections" (*perfectiones, volmaaktheden*) is, accordingly, a term used by the many of the scholastics as an alternative to "attributes" (*attributa, eigenschappen*).[503] It can be understood as the basic conception of the divine essence from which a right understanding of the attributes can be inferred,[504] as a conclusion to be drawn from right consideration of the whole series of divine attributes,[505] or as a corollary or implicate of one or another of the attributes, such as necessity, infinity, independence, immutability, simplicity, and self-existence.[506]

The perfection of God can be argued logically from the other attributes as well as scripturally:

> (1) That which is the chiefest being and Independent is most perfect. (2) That which is infinite in essence can want nothing. (3) The more simple a thing is, the more perfect.[507]

Unlike his creatures, God depends on nothing "from the outside" for his perfection.[508] To this series can be added, therefore, (4) that God is perfect *privatively*, by the removal of all creaturely imperfection: we understand God to be perfect in that all such imperfections as contingency, dependence, limitation, composition, alteration, and multiplication are absent from God: he is necessary, independent, unlimited, simple, unchangeable, and one.[509] In brief, God is called perfect inasmuch as "no perfection is wanting in him" and inasmuch as imperfection is understood as existing *in potentia passiva*, "in a passive power to some act; but God is pure act, and in him there is no power that is passive."[510] There neither is nor can be conceived any perfection that is not in God in a more eminent and excellent way than it is in human beings, or angels, or any other creatures.[511]

Further, a series of arguments parallel to the rational presentation of the doctrine, indicating the ways in which God is understood to be perfect, can be drawn from various biblical texts. First, God is perfect essentially. As Mastricht indicates in his preliminary exegetical discussion, Genesis 17:1, "I am God Almighty (*El Shaddai*)," carries with it a double sense and can also indicate, "I am the sufficient one," having

---

502. Cf. Van Til, *Theol. revelata comp.*, I.ii; Francken, *Kern der Christelijke Leer*, III, q. 24-25 (p. 57); Leigh, *Body of Divinity*, II.vi (p. 183).

503. E.g., Mastricht, *Theoretico-practica theol.*, II.v.7; Brakel, *Redelijke Godsdienst*, I.iii.7; Howe, *Living Temple*, I.iv (p. 87); Ridgley, *Body of Divinity* (1855), I, pp. 79-80; and cf. above, 3.3 (C.2).

504. Walaeus, *Loci communes*, pp. 159-160; Grotius, *De veritate*, I.iv.

505. Ames, *Marrow*, I.iv.66

506. Burman, *Synopsis theol.*, I.xviii.4;cf. Le Blanc, *Theses theol.*, De perfectione et infinitate Dei, i.

507. Leigh, *Treatise*, II.vi (p. 49); Le Blanc, *Theses theol.*, De perfectione et infinitate Dei, i.

508. Brakel, *Redelijke Godsdienst*, I.iii.8; Walaeus, *Loci communes*, p. 160.

509. Leigh, *Treatise*, II.vi (p. 51); cf. Brakel, *Redelijke Godsdienst*, I.iii.8; Grotius, *De veritate*, I.v; Amyraut et al., *Syntagma thesium theologicarum*, I.xiii.22.

510. Walaeus, *Loci communes*, p. 160; Pierre Du Moulin, *A Treatise of the Knowledge of God*, trans. Robert Codrington (London: A. M., 1634), p. 27; Le Blanc, *Theses theol.*, De perfectione et infinitate Dei, ii-iii.

511. Walaeus, *Loci communes*, p. 160.

all goodness and perfection.[512] Similarly, looking to Matthew 5:48, "God is perfect ... essentially; he is Perfect, in and by himself, containing in him all perfections eminently" — or, as it might be said, "He hath all needful to a Deity."[513] As Poole points out with specific reference to Matt. 5:48, "*Perfect* here is not taken in that sense as it is taken in other texts of Scripture, where it signifieth sincerity and uprightness ... but for an absolute perfection ... so much is signified by the proposing of our heavenly Father as our example."[514]

Second, God is perfect in that "nothing is wanting to him; he hath no need of any other thing outside of himself, Job 22:2, 3; Psalm 16:2."[515] "Can a man be profitable unto God," asks the text of Job 22:2 — or, as the exegetical tradition questions, can human beings "add anything to his perfection or felicity?"[516] Reformed citation of Ps. 16:2, "my goodness extendeth not to Thee," in this context reflects a long exegetical tradition in which the Septuagint rendering, "of my goods you have no need," is brought to bear on the text,[517] and draws on the natural association of the Psalm with the teaching of Job 22.[518] Nothing that we can offer, writes Poole, can "add anything to Thy felicity."[519] Similarly, Job 37:16 tells of the perfect knowledge of God.[520]

Third, God is perfect "originally" as the absolutely "first" or "prior" being, the first and the last, the beginning and the end of all things, as testified in Revelation 1:4, 8.[521] So also, he is the cause of all perfection; what hast thou, which thou hast not received? (James 1:17)."[522] As Poole comments on the text, "*And every perfect gift*; the highest degree of good gifts, those that perfect us most; to intimate that all the parts and steps of spiritual life, from the first beginning of grace in regeneration to the consummation of it in glory, are of God."[523]

Fourth, God is perfect "operatively: all his works are perfect, Deut. 32:4."[524] This perfection arises from the will of God and is understood as the divine omnipotence by which God "perfectly" executes his will "in reference to possible things."[525] Thus, in a more practical sense, related to piety, God's works "both of creation and redemption of his people ... are said to be perfect, or unblemished, because there is

512. Mastricht, *Theoretico-practica theologia*, II.xxi.2.

513. Leigh, *Treatise*, II.vi (p. 49); cf. Mastricht, *Theoretico-practica theol.*, II.xxi.3.

514. Poole, *Commentary*, III, p. 26; cf. Calvin, *Harmony of the Evangelists*, in loc. (CTS *Harmony*, I, p. 308).

515. Leigh, *Treatise*, II.vi (p. 49).

516. Poole, *Commentary*, II, p. 975; cf. Henry, *Exposition*, in loc.

517. Cf. Ainsworth, *Psalmes*, in loc., citing the LXX with Calvin, *Commentary upon the Book of Psalms*, in loc. (CTS *Psalms* I, p. 217).

518. Cf. Calvin, *Sermons on Job*, p. 389, col. 1, citing Ps. 16:2.

519. Poole, *Commentary*, II, p. 21; cf. Mastricht, *Theoretico-practica theol.*, II.xxi.3.

520. Mastricht, *Theoretico-practica theol.*, II.xxi.3.

521. Mastricht, *Theoretico-practica theol.*, II.xxi.4.

522. Leigh, *Treatise*, II.vi (p. 49); cf. Le Blanc, *Theses theol.*, De perfectione et infinitate Dei, v-vi.

523. Poole, *Commentary*, in loc. (III, p. 882).

524. Leigh, *Treatise*, II.vi (p. 49).

525. Venema, *Inst. theol.*, vi (p. 159)

no defect, or fault, in any of them" — he is the source and efficient cause of all that is good and perfect in the creation.[526]

For Mastricht, there is a considerable amount at stake polemically in the confession of God's perfection. It is clear to him that the Pelagians and Semi-Pelagians of his day, the Jesuits and Remonstrants, together with the Socinians, attack the notion of divine perfection — not directly, but by the implication of their various other doctrinal assumptions. The doctrine of radically independent choice on the part of human beings, held by all three groups, under the pretext of harmonizing the doctrines of grace, providence, contingency, and free choice, only serves to undercut the perfection of God. When, for example, they argue the independent choice of human beings as providing a prior condition for divine willing, they undermine the perfect independence of the divine will. When they argue that there is in God an unfulfilled or imperfect will, they similarly render God imperfect — as if he cannot produce what he wills.[527] And as for the Socinians, their "implacable hatred" of traditional doctrine of the divine attributes, the deity of Christ, the Trinity, Christ's satisfaction, and our justification according to the righteousness of Christ alone renders their teaching utterly incompatible with a confession of the perfection and sufficiency of an infinite God. Christ's satisfaction, for example, presupposes the essential holiness and justice of God, which they, accordingly, deny. The Trinity points toward ultimate perfection of the most blessed society of divine persons, which they would destroy. And, of course, together with Conrad Vorstius, the Socinians deny divine simplicity, infinity, omniscience, and vindicatory justice.[528]

By way of contrast, affirmation of God's perfection is a strong support of piety, for "We should choose the Lord to be our portion, for in him alone is true happiness, and contentedness to be found; in our wants we should confidently go to him for help, he being perfect can supply them." Since God is the inexhaustible fountain of good things, "we should place all our confidence in God alone, expect all good things from him."[529] This divine perfection also stands in contrast to the "imperfection, insufficiency, and vanity" of all created things, none of which can supply our needs as God can.[530] Scripture also tells us to imitate him, to "be Perfect as our heavenly Father is perfect," to "*let Patience have her perfect work*," and "*let us perfect holiness in his fear*."[531] Quite specifically, Scripture connects the identification of God as the sufficient or perfect one with the command and promise, "walk before me, and be perfect, and I will make my covenant..." (Gen. 17:1-2), so that our belief in God's perfection or sufficiency ought to make us want to walk before him also.[532] Similarly,

---

526. Ainsworth, *Annotations upon Deuteronomy*, Deut. 32:4, in loc.; Walaeus, *Loci communes*, p. 160.

527. Mastricht, *Theoretico-practica theol.*, II.xxi.10.

528. Mastricht, *Theoretico-practica theol.*, II.xxi.9.

529. Leigh, *Treatise*, II.vi (pp. 53-54).

530. Mastricht, *Theoretico-practica theol.*, II.xxi.11.

531. Leigh, *Body of Divinity*, II.vi (p. 186), citing Deut. 18:13; Matt. 5:48.

532. Mastricht, *Theoretico-practica theol.*, II.xxi.15.

This may also serve to comfort the godly in their weakness; God will make his works perfect (Ps. 18:22). He that hath begun a good work in them will perfect it; they should be comforted therefore against all their imperfections to which they are subject in this life, and seek perfection in him. He will supply all their wants, bear with them here, and make them perfect in the other life (1 Cor. 15:28, 40-49; 1 Cor. 13:10).[533]

2. Divine necessity. As in the discussions of divine perfection, so in the discussions of the divine necessity is there remarkable diversity among the Reformed, although all, certainly, agreed on the basic concept of God as necessarily existing. The Reformed orthodox often fail to separate this concept from the doctrines of perfection, independence, sufficiency, aseity, and immutability, and they often identify it as an issue only in the context of the traditional proofs of God's existence.[534] When found among the proofs, it functions as a demonstration of God's existence from the existence of unnecessary or contingent creatures, as the ground of their existence — when found among the attributes, it functions as an explanation of the relation of God to the world: the dual placement serves to reinforce our earlier conclusion that the Reformed theologies of the era of orthodoxy do not function in a purely deductive manner.

The divine necessity is understood as the necessary existence of a first cause: inasmuch as the entire world order is caused and contingent, its existence can only be explained in terms of a first, uncaused, or noncontingent cause. Such a cause will be necessary — "necessarily existing, and always existing without any capability or possibility ever not to be."[535]

> Contingency is found in the essence of every creature: it might not have been, as well as have been; it may not be, as well as be ... there was an equal or greater possibility of its not being, than its being.
>
> God is a necessary essence: it is absolutely necessary that he should be, and he cannot but be and be as he is; and his actions upon himself are altogether and simply necessary, they must be as they be, and cannot but be so.[536]

This sense of necessary existence also appears in Edwards' discussion of the existence of God: he refrains from discussing the proofs in his *Theologia Reformata*, reserving this discussion for apologetics, and discusses existence, not in order "to prove that there is such a thing, but ... under the Notion of an Attribute," indeed, as the "first attribute" of God and the "foundation of all God's other Attributes," given that "it is Natural and Essential to him *to be*": "Existence is necessarily contained in our Notion and Conception of Divine Being."[537] In this sense, "we may conclude from our Idea of him that he is," although "that ingenious Philosopher who argues from the Idea

533. Leigh, *Treatise*, II.vi (p. 54).
534. See above 4.1 (B.1, independence); and below 5.2 (A.1-2, aseity, sufficiency).
535. Charnock, *Existence and Attributes*, I (I, p. 51).
536. Leigh, *Treatise*, II.vi (p. 56).
537. Edwards, *Theologia Reformata*, I, pp. 44, 46.

of God to his Existence" and his followers, "have so stretched" the argument "as to make it Inconclusive."[538]

Pictet offers an extended definition of the divine necessity, arguing "that God is a Being who necessarily exists, is evident" for a series of reasons: first, "necessary existence belongs to the nature of an all-perfect Being, since if it were possible to conceive a most perfect being without necessary existence, it would [also] be conceived without perfection."[539] This, of course, would imply a contradiction. In addition, necessary existence is an implicate of divine simplicity and the identity of essence and existence in God.[540] Furthermore,

> if God is not the necessarily existing Being, he would be capable of not existing — but if this be granted, as evident impossibility will arise; for God did not then derive his existence from another, since we can have no idea of a being so perfect as God, and therefore no being could confer upon another a perfection which it did not itself possess. Neither could he be self-existent (*a se ipso*), if it were assumed that he [at one time] did not exist; it is therefore impossible [that he is not self-existent].[541]

Perhaps more interesting than the argument itself is its clear rootage in the scholasticism of the medieval doctors, looking back to the argumentation of Anselm's *Prosolgion*. Beyond this basic definition, moreover, is the firm distinction that must be made between "necessity of being" and "necessity of operation," inasmuch as the necessity of the being or existence of God is not to be opposed to the freedom of the divine will or the divine "power to act, or forbear." Indeed, the divine necessity implies that God is the foundation of all motion in the universe and the fundamental power of being, having "power over [his] own essence" and the power to bring all finite things into being.[542]

4.4 Divine Infinity, Eternity, and Related Attributes

A. The Divine Infinity

1. Basic definitions and biblical foundations. The Protestant orthodox doctrine of the divine infinity, although at certain points more philosophically stated than the position of the Reformers, retains a considerable affinity for the theology of the Reformation, particularly in its biblicism and in its attention to the ways in which the biblical language of God modifies and redefines the concepts drawn from philosophy, while at the same time drawing on the resources of patristic and, especially, medieval scholastic theology. The great difference between the Protestant scholastics and the Reformers, here, as in the discussion of other attributes, is that they move away from the discursive or somewhat more oratorical style of a Calvin to a clearly scholastic

---

538. Edwards, *Theologia Reformata*, I, p. 46.
539. Pictet, *Theol. chr.*, II.xi.1.
540. Le Blanc, *Theses theol.*, *De Dei simplicitate*, xvii-xviii.
541. Pictet, *Theol. chr.*, II.xi.2.
542. Ward, *Philosophicall Essay*, I.iii (pp. 20-21).

style of exposition, adding to the "religious," "literary," and "practical" purpose noted by Warfield in his exposition of Calvin's doctrine of God a strongly technical and disputative or polemical interest.[543] Of course, even here, the stylistic difference is relative, inasmuch as there are scholastic and disputative elements in Calvin's exposition and there are clear influences of humanist rhetoric and logic in the Reformed scholastic theology.

Calvin and his contemporaries wrote little concerning the divine infinity in the more technical sense: like divine simplicity and spirituality, this is a doctrine that Calvin affirmed without either much explanation or much debate.[544] He also identified God as immeasurable, eternal, beyond any human comprehension, and infinite in various of his attributes, such as power.[545] Virtually all of these arguments remain within the framework of basic statement, exegetical, or homiletical formulation. The burden of scholastic Reformed exposition of the doctrine was to retain the practical side of the doctrine while at the same time adding the technical and philosophical dimension as a means to the end of refuting the problematic views of various adversaries — notably Vorstius and the Socinians. The argumentative structure of the orthodox doctrine, moreover, rests primarily on assumptions taken from a traditionary exegesis of the biblical revelation of God's relationship to the temporal economy rather than from a series of philosophical assumptions about the being of God. The problems encountered and resolved, exegetically, dogmatically, and polemically, by the orthodox in discussing the divine infinity, eternity, immensity, and omnipresence are representative of the orthodox doctrine of the attributes: we see here the entrance of certain philosophical considerations, in particular, the ontological implications of biblical statements concerning the greatness of God in relation to temporal things. The frequent references to Christ and the Spirit manifest the profound connection between the discussion of essence and attributes and the doctrine of the Trinity — and the way in which God relates to the world, both in general in the work of providence and in the "special" work of grace and salvation, remains of paramount interest to the orthodox.

Orthodox Reformed discussion of the *infinitas Dei* varies in form and approach, particularly among the thinkers of the early orthodox era. The concept can be used, like the *simplicitas Dei*, as a way of describing all of the divine attributes,[546] or it can be formulated as one among many attributes.[547] Although, moreover, the Reformed orthodox follow the fathers in understanding God as by nature infinite "in all respects,"[548] there are significant differences in formulation. Some thinkers, like Perkins,

---

543. Cf. Warfield, "Calvin's Doctrine of God," p. 133.

544. Calvin, *Institutes*. I.xiii.1.

545. Cf. Calvin, *Commentary upon the Psalms*, 90:2; 102:24; 145:1, in loc. (*CTS Psalms*, III, pp. 462-463; IV, pp. 120-121; V, pp. 272-273); with *Commentaries on Daniel*, 4:34 (*CTS Daniel*, I, p. 296); *Commentary on Isaiah*, 40:12 (*CTS Isaiah*, III, p. 217).

546. E.g., Twisse, *Discovery*, pp. 69-86.

547. E.g., Turretin, *Inst. theol. elencticae*, III.viii.

548. Cf. e.g, Gregory of Nyssa, *On "Not Three Gods,"* in *NPNF* 2 ser. V, p. 335; Gregory of Nazianzen, *On the Theophany*, vii-viii, in *NPNF* 2 ser. VII, p. 346-347; Augustine, *De civitate Dei*,

present divine infinity in terms of both the divine transcendence of time and the divine transcendence of space,[549] while others, like Trelcatius, tend to explain the concept in terms of God's transcendence of "magnitude" and "multitude" — and therefore as utterly distinct from what is experienced in the temporal and even the mathematical order.[550] Flavel rather nicely points out that the divine infinity or boundlessness ought to be considered in "three respects": first, the divine immensity or according to which the "perfection of his nature; his wisdom, power, and holiness, exceed all measures and limits"; second, the immeasurability of God "in respect of time and place," namely, eternity and omnipresence; and third, "in respect of his incomprehensibleness."[551] These affirmations of orthodoxy stand, moreover, against the claims of seventeenth-century Socinians, who, in their more extreme moments, denied the infinity and incomprehensibility of God.[552]

In both their exegetical and their dogmatic works, moreover, the Reformed orthodox identify a series of biblical approaches to the concept of divine infinity: God is infinite affirmatively and negatively (Psalm 145:3) in himself, and comparatively (Job 11:8; Isaiah 40:12, 15; Daniel 4:34) in relation to creatures.[553] The divine infinity can also be affirmed originally, formally, and virtually: originally, because nothing is prior to God; formally, because the divine essence is absolutely infinite; and virtually, because the *virtus* or strength of God has no limitation, needs no *concursus*, and accomplished all that God wills.[554]

Perkins understands the divine infinity as the primary attribute in the second half of his Ramistic division of the topic of divine perfection (the first half having consisted in simplicity and related attributes). Here, too, he offers a bifurcation of the topic, identifying infinity as consisting either in eternity or in greatness understood as omnipresence:

> The infiniteness of God is twofold: his eternity, and exceeding greatness. God's eternity is that by which he is without beginning and ending (Ps. 90:1-2; Rev. 1:8). ... God's exceeding greatness (Ps. 145:3), is that by which his incomprehensible nature is everywhere present, both within and without the world (1 Kg. 8:27; Jer. 23:24).[555]

This basic bifurcation of the topic into infinity in relation to time and infinity in relation to space is also characteristic of Polanus, Keckermann, the Leiden Synopsis, Le Blanc,

---

XII.18.

549. Perkins, *Golden Chaine*, ii (p. 11, col. 2); cf. Spanheim, *Disp. theol.*, XIII.xi-xiii.

550. Trelcatius, *Schol. Meth.*, I.iii.

551. Flavel, *Exposition of the Assembly's Catechism*, in *Works*, 3, p. 147; cf. Ames, *Marrow*, I.iv.46-48; Turretin, *Inst. theol. elencticae*, III.ix.4; Le Blanc, *Theses theol.*, *De perfectione et infinitate Dei*, xxiv; Edwards, *Theologia Reformata*, I, p. 51.

552. See Biddle, *Duae Catecheses*, II, pp. 26-27; and cf. Owen, *Vindiciae evangelicae*, preface, in *Works*, XII, p. 70.

553. Leigh, *Treatise*, II.iv (p. 33), correcting the citation of Daniel from 4:32; cf. Turretin, *Inst. theol. elencticae*, III.viii.5.

554. Turretin, *Inst. theol. elencticae*, III.viii.8; Spanheim, *Disp. theol.*, XIII.xi.

555. Perkins, *Golden Chaine*, ii (p. 11, col. 2). Perkins cites the Scripture texts entire.

Amyraut, and Mastricht.[556] Latent in Perkins' definition, moreover, is yet another aspect of the Reformed orthodox language that is sometimes the basis of another descriptor of infinity, prior to immensity and eternity, namely, the "greatness of God" or *magnitudo Dei*. In most of the writings of the orthodox, the *magnitudo Dei* is understood simply as an aspect of the basic category of infinity and not separated out, leaving the basic bifurcation of the topic into immensity and eternity.

2. *In se* and *ad extra*: the absolute and relative understandings of divine infinity. The bifurcation of the topic, then, yields an *ad intra* attribute of infinity or greatness (*magnitudo*) that is predicated of God *absolutè*, followed by a pair of *ad extra* attributes, *omnipraesentia* and *aeternitas*, predicated of God *relativè*.[557] In some cases, the paradigm is complicated a bit by the addition of *magnitudo* or greatness as an *ad extra* or relative attribute and by a further distinction between *omnipraesentia* and *immensitas*. "Magnitude" sometimes appears as a positive (*via eminentiae*) synonym for the *via negativa* concept of infinity and sometimes as the *ad extra* understanding of infinitude relative to quantity. "Immensity" can be understood as the characteristic of the divine essence according to which God is "omnipresent," with omnipresence strictly identifying the repletive presence of God in relation to finite creatures, who have a definitive or circumscriptive presence.[558] Taken as a whole, this set of terms identifies a distinction between the infinity of God's essence and nature *in se* and absolutely considered, as indicated in his name and power, and the divine infinity considered in *ad extra* relation to God's works and authority, as evidenced in the exceeding greatness of his acts, judgments, and counsels, a distinction between divine infinity "intrinsically considered" and divine infinity "extrinsically considered."

This distinction of an *ad intra* from an *ad extra* understanding of the attributes related to infinity will be paralleled in other discussions of the divine attributes — including divine grace and justice. It parallels, moreover, such preliminary and foundational distinctions as that between the *theologia archetypa* and the *theologia ectypa*, indicating the fairly constant Reformed concern to argue the grounding of what is known concerning God by revelation in what is true of God according to his essence. The concern for grounding what is known also appears in the discussion of the attributes themselves and their distinction both *ad intra* and *ad extra*: the *ad intra* distinction of attributes is precisely what is at stake in the identification of a divine eternity and immensity apart from the creation of the world.

This distinction, moreover, goes to the very heart of the Reformed doctrine of divine infinity: for although from an etymological perspective the term "infinity" stands among the attributes of the *via negativa*, the attribute carries with it a primary positive significance. This positive, intrinsic significance of the term frames the discussion of

---

556. Polanus, *Syntagma*, Synopsis libri III; Keckermann, *Systema theol.*, I.iv (p. 95); *Synopsis purioris theol.*, VI.xxvii, ad fin; Le Blanc, *Theses theol.*, De immensitate et omnipraesentia Dei, ii; Amyraut, *De mysterio trinitatis*, II, pp. 38-40; Mastricht, *Theoretico-practica theol.*, II.ix-xi.

557. Mastricht, *Theoretico-practica theol.*, Methodica dispositio, fol. **2v.

558. Thus, e.g., Mastricht, *Theoretico-practica theol.*, II.x.6; Rijssen, *Summa theol.*, II.xvi; Turretin, *Inst. theol. elencticae*, III.ix.6.

the main branches of the doctrine of divine infinity, the doctrines of divine immensity and divine eternity, by allowing for the extrinsic relationship between God and the finite order in its spatiality and temporality at the same time that it guards the positive divine transcendence of the order: there is a logically prior concept of intrinsic infinity that qualifies and guards the concept of extrinsic infinity.

In the logically prior sense, God's intrinsic infinity is nothing other than the "bottomless profundity of essence, and the full confluence of all kinds and degrees of perfection, without bound or limit."[559] The divine infinitude follows, therefore,

> from the perfection of God; whatsoever thing hath not an end of its perfection and virtue, that is truly and absolutely infinite. Infiniteness is to be without bounds, to be unmeasurable, to exceed reason or capacity; it is opposed to Finite, which is to bound or limit, to define, to end, or conclude. Infiniteness is such a property in God, that he is not limited to any time, place, or particular nature and being; or it is that whereby God is free altogether from all limitation of time, place, or degrees.[560]

Infinity, intrinsically considered, also follows from the primacy or ultimacy of God: whatever is uncaused is also "without *limit* of being," given that "all limitation proceeds from the cause of a thing, which imparted to it so much and no more."[561] It follows further that all of the divine properties or perfections are also infinite, above all measure and degree. Thus, the infinity of God is a transcendence of all "categories," whether mathematical, metaphysical, or physical.[562] Given that Scripture testifies that God is wise, powerful, and good, infinitely so (cf. Eph. 3:20; Isaiah 40:12, 15, 17), it follows that "His love is infinite, his mercies are infinite, and so is his anger."[563] *Infinitas*, therefore, is a general term "through which the divine nature is conceived as lacking all limit and imperfection" — so that by reason of infinity of essence God, is called "incomprehensible"; by reason of infinity of duration, "eternal"; and by reason of freedom from limit of place, "immense."[564]

3. Issues in debate. The Reformed argue that it is improper — indeed, absurd — to claim an infinite power in God while at the same time denying an essential infinity, as Vorstius, the Socinians, and the Remonstrants do.[565] The Socinian argument had, by the mid-seventeenth century, proceeded to the point of claiming that God is a finite and even circumscribed being who inhabits the highest heaven and only extends his

---

559. Howe, *Living Temple*, I.iv (p. 98); cf. Ames, *Marrow*, I.iv.43; Amyraut et al., *Syntagma thesium theologicarum*, I.xiii.23.

560. Leigh, *Treatise*, II.iv (p. 33); in margin: "Infiniteness is that, whereby God cannot be limited, measured, or determined of anything, being the first cause from whom, and the end wherefore all things were made."

561. Howe, *Living Temple*, I.iv (pp. 90-91); Le Blanc, *Theses theol.*, *De perfectione et infinitate Dei*, xxiv.

562. Amyraut et al., *Syntagma thesium theologicarum*, I.xiii.3

563. Leigh, *Treatise*, II.iv (p. 33).

564. Rijssen, *Summa theol.*, III.xv.

565. Spanheim, *Disp. theol.*, XIII.xii; cf. Owen, *Vindiciae evangelicae*, in *Works*, 12, p. 335.

presence by way of an exercise of power.[566] Volkelius had even argued that the material universe existed eternally as a passive principle on which God, the active principle, exercises his creative power, thus denying both the divine infinity and the divine omnipotence.[567] These opponents of the Reformed, so often enlisted on the side of modernity against the "Aristotelian scholastics" of the seventeenth century, on this particular point take the side of Aristotle against the Reformed: Aristotle had denied that infinity of essence could be a perfection, inasmuch as infinite essence implied dimensive quantity. So, too, did the medieval opponents of an essential divine infinity argue against the doctrine on Aristotelian grounds, while at the same time attributing to God infinite power.[568] Aristotle's view was, moreover, discussed and critiqued at length by seventeenth-century metaphysicians like Campanella as well as by the Protestant orthodox theologians of the era.[569] The point is simply that the seventeenth-century scholastics knew the medieval debate, understood the problematic nature of the Aristotelian view, and ranged themselves with the medievals (and, indeed, with the Cartesians of the seventeenth century)[570] against Aristotle on the issue of divine infinity. Moreover, in disavowing infinity of essence while at the same time allowing infinity of power (presumably on the basis of the divine work *ad extra*), the Socinians refused to acknowledge the prior member of the fundamental distinction between intrinsic and extrinsic infinity and therefore also disobliged the logic of the Reformed position that, in order to be extrinsically infinite in relation to the physical and temporal order, God must be intrinsically infinite in his essence.

Some comment must also be made concerning the character of the scholastic opposition to the Aristotelian notion of infinity in relation to the problems of space and time. Aristotle had denied infinity to God because he understood infinity solely in terms of the endless extension of the categories of finite being — that is, the endless extension of space, time, or quantity. Such infinity belongs as it were to the lower end of the scale of being. All of the arguments of the scholastics, namely, that the divine infinity is not "a magnitude or multitude that cannot be traversed, that it is not "a corporeal quality and extension," and so forth, are in fact denials of the attribution of the Aristotelian notion of infinity to God, given that such infinity belongs to lower and limited orders of being. Like Aquinas and the medieval doctors, the Protestant scholastics define divine infinity not as the endless extension of the categories of finite being, but as the transcendence of those categories. Thus, the understanding of divine immensity and eternity take the concept of God beyond the limits of the finite order

---

566. Crell, *The Two Books ... touching one God the Father*, xxvii; Biddle, *Duae catecheses*, I, cap. Ii (pp. 26-28).

567. Volkelius, *De vera religione*, II.iv.

568. Cf. Sweeney, *Divine Infinity*, pp. 338-340.

569. Tomasso Campanella, *Universalis philosophiae, seu metaphysicarum rerum, iuxta propria dogmata, patres tres* (Paris, 1638; repr. Turin: Bottega d'Erasmo, 1961), Lib. VII.v.1-5 (Pars. II, pp. 139-44).

570. Cf., e.g., Malebranche, *The Search after Truth*, trans. and ed. Thomas M. Lennon and Paul J. Olscamp (Cambridge: Cambridge University Press, 1997), III/II.vi; ix.4; IV.xi.2 (pp. 231, 251, 317-318).

in two of its categories of extension, temporal and spatial — just as the doctrine of divine simplicity, or, indeed, the occasional discussion of a distinct *magnitudo Dei*, takes the concept of God beyond notions of quantitative magnitude.

B. Infinity in Relation to Quantity: The *Magnitudo Dei*

Wollebius defines divine infinity as the attribute according to which "God is known as a being infinitely true and good and devoid of all measure or limit."[571] Since "there can be but one thing infinite in nature," it follows that God is "only one, and that indivisible, not many."[572] Trelcatius similarly concentrates on the problem of infinity over against vast but comprehensible magnitude:

> *Infinity* in God is not a magnitude or a multitude that cannot be traversed, but an incomprehensible power, or an incomprehensibility of act, according to which he is neither internally nor externally finite, but is in himself in his entirety everywhere and at the same time is in all things in his essence and power. Since, according to his essence, God is everywhere, or speaking more properly, he is everywhere itself: that is, being in every place without definition or circumscription, in every time without change, whole in all things ... whole in himself.[573]

This divine greatness is not, therefore, analogous to the greatness of bodily things — as the greatness of mountains or of the sun. Nor is the divine infinity analogous to the apparent infinity of the stars or of the sands of the seashore: "This [greatness] cannot be found in God, who is not a body, but an immaterial essence": the divine greatness or infinity, therefore, transcends the so-called infinity of things that are merely innumerable or incalculable. Rather it is a greatness

> of perfection, worth and virtue, ... abundance of all excellencies ... of whatsoever makes to perfection of being, and this is in God. [Greatness is attributed to God metaphorically and denoteth an incomprehensible and unmeasurable largeness of all his excellencies.][574]

As Rijssen notes, it cannot be objected to this that *beati sunt comprehensores*, for none can ever attain full knowledge of God in the sense of having an "absolute knowledge of God." It ought to be clear that neither men nor angels can ever attain such knowledge inasmuch as *"finitum non est capax infiniti."*[575]

When, therefore, the Protestant orthodox refer to God as infinite, they do not typically posit an analogy between the divine infinity and the infinity of a numerical series. God's essence is not only infinite in relation to our finitude as the numbers of the stars or the depths of the sea are said, *improprìe*, to be infinite, but also *proprìe et in se, categorematica et absoluta.* Even so, the Psalm 145:3 states, "Great is the Lord

---

571. Wollebius, *Compendium*, as cited in Heppe, *Reformed Dogmatics*, p. 65.
572. Perkins, *Golden Chaine*, ii (p. 12, col. 1), citing Eph. 4:5; Deut. 4:35; 1 Cor. 8:4.
573. Trelcatius, *Schol. meth.*, I.iii; cf. Amyraut, *De mysterio trinitatis*, II, pp. 67-68.
574. Leigh, *Treatise*, II.vi (p. 48); cf. Turretin, *Inst. theol. elencticae*, III.viii.2, 14-15.
575. Rijssen, *Summa theol.*, III.xv; cf. Turretin, *Inst. theol. elencticae*, III.viii.10.

and greatly to be praised; and there is no end to his greatness *(et magnitudinis eius finis non est)*." And, similarly Zophar says to Job,

> Can you plumb the depths of God or comprehend the perfection of his powers? It is higher than the highest heaven; what can you do with it? deeper than hades; what can you know of it? longer than the earth in its measure, and wider than the sea.[576]

The problem of an infinite series of finite things is echoed in the problem of an infinite time lapse: this too falls short of the divine infinity inasmuch as the flow of time is not an infinite presence, but a flow from one moment to the next.[577] God, after all, cannot be like either kind of infinite series since he is not composed of parts or moments that could be described as differing in magnitude, location, duration, and so forth — nor ought God to be viewed as occupying an indivisible point or moment, but rather, in his immensity as containing all times and places, having no limit of essential perfection.[578]

The absence of analogy to any infinite series or infinite extension is made abundantly clear in the middle of the seventeenth century by Leigh's definition:

> God truly is Infinite in his nature and essence, actually and simply, by himself, and absolutely... He is not [however] infinite,
> (1) In corporeal quantity and extension, but in essence and perfection
> (2) Not *privativè* but *negativè*: he hath simply no end.
> (3) He is Infinite not according to the Etymon of the word, which respects an end only; for he is both without beginning and end; and although the word be negative, yet we intend by it a positive attribute and perfection.[579]

The infinite essence of God is understood to be "entirely without any *finis* or *terminus*.[580]

Beyond their negative language of infinity, the Reformed scholastics can also, therefore, point toward a positive divine infinity, often called, simply, as in Perkins' *Golden Chaine*, the greatness of God or *magnitudo Dei*. The *magnitudo Dei* refers to the essence and the nature of God, to his works, and to his authority.[581]

> His name is Great, Jer. 10:6; Josh. 7:9; his power is great, Psalm 147:5; his acts are great, Psalm 111:2; his judgments are great, Exodus 7:4; he is great in counsel, Jer. 32:19; and mighty works, Jer. 32:19; Deut. 32:4.[582]

Nor ought the doctrine of divine infinity and magnitude be viewed as a purely speculative element in the orthodox system. The practical implications of the doctrine

---

576. Turretin, *Inst. theol. elencticae*, III.viii.4-5, citing Job 11:7-9.

577. Amyraut et al., *Syntagma thesium theologicarum*, I.xiii.6-7.

578. Amyraut et al., *Syntagma thesium theologicarum*, I.xiii.11, 14-15, 21.

579. Leigh, *Treatise*, II.iv (pp. 32-33).

580. *Synopsis purioris theol.*, VI.xxvii; cf. Le Blanc, *Theses theol.*, De immensitate et omnipraesentia Dei, iii.

581. Perkins, *Golden Chaine*, i (p. 11, col. 2); cf. Leigh, *Treatise*, II.vi (p. 48); Amyraut et al., *Syntagma thesium theologicarum*, I.xiv.19.

582. Leigh, *Treatise*, II.vi (p. 48).

are offered as a central issue in many of the orthodox systems. Thus, the greatness of God's nature ought to lead us to "prefer God above all things" — as the sun outshines all other stars in our estimation or the king all other persons. "We should highly esteem his favor, Isaiah 40:12."

> We should perform all duties to him with the greatest care, diligence and reverence, and in the highest degree; love him greatly, fear him greatly, praise him with all our might, yield unto him a service proportionable to his incomprehensible greatness. *Great is the Lord and greatly to be praised*, Psalm 143:3.[583]

Beyond this, the greatness of God ought to be a great terror to God's enemies.

> God is great in his works, Deut. 4:36. God's perfection stands in an infiniteness of goodness, Matt. 19:17; wisdom, Rom. 11:33; power, Gen. 17:1; perfect wisdom, goodness, righteousness, moderation, holiness, truth, and whatsoever may possibly be required to grace and commend an action, that is found in the whole course and frame of God's actions. The work of creation is a perfect work: [God] made all things perfect in unsearchable wisdom. No man could have found any want of anything in the world which might be reasonably desired; no man could have found there any evil thing worthy to be complained of. The work of providence is perfect, all things are carried in perfection of wisdom, justice, and goodness. So is the work of Redemption likewise perfect. The most perfect measure of justice, wisdom, truth, power, that can be conceived of, doth show itself forth in that work.[584]

The creation itself is a proof of God's infinity, given that it could not have been made by a finite being — whether in terms of the manner of working necessary to bring it about or in terms of the vast array of "genera and species, degrees and modes" of things that it contains. In addition, the concept of a divine decree on which all things depend also demands the concept of immensity or eternity inasmuch as it stands beyond time, having nothing before, whether according to nature or origin: the decree is an act of infinite wisdom that from all eternity comprehends all possibilities, in all of their varieties, modes, and aspects.[585] Logically, a being who is confined to a place or to a time — of whom it could be said "it is necessarily here" — is, certainly, of necessity, not God.[586]

This view of God's greatness as a greatness manifest in God's works raises several questions: Why, if God is perfect, does he work through the agency of others? Why does not God abolish sin, since his greatness, as infinite, can in no way be increased by the glory that comes to him in the work of Christ or in his mercy in pardoning sinners? Why did God not make all things perfect immediately but cause some to grow toward perfection? The answer to the first question, God works through secondary

---

583. Leigh, *Treatise*, II.vi (p. 53).
584. Leigh, *Treatise*, II.vi (p. 50).
585. Amyraut et al., *Syntagma thesium theologicarum*, I.xiii.31, 35; cf. xiv.8.
586. Amyraut et al., *Syntagma thesium theologicarum*, I.xiv.21-22.

causes and means not out of any necessity — as his immediate acts and his use of "contrary means" manifest — "but out of choice and liberty."[587]

It must therefore be added that the infinitude of God's activity and power indicates an infinite manner (*modus infinitus*) of working necessary to an infinite being, but not an infinite effect: the idea of an infinite effect is a *contradictio in adjecto*.[588] The infinitude of divine power correlates with the nature and essence of God but not precisely with the results of God's exercise of his power in his work. From the perspective of the finite and temporal effects of God's willing, it is the case that God is fully able to do what he wills and that he must consistently will and act according to his nature. The results of God's willing, however, as willed or created results *ad extra* are finite.[589]

As for the existence of sin somehow casting doubt on the greatness of God in his work, Leigh writes,

> Because sin is not so great an evil as Christ is good, and therefore God would not have suffered sin, if he could not have raised up to himself matter of honor; God makes an antidote of this poison.[590]

On the issue of God's perfecting of things in the course of their history, having made them imperfect at the first, Leigh comments,

> Those things were perfect *ex parte operantis*: he intended not they should have any further perfection at that time; the essence of no thing can be made better than it is, because it consists *indivisibili*. God makes not our graces perfect in us because he aims at another end.[591]

It is worth noting here the adumbration of Leibniz's "best of all possible worlds": God is required to make an absolutely perfect universe in order to manifest his own goodness and righteousness, given that no finite thing can be absolutely perfect. God makes, of all the possible universes known to him, according to the *scientia necessaria*, a universe of finite things than which no better universe of finite things could exist.[592]

The works of God are so great and unsearchable that we need to stand in awe of the maker and refrain from all foolish attempts to hinder God. Indeed, our inability to comprehend ought to increase in us the awe and reverence that is due to God: "Let us learn often to contemplate God in his works; see his goodness, greatness, wisdom, power in them, and so we shall profit much in the knowledge of him."[593]

---

587. Leigh, *Treatise*, II.vi (p. 50).

588. Spanheim, *Disp. theol.*, XIII.xi.

589. Spanheim, *Disp. theol.*, XIII.xii.

590. Leigh, *Treatise*, II.vi (p. 50).

591. Leigh, *Treatise*, II.vi (p. 51).

592. Cf. G. W. *Leibniz: Theodicy*, intro. by Austin Farrer, trans. E. M. Huggard (New Haven: Yale University Press, 1952), § 20, with *Metaphysics*, I, in G. W. Leibniz, *Discourse on Metaphysics, Correspondence with Arnauld, Monadology*, intro. by Paul Janet, trans. George R. Montgomery (Lasalle, Ill.: Open Court, 1980), pp. 3-7.

593. Leigh, *Treatise*, II.vi (p. 55).

C. Infinitude in Relation to Space: Immensity and Omnipresence

1. Infinitude and presence: a scholastic problem with Reformation resonance. The concept of divine infinity leads the scholastics — both medieval and post-Reformation — to the question of how that infinity ought to be understood in terms of attributes of presence, both spatial and temporal.[594] Thus, discussion of the divine infinity is related, in many systems, to examination of the attributes of omnipresence and eternity. And although this sense of the order and progression of systematic argument is largely absent from the theologies of the Reformers and their immediate successors, the basic doctrine surely is not. Thus, the nominally philosophical discussion of divine infinity that can be found in the medieval debate with Aristotle and the fairly detailed discussion of infinity found in the Reformed orthodox have little parallel in the thought of the Reformers, but the doctrine of divine omnipresence (and, as we will note below, divine eternity) are found in detail in the thought of the Reformers, although the Reformers certainly held the doctrine and held it in the same basic form and content as both the medieval scholastics and the Protestant orthodox.[595]

As one might expect, the section devoted to the divine *praesentia* in Musculus' *Loci communes* is the most developed discussion of the topic found among the early codifiers of the Reformation. His discussion, moreover, is a finely balanced examination of biblical and traditionary materials that carries with it a strong didactic and pastoral overtone. Musculus begins by noting that the biblical language of God's seat or throne in the heavens might give some the impression that God functioned like an earthly monarch, distant from his subjects, who rules by means of emissaries while he remains "in his princely tower." This view, Musculus continues, is "childish" and not at all suited to God: "we do not have a God who is absent," he notes, "but who is everywhere present."[596] The full doctrine of divine presence is taught in such passages of Scripture as Psalm 139, where the Psalmist recognizes that he cannot flee from the spirit of God, whether on the earth or the sea, or even in hell. So too does the prophet Jeremiah teach that God "fills" the heavens and the earth. Scripture therefore teaches that God is never far off, but is always present and, indeed, present in his knowing and willing, so that no place "is destitute of the presence of God." This divine presence, moreover, is not a presence such as is characteristic of finite beings, which do not "fill the places in which they are present" and which, when present in one place, cannot be present elsewhere.[597]

---

594. Cf. Spanheim, *Disp. theol.*, XXI.iv, xiii, xv; Amyraut et al., *Syntagma thesium theologicarum*, I.xiii.2-3. A significant precedent for this grouping of magnitude, omnipresence, and eternity together as each a category of divine infinity is found in Alexander of Hales *Summa theologicae*, in a similar series of attributes is understood as categories of divine *immensitas* and the immensity itself is understood *ad se* as the divine infinity, including *immensitas* as to place and *immensitas* as to duration. See Alexander of Hales, *Summa theol.*, pars. I, tract. II, *De immensitate divinae essentiae*.

595. For a survey and analysis of the doctrine, see Luco Johan van den Brom, *Divine Presence in the World, a Critical Analysis of the Notion of Divine Omnipresence* (Kampen: Kok Pharos, 1993).

596. Musculus, *Loci communes*, liii (*Commonplaces*, p. 1028, cols. 1-2).

597. Musculus, *Loci communes*, liii (*Commonplaces*, p. 1029, cols. 1-2), citing Jer. 23:24.

The text in Jeremiah is, of course, a *locus classicus* for the doctrine of divine omnipresence. Over against the more speculative of the scholastics, the Reformers indicate the need for caution in interpretation lest the theologian lose the import of the text: Calvin notes that the text ought not to be "refinedly explained of the infinite essence of God," although it is certainly true that "his essence extends through heaven and earth, as it is interminable." This particular text, however, directs us primarily toward a consideration of God's "providence and power."[598] Thus, too, for Musculus, the discussion of the *praesentia Dei* is linked intimately with that of the divine providence and, in fact, follows it immediately in the order of his *loci*. Yet Musculus, more than Calvin, perceives the need to provide a more fully developed discussion of the attribute.

There is a series of difficulties in the discussion of the biblical language of God's presence that need to be cleared away: Scripture frequently speaks of God's presence in terms of "the face of God," but certainly does not mean to define the divine presence as a presence to the senses. We must therefore, Musculus indicates, consider "how" God is said to be present. We can distinguish corporal from spiritual, virtual, and contemplative or intellective presence. Corporal presence is usually referred to as "local" presence or presence in a place. Such a conception does not apply to God "in part because God has no body, in part because God cannot be confined in a place" but fills all things.[599] Spiritual and virtual presence, by way of contrast, can indicate a limited, non-corporeal presence in a place, as when the Apostle Paul speaks of being absent in the body but present in spirit (1 Cor. 5:3), or when a monarch who is physically absent from a place in his realm still exercises power there. This understanding of presence is also unsuited to God, whose presence is not limited in any way and cannot be reduced to an exercise of power. Clearly, also, a contemplative or intellective presence, namely, a presence to the mind in thought of something that is absent, is also not suitably applied to God.[600]

A proper understanding of the divine presence, Musculus concludes, must respect the nature of God and thus must refer both to the essential and to the effective presence of God. Musculus thus assumes that the topic or *locus* on the divine presence must offer a fuller definition than that permitted by Calvin in his commentary on Jeremiah 23. God's essence is "not contained in any place" but "cannot be said to be nowhere" — indeed, it is "necessarily" everywhere. This essential omnipresence, moreover, is conjoined to a universal "potential or virtual" presence of God as creator, preserver, and governor of all things: God both "is everywhere" and is operative in and through all things. This presence, Musculus adds, is analogous to the presence of the soul in the body — and, in express disagreement with Lombard, Musculus indicates that it is an insufficient explanation to argue that the divine providence and preservation

---

598. Calvin, *Commentaries on Jeremiah*, Jer. 23:24, in loc. (*CTS Jeremiah*, II, pp. 188-189).

599. Musculus, *Loci communes*, liii (*Commonplaces*, p.1030, col. 1-p. 1031, col. 1); cf. Calvin, *Harmony of the Last Four Books of Moses*, Ex. 3:4 (*CTS Pentateuch*, I, p. 64).

600. Musculus, *Loci communes*, liii (*Commonplaces*, p.1031, col. 1-p. 1031, col. 2).

can be identified merely as the universal presence of the divine power: God fills all things not only virtually but also essentially.[601]

We are also enjoined not to understand this essential omnipresence according to our "narrow capacity" and conclude from the presence of God both in heaven and on earth that he is divisible into parts, as if a part of God were in heaven and another part elsewhere: for God is "neither corporal nor local" — he is neither divided nor does he move from place to place with the finite things in and to which he is present. Such conclusions would be "unworthy of the majesty of God."[602]

Still, there is a sense in which God may be said to present in a special sense to certain people. Musculus notes the importance of the point, inasmuch as the essential and virtual omnipresence of God might become a reason for diminishing or losing entirely the significance of such biblical passages as Exodus 33:5, "the Lord said unto Moses, Say unto the children of Israel ... I will come into the midst of thee in a moment," or Isaiah 7:14 and Matthew 1:23, where the name of Christ is Emanuel, or "God with us." Just as the soul is present essentially and virtually throughout the whole body, working throughout the whole, Musculus argues, but is also present in particular ways in the mind and the heart, so is God present everywhere, preserving and directing all things, but also present in a special way in heaven, according to his full majesty and glory; in grace and love in those who belong to him as his elect.[603]

By way of conclusion to his discussion, Musculus offers a pastoral counsel concerning the "use" of the doctrine: it is important, he notes, on the one hand, to avoid speculative and unprofitable questions about the manner God's presence and, indeed, the manner of the presence of spirits or of the body of Christ in heaven; but equally important, on the other hand, to recognize that God is present everywhere in a manner that is unique to God. It is necessary to faith and piety that we "attribute to God alone and to no creature that which belongs to God's nature alone." For when we recognize that God alone is present everywhere both essentially and virtually, we easily perceive the uselessness and even the idolatry of prayers to "dead saints." So, too, does the affirmation of divine omnipresence lead us to revere God's majesty at all places and in all times, and also to have confidence in him in the midst of any and all dangers and in the face of all manner of evil and death.[604]

2. The Reformed orthodox conception of divine immensity and omnipresence as extrinsic attributions. Although the Reformed orthodox discuss the divine immensity and omnipresence at considerable length, both as a result of their controversies with various adversaries, most notably the Socinians, Lutherans, and Cartesians, they are hesitant to claim that the doctrine can be fully grasped by reason: the manner of God's omnipresence ought not to be discussed curiously or rashly, and full explanation remains impossible.[605] Immensity and omnipresence typically stand

601. Musculus, *Loci communes*, liii (*Commonplaces*, p. 1031, col. 2-p. 1032, col. 1).
602. Musculus, *Loci communes*, liii (*Commonplaces*, p. 1033 col. 1).
603. Musculus, *Loci communes*, liii (*Commonplaces*, p. 1033, cols. 1-2).
604. Musculus, *Loci communes*, liii (*Commonplaces*, p. 1035, cols. 1-2).
605. Pictet, *Theol. chr.* II.x.11.

as the initial branch of the discussion of divine infinity, the other being the divine eternity:

> The attribute of God's being everywhere, is called Immensity, Omnipresence, or Ubiquity. God is immense or omnipresent, Psalm 139:7-10; Josh. 2:11; Job 11:8; Jer. 23:23-24. Immensity is taken (1) largely, so it is the same with Infiniteness, signifying that God is neither measured by place nor time, nor by any other thing, but is in his own nature and essence Infinite and Immense. *Immensum proprie est quod non possis metiri*; (2) strictly, so it differs from Infiniteness as the species from the genus, there being two kinds of Infiniteness, Immensity and Eternity.[606]

Or, following Wendelin, "Immensity is that property of God that excludes all limitation of essence; the divine essence is everywhere in heaven and on earth; but is nonetheless beyond the heavens: and it is so without any expansion or multiplication."[607]

Many of the Reformed orthodox offer clarification of the concept of divine immensity by drawing out its relation to the *via negativa* attributes even as they indicate that its synonym, omnipresence, belongs to the perfections of the *via eminentiae* — creating a distinction between immensity, strictly so called, and omnipresence. Immensity is a largely negative concept:

> According to his immensity, God is certainly *extra mundum*, not however in a positive sense, as we conceive the spaces that are, so to speak, *extra mundum*, spaces that God fills with his presence; but negatively, inasmuch as the spaces of the entire universe cannot exhaust the immensity of God, which contains them all: God is therefore *extra mundum* in and of himself, as he was formerly, before the creation of the world.[608]

While the *immensitas Dei* refers to God in distinction from the created order, the *omnipraesentia Dei* refers to him in positive relation to the world and indicates his "dwelling" in all places in the world.[609] Owen indicates that the omnipresence or "ubiquity of God is the habitude of his immensity to the creation": namely, omnipresence is the disposition of God in relation to things spatially considered.[610] Here also we see the ground of the epistemological connotation of the famous dictum *finitum non capax infiniti*: God is unlike the world and prior to it; he is beyond it in an absolute and ultimate sense and his relation to it is the expression of his will rather than a necessity imposed upon him by proximity.

3. Controversies — against Vorstius and the Socinians; against the Lutherans; against various Cartesians. There is, Rijssen comments, no controversy over the omnipresence of God in his powers and his works (*virtutes et operationes*), but the

---

606. Leigh, *Treatise*, II.iv (p. 36); similarly, Zanchi, *De natura Dei*, II.vi (cols. 90-91).

607. Wendelin, *Christ. theol.*, I.i; cf. Zanchi, *De natura Dei*, II.vi (cols. 89-90); Cocceius, *Summa theol.* III.ix.45; Ward, *Philosophicall Essay*, I.iii (p. 27); Ezekiel Hopkins, *On the Omnipresence of God*, in *The Works of Ezekiel Hopkins, successively Bishop of Raphoe and Derry*, ed. Charles W. Quick, 3 vols. (1874; repr. Morgan, Pa.: Soli Deo Gloria Publications, 1995-98), III, p. 392.

608. Rijssen, *Summa theol.*, III.xix; cf. Spanheim, *Disp. theol.*, XIII.xvi.

609. Rijssen, *Summa theol.*, II.xvi; cf. Turretin, *Inst. theol. elencticae*, III.ix.2.

610. Owen, *Vindiciae evangelicae*, in *Works*, XII, p. 93.

Socinians and Vorstius deny the essential omnipresence of God. In Vorstius' view, God is located in heaven, essentially and personally, and is only omnipresent by *virtus* and *potentia* — on the analogy of the sun and its rays or of a king on his throne who nonetheless exercises authority throughout his kingdom. Indeed, Vorstius examines a series of biblical texts traditionally understood as indicating omnipresence and argues that none of these texts teach of a "immense, non-composite, substance of God" or that God is "present in all places."[611] The Socinian view of the divine attributes here contradicts the tradition: "Immensity, in the sense in which the Scriptures attribute it to God, imports the supreme perfection of his dominion, power, and wisdom, and also of his providence, which extends to all affairs and to all places," without, however, an essential presence everywhere.[612] The implication of the Racovian Catechism is that the divine immensity or omnipresence is an extension of power, not of essence. Biddle could even argue that God is in heaven "as in a certain place," is neither infinite nor immense, and therefore "is not everywhere," with the christological corollary that Jesus cannot be essentially divine, but must rather be a human being invested with the divine *virtus*.[613]

The orthodox, to the contrary, in explicit continuity with the declarations of Musculus and other Reformers, maintain the divine omnipresence *essentialiter*, but not in such a way, as would imply an overweening curiosity into the incomprehensible and infinite divine essence. Thus, the frequent statement of Scripture that "God is in heaven" does not deny his earthly presence but rather reveals the height of divine majesty: the text intends that our eyes and thoughts be drawn away from earthly things and lifted toward heaven in reverence for the throne of God. The language of Scripture is clearly symbolic and is used of God by way of "anthropopathy."[614] The same kind of interpretive strictures apply to such passages as 1 Kings 19:11, where God is said not to be in the wind and to the many places in which God is said to ascend and descend. In the former case, the text speaks of "extraordinary signs" and not of the essential presence of God — and in the second, the issue is also not one of essence but of the various divine acts or operations.[615]

Neither does this omnipresence consist in a multiplication, extension, or corporal diffusion of the divine essence. Nor is it a physical conception of the divine. God stands in intimate relation with all things and is everywhere in the world, without including the world in himself. Omnipresence refers, therefore, to magnitude of the divine substance filling the entire universe and not contained by it.[616] Against Vorstius and

---

611. Vorstius, *De Deo*, p. 212.

612. Racovian Catechism, III.i (Rees, p. 32).

613. Biddle, *Catechismus*, II, IV (pp. 26-27; 46-47); and see Owen, *Vindiciae evangelicae*, in *Works*, XII, p. 90; Edwards, *Theologia Reformata*, I, p. 53.

614. Rijssen, *Summa theol.*, III.xvi, controversia, obj. 1-2; Cocceius, *Summa theol.* III.ix.45; Le Blanc, *Theses theol.*, De immensitate et omnipraesentia Dei, xxxii.

615. Rijssen, *Summa theol.*, III.xvi, controversia, obj. 4-5.

616. Rijssen, *Summa theol.*, III.xvi; Zanchi, *De natura Dei*, II.vi, q. 2 (col. 95); cf. Malebranche, *Dialogues on Metaphysics and Religion*, VIII (p. 132).

the Socinian exegete Crellius, who argued explicitly that all of the scriptural *loci* normally cited to prove the omnipresence of God must be understood not of God's essence but of his power and efficacy, the Reformed argue that the texts imply an essential omnipresence, inasmuch as they explicitly speak of God filling heaven and earth and not merely of his power and efficacy doing so: God is thus immense *per potentiam, praesentiam, & essentiam* or, alternatively, *per operationem, per cognitionem, & per substantiam.*[617] When Scripture indicates that God is on his throne in heaven (Is. 66:1), it does not mean to restrict God to a place any more than when, in the same book, the human heart is called God's throne (Isa. 57:15) — for "the humble Heart is his Throne, in regard of his gracious Presence; and Heaven is his Throne, in regard of his glorious Presence; and yet neither of these Thrones will hold him, for the Heaven of Heavens cannot contain him."[618] The point was maintained, equally strongly, against the Cartesian assumption that divine omnipresence was not spatial but was solely the exercise of power.[619]

Second, against the Socinians, texts like Psalm 139 do not distinguish between the mode of God's presence in heaven and the mode of his presence in the grave or *sheol*: "therefore he is everywhere according to his essence, or nowhere according to his essence." Third, the scope or meaning of the Psalm is to state that nothing can be hidden from God and that there is nothing that God cannot see, "since nothing can be where God is not." Fourth, it also appears that a presence of power presupposes an essential presence,[620] indeed, "magnitude of power corresponds proportionately with magnitude of substance."[621] Here again, we encounter the Protestant orthodox assumption that the language of Scripture, though not itself philosophical and often strictly limited to concrete description of the historical activity and powerful presence of God, nonetheless implies an ontology: the texts of Hebrews 1:2 and Acts 17:27-28, which speak of the work of God in all things, testify to his omnipresence.[622] If the Socinians were correct, that God is spatially in heaven and must descend to be essentially present on earth, then the world would, in effect, be greater than God. The immensity or magnitude of God, moreover, is confirmed by the analogy of faith: were he not infinite, the gravity of our sins would not be so great, the sacrifice of Christ could not have infinite worth, the righteousness of God would not be infinite, his

617. Rijssen, *Summa theol.*, III.xvi, controversia, citing Crellius, *De Deo et eius attributis*; cf. Le Blanc, *Theses theol.*, *De immensitate et omnipraesentia Dei*, vi; elaborated, vii-ix; Amyraut, *De mysterio trinitatis*, II, pp. 84-85; Edwards, *Theologia Reformata*, I, p. 51.

618. Watson, *Body of Divinity*, p. 27.

619. Cf. Gisbertus Voetius, *Nader openinge van eenige stucken in de Cartesiaenische Philosophie raekende de H. Theologie* (Leiden, 1656) with the comments in Van Asselt, *Federal Theology*, p. 87 and McGahagan, "Cartesianism in the Netherlands," pp. 289-295.

620. Rijssen, *Summa theol.*, III.xvi, controversia; cf. Amyraut et al., *Syntagma thesium theologicarum*, I.xiv.13-14; Hopkins, *On the Omnipresence of God*, in *Works*, 3, pp. 391-392. On the hermeneutical significance of the issue of "scope," see *PRRD*, II, 3.4.

621. Amyraut et al., *Syntagma thesium theologicarum*, I.xiv.20.

622. Rijssen, *Summa theol.*, II.xvi.

wisdom and power would have limits, and the faith, love, and adoration due him would be within our capabilities.[623]

Right understanding of divine omnipresence also confutes Lutheran opponents of the Reformed orthodox, with specific reference to the transference of divine ubiquity to finite objects, such as the body of Christ:

> This serves to confute the Lutherans, who hold Ubiquity to be communicated to Christ's body, and therefore they say his body is in the Sacrament, and everywhere else; because it is assumed by God; but this is false: for the reason of God's omnipresence is the infiniteness of his nature, and therefore it can be no more communicated to the body of Christ than the Godhead can; for his human nature might as well be eternal as everywhere. Christ's body is a finite creature, and though it be glorified, yet it is not defied. It is an incommunicable attribute of the Deity to be in many places at one and the same time.[624]

Of course, the fact of Christ "walking about the world" in no way either contradicts his deity, or denies the presence of God in heaven, or implies that Christ dragged his deity around with him from place to place![625] We ought to acknowledge God greater than any creature and therefore not bound by our conceptions of creaturely existence.[626] Polemic against Cartesian conceptions of divine omnipresence varied, given the presence of Cartesian leanings among the Reformed and given also the variety of formulations among those who followed Descartes. Turretin, given his proximity to Reformed Cartesians, makes his point rather obliquely, without naming the adversary — Mastricht, by contrast, argued pointedly against the Cartesians. For Mastricht, the central issue was the Cartesian reduction of substance to thought and extension, and the resulting identification of God as infinite thought and the assumption that omnipresence was merely a matter of external operation or power. Indeed, Mastricht noted that these Cartesians deny divine presence in all places inasmuch as they define such presence as extension and fail to distinguish between circumscriptive, definitive, and repletive presence.[627] Turretin, with considerable caution, notes that "it is one thing to declare and demonstrate a posteriori the presence of God through external operation; another thing to define a priori the presence of God by that operation or to maintain that God is not present except by power and operation" — various modern thinkers, Turretin declares, who follow these arguments are in danger of Socinianism when they take the latter path.[628]

Turretin also warns specifically against rash rejection of this concept of omnipresence or ubiquity through an inaccurate understanding of the traditional language of repletive presence, as if it "may seem to belong properly to a body occupying

---

623. Amyraut et al., *Syntagma thesium theologicarum*, I.xiv.24, 26.
624. Leigh, *Treatise*, II.iv (pp. 39-40); cf. Zanchi, *De natura Dei*, II.vi, qq. 2., 4 (cols. 97, 107-138).
625. Rijssen, *Summa theol.*, III.xvi, controversia, arg. 2-3.
626. Leigh, *Treatise*, II.iv (p. 40).
627. Mastricht, *Theoretico-practica theol.*, II.x.10.
628. Turretin, *Inst. theol. elencticae*, III.ix.21.

place by its extension." The point is clearly anti-Cartesian, given that Descartes' view of substance allows for no immaterial extension: Turretin admits that the traditional conception of repletive presence borrows terms from "finite and corporeal things," but this he indicates is a problem of theological language itself, which has "no proper and accurate terms for explaining the ubiquity of God" but which must nonetheless wrestle with the issue of how an infinite spiritual being can be said by Scripture to "fill heaven and earth, Jer. 23:24."[629] Mastricht's and Turretin's strictures can certainly be applied to the Cartesian meditations of the young Spinoza, who denied extension to God and concluded immensity and an inexplicable divine presence to all finite beings on grounds of the radical *concursus* of God with all things.[630] The critique does not apply to Malebranche, whose arguments follow Turretin's model of a posteriori demonstration: Malebranche placed God beyond both extension and thought and attributed to God an infinite, nonlocal extension — while explicitly denying that omnipresence could be reduced to operation.[631]

4. Omnipresence: positive exposition and philosophical overtones. In the Reformed orthodox view, God is not local, nor can he be circumscribed in any way — whether according to essence, power, or operation — he is neither excluded from nor included in any place: as sometimes said, God is like a circle, the center of which is everywhere, the circumference nowhere.[632] God fills all things essentially (1 Kings 8:27; Isaiah 66:1; Acts 17:27), he is everywhere in "presence," "power and operation," because he "works all in all" (1 Cor. 12:6), and he is present by his knowledge inasmuch as he knows all things in all places as intimately or immediately present to him (Hebrews 4:13).[633] Scripture demonstrates this not only positively but also negatively, insofar as God "is denied to be concluded and comprehended in a certain place" (1 Kings 8:27; 2 Chron 2:6; 6:18; Acts 7:48; 17:24, 27). Thus, when God is said to ascend and descend (Gen. 18:21, 33; 35:13; Ex. 3:8), Scripture refers not to the motion of a body but to the withdrawal or the sense of God's presence: "He departs not in respect of his essence, but in respect of the manifestation of his presence."[634]

The Reformed orthodox agree with the Socinians on one point, namely, "that God is omnipresent by virtue of his power, energy, and operation," but they add that "he works all in all, giving to all the creatures their being, and preserving them, bestowing on all of them their strength and power of action," and insist that this omnipresence of power does not exhaust the concept — indeed, given the nature of God, the omnipresence of God's power is at best a partial conception of omnipresence. Since the attributes of God are not separated from his essence as characteristics in it (i.e.,

---

629. Turretin, *Inst. theol. elencticae*, III.ix.5; cf. Zanchi, *De natura Dei*, II.vi, q. 2.3 (col. 96).

630. Spinoza, *Thoughts on Metaphysics*, II.iii (p. 132).

631. Malebranche, *Dialogues on Metaphysics and Religion*, VIII.vii-viii (pp. 135-137).

632. Spanheim, *Disp. theol.*, XIII.xv; Le Blanc, *Theses theol.*, *De immensitate et omnipraesentia Dei*, iv-v; Amyraut et al., *Syntagma thesium theologicarum*, I.xiii.3.

633. Turretin, *Inst. theol. elencticae*, III.ix.4; cf. Zanchi, *De natura Dei*, II.vi, q. 2.3 on Isa. 66:1 (col. 96); Leigh, *Treatise*, II.iv (pp. 36-37); Watson, *Body of Divinity*, p. 27.

634. Leigh, *Treatise*, II.iv (pp. 37-39).

God is simple — a point denied by the Socinians), the omnipresence of divine power indicates an omnipresence of undivided essence. Scripture speaks of God as ascending and descending, approaching and departing, but this means, not an essential change of location, but a giving testimony to or withholding signs of his presence.[635]

This latter point relates directly to the assumption of a providential *concursus* or concurrence, for "this omnipresence of God is simply necessary, not only for preserving and upholding his creatures in their beings and operations, but necessary to our very beings." God not only *will not* but also "*cannot* withdraw from nor forsake any place or any thing, with which his presence now is" inasmuch as "God cannot contract or lessen himself, nor gather up his essence into a narrow room and compass."[636]

Thus, God is "neither shut up in any place, nor shut out from anyplace, but is immense, everywhere present, he is without place and above place, present everywhere without any extension of matter but in an unspeakable manner."[637] Caryl cites Augustine, "The Divine Essence (as one of the Ancients hath expressed this astonishing mysterie) is whole within all things, and whole without all things, no where included, no where excluded, conteining all things, contained of nothing, yet not at all mingled with the nature of these things, nor defiled with their pollutions."[638] He is everywhere in his power as creator, preserver, and perfecter of the universe: his power is infinite, never failing, being neither augmented nor reduced by its working.[639] God's immensity and omnipresence do not indicate a physical transcendence of physical space, but a categorical transcendence of spatiality. All of these arguments and definitions lead to the rejection of Willis' characterization of the orthodox *finitum non capax infiniti* as a "crudely spatial" concept: the divine immensity and omnipresence place God *extra mundum* in the sense of being beyond all physical limitation, not in the sense of being physically distanced from the world order.[640]

If God's omnipresence does not rest upon material extension (because God is spirit) neither does it rest on principles of multiplication or division: for if by multiplication, there would be many divine essences rather than the One God — and if by division, then one portion of the divine essence would be in one place, and another portion elsewhere. But the divine essence is indivisible and is entirely present everywhere: as Scripture teaches, God is simultaneously in heaven, hell, and the farthest reaches of the sea — he fills the heavens and the earth, and still is higher than the heavens, deeper than the depths, and beyond the farthest reaches of the earth.[641] He is also

---

635. Pictet, *Theol. chr.* II.x.11; cf. Hopkins, *On the Omnipresence of God*, in *Works*, 3, pp. 394-395, 397.

636. Hopkins, *On the Omnipresence of God*, in *Works*, 3, p. 393, my italics.

637. Leigh, *Treatise*, II.iv, p. 36; Zanchi, *De natura Dei*, II.vi.3 (col. 92).

638. Caryl, *Exposition upon the Book of Job*, 22:12, in loc. (VII, pp. 110), citing Augustine, *Ep. 35, Ad Dardanum*; cf. Le Blanc, *Theses theol.*, *De immensitate et omnipraesentia Dei*, ix.

639. Trelcatius, *Schol. meth.*, I.iii.

640. Cf. E. David Willis, *Calvin's Catholic Christology: the Function of the So-Called Extra Calvinisticum in Calvin's Theology* (Leiden: E. J. Brill, 1966), pp. 74-75.

641. *Synopsis purioris theol.*, VI.xxix.; cf. Leigh, *Treatise*, II.iv (p. 38).

essentially "present in and to the whole creation equally, — not by a diffusion of his substance, or mixture with other things ... but by an inconceivable indistancy of essence to all things."[642]

Thus, God's omnipresence does not involve "commixtion, as if he came into composition with any creature":

> he is everywhere effectively with his essence and being; repletively he fills all places, heaven and earth. Yet he fills not up a place, as a body doth, but is present everywhere, by being without limitation of place, so that he co-exists with every creature. Where any creature is, there is he more than the creature, and where no creature is, there is he also; all the sins we commit are done in his presence, and before his face, Isaiah 65:3; Psalm 51:4. ... We should set the Lord therefore always before us, as *David*, Psalm 16:8. We should be comforted in troubles, and patient, Phil. 4:5; a child will not care so long as he is in his Father's presence, Psalm 23:4.[643]

Nor, certainly, does the notion of omnipresence indicate the essential or substantial "inclusion" of all things in God.[644] Rather, the divine essence is "abstracted" from the essences of finite, created things in the sense that it is neither "terminated by ... nor excluded from" finite essences — the divine essence has no limit given to it by the finite order, either in the sense that finite objects provide a boundary for it (i.e., a terminative limitation) or are impenetrable in some sense (an exclusive limit).[645]

The idea of God's omnipresence leads to the concept of his ubiquity — defined in terms of the three scholastic categories of presence, *praesentia repletiva, praesentia circumscriptiva, and praesentia definitiva*. God, according to the orthodox, is ubiquitous in a repletive sense rather than in a circumscriptive manner for the latter reflects a sense of corporeal and spatial presence not applicable to God: God is not to be viewed as present in *loco & spatio* in the way that a thing is commensurate with the *partibus spatii*. Nor is God to be considered as ubiquitous definitively, in the way that spirits and other incorporeal created substances are present — having a definite relation to a particular place insofar as they can be said to be "here" and not elsewhere. God is considered ubiquitous, therefore, repletively in an improper and analogical sense (since, *propriè*, the term can indicate the way in which a body fills space) as testified in Jeremiah 23:24, "God fills heaven and earth."[646]

Still, against the Cartesian notion of substance, the Reformed declare that God's repletive presence "is not to be conceived under the idea of any extension or diffusion of the divine essence through all things." Even so, we ought not to conclude from the biblical association of the divine with the heavenly and of the sinful with the earthly

---

642. Owen, *Vindiciae evangelicae*, in *Works*, XII, p. 93.

643. Leigh, *Treatise*, II.iv (p. 38).

644. Turretin, *Inst. theol. elencticae*, III.ix.13.

645. Turretin, *Inst. theol. elencticae*, III.ix.17; Amyraut et al., *Syntagma thesium theologicarum*, I.xiv.12.

646. Rijssen, *Summa theol.*, III.xviii; cf. Zanchi, *De natura Dei*, II.vi.3 (cols. 92-93); Turretin, *Inst. theol. elencticae*, III.ix.5.

that the doctrine of divine omnipresence implies a contamination of God through contact with the lowly and corrupt:

> the omnipresence of God is not unbecoming the divine majesty, as though God could not be in the most impure places without being contaminated; for since he is a Spirit, he cannot be touched by what is corporeal.[647]

God, moreover, "is not omnipresent by way of contact with the physical, either by some sort of commixture or composition, but rather as the efficient and conserving cause of all things."[648] In addition, if God is not dishonored by the creation of lowly things, God ought not to be dishonored by his continuing presence with them — any more than the presence of the rays of the sun in lowly places degrades the sun.[649]

The orthodox also note a series of ways in which God is present to his creatures. In the first place, God is essentially present to all creatures, inasmuch as he "fills all things with his presence, and is not confined or limited to any space."[650] Nevertheless, this generalized omnipresence "does not prevent [God] from being said to be present in a peculiar manner in certain places and persons, where he gives the signs and effects either of his majesty, or his glory, or his grace."[651] Thus, it can be said as a rule that whereas God is generally present to all things, he is present graciously and specially only to some.[652] He is also present "in heaven, by his Majesty and glory," to the angels and saints — not, of course, to the exclusion of other places, but there in a glorious and eminent manner, and in hell "by his vindictive justice."[653] (Even so, the distance spoken of by Scripture between God and the impious indicates the absence of his special favor and grace, but not the absence of his essence.)[654] So also does he dwell "in the faithful on earth by his Spirit, and in the church by his grace"; and, finally, God is uniquely present in "Jesus Christ, in whom, as the scripture tells us, 'dwelleth all the fulness of the Godhead bodily.'"[655]

D. Infinitude in Relation to Time: Eternity

1. **Approaches and premises.** Just as their discussion of the infinity of God recognized a whole series of biblical and philosophical issues and difficulties at the root of the concept, the Reformed orthodox theologians' presentation of the doctrine of the *aeternitas Dei* evidences a keen awareness of the difficulty of the concept and of the problem of drawing philosophical categories into relation with biblical texts.

---

647. Pictet, *Theol. chr.*, II.x.11.

648. Rijssen, *Summa theol.*, III.xvi, controversia, obj. 2.

649. Rijssen, *Summa theol.*, III.xvi, controversia, obj. 3.

650. Rijssen, *Summa theol.*, III.xx; Pictet, *Theol. chr.*, II.x.11.

651. Pictet, *Theol. chr.*, II.x.11.

652. Rijssen, *Summa theol.*, III.xvi, controversia, obj. 3.

653. Leigh, *Treatise*, II.iv (p. 39); cf. Rijssen, *Summa theol.*, III.xx; Pictet, *Theol. chr.*, II.x.11; Turretin, *Inst. theol. elencticae*, III.ix.13.

654. Rijssen, *Summa theol.*, III.xvi, controversia, obj. 3.

655. Pictet, *Theol. chr.*, II.x.11; cf. Leigh, *Treatise*, II.iv (p. 39), and Rijssen, *Summa theol.*, III.xx.

The scholastic doctrine of the eternity of God does not represent a case of blind appropriation of non-biblical concepts for the analysis of a fundamentally exegetical and non-metaphysical issue. Such claims, although frequently made against scholastic theology, whether medieval or Protestant, do not do justice either to the issues raised by the biblical materials for the theology of past ages or to the care with which the scholastics merge biblical, philosophical, and logical concerns in the work of constructing doctrine and system.

Furthermore, contrary to the statements of some modern writers that Scripture offered traditional dogmatics only minimal attestation to a notion of changeless eternity, and that these texts, rightly understood in their "context," make a "religious" rather than an "ontological" claim,[656] the Protestant orthodox discussion presents a significant series of texts that point toward divine eternity — texts either taken in themselves or understood against the broader background of the biblical message. Nor does the orthodox exegesis ignore the "religious" element in the text: rather it recognizes that religious claims cannot be made without an ontological implication. The orthodox approach is complex, resting both on the exegesis of individual texts and on the collation and comparison of texts for the sake of drawing suitable or "necessary" consequences.[657] In form, these arguments are a doctrinal or dogmatic movement from the exegetical tradition's examination of particular texts toward the development of a *locus* based on a wider range of texts, doctrinal issues, and theological or philosophical distinctions — among the latter, a distinction between eternity in an ultimate sense and everlastingness in relation to the things of the finite and temporal order.

Here again, the Reformed orthodox theology is not at all monolithic: there are different approaches to the problem of divine eternity in the Reformed orthodox systems depending on the question of human comprehension and the placement of the concept of eternity in the context of a *via eminentiae* or a *via negationis*. Cocceius, Turretin, and many of the Reformed orthodox, thus, approach the concept of eternity on the assumption that God's existence is unbounded by time and temporally immeasurable, but always in a positive relationship to the created order, specifically as the ground of the relative permanence that is there. Others, like Brakel, follow a negative pattern of argument, assuming that the concept of eternity is ultimately foreign to human experience and beyond comprehension and, therefore, to be reached by way of the negation of limited attributions of permanence in the created order.[658]

Following a different approach than either Turretin or Brakel, Pictet derives eternity from the divine necessity or self-existence, inasmuch as "what necessarily exists, is

---

656. Cf. Nicholas Wolterstorff, "God Everlasting," in *God and the Good: Essays in Honor of Henry Stob*, ed. Clifton Orlebeke and Lewis Smedes (Grand Rapids: Eerdmans, 1975), pp. 201-202. Ironic here is that Wolterstorff excludes "ontological" meaning on grounds of the "religious" content of the text and then proceeds to draw on the text in order to propound his own ontological conclusions, namely, that God is to be understood, not as "eternal," but as "everlasting."

657. See *PRRD*, II, chapter 7.

658. Cf. Turretin, *Inst. theol. elencticae*, III.x.2, and Cocceius, *Summa theol.* III.ix.37, with Brakel, *Redelijke Godsdienst*, I.iii.9.

incapable of not existing, and therefore can have neither beginning or ending" — this truth, albeit stated logically as a philosophical conclusion, is taught in many places in Scripture, such as Ps. 102:24-28 and 1 Tim. 6:16. The latter text, moreover, explicitly connects God's immortality with his everlasting power.[659] The notion of eternity, therefore, expresses a fundamental and necessary contrast between the uncreated divine existence and the character or nature of the created order: as Augustine had argued, time is no more and no less than the mutability and mutation of the created order.[660] Apart from the existence of the finite order, there can be no time — whereas it is certain that God, as creator, precedes the created order, it is also certain that time cannot precede the creation and that the divine precedence over the created order is a precedence over (or transcendence of) time as well.[661] Thus,

> Eternity, properly so called, such as belongs to God, denotes three things: 1) to be without beginning; 2) without end; 3) without succession. In this eternity we cannot conceive of anything prior or posterior, anything past, present, or future, since God is without beginning or end.[662]

The Reformed orthodox, here, as before, draw on a traditional approach to the logic of divine necessity and eternity rooted in such works as Augustine's *Confessions* and Anselm's *Monologion* and *Proslogion* — an approach that assumed the ultimate agreement of revelation with right reason, and which belonged as much to the exegetical as to the dogmatic tradition. Perhaps more importantly, their conclusion of an unbounded eternity belongs as much to the traditionary hermeneutic of comparing text with text as it does to the reliance on extra-biblical traditionary criteria. Cocceius' and Pictet's assumption is that the received results of exegesis — for the Protestant tradition, exegesis of the text in its original languages — substantiate his position. As Pictet states in the course of his exposition, "what reason teaches, the whole of Scripture far more demonstrates."[663]

Our errors and difficulties of comprehension concerning the relationship of time and eternity, of world and God, arise from the finitude of our mind and from our custom of "conceiving of God along with or after the establishment of the world."[664] On the contrary, however,

> God is Eternal ... a being without limitation of time, or a being without beginning, ending, or succession. Time is the continuance of things past, present, and to come; all time hath a beginning, a vicissitude, and an end, or may have; but God's essence

---

659. Pictet, *Theol. chr.*, II.xi.3.

660. Cf. Tolley, *Idea of God*, p. 109.

661. Cocceius, *Summa theol.* III.ix.39; cf. Ward, *Philosophicall Essay*, I.iii (pp. 14-16).

662. Pictet, *Theol. chr.*, II.xi.4; Le Blanc, *Theses theol.*, *De aeternitate Dei et ejus immutabilitate*, v.

663. Pictet, *Theol. chr.*, II.xi.3; Cocceius, *Summa theol.* III.ix.37.

664. Pictet, *Theol. chr.*, II.xii.7.

is bounded by none of these hedges. Time is *Nunc fluens*, but Eternity is *Nunc stans*, a standing moment.[665]

On this point, the Reformed orthodox offer several forms of statement, differently nuanced: some simply argue that eternity is uniformly present to all of time in such a way that events, which are future and therefore not actual for finite creatures, are not future but present to eternal God and, therefore, are known to him as actual — and others offer the qualification or elaboration, often associated with Scotus, that each moment in time, although always present to all of eternity, is nevertheless not simultaneously existent with any other moment in time, since that would de-temporalize things and remove their succession.[666]

In any case, the doctrine does not imply that, in eternity, all times coexist non-temporally with one another and that eternity is a denial of time — but that eternity, given that it is a duration, coexists with all times without disrupting or confusing the times of individual things.[667]

> He is without beginning; he is before time, beyond time, behind time as it were, and above all circumscription of time. *From everlasting to everlasting, thou are God.* He is what he is in one infinite moment of being, as I may speak. *I am Alpha and Omega,* Rev. 1:8. *In the beginning God made all things*; and he that made all things could not have a beginning himself. What hath no beginning, can have no succession, nor end. We cannot properly say of God, that he hath been, or that he shall be, but he is. To him all things are present, though in themselves they have succession.[668]

This doctrine, as it stands, does not fall precisely into the modern category either of a radically "timeless God" or of an "everlasting God" nonetheless "in time."[669] Eternity is not "timelessness," the term favored in many modern discussions of the issue, but a successionless existence immediately related to all moments of time or, more precisely, a successionless duration directly related to temporal succession: after all, it is defined not as an "absolute" but as a "relative" attribute.

2. Exegetical foundations. Commentators of the sixteenth and seventeenth centuries assume that the text does speak of eternity and that it provides a basis for argumentation toward and within the established theological context of the doctrine of the divine attributes. The words of Scripture in fact attest the eternity of God in

---

665. Leigh, *Body of Divinity*, II.iv (p. 176); cf. Turretin, *Inst. theol. elencticae*, III.x.6, and Flavel, *Exposition of the Assembly's Catechism*, in *Works*, 6, p. 148.

666. Cf. Aquinas, *Summa theol.*, Ia, q. 14, art. 13, and idem, *In Sent.*, I, d. 38, q. 1, a. 5, with Scotus, *Ordinatio*, I, d. 38, q. 2; *Lectura*, I, q. 39; and see the discussion in Adams, *William Ockham*, II, pp. 1117-1130. The possibility remains, however, that Aquinas and Scotus mean approximately the same thing, but that Scotus' explanation clarifies the point: it was probably not Aquinas' intention to de-temporalize the history of the world *sub specie aeternitatis*. It is therefore also quite possible that the seventeenth-century writers understood the Scotist qualification as only a development of the point in detail.

667. Cf. Rijssen, *Summa*, III, xii, controversia, obj. 4, with Turretin, *Inst. theol. elencticae*, III.x.8.

668. Leigh, *Body of Divinity*, II.iv (p. 176); cf. *Synopsis purioris theol.*, VI.xxviii.

669. Cf. Cross, "Duns Scotus on Eternity and Timelessness," p. 8, where this distinction is posed.

several different ways. Leigh enumerates four: 1) by "simple and plain asseveration"; 2) by denial of "time and succession" to God; 3) by the attribution of "eternal properties and operations" to God; and 4) by "metaphorical description" in which days and years are attributed to God, but in a manner different from their attribution to creatures. To these, typically, the orthodox also add a fifth pattern of biblical attestation: the logical inference of eternity as a conclusion from other exegetically derived attributes.

Thus, first, "With a simple and plain asseveration, Gen. 21:33; Isaiah 40:28 and 57:15; Dan. 7:27; Rom. 16:26."[670] In these and other texts, the Reformed orthodox saw the concept of divine eternity firmly established on an exegetical basis — and they were in firm continuity with their predecessors on the point. Calvin could declare, in his comment on Isaiah 40:28. that the prophet calls God "eternal" in order to distinguish him "from all idols, which endure but for a time ... for if God is eternal, he never changes or decays, eternity being uniformly attended by this quality, that it is never liable to change, but always remains the same."[671] "In him," writes Henry, "there is neither beginning of days nor end of life, nor change of time; he is both immortal and immutable."[672] In several of these texts, the translators and commentators vary — sometimes rendering the Hebrew *olam* as "eternal," sometimes as "everlasting"; or in Latin as *aeternum* (eternal), *sempiternum* (everlasting), or *seculum*, this latter term indicating an indefinitely long duration, and sometimes as *perpetuitas*. Yet, in all of these translations, the sense remains: God is not subject to the vicissitudes of time; he endures or has duration without mutation or succession.[673]

So also, eternity appears, second, "By denying to him time and succession, Job 36:26; Isaiah 43:10; Psalm 90:2-5; 2 Pet 3:8."[674] On Job 36:26, Henry writes,

> We know not the duration of his existence, for it is infinite. *The number of his years cannot* possibly *be searched out*, for he is eternal; there is no number of them. He is a Being without beginning, succession, or period, who ever was, and ever will be, and ever the same, the great I AM.[675]

And of Psalm 90:2-5,

---

670. Leigh, *Treatise*, II.iv (p. 41); cf. Turretin, *Inst. theol. elencticae*, III.x.3.

671. Calvin, *Commentary on Isaiah*, 40:28, in loc. (CTS *Isaiah* III, p. 236).

672. Henry, *Exposition*, Isa. 57:15, in loc.; Amyraut et al., *Syntagma thesium theologicarum*, I.xiv.14.

673. Cf. Vulgate, Gen. 21:33, *aeternum*; Isa. 40:28, *sempiternus*; Isa. 57:15, *aeternitas*; Dan. 7:27, *sempiternus*; *The Bible of John Calvin: Reconstructed from the Text of his Commentaries*, comp. Richard F. Wevers (Grand Rapids: Digamma Publications, 1994), Gen. 21:33, *seculi*; Isa. 40:28, *seculi*; Isa. 57:15, *perpetuitate*; Dan. 7:27, *seculi*; Poole, *Commentary*, Gen. 21:33, "everlasting"; Isa. 40:28, "everlasting"; Isa. 57:15, "everlasting"; Daniel 7:27, "everlasting"; Ainsworth, *Annotations upon Genesis*, Gen. 21:33, "eternal"; Trapp, *Commentary*, Isa. 57:15, "eternity"; Henry, *Exposition*, Gen. 21:33, "everlasting"; Isa. 40:28, "everlasting; Isa. 57:15, "eternity"; Daniel 7:27, "everlasting"; and note the comments in Owen, *Vindiciae evangelicae*, in *Works*, XII, pp. 238-239, and Edward Pococke, *A Commentary on the Prophecy of Micah* (Oxford: Printed at the Theatre, 1692), 5:2, in loc (p. 49). Cf. the discussion in PRRD, IV, 6.1 (B.1).

674. Leigh, *Treatise*, II.iv (p. 41); cf. Turretin, *Inst. theol. elencticae*, III.x.3.

675. Henry, *Exposition*, Job 37:26, in loc.; cf. Poole, *Commentary*, in loc.

In these verses we are taught ... to give God the glory of his eternity ... as we may read it, *before thou hadst formed the earth and the world* (that is, before the beginning of time) thou hadst a being; *even from everlasting to everlasting thou art God*, an eternal God, whose existence has neither its commencement nor its period with time, nor is measured by the successions and revolutions of it, but who art *the same yesterday, today, and forever*, without beginning of days or end of life, or change of time.[676]

As will become apparent below, Henry's attribution of "duration" but not of "succession" is far from an accidental choice of terms. Similar usage is found in Poole's comment on 2 Peter 3:8 — "by a synecdoche, a *thousand years* is put for any, even the longest revolution of time; and the sense is, that though there be a great difference of time, long and short, with us, who are subject to time, and are measured by it; yet with him who is eternal, without succession, to whom nothing is past, nothing future, but all things present, there is no difference of time ... nay, all the time that hath run out since the foundation of the world, is but as a day."[677]

The assumption of succession in God would necessarily imply that in God some things are prior, others posterior in order — by implication, subject to change and flux, given what can be called the "foundation" or ground of succession in the movement from prior to posterior.[678] Therefore, against the Socinians and Vorstius, who taught that God had no beginning or end but nonetheless experiences succession of times, Rijssen argues that "the eternity of God" implies an absence of temporal succession and that the biblical text cannot be understood to imply the contrary: when, after all, the Psalmist compares the "foundations of the earth" and the heavens with God and writes that "They shall perish, but thou shalt endure: yea, all of them shall wax old like a garment; as a vesture thou shalt change them, and they shall all be changed: but thou art the same, and thy years shall have no end" (Ps. 102:26-27), it must be clear to all who read that nothing can be said to endure in this fashion that also experiences no succession from past to future.[679]

Thus, Calvin notes that Psalm 102:24 compares God's "eternal existence" with "the brief duration of human life," and subsequently takes comfort from the fact that "God continues unchangeably the same."[680] As Diodati indicates, the divine eternity taught by Psalm 102:26-7 is specifically "not communicated" to creatures except insofar as they are drawn into everlasting fellowship with God.[681] Poole comments of Ps. 102:26

---

676. Henry, *Exposition*, Ps. 90:2-5, in loc.; Amyraut et al., *Syntagma thesium theologicarum*, I.xiv.4.

677. Poole, *Commentary*, in loc.; cf. Boston, *Body of Divinity*, I, p. 84.

678. Spanheim, *Disp. theol.*, XIII.xiv.

679. Rijssen, *Summa theol.*, III.xii.

680. Calvin, *Commentary on the Psalms*, 102:24, 28 (CTS Psalms IV, pp. 121, 123); cf. the comments on Psalm 90:3-4 (CTS Psalms, III, p. 464). So also Dickson, *Commentary on the Psalms*, 102:24-7, in loc.; and Trapp, *Commentary*, in loc. (II, p. 627), where the same conclusion is applied to Christ's divinity.

681. Diodati, *Pious and Learned Annotations*, in loc.

("Of old hast thou laid the foundation of the earth: and the heavens are the work of thy hands"),

> The eternity of God looks backward and forward, it is both without beginning and without end. ... Thou hadst a being before the creation of the world, when there was nothing but eternity, but the earth and heavens had a beginning given them by thy almighty power.[682]

There was hardly a doubt in the minds of the various major commentators of the age — as there was no doubt in the minds of the Reformers, when they encountered this text — that it taught the doctrine of eternity as held in traditional theological system. If the text was the cause of any debate, it was not a debate over the attributes of eternity, omnipotence, and immutability as such, but over whether the text, as belonging to a potentially messianic context, predicated these divine attributes of Christ.[683]

Even so, James writes that "with God there is no change or shadow of change" (1:17).[684] From the statements of Isaiah (41:4) and of the Apocalypse (1:8, 11) that God is the "first and the last," "the Alpha and the Omega," we must infer that he is *principium sine principio*, and "whatever is *sine principio* is also without succession, inasmuch as succession arises *ex principio*." At this point, Rijssen draws consciously on the medieval scholastic tradition and its use of the Boethian definition: the scholastics correctly defined eternity, he writes, as "the simultaneous and perfect possession of life without end." Unlike our life with its succession of times, God exists non-successively: "God is utterly simple and immutable, and for this reason he cannot be said to change temporally."[685] Since eternity is non-successive and indivisible, "indivisibly including all successions of time," it is also the case that "there is no *futurity in Eternity*."[686]

From this perspective, eternity is a corollary of the divine *immensitas*: the first, independent Being stands prior to the finite order in which there is measurement, including the temporal measurement that identifies the succession of one thing after another or of the moments in the life of mutable things.[687] Thus, Poole indicates of Psalm 90:2, "*ever thou hadst formed the earth and world*, i.e., from eternity; which is frequently described in this manner, as Prov. 8:25, 26; John 17:24; Eph. 1:4, because there was nothing before the creation of the world but eternity."[688] Significantly, the Reformed theologians and exegetes do not attempt to understand the biblical text always as directly indicating a concept of eternity in its references to God as

---

682. Poole, *Commentary*, II, p. 157; cf. Hopkins, *On the Lord's Prayer*, in *Works*, 1, p. 197.
683. Cf. Dickson, *Commentary on the Psalms*, II, pp. 212-213.
684. Rijssen, *Summa theol.*, III.xii; cf. Spanheim, *Disp. theol.*, XIII.xiii.
685. Rijssen, *Summa theol.*, III.xii.
686. Baxter, *Catholike Theologie*, I.vi.99.
687. Turretin, *Inst. theol. elencticae*, III.x.5; cf. *Synopsis purioris theol.*, VI.xxvii; Le Blanc, *Theses theol.*, *De aeternitate Dei et ejus immutabilitate*, v.
688. Poole, *Commentary*, Ps. 90:2, in loc.

"everlasting": the full argument for eternity demands the interpretation of Scripture with Scripture and the hermeneutic of drawing conclusions from the juxtaposition of texts. Inasmuch as some passages speak of God as "everlasting" and others of God as "changeless," the everlastingness cannot be understood in successive or temporal terms.[689] The biblical texts, they insist, consistently contrast God's nature to the changeableness of created beings: Calvin notes that "everlastingness" is "referred not only to the essence of God, but also to his providence" for "although he subjects the world to many alterations, he remains unmoved."[690]

Third, Scripture also indicates the eternity of God "by attributing to him eternal properties and operations; [thus] his mercy is said to endure forever, Psalm 103:17; 136:1-26."[691] Of the former text, Poole notes, that "though we decay and perish, yet God's mercy to us does not die with us; but as it was from eternity exercised in gracious purposes, so it will be continued unto eternity."[692] So also in Scripture, "Eternal counsel is attributed to him, Psalm 33:11; eternal Kingdom, Exod. 15:18; eternal Power, Dan. 6:26; eternal glory, 1 Pet. 5:10. His dominion is an everlasting dominion, Dan. 7:14; his righteousness is everlasting, Psalm 119:142; and his truth."[693]

Concerning the eternal counsel or purpose of God, the *Dutch Annotations* indicate in commenting on Ephesians 3:11,

> *eternall purpose*] Eternall, as the Schooles rightly distinguish, is said in a threefold sense; *a parte ante* onely, and so is that which had no beginning, but shall have an end: so are the Decrees of God even of such things as are accomplished in time, and have their period, eternall; and so is that purpose of God eternall, of which the Apostle here speaketh concerning the calling and incorporating of the Gentiles into the mysticall body of Christ and the true Church of God. Secondly, eternal *a parte post* onely, that had a beginning, but shall have no end: so are Angells and the souls of men eternall. Thirdly, eternall *a parte ante, et a parte post*, that which never had a beginning, nor shall have an end; and so God onely is eternall.[694]

As for the kingship and kingdom of God,

> He is an everlasting King, everlastingly powerful, and glorious; as the conclusion to the Lords Prayer showeth. He is called the King eternal, 1 Tim. 5:17; and the eternal God, Rom. 16:26; the Maker of times, Heb. 1:2; he inhabiteth eternity, Isaiah, 57:15. God only is properly and absolutely eternal; Angels and men's souls are said to be eternal

---

689. Turretin, *Inst. theol. elencticae*, III.x.3, citing Genesis 21:33; Isa. 57:15; Ps. 90:1-2 in relation to Ps. 102:26-8; 1 Tim. 1:17; and James 1:17. Cf. Ainsworth, *Annotations upon Genesis*, in loc., noting several ways of rendering the Hebrew, including the Septuagint understanding of "the eternal God," and Calvin, *Commentary on Genesis*, in loc. (*CTS Genesis* I, pp. 557).

690. Calvin *Commentary on Psalms*, Ps. 90:2, in loc. (*CTS Psalms* III, p. 462).

691. Leigh, *Treatise*, II.iv (p. 41); cf. Turretin, *Inst. theol. elencticae*, III.x.3.

692. Poole, *Commentary*, Ps. 103:17, in loc.

693. Leigh, *Treatise*, II.iv (p. 41).

694. *Dutch Annotations*, Eph. 3:11, in loc.; Amyraut et al., *Syntagma thesium theologicarum*, I.xiii.35.

a posteriori or *a parte post*, God *a priori* & *a posteriori*, *ex parte ante* & *post*, since he hath neither beginning, nor succession, nor end.[695]

Fourth, "by a metaphorical description, days and years are attributed to him; but most distinct from our days and years (Job 10:5); he is called *the Ancient of Days* (Dan. 7:9, 22); he is called eternity itself (1 Sam. 15:29); Christ is called the Father of eternity (Is. 9:6), most emphatically, to signify that he is eternity itself, and the author of it."[696] Thus, the concept of divine eternity is also available from the more figurative language of Scripture according to which God is said to experience days and to be most ancient. The passage in Job was of particular importance to the older theological tradition inasmuch as its rhetorical question, "Are thy days as the days of man?" presents a biblical ground for the *via negativa* — Poole notes, "man's time is short and uncertain ... but it is not so with thee, thou art eternal and unchangeable."[697] So too does the exegetical tradition agree that the name "Ancient of Days" (Daniel 7:9) indicates "the eternal Deity himself,"[698] or offers a figure for God as the "everlasting Father."[699] As Trapp comments, "God's eternity and wisdom is set forth by this ... title" just as the white garments, of the text indicate "his majesty and authority," the fiery throne indicates "his just anger and severity."[700]

The attribution of "days" to God is, thus, not stated *propriè* but *anthropopathicè*, given that we human beings, who are immersed in time, can only conceive of things temporally.[701] The psalmist's phrase, that "a thousand years" in the sight of God are "as yesterday when it is past" (Ps. 90:4), reflects the same thought as offered previously, namely, that God is "from everlasting to everlasting": the meaning, therefore, is that the "duration" of human beings cannot be compared to the duration of divine being.[702] The text, therefore, intends no literal comparison of time spans but rather emphasizes the fact that God is not subject to time and that the seeming delay of the fulfillment of his promises or the implementation of his justice in no way detracts from his eternal counsel.[703]

Fifth, beyond the explicit scriptural teaching, the eternity of God also appears by logical argument from other, biblically grounded, divine attributes: God's perfection

---

695. Leigh, *Body of Divinity*, II.iv (pp. 176-177).

696. Leigh, *Treatise*, II.iv (p. 41). N.B. the text of 1 Sam. 15:29, often rendered "the Strength of Israel will not lie or repent" (KJV), has also been rendered "the Eternity of Israel"; similarly, Isa. 9:6, usually translated "everlasting Father" (KJV) is also given as "Father of eternity": see Trapp, *Commentary on the Old and New Testaments*, in loc. (vol. I, p. 444; III, p. 320); Poole, *Commentary*, 1 Sam. 15:29 and Isa. 9:6, in loc.

697. Poole, *Commentary*, Job 10:5, in loc.

698. Cf. Calvin, *Commentaries on Daniel*, 7:9, in loc. (*CTS Daniel* II, p. 31) with Poole, *Commentary*, in loc.

699. Diodati, *Pious and Learned Annotations*, Dan. 7:9, in loc.

700. Trapp, *Commentary*, in loc.

701. Rijssen, *Summa*, III, xii, controversia, objectio 2.

702. Poole, *Commentary*, in loc.; Diodati, *Pious and Learned Annotations*, in loc.

703. Rijssen, *Summa*, III, xii, controversia, objectio 3.

and his independence imply eternity, for if he were not eternal he would be less than the eternal and thus both imperfect and contingent in some sense. So, too, if God is the creator of all things, and therefore also of time, God is without beginning (cf. Heb. 1:2; Rom. 1:20) and transcendent of the temporality of the things he has created: he must therefore be eternal. Since, moreover, he is the author and giver of eternal life, he must have it in himself as the condition for being able to bestow it.[704]

The question arises, however, in relation to these passages, whether, as the Socinians claim, this "everlastingness" of God might be conceived of as an everlastingness only in and through, rather than also transcendent of time and, therefore, as implying succession in God. On the contrary, there is a direct attribution of eternity to God in a series of biblical passages — notably, those that speak of God's existence before the foundation of the world and "from everlasting to everlasting," particularly in relation to other passages that point toward the changelessness of God: the text of Scripture, taken as a whole, cannot be pressed to argue an endless or everlasting existence that is somehow also subject to the category of time.[705] The divine eternity cannot be understood fully by finite creatures — and any attempt to understand the concept by means of temporal categories dishonors God.[706] It therefore becomes necessary to examine the relative use of language of eternity, specifically the scholastic conception of eternity as duration without succession.

Significantly, the Socinian attribution of everlastingness while at the same time denying eternity to God, parallels other aspects of the Socinian and Vorstian alternative to traditional dogmatics: thus, they similarly argue the infinite exercise of divine power while denying essential omnipotence. In both cases, albeit more clearly in the latter, the Reformed response assumes that an exercise or relation *ad extra* implies and, indeed, must be grounded on an essential property *ad intra*. Unlike the Socinian alternative, the Reformed view consistently correlates teaching about the way that God is with teaching about the way in which God acts: for all revealed attributes there is a *fundamentum in re*.

3. Eternity, everlasting duration, and the problem of temporal succession. At the root of the Reformed orthodox argument for divine eternity lie the issues of change and succession and the relationship of unchanging God to things that change and succeed one another: the argument is couched precisely for the purpose of denying change and succession in God while at the same time insisting on a relationship between God and temporal creatures. The historical sources do not offer a doctrine of "timeless eternity" if that is taken to mean a doctrine of eternal being unrelated to time and incapable of dealing with temporal events as temporal — indeed, as already noted, eternity is understood not as an absolute, but as a relative attribute. The Reformed orthodox assume a direct and necessary relationship between God and the temporal order (as ought to be expected given their doctrines of creation, providence,

---

704. Leigh, *Treatise*, II.iv (p. 42); cf. Turretin, *Inst. theol. elencticae*, III.x.5.
705. Turretin, *Inst. theol. elencticae*, III.x.3; cf. Brakel, *Redelijke Godsdienst*, I.iii. 9.
706. Brakel, *Redelijke Godsdienst*, I.iii. 9.

and divine *concursus*)[707] at the same time that they deny change and succession in God. In all of the cited arguments, the denial of change and succession is made for the sake of affirming a specific relationship between God and creatures — indeed, of affirming that both God and creatures have *duration*, the divine duration being *non-successive*, the creaturely duration, *successive*.[708] This in itself ought to make readers of the seventeenth-century documents wary of modern generalizations concerning "timeless eternity." Indeed, the *Synopsis purioris theologiae* indicates that God is without (*expers*) end or terminus, not that he is lacking or without time: his essence is such that he contains or possesses "no limit" of essence, magnitude, places, or times — specifically, in the doctrine of eternity, without "limitation of time" or "circumscription of time."[709]

The notion of eternal or "infinite duration" as a synonym for eternity underlines this issue: eternal duration is *beyond* time in the sense of transcending temporal limitations, but is not descriptive of God as being *without* time, and certainly not as *outside of* time — as if time were an objectively existent container around things. According to the scholastics, God is without change and without succession, but not without duration — the few who deny duration can specify that it is *duratio successiva* that is being denied.[710] The point is important in the high orthodox era, given that Spinoza did deny not only time but also "continuation" or "duration" to eternal substance — arguing that duration is an attribute of actual, contingent things and not a characteristic of essence. For Spinoza, the identification of eternity with necessary existence yields the denial of duration to eternal being. We can tentatively conclude that worry over the concept of divine "duration" and an insistence on the part of many high and late orthodox writers on a distinction between successive and non-successive duration arose in conflict with Spinozism.[711] In the wake of controversy with Spinozists, Edwards specifically defined the divine eternity as the "uninterrupted Duration of his Essence" and Wyttenbach as "duration without succession."[712] A similar understanding can be found in the definitions of eternity offered by Clarke (despite his Newtonian absolutization of time and space), leading to the conclusion that his conception of

707. Cf. *DLGTT*, s.v., *concursus* with the discussion in Muller, *God, Creation, and Providence*, pp. 264-268.

708. Charnock, *Existence and Attributes*, V (pp. 278-279, 303, etc.); Boston, *Body of Divinity*, I, p. 84; Ridgley, *Body of Divinity* (1855), pp. 86-87.

709. *Synopsis purioris theol.*, VI.xxvii; cf. Leigh, *Body of Divinity*, II.iv (p. 176); Turretin, *Inst. theol. elencticae*, III.x.6; Ward, *Philosophicall Essay*, I.iii (p. 27), and Flavel, *Exposition of the Assembly's Catechism*, in *Works*, 6, p. 148.

710. See the discussion in Davies, *Thought of Thomas Aquinas*, pp. 107-109.

711. Spinoza, *Thoughts on Metaphysics*, I.iv; II.i (pp. 120, 127-129); also Spinoza, *Ethics*, I, definition viii (*Works*, II, p. 46); cf. Mastricht, *Theoretico-practica theol.*, II.xi.6; Ridgley, *Body of Divinity* (1855), I, p. 85; Venema, *Inst. theol.*, vi (pp. 142-144); Wyttenbach, *Tentamen theol.*, III, §221-222.

712. Edwards, *Theologia Reformata*, I, p. 55; Wyttenbach, *Tentamen theol.*, III, §221; cf. Cocceius, *Summa theol.* III.ix.44.

a divine duration was not posed, as has sometimes been argued, against traditional orthodoxy, but as he himself indicated in his lectures, against Spinoza.[713]

There are some differences of formulation among the Reformed: some, like Pictet, do not distinguish clearly between successive and non-successive duration and, as a result, do not stress the relationship between God and the temporal order in their discussions of eternity, while others, by far the majority, like the authors of the Leiden Synopsis, Turretin, Charnock, Ridgley, and Rijssen, specifically define eternity as an infinite and successionless duration, standing beyond but nonetheless in relation to time.[714] This latter view appears to echo Aquinas' statement that

> the proportion of eternity to the total duration of time is as the proportion of something indivisible to something continuous; not, indeed, of that indivisible that is the terminus of a continuum, which is not present to every part of a continuum ... but of that indivisible which is outside a continuum and which nevertheless coexists with any given part of a continuum or with a determinate point in the continuum.[715]

Aquinas, whose argument is borrowed by several of the Reformed orthodox,[716] then uses the illustration of a circle: a particular point on the circumference is distinct from other points and cannot "coexist simultaneously" with any of the others, just as points in time are distinct and not simultaneous. The center of the circle, however, coexists simultaneously with all points on the circumference, as eternity is understood to coexist simultaneously with all points in time. The duration indicated by passage through the points on the circumference is a successive duration, in contrast to the nonsuccessive duration of the center is not successive — but the center always remains in relation to the successive duration of the movement around the circumference, indeed it remains always in relation to each of the points on the circumference.[717]

Resident in the scholastic concept of eternity, at least in what appears to be the view of the majority of the Reformed orthodox writers, there is a distinction parallel to that between immensity and omnipresence — namely, between eternity utterly apart from time because prior to the creation of time, eternity strictly so-called; and

---

713. Clarke, *Demonstration of the Being and Attributes of God*, V (pp. 31-33); idem, *Answer to a Seventh Letter*, p. 123.

714. Pictet, *Theol. chr.*, II.xi.5-7; cf. *Synopsis purioris theol.*, VI.xxviii; Turretin, *Inst. theol. elencticae*, III.x.1, 10-16; Charnock, *Existence and Attributes*, V (pp. 279-280); Ridgley, *Body of Divinity* (1855), p. 91; Rijssen, *Summa theol.*, III.xv; cf. the discussion in Davies, *Thought of Thomas Aquinas*, pp. 107-109.

715. Aquinas, *Summa contra gentiles*, I.66.7 (p. 219).

716. Cf. Heidanus, *Corpus theologiae*, II (p. 106), with Hopkins, *On the Lord's Prayer*, in *Works*, 1, p. 196; Turretin, *Inst. theol. elencticae*, III.x.12; Heereboord, *Meletemata philosophica, Disputatio XXV, de aeternitate Dei*, v (pp. 131-132); and Mastricht, *Theoretico-practica theol.*, II.xi.9.

717. Aquinas, *Summa contra gentiles*, I.66.7 (p. 219); note the use of this illustration in Heidanus, *Corpus theologiae*, II (p. 106), Mastricht, *Theoretico-practica theologia*, II.xi.9, and Pictet, *Theol. chr.*, II.xii.8; cf. the discussion in Stump and Kretzmann, "Eternity," in Morris (ed.), *The Concept of God*, pp. 232-236, 239-346. My own reading is that this illustration, given that Aquinas understood time as linear and unrepeatable, actually yields the so-called Scotist modification.

eternity in relation to the temporal sequence, eternity understood as everlasting duration. Thus, Mastricht indicates that the *infinitas Dei* can be considered in two ways, either absolutely and *in se* or in relation to those "other beings" with which God "coexists," whether spiritual or corporeal: the divine infinity is therefore defined either as omnipresence in relation to space or as eternity in relation to time.[718] So also, the Leiden Synopsis: "eternity is the attribute of the duration of the essence of infinite God," and Turretin, "eternity is the essence of God as lacking *terminus* in duration."[719] Ridgley similarly notes that "we firmly believe that God exists *throughout* all the changes of time, and yet that his duration is not measured thereby."[720]

Charnock indicates that eternity, as described in Psalm 90:2, consists in God's "priority" and in the "extension of his duration." God, thus, is "before the world" and exists "from everlasting to everlasting": he "neither began nor ends," and he is "not a temporary ... God." This eternal duration is "the foundation of the stability of the covenant" and refers not only to the divine essence as such but also to the "federal providence" of God. The concept of "eternity" is difficult to comprehend — as Augustine said of time, we know what it is until we are asked to explain it! Surely, we cannot comprehend eternity any more than we can comprehend the essence of God, but we can "comprehend that there is an eternity" just as we comprehend that there is a God. Yet "we may better understand eternity than infiniteness; we can better conceive a time with the addition of numberless days and years, than imagine a Being without bounds." Accordingly, "eternity is a perpetual duration, which hath neither beginning not end; time hath both."[721] Temporal things "grow up by degrees" and have a "succession of parts."

> Time hath a continual succession; the former time passeth away and another succeeds: the last year is not this year, nor is this year the next. We must conceive of eternity contrary to the notion of time; as the nature of time consists in the succession of parts, so the nature of eternity is in an infinite immutable duration.[722]

Nonetheless, the contrariety of the concepts does not demand the absence of relation between eternal and temporal being, inasmuch as God's eternity

> comprehends in itself all years, all ages, all periods of ages; it never begins; it endures every duration of time, and never ceaseth; it doth as much outrun time, as it went before the beginning of it; time supposeth something before it; but there can be nothing before eternity; it were not then eternity.[723]

---

718. Mastricht, *Theoretico-practica theol.*, II.xi.1, 7; the same point is found in seventeenth century philosophers like Malebranche: see his *Dialogues on Metaphysics and Religion*, VIII (p. 132).

719. *Synopsis purioris theol.*, VI.xxviii; Turretin, *Inst. theol. elencticae*, III.v.3.

720. Ridgley, *Body of Divinity* (1855), p. 91.

721. Charnock, *Existence and Attributes*, V, (p. 279); cf. Hopkins, *On the Lord's Prayer*, in *Works*, 1, p. 196.

722. Charnock, *Existence and Attributes*, V, (pp. 279-280).

723. Charnock, *Existence and Attributes*, V, (pp. 2792-80).

The point of the argument concerning duration, therefore, concerns the relationship of God's duration to temporal duration, not the abstraction of God from time.

Another nuance, approved among the English Reformed by Edwards, is found, replete with metaphors, in More's *Divine Dialogues*: although God cannot be called "*successive* properly and formally," he can be viewed as having succession "virtually and applicatively." God's "eternall Duration"

> contains *virtually* all the successive Duration imaginable, and is perpetually *applicable* to the succeeding parts thereof, as being always present thereunto, as the Chanel of a River, to all the water that passes through it; but the Channel is in no such successive defluxion, though the water be. Such is the steddy and permanent duration of the necessary existence of God, in respect of all successive Duration whatsoever.[724]

The key to the point is More's denial of proper and formal distinction of times in the Godhead and his insistence on a virtual distinction that is somehow "applicable" to the distinctions *ad extra*. More's language of a virtual and applicative succession in God echoes the language of the virtual or conceptual distinction of attributes in God: the distinction of times, like the distinction of attributes, belongs to God but is in God in such a way as does not argue division, composition, or any sort of essential mutation. Given, moreover, that God is the source of all being, it follows that there must be, in God (*in re*), a foundation or *fundamentum* for all of the distinctions known *ad extra*: the divine attributes indicate the distinctions of relation between God and things, specifically, in terms of the attributes or predicates of the things. The implication for the traditional doctrine of eternity is that, like all of the divine perfections and like the divine ideas of things, it both contains (virtually or eminently) and provides the foundation for the predicative distinctions in and of things, in this case, the temporal distinctions.

4. Infinity, eternity, and everlasting duration: the *ad intra* and *ad extra* aspects of divine duration and the affirmation of genuine temporality. When the implications of the Reformed orthodox understanding of eternity as a kind of duration are fully drawn out, their distinction between eternity and time does not indicate a categorical incompatibility of eternity with time. Both are kinds of duration, the former without mutation, the latter with mutation.[725] Turretin states quite specifically that God's "eternal duration embraces all time" and that eternity, in a very specific sense,

---

724. Henry More, *Divine Dialogues, containing sundry Disquisitions & Instructions concerning the Attributes of God and His Providence in the World*, 2 vols. (London: James Elesher, 1668), p. 62; cf. Edwards, *Theologia Reformata*, I, pp. 56-57, differing slightly from the original. Note the same metaphor in Hopkins, *On the Lord's Prayer*, in *Works*, 1, p. 196: "as rivers are contained within their banks and flow along by them part after part, without any motion of the banks themselves; so time is contained within eternity and flows along in it without any motion or succession in eternity itself." This is, of course, a classic metaphor — but is remains significant that these writers do not favor the variant of the man sitting on the river bank whose vision is like that of eternity, but stress the duration of the river banks themselves.

725. Turretin, *Inst. theol. elencticae*, III.x.13; cf. Le Blanc, *Theses theol., De aternitate Dei et ejus immutabilitate*, xiv.

"coexists with all the differences of time."[726] Just as in his immensity "God embraces ... all the extended and divisible parts of the world," so in his eternity does God embrace "all divisible times, not coextensively or formally, but eminently and indivisibly."[727] Turretin concludes that "it is not absurd" to teach that "the world and time should be contained in a point of eternity," given that a "point" need not be conceived merely mathematically as "the beginning of a line or of time" or physically as "the shortest extension either of mass or time" but also metaphysically as indicating "the negation of extension and divisibility."[728]

The resultant model, if scanned in the same manner as the first member of divine infinity (viz., immensity and omnipresence), yields a second member of the distinction consisting in eternity and everlasting duration, with eternity as the exact analogue of immensity and everlasting duration as the exact analogue of omnipresence. The distinction, then, is between the infinitude of the divine essence considered in itself, apart from creation, and either the eternity of God as contrasted with the temporal limitation of creation or the everlasting duration of the divine essence considered in its relation to the temporal order. The intrinsic infinitude of God can be understood, extrinsically or *ad extra*, either as the ultimate absence of temporal and spatial limitation, namely, eternity and immensity, or as the everlasting duration and omnipresence of God in his relationship to both time and space.[729] Heidanus indicates as much when he points out that just as, prior to the creation of the world, God cannot be said to be "everywhere (*ubique*)" because there was then no "where" (*quia nondum erat ubi*), just so is it impossible "properly to ascribe duration to God prior to the creation of the world" since there was then "no motion or succession of things": God's *duratio* had neither "before nor after" nor is it "long or short."[730] Similarly, distinction can be made between the eternity and/or eternal duration of God, which "looks backward and forward" and is "without beginning or end," and the sempiternity or everlastingness of things that are in a sense "for ever" and continually "look forward to that which is to come," but which remain "alterable and dependent."[731] In the older theological vocabulary, everlastingness or sempiternity denotes a duration in relation to the ages of the world, whereas eternity and its correlate, everlasting duration, indicate the specifically divine duration, apart from or prior to the existence of finite things and, therefore, capable of transcending the encumbrances of time.

This distinction between infinity and eternity or everlasting duration, like that between infinity and immensity or omnipresence, is *not*, of course, a distinction between attributes: it is a distinction concerning a single attribute made between an intrinsic

---

726. Turretin, *Inst. theol. elencticae*, III.x.6, 8.

727. Turretin, *Inst. theol. elencticae*, III.x.11; *Synopsis purioris theol.*, VI.xxviii.

728. Turretin, *Inst. theol. elencticae*, III.x.12.

729. Cf. Howe, *Living Temple*, I.iv.8, in *Works*, I, p. 98; Leibniz, "Five Letters to Samuel Clarke," V.105-106, in *Philosophical Works*, p. 375.

730. Heidanus, *Corpus theologiae*, II (p. 106).

731. William Jenkyn, *Exposition upon the Epistle of Jude*, ed. James Sherman (Edinburgh: James Nichol, 1863), verse 25, in loc. (p. 359).

and two extrinsic considerations. In terms of the rules for the predication of attributes, everlasting duration and omnipresence stand as descriptions of God grounded in our understanding of God's relation to objects *ad extra*. Such distinctions point us back toward the issues encountered in the initial statement of the problems of predication. Infinity, whether understood over against the finitude of space or of time, is intrinsic to the divine essence and the *fundamentum in re* that establishes the extrinsic attributes as more then mere human rationalization and, more importantly, as genuine relations between God and the world. What is more, the assumption behind the distinction is that these attributes, as intrinsically considered, are distinct *per eminentiam* in the divine essence itself: essentially identical but rationally or conceptually distinct in God and, indeed, to God.

Such a distinction follows from the consideration of the concept of eternity as, in Leigh's words, a "species" of "kind" of infinity, to be, therefore, defined by the language governing the general concept, namely, by the distinction between an intrinsic and an extrinsic infinity. The eternity of God, then, ought not to be defined merely negatively in view of the problem of temporal succession but also positively in view of the necessary relationship between God and the created order, namely, the relation between the infinite source of all good and the vast order of created goods. If this is so, we have once again encountered the phenomenon of a Christianized Aristotelianism, as different here from its ancient philosophical source as the scholastic conception of God as First or Unmoved Mover is different from the original Aristotelian conception. If, moreover, this hypothesis is correct, then it follows that many modern critiques of the traditional concept of eternity as positing a God who cannot relate to time are misplaced, inasmuch as they confuse the relative attribute of eternity and everlasting duration with the absolute attribute of infinity, in effect, addressing only the first member of the distinction and then complaining of a lack of relation to time when there is no time to which to be related — rather than examining the second member, which specifically identifies the way in which an eternal God does relate to time.

Perhaps the obvious point ought to be made that the orthodox tradition, including the Reformers and the Protestant scholastics, held to the Augustinian conception of time as the mutation of the finite order and not as an objective reality or "thing," an assumption which was disputed toward the end of the seventeenth century by various Newtonians.[732] The traditional categories of predication make this point abundantly: time or temporality is not *res* or *substantia* but rather, like quantity, quality, disposition, relation, or spatiality, is a predicate of a thing or substance. And, in the case of God, like all other predicates belonging to this secondary or incidental mode, time cannot be predicated properly of God. The question, then, is not whether God, as an a-temporal (or non-successive) being, can be related to time, but whether God,

---

732. Heidanus, *Corpus theologiae*, II (p. 106); Baxter, *Catholike Theologie*, I.vi.97; cf. Augustine, *Confessions*, IX.27. On the problem of the reification of time in the late seventeenth and early eighteenth century, see Leibniz, "Five Letters to Samuel Clarke," III. 6; IV.15-16; V.44, 55-59, 105-106, in *Philosophical Works*, pp. 335-336, 340-341, 357, 363-364, 375.

as an *a-temporal being* can be related to *temporal being*. This question is analogous to the question of the relation of immaterial to material being or of non-spatial to spatial being — inasmuch as neither materiality nor spatiality are things.[733]

Thus, to say that God is not "in time" or, more precisely, to indicate that temporality is not a divine attribute or property, is not to remove God from contact with an objective reality but rather to say that in his enduring relationship to all *ad extra* objective reality, God does not experience mutation or succession in himself: not that God is "timeless" or "without time," but rather he is "without succession [yet] near to the differentiations of time."[734] Temporal succession is merely the sign of the mutation of the finite order. Duration, by way of contrast, represents a relationship to or presence within the finite order apart from the problem of mutation — or in the case of finite things that endure, a presence within the finite order that is subject to relatively less mutation. Given that the divine relationship to the finite is characterized by duration without succession, there is in the duration itself a ground for conceiving the relationship of God to finite things characterized by duration, albeit with mutation and succession. This understanding of eternity and time quite consciously on the part of the orthodox voids the objection that an eternal being cannot know what is happening in a given moment as distinct from what is happening in another moment.

This recognition of the nature of time as a predicate or attribute of a thing rather than as a thing leads directly to a final consideration of the consequences of identifying God as eternal. Although God is eternal and eternally knows all things, it not necessary, as a logical consequence, that all things be understood as eternal or, alternatively, as out of relationship with God,[735] given that neither eternity nor time are things, but rather different ways in which the attribute of duration is predicated of a thing. Turretin indicates that just as "the immense God embraces in his immensity all the extended and divisible parts of the world, because wherever he is, he is wholly," so also does the "indivisible eternity of God embrace all divisible times."[736] Eternity "embraces" or "comprehends" all time or times because it is not merely an extended divine "time" beyond created time nor is it, strictly speaking, merely the negation of time. Instead, it is a broader and more encompassing kind of duration than temporal or successive duration. Eternity can be said to "coexist" with time and time with eternity — for all temporal things always stand in relation to the being of God, who apprehends them all in their mutation and succession and can even be said to have the succession in himself *virtualiter* or *eminenter* without being himself subject to succession, just as he has all the ideas of things in himself *virtualiter* and *eminenter* without being rendered composite:

---

733. Cf. Mastricht, *Theoretico-practica theol.*, II.xi.7.

734. Alting, *Methodus theol.*, III (p. 77A): "citra successionem juxta temporum differentias."

735. See the discussion of the scholastic background in William of Ockham, *Predestination, God's Foreknowledge, and Future Contingents*, trans., with intro., notes and appendices by Marylin McCord Adams and Norman Kretzmann, second edition (Indianapolis: Hackett, 1983), pp. 54-70.

736. Turretin, *Inst. theol. elencticae*, III.xi.11; cf. Baxter, *Catholike Theologie*, I.vi.99.

Although eternity may coexist with all the differences of time, it does not follow that they equally coexist among themselves. [For eternity] does not coexist with them taken together and existing all at once, but coexists with them existing dividedly and mutually succeeding each other. Thus the past, while it was, coexisted with eternity, the present now coexists with it, and the future will coexist with it. ... Thus all the differences of time agree together in this — that each when it exists, coexists with the whole of eternity. However they ought not therefore to agree among themselves so as to coexist at once because the whole eternity does not coexist with them taken at once, but dividedly as they mutually succeed each other (as the sun and its motion coexist with all the days of the ages; nevertheless it does not follow that they all coexist among themselves because every day coexists in its own order with the sun, which is always the same).[737]

The coexistence of time with eternity, then, is not an "adequated" but an "inadequate" coexistence, given that eternity lacks succession and is, therefore, different in its "nature and duration" from the nature and duration of time.[738] God, who has duration without succession, coexists with the temporal order, which has successive duration: God coexists non-successively with successive things. As Heidanus argues out, the result of this relationship is that from the perspective of his eternity, God truly coexists with all times — but that from the perspective of time, God today coexists with today and does not coexist with tomorrow. For, indeed, today does not coexist with tomorrow.[739] Eternity, as the "scholastics" indicated, "indivisibly embraces in itself, as in a point, the diversity of all times," without detemporalizing temporal things and without in any way disturbing their succession.[740] "Thus we firmly believe that God exists throughout all the changes of time, and yet that his duration is not measured thereby."[741]

E. *Pars Practica*: The "Uses" of Divine Infinity, Omnipresence, and Eternity

The Reformed orthodox writers also indicate several practical consequences that ought to be drawn from the doctrine of God's infinity, omnipresence, and eternity: as is the case with the other topics belonging to the doctrine of God, meditation on eternity was not a matter of philosophical interest or purely rational inquiry for the Reformed orthodox. The doctrine had significant implications for piety, which can be gathered under three specific categories: comfort to the godly; terror to the wicked; and incentive to press on toward the goal of salvation.

---

737. Turretin, *Inst. theol. elencticae*, III.xi.8-9; almost identically, Edwards, *Theologia Reformata*, I, p. 57.

738. Turretin, *Inst. theol. elencticae*, III.xi.10; cf. Mastricht, *Theoretico-practica theol.*, II.xi.9.

739. Heidanus, *Corpus theologiae*, II (p. 106).

740. Heidanus, *Corpus theologiae*, II (p. 106); cf. Mastricht, *Theoretico-practica theol.*, II.xi.9; Baxter, *Catholike Theologie*, I.vi.100; Heereboord, *Meletemata philosophica*, *Disputatio XXV, de aeternitate Dei*, v (pp. 131-132).

741. Ridgley, *Body of Divinity* (1855), p. 91.

First, the issue of comfort. In the promise of salvation, God offers an infinitely valuable reward — "for as God is infinite, such is the Happiness he bestows."[742] From God's greatness or omnipresence, Perkins argues, it follows that he is "the knower of the heart" from whom nothing is hidden.[743] "This omnipresence of God ought to render us sure of his divine assistance in all dangers, and diligent in religion through all our lives, since he is 'not far from every one of us' (Acts 17:27). It is said that he is wise who lives in this world as in a temple, and thinks of God as everywhere present."[744] Thus Leigh similarly states that God's omnipresence has the value of teaching the godly "to be sincere and upright, because they walk before God" (Gen. 17:1). God is present with all people and understands their inmost thoughts: "this should curb them from committing secret sins, and encourage them to perform private duties, Matt. 6:6"[745]

Since it is eternal God and not a temporally limited being who orders and guides all things, believers can be certain that the goal of drawing the world toward "eternal felicity" is within the power of God. Since, moreover, God is eternally the same, he is a constant guide "all the days of their life" who will "after death receive us to the everlasting enjoyment of himself, and revive our dust."[746] In our present condition, consideration of God's eternity provides "a mighty advantage for the strengthening of our faith in pleading with God for the same mercies, which he hath formerly bestowed upon others, because he is *the same yesterday, today, and for ever.*"[747] The contemplation of the eternity of God also draws the mind away from transitory things and points human beings toward their own "capacity of ... endless blessedness" far transcending the limited blessings of the world: "remember, when you are tempted for wealth or honour to wrong your soul, that these are not the eternal riches."[748] "Canst thou not run with patience so short a race," Baxter writes, "when thou lookest to so long a rest?"[749]

Second — the negative side of the doctrine: it cuts against the complacency of the wicked and, if believed by them, fills them with terror concerning their destiny. The wicked, Manton writes, "may outlive other enemies, but they cannot outlive God, who abideth forever to avenge his quarrel against them." For their sin of preferring the creature to the creator, earth to heaven, temporal things to eternal, the wicked are deprived both of the eternal favor of God (which they scorned) and the delights

---

742. Bates, *Harmony of the Divine Attributes*, p. 383.

743. Perkins, *Golden Chaine*, ii (p. 12, col. 1); citing 1 Kg. 8:39, Ps. 139:1-2 on omnipresence and its implications.

744. Pictet, *Theol. chr.*, II.x.11.

745. Leigh, *Treatise*, II.iv (p. 39).

746. Thomas Manton, *Sermons upon Psalm CXIX*, sermon 93, in *The Complete Works of Thomas Manton*, 22 vols. (London: J. Nisbet, 1870-1875), vol. 7, p. 396.

747. Hopkins, *On the Lord's Prayer*, in *Works*, 1, p. 201.

748. Baxter, *Divine Life*, pp. 137, 139; cf. Leigh, *Treatise*, II.iv (p. 43), citing Ps. 48:13, 14; 102:12; Isaiah 46:4; Hab. 1:12, 13.

749. Baxter, *Divine Life*, p. 142.

of the natural order (which they wrongfully desired): "How just is it for God to make them everlastingly to lie under the fruits and effects of their own evil choice!"[750] Eternity "is a terror to the wicked; he shall ever be to make them everlastingly miserable; as heaven is an eternal Palace, so hell is an everlasting Prison."[751] It is a primary mark of the saving knowledge of God that it removes or abolishes vain confidence in the transitory and looks to the eternal and unchangeable God as the foundation of our trust and as the one on whom we can "depend ... in all things."[752]

Third, the concept of eternity offers a practical support and stimulus to the life of faith. Inasmuch as "practical" knowledge directs the knower toward a goal, Christians need to recognize that "the truth of [God's] eternal being is the object of our faith" just as "the apprehension of him as our chief good and felicity is the object of our love."[753] This is so of God's eternity since, in a penultimate sense, our faith seeks as its object "our participated eternity" as the goal of "all our desires and labors ... the expectation of [which] fortifieth us against all the difficulties of our pilgrimage, and so directeth us what to mind, be, and do."[754] "We must carefully and earnestly seek him, place our happiness in him that is everlasting; all other things are fleeting; if we get his favor once, we shall never lose it; he will be an everlasting friend; his truth and mercy remains forever [Psalm 117:2; 146:6]."[755] God's eternity, as an article of our belief (1 Tim. 1:16) and as the ground of our soul's eternal happiness, is a proper subject for daily meditation.[756]

> God's love and election are also eternal, and he will give eternal life to all believers. That which is eternal, is perfect at once; therefore he should be adored and obeyed, his counsel followed.[757]

Negatively, Baxter could argue that "the infidel and ungodly man that looks not after an eternal end, destroys all the mercies of God, and makes them no mercies at all" inasmuch, for example, our creation and continued being is a mercy of God, but only as "it is in order to our eternal end." The denial of God's eternity, Baxter continues, is therefore an assault on the truth and significance of all Christian doctrine.[758]

750. Manton, *Sermons upon Psalm CXIX*, sermon 93, in *Works*, vol. 7, p. 397.
751. Leigh, *Treatise*, II.iv (p. 43).
752. Binning, *Common Principles*, in *Works*, p. 45.
753. Manton, *Sermons upon Psalm CXIX*, sermon 93, in *Works*, vol. 7, p. 399.
754. Manton, *Sermons upon Psalm CXIX*, sermon 93, in *Works*, vol. 7, p. 399.
755. Leigh, *Treatise*, II.iv (p. 43).
756. Cf. Leigh, *Treatise*, II.iv (p. 43), with Baxter, *Divine Life*, p. 125-126, 136-143.
757. Leigh, *Treatise*, II.iv (p. 43).
758. Baxter, *Divine Life*, p. 138.

5

The Attributes of Life, Intellect, and Will

5.1 The Attributes of the "Secondary Order": The Divine Operation and Egress

A. Early Orthodox Models: Perkins and Polanus

The movement from the divine simplicity, immutability, eternity, and like attributes to the attributes of the divine life (*vita Dei*) is variously described by the Reformed orthodox as a movement from the discussion of the essence or nature of God to a discussion of its operations,[1] from the question *quid sit?* (what is it?) to the question *qualis sit?* (of what sort is it?),[2] from the incommunicable to the communicable attributes,[3] or from a primary to a secondary order of attributes.[4] For many of the Reformed, the *vita Dei* is also the basic category which then divides into the two fundamental "faculties" or "internal activities," intellect and will.[5] Perkins makes the transition using the first of these patterns:

> Hitherto we have spoken of the perfection of Gods nature: Now followeth the life of God, by which the divine nature is in perpetual action, living, and mooving in itselfe. ... The divine Nature, is especially in perpetual operation by three attributes, the which

---

1. Perkins, *Golden Chaine*, iii (p. 12, col. 1); cf. Nichols, *Abridgement of Perkins*, pp. 2-4; Pictet, *Theol. chr.*, II.iv; van Til, *Theol. revelatae comp.*, II.C.

2. Mastricht, *Theoretico-practica theol.*, II.xii.

3. Maresius, *Collegium theologicum*, II.xxxvi. Note that others who use this classification do not discuss the *vita Dei*: e.g., Marckius, *Compendium*, IV.xxxiv.

4. Junius, *Theses Leydenses*, viii.27-28; Polanus, *Syntagma*, Synopsis libri II; Wollebius, *Compendium*, I.i.3; Burman, *Synopsis theol.*, I.xx.

5. Cf. E.g., *Synopsis purioris theol.*, VI.xxxii; Burman, *Synopsis theol.*, I.xx.4; Heidanus, *Corpus theol.*, II (p. 112); Van Til, *Theol. revelatae comp*, II.C

do manifest the operation of God towards his creatures. These are his Wisdom, his Will, and Omnipotence.[6]

Polanus, by way of contrast, set out his discussion of *vita Dei* and related attributes with a division between primary and secondary categories:

> The essential attributes or properties of God (*proprietates Dei essentiales*) belong to a twofold order: some are primary, others are secondary...
> The essential attributes of God of the second order are life and immortality (*vita & immortalitas*); blessedness and glory (*beatitudo & gloria*)....
> The goods (*bona*) possessed infinitely and incomprehensibly by God are ... wisdom and will (*sapientia & voluntas*), power and freedom (*potentia & libertas*)
> The essential wisdom of God consists in understanding, knowledge, art and prudence (*intelligentia, scientia, ars & prudentia*).[7]

Polanus' definition is important, not for its enumeration of attributes — his own systematic elaboration of the definition in fact identifies quite a few more attributes of the "second order" that are found in the definition itself — but for its clear demarcation of a set of "essential attributes" different in their character and implication from the attributes belonging to what he has called "the primary order." The "secondary order" refers to the life and "operation" of God and bifurcates into broad discussions of *sapientia* and *voluntas*, or, as most of the later Reformed understood the bifurcation, of *scientia* and *voluntas*.[8] The model is implied in the ascending order that moves from all being, to living being, to living being that knows and wills — and it can be inferred from the work of writers like Musculus and Zanchi, although it was clarified and developed only by the Ramist thinkers of the late sixteenth century.[9] Polanus' argument also echoes the scholastic distinction between the ultimate divine *actus* or actuality and its *operatio* or operation — or, as the distinction can also be stated, between the primary actuality (*actus primus*) and secondary actuality (*actus secundus*) of God, without, however, impinging on the divine simplicity — an issue very clearly noted in Perkins' qualifiers to his language of "operation."

The reason for caution in the use of the primary-secondary actuality distinction became quite apparent shortly after Perkins and Polanus had written. The distinction can also be observed in Arminius' doctrine of God, to a rather different end than in orthodox Reformed dogmatics. In Arminius' theology, essence and life are the two basic categories, with intellect and will standing as attributes subordinate to life. One

---

6. Perkins, *Golden Chaine*, iii (p. 12, col. 1).

7. Polanus, *Syntagma*, Synopsis libri II; cf. Wollebius, *Compendium*,I.i.3, prop. 1-3.

8. Cf. Junius, *Theses Leydenses*, viii.27; Ames, *Medulla*, I.iv.50-52; Cloppenburg, *Exercitationes super locos communes*, II.iii.2; Cocceius, *Summa theol.*, III.x.6-9, 14; Burman, *Synopsis theol.*, I.xx.2, 5.

9. Contra Gründler, "Thomism and Calvinism," pp. 113-117, who describes Zanchi as moving from intellect to will and then indicates that this discussion "necessarily leads to the affirmation of life in God": Zanchi's arrangement is precisely the opposite — life is discussed (*De natura Dei*, II.v) prior to immensity, perfection, and blessedness, while intellect and will follow (*De natura Dei*, III.ii, iv), after the chapter on omnipotence.

possible corollary of such a view, which appears in Arminius' thought, is to create a distinction in the divine nature itself that mirrors the distinction between antecedent and consequent will. Another possible corollary, which was posed not by Arminius but by Vorstius, was the denial of divine simplicity.[10] Such conclusions, clearly, would have been anathema to the Reformed orthodox, who used the distinction between the divine life and its faculties of intellect and will with great care.

B. High Orthodoxy: Cartesian and Anti-Cartesian Approaches

By way of contrast, together with its reflection of a fairly traditional movement from essence to operation, Pictet's derivation of attributes of thought and life from spirituality has strongly logical and philosophical (specifically, Cartesian) overtones and adumbrates the alterations that would take place in theology as it moved into the early eighteenth century:

> We have shown that God is a spiritual substance (*substantiam esse spiritualem*) or a spirit: and the first thing that we conceive concerning a spirit is, that it is a thinking substance (*substantiam cogitantem*) — it is therefore necessary to affirm this concerning God. But it must be observed that God thinks not like men or angels, but in a far more perfect manner, a point which will be explained when we discuss the knowledge of God. Further, since whatever thinks also lives, we must affirm that God is a living substance; and this the Scripture everywhere teaches, calling God "the *living* God": Deut. 32:40 ... Psalm 84:3, etc., thus distinguishing God from idols and the gods of the pagans ... Acts 14:15; 1 Thess. 1:9.[11]

Pictet's argument certainly reflects the logic of the Cartesian *cogito* from thought to existence or life: the relationship between Pictet's theology and Cartesian philosophy here is much like the relationship already indicated between his argument for the oneness of God and the Cartesian form of the ontological argument for God's existence — the philosophical point is not set forth either by or for itself but, rather, in the context of Pictet's more or less biblically determined topic.[12] Nor is it evidence of a fully developed Cartesianism like that found in some of Pictet's contemporaries. Rather is offers evidence of the attempt, on the part of some Reformed thinkers of the late seventeenth century, not to adopt a full-scale philosophical rationalism (which would entail the assertion of reason as the *principium cognoscendi*), but to replace the waning Christian Aristotelianism of the past several centuries with a new philosophical vehicle. By way of contrast, Mastricht, because of the controversies with Socinians, Remonstrants, and Cartesians, preferred to identify the transition as one from the

---

10. Cf. Arminius, *Disputationes publicae*, IV.v, xxviii and idem, *Disputationes privatae*, XVI.ii, iii, with Muller, *God, Creation, and Providence*, pp. 116-126, 187-189.

11. Pictet, *Theol. chr.*, II.iv.1-2; similarly, Burman, *Synopsis theol.*, I.xx.2; cf. Van Til, *Theol. revelatae comp*, II.C.

12. Note also that Pictet's language resonates with the triadic interrelationship of being, thinking, and living found in the Christian doctrine of God since the time of Victorinus and Augustine, although he makes no attempt here to draw out a trinitarian implication.

question "what" to the question "what sort," and defined the divine spirituality in conscious antagonism to the Cartesian philosophy.[13]

5.2 Life, Omnisufficiency, and Divine Blessedness

A. The Teaching of the Reformers

1. The *vita* and *aseitas Dei*. With the significant exception of Musculus, who wrote extensively on the *sufficientia Dei*, the Reformers of the first and second generations did not develop complex *loci* on the life, immortality, and sufficiency of God. There is, nonetheless, a significant continuity in the substance of teaching that appears when exegetical materials are examined, and the Reformed orthodox citation of *dicta probantia* for these attributes reflects their participation in a long exegetical tradition in common with the Reformers and, indeed, with the fathers and the medieval doctors. Thus, on the *locus classicus* for the doctrine of the *vita Dei*, John 5:26 ("For as the Father hath life in himself, so also hath he given to the Son to have life in himself"), Calvin writes, "God is said to *have life in himself*, not only because he alone lives by his own inherent power, but because, containing in himself the fulness of *life*, he communicates *life* to all things."[14] The attribute, for Calvin, as for the later orthodox, is understood both *ad intra* and *ad extra*. Or, in the case of Deut. 32:40, "I live for ever," Calvin indicates that "God swears by his life in a very different sense from men" inasmuch as "here, 'I live,' is tantamount to His swearing by Himself, or by His eternal essence."[15]

Calvin also argues that "to have life in himself" indicates the divine aseity or *aseitas*, an attribute that will be of especial significance to Calvin in his trinitarian teaching. The Godhead, as such, is underived or unoriginate: divinity and the divine essence do not arise from another — so that *aseity*, to be *as se ipso*, or from himself, is an attribute of God. It is also the case that the divine persons are not separated from one another "by a distinction of essence," so that the second Person of the Trinity, "with respect to himself" is called God and, as God, is possessed of an underived divinity or essence — whereas, "with respect to the Father," the second Person is the Son and is begotten or originated from the Father.[16]

Given that God is his own life and is the sole being capable of communicating life to all others, it follows that God is not only living but also immortal. Calvin comments that the identification of God as "immortal" in 1 Timothy 1:17 points toward something beyond the immortality of the angels and the blessed: for such beings are immortal "not of their own nature" but by the divine pleasure. Thus, "not as the angels, nor as our souls are, but as is stated in another place [1 Tim. 6:16], God alone has immortality in himself."[17]

---

13. Mastricht, *Theoretico-practica theol.*, II.xii.1; cf. II.iii.19-20.

14. Calvin, *Commentary on John*, 5:26 (CTS *John*, I, p. 207).

15. Calvin, *Harmony of the Four Last Books of Moses*, Deut. 32:40 (CTS *Harmony*, IV, p. 371).

16. Calvin, *Institutes*, I.xiii.19; reserving discussion of the trinitarian application of the concept for *PRRD*, IV, 5.1 (B.1); 6.3.

17. Calvin, *Sermons on Timothy and Titus*, p. 90, col. 2.

2. The *sufficienta Dei*. "The sufficiency of God" follows the discussion of God's "nature" in Musculus' *loci*, beginning with the interesting note that this and the other attributes might well have appeared at the beginning of the work — unfortunately without further comment on the arrangement of the *loci*.[18]

> ... next after the Essence of the Godhead, and the persons of the holy Trinity, this seems principally to be considered in God's nature, which the Greeks call *autarkes*, the Latins sufficiency, wherein they do scarcely express the strength of the Greek word.... And to the opening of this matter whereof we purpose to speak, we will use these words: Sufficiency (*arkeian*), Sufficiency of itself (*autarkeian*), Sufficiency for others (*heterarkeian*), Sufficiency in all and for all (*panarkeian*), which are always considered in God's nature as peculiar unto it.[19]

Thus,

> First we call Sufficiency, that which excludes all lack, which is so furnished with all abundance of all things necessary, that nothing more can be desired. This the Philosopher terms Sufficiency in itself, and attributes thereunto happiness, and the most high and perfect goodness. But this doth belong to the nature of God only, so that it can agree to no man living. In him there is a continual and an infinite abundance of all good things. ... Universal sufficiency is one, and particular sufficiency is another. The first is in God only: this last is given by God's gift unto men.... The true, full, and perfect sufficiency belongs particularly unto God's nature only: which both has all and has utterly no need of any thing.[20]

We see here scholastic and philosophical elements, but they are bound not to a metaphysical but rather to a didactic and hortatory purpose:

> ... it cannot be said unto God, what has thou but that which thou hast received: he has all, and yet for all that, he has received nothing of any person.... They be fools, yea verily wicked, which say that God provided not the matter and stuff of which the world was made.[21]

Furthermore,

> Secondly, he is in this respect also sufficient of himself, that not only has he all of himself, but he also suffices himself, that he has no need either of any of the things which he has, and which he has made and created. He is sufficient to himself through all things and unto all things.... He should not have been a point the richer, albeit he had created a thousand worlds.[22]

---

18. Musculus, *Loci communes*, xliii (*Commonplaces*, p. 898, col. 1).

19. Musculus, *Loci communes*, xliii (*Commonplaces*, p. 898, cols. 1-2); similarly, Vermigli, *Loci communes*, I.xi.2.

20. Musculus, *Loci communes*, xliii (*Commonplaces*, p. 898, col. 2-p. 899, col. 1).

21. Musculus, *Loci communes*, xliii (*Commonplaces*, p. 899, col. 2).

22. Musculus, *Loci communes*, xliii (*Commonplaces*, pp. 899-900).

Musculus adds a comparison based on Aristotle: he notes that "the Philosopher" shows that a man needs friends both in felicity and adversity, "because the weakness of man's nature is such, that no living man is able to be sufficient to himself, when he is become strong and mighty, much less when he is young and naked, and needy of all things, and new come forth of his mother's womb. But the nature of God is sufficient of itself, that it needeth the help and service of none other."[23]

If God is sufficient, Musculus queries, why then does he use creatures such as angels and men and even creatures and the elements themselves "not only to live, but also to govern?"

> I answer, whereas he uses the ministry of his creatures, he does it not of necessity, as though without them he could not govern the things he made and conserves: for he created the whole mass of Heaven, Earth and Sea by his word only, which is of not less strength and power than it is to govern all that he has made.... But just as he created all things for the declaration of his godly Majesty, so he uses also the ministry of all things, to show himself to be not only the maker, but the Master also of all, and that it might be known to mortal men, for whose sake he made all these things, that all doth depend on the beck of his will, and that there is nothing neither in Heaven, nor in Earth, but (if he list) doth obey and serve him.[24]

The sufficiency or all-sufficiency of God is such that God is providentially bountiful — again, beginning with the human example and application of the term:

> Thirdly, that *heterarkeia*, is when a man is not only sufficient to himself in all things, but yields unto others also plentifully to their use. *Arkein* in Greek signifies to aid, to help, and to relieve; and *arkeisthai*, to be contented, and to have sufficient. Therefore seeing that ... not only ... doth ... he need nothing, but that he doth also liberally and plentifully bestow unto others whereby they may live and be sustained, we may well also attribute unto him this *heterarkeian*.... So that he is absolutely, and in truth rich and sufficient to himself, which needs no other.[25]

Calvin writes similarly in his commentary on Psalm 36:8, "They shall be abundantly satisfied with the fatness of that house," with a strongly soteriological accent — the psalmist here refers to

> the abundance of good things which is not designed for all men indiscriminately, but is laid up in store for the children of God who commit themselves wholly to his protection. Some restrict the expression to spiritual graces; but to me it seems more likely, that under it are comprehended all the blessings that are necessary to the happiness and comfort of the present life, as well as those which pertain to eternal and heavenly blessedness.[26]

---

23. Musculus, *Loci communes*, xliii (*Commonplaces*, p. 900, cols. 1-2).
24. Musculus, *Loci communes*, xliii (*Commonplaces*, p. 900, col. 2).
25. Musculus, *Loci communes*, xliii (*Commonplaces*, p. 901, cols. 1-2).
26. Calvin, *Commentary on the Psalter*, 36:7 (CTS *Psalms*, II, p. 11).

That the divine sufficiency not merely for God, but for all creatures and, specifically, for human beings, is a teaching that the Reformers found clearly stated in Scripture. Calvin's exegesis of the classic *locus*, Jeremiah 2:13, is characteristic:

> the only true God ... in him is found for us a fullness of all blessings, and from him we may draw what may fully satisfy us. When therefore we despise the bounty of God, which is sufficient to make us in every way happy, how great must be our ingratitude and wickedness?[27]

The point is made, somewhat more dogmatically, by Musculus:

> [Fourth] when we consider that universal providence of God, whereby he provides for the necessities of all creatures, we easily perceive that the word *heterarkeias* is not enough to express the full sufficiency of the nature of God, but that we must attribute to it also *panarkeian*, that is to say, the sufficiency whereby all things in general that are in heaven and earth, receive what they need to live and continue.[28]

Even so,

> The one selfsame God is the bottomless fountain of all sufficiency to all things that be created by him, sufficient to all, and alone.... All matter, substance, essence, nature, life, sustentation of life, food, powers, and qualities of soul, spirit and body, all understanding, knowledge, wisdom and foresight, all strength of Imagining, reasoning, judging, remembering, loving, hating, desiring, and refusing, is of him, yea whatsoever things also do outwardly come, either by Angels, either by men, or by beasts, and any creature of his (says Paul to the Romans). And by him and in him, be all things.[29]

Nor does God give life to some things only, but to all: thus the psalmist says many times that we look to God for all things.[30]

3. Divine blessedness or felicity. This attribute is typically not detailed in the more doctrinal works of the Reformers — nor does it occupy a substantial position in the Reformers' exegetical efforts. Even so, discussion of divine blessedness or felicity is not universally present in the systems of the Reformed orthodox. If traced out in terms of the question of continuity and discontinuity, the results are quite mixed. On the one hand, the Reformation discussion, even when the *sedes doctrinae* are examined in the works of the Reformers, evidences a major point of discontinuity with the earlier tradition, in which the blessedness or felicity of God figured fairly prominently, and the reappearance of the discussion in some of the theologies of the Reformed orthodox indicates a moment of some discontinuity with the theological mind of the Reformation and a return to patristic and medieval models. On the other hand, the relative lack of prominence of the discussion among the Reformed orthodox yields also, level of

---

27. Calvin, *Commentary on Jeremiah*, 2:13 (CTS *Jeremiah*, I, p. 94).

28. Musculus, *Loci communes*, xliii (*Commonplaces*, p. 902, col. 1).

29. Musculus, *Loci communes*, xliii (*Commonplaces*, p. 902, col. 1).

30. Musculus, *Loci communes*, xliii (*Commonplaces*, p. 902, col. 2-p. 903, col. 1), citing Psalms 104, 144, 146.

discontinuity with the medievals, particularly with those medieval teachers like Aquinas and Scotus in whose doctrine of God the attributes of blessedness or felicity held a central position.[31]

Beyond Boethius' understanding of blessedness as "*status bonorum omnium congregatione perfectus* (a state perfected by the union of all good things)" and the emphasis on divine blessedness found in Augustine,[32] the tradition had a series of biblical texts that specifically demanded consideration of God as blessed. Thus, 1 Timothy 1:11 reads, "According to the glorious gospel of the blessed God," and 6:15, speaking of Christ, "who is the blessed and only Potentate, the King of kings, and Lord of Lords." The other texts, similarly, predicate blessedness of God and Christ: Romans 9:5, "Christ ... who is over all, God blessed for ever"; 2 Corinthians 1:3, "Blessed be God, even the Father of our Lord Jesus Christ," and 11:31, "the God and Father of our Lord Jesus Christ, which is blessed for evermore." The word translated in all of these places is *makarios*, which can be rendered either "blessed" (*beatus*) or "happy" (*felix*). Although, therefore, the terms "blessedness" (*beatitudo*) and "happiness" (*felicitas*) have slightly different connotations in Latin, the biblical text references are identical and the doctrine of divine blessedness or happiness concerns one attribute, not two.

Elements of these concerns do appear in the relevant places in Reformation era commentaries. In addition, humanist interest in the rhetoric and philosophy of antiquity drew attention to the conception of divine blessedness in writers like Epicurus and Cicero — although the impact of this line of philosophical argumentation was minimal. Luther, certainly, understood eternal blessedness as an attribute of Christ, commenting that "when I possess Him, I surely possess all; for He is pure righteousness, life, and eternal blessedness, and Lord over death as well."[33] On the text of 1 Timothy 6:15, Luther remarked that Paul's intention was to move "from the conditions of praise and thanks to the goodness of God" as manifest in Christ: when the text identifies Christ as "blessed" it sets him apart from humanity but also reveals the truth of salvation that humanity is not blessed except as it is blessed in Christ.[34] Luther also associated the gift of divine blessedness with faithful participation in the Lord's Supper.[35]

Calvin certainly recognized blessedness as a divine attribute, noting that Paul ascribes it to God alone, together with princely power, in order to draw "the eyes of the godly" away from the world's "transitory splendor."[36] But he more typically describes

---

31. Cf. Aquinas, *Summa theol.*, Ia, q. 26, art.1-4; *Summa contra Gentiles*, I.100; Scotus, *Opus Oxoniense*, I, d. 8, q. 4; d. 13, q. 1; IV, d. 13, q. 1. On Aquinas' conception of beatitude, see Patterson, *Conception of God*, pp. 360-363.

32. Cf. Boethius, *De consolatione philosophiae*, III.2;

33. Luther, *Sermons on the Gospel of John*, 6:47, in loc., in *LW*, 23, p. 107.

34. Luther, *Lectures on 1 Timothy*, 6:15, in loc., in *LW*, 28, p. 377.

35. Luther, *That the Words of Christ, "This is my Body, etc., Still Stand Firm,"* in *LW*, 37, pp. 132, 136.

36. Calvin, *Commentary on the First Epistle of Timothy*, 6:15, in loc. (CTS 1 Timothy, p. 167).

blessedness as a gift of God, given only in Christ and in covenant,[37] or in the Psalter, where God is frequently identified as blessed, he understands the ascription as a praise of the goodness and salvation of God.[38] Where Calvin and, at even greater length, Musculus, treat the concepts typically linked by the tradition to the divine blessedness — namely such concepts as the fulness or abundance of the life of God and the absence of any dependence on or need for things outside of himself — is under the rubric of the sufficiency of God, noted immediately above. Indeed, the connection between the attributes of aseity and sufficiency made by both Calvin and Musculus, is paralleled in some of the orthodox writers by a connection between the divine life and divine blessedness.[39]

B. The Divine Life in the Reformed Orthodox Theology

1. The *vita* and *aseitas Dei*. As in the discussions of the other divine attributes, there is a clear double continuity identifiable in the Reformed orthodox doctrine of the life of God — with the older tradition, including its medieval development, and with the thought of the Reformers. On the one hand, the Reformed orthodox doctrine, in a more explicit way than that of the Reformers, relates to the medieval language of divine essence and existence, although it must be observed that the *vita Dei* is not typically one of the attributes discussed by the medieval scholastics. On the other hand, the exegetical foundations of the doctrine relate directly to the biblicism of the Reformation and, indeed, to the specific results of Reformation-era exegesis. What is more, the Reformed orthodox emphasis on the *vita Dei* as a significant issue in the discussion of divine attributes, like their emphasis on the divine names, points to the greater emphasis on exegesis found in their doctrinal formulations as over against those of the medieval scholastics.

In brief, God is "1) a living Being, Gen. 16:14, etc.; 2) he lives to all eternity, Dt. 32:4; 3) is life itself, 1 John 5:20; 4) has life in himself, John 5:26; 5) is the fountain of all life to others; and 6) is most blessed, and the author of all felicity."[40] This set of basic understandings of the divine life has the implication, as already seen in the case of such paired attributes as immensity and omnipresence, eternity and everlastingness and as will be evident in many of the distinctions related to the divine willing, of both an *ad intra* and an *ad extra* dimension — an understanding of God in himself and of God in relation. Thus, inasmuch as God is all-sufficient and is life itself, the *vita Dei* can be defined apart from any and all relationships with the created order. Yet, on the other hand, the *vita Dei* is the necessary foundation of the life of all living things.

---

37. Calvin, *Commentary upon the Book of Psalms*, 48:2, in loc. (*CTS Psalms*, II, p. 220).

38. Calvin, *Commentary upon the Book of Psalms*, 31:21; 41:13; 66:20; 68:19; 72:18, in loc. (*CTS Psalms*, I, p. 517; II, pp. 126-127, 478: III, pp. 27, 118, etc.).

39. Cf. Pictet, *Theol. chr.*, II.iv.7.

40. Pictet, *Theol. chr.*, II.iv.8; cf. Leigh, *Treatise*, II.iii (p. 28).

From an exegetical perspective, the Reformed orthodox here again take as their point of departure a series of biblical predications that exalt the life of God above the life of creatures. The most significant biblical *loci* for this doctrine are Gen. 16:14, Deut. 32:40; Isa. 37:17; Acts 14:15, and other texts that refer to God as "the living God," together with John 5:26, "For as the Father hath life in himself; so hath he given to the Son to have life in himself.[41] Mastricht cites John 5:26 as the exegetical point of departure for his chapter on the "life and immortality of God," and the text figures prominently in discussions of the topic by Gill.[42]

By way of broader definition, the eternal divine life is both intellectual and volitional, consisting in God's "perfect knowing and understanding of himself" in "his willing himself as his own end," and also in "his perfect resting in himself."[43] In Cocceius' words, very simply, "the life of God is to understand and to will."[44] It is, in other words, a self-sufficient spiritual existence that is its own origin and its own fruition and that is therefore capable of being the foundation and source of all other life. The doctrinal conception of the *vita Dei* must, therefore, acknowledge a series characteristics of the divine life and of differences or distinctions between the life of God and the life of creatures — differences, moreover, that point from the *vita Dei* toward other of the divine attributes. These points are variously enumerated by the orthodox.

First, God has life in himself, in a most excellent manner.[45] "His life is his nature or essence; he is life itself, theirs the operation of their nature; he is life, they are but living."[46] To make the point somewhat differently, "the life of creatures is distinct from the creatures themselves, but the life of God is the very essence of God," given that God is fully actualized being.[47] As the medieval theologians from Anselm onward recognized, in God, essence and existence are inseparable — it belongs intimately and irreducibly to *what* God is *that* God is — he is his own essence and he is his own life.[48] God is, therefore, called "the living God," *Deus vivens*, in numerous passages of Scripture.[49]

Second, God is called "life" in the sense of the "source of life" and "the one in whom we live and move and exist."[50] In these texts, Scripture teaches the priority of God's life over all else that lives and, moreover, the relationship between the life of God and the life of all created things: "His life is his own: he liveth of and by and in himself;

---

41. Cf. Burman, *Synopsis theologiae*, I.xx.1; Gill, *Body of Divinity*, I, pp. 73-74.

42. Cf. Mastricht, *Theoretico-practica theol.*, II.xii; Gill, *Body of Divinity*, I, p. 73.

43. Leigh, *Body of Divinity*, II.iv (p. 168, margin).

44. Cocceius, *Summa theol.*, III.x.7.

45. Cocceius, *Summa theol.*, III.x.7.

46. Leigh, *Treatise*, II.iii, Leigh's first point (p. 30).

47. Pictet, *Theol. chr.*, II.iv.5; cf. *Synopsis purioris theol.*, VI.xxxi; Burman, *Synopsis theol.*, I.xx.3; Le Blanc, *Theses theol.*, De vita Dei, iii, xi.

48. Heidanus, *Corpus theol.*, II (p. 111).

49. Mastricht, *Theoretico-practica theol.*, II.xii.3, citing Deut. 5:26, 29; 32:40; Isa. 37:17; Dan. 4:31; Josh. 3:10; Ps. 42:2; 84:3; Jer. 2:13; 5:2; Matt. 16:16; Acts 14:15; cf. Downame, *Summe*, i (p. 10).

50. Mastricht, *Theoretico-practica theol.*, II.xii.3, citing 1 John 5:20; Col. 3:4; Ps. 36:10; Jer. 2:13; Acts 17:28; similarly, Downame, *Summe*, i (p. 10).

their life is borrowed from him: in him we live and move, Acts 17:25, 28. He is life, and the fountain of life to all things."[51] The attribution of "life" to God indicates, therefore, not only or simply "that God lives: but especially that God is the source (*fons*) of life of all things."[52] As such, God is the one who, in the ultimate sense, communicates life — both inwardly, of his very nature and being, and outwardly, through grace, to all living things.

The *ad intra* sense of God as the source of life is fundamentally trinitarian: for life is attributed to God not only essentially but also hypostatically, viz., of individual persons in the Trinity: thus the Father is life (John 5:26); the Son is life (John 5:26; 14:19; Job 19:25) and lives by the Father (John 6:57). So also is the Son the "prince of life" (Acts 3:15), the one in whom life is (John 1:4), the one who is our life (Col. 3:4), who has the power of endless life (Heb. 7:16), who lives and is alive for evermore (Rev. 1:18). The Spirit also is identified with life (Rom. 8:2; 2 Cor. 3:3).[53] In the outward or *ad extra* sense of the communication of divine life, God is to be understood and, indeed, worshiped, as the creator and fountain of all life:

> How the eternal Father *hath life in himself*, is obvious to every capacity; for he is the First Mover, and therefore must have life in and from himself, and not from any other; and he is the First Cause, and therefore that life which floweth from him to all created beings, must be first in him, as in its fountain.[54]

"Their life hath a cause, his none."[55] Thus, the term "life" is not predicated univocally of God and creatures, but "equivocally and analogically."[56]

Third, the differences between God and creatures are also apparent when the divine life is defined in terms of its relationship to the other attributes: "His life is infinite, without beginning or ending; their life is finite, and had a beginning, and most of them shall have an end."[57] Since God is eternal and eternally actualized and fulfilled, "His life consisteth in rest, and he possesseth all his life in one instant." This characteristic of the divine life also stands in direct contrast to the life of creatures, which "is a flux and succession of parts" — "His life is immutable, theirs mutable and subject to many alterations."[58]

Moreover, fourth, God and, therefore, God's life are perfect — unlike the life of things that pass away: "His life is entire altogether, and Perfect, theirs imperfect,

---

51. Leigh, *Treatise*, II.iii, the second point (p. 30); on the use of Acts 17:24-29, cf. *Dutch Annotations*, in loc.; *Westminster Annotations*, in loc.

52. Mastricht, *Theoretico-practica theol.*, II.xii.3; Maresius, *Collegium theologicum*, II.xxxvi.

53. Mastricht, *Theoretico-practica theol.*, II.xii.4; cf. Le Blanc, *Theses theol.*, De vita Dei, xvii-xix, xxi.

54. Poole, *Commentary*, John 5:26, in loc.; cf. Ames, *Marrow*, I.iv.36; Le Blanc, *Theses theol.*, De vita Dei, xii, xv; Mastricht, *Theoretico-practica theol.*, II.xii.5.

55. Leigh, *Treatise*, II.iii (p. 30, margin).

56. Le Blanc, *Theses theol.*, De vita Dei, xvi.

57. Leigh, *Treatise*, II.iii, the third point (p. 30); Maresius, *Collegium theologicum*, II.xxxvi; Burman, *Synopsis theol.*, I.xx.3.

58. Leigh, *Treatise*, II.iii, the sixth point, and margin (p. 30).

growing by addition of days to days. He liveth all at once, hath his whole life perfectly in himself, one infinite moment."[59] To the Reformed orthodox, perfection of life also indicates that, unlike creatures, God does not grow and develop: "Now we must not conceive in God any such imperfect thing as growth or sense, for he is a spiritual, a Simple and Immaterial essence; but his life is to be understood by the similitude of the life of reason, for he is a perfect understanding."[60]

Fifth, by extension from the perfection of the divine life, we may speak of God as "immortal and incorruptible."[61] Scripture describes the immortality and incorruptibility of God both negatively and positively: negatively "when it removes mortality and corruption from God" (Rom. 1:23; 1 Tim. 1:17; 6:16) and positively "when it gives life to God" (Gen. 16:14; Deut. 5:26; Jer. 2:13).[62] Even so, the *Dutch Annotations* infer from Romans 1:23, "the glory of the incorruptible God," that God is "unchangeable ... not only in essence but also in properties" and from 1 Tim. 6:16 that God "possesseth glory and perfection in himself which none can comprehend."[63] This must be so: "because he is void of all composition, therefore he is free from corruption; ... because he is simply, and every way immutable; ... because he is blessed, therefore he is immortal, *Ezek.* 37:14,"[64] — unlike his creatures, whose life "is frail and transitory," and, indeed, subject to corruption, to passions, and "determination of being."[65] Therefore, "when God is said to be *living*, it is not only to distinguish him from the false powers that heathens worship, but from all creatures, who possess only a derived and precarious existence."[66]

Sixth, the *vita Dei* is fundamental to the conception of God and to the reverence accorded him, for if God were not living, all the other attributes would be set aside or undermined, and God would not differ at all from the idols.[67] God is, thus, rightly called "the Living God" (Ps. 84:2; cf. Deut. 32:40; Jer. 4:2; 5:2) — as the "chief title" by which "he is distinguished from all idols."[68] In the case of the first of these texts, "my flesh crieth out for the living God," there is a full denomination of Jehovah as "the living God" in the sense of a name or title, whereas in the others, as in Revelation 10:5-6, the text implies the form of an oath. In Deuteronomy 32:40, "I live forever ... I live unto eternity," as Ainsworth renders the text, it is an oath delivered by God himself, confirming the stability of his promises and threats, given the character of

---

59. Leigh, *Treatise*, II.iii, the fourth point (p. 30).

60. Leigh, *Treatise*, II.iii (p. 30); cf. Mastricht, *Theoretico-practica theol.*, II.xii.5.

61. *Synopsis purioris theol.*, VI.xxxi.

62. Leigh, *Treatise*, II.iii (p. 31).

63. *Dutch Annotations*, Rom. 1:23, in loc.

64. Poole, *Commentary*, 1 Tim. 1:17, in loc (III, p. 776); Leigh, *Treatise*, II.iii (pp. 31-32).

65. Pictet, *Theol. chr.*, II.iv.5.

66. Pictet, *Theol. chr.*, II.iv.6.

67. Mastricht, *Theoretico-practica theol.*, II.xii.5.

68. Ames, *Marrow*, I.iv.37.

the divine life as opposed to the transience of other powers, as the Targum paraphrases, "As I live, so I will not break mine oath forever."[69]

By extension, seventh, it is not merely the case that the divine life is related to and understood in terms of the other divine attributes; the divine life is the actualization of all the other attributes — and, as the actuosity of an essentially spiritual and rational being, it is characterized by intellect and will or knowing and willing.[70] Even as

> our own life is a power, by which we are able to produce lively actions; God's life is that power, whereby he is fit to work or produce all sorts of actions suitable to the perfect essence of his divine Majesty; or it is that, whereby he knoweth, willeth and affecteth, and can do all sort of actions, beseeming his excellent nature.[71]

This pattern of distinction, reflecting the differentiation of primary and secondary actuality (*actus primus* and *actus secundus*), remained characteristic of Reformed theology long into the late orthodox era and was stated with considerable finesse by Gill, without any sign of influence from the newer philosophies:

> Having considered the attributes of Simplicity, Immutability, Infinity, Omnipresence, and Eternity, which belong to God, as an uncreated, infinite, and eternal Spirit; and which distinguish him from all other spirits; I shall now proceed to consider such as belong to him as an active and operative Spirit, as all spirits are, more or less; but he is infinitely so, being *actus, purus, et simplicissimus*; he is all act; and activity supposes life and operations.[72]

Life follows the ultimate essential attributes for the reason that it is not an attribute that radically distinguishes God from creatures — whereas simplicity, immutability, infinity, omnipresence, and eternity are attributes that, when placed as qualifiers into the context of all the other attributes, serve to distinguish them from the analogous attributes of creatures.

The divine life nevertheless, albeit the primary operation of God and, therefore, in a very limited sense *actus secundus*, must be understood as most simple, infinite, and eternal life. Since the life of God, like the divine essence itself, is simple, immutable, infinite, and eternal, the technical discussion of *vita Dei* as "secondary actuality" reflects the problem of predication of the attributes in general: the distinction between primary and secondary actuality in God is not at all a "real distinction" — and since it is not a distinction between attributes, but a distinction between categories of attribute, it is merely a *distinctio rationalis* and not a *distinctio ratio ratiocinata cum fundamento in re*, in Mastricht's words, a distinction between the ultimate *quid sit* of the divine essence and the *qualis sit*, "which we conceive as operation."[73] To press the point as a real

---

69. Ainsworth, *Annotations upon Deuteronomy*, Deut. 32:40, in loc.

70. Van Til, *Theol. revelatae comp*, II.C; cf. Heidanus, *Corpus theol.*, II (pp. 111-112).

71. Leigh, *Treatise*, II.iii (p. 29).

72. Gill, *Body of Divinity*, I, p. 71; cf. Ward, *Philosophicall Essay*, I.iii (p. 24); Turretin, *Inst. theol. elencticae*, III.xii.1.

73. Mastricht, *Theoretico-practica theol.*, II.xii.1.

distinction in God would be to go the way of Vorstius and the Socinians.[74] We can rightly speak of creatures in terms of *actus primus* and *actus secundus*, given that there is a distinction between the essence and the life or operation of creatures — but in God, where essence and operation are inseparable, the terms do not really apply.[75]

Eighth, the divine life itself is fully actualized (*actuosissimus*) and necessary: "He liveth necessarily, they contingently, so as they might not live."[76] God lives *a se* and not from another and his life is realized in knowledge, will, operation, and decretive judgment.[77] That God is *a se*, which is to say "of himself," or "in and of himself," or that "he liveth of and by and in himself,"[78] yields the term *aseitas*, indicating "self-existence." The concept is crucial both to the Reformed doctrine of the divine essence and attributes, where it parallels and reflects the function of divine simplicity, albeit not in quite as philosophical a manner, and to the Reformed doctrine of the Trinity, where it stands, from Calvin's time onward, as a guarantee of the equality of the persons. The term has, moreover, a very specific meaning: it is to understood not positively, as if God somehow "gave being to, or was the cause of himself," but rather negatively, in the sense that God's "being and perfections are underived" and that "they are not communicated to him, as all finite perfections are by him communicated to the creatures."[79] This *aseity* also serves, therefore, to distinguish the life of God fully from the life of creatures: "Creatures have life from another, God from none."[80]

This doctrine can also be inferred from the following reasons, which Leigh summarizes from Zanchi:

> (1) From the effects of life: God understands, wills, loves; therefore he truly lives, for these are all properties of [living beings]; therefore Aristotle often concludes from this, that because God understands all things, he lives a blessed life.
>
> (2) Those things live which move and stir themselves; God doth all things by himself; he is the first and most perfect cause of all; therefore he most properly lives, and that a most blessed life [Acts 17:28].
>
> (3) From his name *Jehovah*: he is *Jehovah*, who is by himself and most perfectly, and of whom all things are which are and live. God therefore so lives, that he is the Author of all life... , and therefore he is called our life, *Deut.* 30:20. [God lives because life is originally in him, *Psalm* 36:9; *John* 1:4: in him was life.][81]

From this it is clear that "God's life differs from the life of the creature."[82] Commentators on such texts as Deut. 30:20 infer from it that God is the "cause" or "Author of

---

74. Cf. Turretin, *Inst. theol. elencticae*, III.v.5-6.

75. Burman, *Synopsis theol.*, I.xx.3.

76. Leigh, *Treatise*, II.iii, the fifth point (p. 30); cf. Van Til, *Theol. revelatae comp*, II.C.

77. Mastricht, *Theoretico-practica theol.*, II.xii.5.

78. Leigh, *Treatise*, II.iii, the second point (p. 30); on the use of Acts 17:24-29, cf. *Dutch Annotations*, in loc.; *Westminster Annotations*, in loc.

79. Ridgley, *Body of Divinity* (1855), I, p. 82.

80. Pictet, *Theol. chr.*, II.iv.5.

81. Leigh, *Treatise*, II.iii (p. 29, text and margin).

82. Leigh, *Treatise*, II.iii (p. 30).

life and length of dayes, for in him we live, move, and have our being, that is, by power and vertue from him."[83] The text indicates our "dependence" on God, who "gives life, preserves life, restores life, and prolongs it by his power, though it is a frail life."[84]

The comforts gained from an understanding of the life of God are profound and are crucial to the Christian existence:

> (1) This comforts all God's people, who have the living God for their friend; who liveth forever, and they shall live eternally with him; the life of God comforted Job (19:25). Let them trust in the living God. This should comfort us against spiritual weakness, and deadness, though we be dull, and dead in Prayer, God is life, and will quicken us.[85]
>
> (2) We miserable men for sin are all subject to death, 2 Sam. 14:14; Psalm 144:4; Psalm 90:6; Job 14:1. Job describes there the brevity, frailty, instability, and manifold miseries of this life; therefore let us place all our confidence and hope in God, who is immortal and incorruptible; our soul is immortal, and made for immortality, it is not satisfied with anything, nor resteth but in God.... A thing may be said to be immortal in two ways: first *Simpliciter, absolutè per se, suaque natura*, so that there is no outward, nor inward cause of mortality; so only God. Secondly, which in its own nature may be deprived of life, yet *ex voluntate Dei* neither dies, nor can die; so the soul and Angels are immortal.[86]

2. The *omnisufficienta Dei*. There is continuity both in dogmatic substance and in practical nuance between the Reformation-era understanding of the divine sufficiency and the Reformed orthodox treatment of the topic. What is more, this corollary of the divine life parallels the exposition of the divine name *El Shaddai*, which is usually understood to mean God Almighty or all-sufficient.[87] Divine all-sufficiency or self-sufficiency is, moreover, closely related to the concept, treated previously, of divine independence — independence indicating, negatively, the difference between God and the world and his transcendence of its limitations, the sufficiency indicating the positive nature or ultimacy of God's being and life. Both attributes also stand as corollaries of the aseity of God.

In approaching the orthodox doctrine, we again, however, note a fair degree of variety in placement and formulation. A majority of the writers treat the *omnisufficientia Dei* in series following the discussions of *vita* and *immortalitate*. Whereas Mastricht placed the *vita Dei* at the beginning of the series of "primitive" or ultimate attributes indicating *qualis*, "what sort" of being God is, he understood *omnisufficientia*, not as an aspect of the divine life, but as a "derivative" attribute to be treated later.[88] Ridgley, following out the line of the Westminster Larger Catechism, places all-sufficiency in

---

83. *Westminster Annotations*, in loc., Deut. 30:20, citing Acts 17:28; cf. Poole, *Commentary*, in loc., citing John 14:6; 17:3.

84. Henry, *Exposition*, in loc.

85. Leigh, *Treatise*, II.iii (p. 32).

86. Leigh, *Treatise*, II.iii (p. 32).

87. See above, 4.2 (B.7).

88. Mastricht, *Theoretico-practica theol.*, II.xxi; cf. the *Methodica dispositio totius operis*, fol. **2.

between the infinity and eternity of God.[89] Zanchi, Leigh, and Binning understood the concept as a corollary of the divine infinity and eternity, with Zanchi equating the concept with divine perfection.[90]

> From God's Infiniteness ariseth his All-sufficiency: he is enough for himself and all things else, to make them happy and perfect in their several kinds; his all-sufficiency is that whereby God is of himself all-sufficient for himself to make himself most blessed, and to satisfy all other things, and make them happy in their several kinds; God hath therefore taken this name upon him [El-Shaddai], and by the commemoration of it did comfort Abraham, and encourage him to be his servant.[91]

Zanchi, moreover, associates the concept exegetically with the divine name *Shaddai*, and (echoing Musculus) interprets it as *autarcheia*.[92] The connection between all-sufficiency and perfection seemed quite evident to the Reformed orthodox: "God is an All-sufficient good, because he is a Perfect good," having sufficient goodness in himself for himself and for all creation, capable of supplying all the wants and satisfying all the desires "of his people both in this life and [in] that which is to come."[93] God is the inexhaustible source of all good and, as such, the cause of all created perfections.[94]

The doctrine follows directly from Genesis 17:1: "I am God Almighty" or "I am the God who is sufficient": there are, he points out, several ways to understand *Shaddai* — as the indicating ultimate power to create or devastate, as the ability to bestow on all whatever they need (given the possible derivation from the word for "breast"), and as a combination of a demonstrative pronoun and a participle, yielding "who is sufficient (*qui sufficit*).[95] So also is it inconceivable that one who is the absolutely first (Rev. 1:5, 8), the ultimate being, *ens per excellentiam, summa entitas*, and as eternal has nothing prior to him or beside him, could be less than perfectly sufficient: this is certainly what John of Damascus meant when he spoke of God as *teleios* and *hyperteles*.[96] The rhetorical questions of Job 22 lead Reformed exegetes to conclude that God "can neither increase nor diminish" and that God is therefore self-sufficient or all-sufficient.[97]

The divine all-sufficiency is preeminently illustrated in the covenant of grace, where God not only promises to be utterly sufficient to all his people's needs but also clearly manifests himself as all-sufficient in the provision and sustenance of Israel during its

---

89. Ridgley, *Body of Divinity* (1855), I, p. 83.

90. Zanchi, *De natura Dei*, II.vii (cols. 138-155); Leigh, *Treatise*, II.iv (p. 34); Binning, *Common Principles*, in *Works*, p. 45.

91. Leigh, *Treatise*, II.iv (pp. 34-35). Leigh indicates that he refrains from an extended treatment of this topic in deference to the popular treatise by Preston: viz., *Life eternall* (London, 1631).

92. Zanchi, *De natura Dei*, II.vii (cols. 138-140).

93. Leigh, *Body of Divinity*, II.iv (pp. 171-172).

94. Zanchi, *De natura Dei*, II.vii, q. 1.2 (col. 140).

95. Mastricht, *Theoretico-practica theol.*, II.xxi.2.

96. Mastricht, *Theoretico-practica theol.*, II.xxi.4.

97. Cf. Calvin, *Sermons on Job*, p. 389, col. 1, with Poole, *Commentary*, in loc. (II, pp. 975-976); Trapp, *Commentary*, in loc. (II, p. 302).

time in the wilderness, where, despite the desolation of the place, they never lacked food, water, or protection.[98] As illustrated by Baxter's *Divine Life*, seventeenth-century Protestants understood discussion of the divine attributes such as self-sufficiency not as a speculative matter but as an eminently practical issue. For the concept of self-sufficiency, like the concept of divine *potentia*, does not indicate a God in isolation but a God who is the gracious source of all things:

> How can we think of such a Fountain-Being, but we must withal acknowledge ourselves to be shadows of his goodness, and that we owe to him what we are, and so consecrate and dedicate ourselves to his glory! How can we consider such a Self-Being, Independent, and Creating Goodness, but we must have some desire to cleave to him, and some confidence to trust in him![99]

Especially when believers experience the assaults of "spiritual enemies" they can hope for victory, trusting in God "because 'his grace is sufficient for them.'"[100]

3. The *beatitudo Dei* in the theology of Reformed orthodoxy. In the era of orthodoxy, however, the topic of divine beatitude and felicity returns to the theological systems, albeit typically only in the large-scale bodies of doctrine and not in the *compendia* or *medullae*: thus the discussion is found in Zanchi, Polanus, Burman, Leigh, Mastricht, Heidegger, Pictet, and Gill,[101] but not in Junius, Perkins, Ames, Maccovius, Trelcatius, the *Synopsis purioris*, Gomarus, Heidanus, Maresius, Hottinger, Turretin, Brakel, or Marckius. The concept of divine blessedness is, moreover, conveyed, not through a single term, but through several predicates that are used almost interchangeably by the Reformed orthodox: blessedness or beatitude (*beatitudo*), joy or happiness (*felicitas*), delight (*delectatio*), and contentment or self-fulfillment (*complacentia*). Indeed, the terms are so interrelated in the discussion and also so dependent on the concepts of divine goodness and self-sufficiency that the discussion of the *felicitas*, *delectatio*, *complacentia*, and/or *beatitudo Dei* appears almost as a conclusion drawn from these other *loci*.

In Polanus' definition, there is both a reflection of Boethius' language and an interest in indicating precisely what categories of "good" God possesses:

> The blessedness of God (*beatitudo Dei*) embraces immunity from all evils (*immunitatem ab omnibus malis*) and the possession of all goods (*omnium bonorum possessionem*).
>
> The goods that the blessed God (*beatus Deus*) possesses are infinite and incomprehensible; however, for the sake of our better and easier comprehension, they

---

98. Leigh, *Body of Divinity*, II.iv (p. 172).

99. Binning, *Common Principles*, in *Works*, p. 45.

100. Ridgley, *Body of Divinity* (1855), I, p. 85, citing 2 Cor. 12:8-9.

101. Zanchi, *De natura Dei*, II.viii (cols. 155-160); Polanus, *Syntagma*, II.xvii; Burman, *Synopsis theol.*, II.xxix.3; Leigh, *Treatise*, II.xv; Mastricht, *Theoretico-practica theol.*, II.xxiii; Heidegger, *Corpus theol.*, III.111-112; Pictet, *Theol. chr.*, I.iv.7; Gill, *Body of Divinity*, I, pp. 175-180.

can be referred to in terms of wisdom (*sapientia*) and will (*voluntas*), power (*potentia*) and freedom (*libertas*).[102]

Similarly, in Pictet's definition, God is said to be "happy" (*felix*) or to have "felicity":

> This life of God is most happy (*felicissima*), since he is more than once called the 'blessed' God by Paul (1 Tim 1:11; 6:15); and the validity of the reference will be clear to anyone who properly considers the concept of true happiness. For who would not call God happy, who is in need of nothing, finds all comfort in himself, and possesses all things; is free from all evil, and filled with all good.[103]

These definitions follow as a consequence of the goodness and sufficiency of God, who alone of all beings finds contentment in himself and whose blessedness is, therefore, the final goal of all creaturely existence: God is both blessed *in se* and the source (*fons*) of all blessedness.[104] He is the *principium supremum* and *causa prima* of all good, who wills to communicate his goodness to his creation.[105] In short, God's blessedness "is that by which God is in himself, and of himself All-sufficient ... that Attribute whereby God hath all fulness of delight and contentment in himself, and needeth nothing out of himself to make him happy." Such blessedness is essential, primary, and original to God. It is also formal, in that God has his own goodness as the object of his contemplation; and objective, in that God is essentially blessed and happy; and effective, given that God "makes his children happy" and is "the author of all blessedness."[106]

Whereas human blessedness consists in the enjoyment of God, the divine blessedness consists "not in [God] enjoying us, but himself"[107] — by way of contrast,

> Man's blessedness is from another, the Lord's is from himself; man's is in grace, God's in nature; man's temporal, God's eternal; man's voluntary, God's necessary, it cannot be otherwise; man's changeable, God's always the same. ... God's glory is never left off, there is no interruption of his blessedness, not a moment wherein he is less happy.[108]

Still, there remains an analogy with human happiness:

> The happiness of a man consists in enjoying himself by virtue of the possession of the greatest good, whereof he is capable, or which is all one, by enjoying the greatest good. ... Accordingly we must conceive God's happiness to be in the enjoyment of himself; he doth perfectly enjoy his being, his life, his faculties, his Attributes, his virtues. ...

---

102. Polanus, *Syntagma*, Synopsis libri II; cf. Burman, *Synopsis theol.*, II.xxix.2.

103. Pictet, *Theol. chr.*, II.iv.7; cf. Zanchi, *De natura Dei*, II.viii, q. 1.2 (col. 156).

104. Mastricht, *Theoretico-practica theol.*, II.xxiii.3; cf. Cocceius, *Summa theol.* III.x.39; Leigh, *Treatise*, II.xv (p. 121); Gill, *Body of Divinity*, I, p. 176.

105. Holdsworth, *Praelectiones theologicae*, II.v (p. 528); II.ix (pp. 555-556).

106. Leigh, *Treatise*, II.xv (pp. 102, 122-123); cf. Zanchi, *De natura Dei*, II.viii (col. 155); Mastricht, *Theoretico-practica theol.*, II.xxiii.4, 6-7.

107. Adams, *Exposition upon Second Peter*, 2:9, in loc. (p. 390).

108. Adams, *Exposition upon Second Peter*, 2:9, in loc. (p. 391); cf. Burman, *Synopsis theol.*, II.xxix.3.

in himself and of himself doth perfectly enjoy himself, and this is his perfect happiness. He liveth a most perfect life, abounds with all perfect virtues, sets them at work himself in all fulness of perfection, and in all this enjoys himself with inconceivable satisfaction.[109]

Thus, the *ad intra* or internal blessedness of God can be described according to several interrelated categories: first, it is the pleasure (*felicitas*) that God has in his own wisdom and goodness and in "the contemplation of his own self-sufficiency." Second, it should be understood as his "comprehension of all happiness; for it is nothing to be blessed and not to understand it ... God's omniscience is his blessedness." Third, grounded in God's knowledge of his own happiness, blessedness is also the "delectation" (*delectatio*) or delight that God takes from this knowledge, "when he knows that there is nothing can offend him." And fourth, blessedness resides in the contentment (*complacentia*) that God receives from his delight — namely, in "having all things fully in himself, that he needs no addition." Thus, God "contemplates his own goodness, and rests in himself with a sweet complacency, as the infinite fountain of all blessedness."[110]

This traditional language of divine blessedness or felicity has a series of significant corollaries: it guarantees the freedom of God. Inasmuch as God is the ultimate source and goal of all good and as both necessary and sufficient in his being, God is in no need of his creatures or of particular acts on the part of his creatures to ensure his happiness. God is, therefore, utterly free in his dealings with the creation — and, above all, utterly free in his bestowing of grace and mercy.[111] There also is an eschatological corollary that relates directly to the analogy of human happiness and to the necessary failure of the analogy. Although perfect happiness is not available on earth, the highest happiness given here is that which is given by God and had through communion with him: "according as he doth communicate himself to no more or less, so are we more or less happy." This conclusion, points toward the intensely practical aspect of the orthodox discussion of this attribute: God's blessedness elicits response from the creature: "God is also to be blessed by us, which blessing adds nothing to his blessedness but is ... required of us that we may ... enjoy his blessedness." As reasonable creatures we ought to "observe and know" the divine blessedness by praising God, applauding his greatness, and outwardly expressing and acknowledging him.[112]

We should 1. see our misery, that being alienated from God [we] must needs be miserable till this estrangement be removed. 2. Set ourselves to get true blessedness by regaining this union and communion with God the fountain of all bliss, and hate sin which only separates between God and us, and hinders us from enjoying the blessed God. 3. We should place all our happiness in him, and in him alone, for he is not only the chief but the sole happiness in him, and in him alone, for he is not only the chief

---

109. Leigh, *Treatise*, II.xv (p. 126).
110. Adams, *Exposition upon Second Peter*, 2:9, in loc. (p. 391).
111. Bates, *Harmony of the Divine Attributes*, p. 143; cf. below, 5.4 (C.2-3) on divine freedom.
112. Leigh, *Treatise*, II.xv (p. 123).

but the sole happiness; we should use the world, but enjoy him, *Psalm* 16:11. We should use the means which may bring blessedness, *Psalm* 1:1; Matt. 5;3-12. ... All the promises of God belong to godly men; they shall be blessed here and hereafter who serve God in sincerity. We must expect and look for happiness only in our union with and fruition of him.[113]

Zanchi emphasizes the blessed life that flows from God into those who receive Christ in faith to their justification, remission of sins, and peace of conscience.[114] Our faith and our hope for the future have a firm foundation when they rest on God, who is "the possessor and author of all perfection, blessedness, and glory."[115]

5.3   The Intellectual Attributes of God: Understanding, Knowledge, Wisdom, Truthfulness, and Faithfulness

A. Intellectual Attributes: The Structure and Content of the *Locus*

Once again, we begin with a set of definitions and divisions taken from Polanus' *Syntagma theologiae*, granting that they offer such a clear picture not only of the Ramist models characteristic of the early orthodox era, but also of the shape and contents of Reformed orthodox theology in general.

> The essential wisdom of God (*sapientia Dei essentialis*) embraces understanding (*intelligentiam*), knowledge (*scientiam*), art (*artem*) and prudence (*prudentiam*).
>
> The knowledge of God (*scientia Dei*), in the first place, is either general or special.
>
> Second, the knowledge of God is both a knowledge of things past and present (*notitia praeteritorum & praesentium*) and a foreknowledge of future things (*praescientia futurorum*).
>
> Foreknowledge is twofold: either universal or particular.
>
> Further, the foreknowledge of God is either theoretical or practical.
>
> Third, the knowledge of God is either a knowledge of vision (*visionis*) or of simple understanding (*simplicis intelligentiae*).[116]

This language consciously reflects categories of knowing found previously in the definitions of theology, given that the essential knowledge of God includes the *theologia archetypa*.[117] There is also, accordingly, variety of formulation at this point in the orthodox systems. Zanchi associates *scientia* and *sapientia*, dealing with the two in a single *locus*.[118] Some theologians, like Maccovius, prefer to focus on the *scientia Dei*; others, like Turretin, on the *intellectus Dei*, and still others, most notably Mastricht, present in series the *intellectus, scientia,* and *sapientia Dei*. The differences in theology caused by these formal divergences are minimal — but they do represent different

---

113. Leigh, *Treatise,* II.xv (p. 124); cf. Leigh, *Body of Divinity,* X.iv, "Of the Last Judgement" (p. 1175); Mastricht, *Theoretico-practica theol.,* II.xxiii.14, 15.

114. Zanchi, *De natura Dei,* II.viii (col. 160).

115. Burman, *Synopsis theol.,* II.xxix.3 ; cf. Mastricht, *Theoretico-practica theol.,* II.xxiii.7.

116. Polanus, *Syntagma,* Synopsis Libri II.

117. See *PRRD,* I, 5.2 (C.2).

118. Zanchi, *De natura Dei,* III.ii (col. 195-198).

ways of addressing the problem of divine knowledge, inasmuch as *intellectus* identifies a faculty whereas *scientia* and *sapientia* do not. In addition, the attention to *sapientia* in some writers relates to a more teleological interest and to the alternative definition of theology as *sapientia* rather than *scientia*. There are also notable differences in the number of distinctions cited and the manner in which they are argued.

B. The Divine Wisdom (*Sapientia*)

1. Teachings of the Reformers. As will also be the case with the post-Reformation orthodox, the Reformers tend to relate the divine knowledge and wisdom, often discussing the two together, but typically defining knowledge in terms of direct understanding of all things and wisdom in terms of the divine purpose or end. Hyperius indicates that wisdom is necessarily attributed to the one who is the cause of all things. Since God is eternal, he has an eternal wisdom concerning those things — a wisdom concerning all things past, present, and future, given the precedence of eternal wisdom over all times.[119] Calvin describes the divine wisdom as an "inscrutable counsel" far beyond human comprehension: indeed, we must always fall short of an understanding of the divine wisdom, given that it is infinite.[120] Still, we can and ought to contemplate the little of God's wisdom that is revealed to us, for although we cannot comprehend the divine wisdom as such, when the word is used to indicate "God's purpose, determination, or intent," we can accept the creation as the "mirror of his wisdom" and we can appreciate the even greater wisdom revealed in the goodness of God toward us.[121] Given the partial revelation and the ultimate inaccessibility of the divine counsel, divine wisdom, indivisible and inseparable from God himself, with respect to us is a twofold wisdom, consisting in "the wisdom which is contained in his word" for our instruction, namely, the "wisdom he communicates to creatures" and the ultimate "wisdom that he keepeth still in himself."[122]

2. Reformed orthodox definitions of divine wisdom. The concept of divine wisdom functions as a necessary corollary in Protestant orthodox theology to the concept of divine omniscience. Some of the orthodox, like Perkins, Ames, Wollebius, and the authors of the Leiden *Synopsis*, make little or no distinction between divine knowledge and divine wisdom.[123] Yet the terms do admit of a distinction: whereas *scientia* is typically defined as a knowledge of first principles and the conclusions that can be drawn from them, *sapientia* is a knowledge of principles and of the ends or goals they imply. Even so, the attribute of *scientia* in God refers more to first causes, while the

---

119. Hyperius, *Methodus theologiae*, I, p. 146.

120. Cf. Calvin, *Commentary on Isaiah*, 40:13 (CTS *Isaiah*, III, p. 218), with idem, *Sermons on Job*, 11:7 (p. 200, col. 1).

121. Calvin, *Sermons on Job*, 11:7 (p. 200, col. 1).

122. Calvin, *Sermons on Job*, 12:13-15 (p. 218, col. 1); and see infra, p. 222, col. 1, the similar distinction between the revealed wisdom of God's law in the rule and order of the world and the hidden ultimate wisdom of God.

123. Thus, Perkins, *Golden Chaine*, iii (p. 12, col. 1); cf. Wollebius, *Compendium*, I.i.3; Ames, *Medulla*, I.iv.52-56; *Synopsis purioris theologiae*, VI.xxxii.

attribute of *sapientia* leads to the consideration of final causality — wisdom is the capacity to order and utilize the knowledge contained in the intellect:

> God's knowledge differs from his wisdom in our apprehension thus: his knowledge is conceived as the mere apprehension of every object, but his wisdom is conceived as that whereby he doth order and dispose all things. His knowledge is conceived as an act; his wisdom as an habit or inward principle; not that it is so, but only we apprehend it in this manner.[124]

Knowledge is opposed to ignorance, but wisdom is opposed to folly or "error in conduct":

> it consists more especially in designing the best and most valuable end in what we are about to do, in using the proper means to effect it, and in observing the fittest season to act, and every circumstance attending it, that is most expedient and conducive thereunto; and also in fore-seeing and guarding against any occurrence that may frustrate our design, or give us occasion to blame ourselves for doing what we have done or repent of it, or to wish we had taken other measures.[125]

Thus, "the *wisdom* or *prudence* and counsel of God" can be defined as the attribute according to "which God rightly perceives the best reason of all things done," resulting in "a most perfect harmony, and beautiful order" and the agreement of all things "both amongst themselves and with God."[126] Wisdom is the specific form of knowing according to which "God knows what is necessary to be done, according to the circumstances of things, and in what order and manner it should be done; by what means he may best attain the end he designs, and thereby display his own glory."[127]

> These ways are unknown, yet they are most righteous, and we must adore, and not curiously examine them. So wonderful is this wisdom of God that it sometimes brings light out of darkness, life out of death, and a blessing out of a curse. To this supreme and "only wise God," be honor and glory forever. Amen.[128]

Beyond the definition of wisdom in its distinction from knowledge, the Reformed orthodox also recognize a distinction between the biblical hypostatization of Wisdom, traditionally identified as the Logos or Word, and the attribute of wisdom often predicated of God in Scripture without any personal implication. They therefore distinguish between the "essential wisdom of God," common to all persons of the Trinity and the "personal wisdom of God," the logos or second person of the Trinity, as referenced in Proverbs 8:1, Matthew 11:19, Colossians 11:3, and 1 Corinthians 1:24.[129]

---

124. Leigh, *Treatise*, II.vii (p. 65).
125. Ridgley, *Body of Divinity*, p. 71, col. 2.
126. Leigh, *Treatise*, II.vii (p. 64).
127. Pictet, *Theol. chr.*, II.v.20; cf. Charnock, *Existence and Attributes*, IX (I, p. 507).
128. Pictet, *Theol. chr.*, II.v.20.
129. Mastricht, *Theoretico-practics theol.*, II.xiii.16; cf. Leigh, *Treatise*, II.vii (p. 65, margin).

Reserving the trinitarian reference of the language to the second part of the *locus*, the Reformed develop first the implications of the essential wisdom of God:

> God is most wise, or infinite in wisdom, or as the Apostle expresses it, he is *the only wise God* (Rom. 16:27). This perfection considered as absolute, underived, and truly divine, belongs only to him; so that the Angels themselves, the most excellent order of created beings, are said to be destitute of it, or charged with folly (Job 4:18).[130]

God is necessarily wise inasmuch as "the notion of wisdom is inseparable from the notion of a Deity." This is, moreover, an "intrinsic and absolute necessity, by virtue of his own essence, without the efficiency of any other, or any efficiency in and by himself."[131] In other words, God does not make himself wise.

Given the identification of wisdom as an essential attribute, it follows, as Scripture teaches, that God's wisdom is

1. Infinite, *Psalm* 136:5 and unsearchable, Job. 11:7.
2. Essential to himself. He is the only wise God, *Rom.* 16:27; 1 Tim 1:17.
3. He is perfectly, originally, unchangeably wise, Isaiah 40:13.
4. The fountain of all wisdom; was there such wisdom in *Adam*, to give names to things according to their natures? and in *Solomon* to discourse of all things? and is there not much more in God?[132]

This understanding of divine wisdom also assumes a distinction between eternity and time, not in the sense of removing a relationship between God and temporal things, but in affirming the nature of their relationship and (as argued above in the discussion of eternity) assuming that God's eternity fully embraces all of time: God foresees eternally but disposes temporally.

> Wisdom hath two principal acts, [1.] foresight, and forecast, by which a man can beforehand see what will be after to make his use of it; 2. disposing and ordering things, by taking the fittest means and opportunities to attain his own good and right ends. This virtue is infinitely in God, for he doth foresee all things eternally; and in time disposeth of them most fitly, by the fittest means and opportunities for the best that can be, to his own glory, which is the highest end that he can and should aim at; for to that which is the best of all things, must all things else be referred; therefore God is the only wise God.[133]

A similar pattern is reflected in the better-known distinction between the decree and its execution.

3. Demonstrations of divine wisdom from the works of God. Keeping the distinction between knowledge and wisdom in view and regarding wisdom as tending toward the disposition as well as the knowing of objects, several particulars concerning

---

130. Ridgley, *Body of Divinity*, p. 71, cols. 1-2.
131. Charnock, *Essence and Attributes*, IX (I, p. 509).
132. Leigh, *Treatise*, II.vii (p. 64).
133. Leigh, *Treatise*, II.vii (p. 65).

the wisdom of God may be observed. The positive relation established in the middle and high orthodox periods between Reformed theology and the older tradition, including elements of a modified Thomism and Scotism as well as the broadly Augustinian philosophy of the Middle Ages, can be seen clearly in the description of the "particulars" of the Divine wisdom. Specifically, God is seen to be wise, first, in the most general terms, in the creation itself:

> In making of this great world, 1 Cor. 1:21. All things therein are disposed in the best order, place, time, by the wisest Architect. How doth *David* in the *Psalms*, admire the wonderful power and wisdom of God, in making the world Psal. 136:5 and 104 *per totum*. Much wisdom and art is seen in the Sun, Stars, creeping things; *Solomon* in all his glory was not comparable to one of the lilies; for that is native and inbred, his adventitious.[134]

An indication of the creative wisdom of God can also be found in the constitution of the human being, the "little world" or *microcosmos*, a point made consistently in the Psalter, in such places as Psalm 139:14, 15.[135] This evidence of divine wisdom incorporates elements of teleology with the principle of plenitude and the concept of a great chain of being.[136] "Nothing" in the created order, "is defective or superfluous."[137]

There is, moreover, a difference between this traditional perception on the part of the Reformed orthodox and Leibniz's more rationalistic use of seventeenth-century "possible world" language in his argument for "the best of all possible worlds." The two perspectives share a general sense of an orderly, rational universe ordered by an all-wise God — a view also characteristic of the "constructive Deism" of the late seventeenth and early eighteenth century — but there are also significant differences. The Leibnizian view, a derivative of seventeenth-century scholastic thought,[138] placed a limit on the divine ability to create that was not present in the more traditional teleological perspective of the Reformed scholastics: the "best possible," for Leibniz, was of necessity less than perfect, given the limitation placed on the divine work by the ideas of things known by God anterior to his knowing and willing.[139] The Reformed placed no such limitation on the divine — and allowed no ideas or forms anterior to

---

134. Leigh, *Treatise*, II.vii (p. 65), citing in the margin, Prov. 3:19, 20; Eccles. 3:11; Prov. 12:12; 13:16.

135. Mastricht, *Theoretico-practica theol.*, II.xiii.16; cf. Leigh, *Treatise*, II.vii (p. 66).

136. Cf. Edward P. Mahoney, "Metaphysical Foundations of the Hierarchy of Being According to Some Late-Medieval and Renaissance Philosophers," in *Philosophies of Existence, Ancient and Modern*, ed. Parviz Morewedge (New York: Fordham University Press, 1982), pp. 165-257; also note E. M. W. Tillyard, *The Elizabethan World Picture* (New York: Vintage, 1942), pp. 91-94.

137. Leigh, *Treatise*, II.vii (p. 66).

138. On the scholastic roots of Leibniz's thought, see Leroy E. Loemker, *Struggle for Synthesis: The Seventeenth-Century Background of Leibniz's Synthesis of Order and Freedom* (Cambridge, Mass.: Harvard University Press, 1972).

139. See in particular, Leibniz, *Theodicy: Essays*, II, § 200-216 (pp. 251-263); idem, *Monadology*, §47, 48 (p. 155).

God's knowledge of them. In fact, this is precisely one of the problems against which the older orthodoxy posed the doctrine of divine simplicity.

Second, the wisdom of God is evident in the general order or governance of things. Scripture calls him "the God of order."[140]

> As it requires infinite power to produce something out of nothing; so the wisdom of God appears in that excellent order, beauty and harmony, that we observe in all the parts of the creation; and in the subserviency of one thing to another, and the tendency thereof to promote the moral government of God in the world, and the good of man, for whose sake this lower world was formed, so that it might be a convenient habitation for him, and a glorious object, in which he might contemplate, and thereby be led to advance the divine perfections, which shine forth therein, as in a glass.[141]

Not only is there an ultimate order in the sense of a chain of being ordered to its end, there is also a temporal order in which all things occur suitably for the achievement of God's ends:

> The wisdom of God appears, in that whatever he does is in the fittest season, and all the circumstances thereof tend to set forth his own honour, and to argue his foresight to be infinitely perfect; so that he can see no reason to wish it had been otherwise ordered, or to repent thereof. For all his ways are *judgment* (Deut. 32:4); to *everything there is a season and a time, to every purpose under the heaven*; and *he hath made everything beautiful in his time* (Eccles. 3:1, 4.).[142]

Even so, "the heavens are said to have a line, which is likewise called their voice, because God by this exact order and art, which he showed in the making of them, doth plainly declare to all the world, his glory and power [Gen 1:31]."[143]

Third, God's wisdom in governance extends to the governance of sinful people, specifically, in his placing of boundaries on the extent of sin to prevent the inundation of all humanity and the "ruin" of all human community in a "deluge of wickedness."[144] God often reveals this aspect of his wisdom "in contriving things by contrary means": He brings about contrary ends, by contrary means; by death he brought life to believers; by ignominy and shame the greatest glory." So, too, "by terrors for sin, he brings the greatest comfort, and leads men by hell to heaven."[145] Along similar lines, the wisdom of God is revealed when he catches the wise "in their own craftiness, Psalm 59; Job. 9:4."[146]

---

140. Leigh, *Treatise*, II.vii (p. 66), citing Ps. 19; cf. Mastricht, *Theoretico-practica theol.*, II.xiii.16.

141. Ridgley, *Body of Divinity*, p. 72, col. 1; cf. Charnock, *Essence and Attributes*, IX (I, pp. 515-516, 525-531).

142. Ridgley, *Body of Divinity*, p. 72, col. 1.

143. Leigh, *Treatise*, II.vii (p. 66).

144. Charnock, *Essence and Attributes*, IX (I, p. 532).

145. Leigh, *Treatise*, II.vii (p. 66).

146. Leigh, *Treatise*, II.vii (p. 66).

Fourth, the wisdom of God is also and perhaps preeminently revealed in the work of salvation, which transcends all human, indeed, even angelic wisdom. God is wise inasmuch as

> The wisdom of God appears yet more eminently, in the work of our redemption; this is that which *the Angels desire to look into*, and cannot behold without the greatest admiration; for herein God's *manifold wisdom* is displayed (1 Pet. 1:12; Eph. 3:10).[147]

This argument undercuts whatever rationalistic tendency might have been present in several of his other arguments on the wisdom of God and indicates the limitation of reason and, therefore, the barrier to rationalism set by the orthodox at the point of transition to soteriological issues: the mysteries of the Christian faith are identified by Paul as the wisdom of God that stands over against the wisdom of this world.[148] Indeed, in the orthodox estimation, the mystery of redemption in Christ overcomes objections that might have been raised to the divine wisdom based on an examination of the Old Testament in isolation:

> This solves the difficulty, contained in a former dispensation of providence, respecting God's suffering sin to enter into the world, which he could have prevented, and probably would have done, had he not designed to over-rule it, for the bringing about the work of our redemption by Christ; so that what we lost in our first head, should be recovered, with great advantage, in our second, the Lord from heaven.[149]

"Here is so much wisdom, that if the understanding of all men and Angels had been put together, they could not have devised a possible way for man's salvation [marg. 1 Cor. 2:7; Eph. 1:8]."[150]

Fifth, the wisdom of God is manifest "in the Church, in the Oracles of Scripture, exceeding all sharpness of human wit; in the original, progress, change and migration of the Church, and other mysteries of the Gospel, the profound and immense wisdom of God's counsel shines [marg. Eph. 3:10; Rom. 11:33; Matt. 11:25]."[151] Thus the preparation and trial of the Church in the centuries before Christ, the coming of Christ at a time of deepest woe and decline of religion, and the preservation of the Church since the time of Christ all manifest the wisdom of God.[152]

Sixth, God's wisdom appears also in the works of his providence by which he works the good of mankind. Examples of this specific providential wisdom can be taken from

---

147. Ridgley, *Body of Divinity*, p. 73, col. 1; cf. Leigh, *Treatise*, II.vii (p. 66); Charnock, *Essence and Attributes*, IX (I, pp. 535-536); for a similar use of 1 Pet. 1:12; also note Calvin, *Commentaries in I Peter*, 1:12 (CTS I Peter, pp. 42-43); Diodati, *Pious and Learned Annotations*, in loc..

148. Mastricht, *Theoretico-practica theol.*, II.xiii.16; cf. Richard A. Muller, "*Duplex cognitio Dei* in the Theology of Early Reformed Orthodoxy," in *Sixteenth Century Journal*, X/2 (1979), pp. 57-61.

149. Ridgley, *Body of Divinity*, p. 73, col. 1; Mastricht, *Theoretico-practica theol.*, II.xiii.16; cf. Leigh, *Treatise*, II.vii (p. 66); for a similar use of 1 Pet. 1:12; also note Calvin, *Commentaries in I Peter*, 1:12 (CTS I Peter, pp. 42-43); Diodati, *Pious and Learned Annotations*, in loc..

150. Leigh, *Treatise*, II.vii (p. 66).

151. Leigh, *Treatise*, II.vii (p. 66).

152. Ridgley, *Body of Divinity*, p. 73, cols. 1-2; p. 74, col. 1.

biblical history of God's people, particularly the ordering of the lives of Jacob and of Joseph in order to bring about the providential bondage and deliverance of Israel in Egypt. The wilderness wandering of Israel was a time of trial and teaching that stands forth as an example of God's providential wisdom, "that he might give them statutes and ordinances, and that they might experience various instances of his preference among them, by judgments and mercies, and so be prepared for all the privileges he designed for them, as his peculiar people, in the land of *Canaan.*" When the Jews were delivered from the evil plans of Haman, "providence turned whatever he intended against them on himself."[153] Leigh similarly notes "the particular passages of his providence to his children, about their outward condition; in taking *David* from the sheepfold to be a king."[154] Ultimately, this divine wisdom will be evident in the eternal counsel or decree of God, specifically in his election of some and reprobation of others, the truth of which will be revealed fully in heaven, when all of God's decrees and promises will be made clear.[155]

4. Practical use of doctrine of the *sapientia Dei*. The doctrine of God's wisdom has also its practical side: for all who would be wise must go to the fountain of wisdom and have God as their Teacher (James 1:5; Psalm 94:10; Job 36:22). We ought to cultivate a fear of God based upon his wisdom and a mistrust in human will (Rom 16:27; 1 Cor. 3:18) and, as a result, "be content with the portion which God gives us ... since he is wisest, and knows best what is fittest for us, and when is the best time to help us." We ought also to hold in admiration the works of God and the unsearchable wisdom on which they are founded — and, as a means to our understanding, we ought to be "constant and diligent in reading, and pondering upon the Scriptures."[156]

From our understanding of this attribute of wisdom, much profit to piety can be derived, for "none can be said to meditate aright on the works of God, such as creation, providence, or redemption, who do not behold and admire his manifold wisdom displayed therein."[157] Our failure to perceive the wisdom of some parts of God's work from some of the dispensations of his will in history can be remedied by viewing the parts within the whole of God's plan. We also may take opportunity as we contemplate God's wisdom to "learn humility, under a sense of our own folly."[158]

> Let us subject our understandings to God, and have a high veneration for his word, in which his wisdom is displayed, which he has ordained, as the means whereby we may be made wise unto salvation; and whatever incomprehensible mysteries we find contained therein, let us not reject them or despise them, because we cannot comprehend them. Since God is infinite in wisdom, let us seek wisdom of him, according

---

153. Ridgley, *Body of Divinity*, p. 72, col. 2-p. 73, col. 1.
154. Leigh, *Treatise*, II.vii (p. 66).
155. Mastricht, *Theoretico-practica theol.*, II.xiii.16; cf. Leigh, *Treatise*, II.vii (p. 66).
156. Leigh, *Treatise*, II.vii (pp. 66-67).
157. Ridgley, *Body of Divinity*, p. 74, col. 2.
158. Ridgley, *Body of Divinity*, p. 74, col. 2-p. 75, col. 1.

to the Apostle's advice, *If any of you lack wisdom, let him ask it of God, that giveth to all men liberally, and upbraideth not; and it shall be given him* (James 1:5).[159]

C. The Divine Understanding (*Intellectus/Intelligentia*) and Knowledge (*Scientia/Omniscientia*)

1. Views of the Reformers. Given the absence of debate over divine omniscience during the era of the Reformation, the Reformers seldom formulate the concept at great length — in contrast to the Reformed orthodox, who encountered both the variant understanding of the concept in Molina's theory of *scientia media* and the subsequent denial of omniscience by the Socinians on what can only be called Molinist principles. Still, it is quite clear from the occasional definition found in a synopsis of theology or from their treatment of the concept in commentaries on Scripture that the Reformers held a traditional view of the divine omniscience. "Scripture frequently attributes *scientia* and *cognitio* to God": the Lord who gives us ears and eyes is a Lord who both hears and sees, who teaches mankind knowledge is a Lord who knows — God knows the inward counsels of his adversaries — he knows all of our needs before we ask him for help — and the Apostle praises the depths of his wisdom and knowledge.[160] Given the eternity of God, moreover, his knowledge is an eternal knowledge of all things, whether past, present, or future. God knows even those things that, from our perspective, are not: for he knows all that is, and he knows as well what once was in the past and what will be in the future, as Scripture tells us, there is not a creature that is not manifest in his sight.[161]

For Calvin, both the divine omniscience and its radical distinction from all human knowing are witnessed in Psalm 139. Human beings frequently

> will not allow [God's] knowledge to be greater than what corresponds to their own apprehensions of things. David, on the contrary, confesses it to be beyond his comprehension, virtually declaring that words could not express this truth of the absoluteness with which all things stand patent to the eye of God, this being a knowledge having neither bound nor measure, so that he could only contemplate the extent of it with conscious imbecility.[162]

God knows all things in the broadest and most general sense — but there is also a close interrelationship between omniscience and providence: Calvin objects strenuously to the view that God knows or foreknows all things but then in some cases "withdraws from the government of the world." Such theories "rob God of half his glory, and ... tear him to pieces." By contrast, Scripture consistently

---

159. Ridgley, *Body of Divinity*, p. 75, col. 1.
160. Hyperius, *Methodus theologiae*, I, p. 146, citing Ps. 94:9-11; Jer. 48; Matt. 6:8; Rom. 11:33.
161. Hyperius, *Methodus theologiae*, I, p. 147, citing Heb. 4:13.
162. Calvin, *Commentary on the Book of Psalms*, 139:6 (CTS *Psalms*, V, p. 210).

joins these two things inseparably; first, God foresees all things, since nothing is hidden from his eyes; and next, he appoints future events, and governs the world by his will, allowing nothing to happen by chance or without his direction.[163]

It is God's omniscience, in conjunction with his providence, that enables God to convey deep and secret knowledge to his prophets. Divine omniscience is also specifically related to God's knowledge of human beings: God is the one who "searches the heart" of all human beings, and "from whose eyes nothing is hidden, that we will observe his law aright."[164]

2. Biblical and rational grounds of Reformed orthodox doctrine of the *scientia* or *omniscientia Dei*. That God has an understanding or knowledge of things follows from the *vita Dei*, specifically from the identification of the living God as a spiritual being. Since God is an infinite Spirit, it follows that his understanding is infinite, beyond all measure: as the Psalmist writes, "Great is our Lord ... his understanding is infinite" (147:5).[165] According to the Reformed orthodox, this doctrine is both biblically and philosophically justifiable, capable of being "proved" from both Scripture and rational argument.

First, the Scriptural proofs: as is the case with the doctrine of the divine attributes in general, Scripture teaches the divine omniscience affirmatively, negatively, and metaphorically or figuratively. In the primary, affirmative, sense, Scripture consistently speaks of the divine knowledge, indicates its vastness, its extent to all things, and its freedom from all deception — as in such texts as Job. 28:24; 1 Samuel 2:3; 16:7; 1 Kings 8:39; Psalm 94:9, 11; 139:1-6, 12; Matthew 7:23; Acts 15:18; 1 John 3:20. Both in their commentaries and in their theological treatises and systems, the Reformed develop this "affirmative" testimony through argument based both on direct biblical statement and on "good and necessary" conclusions drawn from collations of texts by means of the *analogia fidei* or *scopus Scripturae*. Thus, the text of 1 Samuel 2:3, "let not arrogancy come out of your mouth: for the Lord is a God of knowledge, and by him actions are weighed," teaches a present and distinct knowledge of "right, justice, and all mens counsels and actions" as the foundation of God's disposition and governance of events.[166] Nor is this divine knowing analogous to the forms and ways of human knowing, as indicated shortly thereafter at 1 Samuel 16:7: "for the Lord seeth not as man seeth; for man looketh on the outward appearance, but the Lord looketh on the heart." Even so, God knows all things eternally, given that he has ordered and disposed them all according to his eternal counsel, as implied by Acts 15:18, "Known unto God are all his works from the beginning of the world,"[167] and as implied by 1 John 3:20,

---

163. Calvin, *Commentaries on Daniel*, 2:20 (*CTS Daniel*, I, p. 142).

164. Calvin, *Commentaries on Daniel*, 2:22 (*CTS Daniel*, I, p. 147); idem, *Commentary on the Book of Psalms*, 119:168 (*CTS Psalms*, V, p. 244).

165. Cf. Ridgley, *Body of Divinity*, p. 67, col. 2.

166. Diodati, *Pious and Learned Annotations*, 1 Sam. 2:3, in loc.; cf. Poole, *Commentary*, in loc. (I, p. 517).

167. Cf. Marckius, *Compendium theol.*, IV.xxxv; cf. Calvin, *Commentary upon Acts*, 15:18, in loc. (*CTS Acts*, II, p. 69); Rudolph Gualther, *An Hundred, Threescore and Fiftene Homelyes or Sermons*

knows "all things" without limit.[168] The further claim that "He knows from eternity, by one simple act, before all time, before there was a world" is a conclusion drawn from the exegesis by means of collation with other texts — notably those concerned with divine eternity, the priority of God over creation, and the knowledge that God has of all things in his creative work.[169]

The negative argument derives from such texts as Job 42:2; Psalm 139:4; Heb. 4:13. These texts, in other words, do not merely say that God knows all things; they also, to confirm and intensify the point, state that there is nothing that he does not know: thus, "I know that ... no thought can be withholden from thee" (Job 42:2) and "For there is not a word in my tongue, but lo, O Lord, thou knowest it altogether" (Ps. 139:5). Of the latter of these two texts, Poole remarks that it can also be rendered "When there is not a word...," which, he notes is even "more admirable," and paraphrasing, "Thou knowest what I intend to speak ... when I have not yet uttered one word of it."[170] The text of Hebrews 4:13, "Neither is there any creature that is not manifest in his sight, but all things are naked and opened unto the eyes of him with whom we have to do," precisely because of its double negative in the first clause, offers a powerful testimony to the divine omniscience. In Gouge's view, the double negative, grammatically acceptable in Greek, acts as an intensifier of the point and therefore indicates "the impossibility of concealing anything from God."[171]

Finally, the divine omniscience is taught by Scripture, "Metaphorically and figuratively, for when eyes and ears be given to God, his omniscience is signified, 2 Chron. 16:9; Psalm 11:7; when he is called light, 1 John 1:5."[172] The text of 2 Chronicles 16:9, "For the eyes of the Lord run to and fro throughout the whole earth," refers to God's providence, teaching that God governs all things in his infinite wisdom and that all creatures, as in the metaphor, "continually under his eye."[173] In the Psalm, God's "countenance" is said to "approve the upright" — indicating that he sees and judges the deeds of all people.[174] So too is God called "a light" because his understanding knows all things and his will is "pure and holy."[175] There is no ignorance in God.[176] That these texts are read metaphorically is to be emphasized inasmuch as there are

uppon the Actes of the Apostles, written by Saint Luke (London: Henrie Denham, 1572), 15:18 in loc. (p. 601); Le Blanc, Theses theol., De scientia Dei, xxii-xxiv.

168. Maresius, Collegium theol., II.xxxvii; cf. Le Blanc, Theses theol., De scientia Dei, iv-vi.

169. Leigh, Treatise, II.vii (pp. 61-62).

170. Poole, Commentary, Ps. 139:5, in loc. (II, p. 203); similarly, Trapp, Commentary, in loc. (II, p. 680); and cf. Calvin, Commentary on Psalms, in loc. (CTS Psalms, V, p. 209).

171. Gouge, Commentary on Hebrews, IV, §76.

172. Leigh, Treatise, II.vii (pp. 61-62).

173. Henry, Exposition, 2 Chron. 16:9, in loc.; Westminster Annotations, in loc.; Dutch Annotations, in loc.; cf. Trapp, Commentary, in loc. (I, p. 671); also note Bullinger, Decades, IV.iii (p. 138).

174. Poole, Commentary, Ps. 11:7 in loc. (II, p. 17); Westminster Annotations, in loc.; cf. Calvin, Commentary upon the Psalms, in loc. (CTS Psalms, I, p. 169).

175. Dutch Annotations, 1 John 1:5, in loc; cf. Calvin, Commentaries on 1 John, in loc. (CTS 1 John, p. 163).

176. Diodati, Pious and Learned Annotations, 1 John 1:5, in loc.

two kinds of knowledge (*cognitio*): through the senses and through the intellect. Whereas Scripture consistently uses language of sense and sense organs to describe God, it also makes clear that God is incorporeal: he therefore lacks "senses" which are the physical organs of cognition. The texts must be figurative. This argument also applies to the knowledge of Christ, who did have sense knowledge according to his humanity, but not according to his divinity.[177]

Second, the rational argumentation: reason confirms the exegesis of Scripture and proves the omniscience of God in three ways — again echoing the patterns of the divine attributes, this time the more rational patterns of derivation and/or organization, namely, the *via negationis*, *via causalitatis*, and *via eminentiae*. Thus, the divine omniscience can be inferred "by way of negation; ignorance is a defect and imperfection, but God is most perfect; therefore all ignorance is to be removed from him."[178] This point can also be stated positively, as a result either of the idea of God or of the logical relationship of God's knowing to God's infinity and perfection: it follows from the realization that God thinks and understands that he must also be omniscient. That this teaching is generally available to human beings and clearly understood by Christians also follows, inasmuch as "reason itself taught the heathen this truth ... but with greater clearness is this truth set forth through the whole Scripture."[179]

Divine omniscience can also be argued by way of causality, particularly with reference to final causality, given that "God governs all things in the whole universe and directs to convenient ends even those things which are destitute of all knowledge and reason."[180] There can be no sure attainment of the ultimate goal unless the one who brings about the end knows it fully — or, stated in a more logical form, the final goal, although temporally subsequent to the means used to attain it, is necessarily logically prior. Similarly, God's government and justice, therefore, viewed abstractly, presuppose his omniscience: "as the Judge of all, he must be able to discern the cause, or else he cannot determine it, and perfectly know the rules of justice, or else he cannot exercise it in the government of the world."[181] The divine omniscience is also confirmed by way of eminence, given that "By way of eminency. God hath made creatures intelligent and full of knowledge, *viz*. Angels and men; therefore he knows and understands in a far more perfect and eminent manner, Psalm 94:10."[182]

3. Basic definitions and oppositions. On this doctrinal point, as in the case of the divine essence in general, the orthodox of the seventeenth century were in direct conflict with several adversaries. The Socinians simply denied the divine omniscience — with their assumption of the finitude and, according to some of their teachers, the restricted heavenly location of the divine essence, they had no difficulty in arguing that God has a limited foreknowledge of future contingents, indeed, that omniscience

---

177. Zanchi, *De natura Dei.*, III.ii, q. 1.1 (col. 196).
178. Leigh, *Treatise*, II.vii (p. 62).
179. Pictet, *Theol. chr.*, II.v.1-2.
180. Leigh, *Treatise*, II.vii (p. 62); cf. Le Blanc, *Theses theol.*, *De scientia Dei*, vi.
181. Ridgley, *Body of Divinity*, p. 68, col. 1.
182. Leigh, *Treatise*, II.vii (p. 62).

could not be predicated of God.[183] From a different perspective, Molina and the Remonstrants who followed him had added another category to the divine knowing, the *scientia media*, a foreknowledge of future contingents prior to the divine will to actualize them.[184] Eventually, among the Remonstrants, this *scientia media* was modified and understood as a limited foreknowledge of future contingents. In opposition to these views, the Reformed orthodox definition asserted the omniscience of God without qualification: "The divine intellect is the faculty by which God knows all things that are and are not, will be and will not be"[185] — in greater detail, "The object of this knowledge is everything that can possibly be known or understood, whether it be God himself, or all other things which can be conceived in or outside of God (*extra Deum*)."[186] By way of elaboration,

> God is the object of this knowledge: he knows himself, both according to his nature, and according to his perfections: Matt. 11:27, "no man knoweth the Son, but the Father; neither knoweth any man the Father save the Son"; 1 Cor. 2:10-11, "the spirit searcheth all things which are of God. For what man knoweth the things of a man save the spirit of man which is in him, even so no man knoweth the things of God, but the Spirit of God." He also knows his own decrees, and all the actions that he performs in accomplishing his decrees: "Known unto God are all his works from the beginning of the world" (Acts 15:18).[187]

This complete knowledge of himself and of all that is contained in his power and will, as taught by such texts as Matthew 11:27, John 10:15, and 1 Corinthians 2:10-11, 20, is necessary to the divine blessedness and presupposed by the fact of God's revelation.[188]

Second, given the divine self-knowledge as inclusive of all that God wills and accomplishes, there is also the divine knowledge of

> universal and singular; past, present, future; things which neither are, nor have been, nor will be; things necessary and contingent, done and thought of, from the greatest to the least. Here it is said, "His understanding is infinite" (Psalm 148:5) and that "He knoweth all things" (1 John 3:20). Justin Martyr calls him παντων ἐπόπτες [the overseer of all things].[189]

As a third element in their definitions, Reformed orthodox frequently also indicate the difference between divine and human knowing — a difference that stems from

---

183. See Turretin, *Inst. theol. elencticae*, III.xii.7; Owen, *Vindiciae evangelicae*, in *Works*, XII, pp. 115-140, 335.

184. On *scientia media*, see further, below, 5.3 (F).

185. Rijssen, *Summa theol.*, III.xxii.

186. Pictet, *Theol. chr.*, II.v.4.

187. Pictet, *Theol. chr.*, II.v.5; cf. Ridgley, *Body of Divinity*, p. 67, col. 2 - p. 68, col. 1; Cloppenburg, *Exercitationes super locos communes*, II.iii.5.

188. Marckius, *Compendium theol.*, IV.xxxvi.1; cf. Gill, *Body of Divinity*, I, pp. 85-86, 178-179.

189. Pictet, *Theol. chr.*, II.v.4; cf. Turretin, *Inst. theol. elencticae*, III.xi.3; Le Blanc, *Theses theol.*, *De scientia Dei*, xxx.

the identity of God as infinite Spirit and from the radical priority of God over all things. Since God is one and spiritual, the distinctions that we make between "*intellectus*, considered as a faculty ... *scientia*, which is a disposition of the intellect, and ... *cognitio*, which is the action of the faculty springing from its disposition" do not apply to God. "In God, however, all these are one and are distinguished only according to our manner of understanding."[190] In sum,

> The wisdom or knowledge of God, is that by which God doth, not by certain notions abstracted from the things themselves, but by his own essence: nor successively and by discourses of reason, but by one eternal and immutable act of understanding, distinctly and perfectly know himself, and all other things, though infinite, whether they have been or not.[191]

D. The *Scientia Dei*: Its Manner, Objects, and Degree.

1. The mode or manner of divine knowing. These fundamental differences between the divine knower and all finite or created knowers and, therefore, between the nature and extent of divine knowledge and creaturely knowledge fall into three categories — as summarized by Rijssen:

> The knowledge of God differs from that of creatures, 1) in its objects, for God knows all things. 2) In its manner, [since he knows] all things according to his essence. 3) In its degree, [since he knows] all things perfectly.[192]

Maccovius and Brakel could argue the point rather simply on the ground that God eternally knows all things as present to him in a single act of understanding.[193] Reformed writers as diverse as Zanchi, Ames, Leigh, Maresius, Turretin, and Mastricht argue in detail, along traditional Augustinian lines, that God knows all things through his own essence in which the eternal ideas or exemplars of all things reside. For convenience in discussion, we alter the order, moving from the manner or mode of divine knowing to the objects of divine knowledge, concluding with the degree.

First, the manner or mode of divine knowing. The Reformed orthodox analysis of biblical texts concluded that the divine *cognitio* is not a sense knowing but an intellective knowing. Intellective knowing, in turn, occurs in three basic modes: *opinio*, *fides*, and *cognitio*. Clearly, God's knowledge is not opinion, given that this is not an evident knowing, but an affirmation or negation of what is deemed possible in the absence of certainty. In instances of negative opinion, there is an implication of doubt. But God knows evidently and indubitably. Nor is the divine knowing a matter of faith, for as the apostle indicates, faith is a certain knowledge, but of things unseen, an "inevident" knowledge. But God sees all things. Divine knowledge, therefore, is rightly

190. Leigh, *Treatise*, II.vii (p. 60, margin).
191. Perkins, *Golden Chaine*, III (p. 12, col. 1).
192. Rijssen, *Summa theol.*, III.xxiii; cf. Pictet, *Theol. chr.*, II.v.3.
193. Maccovius, *Loci communes*, xx (p. 146); cf. Brakel, *Redelijke Godsdienst*, I.iii.16.

called *scientia*, because it is both certain and evident: God sees all things and knows with certainty what he sees.[194]

Still, *scientia*, as usually defined, does not apply perfectly to God: in creatures, knowledge (*scientia*) is a disposition or *habitus* and can be identified as a "faculty." What is more, it is discursive, knowing principles and drawing conclusions, and therefore moving from potency to act. In God *scientia* is an *actus*, indeed, as is indicated of the divine essence generally, it is *actus simplicissimus*, in which nothing is temporally prior or posterior.[195] Given that God is infinite and knows himself, his knowledge must also be infinite; so too, given that all things exist because of his will, by simply knowing what he wills, God must know all things. Therefore, by way of definition and contrast, with reference both to the objects and the degree of divine knowledge, "Our knowledge is simply finite, but God's infinite."[196] Since, moreover, the *scientia Dei* is immutable, eternal, and perfect, and entirely resting on God himself, God knows all things in himself, specifically in his decree that they exist, without the aid of sense or, indeed, the agency of the things known, "intelligible species."[197] (This point was already implied in the initial comments on the object of God's knowledge, specifically in the radical priority of God as creator over the creation: "For the manner of divine knowledge, God knows all things by his essence, not by species abstracted from the things; for so things should be before the divine knowledge, on which yet they depend.")[198]

The divine eternity also bears on the definition of the mode of divine knowing, given that God's duration is not successive,[199] but encompasses and comprehends all things:

> We understand things successively one after another, with pains of discourse, proceeding from an unknown thing to a known, or from a less known to a more known: but God knows all things together, and by one most simple, immutable, and eternal act of understanding.[200]

The divine understanding is most perfect and always the same (*semper idem*) — it is, therefore, radically different from human knowing, neither discursive nor acquisitive — not dianoetic, but noetic.[201]

---

194. Zanchi, *De natura Dei*, II.ii, q. 1.1 (col. 196).

195. Zanchi, *De natura Dei*, II.ii, q. 1.1 (col. 197); Maresius, *Collegium theol.*, II.xxxvii; cf. Ames, *Medulla theologica*, I.vii.14; Cocceius, *Summa theol.* III.x.8; Mastricht, *Theoretico-practica theol.*, II.xiii.8.

196. Leigh, *Treatise*, II.vii (p. 63).

197. Zanchi, *De natura Dei*, III.ii, q. 10 (col. 211); Marckius, *Compendium theol.*, IV.xxxv; Turretin, *Inst. theol. elencticae*, III.xii.18; Leigh, *Treatise*, II.vii (p. 63); Cocceius, *Summa theol.* III.x9.

198. Leigh, *Treatise*, II.vii (p. 61); cf. Beza et al. *Propositions and Principles*, VII.iii.

199. See above, 4.4 (D.3).

200. Leigh, *Treatise*, II.vii (p. 63).

201. Maresius, *Collegium theol.*, II.xxxvii; Marckius, *Medulla*, IV.xxxv; cf. Voetius, *Selectarum disputationum theologicarum*, I, xiv; Ames, *Marrow*, I.iv.53-54.

God doth not understand by discoursing from a known thing to that which is unknown, in a doubtful and successive reasoning; but by looking on them, and by one most simple and Individual and eternal act comprehending all things. He apprehends by one act of his understanding, and by himself simple things without species, compound without composition and division, syllogisms and consequences without discourse; lastly he most perfectly understands all the multitude of things without distraction, and distance both local and temporal, without distinction of former and later, past or future, according to the beginning, progress, and end, possessing all things together and always present; which with us are reduced in time, Dan. 2:21, 22; 1 Cor. 3:19, 20; Isa. 44:7; Rom. 11:33; Heb. 4:13; Psalm 94:9, 10, 11.[202]

This nondiscursive knowledge of all things can be described as a seeing of all things "as if they were but one" — the simultaneous intellection of the entire universal order, past, present, and future, in all its detail, "all things being represented to him in the pure crystal of his own essence, are but as one individual thing."[203]

"An idea in the human mind, knowledge of which is acquired by *analysis*, is gathered from *the thing* itself, inasmuch as a thing exists first *in itself*, then is perceived by the senses, and only then by the intellect, which conceives an idea of the thing ... God, however, understands all things by *creation*, and does not acquire knowledge by *analysis*."[204] "All things exist first in the mind [of God], subsequently in themselves" inasmuch as "in human knowing, things themselves are the *exemplar*, and our knowledge is the *image*; but in God, the idea is the *exemplar*, and things themselves are the expressed *image*."[205] Indeed, inasmuch as "all things are naked and open" to the eye of God (Heb. 4:13), "God's knowledge doth infinitely differ from ours."[206] (The logic of this point, perhaps not immediately evident to the modern mind, becomes quite clear in the context of creation ex nihilo: in order for God to create all things out of nothing, God must know them prior to their existence — know them, in short, as genuine possibilities for creation, as ideas or exemplars belonging to his *scientia necessaria*.) This is not to deny that God knows particulars in themselves, but only to deny that he knows them *through* or by means of themselves: according to his *scientia visionis*, God knows all actuality as he has willed it to be.

2. The objects and degree of divine knowing. Given that the manner or mode of the divine knowing is utterly different from the mode of human knowing, the objects and degree of divine knowing must be different as well. God knows objects that we do not and cannot know — and even those objects that we know are known differently by God and in a different degree. The order of objects is important, inasmuch as the

---

202. Leigh, *Treatise*, II.vii (p. 61); cf. Wollebius, *Compendium*, I.i.3, prop. 1-3 and canones; Ames, *Medulla theol.*, I.vii.14-25; Turretin, *Inst. theol. elencticae*, III.xii.2; Mastricht, *Theoretico practica theol.*, II.xiii.6-10.

203. Watson, *God's Anatomy*, in *Discourses*, I, p. 148.

204. Mastricht, *Theoretico-practica theol.*, II.xiii.8; cf. Zanchi, *De natura Dei*, III.ii, q.1.2 (col. 197-198).

205. Mastricht, *Theoretico-practica theol.*, II.xiii.8; cf. Ames, *Medulla theologica*, I.vii.14.

206. Watson, *God's Anatomy*, in *Discourses*, I, p. 148.

divine self-knowledge not only precedes all other divine knowledge but is also the determiner of the nature and character of the divine knowledge of all things. At the simplest level, the point can be made that God, as the one who creates all things out of nothing, must have a knowledge of the possibilities for creation and their order and relation prior to the creative act — and, given that creation is ex nihilo, must have a knowledge of those possibilities that does not rest on the creation itself. God's knowledge, moreover, stands in relation to God's power and will, inasmuch as it is God's power or *potentia* that defines the realm of the genuinely possible,[207] while his will or *voluntas* defines the realm of the actual. God, thus, knows "things that are simply possible on the ground of his all-sufficiency, things that he does not will to make," even as human beings, acting freely, know more and can do more than they actually do. God is in no way bound to actualize all of the possibilities that he knows: his will remains free with regard to the objects of his knowledge.[208]

This argument yields a basic division of the divine knowing: God knows, first, himself and, second, all things other than himself. As to the first member of the distinction, God knows himself perfectly: as Scripture teaches, the Father knows the Son and the Son knows the Father — and the Spirit knows all the deep things of God, texts that will be cited again in the trinitarian debates over the full divinity of the Son and Spirit.[209] The second member of the distinction, all things other than God, can be elaborated into a more precise categorization of what God knows — namely, the kinds of objects that God knows. God knows all of the possibilities that arise from his *potentia*, which is to say, all genuine possibilities. He therefore also knows genuine impossibility — specifically, impossibility both with regard to himself and with regard to all things, namely, that which is contrary to their being. Omniscience is, therefore, necessarily concluded from omnipotence[210]

This point is stated by Scripture: God knows and sees all that he has made. By extension, he has an utterly complete knowledge of all "substantial natures" because there are no substantial natures that he has not made. God knows "the substantial natures of all other things; as of Angels, Men, Beasts, Plants; Gen. 1:31, He saw all things which he had made; Matt. 10:29, He is said to take care of Sparrows, which could not be without knowledge."[211] As the older scholastics rightly argued, Maccovius indicates, "Things exist because God knows them — not that he knows them because

---

207. Cf. Stapfer, *Inst. theol. polem.*, I.iii, §324: "Patet inde omnem rerum possibilitatem esse à Deo, & intellectum ejus esse fontem sive radicem omnis possibilitatis" with Ward, *Philosophicall Essay*, I.iii (p. 31).

208. Marckius, *Compendium theol.*, IV.xxxvi.2; cf. Ridgley, *Body of Divinity*, p. 68, col. 2; Le Blanc, *Theses theol.*, De scientia Dei, xvi, xxviii; Greenhill, *Exposition of Ezekiel*, 38:17, in loc. (p. 760). See further below, 5.3 (E.1-2), on the relationship of the divine knowledge of possibility to the divine knowledge of actuality.

209. Zanchi, *De natura Dei*, II.ii, q. 2 (col. 199), citing John 1:18 and 1 Cor. 2:10 ; also see *PRRD*, IV, 6.2 (C.6); 7.3 (B.2).

210. Zanchi, *De natura Dei*, III.ii, q. 3 (col. 200); Maresius, *Collegium theol.*, II.xxxviii; and see below, 6.2 (B) on the divine *potentia*.

211. Leigh, *Treatise*, II.vii (p. 62).

they exist."[212] God not only knows things as individuals, he also knows the immediate circumstances and incidental properties of all things, their actions and passions: Scripture consistently testifies to this when it teaches that God knows the heart, that nothing is hidden from him, that he knows our words and our thoughts.[213] Thus, God also discerns not only the outward works but also the hearts and intentions of all human beings. By implication, he must know all contingents and futures as well.[214]

God knows, then, both the universal and the singular or particular, from the greatest (Psalm 147:4) to the least (Matt. 10:30) of things.[215] This point arises from quite a few texts in Scripture, such as Job 28:24, "For he looketh to the ends of the earth, and seeth under the whole heaven" — God's knowledge, standing in direct relation to his all-encompassing providence, "is infinite and universal, reaching to all places and times, and things, past, present, and to come; whereas the most acute and knowing men have narrow understandings, and see but very few things and small parcels of the works of God."[216] God knows not only angels, human beings, beasts, stars — he also knows their numbers (Ps. 147:4), the planets, and, indeed, the very hairs on our heads (Matt. 10:30).[217]

Pictet further qualifies this concept of omniscience by noting that God, as perfect Being, must know all things, but nevertheless cannot be viewed as immediately effecting or as approving of all things: such a view would make him the cause of sin, degradation, contamination and, thus, imperfect.[218] When, therefore, some passages in Scripture seem to attribute ignorance to God, these refer, not to God's actual knowledge, but to his use of that knowledge and the relation of that knowledge to his will and his justice. The literal reading of such texts by the Socinians, as actually attributing ignorance to God, was viewed by the orthodox not only as an error in exegesis — failing to take a figure of speech as a figure — but as fundamentally abhorrent to Christian theism. As when God vowed to "go down" to Sodom to see what went on there:

> God thus expresses himself, 1) in order to display his justice, that he might not appear hurried on to vengeance under the impulse of a blind fury; 2) to set forth his longsuffering, whereby he is not in haste to punish, though provoked by the obstinate wickedness of man; and 3) to set an example to magistrates in the administration of justice.[219]

---

212. Maccovius, *Loci communes*, xx (p. 146); cf. Zanchi, *De natura Dei*, III.ii, q. 1.3 (col. 198); Brakel, *Redelijke Godsdienst*, I.iii.16; Turretin, *Inst. theol. elencticae*, III.xii.18.

213. Cf. Marckius, *Compendium theol.*, IV.xxxvi, citing Prov. 5:21; 15:3; Job 34:21, 22; Psalm 69:6; 90:8; Jer. 16:17; 32:19; with Turretin, *Inst. theol. elencticae*, III.xii.13; Leigh, *Treatise*, II.vii (p. 62), citing Psalm 119:168; Job. 34:21, 22; 2 Kings 6:12; Psalm 139:4; Matt 12:36; Prov. 15:11; Job 42:2, 4; 1 Sam. 16:7; Psalm 94:11; Gen. 6:5; Psalm 90:8; and Rom 8:27; Rev 2:23.

214. See further, below, 5.3 (D.3 and F.3-6).

215. Marckius, *Compendium theol.*, IV.xxxvi.3; cf. Le Blanc, *Theses theol.*, *De scientia Dei*, ix-xi.

216. Poole, *Commentary*, Job 28:24, in loc. (I, p. 991).

217. Pictet, *Theol. chr.*, II.v.6; cf. Le Blanc, *Theses theol.*, *De scientia Dei*, xvii.

218. Pictet, *Theol. chr.*, II.v.14; cf. Zanchi, *De natura Dei*, III.ii, q. 7 (col. 206-207).

219. Pictet, *Theol. chr.*, II.v.14.

The point is that God does not reveal or communicate all that he knows: he reveals neither "the essential wisdome of his providence , nor that of his secret counsell, by which he hath created and ruleth the universe" — rather, he reveals his law, "by which man ought to govern himself, and not go beyond those bounds."[220]

3. Divine "foreknowledge." If God's knowledge is infinite, it is also eternal, not only comprehending all things and all places, but encompassing all times as well:

> He knows ... all things past, present and to come; open, secret; certain, contingent; that which shall be, which shall never be; we ... understand only those things which are, or at least have been, and we know doubtingly.[221]

God knows the past — although when Scripture speaks of God as "remembering," it means rather his attending to the prayers and needs of the godly while punishing the ungodly. His knowledge of the future is also a complete knowledge of all events,

> not only those which we call necessary, but also those which we term contingent, and which, although determined by God, are really contingent in respect of us, seeing they arise from a concurrence unknown to us of several things together.[222]

Given, moreover, the eternity of God, the way in which God knows things that are past, present, and future to us is unlike the human categories of memory and foresight: "He knows all things which are to come, not as if they were to come; for to him all things are present. God makes this an argument of his Divinity, when he bids them see, if their Gentile Gods can tell what is to come."[223]

During the seventeenth century, the Reformed orthodox were pressed to argue a traditional view of divine foreknowledge against Socinian claims of divine incertitude of future contingencies. The reason given by the Socinians for this conclusion was, moreover, related to a more or less traditionary concern over the nature and circumstances of human free choice.[224] The Reformed viewed such teaching as fundamentally unbiblical in view of the prophetic literature of the Bible, including the Apocalypse: God's prophecies imply a full knowledge of the future.[225] The Reformed orthodox approach to the question proceeds on the further assumption that freedom and contingency are indeed compatible with divine providential willing, and, therefore, future free and contingent acts are fully compatible with the divine knowing. Indeed, they assumed that the divine willing establishes freedom and contingency. According to the *scientia voluntaria* or *libera*, God knows all that he has willed, whether it occurs by necessity, contingency, or the free acts of human beings. There is, therefore, a divine

---

220. Diodati, *Pious and Learned Annotations*, Job 28:28, in loc., citing collaterally Deut. 29:29 and 1 Cor. 4:6; cf. Poole, *Commentary*, Job 28:28, in loc. (I, p. 992).

221. Leigh, *Treatise*, II.vii (p. 63).

222. Pictet, *Theol. chr.*, II.v.8; cf. Ames, *Marrow*, I.iv.5; Marckius, *Compendium theol.*, IV.xxxvi.7.

223. Leigh, *Treatise*, II.vii (p. 62).

224. Cf. Owen, *Vindiciae Evangelicae*, in *Works*, XII, pp. 115-126.

225. Le Blanc, *Theses theol.*, *De scientia Dei*, xxvii.

"foreknowledge" of what, from the human perspective, are "future contingencies." Thus, Ridgley comments that God knows "all things future, namely, not only such as are the effects of necessary causes, where the effect is known in or by the cause, but such as are contingent with respect to us" and which "therefore cannot be certainly foreknown by us."[226] In other words, given the nature of the divine willing of all actuality, all future events are certainly future, whether from a causal perspective they are necessary, contingent, or free, and therefore they are also capable of being known or foreknown by God.[227]

There, moreover, are two related grounds of this absolute divine foreknowledge. In the first place, the Protestant orthodox discussion of the *praescientia divina*, as might be expected, draws heavily on the scholastic tradition, indeed, on that foundation and center piece of the scholastic tradition, the discussion of foreknowledge and freedom found in the fifth book of Boethius' *Consolations of Philosophy*. The concept of foreknowledge is linked immediately by the orthodox to the eternity of God:

> God's *prescience* or *foreknowledge* is that, whereby God foreknew things necessarily, certainly, immutably, and from everlasting. Neither foreknowledge nor remembrance are properly in God; all things both past, and to come, being present before him.[228]

Thus, this attribute is called prescience "not in respect of God but man" as indicated, according to Leigh, by such texts as Genesis 15:16 and 18:10 — the former containing a prophecy to Abraham of the future arrival of Israel in Canaan and the latter containing the promise of children to the barren Sarah — where God, in time, speaks to Abraham of his future.

In the second place, the eternal God encompasses all events, whether necessary, contingent, or freely willed by finite agents, in his decree:

> for things that happen without our design, or forethought, and therefore are not certainly foreknown by us, are objects of his providence, and therefore known to him from the beginning. Thus the fall of a sparrow to the ground is a casual thing; yet our Saviour says, that this is not without his providence (Matt. 10:29). Hence, that which is casual or accidental to us, is not so to him; so that though, we cannot have a certain or determinate foreknowledge of it, it does not follow that he has not.[229]

Foreknowledge itself is not causal: knowledge is related to causality by means of the will. God knows things that he wills directly and immediately, and he also knows things that he wills only indirectly, that arise out of the interrelationship of secondary causality and free choice. God can therefore be said to know with certainly all future contingents and conditionals, whether they eventuate freely as choices of will or as necessities of the consequence, inasmuch as his will actualizes all things and from the perspective of the first cause they happen "immutably and infallibly" — but the manner of his

226. Ridgley, *Body of Divinity* (1855), p. 96.
227. Venema, *Inst. theol.*, vi (p. 150).
228. Leigh, *Treatise*, II.vii (p. 67).
229. Ridgley, *Body of Divinity* (1855), p. 96.

willing of possibles is such that "according to the nature of second causes" they occur "necessarily, freely, or contingently," in the course of time.[230] As for free choices of human beings, the Reformed note that "our liberty is not wholly independent but restricted" Specifically, human freedom is neither absolute nor indifferent — rather it is "spontaneous and dependent on motives" and, in addition on "the direction given to it by God."[231]

The attribute of prescience is also used restrictively to denote the divine omniscience without implying the divine omni-causality: "*Praescientia Dei est cognoscitiva non causativa*, Acts. 2:23; Rom. 8:29; 1 Pet. 1:2."[232] What controversy might have arisen from the definition disappears in the next statement: "Although God's *prescience* bring not a necessity upon events, yet it is necessary for all things to happen so as God hath foretold, because God so foreknows, as he hath decreed and willed it shall be; but his decree gives existence."[233] Thus, foreknowledge does not rest on the things known as if future things co-exist eternally, nor does it rest on the divine infinity — and it certainly is not a matter of conjecture — rather it is grounded in the will of God: God has foreknowledge of "what he wills to exist."[234] It is, in short, identical with the *scientia voluntaria*.

Understood improperly, the concept of omniscience (very much like the concept of omnipotence) can lead to a series of paradoxes and conundrums. If God is truly omniscient, then he must know the entire contents of the human imagination. But how can God know such thoughts as the belief of the atheist that God does not exist? In other words, if God is omniscient, must not God have a vast knowledge of mistakes and impossibilities? Charnock addresses the problem with a qualification of the meaning of omniscience:

> his knowledge extends to things possible, not to things impossible to himself; he knows it as imaginable by man [i.e., that God could lie or cease to be], not as possible in itself; because it is utterly impossible, and repugnant to the nature of God. Since he eminently contains in himself all things possible, past, present, and to come, he cannot know himself without knowing them.[235]

This point is significant. For God to be omniscient, God need not know the entire range of an infinite number of impossibilities — nor need he know all knowables in precisely the way that they are known to creatures. God, thus, knows the atheist's disbelief, but knows it differently from the atheist, inasmuch the latter assumes it to be true.

---

230. Westminster Confession, V.ii; cf. Zanchi, *De natura Dei*, III.ii, q. 15.1-2 (col. 222); Pearson, *Lectiones de Deo*, XIX, in *Minor Theol. Works*, I, pp. 197-205.

231. Venema, *Inst. theol.*, VI (p. 151).

232. Leigh, *Treatise*, II.vii (p. 67, margin); cf. Beza et al. *Propositions and Principles*, VII.iv.

233. Leigh, *Treatise*, II.vii (p. 67); cf. Turretin, *Inst. theol. elencticae*, III.xii.18.

234. Cocceius, *Summa theol.*, III.x.26-29.

235. Charnock, *Existence and Attributes*, I, p. 418; cf. Le Blanc, *Theses theol.*, *De scientia Dei*, xxix.

Similarly, omniscience in no way implies that God knows temporal things temporally, that is, in the way that they are accomplished and known by temporal beings, indeed as they are accomplished in the temporal order. Such knowing would, in fact, imply an imperfection and an incompleteness in God:

> God's perfect knowledge of himself, that is, of his own infinite power and concluding will, necessarily includes a foreknowledge of what he is able to do and will do. Again, if God doth not know future things, there was a time when God was ignorant of most things in the world; for before the deluge he was more ignorant than after; the more things were done in the world, the more knowledge did accrue to God, and so the more perfection; then the understanding of God was not perfect from eternity, but in time; nay is not perfect yet, if he be ignorant of those things which are still to come to pass.[236]

Such limitation of the divine knowledge — making it contingent on temporal events in their temporality — would, Charnock notes, destroy the doctrine of providence, inasmuch as God's "providence hath a concatenation of means with a prospect of something that is future."[237] Providence, in other words, assumes a knowledge of ends and effects as well as of causes and means.

4. **Practical use of the doctrine of divine omniscience.** The relation between omniscience and other attributes yields a rather practical and religious accent to the Protestant scholastic doctrine and offers a point of transition from the somewhat rationalizing definition of the attribute to a description of the use or practical implication of the doctrine. Thus Pictet:

> This attribute of omniscience must *necessarily* be ascribed to God: otherwise there is an end to all religion, since nothing can more powerfully tend to establish it in the mind, than the belief that God continually beholds, and will finally judge our actions. This attribute, moreover, not only teaches us how we ought to regulate our conduct, since nothing escapes the infinite knowledge of God, but it also assures us that we can with confidence address our petitions to him in every place, and commit our cause to him, under the persuasion that the uprightness of our hearts is open before him, and that he will discover it, if not in this, yet at least in the future world.[238]

Such practical application is typical of the orthodox doctrine of the divine omniscience.[239] Even so, God's omniscience is a great terror to the wicked but an immeasurable comfort to believers. "The study of the knowledge of God, and our Lord Jesus Christ, is the highest, noblest, the most soul-perfecting and exalting knowledge that can be; all other knowledge without this will nothing advantage us."[240]

---

236. Charnock, *Existence and Attributes*, I, p. 430.

237. Charnock, *Existence and Attributes*, I, p. 430.

238. Pictet, *Theol. chr.*, II.v.18-19.

239. Cf. Mastricht, *Theoretico-practica theol.*, II.xiii.24-30; Ridgley, *Body of Divinity*, p. 70, col. 2- p. 71, col. 1; cf. Watson, *God's Anatomy*, in *Discourses*, I, pp. 147-171.

240. Leigh, *Treatise*, II.vii (p. 63).

It is necessary for us to be ruled by him, who is full so of knowledge, and to believe all which he saith by way of relating, promising, threatening.[241]

And finally,

This may comfort God's people, *my witness is in heaven*, said Job. If they know not how to express themselves in Prayer, God knows their groans.[242]

According to Manton, Reformed doctrine indicates "that God exactly and perfectly knoweth all things that are in the world, and is more especially privy to the hearts and ways of men." Such doctrine, he concludes, gives "terror to the wicked" and "comfort to the godly."[243]

E. Distinctions in the Divine Knowing[244]

As in their discussions of the divine will, the Reformed orthodox offer a series of distinctions concerning the divine knowledge, none of which indicate a compounded-ness in the divine knowing but rather distinguish God's knowledge in terms of its varied objects.[245] These distinctions are in fact implicit in the definitions given above: divine knowledge can be considered either as God's knowledge of himself or as God's knowledge of finite or created things — and since he knows himself and all things as well, he is said to be omniscient. Given the issues identified by the philosophical and theological tradition, the explanation of neither aspect of the divine knowledge is without complication, and as one would expect, the complications yield distinctions.

1. *Scientia necessaria sive naturalis* and *libera sive voluntaria.* The distinction between "necessary" or "natural" and "free" or "voluntary" knowledge is a distinction between the knowledge that God *must* have and the knowledge that God has freely according to his will — this language, in contrast to that of the very similar distinction between *scientia simplicis intelligentiae* and *scientia visionis*, arises out of a voluntaristic, Scotist approach to the divine knowing.[246] The knowledge that God must have is a necessary knowledge but it is also natural, inasmuch as God has it by nature rather than by imposition from without — the knowledge that God freely has is a knowledge

---

241. Leigh, *Treatise*, II.vii (p. 63).

242. Leigh, *Treatise*, II.vii (p. 64).

243. Manton, *Sermons upon 1 John III*, in *Works*, 21, pp. 174, 181.

244. The following section offers only a brief examination of these distinctions and reserves the detailed consideration of *scientia necessaria* and *libera sive voluntaria*; *scientia simplicis intelligentiae* and *scientia visionis*; and *scientia indefinita* and *scientia definita* for a later section (5.3d) where the debate over *scientia media* is taken up.

245. Mastricht, *Theoretico-practica theol.*, II.xiii.14, provides a basic series of the usual distinctions, as does Maresius, *Collegium theologicum*, II.xxxvii-xlii; Marckius, *Compendium theologiae*, IV.xxxvii-xxxix; and De Moor, *Commentarius*, IV.xxxvii-xxxix. Cf. the discussions in Barth, *Church Dogmatics*, II/1, pp. 567-569 and Heppe, *Reformed Dogmatics*, pp. 72-74.

246. Note that Heppe, *Reformed Dogmatics*, p. 72, is unclear, not identifying *scientia libera* as the other member of the distinction. Heppe's original does not evidence the problem: see *Die Dogmatik der evangelisch-reformierten Kirche*, ed. Ernst Bizer (Neukirchen: Buchhandlung des Erziehungsvereins, 1935), pp. 48, 64-65.

that coincides with his will for the being or existence of all things *ad extra*. Accordingly, the necessary or natural knowledge of God is the knowledge that God has concerning himself and all possibilities *ad extra* or beyond himself. This knowledge of all possibility is typically associated by the orthodox with the *potentia* or *omnipotentia Dei*, given that the divine potency is the potency for the being of all things. The free or voluntary knowledge is a knowledge of all those possibilities that God freely wills to actualize — namely, his creation, whether past, present, or future.[247] This distinction, together with its parallel, the distinction between "knowledge of simple intelligence" and "knowledge of vision," is the conception of divine knowledge most frequently encountered among the Reformed orthodox — perhaps the dominant form, given the likelihood that the distinction between knowledge of simple intelligence and knowledge of vision is, in Reformed systems, integrated with the notion that God freely wills the actual order with full freedom of contrariety.[248]

2. Scientia simplicis intelligentiae and scientia visionis. The divine "knowledge of simple (or pure) intelligence" is identical in its basic implication to the *scientia necessaria*, but defined from a different perspective, namely, that of the divine *intelligentia* or knowledge of first principles.[249] The difference between the two sets of terms arises from the grounding of the language of *scientia necessaria / voluntaria sive libera* in the voluntaristic tradition associated with Scotism and that of the *scientia simplicis intelligentiae / visionis* in the intellectualist or Thomist tradition. In the traditional division of categories of knowing, *intelligentia*, strictly defined, is a knowledge of first principles only, apart from the conclusions that can be drawn from them or the goals toward which they tend. With reference to God, *intelligentia* is a knowledge of all that might be, which is to say, the entire realm of possibility, known without reference to results or goals. This is a knowledge of things and events, some of which God wills into existence, the rest remaining nonexistent. The *scientia visionis* is identical in scope and basic import to the *scientia libera sive voluntaria*, but, of course, with an intellectualist rather than a voluntarist implication: it is the knowledge of all that God "sees" or comprehends as belonging to the realm of divinely willed existence. It is a *scientia intuitiva* inasmuch as God has an immediate and present knowledge in and through his own being of all that he brings into existence — and it is a knowledge that has reference to the results and the goals implicit in each and every possibility willed by God. In other words, God brings into existence only those possibilities that, both in result and in ultimate goal, coincide with his plan and will for the world.[250]

---

247. Cf. Beza et al. *Propositions and Principles*, VII.iii; Greenhill, *Exposition of Ezekiel*, 38:17, in loc. (p. 760).

248. See below, 5.4 (C.2-3), on the divine freedom, and cf. Antonie Vos, "De kern van de klassieke gereformeerde Theologie," in *Kerk en Theologie*, 47 (1996), pp. 106-125.

249. Cocceius, *Summa theol.*, III.x.12, 26.

250. Cf. Heppe, *Reformed Dogmatics*, p. 74. Note that the translation does not clearly indicate the members of the distinction, i.e., "knowledge of simple intelligence" and "knowledge of vision": see Polanus, *Syntagma*, II.xviii; Alsted, *Theol. didactica*, I.xxii, regula 4-5; Owen, *Vindiciae Evangelicae*, in *Works*, 12, pp. 127-128; Pictet, *Theol. chr.*, II.v.16; Rijssen, *Summa theol.*, III.xxiv; and note Michael

In the definitions and explanations of the seventeenth-century Reformed orthodoxy, moreover, the more Thomistic language of *scientia simplicis intelligentiae / visionis* is often explained in a voluntaristic manner, yielding the more Scotistic model under the Thomistic language.[251]

3. *Scientia indefinita* and *scientia definita*. The distinction between "indefinite" and "definite" knowledge mirrors the preceding distinctions between necessary and free knowledge, knowledge of simple intelligence and visionary knowledge. It rests on the identification of possibles as having "indefinite" or "undefined" status and actuals as "definite" or "defined," paralleling the distinction between potency and actuality. Still, God's knowledge is always distinct: he knows possibles or indefinite things distinctly, namely, as distinct possibilities not yet given the "defined" status of actuality.

4. *Scientia practica* and *scientia speculativa sive theoretica*. This distinction is a qualification of the *scientia visionis* according to its two possible relations to the divine decree. The divine practical knowledge is the knowledge of vision or of all actuality understood in conjunction with the divine decree, which, as Maresius puts it, "is not only an act of will but also of intellect."[252] This knowledge is practical inasmuch as it is directed toward the goal of creation; specifically, it is the "cause of things." By way of contrast, there is also the divine *scientia visionis* considered as consequent to the decree — the knowledge of actuals as they have been willed. But this knowledge of actuals is not a knowledge consequent or contingent on the actuals themselves but rather consequent on the decree. In short, it rests on the eternal divine willing of actuality and is a knowledge by which "God knows things *praesenter* in themselves, *antecedenter* in their causes, *supereminenter & idealiter* in himself, [knowing] their *praesentia* when they are being made, their *praeteritio* when they have been made, and their *futuritio* when they are yet to be made."[253] This knowledge is speculative or theoretical and contemplative given that it is noncausal, nondirective, a pure knowledge of all that God wills.

5. *Scientia generalis* and *scientia particularis*. The primary object of omniscience is God himself; and, as the preceding sets of distinctions have all indicated in one way or another, it is in himself that God knows all things:

> God knows all things, because first he knew himself directly in himself, by himself, and primarily, as a most perfect object; which knowledge in God, is of absolute necessity (for he could not exist without the knowledge of himself) and infinite, apprehending an Infinite object, *Psal.* 147:5.[254]

In this prior sense, however, according to which God knows all things in himself, there is first and foremost an ideal or general knowledge of the forms of things: God knows

---

Daniel Bell, "*Propter Potestatem Scientiam, ac Beneplacitum Dei*: The Doctrine of Predestination in the Theology of Johannes Maccovius" (Ph.D. diss., Westminster Theological Seminary, 1986), pp. 98-99.

251. Thus, Owen, *Vindiciae Evangelicae*, in *Works*, 12, pp. 127-128.

252. Maresius, *Collegium theologicum*, II.xli.

253. Maresius, *Collegium theologicum*, II.xli; cf. Barth, *Church Dogmatics*, II/1, p. 567.

254. Leigh, *Treatise*, II.vii (pp. 60-61).

what things are before he decrees and knows *that* they are. Thus, the created order as it actually is in its particulars must be, not the primary, but the secondary object of the divine omniscience — and it is at this point that a series of difficulties arise in relation to the possibility of certain kinds of knowledge and in relation to the causality of knowledge. By way of basic definition:

> God knows all things ... because he knows the creatures, all and singular, *viz.* all things which have been, are, or shall be, might have been, and may be; not only the substances, but all the accidents of creatures, not only things necessary, but also contingent, all good things by himself, and all evils by the opposite good; and that infallibly without error.[255]

An initial difficulty encountered by the Protestant orthodox, as for the medieval scholastics is the question of whether God can know singular or individual things. Much of this problem derived from the assumption held by Aristotelian philosophy that the senses know singular things inasmuch as singulars are individuated by matter and the senses perceive the material order, while reason in and of itself knows only universals — human reason, of course, can deal with singular things, given its relation to sense. In the case of divine knowledge, however, there is utter abstraction from materiality, and in God himself there is no "likeness of singular things" on which to rest an understanding of the singular.[256] Thus, Wendelin argues that although "many philosophers have doubted" that God knows all "singular things as they are: this angel, this man, this plant," it is nonetheless "manifestly true" that God knows individual things, granting that "God created singular things; his judgments are exercised concerning singulars" and, indeed, "he computes the numbers of the stars and calls each one by name."[257]

The point is obviously necessary to Christian theology, inasmuch as the God of the Bible, unlike the strictly Aristotelian First or Unmoved Mover, is the creator of the finite — and is, to borrow on the Aristotelian terms themselves, the first efficient cause and not merely the final cause of all things.[258] Indeed, this is one of several places in the doctrine of God at which all the scholastics distance themselves from an unadulterated Aristotelian perspective. The Reformed orthodox, in particular, see this aspect of the Aristotelian system not only as philosophically unacceptable but also as the source of a series of errors in theology both in and beyond the doctrine of God. It is from this basic error of denying knowledge of singulars to God, writes Mastricht, that the "crassest of Pelagians and Socinians" gain support for their doctrine of the independence and indifference of the human will and for the related claim that

---

255. Leigh, *Treatise*, II.vii (p. 61).

256. Cf. Aquinas, *Summa theologiae*, Ia, q. 14, a. 11, obj. 1-3, citing Aristotle, *De Anima*, ii, with Mastricht, *Theoretico-practica theol.*, II.xiii.17.

257. Wendelin, *Christianae theologiae libri duo*, citing Ps. 47:4; 56:9; Ps. 147; and Matt. 10:30. N.B., Wendelin's definition is also cited by Leigh, *Treatise*, II.vii (p. 61, margin).

258. Cf. Copleston, *History of Philosophy*, I, pp. 314-317.

God knows neither those individuals who will believe nor any future contingents, but merely decrees to save in general any who will believe and repent.[259]

Scripture, moreover, consistently teaches that God knows singular things. Here it is worth noting that Aquinas cites but one biblical text, "All the ways of a man are open to His eyes" (Prov. 16:2) and offers a largely philosophical and rational proof that God does indeed know singulars,[260] while the Reformed scholastics respond to the problem in a primarily biblical and often highly practical manner — to the point that there can be a marked overlap between the dogmatic and the homiletical literature of the age. The Lord, writes Mastricht, is said by Scripture to "know everything" without qualification (John 21:17); "all things are laid bare to his eyes" (Heb. 4:13) — including singulars — inasmuch as he names the stars (Ps. 147:4), counts the troubles of the psalmist (Ps. 56:8), knows the numbers of our hairs (Matt. 10:30), and knows who are his own (2 Tim. 2:19). What is more, Scripture indicates that God knows future contingents (Ps. 139:1-6; Matt. 26: 34-35). Indeed, concludes, Mastricht, if God did not know all singular things, he would not be perfect: moreover, if he created singulars, how can he not know them? If he conserves and governs singulars, can he be ignorant of them? Or how could he know himself, inasmuch as God is *singularissimus!*[261] Voetius proposed a more elaborate dogmatic argument, grounded explicitly in patristic and medieval scholastic theology, indeed, evidencing a clear sense of the Augustinian exemplarist tradition.[262]

6. *Scientia approbationis* and *scientia reprobationis*. Several of the orthodox writers indicate that a distinction must be made between the approving or positive knowledge that God has concerning all that is good, as indicated in the creation narrative of Genesis 1, and the knowledge that God has concerning all that is deficient or evil in his creation, as indicated in Matthew 7:22-23, "In that day ... I will profess unto them, I never knew you: depart from me, ye that work iniquity." As Trapp paraphrases, "I knew you well enough for 'black sheep,' or rather for reprobate goats ... I never knew you with a special knowledge of love, delight, and complacency. I never acknowledged, approved, and accepted of your persons and performances."[263] The text does not indicate an absence of divine knowledge as such but an absence of a particular kind of divine knowledge, namely, a positive knowledge of evil parallel in every way to the divine knowledge of the good: evil, after all, is not an entity or substance, but a defect in a created good. In his "pure intelligence," therefore, God "knows evil by a contrary good, as the light discovers the darkness": he knows sin "so as to hate it, not so as to act or approve it."[264]

---

259. Mastricht, *Theoretico-practica theol.*, II.xiii.17.

260. Cf. Aquinas, *Summa theologiae*, Ia, q. 14, a. 11.

261. Mastricht, *Theoretico-practica theol.*, II.xiii.17; cf. the nearly identical citation of texts and the parallel argumentation in Manton, *Sermons upon 1 John III*, in *Works*, 21, pp. 176-178.

262. Voetius, *Selectarum disputationum theologicarum*, I, 14; V, p. 85.

263. Trapp, *Commentary on the Old and New Testaments*, in loc. (vol. V, p. 134).

264. Watson, *God's Anatomy*, p. 152.

F. The "Necessary" and "Free" Knowledge of God and the Problem of "Middle Knowledge"

1. Basic definitions. The Reformed orthodox inherited from the medieval doctors a set of distinctions concerning the divine *scientia*, granting both the infinitude of divine knowledge over against the finite order and the relation of all things in the finite order, as contingent existents, to the noncontingent or necessary being, knowing, and willing of God. The older scholasticism had distinguished between a knowledge resting on the divine understanding in itself and consisting in all that God must necessarily know, granting that God is God, and a knowledge resting on the divine free willing of the existence of things.[265] The former category of divine knowledge is the *scientia simplicis intelligentiae* or *scientia necessaria*; the latter is the *scientia voluntaria* or *scientia libera*.[266] The scholastics distinguished, therefore, between the eternal, infinite divine knowledge of the divine essence and of all possibility and the divine knowledge of all actuality *ad extra*. Since, moreover, all actualization of possibility or potential existence rests directly on the divine will, the scholastics saw no need for any other category of divine knowing. Although, certainly, there was a need to distinguish between necessary, contingent, and freely chosen events and acts in the temporal order, the divine knowledge of these events and acts was itself in no need of further qualification: contingent and free events and acts have their actuality from the divine will as much as do necessary events and acts.

This distinction between a *scientia simplicis intelligentiae seu necessaria* and a *scientia voluntaria seu libera* carried over directly into the theology of Reformed orthodoxy, although not without some skepticism concerning its usefulness and some qualification of its terms.[267] Rijssen offers a fairly standard statement of the distinction:

> The knowledge of God is commonly distinguished into *simple*, or *natural* and *indefinite understanding*; and *free*, or *visionary* and *definite understanding*. The former concerns merely possible things; the latter concerns things that will be.[268]

The "simple understanding" is sometimes also called *scientia necessaria*, since it is a knowledge that God must necessarily have, given the divine omniscience. It is "natural" because God possesses it according to his nature: it is a knowledge that God has and, in fact, must have simply because God is God. It is an "indefinite" knowledge with regard to things other than the divine essence itself, inasmuch as its objects are possibilities, not actualities. This ultimate divine knowing is typically juxtaposed with

---

265. Cf. Aquinas, *Summa theol.*, Ia, q.14, art.8, with Duns Scotus, *Op. Oxon.*, I, d.39, nota 23; and note also Raymond, "Duns Scot," in *DTC* 4/2, col. 1880.

266. See Heppe, *Dogmatik der evangelisch-reformirten Kirche*, pp. 484-9, cf. 64-65.

267. Cf. Baxter, *Catholike Theologie*, I.iv.41-45, with Alsted, *Theologia didactica*, I.xxii, regula 4-5 (pp. 74-75).

268. Rijssen, *Summa*, III.xxiv: "Scientia Dei vulgo dividitur in *simplicis intelligentiae*, seu *naturalem & indefinitam*; vel *liberam*, seu *visionis & definitam*. *Illa* est rerum merè possibilium; *Ista* rerum *futurarum*." Cf. Owen, *Vindiciae Evangelicae*, in *Works*, XII, pp. 127-128; Gill, *Body of Divinity*, I, pp. 87-88.

scientia libera.[269] Such knowledge is "free" because it rests on the divine freedom, specifically on the freedom of God to will certain possibilities and not others. The Reformed orthodox postulation that God's free or visionary knowledge is definite and certain therefore does not mean that God's knowledge is restricted to certain necessary events and things. It is definite because it refers to actualities. It is certain because it is neither partial nor contingent.

These terms and the issues implied by them are subject to much elaboration and explication in the Reformed orthodox systems. God's knowledge is, in the first place, his perfect knowledge of himself and of all things,

> whereby he knoweth both himself in himself, and out of himself all and singular things by himself, by an indivisible and immutable act. ... and this indivisible and present knowledge of God is unchangeable, as well of things contingent and things necessary, laying the condition of contingency on things contingent, as also the law of necessity on things necessary.[270]

The divine knowledge of the created order is not, therefore, a knowing *ad extra* resting on examination of the individual existents in the finite order, that is to say, neither a contingent knowledge grounded on contingent existences nor an indefinite knowledge, but a knowledge of the possibilites and actualities known and willed by the divine essence itself.[271]

To state the issue from a different perspective, nothing occurs that is not known by God eternally in the "counsel of his will." Since God eternally and immutably decrees what he will "effect or permit," he must also foreknow all things infallibly: "the *praescientia Dei* follows [logically] upon God's decree, and since the decree cannot change, neither can God's knowledge err."[272] What is significant here is the stress on the immutability of the divine knowledge of all things coupled with the notion of a necessary knowledge of all possibility and a voluntary or free knowledge of all actuality. Vos, who roots this volitionally defined version of the conception in Scotus, comments with specific reference to the trajectory of Reformed thought that "during the half millennium between 1300 and 1800," he writes, "it is characteristic of the doctrine of God that the existence and essence of God are said to be immutable and necessary, but that God's acts of knowing and willing are only said to be immutable, but not necessary."[273]

This view of the divine knowing calls forth some words of caution from the Reformed orthodox:

---

269. Cf. Heppe, *Reformed Dogmatics*, pp. 72-74.

270. Trelcatius, *Schol. meth.*, I.iii (pp. 69, 71); cf. Cloppenburg, *Exercitationes super locos communes*, II.iv.1-2, and Francken, *Stellinge God-Geleertheyd*, p. 175.

271. Cloppenburg, *Exercitationes super locos communes*, II.iv.2.

272. Rijssen, *Summa theol.*, III.xxiii, controversia 1, arg. 3.

273. Antonie Vos, "Always on Time: The Immutability of God," in Brink an Sarot (eds.), *Understanding the Attributes of God*, p. 67.

Concerning the manner (*modus*) in which God knows all things, we must speak cautiously and not attribute anything unbecoming or unworthy to the ultimate majesty. Maimonides observes, that *to wish to know the mode of the divine knowledge, is the same as wishing to be God.* Now we must not at all imagine that God knows things in the same manner as men, who understand one thing in one way, and another thing in another way, and the same thing sometimes obscurely and at other times more clearly, and who, from things known proceed to things unknown. The divine knowledge is of such a mode, as not to admit of any discursive imperfection, or investigative labor, or recollective obscurity, or difficulty of application. God comprehends all things by one single act, observes them as by a single consideration, and sees them distinctly, certainly, and therefore perfectly.[274]

Given the "feebleness" of our understanding, we

attribute to God a twofold knowledge: the one, by which he knows things that are possible, called by the scholastics the knowledge of natural and simple understanding (*scientia naturalis et simplicis intelligentiae*); the other, by which he knows things that will be (*res futuras*), called by them free and visionary knowledge (*scientia libera et visionis*). The first kind of knowledge is founded on the power of God (*ipsa Dei potentia*), the second has for its foundation the decree of God (*ipsum Dei decretum*), inasmuch as God knows things that will be because he has decreed that they will be.[275]

There is a highly significant point in the language that associates the natural or necessary divine knowledge of all possibility with the *potentia Dei* and the free or visionary knowledge of all actuality with the *decretum Dei*. The latter issue is simple: nothing can exist unless God in some manner wills its existence (whether directly or through the agency of secondary causes). The former issue demands clarification, inasmuch as the usual translation of *potentia* as "power" misses the sense of the term as "potency": the point is that possibilities or possible existents are *in potentia* — in potency or potential — and the potential *for* their existence is the divine potency or power. Thus, God knows both his power and his will: in his power is the potential for the existence of all that is possible; in his will is the foundation of the existence of all that is actual. This also means that, inasmuch as the potential for the existence of all that is possible is the divine *potentia*, the entire category of the possible is necessarily limited by the *potentia Dei*: there is no genuine possibility beyond the bounds of the divine nature.[276]

Nor is it the case that the Reformed orthodox adopted the distinction between necessary and free knowledge or knowledge of simple understanding and voluntary knowledge without question. Several of the early orthodox writers — Gomarus,

---

274. Pictet, *Theol. chr.*, II.v.15; Cf. Ridgley, *Body of Divinity*, p. 70.

275. Pictet, *Theol. chr.*, II.v.16; cf. Rijssen, *Summa*, III.xxiii, *controversia*, 1, arg. 3; Ridgley, *Body of Divinity* (18550, I, p. 96.

276. On the *potentia Dei*, see further, below, 6.2 (B); this particular argument has affinities with Ockhamist thought: cf. Wolter, "Ockham and the Textbooks," pp. 83-84; Adams, *William Ockham*, II, pp. 1065-1067, 1079-1083 disagrees.

Walaeus, Crocius, and Alsted — were concerned to differentiate a category of divine knowing related to conditional events. Their intention was to divide the category of voluntary knowledge into a knowledge of things directly willed by God as necessary or contingent and a knowledge of things resulting conditionally, as, for example, events or acts permissively willed by God, as the free results of human willing.[277] Thus Alsted can argue three categories: God knows all possibilities; all things existing *ex hypothesi*, that is, conditionals; and all things either necessary or contingent, whether past, present, or future.[278]

The chief issue of debate in the seventeenth century was the location of divine knowledge of the conditional or *ex hypothesi* events. Thus, in a more detailed paradigm, Alsted indicates that God, first in order, knows himself. Second, God knows all possibilities — whether those arising immediately out of his will, or those arising out of his movement, conservation, concurrence, or permissive willing of creatures, or those arising out of the acts of creatures themselves. Third, God knows all beings or existences, whether considered as past, present, or future, whether resulting from direct acts of God, from indirect or mediate acts of God working through creatures, or from acts of creatures themselves. God therefore knows all things and every thing (*omnia & singula*).[279] Alsted does not consider things or events known apart from the divine will, inasmuch as he does not believe that any such things can exist: God knows all things in himself, knowing, as it were, all effects in their omnipotent efficient cause.[280]

2. A seventeenth-century critique of the basic distinctions. Baxter, rather pointedly, expressed his doubts concerning the traditional formulations: "that the Common School distinction of all Gods Knowledge, into *scientia simplicis intelligentiae, & purae visionis*, is not accurate, and the terms are too arbitrary and dark to notifie the thing intended; and that the *scientia media* added doth not mend the matter: And that a fitter distinction is plain and obvious."[281] Baxter objected, in particular, to the typical approach to God's knowledge of "possible" and "future" things. Reflecting, most probably, his appropriation of Campanella's triadic pattern for ontic and noetic distinctions, Baxter offers a triadic approach to "possibility" and then replaces the typical division of divine knowledge into necessary or simple and free or voluntary with his own version of the doctrine — a version that, in fact, reflects more closely the Reformed association of the *scientia necessaria* with the divine power and the *scientia voluntaria* with the eternal decree.[282]

---

277. See Heppe, *Reformed Dogmatics*, p. 79.
278. Alsted, *Theologia didactica*, I.xxii, regula 4 (p. 74).
279. Alsted, *Theologia didactica*, I.xxii, regula 4 (p. 74).
280. Alsted, *Theologia didactica*, I.xxii, regula 5 (p. 75).
281. Baxter, *Catholike Theologie*, I.iv.45.
282. Cf. Richard Baxter, *Methodus theologiae* (London, 1681), praefatio, fol. 5-6, with Campanella, *Metaphysica*, VI.v.1; x.1; xi.1; I owe this point to Carl Trueman, who documents it at length in his "A Small Step Towards Rationalism: The Impact of the Metaphysics of Tommaso Campanella on the Theology of Richard Baxter," in Trueman and Clark, ed., *Protestant Scholasticism*, pp. 147-164.

> The *Power* of God is denominated Relatively *Omni-potency* in three instants to Three several Objects: 1) In the first instant, as to *All things which belong to Power*: And so God *can do all things*, which are hence called *Possible*. 2) In the second instant, to *All things meet* or *Congruous* to the *Divine intellect* to be *willed and done*: And so we say, that God can do *All* that is *meet* to be done, and nothing that is *unmeet*. 3) In the third instant (of reason) as to *All things* which he *willeth to do*: And so we say, that God *can do* whatsoever *he will do*. And so *Possibility* hath various senses.[283]

Given this approach to the possible, Baxter can also frame a threefold definition of the objects of God's knowledge — and, significantly, the middle term is not Molina's *scientia media*:

> Gods Intellect is Relatively denominated *Omniscient*, in respect to three sorts of Objects also in three instants: 1) In the first instant he knoweth all *Possibles*, in his own *Omnipotence*: For to know things to be *Possible*, is but to know *what he can do*. 2) In the second Instant he Knoweth all things, as *Congruous, eligible* and *Volenda*, fit to be *Willed*: And this out of the perfection of his *own wisdom*: which is but to be *perfectly Wise*, and to know what *perfect Wisdom* should offer as eligible to the *Will*. 3) In the third Instant he knoweth *All things willed* by him as such (as *Volita*): which is but to know his *own Will*, and so that they *will* be.
>
> In all of these instances we suppose the Things themselves not to have yet *any Being*: But speak of God as related to Imaginary beings, according to the common speech of men.
>
> These therefore are not properly Transient Acts of God; because it is but *Himself* that is the object indeed, *viz.* His own *Power, Wisdom and Will*.[284]

On these grounds, God's knowledge of "what he *can* do, what he *knoweth* to *be eligible*, and what he *will* do" can be called either a knowledge of "the *Possibility* or *Futurity* of the thing *known*" or — in an ontological sense just as accurately, according to Baxter — a knowledge of nothing.[285] Possibility and futurity, he reminds his readers, "are not accidental notions, or relations of the things themselves; but are *termini diminuentes*, as to the *Things*, and are spoken of *Nothing*." To speak of a thing as possible or as future "is to say that *now* it *is nothing*."[286] It is, therefore an error and a confusion of meaning to claim that "God knoweth things to be future, because they are future; as he knoweth existents, because they exist." "Futurity," Baxter counters, "is Nothing; and Nothing hath no Cause" or causal significance: God cannot be said to foreknow things "*because they will be*; but only that he foreknoweth *that* they will be"[287] — given that God's knowledge of things is not because of things, that is, not caused by the things as if they were prior to God. There can be, Baxter adds, "no effects in God."[288] Of course, Baxter

283. Baxter, *Catholike Theologie*, I.iv.40.

284. Baxter, *Catholike Theologie*, I.iv.41-43.

285. Baxter, *Catholike Theologie*, I.v.70.

286. Baxter, *Catholike Theologie*, I.v.64.

287. Baxter, *Catholike Theologie*, I.v.85.

288. Baxter, *Catholike Theologie*, I.v.71.

has already indicated that all things that were, are, or will be are known by God as *volita*, things willed by him: things are not, in themselves, the cause of God's knowledge of things.

Baxter thus assumes that things happen necessarily, contingently, and, in the case of human choice, freely — but he also assumes that the divine knowledge of these things is both certain and subsequent to the divine determination either to will their existence directly or to concur in their existence by means of free or contingent secondary causes, in the existence of which he also concurs. Much of the difficulty, therefore, he argues, arises from improper discussion of the way in which God knows. It is doubtless true, in a certain way of framing the question, that "God knoweth from Eternity the *truth* of all *conditional propositions that are true*." Even so, granting that true "hypothetical propositions" are as much objects of knowledge as "absolute propositions," they would surely be known to God as well: if the hypothetical proposition is said to be "less perfect" than the absolute proposition, this is no way indicates that "Gods knowledge of it [is] *less perfect*."[289] But Baxter is not quite ready to grant that a hypothetical proposition can be as much an object of knowledge as an absolute proposition.

The problem with all of this argumentation, Baxter comments, is that God is a simple being who does not know by means of propositions — particularly not by means of an ordered series of propositions. There are, in addition, no "propositions from eternity," since propositions are, by nature, of human construction.[290] What is more, since future things — things that will be — do not now exist as far as we are concerned, the truth of their futurity is no more than the truth of a "proposition *de futuritione*," a proposition concerning the future eventuality of something. God can be said to "know the truth of all true propositions of futurity," given that he knows propositions as they are invented in the human mind, and he also knows what he wills.[291] God will also know the falsehood of false propositions of futurity, and know them specifically, as the erroneous thoughts of individuals. Of course, since there is no futurity for God, the question also resolves for the Reformed in the divine knowledge of what is at all times: in his eternity, God knows all time.

By extension, God knows conditional propositions as part of his knowledge of all actuality, inasmuch as he knows all the thoughts of human beings. By further extension, this means that God does not know conditional propositions in the way that we know them: specifically, he does not apprehend the future actuality to which our propositions refer conditionally as conditional in the sense of possibly existing and possibly not existing: for, after all, God knows all possibility prior to his free willing that certain possibilities, including contingents and conditionals, be actualized — and he knows the actual contingents and conditionals not as possibles but as actuals.[292] This critique

---

289. Baxter, *Catholike Theologie*, I.xii.255, 260.
290. Baxter, *Catholike Theologie*, I.v.75-78; xii.262.
291. Baxter, *Catholike Theologie*, I.v.75.
292. Baxter, *Catholike Theology*, I.xii.259 with Ridgley, *Body of Divinity*, p. 70, col. 1.

of the traditional language embodies a high degree of skepticism concerning any speculation about divine knowledge of conditionals — and it precludes many, if not all, claims about the nature of divine knowledge of counterfactuals that fueled seventeenth-century debate over so-called middle knowledge.

3. Middle knowledge: *scientia media.* The Reformed orthodox approach to this distinction requires clarification against the background of late sixteenth-century debate, since the language of the *scientia Dei* is often modified to indicate as a third, mediate knowledge God's indeterminate and non-determinative knowledge of the realm of creaturely possibility, a foreknowledge of events which depend not on his decree but on the liberty or free choice of the creature. This is the *scientia media,* or middle knowledge, was advocated first by the Jesuit theologians Fonseca and Molina, and subsequently by the Remonstrants and Socinians, and it was vehemently denied by the Reformed as it was by the Dominican thinkers of the sixteenth and seventeenth centuries.[293] Rijssen notes with obvious glee that the concept of *scientia media* "aroused such a controversy between the Jesuits and the Dominicans that not even the Pope could make it cease"; what Rijssen rather expectedly fails to note is the profound agreement on the question between the Reformed and the Dominicans![294]

The controversy between the Dominicans and the Jesuits over the relationship of grace and free will had its impact on Reformed orthodoxy particularly following the publication of Luis de Molina's *Concordia liberi arbitrii cum gratiae donis, divina praescientia, providentia, praedestinatiore et reprobatiore* in 1589.[295] In this work Molina posited a divine *scientia media* — a divine knowledge lying between God's indeterminate knowledge of all possibilities and his determinate foreknowledge of the necessary and

---

293. Rijssen, *Summa theol.,* III.xxiv, controversia; cf., at great length, Voetius, *Selectarum disputationum theologicarum,* I, xv-xix. On the seventeenth-century reception of *scientia media,* see Eef Dekker, *Rijker dan Midas: Vrijheid, genade en predestinatie in de theologie van Jacobus Arminius, 1559-1609* (Zoetermeer: Boekencentrum, 1993), pp. 76-84, 102, 232-237; also note idem, "Does Duns Scotus Need Molina? On Divine Foreknowledge and Co-causality," in *John Duns Scotus (1265/6-1308): Renewal of Philosophy,* edited by E. P. Bos (Amsterdam: Rodopi, 1998), pp. 101-111; idem, "The Reception of Scotus' Theory of Contingency in Molina and Suárez," in *Via Scoti,* edited by L. Sileo, pp. 445-54; and idem, "Was Arminius a Molinist?" in *Sixteenth Century Journal,* 27/2 (1996), pp. 337-352; cf. Copleston, *History,* vol. III, part 2, pp. 161-163; the Reformed answer, given above, is much the same as that of Molina's opponent Báñez — giving rise to the Molinist accusation of "Calvinist" against Báñez' Dominican followers; also see Heppe, *Reformed Dogmatics,* pp. 72-75; Barth, *Church Dogmatics,* II/1, pp. 569-86; Vansteenberghe, "Molinisme," in *DTC,* 10/2, col. 2096; and Muller, *God, Creation, and Providence,* pp. 151-166. Not surprisingly, twentieth-century Arminians have also argued a divine *scientia media:* see William Lane Craig, "Middle Knowledge: A Calvinist-Arminian Rapprochement?" in *The Grace of God and the Will of Man,* ed. Clark H. Pinnock (Grand Rapids: Zondervan, 1989), pp. 141-164; and cf. Nash, *The Concept of God,* pp. 51-66.

294. Rijssen, *Summa theol.,* III.xxiv.

295. See Luis de Molina, *Concordia liberi arbitrii cum gratiae donis, divina praescientia, providentia, praedestinatione et reprobatione* (1588), ed. Johann Rabeneck (Onia and Madrid: Collegium Maximum Societatis Jesu, 1953); also, selections in *On Divine Foreknowledge,* trans. with an intro. and notes by Alfred J. Freddoso (Ithaca: Cornell University Press, 1988), and cf. the summary of Molina's teaching in William L. Craig, *The Problem of Divine Foreknowledge and Human Freedom from Aristotle to Suárez* (Leiden: Brill, 1980), chapter 5.

certain effects of his decree. Between the merely possible and the necessary, Molina postulated a category of contingent acts accomplished in the freedom of the secondary causes. These acts God knows as more than merely possible because God knows with certainty just how the human will acts or will act in any given set of conditions — yet this knowledge of God cannot be said to be determinate since God has not foreordained either the wills or the conditions.[296] In short, middle knowledge is a divine foreknowledge of future contingent or conditional acts or events lying outside of or prior to the divine willing.

Molina introduced the concept or, more accurately, developed it further than his predecessor, Fonseca, in order to offer a solution to the problem of human free choice and divine foreknowledge, with particular attention to the problem of grace and election as posed by Calvin and other Protestant theologians of the sixteenth century and by the more soteriologically Augustinian teachers of the Dominican order. His doctrine would, surely, have been viewed as problematic and as an object of polemic by Reformed theologians of the era even had it remained the view of one particular party in the Roman Catholic church. Middle knowledge became a profound problem for Protestantism, however, as it passed rapidly from Jesuit hands into the theology first of Arminius and, shortly thereafter, of the Socinians of the seventeenth century. In Arminius' hands, the idea of middle knowledge retained the direction given to it by Molina and became the philosophical underpinning of Arminius' doctrine of predestination; in Socinian hands, however, it was drawn out in relation to a revised view of the divine essence and attributes, including the claim that there was indeed succession in God, and transformed into a doctrine of limited divine foreknowledge.[297]

It is important to recognize that middle knowledge is not simply the divine foreknowledge of future possibility or contingency. If the issue were simply the divine knowledge of future possibility — even of possibilities arising out of the contingent interaction of finite creatures — it could be easily understood under the rubric of the divine *scientia necessaria* or necessary knowledge of all possibility. If the issue were simply the divine foreknowledge of contingency in the usual sense, namely, a foreknowledge of contingencies arising out of the world order willed or actualized by God, it could easily be understood under the rubric of the *scientia voluntaria*, the divine knowledge of all that God has willed, past, present, and future. *Scientia media*, however, is a kind

---

296. Cf. Copleston, *History*, vol. III, part 2, pp. 161-163; and E. Vansteenberghe "Molinisme" in *DTC*, 10/2, cols. 2094-2187; the bibliography following the text of the article offers an excellent review of earlier literature on the subject; also see F. Stegmüller, *Geschichte des Molinismus* (Munster: Aschendorff, 1935); and Robert Merrihew Adams, "Middle Knowledge and the Problem of Evil," in *The Virtue of Faith and Other Essays in Philosophical Theology* (New York: Oxford, 1987), pp. 77-93.

297. On the history of the problem from a seventeenth-century Reformed perspective, see Turretin, *Inst. theol. elencticae*, III.xiii.2-4. On Arminius' use of middle knowledge, see Richard A. Muller, "Arminius and the Scholastic Tradition," in *Calvin Theological Journal*, vol. 24, no.2 (November 1989), pp. 263-277; idem, *God, Creation and Providence*, pp. 154-166; Eef Dekker, *Rijker dan Midas: Vrijheid, genade en predestinatie in de theologie van Jacob Arminius (1559-1609)* (Zoetermeer: Boeckencentrum, 1993), pp. 76-103; and idem, "Was Arminius a Molinist?" in *Sixteenth Century Journal*, 27/2 (1996), pp. 337-352.

of divine knowing intentionally placed *between* God's necessary and voluntary knowledge. It is a foreknowledge of future conditionals or conditional future contingencies arising from the free choice of creatures prior to the divine willing.[298]

To make the point in another way, if divine knowledge of conditionals and contingencies is considered as belonging to the *scientia necessaria* as possibilities capable of being actualized by God, they represent one of grounds of the divine freedom in creating or not creating the universe or in creating or not creating a particular universal order rather than another. If, on the other hand, divine knowledge of conditionals and contingencies is considered as belonging to the *scientia libera seu voluntaria*, they represent the result of the divine free willing of a particular series of possibilities as the world order. In the first instance, God knows such conditionals and contingencies as mere possibility, in the second, he knows them as actualities — and in both cases, either the purely possible or the actual, God knows the alternative results and counterfactuals as existing in other possible worlds or in what might be called other "concatenations of possible entities" or other "systems of possible things."[299] Middle knowledge adds a different dimension: it understands God neither as simply willing a particular possible world rather than another nor as having willed a particular (actual) world, but as foreknowing and reacting to the result of a finite contingency or conditionality as prior to and apart from his willing.

The extent of the seventeenth-century debate over middle knowledge was vast — as was the significance of the problem it raised in the theology of the day.[300]Nearly

---

298. Turretin, *Inst. theol. elencticae*, III.xiii.5-8; cf. Maresius, *Collegium theol.*, ii.39-43; Venema, *Inst. theol.*, vi (p. 155).

299. Note that I am using the phrase "possible world" in its seventeenth- and early eighteenth-century sense, as found in Leibniz' famous phrase "the best of all possible worlds" — namely, as indicating a possibly or potentially existent universal order of things or world order, and not in the modern semantic sense of a coherent set of propositions. The phrase "concatenations of possible entities" is drawn from Samuel Rutherford, *Exercitationes apologeticae* (Franecker: Johannes Dhüiringh, 1651), II.v.8 (p. 203), "systems of possible things" from Stapfer, *Inst. theol. polemicae*, I.iii, §337.

300. See Sven K. Knebel,"Scientia Media. Ein diskursarchäologisher Leitfaden durch das 17. Jahrhundert," in *Archiv für Begriffsgeschichte*, 34 (1991), pp. 262-294. In addition to the theological systems, the seventeenth-century treatises on the problem include: John Prideaux, *Lectiones novem de totidem religionis capitibus* (Oxford, 1625), Lect. 2; William Twisse, *Dissertatio de scientia media tribus libris absoluta* (Arnheim, 1639); François Annat,*Scientia media contra nouos eius impugnatores defensa. Hoc est contra Guillelmum Tuissium Caluinistam., Auctorem anonymum libri de ordine, &c.*, *Theologum Collegij Salmanticensis., Ioannem à S. Thoma* (Toulouse: Franciscus Boude, 1645); Thomas Ailesbury, *Diatribæ de æterno Divini Beneplaciti circa creaturas intellectuales decreto, ubi patrum consulta, scholasticorum scita, & modernorum placita ad sacræ scripturæ amussim, & orthodoxæ ecclesiæ tribunal deferuntur. Pars prima, quæ est de ipsa ante secula præfinitione, seu proposito Divino* (Cambridge: John Field, 1659); John Stearne, *Animi medela, seu, De beatitudine & miseriâ: illius essentiâ, origine, & ad ipsam methodo: hujus naturâ, causis & remediis, tractatus. In quo quæcunque ad alterutram spectant, explicantur, facilitas cum Beatitudinem consequendi, tum miseriam declinandi, demonstratur; & gravissimæ de libero arbitrio, ratione supplicandi Deo, concursu, causâ & origine mali, Divinâ peccati nonvolitione, scientiâ mediâ, pœnitentiâ, lachrymis, ecstasi, &c. controversiæ enodantur* (Dublin: Gulielmus Bladen, 1658); Voetius, *Selectarum disputationum theologicarum*, I, pp, 264-339 (*De conditionata seu media in Dei scientia, partes IV*);Carolus ab Assumptione, *Scientia media ad examen revocata* (Douai: Joannis

every theologian and exegete of the age touched on the problem and, with the exceptions of the Jesuits, Socinians, and Arminians, response was largely negative, albeit the negatives varied both in content and in intensity. The problem of middle knowledge was, thus, not merely a speculative problem concerning the way in which God knows future contingents and conditionals — it was a broader theological problem concerning the underlying intention of the theory of *scientia media*, namely, the affirmation of a synergistic soteriology, and the use to which the doctrine was put by various groups viewed as heterodox by the Reformed. And whereas Arminius held to the basic form and intention of Molina's argument, the Socinians developed a notion of a limited divine foreknowledge of future contingency on the ground that future contingencies must be "uncertain."[301]

4. Reformed critique of middle knowledge: the problem of Molinism. Among the Reformed, several theologians were willing to acknowledge a need to clarify discussion of the divine knowledge of possibilities and contingencies and, therefore, to draw some limited inspiration from Molina's argument. For example, Gomarus and Walaeus (and later, Baxter), though repelled by the Pelagianizing impact of this view, adapted the argument of Molina to refer, not to a *scientia media* between knowledge of the possible and of the actual, but to a *scientia hypothetica* prior to all of the divine determinations. In this view, God rests his *decretum* upon his knowledge of how the world order is to be constructed in its most minute hypothetical workings. The decree, therefore, establishes the freedom of secondary causes and allows for or permits the eventuality of sin and evil, though only in a hypothetical sense, namely, as events that will occur, given the actuality of the circumstances preceding them. The point, in other words, is not that God learns from or reacts to a future possibility, but that God actualizes a particular concatenation of possibilities in which, given the particular set of circumstances directly willed, certain events will occur by reason of secondary causes, including the exercise of human free choice. The free choices belong, therefore, to the particular world order that God wills to actualize. As for God's "foreknowledge" of all such actual events, it is necessary, certain, and determinate as it follows the decree and rests on the certainty of the divine causality.[302]

The majority of seventeenth-century Reformed theologians saw the notion of *scientia media* as problematic: none denied the divine foreknowledge of future contingency. What they denied was that future contingencies could be construed as sets of

Patté, 1670); idem, *Thomistarum triumphus id est Sanctorum Augustini et Thomae gemini ecclesiae solis summa concordia, I. De scientiâ mediâ, II. De naturâ purâ, seu duplici Dei amore, III. De libertate, IV. De contritione, V. De probabilitate*, second ed., 3 pts. in 2 vols. (Douai: Baltazar Beller, 1672-1674); Gabriel de Henao, *Scientia media theologice defensata*, 2 vols. (Lyon: Laurentius Arnaud & Petrus Borde, 1674-1676).

301. Crell, *De vera religione*, I.xxiv; cf. Owen, *Vindiciae evangelicae*, in *Works*, XII, pp. 116-117; Edwards, *Theologia Reformata*, I, p. 61.

302. Walaeus, *Loci Communes*, p. 174, col. 1-p. 176, col. 1; Cf. the discussion in Barth, *Church Dogmatics*, II/1, pp. 574-576; and note Thomas Gataker, *Antithesis, partim Gulielmi Amesii, partim Gisberti Voetii, de sorte thesibus reposita* (London, 1638), where the author disputes Ames' allowance for "multae ... causae fortuitae" on the ground that "divine providence rules in all things" (pp. 10, 14).

foreknown conditions known by God as other than mere possibilities and yet also known by God prior to God's willing them. As Turretin indicates, the problem was not over "necessary conditional future things, which on this or that given condition cannot but take place," such as "if the sun rises, it will be day" or "if Peter heartily repents, he will be saved." The problem concerned "contingent conditional future things which — the condition posited — can be or not be."[303] To borrow again on the biblical example, "if David had stayed the night at Keilah, he would have been betrayed." According to Molina, God's knowledge of such conditional contingencies belongs to a third category of knowledge: God knows that David would not stay and would not be betrayed, but he knows it without decreeing the condition or willing the contingency. Molina would even go so far as to assert that the divine concurrence enters into the result, leaving the choices of David and the inhabitants of Keilah outside of the divine willing. This particular kind of knowing the Reformed deny, as we will see, on several grounds.[304] Both the Reformed and the Socinians recognized, moreover, albeit from different perspectives, that the notion of a certain divine foreknowledge of future conditionals is a rather unstable concept: in order for God to know the conditional conditionally, God would have to be ignorant of its resolution in actuality. In other words, the "if" of the conditional would have to represent an indeterminacy and uncertainty in God himself. We will return to the Socinian view below.

Furthermore, for Molina's concept to function, the conditions standing prior to the contingent event must be understood as not merely possible, but as having some sort of actuality or quasi-actuality apart from the divine willing — inasmuch as the point is not that God knows various and sundry possible contingencies and knows what would result on condition of their occurrence (viz., given their actualization by him). That would, once again, press back into the divine necessary knowledge. Nor is the point that God knows certain conditions within the realm of actuality that he has willed and also knows what will result from them. That would point toward the divine voluntary knowledge. Rather the point is that God knows what will occur contingently upon certain conditions lying outside of his will: these conditions are not mere possibility nor divinely willed actuality, but foreknown conditions, foreknown as actual apart from the decree, at least for the sake of stating the contingency. Once again, the Reformed deny that there can be such knowledge: "there can be no *scientia media*," Cocceius wrote, "because there can be no being independent of the divine will."[305]

Baxter notes, against some of the more necessitarian of his Reformed brethren, perhaps Twisse, that it is a misconception and hardly a refutation of the idea of middle knowledge to claim that "no futurition can be known but as *Decreed*." This argument errs both in its assumption that all things are decreed absolutely and in its approach

303. Turretin, *Inst. theol. elencticae*, III.xiii.6.

304. Turretin, *Inst. theol. elencticae*, III.xiii.8.

305. Cocceius, *Aphorismi prolixiores*, v.4; cf. Cocceius, *Summa theol.*, III.x33; Turretin, *Inst. theol. elencticae*, III.xiii.10, 19; Greenhill, *Exposition of Ezekiel*, p. 758, cols. 1-2.

to the problem. After all, sin is not decreed directly or absolutely by God, nor does middle knowledge at all concern necessary events:

> The sense of the question *de Scientia Media*, is not *de conditionatis necessariis*, as "If the Sun set, it will be night" ... But of such conditionals as have *some reason* of the *Connexion*, and yet leave the will in an *undetermined power* to act or not. But we know no difference between these *ex parte Dei Scientis*, but only *denominatione extrinseca ex parte obiecti*. ... Therefore, the doctrine of Gods knowledge of such *Conditional propositions*, and *contingents* as so circumstantiated, seemeth *True materially*, (that They are the objects of Gods knowledge;) but *false efficiently* as if there were *any Causes* of his knowledge, (which hath no Cause;) but only extrinsecal denominaters of it in that act.[306]

In other words, God knows the conditional proposition as it is posed extrinsically on the part of its object (or subject), but God's knowledge itself is not conditional, since not resting on the extrinsic denominator as its cause. God knows what we know and knows also the ways in which we know, but the way or mode of the divine knowing itself differs from the mode of our knowing. Baxter also notes that, given the assumption that God's knowledge is not caused by things exterior to God, the concept of middle knowledge is quite useless,

> seeing they use it to shew how God *knoweth that Determinatively*, which he foreseeth but *in Conditionibus sine quibus non*, or in *unnecessary* and not *determining* causes. And their own answer signifieth nothing more to the purpose, but that God can know future contingents by the Infinite perfection of his understanding, which is most true. But that he knoweth them the more from the *supposition of circumstances*, they never prove.[307]

Still, it is precisely at this point that the larger number of the Reformed (and the Thomists) of the seventeenth century press the ontological question and deny the existence in actuality of a particular class of what Baxter identifies as "extrinsic denominators." As Twisse pointed out, the status of middle knowledge, between the knowledge of all possibility and the knowledge of all willed actuality, whether necessary or contingent, rests on one's ability to maintain a distinction between known future contingents such as Baxter has indicated *de conditionatis necessariis* in which there is no indeterminacy, namely, a necessity of the consequence, and apparently indeterminate future contingencies that are not capable of being known "as a thing to come" any more than they can be known "as a thing not to come."[308] The falsity of a notion of middle knowledge and the inability to sustain such a distinction appears,

---

306. Baxter, *Catholike Theologie*, I.xii.264, 267. Baxter, as usual, manifests a vast knowledge of the medieval scholastics, citing marginally Ockham, Gregory of Rimini, Gabriel Biel, Bonaventure, Nicholas of Orbellis, Durandus, Pierre D'Ailly, Duns Scotus, and Joannes Rada throughout his discussion of these questions.

307. Baxter, *Catholike Theologie*, I.xii.267.

308. Twisse, *Discovery*, p. 335. See the discussion of Twisse's debate with Jackson in Sarah Hutton, "Thomas Jackson, Oxford Platonist, and William Twisse, Aristotelian," in *Journal of the History of Ideas*, 39 (1978), pp. 635-52.

according to Twisse, when it is asked, not how such a contingent can be known, but rather how "such a contingent shall exist."[309]

Indeed, in Twisse's view, the proponents of middle knowledge, notably Suárez, consistently beg the ontological question:

> I would know of him ... for example, how it is true that tomorrow it shall rain rather than tomorrow it shall not rain, seeing in itselfe it is no more inclinable to the one than to the other. If the one were true and the other false, then there were no question, but God should know the one to be true and the other to be false. But seeing there is no reason given by Suárez, why the one should be true rather than the other, there is no reason why the one should be known of God to be true more than the other.[310]

The problem with this line of argument, Twisse continues, is that Suárez has given an example of a future contingent without also indicating how the contingent will come into existence: "But had he gone about this worke, which indeed was most necessary, the truth would soone have appeared ... that nothing could be the cause hereof but the will of God."[311]

Reformed exegetes draw out this point in their exegesis of Ezekiel 38:10-13 — "Thus saith the Lord God; It shall also come to pass, that at the same time shall things come into thy mind, and thou shalt think an evil thought: and thou shalt say, I will go up to the land of unwalled villages": God not only knows the thoughts of the wicked, but he knows them with certainty before they entered the mind of their human subjects.[312] Beyond this, "God foreknows and determines things to come, even those things which seem most free and contingent, as the thoughts of men's hearts." Without the divine determination, the free and the contingent could not exist at all: "if God did only permit a thing to come to pass, how could it come to pass without some action, and God's concurrence to that action? for there is no action or cause producing any effect, with which God doth not concur, Lam. 3:37; Prov. 21:1; 16:1."[313]

Furthermore, neither human beings nor God know unknowable things: there is not, Twisse insists, any difference between finite and infinite knowledge on this point. The difference is that "of things knowable, finite knowledge takes notice only of some; infinite knowledge comprehends all."[314] When this point is applied to the case of future contingents, it remains the case that truly unknowable things cannot be known at all, whether by man or by God, whereas genuine future eventualities, although unknowable to human beings, can indeed be known by God. The issue is simply how it is determined that future contingencies will or will not occur:

> Now things contingent, till they are determined to come to passe, or not to come to passe, are not knowable that they shall come to passe, nor are knowable that they shall

---

309. Twisse, *Discovery*, p. 335.

310. Twisse, *Discovery*, p. 336.

311. Twisse, *Discovery*, p. 336.

312. Henry, *Exposition*, in loc.

313. Greenhill, *Exposition of Ezekiel*, in loc. (p. 758, cols. 1-2).

314. Twisse, *Discovery*, p. 338.

not come to passe; and consequently cannot be knowne that they shall come to passe, or knowne that they shall not come to passe.[315]

There must be a causal determination that moves any future contingent from the realm of mere possibility into the realm of actuality: "that which in its own nature is only possible, cannot passe from this condition into the condition of a thing future, without some cause." Ultimately, the cause of the actuality of anything is the will of God. Twisse then denies that this eliminates contingency: God "decreeth a contingent manner of production" when he determines the futurition of contingent things — "as he decreeth that necessary things shall come to passe necessarily, so he decreeth that contingent things shall come to passe contingently."[316]

The same problem obtains with reference to conditionals as with reference to contingencies: in addition to the problem of the actuality of future conditionals, there is also the problem of their knowability. Baxter concluded that much of the problem of "middle knowledge," apart from the ontological problems inherent in the discussion, arises from the notion that God's foreknowledge of a contingent or conditional event arises out of the event itself, as if God's knowledge were caused by the finite order:

> If we may or must say that God from eternity *fore-knew our Propositions* of *future contingents*, which are Conditional, yet we must not say or think that his *knowledge quoad actum* is *conditional*, so as that the Creatures state is the condition of Gods Knowledge in its self: But only that the *object* is a *conditional proposition*, speaking the Condition of the event fore-known: From which Gods Act is denominated conditional only *denominatione extrinseca*, not as *an Act*, but as *This act*. ... Nor doth Gods fore-knowledge that *Adam will sin in such circumstances*, make his understanding depend on the Creature, but only to be terminated on the Creature as an object.[317]

This conclusion also appears from God's eternity, for even the concepts of past, present, and future knowledge are attributed improperly to him: God knows everything that can be known all at once, without succession. Thus he does not see our past, present, and future as his own past, present, and future. Thus the process of discursive reasoning itself cannot be attributed to God.[318]

5. The Socinian problem: limited foreknowledge of future contingency. A further nuance was added to the debate by the Socinians: while it is clear that God has exhaustive knowledge of things directly caused by him, allowing for the category of *scientia media*, can God have unlimited foreknowledge of the contingent results of the free operation of secondary causes? (Indeed, what does it mean to speak of the contingent results of the free operation of secondary causes?) In other words, if he does have foreknowledge of contingent events, is that foreknowledge *indeterminatè tantum & verisimiliter* or *determinatè & certissimè*?[319] The Socinians press the point even

---

315. Twisse, *Discovery*, p. 338 ; cf. Turretin, *Inst. theol. elencticae*, III.xiv.21.
316. Twisse, *Discovery*, p. 338; cf. Turretin, *Inst. theol. elencticae*, III.xiv.21.
317. Baxter, *Catholike Theologie*, I.xii.259; cf. Ridgley, *Body of Divinity*, p. 70, col. 1.
318. Cf. Ridgley, *Body of Divinity*, p. 70, cols. 1-2;
319. Rijssen, *Summa*, III.xxiii, controversia 1; cf. Ridgley, *Body of Divinity*, p. 69, col. 1.

farther than either the Jesuits or the Remonstrants and *limit* God's knowledge of *futura contingentia, actionesque Creaturarum liberarum*. Thus, for God to know conditionals as conditional (i.e., to know them conditionally), he must have a limited foreknowledge of future contingency. The Socinians press the Molinist formula toward a logically stable form by denying divine omniscience.

Many of the Reformed, following the arguments of Voetius and Heidanus, saw this view as turning on itself — namely, as introducing a new form of determinism into the universal order: inasmuch as it claimed to discuss future contingents lying outside of the will of God, it introduced into the concept of a world order events and things not caused by God and, in addition, determinative of the divine will itself. If, moreover, it was the divine will that established all things in their necessity, contingency, or freedom, such events lying outside of the divine will would not only be in some way determinative of God, would not only introduce effects into the divine essence, but would also to the same degree *impede* the divine establishment of all things in their necessity, contingency, and freedom.

Leigh thus commented that the concept of a middle knowledge "is a great dishonour to God, as if he knew the futurition of things by second causes." Such a theory would render God's "knowledge uncertain and dependent on the Creature."[320] Or, as Voetius argued, if there is a middle knowledge in God, dependent on "external objects," then there is an eternal priority of these creatures and creaturely events over God and "creatures will not depend on God alone, but God will instead depend on creatures as his exemplars."[321] This divine dependence, in turn, would argue the absolutely certain existence of future contingents "prior to all divine decrees" and, given the absolute certainty of such contingents, introduces a causal necessity into their effects — that is, the necessity of the consequent, which, from the perspective of the consequent act or thing itself is an absolute necessity. A radical conception of foreknowledge that insists on a divine foreknowledge of conditionals as conditional, in other words, reifies the conditionals, places events and things outside of the divine purpose, and hypothesizes an order of occurrences that, therefore, impinges negatively on the divine willing. Thus, those who "establish future events as prior to the decree of God, introduce Stoic fatalism, namely, an interconnection of things independent of God."[322] This, for Burgersdijk, Voetius, and Heidanus, is the implication of the theory of middle knowledge, especially of the Socinian version. The attempt to gain freedom at the expense of the divine causality results, therefore, in a new fatalism, a replacement of the conception of overarching divine purpose with a model of blind natural necessity.[323]

---

320. Leigh, *Body of Divinity*, II.vii (p. 193), cf. Zanchi, *De natura Dei*, III.ii, q. 4.4 (col. 204).

321. Voetius, *Selectarum disputationum theologicarum*, I, p. 326 (*De conditionata seu media in Deo scientia*, IV.23); cf. Heidanus, *Corpus theol.*, II (p. 224).

322. Van Til, *Theol. comp. naturalis.*, I/I, I.iv.3 (p. 41).

323. Voetius, *Selectarum disputationum theologicarum*, I, pp. 334-336 (*De conditionata seu media in Deo scientia*, iv.29); Heidanus, *Corpus theol.*, II (p. 124); Burgersdijk, *Institutiones metaphysicae*, II.vii.18; also note Barth, *Church Dogmatics*, II/1, p. 574.

Against Socinianism, therefore, the Reformed maintain the absolute omniscience of God, presenting a battery of scriptural proofs and several arguments based on Scripture — God, in Scripture, predicts contingent events in the future: therefore he knows them and knows them infallibly, for otherwise he could not predict them certainly.[324] As, for example, the prediction of King Ahab's death "by an arrow shot at random," an event by all standards contingent (1 Kings 22:17-18, 34); or the bondage and deliverance of Israel in Egypt foretold four hundred years previously or the divine prediction to Moses of Pharaoh's obstinacy (Gen 25:13-14; Exod. 3:19-20) — both of these instances indicate divine foreknowledge of future contingent events. Similarly, God predicts not only the taking of the Syrian crown by Hazael but also the unexpected cruelty of Hazael upon his ascension to the throne, quite contrary to Hazael's own expectation; and the Lord Jesus predicted his betrayal by Judas prior to Judas' decision to commit the crime (2 Kings 8:12-13; John 6:70-71). Even so, Joseph's advancement in Egypt and the events foretold in the various dreams interpreted by Joseph with the power of God were all contingent events.[325] Thus, in sum, "God knows all future events with certainty," including "the contingent and free effects of creatures" — and knows these things in such a way as does not undermine the freedom and mutability of human existence.[326]

Against these points, the Socinians argue that, since future contingent events do not presently have a hard and fast determination of their course and result, there can be no certain and infallible foreknowledge of them. Such an argument would open up the way for a doctrine similar to the Molinist *scientia media* rejected by the early orthodox and opposed, still, in the era of high orthodoxy. Rijssen answers, that whereas "there can be no determination of the truth [of future events] by reason of secondary causality," this is fully available "by reason of the first cause, which decreed their future existence, and which observes all future events as if they were present."[327] Thus the "future contingent" is fully contingent with reference to secondary causality but not "with respect to God," who decrees it: the Reformed point is that liberty and contingency are not absolute but occur within an order that owes its entire existence to God.[328]

By way of example, God's expectation of good fruit from the vine that was Israel (Isa. 5:4) arises not out of a lack of divine knowledge but out of the human form of speaking which seriously commands the people of Israel to do good works: for God

---

324. Rijssen, *Summa theol.*, III.xxiii, controversia 1, arg. 1-2, citing Heb. 4:13; John 21:17; 1 John 3:20; Acts 15:18; Psalm 139:1-7; Jer 1:5.

325. Cf. Ridgley, *Body of Divinity*, p. 69, cols. 1-2.

326. Cocceius, *Aphorismi prolixiores*, V.5-6, 8; cf. Muller, "Grace, Election, and Contingent Choice," in Schreiner and Ware, eds., *Grace of God*, pp. 268-269, 275-277.

327. Rijssen, *Summa theol.*, III.xxiii, controversia 1, obj. 1 and resp; also Ridgley, *Body of Divinity*, p. 69, col. 1.

328. Zanchi, *De natura Dei*, III.ii, q. 4.4 (col. 204); Venema, *Inst. theol.*, vi (pp. 150-151).

does indeed and rightly expect them to obey him even as the vintner rightly expects his vine to bear fruit — even if he knows that his expectation will go unfulfilled.[329]

> Things that happen without our design, or fore-thought, and therefore are not certainly fore-known by us, are the objects of his providence, and therefore known unto him from the beginning: thus *the fall of a sparrow to the ground* is a causal thing, yet our Saviour says, that this is not without his providence (Matt. x.29). Therefore, that which is causal or accidental to us, is not so to him; so that though we cannot have a certain or determinate fore-knowledge thereof, it does not follow that he has not.[330]

Nor does the fact that God tests certain men — like Abraham — go against his foreknowledge of their acts:

> God tests human beings not out of ignorance, but on the grounds of his most wise providence, in order that he might declare what he had previously kept hidden from them. Thus, God tested Abraham, not in order that he might know a faith and obedience of which he had previously been ignorant, when God had already (Gen. 18:17-18) acknowledged that he knew Abraham's piety, but rather that he might manifest to the world and to the church Abraham's remarkable faith.[331]

This explanation appears to be countered by Genesis 22:12, where God says to Abraham, "Now I know that you fear God." The verse is not to be understood *absolutely*, as concerning knowledge that God has obtained, but *transitively*, as concerning knowledge that God provides to others.[332] It is worth noting that most commentators of the sixteenth and seventeenth centuries — from Calvin to Henry — explained the text in a similar way and that here, as in so many other places, the dogmatic use of the text reflects the exegetical tradition:

> God knew the sincerity and resolvedness of Abraham's faith and obedience before and without this evidence, and from eternity foresaw this fact and all its circumstances; and therefore you must not think that God had now made any new discovery: but this is spoken here, as in many other places, of God after the manner of men.[333]

Another way of explaining the various Old Testament texts which seem to deny the omniscience of God is to argue that they refer to God by *anthropopatheia*. This applies in particular to such passages as Genesis 18:21, where God is said to descend to Sodom to inquire concerning its morality: the text indicates that God is a just judge who makes no precipitate judgments.[334] Even so, the text does not indicate that "there

---

329. Rijssen, *Summa theol.*, III.xxiii, controversia 1, obj. 1 and resp.

330. Ridgley, *Body of Divinity*, p. 69, col. 1.

331. Rijssen, *Summa theol.*, III.xxiii, controversia.

332. Rijssen, *Summa theol.*, III.xxiii, controversia, obj. 3 & resp.

333. Poole, *Commentary*, Gen. 22:12 in loc. (I, p. 52); cf. Calvin, *Commentaries on Genesis*, in loc. (CTS Genesis, I, pp. 570-571); Diodati, *Pious and Learned Annotations*, in loc.; *Dutch Annotations*, in loc.; *Westminster Annotations*, in loc.; Henry, *Exposition*, in loc. (I, p. 81).

334. Rijssen, *Summa theol.*, III.xxiii, controversia, obj. 4 & resp.; cf. *Westminster Annotations*, in loc.; Poole, *Commentary*, in. loc. (I, p. 43).

were any thing concerning which God is in doubt, or in the dark; but he is pleased thus to express himself after the manner of men" for the specific purpose of revealing "the incontestable equity of all his judicial proceedings"; indeed, "the decree is here spoken of as not yet peremptory, that room and encouragement might be given to Abraham to make intercession."[335] Nor does any of this reasoning deny the contingent nature of things and events:

> Since it is possible for something to arise necessarily as far as the occurrence is concerned (*quoad eventum*), but contingently according to its manner of being produced (*quoad modum productionis*), future contingents can therefore be necessary according to the immutability of the decree (*immutabilitatem decreti*) and the infallibility of foreknowledge (*infallibilitatem praescientiae*), while remaining genuinely contingent in the secondary causality on which they depend proximately and immediately — which secondary causes are, by themselves, indefinite (*per se indefinitae*).[336]

The Reformed also argue that God's natural faculty of knowing and his unconstrained knowledge of events and things comprise all knowables, given that entities cannot be multiplied without cause: there is nothing that falls outside of the realm of possible and future existents (*nihil enim est, quod non sit possibile aut futurum*), which is to say that the categories of the possible and the actual are exhaustive. Nor is uncertain or indeterminate knowledge ever rightly attributed to God.[337] Inasmuch as "God eternally knows himself and all possible worlds, he therefore knows whatever is knowable" and, since he knows all possible worlds as possible worlds, namely, as systems or concatenations of things in their relation and distinction, "he therefore knows all things distinctly and nothing confusedly."[338]

> All acts of a created will are subject to divine providence, so that nothing is indeterminate; this [line of argument] proves absolutely the interdependence of primary and secondary causality and of the creature and the creator — so that all creatures depend on God not only for their existence (*non tantum in esse*), but also in their activity (*sed etiam in operari*). Therefore, a middle knowledge (*scientia media*) that is supposed to have as its object a free determination of the will dependent upon no higher cause is impossible.[339]

And finally, the most pressing objection against the *scientia media* — it destroys the lordship or sovereignty of God. In Cocceius' view, *scientia media* renders God's knowledge and willing dependent on human actions — in Van Asselt's paraphrase, reducing God to a classical "Jupiter who consults the Fates."[340] Rijssen, unlike several of his early orthodox predecessors, will allow of no divine foreknowledge of things or

---

335. Henry, *Exposition*, in loc. (I, p. 69).
336. Rijssen, *Summa theol.*, III.xxiii, controversia, obj. 5 & resp.
337. Rijssen, *Summa theol.*, III.xxiv, controversia, arg. 1, 4.
338. Stapfer, *Inst. theol. polemicae*, I.iii, §338-9.
339. Rijssen, *Summa theol.*, III.xxiv, controversia, arg. 3.
340. Van Asselt, *Federal Theology*, p. 167.

events that is prior to the decree, not even a so-called hypothetical knowledge.[341] This argument undermines not only the Molinist position but also rejects the concept put forth by Gomarus and Walaeus of a *scientia hypothetica*, as is seen from the first objection and response:

> If David had remained the night at Keilah, he would have been betrayed (1 Sam. 23:9[-13]). Response: The text does not deal with an action that might, hypothetically, have occurred *(de actione ex hypothesi futura)*, but with the plan and intention of the people of Keilah to betray David.[342]

In other words, the text does not point toward a hypothetical future in which David remained the night at Keilah and then claim to know that he actually would have been betrayed rather than somehow delivered from betrayal: the betrayal at Keilah is not a hypothetical future event, but no event at all and, prior to David's decision not to remain there, a pure possibility (belonging, arguably, to the divine *scientia necessaria*). And, as a possibility, the betrayal of David, had he stayed the night, is nothing more or less than an unfulfilled intention in the minds of the inhabitants of the village, in fact, a false proposition of futurition, rendered false by the fact that its eventuality did not belong to the ultimate will or providence of God.[343] There is nothing prior to the decree but pure possibility: God's decree establishes the order of things — it does not proceed from foreknowledge of the order.[344]

The alternative view, that such an event (if this, then that) is not merely in the order of possibilities and must be known by a "middle knowledge," confers a quasi actuality upon the possibility. Then, of course, the ground of the actuality once again becomes a matter of issue: from the Molinist, Arminian, and Socinian perspective, the contingency is known as an event prior to the divine willing — an event, which the Reformed contend, cannot be, inasmuch as all actuality is conferred by God. Nor, given the Reformed assumption of an eternal or successionless duration of God, is it possible to argue a discursive or successive process of knowing and willing in the divine mind, according to which God weighs contingent possibilities in his *scientia necessaria* and then chooses which one to actualize based on his desire to actualize one particular result rather than another. (And even this rejected position would not need a middle knowledge between God's necessary and free knowledge.)

A similar response is given to the indefiniteness of future prophecies in the Old Testament:

> 2 Kings 13:18-19. *If he had struck the ground more frequently, etc.* Response: Elisha said to Joash: "If you had struck the ground five or six times, you would have utterly annihilated Syria," not because this was known to him by means of a middle knowledge,

---

341. Rijssen, *Summa theol.*, III.xxiv, controversia, arg. 5.
342. Rijssen, *Summa theol.*, III.xxiv, controversia, arg. 5. obj. 1; cf. Maresius, *Collegium theol.*, ii.44.
343. Ridgley, *Body of Divinity* (1855), I, p. 96; cf. Maresius, *Collegium theol.*, ii.44; Cocceius, *Summa theol.*, III.x34, 36; Venema, *Inst. theol.*, vi (p. 155).
344. Mastricht, *Theoretico-practica theol.*, II.xiii.22.

but because the prophet inferred this as a condition on the basis of an indefinitely given divine revelation.[345]

In other words, the terms of the revelation were indefinite, and the prophet, who is said by the text to have been angry at the half-hearted effort of Joash, and who himself did not know the number of victories that would be given to Joash drew the legitimate inference that Joash's victories would be as inconsequential as his symbolic act of striking the ground with arrows.[346] The text, therefore, does not indicate any indefiniteness in the divine plan itself prior to the act of the king.

6. **Conditionals, possibles, and counter-factuals: some conclusions.** According to the Reformed writers of the seventeenth century, God can know contingents with certainty — either because he knows them as possible according to his necessary knowledge of all possibility or because he knows them as actual according to his visionary knowledge of all that he has willed. From the Reformed perspective, however, God does not know conditionals conditionally. The conditionality, if it is rightly stated, belongs to our finite and fallible statement of a hypothesis. On the one hand, in order for the conditional, "If David had stayed the night at Keilah, he would have been betrayed," to be known by God as not actualized either to staying the night or not staying the night, being betrayed or not being betrayed, it would have to be known by God as mere possibility. In this case, it would belong under the *scientia necessaria* and would be known as two possibilities, each capable of actualization: that is,, David stays the night and is betrayed, or David does not stay the night and is not betrayed. On the other hand, for the substance of the conditional statement to be known by God as an actuality, it would be known as the actuality of David either staying the night and being betrayed or not staying the night and not being betrayed. But there is only one actuality to be known: David does not stay and is not betrayed. The other member of the conditional, David staying and being betrayed, as an unwilled and unactualized possibility, is not, strictly speaking, knowable as actuality. In other words, the so-called counterfactual of David staying the night and being betrayed does not belong either to the same possible or to the same actual world as David not staying the night and not being betrayed: indeed, its only location is in a possible world that God does not choose to actualize.[347]

If, however, one wishes to press the point of middle knowledge and claim that the conditional is not mere possibility nor divinely willed actuality — namely, that it is something to be considered in actuality but outside of the divine willing — one would need to hold two other assumptions. First, in order to preserve genuine conditionality, one would have to assume that God's knowledge (or foreknowledge) is limited, specifically by being incapable of knowing outcomes either in themselves or in their causes. Second, one would either have to hypothesize partially knowable actualities

---

345. Rijssen, *Summa theol.*, III.xxiv, controversia, obj. 3.

346. Cf. Poole, *Commentary*, in loc. (I, p. 745).

347. These considerations raise issues of the nature of the possible and of the character of divine freedom: see the discussion of the will and freedom of God, below, 5.4 (C).

outside of God's willing or to claim that there are two phases, as it were, of the divine knowing of an event prior to his willing it — namely, that God first knows an entire possible world in an indeterminate way, as containing (possibly!) both an event and its contrary (*scientia necessaria*), and then knows by *scientia media* the outcome of the contingency or free choice were he to actualize that world, with the result that God in (or, indeed, temporally subsequent to) his actualization can also introduce other factors into that world order that are consequent on his knowing of the particular outcome. In this latter view, God acts consequently on the ground of his knowledge of actual events that he has not willed. The first assumption denies omniscience, which is opprobrious — and, in addition, it was not Molina's contention, albeit it was the Socinian conclusion. The latter assumption affirms an ontological impossibility, actualities arising solely out of finite causes. Such

> are not real (*vera*), nor are they capable of being foreknown as real, nor indeed are future contingents real when they are separated from the determination of the divine will, inasmuch as no effect can be known as having been apart from the divine decree.[348]

To state the latter problem in a slightly different way, a so-called future conditional — "if David will stay the night" — when posed as pure possibility, prior to God's decree, is literally "nothing" (or nothing more than a logical hypothesis). It cannot be known or foreknown as actual. Indeed, insofar as it is nothing, it cannot be known at all.[349] Nor does it detract from God's omniscience to state that it is unknowable, because it is not an unknowable something, but simply nothing at all. In other words, contrary propositions standing prior to the decree of God to actualize one or the other are "not entities," and thus are neither true nor false, nor, indeed, knowable — such propositions "are indifferent to truth and falsehood."[350] If it is known as actual, then it is no longer a conditional in an absolute sense (since David has indeed stayed the night!), but merely a contingent event. And if the claim is pressed that it is an actuality, known imperfectly by God as conditional and, although occurring outside the divine will, not an ontological impossibility, then it represents the introduction of an actuality that is by definition ultimately purposeless and therefore the introduction of a fatalism worse than the divine determination of all things that it sought to avoid. This modified and developed but essentially Thomistic solution to the problem of distinctions in the divine knowledge and, specifically, to the problem of the *scientia media* remained standard theological fare well into the era of late orthodoxy and, indeed, became a feature of the Wolffian theology of the mid-eighteenth century. Wyttenbach could argue that "since God can have no other objects of his knowledge" than what is possible

---

348. Rijssen, *Summa theol.*, III.xxiv, controversia, arg. 2.

349. Inasmuch as God does not think discursively, or dividedly by means of propositions, the proposition itself may only exist in the mind of the human being who poses it: there is, in other words, no way for the human mind to invade the divine *scientia necessaria* and determine whether the possibility that it has posed has the status of a genuine possibility capable of actualization: cf. Baxter, *Catholike Theologie*, I.v.75-81.

350. Rutherford, *Exercitationes apologeticae*, I.v.10; cf. Baxter, *Catholike Theologie*, I.v.64.

and what is actual, "it is superfluous to add to this twofold *scientia Dei* the third [category], *scientia media.*"[351]

The Reformed orthodox doctrine of the *scientia Dei* represents, at very least, a vast elaboration of the premisses of the Reformers concerning the knowledge of God. The expansion itself tempts the unwary first glance to declare a fundamental discontinuity between Reformation and orthodoxy brought about, of course, by "scholasticism." Several issues, however, stand against such a conclusion. First, the orthodox insistence on the categories of *scientia necessaria* or *scientia simplicis intelligentiae* and *scientia libera* or *scientia voluntaria* represents, at very least, a determined maintenance of the categories of divine knowing available to the earliest Reformers in their theological education and, therefore, forming the backdrop to any Reformation era discussion of the question of divine knowing. It is relatively certain that Reformers trained in the patterns of late medieval thought — Bucer, Musculus, Vermigli, and Zanchi — knew these terms and concepts. It is also certain that they did not know the concept of a divine *scientia media*, which arose only in the era of early orthodoxy.

The Reformed orthodox were pressed to argue the older categories of *scientia necessaria* and *scientia voluntaria* as the sole proper usage in the face of the rise of an alternative paradigm for understanding the divine knowing — a clear example of the development of doctrine in the context of polemic. The notion of *scientia media*, moreover, was brought to bear on the problem of divine predestination, providence, grace, and human responsibility by various Jesuit theologians and by Arminius. The development of Reformed doctrine on the point belongs to an attempt to maintain the soteriological monergism of the Reformation over against various synergistic theologies — this is not a "speculation" brought on merely by the advent of scholastic method, nor is it an attempt of academic theologians to penetrate the recesses of the Godhead out of pure curiosity. Development of the argument well beyond the level of detail found among the Reformers belongs to a debate over the issues raised by the Reformation — and the Reformed orthodox worked, at this more technical level, to uphold the concept of predestination apart from foreknowledge of works or of faith that was intrinsic to the original Reformed theology. Development and change are certainly evident, but so also is continuity of doctrinal intention.

5.4 Will and Freedom

A. The Will of God in Reformed Theology

1. The state of the question in modern discussion. It is fitting that we begin our discussion of the Reformed orthodox doctrine of the will of God, not with a simple definition, but with a series of distinctions. For the older orthodoxy, particularly when it engaged in the more academic or scholastic forms of exposition, recognized as fully as did the medieval doctors that the discussion of the divine will was necessarily complex, given, as Peter Lombard had long before noted, that the biblical references

---

351. Wyttenbach, *Tentamen theologiae dogmaticae*, III, §250; cf. Bell, "Predestination in the Theology of Johannes Maccovius," pp. 99-104.

to divine *voluntas* were so varied that they could not be understood apart from a series of distinctions in the divine willing.[352] Or, to make the point more positively, given that Scripture uses the word will in a variety of ways, specifically with regard to the varied objects and directions of the divine will, a series of distinctions concerning the divine will are implied in the text itself and must be made explicit simply for the sake of rightly understanding the text of Scripture itself.

Far from being an excessively "speculative" doctrine in the modern sense of the term, the orthodox discussion of the divine will was deeply rooted in the redemptive and historical elements of Christian theology and indicative of the a posteriori character of much Reformed theology in the era of Protestant scholasticism: for the distinctions made by the orthodox concerning the divine willing were not a matter of rational speculation but rather a result of the examination of biblical texts and traditional discussions of the *voluntas Dei*, the latter with particular respect to the needs or concerns of the doctrine of salvation by grace alone. We find here no examination of the recesses of divine willing for the sake of a speculative impulse and no overriding interest in discussion of the divine essence *in se*. Just as in the case of the Arminian discussion of distinctions in the divine willing,[353] here too the discussion reflects the soteriological concerns of the writers, and nearly all discussion of the divine will *in se*, or (more precisely) *ad intra*, serves as a foundation for understanding the divine willing *ad extra*.[354]

The will and freedom of God are natural and necessary correlates in the Reformed orthodox doctrine of God. The will of God is characterized by its absolute freedom from all external constraints, and the freedom of God is illustrated most fully in the unconstrained efficacy of the divine willing and by the genuine contingency of created things.[355] The orthodox conception of the divine will has frequently been misinterpreted: the essential identity of the divine will or decree with God himself has, mistakenly, been taken as removing divine freedom, when in fact this understanding supports and even guarantees the freedom of God.[356] So also, despite the obvious importance of the doctrine of the divine will, the Reformed orthodox never make it the basic category for understanding the essence and attributes of God and insist on understanding the doctrine of God's will as an integral part of the larger doctrine of the attributes — indeed, as a connecting link in the chain or circle of attributes that, together in their unity, provide us with an understanding of what God is and of the way that God relates to his world.[357]

---

352. Lombard, *Sententiae*, I, d. xlv, cap. 5.

353. See Muller, *God, Creation, and Providence*, pp. 167-207.

354. Contra Armstrong, *Calvin and the Amyraut Heresy*, p. 32.

355. Cf. Turretin, *Inst. theol. elencticae*, III.xiv.3, 6-8.

356. See, for example, James Daane, *The Freedom of God: A Study of Election and Pulpit* (Grand Rapids: Eerdmans, 1973), pp. 58-66, 158-160, 168-170, 188-189.

357. Cf. the discussion of the way in which various distinctions and definitions in the language of the attributes address the issue of the God/world relationship in: Muller, *God, Creation and Providence*, pp. 179-183, 204-205, 207, 239-243, 252-267.

In the twentieth century in particular the orthodox equation of God's will with the divine essence (on grounds of the simplicity of God) and the similar equation of the decree with the will of God has become a point of departure for criticism of the orthodox system as a rigid, metaphysical determinism.[358] This mistaken reading of the Reformed orthodox has actually been taken to the extreme of claiming that the identity of the divine decree or will with the divine essence, taken together with the definition of God as fully actualized (*actus purus*), yields the notion of a God who is not free in relation to externals but must create the world, must create it in a particular way, and must also be unable to relate to the individual acts and wills of creatures.[359] What is curious about these contentions is that they are opposed by the most basic of the Reformed orthodox definitions. Another mistaken reading of the materials claims that Reformed recourse to scholastic "voluntarism," specifically to the concept of *potentia absoluta*, in their doctrine of God led to highly inconsistent theological positions, including the problem of positing a God "at odds with himself" who "wills from necessity and freedom, but not always both."[360]

2. Reformation and orthodoxy: the continuity and discontinuity. Apart from the fact that these modern critics of the doctrine have grossly misinterpreted it,[361] there is also, first and foremost to be noted, the continuity not only between the Reformers and the Protestant orthodox on this point, but also the broader continuity between all of the Protestant writers and the Christian tradition in general. Calvin comments on the oneness and consistency of the divine will as resting upon the simplicity of God and, particularly in his commentaries and sermons, used traditional scholastic distinctions to explain difficulties in the biblical language of divine willing. Musculus and Vermigli not only introduced a series of scholastic categories into the Reformed doctrine of the *voluntas Dei* at an early date in its development, they also raised the issue of the relation of will to the other attributes in the simplicity of the divine essence.[362] In making these points, Calvin and Musculus were merely echoing the broad

---

358. Cf. Daane, *Freedom of God*, pp. 7-8, 38-44, 51-57, 152-56, et passim with the summary statement in Philip C. Holtrop, "Decree(s) of God," s.v. in *Encyclopedia of the Reformed Faith*, ed. Donald K. McKim (Louisville, Ky.: Westminster / John Knox, 1992), pp. 97-99.

359. Thus, Daane, *Freedom of God*, pp. 60-65, and Jürgen Moltmann, *God in Creation: A New Theology of Creation and the Spirit of God* (New York: Harper & Row, 1985), pp. 80-81.

360. Stephen Strehle, "Calvinism, Augustinianism, and the Will of God," in *Theologische Zeitschrift*, 48/2 (1992), pp. 233, 236-237; also note the similar arguments in Strehle, *Calvinism, Federalism, and Scholasticism*, pp. 316-317, 389-391. What Strehle does not understand is that necessity and freedom are neither contraries nor contradictories: the contrary of necessity is impossibility; the contrary of freedom is coercion. Strehle does recognize that much of the discussion, whether medieval or post-Reformation stressed the divine freedom— but he, oddly, divorces this interest in freedom of will from the Reformation understanding of its sovereignty: cf. *Calvinism, Federalism, and Scholasticism*, p. 1.

361. See Richard A. Muller, "The Myth of 'Decretal Theology,'" in *Calvin Theological Journal*, 30/1 (April, 1995), pp. 159-167.

362. Cf. Calvin, *Institutes*, I.xviii.3; with idem, comment on Deut. 29:29 in *Harmony of the Four Last Books of Moses*, I, p. 410; *Sermons on Job*, pp. 222, col. 1; 740, col. 2; and with Musculus, *Loci communes*, xlv (*Commonplaces*, pp. 931-932); Vermigli, *Loci communes*, I.xvii.25-44, passim. Some of

consensus of the fathers and the medieval doctors — none of whom saw the essential identity of the divine will with God himself as a ground for determinism: rather it was the foundation of the divine freedom, a characteristic of the doctrine that will become evident in the materials presented here.

The question of continuity and discontinuity between the theology of the Reformers and the theology of Post-Reformation orthodoxy takes on a particular importance in this chapter, inasmuch as the doctrine of the divine will has been one of the points at which a discontinuity has been most pointedly noted. In his often-cited study of Moises Amyraut, Armstrong argued that Protestant scholasticism and orthodoxy evidence

> a pronounced interest in metaphysical matters, in abstract speculative thought, particularly with reference to the doctrine of God. The distinctive Protestant position is made to rest on a speculative formulation of the will of God.[363]

Granting the extensive discussion of the divine will characteristic of many of the Reformed orthodox theologies from Zanchi's *De natura Dei* onward, the question arises whether this interest has roots in the theology of the Reformers or whether it is a direct return to the earlier scholasticism — to what degree does it present and perhaps refine issues raised by the Reformers or to what degree does it introduce traditionary elements into a theology that had, previously, set them aside. For example, the extended comments that various Reformers made concerning the divine will are not consistently different from the views of the Reformed orthodox that have been denominated "speculative" by Armstrong and others. Nor, as noted in an introductory section, are the theses on the *voluntas Dei* proposed at Saumur particularly different from those presented in other centers of the Reformed faith, whether with respect to content or to "speculative" elaboration.[364] (Of course, it must be noted by way of caveat that not all of the Reformed orthodox offer extensive discussions of the divine will: Marckius omits the topic and the vast commentary on Marckius by DeMoor makes little attempt to remedy the situation.)[365] In addition, whatever the historical source of the Protestant orthodox discussions of the divine will, the motivation and the character of the discussion need to be examined — particularly given the exegetical roots of many of the distinctions noted in the will of God by the scholastic tradition, given the question of whether these discussions can invariably be called "speculative" in the modern sense of the term, and given the absence of central dogmas on which entire theological systems can rest from the Protestant orthodox theological perspective.

---

these issues were broached in Percy Linwood Urban, "The Will of God: A Study of the Origin and Development of Nominalism and Its Influence on the Reformation" (S.T.D. dissertation, General Theological Seminary, 1959).

363. Armstrong, *Calvinism and the Amyraut Heresy*, p. 32.

364. Amyraut et al., *Syntagma thesium theologicarum*, IV.viii: cf. the citations of particular theses below, this chapter.

365. Cf. Marckius, *Compendium theologiae*, IV.xl, with De Moor, *Commentarius perpetuus in Joh. Marckii compendium*, IV.xl.

B. The *Voluntas Dei* in the Theology of the Reformers

1. Musculus, Calvin, and Vermigli on the divine will. As is the case with other topics belonging to the traditional discussion of the divine attributes, the *voluntas Dei* received, with the significant exception of the extended exposition in Musculus' *Loci communes*, little discussion as an independent *locus* among the Reformers, but major attention as a collateral issue in other theological topics, notably providence and predestination. There is also a considerable body of exegetical meditation on the subject in the writings of the Reformers — not surprising, given that this was precisely the source of Musculus' *locus* on the divine will, just as exegetical efforts are the source of the various meditations on the divine will found in Vermigli's *Loci*. It is in the exegetical materials that the full extent of the continuity between the Reformers and the Reformed orthodox becomes apparent. What is more, perusal of the Reformers' discussions of the divine will demonstrate both acquaintance with and respect for many of the distinctions made by medieval scholastic theology and, by extension, demonstrate also a continuity with the distinctions made by the Reformed orthodox.

"The order of the subjects," writes Musculus, "seems to require that we ought to place the topic of the will of God after the *locus* of God's omnipotence." Discussion of this topic, moreover, does not attempt to investigate the depths of the divine will but only to treat of the will of God as far as "the measure and reason convenient for godly life and salvation lead."[366] Musculus notes that the medieval scholastics asked such questions as how will can be predicated of God, whether his will and his essence are one and the same, and whether will is the substance of God — but these topics, Musculus continues, are improper insofar as they ask, not what the will of God is toward us, but what it is in itself. He accordingly begins his exposition with a cautious qualifier:

> Let it suffice us to know, that will is not in God in the same way that it is in a human being, in whom will is a motion and affection of the soul, to choose or reject objects without compulsion. Such [a will] cannot be predicated of God.... It is not required of us to search out what God's will is in itself. But it is required of us to understand what it is, not in general toward all the things that [God] created and governs, but toward mankind, and specially toward those who are elect in and faithful to Christ his Son.[367]

Although, moreover, the ultimate will of God remains unknowable, we recognize it to be "the fountain of all righteousness,"[368] and the "highest rule of the highest equity."[369] There is, in other words, no law that constrains God, and God alone sets the standards for justice and righteousness. Still, God has "prescribed to himself that he will do nothing unjustly": when he forsakes the reprobate, he is also forsaken by

---

366. Musculus, *Loci communes*, xlv (*Commonplaces*, p. 919, col. 2).

367. Musculus, *Loci communes*, xlv (*Commonplaces*, p. 920, col. 1).

368. Calvin, *Sermons on Job*, sermon 47 (p. 222, col. 1)

369. Calvin, *Secret Providence*, p. 283; cf. Calvin, *Institutes*, II.viii.5; idem, *Commentary on Acts*, 14:16; 28:26, in loc. (CTS Acts, II, pp. 18, 429).

them — they will to forsake God, and he does not alter their wills. He thus decrees their reprobation justly, according to the standard that he himself has set.[370]

"It is a common saying," notes Musculus, "that nothing occurs without a cause" and that therefore "it is necessary that there be some first and highest cause, by which all things are effected." This is the ground for resolving the question "whether the will of God is the cause of all things."[371] Scripture, indeed, answers the question of the philosophers by declaring that all things belong to God and that God does whatsoever he will. Therefore, it may be seen that the will of God is the cause both of those things done immediately by God and of those things done by God's creatures. "So he is the cause not only of our souls, bodies, and life, but of our will, understanding, purposes, affection, motions, and acts as well."[372]

The ancients and the scholastics, notes Musculus, asked whether it was possible to discern the cause of God's will. To this question Augustine answered wisely that the will of God is the cause of all things. If God's will itself had a cause, there would be something prior it: this is a contradiction that cannot be allowed. Even so, the Master of the Sentences shows that there is nothing prior to the will of God, as it is everlasting, that there is nothing greater than this will, and that it cannot have a cause: thus the question of discerning a cause is vain. Musculus agrees with these opinions but notes the further possible controversy over the assumption that God's will has no cause. We may not search out why God does what he does — but we may at least infer that God does not act "without reason" and that he himself knows why he wills. We know from Scripture that God has good reason for willing particular things: as in sending his Son (John 3:16), where "the efficient cause of his will is love, and the final cause, the salvation of the faithful."[373] Thus we may say that God wills good things because he is good, just things because he is just, kind and merciful things because he is kind and merciful. Ultimately, Musculus refuses to argue a priority of will *ad intra* while insisting that God's will is absolutely free from external influence:

> And whereas Augustine's statement that there is nothing prior to or greater than the will of God is correct if we understand it of those things that are not in God, it may not appear so, if stated absolutely and generally. It is, thus, a doubtful statement and a matter for dispute when he states that there is no cause of the will of God.[374]

Vermigli, similarly, refuses to deal with the question of the relative priority of intellect or will in God: it is enough to recognize that in God there is a power of understanding and a power of willing and that God both knows and wills all things. To argue beyond this is to engage in "needless disputation": and anyone who wishes to do so, Vermigli

---

370. Vermigli, *Loci communes*, I.xvii.33.

371. Musculus, *Loci communes*, xlv (*Commonplaces*, p. 927, col. 2).

372. Musculus, *Loci communes*, xlv (*Commonplaces*, p. 928, cols. 1-2); cf. Calvin, *Concerning the Eternal Predestination of God*, pp. 177-178 and idem, *Secret Providence*, p. 281.

373. Musculus, *Loci communes*, xlv (*Commonplaces*, p. 929, col. 2-p. 931, col. 1); cf. the similar argument in Vermigli, *Loci communes*, part III, p. 12a-b.

374. Musculus, *Loci communes*, xlv (*Commonplaces*, p. 931, col. 2).

comments, ought to consult the Thomists and the Scotists![375] It would be incorrect, therefore, to say that the will of God has a cause in the sense of an efficient cause that brings it about that God will one thing rather than another, but there are, clearly, reasons for God willing in various ways, and such reasons are often revealed in Scripture. What is more, there are also final causes of the will of God, notably the final causes of his decree of predestination, namely, that he might reveal his justice and his glory.[376]

2. **Distinctions in the will of God.** Despite their frequent admonitions against speculation, Calvin, Vermigli, and Musculus recognized that many of the traditional distinctions concerning the will of God were necessary for Christian understanding. Calvin indicates that "in itself" the will of God "is one and simple," but that Scripture reveals it to us by means of a distinction between God's accomplishment of "his secret providence" and his commands of obedience.[377] Indeed, although it is certain that God "does not in himself will opposites," his will is so far beyond our comprehension that he sometimes "wills what now seems to be adverse to his will."[378] Thus, "to our apprehension the will of God is manifold" although in itself it is in fact simple.[379] The reason for this is that the one will of God has diverse objects in the finite order.[380] Musculus, similarly, raises the issue of the divine will *in se* as one, ultimate, and identical with the divine essence, leading him to offer a series of distinctions in explanation of the ways in which God's will can be known by human beings. As his discussion progresses, he appears to have no objection whatsoever to the use of scholastic distinctions, provided that they are finally drawn out of the realm of metaphysics into the realm of Christian instruction. The will of God, he indicates, is to be understood in two ways, as "the Master of the Sentences" pointed out: "first properly of that only, perfect, immutable, and everlasting will, which is in him, and in his essence. Secondly, figuratively of his precepts, prohibitions, purposes, permissions, and works."[381] The distinctions, therefore, arise out of the fact that God has a will and that he reveals his will in his commandments — given that there is a significant difference between the way in which the ultimate will of God is revealed in the commandments and the way that it is revealed in relation to the salvation of human beings. The commandments "express [God's] nature" at the same time that they enjoin all people to be obedient — at the same time that God does not equally enable all people to keep the commandments.[382]

---

375. Vermigli, *Loci communes*, I.xvi.7.

376. Vermigli, *Loci communes*, III.i.16.

377. Calvin, *Harmony of the Evangelists*, Matt. 6:10 (CTS *Evangelists*, I, pp. 320-321); cf. Calvin, *Concerning the Eternal Predestination of God*, pp. 182, 184; *Institutes*, I.xviii.3; and *Secret Providence*, p. 283.

378. Calvin, *Institutes*, III.xxiv.17.

379. Calvin, *Institutes*, III.xxiv.17.

380. Vermigli, *Loci communes*, I.xvii.36.

381. Musculus, *Loci communes*, xlv (*Commonplaces*, p. 920, col. 1).

382. Vermigli, *Loci communes*, I.xvii.25.

This distinction between a "proper" and a "figurative" will yields, almost immediately, a parallel distinction between God's will as "absolute" and as "relative." God's will must be considered absolutely, so that we can "understand how and what he hath determined from evermore in himself concerning our salvation," and then relatively, so that we can know what God would have us do. Even so, God, first, wills us to be saved and, second, requires that we believe in him and do his will. Furthermore, God's will is not indifferent toward human beings, but addresses us individually in terms of "persons, callings, and conditions."[383] From this we infer "that the will of God is the foundation of faith, godly life, and of our salvation," for God indeed wills all men to be saved and to come to a knowledge of the truth (cf. 1 Tim. 2).[384]

> It cannot be doubted that the foundation of our salvation is located in the truth of God's word. But if we look deeper into this matter, we shall find that the first cause of salvation ought to be ascribed to the will of God, according to the purpose whereby he chose us eternally in Christ, and predestined us to salvation.[385]

Even so, the apostle says that God has mercy on whom he will, for mercy belongs to the will of God. The "object and ground" of faith is the "word of promise" as that word is the manifestation of God's will. Thus our minds are blind without knowledge of God's will — and, indeed, can be blinded all the more if we mistake the will of God: Satan appears as an angel of light and his servants as teachers sent from God, "wherefore we must search whereby it may be tried, what is the will of God towards us, that we give no place in us, to such opinions as do reign in Popery."[386]

God declares his will to us by "word, signs, and doings." In the word we receive his threats and promises, comforts and judgments. When God declares salvation to the godly and punishment to the wicked, he manifests his will, first, in his loving regard for us and, second, in the requirements he sets for us.[387] Similarly, God witnesses his will to us in signs — specifically in the sacraments instituted by Christ, baptism and the Lord's Supper. The first, baptism, assures us that it is God's will to accept us as his people "consecrate and consigned unto his name" and the second, the Lord's Supper, assures us of our continuing membership in the company of the redeemed. Finally, in sending the prophets, apostles, evangelists, pastors, and doctors into all the world to call men to repentance, God by deeds shows his good will toward us. Musculus next devotes a section to the requirements of piety, "what it is to do the will of God."[388]

Calvin, similarly, recognized that a distinction needed to be made between the ultimate or "hidden will" (*voluntas arcana*) of God and the "revealed will" (*voluntas*

---

383. Musculus, *Loci communes*, xlv (*Commonplaces*, p. 920, col. 2-p. 921, col. 2).

384. Musculus, *Loci communes*, xlv (*Commonplaces*, p. 921, col. 2-p. 922, col. 1).

385. Musculus, *Loci communes*, xlv (*Commonplaces*, p. 922, col. 1).

386. Musculus, *Loci communes*, xlv (*Commonplaces*, p. 923, cols. 1-2).

387. Musculus, *Loci communes*, xlv (*Commonplaces*, p. 923, col. 2); cf. Calvin, *Concerning the Eternal Predestination of God*, pp. 183-184).

388. Musculus, *Loci communes*, xlv (*Commonplaces*, p. 925, col. 1-p. 927, col. 2).

revelata),[389] but also that we dare not enquire into the hidden will — rather we must ask God only to show us his will "according to our ability."[390] Calvin sees the distinction in such texts as Romans 9:19-20: "Proud men clamor." Calvin writes, "because Paul, admitting that men are rejected or chosen by the secret counsel of God, alleges no cause; as though the Spirit of God were silent for want of reason, and not rather, that by his silence he reminds us, that a mystery which our minds cannot, comprehend ought to be reverently adored, and that he thus checks the wantonness of human curiosity."[391] So, too, in Matthew 23:37, Calvin presses the distinction between the secret and the revealed will of God, noting that the indiscriminate and universal call of the gospel expresses the revealed will of God that all ought to be saved, not the secret will or purpose of God to save his elect.[392]

Musculus next approaches the related issue of whether or not God's will can be hindered or abrogated. The grounds of his position have, of course, already been reached in the preceding remarks, but, as in that discussion, he feels the need to introduce a series of scholastic distinctions into Reformed theology for the sake of clarity. Citing Isaiah, he comments that God can do whatsoever he will. Any other opinion would be contradictory to the doctrine of the divine omnipotence. But this general principle must be treated in terms of the finer distinctions made by the scholastics: "Ockham," Musculus indicates, "makes a distinction between the will of good pleasure *(voluntas beneplaciti)* and the will of the sign *(voluntas signi)*."[393] Vermigli, similarly, notes that the scholastics make such a distinction and that he finds it congenial — as a distinction between the "mighty" and "effectual" will of God that no power can resist and the will of God as revealed in his "judgment and ordinance," "in the law, in the commandments, promises, threatenings, and counsels," in short, the will that we ought to oblige. These "two wills," however, are not distinct as two separate things or faculties in God. Rather, these "two wills" arise from the fact that God does not always reveal the entirely of his counsels to human beings, but only reveals what is necessary for salvation. That which is revealed is called the *voluntas signi*; that which remains secret and hidden in God is the *voluntas beneplaciti*.[394]

Vermigli adds to this set of distinctions a further distinction within the will of God's good pleasure: since the ultimate counsel of God is in part revealed to us, a distinction can be made between the unknown and the known or between the hidden and the revealed will of God. This distinction is significant inasmuch as we are enjoined to conform ourselves to the will of God and we can only know it in part — resulting in situations in which the revealed will of God is displeasing to us even as we obey it.

---

389. Cf. Calvin, *Secret Providence*, pp. 307-308, 310, with idem, *Institutes*, III.ii.14; xx.43; cf. I.xvi.3; III.xxii.4; xxiii.1, 4, 7; xxiv.3 *(arcanum concilium)*.

390. Calvin, *Sermons on Job*, sermon 157 (p. 740, col. 2).

391. Calvin, *Commentary on Romans*, 9:20 (CTS *Romans*, p. 365).

392. Calvin, *Harmony of the Evangelists*, Matt. 23:37, in loc. (CTS *Harmony*, III, p. 109).

393. Musculus, *Loci communes*, xlv (*Commonplaces*, p. 932, col. 1); cf. the discussion in Adams, *William Ockham*, II, pp. 1169-1173.

394. Vermigli, *Loci communes*, I.xvii.38.

For example, when Moses learned, after the incident of the golden calf, that God would demand the deaths of numerous Israelites, he lamented the will of God and prayed for forgiveness — or when Samuel learned that God had rejected Saul, he did not immediately give up hope for Saul's kingship — or, further, Jeremiah knew that it was God's will to destroy Jerusalem and yet lamented its ruin. According to Vermigli, the point of such texts is that the partial revelation of the divine will does not always yield the acquiescence that would follow the full revelation, but the failure to acquiesce fully is not sinful, given that in all the cases noted, the one resisting the revelation was also following the commands of the *voluntas signi*, without, however, implying a contradiction between obedience to the commands of God and the ultimate divine good pleasure.[395]

Given these arguments, Musculus notes, particularly the arguments concerning the irresistibility of the ultimate divine good pleasure and concerning the dependence of all things, including the thoughts and affections of human beings on the divine will, some impious thinkers conclude that either God must be the cause of evil or that God must not be almighty — for if he does not cause evil, then something occurs which is against his will.[396] It is clear, responds Musculus, that God must in some respect will that evil things be done — but this must belong (as Augustine says in the *Enchiridion*) to God's just judgment, yielding a distinction concerning the divine willing.[397] Calvin, similarly, argues, on the basis of Acts 2:23, that God wills the death of Christ, having appointed it from all eternity — but it is still the case that Christ was put to death "by the hands of the wicked." The wicked execute what God has in fact decreed, but they do so out of no intention to follow the will of God. In fact, they act disobediently in transgression of the law of God. Obedience is defined by the divine law and by willing submission to the divine government.[398] Such considerations yield the conclusion that "although the will of God, viewed in itself, is one and simple, it is presented to us in Scripture under a twofold aspect": there is, in other words, a distinction to be made between God's decretive will, which belongs to "the secret counsels of his providence" and cannot be thwarted, and God's preceptive will, which ought to be obeyed but which can be transgressed.[399]

So, too, can a distinction be made between God's effective will and his permission or permissive will. The distinction is necessary given the fact that, if God were to resist the working our of any finite sequence of events, those events would not occur. The divine permission, therefore, "is a certain kind of will."[400] Even Calvin, who polemicized against misuse and misunderstanding of this distinction, was able to affirm it when

395. Vermigli, *Loci communes*, I.xvii.43, citing Ex. 32:32; 1 Sam. 15:35; Jer. 18:6.
396. Musculus, *Loci communes*, xlv (*Commonplaces*, p. 928, col. 2 - p. 929, col. 1).
397. Musculus, *Loci communes*, xlv (*Commonplaces*, p. 929, cols. 1-2); cf. Calvin, *Institutes*, I.xvii.5.
398. Calvin, *Commentary on Acts*, 2:23, in loc. (CTS *Acts*, I, pp. 97-98).
399. Calvin, *Harmony of the Evangelists*, Matt. 6:10=Luke 11:2, in loc. (CTS *Harmony*, I, p. 320).
400. Vermigli, *Loci communes*, I. xvii.15.

the *permissio Dei* was defined as "not unwilling, but willing."[401] Both Vermigli and Calvin cite Augustine's *Enchiridion* on the point: since nothing can occur outside of the divine willing, the category of divine permission is necessary to any understanding of events that appear to contradict God's will. Nonetheless, once this category of divine willing is recognized, there is a further issue: when God permits something, he must permit it either willingly or unwillingly. For the permission to be unwilling, there would have to be a power greater than God, capable of contravening his will. This, of course, is impossible. God therefore permits willingly — or, better, his permission is a kind of divine willing.[402]

Calvin, thus, contends that although God ordained the fall of the angels and of Adam and Eve, he was not the author or active effector of the fall: the fall lies within the divine ordination inasmuch as nothing at all can occur apart from or outside of God's will. Nonetheless, the angels and Adam and Eve acted "contrary to the will of God, to the end that God, by means of their evil will, might effect that which was according to his decreeing will."[403] Thus, there are instances throughout the history of the creation in which "by the very act of ... doing what was contrary to the will of God," disobedient creatures have in fact fulfilled the will of God — yielding the distinction between permissive and effective willing. God ought never to be viewed as an unconcerned or inactive observer of human conduct.[404] When God permits something, therefore, his permission consists in a will not to hinder a particular sinful act but to use the sin to bring about his own ends. Or, it might be said that God wills sin, not as sin, given that his will is always directed toward the good, but insofar as it is a punishment for wickedness.[405]

Vermigli notes also that the distinction between will and permission or between the divine good pleasure and permission, as found in the thought of John of Damascus, also implies a distinction between antecedent and consequent willing in God. The Damascene had argued that God antecedently wills all people to be saved but subsequently punishes them for their faults. This latter divine willing is consequent on the sinful choices of human beings. Vermigli objects to this distinction, albeit mildly, as one that is not quite suitable: it is true, he notes, that God has chosen some for salvation and that there are others, the reprobate, who will be punished for their own fault. But the sins of the reprobate do not fall outside of God's universal providence, and God in fact wills to show his power in the reprobate. His will remains one and

---

401. Cf. Calvin, *Eternal Predestination*, pp. 126, 253, with idem, *Secret Providence*, pp. 286-296, and idem, *Institutes* (1559), I.xvi.8; III.xxiii.8; also see Doumergue, IV, pp. 139-140, and Wendel, pp. 186-187.

402. Vermigli, *Loci communes*, I.xvii.15; cf. I.xvii.36, 39-42, citing Augustine, *Enchiridion*, cap. 101-102.

403. Calvin, *Eternal Predestination*, p. 127.

404. Calvin, *Secret Providence*, pp. 290, 294-295.

405. Vermigli, *Loci communes*, I.xvii.34, 40.

simple, distinguished by its objects, positively willing some things, willingly permitting others. What the Damascene identifies as a consequent will is not, therefore, reactive.[406]

Musculus comes to a similar conclusion in an examination of the medieval scholastic forms of the argument: Ockham, he notes, "further divides the *voluntas beneplaciti* into the antecedent will and the consequent will; and he grants that the antecedent will and the will of the sign may be identified."[407] The Master of the Sentences also handles this subject — and Musculus indicates that this subject is also found in Lombard's *Sentences*: Lombard argues that the passage in 1 Timothy 2 where God is said to will all men to be saved does not contradict the Savior's statement that "he that believeth not shall be condemned," since God wills that all men be saved under the condition that they accept his truth.[408] In fact, God accomplishes all that he determines to do. What intervenes between the "antecedent" and the "consequent" is not a human action to which God reacts, but a divine condition. Thus, if the antecedent will is the *voluntas signi*, namely, the command or precept, it is the consequent will of God that is the effective will: this argument can be applied to the interpretation of 1 Timothy 2:4, given that according to the antecedent will of the sign, all people are called indifferently by the gospel and the conditions of salvation are set forth to all, whereas consequently and effectively God saves those whom he has chosen.[409] There is, therefore, no indication of contrary wills in God. If this explanation is unsatisfactory, says Musculus, we may have recourse to Augustine's exegesis which interprets "all" to mean "all kinds of men, divided in differences of estates and degrees."[410]

We have already seen some diversity among the Reformers in the identification and use of distinctions concerning the divine will — although it is clear that all understood the exercise of making the distinctions to be quite necessary. Both the exercise and the diversity will continue to be characteristic of Reformed orthodoxy, although surely the precision and use of the distinctions will increase under the impact of scholastic method.

C. The Reformed Orthodox Doctrine of the *Voluntas Dei*

1. Basic definitions of the divine will in its unity. After having defined the *scientia Dei* and its various corollaries, the Reformed orthodox typically pass on to discuss the divine will as the next major category of the attributes. Indeed, it is the most exhaustive and detailed category of attributes in many of the systems. By way of introduction and example, Polanus' initial bifurcations:

---

406. Vermigli, *Loci communes*, I.xvii.36.

407. Musculus, *Loci communes*, xlv (*Commonplaces*, p. 932, col. 1); cf. the discussion in Adams, *William Ockham*, II, pp. 1169-1173.

408. Musculus, *Loci communes*, xlv (*Commonplaces*, p. 932, col. 1-p. 933, col. 1).

409. Vermigli, *Loci communes*, III.i.11, 45-46.

410. Musculus, *Loci communes*, xlv (*Commonplaces*, p. 933, col. 2), citing Augustine, *Enchiridion*, cap. 103.

The will of God in reality is one (*unica*), for the sake of this instruction, however it is considered as first, either essential (*essentialis*) or personal (*personalis*).

Second, the will of God is either effective (*efficiens*) or permissive (*permittens*).

Third, the will of God is either absolute (*absoluta*) or conditional (*conditionalis*); the former is called [the will] of good-pleasure (*beneplaciti*), the latter [the will] of the sign or precept (*signi*).

Fourth, the will of God is either revealed (*revelata*) or hidden (*occulta*); the revealed will is, first, either antecedent (*antecedens*) or consequent (*consequens*) and, second, either legal (*legalis*) or evangelical (*evangelica*).

Fifth, the will of God is either of the necessity of nature (*necessitatis naturae*) or free (*libera*).

Sixth, the will of God toward us (*erga nos*) and what he wills to do concerning us (*de nobis*) and all creatures is one thing — and what he wills to do because of us (*a nobis*) is another.

Seventh, if the object of the will is considered, its object is either good (*bonum*) or evil (*malum*)....

The freedom of God (*libertas Dei*) is threefold: from coaction (*a coactione*), from servitude (*a servitute*), and from the burden of suffering (*ab onere miseriae*).[411]

Yet, as these distinctions already indicate, the sheer size and detail of the doctrine does not necessarily suggest either excessive "speculation" or departure from the framework of thought identified among the Reformers. On the one hand, the orthodox retain the Reformers' interest in the direct relation of the doctrine of the divine will to issues of salvation. There is little metaphysical speculation simply for the sake of speculation. Nonetheless, on the other hand, the orthodox do draw Reformed doctrine into a far more consistent dialogue with the scholastic past and work far more concertedly than any of the Reformers, even Musculus, to adapt the medieval distinctions to Protestant use. The size of the exposition has more, certainly, to do with the difficulty of appropriating the materials, with the numerous "affections" belonging to the will, and with the debates of the age between the Reformed and Arminian, Lutheran, Jesuit, and Socinian theologians on all of these issues than it does with a pure metaphysical interest in will.

The Reformed orthodox are far less ready even than Musculus to leave the divine will unqualified, and they almost uniformly set the *locus* of the divine intellect and knowledge first.[412] Following the more Thomistic side of medieval scholastic doctrine, the Reformed orthodox tend to argue, first, that God, as the highest being, must be

---

411. Polanus, *Syntagma*, synopsis libri II.

412. Cf. Turretin, *Inst. theol. elencticae*, III.xii-xiii (*scientia*), xiv-xviii (*voluntas*), with Trelcatius, *Schol. meth.*, I.iii; Ames, *Medulla*, I.iv.53-56 (intellect), 57-61 (will); Polanus, *Syntagma theol.*, II.xviii (*sapientia*), xix-xx (*voluntas*); Maccovius, *Loci communes*, xx (*scientia*), xxiii-xxiv (*voluntas*); Twisse, *Discovery*, II.viii (wisdom), x (the decree), xiii (will); Leigh, *Body of Divinity*, II.vii ("Of Gods Understanding, that he is Omniscient, and of his Will); Pictet, *Theol. chr.*, II.v (*intellectus*), vi (*voluntas*); Mastricht, *Theoretico-practica theol.*, II.xiii (*intellectus*), xv (*voluntas*); and Francken, *Stellinge God-Geleertheyd*, pp. 17417-5.

regarded as having intellect, and, subsequently, that God, understood as having intellect and as knowing himself as the ultimate good, must also have will.

> There must be a will in God, since God must possess everything which belongs to the nature of an intelligent being, and every thinking being must not only have understanding, but also will. The whole scripture teaches this.[413]

In addition, as the definitions indicate, the will is, by nature, a *rational* faculty.

> Will is taken, (1) For a faculty or power of the soul whereby we will; so we say there are these faculties in the soul, the understanding and the will. (2) For the act of willing called *volitio*. (3) The object or thing *willed*, so John 6, *this is the will of my Father*, that is, that which he willeth and hath decreed.[414]

Indeed, Scripture ascribes to God both the faculty of will (*voluntas*) and the basic capacity of willing (*velle*):[415]

> The Scripture often ascribes a will to God, *Isaiah* 46:10; *Rom.* 9:19; *John* 6:39. The will of God is an essential property whereby the Lord approveth that which is good and disapproveth the contrary, *Matt.* 19:17; *James* 1:17; *Psalm* 5:4.[416]

Specifically, it identifies the divine will as the volitional faculty "in itself" in Ephesians 1:11, "all things are accomplished according to the counsel of his will"; as the act of willing particular objects by reference to Revelation 4:11, "by your will all things are made"; and as the result of willing by reference to James 4:15, "if the Lord wills, we shall live."[417]

As to the definition of precisely what will is in God, the Reformed orthodox offer a series of slightly variant definitions: "Will is the active principle (*principium imperans*), by which God, through himself, wills himself, and, beyond himself, wills all things according to himself or to his glory."[418] Mastricht offers as a brief definition the statement that the divine will is God's "propensity toward the good,"[419] and the somewhat longer definition that "will in God is nothing other than his most wise propensity toward himself as the highest goal and toward creatures as means, for the sake of himself," inasmuch as creatures attain the fulfilment of the good not in

---

413. Pictet, *Theol. chr.*, II.vi.1, citing Ps. 115.3; Isa. 46:10.

414. Leigh, *Treatise*, II.viii (pp. 67-68).

415. Wendelin, *Christianae theologiae libri duo*, I.i.18 (1).

416. Leigh, *Treatise*, II.viii (p. 68); cf. Ussher, *Body of Divinity*, p. 54.

417. Rijssen, *Summa theol.*, III.xxv.

418. Wendelin, *Christianae theologiae libri duo*, I.i.18; cf. Zanchi, *De natura Dei*, III.iv, q. 1.3 (col. 246); Francken, *Stellinge God-Geleertheyd*, p. 175. As Deferrari notes in his *Lexicon of Saint Thomas Aquinas*, the term *principium imperans*, literally commanding or ruling principle, is used synonymously with *principium dirigens*, guiding or directing principle, although not, as Deferrari comments of Aquinas, with *principium exsequens*, executing or executive principle. The Reformed orthodox also reserve this latter term for the *potentia Dei*; see below, 6.2 (C).

419. Mastricht, *Theoretico-practica theol.*, II.xvii.4.

themselves but in God.[420] In Perkins' definition, which is echoed in quite a few of the later orthodox, the will of God is a single, eternal, and immutable act "by which he both freely and justly with one act willeth all things."[421] This will approves the good and permits evil according to God's purpose, and because of its "divers objects" God's will has "divers names; and is either called Love and Hatred, or Grace and Justice."[422] By the love of God, Perkins means God's approval of himself and of his creatures insofar as they are good. God delights in his creation — but he also has a hatred or dislike and detestation of the willful faults of his creatures. God's grace is the freely declared favor of God to his creatures either manifest as his goodness or free "exercise of his liberality upon his creatures" grounded in his absolute goodness or as his mercy or free assistance of creatures in their needs.[423]

The orthodox are also concerned to indicate the immutability of the divine will is not only "agreeable to his infinite perfection," and thus intellectually congruent with the understanding of his other attributes, but also a matter of piety. It is certainly true that the outward revelation of God's will may change — with the result that something commanded by God at one time in history may be forbidden or set aside at another: this is certainly the case with the ceremonial law of the Old Testament. Still, God "does not purpose to do a thing at one time, and determine not to do it at another ... for he determines all changes in the external disposition of his providence and grace, without the least shadow of change in his own will."[424] Were this not so, God could not be the "object" of our trust: "for how could we depend on his promises if it were possible for him to change his purpose?" So, too, would the threats of his revealed law become useless, if his will were inconstant. Scripture, however, assures us that "the gifts and the calling of God are irrevocable."[425]

2. The *libertas Dei*: necessary and immutable, spontaneous and unconstrained. The divine will stands in a direct relationship to the other divine attributes, notably, divine immutability, freedom, and goodness — and it is defined in relation to the understanding of God as necessary Being and as necessarily willing according to his own nature. From one perspective, divine necessity and immutability limit the divine will; from another, these perfections of the divine being in no way impede the spontaneity of divine willing nor do they imply an absolute necessity or necessity of coaction imposed on the divine will. What is more, the will, considered as a rational faculty, assumes the known good as its object and, indeed, wills the highest good and all other goods insofar as they participate in the highest good:

---

420. Mastricht, *Theoretico-practica theol.*, II.xv.7; cf. Cocceius, *Summa theol.*, III.x.23-24 and Van Asselt, *Federal Theology*, p. 166.

421. Perkins, *Golden Chaine*, iii (p. 12, col. 2); cf. Ames, *Marrow*, I.iv.58-60; Pictet, *Theol. chr.*, II.vi.3.

422. Perkins, *Golden Chaine*, iii (p. 12, col. 2); cf. Ames, *Marrow*, I.iv.58-60.

423. Perkins, *Golden Chaine*, III (p. 12, col. 2).

424. Ridgley, *Body of Divinity* (1855), p. 90.

425. Ridgley, *Body of Divinity* (1855), p. 90.

[Will is that] by which God freely, immutably, and efficaciously wills and approves of the Good and that only, both the chief and the first, *viz.* himself and his own glory, as the end: and also the secondary, inferior and subordinate good, *viz.* that of the creatures, as far as it hath an image of that chief good, and tends as a means to that ultimate end.[426]

This relationship of the divine will to the other attributes results in the assumptions, already noted in the various definitions cited, that God wills both freely and effectively. This freedom and efficacy are, moreover, to be understood in terms of the interrelationship of the attributes in their essential unity — with the result that the divine freedom is defined in terms of the ultimate necessity that God must will according to his own nature and, therefore, both immutably and for the good:

God wills (1) Most freely; for liberty is essential to every will, so it is chiefly proper to the Divine, ... yet God wills good necessarily with a necessity of immutability; but not with a necessity of coaction, for he is necessarily and naturally Good, and that which he once willed, he always wills immutably and yet freely; (2) God wills efficaciously, for no man resisteth, nor can resist his will, *Dan.* 4:32; *Rom.* 9:19.[427]

Freedom, strictly speaking, is the "faculty of doing what one wills," as opposed to the Arminian sense of freedom as the ability to do or not to do what is necessary, rooted in a fundamental indeterminacy and having to do primarily with actions or movements (*locomotiva*) rather than with rule. The Reformed alternative assumes a *libertas imperativa*, a freedom to do as one wills — an utter freedom, apart from consideration of external circumstances.[428] "God hath a natural *Freedome of Will*, being Determined to Will by nothing without him, nor liable to any Necessity, but what is consistent with perfect Blessedness and Liberty."[429] Quite specifically, not only the act of creation but also the work of redemption is utterly free: redemption is a "free act of the will of God" done apart from any obligation placed on God, not even an obligation deriving "from any of his own properties."[430] The divine freedom, then, is initially defined as a freedom from coaction or coercion, including the freedom from impediment or resistance on the part of the created order. There can be nothing higher than God and nothing below God that can impede or determine his willing.

3. The utter freedom of God: freedom of indifference or contrariety with respect to the finite order. Beyond this basic definition, the divine freedom is also to be

---

426. Leigh, *Treatise*, II.viii (p. 67).

427. Leigh, *Treatise*, II.viii (p. 67).

428. Amyraut et al., *Syntagma thesium theologicarum*, IV.viii.4-5, 7, citing Cicero and arguing that the Arminians follow too closely an Aristotelian definition of freedom. See the discussion of limitations placed on the divine freedom in Arminius' thought in Richard A. Muller, "God, Predestination, and the Integrity of the Created Order: A Note on Patterns in Arminius' Theology," in *Later Calvinism: International Perspectives*, ed. W. Fred Graham, Sixteenth Century Essays & Studies (Kirksville, Mo.: Sixteenth Century Journal Publishers, 1994), pp. 431-446.

429. Baxter *Divine Life*, I.xvi (p. 131).

430. Owen, *Christologia*, in *Works*, I, p. 190.

understood in terms of the relationship of the divine will to the possibilities known to God according to the *scientia necessaria*. (This point also has significant ramifications for the understanding of human freedom.) The structure of the argument, particularly as evidenced in its assumption that willing the good follows from and is in some sense directed by knowing the good, indicates an intellectualist rather than a voluntarist perspective — although, as we have seen in the Reformed distinctions between *scientia necessaria* and *scientia voluntaria sive libera* (and, shortly, between *voluntas necessaria* and *voluntas libera*), a significant element of voluntarism remains in the Reformed model, thereby emphasizing the freedom of God in all his acts.

The relationship between what God knows and what God wills to do is complex: since God knows both the things that are and will be and the things that are not and will not be, the *voluntas Dei* only correlates in part with the *scientia Dei* — there are possibilities known but not willed by God. Thus Rijssen: "the [faculty of] will is that which either wills or does not will that which it knows" — "*voluntas est, quae vult aut non vult id quod novit.*"[431] It is simply not the case that God wills all things by an absolute necessity of his nature: God necessarily but also spontaneously, without coercion or coaction, wills himself and his ultimate glory, "but other things he wills freely because, since no created thing is necessary with respect to God but contingent."[432]

Indeed, God is free to "abstain" entirely from the production of the world, not merely according to a "freedom of spontaneity" but also according to the "freedom of indifference" or "freedom of contrariety"[433] God's immutable willing of the world does not render the objects of his willing absolute necessities, given that when God wills any particular result, its contrary remains possible — namely, remains a resident possibility in the divine *scientia necessaria*. In other words, there is no violation of the law of noncontradiction: God cannot equally will and not will a particular object "in a composite sense" (*in sensu composito*), but "in a divided sense" (*in sensu diviso*) he can will a particular object and know not willing it or willing its contrary as a possibility.[434] In other words, God's will is free in two ways — first, because of the absence of "coaction" or control from without and, second, because none of the external objects of the divine willing are necessary to God and could all be "nilled" or "not-willed." Marckius makes this point explicitly against the notion of a necessary creation that is in some sense coeternal with God. Such philosophy is the source of atheism.[435]

This view of God as possessing a freedom of contrariety with regard to the world renders a whole series of questions concerning the origin and nature of the created

---

431. Rijssen, *Summa theol.*, III.xxv.

432. Turretin, *Inst. theol. elencticae*, III.xiv.5; cf. Zanchi, *De natura Dei*, III.i, q. 11 (cols. 187-188); Beza et al. *Propositions and Principles*, VIII.vii; Wollebius, *Compendium*, I.i.3, prop. 3, canon v.2-3.

433. Turretin, *Inst. theol. elencticae*, III.xiv.6; Maccovius, *Loci communes*, xxxvii (p. 339); Marckius, *Compendium*, VIII.12.

434. Cf. Voetius, *Syllabus problematum*, G1v, with idem, *Sel. disp.*, V, p. 115, as analyzed in Beck, "Gisbertus Voetius (1589-1676): Basic Features of his Doctrine of God," pp. 215-216.

435. Marckius, *Compendium*, VIII.12.

order impossible of purely rational resolution. Ursinus notes that there are philosophical arguments proving "that the world was created" and that this creation was a divine act — but philosophy cannot prove when the world was created, whether it was created "from all eternity or in time," or more precisely, "whether it be an effect of equal perpetuity with its own cause, or had it at some time a beginning, prior to which it had not existence," whether the creation of the world was in some sense necessary, whether once created the world will "endure forever," or, if it endures forever, will it be at some time transformed? None of these questions can be resolved by reason or philosophy, which must attempt to argue them a posteriori, from effect to cause. The philosophical dilemma arises from the radical freedom of God as first cause: the answers to all of these questions "depend on the will of the first mover, which is God, who does not act from necessity but most freely." God, as the utterly free creator, "may either act or suspend his action, at pleasure." Nor can the argument move in an a priori manner, given that "no effect that is dependent on such a cause as acts freely or contingently can be demonstrated from that cause."[436] Since the existence, nature, and duration of the created order depend entirely on the free will of God, knowledge of such matters depends entirely on revelation.[437] Ursinus' arguments certainly reflect late medieval understandings of the *potentia Dei absoluta* and its epistemological implications.

To the objection that the eternity and immutability of God's will restrict its freedom by removing the freedom of contrary choice, Turretin responds that "what is necessary originally on the part of the principle can be free terminatively on the part of the object."[438] God must will and, of course, must will himself — but the divine will is not determined in its objects: the only necessity of willing *ad extra* that is implied by eternity and immutability is the necessity that, given the divine will for the existence of a particular object, that object must be and must be the way that God has willed it to be.[439] But God was under no necessity of willing any particular object in the first place — and in willing a contingent object, he in no way removes its contingency, given that, *in sensu diviso* (in view of the content of the *scientia necessaria*), God can will "a" and "not-a" remain a possibility. Ames can even state that "whatever God wills to produce *ad extra*, he wills, not out of a necessity of nature, but out of a preceding choice (*electione praecedente*): for there is no necessary connection between the divine nature and these actions."[440] "Therefore," Baxter comments, "one part of the Schoolmen maintain, not only that there is *Contingency from* God, but that there could be no *Contingency* in the creature, if it had not its original in God: the Liberty of God being

---

436. Ursinus, *Commentary on the Heidelberg Catechism*, q. 26 (pp. 142-143).

437. Ursinus, *Commentary on the Heidelberg Catechism*, q. 26 (p. 143).

438. Turretin, *Inst. theol. elencticae*, III.xiv.11.

439. Cf. Ames, *Medulla*, I.vii.34-36; Mastricht, *Theoretico-practica theol.*, II.xv.14-15; Turretin, *Inst. theol. elencticae*, III.xiv.3, 5, 6.

440. Ames, *Medulla*, I.vii.36.

the fountain of Contingency."[441] So much for Moltmann's claim that, according to the Reformed doctrine, God lacks freedom and has "no choice"![442]

4. The Reformed orthodox on the distinctions in the divine will. Although the will of God is one and simple, the Reformed orthodox, respecting the same difficulties encountered in the subject by the medieval doctors and the Reformers, discuss it in a series of terminological bifurcations. These distinctions are, of course, bounded by a basic understanding of the nature or character of the divine willing.

> This *will* is not to be conceived of as a *mode* of a faculty, but as *actuality*; and it is the very essence of God, since there is nothing in God which is not God; and hence it is plain that this will is eternal, since the essence of God is eternal.[443]

Thus,

> God's will is his essence, whereby he freely willeth good, and nilleth evil. ... [Thus] the will of God is one and the same: ... every distinction of God's will must be framed *ex parte volitiorum, non ex parte volentis.*[444]

Thus, distinctions in the divine will are not to be understood as separate wills, separate kinds of willing, or as alterations in the divine will. The distinctions are made "on the part of the things willed (*volitiorum*), not on the part of the one willing (*volentis*)." In our finite minds, we divide the will of God, as the Scripture itself does, "according to the diversity of its objects."[445] To make the point as forcefully as possible, the distinctions in the divine will serve the purpose, not of dividing the will, but, explicitly,

---

441. Baxter, *Divine Life*, I.xvi (p. 131). Unfortunately, Baxter does not cite his scholastic point of reference. This kind of argument can be found in Scotus, Bradwardine, and Gregory of Rimini and in many later scholastics: see Scotus, *Contingency and Freedom*. *Lectura I* 39, pp. 23-36; also Jean-François Genest, *Prédétermination et liberté creé à Oxford au XIVe siècle: Buckingham contre Bradwardine* (Paris: J. Vrin, 1992), pp. 147-152; Leff, *Gregory of Rimini*, p. 110; and cf. Beck, "Gisbertus Voetius (1589-1676): Basic Features of His Doctrine of God," pp. 215-217, where Voetius is noted as referencing the *in sensu composito/in sensu diviso* distinction to Diego Alvarez (d. 1635), a Dominican Thomist adversary of Molinism. The distinction is also used in this manner in Bañez's arguments against Molina's theory of *scientia media*: see Robert Sleigh, Vere Chappell, and Michael Della Rocca, "Determinism and Human Freedom," in Garber and Ayers, ed. *Cambridge History of Seventeenth-Century Philosophy*, II, pp. 1203-1205.

442. Moltmann, *God in Creation*, p. 81: Moltmann cites Heppe, *Reformierte Dogmatik*, pp. 107-109 (the chapter on the divine decrees), where on the very same page, Heppe's sources indicate that the divine will is "free." It is also quite curious to claim that the Reformed allow "no choice" in God, given that the Reformed are the most likely to be criticized for their emphasis on precisely that point, viz., that God decrees and chooses, *Deus decrevit et eligit*. Moltmann apparently failed to examine Heppe's other chapter on the relevant subject — creation — where the sources cited uniformly declare that creation is a free act of God, capable of being not willed (cf. ibid., pp. 151, 154).

443. Pictet, *Theol. chr.*, II.vi.2.

444. Leigh, *Treatise*, (p. 68); cf. Wollebius, *Compendium*, I.i.3, prop. 5, canon v; and Cocceius, *Summa theol.*, V.xiv.56.

445. Pictet, *Theol. chr.*, II.vi.3; cf. Zanchi, *De natura Dei*, III.iv, q. 3.2 (col. 253).

of preserving the sense of its unity: it is the Arminian, not the Reformed theology, that argued two wills in God.

These distinctions are of several sorts. First, there are several distinctions that relate to the problem of discussion, the divine will *ad intra* on the analogy of a faculty of mind — such as the divine willing and non-willing of various possibilities known to God. Next, there are a series of distinctions generated by the basic, bifurcatory conclusion, paralleling the definitions of divine knowing, that the divine will "is concerned either with God himself, his life and approbation, or with creatures."[446] In fact, the larger part of the bifurcations point, on the one hand, to the will of God in itself (which no one can know) and, on the other, to the will of God as it is directed toward its objects *ad extra* or as it is perceived and known directly by us. Third, there are several distinctions that can be made concerning the operations of the divine will *ad extra*, such as that between positive or effective and permissive willing. Following out the distinctions we have drawn from Polanus, the essential will of God, understood simply in terms of his transcendent being, is absolute, hidden, natural and necessary, effective or efficient, and free from coaction. Understood in terms of the divine activity in the world, God's will is relative (and sometimes conditional), revealed, free in its acts, sometimes permissive, and free from servitude and the burden of suffering.[447] Rijssen offers a useful summary of the distinctions:

> [the divine will] is distinguished into the decretive and preceptive will, the *voluntas eudokias* and *voluntas euarestias*, the will of good pleasure and the signified will, the hidden and the revealed will. The former terms present what God himself wills to do or to permit: the latter what he wills for us to do. The former is determining, the latter instructs and approves. The basis of these distinctions is provided by those places in Scripture in which the will of God is indicated either as the decree or as a precept: thus, as a decree, Rom. 9:19, "Who can resist his will?" and Eph. 1:11, "All things are accomplished according to his will." Or as a precept, Ps. 143:10, "O Lord, teach me to act according to your will." And there are also places [in Scripture] which indicate both wills of God, such as John 6:38, where Christ says, "I came down [from heaven] to do the will of him who sent me," i.e., to fulfill what was decreed by God and to obey the command of the Father.[448]

Still, these distinctions do not imply actual division of the divine will. "In order that every doubt on this subject may be removed," Pictet notes, "let it be observed, that ... strictly speaking, there is only one divine will, namely, the will of the decree (*voluntas decernens*)."[449]

Here, admittedly, the orthodox line of thought is guided not by a totally open or unbiased exegesis of texts, but by an ontological conception of the immutability of

---

446. Rijssen, *Summa theol.*, III.xxv.

447. Polanus, *Syntagma*, synopsis libri II; cf. ibid., II.xix with II.xxx..

448. Rijssen, *Summa theol.*, III.xxvii (entire, no controversy); also, Turretin, *Inst. theol. elencticae*, III.xv.1-3; and cf. Heppe, *Reformed Dogmatics*, V.25 (pp. 85-88).

449. Pictet, *Theol. chr.*, II.vi.6.

God: this guiding conception in turn leads to an interpretation of Scripture that gives priority to those texts stressing the unchangeability of God over those texts which indicate change, priority to those texts which stress God's otherness over those which indicate emotion, passion, or other kinship with humanity. But this is not a case of rationalism or metaphysical speculation overruling revelation: instead it is an example of one of the many instances in which theology must make a choice concerning its view of God, deciding which aspects of the scriptural view are governing concepts, anthropomorphism or transcendence, the "repentance" of God or the divine constancy.[450] And, in this case in particular, the Reformed orthodox stand not only in the line of the more philosophical arguments typical of scholastic theology but, together with the older scholasticism, in the line of the church's exegetical tradition — and, indeed, in accord with the doctrinal statements and with the exegesis of the Reformers.

Once this underlying point concerning the ultimate oneness and immutability of the divine will has been established, however, the distinctions also serve to argue the case for the relationship of God to the world, specifically, the case for an ongoing, constant, and yet variegated relationality. It is not the case that the immutability of the ultimate divine willing either rules out a notion of relationship between God and world or removes any notion of varied relationship at different moments in time. The distinction serve, in tandem with the scholastic understanding of eternity not as a mathematical point but as an everlasting duration, to indicate the genuine alteration of relationships between God and the world without also indicating a fluctuating divine nature.[451]

In these various arguments concerning the will of God and distinctions in the divine will, we see the continuing interpenetration of the concept of the immutability of the essence of God with the concept of the will, with the conclusion that the will of God also must be, at least in the primary causal and intentional sense, immutable. This would be a highly metaphysical argument divorced from piety were not its underlying concern the consistency of the divine promise of salvation and the priority of grace in the saving work of God. Both in this intentionality and in their use of the standard distinctions, the orthodox stand in a fairly continuous line of development of the doctrine of the divine will: their cautionary stance and their emphasis on the work of salvation place them in continuity with the teaching of the Reformers, despite the significant development and elaboration of the definitions and distinctions — whereas their use of the distinctions themselves evidences not only continuity in development, but also a mediation of concepts through the tradition, from the later Middle Ages through the Reformation into the seventeenth century, together with as consistent effort to retrieve the detail of the tradition in the context of a confessionally defined Reformed Protestantism.

---

450. Cf. the argument in Richard A. Muller, "Incarnation, Immutability and the Case for Classical Theism," in *Westminster Theological Journal*, vol. 45 (1983), pp. 22-40.

451. Cf. the comments in Van Asselt, *Federal Theology*, pp. 56, 168, noting the salvation-historical dimension of the doctrine of the *voluntas Dei*.

D. The *Ad Intra* Distinctions.

1. *Voluntas essentialis* and *voluntas personalis*. This is an admittedly rare distinction, given the Reformed orthodox unwillingness to speculate into the doctrine of the Trinity in a manner like that of the medieval doctors. This distinction parallels, of course, the basic distinction of properties of the Godhead into *proprietates essentiales* and *proprietates personales*. Thus, the *voluntas essentialis* is simply the will of God, understood as an essential property or as a faculty of the divine life. The "essential" will of God can also be termed the *voluntas realis*, namely, will by which God discerns all things existent or nonexistent.[452] The *voluntas personalis*, then, can only relate to the inward begetting and proceeding of the persons of the Trinity, understood as somehow belonging to the divine willing — as such, this language relates also to the concept of a necessary divine will, the *voluntas necessaria*. Thus, God the Father necessarily wills to beget God the Son.

2. *Voluntas necessaria* and *voluntas libera*. In a sense, it can be argued that God must will some things and must will them in a certain way; but it is also true that God wills other things freely. The distinction between this necessary will and the free will of God is determined by the possible objects of God's willing: thus, inasmuch as the good is the object of the divine will, the objects of God's willing can be distinguished into the infinite, uncreated good and the finite, created good.[453] Thus,

> In some instances God wills necessarily, in others freely: he necessarily wills himself, since he is the ultimate goal and the highest good, which he is unable not to will and to love, inasmuch as he can neither cancel his own glory or deny himself. Other things he wills freely, since no created thing is necessary with respect to God, but contingent, inasmuch as he is able to exist without it: he wills all things in such a way as also to be able not to will them.[454]

Nothing is able to influence the will of God in the sense of standing prior to it as a cause. When, moreover, he wills necessarily, it is not by reason of an external compulsion nor is it a contingent willing. This is not to say that God's will is *alogos* but rather that God is not constrained by externals:

> the will of God is the cause of all things, having nothing prior to itself; all other causes are secondary, not primary, regulated, not the rule — a point against the Pelagians and Pelagianizers, who in the discussion of predestination seek causes of the divine will outside of God, in the foreknowledge of faith and in the proper exercise of free will.[455]

---

452. Rijssen, *Summa theol.*, III.xxvi.

453. Turretin, *Inst. theol. elencticae*, III.xiv.1.

454. Rijssen, *Summa theol.*, III.xxviii; Turretin, *Inst. theol. elencticae*, III.xiv.5; cf. Heereboord, *Meletemata philosophica, Disputatio XXIII, de voluntate Dei*, vi-vii (p. 124).

455. Rijssen, *Summa theol.*, III.xxx.

The properties of the divine will, therefore, are its holiness, freedom, eternity, immutability, and efficacy — according to which God wills, necessarily willing his own being and freely willing all things *ad extra* by his eternal decree.[456]

The orthodox can also pose a series of distinctions concerning the freedom of the divine will, the *voluntas Dei libera*. The freedom of the divine willing, in terms parallel to those used to describe the freedom and the bondage of human willing, is threefold: a freedom from coaction, a freedom from servitude, and a freedom from suffering. God's will is both immutable and free: given that God has willed, he cannot will otherwise, but his will — constrained only by his own consistency — is free in that it "is determined by no external power, but by himself only, and because he always acts voluntarily and with reason, which things constitute the highest degree of liberty."[457] The will of God is also to be viewed in the light of the various "affections" attributed to God. These "affections" are, in man, termed emotions or passions and are associated with human weakness and mutability. In relation to God, however, the "affections"

> do not designate any passions or emotions, nor are to be understood as diverse divine wills, for this would imply mutation in God, but as acts of the same will, indicating its different relations.[458]

Of course, the immutability of God, like his being unmoved, describes a God who is also *actus purus*: thus neither concept indicates a divine immobility or quiescence.[459]

The freedom of the eternal divine willing of all finite, created objects and, therefore, the genuine contingency of the entire created order as capable of not being (and capable of not being willed) rests in the Reformed orthodox view on a series of considerations. In the first place, it will be observed that the distinction between the necessary and the free will of God parallels the distinction between the necessary and the free knowledge of God — with the necessary knowledge of all possibility standing prior to the free will of God and the free (or voluntary) knowledge of all actuality subsequent to the free will of God.[460] Thus, God's free willing takes as its possible objects the entire range of possibility. In the second place, as the Reformed insist, the divine *potentia absoluta* stands prior to the free will of God — so that God is understood to be capable of realizing or actualizing any genuine possibility.[461]

If, therefore, God freely wills all finite and created objects, the question of the nature of his free willing focuses on the issue of whether such objects are willed freely merely in the sense of a spontaneous willing, or, in addition, is there a freedom of indifference

---

456. Rijssen, *Summa theol.*, III.xxxi; Turretin, *Inst. theol. elencticae*, III.xiv.1.

457. Pictet, *Theol. chr.* I.vi.8; Heereboord, *Meletemata philosophica, Disputatio XXIII, de voluntate Dei*, vii-viii (p. 124).

458. Pictet, *Theol. chr.* I.vii.1.

459. Contra Barth, *Church Dogmatics*, II/1, pp. 492-493; cf. Louis Berkhof, *Systematic Theology* (Grand Rapids: Eerdmans, 1938), p. 59; Muller, "Incarnation, Immutability and the Case for Classical Theism," pp. 26-28.

460. Cf., above, 5.3 (E.1).

461. Cf., below, 6.2 (B.4).

in relation to finite objects? Here the Reformed note that even the necessary will of God, that by which he wills himself and his own goodness, is free in the sense of spontaneity: God's necessary willing is subject to no external compulsion and is, therefore, characterized by freedom of spontaneity. Such spontaneity must also belong to the divine willing of finite objects — but the Reformed also insist on a liberty of indifference with regard to the created order, "since no created thing is necessary with respect to God, but contingent (since he could do without it), he wills all things in such a way as being able not to will them."[462] Thus, although the pure extent of God's willing, like the pure extent of his knowing, is necessary, namely, extending to all possible objects, the acts of divine willing and knowing are free and, in a sense, contingent, yielding a genuine and even radical contingency of the created order.[463]

3. *Libertas voluntatis antecedens* and *libertas voluntatis concomitans.* This distinction follows directly on the former: antecedently, the divine will is prior to all things willed, as their foundation or *principium*; concomitantly, it is the willing by which God wills all things. In the first sense, God's will is utterly free, bounded only by the divine nature itself, capable of willing all things without constraint: the *libertas voluntatis antecedens* refers to God's will understood absolutely or *simiplciter*. In this ultimate sense, God's will is free antecedently, prior to any willed object — inasmuch as it is "indifferent," not necessarily directed toward any given object. God is not, of course, passively indifferent — but rather actively indifferent, capable of either willing or not willing this or that thing. In the second sense, God's will is free in the act of willing, and therefore concomitantly with his willing of himself and of all things. This willing is no longer indifferent but is to be understood as the eternal *consilium Dei*, determined toward particular objects. The *libertas voluntatis concomitans* refers, therefore, to the divine will understood in relation or *secundum quid*.[464] This distinction, like the preceding and following distinctions, emphasized the Reformed view, over against the necessitarian assumptions of seventeenth-century Platonists, that God, although always (and necessarily) willing according to his nature, is nonetheless free, and antecedently so — free to create or not create, free to create this world or another equally good — not merely free of compulsion from creatures following the act of creation.[465]

4. *Volitio* and *nolitio.* God both wills and wills-not — in God there is both volition and nolition. This distinction builds on the previous conception of the freedom of divine willing and underlines the point that, in not willing a particular thing, God is neither indifferent nor passive. Specifically, there are things that God could will that God does not will or, more accurately, "wills-not," given that his nolition is not a mere

---

462. Turretin, *Inst. theol. elencticae*, III.xiv.5.

463. See Vos, "Always on Time: The Immutability of God," in Sarot and Brink (eds.), *Understanding the Attributes of God*, pp. 66-70.

464. Mastricht, *Theoretico-practica theol.*, II.xv.14.

465. Cf. the discussion of various seventeenth-century options on this point in Stephen M. Fallon, "'To Act or Not': Milton's Conception of Divine Freedom," in *Journal of the History of Ideas*, 49/3 (1988), pp. 425-453.

suspension or cessation of will nor (certainly!) an absence of the faculty of will, but a decisive or intentional non-willing of certain things and events. A distinction must therefore be made between *nolitio* and *non velle* (between intentional nolition and the absence of a willing toward a particular object) just as there is a distinction between *volitio* and *velle* (actual volition and the mere capacity of willing).[466] We have already seen this issue arise in the distinction between *scientia necesaria* and *scientia voluntaria*: God knows all possibilities and also knows those possibilities that he wills to actualize. God does not, in other words, will the actualization of *all* possibilities — nor is he either ignorant of or indifferent to the unactualized possibilities. As Calvin commented, "How many things can He do that He yet wills not to be done; but He wills nothing that He cannot do."[467] Since, moreover, as we have already noted in the distinction between *voluntas necessaria* and *voluntas libera*, the will of God *ad extra* is entirely free, it is clear that God is in no way obliged either by nature or by anything external to him to will effectively all that he is able to will (or to do). Thus, there is in God a non-willing or *nolitio* of an entire range of possibilities. "It cannot be denied," Baxter writes,

> that there is in God a Negation of Volition: that is, that he willeth not some things which he *could will*. As to have made the world sooner, greater, with other sorts of creatures: to have made some men better, wiser, richer, &c. The exterior objects of God's Will are finite, and contingent beings.[468]

Or, by way of further elaboration, in the case of an event "a," God can will "a" or will "not-a" — but he can also "not will 'a'" without any necessity of willing "not-a" and, indeed, he can "not will 'a'" and in the same moment "not will 'not-a.'" This distinction may be yet another example of the Scotist influence found in seventeenth-century Reformed thought.[469]

E. The *Ad Intra* — *Ad Extra* Distinctions.

Many of the Reformed orthodox introduce the main series of distinctions in the divine willing by offering a series of similar pairs of terms: the *voluntas beneplaciti* and *voluntas signi*; the *voluntas decreti* and the *voluntas praecepti*; the *voluntas arcana* and the *voluntas revelata*; and the *voluntas eudokias* and *voluntas euarestias*. The hidden or "secret will" (*voluntas arcana*) of God's "good pleasure" (*voluntas beneplaciti*) can also be identified as "the will of [God's] decree" (*voluntas decernens aut decreti*) according to which the elect are predestinate; the latter is well called "the will of commandment

---

466. Cf. Olevian, *Exposition of the Symbole*, p. 65; with Baxter, *Catholike Theologie*, I.xiii, §297 (p. 48); Amyraut et al., *Syntagma thesium theologicarum*, IV.viii.9; and Turretin, *Inst. theol. elencticae*, III.xiv.6.

467. Calvin, *Secret Providence*, p. 289.

468. Baxter, *Catholike Theologie*, I.xiii, §297 (p. 48).

469. Cf. the discussion in Eef Dekker, "The Theory of Divine Permission According to Scotus' *Ordinatio* I 47," in *Vivarium*, 37/2 (2000), pp. 232-234.

(*voluntas praecepti*)" or the "revealed will" (*voluntas revelata*) of God.[470] Still, there are slight differences in meaning among the several distinctions.

1. Voluntas beneplaciti and voluntas signi. In most of the orthodox systems this stands as the initial or at least one of the basic distinctions — and it is certainly a distinction well established in the older theological tradition.[471] Wendelin and Rutherford comment that the distinction between the will of the divine good pleasure (*beneplaciti*) and the will of the sign or precept (*signi*) is unanimously attested and rightly used by the scholastics.[472] It is, however, omitted by the *Synopsis purioris* and Hottinger.[473]

The biblical texts most frequently examined to support this distinction are Matthew 3:17; 11:25-26; 12:18; Romans 9:19; 12:2; Ephesians 1:5; 5:10; Philippians 2:13; Colossians 3:20. In the first of these texts, Jesus speaks of God as hiding "the mysteries of the gospel" from the wise but revealing them to children because this pattern of revelation seemed good to God: in other words, this revelation rests entirely on the divine "good pleasure (εὐδοκία)"[474] or, stated slightly differently, God's "most wise decree and counsel."[475] Ephesians 1:5 offers the point even more clearly: "having predestinated us unto the adoption of children by Jesus Christ to himself, according to the good pleasure of his will." Thus, the "efficient cause" of predestination is God himself, and the "formal cause" is "the good pleasure of his will."[476] Poole comments that the latter phrase indicates God's "sovereign grace and good will, as the only spring from which predestination issued, God being moved to it by nothing out of himself."[477] The other verses do not so much identify the distinction as confirm the assumption that God does, indeed, have a good pleasure or ultimately good volition.

The terms *voluntas beneplaciti* and *voluntas signi* can be rendered into English in several ways, each conveying only a part of the technical meaning of the terms. Thus, *voluntas beneplaciti* can be rendered as a "willing" or even "wishing" of "good pleasure" or "complacency" and sometimes appears as *voluntas complacentiae*, indicating the resting of the will in its fundamental willing or, simply, the fundamental inclination

---

470. Pictet, *Theol. chr.*, II.vi.3.

471. Thus, e.g., Hugh of St. Victor, *De sacram.*, I.iv.2; Lombard, *Sententiae*, I, d. 45, cap. 5; Alexander of Hales, *Summa theol.*, I, inq. I, tract. vi, q. iii, tit. 1; Bonaventure, *In Sent.*, I, d. 45, a. 3, q. 1.

472. Wendelin, *Christianae theologiae libri duo*, I.i.18 (2); Rutherford, *Exercitationes apologeticae*, II.i.1 (pp. 213-214). Cf. Lombard, *Sent.*, I, d. 46, cap. 1-2; Alexander of Hales, *Summa theol.*, I, inq. I, tract. IV, q. 3, tit. 3, memb. 1-2. Among the Reformed, see, e.g., Heereboord, *Meletemata philosophica*, *Disputatio XXIII, de voluntate Dei*, i (p. 122).

473. Cf. *Synopsis purioris theol.*, VI.xxxiv; Hottinger, *Cursus theologicus*, III.xv & canones A-E.

474. Poole, *Commentary*, Matt. 11:25-26, in loc.; cf. Diodati, *Pious and Learned Annotations*, in loc.; Amyraut et al., *Syntagma thesium theologicarum*, IV.viii.9.

475. Trapp, *Commentary*, in loc. (V, p. 164); Cocceius, *Summa theol.*, III.x41, 47.

476. Trapp, *Commentary*, Eph. 1:6, in loc. (V, p. 598); cf. Calvin, *Commentary on Ephesians*, Eph. 1:5 (CTS, p. 200), who identifies the divine "good pleasure" as the "efficient cause" of predestination; similarly, Diodati, *Pious and Learned Annotations*, in loc..

477. Poole, *Commentary*, Eph. 1:5, in loc.

of the will. In God this fundamental willing or inclination of will must ultimately be identical with all that God wills and, therefore, with all that was, is, and will be: thus the identification of the *voluntas beneplaciti* with the divine decree and the *voluntas propositi*. Leigh indicates that the *voluntas beneplaciti* or the *beneplacitum* of God is in fact the divine "decree, properly so called," and that it "may be either hidden or revealed."[478] So, too, is this will identified as *beneplacitum*, not on the basis of its objects, given that some things and events are good and others are not, but because of the "manner of [divine] willing, since whatever God wills, whether to effect or to permit, has as its cause nothing other than his pleasure."[479]

The term *voluntas signi*, literally, the will of the sign, is closely related to the term *signum voluntatis*, the sign of the will or purpose. It indicates an overt sign or indication that someone wills something and can therefore be understood as a revealed will or, specifically, as a revealed precept or "preceptive will" — thus, what is literally called the "signified will" is a will that God makes known and in effect "signifies" what is commanded. This signified or preceptive will, moreover, does not contradict the will of the divine good pleasure, although the relationship between the two may sometimes be difficult to establish immediately. The *voluntas signi*, therefore, is not a "mere sign" but one that corresponds with something that is truly in God.[480] In the particular sense of a distinction between the *voluntas beneplaciti* as the decree and the *voluntas signi* as the divine command, the distinction is little different than the correctly understood distinction between the absolute and the conditional will of God.[481]

Thus, when the *voluntas signi* is understood as the revealed preceptive will of God, the definition takes as its point of departure the identity of "command" and "will" and then identifies "the commandment of God" as "one of the signs of his will." In this sense, Twisse argues, when God commanded Abraham to sacrifice Isaac or when God commanded Pharaoh to "let Israel go," this is a revelation or pronouncement of the *voluntas signi*. Yet, in both cases, this revealed will was not the ultimate will of God: the *voluntas beneplaciti* or divine good pleasure was that Isaac not be sacrificed and that Pharaoh's heart be hardened to deny Israel's departure. What, therefore, God is said to will according to the "sign," "the same at once he does not will, but rather the contrary sometimes, by his *voluntas propositi*" or *beneplaciti*. Yet, there is not an ultimate contrariety inasmuch as the distinction between these two wills arises only because the "objects" of God's signs or commandments are "are only morall duties, and not the rewards of them, such as is salvation."[482] Nor do the things that God commands always reflect his ultimate purpose — commands may point toward penultimate ends rather than to the ultimate ends identified in the *voluntas beneplaciti*.

478. Leigh, *Body of Divinity*, II.vii (p. 199); cf. Zanchi, *De natura Dei*, III.iv, q. 3.2 (cols. 253-254).

479. Maccovius, *Loci communes*, xxiii (p. 173, col. 1); cf. Beza et al. *Propositions and Principles*, VIII.iii; Mastricht, *Theoretico-practica theol.*, II.xv.22.

480. Cocceius, *Summa theologiae*, III.x.47; Amyraut et al., *Syntagma thesium theologicarum*, IV.viii.20.

481. Leigh, *Body of Divinity*, II.vii (p. 198); Cocceius, *Summa theol.*, III.x47.

482. Twisse, *Discovery*, II.xv (p. 536); cf. Beza, *Christian questions and aunsweres*, pp. 70v-71r.

In the light of such problems, Leigh, Maccovius, and Twisse (very much following the tradition) indicate that the *voluntas propositi* or *beneplaciti* alone is properly called the will of God, "which none can resist, Rom. 9:19," whereas the *voluntas signi* or commandment is only "improperly" called God's will.[483]

A different nuance in the definition is found in Baxter, who states that Twisse's definition is correct in itself but is too narrow, given the full meaning of the distinction. In favor of his own view, Baxter cites Pierre D'Ailly. Inasmuch as God's revelation is true, the *voluntas signi* can never be contrary to the *voluntas beneplaciti* — rather the will of the sign only partially reveals the divine good pleasure, and the revelation can be misinterpreted by human beings.[484] The *voluntas beneplaciti*, according to Baxter, refers to God's ultimate will to effect all "Natural Things and Events as such," whereas the *voluntas signi* is God's will "concerning what is owed or commanded as such." The object of the first is "nature," of the second, law and justice. The partial character of the *voluntas signi* arises out of the fact that it covers only juridical events: thus, God's good pleasure or *beneplacitum* concerns natural things and events, including judicial events. The correct formulation of the distinction, according to Baxter, recognizes that "as Gods *Will de Naturalibus* is his *Beneplacitum*; and the effects of it as the *signa subsequentia* ... so God's will *de Debito* is his *Beneplacitum*, signified by his *Law* and *Judgment*."[485] So too are the signs of God's law both natural and revealed — namely, the natural law or "order of things" and the revealed precepts given directly to human beings. Baxter does agree with Twisse, however, that the commandments or signs of God are only improperly designated as the divine will. We note that Heppe's claim to the effect that the Reformed "disapproved" of the distinction and Strehle's argument concerning an "antithesis" between the *voluntas beneplaciti* and the *voluntas signi* at the heart of Reformed theology are simply not borne out by the evidence from the sixteenth and seventeenth centuries.[486]

2. Voluntas decernens sive decreti seu propositi and voluntas praecepti. This distinction is nearly identical to the preceding and is synonymous with the distinction between the *voluntas eudokias* (will of good pleasure) and *voluntas euarestias* (will of approbation), and it serves to clarify the distinction between God's hidden will and his revealed will against the alternative reading proposed by Arminius and his followers.[487] Even so. we distinguish "one will, by which God decrees what he wills or permits to be done; the other by which he prescribes to men their duty: the former

---

483. Leigh, *Body of Divinity*, II.vii (p. 199); Maccovius, *Loci communes*, xxiii (pp. 172-173); Twisse, *Discovery*, II.xv (p. 536); cf. Lombard, *Sententiae*, I, d.45, c.6; Alexander of Hales, *Summa theol.*, I, inq.I, tract.vi, q.iii, tit.1.

484. Baxter, *Catholike Theologie*, I.xiv, §325-326 (pp. 51-52); cf. Cocceius, *Aphorismi breviores*, V.10-12.

485. Baxter, *Catholike Theologie*, I.xiv, §329 (p. 52).

486. Baxter, *Catholike Theologie*, I.xiv, §332, 340 (pp. 52, 53); contra Heppe, *Reformed Dogmatics*, p. 88, and Strehle, "Calvinism, Augustinianism, and the Will of God," p. 232.

487. Amyraut et al., *Syntagma thesium theologicarum*, IV.viii.16-17, citing Arminius, *Analysis cap. IX ad Romanos, cum Aphorismis*, in *Opera*, pp. 790-792 (*Works*, III, pp. 504-507); cf. Turretin, *Inst. theol. elencticae*, III.xv.8; Leigh, *Body of Divinity*, II.vi (p. 199).

regards the *futurition* and *taking place* of things, the latter is the *rule* of our actions; the one is always fulfilled and cannot be resisted (Rom. 9:19), the other is often violated by men."[488]

> This decretive will has not only determined what shall be done by men, but has also determined what things shall be enjoined upon them, or revealed to them. [Furthermore] the preceptive will (*voluntas praecepti*) is, properly speaking, the execution of a part of the decretive will, namely, that part which has determined what shall be revealed to, or enjoined upon, men in due time.[489]

Even so, the preceptive will of God is identical with the revealed will or with the revelation of the decree. Thus, "God wills nothing by his preceptive will, that he does not at the same time (*simul*) will according to his good pleasure."[490]

The biblical texts examined here are Psalm 143:10; John 6:38; Romans 9:19; 12:2; Ephesians 1:11 — with a view to their juxtaposition and correlation, given as we noted at the beginning of this section, "will" has a variety of meanings in Scripture. Thus, Psalm 143:10 states "teach me to do thy will," a clear reference to the revealed and preceptive will of God, which may or may not be obeyed. On the other hand, John 6:38, "and this is the Father's will ... that of all which he hath given me I should lose nothing," is clearly not a preceptive will, but an ultimate will which must be fulfilled. Similarly, Ephesians 1:11 refers to the eternal "counsel" of God's will that has predestined all things.[491] The entire juxtaposition appears in the Epistle to the Romans, where Paul declares at 9:19, "For who hath resisted his will?" — and at 12:2, "be ye transformed by the renewing of your mind, that ye may prove what is that good, acceptable, and perfect will of God": the former passage indicates an ultimate irresistible will, while the latter, like the Psalm, indicates the preceptive will, revealed in God's Word.[492]

This principle of the fundamental identity of the decretive and preceptive will does not, however, always conform to human perception of the case and needs to be argued by the orthodox: it is clear that God, according to his preceptive will, wills that all people be holy and conformed to the divine law. It is equally obvious, comments Wendelin, "that the greater part of the human race is not holy, not conformed to the divine law." From this fact it can be inferred that the eternal, hidden will or decree of God is not that God will sanctify all people! God does not, in other words, efficiently will that all people be sanctified — and it is also the case that no one can be holy unless God sanctifies him.[493] Does this, then, pose a contradiction between the wills of God

---

488. Pictet, *Theol. chr.*, II.vi.3; Beza et al. *Propositions and Principles*, VIII.iii, v.

489. Pictet, *Theol. chr.*, II.vi.6.

490. Wendelin, *Christianae theologiae libri duo*, I.i.18 (3).

491. Poole, *Commentary*, John 6:38-40; Eph. 1:11, in loc.

492. Cf. Poole, *Commentary*, Rom. 9:19 and 12:2, in loc.; Calvin, *Commentary on Romans*, 9:18 and 12:2 (CTS *Romans*, pp. 362, 454-455).

493. Wendelin, *Christianae theologiae libri duo*, I.i.18 (3).

— or, indeed, as the Arminians claim, a contradiction between those wills as defined by the Reformed?

Wendelin answers that this is hardly a contradiction — rather it points toward a diversity of meanings and cases. Thus, when it is revealed in the Word that God wills all people to be holy, this is not an indication of the divine good pleasure or decree (*non est signum beneplaciti seu decreti*). It is the good pleasure of God — and revealed as such — that God wills that all men understand their duty to be holy. It is equally the good pleasure of God, as revealed "partly in the Word and partly in fact," that the greater part of humanity will not be made holy. The contradiction, therefore, is apparent, not real: and it arises only when the revealed will is incorrectly paired with one aspect of the ultimate will of God.[494]

By Rijssen's time, the sacrifice of Isaac (Genesis 22:1-18) had become a standard text in debate over precisely this issue: it is a false objection to the Reformed insistence on a single, ultimate, and inalterable will of God to claim that, according to Scripture, God first willed the death of Isaac and then afterward willed his life: "God did not will or decree [Isaac's death], rather he commanded it."[495] The distinction between the ultimate will or decree of God and a divine command is significant, since the former refers to the ultimate good pleasure of God, the *voluntas beneplaciti*, while the latter refers to the revealed will of God, the *voluntas signi*: God does not, therefore, "will and not will in the same manner and relation." God thus wills the sacrifice of Isaac according to his revealed or preceptive will in order to test Abraham's obedience — but does not will the sacrifice according to his ultimate good pleasure. Rijssen states categorically, "*Non datur contrarietas in voluntate Dei.*"[496]

3. *Voluntas immanens* and *voluntas transiens*. A distinction can be made between the inward will of God and the divine will as it passes outward toward its effects. As Owen commented, "an eternal act of God's will, immanent in himself, puts no change of condition into the creature."[497] On the one hand, God can be considered as having in himself the faculty of will, apart from any external acts or effects. Will, like intellect, belongs to the nature of God prior to the creation of the world, apart from any consideration of the effects of willing, but will also indicates the effective willing of God or the acts of the divine will that bring about effects in the world order or, indeed, the world order itself. In Baxter's words, "God's will, as it effecteth *Relations ad extra*, is ... *effectively Transient.*"[498]

4. *Voluntas arcana sive occulta* and *voluntas revelata*. The distinction made between the *voluntas arcana* and *voluntas revelata* is similar but not identical with that between the *voluntas beneplaciti* and *voluntas signi*. The *voluntas beneplaciti* refers to the decree of God which can be both hidden (*arcana* or *occulta*) or revealed (*manifesta*): some aspects of the ultimate divine good pleasure, comments Wendelin, are revealed

---

494. Wendelin, *Christianae theologiae libri duo*, I.i.18 (3); cf. Ussher, *Body of Divinity*, p. 51.
495. Rijssen, *Summa theol.*, III.xxxi, controversia, obj. 2.
496. Rijssen, *Summa theol.*, margin at III.xxix.
497. Owen, appendix to *Death of Death*, in *Works*, X, p. 427.
498. Baxter, *Catholike Theologie*, I.xiv, §314 (p. 50).

in the Word, others are not. "The hidden will of God," Wendelin offers, "is the eternal and immutable decree of God concerning the making or permitting of things in the temporal order, of which we are ignorant in the absence of its manifestation."[499]

There is a series of biblical texts that generate this distinction as well: Deuteronomy 29:29; 30:14; Psalm 36:6; and Romans 9:19-20; 11:33-34. It is of this will, Wendelin indicates, that Scripture speaks (Deut 29:29) when it states that "hidden things belong to the Lord your God, but those things which are written belong to you and to your children."[500] On this point of exegesis, the orthodox are in total accord with Calvin: "to me," he writes, "there appears no doubt that, by antithesis, there is a comparison here made between the doctrine openly set forth in the Law, and the hidden and incomprehensible counsel of God, concerning which it is not lawful to inquire."[501] The point made by Moses, Henry indicates, is identical with that made by Paul in Romans 11:33 — "How unsearchable are God's judgments, and his ways past finding out." The text in Deuteronomy divides the issue into two observations, first, that "we are forbidden curiously to inquire into the secret counsels of God, and to determine concerning them" and, second, that "we are directed and encouraged diligently to inquire into that which God has made known; things *revealed belong to us and to our children.*"[502]

There are, Wendelin adds, many things decreed by God of which we remain utterly ignorant before they come to pass — as the apostle James writes (5:13-14), we often arrogantly make plans for tomorrow, when we know nothing of what will happen. Rather, as James advises us, we ought always to add, "if the Lord wills."[503] And here, too, we find a precise continuity in interpretation between the orthodox and Calvin — including the assumption that the text of James 5:15 implies a distinction between the revealed law of God and the hidden counsel "by which [God] governs all things."[504]

In controversy with the Arminians, the Reformed insisted that, albeit there is a necessary correlation between the hidden and revealed wills of God, these cannot be identical in content — as if there were no hidden will of God according to which he can will things concerning the fulfillment of his work of salvation that remain hidden from us and, indeed, not fully comprehended in his commands and promises to us.[505]

The revealed will can be defined in two ways — either as the effects of God's will manifest in the world or as a synonym of the *voluntas signi*. In the latter sense, "the revealed will, properly so called, is not the decree of God, but the revelation

---

499. Wendelin, *Christianae theologiae libri duo*, I.i.18 (3); Heidanus, *Corpus theol.*, II (p. 135).

500. Wendelin, *Christianae theologiae libri duo*, I.i.18 (2); cf. Mastricht, *Theoretico-practica theol.*, II.xv.23, also citing Deut. 29:29.

501. Calvin, *Harmony of the Four Last Books of Moses*, Deut. 29:29, in loc. (CTS *Harmony*, I, p. 410).

502. Henry, *Exposition*, in loc.; cf. Ussher, *Body of Divinity*, pp. 51-2.

503. Wendelin, *Christianae theologiae libri duo*, I.i.18 (2).

504. Calvin, *Commentary on James*, 5:15, in loc. (CTS *James*, p. 341).

505. Amyraut et al., *Syntagma thesium theologicarum*, IV.viii.2-3, 16; cf. Arminius, *Analysis cap. IX ad Romanos, cum Aphorismis*, in *Opera*, p. 791 (*Works*, III, p. 505).

accomplished in the Word, which offers some testimony about the decree": God's revelation is, thus, the "sign and testimony" of the decree, considered both efficiently and permissively — with the result that there can be no contradiction between the decree and the revelation. Indeed, a further distinction can be made within the *voluntas revelata* between the revelation of the law and the revelation of the gospel.[506] In other words, the Reformed orthodox deny that the hidden will or eternal decree of God runs counter to the truth of God's revelation: they do not follow out the late medieval nominalistic line of argument severing the *potentia ordinata* from the divine *potentia absoluta*, that the divinely given order of things stands in no necessary relation to the ultimate being of God, but they nonetheless assume that the revealed will is largely preceptive and promissory, not utterly reflecting the divine good pleasure: in his revealed will, God genuinely calls all who hear the gospel and promises to accept all who answer his invitation — in his hidden will, he determines those to whom the grace will be given that enables response to his calling.[507]

5. *Voluntas absoluta* and *voluntas conditionata*. The distinction between decretive and preceptive will, *voluntas beneplaciti* and *voluntas signi*, relates also to a distinction between absolute will and conditioned will (*voluntas absoluta et voluntas conditionata*). According to the former, God wills and determines that something should occur "without any condition" in the object of God's willing — but the latter, the conditional will, rests upon the fulfillment of a condition in or by the object of the divine will, for example, the will of God to save men upon condition of faith.[508] Maccovius notes, against the Arminians, that the distinction is "utterly vain."[509] Wendelin indicates that this distinction causes some difficulty, but makes perfectly good sense if it is understood solely in terms of the *voluntas signi* — granting that most of the divine precepts, promises, and condemnations are stated conditionally. The distinction is, however, extended improperly to the eternal decree, inasmuch as the decree cannot be "suspended on conditions" — as if God decreed to save those individuals from among the damned who will repent and believe in Christ. Citing Du Moulin, Wendelin argues that language of a conditioned will in God that views the decree as unstable, fluctuating, and dependent on human will is unacceptable: there can be no such thing as a condition serving as a means external to God without which God would be unable to reach a certain goal. It is incorrect to state that God will elect to salvation those who believe and repent, correct to argue that God elects some to salvation through belief and repentance.[510]

---

506. Wendelin, *Christianae theologiae libri duo*, I.i.18 (2); Zanchi, *De natura Dei*, III.iv, q. 2, thesis (cols. 242-243), and see below, 5.4 (F.8).

507. Amyraut et al., *Syntagma thesium theologicarum*, IV.viii.16, citing the Canons of Dort, III/IV.viii; contra the confused account in Strehle, "Calvinism, Augustinianism, and the Will of God," pp. 227-229, 232-233.

508. Leigh, *Treatise*, II.viii (p. 68); cf. Wendelin, *Christianae theologiae libri duo*, I.i.18 (4).

509. Maccovius, *Distinctiones et regulae*, IV.xxxiii.

510. Wendelin, *Christianae theologiae libri duo*, I.i.18 (4), citing Du Moulin, *Enodat. graviss quaest.*, p. 315; cf. Leigh, *Body of Divinity*, II.vii (p. 198); Amyraut et al., *Syntagma thesium theologicarum*,

Even so, Poole can comment on Gen. 22:12, "for now I know that thou fearest God," as the conclusion of Abraham's trial but not as a discovery on God's part:

> God knew the sincerity and resolvedness of Abraham's faith and obedience before and without this evidence, and from eternity foresaw this fact with all its circumstances; and therefore you must not think that God had now made any new discovery: but this is spoken here, as in many other places, of God after the manner of men, who is then said to know a thing when it is notorious and evident to a man's self and others by some remarkable effect.[511]

As in the previous controversies, the rectitude of the distinction depends upon its definition: "it is possible to allow a *voluntas conditionata*" in God "but not in an *à priori* and antecedent sense, as if dependent on a condition, rather in an *à posteriori* and consequent sense, given that some condition in the creature intervenes between the will and its execution"; and then "only to the extent that the condition does not belong to the internal divine act [*à parte actus interni*] or volition [*volitionis*], but to the external object [*à parte obiecti externi*] or thing willed [*rei volitae*]."[512]

In this sense, the distinction can legitimately be applied to the promises associated with God's covenants — whether the natural covenant with its promise of eternal life on condition of perfect obedience, or the covenants of law and gospel, where God's promises are extended conditionally to sinners.[513] In the same sense, Amyraut argued that the eternal decree of election was conditional — executed in individuals on fulfillment, by God himself, of the condition of faith.[514] In other words, the conditional will remains an immutable will, willed eternally by God, but it is understood as being directed toward a contingent or conditional event: the condition, strictly understood, obtains, not in the divine will, but in the temporal event. What is to be rejected is the "Neopelagian" form of the distinction in which an absolute will, independent of all external conditions, is set against a conditional will, "dependent on a condition *extra Deum*": such a concept is repugnant to the independence, wisdom, and power

---

Iviii.32; Owen, *Dissertation on Divine Justice*, in *Works*, X, p. 597.

511. Poole, *Commentary*, I, p. 52.

512. Rijssen, *Summa theol.*, III.xxxi, controversia III; cf. Zanchi, *De natura Dei*, III.iv, q. 3.2 (col. 254).

513. Amyraut et al., *Syntagma thesium theologicarum*, IV.viii.34. N.B., the theses here reflect the Cameronian "threefold covenant" model typical of Saumur.

514. Moyse Amyraut, *Brief Traitté de la predestination et de ses principales dependances* (Saumur: Iean Lesnier & Isaac Desbordes, 1634), ch. vii, xi (pp. 89-90, 131-134, 147): it is not, strictly speaking, this understanding of conditionality per se that caused the controversy — rather the problem was that the divinely bestowed condition, faith, intervened, in Amyraut's view, between an initial divine intention to save all on condition and a subsequent divine act of saving only some on the ground of the fulfillment of the condition. The debated issue was this dual intentionality in God and the "hypothetical universalism" it implied. Still, Amyraut's qualifier that the condition was fulfilled by God through grace alone left his formulation, arguably within the boundaries created by the confessional pronouncements of the Reformed churches, viz., the author of a debated and, in some quarters detested, formula, but not an Arminian and not a heretic in any strict sense: cf. the discussion in *PRRD*, I, 1.3 (B.2-3) and *PRRD*, II, 2.3 (A.2).

of God inasmuch as it renders these attributes "doubtful and uncertain," dependent on the mutable will of human beings, and by extension "ineffective and capable of disappointment."[515]

The Neopelagians object that the divine offer of salvation itself presupposes just such a conditional will, granting that "God wills the salvation of human beings if they believe." The proposition, comments Rijssen, is susceptible of two meanings. It can mean that "God wills or establishes our salvation as contingent on the condition of faith" — so that our salvation, and not the will of God, is conditional. Or, it could mean that our salvation rests "on the condition of faith, established or foreknown to reside in the will of God that confers salvation." This latter meaning must be false inasmuch as "nothing that is temporal can be the cause of that which is eternal."[516]

6. *Voluntas antecedens* and *voluntas consequens*. A problem similar to that of the absolute and conditional will of God arises in the context of the revealed will and is resolved by a distinction between *voluntas antecedens* and *voluntas consequens*. A broad sampling of Reformed theologians — Maccovius, Cocceius, Heidanus, Rutherford, Owen, Turretin, Rijssen — recognized that the distinction itself may be used in a valid way but is also subject to great abuse.[517] Thus, the question "*An voluntas Dei bene distinguatur in antecedentem & consequentem?*" is to be answered negatively against the Socinian and Arminian use of the distinction, inasmuch as the more basic distinctions made between *voluntas beneplaciti* and *voluntas signi*, *voluntas arcanum* and *voluntas revelatum* in no way indicate an alteration of God's eternal will as it manifests itself in time.[518] Turretin comments that this "ulcerous" distinction was probably invented by John of Damascus, then taken up by some of the medieval scholastics and "Neopelagians," and more recently used by "Arminians, Socinians, and other patrons of universal grace."[519] In Owen's view, the Arminian distinction was a "gross Anthropomorphism" that attributes fluctuating passions to God.[520] Others like Cocceius, Heidanus, and Heidegger cite both Chrysostom and John of Damascus as using the distinction and note that this patristic usage was adequate, as distinct from subsequent pelagianizing use of the distinction.[521] To Rutherford's mind, Scotus and Durandus evidence the correct scholastic use of the distinction — namely, not as a reference to an antecedent will in the Godhead itself (*non in se & immediate*), but as a divine will resident

---

515. Rijssen, *Summa theol.*, III.xxxi, controversia III, argumentum.

516. Rijssen, *Summa theol.*, III.xxxi, controversia III, obj. & resp.

517. Cf. Maccovius, *Distinctiones et regulae*, IV.xxxiv; Cocceius, *Summa theologiae*, III.x.44; idem, *Aphorismi prolixiores*, V.14; Heidanus, *Corpus theol.*, II (p. 141-144); Rutherford, *Exercitationes apologeticae*, II.iii.1 (pp. 323-324); Owen, *Dissertation on Divine Justice*, in *Works*, X, p. 611; Turretin, *Inst. theol. elencticae*, III.xvi.19-23; and note the citations in Heppe, *Reformed Dogmatics*, pp. 90-92.

518. Rijssen, *Summa theol.*, III.xxxi, controversia 1; cf. Burgersdijk, *Institutiones metaphysicae*, II.ix.11.

519. Turretin, *Inst. theol. elencticae*, III.xvi.2; cf. 3-4.

520. Owen, *Death of Christ*, in *Works*, X, p. 452.

521. See the citations in Heppe, *Reformed Dogmatics*, pp. 91-92, and cf. Cocceius, *Summa theologiae*, X.xliv; Heidanus, *Corpus theol.*, II (p. 141).

in the antecedent causes from which an effect follows, but not necessarily; so that God antecedently wills that all people be saved, insofar as he gives to all the natural capacity to be saved and in no way impedes the sufficiency of the means; and God wills consequently that which he wills not in the causes but in himself, namely, that believers be saved.[522]

"The distinction of the divine will into antecedent and consequent is used among our theologians," Rijssen comments, as a reference to the decretive and the preceptive will of God. The former "was determined by God from eternity before any created things existed," while the latter will rests upon the *voluntas decreti* as on its proper antecedent. The "Neopelagians" of the age, however, offer a different explanation of the distinction: the antecedent will of God they place, not prior to all creation, but prior to the acts of the creature; and the consequent will they rest not on the *voluntas antecedens*, but on the will of the creature that precedes it in time.[523] Cocceius similarly points out that there can be no cause of the divine will and certainly no conditioning of the divine will by the creature.[524]

The issue for the Reformed is not so much advocacy of a particular metaphysical theory as the soteriological consistency of the divine intention and will with its effects.[525] There is no ground, moreover, for concluding from the frequently conditional nature of the *voluntas signi* that the decree, as an antecedent will, must also be conditioned, if the genuinely conditional nature of the revealed will or precept is to remain in force. The Arminian and Lutheran "adversaries," comments Wendelin, argue "that God decreed to save each and every human being, without distinction, on the condition that they believe in Christ: and this is the antecedent will." God "then decreed to save some only, since he foresaw that these only would believe: and this is the consequent will." An antecedent will such as this is alien to the divine wisdom. And a consequent will defined in this manner indicates nothing less than "divine imprudence" after the fashion of Pelagian teaching — since it grounds faith in Christ on the human will.[526]

In other words, the Arminians can argue on the basis of the *voluntas signi* that the antecedent will of God must oblige the conditions set in God's revelation — otherwise, either the antecedent will is falsified by the consequent or the conditions stated in

---

522. Rutherford, *Exercitationes apologeticae*, II.iii.1 (p. 323).

523. Rijssen, *Summa theol.*, III.xxxi, controversia 1; cf. Zanchi, *De natura Dei*, III.iv, q. 3.2 (col. 254); Turretin, *Inst. theol. elencticae*, III.xvi.3.

524. Cocceius, *Aphorismi prolixiores*, V.13, 15.

525. See further Muller, *Christ and the Decree*, pp. 171-173, 178-182; idem, "Perkins' A Golden Chaine: Predestinarian System or Schematized Ordo Salutis?" in *The Sixteenth Century Journal*, IX/1, (April 1978), pp. 69-81; and cf. Lynne Courter Boughton, "Supralapsarianism and the Role of Metaphysics in Sixteenth-Century Reformed Theology," in *Westminster Theological Journal*, 48 (1986), pp. 63-96.

526. Wendelin, *Christianae theologiae libri duo*, I.i.18 (4), citing Du Moulin, *The Anatomy of Arminianism*, cap. 5; Rivetus, *Disputationibus XIII*, disp. 7, sec. 23; and Maccovius, *Volumen thesium*, pars I, disp, 26, sec. 9.

God's revelation are falsified by the antecedent will.[527] Despite this attempt to harmonize the antecedent will with the consequent and with aspects of the revealed will, the Arminian or "Neopelagian" form of the distinction nonetheless still argues "contrary wills" in God. This is, of course, precisely the problem of the Arminian doctrine of predestination.[528] Thus, God is said antecedently to will the salvation of all people and consequently not to will the salvation of all, but only of some. Since both of these wills are (and must be) eternal, there is a contradiction in God. Even so, God from eternity wills the salvation of Judah, while at the same time knowing that Judah will disbelieve and, on the basis of that knowledge, permits Judah to remain in its infidelity and perish.

Who, questions Rijssen, would be so foolish as to attribute such wills to God? According to this doctrine, God genuinely wills that which he knows will never happen! Such doctrine makes God foolish and impotent, inasmuch as it claims God antecedently intends something and antecedently desires it to happen when it neither will happen nor can be brought about by human ability — all the while that its non-occurrence is guaranteed because God himself, in another manner, does not will it. The *voluntas antecedens*, thus defined, is not a will at all but a wish, an incomplete exercise of the faculty, utterly unworthy of an omniscient and omnipotent being. In this view, Rijssen concludes, the covenant of God with human beings depends entirely on the human will, and, indeed, only those who have chosen God through faith and repentance will, in turn, be chosen or elected by God.[529]

Is it the case, however, that Scripture denies this logic and manifests instances in which the antecedent will of God is in fact disappointed by human choice? It may be argued from the text of Matt. 23:37 — "how often would I have gathered thy children together ... and ye would not" — that Christ willed antecedently and absolutely to gather together all people in general, but consequently and conditionally willed not to do so. Both of these distinctions, that between an antecedent and a consequent will and that between an absolute and conditional will, were favored by Arminius and bound up with the concept of a divine *scientia media*.[530] A consequent or conditional will in God, in this sense, rests as much on the effects of secondary causality as it does on the divine nature — and indeed it assumes the existence of a secondary causality not directly under the divine control and, perhaps, not fully foreknown by God.

Trapp raises precisely this issue when he comes to Matthew 23:37: "How could they perish," he asks, "whom God would have [to be] saved?" He is clearly aware, moreover, of the Arminian claim that God antecedently wills to save all but consequently saves only some, on grounds of faith, and he turns the Arminian distinction on its head:

---

527. Wendelin, *Christianae theologiae libri duo*, I.i.18 (5).

528. See Arminius, *Declaration of Sentiments*, in Works, I, pp. 653-654; cf. idem, *Certain Articles*, in Works, II, pp. 718-719; *Public Disputations*, IV.lix-lxii.

529. Rijssen, *Summa theol.*, III.xxxi, controversia 1, arg. 1-4.

530. Cf. Muller, *God, Creation, and Providence*, pp. 185-189.

It is answered, *Voluntas Dei alia est praecepti, revelata antecedens, alia beneplaciti, arcana consequens*. By the former God willed their conversion, but not by the latter. A king wills the welfare of all his subjects; yet he will not acquit those that are laid up for treason, murder, and the like foul crimes.[531]

The preceptive will of God is revealed antecedently to indicate the promise of salvation to God's obedient children; the ultimate divine good pleasure to allow some to perish is hidden until the event. Thus, the preceptive will appears antecedently in the temporal order, the ultimate will consequently, following out the logical rule and order of means and ends.[532] Rijssen argues similarly that the text does not state that God willed to scatter those whom he had previously willed to gather together, but only that Christ wished to gather those who were his, while the leaders of the people wished otherwise. The leaders of the people did not prevent Christ ultimately from gathering to himself those who were his: Jerusalem must here be distinguished from God's children, granting that the text follows upon Christ's discourse (vv. 13-36) against the scribes and Pharisees who, as Christ himself previously states, would not inherit the kingdom of heaven. Thus, "the will with which this verse is concerned is not the decretive will [*voluntas decreti*], which is one and simple, but the preceptive will, which refers to man's calling and which is often made known publicly."[533]

These seven pairs of distinctions — *voluntas beneplaciti et signi; voluntas decreti et praecepti; voluntas eudokias et euarestias; voluntas immanens et transiens; voluntas arcana et revelata; voluntas absoluta et conditionata; voluntas antecedens et consequens* — raise the question of whether or not there is an antecedent cause of the will of God itself. Of course, comments Wendelin, when the term *voluntas Dei* is used to indicate the object of God's willing, which is to say, something outside of God, there is no controversy: a distinction is made, then, between will understood as *quod vult Deus*, "what God wills," and the *voluntas qua vult Deus*, the "will by which God wills." When the latter is indicated, Wendelin notes, whether it refers to "the primary actuality (*actus primus*) or faculty" or to "the secondary actuality (*actus secundus*) or action," it must be acknowledged that "to the extent that [the will] is in God, it is nothing other than God himself willing (*ipse Deus volens*)."[534]

Granting this assumption, the will of God can have no cause external to it, whether instrumental, or impulsive, or final. After all, God is the cause of all things and is himself uncaused — and there can be nothing prior to or greater than the will of God. So also, is the "will of God" — granting that it is *ipse Deus volens* — "independent being (*ens independens*), which is always in actuality and never in potency: and for anything to be caused, in the proper sense of the term, it must depend on and "be in potency with respect to" the cause. Similarly, there can be no instrumental causality prior to the

531. Trapp, *Commentary on the Old and New Testaments*, in loc. (vol. V, p. 244).
532. Cf. Poole, *Commentary*, in loc., with Calvin, *Harmony of the Evangelists*, in loc. (*CTS Harmony*, III, p. 109).
533. Rijssen, *Summa theol.*, III.xxxi, controversia, obj. 1.
534. Wendelin, *Christianae theologiae libri duo*, I.i.18 (6).

will of God, inasmuch as the will of God is "the immediate, eternal action of God." Any such instrumental cause would have to be either uncreated or created — but it could not be "uncreated, since there is nothing uncreated beside God," not could it be "created, since there is no creature coeternal with God." In other words, an eternal act and action, such as is the will of God, can only be understood as immediate. As for the notion of an external *causa impulsiva*, this causality implies an external impulse to action, which in turn implies change in the being that is impelled, but this too is ruled out in God.[535] The identity of God likewise rules out the possibility of the divine will having an external final cause. God is the first and ultimate unmoved mover *(principium movens immobile)*, and it is clear that anything that itself has a final cause cannot be the final cause of mediate or finite wills: in other words, if God is to be understood in any genuine sense as the final cause of all things, then there can be no final cause of the will of God.[536]

F. The *Ad Extra* Distinctions.

1. *Decretum sive voluntas de futuris* and *voluntas de praesentibus*. The eternal decree of God is not to be distinguished essentially from the divine will — it is not, in other words, a kind of willing in God that differs fundamentally from the divine willing in general, nor does it, considered as an internal work of the Godhead (*opus Dei internum sive ad intra*), stand apart from the *voluntas Dei*. From the perspective of the divine essence, which is to say, of the eternal God who performs his work, all of God's acts are eternal. Yet, from the perspective of their effects and objects, God's acts are temporal — some are past, some present, some future. Thus, some distinction can and must be made between the eternal decree of God concerning all things and events in the temporal order and the will of God concerning actual effects at the moment of their existence in time. As Baxter indicates, "God's decrees *de futuris* and his will *de praesentibus* are in themselves the same, save as to the extrinsick denomination from the divers state of connoted objects."[537] A distinction must be made, therefore, between the divine decree or decrees that determine all things in their necessity, contingency, and freedom and the volition of God that actualizes specific temporal effects in the present.[538] This point is parallel to the point made in the discussion of divine eternity, that God's eternity coexists with all moments in time without rendering those moments coexistent with one another: if, as Turretin indicated, eternity "does not coexist with [all moments in time] taken together and existing all at once, but coexists with them dividedly and mutually succeeding each other," then the divine willing, albeit utterly eternal and undivided in itself can be conceived as also effecting discrete moments in time in an act of willing that, from the perspective

---

535. Wendelin, *Christianae theologiae libri duo*, I.i.18 (6).

536. Wendelin, *Christianae theologiae libri duo*, I.i.18 (6), citing, among others, Aquinas, *Summa theol.*, Ia, q. 19, art. 5, and Zanchi, *De natura Dei*, III.4.11; Tylenus, *Syntagma*, I, disp. 13, sec. 26; and Maccovius, *Volum. thes.*, I, disp. 27, sec. 8.

537. Baxter, *Catholike Theologie*, I.xiii, §274 (p. 45).

538. Baxter, *Catholike Theologie*, I.xiii, §275 (p. 45).

of the temporal moments themselves, can be understood "dividedly and mutually succeeding" itself in its relation to its objects.[539]

2. Voluntas decernens sive efficax and voluntas praecipiens sive moralis. The decretive and effective will of God, in Heidegger's words, is "the deepest cause of events and of the existence of all things"[540] and is always fulfilled. The moral will of God, by contrast, is the rule by which good and evil are distinguished and is often not effective in determining the life or actions of God's creatures. The orthodox insist that the preceptive will of God is effectual in the sense that God does reveal all of his precepts — so that there is no barrier to or limit on the will to reveal or lay down a rule of conduct. God does in fact establish the precepts according to which righteousness is determined and according to which salvation might be merited. Yet, his preceptive will is often ignored by his rational creatures. As Mastricht indicates, the decretive or effective will of God determines events de facto while the preceptive, moral, or legislative will of God establishes the rules of conduct de jure.[541] The Reformed orthodox here cite the passage in Augustine's *Enchiridion* where a contrast is made between a good son who prays for the health of his dying father and an evil son who wishes the death of his dying father: the former is obedient to the preceptive will of God and, unwittingly, out of accord with the decretive will — whereas the latter stands, just as unwittingly, in accord with the decretive will, but is consciously disobedient to the divine precept. The former son is righteous, but the latter is sinful and will be held accountable before God.[542]

3. Voluntas efficax and voluntas inefficax. The problem of an antecedent and consequent will in God raises a further, deeper question, typically debated with the Arminians.[543] An underlying assumption in all of the distinctions accepted by the Reformed orthodox was the consistency and inalterability of the divine willing, an assumption directly at odds the notion of a *voluntas antecedens* and a differing *voluntas consequens*. In refutation of that distinction, the Reformed had announced as one of their arguments the omnipotence of God — but what of the possibility that God's will can be distinguished into *voluntas efficax* and *voluntas inefficax*? This latter distinction is ill chosen, but will stand if it refers the effectual will of God to the decree and the ineffectual will to the divine precepts, the former being incapable of resistance and the latter resisted successfully by all evildoers. If a distinction between effective and ineffective will is sought in the *voluntas decreti* itself, this is repugnant and deeply in error, inasmuch as it attributes to God "moments of willing (*velleitates*) and unfulfilled desires," namely, failures of purpose and unaccomplished intentions. Such attributions, moreover, accuse God either of ignorance or of impotence — for they imply either that he does not know of a particular event or its impossibility or that he is not able

539. Turretin, *Inst. theol. elencticae*, III.xi.8.

540. Heidegger, *Corpus theologiae*, III.74 (cited in Heppe, *Reformed Dogmatics*, p. 88); cf. Witsius, *Exercitationes*, xiii.18, 20.

541. Mastricht, *Theoretico-practica theol.*, II.xiv.8; cf. Heppe, *Reformed Dogmatics*, pp. 88-89.

542. Augustine, *Enchiridion*, cap. 101.

543. Amyraut et al., *Syntagma thesium theologicarum*, IV.viii.2, 22.

"to effect what he intended."[544] The eternal counsel of God is immutable and his will cannot be resisted — as both Isaiah (46:10) and Paul (Rom. 9:19) testify. Furthermore, "an ineffective will cannot be attributed to God, since it would imply either a divine ignorance, which does not know events that are not going to follow, or an impotence, which is not able to effect what it intends."[545] This distinction, Turretin indicates, is in effect the other side of a particularly bad coin — the notion of an ineffectual will fails for the same reason that the notion of an unfulfilled antecedent will fails. Nor, indeed, are the various texts of Scripture used by Arminians and Socinians to support the concept of an ineffective divine willing to the point — not, "unless we chose to adopt the deleriums of the Anthropomorphites!"[546]

4. *Voluntas efficiens sive effectiva* and *voluntas permittens sive permissiva*. The will of God is also distinguished into *voluntas efficiens* and *voluntas permittens*. The first of these is the will by which God directly accomplishes all things, whether through his own efficient causality alone or "coefficiently" operating not only through but with secondary causes; the second, that will of God whereby he permits evil or sin by not impeding their accomplishment and by not withdrawing the divine *concursus* required for the existence of things.[547] The permissive will is, thus, not directly causal, but no sin could occur without it. Heidanus, Rijssen, and others state this division without controversy — though it is surely one point on which the Reformed came to differ with Calvin and to follow the line set forth by Vermigli and others. Heidanus understands this distinction specifically as a distinction in the working of the *voluntas beneplaciti*.[548] Quite simply,

> There are some things which God wills to do, that are good, but others which he neither does nor can do, because they are evil, which, however, he permits to be done, and which he then directs to good ends; thus he permits men to sin, but he is not the author of sin; on the contrary he most strongly forbids it.[549]

This permission, moreover, must not be understood as a direct, albeit negative, willing of evils: "defects are permitted by God, not effects."[550] Thus, specifically,

> to permit doth sometime signifie not to hinder or stop evil when we may, so God is said to permit sin, because he could by his grace, hinder and prevent sins that none should be committed; and yet he doth willingly permit us in our nature to sin: That

---

544. Turretin, *Inst, theol. elencticae*, III.xvi.15; cf. Heidanus, *Corpus theol.*, II (pp. 138, 144); Amyraut et al., *Syntagma thesium theologicarum*, IV.viii.32; Rijssen, *Summa theol.*, III.xxxi, controversia II.

545. Rijssen, *Summa theol.*, III.xxxi, controversia II, argumenta; cf. Maccovius, *Distinctiones et regulae*, IV.xxxvi.

546. Turretin, *Inst. theol. elencticae*, III.xvi.17.

547. Heereboord, *Meletemata philosophica*, Disputatio XXIII, *de voluntate Dei*, ix (p. 124).

548. Heidanus, *Corpus theol.*, II (p. 138); Rijssen, *Summa theol.*, III.xxvi ; cf. Ussher, *Body of Divinity*, p. 51; Hottinger, *Cursus theologicus*, III.xii, canon B (p. 52).

549. Pictet, *Theol. chr.*, II.vi.4.

550. Greenhill, *Exposition of Ezekiel*, p. 758, col. 2.

God doth thus permit sin, it is evident by these places in scripture, Ps. 81:11-12; Acts 14:16. That he doth permit them willingly, and not constrained thereunto, these places do shew, Rom. 9:19; Is. 46:10.[551]

This assumption also creates a contrast between the divine permission and the revealed will of God in the law, but a contrast that must not be absolutized: "These two wills, although they are viewed by us as different, are yet by no means contrary to each other, because they are not directed to the same object."[552] Thus "God had decreed that Abraham should not sacrifice his son, and yet he commanded him to sacrifice his son," the former will of God tending toward his ultimate purpose, the latter for the limited purpose of trying Abraham's faith.[553] The divine permission thus appears as a concept necessary to the understanding of the *voluntas moralis*, but clearly not identical with it: for the moral will of God relates to things external to God which are good and evil, but it does not itself include "permission" to do evil. God discerns the acts of men and permits them to occur freely, although he both commands and directly or effectively wills only the good.[554]

5. *Voluntas efficiens & effectiva* and *voluntas approbans & approbativa*. Maccovius cites this distinction as representing Arminian views and declares it "empty" or "meaningless" in its application to the problem of God's saving will. Thus it is meaningless to argue that God approvingly wills the salvation of all and singular individuals but then effectively wills only the salvation of some — or, alternatively, that God approvingly but not effectively wills the means of salvation to lead the reprobate to salvation.[555] Nonetheless, it bears a certain resemblance to the distinction between *voluntas eudokias* and *voluntas euarestias*, where the former term indicates the effective decree of God and the latter will by which God declares what is approved by or pleasing to him — and, therefore, could be used in a Reformed sense.[556] Rutherford uses such a distinction, identifying God's "will of approbation" as God's willing approval of repentance, obedience, and belief, in contrast to the effective will of God's good pleasure that decrees or appoints all things.[557] Here, in the Reformed approach to the distinction, the *voluntas approbans* is identical with the revealed, preceptive will of God, but is nuanced to indicate the divine relationship to the human objects of the various precepts and commands, over against the Arminian approach to the distinction in which the *voluntas approbans* parallels the *voluntas antecedens* in representing a divine intention that is not fulfilled.

6. *Voluntas ordinans* and *voluntas gubernans*. The *voluntas ordinans*, or ordaining will of God, is the divine will considered as establishing the order of all things,

---

551. Ussher, *Body of Divinity*, p. 59.

552. Pictet, *Theol. chr.*, II.vi.5.

553. Pictet, *Theol. chr.*, II.vi.5.

554. Cf. Rijssen, *Summa theol.*, III.xxxii.

555. Maccovius, *Loci communes*, xxiii (p. 184, col. 1); cf. Maccovius, *Distinctiones et regulae*, IV.xxxv.

556. Cf. Turretin, *Inst. theol. elencticae*, III.xv.8-9.

557. Rutherford, *Covenant of Life Opened*, II.x (pp. 341-342).

specifically, the "interconnections of possible things" — with possibility being understood as the contingent reality of the temporal process. This ordaining will both determines the obligations under which creatures are placed and approves of the virtuous conjunction of human willing with the divine commandments. It thus comprehends the preceptive and the approbative wills of God. It is juxtaposed with the *voluntas gubernans*, the governing will of God that orders and disposes what will come to be: specifically, the governing will of God is the divine decree considered in its exercise.[558]

7. *Voluntas obligationis sive praecepti* and *voluntas euarestias sive approbans.* This distinction, as implied in the foregoing paragraph, stands as a subset of the *voluntas ordinans.* The ordaining will of God comprises both the obligations or precepts that govern the universal order of things and the approbation accorded to the voluntary and righteous obedience to the precepts or fulfillment of the obligations.[559]

8. *Voluntas legalis* and *voluntas evangelica.* A further distinction also appears under the category of *voluntas revelata* — the distinction between *voluntas legalis* and *voluntas evangelica.*

> The revealed will of God is two-fold: the one is that which is properly revealed in the Law, that is, what God requireth to be done of us: and therefore it is called the Law.... The other is the Gospel, which sheweth Gods will towards us, and what he hath decreed of us in his eternal counsel as touching our salvation.[560]

Thus, the *voluntas legalis* or *voluntas moralis* is that by which he commands virtuous life, punishes wickedness, and rewards the good; the *voluntas evangelica* is the saving will of God as revealed in the promises of the gospel.[561]

G. The *Voluntas Dei*: Continuities, Developments, and Uses

Unlike the doctrine of the *scientia Dei*, where for the most part scholastic distinctions hovered in the educational background of the thought of the Reformers, to be revived by the Reformed orthodox in polemic, the Reformed orthodox doctrine of the *voluntas Dei* and the distinctions found in it stand in fairly explicit continuity with the teaching of the Reformers. Not only have we seen distinctions such as the secret and revealed will, the will of divine good pleasure and the will of the sign carry over from the Reformation into orthodoxy, we have also seen a maintenance of the sense of these distinctions, with reference to the insistence on a single divine will, to the use of the distinctions to maintain a monergistic understanding of grace and predestination, and to the understanding of the freedom of God and the contingency and free choice of creatures. Certainly, orthodoxy brought a more philosophical and scholastic discussion of the problem, largely in the interest of precision. Contra the older scholarship, this scholastic development did not result in a system of theology any more grounded in

558. Van Til, *Theol. comp. rev.*, I.ii (pp. 38-39).

559. Van Til, *Theol. comp. rev.*, I.ii (p. 9).

560. Ussher, *Body of Divinity*, p. 52; cf. Zanchi, *De natura Dei*, III.iv, q. 2, thesis (col. 243).

561. Rijssen, *Summa theol.*, III.xxvi.

the divine willing than the theology of the Reformers, nor did it present a theology that was "speculative" in either the sense of the term used by Armstrong or in the sense of the term found in the sixteenth- and seventeenth-century documents. In other words, the scholastic doctrine of the divine will does not contain a significant amount of philosophical or metaphysical elaboration beyond the bounds of the Reformers teaching nor does it imply an interest in either a knowledge to be grasped as an end in itself or an attempt to pry into divine mysteries.[562] The Reformed orthodox, certainly, did add precision to the discussion of the divine will by the elaboration of traditional distinctions. This scholastic precision, however, did not result, either necessarily or typically, in a divorce between theology and piety, doctrinal statement and churchly "use."

God's will is a great comfort to believers in the midst of adversity: since God's will is free and not bound to temporal things, nothing can happen to believers apart from the good pleasure of their heavenly Father. Given this comfort, we are not to endeavor to pry into God's secrets, but rather are to

> be afraid to sin against God, who can punish how he will, when he will, and where he will; God wills seriously the conversion of all men, by the preaching of the word, *voluntate approbationis*, by way of allowance, but not *voluntate effectionis & intentionis*, not effectually, by way of full intention to work it in them.[563]

The will and power of God relate directly to the question of righteousness or holiness. Rijssen poses the question "Whether the will of God is the basic rule of all righteousness," noting as the underlying issue "Whether things are good because God wills, or truly whether God wills things because they are good?"[564] In respect to us the source of all righteousness is the will of God — and, argues Rijssen, in the following sense: "The will of God is the highest rule of righteousness or justice, and therefore whatever God wills is for that reason just and good, because God wills it."[565] The will of God, in turn, corresponds with his most holy nature. This determination of the relationship of will and justice, placing as it does primacy in the will of God, manifests a Scotist or nominalist rather than a Thomist element in the Reformed conception of the divine nature, but it does not, as often claimed in older scholarship, indicate an utter arbitrariness on God's part.[566]

It is precisely this pronounced sense of the continuity between God's intention and will and the execution or revelation of God's intention and will that allows the Reformed orthodox to include a strong a posteriori element in their doctrine of the divine attributes. Since the distinction between an antecedent and a consequent will in God is denied and since the utter sovereignty of will and immutability of purpose

---

562. Armstrong, *Calvinism and the Amyraut Heresy*, p. 32; and see the discussion of the meaning of "speculative" as a modifier of "theology" in *PRRD*, I, 7.3 (B.2).

563. Leigh, *Treatise*, II.viii (pp. 69-70).

564. Rijssen, *Summa theol.*, III.xxxiii.

565. Rijssen, *Summa theol.*, III.xxxiii.

566. Cf. Biel, *Collectorium*, I, d. 43, q. 1, art. 4 cor.

is reflected with precision in the created order, the divine revelation of God's identity and purpose, the divine dispensation of grace and mercy, justice and punishment can become a ground or basis for the discussion of the unity and Trinity, the essence and attributes of God. Without this consistency in will and execution, the entire revelation is placed in doubt and the a posteriori pattern of argument rendered impossible. In short, the Arminian (at least according to the logic of orthodoxy) can know nothing surely of the identity and intention of God, who God is, and what he wills.

6

Attributes Relating to the Manifestation and Exercise of the Divine Will

6.1 The Righteousness, Holiness, Goodness, Truth, and Faithfulness of God

A. The Righteousness or Justice of God

1. The righteousness of God in the theology of the Reformers. Reformed discussion of the justice or righteousness of God also bears out the broad thesis of a continuity in basic theological framework from the Middle Ages into the Reformation and the era of orthodoxy as well as in debate over the ramifications of the doctrine. Like the concept of will in God, the concept of righteousness or justice was explained and nuanced with a series of distinctions, many of which rested on different usages in Scripture as well as on the logical problems involved in relating divine to human righteousness and on the theological problem of divine transcendence. The various issues and problems that are addressed in the course of Reformed discussion of the *iustitia Dei* arise as much out of the exegetical tradition as out of the controversies of the scholastic era of Protestantism. Thus, we find Zwingli meditating on the relationship of God to the righteousness demanded by the law in a way that very nearly places God *ex lex* or beyond the law — and we encounter, in Calvin's theology, a discussion of the *duplex iustitia* or twofold righteousness of God in which the Reformer explicitly denies that God can be *ex lex*.[1] In addition, the problem of the righteousness of God stands at the heart of the Reformation preaching of justification by grace through faith alone and of the Protestant doctrine of the work of Christ and its satisfaction of the demands of divine justice. These doctrinal relationships between the *iustitia Dei*,

---

1. Zwingli, *On Providence*, pp. 168-9; Calvin, *Institutes*, III.xxiii.2; idem, *Sermons sur le Livre de Iob*, in CO, 34, 331-344. See Susan E. Schreiner, "Exegesis and Double Justice in Calvin's Sermons on Job," in *Church History*, 58 (1989), pp. 322-338; and cf. Steinmetz, *Calvin in Context*, pp. 40-52.

justification, and Christ's satisfaction for sin remained at the center of development and debate throughout the era of orthodoxy.

Musculus' substantial discussion of the *iustitia Dei* begins with a brief comment connecting this particular *locus* with those preceding it: proper consideration of the justice or righteousness of God depends on the understanding of the attributes that he has discussed immediately before it, namely, truth, goodness, love, mercy, power, and dominion. He indicates that he does not intend to discuss justice in general, much less the justice or righteousness that belongs to human beings: rather he proposes to offer a discussion of the incomprehensible *iustitia Dei*, which is so transcendent that it cannot be fully understood by any of the angels, not to mention human beings. The topic, therefore, is limited by the small capacity of the human mind and by the requirements of our salvation: we can know no more than we are given to know for the sake of our salvation.[2] Given that the knowledge that God is just does not arise uniformly from the acts of God and that the universal testimony of conscience to the divine justice against sin provides only minimal knowledge, the full revelation of God's justice or righteousness comes only from Scripture. There it is revealed both by direct statement of the doctrine and by a multitude of examples. The Psalms and the Prophets testify explicitly to the *iustitia Dei*, whether the justice of God himself, the justice of his judgments, the justice of all God's works and ways, or the justice of God's commandments to his people.[3] So, too, does the entire order of the universe declare the righteousness of God — given that the order itself would be overthrown if God were not "just in all things."[4]

The definition of the *iustitia Dei*, moreover, depends on an understanding of what precisely it means to be "just" — and when one is "just," one is "sound and upright" in accord with his proper "office and person": thus, a just judge rightly and with impartiality determines guilt and innocence, and a just king administers his kingdom rightly to the support of his subjects. These considerations not only point toward the meaning of the statement that "God is just," they also point toward the fact that a suitable definition of the righteousness of God rests on a right understanding of God himself: unless we know that it means for God to be God and for God to be Lord and Judge, we cannot understand the justice or righteousness of God.[5] Inasmuch as the "office" or work of God is the creation of all things out of nothing, the governance and preservation of the order, the *iustitia Dei* is the power by which God rightly accomplishes these ends — and it stands in intimate relationship with the identification of God as the highest good, from whom all things come and by whom they are preserved.[6]

---

2. Musculus, *Loci communes*, li (*Commonplaces*, p. 997, col. 2-p. 998, col. 1); similarly, cf. Calvin, *Sermons upon the Book of Job*, sermon 58, p. 273, col. 1.

3. Musculus, *Loci communes*, li (*Commonplaces*, p. 998, cols. 1-2), citing Deut. 32:4; Isa. 45:21; Jer. 12:1; Dan. 9:7; Zeph. 3:5; 2 Sam. 23:3.

4. Musculus, *Loci communes*, li (*Commonplaces*, p. 998, col. 2).

5. Musculus, *Loci communes*, li (*Commonplaces*, p. 999, cols. 1-2).

6. Musculus, *Loci communes*, li (*Commonplaces*, p. 1000, col. 1).

Calvin makes a distinction between the justice or righteousness of God in himself and the justice or righteousness of God's works that will be precisely reflected in the Reformed orthodox exposition of the doctrine.[7] He also, however, declaims sharply against any use of the distinction between *potentia absoluta* and *potentia ordinata* to define the divine transcendence as *ex lex*.[8] Such doctrine is "a devilish blasphemy forged in Hell" because it violates the fundamental assumption of the inseparability of the divine attributes: God is not a tyrant whose power can run contrary to his righteousness.[9] There is a divine "righteousness more perfect than that of the Law" — but there is no divine power beyond or outside of the divine righteousness. By way of contrast, "we must say that God has an infinite or endless power which, notwithstanding, is the rule of all righteousness ... for it would be to rend God in pieces to make him almighty without being all-righteous."[10] The divine *potentia* or *voluntas* is the rule of all righteousness and that righteousness issues from God: there is no rule of righteousness prior to God, but inasmuch as his righteousness is essential, it is also consistent and never arbitrary in its exercise, albeit not in the sense that it somehow causes the divine willing. Thus, from the other side of the question,

> the divine will ... is itself, and justly ought to be, the cause of all that exists. For if his will has any cause, there must be something antecedent to it, and to which it is annexed; this it were impious to imagine. The will of God is the supreme rule of righteousness, so that everything which he wills must be held to be righteous by the mere fact of his willing it.[11]

This divine justice, which, like the divine goodness, is utterly one with the essence and operation of God, can be distinguished in relation to the names of God — specifically, the designations God, Lord, and Judge. Thus, the sole justice of God is, in a sense, "manifold." Scripture clearly attributes *iustitia* to God in the specific sense of the goodness and uprightness of the creator and conserver of all things that pronounces the forgiveness of sins to those who repent — as in Psalm 51:14, "Deliver me from bloodguiltiness, O God, thou God of my salvation: and my tongue shall sing

---

7. Cf. Calvin, *Sermons on Job*, 23:1-7; 34:12-15 (pp. 412-413, 611-612).

8. Calvin, *Institutes*, III.xxiii.2: "Neque tamen commentum ingerimus absolutae potentiae: quod sicuti profanum est, ita merito detestabile nobis esse debet. Non fingimus Deus eslegem, qui sibi lex est ... Dei autem voluntas non modo ab omni vitio pura, sed summa perfectionis regula, etiam legum omnium lex est"; cf. the discussion by Steinmetz, *Calvin in Context*, pp. 40-50. On the history of the concept, see William J. Courtenay, *Capacity and Volition: A History of the Distinction of Absolute and Ordained Power* (Bergamo: P. Lubrina, 1990). Cf. Jean Calvin, *Sermons sur le Livre de Iob*, in CO 34, 331-344; cf. John Calvin, *Sermons of Maister Iohn Calvin, upon the Book of Iob* (London, 1574), especially sermon 88 (pp. 412-416); and see the discussion in Schreiner, *Where Shall Wisdom be Found*, pp. 110-120.

9. Calvin, *Sermons sur le Livre de Iob*, CO, 34, cols. 336, 339; cf. Calvin, *Sermons on Job*, pp. 414, col. 1:2-5; 415, col. 1:44-45.

10. Calvin, *Sermons sur le Livre de Iob*, CO 34, cols. 334, 340; cf. Calvin, *Sermons on Iob*, pp. 413, col. 1:31-32; 415, col. 1:42-49.

11. Calvin, *Institutes*, III.xxiii.2 (Beveridge trans.)

aloud of thy righteousness." This justice or righteousness of God, moreover, not only conserves and preserves all things but also, in Christ, is offered to believers through faith alone for their justification apart from any merits or works:[12] "By the righteousness of God ... we are to understand his goodness; for this attribute, as usually ascribed to God in the Scriptures, does not so much denote the strictness with which he exacts vengeance, as his faithfulness in fulfilling the promises and extending help to all who seek him in the hour of need."[13]

God is also just as "Lord and Master." This form or aspect of the divine *iustitia* is revealed in the "dominion, and full power, property, and possession, by which God governs all things in heaven and earth." According to this justice, God freely has mercy on some, hardens others, and wills his pure good-pleasure in all things.[14] There is an overarching dispositive justice of God in the law and governance of all things as well as the justice that punishes sin.[15] It is this *iustitia* to which the apostle Paul refers in Romans 9, when he queries "is there any injustice in God?" and then declares, "God forbid." Because of his perfect "power of proper right and dominion," God cannot be accused of injustice — indeed, the perfection of God's power utterly excludes injustice from his will, his works, and his precepts. Where there is no wrong, Musculus declares, there can be no injustice: whether God loves and saves or hates and destroys, he does so only to what is his own, thus declaring either his "special goodness and mercy" or his "most just power and authority."[16]

Third, God is just as Judge. Again, the Psalms declare this truth consistently — "the heavens declare his righteousness: for God is judge himself" (Ps. 50:6) — and the Apostle Paul also calls the Lord "the righteous judge" (2 Tim. 4:8). Thus, God loves righteousness and hates iniquity, as is evidenced by all of the commandments in the law. God, moreover, judges both in words and in acts, exercising anger against evil and mercy toward the good.[17] The implication of the psalm is that there is a punitive or vindicatory justice in God: "God will make known his righteousness in due time from above, and vindicate it from the dishonors done to it by your wicked inventions."[18] Calvin's numerous comments on the justice or righteousness of God typically identify it as either dispositive or distributive,[19] and he explicitly divided

---

12. Musculus, *Loci communes*, li (*Commonplaces*, p. 1000, col. 2), also citing Ps. 69:10; 116:5; 145:7-8; and Rom. 3:21-22.

13. Calvin, *Commentary upon the Psalms*, 51:14 (*CTS Psalms*, I, pp. 302-3).

14. Musculus, *Loci communes*, li (*Commonplaces*, p. 1001, col. 1-2).

15. Cf. Calvin, *Sermons on Job*, 23:1-7; 34:12-15 (pp. 412-413, 611-612).

16. Musculus, *Loci communes*, li (*Commonplaces*, p. 1001, cols. 1-2).

17. Musculus, *Loci communes*, li (*Commonplaces*, p. 1001, col. 2-p. 1002, col. 2).

18. Calvin, *Commentary upon the Psalms*, 50:6 (*CTS Psalms*, I, p. 265).

19. Cf. Calvin, *Commentary upon the Psalms*, with reference largely to dispositive justice: 36:6; 40:10 (*CTS Psalms*, II, pp. 9-10, 106); with reference primarily to distributive justice: 7:16; 36:10; 71:15 (*CTS Psalms*, I, p. 91; II, p. 13; III, pp. 90-91); with reference to both, viz., as preservation and reward or defense: 5:8; 7:17; 22:31; 48:10; 103:17; 145:17 (*CTS Psalms*, I, pp. 59, 92, 389; II, pp. 229-230; IV, p. 139; V, pp. 280-281).

distributive justice into reward and punishment.[20] (Incidentally, inasmuch as the distinction between a universal dispositive and a particular distributive justice derives from Aristotle's *Nichomachean Ethics*,[21] we see here yet another example of a latent Aristotelianism in the Reformers' thought that stands as a point of continuity with the older tradition and that carries over as a clear evidence of continuity into later Reformed orthodoxy.)

So also, although Calvin did not face the problem posed by the seventeenth-century Socinians, who denied that punitive or vindicatory justice was an essential attribute, he certainly held that God never relinquishes this particular attribute:

> He farther means by this expression, that it is impossible for God to abdicate the office and authority of judge; a truth which he expresses more clearly in the second clause of the verse, *He hath prepared his throne for judgment*, in which he declares that God reigns not only for the purpose of making his majesty and glory surpassingly great, but also for the purpose of governing the world in righteousness.[22]

When the wicked "endeavor, in all the transactions and concerns of their life, to remove him to the greatest distance, and to efface from their minds all apprehension of his majesty," God is then "dragged from his throne, and divested of his character as judge, impiety has come to its utmost height."[23]

2. *Iustitia Dei*: basic definitions of the Reformed orthodox. There was little debate in the seventeenth century over the basic declaration that God is just or righteous. God's justice can be argued from Scripture under five categories: affirmatively, negatively, affectively, symbolically, and effectively.[24] Thus,

> The Scripture proves the justice of God,
> (1) Affirmatively, when it calls him just, a revenger, holy, right, and extolls his justice, *Exod.* 9:27; Psalm 11:7; Jer. 12:1.
> (2) Negatively, when it removes from him injustice and iniquity, respect of persons, and receiving of gifts, and also all the causes and effects of injustice, *Deut.* 32:4; 10:17; Dan. 9:14; Job 8:3.
> (3) Affectively, when it attributes to him zeal, anger, fury, *Exod.* 20:5 & 32:10; Numb. 11:10, which are not in God such passions as they be in us, but an act of the immutable justice.
> (4) Symbolically, when it calls him a consuming fire, Deut. 4:24; compares him to an angry Lion, an armed Soldier, Is. 38:13; [42:13].
> (5) Effectively, when it affirms that he renders to everyone according to his works, 1 Sam. 26:23.[25]

---

20. Calvin, *Sermons on Job*, 9:23 (p. 165, col. 2.59-62)
21. Aristotle, *Nichomachean Ethics*, 1130B-1131A; cf. Copleston, *History of Philosophy*, I, pp. 341-343; G. E. R. Lloyd, *Aristotle: The Growth and Structure of His Thought* (Cambridge: Cambridge University Press, 1968), pp. 223-224.
22. Calvin, *Commentary on the Psalms*, 9:7 (CTS Psalms, I, p. 117).
23. Calvin, *Commentary on the Psalms*, 14:1 (CTS Psalms, I, p. 191).
24. Leigh, *Treatise*, II.xii (p. 92, citing Gerhard's *Loci communes*).
25. Leigh, *Treatise*, II.xii (p. 92).

By definition,

> *Justice* [is the attribute] by which God in all things wills that which is just; or it is the
> Attribute whereby God is just in and of himself, and exercises justice toward all
> creatures, and giveth every one his due, Is. 45:21; Psalm 11:7; Gen. 18:25, Zeph. 3:5;
> Rom. 2:6, 7; 1 Pet. 1:17; 2 Thess. 1:6, 7; 2 Tim. 4:8; 1 John 1:9 & 2:29. Justice in man
> is a settled will to do right in everything to every person, so God hath a settled will
> to do right. *Shall not the Judge of all the world do right?* [Gen 18:25] and *are not my ways
> equal?* God styles himself by this title, and gives himself this Attribute, Zeph. 3:5.[26]

In the precise language of Wendelin, *"Justitia est qua Deus in se sanctus & justus est,
& extra se constanti voluntate suum cuique tribuit"* — "righteousness is [that attribute]
by which God is holy and just in himself, and which is consistently to be attributed
to his will toward externals."[27] Again we encounter the underlying refrain of the
Reformed doctrine of the divine attributes — the *ad intra* identification of a distinct
attribute as the foundation of the *ad extra* manifestation of the divine.

If the scriptural predications were acceptable to nearly all, definitions such as these
raised considerable controversy. The Socinians argued that punitive or vindicatory
righteousness was not an essential property of God but rather a voluntary exercise
of the divine righteousness *ad extra* — indicating, by extension, that God was under
no necessity to punish sin. Against the Socinians, the Reformed were in agreement
that the justice or righteousness of God "is not a quality or accident in him, but his
very nature, essential to him."[28] As with all the attributes, the *justitia Dei* cannot be
really or substantively distinguished from the *essentia Dei*: God may equally well be
said to be "just" and to be "justice" or "righteousness" itself. Thus, by definition, the
divine justice or righteousness is one of the virtues of the divine will, specifically, the
virtue "by which God is in himself holy and just and has the constant will of giving
to each his due."[29] Given the identity between the divine justice and the divine essence,
the identification of righteousness as a virtue in God meets with a qualification: it is
not to be understood as a variable disposition or *habitus*, like a human virtue, but as
a perfection of the divine essence itself. "A man may be a man and yet be unjust; but
God cannot be God and be unjust": since purity and justice are the "very essence and
being" of God, when you attempt to "destroy or deny the purity and justice of God,
... you put God out of the world, as much as in you lies: for he cannot be God, unless
he be both just to others and pure in himselfe."[30] "Absolutely considered," the justice
or righteousness of God "is the universal *rectitude and perfection* of the divine nature

---

26. Leigh, *Treatise*, II.xii (p. 91).

27. Wendelin, *Christianae theologiae libri duo*, I.i.26; and cf. the marginal citation by Leigh, *Treatise*,
II.xii (p. 91).

28. Leigh, *Treatise*, II.xii (p. 92, margin); cf. Voetius, *Selectarum disputationum theologicarum*, I, xix-
xxi; also Caryl, *Exposition upon the Book of Job*, 4:17, in loc. (II, pp. 112-113).

29. Turretin, *Inst. theol. elencticae*, III.xix.1.

30. Caryl, *Exposition upon the Book of Job*, 4:17, in loc. (II, p. 113); cf. Leigh, *Treatise*, II.xii (p. 92,
margin), the maxim repeated verbatim.

... antecedent to all acts of his will and suppositions of objects towards which it might operate."[31] Since this righteousness is prior not to the *voluntas Dei* itself but to all free acts of will (*libera voluntatis actum*), it follows that the divine righteousness or justice is in God prior to his free eternal decree (*ante liberum decretum*). There can, therefore, be no opposition between the decree and the righteousness of God.[32]

A great number of the Reformed writers also remark, with various nuances, the connection between righteousness and holiness: Ridgley states that the two attributes "differ but little," holiness representing "the contrariety of [God's] nature to sin, justice [the] external and visible display of that opposition."[33] For Mastricht, they are related concepts, justice indicating the abhorrence of moral impurity, holiness proclivity to the moral good.[34] For Brakel, "righteousness" in God is the "rightness" or "justice, perfection, and holiness of the divine nature."[35] For Caryl, the direct correlate of justice is purity — and both belong to God essentially, therefore also infinitely and perfectly.[36]

God's justice, moreover, is utterly impartial. He does not hesitate to punish the multitudes of Sodom and Gomorrah or of the Noahic age of the world as well as individual sinners. Nor does he exempt the great and mighty from his judgment or even those who are near to him — as his people, the Jews and their leaders: Moses and David were punished and the nation of Israel was cast off because of its iniquity.[37] Beyond the impartiality of God's justice is its inexorability:

> His justice is ... inexorable: no sinners can escape being punished; the sins of the godly are punished in their surety Christ, and they are afflicted in this life. God is justice itself, justice is essential to him, his will is the rule of justice, a thing is just because he willeth it, and not he willeth it because it is just. He will right the wrongs of his children, 2 Thess. 1:6, 7, 8. He cannot be corrupted or bribed.[38]

As a corollary to this impartiality and absolute essential justice, it can also be asserted that "God is so just, so pure in himselfe, that he neither doth nor can doe wrong to any creature." This claim is true, moreover, both de facto in the sense that God has never done wrong, but also *de posse*, in the sense that God cannot do wrong. God's omnipotence, thus, is defined and limited by his essential justice, inasmuch as God lacks the "naturall power" to do wrong — "this impotencie (if we may so call it) is the strength of God."[39]

---

31. Owen, *Dissertation on Divine Justice*, in *Works*, X, p. 498.

32. Voetius, *Selectarum disputationum theologicarum*, I.xix (pp. 365-366).

33. Ridgley, *Body of Divinity* (1855), I, p. 106.

34. Mastricht, *Theoretico-practica theol.*, II.xviii.1.

35. Brakel, *Redelijke Godsdienst*, I.iii.38 (p. 99): "Rechtvaardigheid. Deze kan men aanmerken of in zichzelve, als de rechtheid, volmaaktheid en heiligheid der natuur Gods."

36. Caryl, *Exposition upon the Book of Job*, 4:17, in loc. (II, p. 112).

37. Leigh, *Treatise*, II.xii (p. 93).

38. Leigh, *Treatise*, II.xii (p. 93).

39. Caryl, *Exposition upon the Book of Job*, 4:17, in loc. (II, p. 114).

According to these definitions, the term "justice of God" has two related meanings, corresponding with the two ways of considering the divine activity in general, *ad intra* and *ad extra*. First, in its "universal" sense, the term *iustitia Dei* indicates the perfection of all God's ways and is virtually synonymous with "holiness." Second, it can also signify "that particular justice by which he gives to every man according to his deeds." This second understanding can, by extension, indicate either "the will of God in punishing sinners, and sometimes for the punishment inflicted by justice" or "the *truth* of God in his promises, or for his kindness (*benignitas*)."[40] Owen, similarly, distinguishes between the *iustitia Dei* considered "absolutely, and in itself" and the *iustitia Dei* considered "in respect of its egress and exercise."[41] With reference to the operation or relations of the divine justice *ad extra*, Maccovius indicates that the *iustitia Dei* "is either that of [God's] absolute rule" or "the vindicatory justice" of the divine judgments against sin.[42] The orthodox typically discuss these several connotations in sequence, beginning with the essential justice and then proceeding to elaborate a series of distinctions.

It is worth noting, however, that within this general consensus, there is considerable variety of formulation found among the Reformed orthodox writers — such as over the question of precisely in what sense punitive justice exists in God, whether it is absolute and necessary, or essential to God but nonetheless related to other attributes so as to receive its exercise on a particular supposition, or utterly free so as to obligate God to no particular response to sin. Owen, thus, notes full agreement with Maccovius, general agreement, with some differences in nuance, with Lubbertus and Piscator, and major differences with the views of Twisse and Rutherford.[43] There are also differences over the precise manner of formulating the relationship of righteousness to will and of both to the revealed law.[44]

B. Distinctions in the *Iustitia Dei*

1. The "essential rectitude ... variously considered": the *ad intra/ad extra* dynamic. The varied connotations of "righteousness" in Scripture and the problems inherent in the discussion of essential and manifest, inward and outward righteousness

---

40. Pictet, *Theol. chr.*, II.viii.1; cf. Polanus, *Syntagma theol.*, II.xxvi; Leigh, *Body of Divinity*, II.xii (p. 219); Hottinger, *Cursus theologicus*, III (p. 53); Turretin, *Inst. theol. elencticae*, III.xix.2; Brakel, *Redelijke Godsdienst*, I.iii.38 (pp. 99-100); Manton, *Sermons upon the Fifth Chapter of 2 Corinthians*, in *Works*, 13, p. 73; Van Til, *Theologiae utriusque compendium ... revelatae*, p. 40; Mastricht, *Theoretico-practica theol.*, II.xviii.1; Gill, *Complete Body of Divinity*, I, pp. 153-154; and Heppe, *Reformed Dogmatics*, pp. 95-96.

41. Owen, *Dissertation on Divine Justice*, in *Works*, 10, p. 498.

42. Maccovius, *Loci communes*, xxi (p. 157).

43. Owen, *Dissertation on Divine Justice*, in *Works*, 10, pp. 586, 589-590, 594 (on Maccovius), pp. 586-594, et passim (on Twisse), pp. 594-602 (on Lubbertus), pp. 594, 603-607 (on Piscator), pp. 607-618 (on Rutherford).

44. Cf. Owen, *Dissertation on Divine Justice*, in *Works*, X, pp. 595-618, comparing the differing views of Sibrandus Lubbertus, Johannes Piscator, William Twisse on the *iustitia punitiva* with Baxter, *Catholike Theologie*, part II, pp. 79-80; and note Heppe, *Reformed Dogmatics*, p. 93-95 on the relationship of will, righteousness, and revealed law.

of God led the Reformed orthodox to argue a series of fairly traditional distinctions in the *iustitia Dei*. They also insist, however, that given the essential character of the divine justice, the distinctions that must be made in order to clarify the concept ought not to be understood as distinctions between attributes or as distinctions in the divine essence itself. Owen emphasizes the point: "here again, reader, I would wish to put you in mind that I by no means assert many species of divine justice, or, so to speak, particular or special justices, as distinct perfections in God, which others seem to do, but one only, — namely, the universal and essential rectitude of the divine nature variously considered."[45]

Thus, as in the case of the divine will or divine decree, which the Reformed consistently define as one,[46] the distinctions that can be made concerning the *iustitia Dei* refer, not to the essential rectitude of God itself, but to the diversity of its objects and, typically therefore, to its exercise *ad extra*. Accordingly, Rijssen clarifies the description of the divine justice or righteousness by distinguishing between the perfection of virtues wherein God is recognized as most just and most holy in himself and the justice of God toward externals. Thus, the divine righteousness is considered either *absolute & in se* or as *relate, respectu exercitii*.[47] The absolute justice or righteousness of God is the "rectitude and perfection of the divine nature" itself, which belongs to God essentially, simply because he is God: this justice is called either the *iustitia Dei* or the *iustitia universalis*.[48] As such, it is intimately related to other "virtues" of the divine will: "God's justice comprehends his righteousness and truth" — considered according to its exercise, the divine will is the ultimate rule of right or justice, intimately related to the eternal wisdom of God and manifest throughout his revelation: "he is just in words and deeds."[49]

2. The problem of "double justice" and the *Deus ex lex*. The nearly inevitable distinction between divine righteousness *ad intra* and absolutely considered and the divine righteousness revealed *ad extra* and in relation to particulars, like the distinction between *voluntas beneplaciti* and *voluntas signi*, raised the problem of "double justice" in God and the question of whether God is in some sense *ex lex*, beyond the law. As in the discussion of God's goodness, the question arises whether the divine *iustitia* is righteousness because God so wills, or whether God is righteous because he wills what is righteous. We see here, moreover, a point of considerable continuity between the Reformed orthodox and the earlier exegetical tradition, given the tendency of certain texts, particularly texts found in the book of Job, to raise these problems.[50]

---

45. Owen, *Dissertation on Divine Justice*, in *Works*, 10, p. 505.
46. See above, 5.4 (C.1, 4).
47. Rijssen, *Summa theol.*, III.xxxviii-xl.
48. Turretin, *Inst. theol. elencticae*, III.xix.3.
49. Leigh, *Treatise*, II.xii (p. 92); cf. Turretin, *Inst. theol. elencticae*, III.xix.3.
50. See Schreiner,"Exegesis and Double Justice," pp. 326-328, 336-337; and idem, *Where Shall Wisdom Be Found?* pp. 91, 94, 106-109, 111-112, 115, 120.

Heppe cites Polanus' parallel statement of two aspects of the problem as an indication of the early Reformed orthodox sense of the absoluteness of God, commenting that "the later dogmaticians let this idea drop":

> 1) Since he passed the law for us, not for himself, God does what by his own law he prohibits us from doing. For example, he does not bring it about that we can commit no sin while living here, though he might most easily have done so. 2) The supreme rule of divine righteousness is his most perfect and infallible will. For God is a law to himself. Whatever God wishes done, is right by the very fact that he wills it.[51]

If Heppe is indeed correct that this precise form of the statement cannot be easily found in later writers, he is certainly wrong to assume that the problem disappeared — just as he is somewhat remiss for not noting how closely Polanus reflected the concern of Calvin. Polanus' statement in fact reflects the long voluntarist tradition to which Reformed theology belongs — with antecedents in medieval Augustinian and Scotist thought and continuing reflections throughout the Reformation and the era of Reformed orthodoxy. Nor does it imply a radical arbitrariness on the part of God: certainly, the rule of righteousness is the will of God, but it is not as if the will of God could be unrighteous, given the interrelation and mutual definition of the divine attributes in the simplicity of the divine essence.

Voetius raises precisely this issue, citing Calvin, Perkins, Polanus, and Twisse: he argues against the "Pelagian antagonists of the present day" that the statement "something is good because God wills it" is not contrary to the claim that "God wills it because it is good."[52] Voetius demands, in short, a resolution of the all-too-easy opposition of categories and a resolution of the problem — what God wills must be righteous, and righteousness must be what God wills. Thus, in view of the essential equality and identity of the divine attributes, Owen was pressed to qualify his original insistence of the priority of the divine *iustitia* over all acts of the divine will or "suppositions" concerning external objects. In its "egress and exercise" the divine righteousness is to be "considered as consequent, or at least concomitant, to some acts of the divine will, assigning or appointing it to a proper object." So too, this egress of divine justice must occur "in a manner agreeable to the rule of [God's] supreme right and wisdom."[53] Voetius similarly indicates that although "nothing is antecedent to the will of God, whether as a rule or an attribute in God ... according to which God is a debtor or obligated to rational creatures either to impede their sinning or to prepare them for glory," it therefore does not follow that the eternal decree of election and reprobation fails to be just.[54] God is *ex lex*, beyond the law in the sense that he is not

51. Polanus, *Syntagma theol.*, II.26, trans. emended from Heppe, *Reformed Dogmatics*, pp. 93-4.

52. Voetius, *Selectarum disputationum theologicarum*, I.xix (p. 371), citing Calvin, *Institutes*, III.xxiii.2; Perkins, *De praedestinatione modo et ordine*; Polanus, *Syntagma theol.*, II.xxvi.4; Twisse, *Defensio Perkinsi contra Arminium*, II.v.2.

53. Owen, *Dissertation on Divine Justice*, in *Works*, X, pp. 498-9.

54. Voetius, *Selectarum disputationum theologicarum*, I.xix (p. 372); cf. the citation in Heppe, *Reformed Dogmatics*, p. 94, which omits this portion of the argument.

bound by the specific precepts of a law that he has ordained as a standard for human conduct — nevertheless, he is not free from the substance of the law and cannot "enjoin or himself make its opposite, as, for example, to believe that he is not God ... in opposition ... to the first precept of the Decalogue."[55]

Even so, the standard Arminian critique of the Reformed conception of the *justitia Dei* misses its mark:

> The Arminians urge, how can God in justice command a man by his word the performance of that which cannot be done by him without the inward help of the Spirit, and yet in the meantime, God denies this inward grace to him?[56]

The Reformed reply that it is not as if God has altered his law or has proposed one standard for human life and then based salvation on another norm entirely —

> God hath not lost his right to command, though we have lost our ability to obey. ... God may without blemish to his justice command man to perform his duty, although he have now no strength to do it, because he once had strength and he hath now lost it.[57]

"A drunken servant," Leigh opines, "is not disobliged from service."[58]

3. Distinctions *ad extra* in summary. The external exercise of the divine justice can be identified under four aspects of the divine work, ranging from the general category of all divine enactment, the temporal execution of God's eternal decree, to the specific works of creation, redemption, and judgment. Thus, God is to be considered just,

> (1) As he is free Lord of all, so his decrees are just, *Rom.* 9:13, 14.
> (2) As he is God of all, and so the common works of preserving both the good and bad are just, I *Tim.* 4:14; Matt 5:45.
> (3) As a Father in Christ, and so he is just in performing his promises, and infusing his grace, and in bestowing the justice of his Son, I John 1:5.
> (4) As Judge of all the world, and so his justice is not only distributive but corrective.[59]

In the early orthodox era, Perkins defined God's justice in a series of distinctions characteristic of developing Reformed orthodoxy:

> God's Justice, is that by which he in all things willeth that which is just.... God's justice is in word or deed. Justice in word, is that truth by which he constantly and indeed willeth all that which he hath said.... Justice in deed, is that by which he either disposeth or rewardeth. God's disposing Justice, is that by which he, as a most free Lord, ordereth rightly all things in his actions.... God's rewarding Justice, is that by which he rendereth

---

55. Voetius, *Selectarum disputationum theologicarum*, I.xix (p. 375); cf. Heppe, *Reformed Dogmatics*, p. 94.

56. Leigh, *Treatise*, II.xii (p. 94).

57. Leigh, *Body of Divinity*, II.xii (p. 221), margin and text.

58. Leigh, *Body of Divinity*, II.xii (p. 221).

59. Leigh, *Treatise*, II.xii (p. 93).

to his creature according to his work ... either his Gentleness or Anger. God's Gentleness, is that by which he freely rewardeth the righteousness of his creature.... God's Anger is that by which he willeth the punishment of the creature offending.[60]

From a formal perspective, the logical bifurcations of the topic and the consistent further division of subdivisions evidences Perkins' Ramism — the content of the divisions, however, evidences a variety of sources, including Aristotle.

4. Justice in word and justice in deed. This distinction, found in such writers as Perkins, Leigh, and Owen, emphasizes the coherence between the divine commandments and exhortations, on the one hand, and the divine enactment of reward and punishment, on the other.[61] In Owens' view, this distinction between word and deed is the fundamental distinction necessary to the discussion of the "egress" of divine justice. In other words, it is the basic *ad extra* distinction from which all other flow and on which they depend for their meaning. It also manifests to which kind of divine perfection the *iustitia Dei* belongs: it is not like the divine power and wisdom, "which create and constitute an object to themselves," nor is it like the affections, mercy, patience, forbearance, and so forth, "which not only require an object for their exercise, but one peculiarly affected and circumstanced."[62] The divine justice both constitutes its objects and receives objects already constituted. It takes as its objects either the commandments or declarations it has delivered *ad extra* or things created by the divine will or constituted as what they are according to the exercise of divine power and wisdom. Still, its exercise is toward any and all objects in the created order — unlike mercy, which requires for its exercise an object deserving of mercy, or unlike patience, which requires an object deserving of patience. God is just toward all things — although, of course, the form that God's justice takes relates directly to the character of its particular objects.

There is, in the first place, a twofold egress of the divine justice: God both speaks and acts — thus the distinction of word and deed. The first of these egresses, word or speech, is "absolute and perfectly free." In this egress, God's justice constitutes or, in a sense, creates "an object to itself" in its promulgation of commands — "in words of legislation" which refer to "equity" and "in words of declaration and narration" which refer to "truth."[63] Accordingly, writes Leigh, "God's justice comprehendeth two things under it,"

> (1) Equity, in that he directs men equally and requites them equally, commanding all and only good things, such as they in reason ought to do, promising and threatening fit and due recompenses of their obedience and disobedience.

---

60. Perkins, *Golden Chaine*, iii (p. 13, col. 1), only citations of Scripture omitted.

61. Perkins, *Golden Chaine*, iii (p. 13, col. 1); Leigh, *Treatise*, II.xii (p. 92); idem, *Body of Divinity*, II.xii (p. 220); Owen, *Dissertation on Divine Justice*, in *Works*, X, pp. 499-500.

62. Owen, *Dissertation on Divine Justice*, in *Works*, X, pp. 499.

63. Owen, *Dissertation on Divine Justice*, in *Works*, X, pp. 499.

(2) Truth, whereby he declareth nothing to them but as the thing is, and fidelity whereby he fulfilleth all that he has spoken.[64]

Given the grounding of God's justice or righteousness in his will, both of these kinds of egress in words "take place absolutely and freely." They are absolute because they do not rest on some antecedent condition — God works all things and wills all things outside of himself according to the counsel of his own will, including the commands and exhortations that he sets forth.[65] Accordingly, "the justice of God is sometimes taken for his faithfulness, which is a doing justice to his word."[66]

The second egress, the divine actions or deeds, is "respective" and "necessary." Given his absolute or unconditioned revelation of the standards of divine justice in words, God exercises his justice with respect to the conduct of his creatures. Since God's necessary egress in divine action or deed refers both to the governance of all things by God and to the legislative rule of God in rewarding or punishing his rational creatures, it yields the next distinction, namely, that between dispositive and distributive justice.[67] This relative or respective justice is necessary in the sense that, given, on one hand, the equity and truth of the *iustitia Dei* and, on the other, both the fundamental goodness of the created order and the sinfulness of rational creatures, God cannot do other than administer the governance of his world and punish sin. In this sense, then, the justice or righteousness of God is quite different from his mercy: "no natural obligation intervenes" between "the act of mercy and its object," given that God is in no way constrained to be merciful; but God is necessarily just precisely because there is a natural obligation "between the act of justice and is object."[68]

5. Dispositive and distributive justice. With respect to its exercise, God's justice is also twofold. Wendelin, Leigh, Turretin, Rijssen, and Pictet expand at length on the distinction, also drawn from the language of law and ethics, between *justitia disponens* or *iustitia universalis* and *justitia distribuens* or *iustitia particularis*, or, sometimes, *iustitia retributativa*. The former terms indicate the universal righteous order according to which God disposes and governs all things — as taught, Wendelin notes (unabashedly citing the Apocrypha!) in Wisdom 11:21, "You rightly order all measures of number and weight." Thus, universal or dispositive justice is God's universal governance and identifies him as the one who rules as *Dominus* and *supremus rerum arbiter*.[69] The latter terms indicate the specific rule or judgment of God both in reward and in punishment and therefore are frequently identified as illustrating the divine gentleness, love, and mercy or, alternatively, the divine anger and hatred. The latter terms are used with the qualification — taught "in all of the theological schools" — that "affections are attributed to God according to [his] effects." God, thus, either

---

64. Leigh, *Treatise*, II.xii (p. 94).
65. Owen, *Dissertation on Divine Justice*, in *Works*, X, pp. 499, 510.
66. Ridgley, *Body of Divinity* (1855), I, p. 106.
67. Owen, *Dissertation on Divine Justice*, in *Works*, X, p. 499.
68. Owen, *Dissertation on Divine Justice*, in *Works*, X, pp. 499, 511.
69. Leigh, *Treatise*, II.xii (pp. 91-92).

wills graciously in his righteousness to effect his promises or he wills angrily in his righteousness to implement punishments, but it is not the case that "imperfections and passions" can be attributed to God. Divine promises and punishments are conditional, indeed, but the conditions are fulfilled by human beings and no mutation is implied in the divine will.[70]

God's dispositive justice is revealed primarily in the "equitable" character of all of God's dealings with his creation, especially in the manifestation of his holiness and goodness in providence — distributive justice is concerned with reward and punishment.[71] In Leigh's summary,

(1) Disposing [justice], by which as a most free Lord and supreme Monarch of all, he disposeth all things in his actions according to the rule of equity, and imposeth most just laws upon his creatures, commending, and forbidding only that which is fit for them in right reason to do and forbear. [Deut. 32:4; Psalm 11:7 & 48:11 & 145:17.] (2) Distributive [justice], which renders to everyone according to his work without respect of persons, *Psal.* 62:12; *Job* 34:11, 19; *Prov.* 24:12; *Jer.* 32:19; *Ezek.* 7:27; *Matt.* 16:27; *Deut.* 16:17; 2 *Chron.* 19:7; *Acts* 10:34; *Ephes.* 6:9; *Gal.* 2:6.[72]

The influence of Aristotelian ethics is apparent in the distinction between universal or "disposing" and particular or distributive, with the distributive later divided into positive and negative categories according to the nature of the reward.[73] Of course, once it is said that the distinction reflects Aristotelian influences, it is also necessary to note that the distinction is taken from Aristotle's *Nichomachean Ethics* and can hardly be associated either with the claim of a "metaphysical" or speculative dimension of scholastic orthodoxy or with the assumption that Aristotelianisms mark a point of distinction between the Reformation and orthodoxy — we have already seen these distinctions offered in detail by Calvin and we have noted the early, Reformation era return of the *Nichomachean Ethics* to Protestant curricula.[74]

The theologians who note the language of *iustitia universalis* and *iustitia particularis* as synonymous with the distinction into dispositive and distributive justice also note that this model allowed the further division, by some theologians, of particular justice into distributive (*iustitia distributiva*) and commutative justice (*iustitia commutativa*). This latter distinction is typically denied by the Reformed.[75] Commutative justice, by way of definition, is a justice of proportionality, grounded in a transfer or exchange

---

70. Wendelin, *Christianae theologiae libri duo*, I.i.26 (2),

71. Ridgley, *Body of Divinity* (1855), I, p. 106.

72. Leigh, *Treatise*, II.xii (p. 91).

73. Cf. Aristotle, *Nichomachean Ethics*, 1131-1132.

74. Thus, above, this volume, 6.1 (A.1) and *PRRD*, I, 8.1 (B.2).

75. Turretin, *Inst. theol. elencticae*, III.xix.2; also Samuel Rutherford, *Exercitationes apologeticae pro divina gratia, in quibus vindicatur doctrina orthodoxa de divinis decretis, & Dei tum aeterni decreti, tum gratiae efficacis operationis, cum hominis libertate consociatione & subordinatione amica* (Franecker: Johannes Dhüiringh, 1651), II.3 (pp. 301-303); Owen, *Dissertation on Divine Justice*, in *Works*, X, pp. 500-502; Brakel, *Redelijke Godsdienst*, I.iii.38 (pp. 99-100).

that is adjudged to restore the equality or proper balance of the two parties in dispute. It is a typical form of justice in human affairs. It cannot, however, be applied to God, inasmuch as "none of our works, however perfect they may be, are by nature something worthy before God; since there is no sufficiency when there is no proportionality between the work and the payment — God is forever free and never the debtor and man can bring nothing of his own before God."[76]

6. Distinctions within distributive justice: justice of reward and justice in punishment. We have already seen one form of this distinction in the general definition offered by Perkins — the division of God's "rewarding justice" into categories of "gentleness" or positive reward and "anger" or punishment. In Leigh's terms, "this distributive justice is also twofold, *premii & poenae*, of reward and punishment,"[77] or as some sources state the distinction, distributive justice is "remunerative" (*remunerativa*) or "vindicatory" (*vindicativa*).[78] Leigh writes that God's distributive justice is

(1) of reward, when God bountifully rewards the obedience of the creature with a free reward, 2 Thess. 1:5, 7; Matt. 10:41, 42; Mark 9:41. God bestows this reward not only on the godly, both by heaping divers mercies on them in this life, and by the fulness of glory and felicity in the life to come, but also on the wicked, whose moral actions he rewards with temporary rewards in this world, as the obedience of *Jehu*, the repentance of *Ahab*.

(2) of punishment, by which he appointeth to the delinquent creature the equal punishment of eternal death for the least sin, Gen. 2:17; Rom. 6:23, which death is begun in this life, in divers kinds of miseries and punishments, which for the most part are proportionable to their sins, Gen 3:17 & 20:18, but is perfected in the life to come, when the full wrath of God is poured upon it, John 3:36; 2 Thess. 1:6.[79]

This latter category, the *iustitia poenae*, refers to "vindicatory justice" (*iustitia vindicatrix*), chastising, punishing, and finally avenging.[80] It was concerning this final division of the topic, the *iustitia poenae* or *vindicatrix*, that the greatest controversy arose in the seventeenth century.

7. Debate over punitive or avenging justice in God. The extent and intensity of the seventeenth-century controversy over the essential character and necessary exercise of divine justice is well catalogued in Owen's *A Dissertation on Divine Justice* (1653), directed largely against the Socinian objections to the doctrine and against those of the Reformed who responded to the Arminian or Socinian teaching with what

---

76. Brakel, *Redelijke Godsdienst*, I.iii.38 (p. 100); cf. Turretin, *Inst. theol. elencticae*, III.xix.2.

77. Leigh, *Treatise*, II.xii (p. 91), citing in margin, 1 Pet. 1:17; Rom. 2:6-12; 2 Cor. 5:10; Col. 3:25; Rev. 22:12.

78. Mastricht, *Theoretico-practica theol.* II.xviii.13-14; cf. Rijssen, *Summa theol.*, III.xl; Ridgley, *Body of Divinity* (1855), I, p. 106; Boston, *Body of Divinity*, I, pp. 106-107; the Latin forms used are *vindicativa* and *vindicatrix*, which can be rendered "vindictive" or "vindicatory" — I hesitate to use the English form "vindictive" because of the negative modern connotation, not at all implied in sixteenth- and seventeenth-century usage: see Owen, *Dissertation on Divine Justice*, in *Works*, X, p. 495, note 2.

79. Leigh, *Treatise*, II.xii (pp. 91-92).

80. Rijssen, *Summa theol.*, III.xxxviii-xl.

Owen took to be an excessively Scotistic approach to the problem.[81] From Owen's perspective, the problem had its roots in Arminius' view of the satisfaction of Christ, but then took a more severe turn in the thought of Corvinus, Episcopius, and the Socinians. In addition, Owen distinguished carefully between the various Remonstrant and Socinian views, on the one hand, and the divergent Reformed approaches, on the other: debate with the Remonstrants and Socinians rested on a twofold problem — the denial of Christ's full penal satisfaction for sin and the related assumption that divine punitive or vindicatory justice was not an essential attribute but a free exercise of will *ad extra*; debate among the Reformed assumed agreement on the doctrine of Christ's satisfaction for sin, but addressed differences over the way in which the free exercise of an essential divine justice ought to be understood. In the former debate, Owen presumes the heresy of his opponents. In the latter, he allows for their orthodoxy, despite his profound distaste for their arguments. These divergent approaches are, thus, determined by the boundaries of confessional orthodoxy — and they illustrate the diversity of confessional orthodoxy.[82]

The Socinians denied an "avenging justice" (*justitia vindicatrice seu ultrice*) in God: this justice, they claimed, was in God, not by nature, but by exigency, for the purpose of punishing sin. By extension, if avenging justice were merely an exigency *ad extra* and not an attribute belonging to the essence or nature of God, then God would not necessarily have to exercise it. The Socinian argument was that God's punitive justice was the result of the free will of God, much like the creation of the world. Just as God was free to will or not will the existence of the world, so is he free to will or not will the enactment of justice and the punishment of sin. By extension and intent, the argument undermined the satisfaction theory of atonement: if the Socinian view were correct, salvation could be grounded in something other than a satisfaction of the divine justice.[83]

In other words, the Socinian polemic was directed not so much toward an abstruse question concerning the divine essence but toward the doctrines of the just punishment of sin, the satisfaction of Christ, and the redemption of human beings — as also was the Reformed counterargument. In Turretin's summary,

> The question comes to this — whether the vindicatory justice of God is so natural to him that, the sinning creature being granted, he cannot but exercise it, and to leave sin would be repugnant to it; or whether it is so free in God that his exercise depends on his will and good pleasure alone. They with whom we debate maintain the latter; we defend the former.[84]

---

81. Owen, *Dissertation on Divine Justice*, in *Works*, vol. 10, pp. 481-624; cf. Trueman, "John Owen's *Dissertation*," pp. 89-92, on the shift in Owen's views.

82. Owen, *Dissertation on Divine Justice*, in *Works*, vol. 10, pp. 496, 504-507, 583-585; cf. the discussion in *PRRD*, I, 1.3 (B.2-3).

83. Turretin, *Inst. theol. elencticae*, III.xix.8, citing Socinus, *De Iesu Christo Servatore*, I.1 (pp. 1-11) and Socinus, *Praelectiones theologicae*, 16 (p. 87).

84. Turretin, *Inst. theol. elencticae*, III.xix.10.

According to Socinus, the *iustitia Dei* is simply the rectitude and equity of God's nature, not a distinct quality or attribute in God, indeed, "only the effect of [God's] will."[85]

In response, the Reformed argued that there must be a fundamental correspondence between the inward and absolute righteousness of God and the external manifestation of his righteousness, both despite the infinite distance between the divine essence and the finitude of revealed law and despite the hiddenness of the ultimate purpose of God over against his revealed demands. This correspondence is illustrated for the Reformed orthodox nowhere as clearly as in the relationship between the divine righteousness and Christ's satisfaction:

> This justice is so essential to God, immutable, and ... inexorable, that he cannot remit the creatures' sin, nor free them from punishment, unless his justice be satisfied; God cannot dispense against himself, because sins do hurt against the inward virtue of God, and the rule of righteousness, the integrity therefore and perfection of God cannot stand, if he satisfy not that; yet through his bounty and goodness he hath found out a way by which due satisfaction may be given thereunto, *viz.* by Christ, who hath borne a punishment equivalent to our sins, for us.[86]

Indeed, the case for an essential vindicatory justice in God is proven by the death of Christ: for God would not have subjected his beloved Son to death had there not been an inward necessity that his righteousness be satisfied by the infliction of punishment.[87] Such adversaries, notes Wendelin, in effect deny the divine justice altogether: "One who is utterly merciful cannot be utterly just; but God is taught by Scripture to be utterly merciful; therefore he is not utterly just." The basic proposition is false, he responds, inasmuch as there is no contradiction between the highest justice or righteousness and the highest mercy — God, after all, is utterly just toward some and utterly merciful toward others, and the utter or highest mercy is revealed in Christ and to those who are in Christ. And it is in Christ that we learn that God does not set aside sin without punishment, for the punishment of sin falls on Christ as Mediator.[88]

Reformed dogmaticians were, moreover, willing to recognize the difficulty of the concept of a freely exercised but nonetheless essential justice — notably Pictet:

> the idea itself of an all-perfect Being indicates that God is a most just, most wise, and most true Being; indeed, it involves a contradiction to conceive of an *unjust* God. Nonetheless it may be inquired, whether that justice by which God punishes sin, and which is termed vindicatory justice, is essential to God himself, and whether it is contrary to his nature to let sin go unpunished.[89]

---

85. Socinus, *Praelectiones theologicae*, 16 (p. 88); cf. the citation in Turretin, *Inst. theol. elencticae*, III.xix.8.

86. Leigh, *Treatise*, II.xii (p. 92).

87. Rijssen, *Summa theol.*, III.xl.

88. Wendelin, *Christianae theologiae libri duo*, I.i.26 (3).

89. Pictet, *Theol. chr.*, II.viii.2; cf. Turretin, *Inst. theol. elencticae*, III.xix.9

Pictet argues that "if the love of holiness, or hatred of sin is essential to God, then his avenging justice will be also," since he could not let sin go unpunished. Specifically against the Socinian alternative, he concludes,

> We must not therefore conceive of God as a creditor who remits debt *de jure*, for even though sins are identified as debts, we are still bound to be punished. Rather, [we should conceive of God] as the supreme Ruler and Judge of the universe, who is bound to preserve inviolate the majesty of his own laws.... If this justice were not an essential attribute of God, there could be no legitimate reason, why he should have delivered up his beloved Son to death; for the perfect wisdom of God will not allow us to say that this was done without reason and extreme necessity.[90]

Against various objections, then, the Reformed insist that *justitia vindicatrice* is naturally and essentially in God, at least in the limited sense that God's righteousness cannot choose to allow sin to go unpunished. Yet, they insist that, although the "egress" of God's justice is necessary, given its essential status, nonetheless, God still must be said to exercise justice freely.[91] This may be argued from Scripture where God necessarily — that is, in order to be truly God — is shown to have a hate of sin (*odium peccati*).[92] Still, this *odium* and the exercise of justice that flows from it arise spontaneously and without any compulsion or coaction, and are therefore free. God's justice, Turretin comments, is therefore not characterized by a freedom of indifference, as if God might punish or not punish, but by a freedom from any compulsion to punish.[93] Drawing on a similar set of concerns, and despite his characterization of "avenging justice" as an "essential attribute," Pictet does not want to speak of punishment as the proper work of God: justice is not opposed to such divine virtues as mercy and long-suffering, for God does not always punish and, indeed punishment is identified by Scripture as his "alien work (Is. 27:21)" — God is "ready to pardon and slow to execute his wrath, (Jer. 18:7, 8; Rom. 2:4; 2 Peter 3:9)."[94]

On this final point, however, there was disagreement among the Reformed, brought on in large part by developments in the debate with the Socinians: Owen, for one, altered his views on the relationship between the divine justice and the divine will absolutely considered and, in his revision, found himself standing against both Twisse and Rutherford. Twisse, arguing against Piscator on the basis of points drawn from Scotus, had argued against the premise that God could not, according to his absolute power, forgive sins without satisfaction. The point made by Twisse belonged to the Scotist critique of the so-called Anselmic theory of atonement. Calvin had argued, against a strict Anselmic approach, that there was no "absolute necessity" to Christ's person and atoning work but that it arose instead from "a heavenly decree on which

---

90. Pictet, *Theol. chr.*, II.viii.3.

91. Turretin, *Inst. theol. elencticae*, III.xix.5

92. Rijssen, *Summa theol.*, III.xl, *controversia et argumenta*; citing Ex. 34:7; Hab. 1:13; Ps. 5:6; Gen. 18:25; Rom. 5:6; 1:18, 31; 1 Thess. 1:6.

93. Turretin, *Inst. theol. elencticae*, III.xix.5

94. Pictet, *Theol. chr.*, II.ix.1-3.

man's salvation depended" — in other words, Christ the mediator is necessary to our salvation, but there is no ultimate necessity that God offer this mediation. God remains utterly free in his willing.[95] In addition, there appears to be an underlying Scotist pattern in Calvin's identification of the decretive will of God as the sole ground of the merit of Christ.[96]

It was not, Twisse insisted, a contradiction in terms not to pardon sin: there is, in other words, no necessity on God's part that sin be forgiven or that sin be forgiven in a particular way. Thus, given the absence of any utter determination of the divine will toward any particular "secondary object," namely, toward a particular solution to the problem of sin, God can "forgive sin absolutely, without any satisfaction received."[97] Owen recognized that this kind of argument could be constructed with a view toward the pure possibility of any occurrence in the world order, when the possibilities and their opposites are construed *in sensu diviso*, in a divided sense, rather than *in sensu composito*, in the composite sense. Thus, whereas it is clearly a contradiction and impossible for God to punish sin and not to punish sin at the same time (i.e., *in sensu composito*), it can be argued, *in sensu diviso*, that while God does will to punish sin, it remains true that it is possible that God may not punish sin. It is to this particular conclusion of Twisse that Owen objects strenuously — with the qualification that Scotus was just a bit more acute than Twisse.[98]

From Owen's perspective, "the non-punishment of sin implies a contradiction, — not, indeed, formally, and in the terms, but virtually and eminently in respect of the thing itself."[99] In other words, in a formal sense, with regard simply to the capacity of the divine will to perform any act that does not involve a logical contradiction, God can will or not will any object or can will any object or its opposite. This is true, comments Owen, "in respect of the egress of those divine attributes which constitute and create objects to themselves."[100] When, however, the question of divine willing or not-willing is asked "virtually and eminently in respect of the thing itself," namely, with respect to the God who is doing the willing and not with respect to the external object, the answer must be different. The divine will may not include opposites, therefore, " in respect of those attributes which have no egress towards their objects but upon a condition supposed." As an example, Owen indicates that "God may justly speak or nor speak with man; but it being supposed that he wills to speak, the divine will cannot be indifferent whether he speak truth or not."[101] Owen's example, moreover,

95. Calvin, *Institutes*, II.xii.1; cf. Seeberg, *History of Doctrines*, II, pp. 156-157 on Scotus, and note Muller, *Christ and the Decree*, pp. 27-28.

96. Wendel, *Calvin*, pp. 227-232.

97. Twisse, *Vindiciae gratiae*, cited by Owen, *Dissertation on Divine Justice*, in *Works*, 10, p. 587.

98. Owen, *Dissertation on Divine Justice*, in *Works*, 10, pp. 587-588.

99. Owen, *Dissertation on Divine Justice*, in *Works*, 10, p. 587. Note that Owen's focus on the virtual and eminent relations or distinctions in the thing itself, as opposed to formal relations or distinctions, indicates immediately his Thomistic approach over against the Scotistic model accepted by Twisse.

100. Owen, *Dissertation on Divine Justice*, in *Works*, 10, pp. 588-589.

101. Owen, *Dissertation on Divine Justice*, in *Works*, 10, p. 589.

does not arbitrarily juxtapose divine speaking as necessarily true with the problem of the necessary exercise of justice — it correlates neatly with the Reformed understanding of divine righteousness in both word and deed.

From Owen's perspective, Twisse has failed to recognize that, although there cannot be any absolute necessity placed on God's will, there are necessities of supposition or necessities of the consequence that can define and determine the divine willing. There is no absolute necessity that God create the world — but on the supposition that God wills to create the world, the creation is necessary. There is also no necessity that God speak, "but it being supposed that he wills to speak, it is impossible that he not speak truly." Similarly, the punishment of sin is not an absolute necessity, but it is necessary, given the "suppositions" that God has willed to create human beings rational and responsible and has willed to permit them to transgress his laws. God cannot have an "antecedent indifference" to sin — although in punishing it he acts freely and "with understanding," not being compelled to punish in the absolute sense nor necessarily punishing "to the extent of his power."[102] Turretin similarly indicates that "we hold the egress of justice to be necessary, yet we do not deny that God exercises it freely" — justice is necessary in an ultimate sense inasmuch as "it is founded in the very nature of God" and is necessarily dispensed given the absence of an "antecedent indifference" to sin. God does not punish or not punish at mere whim: in view of the sinful condition of the creature, God will administer justice. There is, thus, a suppositional or hypothetical necessity. Yet God punishes freely, having a "concomitant liberty" by which God is not under any compulsion to punish either immediately or in a particular degree or, indeed, to punish directly the one who is sinning.[103]

Owen's and Turretin's option, the divine self-determination, resting on a logically prior divine willing — a necessity *ex suppositione* or a necessity of the consequence — is positioned, as it were, between the claim of an absolute necessity that God will something with respect to an object *ad extra* (which all of the Reformed deny) and the claim of an utter freedom of the divine willing, maintained in slightly different forms by Twisse and Rutherford. Owen took particular pains to refute the "great man" Samuel Rutherford, who had contended, with reference to Twisse, "that truly, punitive justice ... is not at all in God by necessity of nature, but freely."[104] Rutherford's chapter, as a whole, was concerned to argue that "God's good pleasure (*beneplacitum*) is the first rule of all moral good in creatures." The particular point at issue in Owen's counterargument was Rutherford's insistence that the graciousness of the divine purpose in willing the death of Christ was inextricably linked to the radical freedom of the exercise of divine punitive justice: given that God wills the death of Christ on

---

102. Owen, *Dissertation on Divine Justice*, in *Works*, 10, p. 589; cf. pp. 596, 604-605.

103. Turretin, *Inst. theol. elencticae*, III.xix.4-6.

104. Samuel Rutherford, *Disputatio scholastica de divina providentia, variis praelectionibus, quod attinet ad summa rerum capita ... Adjectae sunt disquisitiones metaphysicae de ente, possibili, dominio Dei in entia & non entia, & variae quaestiones* (Edinburgh: George Anderson, 1649), xxii (p. 345), citing Twisse, *Vindiciae gratiae, potestatis, ac providentiae Dei*, I.iii.4, digression 1 (pp. 227-228); cf. Owen, *Dissertation on Divine Justice*, in *Works*, 10, p. 608.

the basis of his punitive justice, a necessity of the exercise of justice would remove the fully gracious and loving character of Christ's death. Nor, Rutherford argues, could God transfer the penalty of sin from the deserving sinner to the innocent Christ if he were necessitated by nature to punish sin. Nor, indeed, could God at the same time be necessitated to punish sin, declare the penalty of eternal death for it, and then will, not death, but a future restitution for sinful humanity![105]

In Owen's view, this resolution of the problem of punitive or vindicatory justice, far from merely taking a good argument from Twisse, altered the form of Twisse's point and situated Rutherford's doctrine rather nebulously between the view of Twisse that "the exercise of that justice is free to God" while "justice itself is a natural attribute of God" and the Socinian claim that justice "is only a free act of the divine will."[106] From Owen's perspective, the problem with Rutherford's argument is simply that Rutherford allowed no middle position between absolute necessity and utter freedom — whereas the right understanding of divine justice as an essential attribute demanded both a distinction between absolute and conditional necessity and a distinction between divine attributes that constitute or create their objects *ad extra* and divine attributes that "do not constitute or create objects to themselves" but "have egress" only "towards certain objects particularly modified." Justice, in Owen's view, belongs to the latter category — and once its object has been "constituted by a free act of the divine will," it "must necessarily ... be exercised."[107]

8. Divine justice and human piety: practical applications. The Reformed response to Arminian and Socinian critiques of the doctrine of the divine justice was not merely dogmatic — the Arminian and Socinian views were seen by the Reformed as undermining piety and worship as well as sound doctrine. Owen comments, with some hyperbole, "Whether holiness or purity be an attribute natural to God, and immutably residing in him, has not yet been called in question by our adversaries." "They have not yet," he concludes, "arrived at such a pitch of madness."[108] The Socinian teachings, in his view, as in the thought of other Reformed orthodox writers, are not merely wrong, but dangerous to piety and salvation: denial of the vindicatory justice of God sets aside the utterly "abominable nature of sin," the fact that "sin opposes the divine nature and existence; it is enmity against God, and is not an idle enemy; it has even engaged in a mortal war with all the attributes of God."[109] Recognition of this fact and the resultant praise of God's justice has the effect of rightly glorifying God. The primary practical "use" or application of the confession of God's justice, thus, is doxological.[110]

The positive applications of the concept of the *justitia Dei* to Christian life are many:

---

105. Rutherford, *Disputatio scholastica de divina providentia*, xxii (pp. 345-347).
106. Owen, *Dissertation on Divine Justice*, in *Works*, 10, p. 608.
107. Owen, *Dissertation on Divine Justice*, in *Works*, 10, p. 611.
108. Owen, *Dissertation on Divine Justice*, in *Works*, 10, pp. 512-513.
109. Owen, *Dissertation on Divine Justice*, in *Works*, 10, pp. 512-513.
110. Mastricht, *Theoretico-practica theol.*, II.xviii.17.

[God's justice] reproves such as live in sin, *Exod.* 34:17; *Psalm* 5:5; *Gal.* 6:6; if God be merciful that he may be feared, much more is he just that he may be feared.... We must take heed of justifying the wicked; we should be just in our actions to man, in buying and selling, in rewarding and punishing; Magistrates, Ministers, Masters, Parents should be just. We should not murmur at God's disposing justice in making us poor, and should yield to his directing justice, obeying his Commandments seem they never so unreasonable. We should get Christ's righteousness to satisfy God's justice for us, and to justify us [2 Chron. 2:5; Neh. 9:33; Psalm 119:137; Dan. 9:7; Rom. 3:26].

The consideration of God's justice should affright us from hypocrisy, sinning in secret, keeping bosom sins. It ministers comfort to the godly, who are wronged by the wicked: they shall have an upright and just Judge, who will uphold them in a good cause, *Psalm* 33:24.

It may serve to exhort us to glorify God's justice, both in fulfilling of his promises, and punishing wicked men, *Psalm* 7:18 & 51:15; Rev. 19:1.[111]

C. The Holiness or Purity of God

1. Divine holiness and purity in the thought of the Reformers. Holiness is not a divine attribute that is singled out for separate discussion in any of the systematic works of the major second-generation Reformers — whether Calvin, Vermigli, Musculus, Bullinger, or Hyperius. The idea or theme is certainly present, however, as is the exegetical basis for the doctrine. Calvin, thus, with consistency, comments on the purity of God over against the impurity of the sinful creature and on the inability of sinful human beings to stand before the brightness of the divine majesty.[112]

Although, as we have seen, Calvin had no difficulty referring to the essence of God in the most absolute sense, it remains the case that his reading of Scripture most typically understood its references to divine attributes as identifying the relationship of God to the economy of creation or redemption. This is particularly the case with attributes relating to the exercise of the divine will and its affections. In the case of the divine holiness, such texts as Isaiah 17:7 or Habakkuk 1:12, often used by the later orthodox to identify the essential holiness of God, Calvin will often argue in the opposite direction for the primary meaning of the text: "He therefore calls God *Holy*, not only as viewed in himself, but from the effect produced, because he has sanctified or separated to himself the children of Abraham."[113] As in the case of other attributes, this apparently antispeculative approach of Calvin may relate to the late medieval nominalist assumption that human understanding of the attributes is a reflection on the *ad extra* revelation of God, stated in (or accommodated to) the forms of human knowing as diverse concepts concerning an infinite being. Of course, Calvin does not deny the essential holiness of God; he only points toward its effect as the focus of the revelation.

---

111. Leigh, *Treatise*, II.xii (p. 94).

112. E.g., Calvin, *Institutes*, I.i.3; II.xii.1; III.xii.1-3.

113. Calvin, *Commentary on Isaiah*, 17:7 (CTS *Isaiah*, II, p. 26); cf. Calvin, *Commentary on Habakkuk*, 1:12 (CTS *Habakkuk*, pp. 38-39, 41-42).

Once this approach to the meaning of the attribute is recognized, it is also apparent that Calvin understood the divine holiness as a separation from sin and evil, albeit with specific reference to the divine demands laid on the children of Israel. Thus, God is called "the Holy One" because of the care that he bestows on "his peculiar people": "he is called Holy, because he has chosen and separated a people, that he might consecrate them to himself."[114] Calvin also recognizes that the holiness of God's people cannot approach the holiness of God himself: "in bidding us to be holy like himself, the proportion is not that of equals ... even the most perfect are always very far from coming up to the mark."[115] Still, he does not appear to have grasped — or perhaps simply did not choose to emphasize — the sense of divine holiness as separation over against all worldly and human unworthiness. Rather Calvin associates holiness primarily with reverence and worship: "the name of God," Calvin writes, "is called *holy*, because it is entitled to the highest reverence; and whenever the name of God is mentioned, it ought immediately to remind us of his adorable majesty."[116]

2. The Reformed orthodox doctrine of the divine holiness. The divine holiness occupies a far more prominent place in the Reformed orthodox discussion of the divine attributes and, indeed, in the exegetical analyses of the Reformed orthodox than it does in the work of the Reformers themselves. As already indicated in Wendelin's basic definition of righteousness, many of the orthodox united their discussion of God's righteousness or justice with their discussion of God's holiness.[117] This particular attribute, like the other divine virtues with which it is associated, is for the Reformed orthodox one of the profound attributes of relation at the same time that it describes the inaccessible height of the divine Majesty — and, of course, the divine Majesty itself is an attribute of the divine presence.[118] Scripture calls God "the Holy one" (Job 6:10), "The Holy one of Israel" (Isaiah 41:20; 43:14), "the Holy one of Jacob" (Isa. 49:23) and declares "Holy is his name" (Luke 1:49). In addition, such texts as 1 Peter 1:15-16 indicate that even as God is holy so also ought his people to be holy — indicating "a two-fold holiness":

> 1. Original, absolute, and eternal, in God, which is the incommunicable eminence of the divine Majesty, exalted above all, and divided from all other eminences whatsoever... (Is. 17:7; Hab. 1:12).
> 2. Derived or relative in the things which are his, properly called *Sacra*, holy things... 2 Pet. 3:11.[119]

Thus, in its ultimate or "original" sense, the word "Holy" may simply be a name or term for God himself, since God is "most holy and pure" — or, more precisely, it refers

---

114. Calvin, *Commentary on Isaiah*, 43:14-15, in loc. (*CTS Isaiah*, III, pp. 336, 338).
115. Calvin, *Commentary on I Peter*, 1:15, in loc. (*CTS 1 Peter*, p. 47).
116. Calvin, *Harmony of the Evangelists*, Luke 1:49, in loc. (*CTS Harmony*, I, p. 56).
117. Marckius, *Comp. theol.*, IV.xlv; Rijssen, *Summa theol.*, III.xxxviii-xxxix.
118. See below, 6.3.
119. Leigh, *Treatise*, II.xiii (p. 102. marg.).

to the "essential and uncreated holiness" of God, which, as essential, is God himself,[120] and the "first cause" of all derivative holiness.[121] It is the "primary virtue" of God's will.[122] In summary,

> Holiness is in God, essentially and originally, 1 Sam. 2:2. He is the author of all holiness; all the holiness in Saints or Angels comes from God, and is a quality in the creature. He is holy of himself; men and Angels are sanctified by him; his holiness is a substance, in men it is an accident. The essence of many Angels continues, though their holiness be lost; most men never had holiness, and the man would remain, though his holiness were lost.[123]

In this original or ultimate sense, holiness has, moreover, two implications, both of which are typically stated in relation or in contrast to creatures. First, it can indicate the absolute "moral purity" of God and stand, therefore, in relation to his justice or righteousness. This meaning can be illustrated from such texts as "Ye shall be holy; for I am holy" (Lev. 11:44); "Be ye holy, for I am holy" (1 Pet. 1:16); and "Thou art of purer eyes than to behold evil" (Hab. 1:13). So also in this sense of holiness is God compared to fire or to light: it is "the brightness of all his perfections."[124] Thus, further,

> Holiness is the beauty of all God's Attributes, without which his Wisdom would be but subtlety, his Justice cruelty, his Sovereignty tyranny, his mercy foolish pity.... Holiness is (as it were) the Character of Christ Jesus, the Image of God, the beauty, the strength, the riches, the life, the soul of the soul, and of the whole man. It is a very beam of the Divine light, called therefore by the Apostle "the divine nature."[125]

Second, "the word is also employed to denote God's infinite excellence above all that is low and created"[126] or the quality "whereby God is infinitely opposite to every thing that tends to reflect dishonour or reproach on his divine perfections."[127]

> God's holiness is that excellence of his nature, by which he gives himself (as I may say) unto himself, doing all for himself, and in all, and by all, and above all, aiming at his own pleasure and glory.[128]

Even so, given the eminence, perfection, and absoluteness of the divine holiness, "God is ever equally holy, ever in the same degree and frame of holinesse" and there is "not the least variety or shadow of turning in him."[129]

---

120. Ursinus, Commentary, p. 630).

121. Poole, Commentary, 1 Pet. 1:15, in loc.

122. Cocceius, Summa theol., III.x.52.

123. Leigh, Treatise, II.xiii (p. 102).

124. Brakel, Redelijke Godsdienst, I.iii.31 (Reasonable Service, I, p. 122).

125. Leigh, Treatise, II.xiii (p. 104, text and margin).

126. Venema, Inst. theol., vii (p. 161).

127. Ridgley, Body of Divinity (1855), I, p. 103.

128. Leigh, Treatise, II.xiii (p. 102).

129. Caryl, Exposition upon the Book of Job, 6:10, in loc. (II, pp. 468-469).

As such, holiness stands over against moral impurity or blemish just as the divine omnipotence stands over against creaturely weakness and the divine wisdom and intellect over against creaturely lack of understanding — and it is "not so much one perfection as the harmony of all [God's] perfections, as they are opposed to sin."[130] This second sense of the word can be found in such passages as Isaiah 40:18-25: "To whom then will ye liken God? ... It is he that sitteth upon the circle of the earth, and the inhabitants thereof are as grasshoppers ... that bringeth princes to nothing ... to whom then shall ye liken me, or shall I be equal? saith the Holy One." This holiness identifies God as one to be "feared, glorified, worshiped," as the one in whose sight even the stars are impure and angels are "charged with folly."[131]

Combining the essential and moral definitions, God's holiness may be defined essentially, formally or subjectively, objectively, and as exemplary. Thus,

> 1. Holiness is in him without measure, in the highest degree; man's may be limited, it is in him immutable and infinite like himself, and cannot be lessened or augmented.
> 2. He is holy formally and subjectively: holiness is a conformity to the will of God; how holy then must he needs be when his nature and will are one?
> 3. Objectively, he is the object of all holiness, for there is no holiness but what hath him for the object. [margin: Our holiness is terminated in him. Exod. 28:36.]
> 4. Exemplary, "Be ye holy as I am holy," so Christ bids us to learn of himself for he was meek and humble.
> God is holy in Heaven, holy in earth, holy in hell itself, holy in glorifying Angels, holy in justifying men, holy in punishing devils, holy in his Nature, Word, Works, "Glorious in holiness" (Exod. 15).[132]

God's holiness is in a sense the foundation of all his other virtues or "excellencies" insofar as God must be characterized by this sacred self-regard or reflexive purity if he is to be perfect in wisdom, power, justice, and mercy and if he is to be properly regarded by his creation. His felicity, contentment *in se* and self-enjoyment — in short, his having himself as his own end and highest good — depends upon the fact that he need not look beyond himself, which is to say upon the purity of his nature or holiness.[133] Thus, in the same sense that the scholastic tradition speaks of God willing himself and loving himself, the divine holiness can be understood as "the purest love of his [own] attributes and affections" or as "that perfection of the divine nature which renders every act of his understanding and will consistent with his perfections, and fitted to promote their manifestation."[134]

The divine holiness, therefore, directs out attention to the ultimacy of God both in himself, separate from the world, and in his most intimate relationship to the world.

---

130. Ridgley, *Body of Divinity* (1855), I, p. 103.
131. Venema, *Inst. theol.*, vii (p. 161), citing Rev. 15:4; Job 25:5; 4:8.
132. Leigh, *Treatise*, II.xiii (pp. 102-103).
133. Cf. Leigh, *Treatise*, I.xiii (p. 103).
134. Witsius, *Dissertations on the Lord's Prayer*, VIII (p. 189).

Holiness is a separation both from sin and the world. The will of God is the rule of holiness, as his nature is the pattern of it. See Acts 13:22.[135]

God is holy in these particulars:

1. In his will; whatsoever God wills is holy, whether it be his secret will and purpose, or his revealed will and word.

2. In all his works, Eph. 1. He hath predestinated us to be holy; this is the end of all his graces to make us like himself; this is likewise the end of his Ordinances, his Word and Sacraments are to make us holy; so his works of justice, Christ's death.

3. In his Laws and Commandments, Psalm 19. His Commandments are just and right, and require holiness of heart, not suffering the least sinful notion.[136]

God's holiness thus distinguishes him from all the gods of paganism, as it is the characteristic that distinguishes also between his servants and the servants of the devil, between heaven and hell.

There are two consequences that follow from the divine holiness — one concerning God, the other concerning creatures. The consequence for God is that (as is the case with the other attributes as well) his holiness pervades all of his actions and interprets all of his other attributes. God is, thus, holy in his commandments, and he is never the author or "efficient cause" of sin: for him to be otherwise would be to deny his own nature and to act contrary to it. Even so, he cannot but hate sin and he must act to punish it. Indeed, it is the necessary and natural consequence of his holiness that he will punish sin "in order to give a manifestation of his holiness."[137] By extension, the orthodox view of the divine holiness underscores the conclusion reached against the Socinians in the discussion of divine vindicatory or punitive justice: it is essential to God and must be exercised. Indeed, removal of this aspect of justice would render God less than perfectly holy.

3. Holiness in creatures and the practical use of the doctrine. When the term is applied to created things, it can mean that they have been set apart for a sacred use, "as in the temple at Jerusalem, the altar, the vessels, the priests," are called holy. Or, when referring to the virtues of a rational being, "holiness" refers to their "conformity to God." In believers, this holiness will be made perfect only at the final resurrection — in the holy angels it is complete even now.[138]

The consequence of this attribute with reference to creatures is that they ought to fear, adore, and worship him as holy, and imitate his actions and affections by conforming themselves to his holiness, so that they may reflect his image in themselves and in their life. For he is a perfect pattern to us, the exemplar of all holiness, and

---

135. Leigh, *Treatise*, I.xiii (p. 105, margin).

136. Leigh, *Treatise*, II.xiii (pp. 103-104); cf. Brakel, *Redelijke Godsdienst*, I.iii.31 (*Reasonable Service*, I, p. 123); Caryl, *Exposition upon the Book of Job*, 6:10, in loc. (II, p. 467); Ridgley, *Body of Divinity* (1855), I, p. 103.

137. Venema, *Inst. theol.*, vii (pp. 161-162); cf. Brakel, *Redelijke Godsdienst*, I.iii.31 (*Reasonable Service*, I, p. 123).

138. Ursinus, *Exercitationes catecheticae* (Williard, p. 630).

therefore we should be perfect as he is perfect, Matt. 5:48. Nor can God hold communion except with the holy; for he is a consuming fire to the sinner, Is. 33:14.[139]

This *ad extra* consequence leads, therefore, to the two implications of holiness, now, however, in relation to creatures. In a negative sense, holiness indicates separation from what is low and base. When God is called "the Holy One," this signifies that he is "one separate or set apart from all filthinesse and uncleannesse" — not only is it the case that "no evil dwells with God," it is also true that

> none comes neare him. ... He is so separated from evill, that hee cannot behold evill, or looke on iniquity (Hab. 1:13) except with a vindictive eye.[140]

In a positive sense, holiness may be defined as the purity or "the moral goodness of a thing," so that "Holiness in man is that virtue whereby he giveth and yieldeth himself to God, in doing all for and to Him, in regard of which, the actions he doth are acceptable to God."[141] The foundation and root of all moral good is in God's goodness and holiness, and holiness, therefore can also be called "the brightest part of the image of God in man."[142]

Human holiness, then, "consists in ... conformity unto God," to the attainment of the divine likeness, and, specifically, in "the application of our minds and actions to God."[143] This conformity, moreover, is a conformity both to the nature and to the will of God. The believer is a partaker of God's nature in the sense that his life embodies an "analogical resemblance" to God both in the attributes that we have as created and regenerate in God's image, patience, mercy, justice, faithfulness, truth, love; and in the affections that we display "when we love what God loves, when we hate, what God hates; when, what pleases God, pleaseth us also." Conformity to the will of God, is, in Caryl's definition of personal holiness, a conformity to the "externall will ... signified by his word" — "every action of man is holy or unholy, according to its conformity with or variation from this will."[144]

Christians need learn from this conception of the holiness of God to be wary of hypocrites and profane men who "scoff" at divine holiness, to recognize here the condemnation of the pope "who proudly arrogates" to himself "the Title of the most holy." Holiness ought to be "prized and admired" as the virtue of God which demands worship and which demands, also, a resemblance or analogy in the conduct of God's children. This truth is of greatest comfort and assurance to the saints of God and a great terror to the unholy of the world, who find in themselves their highest good.

---

139. Venema, *Inst. theol.*, vii (p. 162).

140. Caryl, *Exposition upon the Book of Job*, 6:10, in loc. (II, p. 467).

141. Leigh, *Treatise*, II.xiii (p. 102).

142. Ridgley, *Body of Divinity* (1855), I, p. 103.

143. Caryl, *Exposition upon the Book of Job*, 6:10, in loc. (II, p. 469).

144. Caryl, *Exposition upon the Book of Job*, 6:10, in loc. (II, pp. 469-470), marginally noting the *voluntas signi* as distinct from the *voluntas beneplaciti*.

We should labor after holiness, to go quite out of ourselves, and all creatures, and go wholly as it were unto God, making him the ground, measure and end of all our actions, striving above all things to know him, esteem him and set all our powers upon him. This is the felicity of the creature, to be holy as God is holy; this is the felicity of the Saints in Heaven, they care for nothing but God, are wholly and altogether carried to him and filled with him. He is all in all unto them, as he is all in all unto himself. In being thus carried to him, they are united to him and enjoy him and are blessed.[145]

D. The Goodness of God

1.The views of the Reformers. The goodness of God serves two functions among the divine attributes: on the one hand, the *bonitas Dei* serves as an essential attribute, indeed, together with "oneness" or unity as a primary perfection of the divine essence in itself.[146] On the other hand, inasmuch as it is the primary characteristic of all divine relationships with the finite order, it also serves as the primary affection of the divine will. It is in this latter placement, in relation to love, grace, and mercy, that it is most typically found in Reformed theology, although both systematic functions of the doctrine are made clear in many of the larger orthodox systems.[147] These two perspectives on the doctrine and its two corresponding systematic functions are identifiable in virtually all Reformed orthodox discussions in a basic distinction between the divine goodness understood in itself and the divine goodness understood in relation to its objects in the created order. A second distinction, governing the discussion of the relationship of the goodness to its objects, indicates that the goodness of God *ad extra* may be considered either as general or as special.[148]

Once again, these perspectives reflect medieval scholastic theology and were characteristic of Reformed theology from its beginnings. Zwingli, for example, argues that God's being "is as really good as it is being" inasmuch as "it exists alone and of itself" and is "of itself good." This must be so, he continues, granting the goodness of the created order considered both "singly and collectively": "it is clear that their author must be good, and in such a way good as to have his goodness from no other but his own self."[149] We also recognize, however, that this ultimate goodness is "not a thing idle or inert, so as to lie torpid and motionless, moving neither itself nor other things":

this supreme good, which is God, is by nature kind and bountiful ... for He desires to impart Himself freely. For, as He is the fountain-source of all things ... so also is He

---

145. Leigh, *Treatise*, I.xiii (p. 105).

146. See above, 4.3 (D.1) on the universal predicates of Being (*ens, res, unum, verum, bonum*) in traditional metaphysics and note the reflection of this point in relation to the essential goodness of God in Junius, *Theses Leydenses*, IX.2; Arminius, *Disp. priv.*, XV.vii; Mastricht, *Theoretico-practica theol.*, II.xvi.3.

147. Cf. e.g., Turretin, *Inst. theol. elencticae*, III.xx.3-11, with Mastricht, *Theoretico-practica theologia*, II.xvi.1, 7-10; Venema, *Inst. theol.*, VII (pp. 162-165).

148. Cf. Gill, *Body of Doctrinal and Practical Divinity*, I, pp. 132, 134.

149. Zwingli, *Commentary*, p. 64; cf. idem, *On Providence*, pp. 131-12.

unceasingly bountiful to those whom He begot with this one purpose, that they might enjoy his bounty. ... This good is so exhuberantly abundant that it is more than sufficient for the needs of all; for it is limitless and loves to impart itself.[150]

For Zwingli, therefore, the *bonitas Dei* serves as the primary attribute of the divine essence. This understanding of the divine goodness carries over, albeit in brief, homiletically presented forms, into Bullinger's theology: God is good in himself or by nature and the divine goodness is the foundation of goodness of the created order.[151] God, writes Bullinger, "is the everlasting wellspring of all good things."[152]

Calvin and Musculus, however, without denying these arguments, tended to understand "goodness" as one of the divine virtues everywhere manifest, alongside of might, wisdom, righteousness, mercy, and truth.[153] Musculus in particular devoted considerable attention to the concept of divine goodness. He noted the goodness of God as an essential attribute in his initial discussion of the divine nature and returned to it as a separate *locus* following his discussions of the will and veracity of God.[154] The concept of divine goodness, Musculus begins, is widely revealed throughout Scriptures and is highly edifying and comforting to the godly as the foundation of their life and salvation. This biblical and Christian doctrine must be distinguished from such errors as that of Cerdon and Marcion, according to which there are two Gods, an evil creator and a good and merciful Father. Scripture is clear: there is but one good God, who is both the creator and the Father of Jesus Christ.[155]

There are, Musculus adds, an "infinite number of arguments" demonstrating the goodness of God that can be gathered together into three main categories: creation itself, the daily care of God for all creatures (including the wicked), and the consistent testimony of Scripture. Scripture speaks variously of the divine goodness as beneficial, as delightful to the mind, and, as pleasant to the heart. "The Philosopher," Musculus adds, "defines that to be good which all people desire." By identifying God as good, Scripture set him utterly apart from all malice, cruelty, and harshness, shows him to be kind, liberal, worthy of trust, and full of grace toward us.[156] The contrast between the divine goodness and creatures is stated emphatically, moreover, by Christ, who tells the rich young ruler that only God is good. Here, Musculus notes that Scripture itself speaks otherwise — calling Barnabas good, speaking of God's creatures as good, and commanding human beings to be good. The text demands that we make two comparisons: one between God and creatures in general, another between God and human beings. Over against the creation, the goodness of God is "original, perfect,

---

150. Zwingli, *Commentary*, pp. 71-72; also see the extended discussion in Stephens, *Theology of Huldrych Zwingli*, pp. 84-86.

151. Bullinger, *Decades*, III.x (p. 366).

152. Bullinger, *Decades*, II.ii (p. 216).

153. Cf. Calvin, *Institutes*, III.xx.41 with Musculus, *Loci communes*, I (*Commonplaces*, p. 17, col. 1).

154. Musculus, *Loci communes*, I, XLII (*Commonplaces*, p. 17, col. 1; p. 889, col. 2).

155. Musculus, *Loci communes*, XLVII (*Commonplaces*, p. 948, col. 2).

156. Musculus, *Loci communes*, XLVII (*Commonplaces*, p. 950, col. 1).

and most excellent." It is original because God receives it from no other: it is proper to him and has no beginning. It is perfect because nothing can be added to it and nothing more can be desired from it; and it is most excellent inasmuch as it can neither be fully expressed nor fully emulated by any creature, "not even the angels in heaven." God alone is good in the same sense that Scripture indicates he alone is the existent one. The goodness of creation, however, is derived from its creator and is a goodness of degree.[157]

In order to compare the divine with human goodness, Musculus continues, human beings must be considered in four ways. First, when human nature is considered in itself, as given existence by God, it is good in the same sense as the rest of the created order. Second, when human nature is considered in its present condition, as fallen from its original created goodness, it is utterly depraved and falls under Christ's condemnation, namely, that none are good, but only God. Third, human beings can be considered good in and through the redemptive grace of Christ, by which the corruption of their nature is healed and the "image of God's goodness" is restored: but this is not a goodness of which human beings may boast, for it is the goodness of Christ in them. Finally, Musculus also notes a goodness of instruction or upbringing, most evident in the gifts and skills of human beings — but this, again, is not an "absolute" goodness like that of God.[158]

Having stated his case negatively, Musculus moves on to the positive statement of the doctrine: whereas the human heart is changeable and lacks constancy in its dispositions, the goodness of God is changeless, "for God is good, not on occasion or due to external causes, but naturally, of himself."[159] God's goodness, therefore, differs from God's anger: just a a human father can be angry with his son "on occasion" but continually wills the good of his son as a natural affection," so is God angry with human beings "on occasion" for the sake of correcting evil — whereas the blessings of God "proceed without end from his natural goodness." Even so, the goodness of God cannot be overcome or diminished: despite the universal sinfulness of the human race and the "obstinate malice" of the ancient Jewish people, God nonetheless gave "his only begotten Son to be our mediator and savior ... according to his eternal determination."[160]

Musculus next indicates that the goodness of God ought to be understood in two ways — as general and as special. Thus, God manifests his goodness "generally towards all" whether they are good or evil: as Scripture teaches, God makes the sun to shine on the good and the evil and provides for both man and beast, both elect and reprobate.[161] But God is also good "*specialiter et singulariter*" toward his elect, namely, to those who are faithful, godly, and just, of whom the psalmist speaks when he says,

157. Musculus, *Loci communes*, XLVII (*Commonplaces*, pp. 950-951).

158. Musculus, *Loci communes*, XLVII (*Commonplaces*, pp. 951-952).

159. Musculus, *Loci communes*, XLVII (*Commonplaces*, p. 952, col. 2).

160. Musculus, *Loci communes*, XLVII (*Commonplaces*, p. 953, col. 1).

161. Musculus, *Loci communes*, XLVII (*Commonplaces*, p. 953, col. 2), citing Matt. 5:45 and Ps. 145:7-10.

"Truly God is good to Israel, even to such as are of a clean heart." This goodness, Musculus adds, is distinct from the general goodness mentioned in Psalm 145: "such is the character of true goodness, that it wills good to all in general (*in genere bene velit*) and yet at times also bears special favor toward some."[162] The use of this doctrine, Musculus concludes, ought to be clear: all people ought to be moved to commit all their concerns to the providence of God, while believers ought to be especially stirred to look for heavenly blessings and to act so as not to be "found unworthy of such exceeding grace."[163] The practical application of the doctrine now becomes Musculus' primary concern as he enumerates "how many ways we offend against the goodness of God."[164]

2. The goodness of God according to the Reformed orthodox. As already noted, the concept of the *bonitas Dei* has two functions in the theology of Reformed orthodoxy — on the one hand, it is one of the irreducible or transcendental predicates of Being and therefore belongs absolutely to God,[165] while, on the other, it is one of the primary attributes of God's self-manifestation, although it is certainly the latter and not the former point that receives the emphasis in the Reformed systems, as indicated by the placement and use of the *bonitas Dei* in such Reformed thinkers as Wendelin, Leigh, Brakel, Pictet, and Venema. This point is significant inasmuch as there is some correspondence in definition between the Reformed and Thomas Aquinas, but there is very little in terms of the function and location of the doctrine of the *bonitas Dei*: in this *locus*, certainly, the Reformed, unlike Aquinas, are less interested in the absolute Being of God and its transcendent properties than they are in the character and egress of the divine willing. Even so, the Reformed orthodox frequently discuss the divine attributes of goodness, love, grace, and mercy together. Turretin comments that "just as vindicatory justice ... and its adjuncts, hatred (*odio*), wrath (*ira*), and sternness (*severitas*) are concerned with physical evil and the infliction of punishments, so is goodness (*bonitas*), and those virtues belonging to it, namely, love (*amor*), grace (*gratia*), and mercy (*misericordia*), concerned with the communication of good, but in diverse ways."[166] Mastricht, similarly, identifies love, grace, mercy, long-suffering, and clemency as "gracious affections of God" that belong to the communication of the divine goodness.[167] This affective or volitional understanding of divine goodness and related attributes also points away from a Thomistic toward a more Scotistic and *via moderna* Augustinian accent in Reformed orthodoxy on this particular point of doctrine.

God's goodness, with the divine holiness, is an "absolute and original attribute of God, having reference to creatures,"[168] but is nonetheless "the very essence of God's

---

162. Musculus, *Loci communes*, XLVII (*Commonplaces*, p. 953-954).
163. Musculus, *Loci communes*, XLII (*Commonplaces*, p. 954, col. 1).
164. Musculus, *Loci communes*, XLVII (*Commonplaces*, p. 954, col. 2-p. 957, col. 1).
165. Cf. Aquinas, *Summa theol.*, Ia, q. 5, a. 1; q. 6, a. 3.
166. Turretin, *Inst. theol. elencticae*, III.xx.1.
167. Mastricht, *Theroetico-practica theol.*, II.xvii.1, 3.
168. Venema, *Inst. theol.*, VII (p. 162).

Being."[169] Thus, as Leigh writes, "God's *Goodness* is an essential property whereby he is infinitely and of himself good, and the author and cause of all goodness in the creature."[170] Or as Wendelin comments, "*Bonitas Dei est, qua Deus in se maxime perfectus & appetibilis, omniumque extra se appetibilium & bonorum causa est.*"[171] In the philosophical language adopted by orthodoxy — an originally Aristotelian language filtered through Augustine's Neoplatonism and measured against the biblical text — *bonum est id quod omnes appetunt seu quod natura sua appetibile est.*[172] The good is to be desired, and God, as the highest good, is to be desired most of all. "God and [the highest] appetible are convertible," comments Leigh.[173] God and the highest good must be identified, inasmuch as:

> 1. It is *propter se amabile*, to be desired for itself; so only God.
> 2. It is able to satisfy the soul, and that satisfaction which it gives is perpetual: In God there is both satiety and stability; satisfaction of the appetite and continuance of that satisfaction.
> 3. God is causally good, worketh all goodness in the creature, and doth good to them, Psal. 33:5.
> 4. Eminently and absolutely good, the only good. There is a goodness in the creature, its nature is good, but goodness is not its nature; so there is none good but God, *viz.* essentially, originally.[174]

Even so,

> Our Saviour, Matth. 19:17. reproved one for calling him good. Not that he is not so essentially, but because he thinking him to be no more than a Prophet, did yet call him so. God only is good essentially, independently; comparatively to God the creature is not good; as a drop is no water compared to the Ocean.[175]

Indeed, Wendelin adds, drawing together the traditionary and somewhat philosophical point with the biblical materials, Christ himself tells us as much, when he states that none is good but God alone (Matt. 19:17), and when this text is understood in connection with the statement of Paul that all things are from God and in God (Rom. 11:36) and the statements of the Psalmist that the earth is filled with the goodness of God (Ps. 33:5; 103:11), the identification of God as the *summum bonum* has found its biblical ratification.[176] So, too, Leigh passes from the philosophical point to its exegetical ratification: "The Scripture proveth God's goodness," he writes,

---

169. Brakel, *Christian's Reasonable Service*, I, p. 122.

170. Leigh, *Treatise*, II.x (p. 79); cf. Ussher, *Body of Divinity*, p. 61.

171. Wendelin, *Christianae theologiae libri duo*, I.i.20.

172. Wendelin, *Christianae theologiae libri duo*, I.i.20 (1)

173. Leigh, *Treatise*, II.x (p. 79).

174. Leigh, *Treatise*, II.x (p. 79).

175. Leigh, *Treatise*, II.x (p. 79).

176. Wendelin, *Christianae theologiae libri duo*, I.i.20 (1); cf. *Dutch Annotations*, Matt. 19:17, in loc.: "*None is good but one, (namely) God.* Namely, of himself, perfectly, and the Original of all good"; also note *Westminster Annotations*, in loc.

1. Affirmatively, when it affirmeth that God is good, and commends his goodness. Psalm 25:8.

2. Negatively, when it denieth that there is any evil in him. Psalm 92:16; Deut. 32:4.

3. Symbolically, when it celebrateth the riches of his goodness, Rom. 2:4.

4. Effectively, when it affirms that all the works of God are good, Gen. 1:31. It was said of everything particularly when it was made, *The Lord saw that it was good*; and in the conclusion of the whole creation, *God saw all his works that they were good, yea, very good*; that is, commodious for the comfort of man, and all other creatures. He made all things good, therefore he is good himself. This may be proved by the goodness which still remains in the creatures....

5. God is to be loved, honored, praised, and served by man, therefore he is good; or else he were not worthy this respect from the creature.[177]

This goodness of God can be considered *ad intra*, insofar as God is good *in se* apart from any relationship he has to his creation, and *ad extra*, insofar as he is good in his relation to all things outside of himself. And both the goodness *ad intra* and the goodness *ad extra* must be understood as communicable and communicated goodness.[178] In considering God's goodness *ad intra*, it may first be noted that there are, generally speaking, three kinds of good, *bonum utile, bonum jucundum, bonum bonestum* — the useful or profitable good, the good of pleasure, and the exemplar of goodness. As God is the giver of all good things and the one at whose "right hand" there are "pleasures forevermore" (Psalm 34), he is both *bonum utile* and *bonum jucundum* — that is, both of these goods in an ultimate sense. And so he is the highest good and the "author of all holiness," the exemplar of goodness, he is the *bonum bonestum*.[179] Furthermore, this God who is the sum and substance of all goodness *in se* is essentially good and immutably good. From this it follows that God's goodness is not subject to increase: "God cannot be a better God." His goodness is also an independent goodness which is infinite and unlimited. Since God is wholly good, his goodness is unmixed (1 John 1:5).[180]

The Reformed orthodox also recognize that, in view of the trinitarian nature of God, this ultimate goodness ought not to be viewed as monolithic or static: God's goodness *in se* or *ad intra* is communicable. Indeed, writes Wendelin, "God communicates his goodness in two ways *(duobus modis)*, *ad intra* and *ad extra*." "The first of these communications," he continues,

is natural and necessary, by which God the Father communicates his essence eternally to the Son by generation; and the Father and the Son together to the Holy Spirit by spiration. The second communication is free, and by it God communicates his goodness

---

177. Leigh, *Treatise*, II.x (pp. 79-80).

178. Wendelin, *Christianae theologiae libri duo*, I.i.20 (3).

179. Leigh, *Treatise*, II.x (p. 80).

180. Leigh, *Treatise*, II.x (p. 80); cf. John Mayer, *A Commentarie upon the New Testament*, 3 vols. (London, 1631), in loc (vol. 3, p. 178).

to creatures. 1) through creation. 2) through the incarnation. 3) by the grace of adoption. 4) in glory and beatitude. 5) by love and ardent desire.[181]

God is good in all his relations *ad extra* and is the source of all created or finite goodness — to the point that the proper object of the divine goodness can be identified as "the rational creature as such, and considered as good" and the *bonitas Dei* can be defined further as "that amiable perfection in the exercise of which [God] wills and does good to the creatures who are considered by him as good, according to the measure of their goodness relatively to him."[182] The latter phrase is significant, inasmuch as it indicates not only the source of creaturely goodness in God but also the continuance of creaturely goodness in dependence on God. Thus, "all the good of a creature is in God always,"

1. *Eminently*, as you consider it in its kind, without imperfection.
2. *Efficiently*, as he is the Author and cause of all the good the creature has.
3. *Exemplarily*, as he is the rule and pattern of all goodness.
4. *Finally*, as he is the chiefest good of all creatures, so that all terminate their desires in him.[183]

Granting this structure of the divine good in its relation to the world, it is also true that "this highest goodness of God excludes from God and God's works, insofar as they are his works, all evil" including the evil or guilt resulting from "the privation of moral goodness."[184]

Now we call goodness that affection in God, by which he is inclined to communicate himself to his creatures.... The first act of God's goodness in time is *creation*, and because what is produced always depends on what produces it, the second act of goodness is *preservation*.[185]

In this most inclusive sense, the divine goodness can be identified as *benevolentia*, the "inclination of the will to do good as far as it is possible and lawful to do so" or, indeed, as "the love of God towards his creatures" by which he acts to "promote their happiness and perfection."[186] Accordingly, Scripture teaches that "God is love" (1 John 4:8), that he is "good and upright" (Ps. 25:8), that he takes "no pleasure" in the death of his creatures (Ezek. 18:32), would have none perish (2 Pet. 3:9), and "will have all men to be saved" (1 Tim. 2:4).[187]

Furthermore, in a stricter sense, God's goodness is manifest as his "beneficence" toward the created order and toward individual creatures, relative "to the goodness which is in the creatures" — the goodness by which God does not treat all creatures

---

181. Wendelin, *Christianae theologiae libri duo*, I.i.20 (3).

182. Venema, *Inst. theol.*, VII (p. 162).

183. Leigh, *Treatise*, II.x (p. 81).

184. Wendelin, *Christianae theologiae libri duo*, I.i.20 (1).

185. Pictet, *Theol. chr.*, II.vii.2-3; cf. Ridgley, *Body of Divinity* (1855), p. 109.

186. Venema, *Inst. theol.*, VII (p. 163).

187. Cf. Venema, *Inst. theol.*, VII (p. 163), with Turretin, *Inst. theol. elencticae*, III.xx.2, 5.

in the same manner but rather "according to their different states."[188] This beneficence can also be understood in three ways:

> This goodness, moreover, is either *general*, which embraces all creatures, or *special*, which regards *human* creatures, and *most special*, which regards the elect. Nor should it seem strange that God is not equally good towards his creatures, for in this inequality is displayed his sovereign freedom and dominion.[189]

As Scripture teaches, our "daily experience" evidences this general beneficence (Ps. 119:64; 154:15; Matt. 5:45), while at the same time, God's goodness is personally experienced quite differently by the elect and the reprobate (Ps. 51:10; 73:1; Matt. 13:11).[190] Thus God without inconsistency and beyond reproach can "require of men faith and obedience" even as he has decreed to require faith, but only give it to some.[191]

So also, it does not follow (as the Arminians argue) that the goodness of God both *ad intra* and *ad extra* implies that God must will to communicate his goodness to all his creatures in such a way as to save all of them. For God does not will to exercise his infinite justice against all sinners, but wills to save some. God's goodness does not contradict God's justice.

> Notwithstanding God's goodness of nature he suffered man to fall; but yet he was so good that he would not have suffered it, unless he could have showed as much goodness to man another way; and indeed, Christ is a greater good to us by faith, than *Adam's* innocence could have been: but yet since that evil is come into the world, how many calamities might befall thee, did not God's goodness prevent it? That the earth swallows thee not up 'tis God's goodness. The goodness of God is so great, that no creature should suffer punishment, but that the justice of God doth require the same, or else some greater good may be drawn from thence.[192]

Knowledge of God's goodness has also a practical relation to piety: for it manifests to us that God "is the proper object of love" and "ought to be the principal object of all the powers of our souls." Furthermore, we learn from God's goodness to imitate God in cleaving to the good and doing the good and in recognizing the goodness of God as our strong support "in ... calamities, ... poverty, and the fear of death itself." God's goodness also clearly reveals to us the evil of all sinful acts.[193]

E. Truth and Faithfulness

1. **Divine *veritas* and *fidelitas* in Reformed theology.** Reformed theological systems ranging from Musculus' *Loci communes* in the era of the Reformation to such early and high orthodox thinkers as Polanus, Leigh, Charnock, and Mastricht, to Venema's

---

188. Venema, *Inst. theol.*, VII (p. 164).
189. Pictet, *Theol. chr.*, II.vii.3.
190. Ussher, *Body of Divinity*, p. 62.
191. Pictet, *Theol. chr.*, II.vi.6.
192. Leigh, *Treatise*, II.x (p. 82).
193. Leigh, *Treatise*, II.x (pp. 82-83).

Institutes in the late orthodox era all offer a discussion of God's truth or truthfulness in relation to the intellectual attributes. Many of the orthodox theologians also connect the doctrine of the *veracitas Dei* with the faithfulness of God, the *fidelitas Dei* or *constantia Dei*,[194] an association that continued to be characteristic of the theologies of later successors to the orthodox system like Gill and Dick.[195] Others place faithfulness or constancy in relation to the divine immutability or, indeed, to the immutability of the divine willing. Still others, like Maccovius, Brakel, and Turretin, omit mention of the topic, presumably because it could be inferred from or subsumed under the general discussions of divine immutability and divine knowledge.

It is worth noting also that, although the basic doctrine of the *veracitas* and *fidelitas Dei* changes little either in its basic definition or in its exegetical foundation from the time of the Reformers to the close of the era of orthodoxy, its contours were altered by the state of the controversies in which the Reformed engaged. Thus, the early Reformed understanding, as exemplified by Musculus' *locus* on the subject and by the numerous discussions found in the commentaries of the day, had a great deal to do with the truthfulness of God's word and the faithfulness of the divine promises — whereas the later discussion moved toward an encounter with various forms of philosophical skepticism on the one hand and with the rational inference of divine truthfulness (as opposed to a trust in the witness of revelation) characteristic of Descartes' philosophy.

2. The teaching of the Reformers. On the topic of divine truthfulness, its basic definition and implication, and its place among the divine attributes, Musculus wrote:

> Forasmuch as the truth is the foundation of all things that be, and of all things which ought to be believed, known, said, and done, without which nothing can be, nor remain, I think it not unmeet after that which we have spoken of the Nature, Sufficiency, Omnipotence and Will of God, to speak somewhat also of his Truth. For in this the whole certainty and clarity of our faith doth consist, whereby it is cleared from all slander of falsehood, and sundered from all other, arbitrary, and counterfeit religions. ... I intend to stand upon the term of God's truth: not that it can be perfectly conceived by the capacity or understanding of man, whereas it doth infinitely pass and go beyond all our understanding: but because the knowledge thereof is very necessary unto our salvation. Neither is it my mind to enter into that school disputations, whereas they discourse and dispute of the theological truths natural and supernatural, more scrupulously than is meet for the simple searching out of plain truth.[196]

Truth, argues Musculus, is "not all one" — a distinction must be drawn between the truth of God and the truth of creatures. The distinction is made, however, with the initial presupposition that "all truths agree" and "that there is no one truth contrary unto another truth." The difference between divine and creaturely truth is, first, a

---

194. Cf. Ridgley, *Body of Divinity* (1855), pp. 119-123.

195. Thus, Gill, *Body of Divinity*, I, pp. 159-170; John Dick, *Lectures on Theology*, 2 vols. (Edinburgh, 1834), xxvi.

196. Musculus, *Loci communes*, xlvi (*Commonplaces*, p. 935, col. 1).

difference in excellence: "The truth of creatures is not of itself, but from another, and the truth of God is just, and not proceeding of any other, but is in God without beginning." Second, the truth of God is not only the first but also the highest truth, on which all creaturely truth depends. It exceeds creaturely truth "as a matter uncreated excells those things which be created of it."[197] Third, the truth of God is "everlasting and inalterable" in contrast to the temporal and changeable truth of creatures. This being so, the truth of God should be most highly and continually regarded among men — "so for the highest, and chiefest truth of God, we must give up all inferior and later truths."[198]

Musculus next raises the question, "How many kinds of truth are there in God" — in short, the question of explanatory distinctions to be made in the discussion of the *veritas Dei*.

> We do know that there is but one self same truth in God, whereby he is true in himself and in all. But for the exposition thereof, our question is, how many kinds there be thereof. For like as there be not in God many wills, but one and that everlasting, yet for all that a man might not amiss say that there be two, that is one of grace, and the other of wrath: so in my judgment, it shall not be out of the way to say, that the one self same truth of God is of four kinds, of essence, quality, operation, and word.[199]

The distinction can in fact be identified as having two primary members, each of which divides into two parts: thus, the *ad intra* distinction between essence and "quality" or attribute, and the *ad extra* distinction between operation and word.

First the truth of essence and quality: since, in the first place, God is "the true existent and true God" and since "no essence is without truth," we may speak of "a truth of godly essence, in respect of which, false gods being rejected, all honor of Godhead is due unto the One God alone." In the second place,

> there is the truth of quality in God, whereby all those things be true which be reported of him in the holy scriptures. For there be some things reported of his essence, other some of his person, and other some of his nature.[200]

Thus faith apprehends the unity and simplicity of the divine essence, that God is without body or place, incomprehensible, invisible, immutable, indivisible, unspeakable, perfect, and everlasting — and also that the one essence is distinguished into three persons, "Jehovah, Word, and Spirit," or "Father, Son, and Holy Spirit." Concerning God's nature we know that he is "kind, merciful, loving, patient, just."[201] This "quality" of divine truth or faithfulness is also directly related to the constance or immutability

---

197. Musculus, *Loci communes*, xlvi (*Commonplaces*, p. 935, col. 2).
198. Musculus, *Loci communes*, xlvi (*Commonplaces*, p. 935, col. 2 - p. 936, col. 2).
199. Musculus, *Loci communes*, xlvi (*Commonplaces*, p. 936, col. 2).
200. Musculus, *Loci communes*, xlvi (*Commonplaces*, p. 936, col. 2 - p. 937, col. 1).
201. Musculus, *Loci communes*, xlvi (*Commonplaces*, p. 937, cols. 1-2).

of God: by it "we are taught that God continues always the same, and is never wearied of helping us."[202]

Both Calvin and Musculus distinguish between what might be called the *ad extra* manifestations of God's truth, namely, between the truth of "the just and well regulated character of [God's] governance, in which his rectitude is seen to be pure and free from all deception" and the truth or "faithfulness which God manifests in accomplishing his promises,"[203] or, in Musculus' terms, between a truth of "operation" and a truth of "word." A "truth of operation" can also be attributed to God inasmuch as his works, both visible and invisible, are true, none of them being done in vain or with evil or false intent, like the works of the devil. None of God's works, moreover, appear to be one thing while actually intending another.[204]

> Fourthly, there is also in God the truth of word. And we mean by God's word all his promises, all laws and ordinances, all threatenings, all comforts, all oracles and prophesies, set forth either by Angels or by men. In respect thereof the Apostle saith, that God is true in his words, and every man a liar (Rom 3.). And the Prophet David saith, that the word of the Lord is like a silver tried by fire, purged sevenfold.[205]

This point, of course, relates directly to the Reformed doctrine of Scripture, specifically, to the assumption of the absolute veracity of the text as God's Word — as implied also in the Reformed discussions of the "attributes" of Scripture.[206] Calvin makes a similar inference from Christ's grounding of his own righteousness and truthfulness on God: "Let us, therefore, set it down as certain and undoubted, that whatever is from God is right and true, and that it is impossible for God not to be true in all his words.... And if after this the whole world should rise against us, we shall still have this invincible defense, that he who follows God cannot go astray."[207] Musculus notes that the question of truth in God might have been elaborated at great length after the manner of the schoolmen — but that such a statement as supports faith and guides into truth is sufficient, for "in this matter the chief point is the truth of the word incarnate, which is the way, the truth, and life unto all them which were ordained before unto life."[208] The fundamental issue is that "God is true" and therefore "cannot deceive us by his divine promises."[209]

This truth of God is most clear in itself, and it has the effect of enlightening the mind. Only our mortal blindness to truth prevents us from apprehending this. The fault is not with God.

---

202. Calvin, *Commentary on Psalms*, Ps. 40:10, in loc. (*CTS Psalms*, II, p. 106); cf. Psalm 31:5, in loc. (*CTS Psalms*, I, p. 504).

203. Calvin, *Commentary on Psalms*, Ps. 36:5, in loc. (*CTS Psalms*, II, p. 9).

204. Musculus, *Loci communes*, xlvi (*Commonplaces*, p. 937, col. 2-p. 938, col. 1).

205. Musculus, *Loci communes*, xlvi (*Commonplaces*, p. 938, col. 1).

206. See *PRRD*, II, 5.2.

207. Calvin, *Commentary on John*, 5:30 (*CTS John*, I, p. 211).

208. Musculus, *Loci communes*, xlvi (*Commonplaces*, p. 938, col. 1).

209. Calvin, *Commentary on Psalms*, Psalm 54:5, in loc. (*CTS Psalms*, II, pp. 325-326).

It is hard, yea, impossible for any which is born blind to know the light of the Sun, unless he recovers his eyesight by the goodness of God. And it is no less impossible for the carnal man to know the truth of God, unless he receive the heart of understanding by the gift of God.[210]

If the truth of God's oneness, as manifest by the pagan philosophers and confessed by the Jews, is difficult for sinful men to believe, how more difficult is the Christian truth of "Trinity and the word incarnate, hidden from the beginning of the world, his death, resurrection, and ascension, and the whole dispensation of mans redemption purchased by Christ, which our Saviour did express, calling himself the way, the truth, and the life."[211] No carnal man can come to this truth but by the grace of God. These elect are few in number as compared with the blind and lost of mankind: even many of those who recite the catholic faith of the Church do not have hearts enlightened by God's grace unto salvation.

> Albeit that the elect only, and such as be before ordained unto life do come to the knowledge of the truth, and do attain unto it not without the special grace of God, yet for all that there be some certain means without which no man may hope to attain unto it. First there is requisite a heart desireful to know the truth, for the wisdom of God does not admit such as do despise and loath it.[212]

Thus, the scribes and Pharisees, the boastful gentile philosophers of ancient times, prelates and "Seraphical doctors, with other great pontifical Priests" are excluded from the truth because they have no true desire to know it: They are blinded and "provoked into a raging fury against Disciples and ministers of the Truth. ... Secondly, it is needful that the desire to know the truth be ... joined with a care and a study to seek and to learn it."[213]

> Thirdly, it is requisite that we become his scholars, and believe his word, who is the only teacher of this truth, and that is he which said unto them that did believe in him: If you do continue in my word, you be indeed my disciples, and you shall know the truth. So that we must first of all hear the word of truth: secondly, believe it, and thirdly continue in it. Unto them that do this, the knowledge of the truth is promised.[214]

Throughout these arguments, Musculus cites Augustine for support.

God's truth is further characterized by "efficacy and strength."[215] The truth of God, once revealed, drives away the darkness of human ignorance and leaves without excuse those who make pretense of ignorance. God's truth also stirs up men's minds to know of God — in the present time as well as at the beginning of the gospel. It also opens

---

210. Musculus, *Loci communes*, xlvi (*Commonplaces*, p. 938, col. 2-p. 939, col. 1).
211. Musculus, *Loci communes*, xlvi (*Commonplaces*, p. 939, col. 1).
212. Musculus, *Loci communes*, xlvi (*Commonplaces*, p. 940, col. 1; cf. p. 939, cols. 1-2).
213. Musculus, *Loci communes*, xlvi (*Commonplaces*, p. 940, col. 1-2).
214. Musculus, *Loci communes*, xlvi (*Commonplaces*, p. 941, col. 1).
215. Musculus, *Loci communes*, xlvi (*Commonplaces*, p. 942, cols. 1-2).

up knowledge of things previously hidden by the general darkness of mind: true religion, true service, the way of salvation, the will of God, were in large part obscure before the gift of the gospel, but are now made clear to all. Even so does God's truth "find out and reprove the faults of darkness."[216] Having accomplished the latter effect, the truth of God's light grants us freedom from the darkness and from the bondage of sin. Finally, knowledge of God's truth is a knowledge that brings its own conviction making "the faithful person so fast and sure in his confession of faith, that he will not be driven from it."[217]

3. The Reformed orthodox doctrine. The Reformed orthodox discussion of the *veritas* and *fidelitas Dei*, as already noted, differs little in substance from that of the Reformers — like both Musculus and Calvin, the orthodox assume the relationship between the attribution of truthfulness to God and the attributions of omniscience and immutability. Daneau, for one, emphasizes the divine truth or faithfulness by placing them fourth in the order of treatment, after eternity, immortality, and immutability: his point is that, given the divine immutability, specifically the immutability of the divine will, God must be most true (*verissimus*) and most faithful (*fidelissimus*).[218] Indeed, the seventeenth-century orthodox will often argue the attribute in terms of a logical connection with these other points of doctrine — and, therefore, also in terms of their polemic with various adversaries, like Vorstius and the Socinians, they will argue the untenability of a model that affirms divine truth and at the same time denies such attributes as omniscience and immutability.[219]

From the attribution of omniscience and all-encompassing wisdom to God, it follows that God must be conceived of as standing in some relation to all truth. Indeed, the orthodox would state,

> God is *aeterna veritas & vera aeternitas.* ... Truth is originally from God; the first Idea, rule, or standard of truth is God's will, which is *veritas Dei,* whereby he is what he is, essentially, simply, immutably: by which he wills all things to be what indeed they are, and knows them to be such as they are most certainly. *Veritas rei, entitatis,* whereby things are such as God would have them to be, and so are true and good.[220]

Truth, when predicated of finite and temporal things, indicates an agreement in "being and appearance": things are true when they are as they seem to be. This truthfulness, insofar as it relates to both being and appearance, must be twofold; that is, it is both "essential, or of the very substance, of things" and "accidental, of the qualities and actions of things."[221] When predicated of God, truthfulness thus indicates both that he is true *in se* and in his self-revelation and acts *ad extra*: God reveals himself to be as he truly is. God is "in himself the eternal original spring and fountain of all truth"

216. Musculus, *Loci communes,* xlvi (*Commonplaces,* p. 942, col. 2 - p. 943, col. 1).

217. Musculus, *Loci communes,* xlvi (*Commonplaces,* p. 943, col. 2 - p. 944, col. 1).

218. Daneau, *Christianae isagoges,* I.7 (fol. 16r-v).

219. Mastricht, *Theoretico-practica theol.,* II.xiv.8.

220. Leigh, *Treatise,* II.xii (pp. 94-95, margin).

221. Leigh, *Treatise,* II.xii (p. 95).

and therefore also "the only sovereign cause and author of its revelation to us." The truth that is "originally one" in God is to us "of various sorts and kinds, according to the variety of the things which it respects in its communication and use."[222]

The distinctions made by the Reformed scholastics on the basis of such considerations precisely reflect those that we have already seen in the thought of Musculus — God is true in essence, in attributes, in operations, and in word. Thus, Edward Leigh:

> (1) His essence is real and true. He is God indeed, not in imagination alone; the Scripture calls God the true God; *to know thee, saith our Saviour Christ, the only true God*, and *whom thou has sent, Jesus Christ*. ... He hath not an imaginary and counterfeit, but a very real being; he is indeed such as he saith he is; for that which gives being to other things, must needs itself be in very deed. ...
>
> (2) He hath a true, not an erroneous conceit of things; he knows all things most exactly; he is indeed a willer of true goodness.
>
> (3) He speaks nothing but as the thing is, and as he doth conceive it. He means what he promises, and doth what he means: the Lord dissembleth not with men [Matt. 24:35; John 17:17]. He is true in his Word, and his whole Word, wither narrations, promises, threats, visions, or predictions. ... What he promiseth or threateneth to do, he intendeth and will perform, Psalm 89:33, 34; Deut. 7:9; 2 Cor. 1:20; *Promissa tua sunt; & suis falli timeat, cum promittit veritas?* Aug. *Confess.* XII.i.
>
> (4) God is true in his works; they are not done counterfeitly, as those of the Devil, but truely, Psalm 145:17; Rev. 15:3.[223]

Any careful consideration of the nature of God and any examination of the word of God in Scripture manifests God to be true — falsehood derives from "imperfection and wickedness, neither of which is in God." Scripture, accordingly, calls God "the Lord of truth" (Ps. 34:5), identifies his Son as truth (John 14:6), calls the Holy Spirit "Spirit of truth" (John 17:6), and the gospel the "word of truth" (Col. 1:5). The truth of God distinguishes him from "false gods" (2 Chron. 15:3; John 17:3). The truth of God "serves to reprove the wicked" and to prompt Christians to manifest God's truth and to be true in their own words, deeds, vows, and promises (cf. Psalm 45:3; Zech. 8:16). "God loves truth, as in himself, so in his creatures; but abhors dissimulation and hypocrisy, Prov. 12:22." Since God is true, his "true children" may take comfort from his promises. Even so, the church stands firm and safe upon the "pillar of truth," God's Word, knowing that God will not deny himself.[224]

Even as truthfulness is predicated of God, so may be faithfulness, and in much the same sense.

---

222. Owen, *Pneumatologia*, "To the Readers," in *Works*, III, p. 5.

223. Leigh, *Treatise*, II.xii (pp. 95-96); cf. Cocceius, *Summa theol.*, III.x.53, 54; Venema, *Inst. theol.*, vii (pp. 166-167).

224. Leigh, *Treatise*, II.xii (pp. 96-97); Cocceius, *Summa theol.*, III.x.54.

God is *Faithful*, 1 Cor. 19:18; Rev. 19:11. First, in himself, by an uncreated faithfulness. Secondly, in his decrees, Isaiah 14:24, 27. Thirdly, in all his ways and works, Psalm 145:17. ... Fourthly, in all his words and speeches.[225]

The works and words of God, therefore, indicate divine faithfulness as characteristic of all that God does and says: there is a faithfulness in creation (1 Pet. 4:19), in redemption (Heb. 2:17), in justification (John 1:19), in the protection and preservation of the church (Rev. 19:11), just as God's "Commandments are the rule of truth and faithfulness to us (Psalm 19:9), his "predictions are all faithfully accomplished many thousand years after, as Christ's incarnation in the fulness of time" (Gen. 49:10). So also are his "menaces" and his "promises" faithful (Ex. 12:41; Heb. 10:23).[226]

God's faithfulness is distinct from the faithfulness of creatures as a fountain or source is distinct from all derivative things. God's faithfulness, moreover, is unchangeable and is the eternal "rule and measure" of all temporal faithfulness. This appears from the perfection of God in all his ways, from the utterly just and righteous nature of God and from the absence of any imperfection in God that might "hinder" his faithfulness. It follows, then, that "God's faithfulness is the ground of all true Religion" as eminently illustrated in his covenant. We ought, therefore, to be faithful to him and to others:

(1) We must ground all doctrine of faith, all the Articles of faith, all our judgment and opinion in matters of faith, upon this faithfulness of God, and this by holding fast all the faithful word, Titus 1:9; Rom 3:4.

(2) All our obedience of faith must be grounded on this, John 3:33; Heb. 11:11.

(3) All our prayers of faith must be grounded on God's faithfulness, Dan. 9:16; 1 John 1:9; 1 Pet. 4:19, 31; Psalm 1:5.

(4) All sound profession of faith must be grounded on this, Gen 17:1, Psalm 91:4.

(5) All true perseverance in the faith, 1 Cor. 1:8; 10:13; Psalm 91:4.[227]

6.2 The Power, Dominion, Majesty, and Glory of God

A. Divine Omnipotence and Dominion in the Theology of the Reformers

1. The Reformers and the tradition of divine omnipotence. The doctrine of divine power and dominion inherited by the Reformers had been elaborated and debated at length by the medieval doctors and had been developed in several directions, as represented in general by Thomistic thought or the so-called *via antiqua* on the one side, and by Scotist or nominalist thought, identifiable as the *via moderna*, on the other.[228] In addition, the exegetical tradition provided not only numerous meditations

---

225. Leigh, *Treatise*, II.xii (p. 97).

226. Leigh, *Treatise*, II.xii (p. 97).

227. Leigh, *Treatise*, II.xii (p. 98).

228. See Francis Oakley, *Omnipotence, Covenant, & Order: An Excursion in the History of Ideas from Abelard to Leibniz* (Ithaca and London: Cornell University Press, 1984); William Courtenay, "The Dialectic of Omnipotence in the High and Late Middle Ages," in Rudavsky (ed.), *Divine Omniscience and Omnipotence in Medieval Philosophy*, pp. 243-269; Gijsbert van den Brink, *Almighty God: A Study*

on the power and dominion of God, it had labored through a great number of texts bearing different connotations and had developed a background of exegetical discussion for the more philosophical or logical queries of the scholastics. Beyond the general doctrinal agreement of virtually all theologians that God is omnipotent and unlimited in his dominion, there lay the questions of the actual extent of divine power over the order of creation established by God and over all possibilities, including those not realized within the order and those at variance with its laws.[229]

It is true, on the one hand, that a majority of the early Reformers tended to disdain the formalized structures of scholastic theology and to declaim against speculative discussion of scholastic distinctions concerning the power of God — in particular against the nominalist tendency to emphasize the divine transcendence through relatively extensive use of language concerning the divine *potentia absoluta*. It is also the case, on the other hand, however, that the Reformers did have quiet recourse to such distinctions and did tend to frame their thought in relation to the terms of the received doctrine. Luther, for example, despite his strongly expressed epistemological concerns about the character of God's self-revelation and about the inability of speculative reason to identify God rightly and savingly, nevertheless understood the divine omnipotence as a concept of "fundamental significance."[230]

In his fundamentally soteric approach to all doctrine, Luther could teach that a belief in God as the "almighty Maker of heaven and earth" — the credal formula — was necessary to the saving recognition that human beings neither have nor are able to attain anything in and of themselves. Thus, against the radicals, who refused to use such forms as the Apostles' Creed, Luther could not only insist on the teaching of the creed but on the understanding of the first article with its confession of "God, almighty Maker" as the foremost article of the faith.[231] Luther's emphasis on the form of God's revelation in Christ and in Scripture did not militate so much against the traditional language of divine omnipotence as against the way in which that language had been understood and used: Luther was not, in other words, interested in rational speculation about the implications of the identification of God as omnipotent, but primarily in the soteriological meaning of the concept. The approach of Zwingli, certainly in his *De providentia*, can be seen as far less soteriological and far more philosophical than Luther's view — and, indeed, as a position marking the extreme limit of the Reformed view of omnipotence, from which Calvin and most of the Reformed orthodox drew back.[232]

---

of the Doctrine of Divine Omnipotence (Kampen: Kok Pharos, 1993).

229. Gijsbert van den Brink, "Capable of Anything? The Omnipotence of God," in Brink and Sarot (eds.), *Understanding the Attributes of God*, pp. 144-418.

230. Köstlin, *Theology of Luther*, II, p. 281.

231. Cf. Köstlin, *Theology of Luther*, II, p. 214.

232. Zwingli, *On Providence*, I-III (pp. 130-159); and note Calvin's reservations in *Institutes*, III.xxi.1 and, explicitly, in his correspondence with Bullinger, in CO 14, col. 235; trans. in Calvin, *Selected Works*, II, p. 333-334. Also note the discussion in Seeberg, *History of Doctrines*, II, pp. 313-315; and note the more nuanced discussion Stephens, *Theology of Huldrych Zwingli*, pp. 86-97, where

2. Musculus on the power of God. Among the Reformed codifiers, Wolfgang Musculus offered the most developed and extensive discussion of the power and dominion of God. Yet, given that his discussion of the doctrine is the fruit of exegetical labors and, in fact, a *locus* gathered out of his extensive work as a commentator, it is not at all surprising that nearly every point that he makes is echoed in one place or another (albeit not always in strict agreement!) in Calvin's commentaries and sermons — often in relation to the same biblical texts. Calvin rejected the more speculative use of the distinction between the absolute and the ordained power of God but, at the same time, retained elements of the concept as his own theology developed — he certainly assumed that, both in power and in justice, the divine reality far exceeded the limits of the revealed order.[233] The same point can be made concerning the commentaries and sermons of other Reformed contemporaries — Bullinger, Pellikan, Vermigli. And, of course, in the case of Vermigli, we have a set of *loci* gathered posthumously from his tracts, treatises, and exegetical works.

Musculus begins his discussion of divine omnipotence by connecting his doctrine with the concept of divine "sufficiency," which had not only preceded it in the order of his discussion, but which also provided a related concept and natural corollary:

> Next unto the sufficiency of God, we may well place omnipotence. For unless he were also omnipotent and almighty, he could not be sufficient in all things. The Hebrews have no word to signify "almighty," and therefore the Scriptures call God absolutely mighty, full of power and strength. When Job would give unto God the glory of omnipotence, he said: I know that thou art able to do all things.[234]

The usage "God Almighty" in the various versions of Scripture rests, notes Musculus, on the word *Shaddai*, which is best rendered "sufficiency."[235] Similarly, "as we read in Exodus, 'Almighty is his name,' in the Hebrew it is, 'the Existent is his name.'" That God truly is almighty, however, is clear from Christ's statement "All things be possible unto God."[236]

> First, we do make a difference betwixt might, which the Greeks do call *dynamis*, and that which they call *exousian*, whereof we will speak in a place hereafter by itself. For might (*potentia*) standeth in strength, valiant force & c. But power (*potestas*) consisteth

---

the biblical foundations of Zwingli's teaching are balanced with the more philosophical language of the *De providentia*.

233. Cf. Brink, *Almighty God*, pp. 88-90 with Schreiner, "Exegesis and Double Justice in Calvin's Sermons on Job," pp. 322-338; and Steinmetz, "Calvin and the Absolute Power of God," pp. 65-79.

234. Musculus, *Loci communes*, xliv (*Commonplaces*, p. 905, col. 1).

235. Musculus, *Loci communes*, xliv (*Commonplaces*, p. 905, col. 2); cf. Calvin, *Commentary on Genesis*, 17:1 (CTS *Genesis*, I, p. 443) and Calvin, *Harmony of the Last Four Books of Moses*, Ex. 6:3 (CTS *Harmony*, I, p. 126).

236. Musculus, *Loci communes*, xliv (*Commonplaces*, p. 905, col. 2); cf. Calvin, *Harmony of the Last Four Books of Moses*, Ex. 3:14; 6:3 (CTS *Harmony*, I, pp. 73-74, 126-127).

in jurisdiction and authority, wherefore he that is mighty enough to anything that he is able to do, hath not always Authority so to do.[237]

Second, argues Musculus, we recognize two fundamentally different kinds of might, "one which is received from some other and another which is received from none."[238] The former belongs to creatures, the latter to God only — the former is not proper to those that have it, while the second belongs to no other and is proper to God himself. The former power is both a gift and a continuing dependence: "There is no creature heavenly, or earthly which hath so received any strength from God, that it is able afterwards to use the same by its own strength.... So that they themselves be not so much mighty from God, as God is mighty in them."[239] Might that is received is thus "particular and limited." It is particular in that it cannot do all things, which is to say, it is not universal — and it is limited because it exists within certain bounds, which is to say, it is not absolute. Such is the power even of kings and emperors.[240]

> But the might of God, not received but proper unto him, is not particular, but altogether universal. Whereupon it is also called Almightyness, because that there is nothing impossible unto it. And it can have no determination, limitation, nor restraint, but it is utterly free, full, and absolute ... unto God there is nothing impossible, but all possible, and that without all limitation: so that he can do what he will, when, as far forth, and howsoever it pleaseth him to do.... The almightiness of God is continual, unchangeable, and everlasting: for it is not determinable by any process of time, by any change of worlds or matters, neither by any destiny. As long as God himself endureth, who hath neither beginning nor end, so long his almightiness also endureth: so that not only he is everlasting, but his Omnipotency also is everlasting.[241]

Beyond this, God's omnipotence is "most perfect" in that "it dispatcheth speedily what it will, and can have no cause, passion, or impediment." Even so, Augustine states that God is "Almighty, because he doeth what he will, and suffereth not that which he willeth not."[242] This language, moreover, yields a clear distinction between the power and the will of God: the divine omnipotence extends farther than the divine will, given that God can do far more than he wills — as Christ asked, "Could I not require my father, and he would give me more than twelve legions of angels."[243]

---

237. Musculus, *Loci communes*, xliv (*Commonplaces*, p. 905, col. 2). The Latin words *potentia* and *potestas* both translate into English as "power" — the former indicating physical or metaphysical strength, the latter political force or jurisdiction. For the sake of clarity, I have consistently rendered *potentia* as power or potency, *omnipotentia* as omnipotence, *potestas* as rule, and *dominium* as dominion. The sixteenth-century translation of Musculus, which I have followed and emended, tends to render *potentia* as "might," and *potestas* as "power."

238. Musculus, *Loci communes*, xliv (*Commonplaces*, p. 905, col. 2-p. 906, col. 1).

239. Musculus, *Loci communes*, xliv (*Commonplaces*, p. 906, col. 1).

240. Musculus, *Loci communes*, xliv (*Commonplaces*, p. 906, col. 2).

241. Musculus, *Loci communes*, xliv (*Commonplaces*, p. 906, col. 2-p. 907, col. 1).

242. Musculus, *Loci communes*, xliv (*Commonplaces*, p. 907, col. 1).

243. Vermigli, *Loci communes*, II.xv.1, citing Matt. 26:53.

Even though the almightiness of God is beyond comprehension, Musculus continues, there is benefit in considering its "use." God does all things "which do properly appertain to the true God."[244] First, God created the world out of nothing, there being no "matter or stuff" in existence prior to his act. Thus God first created "fire, water, earth and air" as the beginning of his work of creation. This Musculus argues against those who claim that God created the world out of preexistent matter or elements. Such claims would deprive God of his omnipotence.[245] Second, the omnipotence of God is such that it created all things from this matter or elements. Third, God uses his omnipotence to give animals the power to grow and multiply — and fourth, these creatures not only grow and multiply but also are "continued in each kind, during the seasons of all this world."[246] Fifth, "there is required a special might, whereby all things as well in heaven, as in earth be governed, disposed, fed, & preserved": for were all things not so preserved by the omnipotence of God, "they could not continue the space of one minute of an hour."[247]

Sixth, the omnipotence of God serves to heal and strengthen creatures, to bring those that stray back to the right path, to deliver the prisoners, relieve the hungry and thirsty, and to preserve the lives of those in danger:

> He created us such as might fall, hunger, thirst, be sick and sundry wise in dangers, to the intent that we should depend always upon the virtue and aid of his might.[248]

Seventh,

> for as much as he chose unto him such as he would save, and make happy forevermore, before the establishment of the world, there is of necessity requisite the virtue whereby he should regenerate them from above, that they may be partakers of the kingdom of heaven. Thus he doeth by that might, whereby the hearts of the elect, be renewed, and of fleshly, be made spiritual. This work of God's almightiness is performed by the Gospel of Christ, with the working withal of the holy Spirit. Wherefore the Apostle calleth it the virtue of God, to save believers.[249]

Calvin certainly concurs in this point, as is very apparent from his emphasis on the omnipotent redemptive power of God throughout his exegesis of the Gospel of John.[250]

Furthermore (eighth), it is also the work of God "to punish the wicked with just and effectual judgment."[251] Whereas justice is the rule of God's judgment, his almighty

---

244. Musculus, *Loci communes*, xliv (*Commonplaces*, p. 907, col. 2).

245. Musculus, *Loci communes*, xliv (*Commonplaces*, p. 907, col. 2-p. 908, col. 1).

246. Musculus, *Loci communes*, xliv (*Commonplaces*, p. 908, cols. 1-2). Note that Calvin, *Commentary on Genesis*, 1:1-2 (CTS *Genesis*, I, pp. 70, 73-4) not only indicates creation out of nothing but also implies a two-stage creation.

247. Musculus, *Loci communes*, xliv (*Commonplaces*, p. 908, col. 2).

248. Musculus, *Loci communes*, xliv (*Commonplaces*, p. 909, col. 1).

249. Musculus, *Loci communes*, xliv (*Commonplaces*, p. 909, col. 2).

250. E,g., Calvin, *Commentary on John*, 1:12; 3:7; 6:70; 11:9 (CTS *John*, I, pp. 40-42, 115, 280, 428-429).

251. Musculus, *Loci communes*, xliv (*Commonplaces*, p. 909, col. 2).

power is the means by which it is accomplished: Scripture extols this might of God's hand against wickedness. Calvin elaborates this point with considerably greater emphasis on the divine ordination of even the acts of the wicked than can be found in Musculus' exposition, albeit without abolishing either the free will of the wicked or their moral responsibility for freely willed sins.[252]

Ninth, the nature of this judgment, which comes at the end of life, separates the just from the wicked, and is worked through the final resurrection, the gift of eternal life and the punishment of everlasting fire also bespeaks an almighty power which alone can bring the dead to life.[253] Finally, God's omnipotence is also needed for the establishment for eternity of the new heavens and the new earth.[254] Musculus continues by elaborating on these works in which God's omnipotence is to be considered[255] and by discussing the necessity of belief in God's almighty power.[256] Under the latter topic he emphasizes in particular the consolation given to the church and to faith by the knowledge that all things ultimately belong to the will of God.

Many curious questions are asked concerning the divine omnipotence: does it mean that God can do all things — such as be weak, hungry, die, be consumed, sin? In an obvious attack on the most speculative arguments of the preceding two centuries, Musculus comments that those who "take great delight in wickedness" argue that God must be able to do such things or not be omnipotent. Moreover, can God undo what he has done or make the creation over again differently (better or worse) — can he redeem the world according to another plan or do again what he did once as in the incarnation? Or, as Ockham asks, is it that God cannot do the impossible or that the impossible is what God has not done?[257] The Reformers, typically, resist the urge to speculate on such questions after the manner of the late medieval nominalists. Thus, on the text of Luke 1:37, *"For no word shall be impossible with God,"* Calvin first acknowledges the extent of the divine power:

> If we choose to take ῥῆμα, *word*, in its strict and native sense, the meaning is, that God will do what he hath promised, for no hindrance can resist his power. The argument will be, God hath promised, and therefore he will accomplish it; for we ought not to allege any impossibility in opposition to his *word*.[258]

Calvin is also quite willing, given the evangelists' tendency to echo Hebrew idiom in their Greek, to understand "word" as indicating "thing" and to conclude that the

---

252. Cf. Calvin, *Sermons on Job*, sermons 130 and 144 (p. 615, col. 1; p. 675, col. 1); and see above, 6.1 (A-B) on the righteousness or justice of God.

253. Musculus, *Loci communes*, xliv (*Commonplaces*, p. 910, col. 1).

254. Musculus, *Loci communes*, xliv (*Commonplaces*, p. 910, col. 1).

255. Musculus, *Loci communes*, xliv (*Commonplaces*, p. 910, col. 2-p. 913, col. 1).

256. Musculus, *Loci communes*, xliv (*Commonplaces*, p. 913, col. 1-p. 915, col. 2).

257. Musculus, *Loci communes*, xliv (*Commonplaces*, p. 915, col. 2-p. 916, col. 1); cf. Calvin, *Sermons on Job*, sermons 130, 157 (p. 613, col. 1-2; p. 738, col. 1).

258. Calvin, *Harmony of the Evangelists*, Luke 1:37 (CTS *Harmony*, I, p. 45).

text teaches that "nothing is impossible with God." But then he warns his readers against speculation:

> We ought always, indeed, to hold it as a maxim, that they wander widely from the truth who, at their pleasure, imagine the power of God to be something beyond his *word*; for we ought always to contemplate his boundless power, that it may strengthen our hope and confidence. But it is idle, and unprofitable, and even dangerous, to argue what God can do unless we also take into account what he resolves to do.[259]

We surely have here something akin to the language of *potentia absoluta*, although without any speculation — together with a clear demand that we examine the *potentia ordinata* not in juxtaposition with God's absolute power, but instead for the sake of a positive identification of the fact and implication of God's boundless power.[260]

Musculus offers a careful definition in response to the questions, also pointing away from excessive speculation. In the first place, he notes that it does not belong to omnipotence to be able to do deficient things — as, for example, consume itself and thereby undo its own powers. Nor can God undo what he has done, for God's will does not change as does the human will, nor does God's truth alter: all things, even evils, conform to the pattern ordained by God, and to undo them would be to call God's plan a lie or a mistake.[261] Similar reflections are found in the writings of his Reformed contemporaries: Calvin makes virtually the same point when he insists that God's omnipotence can never be severed from his will; God is omnipotent in the sense that he "can accomplish whatever he wills to do."[262] This, Calvin continues, is not a point that "the papists" have yet learned: God will not "darken the Sun" or "make the earth into heaven" or, indeed, turn "bread ... into the body of Jesus Christ" — such acts would "pervert all order" and "rend asunder God's power."[263] So, too, does Bullinger identify the divine nature itself as the sole limitation of God's power: God is true to his nature and cannot do anything contrary to it — still God can do all things, specifically in the sense that he can do anything that he wills, and all that he wills is in accordance with his nature.[264] Even so must God's omnipotence always be understood in relation to his righteousness, goodness, wisdom, and just judgment.[265] Furthermore, there are no contradictions in God: so that it is impossible for things to be other than as they are. As for Ockham's question, this is not a matter of contradictories but of correlatives in logic:

---

259. Calvin, *Harmony of the Evangelists*, Luke 1:37 (*CTS Harmony*, I, p. 45).

260. Cf. Steinmetz, *Calvin in Context*, pp. 47-50, with S. Mark Heim, "The Powers of God: Calvin and Late Medieval Thought," in *Andover Newton Quarterly*, n.s. 19 (1978/79), pp. 156-166.

261. Musculus, *Loci communes*, xliv (*Commonplaces*, p. 917, col. 2-p. 918, col. 1).

262. Calvin, *Sermons on Job*, sermon 157 (p. 738, col. 1).

263. Calvin, *Sermons on Job*, sermon 157 (p. 738, col. 1).

264. Bullinger, *Decades*, V.ix (IV, pp. 451-452).

265. Calvin, *Sermons on Job*, sermons 29, 123, 130, 144 (p. 134, col. 2; p. 581, col. 2; p. 615, col. 1; p. 675, col. 1).

To be absolutely impossible, and to be incapable of being done by God, are correlatives. For whatsoever cannot be done by God is impossible: and on the other hand, whatsoever is absolutely impossible, cannot be done by God.[266]

Finally, we note the diversity of formulations even among the Reformers: Calvin, Musculus, and Vermigli do not, after all, offer exactly identical formulations of the divine omnipotence. Calvin is more prepared than the other codifiers of his generation to identify the divine will as the "rule of righteousness" and to argue, with little instrumental nuance, that God is the "cause of all things." Calvin also strenuously rejects the distinction between *potentia absoluta* and *potentia ordinata* while, at the same time, embodying in his own thought many arguments resembling those of Scotus and Ockham that insist on the freedom of God and the radical contingency of the created order.[267] Yet, the differences over these issues and definitions — which continue into the era of orthodoxy — do not move ineluctably from matters of nuance into matters of substance: all of the thinkers cited assume both the divine freedom and the contingency of creation, both the divine concurrence and the integrity of secondary causality.

B. Divine Omnipotence in Early and High Orthodox Theology

1. Basic definitions. The initial division of many of the Reformed orthodox discussions of the divine omnipotence echoes the distinction we have already seen in Musculus' *Loci communes*: the divine power, understood as potency, must be distinguished from the divine power understood as authority or right:

There is a difference between *dynamis* and *exousia*, [as also between] *potentia* and *potestas*; *exousia* or *potestas* is properly authority, right to do a thing, as a king hath over his Subjects, ... a master over his servants, of which Christ speaks, John 17:2, Matt. 28:18. *Dynamis* or *potentia* is properly strength to do something.[268]

God, therefore, has both jurisdiction and strength or capability — and it is the latter concept, the divine *potentia*, that occupies the larger portion of the Reformed discussion.

The Reformed orthodox view of divine power or omnipotence agrees in substance with the teaching of the Reformers, drawing, as the writers of both eras did, on the exegetical tradition and on the doctrines and distinctions of the patristic and scholastic past.[269] It is even the case that the strong tendency toward piety or the religious "use" of the doctrine carried over from Reformers like Musculus and Calvin into the theology of the Reformed orthodox, perhaps more clearly into the British thinkers, and served

---

266. Musculus, *Loci communes*, xliv (*Commonplaces*, p. 919, col. 1).

267. Cf. Steinmetz, "Calvin and the Absolute Power of God," in *Calvin in Context*, pp. 48-50.

268. Leigh, *Treatise*, II.xiv (p. 109); cf. the same argument in Zanchi, *De natura Dei*, III.i, q. 1-2 (cols. 162, 164); Brakel, *Redelijke Godsdienst*, I.iii.41; Rijssen, *Summa theol.*, III.xxxv; Turretin, *Inst. theol. elencticae*, III.xxi-xxii; Mastricht, *Theoretico-practica theol.*, II.xx.1-5, 10.

269. As a point of entry into the exegetical tradition, cf. Augustin Marlorat, *Propheticae, et apostolicae, id est, totius divinae ac canonicae Scripturae, thesaurus, in locos communes rerum, dogmatum suis exemplis illustratum* (London, 1574), pp. 188-190, on *Deus solus omnipotens*.

to balance the highly objectivistic language of seventeenth-century scholastic theology with an emphasis on subjective application. The early orthodox thinkers, however, did draw out the scholastic distinctions inherent in the received doctrine at greater length and in greater positive detail than did the Reformers. And this movement toward metaphysical cohesion continued into the high orthodox era, where the biblical, philosophical, and religious elements of the doctrine remained in a rather delicate balance despite the obvious difficulties brought by an increasingly text-critical exegesis and a vast reorientation of philosophy.[270]

In the fully developed high orthodox system, Pictet offers a sense not only of the growing precision of definition but also of an interest in the clear structure of system. His basic definition of the divine omnipotence is prefaced by a statement of its relation to the larger category of will. In God, *potentia* is not distinct from will as it is in humans: "since we bring about no thing (*res*) by means of our will," whereas "in God will is power itself."[271] God can do all that he wills: his power does not extend beyond his will, nor his will beyond his power.[272] Given, moreover, the absence of real distinctions among the attributes, the *potentia Dei* is the being of God[273] or, one might say, the being of God understood as conferring being. In its most general sense, therefore, the power of God is called omnipotence, Wendelin notes, "since God can do all things."[274]

The *potentia Dei* is defined by the Reformed orthodox as infinite: there can be, after all, no external constraints placed on the will of God and God is by nature infinite. The point can be argued rationally:

1. His essence (as was said) is infinite, therefore his power.

2. He is most perfect, therefore most powerful.

3. Whatsoever good thing is to be found in any creature, the same is perfectly and infinitely in God. [There is strength in Angels, Men, beasts, and all creatures in their kind, therefore it is much more perfectly and eminently in God from whom they have it.][275]

Significantly, Leigh shows no interest in the nominalist line of argument here — namely, that the divine omnipotence cannot be logically demonstrated — nor even a Thomistic inclination to derive omnipotence from the identification of God as first efficient cause. The derivation from divine perfection echoes the older sensibilities of Anselm and the early scholastics.

This divine *potentia* may be defined as a "virtue (*virtus*) by which God can do whatever is possible to be done."[276] Wendelin offers a more qualified definition, continuing a line adumbrated in his definition of the divine will — "the *principium*

---

270. Cf. Voetius, *Selectarum disputationum theologicarum*, I, xxii-xxv.

271. Pictet, *Theol. chr.*, II.x.1.

272. Zanchi, *De natura Dei*, III.i, q. 4.2 (col. 174).

273. Ward, *Philosophicall Essay*, I.iii (p. 30).

274. Wendelin, *Christianae theologiae libri duo*, I.i.27; Cocceius, *Summa theol.*, III.x.75.

275. Leigh, *Treatise*, II.xiv (p. 107, text and margin).

276. Pictet, *Theol. chr.*, II.x.1; cf. Stapfer, *Inst. theol.*, I.iii, §394.

imperans" or executive (*exequens*) principle, the *potentia Dei*, is that by which God is able to do whatever is not alien to his nature and truth."[277] Another form of the qualification on divine power is offered by the Leiden *Synopsis* — God's will is "absolute, because it has reference to all possibilities, not however to things that are purely impossible"[278] — as many of the orthodox declare, the *potentia Dei* is the source of all possibility, as the *voluntas Dei* is the source of all actuality, there can be no possibilities beyond the divine *potentia*: Heidanus specifically rejects the Scotist identification of the *intellectus Dei* as the source of possibility, grounding possibility in the divine *potentia*, perhaps an Ockhamist solution to the problem, although, equally so, it could be derived from Albert the Great.[279] Of course, the human mind can conceive of impossibilities, of things contrary to the divine nature and truth, and of things "contrary to the essential nature of a creature," but such cannot be attributed to God — nor, indeed is it a sign of God's lack of power, but of human impiety to make such claims.[280] Although the extent of these definitions, in the face of various alternatives found in the seventeenth-century context (namely, various scholastic options found among the Roman Catholic thinkers of the era and a series of alternatives to any traditional understanding brought forth by the Vorstius, the Socinians, and the Remonstrants) goes beyond the statements of most of the Reformers, what remains characteristic of the Reformed orthodox approach to the doctrine is the restraint with regard to more speculative discussion of what God could do — specifically a refusal to go down the path of late medieval speculation.[281]

2. Exegetical issues. This truth is taught throughout Scripture, and it is also rationally intelligible.[282] First, the biblical argumentation:

> The power of God is the faculty by which God is able to effect what he wills and whatever he is able to will: which is taught in Holy Scripture, first, positively, inasmuch as God is omnipotent (Rev. 1:8); second, negatively, because nothing is impossible for him; and third, comparatively, because he can do what no one else can do (Matt. 3:9ff.; 19:26).[283]

---

277. Wendelin, *Christianae theologiae libri duo*, I.i.27.

278. *Synopsis purioris theol.*, VI.xxxvi; cf. the discussion of similar language of limitation in Michael Daniel Bell, "*Propter Potestatem Scientiam, ac Beneplacitum Dei*: The Doctrine of Predestination in the Theology of Johannes Maccovius" (Ph.D. diss., Westminster Theological Seminary, 1986), pp. 95-97.

279. Heidanus, *Corpus theol.*, ii (p. 88); cf. Wolter, "Ockham and the Textbooks," pp. 83-84 and F. L. Catania, "Divine Infinity in Albert the Great's Commentary on the Sentences of Peter Lombard," in *Medieval Studies*, 22 (1960), p. 33; Adams, *William Ockham*, II, pp. 1079-1080 disagrees over Ockham's view of the ground of possibility.

280. Brakel, *Christian's Reasonable Service*, I, pp. 131-132.

281. As described, e.g., in Kennedy and Romano, "John Went, O.F.M. and Divine Omnipotence," pp. 138-170.

282. Wendelin, *Christianae theologiae libri duo*, I.i.27 (1), citing Luke 1:37; Rev. 1:8; 15:3; Matt. 19:26; 1 Chron. 29:12; Ps. 106:5.

283. Rijssen, *Summa theol.*, III.xxxiv.

So also, is the power of God "Essential and Independent" inasmuch as "it is the cause of all power, John 19:11; it reacheth beyond his will, Matt. 26:35."[284] It therefore "extends to all things that are not nor never will be, as to raise up children of stone to *Abraham*, Matt. 3:9; to give Christ more than ten legions of angels."[285]

By citing such texts as Ruth 1:20, 21 ("for the Almighty hath dealt very bitterly with me"); Job 21:15; 27:10; 31:2 ("What is the Almighty, that we should serve him? ... Will he delight himself in the Almighty? ... What inheritance of the Almighty [is] from on high?"), Rev. 15:3 ("marvelous are thy works, Lord God Almighty"), seventeenth-century Reformed theologians could easily establish from Scripture that God is almighty or omnipotent in the most general sense of the term.[286] From the perspective of the shape and organization of the Reformed system, much of this basic effort had been accomplished under the topic of the divine names, even before the attribution of omnipotence had been broached.[287] The issue to be addressed, however, in the discussion of the attribute of omnipotence, was its precise meaning given the diversity of biblical usage and, moreover, given the consistent reflection of the tradition that, in the context of the other divine attributes, the "all" or "omni" in "almighty" or "omnipotent" most certainly did not mean that God could (or, if there is a difference, would) do absolutely anything at all.

Leigh offers a basic categorization of the biblical language, noting that "Scripture confirms the omnipotence of God," in four ways:

> 1. Affirmatively, when it calls God *Abloir*, Job 34:20. *Shaddai*, all sufficient, Gen. 35:11; Deut. 10:17; Psalm 89:13. *Gibbor*, powerful, Deut, 10:17.
>
> 2. Effectively, when it witnesseth, that God can do all things, Matt 3:9 & 19:16; Mark 14:36; Luke 18:26; Eph. 3:20. Hitherto belong all the *works* of the divine power and supernatural miracles.
>
> 3. Negatively, when it denies anything to be difficult to him, much less impossible, Gen. 18:14; Jer. 32:17, 27; Luke 1:37; Matt. 19:36.
>
> 4. Symbolically, when it gives him a strong right hand, a stretched out arm, 1 Chron. 29:12; Jer. 32:17; Ephes 1:19.[288]

Charnock and Mastricht establish an explicit and detailed balance between the logic of system and the demands of an exegetical foundation that leans far more heavily on the biblical, exegetical element. Charnock, in particular, perhaps because his systematic exposition of the attributes belongs to a series of technical sermons, follows out the argument of his text (Job 26:14), including a lengthy presentation of its context in the debate between Job and Bildad: "Bildad," Charnock begins,

> had, in the foregoing chapter, entertained Job with a discourse of the dominion and power of God, and the purity of his righteousness, whence he argues the impossibility

---

284. Leigh, *Treatise*, II.xiv (p. 108).

285. Leigh, *Treatise*, II.xiv (p. 108).

286. Leigh, *Treatise*, II.xiv (p. 107, margin).

287. See above, 4.2.

288. Leigh, *Treatise*, II.xiv (p. 107).

of the justification of man in his presence, who is no better than a worm. Job, in this chapter, acknowledges the greatness of God's power, and descants more largely upon it than Bildad had done.... Job, therefore, from ver. 1-4, taxeth him in a kind of scoffing manner, that he had not touched the point, but rambled from the subject in hand, and had not applied a salve proper to the sore (ver. 2).[289]

Charnock's entire discussion of the attribute not only develops the theme of power by way of an exposition of the text, it also respects the problem posed concerning the divine power and the particular issues and examples raised by the book of Job and, specifically, by the twenty-sixth chapter. The intention of Job, argues Charnock, is to show the superiority of his own conception of the power of God to that of Bildad: the chapter, accordingly, after the four verse introductory comment, "doth magnificently treat of the power of God in several branches" and manifest "more distinct conceptions of it than [Bildad] had uttered."[290]

The chapter, therefore, in its own internal argument and in its distinctions, provides Charnock with the ideal *locus doctrinae* for his discussion of divine power. This is hardly a case of "proof-texting" — rather it is a case of movement from exegesis to contemporary theological formulation on the grounds of the accepted hermeneutic of the day. Charnock sees in the text a pattern of ascent and descent through the created order, examining God's relation in power to finite things: thus, the text begins (vv. 5-6) with a discussion of dead things and "hell" (Sheol) and then "from the lower parts of the world ... ascends to the consideration of the power of God in the creation of the heaven and earth" (vv. 7-8); from there, by means of the language of clouds in verse 8, Job moves on to discuss the abundance of divine power hidden, as it were by the clouds and then by the seas.[291]

The exegetical grounding of the doctrine is reflected in the systematic exposition, evidencing in the larger systems a fundamental interrelationship of the questions raised by the biblical text and various dogmatic questions. Leigh, for example, cites marginally 2 Cor. 6:18; Rev. 1:8; Luke 18:28; Matt. 19:26; and Eph. 1:19 at the outset of his argument, and he notes that Matt. 3:9 and Phil. 3:21 confirm the absolute power of God, while Psalm 115:3 and 135:6 point to the actual or ordained power.[292] Mastricht grounds his doctrinal discussion in an exegesis of Ephesians 3:20-21, "And to him who is powerful above all things, to work abundantly, above all that we can ask or think according to the power that works in us, to him be glory in the church."[293] Turretin anchors his exposition with reference to Psalm 115:3, Matthew 3:9 and 26:53.[294]

---

289. Charnock, *Discourses*, X, (vol. II, p. 5).
290. Charnock, *Discourses*, X, (vol. II, p. 5).
291. Charnock, *Discourses*, X, (vol. II, pp. 6-7).
292. Leigh, *Treatise*, II.xiv (p. 106, margin).
293. Mastricht, *Theoretico-practica theol.*, II.xx.1-2.
294. Turretin, *Inst. theol. elencticae*, III.xxi.3.

3. Distinctions in and limitations of the divine power. The exegetical discussion of the *potentia Dei* provides a basis for such distinctions as that between the absolute and the ordained power of God — implied by such texts as Matt. 3:9 ("God is able of these stones to raise up children to Abraham") and Matt. 19:26 ("with God all things are possible"). Further considerations of the *potentia Dei* yield a series of distinctions and qualifications — distinctions between God's absolute and actual power, God's extraordinary and ordinary power, plus reflections on the limitation of God's power and the exertion of divine power in the form of God's dominion and rule over creation.

First, there is the problem of the term "power" itself: *potentia* is typically contrasted with *actus* — and God is usually understood to be pure *actus*, fully actualized, having in him no *potentia*: strictly speaking, there is in God no passive potency (*potentia passiva*) or possibility.[295] Thus, it may be objected to this language of divine *potentia* that, taken together with the attribution of actuality to God, it indicates composition: "where there is act and potency, there is composition grounded on act and potency."[296] Wendelin responds with another qualification of the language of divine potency: the attribution of potency and act to God in no way implies that these two terms are distinct *realiter* in God, for then the objection would stand and the divine potency would be understood, in distinction from act, as a *potentia ad non esse*. But this distinction does not obtain in God. The divine *potentia* is the full actuality of the powerful God (*potens Deus*), who cannot not exist (*non potest non esse*).[297] Thus, God must be said to have power distinct from its exercise — a power that implies no composition (given that it is not contrasted with the divine actuality) and that is not "exhausted by acting."[298] This is, moreover, an active power (*potentia activa*) as distinct from a passive potency (*potentia passiva*): it is an acting, not a being acted upon.[299]

The connection between divine omnipotence and the concept of genuinely possible things capable of being given actuality is obvious in the Latin term for power, *potentia*: the divine omnipotence is not to be viewed in the rather restricted sense of "power" as a force exerted upon a thing but in the larger and more inclusive sense of an absolute and all-encompassing *potency*. God, of course, is *actus purissimus*, pure or absolute actuality, and is, therefore, in no way potential: there is not potency in God for God to become other than what he is inasmuch as there is no actuality beyond God capable of changing God or of drawing God toward itself. God, in short, is perfect and immutable. But if there is no potency in God for God to become, there is a potency in God for creatures to become, for creatures to be drawn from pure potentiality into actual existence. God's *potentia* is, then, a potency or potential for the being of creatures exerted *ad extra* in view of the range of genuine possibility. "Things known by him

---

295. Zanchi, *De natura Dei*, III.i (col. 159); cf. Amyraut, *De mysterio trinitatis*, I, p. 31; II, p. 81.

296. Wendelin, *Christianae theologiae libri duo*, I.i.27 (3,5); cf. Maccovius, *Loci communes*, XVII (pp. 138-139); Le Blanc, *Theses theol.*, *De Dei simplicitate*, xxiv-xxv.

297. Wendelin, *Christianae theologiae libri duo*, I.i.27 (3,5).

298. Venema, *Inst. theol.*, V (p. 137).

299. Zanchi, *De natura Dei*, III.i, q. 1 (cols. 162-164).

are said to be possible, by reason of his power, whereas the future existence thereof depends on his will."[300]

William Perkins provided a basic early orthodox form of the doctrine in which most of the standard scholastic distinctions were stated or adumbrated:

> God's Omnipotencie, is that by which he is most able to perform every work.... Some things notwithstanding are here to be excepted. First, those things whose action argueth an impotencie, as to lie, to deny his word.... Secondly, such things as are contrary to the nature of God, as to destroy himself, and not to beget his Son from eternity. Thirdly, such things as imply contradiction. For God cannot make truth false, or that which when it is not, to be.[301]

According to Trelcatius' definition, God's power is "that by which he perfectly accomplishes all the things he wills, and by which all things that he can will, he can accomplish perfectly" — it is a power both actual and absolutely considered. Thus God, as infinite, can will an infinite number of things; he does as he chooses, not being bound to a certain order of things, being able to do more than he actually effects, and being in no way limited or impeded by his own creation.[302] Nevertheless, he cannot will things contrary to his nature or things which are self-contradictory: rather, God as all powerful "abides and persists in the best thing" rather than fall into impotence by doing lesser or unworthy acts.[303] Both Perkins and Trelcatius, thus, echo the doctrine found in Musculus' *Loci communes*, particularly in its qualifications. The same is true of the teaching of their early orthodox contemporaries.[304]

So, too, must infinite power be defined in such a way as to safeguard the freedom of God. The essential infinitude of divine power must be carefully defined so as not to give the impression either that God wills all possibilities or that God's infinite will must have infinite effects. Trapp argues, for example, that Matthew 3:9 indicates an absolute power "whereby [God] can do more than he doth" and an "actual" power, "whereby he doth only that [which] he willeth": God could raise up new children to Abraham from the stones of the earth, but he does not will to do so. As for the absolute

---

300. Ridgley, *Body of Divinity*, p. 68, col. 2; cf. Greenhill, *Exposition of Ezekiel*, 38:17, in loc. (p. 760).

301. Perkins, *Golden Chaine*, iii (p. 13, cols. 1-2); Beza et al. *Propositions and Principles*, VI.v; cf. Pictet, *Theol. chr.*, II.vi: (pp. 91-92): "That God's omnipotence is nothing more than his efficacious will, is very evident, because, since God is an all-perfect Being, he acts or works in a most perfect manner ... the object of this power is every thing that God wills, and which does not involve a contradiction, as that *a thing is*, and *is not, at the same time* ... and does not imply sin and imperfection, as *to lie*, *to eat*, *to drink*, to be *hurt*, to *die*, & c. ... God can do many things which we cannot comprehend, as the creation of the world out of nothing; but we ought firmly to believe that God can bestow upon us all things necessary to our salvation."

302. Trelcatius, *Schol. meth.*, I.iii (p. 67); cf. Zanchi, *De natura Dei*, III.i, q. 6.3 (col. 180); Beza et al. *Propositions and Principles*, VI.iv.

303. Trelcatius, *Schol. meth.*, I.iii (p. 68), citing Matt. 3:9; cf. Zanchi, *De natura Dei*, III.i, q. 6.3 (col. 180).

304. Cf. e.g., Polanus, *Syntagma theol.*, II.xxix; Ames, *Medulla theol.*, I.vi.16-20; Walaeus, *Loci communes*, p. 182, col. 2-p. 183, col. 1.

extent of God's power or ability, Trapp adds, "some things he can do, but will not, as here, and Matt. 26:53; Rom 9:18" whereas "some things he neither will nor can, as to lie, to die, to deny himself, 2 Tim. 2:13; Titus 1:2; Heb. 6:18, for these things contradict his essence and imply impotency."[305] Of the divine power to raise up children of Abraham from stones, Trapp notes,

> This he could do, though he will not. And yet he doth as much as this when he takes the stone out of the heart; when of carnal he makes us a people created again, Psal. 102:18. ... This is a work of God's almighty power, the same that he put forth in raising Christ from the dead ... and in creating the world.[306]

This distinction between the inherent possibilities in the *potentia Dei* and its activity or actual extent yields a threefold model: the *omnipotentia Dei* is infinite, "1) *in se* and *per se*; 2) with respect to objects; 3) with respect to the activity according to which it acts or is capable of acting."[307] Thus, first, *in se et per se* the power of God is infinite, inasmuch as it is identical with the divine essence, which is infinite. In other words, the power of God is infinite, "in respect of the Divine essence, since it flows from the infinite nature of God; for it is a most certain rule, that the faculties and powers of the Subject flow from the form and agree with the form. Second, with respect to its objects, the divine power is also infinite, granting that it has innumerable objects that it produces at will: "for God doth never so many and so great works, but he can do more and greater."[308] Still, in Leigh's form of the argument and definition, there is limitation on the divine omnipotence, significantly, one that reflects late medieval debate over the notion of omnipotence and its limits — "we must hold that God cannot make a creature of infinite perfection simply, or creatures indeed infinite in number, for so they should be gods; for the Divine power is so far exercised on the object as the passive power of the object extends itself, but infinite perfection imports a pure act."[309] And, third, with respect to its activity or action since it produces nothing that could be produced in a still more excellent way nor does it act with an intensity or efficacy that could be made more intense or more effective. This active power of God is infinite in its efficacy and exercise, not in the number or extension of its external effects or objects.[310] Thus, "in respect of duration, which is perpetuall as his essence is, therefore this force and power of God is deservedly styled Omnipotence, Job. 42:2

---

305. John Trapp, *Annotations upon the Old and New Testaments in Five Distinct Volumes* (London: Robert White, 1662), reissued as *A Commentary on the Old and New Testaments*, 5 vols. (London: Richard Dickinson, 1856-68), Matt.3:9, in loc.; cf. William Gouge, *A Learned and very Useful Commentary on the Whole Epistle to the Hebrews* (London: A.M., T.W. and S.G., 1655), 6:18, §141.

306. Trapp, *Commentary*, Matt.3:9, in loc.

307. Wendelin, *Christianae theologiae libri duo*, I.i.27 (2); Zanchi, *De natura Dei*, III.i, q. 3 (cols. 166-167).

308. Leigh, *Treatise*, II.xiv (p. 107); cf. Beza et al. *Propositions and Principles*, VI.iv.

309. Leigh, *Treatise*, II.xiv (p. 107); cf. Adams, *William Ockham*, II, p. 1154-1155.

310. Zanchi, *De natura Dei*, III.i, q. 3 (col. 167); Wendelin, *Christianae theologiae libri duo*, I.i.27 (2).

(cf. Luke 1:37). God's power is not only *potentia*, or *multipotentia*, but *omnipotentia*, for degree infinite; *shall any matter be hard for the Lord?*"[311]

Since God's power is original and primary, all other powers are not only derived but also "continued and ordered by him." But, despite this primacy and all-inclusive extension of the divine will even to unactualized possibilities, there is a sense in which the divine will must be described as having limits: "God can do all things, *quae habent rationem factibilitatis, quae contradictionem non implicant*, Titus 1:2; 2 Tim. 2:13."[312] From this basic definition it ought to be clear that objections to the traditional language of divine omnipotence on the ground that it is either logically contradictory or physically impossible for a being to "do anything" are false objections based upon ignorance of the traditional formulation. The identification of God as omnipotent *never* was taken to mean that God can, literally, do anything.[313] Since God can perform only possible acts and the *omnipotentia* extends only to possibles, even "miracles are possibles," not impossibles.[314]

4. *Potentia absoluta* and *potentia ordinata*. This distinction, made central to the theological enterprise of the later Middle Ages by Scotus and the nominalists, passed over into Reformed orthodoxy if not entirely by way of the Reformers themselves, certainly by way of the traditions that they mediated and, in addition, by way of the late sixteenth-century reappropriation of the broader tradition (whether through the reading of medieval theology or through the appropriation of materials from contemporary scholastics like Suárez, Bañez, and Baius.) In Perkins' words,

> God's power may be distinguished into an absolute and actual power. God's absolute power is that by which he can do more than he either doth or will do.... God's actual power, is that by which he causeth all things to be, which he freely willeth.[315]

Leigh offers a fairly standard statement of the distinction between "absolute" and "actual" power:

> there followeth [after the discussion of God's will, affections, and virtues] Power in God, by which God by the bare beck of his will, effecteth all things which he will, and howsoever he will, perfectly without labor and difficulty, and can do perfectly all things which he can will; this is called Absolute Power, by which he can do more things than either he doth or will. Actual power is when God causeth those things to exist which he will have exist.[316]

Here, despite the possible Thomist implication of his ordering of the *scientia* and *voluntas Dei*, Leigh follows Wendelin by adopting a somewhat Scotist or nominalist accent in not only distinguishing between *potentia absoluta* and *potentia ordinata* but also

---

311. Leigh, *Treatise*, II.xiv (pp. 106-107).

312. Leigh, *Treatise*, II.xiv (p. 108).

313. Heppe, *Reformed Dogmatics*, p. 100.

314. Stapfer, *Inst. theol.*, I.iii, §396.

315. Perkins, *Golden Chaine*, iii (p. 13, col. 2).

316. Leigh, *Treatise*, II.xiv (p. 106).

indicating a positive theological use of the concept of an absolute divine power. Leigh also more clearly and positively subordinates power to will than to understanding or knowledge. Of some significance is the replacement of the term *potentia ordinata* with *potentia actualis* by some of the theologians, most probably for the sake of dividing the concept of *potentia ordinata* into two parts, "actual" and "ordinary" power — the "actual" divine power considered as that which establishes all things in their being, corresponding with the *scientia visionis sive libera*, and the "ordinary" divine power considered as that which orders the world and establishes its laws, as distinct from the *potentia extraordinaria* that is active in the realm of the miraculous.

It is clear from Wendelin's repetition of his basic definition in the definition of *potentia absoluta* that he intends this as the basic category of divine power: to his original definition and its qualifier "whatever is not alien to the divine nature and truth," he merely adds, "or which are not contradictories." Cloppenburg can even define this *potentia absoluta* as the ultimate power that is in God prior to and "independent of the decree" and standing as an ultimate, divine sufficiency.[317] Nor ought it to be concluded, Wendelin adds, that God must therefore do or create everything that is possible for him to do. Indeed, the *potentia actualis* is the power "whereby God actually does do what he wills to do."[318] The Reformed point, clearly echoing that underlying the late medieval emphasis on the *potentia absoluta*, is the ultimate freedom of God over against the created order, over and above his own actual willing, and (in Cloppenburg's formulation) above and beyond the eternal decree itself.

It might be objected that, according to such exegesis and argument, the power of God is not as extensive as the divine knowledge and, therefore, cannot be infinite. One form of the objection rests on the doctrine that God knows both all *possibilia* and all *impossibilia*, but wills only the *possibilia*. In response, Wendelin points out that a distinction must be made between the *potentia Dei* considered intrinsically, according to essence, and the *potentia Dei* considered extrinsically, in proportion to the external objects related to its acts: in the former sense, the power of God is identical with the divine essence and, indeed, with the divine knowledge, and is infinite. In proportion to its objects, moreover, the knowledge of God should be defined in terms of "knowables" rather than "possibles" and only the power of God defined in terms of "possibles": then we recognize that the knowledge of God extends to all knowables (*scientia Dei extendit se ad omnia scibilia*) and the power of God to all possibles (*ad omnia possibilia*), both of which are infinite.[319]

---

317. Cloppenburg, *Exercitationes super locos communes*, II.v.5-6. Note how this formulation utterly undercuts the claims of writers like Daane, who hold that the identification of the decree with the divine essence eliminates the freedom of God: see James Daane, *The Freedom of God: A Study of Election and Pulpit* (Grand Rapids: Eerdmans, 1973), pp. 7-8, 38-44, 51-57, 152-156, et passim.

318. Wendelin, *Christianae theologiae libri duo*, I.i.27 (2).

319. Wendelin, *Christianae theologiae libri duo*, I.i.27 (3,5): the assumption here is that God *does not* know absolute unknowables — inasmuch as he does not "think" discursively and, therefore, does not eternally bemuse himself with the contemplation of an infinite range of impossibilities or contradictories. God, in other words, does not know "square circles" and does not will them — although he surely does know the thoughts of silly people who pose self-contradictory propositions to

The *potentia Dei absoluta* is the power of which Psalm 115:3 bears witness: *"Deus noster in coelis est, quicquid vult, facit,"* that is to say the power by which God acts and irresistibly works his will in his own time and manner. The latter indicates God's ability to do other than what he has done: he could have sent Christ twelve legions of angels to guard him from harm in Gethsemane. Rijssen notes that Calvin rejected the idea of *potentia absoluta* — but that this was not a complete rejection of the concept, but only insofar as the medieval scholastics abused it in foolish and irreverent rationalizations, asking, for example, whether God could lie or sin.[320] There must be things that God cannot do: not even according to his *potentia absoluta* could God lie or sin — any more than he could die. Following an Augustinian and Platonic line of reasoning, these things are imperfections and defects and for God to do them would imply, not his power, but his impotence.[321] Neither can God do things which imply contradiction: the object of his potency is the realm of the possible even as the object of his omniscience is the realm of the knowable.

Thus there is no defect in the *potentia Dei* but rather a limitation in the *possibilitas rei*:[322]

> The object of divine power is all things simply and in their own nature possible, which neither contradict the nature of God, nor the essence of the creatures; those which are contrary to these are absolutely impossible; such things God cannot do, because he cannot will them; nor can he will and do contrary things, as good and evil; or contradictory, as to be, and not to be, that a true thing be false, that any thing while it is should not be; God cannot sin, lie, deny, change or destroy himself, suffer; he cannot not beget his Son from eternity: for all these things do *ex diametro* oppose the Divine, Immutable, Simple, most perfect and true essence. God cannot create another God, nor cause a man to be unreasonable, nor a body to be infinite and everywhere, for these things contradict the essential definitions of a creature, of a man and of a body; not to be able to do these things is not impotency but power, for to be able to

---

themselves. Cf. the similar issues raised in the discussion of omniscience, conditionals, and contingencies, above 5.3 (F.2-6).

320. Rijssen, *Summa theol.*, III.xxxvi; cf. Turretin, *Inst. theol. elencticae*, III.xxi.5.

321. Rijssen, *Summa theol.*, III.xxxvii: "haec enim non sunt potentiae, sed impotentiae." Cf. Gouge, *Commentary on Hebrews*, 6:18, §141.

322. Rijssen, *Summa theol.*, III.xxxvii; cf. Turretin, *Inst. theol. elencticae*, III.xxi.6. The notion of limitation resident in the possibilities of things points perhaps in the direction of Leibniz's claim that imperfection is inherent in the world as planned by God. Leibniz asks, "We, who derive all being from God, where shall we find the source of evil?" "The answer," he continues, "is that it must be sought in the ideal nature of the creature, in so far as this nature is contained in the eternal verities which are in the understanding of God independently of his will. For we must consider that there is an *original imperfection in the creature* before sin, because the creature is limited in its essence; whence it follows that it cannot know all, and that it can deceive itself and commit other errors" (*Theodicy*, § 20). In other words, Leibniz recognizes and states (far more clearly and bluntly than Augustine or the scholastics) the limitation of God in his creation of the world: the ideal natures of creatures exist in God's mind, independent of his will. God cannot will that finite things exist without their imperfection — their forms are eternally determined as independent universals.

do opposite things is a sign of infirmity, being not able to remain altogether in one and the same state.[323]

These limitations on the divine power, very similar in their formulation to those argued by various late medieval scholastics, were not universally accepted in the seventeenth century, and the Reformed engaged in controversy over the point. There is, in other words, a significant contextual reason for the Reformed discussion. According to Mastricht, there are three fundamental errors — first, the Socinian claim that God simply cannot do contradictories, on the ground of the finitude and limitation of the divine essence; second, the Weigelian fanatics, who argue that God can do absolutely anything, including contradictories; and third, "Descartes and his colleagues," who "suspend all possibility and impossibility on the will of God" and who misuse the distinction "between impossibilities *ex parte Dei* and *ex parte rei*."[324]

The Cartesian claim was particularly objectionable to the Reformed inasmuch as it appeared to portray God as utterly arbitrary. Descartes had included in the first printed edition of his *Meditations* a series of objections raised by contemporary philosophers and theologians to the circulated manuscript. There he had defended his view of the freedom of God on the grounds of the eternal indifference of God to all that has occurred — given that no conception of which we are capable is either good or true in the divine understanding prior to God's willing. Descartes even illustrated his point with the example of the sum of the angles of a triangle being equal to two right angles: God, he argued, did not know the truth of this proposition as a necessary truth and will triangles; rather, it is because God willed that the sum of the angles of triangles be equal to two right angles that this truth is necessarily so.[325] Thus, that the sum of angles of a triangle be other than equivalent to two right angles is impossible only *ex parte rei*, given the way that God has made the world, but not *ex parte Dei*: Descartes appears to say that there are no conceivable impossibilities *ex parte Dei*. This conclusion presses the *potentia absoluta* even farther than Ockham had pressed it.

In response, the Reformed distinguish between "impossibilities of nature" (*impossibilia naturae*) and "things impossible by nature" (*impossibilia natura*). The former are things that cannot occur in the normal course of nature, such as making something out of nothing, the sun standing still, fire not burning, raising the dead. Nature cannot produce such results: they are impossible *ex parte rei*. But God can (and has) accomplished all of them: they are not impossible *ex parte Dei*. The latter are things or events "repugnant" to nature and in themselves contradictory — such as making something exist and not exist at the same time, in the same place and in the same way, making something that has existed not to have existed, or, indeed, making a substance that has the properties not of itself but of another substance (namely, as

323. Leigh, *Treatise*, II.xiv (p. 108).

324. Mastricht, *Theoretico-practica theol.*, II.xx.21; citing Descartes, *Resp.*, vi.6, and Wittich, *Theol. Pacif.*, §199-201.

325. Descartes, *Objections and Replies*, vi, reply 6, in *Writings*, II, pp. 291-292.

in the case of transubstantiation). These are pure impossibles, impossible even for God, impossible both *ex parte rei and ex parte Dei*.[326] As Wendelin succinctly states, citing 2 Tim. 2:13, "Deus se ipsum negare non potest" — "God cannot deny himself."[327]

> God's omnipotence lies in this (Matt. 3:9), that he is able to do whatsoever is absolutely, simply, and generally possible. A possible thing is that, the doing of which may be an effect of God's wisdom and power, and which being done would argue power and perfection; an impossible that which cannot be an effect of wisdom and power, but if it should be done would argue weakness and imperfection in God. In respect of manner, he doth it with a word, *Let there be light*, said he, *and there was light*. He can do all things of himself without any creature's help. God's power is styled *Might of power*, Ephes 1:19 and it is seen in his works of creation, making all things from nothing... 2. In his works of providence. 3. In his Word, Rom 1:16.[328]

The initial distinction into absolute and actual power, moreover, does not indicate a passivity or potency in God: "Both God's Absolute and Actual power is active only (Eph. 3:20), and no way passive."[329] Indeed, the association of *potentia* with passivity or potency (in the sense of non-actuality) must not be allowed to lead to a denial of *potentia* in God, any more than should the identification of God as *actus purus*. The divine power or potency is to be defined, not in terms of "possible being" in God, but rather in terms of the possibility for being external to God. The divine potency is an active, not a passive, potency: its actuality is the divine essence itself or the capability of the divine essence (*activa in Deo est ipse actus Deus, seu potens Dei essentia*). And the actions attributed to the power of God are the passing over of the divine power into the created order, *actiones Dei transeuntia*. Indeed, it is correct to say, with Thomas Aquinas, that the *potentia Dei* is an "effect without an action."[330] Even so, creation is not a new or a temporal act of God — rather God in eternity wills in order that creatures might come into existence in time, and, as far as the creature is concerned, it is a passive creation.[331]

The Reformed orthodox define the other half of the traditional distinction, the divine *potentia ordinata*, as the power of God, "subordinate to the decree of God" and

---

326. Turretin, *Inst. theol elencticae*, III.xxi.8; Maresius, *Collegium theol.*, ii.58; cf. Heidanus, *Corpus theol.*, ii (pp. 88-89), specifically rejecting the Cartesian notion that God can accomplish logical impossibilities. Also note Leigh, *Treatise*, II.xiv (p. 108 margin, citing Willet on Gen. 18:12); cf. virtually the identical argument in Manton, *Sermons upon Mark 10:17-27* [sermon 15], in *Works*, XVII, p. 86.

327. Wendelin, *Christianae theologiae libri duo*, I.i.27 (3,6).

328. Leigh, *Treatise*, II.xiv (pp. 108-109).

329. Leigh, *Treatise*, II.xiv (p. 106, scripture from margin); cf. *Dutch Annotations*, Eph. 3:20 in loc., where the text is said to refer, not to the "hidden," but to the revealed power of God in its gracious exercise.

330. Wendelin, *Christianae theologiae libri duo*, I.i.27 (3), citing Aquinas, *Summa theol.*, Ia, q. 25, art 1, ad 3.

331. Wendelin, *Christianae theologiae libri duo*, I.i.27 (3).

relative to its ordained effects.[332] This ordained power brings about all that God has willed to bring about and belongs to the order of time (*temporis series*). Within the *potentia ordinata*, however, they also make a further distinction, parallel to the distinction between absolute and actual power: the distinction between *potentia extraordinaria* and *potentia ordinaria*. As Manton indicates, drawing on the traditional *pactum* language of *potentia ordinata*, the "ordinary" power of God is the divine power that operates "according to the course of second causes and [the] law of nature" through which God "preserves the creatures and works by them according to the order which he himself hath established: Ps. 109:91, 'They continue this day according to thine ordinance, for all are thy servants.'" The sun, moon, and stars are preserved in their courses, and all things are sustained in their being by this "covenant of day and night."[333]

Nonetheless, despite this rootedness in the ultimate ordination of God, the *potentia ordinata* can be distinguished into effects that are above or beside the normal order of nature and effects that belong intrinsically to the order of nature. There is, thus, an ordained power that is "extraordinarily and immediately operative" and an ordained power that is "ordinarily and mediately operative."[334] The former power is commonly referred to as the divine omnipotence as it is evidenced in miracles or witnessed in the statements of Scripture concerning the world-encompassing power of God, capable of all things, including the impossible; the latter refers to the power of God in and through the order of nature, moving and sustaining all things.[335] God also thus possesses an "extraordinary power, by which he can suspend the whole course of nature, as he hath done sometimes upon eminent occasions; as when the sun stood still in the valley of Ajalom, Josh. 10:12-13, or when the sun went back ten degrees on the dial of Ahaz, 2 Kings 20:11; his interdicting the Red Sea that it should not flow, Exod. 14:21, 22; his causing iron, which is a heavy body, to swim upon the top of the water at the prayer of Elisha, 2 Kings 6:6."[336] Presumably, this power remains within the *potentia ordinata* because it does not utterly abridge the laws of nature, but allows the world order to continue on around the miraculous intervention.

5. *Potentia*, *potestas*, and *dominium*: the distinction and relation of power, sovereignty, and dominion. Finally, the seventeenth-century scholastics distinguish between the power of God as *potentia* or the power inhering in the divine essence to do as it wills and the power of God as *potestas* or the power of God over things, that is the absolute *jus* and *authoritas* of God to control what is his.[337] The latter, considered as the right of the creator over the creation, is not a category as much elaborated upon as the *potentia Dei*, the "potency" or effective power of God.

---

332. Cloppenburg, *Exercitationes super locos communes*, II.v.5.
333. Manton, *Sermons upon Mark 10:17-27* [sermon 15], in *Works*, XVII, p. 86.
334. Cloppenburg, *Exercitationes super locos communes*, II.v.8-9.
335. Cloppenburg, *Exercitationes super locos communes*, II.v.11, 13.
336. Manton, *Sermons upon Mark 10:17-27* [sermon 15], in *Works*, XVII, p. 86.
337. Rijssen, *Summa theol.*, III.xxxv.

The greatness of God's authority standeth in two things: (1) The universality of it,
God's authority reacheth to all things, the whole world and all creatures in it are subject
to his will and disposing; (2) the absoluteness of it; what he willeth must be done.[338]

This power (*potentia*) of God is also intimately related to the rule or sovereignty
(*potestas*) and dominion (*dominium*) that he exercises. The rule or sovereignty of God
is that

> by which he possesses the right (*ius*) to do all that he does. This rule or dominion of
> God has as its foundation, 1) the dependence of all the creatures on their creator, and
> 2) the eminence and dignity of the divine nature above all others.[339]

God's dominion rests also on his infinite knowledge and wisdom and is manifest in
the benefits he freely bestows upon his creatures: in contrast with the view held by
Arminius, the Reformed understand the dominion of rule of God without any such
qualification as might be drawn from the idea of a divine *scientia media* or from a relaxed
notion of the extent and implication of the divine providential *concursus*.[340] According
to the Reformed, God has supreme dominion over his creatures both in terms of
"jurisdiction" according to which he rules according to his pleasure and in terms of
"propriety" or the right he has over every creature to order it as he pleases.[341] This
dominion, like God himself, is independent of all other powers, it is "full and perfect"
(cf. 1 Chron 29:11, 12) and "it extends to the soul and heart."[342]

The *dominum Dei* may be defined as that power or rule of God according to which
he does with his creatures as he wills.[343] This divine rule Rijssen describes under six
categories, each based upon a scriptural reference. According to this *dominum*, God
1) determines the end of things as he wills, 2) gives life or being as he chooses, 3)
prescribes or commands as he wills, 4) works in and through things as he wills, 5)
permits evil, and 6) owes no one a reason. "The foundation of this divine rule in God
is nothing other than his eminence and primacy" over all things: all creation depends
upon God and his covenant.[344] So, too, the greatness of God's authority appears in
the scriptural attributions to him of kingship and sovereignty. All things are subject
to him as their creator and Lord. Scripture calls him "the most high," the high and
lofty one (cf. Isaiah 57:15).

In his analysis of the rule (*dominum*) or right (*jus*) of God Rijssen makes a distinction
structurally similar to that between *potentia absoluta* and *potentia ordinata*. The *dominum*
or *postestas absolutum* is the power God maintains over all his creatures, established
over them as authority, without injustice; while the *dominum ordinatum* is the order

---

338. Leigh, *Treatise*, II.vi (p. 51).
339. Pictet, *Theol. chr.*, II.x.6.
340. See above, 5.3 (F.1) and cf. Muller, *God, Creation, and Providence*, pp. 235-257.
341. Leigh, *Treatise*, II.vi (p. 52).
342. Leigh, *Treatise*, II.vi (p. 53).
343. Rijssen, *Summa theol.*, III.xlv.
344. Rijssen, *Summa theol.*, III.xlvi.

or principle of rule (*ordo seu ratio justitiae*) which God declares to us in the word of the law and the Gospel.[345] To the former belongs the free will of God by which he chooses some unworthy creatures to be saved and passes over the others without regard to merit. To the latter belongs the order of salvation accomplished by grace through the satisfaction of Christ in which faith is rewarded and sin punished by damnation.[346] Wendelin explicitly distances his own theology from the medieval scholastics on this point: the divine *potestas* or *jus* ought not to be identified as absolute in such a way as to sever it from God's righteousness: divine power and right must be understood in scriptural terms, and "human speculation" ought not to be indulged! Indeed, Wendelin adds, Luther once argued that God, by his absolute power and right could subject the innocent to eternal suffering — to which Calvin had responded that he not only repudiated but also detested the scholastic notion of absolute power, inasmuch as it separated God's righteousness (*iustitia*) from God's rule (*imperium*).[347]

6. *Usus practicus.* The doctrine of God's power is of great practical use, since it gives assurance that whatever God has promised will be fulfilled.[348] And beyond this,

> It serves both for a spur to do well, since God is able to save, Gen 17:1 and a bridle to restrain from evil, seeing he hath power to destroy; we should therefore humble ourselves under his mighty hand, 1 Pet. 5:6; Luke 12:5. ... This ministers comfort to those which have God on their side, they need not fear what man or devil can do against them. He can strengthen them in spiritual weaknesses against sin, and unto duty: all the devils in hell are not able to pluck them out of his hands, Matt 16:18; John 10:28, 29. If a people fall from Him he is able to graft them in again, Isaiah 44:22; Rom. 11:23; they are *kept by his power through faith unto salvation*, 1 Pet. 1:5.[349]

Even so, the commandment to "'be strong in Christ and in his power,' includes a promise that he will give us his power, if we seek to him and rest on him," so that God's omnipotence is an impetus to worship.[350] So also is omnipotence a ground of hope: God promises us that if we call on him in our day of trouble, he will save us — and his power assures that this is possible, confirming all of the promises of God, particularly his *benevolentia* toward his elect, as made effective in Christ.[351]

---

345. Rijssen, *Summa theol.*, III.xlvii.

346. Rijssen, *Summa theol.*, III.xlvii.

347. Wendelin, *Christianae theologiae libri duo*, I.i.27 (4), citing Calvin, *Opuscula*, p. 735; i.e., *Ioannis Calvini Tractatus theologici omnes, in unum volumen certis classibus congesti* (Geneva, 1612), the treatise cited is, *De occulta Dei providentia*. Calvin's remarks are not, however, directed against Luther (this is an aspect of Wendelin's own polemic) but rather against the anonymous "calumnator," in fact, Sebastian Castellio, who had attacked Calvin's teaching on predestination, providence, and divine justice. Calvin did not, however, entirely reject the distinction between a higher, absolute justice and a revealed or ordained justice in God; he merely had refused to separate this justice from the ultimate (and hidden) righteous purpose of God: see Schreiner, "Exegesis and Double Justice," pp. 323-338.

348. Zanchi, *De natura Dei*, III.ii (col. 190); cf. Leigh, *Treatise*, II.xiv (p.109), citing Acts 26:8 and Matt. 22:29.

349. Leigh, *Treatise*, II.xiv (pp. 109-110).

350. Leigh, *Treatise*, II.xiv (p. 110).

351. Zanchi, *De natura Dei*, III.i (col. 191).

By way of conclusion — it is certainly the case that such discussions of the relationship of God's knowledge and power to possibles and impossibles stands in considerable topical and stylistic discontinuity with the theology of the Reformers and, indeed, approaches the kind of argument that the first generation of the Reformation in particular tried to excise from theology. It is, nonetheless, also the case that the Reformers assumed the infinitude of God's power as much as did the later orthodox, and that they shared with the orthodox writers a common exegetical foundation and a similar piety — and that the orthodox used whatever means were available to defend the doctrine, including scholastic means when scholastic objections had been raised. There remains, therefore, a continuity in fundamental doctrinal perspective, served in the era of orthodoxy by an altered method and explained at a level of detail not envisioned by the Reformers — and, arguably, this continuity of basic teaching was mediated through the Reformation with late medieval accents (in this case, not Thomistic ones) that offered the Reformed orthodox writers clues to their own scholastic formulations.

C. The Majesty and Glory of God

1. The place of majesty and glory among the divine attributes. The modern misunderstanding of the traditional orthodox approach to the divine attributes in general and to the divine majesty and glory in particular is nowhere more clearly identifiable than in the discussion offered by Otto Weber. He comments that "older theology speaks of the 'majesty attributes' of God in much greater detail than it does of the attributes of his love" without ever qualifying his comment with the fact that *neither* majesty *nor* love is presented by the older dogmatics as a category for the classification of divine attributes, and that both majesty and love stand coordinated with each and all of the other attributes of God.[352] In other words, the phrase "majesty attributes," and, therefore, Weber's critique as well, is lacking in any substantive relationship to the older dogmatics![353] It is true that the *maiestas Dei* was used both by the Reformers and the Protestant orthodox as one of the attributes that clearly and surely indicated the divine transcendence of human categories and, therefore, the inability of human beings to penetrate the Godhead with their theological reasonings. One does not approach, much less penetrate the divine majesty — as Calvin often said in his prayers, one falls down before it. We do not, in other words, find a listing of "majesty attributes" in the older theology, any more than we find a listing of "love attributes" or "goodness attributes" or "omnipotence attributes" — what we do find is an understanding of the *maiestas Dei* that provides guidelines and boundaries for the interpretation of the doctrine of God in general.

---

352. Weber, *Foundations of Dogmatics*, I, p. 438: in the German original, "*die Majestätsprädikate.*"

353. Note that in the Lutheran orthodox dogmatics, the divine attributes in general are communicated to the humanity of Christ according to the *genus maiestaticum*, but this is not a genus of attributes, but a genus of communication — and by the very fact of the communication is not part of a discussion of the Godhead *in se*, but of its relations *ad extra*. See Schmid, *Doctrinal Theology*, pp. 327-337.

What is more, as the exegetical foundations of the Reformed orthodox doctrine make clear, both the *maiestas* and the *gloria Dei* are most frequently taken as identifiers of the *Shechinah* and of the *kabod Adonai* — namely, the manifestation of the divine presence and of the "glory of the Lord" to the people of Israel.[354] Although, therefore, the majesty and glory of God are revelatory of the divine transcendence, they are fundamentally and categorically *revelatory*, indeed, they are theophanic in their biblical context and are so understood by the Reformed orthodoxy. What is more, the divine majesty is also often understood in a fully trinitarian manner and is one of the points at which the doctrine of the divine attributes relates directly to the doctrine of the Trinity, specifically to God's manifestation in Christ and in the work of the Spirit. Weber's contention that the older theology's emphasis on "majesty attributes" derived from its tendency to develop the doctrine of God as a "concept of God 'in himself'" in contrast to the Christology where "they discussed the concept of 'God for us,'"[355] is some of the most blatant nonsense in the literature — given both Weber's mistake concerning the categories of attribution and his even more egregious reading of *maiestas* as referring to only God *in se* rather than to the divine presence!

2. The Reformers on the *maiestas Dei* and *gloria Dei*. Like the attributes of blessedness and felicity, the divine majesty and glory are seldom given lengthy separate exposition in the doctrinal works of the Reformers but are treated, instead, in considerable depth exegetically. From early on in the development of Protestant theology, a special significance was ascribed to the majesty of God *(maiestas Dei)*. Such usage was characteristic of the theology of Luther, who was concerned to warn against any attempt to grasp the absolute or "naked" Godhead in theological formulae. God in his majesty must be regarded as unreachable, as dwelling in "unapproachable light": God in his majesty, Luther remarks with reference to Hebrews 12:29, is "a consuming fire."[356] It is, however, characteristic of subsequent discussion that Protestant theologians retained Luther's cautions without his sense of paradox: thus, Musculus, Calvin, and many of the later Protestant orthodox, both Lutheran and Reformed, presented lengthy discussions of the attributes of absolute Godhead — with the result that Luther's consideration of the *maiestas Dei* was transmuted into a rule of caution for the presentation of an elaborate discussion. Here again, Musculus' thought appears to be of primary importance to the Reformed tradition — for it was Musculus who used the term "majesty of God" to indicate the ultimacy and transcendence of the divine nature. When analyzing the problem of naming God, Musculus questioned whether the divine majesty could be designated or denominated, granting that denomination belongs to the finite realm of genus and species. Indeed, when speaking of "the essence and substance of [God's] majesty," Musculus appears to use the term as a summation of all the attributions of eminence or perfections of God and, indeed, as a term for the unreachable and unsearchable height of the Godhead considered

---

354. Cf., comments on Ex. 24:17 and Isa. 6:1 — e.g., Henry, *Exposition*, in loc; Poole, *Commentary*, I, p. 172; II, p. 337; Trapp, *Commentary*, III, p. 309.

355. Weber, *Foundations of Dogmatics*, I, p. 439.

356. Cf. Köstlin, *Theology of Luther*, II, p. 280.

in its essence.[357] Musculus returns to the concept of *maiestas Dei* when he raises the problem of attributing love to God. Here he further defines divine majesty as the lordship of God over all things and the freedom of God in all his acts. Right understanding of the divine majesty, furthermore, leads us to refrain from attributing to God anything "servile or vile" and to attribute positively to God all that is "principial, sublime, excellent, free, and divine."[358]

Calvin, similarly, albeit with a somewhat greater pastoral emphasis, understands the majesty and glory of God as a ground of awe — indeed, as the primary foundation for a right consideration of the "lowly condition" of human beings, both in sin and in redemption.[359] The glory and majesty of God shine forth consistently in the created order.[360] For Calvin, as for the later orthodox, the *gloria Dei* is an attribute consistently manifested to the world, "chiefly visible," Calvin writes, "in the fulfillment of what he has promised." This manifestation of the divine glory, moreover, is victorious over all attempts of sinful creatures to obscure it — and, declares Calvin, in almost supralapsarian fashion, this is in fact the foundation for God's unswerving fulfillment of the promises: "He declares ... that he will abide by his promises, because he wishes to vindicate his glory and preserve it entire, that it may not in any respect be diminished."[361] Even so, "the reprobate are ... instruments of the glory of God" and, "in a different manner" it is the goal or "end of our election" to "show forth the glory of God in every possible way," specifically, "to the praise of the glory of his grace."[362]

The category of "majesty" is closely associated with the worship of God and with prayer to God as the "supreme ... maker of heaven and earth" and as the Redeemer made known in Christ.[363] When, moreover, we turn from Calvin's *Institutes* to his commentaries, the *maiestas Dei* receives consistent reflection — indeed, those who have commented, against the older scholarship of a Warfield, that Calvin virtually never appeals to the "sovereignty" of God ought to look a bit more closely at Calvin's frequent references to the divine majesty. Calvin relates the conception of God's majesty to the revelation of God in nature:

> the infinite majesty of God shines forth in the heavenly bodies, and justly keeps the eyes of men fixed on the contemplation of it, yet his glory is beheld in a special manner, in the great favor which he bears to men, and in the goodness which he manifests towards them.[364]

Or, again,

---

357. Musculus, *Loci communes*, xli (*Commonplaces*, p. 875).
358. Musculus, *Loci communes*, XLVII (*Commonplaces*, pp. 957-958).
359. Calvin, *Institutes*, I.i.3.
360. Calvin, *Commentary on Isaiah*, 6:3 (*CTS Isaiah*, I, p. 205).
361. Calvin, *Commentary on Isaiah*, 42:8 (*CTS Isaiah*, III, p. 296).
362. Calvin, *Commentary on Isaiah*, 43:22 (*CTS Isaiah*, III, p. 345), citing Eph. 1:4-6.
363. Calvin, *Institutes*, II.vi.4; cf. I.xiii.13; II.xii.1.
364. Calvin, *Commentary on the Psalms*, 8:3 (*CTS Psalms*, I, p. 99).

David, out of the whole fabric of the world, has especially chosen the heavens, in which he might exhibit to our view an image of God, because there it is more distinctly to be seen, even as a man is better seen when set on an elevated stage; so now he shows us the sun as placed in the highest rank, because in his wonderful brightness the majesty of God displays itself more magnificently than in all the rest.[365]

Even so, "When God is exhibited to us as sitting on his throne to take cognisance of the conduct of men, unless we are stupefied in an extraordinary degree, his majesty must strike us with terror."[366]

Yet, the divine majesty does not simply instill fear, but is also a ground of right worship, for "the service which we owe him is better expressed by the word reverence, that thus his majesty may prominently stand forth to our view in its infinite greatness."[367] In addition, the divine majesty is also an attribute used by Calvin to underline the doctrine of the Trinity: in his commentary on Psalm 2, he cites John 5:22, "He that honors not the Son, honors not the Father which hath sent him," and then adds, "it is of great importance to hold fast this inseparable connection, that as the majesty of God hath shone forth in his only begotten Son, so the Father will not be feared and worshiped but in his person."[368] So also Calvin writes that "as the eternal Word of God, Christ, it is true, has always had in his hands by right sovereign authority and majesty."[369]

3. The Protestant orthodox doctrine of the *maiestas Dei* and *gloria Dei*: definitions. This Reformation-era sense of the divine majesty, conjoined with a similar use of the concept of divine glory, carries over directly into the theology of the Protestant orthodox — albeit the placement of the doctrine varies greatly. Perkins relates God's glory and blessedness to his self-sufficiency.[370] Venema identifies majesty and glory, together with authority and omnipresence, as attributes of relation illustrative of the kingship of God.[371] Edward Leigh specifically uses the *maiestas* and *gloria Dei* as a conclusion to his entire discussion of the attributes —

From all these before-mentioned Attributes ariseth the Glory or Majesty of God, which is the infinite excellence of the Divine Essence, Heb 1:3; Exod. 33:18; Psalm 29:9. This is called *the face of God*, Exod 33:20 and *light inaccessible*, 1 Tim 6:16 which to acknowledge perfectly belongs to God alone, yet the revelation and obscurer vision thereof is granted to us in this life by the ministry of those things which are seen and heard, the clearer in the life to come, where we shall see God face to face, 1 Cor. 13;12; Matt. 18:10.[372]

---

365. Calvin, *Commentary on the Psalms*, 19:4 (*CTS Psalms*, I, p. 315).
366. Calvin, *Commentary on the Psalms*, 14:2 (*CTS Psalms*, I, p. 192).
367. Calvin, *Commentary on the Psalms*, 18:1 (*CTS Psalms*, I, p. 260).
368. Calvin, *Commentary on the Psalms*, 2:2 (*CTS Psalms*, I, p. 12).
369. Calvin, *Commentary on the Psalms*, 2:8 (*CTS Psalms*, I, p. 19).
370. Perkins, *Golden Chaine*, IV (p. 13, col. 2).
371. Venema, *Inst. theol.*, VII (p. 192).
372. Leigh, *Treatise*, II.xv (p. 110-111).

Mastricht, similarly, discusses majesty and glory together, as a conclusion to his discussion of the attributes, followed only by the divine blessedness.[373] Witsius and Pictet speak of the "glory and majesty" of God as the result or sum of the divine perfections.[374] The glory and majesty of God are intrinsic to his nature: "God's glory or majesty, is the infinite excellency of his most simple and most holy divine Nature."[375]

Still, although the attributes of majesty and glory are typically discussed together by the Reformed orthodox, they are not understood as entirely synonymous. Majesty or magnificence are the terms used to translate the Greek, μεγαλωσύνη, which indicates the "admirable highness and greatness, amplitude, splendour, [and] dignity" of the divine — an attribute not only to be predicated of God in general but of all the persons, notably of Christ according to his divinity. Such majesty "appears principally in his works," which are often identified in Scripture as "great" and "wonderful."[376] Thus, among the names and titles given to God by Scripture are such phrases as "God above," "God over all," "God of Heaven," and "the Most High" — all of which are "descriptive" of "the majesty, power, and authority of God," who is glorious and "terrible in his majesty."[377] More specifically, the divine majesty is that greatness and splendor that belong to God as a "royal honor" such as is attributed to "the representative of a whole people" and is manifest either in governance, the enactment of laws, and the execution of judgment according to law or in the protection and defense of a people from their enemies. Majesty, therefore, is a dignity that inspires awe in subjects. It is particularly applied to God, whose throne is in the heavens, who has earth as his footstool, who is "surrounded by an army of angels who are his ministering servants," and who "sends his laws upon earth, executes vengeance upon his enemies, and encompasses his own people with his shield of defense."[378]

Glory, in Venema's view, indicates a still "higher degree of honor" than does majesty — it "denotes all those perfections which render him infinitely superior to all other beings."[379] According to Scripture, "God is and ever shall be exceeding Glorious, Exod. 15:11; Deut. 28:58."[380]

> Glory is sometimes taken for outward lustre and shining, as *one glory of the Sun*; sometimes for outward decking and adorning, as *long hair is a glory to a woman*; but the proper signification of it is, excellent estimation by which one is preferred before others.[381]

Even so, there are several possible implications of the attribution of "glory" to God:

373. Mastricht, *Theoretico-practica theol.*, II.xxii.
374. Witsius, *Dissertations on the Lord's Prayer*, XIV (p. 378); Pictet, *Theol. chr.*, II.xii.5.
375. Perkins, *Golden Chaine*, IV (p. 13, col. 2).
376. Jenkyn, *Exposition upon the Epistle of Jude*, verse 25, in loc. (p. 359).
377. Owen, *Exposition of the Epistle to the Hebrews*, 7:1-3, in loc. (V, p. 311).
378. Venema, *Inst. theol.*, VII (p. 192).
379. Venema, *Inst. theol.*, VII (p. 192); cf. Mastricht, *Theoretico-practica theol.*, II.xxii.5.
380. Leigh, *Treatise*, II.xv (p. 111).
381. Leigh, *Treatise*, II.xv (p. 111).

Glory is used metonymically for that which is the ground and matter of glory, as Prov. 19:11 & 20:29. Sometimes the glory of God signifieth the very essence and nature of God, as Exod. 33:18. Sometimes it is used to signify some of God's Attributes, Eph. 1:12, that is, his grace and good will, by showing forth of which he makes himself glorious. Sometimes it is put for some work of God which is great and marvelous, John 11:40, that is, the grace and powerful work of God in raising up thy brother *Lazarus* unto life again; Exod. 25:16 & 40:35, that is, some extraordinary splendor, as *R. Moses* expounds it, which God created, thereby to show forth his magnificence and glory.[382]

"R. Moses," or Rabbi Moses is, of course, Maimonides, whose *Guide for the Perplexed* offered the Jewish equivalent of Christian Aristotelianism both to the Middle Ages and to subsequent scholasticism. The advantage of Maimonides for Protestant scholastics in the seventeenth century was not merely the fact that he was not a Roman Catholic and that his reputation as a theologian could not be impugned in the same way as the reputations of Roman Catholic scholastics — but also and preeminently that he was a master of the Hebrew Old Testament. Maimonides' comments on the divine glory or *Shekinah* indicated, in the line of the tradition of rabbinic commentary, an effulgence of the divine given forth by God as a self-manifestation, yet also, as perceived by humans, a resplendence standing between the human mind and eye and the ultimate divine majesty that no one can withstand.[383]

The glory of God is correctly understood, argues Leigh, as Aquinas also said, as "the manifestation and shining forth of Excellency. God is said to glorify himself, when he manifesteth his unspeakable and incomprehensible excellency, Num. 14:21; Psalm 72:19; Levit. 10:3."[384] Since God only can know himself perfectly, the fulness of his glory is hidden from his creatures. Thus, when Scripture speaks of the "glory of the Lord" or of the vision of the divine majesty, the implication is that the prophet sees God, "not in his essence, or in the infinite excellency of his majesty, but in some visible model of his glory; like as we cannot see the sun *in rota*, but *in radiis*, [not] in the body of it, but in the beams only."[385]

Since the divine nature itself is "infinitely glorious, exceeding glory" it is therefore inaccessible to human beings, who, as Ezekiel taught, can "in this life" see "but the appearance and likeness of the glory of God."[386] Therefore,

Glory is taken essentially, as it signifieth the nature and attributes of God; or else respectively, as it signifieth the acknowledgement and celebration of his Majesty, and this is called properly glorification. [Angels and men glorify him when they extol his greatness and testify their acknowledgment of his glory, Is. 6:3; Psalm 29:1,2; Luke 2;14; Rev. 4:11.][387]

---

382. Leigh, *Treatise*, II.xv (p. 111).

383. Cf. Maimonides, *Guide for the Perplexed*, I.xxv (p. 34).

384. Leigh, *Treatise*, II.xv (p. 111, margin).

385. Trapp, *Commentary*, Is. 6:1 (III, p. 309), citing collaterally, Ex. 33:20 and 1 Tim. 6:16.

386. Greenhill, *Exposition of Ezekiel*, 1:28 in loc. (pp. 66-67).

387. Leigh, *Treatise*, II.xv (p. 111, text and margin).

This doctrine, therefore, points in two directions: on the one hand, the height of the divine glory and majesty is such that human beings, given their sin and "frailty," are separated from the divine and incapable of bearing or withstanding the full vision of God — on the other hand, the glory and majesty of God are attributes that belong to the revelation of the divine presence and require that God "be reverenced by all that have to do with him."

This truth, moreover, is available both by reason and by revelation. "Faith, reason, and sense" provide enough knowledge of God for us to recognize that God "is great and glorious both in himself and in all his works."[388] Thus, we apprehend some of that glory, though obscurely, in this life by the mind with the help of the senses — it is "a matter of sense, and evident by natural light" that "needeth not so much to be proved as improved." All the works of God display his glory. Moreover, the glory of God it is abundantly testified by Scripture — the Word of God manifests his glory to the mind and to the conscience, while the brightest, fullest demonstration of the glory of God in this life is given in the work of salvation, a work that "ought to raise our minds to holy astonishment."[389] Finally, the vision of his majesty will be more complete in heaven when we see him face to face.

This orthodox explanation of the divine glory and of the nature and limits of human perception of the glory or majesty of God reflects a series of issues and distinctions that we have encountered both in the prolegomena to theology and in the general discussion of the divine attributes. First to be noted here is the fundamental distinction between archetypal and ectypal theology in its relation to the *ad intra* and *ad extra* understanding of the divine attributes: human perception of the divine glory rests on the glory intrinsic to God but only knows it faintly or ectypally in its manifestation *ad extra*. Next, this approach to the problem parallels what we have already seen in the orthodox language of divine infinity, immensity, and eternity: God has these attributes *in se*, absolutely and apart from any relation to the created order, in a way in which they cannot be known — but he also possesses them in their egress and relation to the world. God is thus "glorious in his nature to the exclusion of all other glory and glorious also in his self-manifestation."[390] Finally, both the limits and the stages of human perception of God's glory rest firmly upon the categories of *theologia viatorum* and *theologia beatorum* enunciated as presuppositions of theological discourse in the prolegomena: we see, in other words, the working out of *prolegomena* and *principia* in system rather than, as the nineteenth-century view of orthodoxy would have it, the replacement of enunciated presuppositions and principles with central dogmas.

4. Distinctions concerning the majesty and glory of God. These considerations yield a series of distinctions related to the divine glory: God's glory may be understood either internally or externally — either as "the inward excellence and worth whereby

---

388. Manton, *Transfiguration of Christ*, sermon vii (*Works*, I, p. 404).

389. Witsius, *Dissertations on the Lord's Prayer*, XIV (p. 378); cf. Manton, *Transfiguration of Christ*, sermon vii (*Works*, I, p. 403).

390. Leigh, *Treatise*, II.xv (p. 113).

he deserves to be esteemed and praised" or as "the actual acknowledging of it, for glory is defined as clear and manifest knowledge of another's excellence."[391] Thus, the glory of God is a twofold glory, to be considered internally and essentially or externally or "respectively," efficaciously, and accidentally. Each category, moreover, the internal and the external, can be considered either objectively or formally.

First, then, God's glory is to be understood essentially, as one of the divine attributes but, moreover, as an attribute that eminently reflects and reveals the perfection of all the attributes. The Scriptural revelation consistently extolls God's glory in this "essential" sense "when it calls God, *Great, Most high, Glorious, Acts* 7:2; *The God of glory, King of glory, Psalm* 24:8; *Father of glory, Ephes.* 1:17."[392] Scripture consistently, moreover, praises the infinitude and perfection of God's majesty and speaks of God as magnificent and greatly to be praised.[393] As opposed to an incidental or "accidental" glory, God's essential glory is underived, infinite, and everlasting: "this is called *gloria* [as distinct from *glorificatio*]; it receives neither addition nor diminution by any created power."[394]

Mastricht enumerates four characteristics of *ingredientia* of the *gloria Dei*: it is infinite, it bears an ultimate perfection and eminence, its brightness demands recognition, and it rightly and necessarily is celebrated and glorified in and through its manifestation.[395] It is the very nature of the divine glory and majesty, therefore, that they are intrinsic to God but are also manifest in and for the creation. Since, moreover, these attributes are not isolated perfections, but spring forth from all of the divine perfections together as their "source," and since the attributes are "inseparably connected, and are not opposed to one another," care must be given not to exalt or emphasize one attribute to the neglect or diminution of the others: right understanding of the divine glory, therefore, inculcates, for example, the lesson that divine justice ought not to be exalted over divine goodness and grace.[396]

This internal, essential glory is, as Leigh notes in more detail, twofold:

1) Objective, that glory of God is the excellence of his Divine nature, for such is his Majesty and excellence, that he is infinitely worthy to be praised, admired, and loved of all.
2) Formal, is his own knowledge, love, and delight in himself; for this is infinitely more the glory of God, that he is known and beloved of himself, than that he is loved and

---

391. Leigh, *Treatise*, II.xv (pp.111-112).

392. Leigh, *Treatise*, II.xv (p. 112).

393. Mastricht, *Theoretico-practica theol.*, II.xxii.3, citing Deut. 7:21; 10:17; Neh. 1:5; 4:14; 9:32; Ps. 47:3; 96:4; 113:3; 135, and the Psalter passim; Isa. 12:16; Jer. 10:6; Dan. 11:45; Ex. 15:4 and cross-referencing his discussion of infinity and magnitude, II.ix.

394. Leigh, *Treatise*, II.xv (p. 116; cf. p. 114).

395. Mastricht, *Theoretico-practica theol.*, II.xxii.5-8.

396. Venema, *Inst. theol.*, VII (p. 192). Note that this way of addressing the relationship of glory to other attributes rests on the orthodox assumption that the divine simplicity is defined by the presence of certain kinds of distinctions in the Godhead: see above, 4.3 (D).

praised by all creatures, Men and Angels, because this argueth an infinite worth in God's own nature, that an infinite love and delight is satisfied with it.[397]

The inward glory of God, whether objective or formal, is not a result or effect of God's work: since "God hath this kind of glory objective and formal, most fully even from all eternity," it is not this essential glory that is indicated "when he is said to make all things for himself or his glory" — rather such statements refer to the outward or external glorification of God. By contrast, the inward, objective glory of God flows from "the essential excellencies that are in Him."[398] The "formal internal glory" or contemplation and love by God of God as the object of his contemplation is a ground, in the discussion of the unity of divine essence in its attributes, of one of the typical Augustinian models of the Trinity: the mind which knows itself as object.

In this ultimate, inward sense, the divine glory is incommunicable to creatures. Specifically, in polemic against the Lutheran Christology and its tendency toward a *communicatio idiomatum in abstracto*, the Reformed argue that Christ's humanity is not a bearer of the divine attribute of glory and that the glory that belongs to the Mediator on the accomplishment of his office is distinct from the eternal, essential glory of God:

> *Quest.* Whether the infinite glory which God hath as God, be communicated to Christ's human nature.
> *Answ.* That being a creature cannot have that glory which is due to the Creator. It is true Christ is infinitely to be glorified, because he is God and man, but not therefore his human nature. Our Divines distinguish between a glory merely divine, and a Mediator's glory, which is next to divine, far above all creatures.
> *Ob.* Christ prayed for the glory which he had before the beginning [John 17:5].
> *Sol.* Christ had it in decree and predestination, and that was not God's essential glory, which is a property, for he requires he may have it now, which could not have been if he had it from eternity.[399]

Second, the divine glory may be considered as external, expressed both in the creation and "in divine dispensations toward his church and his people."[400] In particular, this external glory refers to "the manifestation of his perfections by their effects."[401] As in the case of the inward and essential glory of God, this external glory can be divided into objective and formal categories. The former, "objective" is the efficacious glory of God or the divine glory considered respectively or in relation to the created order, the latter, "formal" is the creatures' glorification of their creator. Although there is a "great difference between God's glorifying himself and our glorifying him,"[402] Scripture draws out the connection between the revealed glory of the attributes and works of God and the ultimate, inaccessible light of the essential glory in its references

---

397. Leigh, *Treatise*, II.xv (p. 112).
398. Durham, *Exposition of Revelation*, 4:11, in loc.
399. Leigh, *Treatise*, II.xv (p. 115).
400. Greenhill, *Exposition on Ezekiel*, 1:28 in loc. (p. 66).
401. Venema, *Inst. theol.*, VII (p. 192).
402. Ridgley, *Body of Divinity* (1855), I, p. 4.

to the "face" and the "name" of God — indicating both the "majesty and eminence of the thing itself" and the presence that demands acknowledgment.[403] Thus, among the ways that the divine glory *ad extra* can be considered, there is the glorification

> 1) By way of object, *viz.*, when he made the Heavens and Earth, and all these glorious creatures here below, which are said to show forth his glory, Psalm 19, that is, objectively, they are the effects of his glorious wisdom and power, and so become objects of mens' and Angels' praises of him; and as the glory of men consists in outward ornaments, so God's glory consists in having such creatures, men and Angels to be his followers.[404]

Scripture speaks of God's glory "efficaciously, when it affirmeth that all the earth is full of the glory of God, Is. 6:3, and propounds the glorious and wonderful works of God to be considered by us, Exod. 32:18."[405]

The importance of this external, objective manifestation of divine glory to the Reformed orthodox — quite to the contrary of Weber's claims — appears clearly from Owen's argument that the "representation of [God's] holiness and righteousness among his creatures," manifesting "His eternal power and Godhead ... in the things that are made," is the principle form of the glory of God. For without this manifestation, God "could not be known and glorified as God."[406] This, too, is the foundation, according to Owen, of the creation of human beings in the image of God and of the renewal of the fallen image in Christ: "How glorious and beautiful soever any of the works of creation appear to be, from impressions of divine power, wisdom, and goodness on them; yet without this *image of God* in man, there was nothing here below to understand God in them — to glorify God by them."[407] The point is made confessionally in the Westminster Standards.[408]

God manifests his glory sometimes "extraordinarily" in apparitions, visions, or as in the cloud and pillar of the Exodus (Exod. 16:10; cf. Ezek 1:28) but more commonly or "ordinarily" in his "word and works." Indeed, whatever "glory" inheres in the created order is present there only as a gift and benefit from God, enjoyed by creatures "only to exalt his glory forever."[409] Thus,

> The Law sets forth the glory of his justice [Exod. 9:15], and the Gospel that of his mercy, 2 Cor. 3:8; it is called his glorious Gospel, Luke 2:14.
>
> All his works set forth his glory, both those of creation and preservation or providence, *Psalm* 19; the whole creation must needs show forth his glorious power and wisdom, the sound is said to go over all the world [Rom 10:18; Psalm 19:4], that

---

403. Mastricht, *Theoretico-practica theol.*, II.xxii.7.

404. Leigh, *Treatise*, II.xv (p. 112); cf. Ridgley, *Body of Divinity* (1855), I, p. 4.

405. Leigh, *Treatise*, II.xv (p. 112).

406. Owen, *ΧΡΙΣΤΟΛΟΓΙΑ*, in *Works*, I, pp. 182-183.

407. Owen, *ΧΡΙΣΤΟΛΟΓΙΑ*, in *Works*, I, pp. 183.

408. Westminster Shorter Catechism, q. 1; Westminster Larger Catechism, q. 1; and cf. the extended discussion in Ridgley, *Body of Divinity* (1855), I, pp. 4-9.

409. Diodati, *Pious and Learned Annotations*, Rev. 4:10, in loc.

is, all creatures must needs gather, that if the Heavens be such glorious Heavens, the
Sun so glorious a Sun, how much more must that God be a glorious God who is the
author and worker of them.

God is glorious in all his works upon the hearts of believers: he puts a glory upon
them, so that in this sense he is effectually glorious, *Ephes.* 5 ... ; this glory is grace when
God makes one holy, heavenly minded, meek, zealous; hereafter we shall have glorious
bodies and souls.[410]

Just as God's glory is manifested in all his works, so do all his works redound to his
glory as their proper end: "God's glory is the end of predestination, both reprobation,
Prov. 16:1 and election, *Ephes* 1:5,6; of the creation and administration of all things,
Rom 11:36; of all benefits obtained in Christ, 2 Cor. 1:20; and would be of all our
actions, 1 Cor. 10:35."[411] Even so,

> God glorified himself, John 12:28. Christ glorified him, his whole life was nothing but
> a seeking of his Father's glory, John 17:4. The Saints and Angels spend eternity in
> setting forth his glory, Is. 6:23; Rev. 4:10,11; 7:9,10. All the creatures do glorify God
> in their kind, Psalm 145:10 & 148: the worm is not exempted, therefore that man (saith
> *Chrysostom*) which doth not glorify God, is baser than the basest worm. This is all the
> first table of the Decalogue, and above half the Lord's prayer. The three first petitions
> concern God's glory, and the conclusion likewise hath reference to it. We should glorify
> God in all conditions, in adversity as well as in prosperity, Psalm 50:15; in all the parts
> of our bodies, in our hearts, 1 Pet. 3:15; with our mouths, Rom. 15:6; in our lives, 1
> Cor. 6, cf. Matt. 5:16.[412]

In the second part of the bifurcation, the glory of God manifest *ad extra*, is considered
formally or accidentally — thus, the divine glory is "2) Formal, when men and Angels
do know, love, and obey him, and praise him to all eternity."[413] This external, formal
glory is "accidental, finite, temporary," and is rightly "called *glorificatio*; this ebbs or
flows, shines or is overshadowed, as goodness or gracelessness prevails in the world."[414]
It is, in other words, the subjective contemplation of the divine glory, not by God,
as in its *ad intra* analogue, but by rational creatures: specifically, glory in this sense
refers to "the recognition and celebration of [God's] manifested perfections."[415]

This last category of the orthodox discussion of the divine glory yields a strong
practical application of the doctrine even beyond the obvious implications of the
dogmatic exposition for piety: from this doctrine we ought to learn, above all, to seek
after God's glory, to "labor to partake of God's image, that we might be partakers of
his glory" —

---

410. Leigh, *Treatise*, II.xv (p. 113); cf. Mastricht, *Theoretico-practica theol.*, II.xxii.8-9.

411. Leigh, *Treatise*, II.xv (p. 115).

412. Leigh, *Treatise*, II.xv (pp. 118-119); cf. Diodati, *Pious and Learned Annotations*, Rom. 15:6-7;
1 Peter 3:15; Rev. 7:11, in loc.

413. Leigh, *Treatise*, II.xv (p. 112); cf. Ridgley, *Body of Divinity* (1855), I, p. 4.

414. Leigh, *Treatise*, II.xv (p. 116); cf. Mastricht, *Theoretico-practica theol.*, II.xxii.8-9.

415. Venema, *Inst. theol.*, VII (p. 193); cf. Mastricht, *Theoretico-practica theol.*, II.xxii.8-9, 17-18.

we must earnestly desire that God's glory may be communicated to us, that he would send forth his Spirit of glory to rest upon us, by which means we shall commend ourselves to God, Christ, the Angels and Saints, and to our consciences.[416]

Negatively, God's glory also manifests the vileness and the baseness of the sinful world, which opposes his glory and endeavors, vainly, to obscure it: the wicked only further manifest the glory of God by the contrast. There is danger in profaning or denying the glory and majesty of God! The glory of God will be manifest in the wicked, for "God will gain the glory of them in despite of their hearts by magnifying his justice."[417] Positively, the revelation of God's glory and majesty ought to inculcate humility.[418] All people need, further, daily "to contemplate the glory of God with admiration," that is, to direct their souls toward God in and through the admiration of his external glories as manifest in all God's works. We are led to glorify God by the confession of our sins, "by loving and delighting in him above all things," "by believing and trusting in him," and "by a fervent zeal in his honour," by cultivating out abilities to his glory, "by walking humbly, thankfully, and cheerfully before God."[419] This daily glorification of God — to which we testify in the concluding words of the Lord's prayer — offers profound confirmation of our faith, given the identification of God's glory as the ultimate end or final cause of all things.[420] Above all, our conduct ought — to paraphrase Paul — to recognize that "in the mystery of the Gospel, we behold as in a glass the glory of God." Even so, we ought to long for the final vision of God's glory and "wish earnestly to be in Heaven."[421] We ought to recognize our "highest happiness" as a devotion to the glory of God, just as "our highest rejoicing is to rejoice in the hope of the glory of God."[422] God's glory becomes a great comfort, therefore, "against reproaches and contempt in the world," against death itself, and even against the fear of judgment in the end of time.[423]

6.3 The Divine Affections and Virtues

A. General Considerations: The Problem of Affections and Passions in God

1. The concept of affections and passions: issues and problems. As a preliminary point in addressing the Reformed orthodox doctrine of the divine affections, we return to one of the divisions of Polanus, cited earlier at the beginning of the discussion of the divine attributes.

---

416. Leigh, *Treatise*, II.xv (p. 116).
417. Leigh, *Treatise*, II.xv (p. 116).
418. Mastricht, *Theoretico-practica theol.*, II.xxii.14-15.
419. Ridgley, *Body of Divinity* (1855), I, p. 5.
420. Ursinus, *Commentary*, p. 658.
421. Leigh, *Treatise*, II.xv (p. 116).
422. Witsius, *Dissertations on the Lord's Prayer*, VIII (p. 196), citing Rom. 5:2.
423. Leigh, *Treatise*, II.xv (p. 117).

The divine attributes are, in the first place, either affirmative or negative; in the second, either proper or figurative.[424]

The divine affections, given that they include such opposites as love and hate, mercy and anger, offer some reflection of the first part of Polanus' division, even though the affirmative attributes are usually taken as members of the *via eminentiae* and the negative, of the *via negativa*. The second part of the division, however, that between "proper" and "figurative," is the point of distinction between the affections and all of the attributes discussed previously. For the affections of the divine will or, as they are sometimes called, divine virtues, are attributed to God, not properly, but figuratively — and the question of the *ad intra* distinction of attributes revealed *ad extra* does not apply here, at least not in the same way that it applies in the case of the other, namely, the "proper" or essential attributes.[425] As Ames indicates, "The affections attributed to God in scripture, such as love, hatred, and the like, either designate acts of will or apply to God only figuratively,"[426] with the *ad extra* designation referring to the transient manifestation or the "act" of the essentially changeless divine will or disposition of will in the finite order. The affections are, therefore, either inward and inalterable dispositions of the divine will or figurative attributions based on *ad extra* manifestations. Furthermore, what makes the attribution of an affection to God figurative or metaphorical is its apparent variation, temporality, or alterability.

Significantly, this figurative or metaphorical understanding of some of the divine affections as inward, permanent dispositions and others as *ad extra* manifestations of permanent dispositions in no way lessened the Reformed interest in the topic — nor did it in any way undermine the discussion of the divine affections in the works of popular piety written during the era of orthodoxy. It is even possible to argue the opposite, that the Reformed orthodox reading of the biblical language of divine affections as not indicating alterations of the divine essence but, nonetheless, as descriptive of genuine patterns of relationship between God and his creation, enhanced the interest of theologians, pastors, and authors of treatises of popular piety in the divine affections: in other words, these authors emphasize the constancy of divine love and mercy toward the righteous and the inevitability of divine hatred of sin and anger against the wicked.[427]

---

424. Polanus, *Syntagma theol.*, Synopsis libri II.

425. Venema, *Inst. theol.*, VIII (p. 180).

426. Ames, *Marrow*, I.iv.62.

427. This impression is perhaps most clearly given in writings of Puritans such as John Preston, *Life Eternall, or, A Treatise of the Knowledge of the Divine Essence and Attributes* (London, 1631); William Bates, *The Harmony of the Divine Attributes in the contrivance and accomplishment of man's redemption by the Lord Jesus Christ, or, Discourses: wherein is shewed how the wisdom, mercy, justice, holiness, power, and truth of God are glorified in that great and blessed work* (London: J. Darby, 1674); Richard Baxter, *The Divine Life in Three Treatises: first, The Knowledge of God, and the Impression it Must make upon the Heart ... second, The Description, Reasons, and Reward of the Believer's Walking with God ... third, The Christian's Converse with God* (London, 1664); or in the discussion of divine attributes in works by exponents of the *Nadere Reformatie* such as Brakel: see his *Redelijke Godsdienst*, I.iii.31-48.

The Reformed orthodox doctrine of the divine affections and virtues, although far more elaborate and characterized by a fuller and clearer recourse to scholastic distinctions, also stands in substantial continuity with the views of the Reformers. In particular, apart from differing nuances found in various thinkers throughout the period, the exegetical basis of the doctrine remained much the same: the orthodox systems refer to the same texts that the Reformers had identified as the crucial *loci* and, we might add, had themselves received from the medieval and patristic exegetes as the primary points of reference. Nor, indeed, has the basic doctrinal assumption shifted: like the Reformers, the orthodox assume that God has *affectiones* that characterize his relationship to the world and that some analogy can be drawn between these "divine affections" and the affections that belong to human willing — with the major qualification that, unlike human affections, the divine affections do not indicate essential change in God and that they are permanent rather than transient dispositions. Because of the difficulties inherent in the term "affection," some of the Reformed prefer to speak of the divine "virtues."[428]

The question of the "affections" (*affectiones* or *adfectiones*) and "passions" (*passiones*) of the divine will arises rather naturally as a result of the definition and discussion of the *voluntas Dei*, granting the context of traditional, Christian Aristotelianism and scholastic faculty psychology within which Protestant discussions of mind and will took place, both in the time of the Reformation and afterward.[429] The terminology is itself interesting: the language of affections and passions is typically a language indicating the changeableness of a living being, specifically of the soul, in its sentiments or dispositions. Strictly, an affection or passion is an acquired quality.[430] An affection is usually favorable or positive, whereas a passion is usually negative. Thus, an affection is a disposition of nature or an inclination of will *toward* an object and, as such, it can indicate either a transient disposition (in contrast to a *habitus*) that is caused by an external object or a permanent disposition or virtue.[431] It is the latter sense of the term, as a permanent disposition or virtue, that the orthodox accept. A passion, most strictly, is a form of suffering and would not have the connotation of a permanent disposition and certainly not of a disposition positively directed toward an object. Passions, moreover, indicate a declension from an original or natural condition that is at variance with the fundamental inclination of the individual — and, therefore, a loss of power or self-control.[432] A virtue is, quite simply, a moral perfection — in the case of God, the perfection of his understanding and/or will.[433]

---

428. Thus, Leigh, *Treatise*, II.x (pp. 78-79); Mastricht, *Theoretico-practica theologia*, II.xv.18-19.

429. See Muller, *Unaccommodated Calvin*, pp. 159-173; and idem, *God, Creation, and Providence*, pp. 143-149, 167-169, 191-207.

430. François Brémondy, "Affection," in *Encyclopédie philosophique universelle*, II/1, p. 49.

431. Cf. Heidanus, *Corpus theol.*, II (p. 172); Venema, *Inst. theol.*, viii (p. 180).

432. Venema, *Inst. theol.*, viii (p. 181).

433. Ames, *Marrow*, I.iv.63; note that this understanding of affections and passions reflects the standard categories of predication, in which action and passion denote respectively, the act of a subject and the subject being acted upon: thus, the point of the theological argument is that God act

The Reformed orthodox understanding of God, in accord with the greater part of the Christian tradition, assumes the divine immutability, and, typically, denies change and, certainly, acquired qualities to God. God does not change. Nonetheless, God is not unrelated to the world — and those relations have a certain analogy to human affections and virtues. The basic definitions noted above also offer explanation of why the tradition has settled on the terms "affection" and "virtue" for this particular group of divine attributes of relation and volitional exercise. Owen makes the point, in his refutation of Biddle, that affections are attributed "metaphorically" to God "in reference to his outward works and dispensations, correspondent and answering to the actings of men in whom such affections are." Such an attribution of affections on grounds of the divine works *ad extra* "is eminently consistent with his infinite perfections and blessedness."[434] Here again, the Reformed come into conflict with the Socinians, who, after abandoning the essential infinity and simplicity of God, went on to argue changing affections and passions in the Godhead. From the Socinian perspective, the divine affections and passions are analogous to human affections and passions — and are attributed to God in the proper sense of the terms, as inclinations of will grounded in external objects, albeit better regulated in the Godhead than they are in human beings. The Socinians, moreover, attributed passions to God in the sense of "vehement commotions" to the "will of God, whereby he is directed outward toward the object of his desires."[435]

This view of the divine affections or virtues corresponds directly with the orthodox approach to the divine knowledge of things: God knows things because of himself or in his essence — not because of or by means of the things. Since a passion has its foundation or origin *ad extra* and its terminus *ad intra*, it cannot be predicated of God and, in fact, fails to correspond in its dynamic with the way that God knows. An affection or virtue, by way of contrast, has its foundation or source *ad intra* and terminates *ad extra*, corresponding with the pattern of operation of the divine communicable attributes and, in particular, with the manner of the divine knowing. This understanding of affections and passions corresponds, moreover, with the etymology of the terms: an *af-* or *ad-fectio* from *adficio*, to exert an influence on something — in other words, an influence directed toward, not a result from, something; whereas *passio*, from *patior*, is a suffering or enduring of something — it can refer to an occurrence or a phenomenon and even to a disease.

The attribution of affections or passions to God encounters, still, at least four fundamental problems. First, "affections, considered in themselves, have always *an incomplete, imperfect act of the will* or volition joined to them."[436] This incompleteness or imperfection is seen once it is recognized that the affections of the will are situated between a particular purpose or volition and its execution: in the first instance, the

---

but is not acted upon.

434. Owen, *Vindiciae evangelicae*, in *Works*, 12, p. 108.

435. Crell, *De Deo*, xxix, cited in Owen, *Vindiciae evangelicae*, in *Works*, 12, p. 109; cf. Venema, *Inst. theol.*, viii (p. 180).

436. Owen, *Vindiciae evangelicae*, in *Works*, 12, p. 109.

will has an unfulfilled purpose — in the second instance, the purpose of the will is effected by means of an acquired attraction to or repulsion from a particular external object (namely, the affection or passion). Thus, affections and passions indicate a lack or deficiency in the being who has them: a being who has affections and passions is, therefore, incomplete and neither all-sufficient or perfectly blessed as God is known to be.

The problem underlying the predication of affections understood in this way to God is seen perhaps more clearly in the second point: such description of the divine purpose and its execution indicates dependence on external objects for the completion of the divine willing — indeed, implies "affections" that "owe their rise and continuance to something without him in whom they are." But it is "a most eminent contradiction" to speak of God in this way.[437] Third, "affections are necessarily accompanied with change and mutability"[438] — inasmuch as the will and purpose of the being in question is moved by the object of its affections and, in effect, altered by the attraction or repulsion or, indeed, by the very sequence indicated in affective selection of an object. And fourth, many of the affections, if ascribed to God without qualification as metaphors or anthropopathisms, "denote impotence" in God — by indicating a desire for impossibilities or even disappointments.[439]

2. Exegetical resolutions: the identification of biblical anthropopathisms. Reformed commentators of the era of the Reformation consistently addressed the issue of divine affections and the implication of various biblical texts that God might have changing or conflicting emotions — and consistently offered the same conclusion. At the end of the chapter dealing with the Holy Spirit, Vermigli's editor has placed some material from Genesis and Judges on the attribution of repentance and anger to God:

> it must be considered, that the scripture speaketh of God after the manner of men, for the affect of remembrance declareth the goodness of God: for they which be mindful of their friends in danger, do (for the most part) relieve them. Howbeit, to remember, accordeth not properly with God, seeing it noteth a certain forgetfulness that went before; which to ascribe unto God, were an unjust thing. But of knowing we see there be three kinds, the which are distinguished one from another, according to the difference of time. For if a thing present be found out ... this knowledge is the root of all the other and more sure than the rest. Further, if it respect unto things that be past, it is called memory. If unto things to come, it is foresight. ... Of those kinds of knowledge, none is truly attributed unto God, but the first, seeing all things are present with him: and even as his nature, so his actions are by no means comprehended within the course of time. But yet it is said in the Scriptures, that either he remembered, or that he foresaw; because oftentimes those effects are attributed unto him which they are wont to do that foresee or remember.[440]

---

437. Owen, *Vindiciae evangelicae*, in *Works*, 12, p. 110; cf. Venema, *Inst. theol.*, VIII (p. 181).

438. Owen, *Vindiciae evangelicae*, in *Works*, 12, p. 110.

439. Owen, *Vindiciae evangelicae*, in *Works*, 12, p. 110.

440. Vermigli, *Commonplaces*, I.xii.21.

Similarly,

> when it is said, that God waxed angry, it is not so to be understood as though God
> were troubled with affects; for that belongeth unto men: but according to the common
> and received exposition of these places, we understand it, that God behaved himself
> like unto men that be angry.[441]

Citing Ambrose, Vermigli adds,

> neither is he angry, as though he were mutable. But these things are therefore believed,
> to the intent that the bitterness of our sins may be expressed, which hath deserved
> the wrath of God.[442]

Even so, when God is said to "repent" this signifies no change — no imperfection
or inconsistency — in God, but instead a change in us. Vermigli cites Jeremiah 18:6-10
and concludes,

> these words show, that God is not variable in these kind of promises and threatenings;
> for he speaketh not absolutely and simply, but upon condition. But the fulfilling, or
> making void of the conditions, is looked for in us: wherefore the change must not be
> attributed unto him, but unto us.[443]

The point might just as easily have been cited from Calvin: "the repentance which
is ... ascribed to God," he writes, "does not properly belong to him, but has reference
to our understanding ... for since we cannot comprehend him as he is, it is necessary
that, for our sake, he should, in a certain sense, transform himself." As for the
underlying point that this language is an anthropopathism and "that repentance cannot
take place in God," Calvin adds, "easily appears from this single consideration, that
nothing happens which is by him unexpected or unforeseen."[444] Calvin, moreover,
specifically addressed the problem of the biblical language of divine affections or
passions:

> "Because of these things," says Saint Paul, "the wrath of God comes upon unbelievers"
> (Eph. 5:6). "You have grieved the Holy Spirit," says Isaiah (63:10). "You have
> transgressed against Me," says the Lord in another passage (Isa. 43:27), Again, "The
> Lord has poured out his anger upon him and his wrath has enveloped Israel" (Isa.
> 42:25). I know quite well that God is not subject to human passions. But all these
> passages reveal that He reproves evil and condemns it.[445]

---

441. Vermigli, *Commonplaces*, I.xii.22.

442. Vermigli, *Commonplaces*, I.xii.22.

443. Vermigli, *Commonplaces*, I.xii.23.

444. Cf. Calvin, *Commentary upon the Book of Genesis*, Gen. 6:6, in loc. (CTS *Genesis*, I, pp. 248-
249); cf. idem, *Harmony of the Four Last Books of the Pentateuch*, Numbers 23:18-19, in loc. (CTS
Harmony, IV, pp. 210-212).

445. Calvin, *Against the Fantastic and Furious Sect of the Libertines Who Are Called "Spirituals,"* in
Farley, ed., *Treatises Against the Anabaptists and Against the Libertines*, p. 251.

The Reformed orthodox solution to interpretive problems arising from the biblical texts in which affections, passions, and virtues are attributed to God is virtually identical to that of the Reformers. As Wendelin points out in the thesis that links his doctrine of the will to his discussion of the divine goodness and justice, the divine will is given various names in Scripture, each of which presents a different aspect of the divine willing as a distinct property — the two foremost being, according to Wendelin, goodness (*bonitas*) and righteousness or justice (*justitia*).[446] Of course, this entire approach must be immediately qualified, inasmuch as "affections" or "virtues" do not reside in God in the way that they reside in human beings. The interpretive or hermeneutical question concerns the intention of the references to divine affections and passions in the text of Scripture:

> The words also in the original, in all the places mentioned, express or intimate perturbation of mind, commotion of spirit, corporeal mutation of the parts of the body, and the like distempers of men acting under the power of that passion. The whole difference is about the intendement of the Holy Ghost in these attributions, and whether they are properly spoken of God, asserting this passion to be in him in the proper significancy of the words, or whether these things be not taken *anthropopathos*, and to be understood *theoprepos*, in such a sense as may answer the meaning of the figurative expression, assigning them their truth in the utmost, and yet to be interpreted in a suitableness to divine perfection and blessedness.[447]

The divine affections or virtues are not distinct dispositions or habits that stand as attributes or functions of will, as they do in human beings, but instead are divine perfections that have some analogy to the dispositions or habits of the human will: "for though, properly speaking, there are [no affections] in God, he being a most pure and simple act, free from all commotion and perturbation; yet there being some things said and done by him, which are similar to affections in intelligent beings, they are ascribed to him; as love, pity, hatred, anger &c., from which must be removed everything that is carnal, sensual, or has any degree of imperfection in it."[448] Several writers, most notably Venema, treat these affections not only in relation to the divine will, but also as the affective manifestations of the goodness and holiness of God — with such virtues as love, mercy, long-suffering, patience, compassion, joy, and grace

---

446. Wendelin, *Christianae theologiae libri duo*, I.i.19; cf. the almost identical definition in Turretin, *Inst. theol. elencticae*, III.xix.1. Here we must protest against the tendency of some modern philosophical theologians to argue against what they take to be a traditional notion of divine "impassibility," as if the Christian tradition had simply adopted one of the ancient Stoic approaches to God. Whereas the Christian tradition does clearly state that God does not have or, more precisely, is not subject to *passiones*, few theologians (none of the seventeenth-century scholastics that I have examined) list "impassibility" among the divine attributes. In addition, whereas they strenuously deny *passiones* or negative affections to God, they are nearly unanimous in attributing *affectiones* to God, by way of analogy and in their insistence that God had *virtutes*.

447. Owen, *Vindiciae evangelicae*, in *Works*, 12, p. 111.

448. Gill, *Complete Body of Divinity*, I, p. 112; cf. *Synopsis purioris theologiae*, VI.xxxix; Turretin, *Inst. theol. elencticae*, III.xix.1.

belonging to the goodness of God and hatred, anger, scorn, and jealousy standing under the divine holiness.[449] Wendelin describes the relationship as one of species to genus: "the species or adjuncts of the divine goodness are grace (*gratia*), love (*amor*), mercy (*misericordia*), and patience (*patientia*)."[450] The basis for this understanding is the assumption that affections are not essential attributes or original properties but, rather, are *ad extra* manifestations in which God is known through his effects.

Even so, negative affections, such as untruthfulness and injustice, cannot be properly predicated of God, nor can repentance, fear, sorrow, hope, or desperation.[451] As Venema points out, there is a sense in which (certainly according to the orthodox doctrine of Scripture and its interpretation) Scripture itself "confirms" the conclusion that affections are only improperly or figuratively predicated of God — "when it says in one place that which really does not belong to God which it ascribes to him in another."[452] Thus, Genesis 6:6 states that God repents, while Numbers 23:19 and 1 Samuel 15:29 indicate that God does not repent. The solution to the problem lies both in the clear negative found in Numbers and in 1 Samuel, and in the difference between God and human beings, also noted clearly in both texts. Given that the attribution of repentance to human beings indicates both a detestation of what has been done and an alteration of the path taken by future acts, repentance cannot be applied to God in a literal sense:

> repentance may apply to God, because he sometimes changes his work, and so far does the same thing which men do when they repent. ... this change of work does not imply a change in the mind of God, for by one and the same act of his will he decrees both to do the work, and afterwards to alter it; thus he did at the same time decree to create men, and to destroy them all by a deluge ages after.[453]

Moreover, divine repentance is typically associated in Scripture with divine threats and promises, to which a condition is always attached, as in Jeremiah 18:8, where God states, "if that Nation against whom I have pronounced, turn from their evil ways, I will repent me of the Evil which I thought to bring upon them." The condition is that the nation turn from its evil ways: the divine repentance relates to the human meeting of the condition — "if they Repent, the God Repents," not indicating any change in the divine essence or purpose, but a human meeting of God's condition.[454]

On this point, the dogmaticians offer clear reflection of the exegetical tradition, where Numbers 23:19 — "God is not a man that he should lie, or the son of Adam

---

449. Venema, *Inst. theol.*, VIII (pp. 183-4); Maresius, *Collegium theol.*, II.xlix.

450. Wendelin, *Christianae theologiae libri duo*, I.i.21.

451. *Synopsis purioris theologiae*, VI.xli, citing Num. 23:19; 2 Chron. 19:7; Rom 9:14; Titus 1:2; James 1:13; Rom. 3:5.

452. Venema, *Inst. theol.*, VIII (p. 181).

453. Pictet, *Theol. chr.*, II.vii.11; also note Rijssen, *Summa theol.*, III.xxi, objectiones, 3: under the issue of the divine immutability, Rijssen comments, "*Poenitenti notat mutationem operis facti,*" i.e., not of the *voluntas Dei*; cf. Perkins, *Golden Chaine*, ii (p. 11, col. 2); Klinkenberg, *Bijbel verklaerd*, I, Gen. 6:6, in loc.

454. Edwards, *Theologia reformata*, I, p. 134.

that he should repent: hath he said, and shall he not do? and hath he spoken, and shall he not confirm it?" — had long been a *locus classicus* for the discussion of divine affections. Even Ainsworth, who often simply annotates his translation with philological comments, compares the text with 1 Samuel 15:29 and remarks, "though the scripture speaketh sometime of God, that he repenteth, as in Amos 7:3, 6; Jer. 18:8; yet that is spoken of him according to our capacity, because his work is changed, when he himself continueth unchangeable, for with him there is 'no variableness, neither shadow of turning,' James 1:17."[455] In his annotation on Genesis 6:6, "And it repented Jehovah, that he had made man on earth," Ainsworth similarly indicates,

> The scripture giveth to God, *joy, grief, anger,* &c. not as any passions or contrary affections, for he is most simple and unchangeable, James 1:17, but by a kind of proportion, because he doth of his immutable nature and will, such things as men do with their passions and changes of affections. So *heart, hands, eyes,* and other parts are attributed to him, for effecting such things as men cannot do but by such members. God is said to be grieved for the corruption of his creatures; contrawise, when he restoreth them by his grace, he rejoiceth in them, Isa. 65:19; Psalm 104:31.[456]

3. Doctrinal conclusions: the nature of divine affections and virtues. Drawing on the faculty psychology of the era, the Reformed typically understand the divine affections and virtues as qualities or characteristics of the divine will in its *ad extra* operation. Discussion of the divine *affectiones* and *virtutes* rests upon proper conception of the analogy between divine and human and upon the realization that attribution of such qualities to God rests, not on changes or distinctions in God, but on analogies made between the divine activity in this world and distinctions that can be observed in human beings. Since the human virtues and affections "have their seat ... in the will and affections ... it is not inconvenient *for method's sake* to refer them to the same in God."[457] Thus, the divine affections and virtues are predicated of God analogically, metaphorically, or by *anthropopatheia* and are, therefore, only "improperly" or analogically predicated of God.[458]

Inasmuch, moreover, as the divine affections are understood as descriptive of God's movement or egress toward the finite order, they are not only to be understood as communicable attributes *par excellence*, they are also attributes defined primarily in their relationship to finite objects. It is by these *affectiones* or *virtutes* that God sustains his relations with creatures — they are the preeminent example of the so-called *communicabilia* or relative attributes.[459] In attempting to define the issue still more

---

455. Ainsworth, *Annotations upon Numbers*, Num. 23:19, in loc.

456. Ainsworth, *Annotations upon Genesis*, Gen. 6:6, in loc.; cf. *Dutch Annotations*, Gen. 6:6, in loc., citing Num. 23:19; 1 Sam. 15:11, 29; 2 Sam 24:16; Mal 3:6; James 1:17; and Acts 15:18 in support of the reading.

457. Leigh, *Treatise*, II.x (p. 78), my italics.

458. Mastricht, *Theoretico-practica theologia*, II.xv.18-19; cf. Ames, *Medulla*, I.iv.62; Rijssen, *Summa theol.*, III.xxi, controversia, obj. 3 & resp..

459. Mastricht, *Theoretico-practica theologia*, II.xv.19.

precisely, Owen distinguished between "attributes of Deity which, in order to their exercise, require no determined object antecedent to their egress" and "attributes which can in no wise have an egress or be exercised without an object predetermined, and, as it were, by some circumstances prepared for them."[460] The affections fall, clearly, into the latter category, the virtues into the former: just as in human beings, the term "virtues" is reserved for "excellent and confirmed habits" or dispositions that conduce to the proper use of the faculties, so also in God is the word "virtues" applied to the workings of the divine essence, with specific reference to the disposition and use of the "faculties" of intellect or will. This approach is analogical, given that the divine virtues are not separable from the divine essence as human virtues are separable from humanity. In short, the virtues of God are the divine moral perfections, specifically the goodness and righteousness of the divine willing. These virtues are also the source of all finite or creaturely goodness and righteousness.[461]

In the words of the Leiden *Synopsis*, the divine affections "are nothing other than the ardent (*ardens*) will of God toward us," known in terms of its power and its effects in creatures — known, therefore, by diverse objects, varied effects, and different ways of operating *ad extra*. Such affections are "truly and properly" predicated of God when care is taken to avoid the attribution of any imperfection to the Godhead.[462] This understanding of the divine affections as movements or attractions in some sense defined by their external object is a significant element of the Reformed orthodox system, both in terms of the implications of the concept for the orthodox theology as a whole and in view of the frequently heard claim that the older theology was so caught up in an Aristotelian conceptuality of God as Unmoved Mover that it paid scant attention to the biblical language of God in relation to his world. Quite to the contrary, the orthodox doctrine of the divine essence presses out into the rest of the theological system with the assumption of attributes requiring external objects and capable of being understood only insofar as they are relations *ad extra*. Thus, in summary,

> goodness (*bonitas*) is that act of the divine will, by which he is disposed to self-communication. Love (*amor*), that by which God is moved toward created things and bestows blessings on them. Grace (*gratia*), that by which God is moved to communicate himself to creatures of his own accord, not on grounds of merit or debt. Mercy (*misericordia*) is the disposition of the divine will to help the wretched, not because of any external cause, but solely of the divine goodness. Hatred (*odium*) in God indicates either the disapproval of sin, or the will to punish sinners that follows sin, or the denial of those salutary benefits that flow from the divine will. Longing (*desiderium*) in God indicates that the obedience of human beings is exceedingly pleasing to him, and not without future reward. Hope and expectation (*spes & expectatio*) in God signify that something is owed. God is said to rejoice (*gaudere*) when something is pleasing to him. Dread (*metus*) is sometimes attributed to him, in order to indicate that he desires to

---

460. Owen, *Dissertation on the Divine Justice*, in *Works*, X, p. 503.
461. Leigh, *Treatise*, II.x (pp. 78-79).
462. *Synopsis purioris theol.*, VI.xxxix.

prevent evil. Sorrow *(tristia)* in God indicates something that is exceedingly displeasing to God and contrary to his virtues. Jealousy *(zelotypia)* is the firm will of God that his glory not be given to another and to punish those who do so. Repentance *(poenitentia)* indicates a change in a work performed. Anger *(ira)* the just and free will of God to punish sinners.[463]

B. The Love of God

1. The love of God in Reformed theology: issues and placements of the discussion. The love of God is an attribute stressed in the theology of the Reformed orthodox perhaps more than in the theology of the Reformers. It is, moreover, an attribute that received emphasis in several places throughout the *locus de Deo*. The primary location is certainly among the affections of the divine will, with the understanding that the *amor* or *amicitia* (strictly, the friendship) of God is known through the gracious relationship of God to his world, whether in creation, in redemption, or in the final glorification. Still, given the underlying assumption of classical theism that God delights in his own goodness and ultimately loves himself for what he is and what he wills, love can also be identified as an essential attribute of God, even when the discussion of the attribute typically places it among the affections. This dual understanding can result in a distinction between the natural love of God for himself and the volitional or affective love of God for his creation.[464]

The love of God is also understood by the Reformed orthodox in three profoundly trinitarian ways. First, it appears in the discussion of the *ad intra* relationship between the Father and the Son, defined primarily as love, and its *ad extra* manifestation that provides a foundation for the love of God for all of the redeemed, often with reference to John 17:22-24.[465] Second, understood as the primary affection of the divine will, the *amor Dei* also serves, in some of the Reformed orthodox, to explain the procession of the Spirit from the Father and the Son, echoing some of the medieval elaborations of the inner trinitarian relations.[466] Third, as a development of the discussion of the love of the Father for the Son, the love of God serves as a fundamental concept in the Reformed doctrine of the *pactum salutis*.[467]

2. The love of God in the thought of the Reformers. The interrelationship of divine affections and their grounding in the essential divine goodness can be seen in Reformed theology as early as Musculus' *Loci communes*. Musculus' *locus* on the divine love, albeit presented discursively, bears elements of scholastic form. He begins with the question, "An Deo competat dilectio" (Whether love is proper to God), noting first, by way of transition from his discussion of the goodness of God, the positive answer

---

463. Rijssen, *Summa*, III.xxi, controversia, obj. 3 & resp.

464. Brakel, *Redelijke Godsdienst*, I.iii.33.

465. Thus, Owen, *ΧΡΙΣΤΟΛΟΓΙΑ*, xii, in *Works*, I, pp. 139-146.

466. Keckermann, *Systema theologiae*, I.iii (p. 28-33); Ames, *Medulla*, I.v.16; and cf. *PRRD*, IV, 3.1 (C.3).

467. See Willem J. Van Asselt, *The Covenant Theology of Johannes Cocceius (1603-1669)*, trans. Raymond A. Blacketer (Leiden: E. J. Brill, 2001), pp. 256-257, 315-321.

to his question: it is of the very "nature of goodness" that it "cannot be without love" and that, therefore, the discussion of the divine love (*philanthropia* or *dilectio Dei*) follows as a direct "consequence" on the discussion of the divine goodness.[468]

What follows amounts to a discursively presented scholastic *obiectio*: despite this obvious and seemingly necessary relationship between goodness and love, Musculus queries whether the "affection of love" is suitably attributed to God. Inasmuch as the goodness of God is not separable from the other divine attributes and is conjoined particularly with the majesty of God, it would appear that God ought to be loved and served, not that God ought to love or serve his creatures. So, too, the divine majesty implies that God is independent and utterly free, whereas love implies that the one who loves is "drawn into the service" of the one loved.[469] By way of answer, Musculus notes first that the majesty of God, as an excellence of the divine nature, cannot be understood to "hinder" God in any way from having or doing anything that is agreeable to God; second, that love, as already indicated, stands in "natural and inseparable conjunction with goodness," and that, similarly, as mirrored in the example of a good ruler, love and majesty conjoin. And, Musculus adds, inasmuch as hatred and majesty can be joined in a tyrant, we ought to be careful in the use of the simile to attribute to God only what comports with his goodness! Third, there is the general rule that inasmuch as not all things attributed to human beings can be attributed to God, so also various characteristics of human love, such as its weakness and credibility, ought not to carry over into discussions of divine love. The objections raised to predicating love of God are, therefore, set aside as not obliging the rules of predication: "a discrete and godly person ought wisely to distinguish between those things that are agreeable to the nature of God and those things that are not."[470]

Just as the goodness of God is one and simple, but nonetheless distinguished according to its several objects, so also is the divine love capable of being distinguished. The one God can be understood as Trinity, as creator, and as redeemer: accordingly, the love of God can be understood as the love of the father for the Son, the general love of God for all creatures, his love of human beings, his special love for his elect, and his love of the good or goodness itself.[471] Echoing Calvin's distaste for the more speculative side of Augustine's trinitarianism, Musculus cautions that the "scholastics" were much more interested in searching into the hidden depths of the Trinity and discussing the love of God *ad intra* than in interpreting what Scripture had to say concerning God's love. Their inquiries included such questions as "whether the Father and the Son love each other in the holy Spirit," "whether that love is essential or intellectual," and whether it is "given and recompensed." Musculus notes that Lombard raises the question of the nature of the love between the Father and the Son and then proceeds to declare that he cannot answer it: let this be an incentive to pass over

---

468. Musculus, *Loci communes*, XLVIII (*Commonplaces*, p. 957, col. 1).
469. Musculus, *Loci communes*, XLVIII (*Commonplaces*, p. 957, col. 2).
470. Musculus, *Loci communes*, XLVIII (*Commonplaces*, pp. 958-959).
471. Musculus, *Loci communes*, XLVIII (*Commonplaces*, p. 959, cols. 1-2).

scholastic inquiry and be guided by the "simplicity of the Scriptures."[472] (It is worth noting that, even as he decries "scholastic" excesses. Musculus engages in an exercise that lay at the heart of the scholastic effort — the examination of the text of Scripture with a view to the distinction of meanings in cases of seemingly equivocal usages of words.)

The Gospel of John serves as the most adequate guide to the question of the love of the Trinity: the Scriptures teach, quite simply, that the Father loves the Son and is loved by the Son, and that because of this love the Son was obedient to the Father "unto the death of the cross." Because the Father loves the Son, he has given him all things — and the Son loves those who are his just as the Father has loved him.[473] Calvin, quite similarly, decries excessive patristic speculation into the nature of the love of the Father for the Son and emphasizes the redemptive implication of the Johannine language: "not only does God extend to us the love which is due to the only-begotten Son, but he refers it to us as the final cause."[474]

The second kind of divine love that Musculus identifies is the love of the creator for all his creatures, resting on his creation of all things as good in the beginning. It would be impossible, Musculus notes, given the nature of God, for God to "make evil things and love them after they were made" or to "make good things and not love them when they were made." Nor could it be that God loved his creation in the beginning and subsequently ceased to love it — for God's love is immutable. Nor, again, is God's love hindered by the subjection of the created order to corruption after the fall, for the creation not only remains God's work despite this corruption, but also it was God's own "most wise and unsearchable purpose" that has subjected the entire creation to this bondage and vanity, as the apostle Paul teaches in Romans 8, or indeed as is written in the Wisdom of Solomon, "thou lovest all things that are, and hatest none of the things which thou hast made."[475]

Third, above his love for all creation, God loves humanity in general. This love, Musculus notes, ought to be a source of wonder on our part: we would not be surprised if Scripture were to tell us that God loves his angels, inasmuch as they have a heavenly nature and purity and have been chosen as god's "special ministers." Yet Scripture speaks instead of the surpassing love of God for human beings, made in the image of God and accorded a special dignity "above all other creatures." God has not, moreover, forsaken us after the Fall but continues to care for us with his special providence. Beyond this, God so loves human beings that in the incarnation "God was made man, to the end that man should be advanced into the fellowship of God's nature." There could be no greater indication of the love of God for humanity than this personal union of human nature with the divine nature. So, too, the love of God for all humanity is seen in the death of his Son for our redemption. And finally, the general love of

472. Musculus, *Loci communes*, XLVIII (*Commonplaces*, pp. 959-960).

473. Musculus, *Loci communes*, XLVIII (*Commonplaces*, p. 960, col. 1), citing John 5:20; 10:17; 14:21, and 17:24.

474. Calvin, *Commentary on John*, 5:20; 10:17 (*CTS John I*, pp. 199-200, 409).

475. Musculus, *Loci communes*, XLVIII (*Commonplaces*, pp. 960-961), citing Wisdom, 11:25.

God for humanity is manifest in the universal calling of the gospel.[476] This divine love for the world and specifically for humanity, Calvin writes, is the "first cause ... and source of our salvation."[477]

The fourth *species* of divine love, according to Musculus, is the "special" love of God for those human beings chosen "to the adoption of children, before the foundation of the world," a love not extended to the entire human race, as indicated by the text in Romans, "Jacob have I loved, Esau have I hated." Reflecting definitions from the older scholastic tradition, Musculus indicates that this love "comprehends" all of the other elements of the salvation of the elect, namely, "predestination, calling, the gift of faith and of the Spirit, justification, regeneration, and the renewal of mind and life": all of these things are referred to the goodness and love of God by the apostle in Titus 3:4-8.[478] Calvin also identifies the special, saving love of God as a sign of God's utter mercy, apart from all human works, to save some by grace: "this love was founded on *the purpose of his will* (Eph. 1:5)."[479]

Fifth, there is in God a love of the good, simply because it is good. This love is directed particularly toward all that is "just, honest, gentle, meek, mild, and merciful" and evidences a love of true goodness in human conduct.[480] Musculus enquires how this can be so if we are saved according to God's mercy and not according to our works. The solution to the problem is that "we must consider the love of God toward us in two respects": first, God loves us merely on account of his own goodness. Our salvation has "no cause in us" but arises only out of the goodness of God. By this love we are made good despite our sinful condition. Second, God also loves "good, faithful, and obedient persons: this second form of divine love toward believers, argues Musculus, is in no way hindered or prevented by the former, prior, love, "for he who of his infinite goodness loves us without cause" can love us still more "when we are godly." This divine love of the good in us, Musculus concludes, ought to inspire believers to be "studious in goodness, godliness, and righteousness" and to be thankful toward God for his kindness.[481]

3. *Amor* and *amicitia Dei* in the theology of the Reformed orthodox: basic definition and the *amor naturalis*. The Reformed orthodox describe God's love as an act of the divine will or a movement toward the good — both toward the good in itself and toward the good as it is embodied in the creature. Indeed, the predications of will, love, and goodness conjoin in the basic definition, granting that the divine will is God's propensity for the good that is ultimately the divine essence itself as the

---

476. Musculus, *Loci communes*, XLVIII (*Commonplaces*, pp. 961-963).

477. Calvin, *Commentary on John*, 3:16 (*CTS John*, I, p. 122).

478. Musculus, *Loci communes*, XLVIII (*Commonplaces*, p. 963, cols. 1-2).

479. Calvin, *Commentary on John*, 3:16 (*CTS John*, I, p. 123).

480. Musculus, *Loci communes*, XLVIII (*Commonplaces*, p. 964, col. 1), citing 2 Cor. 9:7.

481. Musculus, *Loci communes*, XLVIII (*Commonplaces*, pp. 964-965). Musculus develops the practical implications of his teaching at length (pp. 965-977).

source of all good — and *amor*, strictly defined, is a propensity for the good,[482] or a desire or "appetite for union."[483] The *amor Dei* can, moreover, be differentiated into *amor naturalis* or *amor complacentiae* and *amor voluntarius*. Much like the orthodox discussions of other attributes, this form of argument, with its bifurcation between natural and voluntary love, observes the pattern of movement from the *ad intra* attribute or the attribute considered in itself apart from any relationship of God (the *amor naturalis*), to the world to the attribute in its relation to the created order or the operation of the attribute *ad extra* (the *amor voluntarius*).

The divine *amor naturalis* or *amor complacentiae* is the attribute considered in itself, apart form the existence of creatures, in terms of its primary object. The "primary object of God's love," like the primary object of God's will, "is himself, for he taketh great pleasure in himself, and is the Author of greatest felicity toward himself"[484] — it is natural, inasmuch as it belongs to God by nature; it is a love of *complacentia* or exceeding pleasure, delight, or contentment inasmuch as it has as its object the ultimate good fully actualized. This inward divine love has, moreover, two aspects, given the two ways in which God in himself can be the object of love. Thus, the "natural love of God" is both the love by which "God necessarily loves himself"or, more precisely, loves the ultimate goodness of his own Being as the foremost and highest object of love — and also "the love by which the Persons of the Holy Trinity love one another."[485] The former aspect, the concept of the necessary love of divine Being for itself, belongs to the doctrine of the essence and attributes, whereas the latter aspect of the *amor naturalis* belongs largely to the doctrine of the Trinity, and to the occasional reflection of the traditional Augustinian and scholastic view of the Spirit as the "bond of love" between the Father and the Son.[486]

The orthodox here follow a traditional pattern of philosophical theology in their understanding of "God is love" in an ontological sense as the foundation of the idea of a *summum bonum*. The "love of God," writes Brakel, "is the love-possessing God Himself [*de liefhebbende God zelf*]," for which reason John states that "God is love" (1 John 4:8).[487] The inability of love to remain static and the necessity of love to give of itself makes understandable God's love as a principle of the Trinity and as the foundation of his relationship with creatures. The distinctions employed are similar to those noted in Scotus, but are used quite differently, not reflecting the Scotistic reference of the *amor complacentiae* to the divine knowledge of all possibility.

---

482. Mastricht, *Theoretico-practica theol.*, II.xvii.3, 4, 6; cf. Brakel, *Redelijke Godsdienst*, I.iii.33. Note the similar definitions in Arminius, *Disputationes privatae*, XX.iii-iv.

483. Heidanus, *Corpus theol.*, II (p. 172).

484. Leigh, *Treatise*, II.viii (p. 71), citing Matt. 3:17; 17:5; John 3:33, 35; 5:20; 10:17; 15:19; 17:24; cf. Wendelin, *Christianae theologiae libri duo*, I.i.23.

485. Wendelin, *Christianae theologiae libri duo*, I.i.23 (2); similarly, Brakel, *Redelijke Godsdienst*, I.iii.33; Leigh, *Treatise*, II.viii (p. 71).

486. Cf. Mastricht, *Theoretico-practica theol.*, II.xvii.8 with idem, II.xxiv.21.

487. Brakel, *Redelijke Godsdienst*, I.iii.33.

4. Amor voluntarius: its nature and objects. The "voluntary love of God" is the love according to which God freely loves his creatures as the secondary object of the divine love.[488] Following the fundamental rule of trinitarian orthodoxy that all of the work of God *ad extra* is the undivided work of the divine persons, orthodox discussion of the *amor voluntarius* belongs properly to the doctrine of the essence and attributes, which the persons have in common. There is also a certain logic of interrelation of attributes in the orthodox presentation of the voluntary love of God for the world — God's propensity to love the finite order rests on the grounding of the finite order in the goodness of God: "From the *goodness* springs the *love* of God, by which God is inclined towards the creature, and delights to do it good, and as it were, to unite himself with it."[489] The love of God, therefore, belongs to the category of affection, arising inwardly and extending outward, and is not to be understood as a passion, arising because of some outward good that it apprehends and desires.[490]

The Reformed orthodox also make a set of distinctions within the category of *amor voluntarius*, dividing it either into two main parts, the *amor benevolentiae* (love of benevolence) and *amor complacentiae vel amicitiae* (love of delight or friendship) and then dividing the *amor benevolentiae* into subcategories of general and special — or, in a more soteriologically specified approach for the purpose of identifying the love of God toward rational creatures, into three parts: the *amor benevolentiae*; the *amor beneficentiae* (love of beneficence or kindness); and the *amor complacentiae vel amicitiae*. The first of these approaches, the *amor benevolentiae*, is defined as an antecedent love resting on the *benevolentia* or good will of God toward all creation — and must be distinguished, like the providence of God, into the categories of universal (or general) "affective" love and special "effective" love,[491] specifically, the universal love of God for all created good and the special love according to which God unequally loves various creatures, given the inequality of the goodness in them — and, beyond this, the special love that he has for Christ and for rational creatures and, among the rational creatures, for his elect:

> God's love to Christ is the foundation of his love to us, Matt. 3:17; Ephes. 1:6.
> God loves all creatures with a general love, Matt. 5:44, 45, as they are the work of his hands; but he doth delight in some especially, whom he hath chosen in his Son, John 3:16; Ephes. 1:6.[492]

The love of delight, in this usage (as distinct from the usage in which it is synonymous with *amor naturalis*), is the consequent love by which God loves his elect in Christ

---

488. Wendelin, *Christianae theologiae libri duo*, I.i.23 (2); similarly, Brakel, *Redelijke Godsdienst*, I.iii.33

489. Pictet, *Theol. chr.*, II.vii.4; cf. Mastricht, *Theoretico-practica theol.*, II.xvii.8; *Synopsis purioris theologiae*, VI.xl..

490. Beza et al. *Propositions and Principles*, IX.viii.

491. Brakel, *Redelijke Godsdienst*, I.iii.33; Maresius, *Collegium theol.*, II.l.

492. Leigh, *Treatise*, II.viii (p. 71).

or, alternatively, loves his creation in its final form, after the work of redemption and final consummation is accomplished.[493]

Given that the primary object of God's love is God himself as the ultimate good and the goal of all things, the secondary object may be more closely defined as the rational creatures, angels and human beings, in whom God will ultimately most fully reveal his goodness and glory: "For though he approve of the goodness of other things; yet he hath chosen that especially [i.e., the goodness of rational creatures], to prosecute with his chiefest love."[494] This more restrictive identification of the secondary object of divine love follows (according to Leigh) for several reasons:

(1) For the excellency and beauty of the reasonable creature, when it is adorned with due holiness.
(2) Because between this only and God, there can be a mutual reciprocation of love, since it only hath a sense, and acknowledgment of God's goodness.
(3) Because God bestows Eternity on that which he loves; but the other creatures besides the rational shall perish.[495]

When thus applied to rational creatures, the *amor voluntarius* of God is further distinguished into three categories: the "love of benevolence" (*amor benevolentiae*), by which God wills in eternity to elect and to save; the "love of beneficence" (*amor beneficentiae*), by which God wills in time to redeem and to sanctify the elect; and the "love of delight or friendship" (*amor complacentiae vel amicitiae*), according to which God rewards those who have become "just and holy" and delights in the ultimate fruits of redemption.[496] Turretin notes that the first two categories, the love of benevolence and the love of beneficence, "precede any actualization of creatures," whereas the third category, love of delight or friendship, follows upon the actualization of creatures and describes the communion that they have with God. This "communion which we have with God" is rightly called "the love of friendship," given how "intimate" and how "accompanied with ... spiritual boldness" it is — it is characterized by "mutual trust" such that Abraham was called the "friend of God" (Isa. 41:8; James 2:23) and those taught by Christ of his Father are called his friends (John 15:15).[497]

---

493. Cf. Brakel, *Redelijke Godsdienst*, I.iii.33, with Burman, *Synopsis theol.*, I.xxiii.10; Maresius, *Collegium theol.*, II.l.

494. Leigh, *Treatise*, II.viii (p. 71).

495. Leigh, *Treatise*, II.viii (p. 71); cf. Leigh, *Body of Divinity*, II.viii; X.ii (pp. 201, 1159). Note that Leigh here implies a doctrine of the *interitus mindi secundum substantiam*, which is not the typical Reformed position, although it is that of the *Synopsis purioris theol.*, lii.60, as well: Turretin, *Inst. theol. elencticae*, XX.v, notes that this is a point on which difference of opinion is permitted, but identifies the more probable conclusion as a renovation rather than an utter destruction of the world order — so also, e.g., Ames, *Medulla*, I.xli.31, 33; Maccovius, *Loci communes*, lxxxvi (pp. 776-778); Brakel, *Redelijke Godsdienst*, II.lix.25-29.

496. Pictet, *Theol. chr.*, II.vii.4; cf. Turretin, *Inst. theol. elencticae*, III.xx.5; also note Bates, *Harmony of the Divine Attributes*, p. 260, as an example of the distinction used in a work of piety.

497. Owen, *ΧΡΙΣΤΟΛΟΓΙΑ*, in *Works*, I, pp. 155-156.

Nonetheless, neither the distinction of categories nor the last category in itself indicate a change in God: for the *amor complacentiae* follows creaturely actuality, not as an effect follows a cause, but "as a consequent follows its antecedent" — simply put, God delights in what he has made, given the reflection of his own being and goodness in the entire creation.[498] This is surely a Scotist accent, although Turretin and the other Reformed writers who evidence these arguments do not precisely follow Scotus in using these categories as his primary descriptors of the freedom of the divine willing.

5. The effects of the divine love. Passing from their discussion of "the object of God's love," the orthodox treat of "the effect or manner of God's love":

> The effect or manner of God's love is, that God makes the person happy whom he loves. For he doth amply reward that joy and delight which he takes in the holiness and obedience of the Elect, while he pours plentifully upon them all gifts, both of grace and of glory [1 John 4:16; John 3:35; Rom 5:8; Mal. 1:2]. This love of God to the elect is (1) Free, Hos. 15:5. He was moved with nothing but his own goodness [1 John 4:10, 19]. (2) Sure, firm, and unchangeable, Rom. 5:8, 10; 1 John 4:10; John 13:1 and 31:3. Infinite and Eternal, which shall never alter, John 3:16. (3) Effectual, as is declared both by his temporal and eternal blessings, 1 John 3:1. (4) Great and ardent, John 3:16 and 15:13; Rom. 5:6, 7. God bestows pledges of his love and favor upon them whom he has chosen, and sometimes he sheds the sense of his love abroad in their hearts [cf. Rom. 5:5; 8:1, 2].[499]

The effect of God's love is the happiness of the creature — and in the instance of the elect, the bounteous gifts "of grace and glory" resulting from God's joy in their "holiness and obedience." The love of God must also be free, for God is "moved by nothing but his own goodness" — indeed, it is the effect and manifestation of God's eternal goodness.[500] It is also unchangeable and certain even as God himself is infinite and eternal. Furthermore, the love of God, in view of its source, must be "effectual" — even as it is an excellent love of God for his creature so does it produce love in the heart of the creature.[501] Thus the love of God for us ought to produce in us a love of God, a desire to do his commandments, and a constant desire to be conformed to Christ — who is the gift of God's love to us:

> We should admire the love of God, 1 John 3.1. For the sureness, greatness, and continuance of it passeth our knowledge, Ephes. 3.19. He hath given his son for a price, his Spirit for a pledge, and reserves himself for a reward.[502]

---

498. Turretin, *Inst. theol. elencticae*, III.xx.5.
499. Leigh, *Treatise*, II.viii (pp. 71-72).
500. Leigh, *Treatise*, II.viii (p. 71); Heidanus, *Corpus theol.*, II, p. 173.
501. Preston, *Life Eternall*, I, p. 171; II, p. 78.
502. Leigh, *Treatise*, II.vii (p. 72).

Even so, God ought to be loved by us, insofar as he is "the only immediate and proper object of love, Psalm 103:1" as Augustine said, *"Beatus qui amat te, amicum in te, & inimicum propter te."*[503]

> We must love God *Appreciativè*, love him above all things, and in all, Psal. 73:24; Matt. 10:37; *Intensivè* and *Intellectivè*, with all our might and strength. *Affectu* & *effectu*, love him for himself, and all things for the Lord's sake. We should express our love to him by our care in keeping his Commandments, 1 John 2:3; John 14:25 and 15:10; and earnest desire of his presence, Psalm 4:2-4.... Our love should be conformed to God's, in loving the saints, Psalm 16:3; Gal. 6:10, and Christ above all, desiring to be united to him, 1 Cor. 5:44; 1 Pet. 1:8.[504]

To this end, we recognize that God is *maximè amabilis*, that he bestows upon us many blessings (Psalm 116:12), desires that we love him (Deut. 10:4; Mark 12:33), and wills to love us eternally. This point raises the question of the eternity of the divine affections, given that they are all *ad extra* relations of the divine essence or nature. Some of the Reformed argue the eternity of all the affections on the ground of the eternity of God's knowledge of all objects of his willing,[505] whereas others indicate that only love and joy are eternal, given that these affections have the triune God itself as their ultimate object.[506]

C. Divine Grace and Favor

1. The grace of God in the thought of the Reformers. Although the Reformers held firmly to a doctrine of salvation by grace alone, virtually none of them wrote a separate treatise on grace — nor, indeed, is there a *locus* on grace in Musculus, Calvin, or Vermigli. Of the major Reformers of their era, only Melanchthon and Bullinger provided topical discussions of the grace of God. Still, the absence of extended discussions of "grace" as a divine attribute does not mark a radical point of discontinuity with the Reformed orthodox. The definitions and the polemics of the Reformers do understand grace in the ultimate sense as lodged or grounded in God — and not merely as a matter of divine favor exercised *ad extra*. Melanchthon's definition is one of the few that refers grace strictly to the economy of salvation, understanding it as "the free remission of sins" or the free unmerited mercy of God.[507] Bullinger, by way of contrast, looks as much to the nature of God as to the work of salvation, defining grace as "the favor and goodness of the eternal Godhead, wherewith he, according to his incomprehensible goodness, doth gratis, freely, for Christ's sake embrace, call, justify, and save us mortal men."[508] Similarly, Calvin (whose full definitions of grace appear, not in the *Institutes*, but in the commentaries) identifies grace as the unmerited or

---

503. Leigh, *Treatise*, II.viii (p. 72, margin).
504. Leigh, *Treatise*, II.viii (p. 72).
505. Preston, *Life Eternall*, II, p. 78.
506. Leigh, *Treatise*, II.viii (p. 72), citing 1 Cor. 13:20ff.
507. Melanchthon, *Loci communes* (1543), VIII.
508. Bullinger, *Decades*, IV.i (vol. III, p. 7).

undeserved goodness of God[509] and insists on the absurdity of certain scholastic definitions of grace that identify it as "nothing else but a quality infused into the hearts of men: for grace, properly speaking, is in God; and what is in us is the effect of grace."[510] In addition, when Calvin understands the biblical text as referring "grace" restrictively to the saving work of God, he can offer the qualification that "the term grace denotes here not the favor of God, but by metonymy, the gifts that he bestows on men gratuitously" — and since "metonymy" is a figure of speech that names the effect for the cause, Calvin clearly assumes that the basic meaning of grace is the *favor Dei* itself.[511]

2. **The Reformed orthodox doctrine of the *gratia Dei*.** Although by far the larger discussion of divine grace belongs to the soteriology of Reformed orthodoxy, the theologians of the late sixteenth and the seventeenth centuries also consistently place the *gratia Dei* among the divine affections. Divine grace, as indicated both in the doctrine of the divine attributes and in the developing Reformed covenant theology of the seventeenth century, is not merely the outward favor of God toward the elect, evident only in the post-lapsarian dispensation of salvation; rather is it one of the perfections of the divine nature. It is a characteristic of God's relations to the finite order, apart from sin, in the act of divine condescension to relate to finite creatures.[512] Beyond this, it is a characteristic of the divine being itself, at the very foundation of God's relationship with finite, temporal beings. God, in other words, is eternally "capable of manifesting His benevolence to creatures apart form any merit" — "even if there were no creature" in existence.[513] As is the case with the other divine attributes,

---

509. Calvin, *Commentary on Isaiah*, 14:21, in loc. (*CTS Isaiah*, I, p. 453).

510. Calvin, *Commentaries on Romans*, 5:15, in loc. (*CTS Romans*, p. 208).

511. Calvin, *Commentaries on 1 Corinthians*, 1:5, in loc. (*CTS Corinthians*, I, p. 56).

512. There is, both in the orthodox Reformed doctrine of God and in the orthodox Reformed covenant theology of the seventeenth century, a consistent identification of grace as fundamental to all of God's relationships with the world and especially with human beings, to the point of the consistent assertion that the covenant of nature or works is itself gracious: see Won Taek Lim, *The Covenant Theology of Francis Roberts* (Ph. D. dissertation, Calvin Theological Seminary, 1999), pp. 40-46; cf. Ernest F. Kevan, *The Grace of Law: A Study of Puritan Theology* (London: Carey Kingsgate Press, 1963), pp. 119-126 et passim. There is no substance to the repeated assertion of J. B. Torrance that the Reformed notion of the covenant of works undermines the notion of the priority of grace or indeed the graciousness even of the divine law: see his "Strengths and Weaknesses of the Westminster Theology," in Alasdair Heron, ed., *The Westminster Confession in the Church Today: Papers Prepared for the Church of Scotland Panel on Doctrine* (Edinburgh: St. Andrews Press, 1982), pp. 40-53; idem, "Covenant or Contract? A Study of the Theological Background or Worship in Seventeenth-Century Scotland," in *Scottish Journal of Theology*, 23 (1970), pp. 51-76; idem, "Calvin and Puritanism in England and Scotland — Some Basic Concepts in the Development of 'Federal Theology,'" in *Calvinus Reformator* (Potchefstroom: Potchefstroom University for Christian Higher Education, 1982), pp. 264-277.

513. Brakel, *Redelijke Godsdienst*, I.iii.33.

God's *Graciousness* is an essential property, whereby he is in and of himself most gracious and amiable, Psalm 145:8. God is only gracious in and of himself, and whatsoever is amiable and gracious, is so from him.[514]

Since grace is in God "affectively" as an affection of the will and its operates effectively in the creatures who are the objects of God's favor, it refers both to the inward *actus* or capacity in God for gracious or favorable relation to the creature and to the outward relationship of God to creatures as characterized by the undeserved divine benevolence.[515] Thus, *gratia Dei* is that perfection or attribute according to which God, out of a totally gracious and unmerited love, is conceived as willing to communicate himself to his creatures.[516] Considered as affective, as *ratione actus interni in Deo*, grace is a propensity of the divine will — while considered as effective it is the gifts of the Spirit graciously given to us by God, either the ordinary gifts of faith, hope, and love or the extraordinary gifts bestowed upon the church for its edification.[517] The former, more fully described, is God's grace

by which he is induced to communicate himself to the creature, freely and of his own accord; not from desert or debt, or any other cause outside of himself; and not to add anything to himself, but for the benefit of the object of this grace. For *grace* is nothing else but unmerited favor; it is always opposed to merit.[518]

The relationship between grace and love is, moreover, made explicit by the orthodox: "Grace is that by which God is capable of being loved in himself and by which he favors and blesses his creatures."[519] This distinction between the inward grace by which God favors the creature and the outward blessing of grace yields, also, a distinction between "decretive" and "executive" grace, modeled on the often-used distinction between the eternal decree and its execution in time, and indicating "the eternal purpose of God concerning our election before the foundation of the world" and exercise or execution in the calling, justification, and sanctification of the elect.[520]

This twofold distinction can also yield a threefold meaning of grace: it can indicate, with reference to the decree or the "affective" inward grace of God, "God's favor, by which he chose us from eternity unto life," and, with reference to the outward executive or effective grace, either the temporal favor granted when God receives us in Christ, or the further effects of grace, namely, the blessings bestowed upon believers in Christ.[521] This latter division of the effective grace of God follows out the breadth of the biblical usage — where the word "grace" has several connotations. These, the Reformed indicate, need to be carefully defined in order to avoid misrepresentation.

514. Leigh, *Treatise*, II.xi (p. 84); cf. Cocceius, *Summa theol.*, III.x.69.

515. Turretin, *Inst. theol. elencticae*, III.xx.7.

516. Rijssen, *Summa Theol.*, III.xliii.

517. Rijssen, *Summa theol.*, III.xliii.

518. Pictet, *Theol. chr.*, II.vii.5.

519. Wendelin, *Christianae theologiae libri duo*, I.i.22.

520. Turretin, *Inst. theol. elencticae*, III.xx.9.

521. Maresius, *Collegium theol.*, II.l; cf. Pictet, *Theol. chr.*, II.vii.5.

The effective grace of God can be divided into two categories — the gift itself and the receipt of the gift. Brakel, without comment, identifies these categories with the older scholastic language of *gratia gratis dans*, grace giving graciously, and *gratia gratis data*, grace graciously given.[522] Fully acknowledging the source of the distinction, Rijssen comments that the "scholastics" describe effective grace as *gratia gratis faciens* and *gratia gratis data*. He indicates specifically that Reformed orthodoxy can appropriate the older vocabulary, redefining it to conform to the principle of *sola fidei*: this grace given by God cannot make us agreeable to God except insofar as the grace and righteousness (*justitia*) of Christ imputed to us does so; or, better said, the *gratia gratum faciens*, "grace working graciously," or, as it is sometimes called, *gratia gratum dans*, is the gracious favor of God that turns toward us, not on grounds of our merit, but because of the gracious work accomplished for us in Christ.[523] The *gratia gratis data*, or "grace graciously given," indicates all of the means necessary to salvation and all of the benefits of Christ that are given to us in this life.[524] Grace can also be distinguished into sufficient and efficient grace, Wendelin notes, but the distinction is disputed by Maccovius.[525]

There is also good ground for concluding that the modern conception of "common grace" finds its root more in the period of Reformed orthodoxy that in the era of Calvin and his contemporaries, given that many of the orthodox theologians were willing to define the *gratia Dei* as a bounty or graciousness extending to all creation.[526] While God is gracious to all, his grace is particularly bestowed upon those who are his in Christ: "God's free favor is the cause of our salvation, and of all the means tending thereunto, Rom. 3:24 & 5:15, 16; Eph. 1:5, 6 & 24. Rom 9:16; Titus 3:5, Heb. 4:16; Rom 6:23; 1 Cor. 12:4, 9. The gospel sets forth the freeness, fulness, and the powerfulness of God's grace to his Church, therefore it is called the *Gospel of the grace of God*, Acts. 20:24." This grace is such that it is given freely without desert and it is "firm and unchangeable, so that those which are once beloved, can never be rejected, or utterly cast off, Psalm 77:10."[527]

God's effective grace given to us indicates all the gifts bestowed by the Spirit. Thus, in Rijssen's analysis, the principle of justification by faith has caused the equation of the scholastic terms *gratia gratis data* and *gratia gratis faciens* — for the orthodox, forensic

---

522. Brakel, *Redelijke Godsdienst*, I.iii.34.

523. Rijssen, *Summa theol.*, III.xliii; similarly, Maresius, *Collegium theol.*, II.l; Heidanus, *Corpus theol.*, II (p. 162).

524. Wendelin, *Christianae theologiae libri duo*, I.i.22; cf. Maresius, *Collegium theol.*, II.l.

525. Wendelin, *Christianae theologiae libri duo*, I.i.22.

526. Cf. Maresius, *Collegium theol.*, II.li; Wendelin, *Christianae theologiae libri duo*, I.i.22; Leigh, *Treatise*, II.xi (pp. 83-84); but note Heidanus, *Corpus theol.*, II (p. 162), who reserves *gratia* for the elect and refers *benignitas* to all creation. For the modern debate, see Abraham Kuyper, *De gemeene gratie*, 3 vols. (Leiden: Donner, 1902); Herman Kuiper, *Calvin on Common Grace* (Goes: Oosterbaan & Le Cointre, 1928); William Masselink, *General Revelation and Common Grace: A Defense of the Historic Reformed Faith* (Grand Rapids: Eerdmans, 1953); Richard Arden Couch, "An Evaluation and Reformulation of the Doctrine of Common Grace in the Reformed Tradition" (Th. D. diss., Princeton University, 1959).

527. Leigh, *Treatise*, II.xi (p. 84).

understanding of justification relates all righteousness to Christ and all virtue in the believer to the imputation of Christ's righteousness and the consequent bestowal of gifts by the Spirit. The medieval categories enter, here, by way of clarification of doctrine: Rijssen both finds them useful as ways of describing the effective grace of God and senses the need for clarifying their application. Had not Rome continued to distinguish between *gratia gratis data* as the initial gift and *gratia gratis faciens* as the subsequent gift contingent on acceptance of just grace, Rijssen might well have omitted mention of the terms altogether: the point of his argument is that the terms are two ways of looking at the same thing.[528]

The Arminians, too, mistake the meaning of God's grace. Leigh calls them "patrons of man's free will, and enemies of God's free grace." They claim that a man can come to merit God's grace and that God gives "effectual grace" to all men, even to "the wicked which shall never be saved, to Judas as well as to Paul." The Arminians, it seems, would forget that "effectual grace" is grace which obtains an effect![529]

The doctrine of God's grace is, therefore, a doctrine of great practical import, in that it moves men to seek God's favor:

> The holy Patriarchs often desired to find grace in the eyes of the Lord. It is better than life to him that hath it; it is the most satisfying content in the world, to have the seal firmly settled in the apprehension of God's goodness to him in Christ. It will comfort and stablish the soul in the want of all outward things, in the very hour of death. It is attainable; those that seek God's face shall find him.[530]

Leigh, even in this presentation of the divine attributes, takes the opportunity to develop a view of Christian life seeking the divine grace. Consciousness of one's own sinfulness, meditation upon the law, consideration of "the gracious promises of God" and of "the grace of God in Christ," confession of sin "with full purpose of amendment," and pray for grace:

> This stays our hearts when we apprehend our own unworthiness.... We should acknowledge that all grace in us doth come from him the fountain of grace, and we should go boldly to the throne of grace, and beg grace of him for ourselves and others, Heb. 4:16. *Paul* in all his Epistles saith, *grace be unto you*. We should take heed of encouraging ourselves in sin, because God is gracious; this is to turn God's grace into wantonness. We should frequent the Ordinances, where God is graciously present, and ready to bestow all his graces on us; the word begets grace, prayer increaseth it, and the Sacraments seal it.[531]

Related to God's grace are a series of other affections that appear variously in the Reformed orthodox theology — patience, long-suffering, compassion, condescension.

---

528. Rijssen, *Summa theol.*, III.xliii; similarly, Venema, *Inst. theol.*, VIII (p. 184).
529. Leigh, *Treatise*, II.xi (p. 86).
530. Leigh, *Treatise*, II.xi (p. 85).
531. Leigh, *Treatise*, II.xi (p. 85).

Patience and longsuffering are the willingness of God to moderate "his anger toward creatures, and either defers punishment or for a moment withholds his wrath."[532]

> God is *Patient*, Psalm 103.8; Job 21:7. God's patience is that whereby he bears the reproach of sinners and defers their punishments; or it is the most bountiful will of God, whereby he doth long bear with sin which he hateth, sparing sinners, not minding their destruction, but that he might bring them to repentance. See Acts 13:18.[533]

Even so God both endures "with much longsuffering" the sins of the reprobate and, at the same time, is patient with the elect prior to their conversion, willing their repentance rather than their immediate destruction because of sin.[534] It is, thus, "the most bountiful will of God not suffering his displeasure suddenly to rise against his creatures offending, to be avenged of them, but he doth warn them beforehand, lightly correct and seek to turn them unto him."[535] The divine compassion, similarly, is the disposition of God to deliver creatures from their misery. It is manifest when "the object of the divine goodness of love [is] involved in misery, such as man who is a sinner and subject to death."[536] God's humility or condescension, "by which God descends to our capacity, and graciously provides for our weakness," is exemplified in "God's familiar conversing and conference with *Moses* and *Abraham* interceding for Sodom, with *David* and others, and especially the incarnation of Christ."[537] The point very much reflects the assumption of the Reformers, particularly evident in Calvin, that God consistently accommodates himself to human capacity, both ontically and noetically: namely, God condescends or accommodates himself in order to relate to finite humanity, and he also does so in the form of his revelation in Scripture. This point of continuity, including its emphasis on the incarnation as the preeminent example of divine condescension, is significant if only because it is typically overlooked by the older scholarship.[538]

D. The Divine Mercy

1. The mercy of God in the thought of the Reformers. The *misericordia*, or *clementia Dei*, is an attribute stressed by Reformers and orthodox divines alike and firmly grounded in their understanding of the exegetical tradition. Just as in the created order, Musculus comments, the natural or essential qualities of things are often interrelated, so much the more in the nature of God are the attributes incapable of being severed from one another. Specifically, the divine mercy cannot be severed in our understanding from the goodness and love of God without doing injustice to the

532. Wendelin, *Christianae theologiae libri duo*, I.i.25; Brakel, *Redelijke Godsdienst*, I.iii.36.

533. Leigh, *Body of Divinity*, II.xiii (p. 299), citing marginally Nahum 1:3 and Isa. 30:18; cf. Cocceius, *Summa theol.*, III.x.67.

534. Brakel, *Redelijke Godsdienst*, I.iii.36.

535. Leigh, *Treatise*, II.xiii (p. 100).

536. Venema, *Inst. theol.*, VIII (p. 185).

537. Leigh, *Treatise*, II.xiii (p. 106).

538. E.g., Jack B. Rogers and Donald K. McKim, *The Authority and Interpretation of the Bible: an Historical Approach* (San Francisco: Harper and Row, 1979), pp. 112-113, 148, 166, 177, 186, 188.

divine nature. Just as we confess God to be good, so also must we confess him to be merciful. Evidencing his humanist as well as his scholastic training, Musculus offers definitions of mercy from Cicero, Seneca, and Augustine. Cicero and Seneca define mercy as a personal sorrow or grief aroused by the misery of another, entailing a willingness to aid the undeserving sufferer. Augustine similarly regards mercy as a compassion toward others, generated by their misery and by a desire to alleviate it.[539] Musculus is quite interested in the etymology of *misericordia* inasmuch as the Latin word connects misery (*miseria*) with the heart (*cor*), implying, literally, a compassion that generates in one's own heart a feeling akin to the feelings of the sufferer. So, too, he notes, does the Hebrew word for mercy, by its derivation from the word for "belly," indicate that one is touched inwardly by the sight of misery and moved to pity and compassion. That God has mercy, Musculus continues, is clear from the fact that God permits a world so full of evils to be spared from day to day. As Moses teaches, the Lord is a merciful God who will never forsake his people, will never utterly destroy them, and will not forsake his covenant. So, too, the psalmist continually praises the mercies of God, who is longsuffering and who pardons the sins of his people.[540] The prophets testify similarly and the apostle calls God the "father of all mercies" and the God of all comfort, rich in mercy," who has saved us by his mercy.[541]

Nonetheless, there are objections raised against this doctrine. Musculus continues by offering a discursive presentation of these objections, drawn largely from the Stoics, one of whom, Seneca, he has already cited in his definition of mercy. How can mercy be attributed to God when it is clear that negative affections, like sorrow or grief, have no place in God? The Stoics, after all, identified mercy, not as a virtue, but as a flaw or passion: thus Seneca distinguished between mercy as a passion belonging to weaker persons and clemency as a rational virtue characteristic of the wise.[542] Here, also, the formal scholastic background is obvious. Musculus' positive exposition begins simply, "Respondeo: Quod" — "I answer that": the classical definitions are in fact faulty, inasmuch as mercy does not imply a negative affection, specifically, a "grief" or "heaviness of heart" that renders the subject as "miserable and wretched" as the object of mercy. Rather, mercy is rightly defined as a consideration of the condition of the poor, the needy, and the wretched that moves one to ameliorate their situation: it is not so much a troubling of one's own heart as "a regard of our heart toward the misery of the wretched."[543] There is, therefore, no contradiction in attributing mercy to God, inasmuch as true mercy does not render the merciful subject miserable or wretched: indeed, when Scripture speaks of the mercy of God, it points, not toward any trouble in God, but to the fruit of God's mercy, the relief given to the wretched.

---

539. Musculus, *Loci communes*, XLIX (*Commonplaces*, p. 978, col. 1).

540. Musculus, *Loci communes*, XLIX (*Commonplaces*, pp. 978-978), citing Exodus 34:7; Deut. 4:31.

541. Musculus, *Loci communes*, XLIX (*Commonplaces*, p. 979, cols. 1-2), citing 2 Cor. 1:3; Eph. 2:4; Titus 3:5.

542. Musculus, *Loci communes*, XLIX (*Commonplaces*, p. 980).

543. Musculus, *Loci communes*, XLIX (*Commonplaces*, p. 981).

Musculus once again has recourse to the majesty of God as a governing concept: according to his majesty, God is most excellent, most righteous and just, and most happy or blessed. "There is no cause of mercy in God that arises from any communication of nature, condition, life, or state" outside of God, certainly not the righteousness or merit of human beings. Instead, the cause of God's mercy, like the source of the divine love, is the "incomparable goodness" of the divine nature. Even so, Scripture often pairs goodness with mercy, and both the psalmist and the apostle Paul explicitly place goodness before mercy when they teach of the grounds of salvation.[544] A distinction, parallel to those made concerning the goodness and love of God, can be made between general and special mercy, the former bestowed on all things even as the sun rises on the just and the unjust, the latter directed toward the sufferings of the righteous and the innocent. This language points, in turn, toward a distinction, between the temporal and eternal mercies of God, the former toward various offenders in this life for the sake of their instruction and amendment, the latter toward believers, in their election, regeneration, justification, and glorification. Musculus explicitly condemns as heresy the claim that God's mercy is so great that no one will ever be condemned to eternal destruction.[545]

2. The Reformed orthodox doctrine of the *misericordia Dei*. The divine mercy is one of the several attributes or affections that belong primarily to the revelation of God as Father and Savior under the covenant of grace, inasmuch as human beings prior to the fall were not a "qualified object" for mercy — mercy, in other words, is an attribute or affection that depends for its revelation or manifestation on the temporal economy of salvation.[546] That God is merciful is made clear by numerous texts of Scripture: in his revelation to Moses, God identifies himself as merciful (Ex. 34:6) and Christ commends mercy to believers as an attribute of God that they ought to imitate (Luke 6:36). Even so, God is called "the father of mercies" (2 Cor. 1:3) and "abundant in mercy" (1 Pet. 1:3), and "rich in mercy" (Eph. 2:4). "He hath a multitude of mercies, Psalm 51:1 is said to be *of tender mercy*, Luke 1:58, to have bowels of mercy, Psalm 40:12. God's mercy in Scripture usually hath some epithet: *Matchless*, Jer. 3:1; *Great*, Neh. 13:22; *Everlasting*, Ps. 25:6; Luke 1:50; *Free*, Eph. 2." In his mercy, God

---

544. Musculus, *Loci communes*, XLIX (*Commonplaces*, p. 983).

545. Musculus, *Loci communes*, XLIX (*Commonplaces*, pp. 986-987); note the recurrence of a logically argued doctrine of apocatastasis, resting on the nature of God, in the theology of the seventeenth-century Cartesian rationalist and mystic Pierre Poiret: see his *L'Oeconomie divine ou système universel et démontré des oeuvres de des desseins de dieu envers les hommes. Où l'on explique & prouve d'origine, avec une évidence & une certitude métaphysique, les principes & les vérités de la nature & de la grace, de la philosophie & de la théologie, de la raison & de la foi, de la morale naturelle & de la religion Chrétienne: et où l'on resoud entièrement les grandes & épineuses difficultés sur la prédestination, sur la liberté, sur l'universalité de la redemption, & sur la providence, &c.*, 7 vols. (Amsterdam, 1687); Latin trans., 2 vols. (Frankfurt, 1705); and note Richard A. Muller, "Found (No Thanks to Theodore Beza): One 'Decretal' Theology," in *Calvin Theological Journal*, 32/1 (April 1997), pp. 145-151.

546. Patrick Gillespie, *The Ark of the Testament Opened: or, the Secret of the Lords Covenant Unsealed in a Treatise of the Covenant of Grace* (London: R.C., 1661), I.vi.6 (p. 237); cf. Boston, *Body of Divinity*, I, p. 122.

overlooks the faults and infirmities of the church and provides for her needs. As the etymology of the word itself indicates, *misericordia* or mercy is directed toward the alleviation of *miseria*, misery — so that, in the proper sense, "Mercy is a disposition toward the creature considered as sinful and miserable by his sin." It is not directed toward those who are not immersed in *miseria*: "it is a readiness to take a fit course for the helping of the miserable, or it is an Attribute in God whereby the Lord of his free love is ready to succor those that be in misery, Judges 2:18 & 10:26."[547]

This pattern of definition results in the understanding of mercy as an affection, although there remains among the Reformed orthodox the assumption that the inclination to aid the creature is so intrinsic to the divine nature that mercy also can be understood as an essential attribute of God: the disposition belongs to God essentially, although its transient revelation belongs to the category of affection.[548] Therefore, the divine attribute, which appears to mirror a human affection or passion, does not belong to God in the same way that the attribute of mercy is possessed by human beings. "Mercy in God and in us differ," inasmuch as

1. It is in him essentially, in us as a quality.
2. In him primarily, in us secondarily. God's mercy is the cause of all mercy, it is without motive or worth in us, naturall, free, Rom. 9:18, boundless, extends to a man's soul, body, this life, the next; to a man and his posterity, Exod. 34:6, 7. it is above all his works, Psalm 145:9.[549]

The divine mercy is not a passion like human passions, which are qualities that alter in relation to their objects, that begin or cease to be — God's mercy, like the other attributes, is the essence itself. It is infinite, perpetual, and unfailing. The mercy

concerning which the Psalmist speaks (Psalm 103:8; 145:9; also Lament. 3:22, 23) ... as existing in God, is not a sorrow or sadness of mind arising from the miseries of others, but a ready disposition to succor the miserable. It does not spring from any external cause, such as usually stirs up this emotion in human beings, but from the sole goodness of God.[550]

God's mercy does assume, or even in a sense, require misery in its object but "only as holding the relation of condition and quality and not of a cause."[551] So also,

the greatness of this *mercy* is shown, 1. by the extreme unworthiness of those who are the objects of it, compared with his majesty, by the number of the sins they have

---

547. Leigh, *Treatise*, II.xi (p. 87); cf. Wendelin, *Christianae theologiae libri duo*, I.i.24; Turretin, *Inst. theol. elencticae*, III.xx.10; Brakel, *Redelijke Godsdienst*, I.iii.35.

548. Cf. Brakel, *Redelijke Godsdienst*, I.iii.35.

549. Leigh, *Treatise*, II.xi (p. 87); Polanus, *Syntagma theol.*, II.xxiii; and cf. Barth, *Church Dogmatics* II/1, pp. 370-371.

550. Pictet, *Theol. chr.*, II.vii.6; cf. Turretin, *Inst. theol. elencticae*, III.xx.10-11.

551. Turretin, *Inst. theol. elencticae*, III.xx.11.

committed, and the greatness of their misery; 2. by the severity of the divine justice; 3. by the eternal duration of this pity; and 4. by its innumerable effects.[552]

The attribute of mercy became, in the orthodox period, a point of polemical contention between the Reformed and the Lutherans, the latter having claimed that "the Calvinists affix utter mercilessness and cruelty to God."[553] From Wendelin's perspective, the erroneousness charge was exacerbated by a further claim that, in such doctrinal points, the Reformed found Beza to be a sufficient authority for their doctrine. "We are baptized, not into Beza, but into Christ," he responded — and our doctrine belongs uniformly to the French, English, Palatine, Brandenburg, Hessian, Swiss, and Belgian confessions, not to mention the teaching of the *Synodus Belgicae* against the Arminians. Indeed, Wendelin adds, Boquinus and Rennecherus (both German Reformed) also concur in these teachings with Calvin, Beza, Martyr, and Piscator — and none attribute mercilessness and cruelty to God.[554] The issue addressed by the Lutherans is the Reformed teaching that the decree of reprobation is absolute, without respect to anything in the creature, even sin. This is hardly merciless, Wendelin counters, taking the infralapsarian view of the confessions and most of the theologians noted, granting that God's election saves sinners who are fully deserving of damnation — and hardly cruel, given that God's absolute decree of reprobation is to leave some in their sins and not to have mercy and, in the same divine will, to execute justice justly. Such, indeed, is the teaching of Martyr, Piscator, and Rennecherus.[555]

From the purely historical perspective, Wendelin's point also serves to counter Heppe's construct of a German Reformed theology standing distinct from the other forms of Reformed thought. Wendelin's German Reformed approach is no less predestinarian than that of other branches of the Reformed faith, and, more importantly, Wendelin himself looked to a broad, international confessional consensus. Both here and in other instances of debate among the Reformed, it is difficult, if not impossible, to claim divisions along geographical or national lines.

The interrelationship of the divine attributes as understood by the Reformed is such that attributes like mercy and clemency serve to

> moderate [God's] anger, that it doth not exceed, yea it doth not match the heinousness of the offence; or it is a property, whereby the Lord in judgment remembereth mercy, not laying such grievous punishments, or of so long continuance upon his creatures, as their sins deserve..., 2 Sam 7:14; Jer. 3:5; Joel 2:13; John 3:9, 10.[556]

---

552. Pictet, *Theol. chr.*, II.vii.6.

553. Wendelin, *Exercitationes theologicae*, V.i, §1.

554. Wendelin, *Exercitationes theologicae*, V.i, §2, 4, 6; cf. Wendelin, *Christianae theologiae libri duo*, I.i.24 (2).

555. Wendelin, *Exercitationes theologicae*, V.i, §6, citing Peter Martyr Vermigli, *Ad Romanos*, cap. 9; Johannes Piscator, *Disputationes*, loc. 19, thesis 16; and Hermann Rennecherus, *Catena salutis*, pp. 37-38; cf. the translation, Hermann Rennecherus, *The Golden Chaine of Salvation* (London: Valentine Simmes, 1604), cap. 6 (pp. 23-34).

556. Leigh, *Treatise*, II.ix (p. 77); cf. Ursinus, *Commentary*, p. 127.

Not only, therefore, is God not merciless; even in those cases in which the special mercy of God toward his elect is not evident, there is a broader kindness and mercy of God manifest in restraint. Since God in general does not punish sin to the immediate extent it deserves, even where he is not overtly merciful in the ultimate sense, he is far from cruel and does in fact extend a certain degree of mercy toward all.

3. **Distinctions in the divine mercy.** Granting such controversy, the Reformed orthodox were led to note distinctions in the divine mercy similar to those noted in the divine will and grace, most notably a distinction between *misericordia universalis* and *misericordia specialis*. The former refers to the divine relationship to all creatures suffering temporal miseries; the latter refers specifically to the divine mercy on the elect, the "vessels of mercy" chosen by God, and therefore refers to a saving and eternal blessing.[557] Thus, first,

> There is a mercy of God which extends to all his creatures, Psalm 145:9; Luke 6:35. God is merciful unto all men, but especially to some men (Exod. 20:6) whom he hath chosen unto himself. ... All blessings Spiritual and Corporeal are the effects of God's mercy. Common blessings of his general mercy, special blessings of his special mercy.[558]

The universal mercy of God offers food to hungry creatures, water to the thirsty, restored health to the sick, consolation to the sorrowful, freedom to the captives — as the Psalmist often teaches. Second, the special mercy refers directly to the divine relationship to those sinful human beings elected in eternity, called, justified, sanctified, and glorified in time. It is, therefore, a mercy that is extended to the church and bestowed specifically on those members of the church who receive Christ and believe in him — and it is manifest in the gift of Christ, the Word, justification and sanctification, the gift of the Spirit as comforter, and the sacraments.[559]

These effects of mercy, together with the distinction between general and special mercy, correspond closely with the effects and the formal description of God's grace, just as they overlap somewhat with the analysis of other divine attributes and affections. There is, of course, a reason for this correspondence:

> Mercy must accord with wisdom, justice, and truth; therefore those that stoop to justice by acknowledging their offense, and worthiness to be punished for it, and are sorry they have so offended, and resolve to offend no more, and earnestly also implore God's mercy, shall partake of it.[560]

Mercy and justice neither cancel nor impede one another, nor is it the case — as Arminius had argued — that the divine mercy sits on a higher throne than the divine

---

557. Wendelin, *Christianae theologiae libri duo*, I.i.24 (2); Turretin, *Inst. theol. elencticae*, III.xx.12; cf. Mastricht, *Theoretico-practica theol.*, II.xvii.23; Ridgley, *Body of Divinity* (1855), I, p. 109.

558. Leigh, *Treatise*, II.xi (p. 88).

559. Wendelin, *Christianae theologiae libri duo*, I.i.24 (2), citing as examples, Psalms 140 and 147; Leigh, *Treatise*, II.xi (p. 88).

560. Leigh, *Treatise*, II.xi (pp. 88-89).

justice.[561] "Profane people conceit God to be all of mercy, and cannot endure to hear of his justice; or if they be convinced to acknowledge him also just, yet they measure it by the poverty of their own judgement."[562] On the contrary, God is said to be both most just and most merciful:

> Mercy and Justice may be considered 1) *ad intra*, as they are essential properties in God, and so he is equally just as well as merciful. 2) *Ad extra*, as he puts himself forth into the outward exercise of mercy and punishment. In this latter sense, we must distinguish between the present time, where mercy triumphs against judgment, Jam. 2:13, and the day of judgment, that is a time of justice and retribution to the wicked, and so *David* speaking of this present time, saith, *All thy ways are mercy and truth*, Psalm 25, and that of the Schools is true, *remurerat ultra condignum, punit infra* [he rewards more than is merited and punishes less].[563]

Thus, "*Misericordia & justitia Dei in se & quatenus in Deo sunt, pares sunt; respectu effectorum & objectorum major est misericordia* — Mercy and justice are equal in themselves and in God, [but] with respect to their effects and objects, mercy is the greater."[564] God is more merciful to the saved than he is just to the damned.[565] Still, there is "no conflict between mercy and justice ... nor any naturall desire in God to have all Angels and men saved, which is hindered by his justice," inasmuch as the plan of salvation reveals and gives full and equal glory to a host of attributes, namely, "justice, truth, mercy, peace, grace, power, wisdom."[566]

4. Practical considerations. Of course, there is great practical benefit in meditating upon the divine attribute of mercy:

> 1. We should believe this point, labor to be fully persuaded in our hearts that God's mercies are great and many; he hath preventing mercies; how many sins hath he preserved thee from? 2. sparing mercies, Lam. 3:22, behold God's severity toward others, and mercy toward thee; 3. renewing mercies; 4. pardoning mercies. He is willing and ready to help us out of misery. Therefore we should praise him for this attribute; how excellent and desirable a thing is mercy, therefore give him the glory of his mercy.[567]

And although mercy and justice are "both infinite" and are each distributed duly, God rightly desires "to be magnified by his mercies above all his works": he is called "Father of mercies," not "Father of judgments." This is true because mercy is more ultimate in its grounds and immediate cause than vengeance: the divine mercy on sinners arises

---

561. Cf. Rutherford, *Covenant of Life Opened*, II.vii (p. 303), contra Arminius, *The Priesthood of Christ*, in *Works*, I, p. 413, where the pattern of salvation is described as justice yielding to mercy.

562. Adams, *Commentary on Second Peter*, 2:9, in loc. (p. 383).

563. Leigh, *Treatise*, I.xi (p. 89).

564. Wendelin, *Christianae theologiae libri duo*, I.i.24; cf. Turretin, *Inst. theol. elencticae*, III.xx.13.

565. Leigh, *Treatise*, I.xi (p. 89).

566. Rutherford, *Covenant of Life Opened*, II.vii (p. 304).

567. Leigh, *Treatise*, II.xi (p. 89).

from God "himself and his goodness" while the vengeance against sin is caused directly by the sins we commit.[568]

Because of the mercy of God, the children of God need never be dismayed — not even with their own imperfections. Not even the devil can contravene the divine mercy: "for God is more merciful to help ... than the devil can be malicious to hurt." We must be encouraged to seek the divine mercy: "There is an infiniteness of mercy in God, so that whatever my sins have been, if now I will turn he will accept me; if I strive to turn he will enable me." Furthermore, having been granted the mercy of God, we should praise it all the more and in our own lives imitate the divine mercy in being "merciful to the afflicted and distressed."[569] God's mercy, then, "is an asylum for the penitent and pious, but not a refuge for the impenitent and impious."[570]

E. *Ira* and *Odio Dei*: The Anger and Hatred of God and Related Affections

1. The views of the Reformers. As in the case of the other divine affections, the Reformers identify such negative attributions as anger, hate, scorn, or jealousy as metaphors and anthropopathisms, applied to God or even in a sense "assumed" by God by way of revelation and accommodation to us — as in the case of the anger of God against a "stiff-necked" Israel in Exodus 32:10, it is not "as if God learned by experience" that Israel was recalcitrant. References to God's emotions identify his way of approach to human beings who otherwise could not understand him.[571] Thus, in his wrath against Babel, "God complains of a wickedness in men so refractory, that he excites himself by righteous grief to execute vengeance" — to which he adds "not that [God] is swayed by any passions." Rather the text intends to teach that God is "not negligent of human affairs."[572] Of course, Calvin's approach to these texts, like the approaches of various of his contemporaries and successors, was not uniform. He does not, invariably, indicate the presence of the metaphor or accommodation in the reference to God's wrath or anger — alternatively, Calvin can place the accommodation in reference to the divine seeing or hearing of a human event that results in a display of anger.[573]

Alone of the early codifiers of Reformed theology, Musculus saw fit to discuss the *ira Dei*, or anger of God, as a separate topic. The topic, he notes, offers a salutary reprimand to those who have heard of the goodness, love, mercy, providence, and presence of God but who remain unconcerned and careless in their sinful state: such sluggards may be awakened to the fear of God by a notice of the divine anger. This topic, moreover, stands over against the philosophers who declare that God is neither angry nor favorable toward human beings, but rather remains happy and incorruptible,

---

568. Adams, *Exposition upon Second Peter*, 2:9, in loc. (p. 383).

569. Leigh, *Treatise*, II.xi (p. 89).

570. Turretin, *Inst. theol. elencticae*, III.xxi.14.

571. Calvin, *Harmony of the Last Four Books of Moses*, Ex. 32:9f (CTS *Harmony*, III, p. 341).

572. Calvin, *Commentary on Genesis*, 11:6, in loc. (CTS *Genesis*, I, p. 329).

573. Thus, e.g., Calvin, *Commentary upon the Psalms*, 78:59, in loc (CTS *Psalms*, III, p. 270).

all-sufficient unto himself. This is the view of the Stoics, who understood anger and fury to be lower emotions, suitable only to the beasts.[574] Yet, there is another kind of anger: anger can be understood not only as a deficiency, fault, or base emotion, but also as an affection related to virtue — inasmuch as virtue must be angry against injustice. The rational argument, however, that sets philosophers against philosophers is less than conclusive in matters pertaining to God. The correct view of God derives from Scripture, which "everywhere testifies to the anger of God ... the writings of both testaments testify that the one true God, from whom we have both our life and our salvation, is angry with evil and lovingly embraces the good."[575]

Given the problems attending the attribution of anger to God, particularly the fact that certain kinds of anger are unworthy of God and that all discussion of God and his attributes must respect both the majesty of God and the truth of Scripture, Musculus devotes a fair amount of attention to the question of "how anger is attributed to [God]." There is, in the first place, an analogy to be made with other divine affections: God does not repent as human beings do, not does he have mercy or evidence zeal in a human manner, yet Scripture attributes repentance, mercy, and jealousy to God. Thus,

> his repentance is not with sorrow, nor after any error; his mercy contains no anger nor does it make his heart miserable; his jealousy is without excess.... He is said to repent when he alters, for reasons unknown to us, some part of his work; he is said to have mercy when, out of his goodness, he aids the afflicted; he is said to be jealous, when he punishes his people for their attraction to false Gods.[576]

Similarly, God is understood to be angry when he punishes sin, but this is not an anger like the anger of human beings, for God "does with judgment what we do with rage and tumult of mind." Yet, even some tumult or commotion of mind may in fact be attributable to God — as is attributed to God in Lactantius' treatise, *De ira Dei*. There are, after all, many acts of human beings that are necessarily displeasing to God, and it is necessary that God be justly angry at sin and move to punish it. We must recognize, Musculus concludes, that "God is not moved or changed in the way a human being is moved and changed" but that still God may become angry. This is not a subject that we ought to investigate with great curiosity inasmuch as it "surpasses our capacity."[577]

The *ira Dei* can also be distinguished into three kinds — general anger or wrath, temporal anger, and everlasting anger. God's "general" anger is divine wrath against sin, to which the entire human race has been subjected since the fall of Adam. As the Apostle says, we are by nature "children of wrath" without exception inasmuch as we all partake of the sinful nature of humanity. The sign of this wrath is the

---

574. Musculus, *Loci communes*, liv (*Commonplaces*, p. 1035, col. 2-p. 1036, col. 1).

575. Musculus, *Loci communes*, liv (*Commonplaces*, p. 1036, col.2-p. 1037, col. 1).

576. Musculus, *Loci communes*, liv (*Commonplaces*, p. 1037 cols. 1-2).

577. Musculus, *Loci communes*, liv (*Commonplaces*, p. 1037, col. 2; p. 1039 col. 1); cf. Vermigli, *Loci communes*, I.xi.22.

"wretchedness" of the human condition, both in flesh and in spirit; and its result is the general condemnation of all humanity.[578]

God's temporal anger stands over against the sins both of the wicked and the godly and is revealed in the earthly punishments meted out to sinners. Here, frequently, God defers punishment and "suspends" his anger against the ungodly in order to demonstrate his willingness to pardon sin — but neither does he tolerate the abuse of his patience.[579] Still, some distinction must be made here between the divine anger that is directed against the sins of the godly or elect and the anger that is directed against the ungodly or reprobate: God "is angry with the former as a father with his beloved children, with the latter as a Lord or Prince with enemies and rebels." Thus, God's temporal anger against the elect serves as chastisement for the sake of reformation and salvation, rooted in "fatherly love and discipline." By way of contrast, God's anger against his enemies, namely, the reprobate who blaspheme against his name and who oppress his people, takes the form of revenge and punishment — as has been seen in the cases of the Egyptians, Assyrians, Babylonians, Greeks, and Romans.[580]

God's everlasting anger is "that whereby the reprobate and unbelievers are condemned in eternity," called by the apostle "the wrath to come" on the day of judgment. Scripture therefore also calls the day of judgment "the day of wrath." This anger, moreover, does not merely begin on the last day: it has been "charged" to the reprobate since the beginning; it is in this sense that the apostle Paul refers to them as "vessels of wrath made for destruction." Thus, the reprobate have "no hope of pardon" or of escape from the hand of God.[581] God's anger, therefore, in an ultimate sense, if (as Vermigli notes) we can accept the understanding of anger found in Aristotle's *Rhetoric*, is an inherent propensity to punish, grounded in contempt (*appetitus ultionis propter contemptionem*).[582]

In each of these forms, the divine anger is just and suited to its object: whereas the philosophical objections to anger consistently identify it as arising on occasions where it is unjustified and as being excessive, Scripture consistently teaches that God is slow to anger. The psalmist and the prophets often "borrow" this language from the declarations of Moses in Exodus 34.[583] Nonetheless, God's anger is heavy and grievous when it is exercised. Scripture also testifies to the power of God's judgment

---

578. Musculus, *Loci communes*, liv (*Commonplaces*, p. 1039, cols. 1-2).

579. Calvin, *Commentaries on Nahum*, 1:3, in loc. (CTS *Minor Prophets*, III, p. 422).

580. Musculus, *Loci communes*, liv (*Commonplaces*, p. 1039, col. 2).

581. Musculus, *Loci communes*, liv (*Commonplaces*, p. 1040, col. 1); Calvin, *Commentaries on Nahum*, 1:3 in loc. (CTS *Minor Prophets*, III, p. 423).

582. Vermigli, *Loci communes*, I.xi.22.

583. Musculus, *Loci communes*, liv (*Commonplaces*, p. 1040, col. 2), citing Exodus 34, *passim*; Num. 14:18-21, 27-31, et passim; Neh. 9:17; Ps. 86:5; 103:8; 145:8; Joel 2:13; Jonah 4:2; Nahum 1:3; Calvin, *Commentaries on Joel*, 2:12-13, in loc.; cf. idem, *Commentaries on Nahum*, 1:3, in loc. (CTS *Minor Prophets*, II, p. 60; III, p. 421). Here Musculus' *loci communes* are clearly topical sections based on Musculus' commentaries: each text is developed at some length.

on the reprobate — God himself speaks of his wrath as fire.[584] Yet, the temporal anger of God may be appeased by the "amendment of life" and by contrition, given that God's natural or essential goodness consistently leads him to mitigate his anger.[585] God cannot "divest himself of his mercy, for he remains ever the same." Indeed, God works toward the salvation of the human race at the very same time that he is angry at sin: the ground of our hope of mercy and pardon is, therefore, the "infinite and inexhaustible" goodness of God, who does not respond in anger to the constant provocation of sinful humanity.[586] This goodness is, indeed "the principal cause" of the lessening of divine anger toward those who repent — a truth that we must keep consistently before us in order that we do not attribute any appeasement of divine anger "either to our virtues or to the satisfaction that arises from the punishment of our sins." There is, however, no way to appease the everlasting anger of God, which is as incomprehensible and vast as his grace.[587]

2. The teaching of the Reformed orthodox concerning the divine anger. The orthodox recognize that Scripture opposes a series of negative affections to the positive affections of God — the latter, which can be broadly described as God's "desire," are opposed or contrasted with God's "aversion":

> Now it is the absence of good which excites desire; but since God enjoys all good, it is plain that desire cannot properly apply to him; yet it is frequently attributed to him in scripture. ... Therefore this desire in God denotes, that man's obedience is highly pleasing to him, and that he will not pass it by unrewarded; at the same time it points out man's duty, and his great wickedness in not discharging this duty. To this desire is opposed *aversion*, by which God is said to loathe sin, and to have no pleasure in the destruction of the creature.[588]

Thus, anger or hatred, like its contraries, love, complacency, and gentleness, are said to be in God — yet, they are attributed to God "metaphorically" or by "anthropopathy," as belonging to him not "properly" but "improperly":

> for he is neither pleased nor displeased; neither can a sudden perturbation or tranquillity agree to God; but by these the actions of God are declared, which are such as those of offended and pleased men are wont to be, *viz.* God by an eternal and constant act of his will approves obedience and the purity of the creature, and witnesseth that by some sign of his favor, but abhorrs the iniquity and sin of the same creature, and shows the same by inflicting a punishment not less severe but far more just than men are wont to do when they are hot with anger.[589]

---

584. Musculus, *Loci communes*, liv (*Commonplaces*, p. 1043, col. 2-p. 1044, col. 2), citing Deut. 32:22ff.

585. Musculus, *Loci communes*, liv (*Commonplaces*, p. 1051, col. 2).

586. Calvin, *Commentaries on Jonah*, Jonah 4:2, in loc. (*CTS Minor Prophets*, III, pp. 123, 125).

587. Musculus, *Loci communes*, liv (*Commonplaces*, p. 1051, col. 2).

588. Pictet, *Theol. chr.*, II.vii.9.

589. Leigh, *Treatise*, II.ix (pp. 74-75), citing Exod. 32:10, "Now therefore, let me alone, that my wrath may wax hot against them, and that I may consume them, and I will make of thee a great

Recognizing these restrictions on the concept of divine anger, the *ira dei* may be defined as follows:

> God's *Anger* is an excellence of his own essence, by which it is so displeased with sin, as it is inclined to punish the sinner; or a settled and unchangeable resolution to punish sinners according to their sins.
>
> God is greatly moved to anger against all impenitent sinners, especially the unjust enemies of his people, Rom. 1:18 & 2:8, 9; 1 Cor. 10:22; Ephes. 5:6; Col. 3:6; Deut. 32:21; Psalm. 106:40, because such wrong God; He cannot be hurt, for that were a weakness; but he may be wronged, for that is no weakness, but a fruit of excellency, seeing nothing is more subject to be wronged than an excellent thing or person: for wrong is any behaviour to a person or thing not suitable to his worth.[590]

Thus, the divine anger denotes, not a change of emotion in God, but his constant purpose of punishing sin.[591] In a more precise and scholastic vein,

> anger is given to God, *Non secundum turbationis affectuum, sed secundum ultionis effectuum* [Not in the sense of disordered affections, but in the sense of punishments executed], say the Schoolmen. God's wrath is his revenging justice; which justice of God, as it simply burns against sin, the Scripture calls his *anger*: when it doth most fiercely sparkle out, it is called his *wrath*; the same justice when it pronounceth sentence is called his *judgment*; when it is brought into execution, it is called his *vengeance*.[592]

And further,

> God's anger signifieth three things. (1) The eternal decree, whereby God hath purposed in himself to take vengeance upon all evil doers, John 3:36; Rom. 1:18. (2) His menacings or threatenings, Psal. 6:1; Jonah 3:9; Hos. 11:9. (3) It is put for the effects of his anger, for punishment and revenge, Rom. 3:5; Matt. 3:7; Ephes. 5:6.[593]

In the first instance, the divine anger reflects the essential attribute of the *iustitia Dei*, which, in the Reformed view, includes the vindicatory or punitive justice of God — an attribute denied by the Socinians. Sin "offends" the honor and majesty of God and brings forth anger in response.[594] God's authority is wronged by sin insofar as he is the governor and ruler of all things who has ordered the universe according to his Law. Furthermore, sin dishonors God's name and dignity in "denying ... his perfect wisdom and justice"; it wrongs his person by "being offensive to the purity of his holy

---

Nation." Cf. Calvin, *Harmony of the Four Last Books of Moses*, Ex. 32:9f (CTS *Harmony*, III, p. 341); *Dutch Annotations*, Ps. 78:21, in loc..

590. Leigh, *Treatise*, II.ix (p. 75).

591. Pictet, *Theol. chr.*, II.vii..11-12; cf. Mastricht, *Theoretico-practica theol.*, II.xv.20.

592. Leigh, *Treatise*, II.ix (p. 74, margin, citing "Mr. Marshall on II Kings 23:26"); cf. Pictet, *Theol. chr.*, II.vii.12.

593. Leigh, *Treatise*, II.ix (p. 75, margin, citing "Dr. Benfield's Sermon 10, on Heb. 10:30").

594. Venema, *Inst. theol.*, VIII (p. 183).

person"; and it wrongs his creation by abusing what is God's and seeking dishonorable ends.[595]

Since God himself never changes, and since his anger is best defined *secundum ultionis effectum* or in terms of his relations *ad extra*, its character more clearly appears in terms of its "properties":

> (1) It is terrible; he is called ... the Lord of Anger, Nahum, 1:2. His wrath is infinite like himself. If we consider it, (i) in regard of its intention, for God is called a consuming fire, Heb. 12:29, it pierceth the soul, and the inmost part of the spirit. (ii) In respect of its extension, it comprehends in it all kinds of evil, Corporeal, Spiritual, in life, in death, after death; it reacheth to Kingdoms, as well as to particular persons or families; to the posterity, as well as to the present generation. (iii) In respect of duration, it continueth to all eternity, John 3:36; it is unquenchable fire.
>
> (2) Irresistible; compared to a whirlwind.[596]

3. The *odio Dei*. God's "hatred" (*odio Dei*) may be defined as "an act of the Divine will, declining, disapproving, and punishing of evil" that is found "prevailing and reigning in the reasonable creature."[597] This divine hatred is an affection of displeasure that, in the case of God, "denotes 1) the disapprobation of sin, 2) the purpose of punishing the sinner, following upon the sin, 3) a withholding of those blessings that flow from his goodness."[598] Divine hatred, then, is the contrary of divine love and the corollary of divine justice. Aversion is its immediate effect: one who loves felicity and justice cannot but hate infelicity and injustice, and hatred results in deep aversion.[599] Thus, the idea of a divine hatred primarily expresses the separation or rupture between God and creaturely evil (cf. Ezek. 33:11; Rom. 9:14; Ps. 45:7 and 5:6; Isa. 1:14). The greatest hatred of God appears in the punishment or "eternal death" of the damned. This doctrine is tempered somewhat, however, by the insistence of the orthodox, by way of texts like Ezekiel 33:11, that God takes "no pleasure in the death of the wicked," who are ultimately the cause of their own destruction.[600]

Perhaps a better terminology is Baxter's identification of a "dreadfulness or terribleness" of God toward the "objects of his wrath." Here again, this is not an ultimate attribute of the divine being but "the result of his other Attributes, especially of his Holiness, and Governing Justice, and Truth in comminations" in their relation to the unholiness, injustice, and untruthfulness of fallen human beings.[601] In speaking of these negative *affectiones* of God, three things need to be noted: their cause, their object, and their effect. The cause of God's hatred is the sin or evil of an utterly

---

595. Leigh, *Treatise*, II.ix (p. 76).

596. Leigh, *Treatise*, II.ix (p. 76); cf. Poole, *Commentary*, Nahum 1:3, in loc.: "This is spoken after the manner of men and must be applied as beseems God."

597. Leigh, *Treatise*, II.viii (p. 73); cf. Venema, *Inst. theol.*, VIII (p. 183).

598. Pictet, *Theol. chr.*, II.vii.8.

599. Heidanus, *Corpus theol.*, II (p. 174).

600. Heidanus, *Corpus theol.*, II (p. 174); cf. Leigh, *Treatise*, II.viii (p. 73); Greenhill, *Exposition of Ezekiel*, 33:11, in loc (pp. 667-670); *Dutch Annotations*, Ezek. 33:11, in loc..

601. Baxter, *Divine Life*, I.xxi (p. 148).

"delinquent creature." Second, the object: given that God hates sin and evil, the object of his hatred can only be a "reasonable creature" that persists in sin and evil and, in so doing, acts contrary to the nature, law, and honor of God. The ultimate effect of God's hatred of sin is the divine rejection and just judgment on the impenitently sinful creature. Leigh concludes, "Hatred in God is a virtue, and the fruit of his justice, and not a vicious passion."[602] Nor ought it ever to be forgotten that the deepest manifestation of "the Aversion of God's Wrath" against sin is the death of Christ as propitiation and that, because of it, God does not exercise his hatred and wrath against the faithful, despite the remnants of the sinful nature in them.[603] Even as, therefore, we recognize the rectitude of the divine hatred of sin, so ought we to hate sin as "the first, principal and most immediate object" of our hatred.[604]

The scorn or derision of God (*irrisio Dei*) is also a corollary of his holiness — in that he can be "represented as delighting in the calamities that befall the wicked, Prov. 1:26."[605] The biblical language of God laughing and mocking is, of course, figurative, albeit eminently weighty in its significance:

> when the Scripture speaks of God's laughing and mocking, it is not to be understood literally, but after the manner of men: but this may suffice us, that it will be such an act of God to the tormenting of the sinner, which he cannot more fitly conceive or express under any other notion or name, than these.[606]

This negative affection appears particularly in the derision of the proud (Ps. 2:4-5), such as the king of Babylon (Isa. 14) and Adam (Gen. 3), and the idolatrous (cf. Judg. 10:4; Jer. 2:28; Isa. 47:13; Hos. 3:10).[607] Thus God "shall both despise and deride" the kings of the earth "and all their crafty devices, which he shall manifest to the world to be ridiculous and contemptible follies."[608] In an ultimate sense, too, God can be said to delight in his "justice and revenge" against the wicked, for, although "he desire not the death of him that dieth, but rather that he doth repent and live; yet, when he will not repent and live, God doth desire and delight in the execution of justice conditionally."[609]

God can also be described as "jealous" or as exhibiting "jealousy," yet in such a way as it represents "the most constant will of God"[610] to avenge any impugning of

---

602. Leigh, *Treatise*, II.viii (p. 73), citing Ps. 5:6; 11:5; 45:[7]8; 78:59; Hab. 1:13; Prov. 11:1 and 16:5.

603. Bates, *Harmony of the Divine Attributes*, p. 255.

604. Leigh, *Treatise*, II.viii (pp. 73-74).

605. Venema, *Inst. theol.*, VIII (p. 184).

606. Baxter, *Saints' Everlasting Rest*, III.iv.4.

607. Burman, *Synopsis theol.*, I.xxiii.32.

608. Poole, *Commentary*, Ps. 2:4, in loc., with collateral citations of 2 Kg. 19:21; Ps. 37:13.

609. Baxter, *Saints' Everlasting Rest*, III.iv.4. The "condition," of course, lies in the creature as a subordinate cause intervening between God's will and its execution — not that God's will itself is conditioned. See above, chapter 5.4 (E.5-6)

610. Pictet, *Theol. chr.*, II.vii.10.

his glory or any attribution of his glory to another[611] — for God's jealousy is that divine virtue

> by which he will have all due glory given to him, and suffers not the least part of it to be communicated to the creature. This care of his honor and fame is manifest by the grievous punishments inflicted on those who have dared to arrogate part of the Divine glory to themselves, as on the builders of Babel, Gen. 11:4; the Bethshemites, 1 Sam 6:19; Nebuchadnezar, Dan 4:29, 30; and Herod, Acts 21:22, 23.[612]

God is also said to be sorrowful — in the sense that some act of the creature "displeases him and is contrary to his virtues."[613]

The orthodox writers, like the Reformers, drew lessons from their reading of the divine affections. Thus, from the doctrines of the *odio* and *ira Dei* and the various related affections, Christians should learn to repent and to reform themselves, to pray earnestly to God that, in view of their repentance, his anger might be turned aside. Beyond this, believers can learn to "take heed of sinning, and so provoking God to anger."[614] Baxter, Charnock, Mastricht, and Brakel especially indicate the positive effect of a knowledge of these negative attributes. For Baxter, the "dreadfulness" of God teaches us that "his children ... must be kept in a holy awe" and taught to serve God "acceptably with Reverence and godly fear, because our God is a consuming fire."[615] Charnock and Brakel refer to the negative affections primarily in their discussions of the patience and justice of God, where they stress the divine forbearance in passing wrathful or angry sentence on sinful creatures.[616]

As for the understanding of divine affections generally, we have seen little discernible movement or development from the Reformation into the era of orthodoxy. The basic understanding of what divine affections are, namely, *ad extra* relations, not indicative of a change in God, together with the exclusion of "passions," belongs in common to the Reformers and the orthodox. There are, to be sure, variations in emphasis and in exegetical explanation of difficult texts, but these are hardly indicative of major differences in opinion — indeed, there is far less change of teaching here than on such issues as divine simplicity or the divine *scientia*, where orthodoxy witnessed a major expansion of discussion. In sum, the Reformed interpretation of the divine affections was in the interest, not of a metaphysical structure, but of a consistent view of the way God relates to the human race. The method by which the interpretation was achieved, moreover, reflects the general hermeneutics of the era: the argument did not consist in the direct application of a philosophical theme of transcendence or

---

611. Diodati, *Pious and Learned Annotations*, Ex. 20:5, in loc.; cf. Poole, *Commentary*, Ex. 20:5, in loc. (I, p. 158); *Dutch Annotations*, Nahum 1:2, in loc.

612. Leigh, *Treatise*, II.xiii (p. 106).

613. Pictet, *Theol. chr.*, II.vii.10.

614. Leigh, *Treatise*, II.ix (p. 77).

615. Baxter, *Divine Life*, I.xxi (p. 148), citing Heb. 12:28-29; cf. Mastricht, *Theoretico-practica theol.*, II.xvii.39

616. Cf., e.g., Charnock, *Discourses*, II, pp. 490-498; Brakel, *Redelijke Godsdienst*, I.iii.39.

immutability to a particular biblical text, but in a recourse to the general principles of the *analogia fidei* and *scriptura sui interpres* by way of drawing conclusions from the juxtaposition of biblical texts.

Index